Peter Wingate was born in 1920 and educated in Switzerland and England. He qualified at Bart's and after three years of general practice in London joined the Colonial Service. During eleven years as a medical officer in Zambia and Malawi his duties ranged from school inspections to major surgery and from psychiatry to epidemiology and health education. He spent four years as a medical adviser to a large drug company in Basle and a year and a half on the editorial staff of the *Lancet*. He later worked in postgraduate medical education, firstly with the BBC's programme for doctors, *Medicine Today*, and later with *Medicovision*, a series of closed-circuit video programmes (sponsored by Hoffman La Roche). His novel *Rain Doctor* (1957) had an African background, and a historical novel *The Heretics* (1975) is a spin-off from research for this encyclopedia.

Richard Wingate followed his father at Malvern College and later at St Bartholomew's Hospital, where he qualified in 1972. After his internships he demonstrated anatomy for a year. As a surgeon in the Royal Navy he worked for a time on the medical problems associated with diving before returning to his chosen speciality, ophthalmology. After leaving the Navy he emigrated to Australia, where he now works as a consultant eye surgeon. In addition to general ophthalmology he is especially concerned with the use of lasers in this branch of medicine, and with applying one of his hobbies, photography, to the internal examination of the eye. In 1993 he was awarded first prize in a photographic competition organized by the Australian Institute of Medical and Biological Illustrators for a presentation of novel techniques in retinal imaging. He has also had several photographs published in various surfing magazines.

THE PENGUIN MEDICAL ENCYCLOPEDIA

FOURTH EDITION

Peter Wingate with Richard Wingate

PENGUIN BOOKS

PENGUIN BOOKS

Published by the Penguin Group
Penguin Books Ltd, 27 Wrights Lane, London W8 5TZ, England
Penguin Books USA Inc., 375 Hudson Street, New York, New York 10014, USA
Penguin Books Australia Ltd, Ringwood, Victoria, Australia
Penguin Books Canada Ltd, 10 Alcorn Avenue, Toronto, Ontario, Canada M4V 3B2
Penguin Books (NZ) Ltd, 182–190 Wairau Road, Auckland 10, New Zealand

Penguin Books Ltd, Registered Offices: Harmondsworth, Middlesex, England

First published by Penguin Books 1972
Second edition 1976
Third edition 1988
Fourth edition 1996
3 5 7 9 10 8 6 4 2

Set in 8¼/10 pt Monotype Times
Typeset by Datix International Limited, Bungay, Suffolk
Printed in England by Clays Ltd, St Ives plc

INTRODUCTION TO THE FOURTH EDITION

The rapid advance of scientific medicine noted in previous introductions to this book has continued unabated. Surgeons repair or replace damaged organs that would have been untreatable a generation ago. The successful transplantation of live organs has called for new drugs to protect them from being rejected as 'foreign' by the body's immune system, and the same drugs have found a place in the treatment of certain immune reactions to the body's own tissues, and also of some cancers.

Though heart disease still heads the mortality tables, new drugs, while not conferring immortality, enable people who would formerly have been invalids to lead normal, active lives.

New methods of diagnosis such as CT and MRI scan provide information that could otherwise be had – if at all – only by exploratory surgery: open him up and have a look.

Doctors and nurses now tell their patients what is being done for them and why, and there is hardly a limit to the explanatory leaflets and other available literature. Even the illegible prescriptions for remedies labelled 'The Mixture' or 'The Pills', hallowed by tradition, have mercifully vanished.

Yet one of the most spectacular developments in recent times has been the proliferation of alternatives to orthodox practice, ranging from the serious and professional approach of some to the blatantly commercial quackery of others. This trend repeats what happened in the eighteenth century, a golden age for quack doctors and their alleged cures – and to some extent the reasons for it may be similar. Although the eighteenth century could boast of some of the greatest names in British medicine – Withering, Bright, Pott and Hunter – it also spawned a generation of physicians whose remedies were often worse than the diseases that they were meant to cure. They were 'natural' medicines, to be sure, for there were as yet no chemical laboratories to produce synthetic ones, but, in the prescribed doses, as lethal as any of our modern drugs. Not surprisingly, people sought cures elsewhere, as they are doing today in reaction to the ever more powerful drugs that appear. Other possible reasons for the flight from orthodoxy include the spiralling cost of it and, paradoxically, the welcome spread of information that has banished the mystery that in their hearts many people expect of their physicians. Perhaps most of all it is more and more difficult for a scientific physician to find time to be a *good doctor* in a sense that a reminiscence from half a century ago may illustrate.

We were following one of the greatest teachers of the time, Geoffrey Evans, round his wards. Each of us had to study his allotted patients and, as though already a real doctor, present his diagnosis and suggested treatment. One of us had correctly diagnosed an incurable complaint.

'No treatment,' he announced.

'No treatment, *doctor*?' Evans growled. '*What are you going to do about his corns?*'

Of course the patient had worries enough without the misery of not being able to walk in comfort. He had probably never heard of a chiropodist, and he had taken his corns for the price of ageing, not worth mentioning.

Hippocrates would have noticed the corns and the need to relieve them. So, no doubt, would Avicenna, Chauliac, Paré, Paracelsus, Sydenham, Withering, Hahnemann (an eighteenth century 'heretic') and Jenner, all with entries in this book, and countless others. Today there is a danger that medicine will become so much a pure science, and its practitioners academic scientists, that the corns will be forgotten. But we shall still need the old-fashioned, country-style doctor who understands the family and its problems, and almost instinctively hears an unspoken call for help.

Once more I have to thank Dr Richard Wingate for his help and encouragement, and to say that although I have relied on him for many matters of fact the opinions that pervade this book are all my own.

From the Introduction to the First Edition

This book is concerned mainly with the scientific background to current medical opinion, and how it has evolved. In selecting the material I have put scientific interest before practical use. Books cannot teach much about the diagnosis and treatment of individual cases, but they should be able to explain the principles involved. Many statements are qualified with 'perhaps', 'probably', or 'it seems'. There are still not many certainties in medicine, and much of the book expresses no more than my opinion at the time of writing.

Note to the Second Edition

I wish to thank the many people who have suggested improvements, in particular Mr F. D. Allen for advice about drugs and other matters, and Dr Penelope Leach, who helped to revise the whole book.

Note to the Third Edition

I began the introduction to the first edition by mentioning the remarkable changes that medical practice had undergone during the previous thirty years.

It has changed as much again in the past fifteen years, and I am delighted to have my son, Richard Wingate, who in his final student year assisted at the birth of the book, to help me with the present edition. A detailed page-by-page commentary by Dr Paul Siklos has been of inestimable value; I am most grateful to him.

Only a handful of the remedies used a generation ago are still used today, and new drugs are superseded almost as soon as they are generally accepted. Although I have mentioned and discussed drugs frequently in this book I have made no attempt to deal with more than the examples of the various types, and as in the earlier editions I have not mentioned trade names at all. The subject is now so large that it needs a book to itself, and fortunately it has one. *Medicines: A Guide for Everybody* by Peter Parish, and published by Penguin, gives clear and accurate answers to sensible questions that anyone is likely to ask about drugs.

A

abdomen (belly). The enclosed space below the ▸*thorax* (chest) and above the ▸*pelvis*. Its roof, separating it from the thorax, is a dome-shaped muscle, the ▸*diaphragm*. There is no clear demarcation between abdominal and pelvic cavities. The combined cavity is supported below by the muscles spanning the ring of bone at the lower outlet of the pelvis, perforated by the digestive, urinary, and reproductive tracts. Behind, the abdomen is protected by the backbone with massive blocks of muscle on either side, as seen in a sirloin. The front and sides of the abdominal wall are thin sheets of muscle covered with fat and skin, a flexible arrangement that facilitates breathing, eating, pregnancy etc. The weakest points are the groin, where the abdominal muscles meet those of the front of the thigh, and the openings in the diaphragm for the gullet and other structures (▸*hernia*).

Immediately in front of the backbone are two huge blood vessels, both lying vertically: the *aorta*, and to its right the *vena cava*. Each forms an inverted Y at the entrance to the pelvis to provide vessels for the legs. The two *kidneys* lie on the muscles to either side of the backbone; from each a thin pipe (*ureter*) runs down to the urinary *bladder* in the pelvis. A broad strip of soft glandular tissue, the *pancreas*, stretches from kidney to kidney across the front of the aorta and vena cava. Two smaller glands, the *adrenals*, perch on the kidneys, one to each side. All these structures are behind rather than within the cavity of the abdomen.

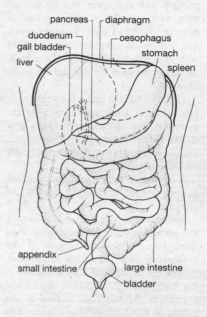

Abdominal organs from the front

The abdomen proper is lined with a fine slippery membrane, the ▸*peritoneum*. The abdominal organs grow into the cavity from behind, pushing a layer of peritoneum before them. Thus each organ acquires a smooth coat and can slide around without significant friction. This is as well, since the diaphragm pushes the organs down with every breath.

The digestive tract begins at the mouth, forms the *pharynx* in the throat, and passes down through the chest, behind the heart, as the *oesophagus*. It enters the abdomen through a hole in the diaphragm, and at once expands in the shape of a bagpipe to form the *stomach*. This lies directly under cover of the diaphragm and the lower ribs of the left side. At the outlet of the stomach, or *pylorus*, the long and tortuous intestine begins. It occupies almost all of what is obviously the belly: the part of the cavity between the ribs and the pelvic bones.

The *liver* fills the space below the right side of the diaphragm, down to the margin of the rib-cage, extending a little to the left of the mid-line. On the left, the *spleen* is tucked under the ribs beside the stomach.

A curtain of fatty tissue, the *omentum*, hangs from the stomach in front of the intestine.

Abdominal pain or belly-ache is among the commonest of all symptoms. Pain from many abdominal organs is felt around the navel regardless of the position of the organ itself. This is because in the embryo all the digestive organs first appear in the mid-line, and as in the course of development they migrate their nerves follow them, like telephone lines in a scattered community all leading back to the exchange. Although the stomach lies in the upper part of the abdomen on the left, the appendix in the lower part on the right, and the large and small intestines all round, pain from any one is felt in much the same central area. Their sensory nerves, all in their peritoneal coats, respond only to stretch such as the swelling of inflammation. This is perceived as central abdominal pain. But inflammation of the peritoneal lining of the abdominal wall is felt at the site of irritation. Thus an inflamed appendix causes pain first around the navel and only later over the appendix as the inflammation spreads to the overlying abdominal wall.

The *kidneys* lie behind the main cavity of the abdomen, and pain from them is usually felt in the back below the lowest rib. Pain from the *liver* and *gall bladder* is felt over the organ or centrally, or it may be ►*referred* to the shoulder.

Hernia or protrusion of an organ into a compartment of the body where it does not belong may appear at a weak point in the muscular walls of the abdomen. Common sites include (1) the groin, where vessels and nerves pass from the pelvis to the thigh and the scrotum, (2) the gap in the diaphragm for the passage of the oesophagus into the stomach, (3) at or near the navel where once the umbilical cord served as lifeline to the foetus, and (4) the scars of wounds where healing has been impaired, e.g. by infection.

Peritonitis or inflammation of the lining of the abdomen is usually caused by bacterial infection, of which the commonest sources are perforations of the appendix, peptic ulcer or obstructed intestine, and penetrating injuries. Irritants such as escaped bile or urine can also cause a sterile peritonitis, but in these cases the inflamed tissues soon become infected. Before the advent of aseptic surgery in the late 19th century the risk of fatal peritonitis made abdominal operations very hazardous.

Abdominal *injuries* can be either *blunt* or *penetrating*. Blunt injuries include blows from fists, boots, falling objects and the like, accidental falls, and the all-too-common impact of a dashboard or a steering-wheel. The solid organs are especially vulnerable to blunt injury: the liver on the right, the spleen on the left and the kidneys behind. Penetrating – e.g. gunshot and stab wounds – are as likely to injure the hollow organs: stomach, intestine or bladder. These also risk damage from blunt injuries if they are full at the time. Any injury more than simple bruising of an abdominal organ is likely to need prompt surgery. ▸acute abdomen.

abortion. Ending of pregnancy before the child has a reasonable chance of survival; delivery after this time but before full term is *premature*. The division between abortion and premature stillbirth is arbitrary; in the UK it is taken as the 24th week of pregnancy; in the USA as the 20th.

The distinction between *abortion* (up to 16 weeks) and *miscarriage* (16–28 weeks) is obsolete. Both are technically abortion, but social convention commonly calls accidental or spontaneous cases miscarriages and deliberately induced ones abortions.

1. ACCIDENTAL ABORTION (MISCARRIAGE)

Nobody knows how many pregnancies end in miscarriage, if only because an early miscarriage can be mistaken for a delayed period. Estimates vary between 10 and 20 per cent of all pregnancies.

The commonest reason for miscarriage is something wrong with the development of the baby; if the baby dies during pregnancy it ceases to produce the hormones that keep pregnancy going, and the uterus automatically empties itself. The trouble may start with an injury to the mother, or an acute illness that also harms the baby; and general ill health or a structural defect can make it difficult for a woman to maintain pregnancy.

Known cases occur most often in the 3rd and 4th months of pregnancy.

The first symptom is bleeding, some-times with pain. At any stage of pregnancy these symptoms need immediate attention, firstly because bleeding occasionally becomes severe, secondly because there may be a chance of continuing the pregnancy, and thirdly because the symptoms may have some other cause. At this stage abortion is said to be *threatened*. With rest and sedation all may still be well. Hormones (e.g. progesterone) are often given but their value is uncertain.

If the bleeding continues an abortion sooner or later becomes *inevitable*. The foetus (embryo) is too small to live independently and is no longer being kept alive by the mother's circulation. The only course is to get it over, with as little further bleeding as possible. In most cases the pregnancy ends with little more trouble than an ordinary period, but if the embryo is not entirely detached bleeding can become serious and the abortion has to be completed surgically. The other possible danger is infection (of the same kind as ▸puerperal fever). This is now rare except after unskilled interference.

Habitual abortion (defined as three or more consecutive miscarriages) may be due to remediable disorders of the uterus or of the endocrine glands (e.g. thyroid), or to chronic ill health of any kind. But in many cases no cause can be found. Treatment then has to be empirical. Hormones are often given and may help, but complete rest, especially during the hazardous 3rd and 4th months, seems to give the best chance of a live baby.

2. DELIBERATE ABORTION

Most drugs with a reputation for procuring abortion are either ineffective or dangerous. Some that are, or have been, used to stimulate natural labour at full term have no effect at any other stage of pregnancy. Of those that have sometimes, apparently, worked, most can have done so only by poisoning the foetus, and at the same time poisoning the pregnant woman. For many years, until safer remedies were found, quinine was the accepted drug for preventing and treating malaria. Its popular reputation for ending unwanted pregnancies may well have arisen from mistaking the effects of malaria (which might well cause abortion) for those of the drug. If quinine ever worked, it would have done so only in dangerous overdoses. On the other hand, some ►*prostaglandins*, and in the first few weeks ►*mifepristone* are effective abortifacients. However, even in experienced hands they can have unpleasant effects, and without adequate supervision they are dangerous.

The desperate old-wives' tales of the recent past, such as falling downstairs, were not far from attempted suicide. Direct interference with the inside of the uterus, the method of the back-street abortionist operating with a dirty knitting-needle, threatens the woman's life twice over: firstly a pregnant uterus is as well adapted to the breeding of lethal germs as of babies, and secondly the woman can easily bleed to death before infection sets in.

There is no place here for discussing the theological and moral aspects of abortion, but now that in most countries the laws against it have been relaxed doctors can be thankful that they seldom face the wretched results of unskilled intervention.

Under hospital conditions, abortion during the first 3 months of pregnancy is no more free from danger than most other interferences with natural processes, but the risk is much less than that of childbirth. American statistics show the mortality with early abortion to be about 1:50,000, against mortality in childbirth about 1:10,000. The usual method at this stage is to empty the uterus mechanically, either with a suction apparatus or with a surgical instrument passed through the natural outlet of the uterus.

Later in pregnancy the risk increases, as do the legal restrictions. The methods include injections directly into the uterus, and the use of prostaglandins by direct injection, by infusion into a vein, or, less reliably, by mouth.

Excluding patients who live abroad and visit Britain for their abortions, about 100,000 abortions are performed annually in the UK. This gives a ratio of abortions to live births of a little less than 1:6, compared with 1:3 in West Germany, nearly 1:3 in the USA, and 1:2 in East Germany. Despite the large number of abortions, it is not true that the law in Britain allows indiscriminate terminations. Current laws differ from earlier ones mainly in degree. A second medical opinion is still needed, as are reasonable grounds for terminating pregnancy. These include risk to the life or health (physical or mental) of the woman, as before, and also risk to the well-being of existing children, or of serious defects in the unborn child, such as those caused by an attack of German measles early in pregnancy.

abrasion. A graze; an injury caused by rubbing or scraping. ►*wound*.

abreaction ►*psychoanalysis*.

abscess. A collection of pus, a result of infection by bacteria. It represents an advanced stage of ►*inflammation*, which is itself a defensive reaction to infection.

The formation of an abscess means that the defence has been partly successful. When the defence is more successful, bacteria are destroyed quickly and the inflammation proceeds straight to healing; when the defence completely fails, the infection spreads widely. An abscess represents an intermediate stage: it is surrounded by actively growing tissue like that of a healing wound, but the walls cannot grow together because of the pus in the centre, where bacteria are free to multiply and damage the surrounding tissue; the damage keeps pace with the attempt at repair.

An established abscess cannot heal until the pus has been released either by finding its own way to the surface and bursting through or by surgical operation.

The balance between infection and healing is not static. If tissue is destroyed faster than it can be replaced the abscess grows. Or with chronic (prolonged) infection such as tuberculosis healing may outpace damage, and a mass of unwanted new tissue is formed – a *granuloma*.

Abscesses cause symptoms locally by pressure on neighbouring structures. Other symptoms such as fever are due to poisons formed by bacteria and by damaged tissue.

In some places, notoriously between the liver and the diaphragm (*subphrenic abscess*), an abscess has room to expand without any local disturbance. An exact diagnosis is then difficult. The fever and the increase of white cells in the blood suggest that pus is being formed somewhere, but there is nothing to show precisely where. In other places the local effects of pressure are all-important. For instance, the skull cannot expand, and the great danger of an abscess there is injury to the brain by pressure. More familiar examples of abscesses confined by rigid walls, with no room for expansion, are small collections of pus in a tooth socket or inside the ear-drum, both excruciatingly painful.

In essence the treatment of all abscesses is the same: to release the pus, and to provide free drainage so that the opening does not heal before the walls have had time to grow together. If the second step is omitted, the abscess reforms.

Antibiotic drugs have greatly improved the treatment of abscesses. If they are given in the early stages the infection may be overcome without any need for surgery, and in the later stages they at least prevent the infection from spreading.

The time-honoured ➤*poultice* is useful only with abscesses very near the surface (➤*boil*).

abstinence syndrome. Unpleasant symptoms experienced when a person stops taking a drug to which he is accustomed, ranging from serious illness after withdrawal of opium narcotics to the highly disagreeable but not dangerous effects of giving up smoking that some (but not all) smokers suffer for a time (➤*drug dependence*).

accidents. On an average day in Britain 12 people are killed on the roads, and another 20 in other accidents, including two at work. For every death on the road, 50 people are injured. For every accidental death at work, 200 are injured. Comparable figures in the USA show that road accidents cause twice as many deaths per head of population, while the rates with other accidents are similar to the English rates.

More young men die in accidents than from all other causes together, and among them the motor cycle is the commonest single cause of death. Apart from road accidents, accidental death is commonest among the very young and the old. In babies, suffocation is the main cause; in old people, falls.

More than twice as many males die from strokes as from accidents. But the average age of death is 73 with strokes and 75 with the heart diseases; it is 46 with accidents. Thus accidents account for more *lost years* than either of the other two causes. The prevention of accidents has become a major problem in public health.

The very word accident is dangerous, because it implies an event governed by chance and therefore inescapable. Yet in retrospect it is clear that few accidents could not have been prevented.

1. DANGEROUS SITUATIONS

Much research has gone into such matters as building safer homes and vehicles, removing hazards from nurseries and old people's homes, and safeguards in industry. Government departments and private organizations have published numerous reports on accident prevention. These are mainly concerned with reducing the number of situations where accidents become likely – with making the environment safer. In some cases, predisposing causes are actually outlawed: drunken driving, unprotected machinery, and inflammable night-dresses for children are illegal. But the precipitating cause of most accidents is human error, which neither advice nor legislation eliminates.

2. ACCIDENT-PRONENESS

If accidents really happen by chance, some people are remarkably unlucky, for with all classes of accident a few people suffer far more than their fair share. They are not necessarily clumsy or stupid; they are accident-prone. Against the concept of accident-proneness it has been argued that the number of serious accidents is not large enough for the statistics to mean anything – but if accidents are really not very common it is all the more remarkable that so many of them should involve so few people. Again, it has been said that people are not really accident-prone, but the after-effects of injury make them more liable to further accidents – but that is a possible explanation of accident-proneness, not an argument against it.

Personality is the primary factor. Hesitancy and aggression are easily recognized as dangers on the road and elsewhere, and either could be made worse by the memory of previous accidents. Aggression is closely linked to the male sexual drive, as are all forms of showing-off. Daring is a part of courtship, and the young Londoner's motor cycle is as much a symbol of virility as the young Zulu's spear. Young men who take unnecessary risks are not always trying to impress girls; they are as likely to be convincing themselves. At the opposite extreme is an urge to self-destruction. American police reports suggest that some road accidents are poorly disguised suicides. A subtler and commoner danger is a frame of mind where a person does not openly wish to kill himself but does not greatly care about surviving. Guilt with a desire for punishment and expiation is an important factor here.

These are all attitudes of normal people. In everyone there are dangerous forces that need expression, and society's problem is to find safe outlets for them.

Sport, then, may be more than the pursuit of physical fitness.

Even slight and apparently harmless mental disorder adds greatly to the risk of accidents. The effects of alcohol are well known, but many other drugs can also impair judgement. Fatigue and minor illness can be dangerous, and the risk increases when external influences on the mind are combined. A couple of aspirins and a small whisky at the start of a cold can make a man as accident-prone as serious drinking at another time. Some women are especially vulnerable just before or during a period: >premenstrual syndrome.

Psychopaths (roughly speaking, people with underdeveloped consciences) are a small but important group in this context. American records show two distinct classes of road accident. Firstly, most accidents seem due to misjudgement, a moment's inattention, or bad luck; and the people involved are a cross-section of the public (except that some are more prone than others). Secondly, a few accidents are due to breach of rules (e.g. disregard of signals, selfish overtaking); and a large number of these road-hogs are people who defy the law in other ways.

This account has dealt mainly with road accidents because there is most information about them, but the principles of cause and prevention are the same with all classes of accident. The personal factor has been emphasized because of its medical overtones, but accidents pose equally important problems for employers, engineers, lawyers and many others.

accommodation. Focusing the eye. At rest a normal eye is focused at infinity, i.e. for distant vision. For near vision the *ciliary muscle* round the lens contracts, and the lens becomes rounder and optically more powerful. (A camera is focused by moving the lens; the eye, by adjusting the strength of the lens.) The lens begins to lose its flexibility quite early in life, and accommodation declines (>*vision*).

ACE. 1. Angiotensin-converting enzyme (>*angiotensin*). **2.** The 3 antioxidant vitamins (> *oxidant*).

acetabulum. Hemispherical socket in the bone at either side of the pelvis to fit the rounded upper end of the femur (thighbone). This ball-and-socket arrangement gives the hip joint great stability with a useful range of movement.

acetyl choline. An ammonium derivative found in animals and plants. It is one of the >*neuro-transmitters* released at the ends of nerve fibres to set off an impulse in an adjacent nerve cell. Acetyl choline is also released by motor nerves to stimulate muscle fibres. (All nerve fibres outside the brain act by releasing acetyl choline, except sympathetic nerves, which release adrenaline and related compounds; there may well be other chemical transmitters in the brain.)

In 1914 (Sir) Henry Dale described some of the effects of acetyl choline, which he had extracted from ergot, on living organs. Many of them resembled the effects of stimulating the *vagus nerve*. In 1921 Otto Loewi slowed the beat of a frog's heart by stimulating its vagus nerve, and found that fluid passing through this heart picked up a substance that slowed a second frog's heart. The substance was later shown to be identical with Dale's acetyl choline. Dale and Loewi shared the Nobel Prize for Medicine in 1936.

Acetyl choline sets off electrical impulses in nerve and muscle cells by making them permeable to electrically active atoms of sodium. The effect is very short-lived, because acetyl choline is rapidly destroyed by an enzyme, choline esterase. The drug *eserine* interferes with this enzyme and so prolongs the effect of acetyl choline. On the other hand, *atropine* (belladonna) prevents the access of acetyl choline to various organs (e.g. heart; digestive system), and *curare* paralyses muscles in the same way.

acetylsalicylic acid ➤*aspirin.*

Achilles tendon. Large tendon behind the ankle, formed from the soleus and gastrocnemius muscles in the calf and attached to the heelbone (calcaneum). It is subject to great stresses, and despite its strength it is occasionally torn and has to be repaired surgically. Traditionally, Achilles' mother grasped him by this tendon when she dipped him in the waters of the Styx to protect him from injury, leaving this as his only vulnerable point.

achlorhydria. Lack of hydrochloric acid in the stomach. The digestive juice secreted by a normal stomach is strongly acidic (0.4 per cent hydrochloric acid) for the digestion of protein. The ability to form acid is lost with chronic diseases of the stomach, including pernicious ➤*anaemia* (B.2). Various symptoms of indigestion are ascribed to achlorhydria; but some healthy people form no acid yet suffer no symptoms.

acholuric jaundice. ➤*Jaundice* without bile in the urine. ➤*anaemia* (A.2).

achondroplasia (Gk = 'non-growth of cartilage'). A hereditary disorder of the skeleton, transmitted as a *dominant* character (➤*genetics* (2)). Bones formed in the embryo from simple connective tissue – those of the trunk and most of the skull

– grow normally. But the bones of the limbs and the floor of the skull are first formed in cartilage, later converted to bone, and their growth is defective. This causes a characteristic type of dwarfism, with a protruding forehead (because the vault of the skull grows ahead of the face), a well developed trunk, and very short but strong limbs. Apart from their unusual bodily proportions these people are perfectly normal.

acidosis. Alteration of the acid/alkali balance of the blood and tissue fluid towards acidity. Even with severe acidosis these fluids do not become strictly acidic, but they become less alkaline than they should be. In health the slight alkalinity is held constant by the balance of dissolved carbon dioxide (acid) and sodium bicarbonate (alkali). The balance is regulated partly by the kidneys, from which acid or alkaline urine is secreted to correct any excess in either direction, and partly by the lungs, from which excessive carbon dioxide is eliminated by deeper breathing. Heavy breathing after exertion is a reflex response to the formation of acid in working muscle. The kind of acid does not matter; removing carbon dioxide (carbonic acid) by the lungs compensates for an excess of lactic acid in muscle, or an excess of any other acid.

Acidosis follows:

1. failure to eliminate carbon dioxide because of disorders of the lungs or muscles of breathing;

2. failure of the kidneys;

3. severe diarrhoea with loss of sodium bicarbonate through the intestine, leaving a relative excess of acid;

4. abnormal formation of acid through incomplete combustion of fat, with diabetes or malnutrition;

5. poisoning by overdosage of drugs such as aspirin.

The condition popularly known as 'acidity', which is indigestion with regurgitation of acid from the stomach, has nothing to do with acidosis; nor has the excessive formation of acid in the stomach associated with duodenal ulcers. If anything, the formation of acid in the stomach tends to deplete the blood of acid; with severe vomiting this acid is lost and leads to the opposite state, *alkalosis*. Contrary to a common belief, children are not very prone to acidosis.

The alkalinity of the blood is easily measured in a hospital laboratory. The level can be adjusted with exact doses of sodium bicarbonate; but essentially the treatment of acidosis is the treatment of its cause. True acidosis is a dangerous condition in its own right, and treatment is a matter of some urgency.

acne. The term is or has been applied to various disorders characterized by spots on the face, including ►*rosacea* (acne rosacea), but is generally understood to mean acne vulgaris, a condition so common that it might be regarded as a normal state in adolescence. Basically, it is an excessive or perhaps abnormal activity of the sebaceous (grease) glands. The glands are most numerous in the skin of the face and back. At puberty they undergo rapid growth and may form so much grease that it blocks their openings. A characteristic sign of acne is a plug of partially dried greasy material in the opening of a sebaceous gland – a *comedo* or blackhead. In more severe cases, sebum trapped in some of the glands leaks between layers of the skin and forms rubbery lumps. These sheltered collections of inert matter are liable to incubate bacteria – sebum has antiseptic properties but certain fairly innocuous species of bacteria seem to thrive on it. They include *Staphylococcus albus* (found on most people's skin) and *Bacillus acnes*, once thought to be the cause of acne, but probably an innocent bystander. These bacteria may produce small superficial abscesses (pimples). Occasionally the infection extends to the deeper layers of the skin and leaves scars.

Acne nearly always disappears when puberty and growth are over and the various endocrine glands have settled into their adult pattern; but this balance may be disturbed by hormone treatment of other disorders so that acne reappears in adult life. In some women menstruation has a similar effect.

In the more serious cases a hereditary factor appears to make the sebaceous glands over-sensitive to the influence of hormones.

Emotional stresses may aggravate acne, but more important is the emotional stress that acne *causes* to young people, and not only girls: adolescents of either sex can be acutely sensitive about their appearance. Their misery is often made worse by old wives' (or young boys') tales about the causes of acne.

The first point to be made about treating acne is that no remedy works quickly: the patient may need to wait weeks or even months for really significant improvement. Of the simple measures to be taken, washing the skin with ordinary soap and water once or twice a day is helpful, but more frequent washing is not. Squeezing pimples and blackheads only increases the risk of scarring. Blackheads can, however, be safely removed with Schamberg's loop, a small instrument which presses evenly around the affected pore. Natural sunlight often seems to improve acne, but the effect of artificial sunlight is rather disappointing. Diet makes little if any difference to acne.

For many years, sulphur ointment was the standard treatment, but it was unpleasant and many patients lost heart and gave up using it too soon. Now, in addition to countless patent lotions and ointments of uncertain value, preparations of *benzoyl peroxide* are highly effective, and *retinoic acid*, a derivative of vitamin A, is especially useful against blackheads. All these applications are mildly irritating, especially at the start of treatment. This need cause no alarm, but they must always be kept away from the eyes.

Although bacteria do not cause acne they aggravate it, and in severe cases an antibiotic, such as *tetracycline*, is needed. This is sometimes applied in an ointment, but is more often given by mouth. Relatively small doses are used, but they have to be continued for six months or more.

For female patients with severe acne, hormone treatment may help by boosting 'female' at the expense of 'male' hormones; despite their names these hormones are found in both sexes. Some contraceptive pills help acne in this way. This treatment is not used with male patients, on whom it would act as chemical castration.

Isotretinoin, taken by mouth, can help in severe cases, but needs expert supervision. Because of possible damage to the foetus its use is proscribed during pregnancy.

acquired. (Disorders) not present at birth, as opposed to *congenital*.

acro-. Prefix = 'extremities'; hands and feet.

acromegaly. The term refers to the enlargement of the hands and feet which is one symptom of the disease. Acromegaly is a disorder of growth in adult life, i.e. of the process by which worn-out tissues are constantly replaced. It is due to an excess of growth hormone from the pituitary gland. (A similar excess in childhood causes the child to grow into a ▸*giant*.) The bones cannot be made to grow longer when once growth has ceased, but growth hormone causes thickening of the skull, face, hands, and feet, and enlargement of various internal organs. There may be an excess of other pituitary hormones with complications such as diabetes and impotence. Acromegaly is treated by X-rays or surgery to the pituitary gland.

ACTH. Adrenocorticotropic (-trophic) hormone; corticotrophin. Hormone formed in the anterior lobe of the ▸*pituitary body*, acting on the cortex of the ▸*adrenal* glands to promote the secretion of ▸*corticosteroids*. ACTH is sometimes used medicinally so that the patient, instead of being given corticosteroids directly, is stimulated to produce his own. Synthetic ACTH is less apt to cause allergic reactions than natural ACTH prepared from animal pituitary extracts. A solution of the hormone can be so prepared that it is only slowly assimilated from the site of injection. In this way a single dose can be made to last for several days.

actinomycosis. An uncommon disease due to infection with *Actinomyces*, a microbe intermediate between bacteria and fungi. The infection usually enters by the mucous membrane of the mouth (according to an ill-founded tradition, from sucking straws) and causes a chronic discharging abscess in the region of the jaw, or more rarely in some other part of the body. The infection responds slowly to penicillin.

'Lumpy jaw' is a similar and commoner disease of cattle.

acupuncture. Treatment of diseases by inserting needles through the skin at determined points, often remote from the actual disorder but said to affect it. ➤*Chinese medicine*.

acute. (Disease) of rapid onset and generally of short duration, as opposed to ➤*chronic*. Neither term describes the severity of a disease: the common cold and smallpox are both acute infections, and athlete's foot and leprosy are both chronic.

acute abdomen. Hospital jargon for any abdominal disorder needing urgent operation. It is a convenient diagnosis because the symptoms may not show precisely what is wrong. Hours could be wasted in trying to distinguish between a ruptured appendix and a perforated duodenal ulcer, but since in either case the abdomen has to be opened, the exact diagnosis can well wait until the surgeon actually sees the affected organ.

acute rheumatism = ➤*rheumatic fever*.

acyclovir. An antiviral drug, used in the treatment of ➤*herpes*.

addiction. There is some confusion between the terms addiction, habituation, dependence and drug abuse. In accordance with current practice the whole subject is considered under ➤*drug dependence*.

Addison, Thomas (1793–1860). Physician at Guy's Hospital, one of the brilliant team led by Cooper. He described numerous diseases in terms of abnormalities of affected organs and not merely, as

had been the custom, of symptoms. His is among the earliest recognizable accounts of appendicitis. He made a valuable study of the actions of poisons.

Addison is chiefly remembered for his descriptions of pernicious or Addisonian anaemia (➤*anaemia*, B.2), and of failure of the adrenal glands (Addison's disease).

Addison's disease. Deficiency of the adrenal glands. In 1855, when Addison's paper was published, the function of the adrenal glands (suprarenal capsules) was quite unknown. For years he had been studying 'a very remarkable form of general anaemia, occurring without any discoverable cause whatever' (pernicious anaemia), and 'whilst seeking in vain to throw some additional light upon this form of anaemia ... stumbled upon [several cases of] anaemia, general languor and debility, remarkable feebleness of the heart's action, irritability of the stomach, and peculiar change of colour in the skin, occurring in connection with a diseased condition of the "suprarenal capsules"'. No more need be said about the symptoms of Addison's disease.

The ➤*adrenal* is in two parts: the *medulla*, secreting adrenaline, and the *cortex*, secreting several hormones. Failure of the medulla does not matter because there are other sources of adrenaline. The symptoms are due to failure of the cortical hormones, which govern the rate at which sugar is made available, the amount of salt lost in the urine and other processes. The weakness is due both to deficiency of sugar in the blood and to disturbed balance of sodium and potassium through loss of salt. But loss of salt leads to loss of water, which in turn reduces the volume of blood; the circulation is then defective, while the heart itself is weakened like all the other muscles. Vomiting and diarrhoea, of which the cause is not clear, add to the dehydration. Anaemia, a shortage of red blood cells, may be due simply to reduced demand for oxygen and for the blood cells that carry oxygen. The pigmentation may be uniform (one of Addison's cases 'might have been mistaken for a mulatto'), but usually it is patchy. It is due to over-activity of the pituitary in an attempt to stimulate the adrenals.

Only about four people in a million develop Addison's disease today, and in three of them no cause can be found; their adrenals simply stop working. ➤Auto-immunity has been suggested but not proved. The few remaining cases are mostly due to tuberculosis of the adrenal glands. Tuberculosis other than that of the lungs is now a rare disease, of which this is an unusual form. But in the past all forms of tuberculosis were extremely common, and one can assume that most of Addison's cases were tuberculous.

The disease is effectively treated by replacing the missing hormones. Like a diabetic, the patient can lead a normal life if he has his daily injections. The only difficulty is that the demand is greatly increased in times of ➤stress. If the patient has an injury or infection, his dose of hormones needs to be adjusted at once.

aden(o)-. Prefix = gland; glandular. *Adenitis* = inflammation, *adenoma* = tumour of a gland.

adenoid. Tissue resembling a lymph gland (lymph node) at the back of the nose, above and behind the soft palate (➤*pharynx*).

adenovirus. A common type of virus, first discovered in adenoids removed surgically, a cause of sore throat and other symptoms of the common cold (➤*virus*).

ADH. Anti-diuretic hormone. ➤*kidneys* (2).

adhesion. Sticking together of membranes as a result of inflammation.

Inflammation is both a defensive reaction to infection and the process by which healing takes place. The fluid in an inflamed region is derived from blood, and like blood can form a clot; connective tissue then grows into the clot. By this means moving surfaces such as those of joints, lungs or abdominal organs may become bound by *adhesions* if they have been inflamed.

adipose tissue. Connective tissue containing deposits of fat, forming a thick layer under the skin and serving as both insulator and fuel store (➤*fat*).

adiposity. Excess of adipose tissue; fatness (➤*obesity*).

Adler, Alfred (1870–1937). Austrian psychiatrist (➤*psychoanalysis*).

adnexa. Appendages, especially those of the uterus (Fallopian tubes and ovaries).

adrenal. The adrenal glands (suprarenal bodies; suprarenal capsules) are a pair of small organs (each about 4 g) at the back of the abdomen, against the upper ends of the two kidneys. An adrenal gland consists of two distinct organs: the *medulla* surrounded by the *cortex*. Their association is an accident of anatomy.

1. ADRENAL MEDULLA

The adrenal medulla is a unit of the ➤*sympathetic* nervous system. Sympathetic nerves act by releasing minute amounts of *adrenaline* and *noradrenaline*. The effects include diversion of blood from skin and digestive organs to muscles, increased action of the heart, increased blood pressure, release of glucose (as ready fuel) from the liver into the blood-stream, and slowing of digestion. As a rule, the amount of adrenaline released at any one site is too small to affect other organs.

But when the adrenal medulla is stimulated by its sympathetic nerves, it pours a relatively large amount of adrenaline into the blood-stream. This circulates and produces 'sympathetic' effects throughout the body. In sum, these effects prepare the organs for physical effort. The muscles are supplied at the expense of functions such as digestion that can wait until the emergency is past. Although not strictly essential to life, the adrenal medulla has evolved as a useful mechanism in the struggle for survival.

Over- and under-activity of the adrenal medulla seem to play some part in emotional disorders; whether as cause or effect is not clear (▸e.g., *anxiety*).

A rare tumour of the medulla (*phaeochromocytoma*) produces large quantities of noradrenaline, causing sudden attacks of very high blood pressure. The condition is cured by removing the tumour.

2. ADRENAL CORTEX

The adrenal cortex is an endocrine gland unconnected with the nervous system. It forms numerous hormones. Chemically, these are all ▸*steroids*. They include some ▸*sex hormones* which, as a rule, are not important in this context because normal function depends on sex hormones formed by the testes or ovaries. Adrenal sex hormones are important only in some rare disorders of the glands. They probably represent an intermediate stage in the synthesis of *corticosteroids*, of which the main natural representative is *cortisol* (hydrocortisone). These promote

the synthesis and storage of glucose (thus balancing the effect of insulin), regulate the distribution of fat in the body, and – most importantly when they are given as medication – suppress inflammation. A second type of action is concerned with the balance of sodium and potassium in the body: it inhibits loss of salt and water through the kidneys. When this effect is excessive the tissues tend to become waterlogged, which in turn strains the heart. Cortisol has these actions in equal measure. Another natural corticosteroid, *aldosterone*, is almost entirely concerned with salt. Numerous related drugs have been synthesized to suppress inflammation without causing salt and water to be retained in the body.

Cortisol and aldosterone are essential to life. Hormones of this type (▸*corticosteroids*) have a direct or indirect influence on many chemical processes in the body. The sum of their effects is to maintain the chemical *status quo* in a changing environment. Living tissue does not tolerate much change in its immediate surroundings, and the action of these hormones is important in preventing body chemistry from being disturbed by external influences or 'stresses'. In this context 'stresses' has a very wide meaning; it includes illness, injury, mental strain, and severe exertion. Without the adrenal cortex such stresses are lethal.

Some effects of cortisol seem paradoxical. Inflammation is a defensive reaction to infection and also the means of repairing injury, yet cortisol suppresses it. But inflammation becomes harmful if it runs riot, and cortisol keeps it within proper bounds. While other mechanisms deal with local problems, the adrenal cortex is concerned with the organism as a whole. Healthy functioning of the body

13

is a balance between these (and many other) opposing forces.

The activity of the adrenal cortex is governed mainly by a hormone, ACTH, from the pituitary gland. By one of the many feed-back mechanisms of the body, secretion of ACTH is stimulated by a shortage of corticosteroids in the blood and suppressed by a surfeit. Stress evokes cortisol by stimulating the pituitary to secrete ACTH. (Aldosterone is regulated not by ACTH but by variations in the volume and salt content of body fluids.)

Corticosteroids and ACTH are widely used in medical treatment: ➤*corticosteroids*.

3. Disorders

Deficiency of the adrenal cortex leads to ➤*Addison's disease*, a fatal disorder if untreated, but remediable with regular doses of corticosteroids.

Three types of *over-activity* are described, due to excess of cortisol, aldosterone, or adrenal sex hormones; in practice these often overlap.

Excess of cortisol (*Cushing's syndrome*) may arise from overgrowth of the adrenal cortex, abnormal secretion of ACTH from a pituitary tumour, or prolonged medication with corticosteroids. The symptoms vary greatly. Since fat and carbohydrate are formed and stored at the expense of protein, there is loss of muscle and increase of fat. The fat has a characteristic distribution over the trunk but not the limbs; the neck is heavy and the face rounded. Bones and skin are both weakened. The disturbance of sugar chemistry sometimes goes as far as frank diabetes.

Excess of aldosterone alone (*Conn's syndrome*) causes retention of sodium and water with loss of potassium: the volume and pressure of the blood increase, and lack of potassium disturbs the working of muscle including heart muscle. This rare condition is due to a small tumour, which can be removed. More often the symptoms of Cushing's and Conn's syndromes are mixed.

Adrenogenital syndrome is another rare condition. The synthesis of corticosteroids is held up at the intermediate stage of sex hormones, which are secreted in great excess, and cause precocious sexual development with a tendency in either sex to develop male characters. Since there is a deficiency of cortisol, the adrenals are under constant stimulation by ACTH, and they can only respond by forming more and more sex hormones in an attempt to form cortisol. The disorder is corrected by giving corticosteroids.

Some forms of over-activity are cured by removing a tumour, which may be in the adrenal cortex and secreting corticosteroids, or in the pituitary and secreting ACTH. Others can be suppressed by X-ray treatment of the pituitary. As a last resort it may be necessary to remove the adrenals and then treat the resulting Addison's disease in the usual way.

adrenaline (known in the US as **epinephrine**; 'Adrenalin' is a registered name). The first ➤*hormone* to be discovered (Schäfer and Oliver; University College, London; 1894). An extract of adrenal gland caused a dog's blood pressure to rise. Adrenaline was isolated from these extracts and, in 1901, synthesized. It reproduced many of the effects of stimulating ➤*sympathetic* nerves, and for a time these nerves were thought to act simply by releasing adrenaline. In fact, a closely related substance *nor*adrenaline is released from most sympathetic nerve-endings, together with smaller amounts of adrenaline and probably of other similar substances.

Adrenaline stimulates the heart action and raises the blood pressure, releases glucose and increases its consumption, increases the circulation of blood in the muscles, relaxes the air passages and stimulates breathing, and produces a sense of excitement. In short, it prepares the body for physical action. At the same time it inhibits digestion and excretion, and reduces blood flow except in the muscles and heart.

Noradrenaline (arterenol) behaves a little differently. Whereas adrenaline causes some structures to contract and others (e.g. blood vessels in muscles) to relax, noradrenaline is almost entirely concerned with contraction. Broadly speaking, noradrenaline does the routine jobs such as maintaining an even blood pressure (by adjusting the resistance of the small arteries) and adrenaline deals with emergencies, when it can be released in large amounts from the adrenal glands.

These and similar substances are active in the ➤*brain*, where they appear to affect mood and emotion.

Adrenaline is a valuable drug in certain emergencies such as severe ➤*allergy*. It gives rapid relief from bronchial asthma. Since it is destroyed in the stomach it has to be injected, and its action is short-lived. It has to be given with great care, because an injection of adrenaline disturbs many organs other than the one that is being treated. For instance, while relieving asthma it causes disagreeable or even dangerous over-activity of the heart. Drugs with similar but fewer actions can often be used instead (➤*sympathetic*).

Aëdes. A genus of mosquito able to transmit several tropical virus diseases, including yellow fever.

aerobic. Living or taking place in the presence of air or oxygen; e.g. aerobic bacteria need air, whereas anaerobic bacteria thrive without it and may actually die in its presence. Similarly, in human muscle, energy is normally provided by the combustion of glucose with oxygen (aerobic), but for a short time the muscle can do without oxygen (anaerobic) (➤*muscle* (1)).

aerophagy. Air-swallowing; a mildly neurotic habit which commonly causes discomfort from flatulence.

aetiology. The branch of pathology that deals with the causes of disease.

affect. The state of mind produced by an emotion. The emotion itself is here regarded as a process; affect as its effect. For instance, fear is an emotion with certain physical manifestations; its effect is usually but not necessarily unpleasant, for some fear is exhilarating. In mentally normal people, emotion and affect are related in more or less appropriate ways, but in some types of mental disorder they are not. Among serious disorders, *schizophrenia* is characterized by extreme poverty of affect, i.e. the patient evinces little or no response to his own emotions. On the other hand the patient with *affective* (manic-depressive) psychosis is carried away by his emotions; at different times he may be wildly elated or utterly dejected.

aflatoxin. A poison found in spores of the mould *Aspergillus flavus* (hence the name: A-fla-toxin), known to be carcinogenic in some animals. In hot, humid conditions stored foodstuffs such as groundnuts are often contaminated by the mould, causing a kind of food poisoning. It may contribute to primary cancer of the liver, which is common in some tropical countries.

afterbirth = ►*placenta.*

after-pains. A symptom that troubles some women after the end of labour. Labour pains are due to contraction of the muscle of the uterus. Rhythmic contractions of this muscle continue when labour is over; this ensures that all bleeding stops, and begins the process of involution by which the uterus regains its non-pregnant shape and size. After-pains are an unpleasant awareness of this necessary function. The uterus cannot safely be discouraged from contracting, but the painful sensation can be relieved with analgesics.

ageing. There is no apparent reason why cells should not live indefinitely if they are provided with enough water and oxygen and a few simple nutrients such as glucose, amino-acids and salts. When a living cell reaches a certain stage of maturity it splits into two new young cells. In a sense, the cells of all creatures now living have been alive for a few hundred million years, for they are the products of repeated splitting of the first living cells.

In the laboratory, portions of tissue or even whole organs can be kept alive beyond the life-span of the animal from which they were taken. A heart, for instance, seems able to go on beating for as long as an adequate circulation of essential nutrients is maintained in its vessels, and waste products are removed. Yet the life of a complete animal is limited. A man who manages to escape every sort of illness or injury is still very unlikely to live beyond a hundred.

A substance that seems bound to de-

generate is *collagen*, which forms the scaffolding between the cells of the body. Its slender fibres gradually lose their strength, and the accompanying elastic fibres harden.

In the nervous system, worn-out cells are not replaced when they die, because unlike other cells they cannot reproduce themselves. If only for this reason an old brain is less efficient than a young one.

In the arteries, a kind of degeneration (►*artery* (1)) probably begins in childhood and ultimately causes the arteries to harden. On its own, atheroma may not be very harmful but when it is combined with civilized habits such as lack of exercise and overeating it becomes the leading cause of ill health and death in middle and old age.

The joints stiffen partly because of changes in the fibrous tissue and partly because the wear and tear of a lifetime inevitably causes some ►*osteoarthritis.* Old bones begin to lose their substance (►*osteoporosis*), but this process may not be as inevitable as it has seemed.

Finally, there is the statistical truism that the longer one lives the greater the chance that something will go seriously wrong.

►*senility.*

agglutination. Clumping together of bacteria (an effect of some ►*antibodies* which inactivate bacteria in this way) or of red blood cells (a similar effect is seen when bloods of different groups are mixed; this is different from clotting, which is solidification of the fluid part of blood).

agranulocytosis. Lack of white blood cells (►*blood* (3)).

ague. Violent shivering (*rigor*) at the beginning of a fever; malaria (tertian ague – malaria with shivering on first and third days; quartan ague – on first and fourth days).

AIDS (acquired immune-deficiency syndrome). Failure to resist certain types of infection and cancer caused by a virus known as human immunodeficiency virus (HIV) and previously known as human T-cell lymphotrophic virus type III (HTLVIII) or lymphadenopathy associated virus (LAV).

The virus enters the body and invades T-lymphocytes, a type of white blood cell on which cellular immunity depends. HIV-infected people produce antibodies (anti HIV) and are said to be 'antibody positive'. These antibodies do not help the patient fight the disease, but do indicate that he/she may be infectious. Anti HIV is usually detectable in the blood, but not always. In the majority of cases patients develop anti HIV within three months of exposure, a few take a lot longer, up to a year or so, while a small number of people who have acquired the virus and who are infectious never develop the HIV antibodies.

People with HIV may have no symptoms at all (and may lead a perfectly normal life); PGL (persistent generalized lymphadenopathy – chronic swelling of the lymph glands); ARC (AIDS-related complex – PGL plus night sweats, diarrhoea, weight loss and malaise); or AIDS. AIDS is diagnosed when the weakened immune system allows in opportunist infections by organisms that normally do little harm, e.g. protozoan agents such as *Pneumocystis carinii* (which causes a pneumonia known as PCP), or tumours such as ▶*Kaposi's sarcoma* and some tumours of lymph nodes (lymphomas) probably caused by viruses, such as ▶*Burkitt's tumour*. There may also be nervous

system involvement; early signs include personality changes and memory disturbances. Later on fits may occur and also dementia (AIDS-related dementia). There is no definite time interval ('incubation period') between the acquisition of the virus and the development of AIDS but it may be several years.

Viruses similar to HIV have probably existed for many years and from time to time have infected various animals. However, in the early 1970s primates in Central Africa became infected with the virus as it began to change its genetic make-up to become infectious to humans as well. The date that the virus first appeared in humans can be pin-pointed with relative accuracy. Blood samples taken during the course of normal medical procedure (e.g. before an operation) and held for years in the interests of research show no signs of HIV prior to 1971. It is thought that migrants from Central Africa took the virus to the Caribbean, from where it spread internationally. At present, high-risk areas (where the similarly transmitted hepatitis B is also prevalent) include parts of tropical Africa (in 1984, 50 per cent of prostitutes surveyed in Kenya carried HIV), the Middle East and the Caribbean. Contributory factors include failure owing to expense or lack of facilities to screen blood before transfusion, and customs such as anal intercourse – sometimes used as a form of birth control – and sharing needles for injecting drugs.

The first victims of AIDS, recognized in 1981, were either male homosexuals or drug abusers, and the disease was wrongly thought to be confined to these two groups. In fact men and women, homosexual or heterosexual, are equally likely to become infected. People differ only in the risks that they run.

17

A person infected with HIV, regardless of whether or not he or she will ever have symptoms, carries the virus in his or her blood and body fluids (e.g. semen or cervical secretions). The virus enters the skin via tiny cuts and abrasions, which are quite common on the delicate tissues of the sexual organs and the anus, or can be injected directly into the blood-stream if the needle of an HIV-infected drug abuser is shared.

Before blood for transfusion or use in the treatment of haemophilia could be screened for HIV, it was possible for the patient to receive blood donated unwittingly by a carrier. Most countries with up-to-date facilities now screen for HIV.

Of the body fluids other than blood and semen, milk has been suspected of infecting breast-fed babies and mothers carrying HIV are now advised against breast feeding. There is also a greater risk that the baby of a carrier will be infected before birth via the blood-stream.

With so much yet to be learned about the nature of HIV there is still some controversy about how it is transmitted. While it is agreed, at present, that insects such as mosquitoes do not spread infection, there is less certainty about how much at risk a person is if he or she shares the toothbrush or razor of a carrier. Some experts maintain that these objects should not be shared while others view such warnings as the work of scaremongers. On the other hand, most will agree that the virus is very unlikely to be transferred as a result of deep kissing. Most important of all, HIV, and consequently AIDS, is *not* transmitted by ordinary social contact, even in a crowded environment such as a school. Failure to accept this simple truth has caused much needless cruelty.

Treatment is still unsatisfactory. A vaccine seems to be a long way off if only because the virus (like that of influenza) readily modifies its structure to form new strains, of which a vaccine attacks only one. Some of the infections and tumours to which AIDS makes people susceptible can be treated with conventional drugs, but because anti-infective drugs tend to support rather than replace natural immune responses the results may be disappointing. Treatment with zidovudine (ZDU, formerly AZT) is not curative but may prolong life. It impedes replication of the virus, but its usefulness is limited because it also interferes with the formation of blood cells. Patients who do not tolerate ZDU may do better with didanosine or zalcitabine.

For the time being, though, prevention is the mainstay, and effective precautions can be taken against all the known ways of catching or passing on the virus. 1. Blood and blood products, e.g. for treating haemophilia, can be effectively screened. 2. Needles for injecting drugs are never shared. 3. A woman carrying HIV avoids pregnancy. If she should have a child who escapes infection (an even chance) then she should avoid breast feeding. 4. Visitors to high-risk areas should be aware of the dangers and should avoid behaviour which might expose them to the virus. 5. AIDS is primarily a sexually transmitted disease. Promiscuity is the most important single factor in its spread, and, as with any STD, couples who from the start confine their sex to each other do not contract AIDS. However, it only takes one infected person in a chain of relationships to pass the virus on to many more than the initial partner; given the indeterminable 'incubation period' the virus may be passed unwittingly between faithful partners in an established relationship. 'Safe' sex, which includes any activity that does not involve the transfer of a body fluid, is one way in which couples can avoid infection. The use of condoms to prevent the transfer of semen is the one available active defence. Condoms greatly reduce the risk of infection, but they cannot abolish it completely any more than they completely abolish the chance of becoming pregnant.

air. A mixture of nitrogen (about 78 per cent), oxygen (21 per cent), small amounts of carbon dioxide and other gases, and a variable amount of water vapour.

Nitrogen has no biological action, but the human body is adapted to live in diluted oxygen and functions better in air than in pure oxygen. (But nitrogen under pressure has some importance: see ►*compressed-air sickness*.)

Oxygen is essential to all forms of life except certain (anaerobic) bacteria. All activity depends on a source of energy, and the usual source is combustion, i.e. combination with oxygen of fuels such as fat and sugar. Oxygen is taken up in the lungs by the blood, and for this to take place satisfactorily a sufficient *pressure* of oxygen is needed. At sea level the pressure of the oxygen in the air is about 150 mm of mercury – 3 lb per square inch – which provides all the oxygen that the blood can carry. At the top of a mountain the air still contains 21 per cent of oxygen but at a lower pressure. A reduction of pressure by about a third is fairly well tolerated but below this the shortage begins to be serious. At an altitude of 3 miles the pressure is only half that at sea level and the blood is able to take up much less than the required amount of oxygen, and conditions are distressing. Many alpine resorts are a

mile or more above sea level. A visitor may notice the reduced pressure of oxygen if he exerts himself, but he soon becomes acclimatized. Shortage of oxygen is a real hazard only at very high altitudes and in confined spaces (where accumulation of carbon dioxide is an even more pressing danger). It is not the essential objection to poor ventilation (►'Fresh Air', below).

Carbon dioxide forms a very small proportion of the air. Plants are able to use it as a food, combining it with water to form carbohydrates and oxygen. Animals convert these products back to carbon dioxide and water, which they exhale. A man breathes out a volume of carbon dioxide equal to about 80 per cent of the volume of oxygen he takes in. In a confined space with no sort of ventilation, a poisonous concentration (6 per cent) of carbon dioxide is reached before the oxygen falls to a dangerous level.

1. FRESH AIR

Enough air to support life (some 15 cu. ft per hour) will leak into the worst ventilated of rooms; but this is far short of adequate ventilation. For comfort, the air in a room needs to be replaced once or twice an hour, depending on the size of the room and the number of occupants. The unpleasantness of an ill-ventilated room arises from lack of air movement and excessive water vapour, both of which impede the evaporation of sweat; from disagreeable smells; and often from irritant smoke. These may look like minor annoyances, but it is on just such apparent trifles that health (as against absence of obvious disease) depends. That their effect may be psychological is beside the point, for psychological influences profoundly affect physical health.

Good ventilation greatly reduces the risk of air-borne infection. The outside air is exposed to the strongly antiseptic action of ultraviolet radiation from the sun. For this reason the air in sickrooms and hospitals needs to change rapidly: the official recommendation is 10 times per hour.

Central heating without ventilation removes too much water from the air and causes the mucous membranes of the nose to dry out. In very cold climates where windows have to be tightly closed some form of humidifier is needed.

Defective gas-taps and inefficient oil or gas burners provide a grave hazard, because small amounts of carbon monoxide are lethal unless ventilation is good. Every year there are several hundred deaths from accidental carbon monoxide poisoning in Britain, mostly among old people who feel the cold and seal off every possible source of fresh air. ➤*dampness.*

2. TOWN AND COUNTRY

The air of most towns is unfit for human consumption. Soot cuts out sunlight; this effect coupled with poor diet was responsible for the rickets of industrial England in the 19th century. Loss of sunlight causes more than rickets. It increases the chances of bacteria at the expense of humanity and, perhaps worst of all, it makes life less pleasant and therefore less healthy.

The danger of air-pollution by smoke was recognized in the 13th century, and a half-hearted law was passed against the use of coal in London. Since there was no other means of keeping warm, the law was never observed. The recent Clean Air Act has been more successful, but it deals with smoke only in terms of soot. Probably the most harmful component of smoke is sulphur dioxide, which is invisible. This gas is an even worse irritant than soot, and is probably the main reason why chronic bronchitis is many times more common in large towns than in the country.

Air-pollution comes next to cigarette smoking as a cause of lung cancer. Coal smoke and oil and petrol fumes contain various substances known to cause cancer.

The virtue of clean air away from towns is simply that it is clean. It has no positive health-giving properties, but it puts no obstacles in the way of health. There is no evidence that sea air or mountain air have special merits except that one or the other may be free of something to which a particular person is allergic. A 'change of air' brings change of occupation, company, diet, and scenery, any or all of which may be beneficial. The value of a holiday is not measured by analysing the atmosphere.

air embolism. Blockage of a blood vessel by an air bubble. Air entering a vein is carried to the heart and pumped into the arteries. Small quantities have no effect, but a large quantity can form an air-lock and stop the circulation in a vital area such as brain or heart muscle. The danger of air embolism arises with wounds of the neck, where the negative (less than atmospheric) pressure in the veins may suck in air, causing sudden death. The risk of air embolism from hypodermic syringes is a myth, because the quantity is too small.

air sickness ➤*travel sickness.*

air-swallowing = ➤*aerophagy.*

alastrim (variola minor). A mild form of ➤*smallpox.* Whether this was really a separate entity was always open to doubt; in any case, the matter is now obsolete, given that vaccination has eradicated smallpox.

albino. Person in whom normal body-pigment is not formed. Albinos lack an enzyme needed for the synthesis of the brown pigment *melanin*, normally found in the hair, skin, and eyes. They have white hair, bright pink skin (strictly, dead white skin that does not modify the colour of the blood flowing through it), and pink instead of blue or brown eyes. Lacking protective pigment, their skin is very sensitive to sunlight – it cannot develop a tan – and their vision is impaired by over-illumination and, in many cases, a flickering movement of the eyes (*nystagmus*). Most albinism is inherited as a recessive character, but a rare variety affecting only the skin is dominant; another, confined to the eyes, is sex linked (►*genetics*).

albumen. White of egg.

albumin. The most abundant of the proteins dissolved in blood, the principal factor in maintaining the osmotic pressure of blood (►*osmosis*).

Alcmaeon. Greek physician, *c.* 500 BC, practising at Croton in Calabria. He regarded health as a balance and disease as an imbalance of opposed factors within the body, reminiscent of the yin and yang of Chinese philosophy. More importantly, he was a pioneer in anatomy and embryology, relying on observed fact rather than empty speculation. He distinguished veins from arteries, described the trachea, the eustachian tubes and the optic nerves, and well ahead of his time he recognized that the brain was a control centre rather than the repository of mucus for cooling the heart that his successors (►*Aristotle*) thought it.

alcohol. Any of a large group of organic hydroxides; only two need be considered here – ethyl alcohol and methyl alcohol (►*methanol*).

1. ETHYL ALCOHOL

Ethyl alcohol (ethanol, C_2H_5OH) is a colourless, almost tasteless liquid formed during the fermentation of sugar by yeast, known simply as *alcohol*. In medicine it has been widely used as a solvent (a *tincture* is an alcoholic solution of a drug) and as an antiseptic. Pure alcohol is an inefficient antiseptic; a 70 per cent solution in water is better.

The effects of alcoholic drinks can be considered as *acute* (immediate) and *chronic* (effects of habitual drinking).

Acute effects. Alcohol reaches the bloodstream rapidly. It can be absorbed from the mouth, and in the stomach it passes quickly through the mucous membrane to the blood. On the way through, it irritates the mucous membrane and sets up inflammation; the increased flow of blood accelerates absorption. Dilute alcohol, e.g. beer or light wine, is less irritating and less rapidly absorbed than spirits. Food in the stomach further reduces irritation and rate of absorption. A mealtime drink may improve appetite and digestion by irritating the stomach and so promoting the flow of gastric juice, and by suppressing the anxiety that so often impairs appetite; on the other hand neither alcohol nor anything else improves a perfectly healthy appetite. The habitual appetizer sets up a conditioned reflex, and then appetite fails without a drink.

After absorption, alcohol depresses the function of all living cells. The brain is more sensitive than other organs, and at every stage from the first drink to unconsciousness the effect of alcohol on the brain is to lessen activity. A few drugs have a double action, first stimulating, then depressing; but alcohol is not one of them. First to last, it is an anaesthetic like chloroform.

The most refined faculties are the first to suffer: judgement, concentration, self-control. Moderate drinking is mistaken for a stimulant because it deadens anxiety and self-criticism. It enlivens conversation by relieving shyness. The subject often thinks that manual skills, such as handling the controls of a car, are improved; but all objective tests show that this is an illusion. Reactions are slowed and muscular coordination is impaired, but alcohol makes a man less critical of his own performance.

The amount needed to produce a given effect depends mainly on the size of the person. Alcohol spreads rapidly through the body fluids, which account for some 70 per cent of the body weight, or in an average man to 40 litres of water. 32 g of alcohol in 40 litres gives 0.8 g per litre or 80 mg per cent, which is the legal limit for drivers in Britain. For an average person, this corresponds with drinking 35–40 g pure alcohol, which is the equivalent of 100 ml (about 3½ oz) of ordinary spirits, or half a bottle of table wine, or 1 litre (1½ pints) of beer. Some spirits, wines and beers are stronger than this, and less of them would attain the 80 mg limit. An experienced drinker can behave himself perfectly at this level; socially speaking he is sober. But his reactions are demonstrably slowed. Most people become dead drunk at a concentration somewhere between 250 and 350 mg per cent, and the lethal dose is not much higher. Death from acute alcoholic poisoning is rare because vomiting and coma limit drinking, but the drinker may drown in his or her vomit.

Alcohol is eliminated at a constant rate which reduces the level in the blood by 15–20 mg per cent per hour, regardless of the amount drunk. Some is excreted unchanged in urine, breath, and sweat, but most is broken down in the liver. To eliminate half a bottle of whisky takes about 12 hours. Hence a man who goes to bed drunk may not be quite sober in the morning, and on the other hand a chronic alcoholic who drinks steadily round the clock may keep pace and stay more or less sober.

Chronic effects. Everything absorbed from the stomach passes first to the liver by way of the portal vein, and the liver bears the brunt of habitual drinking. After some years of continuous low-grade inflammation the lining of the stomach and the whole of the liver are gradually converted to fibrous scar tissue (this is the end-result of sustained inflammation of all kinds anywhere in the body). In clinical terms, the chronic alcoholic has chronic gastritis and cirrhosis of the liver. In time the kidneys and heart muscle are also affected, the heart by deposition of fat in place of muscle.

Vitamin deficiency (mainly vitamin B_1) is common, partly because alcoholics neither attend to their diet nor digest properly what they do eat, and partly because alcohol makes special demands on the supply of vitamin B_1. Because alcohol supplies ready energy and takes precedence over normal fuel, fat and carbohydrate are stored instead of being burnt and the drinker puts on weight.

The chronic effects on the nervous system are serious and progressive. No part of the body is immune to damage by alcohol, and the nerves and brain are more sensitive than most. Various forms of neuritis are common. Habitual heavy drinking impairs concentration and efficiency, in time to the point where the drinker becomes unemployable. Fits of bad temper, jealousy and unreason, disrupting home life, can herald hallucinations, paranoid delusions, indeed almost any kind of mental disorder. Drinkers who develop addiction or physical dependence on alcohol may develop withdrawal symptoms if they stop drinking. These may be mild and fleeting, but can include epileptic fits. The worst of withdrawal symptoms are to be seen in *delirium tremens*: they may include sweating, fever, hallucinations, anxiety amounting to terror, shaking and total disorientation. Although most patients recover within a few days, delirium tremens is sometimes fatal.

While *cirrhosis* and, ultimately, complete failure of the liver are the best-known dangers of heavy drinking, and brain disturbances obviously cause the social problems, *all* tissues and organs are vulnerable. Blotches and other skin blemishes are common. Alcoholic neuritis, like any other damage to nerves, weakens the muscles in the affected zones; alcohol also directly injures muscle fibres, in particular those of the heart. In turn, disease of the heart and blood vessels is aggravated by obesity.

The amount of alcohol that can be taken without any risk at all varies widely. As with the amount required before its effects are felt, the rate of damage depends on body weight and on individual constitution. Women appear to tolerate, on average, less per unit of body weight than men; yet, for some reason, more men tend towards alcoholism. Extensive recent studies suggest that surprisingly small amounts of alcohol taken regularly over the years will harm at least some people. A law-abiding drinker who ensures that he does not consume more than the legal limit will not display any symptoms at all if this amount is taken quietly during the course of the day. However, taken daily over a number of years, it seems that this may be enough to cause serious, permanent damage.

There is, however, some consolation to be gained from research aimed primarily at identifying compatible donors for organ transplants which is based on the same principle that governs the testing of blood groups for transfusion. Certain tissue types have been found to be linked to an increased liability to certain diseases (for example, duodenal ulcers are slightly more common with some blood groups than with others). A statistical link has been found between some tissue types and alcoholic cirrhosis of the liver. It is too soon to draw definite conclusions, but this offers a hope that it may be possible in time to identify people with a genetic predisposition to this serious complication. Similarly, some people can drink heavily over a long period, yet are able to break the habit. Others, after much less drinking, become true alcoholics as described in the section on ►*alcoholism*: perhaps we shall learn to identify and warn them before it is too late.

2. METHYL ALCOHOL

Methyl alcohol (methanol, wood spirit, CH_3OH) is a highly poisonous substance used as a solvent and as an ingredient of methylated spirit, which destitute alcoholics drink because it is cheap. Illicit alcohol may be contaminated with methanol. Methyl alcohol produces stupor and unconsciousness without elation. The lethal dose is only one tenth as large as that of ethyl alcohol. It has a special affinity for the optic nerves, and a single bout of drinking can cause temporary or permanent blindness.

Alcoholics Anonymous. This remarkable venture has grown from its conception in 1934 to a world-wide organization, consisting of self-supporting and practically autonomous local groups of people who – as the sole requirement for membership – wish to stop drinking. Members learn to accept that alone they were powerless over alcohol, and that a power ('God *as we understand Him*') greater than themselves can restore them. This, they learn, requires very detailed self-analysis and close fellowship. The members help each other with the special problems that a recovering alcoholic has to face. AA avoids all publicity and controversy. It declines outside contributions, as a part of a general policy that members themselves support their group.

There is no doubt that AA achieves many more lasting cures than any other system of treatment. Its insistence that it is non-professional does not deafen it to informed outside opinions, and in any case its membership includes many professional people. Two offshoots of AA, Al-Anon and Al-Teen, help adult and young relations of alcoholics respectively.

The success of AA has inspired the formation of numerous analogous organizations such as Narcotics Anonymous and Gamblers Anonymous.

alcoholism. There has been much argument over the exact meaning of this term. It has been applied, quite logically, to any kind of ill effect caused by taking alcohol, but many effects are better named specifically, e.g. alcoholic neuritis. This leaves the term 'alcoholism' for a pattern that distinguishes alcohol from any other poison.

Alcoholism, then, is a chronic, progressive, relapsing, and eventually fatal disease, characterized by excessive and compulsive drinking. In Western society, a majority of people drink at least some alcohol regularly and as many as 10 per cent of them are likely, sooner or later, to suffer in some degree from alcoholism. Three times as many people may suffer indirectly from the patient's problem.

Fully developed alcoholism affects every aspect of the patient's existence: physical, mental, emotional, spiritual and social. By no means all alcoholics reach this stage.

Physical and mental effects have been outlined in the previous section (>*alcohol* (1)). The emotional state is highly unpredictable; angry, sometimes violent outbursts may alternate with introspection, gloom and inordinate feelings of guilt, though not enough guilt to make amends. 'Spiritual' is an ill-defined and perhaps unsatisfactory term. Here it is used to represent whatever beliefs the patient held about guiding principles or forces outside and greater than himself. Any such belief deteriorates under alcohol, until the patient comes to behave as if he were above any such principle or force – even ministers of religion are not exempt from the disease.

The social consequences which accompany an increasing dependence on alcohol are likely to be disastrous. Though initially the potential alcoholic may be the life and soul of the party, in time his friends can no longer keep pace with his drinking. He starts to feel guilty about the amount that he now *has* to drink, and so becomes a secret drinker. He is physically dependent on alcohol: if he stops, he is ill, and he knows that a drink will relieve all his symptoms. He shuns the few friends who have not already shunned him. His marriage is almost certain to fail, he loses his job; sooner or later he will probably be in trouble with the police. Suicide becomes a very real risk. (The patient has been referred to as 'he' partly because the condition is still much more common among men, and partly because affected women tend to destroy themselves more discreetly than men.)

Until alcoholism was recognized as a disease like any other, and not a moral lapse of the patient's own making, treatment was bound to fail. Certainly, many people drink more than is good for them but can stop with no great distress if they can be brought to see why they feel unwell. These are not alcoholics in the present sense. The point is that many people (though not the majority) will, if they drink regularly, reach the stage where they *cannot* stop of their own free will, if only because the craving for alcohol has taken the place of free will.

Merely telling an alcoholic that it is up to him to stop drinking achieves nothing; and no treatment of any kind does any lasting good unless the patient fully understands why he must stop, and wishes to do so. He also has to accept that by the very nature of the disease he needs outside help. For these reasons, ordinary medical treatment is of limited value. Drugs such as disulfiram which affect the metabolism of alcohol to produce unpleasant (and sometimes dangerous) effects if the patient drinks, or other forms of aversion therapy, such as trying to teach him that he gets an electric shock or is made to vomit in response to alcohol, are at best successful for only a while as nearly all these patients soon relapse. Gentler forms of psychotherapy, including hypnosis, may succeed, and

some alcoholics recover through the help of their religion.

However, conventional methods have an important place in the early stages of treatment. When the patient stops drinking he is almost certain to need some kind of tranquillizer to take the place of alcohol for a while, otherwise the symptoms of withdrawal may be intolerable. The drug needs close supervision as the alcoholic may simply be turned into a drug addict as well. Since he is almost certain to have some degree of malnutrition (accounting for some of the physical symptoms), his diet will need close attention. All of this means that at first he must be treated in hospital.

When this initial, acute phase of treatment is over the long climb back to normality begins. A return to moderate, 'sensible' drinking looks like a worthy aim, but experience has shown that it is seldom if ever achieved with true alcoholics. The patient has to accept that he is constitutionally unable to take any alcohol at all: a single drink will lead to another and to a total relapse. He has to accept also that by the very nature of the disease he cannot overcome it without support, be it from priest, family doctor, or analyst. The best chance of success is for the patient to join an organization claiming neither medical nor religious status (►*Alcoholics Anonymous*).

Although statistically the outlook for established alcoholics is not good, there are two bright rays of hope. The first is that almost up to the end, the poisonous effects of alcohol are to a great extent reversible. Livers regenerate and grave disorders of emotion and personality can return to normal. The second is that although first attempts often fail, the patient may, in fact, succeed in giving up alcohol (for life, because his constitutional anomaly will not change). He may not believe this, but companions must do so on his behalf.

alderman's nerve. An anatomical absurdity: it is a small twig of the ►*vagus nerve* to the skin of the ear. A more important branch of the vagus nerve controls the stomach, and a drop of cold wine behind the ear is said to stimulate the stomach by reflex action and help the alderman to digest his share of the banquet.

aldosterone. A hormone of the ►*adrenal* cortex responsible for regulating the excretion of salt by the kidney.

alimentary canal. The digestive tract: mouth, pharynx, oesophagus, stomach, and intestine.

alkaloid. An organic substance with certain chemical properties of an alkali, and medicinal or poisonous effects. Many drugs obtained from plants are alkaloids, e.g. atropine (nightshade), morphine (poppy), quinine (cinchona).

alkalosis. A shift in the ratio of acid to alkali in the blood and tissue fluid towards an excess of alkali (cf. ►*acidosis*). It can be caused by loss of acid from the stomach through vomiting, overdosage of alkalis such as sodium bicarbonate (or both when the one is treated with the other), or excessive elimination of carbon dioxide (carbonic acid) by overbreathing. The most important symptom is exaggerated reactivity of the muscles, which may go into cramp-like spasm (►*tetany*).

Alkalosis is treated by eliminating its cause. Antacids such as magnesium trisilicate or aluminium hydroxide are as effective as sodium bicarbonate in the stomach without altering the alkalinity of the blood. Overbreathing is usually a neurotic symptom.

allergen. A substance capable of provoking allergy.

allergy. The Austrian paediatrician Clemens von Pirquet devised this word in 1905 to mean 'altered reactivity', or abnormal response, such as coming out in a rash after eating perfectly good strawberries, or developing hay fever from grass pollen. The relation of such reactions to the normal processes of resisting infection was recognized from the start: innocent substances differing from the body's own constituents were being treated as dangerous germs, often with more violent and unpredictable effects than those of healthy resistance. Thus the term 'hypersensitivity' was introduced to mean over-reactivity, and for half a century the two rival terms each had their adherents. In the meantime the young science of immunology developed rapidly, revealing the intricate processes by which the body attempts to resist invasion, and also more and more ways in which these processes can go astray. Research was consistently ahead of nomenclature, and there is still disagreement about the precise meanings and limits of allergy and hypersensitivity. At least five different types of adverse reaction are known, each with subdivisions. They are further discussed under ►*immunity*.

For the present, the most useful convention is to limit the term 'allergy' to type I hypersensitivity (also called *anaphylaxis*), which represents immediate reactions to substances to which a previous exposure has made the subject abnormally sensitive. These reactions include localized responses, e.g. in the skin (*urticaria*), the nasal passages (*hay fever*), the intestine (food allergy) or the lungs (*asthma*). Collectively, these reactions are sometimes called *atopy* – another near-synonym lacking an agreed definition. Type I hypersensitivity also includes a generalized reaction, *anaphylactic shock*, an uncommon but dangerous condition with a rapidly falling blood pressure, spasm of the bronchi, and swelling of the mucous membranes of the throat. The symptoms are due mainly to a sudden release of *histamine*, but antihistamine drugs, which obstruct the access of histamine to the susceptible tissues, do not act quickly enough. Adrenaline, which instantly counteracts the effects, can be lifesaving. ►*Corticosteroids* also arrest allergic reactions.

allopathy. Treatment of disease with drugs having opposite effects to the symptoms; a term coined by Hahnemann to describe orthodox medicine as against his own system ►*homoeopathy*.

allopurinol. A drug used for treating ►*gout*, a condition arising from an excess of uric acid in the blood. Allopurinol closely resembles a natural precursor of uric acid. The enzyme responsible for forming uric acid from the precursor occupies itself with allopurinol instead, so that less uric acid can be formed. With this treatment, gout can be almost completely suppressed.

aloes. Subtropical plants, some of which yield laxatives of the same type as senna and cascara.

alopecia. Loss of hair. ►*baldness*.

alternative medicine. This is one of the many names applied to a group of widely different, sometimes contradictory doctrines. Other names include complementary, traditional, fringe, marginal, natural and holistic, but none really applies to all of a very mixed bag. Some are not alternatives to orthodox practice but additions to it; they are complementary. Various kinds of manipulation and of psychotherapy are of this kind.

WHO favours the term *traditional*, which fits ancient arts such as herbalism but hardly applies to more recent innovations such as chiropractic; neither can acupuncture or shiatsu claim to be traditional outside China and Japan. *Fringe* and *marginal* both sound slightly derogatory, and *natural* makes unwarranted assumptions about some of the doctrines: what is natural about a theory claiming, in defiance of the known facts of anatomy, that every organ in the body communicates with its chosen spot on the external ear, and that pricking the spot will put the organ to rights?

Holistic medicine means that it deals with the patient as a whole, and not merely with his ailments – which doctors from the time of Hippocrates have been taught to do. But it is sadly true that the advance of medical science has tended to obscure this principle and leave little time to consider the patient as a person. This is one reason for the popularity of alternative care; another is that the array of versatile and powerful drugs now available tempts doctors to prescribe, and patients to demand, more than is really needed. If massage relieves stress it is surely preferable to a drug that could be addictive.

Many kinds of alternative medicine are based on speculation unsupported by evidence, as was orthodox practice during all the centuries when the theories of Aristotle and Galen were not to be questioned. The mysterious East has always fascinated the West, and the ancient Chinese and Indian (Ayurveda) methods are now widely practised. Both accept the theory first formulated in Greece in the 5th century BC (>*Empedocles, Aristotle*) and not abandoned in Europe for 23 centuries, that the universe is made up of 4 or 5 elements guided by two opposed principles: positive and negative, light and dark, yin and yang. Untenable as the theory may be, the practice is frequently sound. To be sure, traditional medicine in China prescribes tiger's penis and in India rhinoceros horn to enhance virility, but against such absurdities may be set countless effective remedies. One of these, acupuncture, appears to depend on superstition, but there are too many witnesses to its successes to be discounted. Its working is the subject of intensive research in Chinese and other universities.

>*Paracelsus* dosed anaemic patients with iron because he associated iron with the planet Mars, and the red colour of the planet with that of blood; but that in no way detracts from its efficacy. Many current alternative theories may be untenable, but that does not make the practice ineffective. This also applies to much of orthodox medicine.

Many alternative therapies promote relaxation. They include various applications of massage, >*autogenic training*, and the soothing effects of music, colour and aroma. The effects on health of tension or stress, and its relief, are far-reaching. >*placebo* is discussed under that heading, and a few kinds of of alternative or complementary therapy are briefly considered under >*autogenic training, biofeedback, Chinese medicine, chiropractic, homoeopathy, naturopathy* and *osteopathy*.

alveolus. Small cavity or socket: toothsocket: air-pocket in the lung where oxygen diffuses into the blood and carbon dioxide escapes.

Alzheimer's disease. (Alois Alzheimer, 1864–1915, German neurologist.) A kind of dementia described by Alzheimer in 1906. Patchy degeneration of brain tissue leads to progressive loss of memory and later to disordered reasoning and patterns of behaviour. Alzheimer described it as a presenile condition, i.e. one occurring in late middle rather than old age, but in fact much senile dementia is due to the same condition. So far no effective treatment has been found (>*dementia*).

amanita. A genus of >*mushroom* (toadstool) of which several species are poisonous.

ambivalence. Conflicting emotions as a source of neurosis. ('Mixed feelings' is the same thing but without the suggestion of unresolved conflict and turmoil.)

amblyopia. Loss of vision – partial or complete, temporary or permanent – without apparent disorder of the eyes themselves; e.g. as a result of a stroke. Several forms of chronic poisoning can cause *toxic amblyopia*. The poisons include lead, arsenic, and benzene; the commonest are alcohol and tobacco.

amenorrhoea. Absence of menstrual periods. Literally, the term includes the state of girls before puberty and women after the menopause, but it is more sensibly confined to women of childbearing age who do not menstruate. *Primary* amenorrhoea means that menstruation has never begun: perhaps the most important point here is that some girls start late; but each case needs full investigation because some defect of structure or hormone balance may need attention.

Secondary amenorrhoea means that the patient who has previously had periods has stopped having them. The obvious and usual reasons are pregnancy and the menopause (which can be unexpectedly early). Otherwise the condition can be a symptom of all kinds of illness, including emotional upsets.

Amenorrhoea is not an illness but a symptom, and it is harmful in itself only because the feeling that she is not behaving normally disturbs the patient.

amentia. A word formerly used in psychiatry as a counterpart to *dementia*, to signify inborn mental defect as opposed to deterioration of a mind that was once healthy.

amino-acids. Chemically simple substances of which ➤*proteins* are composed. Hundreds of amino-acid molecules are linked together (➤*polypeptide*) to form a single molecule of a protein. Human proteins contain about 22 different kinds of amino-acid. Nine of these, the 'essential' amino-acids, cannot be synthesized by the liver and must be provided ready-made in the proteins of the diet. Animal proteins (meat, milk, eggs etc.) contain all the essential amino-acids, and are known as first-class proteins. Any good mixed diet contains enough of them to supply all the amino-acids that are needed. But in many poor parts of the world, the standard diet lacks not only protein in general, but first-class protein in particular. Children are especially vulnerable, and the malignant form of malnutrition ➤*kwashiorkor* is common where the miserable ration that they get is not even of good quality.

Lack of the amino-acid tryptophan is a factor in *pellagra*, a kind of malnutrition among people who live on maize.

Unwanted amino-acids are broken down by enzymes in the liver to sugars, which are consumed for energy, and nitrogenous waste, which is excreted by the kidneys. Patients whose kidneys are not working can be given a diet in which protein is replaced by measured quantities of the right amino-acids, so that there will be no surplus waste to burden the kidneys or to accumulate in poisonous amounts because the kidneys cannot excrete them.

➤*Phenylketonuria* is a hereditary disorder in which the enzyme for breaking down the amino-acid phenylalanine is lacking.

aminophylline. Theophylline-ethylene-diamine; a synthetic compound of the natural alkaloid theophylline, used to dilate blood vessels (e.g. with angina) and to relieve asthma.

amnesia. Loss of memory. The term is not applied to forgetfulness or the gradual deterioration of memory as one grows older, but to sudden and complete loss of memory over a particular time or particular events. Only two types are at all common: 'found wandering, suffering from loss of memory' is nearly always a kind of acute neurosis; the patient may forget his name, where he lives and so on, but in fact his memory is suppressed, not lost. A severe emotional shock, more than he can bear to remember, is a likely cause. Investigation and psychotherapy are needed. The second type is *retrograde amnesia* after an injury to the head. Here, the patient has no memory of events leading up to the injury, and in this case the loss is real and permanent. It has been suggested that some time must elapse before memories are put into storage, and concussion during this time interrupts the process – so these 'lost' memories were never stored, never reached the stage of being true memories. Concussion does not affect earlier memories.

amniocentesis. Taking a specimen of amniotic fluid, to be examined as a guide to the condition of an unborn baby. Towards the end of pregnancy, the specimen can be taken from below, through the cervix of the uterus. Chemical and microscopical examination may indicate, for example, that the baby is undernourished and should be brought into the world as soon as possible for treatment before irreparable damage is done. Amniocentesis can also be carried out early in pregnancy if the family history suggests a strong possibility of serious congenital disease, which may be indicated by defects in the cells shed from the baby's skin into the fluid. At this stage the specimen may be taken through the abdominal wall. The needle is guided with the help of an ultrasonic echo device, on the principle of a marine depth-sounder, which indicates the position of the baby in relation to the needle. If the examination shows that the baby is certain to be grossly abnormal, there is no need to let the pregnancy go any further. Scanning, especially with ultrasound (►*scan*), gives more detailed information than X-ray examination, without risk to the baby. There is every hope that in future many couples who would have avoided pregnancy because the risk of a serious congenital defect was too high will be able to have children of their own, knowing that they can be told whether the foetus is affected or healthy at an early enough stage for an abortion to be easy and safe. ►*genetics*.

amnion. Membranous bag containing amniotic fluid, a watery liquid in which a baby floats in the uterus until birth.

amoeba. A very simple animal; a kind of ►*protozoon*. The species *Entamoeba histolytica* causes amoebic dysentery.

amphetamine. A drug related to adrenaline; it has been used to relieve nasal congestion, for slimming (by suppressing appetite) and to combat lethargy and depression. There are safer ways of doing all these things. Amphetamine, which has taken the place of cocaine among drugs of addiction, can injure the heart and cause serious mental derangement if taken habitually.

Amphetamine first became popular in the 1930s, mainly in the form of an inhaler for relieving congestion in the nose. It was not very efficient because, although it gave instant relief, when the effect wore off the congestion became worse than it had been before. Tablets of this or one of the related drugs were also widely used as a mental stimulant or pick-me-up, and later for suppressing appetite. The tablets were subjected to restrictions in the same way as sulphonamides and other drugs thought to be potentially harmful but not liable to deliberate abuse. Drug addicts seem to have noticed before most doctors that the effect of amphetamine drugs on the brain is like that of cocaine. In Britain, thanks largely to the initiative of the Pharmaceutical Society, these drugs are now as strictly controlled as heroin and cocaine, and they are seldom prescribed.

ampicillin. A synthetic derivative of penicillin, effective against a wider range of infections than the natural penicillins, and fully active when taken by mouth.

amputation. Surgical removal or accidental loss of a limb. Until the discovery of anaesthetics and antiseptics in the second half of the 19th century amputation was probably the commonest surgical operation. It was dangerous but offered the only hope of preventing fatal gangrene after major injuries to limbs.

As recently as the First World War amputation was the routine treatment for compound fractures (those where the broken bone was exposed in a wound and infected).

With the advance of plastic surgery, including the repair of severed blood vessels, and the use of antibiotics to overcome infection, amputation is now much less often needed; and although it remains the surgeon's last resort it has been made less deplorable than it was by the ingenuity of modern artificial-limb makers.

The usual purpose of amputation is to save life, but in some cases where there is no immediate danger to life a limited amputation done soon may save a more extensive operation later: for instance, gangrenous toes cannot be restored, but removing them may save the rest of the limb.

amyl nitrite. A drug used for treating angina pectoris (▸ *ischaemic heart disease*).

amyloid disease (amyloid degeneration, amyloidosis, lardaceous disease). A gradual change in living cells, usually a result of severe and long-standing infection elsewhere in the body, and presumably a sort of slow poisoning. Affected organs have a pale, waxy (lardaceous) appearance. The name *amyloid* (starch-like) was given because affected tissue forms a dark stain with iodine, as does starch. The function of such organs (liver, kidneys, heart) gradually deteriorates. The usual causes are tuberculosis, chronic lung disease, and chronic infection of bone. But since these diseases have to be active for a long time before amyloidosis sets in, and they can now be controlled with antibiotic drugs, amyloidosis is no longer the common condition that it used to be.

Amyloidosis cannot be treated directly, but it may be arrested or even reversed when the underlying infection is cured.

anabolic steroids. Derivatives of the male sex hormone testosterone introduced in the 1960s as body-builders for patients emaciated, e.g., by prolonged illness. Thought at the time to be true tonics (when all existing alleged tonics were anything but true), their popularity declined when despite exhaustive trials the benefits were overshadowed by side-effects, especially virilization in women and liver damage in either sex. At present they are used mainly in certain types of anaemia to increase the formation of blood cells, and, illicitly, by athletes hoping to strengthen their muscles.

anabolism. Chemical synthesis of new substances in the body.

anaemia. Literally, anaemia means lack of blood, but in fact it is shortage of ▸ *haemoglobin*, the oxygen-carrying pigment of the red blood cells (▸ *blood* (2)). The effects of anaemia are due to shortage of oxygen throughout the body.

Symptoms are vague (though very real) unless the anaemia is severe and the concentration of haemoglobin is reduced to, say, half the normal value. Acceleration of the heart beat keeps the available haemoglobin circulating more quickly and to some extent compensates for the deficiency; in time, untreated anaemia can overtax the heart. The patient feels weary and inefficient, looks pale, and may suffer headache, slight fever, and physical weakness. But anaemia is itself only a symptom and not a disease in its own right, and symptoms ascribed to anaemia are often due to the underlying disorder which is causing the anaemia.

Anaemia may be due either to abnormal loss of haemoglobin or to defective production. The types to be considered are:

A. Abnormal loss, due to
  1. bleeding;
  2. excessive destruction of red cells
B. Defective production due to
  1. iron deficiency;
  2. vitamin deficiency (including pernicious anaemia);
  3. other causes

A. EXCESSIVE LOSS OF HAEMOGLOBIN

1. *Bleeding.* The danger of severe and rapid bleeding is not anaemia but death from ▸*shock*. If someone suddenly loses a quarter of his blood he still has 75 per cent of his haemoglobin, which is more than enough to keep him going, but the loss of a quart from the total volume of a gallon may reduce his blood pressure to a dangerously low level. Blood transfusion is needed after a sudden haemorrhage to combat decreased volume of blood rather than anaemia.

The first response to bleeding (apart from purely local effects such as clotting) is reflex constriction of blood vessels in the less vital parts of the body such as the skin, which reduces the space to be filled with blood and so maintains the pressure. In the next few hours the remaining blood is diluted with water from the tissues to restore the volume, and in the next few weeks the lost red cells and haemoglobin are restored. If the bleeding is spread over, say, 24 hours, so that the volume of blood can be maintained by dilution, a man can survive the loss of half of his blood. He will be severely anaemic for a time, and he will be all the better for a blood transfusion, but his case need not be desperate.

Continuous slow bleeding, or repeated losses of small amounts of blood, deplete the body's reserves of iron until the lost haemoglobin can no longer be replaced (▸B.1, below).

2. *Excessive destruction.* Healthy red cells live about 4 months. When they die they are treated as foreign bodies and digested in the same way as bacteria, by white cells in the spleen, liver and elsewhere. They are replaced by new cells from the bone marrow, which has no difficulty in meeting reasonable demands. But if the destruction of red cells (*haemolysis*) increases beyond about six times the normal rate, the marrow cannot keep pace; demand exceeds supply and a *haemolytic anaemia* develops.

When haemoglobin is broken down by haemolysis, its iron is stored for future use, leaving a yellow pigment, *bilirubin*, which passes through the liver into the bile to be excreted by way of the intestine. If there is too much haemolysis, bilirubin accumulates, and the complexion is tinted yellow. Thus ▸*jaundice* is often seen with haemolytic anaemias.

Haemolytic anaemia can be due to an abnormality that makes the red cells unduly fragile. Two such abnormalities – sickle-cell anaemia and Cooley's anaemia – are described under ▸*haemoglobin*. In pernicious anaemia (▸B.2, below), not enough red cells are formed, and those that are formed are liable to early haemolysis; so this is a case of deficiency anaemia with haemolytic anaemia added.

Many poisons damage red cells and cause haemolytic anaemia. They include lead, various derivatives of benzene, and some kinds of snake venom. Some people become sensitized to a drug that would otherwise be harmless, and may develop haemolytic anaemia if they take the drug again. In people whose red cells lack the enzyme G-6-PD, numerous drugs and also some foods (fava beans) cause severe haemolysis. This defect is commonest around the Mediterranean, or in people with Mediterranean ancestors.

Much the commonest cause of haemolytic anaemia around the world is >*malaria*, because malaria parasites enter and destroy red blood cells.

Outside the tropics, most cases of haemolytic anaemia are due to >*autoimmunity*: the body treats its own red cells as foreign matter and destroys them in the way that it destroys bacteria. A variant of this kind of anaemia occurs in unborn babies whose blood is incompatible with the mother's (>*rhesus factor*).

Only severe episodes of haemolytic anaemia call for treatment other than the treatment of the cause when it is known (e.g. treating malaria, avoiding an offending drug). With the more obscure types, haemolysis tends to come in waves, when for a time the patient becomes very anaemic, and needs transfusions of healthy blood. A curious complication of the disease and its treatment is overloading with iron, because haemolysis involves no loss of iron from the body and repeated transfusions put more and more in. After scores of transfusions enough may be stored to be harmful; the excess can, however, be removed chemically (>*iron*).

B. DEFECTIVE PRODUCTION

1. *Iron deficiency*. The complication just described arises because the body hoards iron regardless of need, presumably because iron is difficult to absorb and the diet seldom contains an excess. When red cells break down after a normal life of 3 or 4 months, their iron is stored for use in new cells. The diet has only to replace small amounts lost in cells shed from the skin and intestine (>*iron*).

A man's 5 litres of blood contains 2.5 g iron, and the reserve, stored mainly in the liver, is about half this amount. If he bleeds, the bone marrow replaces the lost blood cells quite quickly, but the cells can be given their full complement of haemoglobin only while the stores of iron last. Iron lost by slow bleeding can be replaced in the diet only at a rate corresponding to a few ml of blood daily. Even slight losses of blood from, say, piles or a duodenal ulcer will cause anaemia if the bleeding continues long enough.

One of the commonest causes of unsuspected anaemia is bleeding into the stomach from abuse of aspirin (>*analgesic*).

Women are much more vulnerable than men. An average Western diet barely keeps pace with even an average monthly loss, and if the loss is excessive, or other bleeding is added to it, a woman is liable to become anaemic. The 'normal' percentage of haemoglobin in the blood is often said to be lower in women than men, but here 'normal' may be confused with 'average', which is not the same. It has been shown in some large surveys that about a sixth of the adult women in Britain are anaemic, and a further third (making 50 per cent in all) have virtually no iron in reserve to meet emergencies.

There is a special risk of iron deficiency at certain times. During the years of growth a child needs iron not only to maintain the blood but to increase it and this leaves little chance of building up any reserves. When a girl reaches puberty she may have no stored iron, and with the onset of menstruation she becomes anaemic. The underfed factory girls of the 19th century developed a gross iron-deficiency anaemia known as *chlorosis* (from the yellowish complexion).

During pregnancy and while feeding a baby a woman has to provide for the baby's needs from her own iron stores, but the fact that she is not menstruating compensates to some extent for this loss. However, the milk provided by the mother contains no more than just enough iron for the baby's needs. When weaning begins, cereal foods provide a better source.

Symptoms are apt to be more severe with iron deficiency than with the same degree of anaemia from some other cause. This is because small amounts of iron are needed by many tissues other than blood. Cracked lips and deformed fingernails are caused by shortage of iron-containing enzymes, and some part of the general unfitness may arise in the same way.

Iron deficiency is usually due to bleeding. Poor diet is seldom the sole cause, but inability to absorb iron from the food may be, particularly after major operations on the stomach and small intestine.

The best sources of iron are meat, eggs, cereals and leguminous vegetables such as beans. Vitamin C, in fresh fruit and vegetables, is needed for iron to be assimilated from the food. A good mixed diet meets the normal demands. But when the stored iron has been depleted, a medicinal supplement is needed. Ferrous sulphate is the most widely used, but many other iron salts are suitable. Only a small amount can be assimilated at a time, and if the case is urgent (e.g. at the end of pregnancy) the iron can be given by injection instead of by mouth.

The symptoms of iron deficiency im-prove almost as soon as treatment is begun, and the patient, feeling better, often stops taking the preparation. In fact, she may need several months of treatment to build up adequate reserves. Sydenham, the first person to use iron systematically, treated his anaemic patients for as long as a year.

2. *Vitamin deficiency and pernicious anaemia.* Anaemia can be a symptom of most forms of malnutrition, because most of the components of a good diet play some part in the formation of blood. Two vitamins are especially involved: vitamin B_{12}, and folic acid. Although they are chemically unrelated, deficiency of either has the same effect on the blood: the development of red cells is arrested. Too few cells are formed, and those that are formed are misshapen and fragile, so that a haemolytic anaemia is added to the primary disorder. Lack of folic acid causes only the anaemia, but lack of vitamin B_{12} affects other tissues, in particular the nervous system. Severe and prolonged B_{12} deficiency can lead to partial paralysis of the limbs.

Folic acid deficiency can be due to lack of vegetables, to poor absorption in states of chronic diarrhoea (e.g. ►*sprue*), or to increased demand (e.g. in pregnancy).

Vitamin B_{12} deficiency is nearly always due to failure to absorb the vitamin. To be absorbed it has first to be combined with *intrinsic factor*, a protein formed in the stomach. After very drastic operations on the stomach there is sometimes a shortage of intrinsic factor and therefore defective absorption of vitamin B_{12}.

But much the most important disease of this class is *pernicious (Addisonian) anaemia*. It was first described in 1849 by Addison, of Guy's Hospital, London, as 'a very remarkable form of general anaemia, occurring without any discoverable cause whatever'; it was invariably fatal. In 1872 Biermer of Zürich called it 'pernicious anaemia'; in some countries it is now known as Biermer's anaemia. It remained hopelessly untreatable until 1926, when G. R. Minot and W. P. Murphy, following work on dogs by G. H. Whipple, showed that raw liver cured the disease. These three American physicians shared a Nobel Prize in 1934. The curative factor, vitamin B_{12}, was isolated in 1948, and its structure was established in 1955. Pernicious anaemia is now treated with regular doses of the vitamin, which completely control it.

The fundamental disorder in pernicious anaemia is in the stomach and not the blood. Why the lining of the stomach should stop producing the intrinsic factor (and, incidentally, acid) is not known; an autoimmune process has been suggested (>autoimmunity).

3. *Other causes.* All chronic infection (tuberculosis etc.) leads to some degree of anaemia; nobody knows why, or how to treat the anaemia apart from curing the infection. Anaemia is, not surprisingly, a symptom of leukaemia, but it is also common with other types of cancer, more than can be explained by bleeding: indeed, some cancers do not bleed at all, yet cause anaemia.

Advanced kidney disease causes anaemia, perhaps because the hormone erythropoietin, which promotes red-cell formation, is secreted by the kidneys, and diseased kidneys fail to secrete it.

Certain poisons affect the bone marrow. Suppression of all blood-cell formation leads to *aplastic anaemia*, an uncommon but highly dangerous state; one can only keep the patient alive with blood transfusions, and hope that the marrow will recover in time. The causes of aplastic anaemia are the same as those of lack of white cells (leucopenia) >blood (3).

anaerobic. Living without air (oxygen). >aerobic.

anaesthesia. Absence of sensation, either in the whole body (general anaesthesia) or in a part (local anaesthesia). Anaesthesia may be induced by drugs or other means (>anaesthetics), or it may be a symptom of a defect in the nervous system.

Sensation means awareness in the brain of change elsewhere in the body. Impulses are conveyed along nerves to the spinal cord and then by several relays to the higher centres of the brain and consciousness. Different kinds of sensation are conveyed separately and are not necessarily all lost together. When a nerve is compressed the sense of touch is lost before that of pain, whereas local anaesthetic drugs abolish pain first. Sensation is abolished or diminished by obstructing the impulse at any point on its path. Since nerves contain sensory fibres carrying impulses to the brain and motor fibres carrying impulses to muscles from the brain, damage to a nerve impairs movement as well as sensation. Typical causes are wounds, infection (a notorious example is leprosy), and compression (as when a foot 'goes to sleep' from pressure on the sciatic nerve by the edge of a chair). An impulse in a nerve is a small electrical charge resulting from movement of potassium out of the nerve fibre and sodium into it; the original balance is restored as soon as the impulse has passed on. Local anaesthetics prevent sodium from entering the fibre, 'blocking' the nerve by making it unable to hold an electrical charge.

In the spinal cord and brain, sensory

and motor nerve fibres are in separate bundles, and one may be impaired while the other is intact, or only a particular type of sensation may be lost. It has even been possible to relieve pain that responded to no other treatment by operating on the spinal cord to interrupt pain fibres from the affected region without disturbing others.

General anaesthesia follows blockage of impulses in the brain. It is seen in all forms of coma (injuries, epilepsy, stroke, intoxication etc.). How anaesthetic drugs work in the brain is not known. Some drugs (e.g. morphine in small doses) appear to affect the attitude to pain rather than prevent the impulses from reaching consciousness – pain is perceived but the subject does not mind. Whether pain that does not hurt can still be called pain is a question of philosophy rather than physiology. It is an important question, because in some cases of hysteria there is total anaesthesia of part of the body without any apparent disorder of conduction in nerve fibres. A hypnotist can abolish pain by suggestion, and most people have experienced injuries that ought to have hurt but did not because they were preoccupied. In other words, awareness of pain can sometimes be suppressed in the same way as awareness of the ticking of a clock, or awareness of the touch of clothing.

anaesthetics (➤*anaesthesia*). Anaesthetic drugs abolish sensation either in a restricted area (local anaesthetics) or in the whole body (general anaesthetics).

1. LOCAL ANAESTHETICS

The cola plant (*Erythroxylon*) is a traditional drug of addiction among Peruvian Indians. In 1860 Niemann isolated the active principle *cocaine* from cola leaves, and in 1884 Koller used the drug for painless surgery of the eye. Cocaine is rapidly absorbed by the mucous membranes around the eye, in the nose and mouth and elsewhere, producing complete numbness. It was also given by injection. But cocaine has many undesirable effects and in 1905 it was largely superseded by a synthetic drug, *procaine*, that could safely be injected into the area of an operation. Numerous drugs related to procaine are now in use. They can be injected into the immediate area of operation, or around nerves carrying impulses from the area, e.g. inside the angle of the jaw to anaesthetize the lower teeth. For some operations on the lower half of the body a local anaesthetic is injected around the spinal cord in the small of the back.

2. GENERAL ANAESTHETICS

From very early times surgeons have used drugs to lessen pain during operations. Substances extracted from two of the oldest pain-killers (morphine from poppies, hyoscyamine from henbane) are still used to prepare patients for general anaesthesia, but not for anaesthesia itself. Such drugs dull both perception and memory of pain, but doses large enough to abolish pain are apt to be lethal. The same applies to alcohol. One could do painless surgery on a man who was dead drunk, but one could not predict the appropriate dose (even if it did not make him vomit). The time-lag while alcohol takes effect adds to the danger, for there is no way to tell how much more effect is still to come and no way of keeping the effect within the bounds of safety.

Many good anaesthetics act like alcohol but with a different time-scale.

They are very quickly absorbed by inhalation of their vapour, and since they act within seconds their effect can be held up at any stage by giving no more. Anaesthesia is rapidly induced and then kept at the desired level with a mere trickle of vapour. Recovery begins as soon as the anaesthetic is stopped. *Ether* (diethyl ether) is a drug of this type. It was used for the first operation under general anaesthesia by an American surgeon, C. W. Long, in 1842, and became generally accepted after demonstrations in 1846 by W. T. G. Morton in Boston, Mass., and Robert Liston in London.

A year later (Sir) James Young Simpson, an Edinburgh gynaecologist, showed that *chloroform* was easier to use and less unpleasant for the patient. It caused less agitation in the preliminary stage of anaesthesia, less coughing, and less nausea. For many years chloroform was the most widely used general anaesthetic, but in the end it became clear that ether, for all its disadvantages, was a safer drug for long operations. Chloroform held its place for very short operations.

Nitrous oxide ('laughing gas') was first used by an American dentist, Horace Wells, in 1844. It is still the safest and easiest means of inducing light anaesthesia for small operations such as dental extraction, and for major operations it can be mixed with more powerful agents.

Many drugs related to ether or chloroform have been tried; so far the most successful has been *halothane*. Even this, though safer and more reliable than other drugs of its class, shares with them the disadvantage that it occasionally damages the liver, especially if used repeatedly on the same patient.

Some important anaesthetics are injected into a vein. The first were *barbiturates*, closely related to drugs used to promote sleep but with a much more rapid and transient effect. The patient slips into unconsciousness in a few seconds, without preliminary agitation. The earliest of these, *hexobarbitone*, was introduced in Germany in 1933. The most widely used has been *thiopentone*. Recently some short-acting anaesthetics given by injection have come into use, e.g. *propofol*, which has the advantage that it leaves no hangover, and *ketamine*. Benzodiazepines such as *midazolam* act rapidly enough when injected to make them useful as anaesthetics.

3. SUPPLEMENTARY METHODS

In the past, the early stages of an anaesthetic were apt to be stormy. Until the patient lost consciousness he could suffer a spell of excitement amounting to delirium, and it was common practice to anticipate this by strapping him down. A narcotic such as morphine injected beforehand calmed the patient and also served to reinforce the anaesthetic.

An additional hazard was excessive secretion of saliva and of fluid into the lungs when the anaesthetic had suppressed the cough reflex, which could lead to post-operative pneumonia. A drug such as *atropine* or *hyoscine* added to the narcotic diminishes these secretions and their attendant risks.

The anaesthetics now in use are much less prone to these complications than the old ether and chloroform, but premedication remains an important part of an anaesthetist's practice. There is still a place for the traditional morphine and hyoscine, but sedation with one of the benzodiazepines, e.g. diazepam, may be all that is needed. In general it may be said that modern anaesthetists take each case on its merits, using quick-acting drugs as the need arises rather than giving them in advance as used to be customary.

Controlled respiration, or rhythmic inflation of the lungs without the patient's help, has made anaesthesia safer and greatly extended the scope of surgery. Given a simple apparatus it no longer matters if the patient ceases to breathe of his own accord, and the chest can be as safely opened as the abdomen.

The practice of controlled respiration made possible a very important advance in anaesthesia, namely the use of *curare*. The action of this drug, which prevents muscles from responding to their motor nerves, was described by Claude Bernard in 1856, but curare was not used with anaesthetics until 1946. For many operations the surgeon needs the patient's muscles to be relaxed. He generally has to work in a gap between muscles, and he cannot see what he is doing unless the muscles are lax enough to be separated. The more powerful anaesthetics cause muscles to relax, but only at an advanced stage of anaesthesia. If curare has been given, only enough anaesthetic to abolish sensation is needed, and this means a very much smaller and safer dose. With effective methods of inflating the lungs artificially the action of curare on the muscles of the chest does not matter.

To former generations of surgeons, the inside of the heart seemed to be an impregnable barrier. A very few smash-and-grab operations were possible, but anything that interrupted the flow of fresh blood from the heart for more than 3 minutes was believed to cause irreparable damage to the brain. It was then observed that when working at lower temperatures the brain could function without fresh blood, or fresh supplies of oxygen carried from the lungs in the blood, for much longer. Lowering the body temperature from the normal 37 ° to 28 °C increases the period of grace from 3 to 10 minutes; with very elaborate apparatus the temperature can be lowered to 10 °C, giving the surgeon a whole hour.

A second method is a cardiopulmonary bypass: a machine to take over the work of the lungs in oxygenating the blood, and of the heart in pumping it round the body. In theory, this method sets no time limit to keeping the heart out of action, and it has made possible such operations as heart transplants.

analeptic. Restorative, especially as applied to drugs given to stimulate breathing. In the past analeptic drugs enjoyed a better reputation than they deserved, and were given to almost anyone who collapsed. *Picrotoxin*, in regular use for a century or so despite its toxicity, was superseded by *nikethamide* in the 1930s, but this, too, is no longer favoured. The problem with these drugs and many others that have been tried and rejected is that an effective dose is dangerously near to a toxic one. A few, notably *doxapram*, still have a place, but only under close supervision, e.g. during recovery from an anaesthetic.

Respiratory failure is generally best treated by some form of assisted ventilation.

analgesia. Absence of the sense of pain, as opposed to *anaesthesia*, absence of all sensation.

Patient-controlled analgesia (PCA) is a boon to patients liable to severe pain, including pain immediately following major surgery. A PCA device allows the patient to inject a dose of a drug such as morphine as soon as he feels the need; after a set interval he can repeat the dose. Most patients give themselves *less* of the drug than would normally be prescribed.

analgesic (analgetic). (1) lacking the sense of pain. (2) relieving pain; drug used to relieve pain.

Many drugs have analgesic effects, including all >*anaesthetics* and >*narcotics*, which were formerly the only effective drugs for relieving pain (e.g. alcohol; opium), at the cost of stupefying the patient. Tranquillizers and hypnotics, taken in the usual doses, relieve mental turmoil or promote sleep but have little direct effect on pain except, perhaps, to make the patient more able to bear it. But all these classes of drugs overlap: thus the barbiturates are primarily hypnotics, but very small doses calm the patient without putting him to sleep and large doses are anaesthetic. Some drugs act at the source of a pain: for instance, *atropine* relieves intestinal colic by relaxing the painful spasm of the intestinal muscles. But analgesia is taken to mean blunting the conscious perception of pain. The drugs to be considered here, known as non-narcotic analgesics, are used to relieve pain regardless of its source, without impairing other faculties. These drugs are nearly all related to one of three substances discovered in Germany in the 19th century, namely *salicylic acid* (1874), *phenazone* (1883), and *phenacetin* (1887). In addition to dulling pain they are all antipyretic, i.e. they lower raised body temperature, and most of them reduce inflammation. The actions on pain and temperature take place in the brain. There is no effect on a normal temperature, but if the temperature is high the drugs act on a centre in the brain which controls sweating. The action on inflammation is most noticeable with rheumatic diseases. According to the use to which they are put, these drugs are known as analgesic, antipyretic, or anti-inflammatory.

Only the analgesic effect need be considered here. The antipyretic effect, though formerly much esteemed, is seldom useful, because lowering a raised body temperature without investigating the cause of the fever might do more harm than good. The value of these drugs with minor infections such as common colds lies not in lowering the temperature but in allaying headache and other miseries. The anti-inflammatory effect, shared with some other drugs, is discussed under >*anti-inflammatory*.

Salicylic acid, though useful in ointments, irritates the stomach too much to be given by mouth. Its salt *sodium salicylate* is better, and used to be given routinely for rheumatic fever, but by far the most widely used derivative is >*aspirin* (acetylsalicylic acid). This versatile drug is considered under its own heading.

Phenazone and its derivative *aminophenazone* (*amidopyrine*) were used in the same way as salicylates in some countries, though not in Britain, where early reports of serious damage to the blood cells discouraged their use. A much more recent derivative, *phenylbutazone*, has much enhanced analgesic and anti-inflammatory effects, but has inherited the same threat to the blood cells.

Phenacetin was in general use for three-quarters of a century before anyone proved that taken over a long period it poisons the kidneys. It has been superseded by *paracetamol*. The analgesic effect of phenacetin is due to paracetamol, which is separated by digestion from para-phenetidin, the substance that injures the kidneys. But neither is paracetamol as safe as at first it was thought to be. Overdoses can cause irreversible and potentially fatal damage to the liver. Phenacetin and paracetamol have little anti-inflammatory action.

Codeine really belongs to the group of narcotic analgesics, because it is a natural component of opium and closely related to morphine. In very small doses, however, and combined with agents such as aspirin, it is used as a minor analgesic. Codeine is also used to control troublesome coughs. A drawback is that it causes constipation. Several other drugs are on the borderline between simple analgesics and narcotics, e.g. *pentazocine* and dextropropoxyphene. Pethidine, once thought to be in this class, has fewer side-effects than morphine, but is almost as liable to cause addiction.

Some other pain-relieving drugs are classified as ➤*anti-inflammatory*.

analogous. Having similar function but different origin (of anatomical structures); e.g. lungs and gills, as opposed to *homologous* organs with different function but similar origin, e.g. arms and wings.

anamnesis. Account of previous illnesses, an aid to the diagnosis of the present condition. (The word is more often used in other languages; 'case history' is commoner in English.)

anaphylaxis ➤*allergy*.

anaplasia. A tendency of cancer cells to resemble the cells of an embryo rather than adult types. Whether this represents a survival of embryonic cell-types into adult life or a reversion of adult cells to an earlier type is not known.

anastomosis. 1 (anat.). Direct communication between two arteries, or between an artery and a vein without an intervening capillary network. Most arteries communicate with other arteries, and if one is obstructed others can take over its work. An *end artery* is one without anas-

tomoses. If it is blocked, e.g. by a blood-clot, the tissue beyond it is likely to die. Many of the terminal branches of the arteries in the brain, kidney, and intestine are end arteries, and the coronary arteries of the heart do not have enough effective anastomoses to deal with a sudden blockage. Arterio-venous anastomoses are between very small branches, e.g. those of the ➤*renal* artery in the kidney.

2 (surg.). Artificial opening between two tubular structures; operation to establish this. The commonest surgical anastomoses are between the cut ends of stomach or intestine when a part has been removed.

anatomy. In former times the word was used in its literal meaning of dissection or cutting apart; but it has come to mean the knowledge gained by dissection of the structure and arrangement of the various parts of the body. It is the primary discipline of scientific medicine, for without knowing something of the structure of an organism we cannot begin to understand how it works (*physiology*), or what can go wrong with it (*pathology*).

The earliest attempts to study anatomy of which any record remains were by the Greek physician ➤*Alcmaeon* (*c.* 500 BC). He was followed a century later by ➤*Aristotle*, who of all the ancients had the greatest influence on the later development of science.

The first real anatomist seems to have been Herophilus of Alexandria, around 300 BC. He described what he saw in dissections of bodies, not what prevailing theories said he ought to see. In this respect he had no known predecessors and not many successors. Herophilus described the nervous system and brain and their function, most of the abdominal organs, and the major blood vessels. He distinguished arteries from veins and insisted, contrary to current opinion, that the arteries contained blood and not air.

The greatest anatomist of antiquity was Galen in the 2nd century AD, who was to be the last for many centuries. He described the structure of the body in great detail but with two kinds of mistake: much of his human anatomy was inferred from his study of animals; and if facts did not fit theories then the facts had to suffer. Galen's mistakes would not have mattered if they had not been enshrined for the next twelve centuries and more. The Church approved of Galen and Aristotle. Their Stoic philosophy with its suggestion of divine planning was easily adapted to Christian teaching (also to Jewish and Moslem teaching). Because the Church approved, nobody dared to question Galen's authority – besides, theology was the one true science and nobody thought the human body worth studying.

Even Galen's work would have been lost if it had not been nurtured by Moslem scholars. When learning at last revived in Europe, Avicenna's Arabic translation of Galen became a standard text. Even then, professors of anatomy were still content to teach by intoning ancient doctrines; the few dissections were done by menials to whose work scholars paid little attention – if the facts shown in the body disagreed with approved authority then the body must be wrong. The first exception was Mondino, professor at Bologna, whose *Anatomia* (1316) was at least partly based on his own observations. His example was not followed until two centuries later when the artists took a hand. Leonardo's drawings of his own dissections are without

equal. But his concern was beauty of design, not medical progress, and his many discoveries did not reach the doctors of the time. It was left to Vesalius, a generation later, to establish anatomy as a science.

Vesalius published *De humani corporis fabrica* in 1543. He was then 29 years old, and had held the chair of anatomy and surgery at Padua for six years. This work is the beginning of modern medicine. It is a precise record of observed facts, where all earlier authors had recorded opinion and speculation.

Before Vesalius, doctrines had been judged by the personal authority of the teacher. What Aristotle or Galen or Avicenna had said was taken for revealed truth, not to be questioned. Vesalius asked nobody to believe anything simply because he had said so; he asked them to look for themselves. Therefore his errors and omissions were not perpetuated. The great anatomists who followed him at Padua had only to make further dissections to complete the work that Vesalius had so brilliantly started, and by 1600, when Harvey was a student at Padua, anatomy had progressed almost as far as the naked eye could take it. By discovering the circulation of the blood Harvey founded modern physiology – the study of how the body works based on the knowledge of how it is constructed.

In the 17th century the focus moved from Italy to Holland. The University of Leyden, under the influence of Boerhaave, took the lead from Padua, and the next great advance in anatomy – the use of a microscope – was introduced by the Italian Malpighi and developed by Leeuwenhoek and numerous other Dutchmen. *Histology*, the microscopical study of tissues, became even more important to physiologists than to anatomists; and in the 19th century, under the influence of Virchow, was the basis of a completely new approach to the study of disease. The microscope also revolutionized ➤*embryology*.

In the 18th century, mainly under the influence of ➤*Bichat*, interest moved from entire organs to their component tissues (*histology*). A century later the German pathologist ➤*Virchow* took histology further by considering cells – the building blocks of tissues and organs – and their components (*cytology*). Beyond cytology *biochemistry* takes over from anatomy to study molecules and atoms, and their interplay in the living body.

Present-day anatomy also studies development from conception to birth (*embryology*) and compares the structure and evolution of different species (*morphology*). This book offers brief summaries under the headings of regions of the body, of organs and of systems (digestive, nervous, etc.).

Ancylostoma (Ankylostoma). Hookworm (➤*worms*).

androgen. Any substance acting as a male *sex hormone*.

androsterone. One of the male sex hormones.

anencephaly. Failure of the brain to grow in an embryo, a rare and lethal defect.

aneurin = *vitamin B₁* (thiamine).

aneurysm. A bulge at a weak spot in the wall of an artery. Arteries carry blood at a considerable pressure, and their walls need to be tough.

An aneurysm need not cause any trouble unless it is large enough to interfere with neighbouring organs; but there is a danger that the bulge may give way and lead to serious internal bleeding.

The commonest cause of aneurysm used to be *syphilis*, which usually affected the upper part of the aorta. At present *atheroma* is a more usual cause; it most often affects the lower part of the aorta. Considering that most of us develop atheroma in time, these aneurysms are not very common. A few aneurysms are due to a congenital weakness in the wall of the aorta. Other possible causes are injuries to blood vessels (especially if they create a short-circuit between an artery and a vein) and bacterial infection.

Small but dangerous aneurysms occur in the arteries at the base of the brain. They are due to a hereditary defect of the connective tissue of the arteries, but there is seldom trouble in early life. These aneurysms may cause symptoms by compressing nerves, or they may bleed and cause a stroke.

Only surgical treatment has any effect on aneurysms. John Hunter (1728–93) was, as in so much else, the pioneer. If an aneurysm is shaped like a balloon (saccular aneurysm) it may be possible to tie a thread round its neck and remove it. If, as is more likely, the bulge extends along an artery, the artery itself must be sealed above and below the aneurysm. With a small artery, neighbouring vessels can supply blood to the region, but with a main artery the flow has to be restored. In the past the problem has sometimes been solved by leaving the aneurysm and reinforcing its walls with fibrous tissue taken from another part of the body, but the method is not reliable. Arteries could be grafted in the same way as skin, but the patient has no large arteries to spare. Veins are expendable and can be used as grafts, and in time the transplanted vein takes on the structure of an artery. Another method is to insert a tube of synthetic fabric. Even a defective length of aorta can be replaced in this way. A smooth plastic tube does not work as well as a finely woven fabric which can become impregnated with the patient's own living tissue.

angina. 1. A sense of suffocation. **2.** Acute infection in the throat or mouth such as a *quinsy* (abscess around a tonsil), or *Vincent's angina* (trench mouth). **3.** *Angina pectoris*: pain, usually in the chest, or a sense of suffocation, brought on by exertion, excitement, etc. (the usual sense of angina). The pain may radiate to the neck, jaw, arms or upper abdomen; occasionally it is confined to one of these places and obscures the diagnosis. Characteristically it passes off within minutes of stopping the activity that brought it on.

The immediate cause is an insufficient supply of blood and therefore of oxygen to the heart muscle. This can be due to a defective heart valve, or even to severe anaemia; but angina is usually a symptom of arteriosclerosis of the coronary arteries complicating *atheroma*. The pain probably arises from irritant acids that accumulate in any muscle deprived of oxygen.

Angina is only a symptom, and its treatment is symptomatic. The value of certain nitrogen compounds has been known for over a century. *Amyl nitrite*, formerly much used, is a volatile liquid, dispensed in capsules to be crushed so that the vapour can be inhaled. *Glyceryl trinitrate* can be absorbed from under the tongue, injected intravenously or applied to the skin in an adhesive patch for a sustained effect. They relieve angina mainly by dilating blood vessels elsewhere to reduce resistance to flow and ease the burden on the heart. They are best used to anticipate an attack, for instance *before* climbing a flight of stairs that has previously brought on the pain. *Isosorbide dinitrate* has a similar but more lasting effect.

Beta-blockers and *calcium-channel antagonists* can reduce the frequency and severity of attacks. Still more important is to tackle the underlying disorder; ➤*atheroma*.

angiography. A technique for showing defects in blood vessels by means of X-rays: an iodine compound which casts a shadow is injected into the suspected artery or vein immediately before the film is exposed.

angioma. A tumour composed of blood vessels: a *naevus*. Angiomata are generally harmless, and most are congenital malformations of blood vessels rather than true tumours. An angioma inside the skull may interfere with the surface of the brain and have to be removed. ➤*birth-mark*.

angioneurotic oedema = severe ➤*urticaria*.

angiotensin. A polypeptide formed by the action of the hormone renin (➤*circulation* (1)). Of its two forms, angiotensin I is inactive, but when changed to angiotensin II by the action of *angiotensin-converting enzyme (ACE)* it raises blood pressure by constricting small arteries. Several chemically related drugs (all with generic names ending in -pril) are used to inhibit ACE in the treatment of high blood pressure and of heart failure.

aniline. A poisonous coal-tar derivative, the basis of most synthetic dyes and of a few drugs. It poisons by inactivating haemoglobin, the blood-pigment responsible for the transport of oxygen. The dye methylene blue is an antidote, but with severe aniline poisoning transfusions of healthy blood may be needed. Children are highly susceptible to aniline, and may not tolerate phenacetin, a drug derived from it.

ankle. The ankle is a simpler joint than the wrist. Only one bone of the foot, the *talus*, takes part, and movement is only in one plane.

The talus rises above the other bones of the foot. Its summit is shaped like half a drum. The under surface of the tibia is arched to roll over the talus, and the two *malleoli*, the knobs at either side of the ankle, clasp the faces of the drum. The inner malleolus is an extension of the tibia, and the outer is the lower end of the fibula. Thus the talus is clasped in a square mortice. Strong ligaments radiating from the malleoli to the bones of the foot support the joint on each side.

The only possible movements of this joint are to straighten, i.e. to point the foot (plantar flexion) and to draw it up towards the shin (dorsiflexion). The side-to-side movements of the foot are made at the tarsal joints (►*foot*). The feet are turned in and out from the *hip*.

Plantar flexion is a very powerful movement for pushing away from the ground in walking or jumping, and the calf (gastrocnemius) muscles are large. Dorsiflexion is much less important, and the extensor (tibial) muscles beside the shin are accordingly weaker.

A *sprain* of the ankle is among the commonest of all injuries. Usually the anterior fibres of the ligament at the outer side are torn; a sprain at the inner side is unusual.

Few sprains are serious, but there is no clear line between a sprain and a tear large enough to make the joint unstable. A very extensive tear may need surgical repair, but such injuries are nearly always associated with a fracture.

Because the talus is held in a mortice, dislocation is hardly possible without fracture of one or both of the leg bones. Fracture-dislocation of the ankle is known as ►*Pott*'s fracture.

ankylosing spondylitis ►*spondylitis.*

ankylosis. Loss of movement in a joint, usually from severe arthritis or injury, especially fractures involving joint surfaces. With complete ankylosis the moving parts 'heal' together in the same way as the broken ends of a healed fracture. Prolonged immobility can lead to ankylosis of a joint from shrinkage of the surrounding tissues; when a limb is out of use, good nursing includes keeping the joints supple. ►*arthrodesis.*

Ankylostoma. Hookworm (►*worms*).

Anopheles. A genus of mosquito, responsible for transmitting malaria.

anorexia. Loss of appetite.

anorexia nervosa. A serious illness of which almost the only symptom is that the patient either refuses food or, under protest, eats and then secretly vomits. This in time leads to undernourishment, starvation, and occasionally death. Nearly all the patients are adolescent or young adult girls, among whom *amenorrhoea*, the absence of menstrual periods, is a not uncommon consequence of this illness; only rarely does it affect boys or older patients.

Anorexia nervosa is evidently a severe neurosis in which unconscious refusal to accept puberty and adult sexuality is an important factor. Despite the relaxation of sexual taboos of modern times, this illness appears to be on the increase. This may be partly due to exaggerating the popular insistence that slender is beautiful and healthy. The patient usually insists that she eats enough and any more would make her fat.

These patients need experienced psychiatric help, and often a course of treatment in hospital under close supervision.

anoxia. Shortage of oxygen in the body, from breathing deficient air (e.g. at high altitudes), from failure to transport enough oxygen from the lungs (e.g. anaemia), or failure to assimilate oxygen in the tissues (e.g. cyanide poisoning). It differs from *asphyxia* (suffocation): with asphyxia, carbon dioxide accumulates in the blood and stimulates deeper breathing. Pure anoxia, lacking this defensive stimulus, is more dangerous than asphyxia; the victim is unaware of anything wrong and quietly passes out.

antacid. A drug given to counteract excessive acid in the stomach for treating gastritis and peptic (gastric or duodenal) ulcer. Loosely, the term means the same as 'alkali', but not all antacids are alkalis in a strict chemical sense. *Sodium bicarbonate* is the most popular, but it causes uncomfortable distension by releasing carbon dioxide, and some of it is absorbed from the stomach and disturbs the acid/alkali balance of the blood. Preparations which have neither of these disadvantages can be had, e.g. *aluminium hydroxide* or *magnesium trisilicate*.

antenatal care. Over recent years the medical care of expectant mothers and their unborn children has come to be regarded as the most important part of obstetric practice. Whereas obstetricians used to pride themselves on their conduct of actual confinements, they now concentrate on sending mothers into delivery rooms in the best possible condition for uneventful parturition, resulting in unscathed mothers and mentally and physically healthy babies.

Antenatal care should begin as soon as pregnancy is suspected. The fact of the pregnancy and the date of conception must be established. Once the obstetrician knows when the pregnancy has begun he can monitor the foetus's growth, comparing it, at every stage, with what he expects of a normal foetus, and therefore quickly noticing any major deviation from that norm. In the last stages of pregnancy the date at which it began becomes even more critical. It is on the basis of this date that the obstetrician may have to decide whether a baby that seems very small or very large is likely to be in difficulties. ➤*prematurity*; *postmaturity*.

The mother's general health needs careful attention throughout pregnancy as even minor disorders can become a serious threat either to her or to her child. Problems such as poor nutrition, abnormal blood pressure, subclinical urinary infections and latent diabetes are watched for from the beginning. Supplementary vitamins and iron will probably be prescribed, and the mother will be advised on how to feed her unborn child adequately without laying down unwanted fat herself.

These regular medical checks, together, perhaps, with the mother's previous obstetric history, may suggest that special care will be needed. Trouble that is foreseen can always be better dealt with than trouble that presents itself as an emergency. This is why a Caesarean section may be suggested in advance, rather than being carried out as an emergency operation, and why bed rest may be suggested at the first signs of a ➤ *toxaemia of pregnancy*, without waiting for the disorder to become serious.

Even with expert antenatal care, and a problem-free pregnancy, a confinement makes heavy physical and emotional demands on a woman. A programme of antenatal training, designed to prepare both the muscles and the mind, can do much to facilitate childbirth. ►*amniocentesis*.

antepartum. Before childbirth. *Antepartum haemorrhage*: bleeding from the uterus before delivery of the child, commonly because the placenta lies below the baby and becomes dislodged at the beginning instead of the end of labour.

anthracosis. Deposition of coal-dust in the lungs. ►*pneumoconiosis*.

anthrax. An infectious disease of farm animals occasionally transmitted to man, either as a severe localized inflammation of the skin (*malignant pustule*) or as a fulminating pneumonia (*woolsorter's disease*). Without treatment, the former is dangerous and the latter nearly always fatal. Serum treatment, for many years the only hope, often failed, but penicillin and other antibiotics are effective.

The anthrax bacillus was the first bacterium to be identified (F. A. Pollender, 1849), and in 1881 Pasteur successfully vaccinated sheep against the disease. Anthrax is now rare in W. Europe and N. America, and imports of potential sources of infection such as hides are controlled.

antibiotic. A class of drug used to treat infection. Biologists of the 19th century knew that one type of microbe might oppose the growth of another. This antagonism was called *antibiosis*.

In 1928 (Sir) Alexander Fleming noticed that bacteria would not grow on a culture-medium accidentally contaminated with a mould, *Penicillium notatum*. Evidently the mould produced something poisonous to bacteria, which Fleming called *Penicillin*. An antibiotic is either a substance such as penicillin, produced by one mould or bacterium to destroy others, or a synthetic analogue.

Fleming's discovery could not be used in medicine until penicillin had been isolated and tested by Florey and Chain at Oxford. The first patients were treated in 1941, and the three men shared a Nobel Prize in 1945.

A few people become sensitive to penicillin and may have severe allergic reactions, but otherwise penicillin is a very safe drug. It destroys various common and dangerous bacteria, including streptococci, staphylococci, and the spirochaetes of syphilis and other diseases. It has no effect on tuberculosis or virus infections, except by overcoming the secondary bacterial infection which often complicates virus diseases – e.g. pneumonia with measles.

Many different penicillins, all members of the same chemical family, have been prepared. Some can be taken by mouth, others work only by injection. Some act quickly, others slowly but for much longer. Some of the newer penicillins act against a wider range of bacteria than the original preparations.

Since 1941 antibiotics have been prepared from many other moulds (fungi). Some are effective against diseases which penicillins do not cure. The first to be discovered was *streptomycin* in 1944. This was an important breakthrough because for the first time the bacillus of tuberculosis could be attacked directly. Streptomycin was the first of a group of antibiotics, the aminoglycosides. Some of these, e.g. *kanamycin*, can be used to treat tuberculosis resistant to streptomycin. Others, such as *neomycin*, are mainly used externally; neomycin should not be taken internally over a prolonged period as it can cause deafness (a complication which hinders, to some degree, the use of all drugs in this group). Neomycin is taken orally only in preparation for abdominal surgery to prevent infection from escaped intestinal contents. *Chloramphenicol* is an effective antibiotic, but because it is apt to damage the white blood cells its use is limited to typhoid fever and some less common infections. *Tetracyclines*, derived from a fungus related to that of streptomycin, are 'broad-spectrum' antibiotics, i.e. they act against a wide range of bacteria; however, they are rather more prone to side-effects than some of the newer penicillins with similar activity. This list, which cannot possibly cover the scores of antibiotics now available, must close with a mention of the *cephalosporins*, of which the greatest value has been as alternatives for infections that resist other antibiotics.

Antibiotics act by obstructing a chemical reaction vital to the bacterium, i.e. by interfering with an enzyme. Penicillin prevents the formation of the protective cell walls of bacteria, and streptomycin that of the inner lining. Chloramphenicol and tetracycline disturb the formation of proteins within the bacteria. Clearly a useful antibiotic must not obstruct a reaction that human cells also need, at least not in the doses used against infection. One of the earliest, actinomycin-D, was rejected because it did damage human cells, but was later used in the treatment of certain cancers, more susceptible to it than healthy tissue.

Most antibiotics can, at times, have unpleasant effects, and so need to be used with caution. On the other hand, underdosage carries the hidden danger that it may encourage strains of bacteria that will in future resist the drug: a course once started should, unless the patient responds badly to it, be seen through. Penicillin is among the least toxic of antibiotics, indeed of all drugs, but some people become sensitized to it and may then have dangerous allergic reactions if it is given to them again. The point is, of course, that these are life-saving drugs, and the risk of injury has to be weighed against the risk of not giving them.

Laboratory tests show which antibiotics are likely to work in a given case, and the safest can then be chosen.

1. RESISTANCE TO ANTIBIOTICS

On the whole, antibiotics have lived up to the hopes aroused when penicillin first appeared. The one great disappointment is that more and more bacteria have come to the fore which can resist them. In the early days penicillin nearly always worked against staphylococci (the commonest cause of blood-poisoning) and against gonorrhoea. Now, three quarters of the staphylococci in some hospitals, and more than half the cases of gonorrhoea in large towns, cannot be cured with penicillin. Natural selection has favoured the few resistant strains, once an insignificant minority, at the expense of the others.

Resistance is most likely to develop when antibiotics are given indiscriminately and when, in individual cases, not enough is given. Often the symptoms of infection are rapidly controlled; if treatment is then stopped a few bacteria will survive. A later infection with these survivors may not respond to the antibiotic, and another, usually of a different type attacking a different part of the bacterium, has to be used. For instance, penicillin-resistant gonorrhoea responds to tetracycline, and the sulphonamide drugs, which were rather neglected in the early days of penicillin, may come to the rescue.

Some of the newer penicillins will deal with resistant strains. In particular, staphylococci elaborate an enzyme, penicillinase, which inactivates penicillin. But clavulanic acid inactivates this enzyme. Added to amoxycillin, a semi-synthetic penicillin, it exposes resistant staphylococci to the action of the antibiotic.

Sometimes an antibiotic is too effective. The healthy lungs and intestines contain many harmless bacteria. Some are even useful: they synthesize vitamins such as B_{12} and K. A powerful antibiotic can destroy these along with the germs under attack, leaving the way clear for microbes which had never before had a chance of causing disease. The new infection is sometimes more serious than the old. This 'super-infection' is fortunately rare, but it is a distressing development.

Some antibiotics such as *doxarubicin* are too toxic for treating infection, but like actinomycin-D can be used to inhibit the growth of cancer cells.

antibody. An important part of the body's defence against infection. Antibodies are formed by *lymphocytes* (a class of white blood cells circulating round the body). They are proteins classified as gamma-globulins, of which thousands of varieties each act specifically to inactivate one kind of invader. Substances recognized as invaders in this way are called *antigens*, ►*immunity*.

anticoagulant. (Drug) that impedes the clotting of blood. Clotting is a complex process, the result of a chain of chemical reactions involving a dozen or more reagents (►*blood* (4)). Interference at any stage prevents blood from clotting, but

of the many methods of keeping blood liquid in a test-tube only a few are safe in the living body.

Heparin is found in various tissues, especially liver, lung, and peritoneum. It inhibits several of the intermediate stages of clotting.

Coumarin, found in sweet clover, is the basis of several compounds that prevent clotting by displacing vitamin K (one of the essential reagents). Their action was discovered by studying animals poisoned by spoiled clover.

These drugs are used in conditions where blood-clots occur in veins or arteries (phlebitis, coronary thrombosis, certain types of stroke). Heparin acts promptly; coumarin compounds have a slower but more prolonged effect. Close supervision is needed to avoid abnormal bleeding. Heparin can be neutralized with protamine, a substance derived from fish, and the other drugs with vitamin K.

Aspirin inhibits the action of platelets (►*blood* (4)) and so reduces the risk of clotting. Small regular doses are increasingly prescribed as a safe prophylactic after arterial surgery, heart attacks or any other threat of clotting.

antidepressant. ►*depression*.

antidote ►*poison*.

antigen. A substance treated as alien to the body's natural components and invoking the action of an *antibody*. ►*immunity*.

antihistamine ►*histamine*.

anti-inflammatory drugs. Inflammation is essential to the healing of injuries and to combating infection, but it also arises without useful purpose, e.g. in allergic reactions. Of the many drugs used to suppress such inflammation the most powerful are the ►*corticosteroids*, highly valuable when needed but not suitable for general use.

Drugs of which the main if not the only use is the control of inflammation are classed as non-steroidal anti-inflammatory drugs (NSAIDs). The oldest is *aspirin*, in use since 1899 and still the most popular. Though paracetamol is as good for the relief of pain it has little effect on inflammation; but a compound of these two, *benorylate*, is a good anti-inflammatory and less apt to upset the stomach than aspirin. The value of *phenylbutazone*, introduced in the 1950s, is limited by a risk of damage to the blood-forming tissues. Newer and safer NSAIDs include *indomethacin*, *ibuprofen*, *diclofenac* and many others.

All NSAIDs act by inhibiting ➤*prostaglandin* hormones involved in the inflammatory process. None is free of some risk of side-effects, and apart from special cases such as rheumatic fever, *aspirin is unsuitable for children under the age of 12.*

antimony (stibium). An element with chemical properties and poisonous effects similar to those of arsenic. It has been used medicinally since early Egyptian times. Many of its compounds cause vomiting (e.g. *tartar emetic*), and since vomiting was considered a good way to get rid of disease antimony was an esteemed remedy until quite recently. Compounds of antimony still find some use against certain tropical parasites (bilharzia, leishmania).

antioxidant ➤*oxidant.*

antipyretic. Reducing fever, i.e. lowering a raised body temperature. The antipyretic drugs chance to be the same as those commonly used for relieving pain: ➤*analgesic.*

antiseptic. Chemical used to destroy microbes. The terms *antiseptic* and *disinfectant* both describe this sort of chemical, with the difference that antiseptics can be more or less safely applied to the body whereas disinfectants cannot. The distinction is often vague. The first antiseptic, phenol, is too poisonous to be anything but a disinfectant, and safe modern antiseptics are excellent as disinfectants in all but price.

An ideal antiseptic would kill all types of bacteria without damaging human tissues; it would work in the presence of blood, pus etc.; and it would be convenient to handle. No such substance exists, but a suitable one can usually be found for a particular purpose. Hundreds of antiseptics have been used. A few examples of different types can be given.

Phenol (carbolic) is of historical importance, because it enabled Lister to introduce modern surgery. It was soon discarded because it is almost as poisonous to man as to microbes. By present standards it is not even an efficient disinfectant.

Simple modifications greatly enhance the efficiency of phenol without making it more poisonous; these modified compounds still work when they are sufficiently diluted to be harmless, and many of them are less poisonous than phenol even before dilution.

The older compounds of this type include *cresol* (methyl-phenol), *thymol* (isopropyl-methyl-phenol), and *xylenol* (dimethyl-phenol). Chlorination of these substances to *chlorocresol* etc. provides more powerful but safer antiseptics. *Hexachlorophane*, an effective skin cleanser, is a recent example. It is about 100 times more potent than phenol. This is not considered a safe antiseptic for babies, with whom there is some risk of toxic effects from absorption through the skin.

Chlorine gas is used for destroying bacteria in water. Concentrations below one part per million are effective. *Iodine* is equally powerful. For many years it was used in wounds, but it injures exposed tissues and is itself inactivated by blood. It is still used to prepare the intact skin before surgical operations.

All oxidizing agents are antiseptic. *Potassium permanganate* is effective but messy. *Hydrogen peroxide* is *activated* by blood and tissues generally, and in dirty wounds the bubbles of oxygen help to dislodge debris.

Soap is among the most convenient if not the most powerful antiseptics, and some detergents, such as *cetrimide*, are especially suited to the cleansing of minor wounds and of the skin around major ones. They are almost completely non-poisonous. But they are easily inactivated, e.g. by pus. Household detergents are not suitable antiseptics.

Alcohol is a poor antiseptic. A 70 per cent solution in water is better than pure alcohol. It is, however, a good fat solvent. It physically removes bacteria from the skin by removing the layer of grease in which they are embedded.

Many *dyes* are effective and fairly harmless antiseptics. Brilliant green and crystal violet are also effective against some types of ringworm, and acridine dyes such as acriflavine are widely used for wounds.

The list might be continued almost indefinitely. Scores of antiseptics have particular uses, and none is suitable for all occasions. There are times when special antiseptics are much needed, but for most ordinary domestic purposes soap and sunlight seem as good as any.

antiserum. Serum extracted from the blood of a person or animal immune to a particular infection, therefore containing antibodies against that infection. Antisera are used in the laboratory for identifying bacteria and in clinical practice for treating certain types of infection. Serum can provoke severe allergic reactions, and antisera directed against bacteria have given way to antibiotic drugs. But sera against bacterial and some other poisons are still used (▸*antitoxin; antivenene*).

antitoxin. Antidote to bacterial poisons, formed naturally in the body. Most harmful bacteria directly injure tissues in their own vicinity, but a few cause disease by releasing poisons (*toxins*) into the blood-stream. The bacteria of tetanus and diphtheria do little if any local damage, but their toxins are highly poisonous to nerve cells; diphtheria toxin also damages the heart. These toxins are *antigens*, and in time *antibodies* are formed against them. Serum containing such antibodies or antitoxins is used in the treatment of these diseases.

antivenene (antivenin). Serum containing antitoxins against animal poison, e.g. snake, scorpion, or spider venom.

antrum. A natural cavity in the body, especially the *maxillary antrum* (*sinus*), the cavity of the upper jaw, a hollow space between the floor of the orbit and the root of the mouth, with a narrow opening into the side of the nose.

anus. The last inch of the intestine. It is closed by a system of muscular rings under partly voluntary and partly reflex control. It is lined with mucous membrane above and ordinary skin below. The upper part is sensitive to distension, and the lower part to the usual sensations of skin. The network of veins under the lining is liable to become engorged or varicose, a condition known as *internal piles* (►*haemorrhoids*).

Two common and painful disorders are *fissure*, a small crack in the skin of the anus; and *external piles*, a blood blister at the outer margin of the anus. Both are caused by straining, and are among the few troubles that can confidently be ascribed to constipation.

Itching (*pruritus ani*) is a distressing symptom. It can be due to minor disorders of the anal skin, but more often it is a kind of neurosis. Scratching does enough damage to give the itch an obvious physical cause.

anxiety. In a biological sense, anxiety is the same as fear. It is the normal response of the body to recognized danger. Numerous reflexes are involved, and they have presumably evolved with the species by the usual process of natural selection.

An animal survives physical hazards either by fighting or by fleeing. The same preparation is needed in either case: the body is geared to athletic performance at the expense of all other functions.

The supply of blood to the muscles is greatly increased, partly because the heart beats more rapidly and strongly, and partly because the blood vessels of the muscles dilate while those of many other organs constrict, diverting the flow to where it is most needed. The muscles themselves are tensed. Breathing is deeper and more rapid. The mind becomes more alert. The pupils dilate, admitting more light to the eyes. Some of the reflexes may serve to frighten an adversary, such as baring the teeth and raising the hairs by small muscles in the skin.

There are also negative components.

At the start the bladder and rectum may be emptied, but then excretion and digestive functions are suppressed. Fear removes appetite.

In the wild, all these reflexes enhance an animal's fitness for survival, just as much as protective colouring, powerful claws, or an efficient brain.

Modern man has inherited the response to danger that served his wild ancestors so well. On rare occasions when he must fight or flee for his life it still serves its old purpose. In more ordinary circumstances anxiety is still useful. An athlete who feels 'the needle' – nervousness before a contest – is more likely to win than one who is quite unconcerned, and a touch of stage-fright animates an actor. Anxiety, whether fear of criticism or of dismissal or of self-reproach, is a necessary motive for good work, and also makes good work possible by keeping a man alert and improving his mechanical performance.

Though in sum the reflexes of fear act as a useful spur, individually many of them can be a nuisance. Increased alertness helps a man during an alarming interview, but muscular tension and rapid breathing do not. The hair reflex, shown as goose-flesh, lost its purpose thousands of generations ago.

1. ANXIETY DISORDERS

Anxiety and its effects can become an obstacle to mental and physical health. They can be recognized in most if not all *neuroses*, i.e. mental and emotional anomalies of otherwise sane people, now often classified as *anxiety disorders*.

Like any other reflexes, symptoms of anxiety are automatic responses to particular stimuli, in this case those seen as threats of danger. But reflexes may be either inborn or acquired. A sudden noise may act as alarm signal when first encountered and set off an inborn reflex. The sight of a naked flame is not in itself alarming: it is the burnt child that fears fire. The lesson may create an acquired or *conditioned* reflex. Early conditioning may later lead to unwarranted symptoms of anxiety, the victim having forgotten the original cause. According to one theory many neuroses are based on faulty conditioned reflexes; ►*neurosis*.

2. TREATMENT OF ANXIETY

Some anxiety is healthy and indeed necessary. There can be no clear distinction between what is normal and what is abnormal. Anxiety does not call for any treatment unless it is a nuisance, and even then the object of treatment is to keep it within reasonable bounds rather than to suppress it entirely. A patient relieved of all anxiety is unlikely to hold down his job.

The people who most need attention are those whose fears have ceased to serve any useful function and make them ill without enhancing their efficiency. Continued anxiety upsets the balance between the various bodily functions, which is harmful, and it actually impairs efficiency because the patient's concentration becomes centred on the fears themselves, with which he cannot deal because they are not under conscious control, instead of on their original object.

The most important step is for the patient to understand why he has his symptoms. Even if they persist, they are more tolerable when he knows that they have a rational explanation.

Psychotherapy may be needed. This is a very wide term. Sometimes intelligent reassurance is enough (and this is a form of psychotherapy). Certain types of anxiety have been cured by behaviour therapy. In essence, this means that the patient is helped to unlearn his troublesome conditioned reflex. The original process by which he learned it is put into reverse. The unconscious stimulus to fear is brought to consciousness, and the patient acquires a new habit of accepting it without disagreeable effects.

Drugs for suppressing the symptoms of anxiety are classified as *anxiolytics*. In terms of chemistry those prescribed at present are nearly all benzodiazepines. Like their predecessors the barbiturates, drugs of this class serve also as hypnotics (sleeping draughts) and anaesthetics, depending on the speed of action of the particular drug and the dose. Although benzodiazepines are less toxic than barbiturates they are as apt to be addictive. They are therefore more suited to tiding a patient over a difficult period than for long-term use, which can cause trouble. Benzodiazepines offer the advantage over other anxiolytics that they help tense muscles, a common symptom of anxiety, to relax. Good drugs are a priceless adjunct to other forms of treatment, but the anxious patient is cured only by learning to redirect his fears in more profitable directions.

aorta. The principal ►*artery*: an elastic tube about an inch in diameter. Blood from the lungs enters the left atrium of the heart, passes to the left ventricle, and is pumped into the aorta to be distributed. The aortic valve at the origin of the aorta is discussed under ►*heart*. As it leaves the heart the aorta points upwards. It curves back in a hairpin bend, the *aortic arch*, and runs straight down, directly in front of the backbone, to the 4th lumbar vertebra. It then divides into the two common ►*iliac* arteries, which supply the pelvis and lower limbs.

The two ►*coronary arteries* leave the aorta just above its origin and spread themselves over the heart. Three large branches from the summit of the arch supply the head and upper limbs. These are the ►*innominate* artery, which divides into the right ►*carotid* and ►*subclavian*, and the left carotid and subclavian arteries. The branches in the thorax include the ►*intercostal* and ►*bronchial* arteries and several vessels to the oesophagus. The abdominal branches include the ►*coeliac* and mesenteric (►*mesentery*) arteries to the digestive organs, the ►*renal* arteries to the kidneys, separate arteries to the adrenal and reproductive glands, and branches to the abdominal muscles.

The veins corresponding with the aorta are the superior ►*vena cava* above, the azygos vein in the middle, and the inferior vena cava below.

1. DISORDERS

Coarctation is a congenital narrowing of a section of the aorta beyond the origins of the carotid and subclavian branches. The blood pressure is high in the head and arms and low in the rest of the body, sometimes too low to maintain adequate circulation. The narrow section can be removed surgically.

Atherosclerosis (►*artery* (1)) is the commonest disease of the aorta. Other arteries, e.g. coronary, are often involved. ►*Aneurysm*, a bulge at a weakened part of the vessel, may compress neighbouring structures (veins, nerves, trachea, oesophagus). Syphilis used to be the commonest cause of aortic aneurysm, but the aneurysms seen today are mostly due to atherosclerosis. The affected part can sometimes be replaced with an artificial tube.

Cases are described of an ill-defined 'aortitis', with narrowing of the aorta, and sometimes of its branches, and defective circulation in the afflicted region.

The condition may be related to the connective-tissue diseases.

aperient = ►*purgative.*

Apgar rating. (Virginia Apgar, 1909–74, American anaesthetist.) A numerical system of assessing the fitness of a newborn infant within 60 seconds of birth. Points are scored for respiration, heart rate, muscle tone, reflex irritability, and colour. A low score serves to warn that urgent attention is needed, and progress can be monitored by repeated ratings.

apomorphine. Emetic drug from opium, chemically similar to morphine. Whereas morphine occasionally causes vomiting, apomorphine invariably does so. Like other emetics, it is now seldom used.

apoplexy = ►*stroke.*

apothecary. Pharmacist or druggist, a person who prepares and supplies medicines. In England, the Society of Apothecaries was an offshoot of the Grocers' Company. Until the 19th century nobody distinguished drugs from spices. The few doctors of medicine in the Middle Ages left surgery to the barbers and drugs to the apothecaries; they concerned themselves mainly with theories and fees. The apothecaries came to know more about the realities of medical practice than the physicians. Since 1815 the Society of Apothecaries has conferred medical diplomas, which like all medical qualifications are now supervised by the General Medical Council.

appendicectomy. Surgical removal of the appendix. (Most American writers prefer 'appendectomy'.)

appendicitis. Acute inflammation of the appendix; the commonest emergency in abdominal surgery. It is extremely dangerous, because the appendix may burst and cause a fatal spread of infection (*peritonitis*); though there is a fair chance that in the early stages the inflamed peritoneum around the appendix will stick together and limit the infection to a localized abscess. Even this is bad enough, but it is much better than widespread infection in the abdomen.

The appendix is part of the intestine, and all intestinal pain is ➤*referred* vaguely to the middle of the abdomen. The first symptom is thus an indeterminate bellyache. Some nausea is usual, and vomiting not uncommon; it is a reflex response to stretching of the intestine (in this case by inflammatory swelling). As with any infection, the temperature is likely to rise, and the number of white blood cells to increase. If the appendix happens to lie anywhere near the wall of the abdomen, then in due course the inflammation will irritate the lining of the wall; and this pain is felt directly over its origin, below the level of the navel on the right side. It is generally severe enough to obscure the pain from the appendix itself; hence the pain is said to shift from the mid-line to the right side. If peritonitis follows, the pain may shift back to the mid-line.

The diagnosis is easy if the symptoms follow this pattern. From the earliest stage light pressure on the appendix is painful. But the appendix is a mobile organ, and its inflamed tip may be far from its text-book position. If it lies behind several loops of intestine there may be no local pain; if it hangs down into the pelvis the characteristic tenderness can be shown only by examining the rectum. The diagnosis may be in doubt until the appendix is inspected at operation.

The standard treatment of appendicitis is early operation. The appendix is easily removed, and even a healthy appendix is useless. The alternative is to nurse the patient in a half sitting position so that if an abscess forms it will gravitate to the pelvis where it can do least harm, withhold food, and give antibiotics; but this is done only when surgery is impossible or, rarely, if it is certain that an abscess has already formed, when it may be easier to operate later. Uncertainty of diagnosis is not generally considered a good reason for delay, because several of the alternative diagnoses also need operation, and it is very much safer to remove a healthy appendix than to leave an inflamed one even for a few hours.

It is easy to say that appendicitis is caused by infection. The appendix is full of bacteria – but so is the whole of the large intestine, and no other part of it suffers in this way. But the appendix is a slender tube with a rather precarious blood supply. It may be that inflammation mild enough to pass unnoticed elsewhere is enough to block the tube and prevent mucus from escaping (much as a cold in the nose can cause trouble by blocking the sinuses); and that the increased pressure obstructs the flow of blood. This would damage the lining and give bacteria a foothold in the tissues of the appendix. Quite commonly the appendix is found to be blocked by a small hard fragment of faeces (or traditionally, but in fact very rarely, a grape-pip). This sort of obstruction could cause inflammation, or it could be an effect – inflammation inhibiting the muscle of the appendix and preventing it from emptying itself.

Nobody knows why appendicitis suddenly became a common disease at the end of the 19th century. There are earlier descriptions, e.g. by Celsus in the 1st century, Fernel in the 16th and Addison in the 19th, but they are very few. Even Rokitansky, who meticulously described 30,000 post-mortem examinations between 1827 and 1866, gave no account of it. The first successful appendicectomy was done in 1887, and within 20 years the operation was commonplace. This was not simply a new fashion. Acute appendicitis is unmistakable at operation or postmortem examination, and in a large hospital it is almost a daily occurrence. Yet until the 20th century it was practically unknown, and it is hardly possible that the many observant pathologists of the time would have failed to notice it, unless it was in fact rare.

Chronic appendicitis – the 'grumbling appendix' – is another matter. There is not much evidence that such a disease exists, or, if it does exist, that it causes trouble. As a fashion it was at its height around 1930. Whether reality or myth, it has served a useful purpose. When persistent abdominal symptoms cannot be explained an exploratory operation may be needed to ensure that nothing serious is overlooked. A provisional diagnosis reassures both patient and surgeon. In many cases the reassurance probably does more good than the loss of the appendix.

appendix (vermiform appendix). A wormlike protrusion of the large intestine. It opens off the *caecum*, and is closed at its far end like the finger of a glove. It is usually about 8 cm long. Any purpose that it may have served in some remote ancestor has vanished in the course of evolution.

It is important only as the site of appendicitis.

appetite. Appetite is a conditioned reflex – a learned response to sensations or thoughts associated with food. The physical effects are secretion of saliva and of digestive juice in the stomach; the sensation is agreeable. It is not the same as hunger, which is an inborn response to variations in the concentration of sugar in the blood. The main effect of hunger is rhythmic contraction of the stomach, which is not necessarily a pleasant sensation.

arachnoid (arachnoid mater). A gossamer-like membrane covering the brain and spinal cord, the innermost of the ➤*meninges*.

arcus cornealis (arcus senilis). Opaque ring in the perimeter of the cornea, framing the iris in elderly eyes. In younger people, it indicates a high level of cholesterol in the blood together with a predisposition to heart disease.

areola. Pigmented skin around the nipple.

areolar tissue. Kind of ➤*connective tissue*.

Aristotle (384–322 BC). The son of a Macedonian physician. The impetus he gave to scientific thought, especially by his treatise on logic and by his insistence that theory must be based on observation, still endures. The scientific renaissance a thousand years later was inspired more by Aristotle than by any other classical writer: partly because his work was congenial to Christianity and so survived the Dark Ages, but mainly because if anyone 'invented' the scientific method it was he. This, rather than any particular discovery, is his great importance to medicine. He made detailed studies of the anatomy of animals, though not of man, and his classification of animals is only a short step from a theory of evolution.

His account of ►*embryology* leads in the same direction, for he showed in chick embryos that the organs are formed successively in the order of their importance to life. The first organ to be distinguishable is the heart, which Aristotle therefore supposed to be the seat of the mind (soul?) and of life itself. This fallacy was soon dispelled by ►*Herophilus*. It remained for others to describe the anatomy of the human body, but Aristotle had paved the way to an understanding of what anatomy means.

►*teleology*.

arm. In descriptive anatomy the arm extends only from the shoulder to the elbow, beyond which is the *forearm*.

The skeleton of the arm is the ►*humerus*. Three muscles make the contours: ►*deltoid* over the shoulder, ►*triceps* behind, and ►*biceps* in front. The nerves are all branches of the ►*brachial* plexus. The main artery is the ►*brachial*, but most of the blood to the arm comes from a branch of this, the *profunda brachii*. Veins accompany the arteries, and in addition two large veins lie under the skin – the *basilic* vein on the inner side and the *cephalic* on the outer side.

Movements are described under ►*shoulder*; ►*skeleton*.

arrhythmia. Any disturbance of the natural rhythm of the ►*heart*. The word is inaccurate, for it means absence of any rhythm, and with most arrhythmias the heart still has a rhythm, though not the right one. 'Dysrhythmia' would be better.

Sinus arrhythmia is no disturbance, but the natural variation of the heart rate caused by breathing. The heart beats faster during inspiration and slower during expiration, with an effect like *tempo rubato* in music. In some children the difference is great enough to suggest a real abnormality, but it has no significance.

The second commonest arrhythmia is the *extrasystole* (ectopic beat; dropped beat). A contraction wave starts in some area of heart muscle other than the natural pacemaker. The beat is premature and ineffective. When the next normal impulse arrives the muscle is still recovering from the extrasystole and does not respond. The sensation of a missed beat may be disagreeable or even alarming, but in an otherwise normal heart extrasystoles are unimportant. Smoking appears to be one of the causes. This arrhythmia is similar to *syncopation* in music.

Heart-block is a failure of the conducting fibres which carry the impulse from the atria to the ventricles. In a normal heart, when the contraction wave has spread through the receiving chambers (atria) it stimulates the conducting fibres (bundle of His) which convey the impulse to the pumping chambers, the ventricles. By this means the ventricles are ready to contract just when they have been filled by the atria. Conduction in the bundle of His takes about ⅙ second. There is no other path for the impulse, because the muscle fibres of the atria and ventricles do not communicate. Degeneration of the conducting fibres impairs or prevents conduction, and some or all the impulses fail to reach the ventricles. Various degrees are possible. An occasional missed beat resembles extrasystole. Sometimes only 3 beats in every 4, or 1 in 2 reach the ventricle (4:3 or 2:1 heart-block). If conduction fails entirely the atrium beats at the proper rate, while the ventricle takes up its own rhythm, about 30 beats per minute. This may not be enough to maintain efficient circulation, and the patient is liable to fits of unconsciousness (Stokes–Adams attacks) which may be fatal. An artificial pacemaker, giving regular electric pulses at the rate of a healthy heart, can be implanted in the ventricle if adrenaline and similar drugs fail.

Paroxysmal tachycardia is a sudden acceleration of the heart to a rate between 150 and 250 beats per minute. The paroxysm may last anything from a few minutes to several days. The rapid rhythm usually arises from some over-irritable area of heart muscle other than the natural pacemaker in the right atrium. A paroxysm may sometimes be shortened by simple measures such as holding the breath, pressure on a carotid sinus, or vomiting, presumably by stimulating the vagus nerve which in turn inhibits the heart muscle.

Flutter is akin to paroxysmal tachycardia with partial heart-block. The abnormal rhythm of the atrium is so rapid that even with an intact conducting mechanism the ventricle cannot keep pace; consequently only every second or third impulse is effective.

Fibrillation is a state of continuous and unco-ordinated activity of the heart muscle: instead of beating, it quivers, and ceases to act as a pump. Contraction of the atria is not essential to life, because filling of the ventricles is largely passive. The blood simply flows in as the ventricles relax between beats. But with atrial fibrillation the effective impulses reaching the ventricles are haphazard, and the response is irregular both in time and in intensity. Fibrillation is the only complete arrhythmia, i.e. absence of any rhythm. It may occur in the course of most kinds of heart disease, and it precipitates ►*heart failure* because the rapid irregular contraction of the ventricle is extremely inefficient. The effect of the drug ►*digitalis* is to slow the ventricle so that it has time to fill between beats. The fibrillation remains, but the heart becomes reasonably efficient. In some cases, ►*quinidine* restores normal heart action. Fibrillation of the *ventricles* is rapidly fatal because the circulation stops. Immediate cardiac massage or, better, stimulation of the ventricle by an electrical 'defibrillator' can be life-saving.

►*resuscitation.*

arsenic. A metallic element found in many minerals, used from early times as medicine and poison. Mithridates of Pontus (*c.* 100 BC) protected himself against poisoning by taking regular small doses.

Compounds of arsenic poison all living cells. In many the primary damage is to capillary blood vessels, which are so weakened that blood simply distends them and stagnates instead of flowing through; thus the affected tissue is deprived of a free circulation and is poisoned by its own waste products. Plasma leaks from the damaged vessels and the blood in them becomes more viscous. The first tissue to be affected is nearly always the lining of the stomach and intestine. The symptoms – violent diarrhoea and vomiting, dehydration, circulatory failure – are like those of a fulminating bacterial infection such as cholera. The symptoms do not start soon enough for the diarrhoea to eliminate much of a dose. If the victim survives this stage he may still die from widespread effects on the nervous system.

Like lead and other heavy metals, arsenic remains in the body for a long time; it is only gradually eliminated in shed

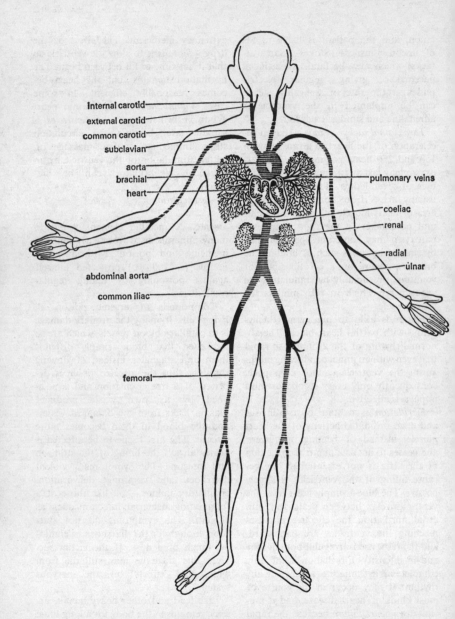

- Internal carotid
- external carotid
- common carotid
- subclavian
- aorta
- brachial
- heart
- pulmonary veins
- coeliac
- renal
- radial
- ulnar
- abdominal aorta
- common iliac
- femoral

Arrangement of principal arteries

skin, hair, and nails. A small regular intake, e.g. from industrial exposure to arsenic, adds up in time to a poisonous amount. The tissues become tolerant to arsenic (as with Mithridates, above), but this only means that a larger dose is needed to poison an habitué than a new-comer to arsenic. An early sign of slow poisoning is thickening and darkening of the skin. This tanned, weather-beaten appearance must account for the use of arsenic as a tonic until very recent times.

Ehrlich's discovery in 1910 of *arsphen-amine* (Salvarsan; 606) was a turning-point in the history of drug-treatment, for it was the first drug to be manufac-tured as a specific remedy for a par-ticular disease. It was a compound in which arsenic was rendered compara-tively harmless to man but remained poisonous to the germs of syphilis. It was not quite harmless enough, and in 1914 Ehrlich replaced it with neoarsphen-amine, which was the standard treatment of syphilis until the advent of penicillin.

The treatment of arsenical poisoning was very unsatisfactory until the dis-covery of BAL (British Anti-Lewisite; dimercaprol), which obstructs the chem-ical combination of arsenic in the tissues and enables it to be eliminated from the body.

arteriography. X-ray examination of ar-teries; ➤*angiography*.

arteriole. Small twig of an artery, leading to still smaller *capillary* vessels.

arteriosclerosis. Hardening of arteries: ➤*artery* (1).

artery. Any vessel carrying blood away from the heart. Arteries sustain consider-able pressure, and are stoutly built tubes. Their walls are reinforced with elastic fibres and muscle. When the muscle con-tracts under the influence of *sympathetic nerves* the artery narrows and increases the resistance to flow. Contraction and relaxation of these muscles regulates the blood pressure, and the distribution of blood amongst the various organs. During exercise the arteries of the limbs relax to admit more blood, at the ex-pense of digestive and other organs whose arteries contract. The arteries of the skin regulate the amount of blood exposed to cooling near the surface of the body, an important mechanism for keeping the body temperature constant.

Excepting the *pulmonary arteries*, which carry blood to the lungs to receive oxygen, all arteries are ultimately branches of the *aorta*, a huge vessel opening off the left ventricle of the heart and running down the centre of the trunk immediately in front of the backbone.

The main branches of the aorta in-clude the following arteries: *coronary* to the heart muscle; *carotid* to the head; *sub-clavian* (continued as *axillary*, then *bra-chial*) to the neck and arm, dividing at the elbow into *radial* and *ulnar*; *coeliac*, *renal*, and *mesenteric* in the abdomen. In the lower part of the abdomen the aorta divides into two *iliac* arteries with branches to the pelvis and thighs (*femoral*).

Arteries divide like trees into smaller and smaller branches ending in countless twigs or *arterioles* leading to the mesh of microscopic *capillary* vessels in which all the work of the blood is done.

Numerous links (anastomoses) be-tween branches ensure that if an artery is blocked there is usually an alternative route for the blood. An *end artery* is one without communicating links; if it is blocked the tissues that it supplied are deprived of blood and die. This is the case with some of the arteries in the brain and kidneys.

1. DISORDERS

Arteries are tougher and as a rule further from the surface of the body than veins; they are therefore less often wounded. A cut artery is recognized by the bright colour of the blood and the force with which it is ejected. The jet pulsates with the heart beat. When an artery is cut through, its muscle contracts tightly, and the bleeding is much less than from an incompletely severed vessel, where the muscle tends to hold the wound open. Bleeding can always be stopped by direct pressure over the cut ends of the artery. Most of the bleeding is from the end nearer the heart, but where there are efficient links with other arteries it can be brisk from both sides of the wound, e.g. in the scalp and the palm of the hand. Most small arteries are expendable and can safely be sealed with a ligature after injury. Where there are not enough other arteries to take over the work, cut arteries can be repaired, or even replaced with synthetic tubes.

An artery is the life-line of a tissue. About a third of all deaths in Britain are due to failure of an artery either in the brain (*stroke*) or the heart muscle (*>ischaemic heart disease*). Disease can weaken an artery and cause a bulge (*aneurysm*) or bleeding; or it can lead to narrowing (*stenosis*) or complete blockage. An artery can be blocked by stagnation and clotting of blood (*thrombosis*) or by a solid fragment, e.g. of a clot elsewhere, carried in the bloodstream (*embolism*).

Diseases as totally different as *diabetes* and *syphilis* cause most of their chronic effects by damaging small arteries and so jeopardizing the blood supply of tissues.

Some relatively uncommon arterial diseases are *>Buerger's disease*, *>polyarteritis nodosa*, and *temporal arteritis*, which is usually associated with *>polymyalgia rheumatica*.

Arteriosclerosis is by far the commonest arterial disease. The walls of arteries are thickened at the expense of the channels, restricting the flow of blood and so depriving the affected tissues of oxygen. The elasticity that should adapt flow to demand is also lost. The effects include heart attacks and strokes – which are the leading causes of death in Western countries – and the disabling effects of poor blood supply to the brain, legs (*>claudication*), kidneys, eyes and other organs. The inner walls of the arteries lose their duck's-back linings, so that blood tends to stick and clot there (thrombosis).

Arteriosclerosis is almost always linked to *>atheroma*; the predisposing causes of atheroma are discussed under that heading.

There are many ways of examining arteries. Feeling the pulse gives information about elasticity and flow, and listening with a stethoscope may reveal sounds indicating an obstruction. Small arteries inside the eye are clearly visible with an ophthalmoscope. X-rays sometimes reveal chalky deposits with arteriosclerosis. A contrast medium, opaque to X-rays, can be injected to provide a silhouette (angiogram) that shows the site and extent of any obstruction. The flow of blood in an artery can be measured from the change in wavelength of an ultrasound signal reflected from it (Doppler shift). Tests such as these are essential to planning treatment, in suitable cases perhaps by dilating (angioplasty), stripping (endarterectomy), renewing or bypassing affected arteries.

arthritis. Inflammation of a joint. The term has been applied to many types of joint disease, not always correctly because with some types there is no real inflammation. The common factors are pain – ranging from an occasional dull ache with osteoarthritis to the sharp stab of gout – and restriction of movement.

The common cause of inflammation in most parts of the body, infection, is no longer among the leading causes of arthritis, since the two infections most likely to settle in joints, tuberculosis and gonorrhoea, are prevented from doing so by treatment with antibiotics. Similarly rheumatic fever, where arthritis follows infection though not directly caused by it, has become rare since the discovery that streptococcal sore throats were quickly cured by penicillin.

The three common types of arthritis, ►*rheumatoid arthritis, osteoarthritis* and *gout*, are discussed under their own headings.

arthrodesis. Surgical operation to fix a joint in one position. If the moving surfaces of a joint are stripped of their smooth coating of cartilage, the exposed ends of bone join in the same way as a broken bone; e.g. if the knee is treated in this way the femur and tibia join to form a single bone from hip to ankle. The operation is a valuable last resort for painful joints that do not respond to less drastic measures. A rigid joint is painless and is not disturbed by movement at other joints. The effect of successful arthrodesis is to make the limb as a whole more mobile than before, because the patient is no longer afraid to move neighbouring joints, and the affected joint had already lost any useful movement.

arthroplasty. Surgical reconstruction of a joint – the opposite to arthrodesis. An old method depends on the fact that if a broken bone is not splinted the broken ends become hard and smooth and a false joint is eventually established. If a joint has become completely fixed by injury or disease it may be possible to cut through the bone and keep some movement between the cut ends. A more satisfactory method is to implant an artificial joint of material that is not corroded by body fluids.

artificial respiration. Any method of getting air into the lungs when natural breathing is suspended. In the widest sense, the term covers mechanical aids ranging from the elaborate respirators ('iron lungs') to a simple hand insufflator that is no more than a modified bellows. In principle, a large respirator is a box in which the patient lies with his head on the outside through an airtight collar. The pressure inside the box fluctuates: when it falls below atmospheric pressure, air is drawn into the patient's lungs, and when it rises air is driven out. But in the more usual sense, artificial respiration is a first-aid procedure needing no equipment.

The oldest, most obvious, and easiest method is also the most efficient. This is the mouth-to-mouth technique mentioned in 2 Kings iv, 34.

The patient is laid on his back.

The head is tilted back by drawing the chin upwards and forwards to keep the tongue away from the back of the throat.

The helper looks inside the mouth and runs a finger round the back of the tongue to ensure that there is no obstruction to the airway by food, weeds, false teeth etc.

He pinches the patient's nose so that the air will not leak, takes a deep breath, and blows steadily into the patient's mouth. The chest is seen to rise as the air flows in.

The helper raises his head and watches the patient's chest fall as the air is passively expelled.

These breaths are repeated every 5 or 6 seconds.

If the method is to be used with a baby the quantity and pressure of air have to be much reduced. This can be done by inflating the cheeks and puffing air in by the mouthful. The helper's mouth covers the baby's mouth and nose together. The rate of breathing should be rather fast, about a puff every two seconds.

Although expired air contains less oxygen than atmospheric air, it provides enough for the patient's needs.

Many other methods have been used. With Schaefer's method the patient is laid on his face with the head turned to one side, and the helper kneels beside or astride him and rhythmically presses the lower ribs with the flat of his hands. It is tiring and not very efficient. With the Holger Nielson method, the patient is in the same position but with the head resting on the hands. The helper kneels at the head and draws air into the lungs by raising the patient's elbows, then expels it by pressing the lower ribs. Lastly, Eve's method is to lay the patient on an improvised see-saw and tilt him up and down, so that the weight of the abdominal organs provides a piston-like action. These methods are no longer recommended.

If artificial respiration is needed at all it is needed at once. A person who stops breathing has only three or four minutes to live unless something is done about it.

Three common situations where lives are saved by prompt action are drowning, gas (carbon monoxide) poisoning, and electrocution.

With drowning, trying to get the water out of the lungs is a waste of precious seconds. As in other situations the mouth has to be cleared of obstructions, then mouth-to-mouth respiration begins at once.

With gassing, fresh air is needed, or artificial respiration will be useless and the helper will become another casualty.

With electrocution, helpers have lost their own lives by forgetting to switch off the current before touching the patient, or at least to drag him clear with a stick, an article of clothing or any non-conductor.

➤*resuscitation.*

asbestosis. Chronic disease of the lungs from inhaling asbestos dust; a kind of ➤*pneumoconiosis.*

ascaris. Roundworm; the species *Ascaris lumbricoides* is a parasite of man in many parts of the world. ➤*worms.*

ascorbic acid = ➤*vitamin C.*

asepsis. Exclusion of bacteria from the site of surgical operations, injections, wound dressings etc.

The technique was evolved soon after Lister's discovery that surgery could be freed from the danger of infection by using a carbolic spray to kill germs in the air, and applying carbolic dressings to wounds. It soon became clear that there was no need for the carbolic if everything that was to come into contact with the patient's tissues was first disinfected, and Lister's antiseptic surgery gave way to the present practice of aseptic surgery.

➤*Lister, surgery.*

aspergillus. A common fungus; one species is the familiar and harmless mould which grows on jam. Another species sometimes causes asthma. What appear to be cases of severe infection (*aspergillosis*) are sometimes found; a few may be genuine, but most are probably other diseases (e.g. virus pneumonia) with aspergillus incidentally, and harmlessly, in the lung. Aspergillosis is common and dangerous in birds, including poultry, but used to be rare in man. However, if the immune system is suppressed, either with drugs to prevent the rejection of transplants or by infection with AIDS, aspergillosis becomes a hazard.

asphyxia. Suffocation; interference with *respiration* so that tissues neither receive enough oxygen nor get rid of carbon dioxide. It is rather less dangerous than simple lack of oxygen (*anoxia*) because accumulation of carbon dioxide provokes compensatory responses: it deepens breathing, and dilates blood vessels to improve the supply of oxygen to deprived tissues. General asphyxia is due to obstruction of the air-passages, e.g. by strangulation or disease of the lungs. Local asphyxia is due to impaired circulation, which may be widespread as with heart failure, or restricted as with blockage of a blood vessel.

aspirin. Acetylsalicylic acid, one of the earliest synthetic drugs. It was introduced in 1899 in order to get the known effects of salicylic acid (relieving pain and lowering raised body-temperature) in a form that could be taken by mouth. It has proved to be a valuable remedy, both for relieving everyday aches and pains and for the distressing and useless inflammation of rheumatic diseases. But like any other effective drug, aspirin has its drawbacks. Even standard doses are very apt to cause some bleeding in the stomach, and larger doses have adverse effects on numerous organs. Severe aspirin poisoning can be fatal, and aspirin accounts for many cases of overdosage of drugs – accidental or deliberate – admitted to hospital. It is not a drug of addiction, but regular abuse of aspirin has been a prevalent bad habit for the best part of a century. In people unduly sensitive to it, aspirin may trigger allergic responses such as asthma. Cases of *Reye's syndrome*, a rare form of brain damage in children, have been associated with the use of aspirin in virus infections, and aspirin is therefore to be avoided with young patients.

A novel and unexpected use for aspirin is for preventing strokes and heart attacks in people known to be susceptible; it discourages the formation of blood clots that might block arteries in the brain or heart.

Aspirin probably lowers temperature and dulls pain by effects within the brain. On the other hand, the anti-inflammatory and anti-clotting actions are both due to interrupting the formation of ▸*prostaglandins*. These are a group of hormone-like substances formed in many parts of the body, with numerous different effects. Two are directly concerned with inflammation; others are concerned in various ways with *platelets*, the small blood cells that activate clotting. One prostaglandin inhibits, another promotes platelet activity. Very small doses of aspirin are thought to favour one; larger doses, the other. Many cardiologists now recommend regular small doses to patients known to be at risk from arterial disease.

asthenia. Weakness.

asthma

1. BRONCHIAL ASTHMA

The original meaning of asthma is heavy

or difficult breathing, but now the word is taken to mean a particular kind of difficulty arising from spasm of involuntary muscle around the small branches of the air-tubes (*bronchi*) in the lungs. As these muscle fibres contract they squeeze the tubes and impede the flow of air. The effect is partly counteracted by breathing in, because expanding the chest creates a partial vacuum and tends to widen the tubes; but breathing out raises the pressure around them and increases the constriction. Therefore the prime symptom of asthma is difficulty in breathing out, and it is then that the characteristic wheeze or whistling sound of asthmatic breathing is loudest. During an attack the asthmatic uses the muscles of his shoulders to help him to force air out of his lungs (➤*respiration* (1)). The spasm makes it difficult to cough away mucus, which collects in the small bronchi and further impedes breathing. The mucus itself is abnormally tenacious. It takes on almost the consistency of a contact adhesive, and the little that the patient manages to cough up during an attack is often in the form of beaded threads, still keeping the form of the bronchi in which they were lodged. Sometimes asthma is precipitated by bronchitis. Then the mucus is infected, i.e. contaminated with pus, from the start. In other cases, the clear mucus trapped in the bronchi by persistent asthma is an ideal incubator for bacteria, and then bronchitis is an effect instead of a cause of asthma. The irritation of bacterial infection causes further spasm of the bronchial muscles, and a vicious circle is set up. With all attacks of asthma, and especially those complicated by bronchitis, the mucous membrane lining the bronchi is congested and swollen, like the lining of the nose with hay fever or a common cold.

Thus three factors contribute to difficult breathing: muscle spasm, blockage by mucus, and narrowing of the bronchi by their swollen lining.

Underlying causes of asthma. All bronchial asthma is an anomalous reaction of the bronchi to a variety of stimuli. These may, in individual cases, include physical exertion, infection of the air passages, exposure to substances such as pollens or particular foods to which the patient is sensitive, sudden exposure to cold, irritant smoke or vapour. These 'stresses' were once regarded as different causes of asthma, but in fact they only trigger off a reaction that perfectly healthy lungs would not show; exertion, for instance, should cause the bronchi to widen and let in extra oxygen. Many cases of asthma (in the opinion of some authorities, all cases) are linked with *atopy*, a type of allergic reaction discussed under ➤*allergy* and ➤*immunity* (6). But in many sufferers, atopy is expressed as a skin rash, or as hay fever, without asthma. Why in some people the bronchi should respond in this perverse manner is still not clear, but it may be that the fundamental defect is a biochemical imbalance between the transmitters released at nerve-endings in the bronchi to regulate their calibre. The idea of asthma as a psychosomatic disorder needs to be forgotten. Certainly, emotional stress may precipitate an attack in someone already subject to asthma, and some asthmatics may appear to bring on an attack (but the same applies to numerous perfectly real chronic or recurrent ailments). In considering anxiety neurosis in relation to asthma it must be remembered that a severe attack is itself a grave source of anxiety to both patient and family.

Course. Asthma is unpredictable. Some patients, for no apparent reason, stop having attacks, while others get worse. The time-honoured doctrine that asthma was never fatal is, sadly, untrue: although most attacks last only a few hours or, if they drag on, lessen in intensity, a few keep the patient in serious distress for a day or more (*status asthmaticus*) and threaten life. On the other hand, even very severe asthma in early life often improves as the child grows up; in some cases it practically disappears, though the *tendency* remains.

Treatment is designed firstly to overcome acute attacks, and secondly to prevent further attacks, or make them less frequent or severe.

The first line of medical treatment is to dilate the constricted bronchi with adrenaline or, more often, a related drug. This reinforces the dilating action of the sympathetic nerves, which themselves release adrenaline. The second line is theophylline, generally in the form of aminophylline. This prevents the destruction by enzymes of the body's own adrenaline, thus prolonging its action. (Although both adrenaline and theophylline were known by the end of the 19th century, their value in the treatment of asthma was unrecognized for many years. Instead, extracts of plants such as belladonna or their active principles, such as atropine and hyoscine, were used. They relaxed the bronchi by suppressing the constricting action of the parasympathetic nerves, but simultaneously dried mucus secretion, making the sputum even more tenacious and difficult to clear. Apart from patent medicines they are no longer used for asthma.)

Adrenaline itself works only by injection, which needs to be administered with great care to avoid over-stimulation of the heart. Derivatives such as *terbutaline* and *salbutamol* have much less effect on the heart, and can be inhaled from a bronchodilator nebulizer. These nebulizers, pocket inhalers, have become the standard everyday treatment. They have to be used correctly: the patient breathes out as far as he can, puts the nozzle in his mouth, holding the nebulizer upright, and while he breathes in takes a single puff. After waiting a minute, he may need to complete the dose with a second puff. As a rule, these bronchodilators are used not more than four-hourly, but whatever dose has been ordered must not be exceeded without further advice. Any temptation to do so is a clear warning that some other form of treatment is needed.

A more severe attack is often arrested by an injection of adrenaline, or of aminophylline. Aminophylline may also work in the form of a suppository. For some patients, slow-acting derivatives of theophylline taken regularly enhance the action of their nebulizers.

With very severe asthma, *hydrocortisone* by intravenous injection generally brings rapid, even dramatic relief. When the worst is over, the patient continues to take a corticosteroid by mouth. As always with these drugs, the dose is gradually reduced and if possible discontinued, although some asthmatics have to continue this kind of treatment. Though some may have to take the drug by mouth, accepting possible side-effects as the lesser of evils, many can control symptoms with a steroid nebulizer. By confining the drug to the air passages, this method overcomes much of the risk. It is used as well as, not instead of, the bronchodilator nebulizer.

Fluid intake becomes important if an attack is prolonged, for breathing can be so impaired that the patient cannot swallow even sips. At the beginning of an attack nobody knows how long it may last, or how serious it may become, so the patient should try to drink more than he thinks he needs. In status asthmaticus, i.e. a prolonged and severe attack, intravenous fluids are needed.

Infection, which may precipitate an attack, can also complicate one; the stagnant sputum that the patient cannot cough up serves as an incubator. Then antibiotics become an essential addition to the treatment. Any kind of bronchial infection needs energetic treatment.

A physiotherapist can often teach a patient to breathe more efficiently, and can also help him to bring up sputum.

A class of drugs that has not been mentioned is the antihistamine group. They are often helpful with seemingly related allergic disorders, but do not relieve asthma.

Prevention. If any avoidable allergens or irritants can be identified, such as a particular item of food or clothing, then obviously it should be avoided. With a specific allergen that cannot be avoided easily, a course of desensitization may be worth trying, but it takes a long time and success cannot be guaranteed.

Psychiatric treatment is of only limited value. The emotional factor in asthma has been much overstated. More often than not the anxiety affecting not only the patient but his family is more effect than cause, and it has no surer remedy than evident relief of symptoms. Tranquillizers or sedatives are probably better avoided, especially during an attack when the patient needs to be as alert as possible.

Finally, one form of treatment is a true prophylactic. While bronchodilators and, if need be, steroids, generally mitigate asthma if used regularly, between as well as during attacks, *sodium cromogly-cate* anticipates attacks by suppressing a stage of certain allergic reactions. It has no effect on an actual attack, but taken regularly it often reduces both frequency and severity of attacks, and though the usual drugs may still be needed, cromoglycate often allows the dosage to be reduced. It does not help all asthmatics, but for some it virtually abolishes attacks. The patient takes cromoglycate from an inhaler, though not as a mist of droplets but as a puff of very fine powder.

2. CARDIAC ASTHMA

A condition with symptoms resembling those of ordinary bronchial asthma but quite unrelated to it: cardiac asthma is a symptom of inadequate performance by the heart (►*heart failure*).

astigmatism. A common defect of vision: the transparent *cornea* at the front of the eye should be a section of a perfect sphere, but with astigmatism it is a section of a spheroid, i.e. the radius is greater in one plane than another, and when a line is seen in focus another line at right angles is blurred. Astigmatism is corrected by a lens in which a similar fault is set at right angles to that of the cornea.

astragalus = ►*talus*.

astringent. (Ointment, lotion etc.) causing shrinkage and drying of surface membranes; e.g. silver nitrate, aluminium salts, hamamelis (witch-hazel), tannin.

ataxia. Failure to co-ordinate the actions of the various muscles involved in performing a movement. The conscious brain directs the result of a movement (I will pick up a pin; I will place my foot there), but the choice of muscles and the balance of their actions depends on unconscious reflexes. Ataxia is a disturbance of these reflexes. There are several rare hereditary forms.

Locomotor ataxia = ➤*tabes dorsalis* (syphilis of the spinal cord).

atelectasis. Incomplete expansion of (part of) a lung. A lung is a spongy structure and should contain a good deal of air even after breathing out as much as possible. Until birth there is no air in the lungs, but after the new-born infant's first breath his lungs should contain air for the rest of his life. Breathing varies the amount of air in the lungs but does not exhaust them.

Atelectasis may be present from birth, when the infant fails to breathe and the lungs have no chance to expand, or it may arise after birth if the lungs, having expanded, promptly shrink and lose their air (➤*hyaline-membrane disease*).

After infancy, atelectasis is generally due to blockage of an air-passage, e.g. by an inhaled foreign body, a plug of mucus, or a tumour. The air in the part of the lung beyond the block is absorbed into the blood-stream and cannot be replaced. Alternatively, air in the pleural cavity, between the lung and the chest wall (*pneumothorax*), or fluid (*pleural effusion*) will cause a lung to deflate.

Many medical writers restrict the term atelectasis to the infantile types and describe the others as *collapse of lung*.

Atelectasis due to failure to breathe is treated by artificial ventilation of the lungs through a tube passed down the windpipe. With other types, the lung expands when the cause is removed.

atheroma. Arteries show the first signs of ageing in childhood, with the appearance of fatty streaks in the lining of the aorta and later of other vessels, composed of *foam cells*. These are scavenger cells laden with *lipids* (fats, cholesterol) that have strayed from the blood and settled in the arterial wall. This innocent condition may later be followed by accumulation of muscle cells and connective tissue, forming a plaque in the lining that in time can gradually block the artery. As the plaque grows calcium salts are deposited like fur in a kettle. These changes result in arteriosclerosis (*atherosclerosis*).

Blood does not clot on a healthy lining but can do so to block a damaged one (*thrombosis*) and cause a heart attack or a stroke. Or the weakened wall can bulge to form an ➤*aneurysm*.

Whether or not lipids are dumped in the arteries rather than being properly disposed of depends largely on the nature of the proteins to which they are linked. Low-density lipoproteins (LDL) favour dumping, and high-density lipoproteins (HDL) favour disposal (➤*cholesterol*).

Whether an individual develops atheroma depends largely on heredity, which he cannot change. But the risk of serious complications can be greatly increased by *smoking*, *overeating*, especially of saturated (animal) fat, and *physical inactivity*, all of which are under his control. Other factors are *high blood pressure*, *diabetes* and *gout*, all of which can be treated. The effect of each is to lower HDL and raise LDL levels.

Current research strongly suggests that *oxidation* of LDL accounts for its involvement, and that *antioxidants* (➤*oxidant*) such as vitamin E may help to protect arteries from atherosclerosis.

athetosis. Uncontrolled, purposeless movements, seen in one type of congenital ➤*spastic paralysis*.

athlete's foot. Ringworm of the feet; infection of the skin, especially between the outer toes, with a microscopical fungus. The only association with athletics is that the changing rooms of schools and sports clubs are likely places for the infection to be passed on. ►*ringworm*.

atopy. Allergy; allergic reaction in a part of the body other than the point of entry of the irritant. For instance, two forms of skin allergy are *contact* eczema, a reaction confined to the area of skin in contact with the irritant, and *atopic* eczema, a reaction to irritants applied elsewhere – perhaps swallowed.

ATP. Adenosine triphosphate, a substance essential to the storage and transfer of ►*energy* in living cells.

atrium. Antechamber of the ►*heart*: the left atrium receives blood from the lungs; the right atrium from the rest of the body.

atrophy. Shrinkage, wasting of an organ or tissue. Atrophy may be due to undernutrition (the literal meaning), especially if the blood supply is impaired by disease; or it may be a result of disuse – e.g. the wasting of muscle in a limb that has been splinted because of a fracture.

atropine. Alkaloid extracted from belladonna (deadly nightshade); this drug abolishes most actions of the parasympathetic nerves by chemically obstructing *acetyl choline*, the substance released at the ends of these nerves. When the parasympathetic nerves are put out of action, the sympathetic nerves are left unopposed; thus atropine mimics some actions of sympathetic nerves and of adrenaline. In this way it causes acceleration of the heart, and also the effect from which belladonna gets its name – widening of the pupils. Its most useful

action is the relief of colic (painful overactivity of the muscles of the intestine and other abdominal organs) by preventing stimulation of the intestine by acetyl choline. Given before an anaesthetic, it inhibits the secretion of mucus in the lungs, and of saliva, which the anaesthetized patient cannot cough up.

Although large doses can be lethal, atropine is less dangerous than many alkaloid drugs. Drugs such as eserine, which reinforce acetyl choline, serve as antidotes to atropine.

Atropine eye drops have virtually no effects on the body as a whole. They are sometimes used to treat iritis, and also when testing the sight of small children.

ATS. Anti-tetanus serum; ►*tetanus*.

Auenbrugger, Leopold (1722–1809). Viennese physician, the inventor of diagnosis by ►*percussion* of the chest – assessing the texture of underlying organs from the resonance when the surface is lightly tapped. Auenbrugger showed how to plot the outlines of the heart and lungs by percussion and recognize diseased areas of lung, repeatedly confirming his opinions by postmortem examination. His book *Inventum novum* (1761) seems to be the first ever devoted entirely to diagnosis, and the first to be based on an objective sign of disease (as opposed to subjective symptoms, coloured by the feelings of patient and doctor).

Nobody paid much attention until ►*Corvisart* (1755–1821) translated Auenbrugger's method in Paris and passed it on to his students.

aura. Sensation at the beginning of an attack of illness such as epilepsy or migraine, before more definite symptoms set in. An epileptic attack is a wave of abnormal electrical activity spreading over the brain. If the spread is rapid the patient loses consciousness with little warning, but if the wave spreads more slowly from a part of the brain concerned with a sensation, then the patient feels that particular sensation as a sort of premonition. The aura can warn the patient to lie down and put a pad between his teeth to avoid hurting himself in the coming attack; some people say that they can abort the main attack by keeping perfectly quiet from the moment when the sensation begins.

The aura of migraine is visual, often an illusion of flickering light. It is not a constant symptom.

aural. Of the ear.

auricle. 1. The visible part of the ear. **2.** A pocket protruding from either ➤*atrium* of the heart. **3.** Formerly the atrium itself.

auscultation. Diagnosis by listening, e.g. to heart or breath sounds. *Immediate auscultation* is by putting an ear to the patient's body; *mediate auscultation* is by means of a ➤*stethoscope*. ➤*Laënnac*.

autism. A serious mental disorder seen in children, usually apparent from early infancy but occasionally only later. The typical picture is of a child totally wrapped up in himself as though cut off from the rest of the world. He appears to see without looking and to hear without listening. This alone makes him a slow learner, but in addition the intelligence of many autistic children is low (but their inability to communicate with others makes their IQ hard to test). Strange repetitive movements and speech patterns are common symptoms. Occasional outbursts of rage may be the only signs of emotion. A few autistic children, though in most respects mentally retarded, are brilliant in a single faculty such as arithmetic.

Until Kanner described autism in 1943 it had passed for a variant of schizophrenia, or for a result of faulty upbringing. It is now generally accepted as an organic disease. Numerous causes have been suggested, including virus infections and metabolic disorders, but none applies to more than a fraction of cases. Patient and skilled psychotherapy, especially speech therapy, helps many of these children. Drugs may occasionally be prescribed, but only to control outbursts of violence. They do not change what is only seldom a good prognosis.

autogenic training. A form of psychotherapy in which the patient is taught to be his own hypnotist (➤*hypnosis*).

autogenous vaccine. A vaccine prepared from bacteria with which a patient is afflicted and given to immunize the patient against their effects. If the patient has not developed immunity to the living bacteria it is not obvious that the dead bacteria in the vaccine will help, and the evidence that they in fact do so is rather thin.

autoimmunity ➤*immunity* (7).

autonomic. Outside conscious control. The *autonomic nervous system* regulates bodily functions other than voluntary movement and conscious sensation, by ➤*reflex* action.

The autonomic system is composed of the ➤*sympathetic* and ➤*parasympathetic* nervous systems, which are both ramified throughout the body. Many of their actions are mutually opposed, e.g. the former accelerates, the latter slows the heart, while on the intestine they work the other way round. Between them, in a healthy body, their effects are constantly balanced.

Avicenna (Ibn Sina) (980–1037). Persian physician and philosopher. He was born at Bokhara, and practised and taught at Baghdad. He was the most celebrated of the Moslem physicians, the only practitioners of rational medicine in an age when Europe had rejected all learning except theology. These men kept alive the spirit of inquiry that had died in Europe at the end of the 2nd century with Galen, and they preserved and translated the great medical books of antiquity.

Avicenna's *Canon* was for centuries the standard if not the only accepted textbook of general medicine. Much of it was derived from classical Greek sources, of which even the worst were better than anything that the Europe of the time had to offer. But Avicenna was no mere compiler; he was a doctor in the tradition of Hippocrates, learning from his patients and recording what he observed.

Until the 16th century and later, the physicians of Europe idolized Avicenna, placing him second only to Galen – not, sadly, for his clinical wisdom but for his loyalty to the approved doctrines of Galen and Aristotle.

axilla. Armpit: space between the upper part of the arm and the side-wall of the chest, enclosed by the pectoral muscles in front and the latissimus dorsi muscle behind.

In addition to the blood vessels and nerves of the arm, the axilla houses an important group of lymph nodes.

azathioprene. A drug used to suppress undesirable immune responses such as rejection of a transplanted organ. It may be used against rheumatoid arthritis and lupus erythematosus, both regarded as manifestations of *autoimmunity* (>*immunity* (7)), but its value is limited by a risk of serious side-effects.

AZT. Azidothymidine, an antiviral drug now known as zidovudine, used in the treatment of >*AIDS*.

B

bacillus. A rod-shaped ➤*bacterium*. The many diseases caused by bacilli include ➤*anthrax*, ➤*diphtheria*, a kind of ➤*dysentery*, gas ➤*gangrene*, ➤*tetanus*, ➤*tuberculosis* and ➤*typhoid*.

backache. Pain in the lower part of the back is among the commonest of all symptoms. There are many possible causes, most of them mechanical. Faulty posture can put undue strain on muscles and ligaments and lead to a low-grade nagging ache. The human back is stable when upright or lying down, but not when suspended cantilever-style in the position of someone bending forward to tuck in a sheet on the far side of a bed or to pick up a weight – which should be done with bent knees and the back upright. The unaccustomed burden of pregnancy readily causes backache, and obesity can have a similar effect. All joints, including those of the backbone, depend on muscles as well as ligaments for support; muscles weakened by lack of exercise leave too much work to ligaments and so strain joints.

Pressure on the roots of the nerves branching off the spinal cord causes pain in the area to which they are destined. This may arise from narrowing of the spaces between vertebrae by degeneration of the spinal joints (spondylosis) or from a 'slipped' intervertebral disc, or both. Pain from the lumbar nerves extends to the buttock and down the leg (sciatica).

The structures of the backbone suffer the same afflictions as any other part of the body: congenital defects such as stenosis (narrowing) of the spinal canal, injuries, tumours, infection, rheumatic diseases and disorders peculiar to bone, such as Paget's disease and osteoporosis. Any can give rise to backache. Sometimes pain from abdominal organs or elsewhere is referred to the back, and for no obvious reason backache is often an early symptom of a fever.

Some backache is said to be psychogenic ('all in the mind'), but (malingering apart) the pain is unlikely to be altogether imaginary. Both the muscular tension of anxiety and the slouch of depression express emotional disturbances, and either can contribute to a backache. Neurotic patients may well exaggerate the severity of the pain, but they are unlikely to invent it. Malingerers may feign backache because it is hard to disprove, but a pain for which no cause can be identified is no more necessarily due to malingering than to neurosis: 'cause unknown' need not mean imaginary.

Though the history of the complaint and routine clinical examination may suffice to determine the cause of a backache, with so many possibilities diagnosis can be difficult. X-ray examination helps, but a CT or MRI scan may be needed.

Treatment obviously depends on the cause. Rest, analgesic or anti-inflammatory drugs and physiotherapy may at least relieve symptoms. Flabby muscles can be retrained and faulty posture corrected. Many backaches improve with sleeping on a firmer mattress than usual. The bulge of a herniated (slipped) disc often recedes with rest; the symptoms then disappear. The value of manipulation depends on careful selection of cases and the skill of the operator. Causes such as spinal tumours call for surgery, as may persistent pressure of a slipped disc or a narrow canal. Retention or incontinence of urine from pressure on nerves is a surgical emergency.

backbone. The vertebral column or spine. ►*skeleton* (4); *vertebra*.

bacteriophage. A virus that infects bacteria; ►*virus* (3).

bacterium. A living creature too small to be seen without a microscope is a microorganism or *microbe*. The microbes of medical importance include various kinds of minute animal (►*protozoon*), e.g. the parasite of malaria; and some simple forms of plant or vegetable life (►*fungus*), e.g. the moulds which cause 'ringworm'. Bacteria are smaller than either, and they hold an intermediate position between animal and vegetable microbes. A still smaller form of life, the ►*virus*, is on the border between living and non-living matter.

1. STRUCTURE

A large bacterium is about 1/100 mm by 1/1000 mm; a small one is about 1/1000 mm each way. A group of bacteria big enough to be seen with the naked eye contains millions of individual microbes.

Under an ordinary microscope a bacterium does not appear to have any structural elements (nucleus etc.). It is simply a speck of living matter. With the much greater magnification of the electron microscope a certain amount of cell-architecture can be seen. Every bacterium has a strong cell-wall, a protective shell to prevent it from becoming waterlogged and bursting. A few species have fine motile hairs (flagella) by which they are able to swim. The corkscrew-shaped *spirochaetes* can move quite briskly. But most species of bacteria are static.

Apart from the spirochaetes, bacteria are either rod-shaped (*bacillus*) or spherical (*coccus*). Bacilli can be slender, e.g. tubercle bacillus, which causes tuberculosis, or short, more or less oval, e.g. *Haemophilus influenzae*, which does not cause influenza. Cocci include *streptococci*, growing in chains, and *staphylococci*, growing in clumps.

2. FUNCTION

The chemical components of bacteria are like those of other living creatures – protein, fat, carbohydrate etc. At one end of the scale are bacteria that can synthesize these substances from inorganic, 'mineral' sources in the manner of plants. Those of the genus *Rhizobium*, which live in the roots of leguminous plants (clover, beans etc.), can use the nitrogen of the air as a food, providing the plant with essential compounds which it could not synthesize for itself. Leguminous plants can be used, thanks to these bacteria, to replace nitrogen compounds in soil impoverished by other plants, an important factor in crop rotation. They are also, of course, valuable foods.

Other bacteria have a similar economy to animals, living off organic foods synthesized by other creatures. All the bacteria involved in human disease are of this type; they are parasites living off human hosts.

Not all parasitic bacteria cause disease; in fact it is against the interests of a parasite to do so, because if the host dies the parasite must either find another host or die itself. The skin and the various openings of the body teem with harmless bacteria which prevent the growth of harmful species, and some of the bacteria of the intestine synthesize vitamins. Hence drugs which destroy bacteria indiscriminately can be a mixed blessing (>antibiotic, penultimate paragraph).

Bacteria reproduce simply by growing until they are large enough to split into two. Under ideal conditions of humidity and temperature, and given unlimited supplies of food, they can do this at an almost incredible rate. Some species are ready to split again within half an hour of reproduction. If the number is doubled every half hour a single bacterium will have increased to over a thousand in five hours and a million in ten hours. Even in the laboratory this rate cannot be kept up for more than a few hours, and in the body it is slowed or stopped by natural defences (>immunity). But the body can succumb very rapidly to an infection to which it has no resistance. The accounts of medieval plagues in which people died within a few hours of falling sick were not exaggerated.

Like all other living creatures, bacteria produce numerous >enzymes. These are substances which promote the various chemical changes necessary for sustaining life. Some of the effects of infectious disease are due to enzymes which promote changes unfavourable to the host. Enzymes from various types of bacteria and microscopic fungi (yeasts and moulds) are responsible for all kinds of decay and putrefaction. Frozen food stays fresh because bacteria cannot multiply at low temperatures. Boiled milk will not turn sour if it is protected from further contamination, because boiling destroys bacteria. Creosote preserves wood by killing the moulds that would cause it to rot. Over a century before bacteria were first seen, and three centuries before their role in disease was recognized, Fracastorius said that contagion and putrefaction were the same thing (>infection).

3. IDENTIFICATION

Bacteria are classified in the same way as other creatures, but the distinctions between different groups are very unsure and the classification is constantly having to be revised. With so little known of their detailed structure and behaviour it is all too easy to make the sort of mistake that would include bats among birds or whales among fish. The characteristics to be studied include shape and size, ability to take up various dyes, presence of particular enzymes, e.g. those that will ferment one or other of a selection of sugars, and patterns of growth under various conditions in the laboratory. A few can be identified by their ability to cause a known disease, e.g. tuberculosis, in laboratory animals. Exact identification usually depends on the fact that a person or animal infected with bacteria forms protective antibodies (>immunity) which will inactivate that species but no other. The antibodies can be isolated and kept, and bacteria can be identified by the antibodies which react with them.

As a rule, rough identification by simple tests gives enough information for diagnosis and treatment of an infected patient. For instance, if a patient with diarrhoea is found to be passing bacilli of the genus Shigella, then he has bacillary dysentery and suitable treatment can be prescribed. But in order to identify the source of his infection and control an outbreak of dysentery, much more precise information is needed. There are four species of Shigella and over two dozen sub-species, and the public health officer needs to know exactly which one he is looking for.

In practice, the bacteriologist does not have to go through the whole gamut of tests. He knows from the clinical history what types of bacteria he is likely to find, and he provides an appropriate medium for their growth (some species will grow in one medium, others in another). If a sufficiently dilute suspension from the specimen (blood, urine, pus, sputum etc.) is spread over a solid medium such as agar jelly, small colonies will grow from single bacteria, and the type of colony gives useful information about the species.

Bacteria are stained before being examined under the microscope. The original reason was to make them easier to see, but it was soon found that different species had affinities for particular dyes. Gram's method, using two dyes, divides bacteria into two classes – Gram-positive, stained purple, and Gram-negative, stained pink. Together with the general appearance of the bacteria this stain sometimes gives all the information that is needed. Another technique, the Ziehl-Neelsen stain, uses the red dye fuchsin. The dye is washed out of the stained specimen with acid and alcohol, but the bacilli of tuberculosis and leprosy hold the colour and stand out as crimson rods against a neutral background. It is important to have a selective stain for these two closely related species, because it is very difficult to grow tubercle bacilli in an artificial medium and impossible to grow leprosy bacilli. Most other bacteria will form colonies in a suitable medium, and the colonies can then be identified by chemical and other tests.

4. BACTERIA AND DISEASE

(➤*infection*)

Bacteria can be found almost anywhere – in the soil, in the air, on healthy skin. They are very abundant on warm, moist surfaces such as the linings of the nose and mouth and of the large intestine. In commonsense terms intestinal bacteria are inside the body, but the digestive tract is a corridor through the body; bacteria in it are walled off from the body proper almost to the same extent as those on the skin.

Only a few of the many species of bacteria are *pathogens*, i.e. can cause disease. Those which do must first penetrate the surface of the skin or mucous membrane. Any kind of wound allows them to do so; an invisible scratch may suffice. A few species seem able to cross an intact mucous membrane, and some others force an entry by damaging a mucous membrane. They may be able to attack one type of mucous membrane but not another. Typhoid bacilli regularly enter the body by way of the small intestine, gonococci (gonorrhoea) by way of the eyes and reproductive organs, but not elsewhere, and many bacteria by way of the pharynx. The harmless bacteria of a healthy intestine, which breed there throughout life without ever crossing the mucous membrane, cause serious trouble if they contaminate the lining of the urinary system.

Having entered the body, a pathogen must be able to meet the next line of defence, the white blood cells. Harmless bacteria which find their way in by chance are promptly engulfed by white cells and destroyed. Pathogens either resist destruction or actually destroy the white cells.

The symptoms of infection arise mainly in two ways. Firstly, bacteria produce *toxins*, highly poisonous substances. Some toxins (endotoxins) are an integral part of the bacterium and are released into the surrounding tissues when the bacterium is destroyed. Others (exotoxins) are much more dangerous; they are released by living bacteria and diffuse into the circulation, producing their effects far beyond the site of infection. Diphtheria bacilli in the throat can release toxins which injure the nervous system, and tetanus bacilli in a wound have a similar and even more dangerous effect. With certain types of bacterial ►*food poisoning* there is no actual infection – the bacteria themselves do not invade the body, but they release toxins into the contaminated food.

Secondly, symptoms are caused by the body's own defences. Fever and its accompaniments are part of the body's response to infection – anyone with pneumonia but no fever is in a bad way, and debilitated old people may die of an infection without ever feeling ill. The process of ►*immunity* is akin to ►*allergy*, and with chronic (i.e. prolonged) infectious diseases such as tuberculosis the symptoms produced in this way can be as bad as those produced directly by the infecting bacteria. Certain diseases are associated with infection but are not direct results of it. Rheumatic fever, for instance, is regularly preceded by a streptococcal infection such as tonsillitis, but does not come until after the infection has subsided. It is possible that antibodies formed to destroy the streptococci also damage the body's own tissues, but there is still some mystery about it. ►*immunity* (6).

5. CONTROL OF BACTERIA

If all bacteria were to be destroyed, many if not most other forms of life would disappear because in the course of evolution so many essential jobs have become delegated to microbes. Bacterial decomposition of dead organisms is essential to fertile soil. Herbivorous animals, on which carnivores feed, rely on bacteria in their digestive organs to break down the cellulose of plants into digestible sugars – man, lacking any such bacteria, cannot live on grass. Thus bacteria must not be destroyed wholesale. On the other hand, selective destruction is often necessary to health.

Polluted water can be made fit to drink by filtration.

Most bacteria are killed by ultraviolet radiation, either artificial or from direct sunlight. All bacteria are destroyed by heat. Boiling water quickly kills nearly all of them, but certain spores can survive prolonged boiling. A spore is a sort of hibernating form adopted by a few species under unfavourable conditions. In hospitals, surgical dressings and instruments are completely freed of bacteria, including spores, with compressed steam in an *autoclave*.

Refrigeration prevents bacteria from multiplying but does not usually kill those that are already present.

Chemicals which kill bacteria are roughly divided into *disinfectants*, noxious to any living matter, and *antiseptics*, which kill bacteria without greatly damaging human tissues. But these categories overlap and are hardly worth distinguishing; one needs to know the exact purpose of the substance. An antiseptic that would be quite safe on intact skin may be harmful to an open wound, or it may be inactivated by blood. There is no satisfactory all-purpose substance for killing bacteria.

The discovery of drugs that kill or inactivate bacteria in the body must be counted the most important medical advance of the present century. They include ►*sulphonamides* and ►*antibiotics*.

►►historical note under *microbe* (1).

Baer, Karl Ernst von (1792–1876). German biologist; the greatest modern embryologist (►*embryology*).

Von Baer's law, the biogenetic law, only confirms what earlier embryologists (e.g. Harvey) had suggested: that the embryos of widely different species resemble one another. It is an important argument in favour of evolution. The law is sometimes restated: the development of the individual recapitulates the development of the species. But this presupposes evolution, of which von Baer knew nothing, and is not quite true. A human embryo never resembles a fish, but only a fish's embryo.

bagassosis. An inflammatory disease of the lungs caused by allergy to the dust of sugar-cane fibre (bagasse).

Baghdad button = ►*oriental sore.*

BAL. British Anti-Lewisite; dimercaprol. It was evolved as an antidote to the arsenical war-gas lewisite. BAL prevents arsenic from becoming chemically bound in the tissues and so enables it to be eliminated from the body. It is also effective against lead and other poisonous metals which otherwise become fixed in the tissues.

balanitis. Inflammation of the glans penis.

balantidium. A parasitic ►*protozoon*, one of the rarer causes of dysentery.

baldness (alopecia). Most other mammals shed hair seasonally, but human hair moults throughout the year. An average rate might be 100 hairs a day. The rate increases in various types of symptomatic baldness (see below), and these are likely to recover as the rate of moulting returns to normal. But much the commonest kind of baldness arises not from shedding hair, but from a change in its character. The adult hair follicles regress and instead of producing normal hair they produce a kind of *vellus* or baby hair, which gives the usual type of bald pate a velvety look in a cross light. As far as anyone knows at present, the change is irreversible. The tendency is hereditary. The loss of normal hair, spreading from the temples and crown, often starts to affect males very early in adult life. A similar condition in women usually starts later and seldom goes beyond thinning rather than extensive loss of hair. In women, this or a similar condition can arise from defective function of the ovaries, e.g. at the menopause, and such cases may respond to hormone treatment. Otherwise, common baldness is a normal condition.

Some baldness is symptomatic of a known or suspected cause. *Scar tissue* carries no hair follicles and so remains irreparably bald. Thus burns and certain infections of the skin can leave permanently bald patches. The fashion of wearing wigs in the 17th century is said to have been adopted to hide scars caused by syphilis.

The stress of an acute infection such as scarlet fever, or difficult childbirth, or, rarely, extreme emotional upset may disturb the normal cycle of growing and later shedding hair, so that in a period of some three months most of the hair is shed. After a time during which the patient may need a wig, normal growth is resumed. Some forms of *chemotherapy*, i.e. drug treatment for cancer, damage new hairs so that they fall out as soon as they appear. The hair may be expected to recover when the drugs are discontinued.

Alopecia areata usually appears as patchy baldness, but occasionally causes all hair to be lost. An association with certain abnormal antibodies suggests that this may be an autoimmune reaction (>*immunity* (7)). Although total baldness of this kind is often lasting, most patients recover from the much commoner patchy form. The only effective treatment of alopecia areata is by local injection of corticosteroids – steroid ointments do not work – and even then the effect is not lasting.

Some cases of baldness may be improved by grafting patches of hair-bearing skin to the bald areas.

bandage. Bandages have several uses: (1) covering wounds to exclude contamination; the bandage holds a clean or antiseptic dressing in place; (2) stopping wounds from bleeding; the bandage is not a tourniquet to prevent blood from reaching the wound but simply keeps the dressing still enough to provide a scaffolding for a firm blood clot; (3) splinting injured tissues, which hurt and will not heal if they are constantly moving; (4) supporting weak structures such as varicose veins.

The gauze roller-bandage is the most widely used but it needs considerable skill. If it is too loose it falls off, and if it is too tight it does more harm than good. In non-expert hands, sticking plaster is a better means of holding a dressing, and if the plaster goes only halfway round a limb it cannot obstruct the circulation. Unfortunately some people's skin does not tolerate sticking plaster.

Crêpe bandages give excellent support. They are easily put on too tightly, especially if elegant figure-of-eight turns are used.

Any bandage that feels too tight probably is too tight. Swelling below a bandage is a warning to loosen it at once.

For anyone without special training, by far the most useful bandage is the triangular bandage, which can be adapted to almost any purpose. The standard first-aid manuals describe its use in detail.

Banting, Frederick (1891–1941). Canadian physiologist who, with C. H. Best, isolated >*insulin* in 1921, for which he (though, by a quirk in the rules, not Best) received a Nobel Prize in 1923.

Banting, William (1797–1878). English undertaker who in 1863 addressed to the public a 'Letter on Corpulence' about a diet that had been recommended to him, based on meat, fish and fruit at the expense of starch, sugar and fat, on which he had shed 46 lb (21 kg). His name became synonymous with 'slimming', and for many years a new verb 'to bant' was in vogue.

Banti's disease. (G. Banti, 1853–1925, Italian physician.) Splenic anaemia; not a specific ailment but simply enlargement of the spleen as a result of back-pressure in its vein from constriction of the *portal vein*, of which the splenic vein is a tributary. The usual cause is cirrhosis of the liver.

barber's itch (barber's rash). Bacterial infection around the roots of the beard. Antibiotic treatment usually clears it up and prevents it from becoming chronic and producing unsightly scars. Growing a beard or changing to an electric razor often cures it.

barbiturates. A group of chemically related drugs introduced in 1903 and for many years the most widely used sedatives. They are no longer recommended

77

for promoting sleep or allaying symptoms of anxiety, having been superseded by benzodiazepines. But very short-acting barbiturates such as thiopentone are still in use as anaesthetics (by intravenous injection), and one of the longest-acting, phenobarbitone, has retained a place in the treatment of epilepsy.

barium sulphate. A substance opaque to X-rays; since it is not absorbed from the intestine it can safely be given by mouth (*barium meal*) or by the rectum (*barium enema*) to outline the digestive tract under X-rays.

barotrauma. Injury by change of pressure (e.g. explosion; diving) illustrated by painful ears in aircraft. Any part of the body can suffer, but ear-drums, sinuses and lungs are the most vulnerable. The fall in pressure as a shock-wave passes by or a diver surfaces, leaving compressed air in the body, is as harmful as the previous rise. Torn ear-drums can lead to infection and deafness, and burst lungs to fatal ▸*air embolism.* (▸*decompression sickness.*)

basal ganglia (basal nuclei). The core of grey matter (nerve cells) at the centre of cerebral hemispheres. The basal ganglia serve movement in the same way as the *thalamus* serves sensation, i.e. they are a relay station immediately below the level of consciousness.

Various types of purposeless involuntary movement are due to disease of the basal ganglia, of which by far the commonest is ▸*parkinsonism* (shaking palsy; paralysis agitans).

basal metabolism. Chemical turnover in the body at complete rest; it represents the chemical energy provided for vital processes such as breathing, circulation and digestion. It is assessed from the rate at which oxygen is consumed when the subject is warm and still, in bed. The result can be expressed as energy produced in a given time; for an average man basal metabolism (basal metabolic rate; BMR) is about 1,700 cal. per day (7.2 kJ). Or it can be expressed as a percentage of the calculated normal rate for the subject's height and weight.

The rate is regulated mainly by the thyroid gland. With an over-active thyroid (toxic goitre) it is above normal; with a defective thyroid (cretinism, myxoedema) it is below.

baths. The main value of bathing is aesthetic rather than medical. People who wash are pleasanter to know and more comfortable than people who do not, but except that they are less liable to be infested with lice, etc., it is doubtful whether they are much healthier.

A skilful bed-bath works wonders for the morale and comfort of anyone confined to bed.

Very hot baths raise the body temperature and can be dangerous. Cold baths are doubtless a moral tonic, but are not known to do any physical good.

Certain diseases affecting large areas of skin can be treated with medicated baths.

The success of spa treatment (▸*hydrotherapy*) depends at least as much on the regimen of controlled diet, exercise and relaxation as on the special virtues of the water. But baths have a special place in the treatment of rheumatic disease, and of all disorders involving stiff or painful joints or weak muscles. Buoyancy allows movement that would be impossible in air, and the warmth of the water may ease pain. Gentle exercise under water is among the best ways of re-educating limbs that have been out of action.

Batten's disease. A genetic disorder of the same kind as ►*Tay-Sachs* disease, with irremediable damage to the nervous system.

battered-baby syndrome ►*child abuse*.

BCG (bacille Calmette–Guérin). A vaccine against ►*tuberculosis* (4), introduced in 1906 by Léon Calmette and Camille Guérin, to prevent tuberculosis. In France it has been used for human vaccination since 1922, but in Britain it was not accepted for many years. It is now offered to children shown to lack immunity to tuberculosis and to adults exposed to infection.

beat elbow (beat knee; beat hand). Chronic, often severe inflammation from continuous pressure on a small area of skin, sometimes with *bursitis*; a scheduled industrial disease of miners and some other workers.

Bedsonia ►*Chlamydia*.

bed-sore (decubitus ulcer). Damage to skin and underlying tissue by constant pressure which prevents blood from circulating and deprives the area of its oxygen supply. Any sustained pressure, e.g. from a badly fitting plaster cast, can destroy skin; and since pressure also interferes with conduction in nerves the patient may be unaware of what is happening. Bed-sores arise in areas where skin is compressed against bone when a patient lies still in bed (buttocks, hips, ankles, heels). They are most likely to affect paralysed or debilitated people who do not move in bed, and are promoted by slight injury or infection of the skin. The first warning sign is a reddened area of skin; unless pressure is relieved this rapidly forms an ulcer that can be difficult to heal. Bed-sores are almost entirely prevented by good nursing. This includes regular changes of the patient's position, cushioning of pressure points and scrupulous hygiene of the skin.

bed-wetting (enuresis). Some children continue to pass urine in their sleep after the third year (by which time most children are dry) because of physical irritation, e.g. inflammation in the urinary passages; but in most cases there is no obvious cause and the condition is thought to be emotional. Training has to be based on encouragement; scolding makes matters worse. Aids to training include various drugs, and an electric alarm that wakes the child when the first drops of urine close the circuit.

bee sting. Bees, wasps, and hornets inject venom which, like viper venom, interferes with the clotting of blood; but the amount is too small to be significant when they sting man. The only danger is to a few people who are allergic to the stings and may react violently (►*allergy*). Bee-handlers become immune to bee stings. Allergic people may need to carry adrenalin for emergencies.

Alkaline solutions such as sodium bicarbonate or dilute ammonia help to neutralize the venom, and antihistamine drugs relieve most of the symptoms.

Bees often leave their stings in the skin. If the sting can be seen it needs to be removed gently.

behaviour therapy. A form of psychotherapy for treating neuroses and oddities of behaviour which are thought to represent abnormal conditioned reflexes. A conditioned reflex is a *learned* response that has become automatic or unconscious (as opposed to an inborn reflex that does not have to be learned). A flow of saliva while actually eating is an inborn reflex, but salivation at the sight of food is conditioned – one has first to learn what food looks like and associate it with the act of eating. The response (salivation) is then transferred from the inborn stimulus (taste) to the learned stimulus (sight). But the process can be put into reverse. If a child tries to eat an addled egg he may afterwards be sickened by the sight of an egg. More subtly, if he associates a particular dish with unhappiness he may become unable to stomach it. Thus a conditioned reflex can be unlearned.

It has been suggested that many disorders such as symptoms of irrational anxiety and abnormal or defective sexual responses are conditioned reflexes that can be unlearned, either by giving them disagreeable associations or by establishing pleasant associations with more normal responses. Behaviour therapy, in short, is a refinement and rationalization of two ancient teaching aids: the stick and the carrot. The 'stick' principle is exemplified by *aversion therapy*, which builds up unpleasant associations with a habit that the patient wishes to break such as alcohol or an anomalous sexual urge. Thus an alcoholic may be given a drug to make him vomit when he drinks, in the hope of establishing a conditioned reflex that makes alcohol nauseating to him.

A more amiable form of behaviour therapy has been named *desensitization* because it is like desensitizing a patient to an allergy by getting him to tolerate gradually increasing doses of the offending substance. Here, a well-defined anxiety is treated by getting the patient to relive, in fact or in imagination, the kind of situation that troubles him, starting with mildly alarming scenes and building up over a series of treatment sessions to situations that would formerly have terrified him.

bejel ➤*yaws*.

belladonna. Extract of deadly nightshade; used internally to correct overactivity of the stomach and to relieve spasm of involuntary muscle in the bronchi and digestive tract, and externally, as belladonna plaster, without any apparent effect. Its active principles are the alkaloids *atropine* and *hyoscyamine*.

Bell's palsy. Paralysis of the facial nerve, described in 1828 by Sir Charles Bell (1774–1842), a Scottish surgeon.

The facial nerve is unusual in that it carries no conscious sensation; it only activates the muscles of the face. (The sensory nerve of the face is the trigeminal.) Therefore disorders of this nerve, unlike those of any other nerve, affect movement but not sensation. The lop-sided appearance of the face is unmistakable.

Bell's palsy might arise from any kind of damage to the nerve – head injury, infection, stroke, etc. – but the term is often restricted to paralysis with no obvious cause and a tendency to recover spontaneously. The nerve passes through a long and narrow tunnel in the base of the skull, around the inner ear, and may be compressed by slight inflammation in this area. An abnormal response to cold is sometimes blamed. In a few cases the pressure on the nerve can be relieved surgically.

bends ➤*compressed-air sickness*.

benign. A term applied to various diseases to distinguish a relatively mild form from a *malignant* or dangerous form. A benign tumour does not disseminate itself to other parts of the body, whereas a malignant tumour or cancer does. *Benign tertian* fever is the form of *malaria* caused by *Plasmodium vivax*. It does not have the lethal complications of malignant tertian fever, caused by *P. falciparum*.

benzodiazepines. A large group of closely related drugs in use since about 1960, since when they have practically displaced barbiturates as sedatives. The prototype is *chlordiazepoxide*; most of the later introductions have names ending -*azepam*. They are now among the most widely prescribed of all drugs. *Diazepam* is used for the relief of anxiety and the countless symptoms that may arise from it, and also as a muscle relaxant. In Britain, *nitrazepam* is much used as a sleeping pill; in other countries *flurazepam* and *bromazepam* may be preferred. These drugs are also a valuable adjunct to anaesthetics, and they also have a place in the control of epileptic convulsions.

The differences between the effects of the various diazepines are slight: the principal one is the duration of action. Although they are not nearly as addictive as the barbiturates, patients can become dependent on them. They may induce some withdrawal symptoms, especially the longer-acting ones. They are, in general, much less toxic than any of their predecessors.

benzyl benzoate. An oily fluid used to treat ▸*scabies*.

beriberi. A form of malnutrition seen mainly in the Far East, due to deficiency of vitamin B_1 (thiamine). Outbreaks have been traced to eating polished rice (from which the husks are removed) in a diet with no other source of thiamine than rice husks. The principal symptoms are *neuritis*, with disturbed sensation and loss of muscle power, and *heart failure*.

Bernard, Claude (1813–78). Professor of physiology at the Sorbonne and of medicine at the Collège de France; the greatest of all physiologists. His sole aim, he said, was to establish scientific method as the basis of medicine. He dismissed as sentimental nonsense the idea of a 'vital spirit' directing the affairs of living bodies according to its own laws, and insisted that living bodies are bound by the same natural laws as inanimate matter. Like Descartes before him, he took nothing for granted, but trusted logical conclusions drawn from proven facts. Unlike Descartes, he pursued an argument no further than could be confirmed by experiment. That is, he would draw conclusions from the result of an experiment, and then devise new experiments to test the conclusions; these in turn became the basis of fresh conclusions and experiments.

His first practical contribution was to show that animals, like plants, could synthesize new material and were not confined to breaking down vegetable products. He later discovered several functions of the liver; the digestive action of the pancreas; the control of blood vessels by nerves; the carriage of oxygen by red blood cells and the abolition of this function by carbon monoxide; the nature of curare poisoning and its implications as regards the control of muscles by nerves; new facts about the brain and spinal cord and the behaviour of secreting glands and of the kidneys. If Nobel Prizes had existed, Bernard could hardly have won fewer than four.

Even more important than Bernard's many particular discoveries was his concept of internal environment (*milieu intérieur*). The external environment – the world around us – constantly changes; but the delicately balanced mechanisms of our bodies are not affected, although all natural processes are extremely sensitive to change of any kind. Bernard realized that a highly developed organism such as the human body is not a unit continually adapting itself to a changing environment, but a community of living cells in an unchanging environment – the blood and tissue fluid in which each cell lives as an aquatic creature. Most bodily functions are directed to keeping this *milieu intérieur* stable in the face of external change – to keeping constant the amount of water, temperature, oxygen supply, pressure, and chemical composition. For instance, in hot weather, the skin flushes and then sweats, preventing the temperature of the blood from rising. Or if muscular work threatens to deplete the blood of glucose, the liver puts more into the circulation. Physiology is largely the study of how each organ helps to maintain a constant environment for all the others, and medicine of how the process goes wrong.

Much of Bernard's experimental work was done with animals. He had an almost unerring sense of how far the results applied to man, and of when human experiment was necessary and justified. He insisted that morals did not forbid doing experiments on people, but only doing people harm.

Bernard's *Introduction à l'étude de la médecine expérimentale* is nothing less than a charter for 20th-century medicine. It is incidentally among the most readable of medical classics, and a smattering of general science is enough to keep abreast of the argument. An English translation has been published.

beta-blockers. Drugs which oppose certain actions of the ►*sympathetic* nervous system (beta-effects), in particular stimulation of the heart. The net effect is to reduce the rate and force of the heart beat, especially in response to effort or excitement. Given to patients with angina it helps to keep the work of the heart within the limits imposed by its deficient supply of blood and oxygen. Similarly, patients endangered by high blood pressure are relieved. These are the two principal uses of beta-blockers, but the drugs also have a place in the treatment of various other conditions in which the pulse is liable to race; these may originate in the heart itself, or from glandular or emotional disorders.

However, beta-effects extend far beyond the heart, and occasional side-effects of the drugs include lethargy, constriction of the smaller air-passages, aggravation of asthma, spasm of arteries in the legs to worsen pain on walking (claudication), and even, though rarely, spasm of the coronary arteries to worsen the very angina that the drug was supposed to prevent.

The prototype of the group, *propranolol*, is still widely used but if side-effects should occur, or seem likely, various other beta-blockers with modified ranges of activity are available. These include *metaprolol*, *pindolol*, *acebutolol*, *timolol* and numerous others. Timolol has been successfully used for treating selected cases of glaucoma (increased pressure within the eyeball) by reducing the secretion of fluid in the eye.

Although the list of possible adverse effects looks formidable, in practice most patients benefit from these drugs without discomfort. For the few who do suffer from side-effects, there are good alternatives.

bezoar. A mass of indigestible matter in the stomach, a rare cause of obstruction. The mass is usually composed of hair; the patient may be an emotionally disturbed girl with the habit of chewing and swallowing her own hair.

biceps. Two-headed: strictly speaking the word is an adjective to describe a Y-shaped muscle formed of two muscles that remain separate in their upper parts but are fused in their lower parts, so that the muscle is attached to the skeleton by two tendons above and a single tendon below. Thus *musculus biceps brachii* = the two-headed muscle of the arm.

Biceps femoris is a similar muscle at the back of the thigh.

Bichat, Marie-François-Xavier (1771–1802). French physician and scientist, the founder of ►*histology* – the study of *tissues*, which he was the first to describe. Working without a microscope, an instrument which he apparently despised, Bichat showed by dissection and the use of chemical solvents that the organs of the body were composed of various kinds of fabric (*tissu*). Diseases, he maintained, attacked not whole organs but particular tissues. This idea set pathology in a completely new light, and led directly to the study of the constituent cells of tissues which is the basis of modern pathology (►*Virchow*).

Biermer's anaemia ►*anaemia* (B.2).

bile (gall). The secretion of the liver, a viscous yellow-brown fluid with rather the appearance of motor oil. The daily output of the liver is about a litre of fluid, but the effective volume of bile is less because it becomes concentrated in the ►*gall* bladder, where much of its water is returned to the blood. Bile accumulates in the gall bladder until after a meal. Fats and the like stimulate contraction of the gall bladder, which injects bile into the duodenum, the first part of the intestine.

The active functions of bile depend on the *bile salts*, formed in the liver from *cholesterol*. These salts enable fat to be digested by making an emulsion of it; unemulsified fat simply passes down the intestine. The fat-soluble vitamins A, D, and K are also poorly assimilated in the absence of bile salts. In addition, bile salts activate certain digestive enzymes.

Bile is also a vehicle for excreting waste products from the liver, such as *bile pigments*, excess cholesterol, and various drugs. The bile pigments are derived from the haemoglobin of destroyed red blood cells; they are what remains when the protein fraction has been put back into circulation and the iron has been stored. ►*jaundice*; *liver*.

bilharzia (schistosoma). A small fluke (flatworm, trematode), parasitic during one phase of its life-cycle to water-snails and during another to man. Three species cause human disease. *Schistosoma haematobium* is found in most of Africa and in parts of Spain and the Middle East; *S. mansoni* in Africa and South America; *S. japonicum* in the Far East.

The eggs hatch in fresh water, and the emerging embryos or *miracidia* invade the bodies of snails; there they grow into larvae or *cercariae* and return to the water. Cercariae penetrate intact human skin, enter the circulation, and grow in the veins of the liver. The adult worms settle in the veins of the urinary bladder (*S. haematobium*) or the intestine (*S. mansoni*, *S. japonicum*). Their eggs, each armed with a sharp spike, set up irritation in the affected organ, and leave the body in the urine or stools. If these contaminate water in which there are snails the cycle begins again, and anyone who enters the water can become infected.

Soon after infection, while the cercariae are circulating, there is a transient fever and skin rash (snail-fever). There are no more symptoms for weeks or even months; then symptoms arise from the site of the adult worms – bleeding into the urine, or dysentery. Eggs may be carried to the liver from the intestinal veins or to the lungs from the bladder. In whatever tissue they are embedded the eggs provoke a mild but relentless inflammation, and normal structures are gradually (over many years) replaced by scar tissue. Thus the bladder becomes rigid and shrunken, and cirrhosis of the liver may develop, in turn causing enlargement of the spleen. By no means all cases go so far; the disease can burn itself out before any serious permanent damage is done. But it is still a serious problem in many hot countries, affecting whole populations with anaemia, discomfort, and general ill health. Often the same people are affected with malaria and other infections.

For many years the only treatment was with compounds of *antimony*, which have unpleasant effects and may have to be given for a long time. *Lucanthone* does not contain antimony but it, too, causes vomiting and is not always effective. A newer drug, *niridazole*, is more satisfactory, at least for treating *S. haematobium* infestation, but these have all been superseded by *praziquantel*.

In theory, bilharzial disease can be eradicated in several ways: (1) successful treatment of every case, for which there are neither the drugs nor the means of administering them; (2) adequate sanitation and education in its use, so that water would not be contaminated; (3) eradication of snails by clearing river banks of the vegetation in which they breed, or chemical treatment of the water, or the use of sluices to keep changing the water level and dislodge the snails from their breeding places. In practice, the expense and difficulty are very great.

bilirubin; biliverdin. Two closely related pigments, one orange, one green, found in bile. ▸*jaundice*.

Billroth, Theodor (1829–94). Professor of surgery in Zürich, later Vienna; one of the first surgeons to recognize the full significance of Lister's discovery that infection after operations could be prevented, and to venture into parts of the body that had previously been too dangerous to touch, particularly the abdomen, where the old methods would inevitably have caused a fatal peritonitis. Many of today's standard operations on the stomach, intestine, and thyroid gland were devised by Billroth.

bioavailability. The rate and extent to which a dose actually reaches its destination in the body. First, the same dose might be given by mouth or rectum, injected under the skin or into a muscle or a vein, rubbed into the skin, or inhaled, and in each case the effective amount might be different. Second, people differ, so that one person may absorb a drug rapidly or fully, and another only slowly or partly; and the same person can differ at different times. Third, different preparations of identical doses may differ in their availability.

biochemistry. The chemistry of living processes, a young but already very extensive science.

Biochemical reactions follow the same laws as other chemical reactions, but they are nearly always activated by biological catalysts – *enzymes*. A few important reactions are briefly mentioned under ➤*energy*, ➤*enzyme*, ➤*fat*, ➤*carbo-hydrate*, ➤*protein*, ➤*vitamin*.

biofeedback. A method of bringing under some measure of conscious control functions, such as blood pressure, usually considered to be independent of any volition. To some extent ➤*feedback* is involved in the regulation of blood pressure: an increase of pressure stimulates the natural mechanisms for decreasing it and vice versa. The process is entirely unconscious. Now, breathing is also under reflex control, but we are aware of it and within limits can choose to breathe more or less rapidly or deeply. With a small electronic device, a patient liable to spells of high blood pressure can become aware of them and of the conditions in which they occur and with practice may learn to forestall them. The technique has been applied to other functions, including pulse rate and normally unconscious activity, also migraine and Raynaud's disease.

biopsy. Diagnosis by removing a portion of living tissue for examination.

birth. The process is considered from the mother's point of view under ➤*labour*.

Until birth, the *foetus* (unborn infant) has only one task – growth. The work of maintaining a constant environment (*milieu intérieur*: ➤*Bernard, Claude*) is done by the mother by way of the placenta and umbilical cord. Almost the only contribution the foetus has to make is to maintain a circulation of its own blood for the distribution of supplies and the return of waste products to the mother's circulation.

The newborn infant suddenly finds itself in a completely strange environment to which its organs must adapt. Some, such as the liver, kidneys and endo-crine glands, need little adaptation. They have gradually begun to work in the womb, in conjunction with the mother's glands. The digestive apparatus has no work to do until after birth, when it has to begin to deal with food, in particular milk. At this stage the stomach forms no acid, and in place of the protein-digesting enzyme *pepsin*, the baby has *rennin*, which starts the digestion of milk protein without the help of acid. The muscular system is well developed at birth but its function is very limited because it depends on the nervous system, which is, comparatively speaking, still rudimentary: it is capable of no more than reflex actions, such as sucking and grasping. Many functions that we regard as inborn and automatic are in fact learnt after birth. Some of the nerve fibres in the brain and spinal cord have not yet acquired their insulating myelin sheaths and are therefore not in working order. As a result, functions that will appear later are still dormant, and some of a baby's reflexes differ from those that will develop later as fresh nerve-pathways come into action. The reflexes of a new-born baby vividly suggest a need to clutch at branches in an emergency (➤*Moro reflex*); this is one of the many pieces of evidence that our early ancestors lived in the trees. The long, arduous apprenticeship of the human child before it becomes independent of its elders is arguably a reason for the intellectual superiority over other animals that it will finally achieve.

But certain functions have to be established at once if the infant is to survive: provision of oxygen and of warmth.

Two processes are needed to supply oxygen: breathing to get oxygen into the lungs, and circulation of blood to distribute the oxygen to the rest of the body. The movements of breathing begin in a small way before birth and draw water into the lungs; this is added to fluid actually produced by the lungs. During birth the baby's chest is firmly squeezed – wrung out – and if he is born in the usual way, head first, the recoil draws some air in. More important, the impact of cold air causes the baby to gasp. This first gasp apparently brings in enough oxygen to activate the respiratory centre at the root of the brain and start automatic rhythmical breathing.

The lung fluid has an unexpected but vital function. If the inside of the lungs were moistened with pure water, the surface tension around the thousands of tiny air-pockets would empty the lungs of air as effectively (and by the same mechanism) as pricking a bubble. But the lung fluid contains a surfactant to lower the surface tension to a point where the lungs easily hold air. With a *premature birth* this property may not have developed and the infant cannot then breathe (►*hyaline-membrane disease*).

The circulation of the foetus is arranged to transport oxygen from the placenta, and the lungs, having no function, are bypassed. At birth, blood is diverted to the lungs by changes described under ►*heart* (1).

The urgency of starting to breathe is rather less than it might be, firstly because converting glycogen to lactic acid provides energy without oxygen for some minutes, and the infant has a large store of glycogen; secondly, because the haemoglobin (the blood-pigment that conveys oxygen) in an infant is different from adult haemoglobin and works at a lower concentration of oxygen. But *premature* babies have little stored glycogen and therefore less time to spare.

Next to oxygen, the infant's most urgent need is warmth. At all times a baby has to work harder than an adult to keep warm. Roughly speaking, a body loses heat in proportion to its surface area and can create heat in proportion to its mass or volume. Thus a body twice as tall as another can lose heat at $2^2 = 4$ times the rate, but can generate heat at $2^3 = 8$ times the rate of the other. But although a baby loses much more heat in proportion to its size than an older child, a healthy newborn baby emerges from its natural incubator, the uterus, and maintains its body temperature without even shivering. It does so by virtue of a large store of fat, mostly in the neck and down the front of the backbone, in a special form (►*brown fat*) that is rapidly burnt. Premature babies, on the other hand, have little fat of any kind.

birthmark. A congenital blemish of the skin, of which there are several types. Birthmarks include the *pigmented naevus* or mole, which is a conglomeration of pigment cells resembling those scattered throughout the skin, and several types of *vascular naevus* composed of small blood vessels. The commonest vascular naevus is the *strawberry mark*, bright red and slightly raised, with a tendency to grow larger before shrinking and finally vanishing. The *port-wine stain*, seen most often on the neck, does not change. An unusual type is the *cavernous haemangioma*, composed of much larger vessels but also harmless, though it may be a clue to a similar collection inside the skull and needing removal.

Unless there are very strong cosmetic reasons for interfering most birthmarks are best left alone. Strawberry marks in any case disappear in time, and no treatment of port-wine stains obliterates them without the risk of an equally disfiguring scar.

bismuth. A heavy metal, formerly much used in the treatment of syphilis. Some of its compounds are insoluble and biologically inert, and can be applied to body surfaces as a protective barrier.

Black Death. Bubonic plague, so called either from the dark bruises of spontaneous bleeding into the skin or from the blue-grey complexion of patients with the pneumonic form of the disease. ►*plague.*

blackhead (comedo) ►*acne.*

blackout. Momentary loss of consciousness, especially when due to rapid acceleration, which propels blood away from the head and leaves the brain without enough oxygen. Similar symptoms, especially in older patients, can be due to compression of arteries while the neck is in an awkward position (vertebrobasilar insufficiency), or to a minor, transient ►*stroke.*

blackwater fever. A rare complication of ►*malaria*: red blood cells are rapidly destroyed. The liberated pigment passes through the filters of the kidneys (which are much too fine to let intact cells through) and, in an altered form, blackens the urine. It may block the fine tubes of the kidney and stop the flow of urine. It occurs only in *subtertian* malaria, and seems to be brought on by quinine.

bladder. Several receptacles in the body are called bladders; the two important ones are the ►*gall* bladder attached to the liver, and the *urinary* bladder, generally known simply as the bladder and described below.

The bladder is a flexible muscular bag.

It receives a continuous dribble of urine from the kidneys, which gradually stretches its walls. But this is not like inflating a rubber bladder in which the pressure steadily increases. The muscle fibres of the bladder remain at rest through a considerable range of distension. They simply adapt themselves to the volume of stored urine, and show signs of stretch only when this volume is considerable. They then begin to resist, and the sensation of need to pass urine is felt. In an infant, this sets off reflex emptying of the bladder. After training the reflex can be suppressed; the muscle relaxes and the bladder can be further distended before giving a further signal. The cycle can be repeated several times before reflex emptying supersedes voluntary control. An average bladder will hold at least a pint without serious discomfort. Emptying is usually complete: if the muscle is allowed to contract it does so until the bladder is empty.

The bladder is in the ►*pelvis*, immediately behind the pubic bones. As it fills, it protrudes into the lower abdomen.

The two *ureters*, carrying urine from the kidneys, enter the back of the bladder. Their openings are guarded by valves which prevent urine from flowing back towards the kidneys when the bladder is full. Failure of these valves is probably a cause (but possibly an effect) of bacterial infection ascending to the kidneys from the bladder.

The *urethra*, by which the bladder empties, opens from the lowest point. It is guarded by a tight ring of muscle (a *sphincter*) which relaxes when the main muscle of the bladder is allowed to contract. The female urethra is little more than an inch long and is not a very efficient barrier to bacteria from outside, whereas the male urethra passes through the *prostate* gland and then runs the length of the penis.

1. DISORDERS

Because the bladder lies on the bone it may be torn when the pelvis is fractured; an empty bladder is seldom injured in any other way, but a full bladder can be ruptured by a blow on the abdomen. According to the site of injury, urine is spilt into the peritoneal cavity and causes peritonitis, or between the layers of the abdominal wall,where it also causes dangerous inflammation. In either case, surgical repair is imperative. The bladder heals surprisingly well when it is stitched up, considering that urine prevents healing in other tissues.

Injuries to the spinal cord commonly paralyse the bladder. If nervous pathways below the injury are intact, though no longer controlled by the brain, a simple reflex automatically empties the bladder as soon as the pressure of urine begins to rise, and the patient only needs a receptacle. But if reflex emptying fails, the bladder has to be regularly emptied with a tube (*catheter*) passed up the urethra, in order to prevent stagnation and infection of the urine.

Obstruction to the outlet causes *retention of urine*. If the obstruction is sudden and complete the patient is acutely distressed. Passing a catheter brings prompt relief. Acute retention of urine due to spasm of the sphincter muscle is not uncommon after surgical operations – not necessarily those involving the bladder. Or the outlet can be blocked by a ➤*calculus* (stone). Small stones may pass on but larger ones need surgical removal.

In middle-aged and older men the urethra may be blocked by enlargement of the ➤*prostate gland*. Narrowing of the urethra used to be a common complication of gonorrhoea before the days of antibiotic treatment.

Cystitis – inflammation of the bladder – is very much commoner in women than men because the urethra is so much shorter and therefore less of a barrier to bacteria. Stone in the bladder is often associated with cystitis; one is not always sure which came first.

Tumours of the bladder generally make their presence known by bleeding into the urine. They need prompt attention because they are generally curable if taken early but tend to do badly if neglected. Some bladder tumours are known to be caused by exposure to *naphthylamine* and other chemicals in the dyestuff and rubber industries. A very high incidence of bladder cancer in Egypt suggests that *bilharzia* may be another cause. There also appears to be a link between smoking and bladder cancer, from inhaled carcinogens excreted into the urine.

The bladder can be directly examined with a *cystoscope*, an optical instrument passed up the urethra.

For surgical operations the bladder is easily approached by way of the lower abdomen. Until the time of Lister the abdomen could not be opened without courting a fatal peritonitis, and the very ancient operation of lithotomy (cutting for stone) was done by opening the bladder from below, through the perineum.

blastomycosis. A group of rare and dangerous fevers caused by infection with fungi of the genus *Blastomyces*, confined to North and South America. Blastomycosis was generally fatal until the discovery of the antibiotic *amphotericin-B*.

blastula. A hollow cluster of cells, representing a very early stage in the development of an embryo.

bleeding (haemorrhage). Blood is essentially a means of transporting oxygen and other raw materials around the body. When it leaves the network of blood vessels it is as useless as a derailed train. Bleeding is loss of blood from the circuit of tubular vessels – arteries, capillaries, veins. Whether it actually escapes from the body does not matter. A quart of blood between the muscles around a broken thigh-bone is as much lost as a quart of blood from a cut throat. One can bleed to death from a blow over the spleen without appearing to lose a drop of blood.

The effects of bleeding are described elsewhere. Rapid profuse bleeding causes ➤*shock*. Slow sustained bleeding causes ➤*anaemia* (A.1).

Slight loss of blood has no ill effects, though the associated injuries may. But 'slight' is relative. A person in reasonable health can lose 15 per cent of his blood with impunity. In a grown man, this means 15 per cent of a gallon; in a 10-year-old, of half a gallon; in a 3-year-old, of a quart; in a 1-year-old, of a pint.

Bleeding reduces the total volume of blood, but after 'slight' bleeding the vessels automatically contract enough to maintain the blood pressure. It is this, and not sudden anaemia, that causes the pale skin after bleeding.

The normal volume of blood is restored within a few hours of bleeding by dilution with water from the tissue spaces, and the lost plasma proteins (➤*blood* (1)) are restored in a few days. It takes several weeks to replace the blood cells.

The natural mechanisms to stop bleeding include reflex shrinking of cut blood vessels, and clotting of blood (➤*blood* (4)). These processes can be helped by firm pressure over the wound, such as that of a padded dressing. The pressure reduces the flow of blood, and the dressing provides a scaffolding for the clot.

Blood from a cut artery is bright scarlet, and comes in spurts like water from a stirrup pump. It can sometimes be stopped by pressure on a 'pressure point', where the artery runs near enough to a bone to be flattened against it. The pressure point must obviously be between the heart and the wound.

Blood from a vein is much darker, and it flows smoothly. There is no positive pressure in veins at or above the level of the heart. Bleeding from a vein in a limb stops when the limb is raised, and increases if the limb is allowed to hang. The effect can be seen in the veins at the back of the hand: they empty when the hand is raised and fill when it is lowered.

bleeding disorders. The bleeding or haemorrhagic disorders form a small group. They do not include the hundreds of diseases in which bleeding from damaged tissues is a symptom. They are abnormalities – most of them rare – of bleeding itself. Either bleeding starts too readily, or it does not stop as quickly as it should. They are defects of one or more of the mechanisms by which bleeding is normally stopped, described under ➤*blood* (4). Three categories are described: defects of the small blood vessels, defects of blood platelets (particles in the blood which block breaches in vessels), and defects of clotting.

The symptoms of all bleeding disorders are similar. Wounds bleed for too long, and spontaneous bleeding can occur anywhere – under the skin, into joints, from the kidneys into the urine.

Purpura, a usual symptom, is bleeding under the skin or mucous membranes, giving scattered unprovoked bruises. Pinpoints of bleeding from capillaries are called *petechiae*.

1. BLOOD-VESSEL DEFECTS

Some infectious fevers can cause purpura. The rashes of severe forms of typhus and epidemic meningitis (spotted fever) are of this type. The bleeding is mainly due to bacterial poisoning of the capillaries, but platelets may be affected too. (➤*Black Death*.)

An uncommon type of *allergy* weakens the capillaries and causes purpura with bleeding into the intestine. It was first described by the Berlin paediatrician E. H. Henoch in 1874. The patients are mostly young. Henoch's purpura nearly always clears up in a few weeks, but there may be one or two recurrences.

Vitamin C is necessary to the health of all connective tissue. Lack of vitamin C (➤*scurvy*) shows mainly as weakness of the bonds between the cells of capillary blood vessels, which become very fragile and bleed with the least provocation.

2. PLATELET DEFECTS

Anything that suppresses the formation of white blood cells (➤*blood* (3)) can also suppress platelets. Thus radiation, poisoning of the bone marrow, and diseases such as leukaemia can cause abnormal bleeding.

In some cases the number of platelets falls for no apparent reason, while the other blood cells remain normal. Surgical removal of the spleen sometimes cures the trouble, also for no apparent reason.

3. CLOTTING DEFECTS

The clotting of blood is a complex reaction (➤*blood* (4)). It involves about a dozen reagents or 'factors'. If one is absent, clotting is delayed.

Vitamin K is needed for the synthesis of certain clotting factors. This vitamin cannot be absorbed from the intestine in the absence of bile. When the flow of bile is obstructed, in some types of ➤*jaundice*, vitamin K is not absorbed and clotting is impaired. The danger is greatest in jaundiced new-born babies, and in adults who need an operation for obstructive jaundice but would bleed excessively if the operation were done. In either case the vitamin can be injected.

The best known of all bleeding disorders is ➤*haemophilia*, due to congenital absence of one of the factors. It is a rare disease, but one of great interest to historians because of the people who have suffered from it, and to biologists because of its peculiar mode of inheritance. A number of similar and even rarer diseases, due to absence of different clotting factors, have been described.

blennorrhoea. 1. Excessive secretion of mucus. **2.** = ➤*gonorrhoea*.

blephar(o)-. Prefix = 'of the eyelids'; e.g. *blepharitis*, inflammation of the eyelids, bacterial or allergic.

blindness. Although literally blindness means the inability to see at all, a relative loss of vision can be socially and economically as disabling. In Britain there are separate registers of 'blind' and of 'partially sighted' people. 'Blind' means so blind as to be unable to perform *any* work for which eyesight is essential (not just the work to which the person is accustomed). 'Partial sight' means that the person's vision is poor enough to be a substantial handicap. About 100,000 people, or 0.2 per cent of the population, are registered as blind, and about half as many as partially sighted. Cataract and retinal disease associated with ageing account for some two-thirds of the blind population; most of the remaining third are 'blind' due to *diabetes*, *myopic degeneration* and *glaucoma*.

In developed countries, the commonest causes of blindness depend on genetic factors or degenerative diseases. World-wide, infection, injury, and untreated cataracts are more important. The commonest infectious cause is probably ►*trachoma*.

blood. A grown man has about 4.5 litres of blood. More precisely, the blood makes up one fourteenth of the body weight. The blood is contained in a closed system of tubes or blood vessels: arteries, capillaries, and veins. The arteries and veins are waterproof, but the capillaries, the minute vessels by which blood crosses from arteries to veins, allow water and other small molecules to leak into the tissues. Since water leaks into the capillaries as fast as it leaks out (►*osmosis*), the total volume of the blood remains constant.

Like bone or muscle, blood is a ►*tissue*, and like other tissues it is composed of living cells set in unformed groundsubstance. The peculiarity of blood is that its ground-substance is liquid, and more abundant than that of most tissues. Blood consists of *red cells* and *white cells* floating in a pale yellow, clear fluid, *plasma*. The cells occupy about 45 per cent of the volume, so that in 5 litres of blood we have rather less than 3 litres of plasma. The plasma and the two kinds of cells are best regarded as three

separate organs, each with its own function and each with its ailments.

1. PLASMA

Plasma is a sticky, pale amber liquid with a faint sickly smell. It is a solution in water of proteins (7 per cent), salt (0.9 per cent), glucose (0.1 per cent), and various substances in transit from one part of the body to another. Plasma is a vehicle for all the raw materials of the tissues: water, oxygen, glucose etc., and for removing waste products.

The molecules of protein are too big to pass through the walls of the capillaries, but the other constituents of plasma are free to do so. Their tendency to escape into the tissues under the pressure of the heart's pumping action is counteracted by the osmotic pressure of the protein molecules, which cannot escape; this is the first function of the plasma proteins.

Plasma proteins (albumin, globulin, and fibrinogen) are all formed in the liver from digested amino-acids, except gammaglobulin, which is formed in the lymphoid tissue of the spleen, lymph nodes and elsewhere. Gamma-globulin carries immunity to infectious diseases, some of which is inherited and some acquired as a result of infection. Hence gammaglobulin from someone known to have had a particular infection can be used to immunize others against that disease.

Plasma proteins, especially albumin, may be deficient because of liver disease (not enough formed), kidney disease (loss of albumin in the urine), or starvation. If the amount in the plasma falls below a critical level the osmotic pressure is too low to prevent an excess of water from leaking into the tissues (►*oedema*).

Fibrinogen is responsible for the

clotting of blood (>'Platelets and Clotting', below).

Serum is not quite the same as plasma. It is the fluid which separates from clotted blood, namely plasma without fibrinogen and other components of clot.

2. RED CELLS (ERYTHROCYTES)

A red blood cell is a parcel of the pigment >*haemoglobin*, which conveys oxygen from the lungs to the rest of the body. Its diameter is about 7.2 microns (1/3000 in) and its greatest thickness is 2 microns. A cubic millimetre of blood (not much larger than a pin's head) contains 5 million red cells, and the whole 5 litres of blood contains 25 million million.

Since haemoglobin represents about a third of the mass of the red cells, which make up 45 per cent of the blood, the normal concentration of haemoglobin in the blood is about 15 per cent. The actual concentration indicates the capacity of the blood for oxygen (i.e. the presence or absence of anaemia). Most of the tests in routine use measure the shade of red of the blood against a standard, and the result is given either in grams per 100 ml or as a percentage of an arbitrary 'normal'.

Red cells are derived from unspecialized cells which may also be the precursors of white blood cells. These primitive blood cells can multiply very rapidly. In the process of development, cells destined to become red cells lose their nuclei and with them their ability to reproduce themselves, and they acquire their load of haemoglobin. Haemoglobin cannot be formed without a supply of iron, and the red cells cannot mature without vitamin B_{12} and certain other factors. The rate at which red cells are formed is governed by a hormone, erythropoietin, derived from the kidneys. If the body is short of oxygen, for instance through living at a high altitude or with defects of the lungs, the number of red cells is increased. The life-span of a red cell is 3 to 4 months.

An abnormal excess of red cells is a fairly rare disorder known as >*polycythaemia*.

Deficiencies of the red cells, of which there are many types, are known collectively as >*anaemia*. (>*haemoglobin*.)

3. WHITE CELLS (LEUKOCYTES)

The 'white' blood cells are colourless bodies, larger than red cells. There are normally about 10,000 of them in a cubic millimetre of blood during childhood, and rather fewer in adult life.

When a thin film of blood is stained with a standard mixture of dyes and examined under a microscope, several types of white cell can be identified. All have darkly stained nuclei. In about 70 per cent, small granules are scattered throughout the cell; these cells are *granulocytes*.

The nuclei of *neutrophil* granulocytes are segmented, like a string of sausages or a map of the Great Lakes; hence they are also called polymorphonuclear cells, or simply *polymorphs*. They are called neutrophil because the granules have no affinity for any particular dye. A less common type of granulocyte is the *eosinophil* (acidophil), whose granules take up the red acidic dye eosin. The rarest type is the *basophil*, whose granules take up the basic (alkaline) dye methylene blue from the conventional mixture of stains.

Neutrophils, like all the white blood cells, can insinuate their way through the walls of the smallest blood vessels into the tissues and act as scavengers. They can engulf and destroy invading bacteria (*phagocytosis*). The function of *eosinophils* is less clear. They are prevalent with parasitic (e.g. worm) infestation, and also with allergic disorders such as asthma. They are thought to attack parasites, and may also be involved in the process of inflammation. *Basophils* inhibit the clotting of blood, which would interfere with the defensive action of inflammation. Almost identical in appearance to basophils, but seemingly of different origin, are *mast cells*, which in addition to inhibiting clotting with *heparin* also release *histamine* and perhaps other substances to initiate inflammation and the undesirable effects of allergy.

Lymphocytes circulate constantly throughout the body, using the blood flow to reach the periphery and returning by the lymphatic vessels. Two kinds are distinguished: T cells, associated with the thymus gland, and B cells, connected with bone marrow. The function of lymphocytes is to patrol the body and to respond to any alien substance (such as a bacterium or virus) by adapting themselves to repel the invader (➤*immunity*).

Granulocytes, not having to adapt themselves to a particular invader, multiply at the early stage of an infection. An increase of the number circulating in the blood is easily recorded, and may be a useful pointer to diagnosis. For instance, with an ill-defined bellyache an abnormal concentration of white blood cells might suggest appendicitis rather than green apples. Lymphocytes need more time to respond.

White cells are formed alongside red cells, in the bone marrow. Lymphocytes are also formed in the thymus, spleen, and lymph nodes. Hormones of the adrenal cortex suppress lymphocytes and eosinophils. The factors which stimulate the formation of white cells are unknown.

Proliferation of white cells is a healthy response to infection. During an acute bacterial infection their number in the blood may increase three- or four-fold.

Like the cells of other tissues, the white cells occasionally multiply regardless of the body's needs. This produces a cancer-like disorder, ➤*leukaemia*. The lymphocytes are involved in a somewhat similar disorder known as ➤*Hodgkin's disease*.

lymphocyte

granulocyte

0·01mm.

red corpuscle

Blood cells

93

Bone marrow is the most sensitive of all tissues to agents such as radiation and poisons which hinder the reproduction of cells. In aplastic ►*anaemia* (B.3) the formation of all types of blood cell is suppressed. More often the white cells are more affected than the red. Shortage of white cells is *leukopenia*. Complete absence of granulocytes is *agranulocytosis*. A few poisons regularly cause leukopenia, as does an excess of radiation. Others, including a number of widely used drugs, affect a few unfortunate people who are sensitive to them. Leukopenia is serious, because it leaves the patient without his first line of defence, and he may succumb to what would ordinarily be the most trivial infection. Before the discovery of antibiotics, severe leukopenia was usually fatal. With antibiotics and strict precautions to avoid chance infection, most patients can now be tided over while the bone marrow recovers.

4. PLATELETS AND CLOTTING

Bleeding, or *haemorrhage*, means loss of blood from the circulation; the blood need not escape from the body. The general effects of rapid bleeding are discussed under ►*shock*, and those of sustained bleeding under ►*anaemia* (A.1).

The natural course is for bleeding to stop, and this involves several mechanisms (►*bleeding*).

The *blood platelets* (thrombocytes) have various effects on bleeding. The platelets are small particles – much smaller than red cells – extruded by large bone-marrow cells. A cubic millimetre of normal blood contains about a quarter of a million of them. When a vessel is damaged, platelets stick to each other and to the site of injury and plug the breach. This is one of the ways in which

unhealthy arteries, of which the walls are no longer smooth, become blocked (►*thrombosis*).

Shed blood tends to clot. Clotting is primarily a chemical change in one of the plasma proteins, *fibrinogen*. Fibrinogen is dissolved in the plasma, but after bleeding it is converted into threads of an insoluble protein, *fibrin*. The threads enmesh the blood cells to form a semi-solid mass. The fibrin mesh then contracts, squeezing out a clear yellow fluid, *serum*, and leaving a firm clot.

A dozen or more factors are concerned in the conversion of fibrinogen to fibrin. Most of them are present in circulating blood, but they are ineffective until acted on by other factors released from injured tissue, especially from the platelets when they stick to each other.

Platelets also release a hormone, ►*serotonin*, which encourages blood vessels to contract.

For disorders of clotting etc., ►*bleeding disorders*.

5. BLOOD GROUPS

A red blood cell has a thin shell, of which the chemical structure differs slightly in different people. Several components of the shell vary. A component and its variants form a *system*. People whose red cells have the same variant belong to the same blood group as regards that particular system.

At least 14 systems have been described. Since they are independent of each other there are many possible combinations. Although blood groups cannot yet be used like finger-prints for positive identification, they can often prove that two samples of blood are not from the same person. And since they are inherited, they may prove that someone is not the child of particular parents. They are sometimes a valuable tool for research into other supposedly inherited states: for instance, an association of duodenal ulcer with a particular blood group would strongly suggest a hereditary factor behind duodenal ulcer. The prevalence of blood groups in different populations has been used to study such matters as early migrations.

The great importance of blood groups in medicine is that chemical compounds different from those of an individual are treated as 'foreign' by his body defences. If red cells of a foreign group enter his blood, they are liable to be destroyed as though they were infecting bacteria.

The most important of the blood-group systems, the ABO system, was discovered in 1900 by Karl Landsteiner, in Vienna. 'Blood group' normally means the ABO group (A, B, AB, or O). Until Landsteiner's discovery, blood transfusion was most hazardous, because if a patient is given blood of the wrong ABO group his own blood may destroy its cells, and in the process he becomes dangerously ill.

Another system of blood groups (>rhesus factor) was discovered in 1940, again by Landsteiner, who had had a Nobel Prize in 1930. Some dangerous illnesses of newborn babies are due to their belonging to a different rhesus group from their mothers.

These two groups are usually enough to show if a blood transfusion is appropriate: the occasional incompatibility of blood with similar groups is shown by crossmatching a sample of each in the laboratory before deciding to transfuse. However, several systems of differing groups that need not affect transfusion, such as the MNS groups and others, are used in forensic laboratories, e.g. in paternity suits or to identify blood stains.

Blood transfusion is the easiest of transplants. Organs such as kidneys and hearts need far more accurate matching. The four groups of the ABO system represent only six genetic types of red cell. The compatibility of an organ such as a kidney is checked by an analogous system (>HLA) representing thousands of types of lymphocyte. (>transfusion; immunity.)

blood count. Number of cells per cubic millimetre of blood.

blood group >blood (5).

blood-letting. A very ancient method of treating disease, probably based on the idea that ill health is due to imbalance of the four humours (blood, yellow bile, black bile, phlegm). Many symptoms were ascribed to surfeit of blood or plethora.

Blood-letting still has a place in the treatment of polycythaemia, a condition in which blood cells are formed too profusely, and the blood does not flow as freely as it should. In congestive heart failure blood-letting gave temporary relief by reducing the load on the circulation, but this treatment has been supplanted by diuretics.

blood-poisoning. A non-technical term used to describe at least three conditions: (1) toxaemia (the literal sense of blood-poisoning), the spread of poisons formed by bacteria such as the toxin of tetanus, which affects the whole nervous system although the actual bacteria are confined to the region of a wound; (2) cellulitis, the spread of bacteria (usually streptococci) from a wound into neighbouring tissues; (3) septicaemia, dissemination of virulent bacteria by the blood-stream.

blood pressure (BP). The pressure at

which the heart pumps blood into the major arteries. Subject to some individual variation, a normal BP fluctuates with the heart beat between about 120 mm of mercury (systolic pressure), and 80 mm (diastolic pressure). The main arteries are wide enough not to impede the flow significantly, so that the pressure in the brachial artery of the arm, where BP is normally measured, is nearly the same as at the outlet from the heart. But the small branches of arteries (arterioles) are narrow enough to exert considerable resistance, and the blood loses much of its pressure in flowing through them. When blood reaches the capillaries the pressure has fallen to about 32 mm, which is enough to oppose back-pressure from the tissue fluid (>osmosis) and carry the blood through to the veins. On the return journey to the heart, the BP in the veins is so low that the blood has to be helped on its way by neighbouring muscles.

Elaborate nervous and chemical controls adjust the circulation to the demands of the moment. The total flow is determined by the volume and rate of the heart beats. The flow to a particular organ, e.g. the leg muscles during exercise, or the stomach after a meal, is increased by widening its arteries, with compensatory narrowing of arteries elsewhere. But the demands of the brain do not vary. At work or idle it needs about 750 ml of fresh blood per minute. The function of the blood pressure is to maintain this constant flow of blood to the brain. Anyone who has ever fainted knows what happens if the pressure is momentarily lowered.

While insufficient pressure deprives the brain of its supplies, excessive pressure over-taxes the heart and blood vessels. Therefore the BP has to be kept within narrow limits.

Pressure is determined by rate of flow and resistance to flow. But the rate of flow is adapted to the constantly varying demand, between 5 litres per minute at rest and 30 or 40 litres in an athlete at full stretch. Therefore the BP can be kept constant only by adapting resistance to rate of flow.

Resistance has two components: the viscosity of the blood, which apart from increasing during exercise does not fluctuate, and the size of the arterioles, of which the diameter is varied by contraction and relaxation of their muscular walls. At constant pressure, the flow in a pipe varies with the fourth power of the diameter; thus doubling the diameter of the pipe increases the flow sixteen-fold. Only small changes in the arterioles are needed for large effects. With a 6:1 increase of blood flow, the average diameter of the arterioles has to increase by only 3:2 in order to keep the BP steady.

If the arterioles fail to expand, then either the flow must decrease or the pressure must rise. But the heart is geared to maintain an adequate flow for as long as possible, and if the resistance to flow is increased it simply works harder; the flow is maintained and the pressure rises.

The regulation of blood pressure by the sympathetic nervous system and by a hormone (renin) from the kidneys is discussed under >circulation.

Blood pressure is measured with a sphygmomanometer, invented in 1896 by the Italian physician Riva-Rocci (who is commemorated in some countries by the symbol R-R for blood pressure). The instrument is a column of mercury supported by the air pressure in an inflatable cuff. The cuff is wrapped round a limb. The sound of the pulse is detected with a stethoscope over an artery, or by a built-in microphone. The highest pressure at which a pulse is heard is a systolic pressure; the lowest, the diastolic. A useful modification is a small aneroid manometer, which is less cumbersome than the mercury-based instrument.

1. HIGH BLOOD PRESSURE

It is normal for the systolic BP to rise in response to exertion or emotion, but it does not vary by more than about 50 per cent even when the rate of flow increases by 300 per cent or more. The diastolic pressure, between beats, hardly changes. After exertion the BP quickly returns to its resting level.

The normal blood pressure is said to increase with age. It may do so to some extent, but what increases greatly is the *average* BP in the population, which is not the same thing. People with perfectly healthy blood vessels show little if any increase of BP as the years go by; but in civilized communities they are a minority. The unhealthy majority puts up the average.

Most diseases of the kidneys can cause hypertension, by interfering with the blood-flow through the kidneys and so causing the hormone *renin* to be released; this in turn promotes the formation of *angiotensin*, which stimulates contraction of arterioles.

A very rare tumour of the adrenal glands, phaeochromocytoma, secretes noradrenaline, with the same effect as stimulation of sympathetic nerves – contraction of arterioles, increased resistance, raised BP.

Excess of blood cells (polycythaemia) increases the viscosity of the blood, and therefore the resistance and the pressure.

But most high blood pressure has no recognized cause, and is known as primary or *essential* hypertension. This condition cannot be properly defined because there is no clear division between the ranges of normal and abnormal pressures. Essential hypertension probably includes various unidentified disorders. It need not cause any symptoms at all, in which case one cannot really describe it as a disorder. But a blood pressure that is persistently higher than would be expected is a warning; the records of insurance companies show that it lessens the chance of living to an old age.

The symptoms – if there are any – are vague and might or might not be really due to hypertension: fatigue, dizziness, headache and the like. With severe hypertension the heart first enlarges to meet the added demands, as does any hard-worked muscle, but may later be overtaxed and fail to keep up an adequate circulation (▸*heart failure*). Very high blood pressure injures the kidneys, and a late stage of hypertension, with impairment of the kidneys as an effect, is indistinguishable from a late stage of chronic kidney disease with hypertension as a symptom. This is a vicious circle, since kidney disease causes high BP and vice versa.

Hypertension aggravates other disorders arising from unhealthy arteries. It increases *atheroma* (the underlying defect with most arteriosclerosis) and the likelihood of suffering coronary thrombosis or a stroke.

To a limited extent a tendency to hypertension may be inherited. For instance, some sufferers are not able to deal with any excess of sodium, so that surplus salt in the diet may raise their blood pressure. But factors that can be controlled are more significant: obesity, heavy drinking and the day-to-day stresses of life in an affluent society.

The rational *treatment* of any illness is to tackle its cause, but this can be done in only a minority of cases of hypertension. The cause of essential hypertension is still unknown, and the symptom has to be treated as though it were the actual disease. Regardless of cause, there is no doubt that raised blood pressure shortens life: the higher the pressure, the greater the risk. It is also certain that lowering the pressure reduces the risk of lethal complications such as strokes, heart attacks and failure of the kidneys. There is no precise level at which hypertension begins, but a diastolic pressure of 95 or more is generally taken as an indication for treatment.

Until 1947 there was no available safe and reliable way of lowering the blood pressure. Since then, numerous *ganglion blocking* drugs have been discovered. They prevent the relay of impulses in sympathetic nerves, and so prevent arterioles from being stimulated to contract. But these drugs act indiscriminately on the sympathetic and parasympathetic nervous systems, with many unwanted effects. Some of the newer drugs suppress the action of sympathetic nerves without other effects, mostly by interfering with noradrenaline, the substance released by sympathetic nerves to constrict arterioles. For instance, ►*rauwolfia* (introduced to Western medicine in 1953) removes noradrenaline from nerve-endings, *guanethidine* (1960) prevents its release, and *methyl-dopa* (1963) interferes with its synthesis. *Hydralazine* appears to act directly on blood vessels, causing them to dilate and so reducing resistance and pressure. It had been known for some time before its value was recognized; after a brief vogue it was in disfavour because of the associated side-effects. Recently it has been combined with other drugs and used in smaller doses than before.

Except in emergencies, the original ganglion-blockers have been superseded by *beta-blockers*. The action of these drugs is confined to the beta-receptors of the ►*sympathetic* system, thus avoiding many unwanted effects of their predecessors. Even so, the first drugs of this class, such as *propranolol*, are unsuitable for asthmatics, in whom they can precipitate attacks. This problem may be overcome with selective beta-blockers such as *acebutolol*, which act on the heart and blood vessels but not the lungs.

Before any of these drugs, none of them free from undesired effects, is called in, mild cases of hypertension often respond to *diuretics*, which promote the flow of urine and the elimination of sodium. These may be effective enough on their own, and when more powerful drugs are needed a diuretic enhances the action of smaller and safer doses.

Without taking any drugs at all, people with high blood pressure can often improve their condition by cutting down alcohol if they drink, losing weight if they are overweight, and restricting their intake of salt. Systematic relaxation, especially with the help of special techniques such as ►*biofeedback*, can also play a useful part in controlling blood pressure.

Since 1980 several new ways of lowering blood pressure have appeared. These include calcium antagonists such as ►*nifedipine*, which impede the stimulation by calcium of the heart muscle and of the muscle fibres that constrict arteries (these drugs are also used in the treatment of angina pectoris). Some of the ►*prostaglandins* lower blood pressure by relaxing small arteries, apparently without impairing the flow of blood through the kidneys, a disadvantage of some other forms of treatment. *Capto-*

pril interferes with the activation of angiotensin, a hormone originating in the kidneys which raises blood pressure. This type of drug has a place in the management of severe hypertension that does not respond adequately to less drastic methods.

2. Low Blood Pressure

Apart from rare disorders such as Addison's disease, with which the patient has more serious worries, it is very doubtful whether people really suffer from persistently low BP, though the diagnosis is quite popular in some countries, perhaps as a change from 'neurasthenia'.

Some people feel dizzy if they suddenly stand up from a chair or when they get out of bed. This is simply because the reflexes that adjust the BP to the standing posture do not act at once, and gravity carries blood away from the head before the blood vessels of the lower half of the body have time to contract enough to oppose gravity. A faint is a similar event produced by sudden relaxation of these vessels.

►*Shock* is a dangerous state following severe injury etc., with the blood pressure so low that the circulation may fail.

blood tests. Hundreds of different blood tests are occasionally used in diagnosis; scores of them are matters of routine in any medical laboratory. There are three main groups.
1. *Haematology*. Tests of the state of the blood itself for the diagnosis of anaemias etc., e.g. number and condition of blood cells, amount of haemoglobin; blood group; clot formation.
2. *Blood chemistry*. Tests reflecting chemical functions elsewhere in the body, e.g.

various enzymes (bone, liver, muscle); sugar (pancreas); urea (kidney disease); uric acid (gout).
3. *Microbiology*. Detection of actual microbes (e.g. malaria, typhoid); detection of immunity (antibodies) as evidence of past or present infection – many types of infection can be recognized in this way.

blood vessel. Tube – ►*artery*, ►*capillary*, or ►*vein* – carrying blood (►*circulation*).

blue baby ►*heart* (4).

BMR ►*basal metabolism.*

Boerhaave, Hermann (1668–1738). Dutch physician; the most celebrated medical teacher of modern times. More than anyone else, Boerhaave established the method of learning from actual patients rather than from lectures and texts. Under his influence, Leyden became the leading medical school of the day. Several other schools rose to greatness under his pupils: Edinburgh (Alexander Monro), Vienna (Gerard van Swieten), Berne (Albrecht von Haller).

boil. Small abscess around the root of a hair, or in a sweat gland. Single boils are painful for a day or two but as a rule take care of themselves; they extrude a core of dead tissue and heal. The process is accelerated by warm applications (poultices). Occasionally a boil has to be opened surgically, but otherwise physical interference is more likely to spread the infection than cure it. Squeezing boils is unhelpful and can be dangerous. Antiseptics are useful for discouraging infection of neighbouring sweat glands.

Boils on the face need more care than others because infection can be carried by the veins into the skull. They may call for treatment with antibiotic drugs.

bone

1. STRUCTURE

The adult skeleton is made almost entirely of a hard, rigid tissue, bone, which consists like other tissues of living cells suspended in an inert ground-substance. But in bone the cells are scanty. The ground-substance gives bone its characteristic properties. It is a network of protein fibres with insoluble mineral salts, mostly phosphates of calcium, deposited among them. The fibres confer resilience and the salts hardness. If the fibres are destroyed, e.g. by bacterial action after death, the remaining bone is brittle; if the salts are dissolved with acid the bone becomes rubbery.

All bones have a hard, dense shell of *compact bone* traversed only by very fine channels, the *Haversian* canals. Inside this shell the bone is porous (cancellous), or hollowed out and replaced with soft blood-forming tissue, ➤*marrow*. There is a hole in the shell (usually only one) for the passage of blood vessels, of which small branches reach the periphery by the Haversian canals. A fibrous membrane, the periosteum, tightly surrounds the bone. It has a network of nerves and blood vessels, which penetrate only the outermost layer of the bone. *Sensation* from bone is really from the periosteum; bone itself is insensitive.

2. DEVELOPMENT AND GROWTH

Bone, like muscle, connective tissue, and blood, is formed in the embryo from ➤*mesoderm*. With a few exceptions, prototypes of the bones appear as a modification of the mesoderm to cartilage. Towards the end of the 2nd month of pregnancy *ossification* begins: an island of true bone is formed in each unit and spreads until all the cartilage has been replaced. The process is not complete at birth. Some small bones of the hands and feet are still entirely cartilaginous. At the end of the 'long' bones (➤'Anatomical Classification', below), at various protrusions where powerful muscles are attached, and at the sites of certain atavistic bones, *epiphyses* are formed. An epiphysis is a part added to a bone in which ossification begins late. Of about 100 epiphyses in the body only those at the knee contain bone at birth. The others remain cartilaginous until a time, roughly predictable for each, between birth and adolescence. After ossification the epiphyses are attached by cartilage which is not converted to bone until the bones reach their adult length.

The exceptions mentioned are the clavicle and most of the skull, which start as bone without first being formed in cartilage.

The stage of ossification indicates the age of a skeleton, and may be a useful guide in identifying human remains.

Bone grows by the activity of *osteoblasts*. These cells produce an enzyme which causes insoluble calcium phosphate to be precipitated from the soluble phosphates in the blood. They are active only under the periosteum and at the ends of bones where the epiphyses join them. Thus bones grow thicker by the addition of new tissue at the outside, and longer by addition at the ends. Injury to the end of a young bone may interfere with its growth.

Simultaneously, the core of a growing bone is eroded; there, *osteoclasts* produce an enzyme with the opposite action to that of the osteoblasts.

The general shape of a bone is determined by hereditary factors, but its details are modified by the pull of muscles, which stimulates bone formation.

Growth is stimulated by the growth hormone of the ▸*pituitary*, and by the ▸*sex hormones*, which also promote the fusion of the epiphyses with the rest of the bone. Since growth stops when this fusion is complete, the sex hormones may also be said to inhibit growth. Thus although sex hormones may be given to undersized children, they defeat their own object unless the dose is carefully regulated, because although they accelerate growth they may stop it too soon.

The ▸*parathyroid* glands are indirectly concerned with bone growth, because they regulate the amount of calcium in the blood. If the level falls, calcium is drawn from the bones by the action of parathyroid hormone.

Healthy growth of any tissue needs a proper diet. Any reasonable diet includes the essential elements of bone, but there may be a lack of vitamin D and consequent ▸*rickets*. Vitamin D was formerly thought to stimulate the actual formation of bone, but it now appears to act only indirectly, by increasing the absorption of calcium from the food into the blood and perhaps by decreasing loss of calcium from the kidneys: if enough calcium is available to them, the osteoblasts will do their work.

3. ANATOMICAL CLASSIFICATION

Bones are described as *long*, *short*, or *flat*. *Long bones* are cylindrical or prismatic, usually hollow, with a knob at each end. *Short bones* are simple blocks of cancellous (spongy) bone with a thin, compact shell. *Flat bones* consist of two parallel sheets of compact bone with a spongy layer between.

The *carpal* and *tarsal* bones in the hand and foot are 'short'; all the other limb bones, including those of the digits, are 'long'. The vault of the skull, the sternum, the scapula, and part of the pelvis are 'flat'. The end of a rib joined to the spine is 'long', but the rest is flat. The body of a vertebra is a compressed long bone. A few irregular bones in the base of the skull and elsewhere remain unclassified.

Sesamoid bones are not really parts of the skeleton. They are imbedded in tendons subject to excessive friction, and are usually very small. Only one is important: the *patella*, in the tendon at the front of the knee.

Supernumerary bones are usually epiphyses which have failed to join their principal bones. They often correspond with bones which are normally separate in other animals.

4. DISORDERS

Bone is subject to the same kinds of trouble as any other tissue, but its physical peculiarities modify the effects of disease.

Bone is very strong, but also rigid. If it yields at all it does so completely (▸*fracture*). And whereas in most other tissues an ▸*abscess* can close once the pus is released, the rigid walls of an abscess in bone cannot fall together; thus the infection persists. Nor can bone expand to make room for inflammation (▸*osteitis*). The increased pressure in an inflamed or injured bone may interfere with the circulation and kill part of the bone. Dead bone, being largely insoluble, is not readily broken down and absorbed as are other dead tissues. It therefore remains, cut off from the defensive elements of the blood, as a focus of infection where microbes can breed without hindrance.

The arteries in bone do not communicate freely with each other: if one is blocked the area it feeds may have no alternative supply. Where an epiphysis joins a bone there is no communication across the line of fusion, which is therefore a bulkhead against the spread of disease.

Sensation is confined to the periosteum, so that unless this outer membrane is involved disorders of bone are painless. But pain is severe if the periosteum is even slightly stretched, e.g. by inflammation or bleeding.

Except at the ends of young bones, growth of new bone depends on the osteoblasts in the periosteum. If the periosteum is destroyed an injured bone does not heal.

Various kinds of tumour (►*osteoma*) arise in bone. Cancer of bone is discussed at ►*sarcoma*.

►*cartilage*; *skeleton*.

booster dose. Supplementary dose of a vaccine to meet a special emergency, such as entering the area of an epidemic, or to reinforce the effect of an earlier vaccination as this begins to wear off. ►*immunization*.

boracic (boric) acid. $H_3B\ O_3$; a mild antiseptic used as a dusting powder, and in various solutions for treating infections of skin and mucous membranes.

bordetella. A kind of very small bacterium. One species, *Bordetella pertussis*, is the germ of ►*whooping cough*.

Borellia. A kind of spiral bacterium or spirochaete. *B. vincentii* is a normal inhabitant of the mouth; very rarely it provokes severe inflammation of the mouth and throat (Vincent's angina). Other species of Borellia can cause *relapsing fever* and *Lyme disease*.

Bornholm disease (epidemic myalgia; epidemic pleurisy; devil's grip; pleurodynia). A virus infection with fever and pain in the muscles of the ribs and abdomen. The disease was first observed in the island of Bornholm, but there have been outbreaks in many parts of the world. An attack lasts a day or two and is sometimes repeated a few days later. Complications are extremely rare.

bothryocephalus (Diphyllobothrium). A kind of tapeworm found mostly in Finland and Japan, causing severe anaemia (►*worms*).

botulism. A rare but exceedingly dangerous type of ►*food poisoning*, caused by a toxin formed by the bacterium *Clostridium botulinum*. This common microbe seldom infects man, but it may contaminate badly preserved food. It multiplies only in the complete absence of air, as in a preserving can. Minute doses of the toxin paralyse the nervous system and are commonly fatal.

Most reported outbreaks have been in the United States, where homecanning is (or has been) popular. Factory-canned foods are safe because the high temperatures destroy any bacteria.

Cooking destroys the toxin; so does the acid of uncooked fruit. Homecanned vegetables have been the greatest hazard.

As breathing and swallowing may be paralysed, botulism requires intensive treatment in hospital, where vital functions can be maintained artificially. An antitoxin to neutralize the toxin is available.

Clostridium botulinum can also infect wounds in the same way as the closely related germs of tetanus and gas gangrene; and it occasionally causes intestinal infection in infants.

bowel = ►*intestine*.

brachial. Of the arm (usually in the strict anatomical sense of upper arm).

The *brachial artery* is the main blood vessel of the upper limb, a continuation of the *axillary* artery. It runs down the inner side of the humerus, where its pulsation can be felt in the groove between biceps and triceps muscles, and where it can be compressed to stop bleeding lower down. In front of the elbow the artery divides into the *radial* and *ulnar* arteries of the forearm.

The *brachial plexus* is a leash of nerves with various intercommunications, arising from the spinal nerves in the lower part of the neck. Its branches provide the nerves of the shoulder-girdle and upper limb. The plexus is sometimes injured during birth, and this causes a temporary paralysis of the arm. In adult life the nerves of this plexus may be subject to irritation or pressure from disorders of the neck such as arthritis of the vertebrae or a slipped disc. ➤*vertebra* (1).

brain. The part of the central nervous system enclosed by the skull. Like its continuation the spinal cord, the brain starts life as a simple tube. But whereas the spinal cord retains this form throughout life, the brain grows into a complex system of bulges and folds.

At an early stage of embryonic life, three bulbous swellings appear at the front end of the tube that is to form the central nervous system, and these develop into the three main divisions of the brain: the *hindbrain*, the *midbrain*, and the *forebrain*.

The original tube is still recognizable in the adult brain as the *brain-stem*, seen as an extension into the skull of the spinal cord. It is a central core from which the larger portions of the brain (cerebellum and cerebrum) grow.

Very roughly speaking, the further from the spinal cord the more advanced the function, progressing from reflexes for maintaining vital functions such as the circulation of blood and breathing in the lower part of the hindbrain to the processes of intelligent behaviour in the outer layers of the forebrain. But structure and function are only loosely related, for the whole nervous system works as an integrated unit.

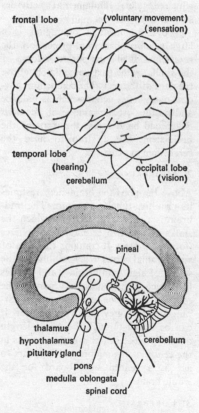

Parts of the brain: (above) *left side,* (below) *mid-line*

1. HINDBRAIN

The spinal cord continues into the skull as the *medulla oblongata*. In the cord, the nerve cells form a fluted rod (grey matter) surrounded by nerve fibres (white matter). In the medulla the grey matter is gathered into more or less distinct groups of cells or *nuclei*; this tendency increases further up the brain. These nuclei include the cells of several cranial nerves and also the *vital centres* which regulate fundamental activities such as the heart beat.

Above the medulla oblongata is a large, rounded, backward projection, the *cerebellum*. It fills the posterior fossa of the skull, i.e. the part immediately above the nape of the neck. The cerebellum governs many reflex actions such as balance and posture. At the same level, the *pons* is a broad band across the front of the brain-stem, like a strap to hold the cerebellum in place.

2. MIDBRAIN

Above the pons the brain-stem resumes its primitive tubular structure. The midbrain is a short cylinder from which the stalks of the two cerebral hemispheres (forebrain) arise. It contains the cells of some cranial nerves, relay stations for the senses of sight and hearing, and centres for the coordination of movements. The *reticular formation* is a criss-cross arrangement of grey and white matter. It can be traced through the whole length of the brain-stem but is most obvious in the centre of the midbrain. It appears to act as a central switchboard for the whole brain.

3. FOREBRAIN

Above the midbrain the brain-stem bends sharply forwards, and the narrow central canal widens to a deep vertical cleft, the third ventricle. At each side of the ventricle is a mass of grey matter, the *thalamus*. Sensation of all kinds is received here and distributed to reflex pathways or to the cerebral cortex and consciousness. Crude sensation, particularly pain, is perceived in the thalamus itself. Below is the *hypothalamus*, the highest centre of the autonomic nervous system, from which is suspended the ➤*pituitary* gland. Behind is a small protrusion, the *pineal body*. The whole complex, representing the headward end of the brain-stem, is sometimes called the tween-brain.

Projecting from either side of the tween-brain and completely enclosing it are the relatively huge *cerebral hemispheres*, which make up the greater part of the human brain. It is only through the development of the cerebral hemispheres that a man's brain is relatively larger than a monkey's or a monkey's than a dog's. (An elephant's brain is about four times as large as man's, but in relation to the size of the animal it is much smaller.)

The central cavity of a cerebral hemisphere, the lateral ventricle, opens by a narrow isthmus (foramen of Monro) into the third ventricle. It is surrounded by masses of grey matter, the *basal ganglia*, which are concerned with muscle action immediately below the level of consciousness. Disorders of the basal ganglia cause *parkinsonism* – shaking palsy. The surface of the hemispheres is covered with a layer of grey matter, the *cerebral cortex*. Between the cortex and the underlying basal ganglia and thalamus is a broad zone of white matter, composed of nerve fibres to and from the cells of the cortex.

Definite functions can be ascribed to

certain areas of the cerebral cortex. The areas for voluntary movement and for most types of sensation have been plotted in detail, but no particular area can be allotted to such functions as reason or memory.

4. SUPPORTING STRUCTURES

Nervous tissue needs a large and constant supply of oxygen and glucose, waking or sleeping, thinking or idling. It ceases to work after a few seconds if the supply is cut off, and irreparable damage is done in a few minutes. The rate of circulation in other organs varies widely but the brain receives about 750 ml of blood per minute, by the carotid and vertebral arteries, regardless of what is going on elsewhere. The complicated mechanisms for maintaining the blood pressure serve mainly to keep up this supply.

The brain is enclosed by fibrous membranes, the ➤meninges, and by the ➤cerebrospinal fluid.

The behaviour of nervous tissue, of which the brain is composed, is discussed under ➤nervous system.

5. DISORDERS

Numerous kinds of defective or faulty development account for most of the severe cases of congenital mental handicap. A relatively small defect sometimes obstructs the circulation of the cerebrospinal fluid through and around the brain, causing a dangerous accumulation of fluid under pressure within the skull (hydrocephalus). This can often be corrected surgically.

Injuries to the brain are never to be taken lightly. The mildest recognizable injury is concussion, and even the briefest loss of consciousness represents some permanent damage. Brain cells, once damaged, have no powers of recovery or regeneration. The effects of repeated concussion, such as professional boxers can incur, are cumulative and can lead to gross disturbance.

Surprisingly, bacterial infection of the meninges (➤meningitis) does not very often spread to the brain, but the associated inflammation and swelling can seriously injure it. Abscesses of the brain usually arise from the spread of infection from the ears or nasal sinuses, or by material carried in the blood-stream from severely infected lungs, or, of course, from infected head injuries. They need urgent attention in order to relieve the pressure within the inflexible skull as soon as possible.

As mature brain cells have no power of regeneration, so they do not form tumours. The connective tissue of the brain (neuroglia) can and does form tumours, and although they have no tendency to set up secondary tumours in other parts of the body they can spread widely and insidiously within the brain; those that do so cannot be treated surgically. Those that remain localized may be operable, and tumours which arise in the meninges and press on the brain are usually curable. Recently developed techniques of ➤scanning greatly facilitate the diagnosis of these and other lesions in and around the brain.

Disturbances of the blood supply to the brain (➤stroke) are among the most prevalent diseases of developed countries. In Britain they rank second to heart attacks as a cause of death, though if all types of cancer are counted together, strokes take third place. There has been a steady decrease since the 1960s. This may be due to the great improvement in the treatment of high ➤blood pressure, a major cause of strokes. The other cause, closely linked to blood pressure, is *arteriosclerosis* (►*artery* (1)).

Numerous hitherto mysterious disturbances of brain function, including mental disorders, are likely to be explained with the advances that are being made in the extremely complicated chemistry of the nervous system; we can await developments with some confidence. ►*dementia*.

brain-stem. The direct upward extension of the spinal cord into the skull, composed of *medulla oblongata*, *pons*, and *midbrain*. The major portions of the brain, *cerebellum* and *cerebral hemispheres*, project from it.

breakbone fever ►*dengue*.

breast. The breasts (mammary glands) develop in the fatty tissue under the skin as columns of cells radiating from the nipples; these columns later become ten or twenty tubes or *ducts*. Thus far, their development is the same in either sex. In a girl (and in a few perfectly normal boys) the ducts branch out at puberty, under the influence of sex hormones from the ovaries (or testes), and a very variable amount of fat is deposited. The size of the breasts depends on this fat and is therefore not related to their efficiency: small flat breasts are as likely to feed twins – and their owners to bear twins – as 'well-developed' breasts and their owners.

During pregnancy the breasts change rapidly under the influence of hormones from the placenta. The ducts proliferate and milk-forming tissue grows around their ends. Towards the end of pregnancy hormones from the pituitary gland stimulate the secretion of milk.

Suckling stimulates the nipple, and this, by an unknown mechanism, causes the release from the pituitary of a hormone, *oxytocin*, which acts on the breast to eject milk and form more milk. Oxytocin also stimulates the uterus to contract and regain its resting size and shape after pregnancy (it does so without this stimulus, but suckling probably accelerates the process). When the baby is weaned the stimulus of suckling is withdrawn and milk soon ceases to be formed. Thyroid hormone is also required for milk production.

The adult female breast is comma-shaped: in addition to the obvious dome of tissue over the pectoral muscles it has a tail-like extension towards the armpit.

Rudimentary breasts may develop anywhere along a line from the armpit to the middle of the groin. They have no significance except as evolutionary curiosities.

1. DISORDERS

Serious deficiencies of the breast are unusual. Complete inability to form milk is very rare, because the breasts develop with the other reproductive organs, and if a woman is capable of having a child at all she is likely to be able to feed it at least for a time. Inadequate (as opposed to absent) milk supply has many causes, including almost any kind of ill health after childbirth. It is the quantity rather than the quality of the milk that suffers. The influence of suckling on the pituitary gland can be disturbed by emotional factors, of which not wishing to feed the infant is among the most important. The commonest physical cause of poor milk supply is a sore or cracked nipple, which destroys the pleasure of suckling and inhibits the formation of milk. Much of this kind of trouble is avoided by antenatal care of the nipples.

Mastitis – inflammation of the breast – is generally due to bacterial infection from a cracked nipple. Antibiotic drugs usually clear it up quickly, but sometimes an abscess forms and has to be relieved surgically. Such complications nearly always mean that breast-feeding has to be interrupted, and often it cannot be successfully resumed.

Various apparent abnormalities of the breast appear around puberty as the gland attains its adult state, and around the menopause as it regresses into inactivity. These used to be classified as chronic mastitis; this was a misnomer, since there was no inflammation, and an indiscretion because it made a harmless anomaly sound like a disease (an objection that equally applies to other names such as fibroadenosis and cystic disease). The term ANDI (Aberrations of Normal Development and Involution) is now preferred; involution being the process of running down with advancing years. Symptoms of ANDI may include a lump, or more often a patch with the feel of a kapok pillow that needs plumping up, or a dull ache. The condition can be regarded as a harmless phase requiring no special treatment, but like any oddity in a breast it should be reported and investigated at once to exclude anything more serious.

Cancer of the breast is the commonest form of cancer in women, and one of the easiest to detect. The first sign is nearly always a lump in the breast, which the patient can be taught to feel for herself and *report at once*. Some 75 per cent of cases treated as soon as a lump appears, before it has time to spread, can be cured as judged by 10-year follow-up studies. If treatment is delayed the success rate declines quickly.

The mainstays of treatment, at least in the early stages, are surgery and irradiation. The extent of the operation is still disputed, each surgeon naturally prefer-

ring the methods that in his hands have given the best results. If it can be shown that the lymph nodes in the armpit are not involved surgeons of one school of thought remove only a part of the breast, but if the tumour has spread to the nodes they have to be removed along with the whole breast. In either case the operation is usually followed by a course of irradiation. Some women may choose to accept the added risk of preserving a good part of the breast; others would rather play safe, and settle for an artificial substitute, either external or implanted surgically. In any case the loss of a breast is a far more traumatic experience than that of, say, a kidney or a length of intestine, which has no symbolic or emotional significance.

It has been known for many years that hormones play a part in the growth of breast tumours, and operations to remove ovaries, adrenals or pituitary have all been used with some success. But drugs now available often obviate the need for such drastic treatment, e.g. *tamoxifen* to oppose the effect of female sex hormones, and *aminoglutethimide* to inhibit their formation in the adrenals. In the later stages of the disease, including cases where surgery is inappropriate, cytotoxic drugs can be used to inhibit the growth of the tumour.

breath-holding. Breathing is essentially a reflex action, but unlike other reflexes it can be transferred for a while to conscious control. When the breath is deliberately held, carbon dioxide accumulates in the blood, stimulating the respiratory centre in the brain until reflex action overrides volition and a breath must be taken.

Small children sometimes acquire the trick of breath-holding to get attention; they can actually lose consciousness for a second or two, giving a fair imitation of epilepsy.

breathing ►*respiration*.

breech = buttocks; *breech delivery* is the birth of a baby buttocks first instead of the usual head first. It adds to the difficulties of both mother and child, and is usually avoided by turning the baby to a head-down position before confinement. When breech delivery cannot be avoided, it is facilitated by bringing the baby's feet down so that his legs are born straight and not bunched in front of his belly.

Bright, Richard (1789–1858). Physician at Guy's Hospital, London, and a member of one of the most brilliant groups in the history of medicine, led by the surgeon Sir Astley Cooper, and including another physician, Thomas Addison, and a pathologist, Thomas Hodgkin. All these are household names in the language of medicine.

Although mainly concerned with the living, Bright paid great attention to postmortem examination of patients who died in the hospital, and the relation of structural changes seen after death to the symptoms of the patient in life.

Bright's *Reports of Medical Cases* include accurate accounts of abdominal tumours, diseases of the liver, and many other conditions, several of which he was the first to describe. He made a special study of dropsy (►*oedema*), which he showed to be not a disease in its own right, but a symptom of various kinds of disease. Dropsy associated with abnormal kidneys could be distinguished from other types by examining the urine, which with kidney disease was 'coagulable'. (Damaged kidneys allow protein to leak from the blood into the urine, which therefore curdles when heated.) Bright

pointed out that the kidney disease now known as glomerulonephritis (►*kidneys*) might be the cause of the dropsy or only a consequence of some other disease – a kind of scientific caution that is all too rare.

bromide. Any salt of hydrobromic acid. The bromides of sodium and potassium were very widely used as ►*hypnotic* (sleep-inducing) drugs, and in smaller doses as day-time sedatives and for the control of epileptic attacks. They have various unpleasant effects such as mental sluggishness, skin rashes, and digestive disturbances, and are no longer much prescribed. More modern hypnotics such as the *benzodiazepines* are not more toxic or habit-forming than bromides and they have fewer unwanted effects. For the daytime treatment of emotional disorders bromides have given way to tranquillizers, which allay symptoms of anxiety without dulling the mind. Epilepsy is treated with carbamazepine, phenytoin and other drugs.

bronchial. Of the bronchi, the air-tubes of the ►*lung*.

bronchiectasis. A chronic disease of bronchi: severe infection such as a prolonged attack of whooping cough in childhood weakens the bronchi, which then stretch and lose their elasticity and their ability to clear themselves of secretion. Affected bronchi offer a permanent base for infecting bacteria. Any severe sustained infection can cause bronchiectasis, which in turn leads to indefinitely prolonged infection. This disease has become much less common since the discovery of antibiotics, which usually clear up the initial infection before lasting damage is done. Antibiotics have also much improved the treatment of established bronchiectasis.

Other useful measures are physiotherapy to help bring up infected sputum, and in cases where the defect is severe but confined to one zone of a lung the affected zone can be removed surgically.

bronchiole. A very small branch of a bronchus.

bronchiolitis. A pneumonia-like affection of infants caused by the ➤*respiratory syncytial virus*.

bronchitis. Inflammation of the air-passages in the lungs, either acute or chronic.

1. ACUTE BRONCHITIS

Most cases are due to spread of a virus infection from the nose and throat – 'a cold settling on the chest'. Bacterial infection usually follows. The bronchi are much more vulnerable to infection when they are irritated by smoke, noxious fumes or, in susceptible people, cold air.

Most attacks are mild and last only a few days. Characteristically a dry, uncomfortable cough develops after a cold in the nose or a sore throat, and the patient feels feverish and unwell. The inflammation causes rapid secretion of mucus from the lining of the bronchi; this gives the patient something to cough up and makes coughing much less of a burden. A cough may persist for some time after an attack, especially in winter.

The virus infection runs its course regardless of treatment, but much can be done to keep the patient comfortable and to minimize secondary infection by bacteria. For both these reasons cold air, smoke, and exertion are avoided. Steam warms and moistens the inspired air and is especially comforting in the early stage when the cough is dry and painful. Menthol, friar's balsam etc. add a reassuring medicinal smell. Various ➤*cough medicines* relieve the main symptom. Medications rubbed into the chest redden the skin but do not affect the bronchi. Antibiotic drugs deal effectively with bacterial infection, shortening the attack and preventing serious damage to the bronchi.

2. CHRONIC BRONCHITIS

Chronic bronchitis has become the new 'English disease' (the old one was rickets). It accounts for well over 20,000 deaths per year, a much higher rate than in other countries. Exact comparisons are impossible because there is no international agreement about what chronic bronchitis means; but the death rate from what in Britain is called chronic bronchitis is higher than the rate from all related diseases anywhere else.

The characteristic symptom is a regular cough with sputum. The smoker's morning cough is an example; bringing up a little phlegm in the morning is not, as he thinks, normal but evidence of inflammation. It is due in the first place to over-production of mucus; later the lining of the bronchi loses its ability to keep mucus on the move because the *cilia* – hair-like structures that normally maintain a wave motion – are smoothed over. In healthy bronchi the cilia sweep the small amount of mucus up to the throat, where it is swallowed with the saliva. With bronchitis there is more mucus, and it is moved only by coughing.

Recently much of the confusion over nomenclature has been resolved by adopting the expression *chronic airflow obstruction* (or chronic obstructive pulmonary disease), which can include elements of inflammation (bronchitis), permanent damage to lung tissue (emphysema) and spasm of the smaller air passages (asthma), in varying proportions. The net effect of all three is to reduce the efficiency of the lungs, finally to the point where the patient can no longer maintain the necessary level of oxygen in his blood.

The most important causative factor is tobacco smoke. Why some heavy smokers get away with no more than an annoying cough while others destroy their lungs is not clear. The polluted air of all industrial towns is an additional factor, and though the Clean Air Act in Britain deals with soot it does not affect sulphur dioxide, a dangerous irritant. The cold, damp, misty weather so typical of Britain also contributes.

While nothing can be done to restore tissue destroyed by emphysema, infection can be treated, with much improvement in the patient's condition. Antibiotics play an important part here, and some doctors leave a supply of an appropriate antibiotic with the patient so that he can start treatment at the first sign of infection (yellow sputum). Alternatively, small doses of an antibiotic are given throughout the winter months, but there is some disagreement about the value of this.

There is nearly always an element of asthma-like spasm (reversible obstruction) which can be relieved with some of the drugs that asthmatics use, notably bronchodilators inhaled as a spray from a pocket inhaler. The value of corticosteroids, which can be life-saving in severe attacks of ordinary asthma, is limited. But aminophylline is a useful alternative to inhaled bronchodilators such as salbutamol.

Physiotherapy can greatly improve the patient's breathing and his ability to bring up sputum. In spite of the symptoms, he may need a great deal of encouragement and support in his efforts to give up smoking. The sight of a severe bronchitic struggling to find enough breath to draw in his next puff of smoke is all too familiar. If people living with him cannot break their own habit, they should at least avoid smoking in the patient's presence.

The individual has little if any control over some of the factors predisposing to bronchitis. He can seldom move to a warmer or less smoky climate. But if some factors are eliminated others lose most of their effect. Even in the worst towns non-smokers do not have much bronchitis, and in most cases the most effective treatment is not to smoke. Fog can be kept at bay by shutting windows. Episodes of acute bronchitis on top of chronic bronchitis are particularly harmful; they drag on because the chronic bronchitic has a residue of sputum that he does not cough up, and after each acute attack the chronic state tends to be a little worse than before. Antibiotics, e.g. tetracycline, deal with these attacks and greatly improve the health and prospects of bronchitics. Influenza vaccine protects against an important source of acute episodes.

bronchodilator. Drug used to relax spasm of the bronchi in the treatment of asthma and bronchitis. The muscles of the bronchi are constricted by parasympathetic nerves and relaxed by sympathetic nerves. Bronchodilators are of two types: drugs that suppress parasympathetic action, such as belladonna and the derivatives of atropine, and drugs that enhance or imitate sympathetic action, such as adrenaline, ephedrine and isoprenaline. These drugs have the disadvantage that they stimulate the heart, sometimes dangerously. Some of the newer bronchodilators such as salbutamol and terbutaline, either swallowed or inhaled, are much safer in this respect. Aminophylline, given by slow intravenous injection, often relieves a severe attack of asthma.

bronchopneumonia ➤*pneumonia*.

bronchoscope. Lighted tube passed down the trachea for direct examination of the main bronchi.

bronchus. Air-passage in the lungs: the bronchi (bronchial tubes) are branches of the windpipe (trachea) and are arranged like branches of a tree, of which the twigs correspond with the *bronchioles* (➤*lung* (1)).

The bronchi and all but their smallest branches are held open by incomplete rings of cartilage in their walls. The rings are completed by involuntary muscle, which contracts under the influence of the ➤*vagus nerves*, reducing the volume of *dead space* during shallow breathing. Over-activity of these muscles narrows the bronchi, an important factor in ➤*asthma*.

The lining membrane of the bronchi resembles that of the trachea.

Some common disorders of the bronchi are listed under ➤*lung* (5).

bronzed diabetes ➤*iron* (2).

brown fat (brown adipose tissue). This tissue looks like the layer of fatty tissue under the skin, but under the microscope the fat is scattered through the cells in tiny droplets instead of forming a single large drop in each cell. 'Brown' refers to the supporting tissue, not to the fat itself. The cells are equipped for immediate combustion of the fat to provide heat (whereas ordinary fatty tissue releases fat into the circulation to be used in the liver

as a source of chemical energy). In hibernating animals, brown fat is used to raise the body temperature after hibernation. In man, it is the new-born baby's source of heat. The discovery of deposits of brown fat around the back-bone answered the question: how does a baby suddenly exposed to the air keep warm without shivering? A *premature* baby has little fat of any kind, and unless it is artificially kept warm its temperature quickly falls to a dangerous level.

Brucella. A genus of bacteria, causing contagious abortion in cattle, sheep, and pigs; in man these bacteria cause ➤*undulant fever*.

brucellosis. Infection with ➤*Brucella*.

bruise (contusion). Bleeding into injured skin. The spilt blood is gradually decomposed and absorbed; in the process the red pigment haemoglobin turns blue as it loses its oxygen, and is later broken down to green and yellow bile pigments. Bruises seldom need treatment. A large collection of blood (*haematoma*) may have to be drawn off with a needle. Expert technique is needed because any contamination of stagnant blood – an ideal environment for bacteria – can lead to serious infection.

bubo. A swelling in the groin due to inflamed lymph nodes.

bubonic plague. The usual type of ➤*plague* with enlarged lymph nodes.

Buerger's disease (thromboangiitis obliterans). (Leo Buerger, US physician, 1879–1943.) Narrowing of arteries and veins, especially in the legs, with a tendency for vessels to be obstructed by blood clot. It causes symptoms of inadequate blood supply: muscular pain on exertion, cold skin, poor healing. Symptoms usually start before the age of 40, and the patients are men who smoke heavily. The outlook depends mainly on whether the patient gives up smoking: if he does, the circulation can be expected to improve; if he does not, he may need an amputation in time. The blood flow can sometimes be improved by drugs to dilate the vessels.

bulimia. Compulsive overeating, usually a symptom of emotional disturbance, commonest in adolescent girls. Typically the patient follows a burst of overeating by self-induced vomiting or purging and recrimination, for despite appearances she is genuinely worried about putting on weight though unable to control her eating habits. Bulimia often accompanies anorexia nervosa, binges of mindless gluttony alternating with spells of deliberate starvation. Though on its own bulimia does not carry the risk to health and life of anorexia it is a distressing complaint. Treatment, by highly specialized psychotherapy, may be reinforced by antidepressant medication.

bunion. A deformity of the joint at the base of the big toe with a tender ▸*bursa* over the protruding 'knuckle'; due solely to wearing unsuitable shoes. Chiropody, splinting, and a change of shoes may suffice, but a severely deformed joint may need a surgical operation to straighten it.

Burkitt's tumour. (D. P. Burkitt, 1911–, British surgeon.) A cancerous growth of lymphatic tissue, usually originating around the jaw, affecting young patients. In the early stages it is often successfully treated with cytostatic drugs such as cyclophosphamide. As far as is known the tumour is rare outside East and Central Africa. Burkitt reported it in Uganda, where the distribution of cases strongly suggested an infectious origin. This was an observation of the very first importance, because for the first time it offered a possible link between cancer and infection, with the hope of some kind of immunization in the future. It now seems likely that the Epstein-Barr virus of glandular fever also causes Burkitt's tumour in people whose immunity to infection is sapped by malaria, malnutrition or other factors prevalent in East Africa. Significantly, in countries where these tumours were almost unknown, people whose immunity is destroyed by ▸*AIDS* are now dying of Burkitt's tumour.

burn. True burns need not be distinguished from many other kinds of injury that are called burns though they have nothing to do with fire. Protein, the chief material of living tissue, is unstable. Quite small changes in its environment alter its properties by changing the shape of its molecules. This process, *denaturation*, hardly affects the chemical properties of a protein but abolishes its biological properties – in other words, kills it. Raw white of egg is a solution of a protein in its natural state. Hot water completely changes its character. Curdling of milk is another example of denaturation. The type of injury called a burn is denaturation of tissue proteins. Boiling water – which cannot literally burn anything – works as well as a naked flame, as do electric currents, and acids, alkalis and other corrosive poisons.

In addition to the immediate damage to burnt tissue, burns cause blood vessels to leak *plasma*, the fluid part of blood. The blood cells remain in the vessels. With small burns the only effect of the leakage is swelling or blistering in the area, but with extensive burns the volume of blood is reduced enough to impair the circulation, while the proportion of solid to liquid in the blood increases enough to slow down the flow still further. Failure to keep up an adequate circulation is the basis of ►shock, and this is a much more serious matter than the loss of burnt tissue. The amount of fluid that leaks from the blood into the tissues, and hence the severity of shock and the immediate danger to life, depend on the area and not the depth of the burn. Burns involving 15 per cent of the skin area in an adult or 10 per cent in a child are likely to cause shock severe enough to need hospital treatment. The leakage is not necessarily rapid, so that shock can develop over some hours. The essential part of treatment is to restore and maintain the volume of the blood (►shock).

The treatment of the damaged tissue – of the burn itself – depends on the depth of the burn. Very complex classifications were devised in the 19th century, with as many as seven degrees of burn. They have no practical value, and surgeons now recognize three degrees, as suggested by Fabricius Hildanus in about 1600.

First-degree burns damage only the inert surface of the skin, which in any case is due to be shed and replaced. The burn itself needs no special attention, though the patient may need treatment for shock.

Second-degree burns destroy living tissue, but leave enough of the growing layer of the skin for the surface to be fully restored provided that no further damage is done, e.g. by infection.

Third-degree burns involve the whole thickness of the skin. New skin can only grow from the edges of the burn, unless the defect is covered by skin-grafting. Some scarring is inevitable. Skin-grafting

hastens recovery, reduces the risk of infection, and prevents deformity from shrinkage of scar tissue. It also improves the final appearance; this was the original object of skin grafting, but the experience of two World Wars taught that skin-grafts had even more important uses.

All burns are painful, and pain contributes to shock; drugs to mitigate pain and distress contribute to safety as well as comfort. The loss of nerve-endings in the deeper layers of the skin often makes 3rd-degree burns less painful than 1st or 2nd-degree.

The best way to dress burns is still disputed. Only 1st-degree burns present no problem: they can be left to their own devices. Applications that form a crust, such as tannin and some antiseptic dyes, delay healing and prevent any assessment of the damage; they are now seldom used. Plain, sterile gauze would be ideal if it were not apt to stick, and nonadherent (petrolatum) gauze is more often used. Dressings prepared from skin, not the patient's own, give satisfactory cover for some burns. They are not expected to 'take' as grafts, but merely to afford temporary protection. Proper grafting from the patient's own skin may follow later. Since the object is to interfere with healing as little as possible, some surgeons use no dressings at all, but leave the burns exposed. This method is especially suitable for burns of the head and neck, but is also used for other parts of the body. It needs a specially ventilated and equipped hospital unit. A remarkable extension of open treatment is an air-bed – not like the inflatable mattress that one takes to the beach, but a device whereby the patient virtually floats on a cushion of warm air.

With corrosive burns, the area should

be flushed with cold water at once. There is no point in trying to neutralize the substance, e.g. by bathing an acid burn with a weak alkali, for the interaction of the two generates heat and could make matters worse. The corrosive needs to be washed away, preferably under a running tap.

Immediate bathing in cold water is also good first-aid for true burns and scalds. The tissues retain heat, causing the damage to spread for some little while after the actual injury has taken place. This delayed damage is prevented by immediate cooling, which also helps to relieve the pain.

Apart from the direct consequences of the injury, the main risk with any burn is infection, because the damaged tissue is a perfect incubator for bacteria. Closed blisters are free from infection. It is highly dangerous to puncture them except under strict surgical *asepsis*, which in practical terms means that a burn-blister is best left alone until the patient is in trained hands. The best first-aid dressing is a simple pad of sterile gauze. A sterile adhesive dressing is suitable for small burns. For a larger area, the inner surface of a freshly laundered and ironed handkerchief is as sterile as anything in an average household. No dressing at all is better than a contaminated one.

Except with really trivial burns and scalds it is a wise precaution to get professional advice early, because the appearance does not always indicate the severity. Electric burns are especially misleading: they are nearly always worse than they look because the damage extends for some depth below the skin.

bursa. A pocket of fibrous tissue lined in the same way as a joint with a slippery synovial membrane. Bursae reduce friction, for example where tendons or ligaments move over bones. Some bursae are standard anatomical structures. Others develop in response to unusual pressure and friction.

bursitis. Inflammation of a bursa; sometimes bacterial, sometimes rheumatic, but usually a result of repeated pressure, friction or other injury. Bursitis is often due to wear and tear arising from a particular trade, e.g. housemaid's or clergyman's knee, dustman's shoulder, miner's elbow, weaver's bottom.

buttock ➤*thigh*.

byssinosis. Chronic disease of the lungs from cotton dust, a form of ➤*pneumoconiosis*. In the early stages the symptoms are troublesome only after a day or two without exposure to cotton, and the disease is known as 'Monday fever'.

C

cachexia. Loss of weight and general bodily deterioration from chronic disease.

caecum. First part of the large intestine, situated low down on the right side of the abdomen. The *appendix* opens off it. ➤*intestine* (1).

Caesarean section. Surgical operation: at a late stage of pregnancy the abdominal wall is opened and the incision is carried through the front of the uterus; the baby is lifted out, and the layers of the incision are stitched. Caesarean section is used when the birth-passage is too narrow for the baby, or when the placenta lies across the passage from the uterus and would be liable to bleed dangerously during natural labour, or in any situation where the health of mother or infant requires immediate delivery.

Legend has it that Julius Caesar was born in this way, but the operation may be named from an ancient law, restated by Caesar, that a woman dying in labour must be cut open in the hope of saving the child.

caffeine. Alkaloid drug extracted from coffee, identical with *theine* from tea. It has numerous effects, not unlike those of adrenaline. Caffeine increases alertness for a time if the subject is drowsy beforehand, but not if he is already wide awake; it also interferes with normal sleep. It dilates blood vessels and stimulates the heart. It increases the flow of urine. It relaxes the bronchi.

Caffeine is not a particularly efficient drug in any of these respects, and if it is given for the sake of one effect the other effects are a nuisance.

The effects of drinking too much coffee, or even strong tea, are well known: insomnia, palpitations, disturbed heart rhythm, 'nervousness', etc.

caisson disease ➤*decompression sickness* (caisson: a chamber kept at high pressure for working under water).

Cal. (abbreviation) = ➤*Calorie.*

calamine. Zinc carbonate or zinc oxide coloured pink with ferric oxide, used on the skin to allay itching and as a mild astringent.

calcaneum. The bone of the heel. ➤*foot.*

calciferol ➤*vitamin D.*

calcitonin. Hormone antagonistic to the action of *parathyroid* glands, formed by the thyroid gland.

calcium. Metallic element: its compounds are very widely distributed in mineral (e.g. chalk) deposits and in animals and plants.

In man, calcium salts resembling the mineral apatite (a compound containing calcium, fluorine, and phosphorus) form the hard framework of bones and teeth.

The blood carries about 0.01 per cent of calcium in solution, and this small amount is essential to life. Deficiency or excess of calcium in the blood seriously disturbs the function of nerve cells and muscle fibres. The correct concentration is maintained by the action of hormones (➤*parathyroid*).

Calcium is also necessary to the clotting of blood.

If the hormones are working properly, the vital calcium of the blood is kept constant by adjustments to the very large quantity stored in the skeleton. If there is a deficiency of calcium in the body the blood remains normal but the bones are weakened (>rickets; osteoporosis). In the much less common event of a surplus, e.g. with a grossly excessive intake of vitamin D, calcium may be deposited in tissues other than bone.

Calcium salts are sometimes deposited in tissues affected by injury or disease, e.g. in the walls of ageing arteries, or in scars where healing has been unduly slow. X-rays commonly show small calcified scars in the lungs, evidence that at some time in his life the patient was infected with tuberculosis and recovered – often with little or no obvious illness.

Insoluble compounds such as calcium phosphate may form stones in hollow organs (>calculus).

An average person needs about 1 gram of calcium in his daily diet; growing children, pregnant women and nursing mothers need rather more. Milk is the best source, but any good mixed diet contains enough calcium. Old people who live alone and lose interest in their diet are apt to be short of calcium; a pint of milk daily would supply their needs.

calcium channel blockers (calcium antagonists). A group of drugs that impede the passage of calcium ions into the muscle cells of the heart and arteries and thereby tend to decrease over-activity. Conditions in which they are effective include selected cases of high blood pressure, angina and irregular heart beat.

calculus. 1. Chalky deposit ('tartar') on teeth, mainly precipitated from saliva.

2. Hard insoluble mass ('stone') in any hollow organ. The common sites for stones are the urinary tract (kidneys, bladder) and the biliary system (gall bladder, bile ducts). The stones are made of substances normally dissolved in the fluid contents of the organ, which for some reason form a precipitate like the fur in a kettle.

Urinary stones are commonly of calcium phosphate or calcium oxalate. They are often associated with infection of the kidney or bladder. Infection may help to cause them, though it is difficult to see how; and the presence of a foreign body such as a stone helps to keep infection going. The only easily explained stones are of substances passed through the kidneys in greater quantities than can be dissolved, such as uric acid in people with gout.

Gall stones are of cholesterol, bile pigment, or both together with calcium salts. They, too, are often associated with infection, but they have not been satisfactorily explained.

Stones can also form in other places, such as the salivary glands.

Stones that cause symptoms generally have to be removed surgically. Small ones may find their own way out. Occasionally a stone can be dissolved: uric acid stones in the kidney can be dealt with by keeping the urine alkaline, some >gall stones can be treated by giving chenodeoxycholic acid, and ultrasound has been used to break down calculi. Some bladder calculi (probably originating in a kidney) can be removed via the urethra, using a cystoscope.

callosity. Thickening and hardening of the outermost layer of the skin in response to pressure or friction.

callus. 1. = >callosity. **2.** Hard tissue

formed at the site of a broken bone, gradually converted into new bone (➤*fracture*).

Calorie. Unit of energy expressed as the heat required to raise the temperature of 1 gram of water by 1 °C. The unit of the diet charts is 1000 calories, the kilocalorie (kcal.) or Calorie with a capital C. In general science (and increasingly in dietetics) the kcal. is now superseded by the *kilojoule* (kJ). This unit is equivalent to 0.239 kcal.; thus 1 calorie = 4.187 joules.

camphor. A crystalline substance obtained from the camphor tree or from turpentine, formerly used to promote coughing and sweating and to stimulate vital centres in the brain; it survives as an ingredient of *paregoric* (camphorated tincture of opium) and of *camphorated oil*.

camphorated oil. A solution of camphor in cotton-seed oil used as a liniment. ➤*counter-irritation*.

cancellous bone. Porous, spongy bone inside the solid casing of *compact* bone.

cancer. A disorder of cell growth. The millions of cells of the body are all derived from a single cell, the fertilized ovum, by a process of duplication and reduplication. All cells (except perhaps those of nerve and voluntary muscle) are capable throughout life of reproducing themselves by splitting into two.

At first, an embryo is a cluster of identical cells, of which the number is repeatedly doubled. Any one of these cells could grow into a complete organism. As growth proceeds, cells become less versatile: they are *differentiated* or specialized for the functions of particular tissues or organs. In general a differentiated cell can do three things: (1) perform a special task – e.g. one kind of cell lays down bone, another stores fat, another makes saliva; (2) look after its own nutrition; (3) replace exhausted cells by dividing to form two new cells.

At birth the nervous system has its full complement of cells, and they are so highly differentiated that they have lost the ability to replace themselves and they rely on supporting (glial) cells for their nutrition. They have to last for a lifetime. The cells of voluntary muscle do not as a rule reproduce themselves. A muscle grows by increasing the size, not the number, of its cells.

All other types of cell continue to multiply. The rate gradually slows; when growth is complete it just keeps pace with the continuous degeneration and loss of cells (in old age or times of illness it may not keep pace). How this rate is adjusted is unknown. In most organs it can be increased to meet added demands, so that lost tissue is at least partly replaced.

Cancer begins in a group of cells, or perhaps a single cell, that divides regardless of need. Although some cancer cells keep the special function of their cell-type, most tend to lose it; in fact they regress towards an embryonic type with less differentiation. The rare cancers of infancy may well arise from cells that have failed to outgrow the embryonic state, but this is no longer thought to explain adult cancer. For convenience, cancers are often classified according to the embryonic tissue they resemble, but this is no more than a useful convention. It seems clear that cancer cells arise from normal, differentiated adult cells that have changed their nature. The change is fixed: it persists in the descendants of the affected cells.

In effect, a cancer is a parasite formed from the patient's own tissues. It is a family or tribe of cells that has become alienated from its neighbours; it no longer serves as part of the integrated community of cells that is a healthy body; it is not subject to the normal control by nerves and hormones; it draws on the general supply of nutrients and contributes nothing in return.

Because they are subject to no control, and because they have nothing to do but reproduce themselves, cancer cells in time outnumber the healthy cells in their neighbourhood. They tend to spread beyond the limits of their original organ, and groups of cells may be carried in lymph vessels or veins to other parts of the body where they form *metastases*.

It is very rare for a cancer to replace so much of a vital organ that life becomes impossible, except that any kind of intruder in the brain can be fatal (a blood clot or an abscess can do harm out of all proportion to its size). It is also unusual for cancer to kill by invading a major blood vessel and causing fatal bleeding, or indeed to do anything obviously lethal. In the great majority of cases, the progressive loss of health is a complete mystery. True, the cancer competes with working tissues for food and oxygen, but its demands should not be enough to cause serious deprivation elsewhere; yet this is the ultimate effect unless the cancer can be treated.

1. Causes of Cancer

Cancer is probably no more a specific disease with a single defined cause than, say, bleeding or heart failure. It is an alteration in the behaviour of cells in response to various harmful factors, some known, many unknown; often different factors work together (rather as overeating,

anxiety and lack of exercise may together cause heart disease when none of them would do so alone).

Inherited constitution plays some part: people with a family history of cancer are rather more liable to the disease than others; but only in a few types of cancer is the hereditary factor the most important. Hereditary factors may predispose to cancer, but they are seldom if ever the sole cause.

Repeated simple injury – 'chronic irritation' – has been invoked more than any other factor; it has even been called the sole cause of cancer. But the evidence is very poor, and it is now doubtful whether cancer ever arises in this way. On the other hand, many special types of injury can certainly cause cancer. If they have anything in common, it is that they can all *prevent* cells from dividing if the dose is large enough. It is as if some critical dose interfered with the process of cell division just enough to take the brake off. Presumably they alter the genetic make-up of a cell – cause *mutation* – so that not only the reproductive behaviour of the cell is disturbed but also that of its progeny. The altered cell breeds true.

The known physical and chemical agents of cancer include *ionizing radiation*, and many chemical poisons.

Many of the pioneers of X-ray work developed cancer in exposed skin. Excessive exposure to strong sunlight can also cause skin cancer, and strict precautions are needed in industries that use radioactive substances. The atom bombs in Japan caused an outbreak of leukaemia (blood cancer) among the survivors.

A chemical cause of cancer was first recognized by the London surgeon Pott in 1775; he showed that soot caused cancer in chimney-sweeps. Many substances able to cause cancer (*carcinogens*) have been extracted from coal, and some lubricating oils have also been incriminated. Other carcinogens are arsenic and some intermediate products in the synthesis of dyes. None of these poisons causes cancer by occasional contamination; the trouble comes from daily exposure, month after month.

By far the most significant chemical carcinogen is ►*tobacco* smoke.

Several types of cancer in animals are caused by infection with viruses. A virus is little more than a parcel of genetic material, and it would not be remarkable for some of this material to become incorporated with the cell's own material and cause the kind of mutation that would lead to cancer. No virus infection has been positively identified in human cancer, but there is evidence that ►*Burkitt's tumour* and ►*Kaposi's sarcoma*, both associated with AIDS, may be caused by viruses.

International statistics show that wholly unsuspected causes must still await discovery. Cancer of the rectum is twice as common in Denmark as in Norway. Finland has one of the highest rates of stomach cancer yet one of the lowest of cancer of the intestine. When facts such as these are explained more will be known about causes, and therefore about what to avoid in order to prevent cancer.

2. MANAGEMENT OF CANCER

One cannot exaggerate the size of the problem. In Britain and many other countries, one death in five is from cancer. Even the best treatment is destructive. Taken reasonably early, some 75 per cent of breast cancers can be cured, but at the cost of a breast. It is the same with many other types of cancer:

the best chance of permanent cure is complete removal of the cancer and any neighbouring tissue that might be involved. As long as this remains the best chance there is no sense in haggling, but nobody can pretend that wholesale removal is the ideal treatment of a disease. And there remain the inaccessible cancers and the cases recognized too late for even drastic surgery to cure.

X-rays and radioactive material are used in several ways. They completely cure some surface cancers, where the radiation can be directly applied without passing through healthy tissue. They are a valuable adjunct to surgery: irradiation may pick off stray cancer cells that the knife has missed, or at least retard the progress of disease that is no longer curable. The results of irradiating accessible cancers show that this treatment can cure; but if the cancer is deep or widespread the patient may be unable to tolerate a large enough dose. Techniques are evolving for confining the rays to their target with less damage to healthy tissue. Some cancers can be made more susceptible to radiation by increasing their supply of oxygen.

Many drugs that suppress division of cells have been used against cancer. Some are derived from the mustard gas of the First World War. A common plant, the periwinkle (*Vinca*), contains alkaloids able to retard some forms of cancer. Antibiotics are primarily drugs for treating bacterial infection. They prevent bacteria from multiplying; and a few, e.g. actinomycin, mithramycin, have a similar effect on cancer cells. Drugs are most used in the treatment of cancers of the lymphatic system (Hodgkin's disease) and blood (leukaemia).

Both radiation and these drugs suppress cell division in general. They work because cancer cells are much more actively engaged in reproducing themselves than normal cells. The appearance and behaviour of cancer cells are distinctive, but no chemical difference from normal cells is yet known. When one is found it should be possible to attack cancer cells specifically.

Some cancers of sex organs (e.g. breast, prostate) are influenced by sex hormones and are sometimes successfully treated with a hormone of the opposite sex.

Since cancer cells differ from normal cells, they are foreign to the rest of the body, and one would expect them to provoke the same kind of response as any other foreign living matter. They should act as ➤antigens, stimulate the production of ➤antibodies, and so cause their own destruction by the reactions of ➤immunity. This possibility has opened up a promising field of research. It has already been shown that many cancers do in fact form antigens, even though the resistance they provoke is not enough to destroy them. Once an antigen is known, it can be identified in the laboratory, so in future it may become possible to diagnose cancer by simple blood tests in the same way as an infection such as typhoid fever. And beyond this, given the presence of antigens it becomes logical to seek ways of increasing the body's response to them or immunizing the patient. This research is still only at an early stage of guarded optimism.

Treatment, then, offers much hope; cancer is by no means the incurable disease that many people think it. The picture looks gloomier than it is because one does not hear much of the many cures. When a surgeon is fairly sure that he has cured a cancer he may decide that to tell the patient the diagnosis would be pointless cruelty, because few people, knowing that they have had a cancer removed, can simply forget it. Nor do people who know necessarily wish to talk about it.

Prevention is mainly of two kinds. The first is to avoid known causes: smoking is far the most important. The second is to recognize cancer early enough for it to be cured. Screening tests for routine checking of large numbers of people are now quite extensively used. Health education may be more important than mass examination. The Metropolitan Life Insurance Company of New York has widely publicized seven 'warning signals' that people should have investigated as soon as they appear:

1. any sore that does not heal;
2. a lump or thickening in the breast or elsewhere;
3. unusual bleeding or discharge;
4. any change in a wart or mole;
5. persistent indigestion or difficulty in swallowing;
6. persistent hoarseness or cough;
7. any change in normal bowel habits.

cancrum oris ➤*noma*.

Candida (Monilia). A fungus related to the yeasts, a normal inhabitant of the mucous membrane of the mouth and intestine which occasionally sets up infection with characteristic white patches known as *thrush*. As a rule, simple mouthwashes clear up thrush, but in obstinate cases antibiotics (nystatin, amphotericin) may be needed. The vagina can also be affected.

Bacteria normally suppress *Candida*; it is apt to proliferate when bacteria are eliminated by intensive treatment of infection with the more versatile antibiotics; a further antibiotic is then needed to control the *Candida* until the normal bacteria of the body are re-established.

cannabis (hashish, etc.) ➤*hemp*.

cantharidin. An irritant of no medical value, extracted from a small beetle, the *Spanish fly*. Its reputation as an aphrodisiac depends on irritation of the whole urinary system, which has been known to cause failure of the kidneys and death.

canthus. Either corner of the eye.

capillary. Smallest blood vessel: blood leaves the heart in arteries and returns in veins, crossing from arteries to veins in minute vessels, the capillaries, with a diameter of about 1/100 mm. Thus capillaries are at once the least twigs of the arteries and the least tributaries of the veins.

There are many more capillaries than can be filled with blood at one time. The amount of blood circulating through an organ is adapted to the demand for oxygen and for removal of carbon dioxide by opening the entrances to an appropriate number of capillaries. The skin is exceptional; here the flow is adapted to ➤*temperature*. A capillary is opened or closed by a minute ring of muscle in the wall of the parent arteriole. There is no muscle to be seen as a rule, yet it seems that capillaries are able to contract to some extent.

The small arteries (arterioles) and veins (venules) are impermeable. Exchange of materials between the blood and the tissues takes place entirely across the walls of the capillaries, which allow free passage to small molecules such as water, salts, glucose, and amino-acids, but not to proteins (➤*tissue fluid*). Solid particles, including blood cells, have been shown by electron microscopy to pass through the cells of the capillary walls.

capsule. Fibrous sheath enclosing an organ; especially the tough, flexible casing of a joint, strengthened with fibrous bands (*ligaments*) and lined with a slippery *synovial membrane*.

caput succedaneum. Fluid swelling in the scalp of a new-born baby caused by pressure during birth; often a source of anxiety to a woman with her first child unless she has seen other new-born babies. The swelling disappears in a few days.

carbachol. Synthetic drug related to acetyl choline; it has similar effects to acetyl choline but is more slowly destroyed in the body. It is used to stimulate the intestine, bladder and other organs normally activated by acetyl choline.

carbohydrate intolerance. It sometimes happens that an enzyme needed for converting a disaccharide to monosaccharides (➤*carbohydrates*) is missing from the intestine. The enzyme is most often *lactase*, which converts milk sugar to glucose and galactose, but failure to break down maltose and sucrose also occurs. The deficiency may be congenital or it may arise in adult life.

Disaccharides are not adequately absorbed from the intestine. If they cannot be converted to absorbable monosaccharides they remain in the intestine and attract water by *osmosis*, which causes diarrhoea; in fact unabsorbable carbohydrates can be used as purgatives. If one has no lactase, a glass of milk acts as a dose of salts. Bacterial fermentation of unabsorbed sugar in the large intestine causes flatulence and discomfort.

carbohydrates. A large class of compounds of carbon, hydrogen, and oxygen, including sugars and starches. They are found in all living cells; the ultimate source is green plants which synthesize them from carbon dioxide and water under the influence of sunlight; ➤*energy*.

The simplest form of carbohydrate is a *monosaccharide* – a simple sugar. There are two groups of these in human chemistry: the *pentoses* with the general formula $(CH_2O)_5$ and the *hexoses* $(CH_2O)_6$. Much the most important pentose is *ribose*, a component of *nucleic acids* (DNA and RNA), which are the chemical basis of life itself.

Apart from ribose, the carbohydrates of the body are either hexoses (*glucose, fructose, galactose*), or compounds of two or more hexoses. Two hexoses form a *disaccharide*. A chain of disaccharides forms a *polysaccharide*.

The three disaccharides of the diet are *maltose* (glucose + glucose), *sucrose* or cane sugar (glucose + fructose), and *lactose* or milk sugar (glucose + galactose).

The only important polysaccharide in the human diet is *starch*. Its molecules are long branched chains of maltose; it is converted to maltose by enzymes in saliva and pancreatic juice. A very similar compound to starch, widely distributed in plants (e.g. grass), is *cellulose*, which is useless as human food because man has no enzyme for converting cellulose to maltose. (Nor has a cow, but a cow's stomach contains bacteria that break down cellulose.)

All the 'human' carbohydrates can be converted by enzymes to glucose.

Carbohydrate is broken down to monosaccharides in the intestine before it can be assimilated into the blood stream. It passes to the liver, where most of it is stored as a polysaccharide, *glycogen* (animal starch). Muscle also contains a store of glycogen. As glucose is used up in the tissues to provide energy, the concentration of glucose in the blood (about 0.1 per cent) tends to fall. This stimulates the breakdown of enough glycogen to restore the level.

The ultimate fate of carbohydrate is combustion of carbon dioxide and water with release of energy (a reversal of the photosynthesis by which plants make carbohydrate). One gram of carbohydrate yields 4.1 Calories. With very few exceptions (e.g. Eskimos) carbohydrates provide most of the energy of a diet, but a mixture of different classes of food is essential to health (➤*diet*). One of the ways to reduce weight is to cut down carbohydrate and leave other foods to look after themselves.

Since all dietary carbohydrates end as glucose, the choice ought not to matter. Yet there is evidence that refined sugar (sucrose) contributes to disease of the arteries (➤*artery*), whereas other carbohydrates do not.

carbon dioxide. Colourless gas, a component of air (0.03 per cent), assimilated by plants for the synthesis of carbohydrates, and given off by all living organisms (animal and plant) as the end-product of respiration.

Carbon dioxide is formed throughout the body and carried by the veins to the lungs. Some is dissolved in the plasma but most is carried in the red blood cells. In the lungs, carbon dioxide is released from the blood. Inspired air contains only 0.03 per cent, but expired air contains about 4 per cent.

The concentration of carbon dioxide in the blood is the main stimulus to breathing. The excess formed during exertion reinforces the reflexes controlling rate and depth of breathing, so that carbon dioxide is eliminated more quickly. This has the effect of supplying more oxygen, which is needed because oxygen uptake and carbon dioxide output are exactly balanced. An excess of carbon dioxide in a tissue also increases the flow of blood.

Carbon dioxide (about 5 per cent in air or oxygen) is sometimes used to stimulate breathing.

Although not as deadly as carbon monoxide, carbon dioxide is poisonous in concentrations over about 6 per cent. It leads to over-stimulation of the heart, depression of reflexes, and finally unconsciousness and death. But except in case of asphyxia, carbon dioxide poisoning is unusual because it tends to right itself by increased breathing. Slight symptoms of poisoning are common with severe chronic disease of the lungs, e.g. chronic bronchitis, because breathing is impaired to the point of slight asphyxia. The patient may get used to a high concentration of carbon dioxide and no longer respond by breathing more deeply.

carbon monoxide. A poisonous component of coal gas, exhaust fumes, and most smoke.

It combines with the haemoglobin of the blood in exactly the same way as oxygen; but it does so 300 times as readily as oxygen. From a mixture of 300 parts oxygen to 1 carbon monoxide the blood will take up equal quantities. Air contains only 1 part in 5 of oxygen; therefore a 1:1500 concentration of carbon monoxide will displace half the oxygen of the blood. The effect is worse than losing half the blood, because the oxygen that remains is not given up in the tissues to be used. So a concentration of 1:1500

is likely to be lethal, and very much lower concentrations cause severe illness.

Carbon monoxide poisoning differs from ordinary asphyxia in the patient's bright pink complexion, instead of the blue of asphyxia. It is treated by giving pure oxygen if possible, or otherwise fresh air, which gradually displaces the carbon monoxide from the blood. ➤*Artificial respiration* may be needed.

carbuncle. Bacterial infection (usually by staphylococci) in the skin, of the same kind as a boil but larger and deeper; a carbuncle can be regarded as several boils run together. The back of the neck, where the hair roots are especially liable to infection, is the commonest site. The principles of treatment are the same as with a ➤*boil*, except that surgery and antibiotics are more often needed.

carcinogen. Any substance liable to cause ➤*cancer* (1).

carcinoid. A cancer-like proliferation of cells that produce ➤*serotonin* and other hormones affecting the behaviour of blood vessels; the disease arises most commonly in the intestine but is liable to spread to the liver. The symptoms may be widespread and may include diarrhoea, asthma, flushing and heart disease. Numerous drugs are used to suppress symptoms, but none is curative.

carcinoma. Literally = ➤*cancer*, but used only of cancers arising in covering and lining membranes (cf. ➤*sarcoma*).

cardiac. Of the heart (also: of the part of the stomach nearest the heart).

Cardiac massage has become an important method of resuscitation, as an adjunct to *artificial respiration*, in cases where breathing and heart beat have stopped. Firm pressure on the lower half of the sternum is applied with the heel of the palm once a second. In an adult the sternum is depressed about an inch by leaning on both hands. In children light pressure with two fingers is enough, and the rate is rather faster. Because cardiac massage has been known to break ribs of people who did not need resuscitation there has been some opposition to teaching it to otherwise untrained people, but against this view is the fact that if cardiac massage is needed at all it is needed at once. If the heart is out of action for more than a very few minutes there is no chance of survival.

cardiology. Branch of physiology and medicine concerned with the heart.

cardiomyopathy. Disease of the heart muscle. By decreasing the efficiency of the heart it causes symptoms such as shortness of breath on modest exertion, angina pectoris and fluid retention. The many causes include virus, bacterial and other infections, poisons such as alcohol and numerous drugs, malnutrition, diabetes and thyroid disease. A similar condition can arise from shortage of blood and thus of oxygen with coronary artery disease, from defective valves which put an excessive strain on the heart muscle, and from congenital defects.

cardiovascular system. The heart and blood vessels considered as a functional whole; the circulatory system.

caries. 1. Dental decay; ➤*teeth* (3). **2.** Tuberculosis of bone.

carotene. Orange pigment of carrots and many other vegetables, also found in egg yolk and milk; converted in the body to vitamin A.

carotid artery. Main artery of the head. The two common carotid arteries run straight up the neck at either side of the trachea, under cover of the sternomastoid muscles. Above the level of the Adam's apple the common carotid divides into external and internal carotid arteries.

The external carotid sends branches to the neck, face and scalp. Only one small branch, the middle meningeal artery, enters the skull. It lies in a deep groove on the inner surface of the side of the skull, and is readily torn if the bone is fractured. Bleeding from this vessel is one of the most important hazards of head injuries. It requires prompt surgery.

The internal carotid arteries pass through the floor of the skull to the brain, of which they supply the top and front with blood. The rest of the brain is supplied by the ➤*vertebral* arteries. Although all these arteries meet at the ➤*circle of Willis* to provide an alternative supply if one is blocked, this is not an efficient system and the brain can be injured by interference with any one of its arteries. Partial blockage of a carotid artery by ➤*atheroma* is a common precursor of a ➤*stroke*. Sometimes the blockage can be cleared surgically.

carotid body. Small gland in the angle between the external and internal carotid arteries. It is sensitive to changes in the concentrations of oxygen and carbon dioxide in the blood, and responds by releasing hormones that act on the parts of the brain controlling respiration.

carotid sinus. Bulge in the wall of the carotid artery at its division into external and internal branches. It contains nerve-endings sensitive to changes of pressure, and is concerned in maintaining a steady pressure of blood, above all to the brain. If the sinuses are squeezed, e.g. by a judo stranglehold, the blood pressure falls by reflex action and the victim may lose consciousness.

carpal tunnel. A fibrous bridge, the *flexor retinaculum*, spans the small bones at the base of the palm of the hand. The carpal tunnel is the opening between the flexor retinaculum and the bones. The flexor tendons to the fingers pass through this tunnel, enclosed in slippery synovial sheaths which prevent friction in this narrow space. Between the tendons is the ➤*median* nerve.

The *carpal tunnel syndrome* arises from compression of the median nerve in the tunnel. In the hand, the median nerve carries motor fibres to the muscles of the ball of the thumb and sensory fibres from the thumb and the index, middle, and ring fingers. Pressure on the nerve causes pins-and-needles, numbness, or pain in this area, and sometimes weakness of the thumb. Arthritis or injury of the wrist may produce this syndrome, but usually there is no obvious reason for it. The fact that it is commonest in middle-aged women and during pregnancy suggests a glandular disturbance. The symptoms are often worst after lying down. Some cases respond to splinting the wrist at night. Injection of hydrocortisone usually gives at least temporary relief. If these simple measures fail, the condition is often cured by cutting the constricting fibres of the retinaculum.

carpus. Base of the ➤*hand*; of its eight small carpal bones three articulate with the forearm to form the wrist-joint.

carrier. Person who harbours an infectious microbe without ill effects. About 10 per cent of healthy people carry dangerous streptococci in their noses, and as many as 50 per cent carry staphylococci; unless they take precautions such as wearing a mask when treating patients with open wounds they may convey serious infection.

Some people recover from infection without completely eliminating the bacteria: they establish a sort of truce, by which they and the bacteria tolerate each other, but at any time they may infect others who have not yet had the disease. Diphtheria and typhoid fever can be carried in this way.

Subclinical infection is like a temporary carrier state. One may actually have a disease without any obvious symptoms; for instance most people with poliomyelitis suffer no more than a mild stomach upset but during the attack – which passes unrecognized – others can contract the serious form of the disease with paralysis from them.

cartilage. Gristle; the tough, smooth, milk-white tissue which coats the moving surfaces of the joints; called *hyaline* cartilage to distinguish it from fibrocartilage and elastic cartilage (see below).

Apart from the clavicles and most of the skull the whole skeleton of the embryo is formed in cartilage, which is gradually replaced by bone. At birth the shafts of the principal bones are of real bone but the expanded ends are still cartilaginous. When growth is complete only thin sheets of cartilage remain.

Unlike bone, cartilage has no blood vessels. It therefore lacks many of the properties of other living tissues. It cannot become inflamed, and cannot heal if it is cut or broken. It has few diseases, but those few tend to be irreversible. ➤*Achondroplasia* is a hereditary defect of embryonic cartilage: all the bones that are preformed in cartilage remain underdeveloped. In ➤*rickets* the replacement of cartilage by bone fails.

In the two most important diseases of joints, ➤*osteoarthritis* and ➤*rheumatoid arthritis*, the cartilages at the ends of the bones are eroded and roughened.

The living cartilage cells, embedded in their plastic ground-substance (➤*tissue*), can form a tumour – a *chondroma* – which is usually slow-growing and harmless apart from the mechanical nuisance of any abnormal lump in a tissue.

Fibrocartilage is not so much cartilage as exceedingly dense and tough fibrous tissue. It is the material of the intervertebral discs between the ➤*vertebrae* – the shock-absorbers of the backbone – and of the pads, like washers, between the bones of certain joints such as the *knee. Elastic cartilage* is the rubbery tissue of the ear.

cascara sagrada. Dried bark of *Rhamnus purshiana*, an American tree; it contains various anthracene compounds that act as *purgatives* by irritating the large intestine.

castor oil. = Ricinus oil; extracted from the seeds of a subtropical bush, *Ricinus communis.* ➤*purgative*.

CAT. Computerized axial tomography; ➤*scan*.

catabolism. Chemical breakdown in the body of complex substances to simple ones (e.g. proteins to amino-acids); the reverse process is *anabolism*.

catalepsy. A kind of hysterical or self-induced trance, in which the patient remains fixed in even the unlikeliest position, as in the children's game 'statues'.

catalyst ➤*enzyme*.

cataplasm = ➤*poultice*.

cataract. Opacity of the lens of the eye, causing dimness of vision; if the cataract progresses, useful vision is completely lost, though light and dark can be distinguished. The defect is confined to the lens; when this is removed vision returns and only the ability to focus is lost. The front of the eye is a powerful compound lens of which the 'lens' itself is only a minor component for altering the focus. Most of the strength of the compound lens is provided by the curved front of the eye, which is not affected by cataract and remains after the lens has been removed. Restoration of sight by this comparatively simple operation is one of the most dramatic and rewarding events in the whole practice of medicine. Often an artificial lens is implanted in place of the natural one that has been removed.

Most cataracts are a result of ageing, but some are a result of injury and some, occurring in infancy, are due to faulty development of the lens. Diabetes is also an important cause of cataracts.

catarrh. Any inflammation of a mucous membrane with excessive formation of mucus. As a technical term, catarrh is almost obsolete, but it is still in general use for inflammation of the mucous membrane of the nose – *rhinitis* (➤*nose* (1)).

Vernal catarrh is an allergic type of ➤*conjunctivitis*, occurring mainly in spring and summer.

catatonia. A severe form of schizophrenia: during an attack the patient seems wholly out of touch with his surroundings. He may show purposeless excitement, or pass into a kind of trance when he is as still as a wax dummy. Between attacks he may behave normally. A similar condition can be seen in a deep hypnotic trance.

catgut. Surgical catgut is similar to that

used for stringed musical instruments. It is the fibrous layer of sheep's intestine, toughened with chromic acid. Catgut ligatures are easy to handle, and they are slowly digested in the tissues, finally disappearing without trace.

catharsis. Cleansing; purging – either of the intestine by *cathartic* drugs (>*purgative*) or of the emotions by psychoanalysis, when a suppressed memory, the hidden cause of emotional conflict and illness, is brought into the open. In principle this is similar to the catharsis that Aristotle said was the purpose of the theatre.

catheter. Usually, a tube specially adapted for passing up the urethra to drain the urinary bladder, secure an uncontaminated specimen, etc. Also a tube inserted into any other organ, e.g. by way of a blood vessel to the heart.

cat-scratch fever. Infection transmitted by cats: a small abscess appears at the site of the scratch after an interval of a week; there is some fever, and lymph nodes are enlarged all over the body (neck, armpits, groins). The original sore may take some time to heal, but otherwise recovery is rapid and complete.

cauliflower ear. Deformity of the ear due to bleeding or infection between the supporting cartilage and its covering membrane; this separates the cartilage from its blood vessels and causes it to degenerate, while an irregular mass of fibrous (scar) tissue is formed as a result of persistent inflammation.

cautery. The branding-iron or cautery is a very ancient tool for the treatment of disease. It was used in ancient Egypt to stop bleeding, and Hippocrates advised treatment by fire as a last resort when medicine and surgery had failed.

The medieval use of cautery to burn out such conditions as epilepsy was pure superstition, but cautery to treat wounds, ulcers and cancers was rational if cruel. It stops bleeding and kills bacteria and also the patient's tissues. But the burnt tissue is an ideal haven for the next bacteria to arrive; in it they can breed without interference from the natural defences of living tissue, and in the long run a cauterized wound is worse infected than a wound left to itself. As long as pus was considered 'laudable' surgeons positively sought infection, and the cautery was not seriously challenged until the 16th century, when Ambroise Paré showed that wounds did better without it.

A kind of electric cautery is used in modern surgery. It produces an almost microscopically small burn. It coagulates bleeding points too small to be closed with ligatures, and used as an electric knife it cuts delicate tissue bloodlessly, sealing the cut edge as it goes. Sometimes the light-sensitive membrane of the eye (*retina*) becomes detached from the inside wall of the eye, and a form of cautery is used to stick it in place. A laser beam – a concentrated form of light – serves this purpose well, and lasers are now finding many other applications in surgery. Extreme cold, e.g. from liquid nitrogen, also 'burns' tissue and can be used as a cautery.

CDH. Congenital dislocation of the >*hip*.

cell. The smallest unit of the body that is capable of independent life. The whole body is a community of individual cells of which the primary function is to maintain a suitable environment for themselves and for each other. Physiology – the study of normal function – shows how each type of cell contributes to the task of preserving constant conditions within the body in the face of constant change outside it. Pathology – the study of disease – shows what happens when the balance is disturbed.

A cell is a blob of jelly, the *cytoplasm*, mainly a solution of protein, in a fine but strong container, the *cell membrane*. Most cells have a dense kernel, the *nucleus*, which directs the activity of the rest of the cell, and various *organelles* that can be discerned only with an electron microscope. Even these tiny structures have enclosing membranes, which can hardly be more than a molecule thick. Among the organelles found in all cells are *mitochondria*, where combustion takes place to provide energy for the cell's activities, and *ribosomes* for the synthesis of proteins. With few exceptions cells can reproduce themselves by dividing into two cells, each an exact replica of the original one. (In an embryo, successive generations of cells are not identical: they are modified to form different tissues and organs.)

In a suitable environment, a cell remains alive on its own; but the conditions have to be exactly right. Isolated cells from every part of the human body have been kept alive in tissue cultures, under carefully regulated conditions of temperature and chemical supplies, and most kinds of cell have been persuaded to multiply. But tissue culture is a most laborious business. Slight changes in the environment are enough to kill the cells.

Robert Hooke recognized the cellular structure of plants in 1665, but it was not until 1839 that Theodor Schwann showed that the structure of plants and animals was fundamentally the same. Schwann thought that cells arose spontaneously in a formless ground-substance, but within the next twenty years it was shown that the ground-substance was produced by cells, and that every cell was the offspring of a cell. Each of the millions of cells in the body has arisen by division and subdivision from the single cell formed at conception. ➤Virchow.)

The largest cell of the human body – the *ovum* – is just visible to the naked eye. Most human cells are much smaller, about 0.01 mm. in diameter.

cellular pathology. The doctrine that the processes of disease are to be studied in the changes undergone by individual cells. It is the title of Rudolf ➤*Virchow*'s great masterpiece, published in 1858.

cellular tissue. Loosely woven connective tissue, allowing movement between adjacent structures, e.g. the tissue beneath the skin, which allows a good deal of play between the skin and the underlying bundles of muscle.

cellulite. A late arrival to the list of possible diseases. Advocates of alternative therapy complain that some doctors refuse to accept its existence, but in fact they deny, not that cellulite exists, but that it is a disease.

In French *cellulite* originally meant cellulitis, a dangerous infection, but now it has taken on a second meaning for which English has adopted the French term. It applies to the deposit of fat around the upper thighs and buttocks of many women, *culotte de cheval* as the French indelicately put it, usually with some dimpling of the overlying skin.

Fashion has decreed that this is unsightly, and industry that it is unhealthy. It is even accused, without evidence, of being a dumping ground for (unspecified) toxic waste.

'Cures' for this innocent condition are especially popular in France and other Mediterranean countries, where women are most prone to put on weight around the hips.

In conclusion it may be pointed out that in many cultures this condition is esteemed as a mark of great beauty.

cellulitis. Inflammation of cellular tissue, commonly due to infection by streptococci from contaminated wounds. The open structure of cellular tissue allows the infection to spread, and cellulitis was always very dangerous until the discovery of drugs (sulphonamides; penicillin) that effectively control streptococcal infection.

Celsus, Aulus Cornelius (1st century AD). Author of the earliest Latin medical treatise (and also of books now lost on veterinary medicine, agriculture, and philosophy). The eight surviving volumes are a survey of medical history and practice. They represent all that was best in Graeco-Roman medicine. Celsus advocated sensible and humane treatment in the manner of Hippocrates. He described surgical operations of remarkable difficulty, including one for removing a goitre.

He is particularly remembered for his account of the signs of inflammation: redness and swelling, with heat and pain. Celsus's books were neglected during the Middle Ages, but with the Renaissance they became the first medical works to be printed (Florence, 1478).

cephalosporins. Broad-spectrum antibiotics, used mainly against bacterial strains resistant to other antibiotics. Some patients allergic to penicillin may also be allergic to cephalosporins.

cerebellum. Part of the brain occupying the hindmost part of the floor of the skull. Its surface, like that of the cerebral hemispheres, is covered with grey matter and thrown into folds or *convolutions*, but the folds are much narrower. The cerebellum is mainly concerned with the reflex adjustment of voluntary movements, with muscle tone, and with balance.

A voluntary movement (turning a screw-driver) is described under ►*muscle* (2). The kind of movement to be made is 'decided' by cells in the cerebral cortex, but the technical details such as which muscles are to contract and which to relax are left to the cerebellum. If the cerebellum is injured the muscles lose their normal tone (i.e. they become flabby) and all movement becomes inaccurate in both force and direction. The gait is unbalanced and all deliberate movements are shaky instead of smooth. The gaze cannot be fixed: it wanders and has to be repeatedly brought back. This oscillation of the eyes is called *nystagmus*. Even the muscles of the larynx are affected so that each syllable has to be spoken as a separate word. The whole picture is reminiscent of drunkenness.

Cerebellar function can be disturbed by injuries, arterial disease, tumours, and alcohol and other poisons. It can also be involved in *multiple sclerosis*.

cerebral cortex ►*cerebrum.*

cerebral hemisphere ►*cerebrum.*

cerebral palsy = ►*spastic paralysis.*

cerebrospinal fever. Epidemic meningitis, a bacterial infection due to the *meningococcus*, a microbe that many healthy people carry in their throats. Outbreaks of illness seldom occur unless people are overcrowded, e.g. in barracks or at sea.

There are three grades of infection. 1. Most people get rid of meningococci without serious symptoms, or they simply harbour them without suffering infection (>carrier). 2. Infection spreads from the nose and throat to the bloodstream, causing fever with a characteristic rash (*spotted fever*). 3. In the most serious form, infection lodges in the *meninges* – the membranes covering the brain and spinal cord. This is the real cerebrospinal fever.

Meningococci are very sensitive to sulphonamide and antibiotic drugs, and what used to be a most dangerous disease can now almost always be rapidly controlled.

➤*meningitis*.

cerebrospinal fluid (CSF). A watery fluid surrounding the brain and spinal cord, filling the space between two layers of the ➤*meninges* and also the ventricles of the brain and the narrow central canal of the spinal cord. CSF is derived from the blood in the *choroid plexuses*, networks of small blood vessels protruding into the ventricles of the brain. It circulates through the ventricles, which communicate with the space between the meninges by small openings in the fourth ventricle, between the cerebellum and the brain-stem. It is reabsorbed into the veins of the skull and backbone. The formation and absorption of CSF are balanced to maintain a constant pressure.

The CSF serves the brain and cord as a shock-absorber.

The passages between the ventricles and from the ventricles to the meninges are narrow. If one is congenitally defective or blocked by inflammation the pressure of fluid inside the brain rises. In infants the skull, which is still plastic, may become greatly enlarged (➤*hydrocephalus*). With a rigid adult skull increased pressure is a surgical emergency.

Examination of the CSF is important in the diagnosis of disorders of the brain and meninges. Normal CSF is a clear solution mainly of glucose and salts. Blood-stained fluid indicates bleeding, and pus cells and bacteria indicate infection. Minor changes in the chemical composition may be equally important clues.

➤*lumbar puncture*.

cerebrovascular disease. Disease affecting the arteries of the brain, usually *arteriosclerosis* (➤*artery* (1)). By far the commonest manifestation is ➤*stroke* of one kind or other: brain haemorrhage, thrombosis or embolism, or the kind of fleeting stroke with complete recovery now called *transient ischaemic attack* (TIA). Much less often, cerebrovascular disease causes *multi-infarct dementia*, a condition in which mental deterioration might be taken for early onset of senility, except that the decline is not steady but in steps corresponding with small but irreversible strokes. *Hypertensive encephalopathy* is a direct result of high blood pressure rather than of the underlying arterial disease.

cerebrum. The largest and most highly evolved part of the brain. It consists of two large outgrowths from the forward or upper end of the brain-stem, the *cerebral hemispheres*. Each hemisphere has a central cavity (ventricle) filled with cerebrospinal fluid. Around the cavity are clusters of nerve cells or grey matter, the *thalamus* and *basal ganglia*, concerned with more or less instinctive behaviour. These are connected by a zone of nerve fibres or white matter with an outer coating of grey matter, the *cerebral cortex*.

The cortex forms most of the surface of the brain. The area is large because the whole surface is thrown into folds (a fold is a *gyrus*; a cleft between gyri is a *sulcus*). The nerve cells of the cortex are concerned with the conscious and intelligent activities of the nervous system.

Neither voluntary movement nor conscious sensation depends wholly on the cortex. Semi-automatic actions such as walking, once they have been thoroughly learnt, seem to be delegated from the cortex to lower centres; the cortex is then needed only to direct them. Skilled, dexterous movements do, however, depend largely on the cortex. Nor does damage to the cortex lead to anaesthesia of the corresponding part of the body; rather it dulls sensation and makes it impossible to interpret what is felt. Hearing, though impaired, is not entirely lost if the auditory area of the cortex is destroyed. On the other hand destruction of the visual area does cause total blindness. Briefly, the cortex plays an important part in consciousness but not the only part. Consciousness itself depends on the reticular formation in the brain-stem; the emotions are largely a function of the hypothalamus; movement and sensation are both possible without the cortex. Its function seems to be to refine the activities of the lower centres, which is as much a matter of suppressing activities as of initiating them.

Willis, in 1664, suggested that the cerebrum might be concerned with voluntary, the cerebellum with involuntary actions. This was confirmed experimentally by Rolando in 1809. At the end of the 18th century Gall made important studies of the location in the brain of different functions but then allowed himself to be diverted into the absurdities of phrenology. A century later Hughlings Jackson identified the area of the cortex concerned with movements. Considerable areas have now been plotted, thanks largely to the work of Penfield. Adjacent to each of the clearly defined areas (vision, general sensation, particular movements etc.) is an *association area*, in which the specific function is co-ordinated with others. One such area is especially important: the speech centre next to the area for movements of the mouth and throat, usually on the left side. In general, one side of the cortex (and of the whole brain) is concerned with the opposite side of the body, but many functions are represented on both sides. This often allows some return of lost function after damage to the cortex, e.g. from bleeding; the opposite side of the brain learns to deputize.

cervical. 1. Of the neck. **2.** Of the *cervix uteri*.

Cervical screening is microscopical examination of cells shed from the *cervix uteri*; by this means the earliest stage of cancer of the cervix can be detected and eradicated before it has any chance to spread.

cervix uteri. Neck of the womb; the part of the ►*uterus* that projects into the upper part of the vagina. It is a powerful ring of muscle, closed at most times but able to expand widely during childbirth.

Cesalpinus (Andrea Cesalpino) (1524–1603). Pupil of ►*Columbus*; physician; professor of botany at Pisa. He is said by some historians to have anticipated Harvey's discovery of the circulation of blood, but the claim is not well founded. Cesalpino had learnt from Columbus that blood circulated through the lungs, and from his own observations that blood in the veins flowed towards the heart. But he did not recognize that the heart was a pump, or that the blood flowed continuously. In fact he thought it flowed outwards in the arteries by day and back in the veins by night as a result of cooling.

Cesalpino's undisputed claim to immortality is as the founder of systematic botany.

cetrimide. An ➤*antiseptic* of the detergent type, suitable for cleansing the skin.

Chagas' disease. South American variety of *trypanosomiasis* (➤*trypanosome*).

chancre. Localized inflammation at the point of entry of an infection that later produces its main effects in other parts of the body; the earliest sign of ➤*syphilis*. The syphilitic chancre is a small painless lump that may pass unnoticed unless it forms an ulcer. It usually recovers quickly, and for some time the patient has no symptoms at all; but in due course the signs of widespread infection appear.

Some other infectious diseases are heralded by a chancre, e.g. sleeping sickness.

chancroid (soft sore). A venereal disease, less common than gonorrhoea or syphilis, caused by Ducrey's bacillus. The usual symptom is a painful and persistent ulcer, often with swelling of lymph nodes in the groins. The infection responds well to antibiotics.

charcoal. Activated charcoal holds to its surface (adsorbs) many substances including some poisons. It is therefore commonly given as an antidote. It is also used for the relief of flatulence.

Charcot, Jean-Martin (1825–93). French physician and pathologist, a pioneer in the detailed study of the nervous system and its disorders. His many disciples included Freud, who was interested in Charcot's studies of hypnotism.

Chauliac, Guy de (*c.* 1300–1370). Physician and surgeon at the papal court in Avignon. His account of the treatment of wounds and fractures became the standard text. He recognized the need to cleanse wounds, bring the edges together and hold them in place, and protect them from further damage; but like most of his contemporaries he thought that pus was to be encouraged. He gave narcotic drugs before operating on patients.

Guy de Chauliac wrote classic accounts of the plague (he survived an attack of the Black Death) and of leprosy.

chelating agent. Substance of which the molecules can engulf molecules of a metal. The red pigment of the blood holds its atoms of iron by chelation: each is enclosed by a ring of porphyrin molecules to form *haem*, which in turn is linked to the protein *globin*. The plant pigment chlorophyll has a similar structure but with magnesium in place of iron. Synthetic chelating agents are used to treat poisoning by metals such as lead.

cheloid ➤*keloid*.

chemotherapy. Treatment of infection with drugs (originally synthetic, but now including natural antibiotics) that poison the infecting microbes without serious harm to the patient.

To this earlier definition is now added the treatment of cancer by chemical means, in general with drugs to which the abnormal cells of the cancer are more sensitive than healthy cells. ➤*cytotoxic agents*.

chest ➤*thorax*.

Cheyne–Stokes respiration. (John Cheyne, 1777–1836, and William Stokes, 1804–78, physicians in Dublin.) A pattern of breathing common in severe illness: instead of the normal rhythm, successive breaths are deeper, then shallower until breathing seems to stop; then the cycle is repeated. Some 23 centuries before Cheyne and Stokes, Hippocrates perfectly described it as like a person 'remembering to breathe'.

chickenpox (varicella). The most infectious and one of the commonest of virus diseases. Since an attack generally confers life-long immunity, chickenpox is seen mostly in children. After an incubation period of a fortnight, the temperature rises and an itchy rash appears almost at once. It consists of small raised spots, later turning to inflamed blisters. Fresh spots develop for several days, first on the trunk, later on the face and limbs. Scarring is unusual. The patient recovers in a few days, but is considered infectious until the last spot has formed a scab and flaked off.

The same virus causes ►*herpes* zoster or shingles.

chigger. 1. *Sand-flea*, a small insect common in hot countries; it burrows into the skin and causes severe itching. **2.** *Harvest mite*, another small insect with an itchy bite.

chilblain. An exaggerated response to cold. In everyone, the flow of blood through the skin decreases when the skin is chilled; in this way the body is protected from losing too much heat. In people whose skin is abnormally sensitive to cold, the blood vessels of the skin contract so much that the skin is deprived of blood and oxygen. This causes swelling, itching, and a characteristic burning sensation, usually confined to the fingers and toes but sometimes affecting the ears and other parts. Prevention, by keeping the sensitive areas warm, is much more effective than treatment. Smoking further reduces the circulation of blood in the skin; alcohol improves it.

child abuse. This is taken to mean ill-treatment of children by parents or guardians. The abuse may be by default (child neglect) or by design, which can include *emotional cruelty*, such as locking a child in a cupboard without causing physical injury, *sexual offences* and *physical assault* culminating in the *battered-baby syndrome*. These categories overlap. The first point is that all are far more prevalent than one might guess. Parents do not report their own failings. Neighbours tend to stay clear of trouble, and near relations may try to avoid the implicit social stigma. Statistics are therefore unreliable, but a respected American source suggests that well over a million children may be affected annually in the USA, and that some 2,000 die from abuse or neglect.

In the majority of cases, victims of the battered-baby syndrome are subjected to ill-treatment during the first three years of life. Characteristic injuries include bruising, burns, broken bones and internal injuries of all kinds. The different stages of healing are a definite indication that the child has been injured repeatedly. In Britain about a hundred children are known to be killed annually in this way. This clearly defined clinical picture cannot be new, yet it was not until 1966 that the first account of it was published.

While it is obvious that criminal acts are involved, in the present context child abuse has to be seen as a medical and social problem as well. The parents are usually young, but most show no obvious mental disorder apart from this one. Often, but by no means always, the baby is unwanted. While simple neglect may be the problem, one or both parents may be mentally incompetent to look after an infant or may be unsuitably housed, suffering from depression, chronically unemployed, overwrought and tired, addicted to alcohol or drugs, or they may have fallen prey to a combination of these and other contributing factors. However, the parents may also appear to be mentally and socially stable and to enjoy the privileges which one would assume would preclude them from abusing their child. The one common factor is that often the parent was illtreated as a child, which evokes the distressing thought that the condition may be self-perpetuating, generation to generation.

The management of this problem is not primarily medical. The doctor, who may be the first person to know what is happening, is responsible not only for treating the baby's injuries, but also for establishing whether or not the parents require psychiatric attention (as do the minority of cases). However, any longterm solution calls for close co-operation between several kinds of social service. Few people like to feel that they are interfering with, or spying on, their neighbours or family, but unless somebody gives the competent authorities a chance to investigate, a child may die or suffer irreparable injuries.

childbirth. ►*labour* as regards the mother, and ►*birth* as regards the baby.

chill. Shivering attack (*rigor*) due to illness (nearly always infection): the im-

mediate cause of raised bodytemperature.

Chinese medicine. The traditional medical practices of China are very ancient: they have persisted almost unchanged for five millennia. Only a few broad generalizations can be made here, for the whole concept of Chinese medicine is alien to Western thought. It is based on philosophical speculation, in which neither observed events nor deductions play any part. To discuss it in the terms of Western science or even, perhaps, in a European language is like trying to explain poetry by algebra.

The body, like everything else, is governed by the two essences yin and yang, which are at once opposed and complementary. Health is a perfect balance of the two. Yin is female. It dominates earth, moon, winter, water. Yang is male and dominates heaven, sun, summer, and fire.

There are five elements (wood, fire, earth, metal, and water) and likewise five of many other things. Five solid yin organs correspond with five hollow yang organs, and each pair responds to a tissue. The triads are as follows. Lungs (yin) and large intestine (yang) respond to skin; heart and small intestine to arteries, liver and gall bladder to ligaments, spleen and stomach to muscle, kidney and bladder to bone or hair.

Yin and yang are stored in three receptacles called burning spaces, from which they are conveyed through the body by twelve meridians. Neither the burning spaces nor the meridians actually exist in any physical sense, but since yin and yang are invisible essences they do not need visible structures for their storage and transport.

Disease is a disturbance of the balance

between yin and yang by influences such as emotion and weather. The diagnosis is made by examination of the pulse at both wrists. Each organ has its characteristic effect on the pulse, and the examination may take a long time. Its object is to determine the exact site of the harmful excess of yin or yang.

Two methods of treating such an excess are well enough known to have been used beyond China. These are *moxibustion* and *acupuncture*.

Moxibustion is setting fire to a small heap of dried mugwort on the skin over the affected meridian.

Acupuncture is the insertion of needles at precisely determined points on the meridians, to allow the harmful accumulations to escape. This encourages the blood to circulate, moistens the bones and ligaments, and lubricates the joints.

There are several points of resemblance to Western beliefs, past or present. Three of the four Greek elements (earth, fire, and water) are among the Chinese five, and there is a clear resemblance between the Greek ►*humours* and Chinese theory. In all Romance languages earth, moon, and water are feminine, and sky, sun, and fire are masculine nouns. But nothing in the foregoing account has ever been verified; indeed none of it is open to verification. It must be taken on trust, or rejected.

If the almost mystical theories of Chinese medicine cannot be reconciled with Western scientific method, there is still much to be learnt from the practice. The most revered physician in the history of Europe, Hippocrates, based his practice on wrong ideas of bodily functions, yet nobody doubts his professional competence.

Chinese doctors practised inoculation against smallpox centuries before anyone else. They saw the importance of cleanliness (which is by no means obvious) and the therapeutic value of bathing. Their extensive materia medica includes drugs later adopted by Western medicine. A good example of these is *ma huang* or ephedrine.

Certain principles of Chinese medicine deserve close study everywhere. Its first object is the prevention rather than the cure of disease – ensured by paying the doctor only while his patient remains well. Its underlying theories emphasize the dependence of one part of the body on the rest, and of the patient on his surroundings. Scientific medicine, by analysing the whole into its parts and by encouraging the specialist, is apt to lose sight of these things.

In modern Chinese hospitals students have to learn traditional as well as scientific medicine, and practitioners of both kinds work side by side, each studying the other's methods. By all accounts the system works well.

chiropractic. A system of treatment mainly by manipulation of the backbone, said to relieve pressure on nerves to allow them to function freely so that the body can restore itself to health. Chiropractic is one of several systems that appeared in the United States during the 19th century. It was invented by D. D. Palmer, who had no formal scientific training but had considered the problems of ill-health for some years before this idea came to him. Superficially the methods resemble those of ►*osteopathy*, but the theory is quite distinct. ►*manipulation*.

Chlamydia. A microscopical parasite, formerly known as Bedsonia. More elaborate than a virus (although like a virus it can multiply within living body cells), in most other respects it is more like a very small bacterium. Chlamydial infections include *psittacosis*, an infection of parrots that can cause human pneumonia, and a group of infections including *trachoma*, which affects the eyelids, and several sexually transmitted diseases. They can be treated with sulphonamides or tetracyclines.

chloral hydrate. Synthetic drug for promoting sleep; introduced in the 19th century as an alternative to bromides, it was generally supplanted in the 20th by the barbiturate hypnotics. It has a very disagreeable bitter taste, but it is safer than most hypnotics, especially for children, and has never completely lost favour.

chloramphenicol. An antibiotic, originally extracted from the fungus *Streptomyces venezuelae* but now synthesized. It is effective against a wide range of infections, including typhoid and typhus fevers and whooping cough. As it is liable to interfere with the formation of blood cells, this antibiotic is used only for infections that respond poorly or not at all to safer drugs, and then under close supervision.

Local application of chloramphenicol in the forms of eye ointment and ear drops is, however, acceptable for more general use.

chlorine. Chlorine gas is a corrosive poison. Inhalation (e.g. by troops gassed in the First World War) causes a violent bronchitis which may be rapidly lethal or may leave permanent damage to the lungs by replacement of normal lung tissue with useless scar tissue. Strong solutions are poisonous when swallowed, e.g. as bleaching powder. It injures or destroys the mucous membranes of the

mouth, throat and stomach. Sodium thiosulphate (photographer's hypo) is to some extent an antidote.

Chlorine is a valuable antiseptic, especially for making water safe for drinking.

chloroform (trichlormethane). $CHCl_3$; discovered in 1831 and first used as an ►*anaesthetic* in 1847.

chloroquine. Antimalarial drug, introduced in 1946 as an alternative to quinacrine. It cures attacks of malaria, and taken weekly it suppresses attacks. It is also effective against amoebic infection of the liver (►*dysentery* (1)).

Chloroquine sometimes suppresses symptoms of rheumatoid arthritis and some skin diseases. The mechanism is not known.

chlorosis. Very severe anaemia with yellow or greenish pallor, formerly common among young women, due to lack of iron. ►*anaemia* (B.1).

chlorpromazine. A powerful drug used as a ►*tranquillizer*: introduced in 1954, it is the prototype of the *phenothiazine* group.

chol(e)-. Prefix = 'of the ►*bile*'.

cholecyst(o)-. Prefix = 'of the ►*gall* bladder'.

cholera. An acute infection caused by *Vibrio cholerae*, a short, curved bacterium ('comma bacillus'); contracted from food or drinking water contaminated by human faeces. The disease is transmitted by people with cholera or about to develop symptoms or very recently recovered. There are no unaffected carriers of these bacteria (as there are, for instance, of typhoid bacilli).

After a short incubation period (1–6 days) during which the bacteria multiply rapidly in the duodenum, violent diarrhoea sets in. Within hours of the onset the patient is so thoroughly purged that his motions are no more than water with dissolved salts and flakes of shed mucous membrane. In an extreme case the amount of water passed from the intestine in 24 hours may be a quarter of the total body weight. Loss of alkali (bicarbonate) causes ►*acidosis*, and loss of potassium salts disturbs the conduction of electrical impulses, especially in the heart. Any of these three effects – dehydration, acidosis, loss of potassium – can be rapidly lethal. The mortality of untreated cholera is over 50 per cent.

The infection never spreads beyond the intestine, and it has no important effect other than diarrhoea. Cholera, more than any other serious illness, is a disease of one symptom. If the losses of water, alkali and potassium are made good then complete recovery is the rule. Early in this century Sir Leonard Rogers reduced the mortality among his patients in India from 50 per cent to 5 per cent simply by replacing salt and water.

Antibiotics probably hasten recovery but they are of secondary importance; it is by maintaining the chemical balance of the body fluids that lives are saved.

Vaccination against cholera is no longer recommended. It confers at best only limited immunity, and that for no more than a few months. Travellers to endemic areas are better protected by strict personal hygiene and avoiding uncooked foods.

Cholera is overcome by prevention rather than treatment, and since human excrement is the only source of infection, adequate sanitation eradicates the disease: if nobody with the infection contaminates food or drinking water, cholera cannot spread. This was first recognized in 1849, by John Snow. Snow was a London doctor, a pioneer of anaesthesia. Five years later, Snow showed that all the victims of an outbreak in London had drunk water from the same pump in Broad Street, and he inferred that the pump had been contaminated with sewage. The pump-handle was removed, and the outbreak stopped. This was 27 years before Koch's discovery of the germ of cholera, and in fact years before any disease could be definitely ascribed to bacteria.

cholestasis. Stagnation of bile in the liver due to obstruction of the bile passages, a common cause of ►*jaundice*.

cholesteatoma. A complication of perforation and chronic infection of the eardrum: skin from the outer ear grows inwards, is shed in the ordinary way, but cannot escape. It causes damage by pressure and harbours infection, and needs surgical removal.

cholesterol. A waxy substance, first observed in gall stones (*chole* = gall, bile; *stereos* = solid). It is an essential component of the cell membranes of most tissues, and the chemical precursor of sex hormones and steroid hormones. In excess, however, it is also a key factor in the blockage of arteries by ►*atheroma*, leading to heart attacks, strokes and other serious disorders.

Cholesterol is closely associated in the body with fat, and like fat is carried in the blood attached to protein molecules as *lipoproteins*. These are classified as high-density (alpha) and low-density (beta) lipoproteins (HDL, LDL). Cells in the liver and elsewhere are adapted to receive lipoproteins and safely dispose of them. But some LDL bypasses these receptors. It is assimilated by wandering white blood cells, which deposit the cholesterol in the walls of arteries. Atheroma begins with these deposits.

The risk of developing serious arterial disease in this way is related to the ratio of LDL to HDL. A preponderance of LDL increases the danger, and one of HDL decreases it. Several known risk factors, including obesity and smoking, raise LDL levels, while regular exercise and moderation in eating and drinking lower them. Although much of the body's cholesterol is synthesized in the liver, cutting down the amount in the diet (egg yolks, red meat) does tend to reduce the amount in the blood. Drugs to lower the levels of circulating cholesterol were greeted very enthusiastically when they first appeared, but they are now generally reserved for patients at special risk.

choline. An organic compound of ammonium hydroxide; it is essential to life and is sometimes counted as a vitamin of the B group. But unlike a true vitamin, choline can be synthesized in the body. Deficiency arises only when the diet is so poor that the raw material for choline synthesis is not provided; this is characteristic of *kwashiorkor*, a grave form of malnutrition seen in the tropics. Lack of choline interferes with the disposal of fat and damages the liver.

The compound ►*acetyl choline* is released at the ends of nerve fibres to stimulate adjacent nerve or muscle cells.

choline esterase. An enzyme responsible for the formation and decomposition of acetyl choline. Drugs such as eserine inhibit this enzyme and so prevent acetyl choline from being destroyed as soon as it has acted. This reinforces the action of nerves that release acetyl choline, particularly those of the *parasympathetic* system.

chondr(o)-. Prefix = 'of ►*cartilage*'.

chorea. Abnormal muscular activity in the form of purposeless twitching and convolution. **1.** *Sydenham's chorea* (chorea minor; St Vitus's dance) is a disorder of children, usually associated with rheumatic fever, characterized by uncontrolled jerky movements, which may involve any part of the body. Unlike a *tic* or habit spasm, which is repetitive, the movement of chorea has no pattern. Mild cases are often dismissed as fidgeting. The cause is not known. The condition clears up spontaneously in two or three months.

2. *Huntington's chorea* (chorea major) is a rare hereditary condition. Although the tendency is inherited as a dominant character, symptoms do not appear until adult life. In addition to the uncontrolled movements of chorea there is progressive mental disorder. Sedative drugs relieve the symptoms to some extent, but no cure is known.

chorion. The outer layer of the membrane surrounding the foetus.

chorionepithelioma. An extremely rare form of cancer derived from the chorion.

choroid (chorioid). Network of small blood vessels in the eye, immediately outside the retina.

choroiditis. Inflammation of the choroid, sometimes due to identifiable infection but usually of unknown cause. It may disturb vision, but complications such as detached retinae and glaucoma are more serious effects. As a rule, corticosteroid drugs are the most effective treatment.

choroid plexus. Networks of blood vessels in the ventricles of the brain in which cerebrospinal fluid is formed.

chromium. A white metal with many industrial uses. Chromium and its salts can cause various types of skin disease.

chromosome. A particle seen in the nucleus of a cell during cell division (i.e. splitting to form two new cells), but not seen in a resting cell. A chromosome is a collection of a large number of *genes*; each gene determines one element in the hereditary make-up of the body.

The nucleus of a resting cell contains a jumble of genes. When the cell is about to divide, this material is organized as a set of X- or V-shaped chromosomes; there are 23 pairs in the human set. The members of a pair are similar excepting the pair of sex chromosomes in the male. In the female, the 23rd pair consists of two large X chromosomes; in the male, of one X chromosome and one small Y chromosome. ►*genetics*.

chronic. (Disease) of long duration, often of gradual onset (cf. ►*acute*).

chrysotherapy. Treatment with salts of gold, now practically confined to rheumatoid arthritis.

chyle. Milky fluid in the lymph vessels of the small intestine: it is an emulsion of tissue fluid and the fat absorbed from food, which is taken up by the lymph vessels (lacteals) and not, like other components of food, by the veins.

chylomicron. Minute droplet of fat suspended in blood.

chyme. Fluid, partly digested contents of the small intestine.

cilia (pl. of *ciltum*). **1.** Eyelashes. **2.** Fine hair-like structures, like the pile of velvet, on the surface of some cells, e.g. those of the air-passages. Their constant undulation sweeps mucus and dust particles upwards to be coughed or sneezed away or swallowed.

ciliary muscle. Muscle encircling the lens of the eye for focusing.

cinchona. *Peruvian (Jesuit's) bark*, the natural source of *quinine*, introduced to Europe from South America in the 17th century as a remedy for malaria, then a common disease throughout Europe (which cinchona cures), and for many other fevers (which it does not affect).

circle of Willis (circulus vasculosus). (Thomas Willis, 1621–75, English anatomist and physician.) A circular system of arteries at the base of the brain: blood is carried into the skull by the left and right internal carotid arteries and the basilar artery (formed by the union of the two vertebral arteries), of which communicating branches form a ring. To a limited extent this provides an alternative supply if one artery fails, but the main function of the circle is to balance the pressure of blood delivered to the brain.

circulation. Constant flow of blood and other body fluids. An average man contains about 45 litres of water (70 per cent of body weight). The cells contain 30 litres. Three litres are in the *plasma* of the blood (the suspended cells make the total volume of blood up to 5 litres). The remaining 12 litres fill the spaces between groups of cells. This *tissue fluid* bathes all the cells of the body except those of the liver and spleen, which are directly in contact with the blood. The *cerebrospinal fluid* of the brain and spinal cord is separate from the rest of the tissue fluid. All the substances necessary for life filter into the cells from the tissue fluid, in exchange for waste products. By filtration from the ►*capillary* blood vessels the tissue fluid receives fresh supplies and gives up waste. For the system to work, the blood in the capillaries must be continually replaced with fresh blood; otherwise supplies would run out and waste would accumulate. The most urgent need is oxygen. The 5 litres of blood in the body can hold at the most 1 litre of oxygen, which is enough to keep a man alive for 4 minutes at rest, or less than a minute during exercise. Nor can the blood give up all its oxygen to the tissues. Thus the blood must circulate rapidly. At rest, it is pumped at the rate of 5 litres every minute, and this can be increased to every 10 seconds.

The heart is two separate pumps, right and left. The right side pumps blood through the lungs, where the oxygen content is restored. This blood returns to the left side of the heart to be sent round the body again. Part of it is diverted to the kidneys for removal of waste products. Another part goes first to the stomach and intestine, where it takes up foodstuffs, and from there to the liver, where these are processed. All the blood then returns to the right side of the heart to be sent through the lungs again. (*>heart*.)

Blood flows from the heart to the periphery in *arteries*, which divide into smaller and smaller branches and finally into *capillaries*, where the work of the blood is done. The capillaries enter small *veins*, which join to form larger and larger vessels on the way back to the heart. The blood is ejected from the heart in spurts; between beats the pressure falls to zero. But the arteries are elastic. They are stretched with each beat, and their recoil maintains the pressure and flow between beats. Instead of falling from 120 mm of mercury to zero, the pressure in the arteries fluctuates between 120 and 80 mm. It is this smaller difference which is felt

as the *>pulse*. The resistance to the flow is greatest in the smallest arteries (*arterioles*), and in them the pressure falls to about 30 mm., while the pulse disappears. The capillaries are even smaller, but they are so numerous that they offer less resistance. The pressure in the veins is very low. Muscular activity keeps the blood moving in the veins, and one-way valves ensure that the flow is in the right direction.

1. REGULATION

The circulation is regulated primarily by the rate at which the heart pumps. The calibre of the vessels is adapted to the needs of the moment, partly by local mechanisms but mainly by the *vasomotor centre*, a group of nerve cells in the lowest part of the brain, close to the cardiac and respiratory centres. A continuous stream of impulses from the centre, carried in *>sympathetic* nerves along the vessels, keeps the muscle fibres in the vessel walls partially contracted. If the blood pressure rises because of increased flow from the heart, the nervous impulses decrease, the vessels dilate, and the normal pressure is restored. If the pressure begins to fall, the vessels contract. This reflex originates in nerve-endings sensitive to pressure in some of the large arteries. Impulses in these nerves inhibit the centre. Other factors influencing the centre are the same as those which influence the cardiac centre (*>heart* (3)). The two centres are coordinated to keep the blood pressure within reasonable limits. Emotion affects the state of the blood vessels even more than it does the heart.

The vasomotor centre affects the circulation as a whole, but the varying needs of particular organs are met by local mechanisms. For instance, the carbon dioxide which accumulates in an active muscle causes vessels in that muscle to dilate, so that it receives more blood at the expense of other organs. *Cramp* is a failure of this response. When the activity of the heart is increased, the lowered concentration of oxygen causes the ►*coronary arteries* to dilate and admit more blood and oxygen. The cramp of an inadequate blood supply to the heart is *angina pectoris*.

The *kidney* has a unique means of maintaining its blood supply. Defective circulation in the kidney causes an enzyme, *renin*, to be released. This reacts with a substance in the blood to form *angiotensin*, which directly stimulates the arterioles to contract and so raises the blood pressure. High blood pressure is a common complication of kidney diseases.

The small blood vessels in the *skin* are the principal means of regulating the body ►*temperature*. If they relax, blood is cooled at the surface of the body, and if they contract heat is retained.

Various disorders involving the circulation are discussed under ►*artery*; *blood pressure*; *heart failure*; *oedema*; *shock*; *vein*.

2. HISTORY

The circulation of the blood is one of the fundamentals of physiology. Until it was understood the workings of the body made little sense. Many of the most important discoveries in medicine were the result of advances in other sciences: for example, the processes of disease could not be studied until the microscope had been invented. But Harvey's discovery that the blood circulated, announced in 1628, could have been made at any time in the preceding 2,000 years. ►*Harvey* had no more idea than ►*Hippocrates* of

how blood passed from arteries to veins, for he had no microscope. But he deduced that it must somehow do so from facts which the ancient Greeks could have observed.

The valves of the heart and their effect were described in the 4th century BC by an adherent of Hippocrates, but the real significance of their permitting flow in only one direction was missed. The arteries of a dead body are empty, all the blood having stagnated in the capillaries and veins. If an artery is opened after death it appears to contain air – as indeed it does after it has been opened. The physicians of antiquity assumed that the arteries were for the transport of air, mysteriously transformed into 'vital spirit'. But for this fallacy ►*Herophilus* and ►*Erasistratus*, working in Alexandria, would probably have discovered the circulation in the 3rd century BC. Herophilus distinguished veins from arteries, but thought that the pulse was a property of the arteries themselves. Erasistratus observed that an artery would bleed if it were cut during life, because, he said, the escaping air was replaced with blood which entered by very small vessels between the veins and arteries. He was postulating capillaries, admittedly with the flow in the wrong direction. If this idea had been related to what was known of the heart valves the puzzle would have been solved.

In the 2nd century AD ►*Galen* went a step further by proving that the arteries carry blood and not air, but he rejected Erasistratus' view that the heart was the terminus of both veins and arteries, and ignored his theory about capillaries. Instead, Galen described the veins and arteries as two separate trees. The veins originated in the liver, where blood was formed from materials brought by the portal vein from the liver. Similarly the arteries originated in the lungs. The arteries were still primarily concerned with the transport of vital spirit. Their blood came from the veins through holes in the wall between the two sides of the heart. In both veins and arteries blood simply ebbed to and fro.

In 1268 ►*Ibn an-Nafis* of Cairo said that there were no holes such as Galen had described, and the blood must reach the left side of the heart from the right by passage through the lungs. In 1552 ►*Servetus* said the same thing, and at about that time ►*Columbus* proved it. In 1603 ►*Fabricius ab Aquapendente* described the valves of the veins, without recognizing their function.

Finally, in 1628 Fabricius's pupil Harvey described the continuous circulation of blood through the body as we should describe it today, and in so doing marked the transition from ancient to modern medical science. It only remained for ►*Malpighi*, with the help of a microscope, to demonstrate the actual channels – first suggested 20 centuries earlier by Erasistratus – which complete the circuit.

circumcision. Surgical removal of part of the foreskin (prepuce) of the penis. The medical value of circumcision has been overstated. Infants seldom need the operation, and those who do are often suffering from ill-advised attempts to draw the foreskin back. In fact, an adherent foreskin is normal in infancy, and only later does the foreskin become loose.

There is, however, evidence that cancer of the penis (an uncommon disease in any case) is even rarer in circumcised men. The difference could be due to bacterial growth under the intact foreskin. Wives of circumcised men are rather less liable to cancer of the cervix of the uterus than other women, according to some authorities, but the evidence is open to question.

cirrhosis. A disorder of the liver, in which healthy liver tissue has at some time been damaged and replaced by fibrous scar tissue. The changes involve the whole organ. The fibrous tissue hardens the liver. Clumps of new liver cells give the organ a lumpy surface, and their yellowish colour gives the condition its name (Gk *kirrhos* = tawny).

The normal liver has a great facility for regeneration, but in a cirrhotic liver lost tissue is unlikely to be all replaced. The mere loss of functioning tissue would not matter until a great deal was destroyed, because the normal liver has a substantial surplus. A more immediate source of trouble is compression by fibrous tissue of the blood vessels in the liver. A large volume of blood is carried in the *portal vein* from the stomach, intestine, and spleen to the liver, to be chemically processed before returning to the heart by the *inferior vena cava*. When the circulation through the liver is impaired by cirrhosis the blood is dammed and finds other routes to the heart. There are small communications between the normal portal vein and the ordinary veins around the oesophagus and rectum: with severe cirrhosis these are distended and liable to bleed. Similar veins at the umbilicus are distended, and the spleen is congested and enlarged. Jaundice, and poisoning by substances that ought to be neutralized in the liver, are other possible effects. But in most cases, cirrhosis causes no symptoms at all: it is only at an advanced stage that there is a risk of serious bleeding or failure of liver function.

Various chemical poisons can cause cirrhosis; overwhelmingly the most important of these is *alcohol*. In addition to the direct effect of heavy drinking, malnutrition may be a contributory factor in alcoholic cirrhosis, for chronic alcoholics are usually undernourished. This is partly because they take alcohol instead of food, and partly because damage to the stomach and pancreas impairs digestion of the food they do take.

The other common known cause of cirrhosis is viral ►*hepatitis* (type B). Some cases with no evident cause may be due to hepatitis that passed unnoticed at the time of the original mild attack.

Heart failure with stagnation of blood in the liver, and various chronic disorders of the liver itself, can lead in time to cirrhosis.

Although cirrhosis advanced enough to cause ill health is a serious disorder it is by no means the hopeless condition that it was once thought to be. Even a liver severely damaged by alcohol may recover considerably if the patient stops drinking. An exactly regulated diet improves most cases. Badly impaired circulation in the liver may be improved by a by-pass operation (►*liver* (3)).

cirs(o)-. Prefix = 'varicose'. *Cirsoid aneurism* is a rare tumour, usually on the scalp, composed of tortuous, distended blood vessels.

citric acid. A weak organic acid readily extracted from lemons and other fruit: in the human body it is an intermediate product in the combustion of foodstuffs. The *citric acid cycle* (Krebs cycle) is a series of chemical reactions in which carbon dioxide and water are formed with release of the energy; it is common to carbohydrate, fat and protein combustion, since citric acid is formed from any of them.

claudication. Limping – usually *intermittent claudication*, a cramp-like pain in the legs during mild exercise, due to inadequate supply of blood to the muscles from defective arteries. It is a similar disorder in the legs to angina in the heart, and the usual reason for either is atheroma.

Smoking aggravates the condition; giving up the habit improves it. Drugs to dilate the arteries are of little value because the diseased vessels cannot respond to them. Regular exercise, on the other hand, helps to maintain the existing circulation and promote the formation of alternative (collateral) pathways for the blood. For the more serious cases surgical methods of clearing the obstruction or else of bypassing it are often used with success.

Pressure on nerves by narrowing of the passages where they leave the spinal column can cause symptoms very like those of intermittent claudication.

clavicle. The collar-bone, a bar joined at its inner end to the breast-bone (*sternum*) and at its outer end to the shoulder-blade (*scapula*). The two joints are bound by very tough ligaments, stronger than the bone itself, so that an injury is much more likely to break the bone than dislocate either of its joints.

The clavicle is more often broken than any other bone: almost any kind of fall involving the upper limb can cause a fracture of the clavicle because it is no more than a light strut and cannot withstand a heavy load. The patient almost announces the diagnosis by supporting the elbow of the injured side with his good hand. Since the whole length of the clavicle lies just below the skin, the fracture is usually obvious.

A bandage to brace the shoulders back reduces (sets) the fracture, and the clavicle heals quickly. Another method, said to give the best cosmetic result, is to keep the patient flat on his back with a pad between the shoulder-blades, so that the weight of the shoulders pulls the fragments into place; this method is described in the Edwin Smith Papyrus of the 17th century BC.

In the rare event of a dislocation of the joint at the outer end of the clavicle, the damage may need surgical repair.

climacteric. Change of life; in women it is the same as the ⊁*menopause*, but the male climacteric is a nebulous concept, for although male fertility gradually declines over the years the change is quantitative rather than qualitative.

clinical. Of the sick-bed or its occupant – e.g. *clinical diagnosis* is recognition of disease at the bedside from the patient's symptoms and signs, as opposed to diagnosis by laboratory tests, X-ray examination etc.

clitoris. A small protrusion at the front of the vulva, sensitive to sexual excitement: its development in the female corresponds with that of the penis in the male.

clofibrate. A drug used to lower the concentration of cholesterol and other lipids in the blood in order to lessen the risk of arterial disease and its complications. When it first appeared in the 1960s it was widely seen as a prophylactic for everyone over the age of about 50 to take regularly, but time has shown that its value is limited: ⊁*cholesterol*.

clomiphene. A synthetic drug able to stimulate the ovary in the manner of the gonadotrophic hormone of the pituitary gland, used for treating certain types of female infertility (⊁*fertility*).

clostridium. A genus of bacteria, including those of *tetanus, botulism* and *gas gangrene*. They thrive in the absence of air. Most are by nature soil-dwellers and infect man only by mischance.

clot ⊁*blood* (4).

club-foot (talipes). Deformity of the foot, generally a result of faulty development before birth, but the term may also include the results of any interference with natural growth such as infection of bone or injury to nerves. Taken early, some types do well with simple treatment such as manipulation and splinting. Others need surgical reconstruction of the joints of the foot. Even early treatment may not obviate the need for special footwear, but at least it improves performance.

cluster headaches. Localized headaches usually centred round one eye; a kind of ⊁*migraine* occuring in 'clusters' of daily attacks for 2 or 3 weeks, with intervals of many months between attacks.

CMV ⊁*cytomegalovirus*.

coagulation. Clotting; ⊁*blood* (4).

cobalt. A metal involved in human chemistry as a component of cyanocobalamine (vitamin B_{12}). A radioactive ⊁*isotope* of cobalt is used in the treatment of some types of cancer.

cocaine. An alkaloid extracted from the South American coca plant, formerly much used as a local anaesthetic. It also has effects like those of adrenaline: the constriction of arteries helps the surgeon by discouraging bleeding, but the stimulation of the heart can be dangerous. It is a notorious drug of addiction, causing temporary elation and hallucinations; habitual use causes grave deterioration of personality and sometimes frank insanity.

coccidioides. A microscopical fungus: an uncommon cause of serious infection of the lungs.

coccus. A spherical or roughly spherical ▸*bacterium*. Several types can cause disease, including *streptococci* (growing in chains) and *staphylococci* (growing in clumps); these two are the usual causes of pus formation. *Diplococci* grow in pairs. They include *gonococci* (causing gonorrhoea) and *meningococci* (causing epidemic meningitis).

coccyx. The lower end of the backbone; a small triangular bone projecting beyond the sacrum. It consists of four tiny vertebrae fused together, and is all that remains of a human tail. It is liable to be broken by a direct blow between the buttocks. The fracture is painful but seldom serious.

cochlea. Spiral cavity, like a snail-shell, containing the hearing apparatus (organ of Corti) of the inner ▸*ear* (3).

codeine. Alkaloid drug from opium, closely related to morphine but less powerful and probably less habit-forming. It is used to relieve pain, generally in small doses mixed with other drugs such as aspirin, to suppress unnecessary cough and sometimes to suppress diarrhoea.

coeliac artery. A branch of the aorta, carrying blood to the stomach, liver, pancreas, and spleen.

coeliac disease. A disorder of the small intestine in which the assimilation of essential dietary ingredients is impaired (malabsorption). The mucous membrane lining the intestine does not tolerate *gliadin*, a component of the protein *gluten* found in wheat, barley and rye. Characteristic changes in the membrane can be seen under the microscope, and diagnosis can be confirmed by examining a fragment of it. The effect is that the patient develops malnutrition with bloating and diarrhoea, since fat is poorly assimilated. Symptoms commonly appear after a previously healthy infant starts to eat bread. Stature may be stunted, and the child may be pale, potbellied, and fretful. Vitamin deficiencies may become apparent. In some cases, symptoms are not recognized until adult life, although the defect may have been present in a mild form since childhood.

The only remedy is to avoid gluten, which means a diet with no bread or products containing flour from the guilty cereals. This usually calls for the advice of an expert dietitian. The patient can be expected to thrive when the diet is correctly adjusted; however, although some children may appear to grow out of their intolerance to gliadin (which would need laboratory confirmation), patients should be prepared to continue their restricted diet indefinitely.

coeliac plexus (solar plexus). Network of nerves behind the stomach, derived from the sympathetic and vagus nerves, supplying branches to regulate the stomach, intestine and other abdominal organs.

co-enzyme ▸*enzyme* (4).

coitus interruptus ▸*contraception*.

145

colchicum. The root of *Colchicum autumnale*, the autumn crocus, provides an alkaloid, colchicine, which is an effective remedy for attacks of gout.

cold. 1. Acute inflammation of the mucous membranes of the nose and throat due to a virus infection, or a similar condition due to allergy. ►*common cold.* The effects of cold environment on the body are *local* and *general.*
2. *Local effects.* The usual response is contraction of small arteries in the skin: this decreases the flow of blood at the surface of the body and prevents loss of heat. It is one of the principal mechanisms for regulating body ►*temperature.* The arteries of the fingers, toes, and ears tend to contract less than other superficial arteries, so that frostbite is less common than it would otherwise be. Unlike the small arteries, the minute capillary vessels are dilated by cold, and blood stagnates in the affected skin, which becomes blue as oxygen is consumed. But with extreme cold the tissues cease to use oxygen and the blood in them remains red. ►*Raynaud's disease* is an exaggerated response to cold, the arteries contracting so much that the affected parts (usually the hands) are severely deprived of blood. ►*Chilblains* are more like an allergic reaction to cold. ►*Trench foot*, as suffered by soldiers standing in cold water, is an instance of local exposure to wet cold. ►*Frostbite*, caused by exposure to temperatures below freezing point, illustrates the damage dry cold can cause. In true frostbite ice crystals form in the tissues, resulting in serious injury. The first change to the tissues is reddening, then numbness of the affected skin is experienced. If exposure continues this is followed by blistering and, finally, by gangrene with gross loss of tissue.

Cold prevents nerves from conducting impulses and so blocks sensation. It has a limited use as a local anaesthetic; for instance, a spray of ethyl chloride evaporates so rapidly on the skin that the nerve-endings are chilled to numbness and a small abscess can be opened without pain.

The more destructive effect of extreme cold is also put to good use. Carbon dioxide snow is sometimes used to destroy warts and moles. Pin-point application of cold (cryosurgery) is now replacing heat (cautery) in several branches of surgery; it has much the same effect as a localized burn with less risk of harm to surrounding tissue. A cold 'burn' can be used to stick the retina – the sensory membrane of the eye – in place if it becomes detached.
3. *General effects.* Acting through the hypothalamus in the floor of the brain, cold causes increased secretion of thyroid hormone and adrenaline, which in turn increases the rate at which heat is produced by combustion of fat and carbohydrate. Shivering is a means of converting the energy of muscle contraction to heat instead of to work. The local effect of cold on blood vessels is reinforced by reflex action starting in the hypothalamus and causing contraction of small arteries near the surface of the body generally. After prolonged exposure to cold the mechanisms for maintaining body temperature are overcome and the body cools rapidly. The victim falls asleep; all his bodily functions are slowed, and he is apt to die when his temperature has fallen below 20 °C (68 °F).

Babies and old people have difficulty in keeping warm, and conditions that would be merely uncomfortable to others are dangerous to them. Heat is produced in the mass of the body and lost from the surface. The amount that can be produced varies with weight, and the amount lost with area. A baby weighing 10 kg has a surface area of about half a square metre. A man weighing eight times as much has only four times the area. Exposure to cold is therefore much less risky for the man, until he grows old and his ability to generate heat begins to fail. Old people living alone in cold houses, or even in surroundings that a fit person might not think cold, can die of exposure. ➤*hypothermia*.

As with local cold, general exposure to wet cold is far more dangerous than dry: immersion in the sea even at temperatures well above freezing rapidly causes a fall of body temperature, heart failure and death (➤*drowning*).

Apart from its direct effect, cold seems to aggravate various chronic illnesses; how it does so is not known.

Controlled cooling of the body is successfully used in surgery of the heart to slow body chemistry and so reduce the need for oxygen. At a temperature of 25 °C (77 °F) the circulation can be stopped for ten minutes without harming the brain. Cooling may prove useful in treating illness such as shock, where the circulation is temporarily jeopardized.

cold abscess. An abscess, usually tuberculous, developing so slowly that the signs of inflammation are scarcely noticed.

cold sore = ➤*herpes* simplex.

colic. Intermittent pain, often severe, arising from internal organs. It is due to powerful contraction of involuntary muscle, which stretches the sensory nerve-endings. (Organs liable to colic are usually insensitive to other stimuli: e.g. burning or cutting the intestine is painless.) Colic is a symptom either of inflammation, which both stimulates contraction and sensitizes nerve-endings, or of obstruction, when the muscle pushes against resistance. Typical examples are inflammation of the intestine with food poisoning, and obstruction of a bile duct by a gall stone.

coliform. A group of bacteria, not strictly classified, including the normal inhabitant of the large intestine *Escherichia coli*, and several species causing disease of the intestine.

colitis. Inflammation of the *colon* (large intestine, lower bowel). The common causes are bacterial food poisoning and the various types of dysentery.

Ulcerative colitis is a severe, chronic inflammation of the colon of which the cause is still unknown. Bacterial infection plays a part, but the bacteria invade mucous membranes already damaged by some other process. At present the most likely explanation is an allergic reaction in which some component of the mucous membrane is rejected as though it were an extraneous substance (➤*autoimmunity*). Emotional disturbance is often cited as a secondary cause and sometimes as a primary cause. It is true that emotion affects the intestine – the association of fear with diarrhoea is almost proverbial – but equally the uncontrollable diarrhoea and incapacity of severe colitis must be a potent cause of emotional upset. Probably emotion plays a similar part to infection in aggravating the primary defect.

Ulcerative colitis is dangerous because the continued diarrhoea leads to various chemical disturbances, dehydration, and ultimately severe emaciation. Loss of blood in the stools causes anaemia. Some patients recover completely from an attack and have no further trouble, but most need prolonged treatment.

Antibiotics, or the sulphonamide sulphasalazine, to control infection, and some form of psychotherapy both have a place in the treatment, in order to combat secondary aggravating factors. The dietitian may have some difficulty in choosing a diet to combat the malnutrition without contributing to the symptoms.

Corticosteroids generally bring some improvement and sometimes put a stop to all symptoms, though they cannot be expected to cure the underlying disease. In many cases the only effective treatment is to remove the whole of the affected part of the intestine. Since the rectum is nearly always involved, this means providing an artificial opening to the small intestine above the site of inflammation (ileostomy) through the front of the abdomen. This is very drastic treatment, but the results justify it. Patients in whom every detail of the skeleton could be made out are returned to a normal life, with the ileostomy no more than a minor nuisance. It is far from being an ideal form of treatment, but until much more is known about ulcerative colitis it is likely to be the best that can be offered in severe cases.

collagen. An insoluble protein, or group of proteins, of which the molecules form long fibres. It is the principal fibrous component of ►*connective tissue*.

Most of the chemical components of the body are regularly broken down and resynthesized, but when collagen is degraded there is little regeneration. This is why it has been said that ageing is mainly a property of the connective tissues. Dis-

eases recognized in the 1950s as having degeneration of collagen in common, and named 'collagen diseases', are now more often called *connective tissue diseases*.

Several genetic disorders of collagen synthesis are known: the rare conditions of *fragilitas ossium* (of which the main symptom is that slight injuries cause fractures) and similar defects of the skin, and, by no means so rarely, a weakness of the connective tissue of the arteries leading to ►*aneurysm* of an artery at the base of the brain with a risk of haemorrhage.

collateral. Alternative route for blood-flow, provided by secondary blood vessels when a primary vessel is obstructed.

Colles' fracture of the radius

Colles, Abraham (1773–1843). Professor of anatomy and surgery, Dublin. Colles wrote an important treatise on surgical anatomy, which includes a description of the fascia of the abdomen and perineum still named after him (1811). He was a bold and skilful surgeon, best remembered for his paper 'On the Fracture of the Carpal Extremity of the Radius' (1814).

Colles' fracture. Colles described a fracture 1½ inches above the wrist, but the much commoner injury now named after him is nearer to the joint. After a fall on the palm of the hand the lower end of the radius is broken off and displaced backwards, carrying the hand with it (the wrist joint is intact). Since the radius and ulna are joined at the wrist by a strong band of fibrocartilage, there is always a concomitant injury at the ulnar side of the wrist: the fibrocartilage or a ligament is torn, or the tip of the ulna is broken off. In a severe case there may be other fractures or dislocation, and the median nerve may be compressed against the shaft of the radius. These fractures usually do well after manipulation and a few weeks in plaster, but with a bad one the wrist sometimes remains stiff.

coloboma. Congenital absence of a sector of one of the tissues of the eye, usually the iris, giving the pupil the shape of a keyhole. It is much more noticeable to the patient than to anyone else.

colocynth. A sort of wild pumpkin from which a powerful purgative has been extracted since ancient Egyptian times.

colon. The large intestine (lower bowel), excluding the caecum and the rectum; ►*intestine* (1).

colostomy. Surgical operation to take over the natural function of the rectum: a loop of the colon is brought through the muscle and skin of the abdomen, and an artificial anus is made; a flexible bag is worn against it. A temporary colostomy is needed during convalescence after various operations on the intestine. If the rectum has to be removed because of cancer, the colostomy remains. Although the idea is very distasteful, in practice colostomies generally work well. With a well-fitted appliance they give no offence or discomfort, and many patients have them completely under conscious control.

colour blindness. Inability to distinguish between certain colours. Normal eyes see colours as various mixtures of three primary colours, each served by a particular kind of nerve-ending. In much the same way, colour photography records the whole spectrum as various mixtures of three primary dyes.

Several anomalies are possible in this system, but only one is at all common: absence of specific nerve-endings for recognizing red. People with this defect cannot distinguish red from the next primary colour, green. Red-green colour blindness (Daltonism) is a sex-linked character (►*genetics*), i.e. one that women may transmit to their sons without themselves being affected. Women can have red-green colour blindness only if they have an affected father and a mother who 'carries' the defect. The rarer forms affect both sexes equally often.

The disability from colour blindness is so slight that many affected men are not aware of their condition until they are examined for a job on the railway or at sea where coloured lights have to be distinguished.

colp(o)-. Prefix = 'of the *vagina*'.

Columbus (Realdo Colombo) (*c.* 1516–59). Professor of anatomy and surgery at Padua 1544–59; pupil and successor of Vesalius. His text-book, *De re anatomica*, repairs some of his great teacher's omissions. He was the first man to describe the lens towards the front of the eye and not at the centre. He showed that the arteries expand when the heart contracts – all earlier anatomists, unaware of the circulation of the blood, had supposed that both contracted simultaneously. He recognized the function of the valve at the root of the pulmonary artery in preventing reflux of blood into the heart, and demonstrated that blood flows from the heart through the lungs.

These discoveries were a step towards the description of the whole circulation by Harvey, who studied at Padua 50 years later.

coma. Unconsciousness from which the subject cannot be roused (as he can from natural sleep); the activity of the brain as a whole is depressed, and reflexes such as coughing that are unaffected by sleep are suppressed. A principal danger of coma is that saliva or vomit may be inhaled and prevent breathing because there is no cough to remove it. When the cause of the coma is increasing (e.g. continued bleeding in the brain; continued absorption of poison) the coma may deepen until the brain ceases to act at all and the subject dies. Even when the cause is stationary or receding a person in coma needs constant supervision to ensure that breathing continues.

The many causes of coma all involve some kind of insult to the brain. They include direct *injury*, *pressure* (bleeding, abscess, tumour), *infection* (meningitis, encephalitis), *poisoning* (alcohol, drugs; also poisons formed within the body as in uncontrolled diabetes or failure of liver or kidneys), *lack of oxygen* (suffocation, obstruction of blood vessels, failure of circulation as in shock), *lack of sugar* (overdose of insulin). An important cause of transient coma, epilepsy, is unexplained.

comedo. Blackhead (▸*acne*).

commensal. Creature living in or on another species without harm to either, e.g. the normal bacteria of the skin and intestine.

common cold. A virus infection of the mucous membranes of the nose and throat. The familiar symptoms – tickling throat, sneezing, running eyes and nose,

cough, headache – set in about a day after exposure and rarely last as long as a week. Inflamed mucous membranes are susceptible to added infection by bacteria, which delays recovery and may lead to bronchitis and other complications; but considering the prevalence of colds, complications are not very common. Immunity is short-lived and is confined to the particular strain of virus that caused the attack – and at least 30 different viruses can cause colds.

For his own comfort and to avoid spreading his cold, the patient is well advised to stay warm and at home. A simple analgesic such as aspirin may relieve any headache arising from congested sinuses, and nasal decongestants give temporary relief, although continuous use is undesirable. A simple cough linctus is often comforting though probably no more so than the time-honoured lemon, honey and hot water, with or without a tot of whisky. None of these, nor any of the popularly vaunted 'remedies', does anything to cure or even shorten a cold; they help to make it more tolerable. ▸*interferon*, a link in the chain of natural immunity to infection, has been shown to help, as have drugs which promote its formation in the body.

The idea of 'catching cold' is found in many languages, and the belief that one literally does so is likely to die hard. In fact, wet feet, sitting in draughts and the rest do not cause colds; only infection with one of the viruses can do that. But *feeling* cold is often the first symptom of the infection, and is easily blamed for the later symptoms. Secondly, in cold weather people are crowded together in the few warm places such as cinemas and underground trains, where they infect each other. Thirdly, some people react to cold air as others react to pollen; they sneeze and their eyes water. The same kind of thing troubles people with chronic bronchitis, and cold damp air aggravates their wheezing and coughing. But if the common cold were really due to cold and dampness it is hard to believe that sports such as skiing and yachting would keep their well-earned reputation for promoting health. Mountaineers and sailors face many hazards, but this is not among them.

compressed air sickness >*decompression sickness*.

computers. The most obvious use of computers in medicine is to ease the burden of maintaining accurate clinical records, a task that good medical practice requires. In the 1960s some doctors expressed concern about a seeming threat that computers might extend their activities to the diagnosis of diseases, for however much information a computer might devour it could never acquire the clinical judgement to assess individual cases.

In fact the great value of a computer in this respect is in its power of recall, which enables it to serve as an instant reference library. Extensions of this facility include feeding a computer with expert data about, say, electrocardiograms, so that someone conducting them but unsure about interpreting them can get an instant reading by telephone. This does not take the place of a specialist's report, which will follow, but reassures a non-specialist that he is not overlooking something important.

Further diagnostic uses of computers include more than one type of >*scan*.

concussion. Shaking of the brain, as by a blow to the head or a jolt to the neck, with temporary disturbance of conscious-

ness. In every case, concussion probably puts some of the millions of nerve cells in the brain permanently out of action, and repeated concussion, such as professional boxers may suffer (a knock-out is concussion), causes serious deterioration. Events immediately before concussion are usually not remembered (retrograde amnesia). Anyone who has just recovered from concussion still needs observation, because symptoms of more serious damage may be delayed for several hours.

conditioned reflex. A *learnt* response to a stimulus, as opposed to an inborn one; >*reflex*.

conditioning. Establishing a conditioned reflex, such as aversion to a bad habit, by >*behaviour therapy*.

condyle. Rounded end of a bone, e.g. a knuckle.

congenital. Present from birth: not necessarily *hereditary*; for example, a child may suffer an injury before birth, which is then congenital though not hereditary.

congestion. Surplus of blood in a part of the body, either from increased supply (e.g. inflammation) or inefficient removal (e.g. heart failure).

conjunctiva. Delicate membrane covering the inside of the eyelids and the front of the eye.

conjunctivitis (pink-eye). Inflammation of the conjunctiva, due to infection with bacteria or viruses. The contagious 'swimming bath conjunctivitis', like the tropical conjunctivitis >*trachoma*, is due to a virus-like parasite, Chlamydia, that (unlike true viruses) responds to treatment with antibiotics. >*ophthalmia*.

connective tissue. The packaging material

of the body, separating, protecting and supporting the various organs. Like all tissues, the connective tissues live by the cells they contain, but the importance of connective tissues lies in the inert ground-substance that surrounds the cells. The least specialized of these tissues is *areolar tissue*. Its soft ground-substance contains a loose tangle of slender fibres. Layers of areolar tissue between organs keep them more or less in place while allowing considerable freedom of movement, e.g. between muscles and skin. *Adipose tissue*, the main store of fat, is like areolar tissue with droplets of fat in its cells. In *fibrous tissue* the fibres of collagen are systematically arranged in bundles or sheets. This is the stuff of ligaments and tendons. *Elastic tissue*, found in the walls of large arteries and in some ligaments, is fibrous tissue modified by the presence of numerous elastic fibres. A highly specialized connective tissue forms *cartilage*. To include bone, muscle and even blood among connective tissues, as some anatomists have done, may be logical in view of their common origin in the embryo, but confuses more than clarifies.

In the tissues called connective here, the ground-substance has two kinds of component. These are fibres of protein (►*collagen*, and much smaller amounts of *elastin*) which are embedded in a mass of soluble material (mainly carbohydrate), an arrangement that has aptly been likened to reinforced concrete. The soluble mass in areolar tissue is liquid, whereas in cartilage it is resilient.

In the 1950s, degeneration of collagen was recognized as a factor common to a group of diseases including lupus erythematosus, polyarteritis nodosa and rheumatoid arthritis, which were therefore named 'collagen diseases'. It has

since become clear that the soluble mass, which protects the fibres, has to be damaged before the disease attacks the fibres, so the term *connective tissue diseases* is now preferred. This name may not last long either, because the above all appear to be *autoimmune* diseases (►*immunity* (7)), a group now due for a new classification.

constipation. This symptom is not easily defined. Life-style, diet, and individual constitution all affect bowel habits; also informed opinions of what is or is not normal differ.

The first point is that constipation *is* a symptom and not a distinct disease. Like any other symptom, it is merely a pointer to an underlying disorder that should, if possible, be identified and corrected, rather than simply tackling the symptom itself (in this case with indiscriminate use of laxatives).

If we say that normal bowel action is complete, regular and easy evacuation of the waste products in the intestine, then constipation can be defined as inadequate bowel action. The idea so prevalent a generation or two ago that the action should occur once daily does not come into it. Some perfectly healthy people open their bowels two or three times a day; others two or three times a week. But however often the bowels act, if the faeces are not completely evacuated there is constipation. Even complete passage of faeces that have stagnated and hardened, and are thus difficult or even painful to pass, is also constipation.

There are many mechanical causes of constipation. Certain rare congenital defects of the bowel make defecation impossible, e.g. ►*megacolon*. Later, any kind of intestinal obstruction obviously includes constipation among its symptoms. With a complete obstruction, such as a strangulated hernia, constipation is the least of the patient's worries; a partial obstruction is more insidious, and in adult life any altered bowel habit needs to be investigated without delay, if only because the possible causes include tumours at a curable stage, which have to be distinguished from relatively harmless diverticular disease. Disorders of the anal canal such as piles and fissures cause constipation, as the discomfort inhibits the normal reflexes. Failure of the intestinal reflexes, e.g. after spinal injury or as a result of old age, results in constipation.

Other readily identifiable causes include drugs, the worst offender being morphine and its derivatives, such as *codeine*. Some drugs used for controlling high blood pressure and some antidepressants can also constipate.

This still leaves a majority of cases with poorly defined causes and often the symptom itself is vague. The sufferer, seeking relief, takes laxatives. However, if the bowel is accustomed to the repeated goad of laxative medicines, it becomes like a needlessly whipped horse and responds to no other stimulus. The regular dosing of children 'to cleanse the system' must have caused millions of people to suffer chronic constipation later in life.

True constipation may sometimes be a symptom of neurosis, but more often a neurotic person merely thinks he is constipated, takes needless laxatives, and as a result actually becomes constipated in time. *Spastic* or *irritable colon* is perhaps the commonest type of constipation. Its precise relationship to anxiety or emotional stress is debatable, because although anxiety can lead to constipation (or to diarrhoea), disturbed bowel action can just as readily cause anxiety. The

symptoms include belly-aches and constipation that often alternates with episodes of diarrhoea. Indeed, constipation of one kind or another is a common cause of diarrhoea in the form of watery stools provoked by the irritation of a mass of hard faeces remaining.

Much constipation results from failure to develop regular habits, lack of exercise or, perhaps the most important in the wealthier countries, an over-refined diet lacking ▸*fibre*, or combinations of these. The obvious and correct remedy is to take exercise and improve the diet, while trying to cultivate a regular bowel habit by such means as having breakfast early enough to leave time afterwards for the bowels to act.

In perfect health, the last few inches of intestine, the *rectum*, contain nothing for most of the time. Faeces remain higher in the colon until they are due to be evacuated, when they begin to move down. The presence of faeces in the rectum stimulates nerves that transmit the urge to defecate and, when opportune, initiate the reflex component of defecation, which, of course, is subject to the voluntary component until the urge becomes irresistible. The chronically constipated patient carries faeces in the rectum without feeling any urge, suggesting some damage to the nerves of the rectal wall.

Nobody doubts that constipation is a symptom to be taken seriously until a clear diagnosis is made, because it may be an indication of some underlying condition that can and should be treated. But when that has been done, there are still differences of opinion about how much constipation matters itself. People have always been very much aware of any apparent disorder of their bowels, and their medical advisers have always been ready with advice and remedies. Faeces are obviously nasty, so in all cultures getting rid of them has seemed a good and healthy thing to do, and (so the argument has gone) the sooner the better. Purges, enemas and the rest are as old as medical practice. With the discovery of harmful bacteria came the suggestion that those in the bowel, which teems with them, might be harmful, and in the early 20th century there was much talk of 'toxic absorption'. In time this fear subsided, and by the middle of the century constipation, once diagnosis was clear, was considered of minor importance. Now, especially in the light of recent studies of the value of dietary fibre, it is again taken more seriously. Not only piles, where the association is obvious, but diverticular disease, hiatus hernia, appendicitis and even cancer have been mentioned, and toxic absorption has reappeared in the guise of products contributing to heart disease if their passage through the intestine is delayed. (➤*fibre*.)

consumption. Any disease causing serious loss of weight; in particular tuberculosis of the lungs.

contact lenses. Lenses serving much the same purpose as spectacles but made to lie directly on the front of the eyeball. Leonardo da Vinci suggested something of the kind in the 16th century, but the idea was first applied in the late 19th century by Zeiss in Germany. The glass lenses were so difficult and expensive to make, and created so many problems for the wearer, that contact lenses fell into abeyance for the next 50 years. When a suitable plastic (Perspex) became available in the 1930s, the Hamblin/Dallos lens was introduced in London. This was the first commercially successful contact

lens, and in a modified form is still in use: this is the 'hard' lens. A much newer type, made of a flexible plastic, is the 'soft' lens.

A hard lens is smaller than the iris and floats on a film of tears. A soft lens is larger and moulds itself to the eye. A hard lens is easier to look after and to handle (apart from its smallness) and is cheaper to make; however, a soft lens is usually easier to wear. Patients with either type are advised, as a rule, to remove them at night, but soft lenses are much less likely to do any harm if they are left in. There are now 'permanent wear' lenses made to be left in for 3 months at a time; these are especially suitable for patients who for some reason, such as arthritis of the hands, cannot manipulate them with ease.

Used instead of spectacles, contact lenses often provide better vision. Some patients consider the invisible nature of lenses an important advantage. Additional advantages include protecting the front of the eye in various conditions where spectacles could not help, and assisting in the application of medication which would otherwise be washed away by tears.

The drawbacks of contact lenses as opposed to spectacles include the following: (1) they need regular professional supervision; (2) they also need careful attention by the patient, especially the soft kind, which not only have to be kept clean but may become brittle and fragile if allowed to dry out; (3) any lack of care may cause superficial injury to the eye, which is an unpleasant nuisance even though the damage is seldom lasting; and (4) the older types of lenses are impermeable to air. Since a healthy cornea has no blood vessels (which would obstruct vision), it relies on direct access to air for oxygen. As the latest types of lenses are permeable, this problem no longer arises.

Contact lenses are especially suitable for very short-sighted people, for those whose natural lens has been removed for cataract and for people who otherwise would need very thick and inefficient spectacles.

contagion. Transmission of infectious disease by direct contact (as opposed to airborne or water-borne infection etc.).

contraception. Birth control; preventing sexual intercourse from leading to pregnancy. Some methods are designed to prevent the male sperm from fertilizing the female ovum, and others to prevent the already fertilized ovum from developing.

Three methods in common use require no artificial aids. The first, withdrawal, or *coitus interruptus*, is simply withdrawing the penis from the vagina before orgasm. Some people may find this form of anti-climax tolerable, but it is certainly not reliable. Even with careful timing, a few sperms escape before orgasm, and a single sperm is enough.

The second is the safe-period or rhythm method, which depends on the fact that both ova and sperms are short-lived, so that conception is possible only within a few days of ovulation. If intercourse is avoided for five or six days about half-way between menstrual periods, pregnancy is unlikely. For this method to be reliable, one has to know when ovulation is going to take place, which is a fortnight *before the next* period, rather than after the last. Some women are so regular that they can predict quite accurately, but others are not, and for them a temperature chart kept throughout the month is the only guide. The virtues of this technique are theological rather than physiological.

The third is not really a method; it is to apply the fact that when an ovum has been fertilized, i.e. a pregnancy has begun, no further ovum is released until some time after the end of pregnancy, and sometimes not until breast-feeding is over. Once pregnant, a woman cannot conceive again and carry twins of different ages. It has been suggested that the relative infertility of a nursing mother is one reason why breast-feeding is continued for as long as two years in some parts of the world, as a simple means of birth control.

Physical barriers between the sperm and ovum include the sheath or condom worn by the man, and several types of occlusive pessary which close off the opening of the uterus high in the vagina. Condoms are easy to get and to use and are fairly reliable, but either partner may find them aesthetically objectionable. A pessary, e.g. a diaphragm or a Dutch cap, is better in this respect, but professional help is needed in the original fitting and the woman has to learn how to insert and remove the device.

The intrauterine device (IUD) is a little spring, placed in the cavity of the uterus and left there. It does not prevent the ovum from being fertilized, but with an IUD in place a fertilized ovum cannot establish itself and grow: the uterus rejects it. Complications are unusual, and the method has been used in some large-scale birth-control campaigns designed to check over-population.

Various chemical preparations for insertion into the vagina just before intercourse are supposed to kill sperms. They are more effective than attempts to kill the sperms afterwards, but on their own they are far from reliable. They may help as an adjunct to a condom or a pessary.

Oral contraceptives – 'the pill' – are

hormone preparations that prevent the ovaries from releasing ova in the same way as natural hormones prevent this during pregnancy. They are the most reliable of all contraceptives provided that the woman strictly follows the prescribed schedule. This is usually one pill daily for three weeks, followed by a week's rest during which there is a period of bleeding like a menstrual period. There are certain drawbacks to the method. Some women feel sick, and some put on weight. Thrombosis (the formation of a blood-clot in a vein) is a rare but serious complication. In short, the complications of taking the pill can also be complications of pregnancy: they arise from the same alteration in the balance of hormones. Hence the dictum that it is safer to take the pill than not to. The method is safer now than it was when it was introduced in the early 1960s, because the required dose is less than was at first thought. Most preparations are a mixture of an oestrogen and a progestogen (>*sex hormones*). Instead, the components can be taken during alternating phases, which is said to be more natural, or a progestogen can be taken alone, which causes fewer complications but occasionally allows an unintentional pregnancy.

Emergency contraception, i.e. afterwards, is possible with some hormone preparations taken within 3 days, or an IUD inserted within 5 days.

Lastly, in either sex there is the possibility of >*sterilization* by a simple operation.

contracture. Shrinkage of connective tissue or scar. All scars tend to contract. With extensive scars, e.g. from burns, this may restrict movement, and in extreme cases plastic surgery may be needed to restore function. If a limb is immobilized by paralysis or plaster, fibrous tissue around joints may contract and restrict movement unless regular physiotherapy is given.

Dupuytren's contracture of fibrous tissue in the hand is described under its own heading. *Volkmann's contracture* is scarring and shrinkage of muscles from deficient blood supply when a plaster cast is too tight.

contrecoup. Injury to one side of the brain from a blow on the opposite side of the skull.

contusion >*bruise*; injury to deeper tissues through intact skin.

convulsion. Involuntary unco-ordinated contractions of muscles; fit; seizure. (>*epilepsy.*) A convulsion is a symptom of irritation of nerve cells. One of the commonest causes is fever in childhood.

Cooley's anaemia. (T. B. Cooley, 1871–1945, American physician.) >*haemoglobin; genetics.*

Cooper, Sir Astley Paston (1768–1841). A distinguished London surgeon and anatomist, and above all the inspiration of a great school of medicine. He taught at St Thomas's Hospital, of which Guy's, founded in 1725, was a sort of annexe. After a disagreement with St Thomas's, Cooper became the leader of a new school at Guy's, and Guy's Hospital separated from St Thomas's. (At that time the two hospitals were both near London Bridge.)

Cooper taught that clinical observation – the recording of symptoms – must be related to postmortem study of the actual changes in the affected organs. In other words, practical medicine needs a scientific basis of anatomy and pathology. This doctrine was brilliantly applied by his young colleagues Bright, Addison, and Hodgkin, under whom Guy's was the leading school in England if not in the world.

cord ➤*spermatic cord*; *spinal cord*; *umbilical cord*; *vocal cord*.

corium (dermis; cutis vera). Inner layer of the skin, containing fibrous tissue, blood vessels, nerves, sweat glands; covered by the outer skin or epidermis.

corn. A cone of horny dead tissue in the outer layer of the skin formed in response to localized pressure from an ill-fitting shoe, and causing pain by irritating nerve-endings in the corium.

cornea. Circular window at the front of the eye, through which the iris and pupil may be seen. The cornea has no blood vessels, and its nerves transmit only the sensation of pain. A very lively reflex shuts the eyes at the least stimulation of these nerves.

Next to blood transfusion, grafting of a cornea from somebody else is the most successful of all operations in which tissues are transferred from one person to another; it is perhaps because the cornea receives no blood that a foreign one is not rejected. It is for this purpose that eyes are bequeathed to hospitals.

coronary arteries. Two branches of the aorta supplying blood to the heart muscle, which consumes a large amount of oxygen and needs a good supply of blood. The heart can make little use of the blood passing through its cavity, which has a waterproof lining. The arteries encircle the heart and distribute twigs throughout its muscle.

The flow through the coronary arteries is adapted to the needs of the moment by a mechanism independent of the control of arteries in general: if the heart works harder more oxygen is used and more carbon dioxide is formed. The coronary arteries respond to carbon dioxide by dilating to let in more blood and so more oxygen. If a point is reached where the heart is still short of blood and the arteries can dilate no further a severe pain develops; this is ➤*angina*. Various drugs can be used to dilate the coronary arteries. Their value is limited, because if there is angina the arteries are probably as widely open as they can be. The whole trouble is that they are abnormal and cannot be fully dilated by any means.

It is possible to inject an opaque fluid into the coronary arteries by way of a tube introduced through an artery of the arm or leg, and then study the arteries with X-rays. This allows blockages to be located with a view to surgical treatment.

coronary thrombosis. Literally, blockage of a coronary artery by blood clot. Until lately, the term was almost synonymous with heart attack, because clotting was always supposed to cause the attack by abruptly cutting off the blood supply to the affected area of the heart muscle. In fact, not all attacks are preceded by thrombosis. A coronary artery can become so narrowed by sclerosis (or perhaps spasm) that it cannot deliver enough blood for the needs of an area of muscle, which therefore degenerates; this is called *myocardial infarction*. The subject is considered under ➤*ischaemic heart disease*.

corpus luteum (yellow body). A small, yellowish structure formed in the ovary at the site of a released ovum. It forms several hormones, including *progesterone*, which stimulates the lining of the uterus to grow in readiness for pregnancy. If the ovum becomes fertilized, the corpus luteum persists; if not, the corpus luteum withers and the lining of the uterus is shed, i.e. menstruation occurs.

corpuscle. A small body; a small well-defined structure within an organ or tissue; a blood cell.

cortex. Distinct outer layer (shell) of an organ, e.g. *cerebral cortex*, the layer of nerve cells (grey matter) on the surface of the brain.

corticosteroid. Any of several hormones formed in the cortex of the adrenal glands, with the ►*steroid* chemical structure and effects on body chemistry that are essential to life; or a synthetic derivative with similar effects to the natural hormones.

The actions of these hormones are considered under ►*adrenal* (cortex), and the effect of deprivation under ►*Addison's disease*.

Until the present century the adrenal cortex was not known to have any function. In 1910 it was shown that animals could not survive without it, and in 1934 E. C. Kendall isolated a hormone from it. (Kendall had isolated thyroid hormone in 1914.) For some time, the only known use of the hormone was for treating Addison's disease. In 1949, Kendall, T. Reichstein, and P. H. Hench described much wider uses; in the following year they shared a Nobel Prize. They had shown that corticosteroids would suppress the symptoms of inflammation and allergy. These two reactions (they are variants of the same fundamental process) occur in a very wide range of diseases – a current handbook lists over a hundred conditions in which corticosteroids may be used to suppress one or the other.

For a short time the new preparations were widely acclaimed as the greatest of wonder-drugs, despite warnings from the discoverers that the practical uses would be limited.

There are grave objections to these drugs, and the disadvantages often outweigh the possible advantages. Inflammation has unpleasant and sometimes dangerous effects, but it is fundamentally a defensive reaction. To suppress it indiscriminately is like abolishing the fire brigade to stop it from breaking windows and doors. Again, allergy is a misapplication of the process by which immunity to infection develops; if allergy is suppressed with corticosteroids, so is immunity. Many of the symptoms of infection arise from these defensive reactions. They can be promptly relieved by corticosteroids, but the infection itself is then unopposed and likely to kill the patient.

In the second place corticosteroids, affecting as they do many of the chemical processes of the body, have numerous undesirable effects if they are given over long periods. Healing, which depends on inflammation, is impaired, and wounds, gastric ulcers and the like become very troublesome. Bone and fibrous connective tissue are weakened, the patient puts on weight (much of it retained water), his blood pressure rises. As one would expect, the symptoms of prolonged treatment with large doses of corticosteroids are like those of over-activity of the adrenal glands (Cushing's syndrome).

In the third place, after a time corticosteroids suppress the natural activity of the adrenal cortex. If the treatment is suddenly stopped the patient is left with no adrenal hormones and develops symptoms of Addison's disease.

If the adrenal cortex is healthy the effects of corticosteroid treatment can be produced indirectly by giving ACTH, the pituitary hormone that stimulates the adrenal cortex. The patient is thus treated with his own corticosteroids. The same complications can arise, with the one difference that it is the pituitary that is suppressed: when treatment is stopped the patient does not form enough of his own ACTH to keep his adrenals working.

In spite of this disheartening catalogue, corticosteroids are extremely valuable drugs. Short courses of treatment are practically free from risk, but with long courses the dose has to be exactly regulated, and at the end the drug has to be withdrawn gradually enough for the patient's own adrenals to have time to recover.

Apart from their obvious value in diseases of the adrenal glands, corticosteroids may be life-saving in conditions of violent stress such as shock after extensive injuries or burns (interference with healing is relatively unimportant because the drug is used only to tide the patient over a short period of acute danger). Similarly they can be life-saving with severe attacks of ➤asthma. Their widest use is in controlling the many kinds of inflammation that are not due to infection, including several rheumatic disorders and a whole range of skin diseases. Many of the diseases that respond to this treatment are probably examples of ➤auto-immunity, where inflammation arises from a kind of allergy to some natural component of the body itself. A few of these conditions can be lethal unless corticosteroids are given. The drawbacks of the treatment are then of minor importance. Far more often the disease is more a nuisance than a danger, and the benefits of treatment have to be weighed against the drawbacks. The decision whether or not to use corticosteroids is among the most difficult in current medical practice. A patient with rheumatoid arthritis who has once experienced the immediate improvement that corticosteroids can bring may take a deal of persuading that on balance her particular case is better treated without them.

The risk of harmful side-effects is much less if the corticosteroid can be applied directly to the trouble spot. Examples are steroid ointments and creams for a wide range of skin disorders; eye drops; injections into inflamed joints; enemas for flare-ups of ulcerative colitis; and inhalations for hay fever and asthma.

Corticosteroids are also used to suppress the reaction to 'foreign' tissue that causes organs grafted from other people to be rejected.

corticotropin (corticotrophin). Pituitary hormone, stimulating the adrenal cortex; ACTH.

cortisol; cortisone. Two of the ➤cortico-steroid hormones.

Corvisart, Jean-Nicolas (1755–1821). Napoleon's personal physician; author of an important treatise on diseases of the heart (1806). His most influential work was a French translation of Auenbrugger's book on percussion of the chest as a method of diagnosis. More than anyone else it was Corvisart who shook off the scholastic shackles that impeded progress in the Paris school of medicine; under his influence Paris was to lead the rest of the world in scientific medicine. His best known pupil was Laënnec, the inventor of the stethoscope.

corynebacterium. A genus of bacteria, including the diphtheria bacillus.

coryza. Running nose; common cold.

Cos. Aegean island, birthplace of Hippocrates (*c.* 460 BC) and seat of the most influential medical school of antiquity.

costal. Of the ribs.

cot death (SIDS, sudden infant death syndrome). Seemingly fit children aged under 2 years, mostly between 2 and 4 months, are distressingly often found dead in their cots, though no cause can be found even by thorough postmortem investigation. Such deaths are commonest with infants who were prematurely born, whose mothers smoked during pregnancy or were addicted to narcotic drugs, who habitually slept face down; also after recent virus infections; and during cold weather. But these are no more than concomitants; none indicates an actual cause.

couching. The simplest operation for ▸*cataract*: instead of being removed as in the modern operation, the diseased lens of the eye is simply displaced so that it no longer impedes the passage of light.

cough. Explosive release of air from the lungs: the pressure is raised by attempting to breathe out while the vocal cords are closed; then the cords are suddenly relaxed. It can of course be done deliberately, but essentially it is a reflex action provoked by irritation of the larger air-passages. Mucus or an inhaled foreign body is expelled in the same way as a shot from an air-gun – and at a comparable muzzle-velocity. This is a useful function, but coughing is also provoked by inflammation of the mucous membrane of the trachea or bronchi even when there is nothing to expel, and by pressure from outside the bronchi (e.g. by enlarged lymph nodes with whooping cough).

cough medicines. A useless cough is suppressed by drugs such as codeine that diminish the response to irritation, or in some cases by damping sensation at the back of the throat. A *linctus* is a syrupy preparation with, as a rule, both effects.

An *expectorant* mixture stimulates the glands in the mucous membrane of the bronchi to dilute and loosen the sticky material that accumulates with bronchitis, to make coughing easier and more useful. Most of the drugs used are *emetics* given in doses too small to cause vomiting. Their value is questionable.

counter-irritation. Relief of minor symptoms by applying heat or mild irritants to the skin. Liniments are used to ease pain and stiffness in joints and muscles and (with less reason) to soothe hacking coughs; hot-water bottles are laid on aching stomachs; poultices and fomentations are supposed to draw out deep-seated inflammation. African herbalists treat most illness by making cuts in the skin and rubbing in irritant powders, and the acupuncture and moxibustion of traditional Chinese medicine appear to be refinements of the same method.

All these forms of treatment stimulate nerves in the skin, and by reflex action this dilates blood vessels and increases the flow of blood in the affected skin. Why reddening the skin – the only demonstrable effect – should help is not clear. Hippocrates pointed out that one kind of discomfort relieved another. A poultice on a boil is a special case because it increases the circulation at the site of the trouble. A potent effect of any form of counter-irritation is that the patient sees something positive being done, but the release of ▸*endorphins* may be more important.

cowpox (vaccinia). A virus infection of cattle transmitted to man, resembling smallpox but much milder. An attack confers immunity to smallpox; this is the principle of vaccination.

Coxsackie viruses. Kinds of small virus, first identified in Coxsackie, New York (1948). They are a versatile group: between them they are responsible for (1) ➤*Bornholm disease*; (2) an assortment of fevers, variously accompanied by skin rashes, inflammation of the heart (myocarditis) or the interior linings of the skull (meningitis), blisters in the mouth (herpangina) and sometimes also on hands and feet – this last (hand, foot and mouth disease) is reminiscent of the well-known Coxsackie infection of cattle, but by no means as serious. Indeed, except with very young patients all these fevers tend to clear up spontaneously within a short time. But some Coxsackie viruses occasionally cause a kind of poliomyelitis.

cramp. Painful spasm (sustained contraction) of muscles. The known causes include shortage of salt from excessive sweating as in miner's or stoker's cramp or heatstroke, for which the remedy or preventive is to take more salt. Deficient blood supply is another cause: if the arteries of the legs are narrowed they do not admit enough blood for the demands of exercise, and a characteristic pain in the calves develops with walking and passes off with rest. This type of cramp is *intermittent* ➤*claudication*. *Angina pectoris* is a similar event in the heart muscle. Swimmer's cramp has been ascribed to spasm of the limb arteries together with diversion of blood to a full stomach.

Occupational (e.g. writer's) cramp is thought to be a kind of neurosis, because it is brought on not by using a particular group of muscles but by applying them to a particular job.

There is no satisfactory explanation of the familiar kind of cramp that comes on at any time, even during sleep, and behaves as though the muscle were squeezing and stimulating its own nerve to set up a vicious circle. This cramp is relieved by stretching the affected muscle – e.g. if it is in the calf by pushing the heel down and the toes up. *Quinine* may help by a similar restraining effect to that of a related drug ➤*quinidine* on the heart.

cranial nerve. Nerve arising directly from the brain and passing through one of the holes in the skull (cf. ➤*spinal nerve*, arising from the spinal cord). Twelve pairs of cranial nerves are described, but they are not an orderly series like the spinal nerves. Their names and functions are as follows:

I. *Olfactory*; sense of smell.

II. *Optic*; vision.

III. *Oculomotor* ⎫
IV. *Trochlear* ⎬ eye movements.

V. *Trigeminal*; ordinary sensation from the face and scalp, movements of the jaw.

VI. *Abducent*; eye movement.

VII. *Facial*; movements of the face.

VIII. *Auditory* (acoustic); in two parts: *cochlear* (hearing) and *vestibular* (balance).

IX. *Glossopharyngeal*; sensation from the back of the mouth.

X. *Vagus*; digestive organs, heart, air-passages.

XI. *Accessory*; sternomastoid and trapezius muscles.

XII. *Hypoglossal*; movements of the tongue.

cranium = ➤*skull*.

creatine. A nitrogenous compound in muscle. Chemical energy is stored by the formation of creatine phosphate and released for muscle contraction by the decomposition to creatine.

crepitus. A crackling sound heard with a stethoscope over inflamed lungs; also the grating sound and sensation over the broken ends of a bone.

cretin; cretinism. Cretinism is congenital deficiency of thyroid hormone, retarding mental and physical growth; a cretin is a person so affected. ➤*thyroid gland* (2).

Creutzfeld–Jakob disease. Spongiform encephalopathy, infection of the brain by a ➤*slow virus* leading to gross mental deterioration; at present it is always fatal. It is a similar condition to ➤*kuru* and bovine spongiform encephalopathy ('mad cow disease').

cricoid cartilage. The uppermost ring of cartilage around the ➤*trachea*; it is the principal support of the ➤*larynx*.

crisis. Time of decision; turning-point or sudden exacerbation during an illness; change for the better.

Crohn's disease. An inflammatory condition of the digestive tract, first recognized in the last segment of the small intestine and called *terminal ileitis*, but renamed *regional enteritis* when it was known to affect a segment or more anywhere in the intestine. In fact, it can on occasion arise anywhere in the tract. It is characterized by a thickening of the intestinal wall, leading to a narrowing of its canal and loss of its natural elasticity; ulceration and consequent scarring, and perforation of the intestine requiring surgical repair may occur. The symptoms in some cases mimic acute appendicitis, but chronic diarrhoea and loss of weight are more usual. Some patients are first seen with intestinal obstruction. Inflammation or ulceration around the anus are not uncommon, and rheumatic diseases are often associated with it.

There is no known cure, but since in time some degree of malnutrition is likely, an adequate diet is needed. Since the lesions are easily complicated by bacterial infection a drug such as *sulphasalazine* may be needed to control this; some physicians use it prophylactically. *Corticosteroids* suppress most of the symptoms, and in some cases keep the disease under satisfactory control when given continuously in small doses. At one time surgical removal of an affected segment of intestine was common practice, but relapse was usual and surgery is now kept for emergencies such as obstruction.

In many ways this strange condition behaves as an autoimmune disease (➤*immunity* (7)), but this is still a matter for conjecture. So is the relation of Crohn's disease to *ulcerative colitis*, a rather similar affliction of the large intestine.

cromoglycate. Sodium cromoglycate is used for treating some allergic diseases, in particular asthma and hay fever. It prevents the release in affected tissues of the toxic substances that cause symptoms. The treatment is continuous. Its purpose is to prevent attacks, not to cure them.

croup. Strained, noisy breathing and harsh cough, as a rule in children. The causes include retarded growth of the larynx (which corrects itself in time), allergy, virus infection, and bacterial infection such as diphtheria (membranous croup).

crush syndrome. A combination of surgical shock with kidney failure after severe injuries to muscle. The pigment *myoglobin* (muscle haemoglobin) stores oxygen reserves in muscle, but if an injury releases it into the general circulation it somehow poisons the kidneys. A period of dialysis while the kidneys recover may be needed to avert the threat to life.

cryptococcosis = ►*torulosis.*

cryptorchism. Retarded descent of the testicles from the abdomen to the scrotum. ►*testis.*

CSF = ►*cerebrospinal fluid.*

CT = computerized tomography ►*scan.*

cubital; cubitus. (Of the) forearm, elbow, or ulna.

Culex. A kind of mosquito found in most parts of the world; it is generally harmless but in parts of West Africa may transmit the threadworm that causes tropical elephantiasis.

culture. Artificial breeding of bacteria for identification, preparation of vaccines etc. ►*microbe.*

curare. Ancient South American arrow-poison extracted from various plants (species of *Strychnos* and *Chondodendron*). It causes rapid paralysis of muscles throughout the body.

Curare was used in hunting. An animal wounded with an ordinary arrow had only to go a short distance to be lost in the dense forest. A slight wound from a curare-tipped arrow was enough to prevent it from escaping, so that it could be dispatched with a hunting knife. When the wound had been cut away the flesh was safe to eat. An incidental advantage to the hunter was that the animal died silently, without frightening the rest away.

The arrow-poisons described by early pioneers (including Raleigh) were battle-poisons, unrelated to curare. The first true accounts were by 18th-century explorers. In 1813, an English naturalist, Charles Waterton, made the important discovery that a poisoned animal could be kept alive by artificial respiration until the effects of the curare had worn off; for curare kills only by paralysing the muscles of breathing. A veterinary colleague, Sewell, suggested that curare might be used to relax the dangerous muscle spasms of tetanus. More than a century later this method was successfully adopted.

In 1850 Claude Bernard published the first of his papers on the action of curare, proving that its action was to prevent impulses from crossing from nerve-endings to muscle fibres. Bernard recognized the potential value of curare in medicine, but insisted that it could not be used until it could be purified and studied in more detail than was then possible. His point was proved by others who tried to use it and found it unreliable.

A pure alkaloid, *d*-tubocurarine, was isolated in 1935. Since 1942 this and other related drugs have been used during surgical operations. Breathing is regulated artificially, and curare provides complete muscular relaxation – a most important aid to the surgeon – while the dose of anaesthetic is kept to a safe minimum. This technique has removed one of the principal risks of major surgery – that a large enough dose of a conventional anaesthetic to relax the muscles may be dangerously large.

Cushing, Harvey (1869–1939). American neurologist, a pioneer of brain surgery. He was both a distinguished scientist and one of the most skilful of surgical technicians – a rare combination but essential to his chosen speciality.

Cushing's syndrome. A disorder of body chemistry, with retention of salt and water, obesity confined to the face and trunk, high blood pressure, weakening of bone and connective tissue, and sometimes diabetes and other symptoms. It is due to excessive production of steroid hormones by the cortex of the adrenal glands or to prolonged treatment with such hormones (►*adrenal; corticosteroid*).

cutaneous. Of the skin.

cuticle. The outer layer of the skin; epidermis.

cutis (cutic vera) = ►*corium.*

cyanide. Cyanides are the quickest acting of all poisons. Inhaled fumes of hydrogen cyanide (prussic acid) kill almost instantaneously; swallowed cyanides in a very few minutes. A victim who survives as long as half an hour is likely to recover.

These poisons inactivate enzymes responsible for the transfer of oxygen from the blood to the actual chemical processes on which life depends. The result is a sort of chemical paralysis of the whole body. It is like suffocation, but instead of the victim's being deprived of oxygen he is unable to use the oxygen that he has.

Among the antidotes used, nitrites and methylene blue permit the haemoglobin of the blood to form a relatively inert compound with cyanide; sodium thiosulphate (photographer's hypo) forms a thiocyanate and ferrous sulphate a ferrocyanide. In all cases, the object is to prevent the cyanide from combining with the iron of the respiratory enzymes.

cyanocobalamine. Vitamin B_{12}.

cyanosis. Bluish complexion from lack of oxygen in the blood circulating through the skin, due either to inadequate intake in the lungs, e.g. pneumonia, or to stagnation of blood in the circulation, e.g. heart failure. Local disorders such as chilblains cause localized cyanosis.

cycloplegia. Paralysis of the ciliary muscle of the eye.

cyclopropane. An anaesthetic gas.

cyst. 1. Bladder (mostly in compound words, e.g. cystitis).

2. Abnormal swelling, containing fluid. Cysts are of several kinds. Some are tumours with cells that form mucus or other fluids with no way of escape; some are composed of normal fluid-forming (glandular) cells that have become displaced in the course of early development; some are ordinary glands, e.g. grease glands in the skin, of which the outlets have become blocked. Cysts appear most often in the skin and in the ovaries, where they may grow very large unless removed.

cysticercus. Larval form of tapeworm: the adult worm lives in the intestine, but cysticerci may be widely scattered in the body.

cystic fibrosis. An uncommon hereditary defect of numerous glands, including the mucous glands of the bronchi, the sweat glands, and the digestive glands. It is a recessive character – both parents carry the abnormal gene without showing signs of the disease, and there is a 1:4 chance that a child of the marriage will inherit the gene from both parents and develop cystic fibrosis. Formerly, none of the 400 affected children born yearly in Britain would have survived, but with treatment now available about half of them can expect to reach the age of 20 or over. If two sufferers marry, all their children must be affected, and few of the males will be fertile.

The symptoms include severe digestive disorders, difficulty with breathing and lung infections (because of blockage by thick mucus), and a tendency to heatstroke (because the sweat glands pour out too much salt).

Digestion is maintained by an exactly calculated diet with supplementary enzymes. The lungs are kept clear by drugs and physiotherapy to loosen and drain mucus, by prompt treatment of infection with antibiotics, and by providing a fine mist with a nebulizer for the patient to breathe at night – this keeps the mucus in his lungs so wet that he can cough it up.

cystine. An amino-acid; one of the components of protein. It occasionally accumulates in the urine and forms stones in the bladder.

cystitis. Inflammation of the urinary bladder, usually from bacterial infection, but sometimes from mechanical irritation from crystalline deposits in the urine.

Urine is normally free from bacteria. The conditions in which it may become infected are discussed under ➤*pyelitis* (inflammation at the outlets of the kidneys, commonly associated with cystitis), and the treatment is similar. The symptoms of cystitis – frequent and painful passage of urine – arise from over-sensitivity of the bladder and its outlet.

cystoscope. Optical instrument for examining the inside of the urinary bladder. It is simply a lighted tube with a system of lenses, slender enough to be passed up the urethra into the bladder. A local an-

aesthetic is usually instilled before the instrument is passed.

cytochrome. Group of compounds related to the haemoglobin of blood, found in all tissues and concerned with the transfer of oxygen from the blood to the cells.

cytology. Study of cells. ➤*histology*.

cytomegalovirus. Adults infected with this herpes-type virus usually remain symptom-free and unaware of its presence. Only a few develop illness such as hepatitis or a fever resembling glandular fever. (If immunity is impaired, e.g. by medication to protect an organ transplant, or AIDS, the risk is much greater.) The worst of this virus is that it is readily passed on to babies, either during pregnancy via the placenta, or at the time of birth. This can cause serious congenital defects, especially in the nervous system.

cytotoxic agents. Drugs that suppress cell reproduction or ➤*mitosis*, i.e. they stop the growth of tissues and the normal replacement of degenerated cells. A drug with this property must, in large enough doses, be a general poison. The drugs are useful because rapidly growing cells such as those of cancer are much more susceptible than normal cells, so that a small dose may inhibit a cancer without damaging healthy tissues. In practice, though, an effective dose is likely to be unpleasant, and these drugs are given only with great caution. Not all cancers respond equally well to cytotoxic treatment. Among those that do best are Hodgkin's disease and some types of leukaemia.

Apart from the treatment of cancer, these drugs are sometimes used to suppress the rapidly growing white blood cells that are concerned with ➤*immunity*, for example to prevent a recently transplanted kidney from being rejected as 'foreign' matter, or to relieve severe symptoms of ►*auto-immunity*.

Many widely different substances are in one way or another cytotoxic. They include derivatives of nitrogen mustard, alkaloids derived from the periwinkle, and antibiotics such as actinomycin.

D

dacry. Gk (Lat., lacrima) = tear; as dacryocystitis, inflammation of the lacrimal sac at the inner corner of the eye into which tears are drained.

Daltonism. Colour blindness, especially the red-green type, from which the chemist John Dalton (1766–1844) suffered.

D and C = ▸*dilatation* and curettage.

dampness. A damp surface loses heat by evaporation at a rate of about 600 calories per litre of water on a cold day. The primary fault of a damp house is that it is cold. But damp walls suggest other defects such as poor ventilation and rotten woodwork; in extreme cases the house may be structurally unsafe. The moist air and unpleasant smell add to the occupier's discomfort. If the walls are permanently damp, nothing else in the house is ever quite dry, and this includes clothing. Dry air enmeshed in cloth does not conduct heat, and therefore the body does not lose heat through it. But if the enmeshed air is damp it becomes a worse insulator, and the body does lose heat through it.

The direct ill effects of dampness on health can be ascribed to the difficulty of keeping warm. Also, moulds that thrive in damp places can provoke allergies such as asthma.

In very hot surroundings, dampness has the opposite effect. If the air is very moist it will take up no more water vapour; sweat will not evaporate from the skin and one cannot keep cool.

dandruff (pityriasis capitis). This very common condition of the scalp, with shedding of fine scales and sometimes itching, may be due to infestation of hair follicles by a yeast-like organism, *pityrosporum*. It is the earliest and often the only symptom of seborrhoeic ▸*eczema*. The many effective lotions and shampoos include preparations of coal tar, pyrithione, sulphur, selenium, lithium or occasionally corticosteroids.

Cradle cap is a similar affliction of babies.

dapsone. A sulphone drug, at present the standard treatment for leprosy.

Darwin, Charles Robert (1809–82). British naturalist. Together with A. R. Wallace he first suggested (1858) that evolution had come about by natural selection, i.e. that the individuals best adapted to their environment stood the best chance of survival and so the best chance of breeding to establish their type. His work aroused great controversy, mainly because it appeared to attack religious beliefs. In fact Darwin did not deny the Creation; he only pushed it further back in time, and suggested a way in which the earliest creatures might have developed into different and more complicated types. Also, people resented the idea that they were descended from monkeys. This is not quite what Darwin said. According to his theory, men and apes have a common ancestor less highly developed than either.

The direct importance of Darwin's work to medicine is the light it sheds on anatomy and embryology. Its indirect and much greater importance is that Darwin was the first biologist to discuss life in scientific terms, without any preconceived notion that things are so because it is right that they should be so. In other words, he was the first to shake off the fetters of teleology and make a purely objective study of life.

DDT (dichloro-diphenyl-trichloroethane). A contact insecticide discovered in Switzerland during the Second World War. It was much more effective than earlier insecticides, and became a major weapon against insect-borne disease, especially in the tropics. The few insects that survive unfortunately tend to produce offspring that resist DDT – a highly condensed example of evolution by survival of the fittest.

dead space. Air passages (nose, pharynx, trachea, bronchi) through which inspired air passes on its way to the working areas of the lungs. The air in this space takes no part in respiration, and a breath must be deep enough to remove it in order to be effective. Breathing through a tube, e.g. under water, increases the space, and if the tube is long enough effective breathing is impossible and the subject suffocates.

deafness. Hearing depends on a chain of events, and can be impaired or lost through disorders of any link in the chain (►*ear*).

The *external* or visible ear carries vibration in the air to the ear-drum. The *middle* ear transmits vibrations of the drum through a series of tiny bones to the *inner* ear, where vibrations are translated into nerve impulses. The *auditory nerve* transmits these impulses to the brain, where they are analysed and recognized as sounds.

The skin of the external ear secretes wax from modified sweat glands. Blockage by accumulated wax is perhaps the commonest cause of deafness; it is cured by washing out the wax – which may first have to be softened with oil.

Sound waves are small, rapid changes of air pressure, which cause the ear-drum to vibrate and stimulate the amplifying mechanism of the middle ear to pass on the message. The efficiency of the middle ear depends on the constant adjustment of the air pressure in it through the Eustachian tubes, the communicating channels between the ears and the back of the nose. If the tubes are blocked by inflammation, the air trapped in the middle ear acts as a damper and hearing is dulled, as often happens with a cold or sinusitis. Blockage of the tubes also encourages infection within the middle ear (►*otitis media*), of which deafness is a symptom. The surgery sometimes needed to treat otitis media, or to prevent dangerous complications, such as the spread of infection towards the brain, can also cause deafness, but the damage to the ear-drum by infection or surgery can usually be repaired by plastic surgery (tympanoplasty = myringoplasty).

Otosclerosis is a formation of unwanted bone in the middle ear. Hearing may begin to fail in early adult life. The cause is not known. Many of these cases respond well to surgical reconstruction.

The inner ear and auditory nerve can be damaged by physical injury, infection etc. The efficiency of the nerve deteriorates throughout adult life. Numerous poisons and drugs can affect the nerve.

Occupational deafness is an important industrial hazard for people whose work exposes them to loud noise: the classic instance is boiler-makers' deafness, but aircraft engines, gunfire and noisy machinery can all deaden the nerve-endings to a range of frequencies. As a rule, the range of lost sounds begins at about 4,000 cycles, say the top note of a piano, then spreads to lower frequencies. There is often tinnitus or ringing in the ear at a still higher frequency.

Deafness from birth can be caused by virus diseases (notoriously German measles) in early pregnancy and by various difficulties during labour. A child that cannot hear does not learn to speak; deaf-mutes are mute only because they are deaf. By dint of extraordinary skill and patience, specialist teachers are nevertheless able to get many of these children to speak intelligibly.

The external ear, the ear-drum, and the opening of the Eustachian tube at the back of the nose can be inspected. The rest of the apparatus can be studied only indirectly and by inference.

The distance at which the patient hears a watch or a whisper with one ear closed is a very rough though useful guide. Tuning forks have special uses. If the base of the fork is applied to the skull sound is conducted by the bone as well as in the usual way by air. Defective air-conduction can be distinguished from defective bone-conduction and sometimes from nerve-deafness. This information is often important in the choice of a hearing-aid, since hearing-aids are of two types – those inserted into the ear to amplify air-conducted sound, and those placed behind the ear for bone-conduction.

A *pure-tone audiometer* emits a note of any chosen pitch (frequency) and volume (intensity). From the volume needed for the patient to hear notes of various frequencies a chart of his hearing can be made. Throughout adult life the ears become less sensitive to high-pitched notes: for instance, few adults can hear the cry of bats, though most children can. Deafness in old age is often only loss of the upper range. Such people suffer as much as anyone else from loud noises, and they can hear that they are being spoken to, so nobody believes that they are deaf. But they cannot distinguish consonants – which are high-pitched sounds – and cannot therefore understand what is said. With occupational deafness in very noisy jobs it is the frequencies that have assailed the ear that are ultimately lost.

Like blindness, deafness is not often total. What matters is whether the remaining sensation is useful.

decidua. Lining of the uterus, shed during a menstrual period or after the birth of a child.

decompensation. A defect of the heart (e.g. an inefficient valve) is said to be *compensated* when the beat is strengthened enough to maintain a normal circulation, and *decompensated* when the circulation is impaired, i.e. when there is a degree of ►*heart failure*.

decompression. 1. The very gradual return to atmospheric pressure of people such as deep-sea divers who work under high pressure, to avoid ►*decompression sickness*.

2. Relief of raised pressure inside an organ by an operation to release excessive fluid; especially release of cerebrospinal fluid or blood through a burr-hole in the skull, e.g. after head injury.

decompression sickness (caisson disease; dysbarism). A hazard of diving: adverse effects of pressure changes, including 'the bends', ►*barotrauma*, and nitrogen narcosis.

Water pressure at 1 atmosphere for each 10 metres of depth forces gas, mainly nitrogen, to dissolve in the body fluids. These may froth when the pressure falls during the ascent. The bubbles cause symptoms by forming tiny airlocks which block small blood vessels and cut off the blood supply to the affected tissues. Symptoms range from itching, cramp-like pain and vertigo to paralysis, suffocation and coma. By surfacing in timed stages according to established rules the diver lets the gas seep safely away through his lungs. These rules are for experts in perfect physical condition: others need much wider safety margins. Time is as critical as depth: it takes as long to surface from a protracted shallow dive as from a brief deep one.

Barotrauma (physical injury) ranges from nose-bleeds to grave lung injuries. Ears are very vulnerable, and nobody with ear or sinus infection should dive.

Any highly concentrated gas (again mainly nitrogen) can affect the brain as a narcotic like alcohol, dangerously impairing a diver's judgement. In this and some other respects it is safer to use helium to dilute the oxygen than nitrogen. Undiluted oxygen is toxic under high pressure.

The bends are treated by recompression to dissolve the bubbles and decompression over many hours. Symptoms may be delayed and also deceptive. *Any* symptom within 24 hours of a dive needs expert care at once; otherwise a chance of preventing permanent damage may be lost. The doctor must be told that the patient has been diving.

Dysbarism adds to the risk of diving by impairing balance (ear injury) and co-ordination. *Nobody* should dive alone, and any beginner needs professional supervision.

decubitus. 1. Lying in bed; position when lying. **2.** Decubitus ulcers are formed by pressure of lying in one position; ➤*bedsore.*

defibrillation. Restoration of rhythmical heart beat by electrical stimulation in case of fibrillation (a completely irregular beat: ➤*arrhythmia*).

degeneration. Alteration of body cells towards less specialized cell-types as a result of defective blood supply, infection etc. As a result of degeneration muscle or liver cells tend to lose their special functions and resemble the cells of fatty or connective tissue.

dehydration ➤*water.*

déjà vu. The false impression of having previously seen things that one is seeing for the first time; occasionally a symptom of epilepsy and other disorders. But many normal people experience it at times.

Delhi boil = ➤*oriental sore.*

delirium. Disturbance of the brain by injury, fever, poisoning etc., with confusion, often hallucinations, excitement and other symptoms of disorganized and exaggerated mental activity.

Delirium tremens is a kind of delirium affecting heavy drinkers, especially after injuries or during sudden illness. The attack may be heralded by a period of depression, insomnia and mental instability; at its height frightening hallucinations, irrational overactivity and sweating are usual. In the 19th century it was thought that delirium tremens was experienced by heavy drinkers when withdrawing from alcohol. Then this idea was rejected for a long time, and only narcotics were said to be associated with a true withdrawal syndrome (implying that drinkers and smokers could stop if they chose). Now, most people have reverted to the earlier idea and accept that delirium tremens, though it can afflict someone still drinking, can also arise following the withdrawal of alcohol from a physically addicted drinker.

delivery. Childbirth ▸*labour*. It is the mother who is delivered of the child, and not, as some medical jargon would have it, the child that is delivered (like a parcel at the door).

deltoid. Triangular muscle covering the shoulder. The base of the triangle is the broad attachment to the clavicle and scapula; the fibres converge on the narrow apex half-way down the outer side of the humerus. The muscle abducts the shoulder, i.e. raises the arm sideways.

delusion. An unshakeable belief which a normal person of the same intelligence and background would recognize as obviously wrong and unreasonable. The extreme delusions of grave mental disorder, especially schizophrenia, are easily discerned, but there is no clear line between mild delusion and simple error. In fact it is almost impossible to define delusions without calling one's political and religious opponents insane.

Most delusions are harmless except as pointers to mental illness. Some are dangerous: a man who thinks he is the Emperor of Atlantis may also think he has the right to cut off people's heads; or (a much commoner danger) one who thinks he is persecuted may take violent steps to defend himself.

dementia. Originally, mental disorder involving loss of intelligence, as opposed to *amentia*, where intelligence is retarded from birth. Thus *dementia praecox*, premature dementia, now known as schizo-

phrenia. Dementia is now generally taken to mean mental deterioration as a result of physical changes in the brain, e.g. from infection, chronic poisoning, injury, arterial disease. The distinction between these 'organic' disorders and mental disorders without organic change in the brain or evident physical cause may be artificial: it may be simply that in the latter case the changes and causes have not been identified.

Although dementia is often an irreversible manifestation of old age, its symptoms (the progressive loss of memory, of concentration, of the ability to think clearly and of the wish to do so, followed by confusion, apathy, hallucinations and other symptoms more suggestive of psychosis) should not be accepted without further enquiry as some dementia may be susceptible to treatment. These include some brain tumours and other operable lesions within the skull, malnutrition, thyroid deficiency (myxoedema), high blood pressure associated with the release of small blood-clots into the circulation of the brain, and unsuspected poisoning (including undiagnosed alcoholism). Therefore, dementia calls for investigation, including a brain scan.

It is characteristic of the nervous system that lost brain-cells cannot regenerate, and characteristic of all tissues that cells do not last for ever. Therefore over the years some deterioration is inevitable, though with some people this may hardly be noticeable until extreme old age. With others, the change is more obvious and more abrupt: between 5 and 10 per cent of people over the age of 65 show a clear lessening of mental capacity. The commonest type of physical change is seen in *Alzheimer's disease*, where nerve tissue throughout the brain withers and dies. Alzheimer (1864–1915) described characteristic changes in the brains of patients who had died with 'presenile' dementia, i.e. people in their 50s and 60s. This is an uncommon disease, but similar changes in older people are common and account for many if not most cases of 'senile' dementia.

A much rarer condition, *Pick's disease*, also affects younger people. The changes affect mainly the frontal lobes.

denaturation. Altering the structure and properties of a protein by changing its environment, e.g. 'setting' egg-white by warming.

dengue. A virus infection occurring throughout the tropics, transmitted by the mosquito *Aëdes aegypti*. Symptoms arise about a week after infection; they include fever, skin rash, nausea, headache, and severe pain in joints ('break-bone fever'). The symptoms often subside about the third day but return after a short interval. After the second, usually milder episode the patient recovers completely, though he may need several weeks to get back his strength.

No treatment shortens the illness, but drugs such as aspirin, codeine, and tranquillizers may ease the symptoms. A vaccine is available, but better still the disease can be eradicated by mosquito control.

dentine (dentin). The main substance of a tooth; ivory. ➤*teeth* (1).

dentistry. There are pre-Roman specimens of artificial teeth, held in place by wires or metal bands attached to the remaining sound teeth. An Egyptian papyrus of about the 16th century BC describes filling cavities and splinting loose teeth with gold wire. Greek surgeons carried these skills to the Roman Empire.

Along with the rest of medical science,

good dentistry was lost in the Middle Ages. The Renaissance surgeons who revived it include Paré in France and Fabricius ab Aquapendente in Italy. Fabricius seems to have been the first to drill and cleanse cavities before filling them.

Pierre Fauchard (1678–1761) was the first specialist in dentistry and the author of the first treatise on the subject (*Chirurgien dentiste*, 1728). He made complete removable sets of false teeth, fitted artificial crowns, and improved Fabricius's method of treating decay, incidentally refuting the current belief that decay was due to worms.

But apart from the few surgeons who happened to be interested in it, dentistry remained in the hands of men with little if any special training. A few jewellers made false teeth; for the rest, dentists were itinerant tooth-pullers. Dentistry as a profession was hardly known until the middle of the 19th century. Then in 1844 Wells gave the first dental anaesthetic. In 1848 (Sir) John Tomes published a most influential work: *Dental Physiology and Surgery*. In the 1850s professional examinations were introduced in many countries – first in America, which in modern times has consistently led the way in the various branches of dentistry.

Recent developments include vastly improved apparatus, the growth of orthodontics (the correction of deformities of the teeth), of preventive dentistry, and of co-operation between dental and general surgeons in the treatment of injuries and diseases of the mouth and jaws.

In some countries there are two professional grades – licensed dentists and graduate dental surgeons, with various auxiliary grades. The profession was unified in Britain with the formation in 1921 of the Dental Board, associated with the General Medical Council. In 1956 the

Board was replaced by an independent General Dental Council.

deodorant. (Means of) removing smells. Unpleasant smells are often due to the action of bacteria: thus fetid breath is generally caused either by bacterial decomposition of food left between the teeth or by bacterial infection of the gums, and strong body smells are due mainly to bacterial decomposition of sweat, rather than to an excess of sweat. Hence careful cleaning of the teeth and dental attention generally deal with the former, and soap (which deals well with most skin bacteria) with the latter. Body deodorants act partly by decreasing the secretion of sweat and partly as disinfectants, i.e. by killing bacteria.

depilatory. (Means of) removing hair. Various chemicals, e.g. barium sulphide, cause hair to fall. They need to be prepared and used with care to avoid injuring the skin. X-rays are also effective; this method was formerly much used in the treatment of resistant cases of ringworm of the scalp, but with newer remedies, particularly griseofulvin, depilation is now seldom needed.

depression. In general: a disorder of mood; protracted and disproportionate melancholy. In a more technical sense: the same exaggerated misery accompanied by impairment of all mental processes and of physical functions such as appetite, sleep, sex, and work.

In some circumstances, melancholy is a normal response. After bereavement, for instance, its absence might imply mental illness. Some people are gloomy by nature but cannot reasonably be called abnormal, and everyone at times feels dejected for no good reason. What distinguishes depression as an illness from a normal fluctuation of mood is that it is deeper and lasts longer than one would expect of the particular person affected. A close friend or relative may notice the early symptoms more easily than a specialist who has not known the patient before. The point is worth making because the sooner the patient is treated the better. Effective treatment not only prevents needless suffering; it can be life-saving, because untreated depression can end in suicide.

To outward appearances there are two kinds of depression. The first looks like a reaction to external events that would upset anyone to some extent, and counts as an illness only because the patient's reaction is greater, in degree and duration, than the circumstances warrant. This can be called *reactive* depression. The second kind, where there seems to be no good reason for misery, can be said to have arisen within the patient himself, and this kind, often associated with the other symptoms of the second definition above, can be called *endogenous* depression. The distinction is useful if only for the sake of discussion, even if reactive and endogenous depression are not so much two distinct illnesses as two factors contributing to the same symptom.

The actions of various drugs support the idea that at least some depression may be endogenous, arising from a disturbance within the patient's own nervous system. Reserpine, a kind of tranquillizer formerly used for the control of high blood pressure, acts by suppressing the action of certain substances that transmit nervous impulses in the brain. It had the drawback that in some patients it caused severe depression. On the other hand, drugs that enhance the activity of these transmitters (MAO inhibitors, see below) relieve depression. Thus, depression might be merely a symptom of deficiency in some part of the brain of one of these transmitters, probably *serotonin*. Unfortunately for this theory, the deficiency might be only a result of depression and not a cause; the question is still open. Exactly the same problem arises with other mental illnesses: does alcohol make people neurotic, or do people drink because they are neurotic? ➤*schizophrenia*.

A clinical or symptomatic classification is as elusive as one based on causes. Some depression is only a kind of personality at the dark end of a spectrum that leads by way of 'average' personalities to the overwhelmingly merry and ebullient. As with the spectrum of political opinion, the two extremes can be very close to each other. The mood of people with *cyclothymic* personalities alternates between gloom and elation. This looks like a small-scale model, still within normal limits, of the serious disorder known as manic-depressive psychosis, but the relation of one to the other is not clear (➤*schizoid personality*, in relation to schizophrenia).

Depression may take the form of a *neurosis*, i.e. the patient has understandable reasons for being miserable, and himself understands the nature of his illness: it is the degree and duration of his misery that are abnormal. This is the type that has been called *reactive depression*. Many psychiatrists no longer accept such a diagnosis, feeling that there is more to these cases than a simple neurosis. On the other hand, depression is sometimes a symptom of an anxiety state, which is certainly a neurosis.

Severe depression may be a component of ➤*manic-depressive psychosis*. Though many people with this psychosis have episodes of mania as well as of de-

pression, some suffer only depressive attacks, and in the early stages at least these may appear to be neurotic or 'reactive', as described above. But the patient is not completely rational, and is liable to have other symptoms of endogenous depression, such as insomnia and loss of weight. Depression of the same type starting in middle age, *involutional melancholia*, is described by different psychiatrists as a disorder on its own or as a variant of manic-depressive psychosis.

The risk of suicide cannot be judged by the apparent depth of depression. The safest course is to regard all depressives as potential suicides. Next to preventing suicide, the object of treatment is to re-establish the patient in society and in his own esteem. He cannot be talked out of his depression: he may not even be interested in the possibility of a cure because he does not consider himself worth saving. But the drugs now available not only relieve the symptoms but get the patient into a frame of mind where he can discuss his illness and listen to advice. Antidepressant drugs brighten the patient's mood, but paradoxically the treatment of a severe case may have to begin with a tranquillizer. Loss of sleep and of weight form vicious circles with depression. They can be difficult to treat at home; the patient needs to be watched because of the suicide risk, and some of the more powerful drugs need close supervision. Therefore severe depression is usually treated in hospital. Some very ill patients lack the initiative and energy to kill themselves, but they may make an attempt to do so as they begin to recover under treatment.

There are two main groups of antidepressant drugs. The first, the monoamineoxidase inhibitors (MAOIs), was discovered in the early 1950s when the drug *isoniazid*, given for tuberculosis, was found to raise the patient's spirits, sometimes alarmingly. Chemically related drugs were then successfully used to relieve depression. These drugs inactivate MAO, an enzyme that serves to destroy some of the substances (noradrenaline; serotonin) that are released at nerve junctions in the brain to transmit impulses. If these transmitters were not destroyed as soon as their work was done they would accumulate and set up uncontrolled activity in the nervous system. The net effect of MAOIs is to increase the available noradrenaline and serotonin. But MAO has the secondary function of activating other potentially dangerous substances. The standard doses of various drugs become highly poisonous to a patient taking MAOI. And *tyramine*, found in cheese, yeast extract and some other foods (it is probably the ingredient of cheese that can disturb sleep), also becomes poisonous with MAOIs. Since a depressed patient may not care much about being poisoned, these drugs need the closest supervision.

A second group of drugs, the tricyclic antidepressants, appear to enhance the action of noradrenaline and serotonin by some means other than interfering with MAO, thus avoiding the dangerous interactions with cheese and other substances that create problems with MAOIs. The two groups of drugs are not compatible with each other, and so cannot be used together. Like any effective drugs the tricyclic antidepressants can cause unwanted side-effects; some people do not tolerate them well; they are not always effective. But they tend to give less trouble than the MAOIs, which are now kept in reserve for patients whom the tricyclics for one reason or another do not suit.

The rather ponderously named *selective serotonin re-uptake inhibitors* (SSRIs), a more recently introduced group of drugs, act, as the name suggests, by prolonging the active life of serotonin. With their different mode of action they are a valuable alternative to the older drugs.

Apart from a possible deficiency of serotonin, depression is also associated with an excess of sodium in certain brain cells. Lithium salts displace sodium, and have been used for treating manic-depressive psychosis. They appear to be more effective with the manic than the depressive component.

Some of the most rapid and dramatic recoveries from severe depression are achieved by ►*electroconvulsive therapy*, which is the application of small electric shocks to the brain. Nobody knows how the method works, but it is a most valuable stand-by, especially with patients who are so ill that their treatment is an emergency.

The value of surgery in the treatment of depression, *psychosurgery*, is still hotly disputed. The operations proposed are empirical because they involve parts of the brain that are not fully understood, but it does appear that in cases where less drastic remedies have failed, severe depression has been relieved by interrupting one or other of the pathways in the brain that are concerned with mood and emotion.

dermatitis. In its literal sense (inflammation of the skin) this term might mean almost any skin disease, but in practice it is applied to inflammation confined to the skin, with itch, vesicles or bullae (small or large blisters) that may exude fluid, and formation of scales. Inflammation due to infection by viruses, bacteria or fungi (e.g. herpes, impetigo, ringworm) is not included.

Many authorities, followed in earlier editions of this book, make no distinction between dermatitis and *eczema*. But because dermatitis is apt to suggest an industrial disease some others distinguish *contact dermatitis*, caused by an external agent, from ►*eczema*, which includes all the other varieties.

Contact dermatitis may be caused by irritants such as acids and alkalis, solvents, petroleum derivatives and detergents. These can inflame anybody's skin.

Many other substances, not in themselves harmful, affect a susceptible person, so that later exposure sets up an immune reponse. The resulting rash, though usually at the site of contact, may also appear elsewhere, perhaps only a few days after the original contact but sometimes not until years later. A metal watchstrap may be the obvious cause of a rash on the wrist, but a seemingly harmless substance with which the patient has worked for years without trouble can be very difficult to inculpate. Possible agents include many drugs, metals such as nickel and chromium and their compounds, epoxy resins, rubber, dyestuffs and plants such as chrysanthemum, primrose and poison ivy. Successful treatment depends on finding and excluding the causative agent.

(►*immunity* (6, hypersensitivity, type IV).)

dermatology. Study of the skin.

dermatophyte. Any of a group of microscopical fungi infecting the skin and causing ringworm and other troubles.

dermatosis. Any affliction of the skin (an even vaguer term than dermatitis).

dermis = ►*corium*.

dermoid. A kind of cyst formed by the growth of a displaced fragment of skin, isolated from the surface either by an accident of prenatal development or, rarely, by injury.

Descartes, René (1596–1650). Although his direct contribution to medical knowledge was small, Descartes has an important place in medical history, because more than anyone since Aristotle he taught scientists to think clearly. Pure science (on which biology and medicine should be based) is today mainly concerned with reducing to a minimum the 'facts' from which natural laws are derived, and of course with ensuring that they are true facts. This attitude to nature springs from Descartes's doctrine that nothing is so obvious that it can be accepted without question. Most errors in science have arisen – and still arise – from neglecting this simple rule, from taking things at their face value. There are good examples in Descartes's own writings. In considerable detail he deduced the workings of the human body, but he argued from wrong data and therefore came to wrong conclusions. Although he had read and praised Harvey's clear proof that the heart muscle pumped blood round the body, Descartes stated as a self-evident fact that the heart heated and distilled the blood. From this he argued with inexorable logic that the heat expanded the blood, forcing it into the arteries, that the most refined fraction of the distillate rose highest, to the brain, whence this 'subtle fluid' was carried by the nerves (which must therefore be hollow) to the muscles. 'And how could digestion take place in the stomach, unless the heart sent heat there by the arteries, with some of the more fluid parts of the blood, which help to dissolve the food that is put there?' The purpose of breathing was to cool and condense the blood, making it fit to return to the heart and feed the fire there. The account is grotesquely wrong at every point. It was almost bound to be, for the role of logic is to interpret facts, not to replace them. John Hunter stands far below Descartes intellectually, but he was a much better biologist: he worked on the principle 'Why think? Why not try the experiment?'

On the other hand, Descartes guessed the nature of reflex action long before anyone else, though he thought it occurred only in animals, which had no soul. He has been much criticized for giving the soul an exact anatomical position – in the pineal body, a small gland in the middle of the brain. But his definition of the soul ('that part of the body of which the nature is simply to think') could as well be applied to the mind, of which the brain is surely the centre if anything so elusive can have a centre. An understanding of sensation and psychology is much facilitated by Descartes's doctrine that qualities such as sounds, colours, or textures are events in our brains rather than inherent properties of the world around us.

Much of the development of modern physiology has taken place in France, and this may be largely due to the influence of Descartes on French thought.

desensitization. A method of treating ➤*allergy*: first, the substance(s) to which the patient reacts (the *allergen*) has to be identified by showing that it causes allergic inflammation in the skin; the allergen is then injected in gradually increasing doses until the patient is immune to its effects.

In psychiatry; a method of treating cer-

tain neuroses. The source of his anxiety having been identified, the patient is exposed in reality or imagination to situations that are increasingly alarming to him, and learns to relax at each stage.

desquamation. Shedding of the outer layer of the skin (a continuous, normal process); peeling after sunburn, scarlet fever etc.

detergent. Cleansing agent, especially one that acts by lowering surface tension – this enables water to penetrate better and remove grease by forming an emulsion. Some detergents are used as ➤*antiseptics* for the skin. Their action depends on an opposite electrochemical effect to that of soap, so that the two cancel each other and should not be used together.

The detergent action of *docusate* is used to lower surface tension in the bowel and so admit more water to soften the faeces and ease the opening of the bowels. Docusate is also used to loosen ear wax.

devil's grip = ➤*Bornholm disease*.

dextran. Carbohydrate, chemically like starch and cellulose, of which a solution can be injected into a vein to restore the volume of the blood in severe ➤*shock*, e.g. after extensive burns, where fluid has leaked from the blood-stream into the damaged tissues. A solution of sodium chloride can be used in the same way, but quickly leaks away. Dextran molecules are too large to escape from the blood vessels, so they retain the necessary water by ➤*osmosis*.

dextrocardia. An unusual arrangement of the heart with the apex on the right, the mirror-image of the common arrangement; sometimes all the other organs are also transposed – liver on the left, spleen on the right etc. – and the condition is then called *situs inversus*. It has no medical significance.

dextrose. Grape-sugar; glucose.

diabetes. Abnormal excess of urine. The two kinds of disease described below have only this symptom in common.

diabetes insipidus. An uncommon disorder, in which a large volume of urine is formed regardless of the state of the body's store of water. In healthy people the flow of urine from the kidneys is regulated to keep the dilution of the blood constant. Diabetes insipidus is a breakdown of this mechanism, usually from failure of the pituitary gland to secrete antidiuretic hormone (ADH). The primary defect may be in the pituitary itself, or in the hypothalamus, the part of the floor of the brain that governs secretion of the hormone in response to changes in the dilution of the blood. The defect is remedied by giving ADH by injection or in snuff or nasal drops. (An extremely rare form of diabetes insipidus is due to congenital inability of the kidneys to conserve water.)

In extreme cases, the daily amount of urine, and therefore the amount of water to be made good by drinking, has amounted to more than half the patient's body weight.

diabetes mellitus. A syndrome or group of symptoms arising from failure to regulate the metabolism of glucose by means of the hormone insulin; usually simply called *diabetes*. The immediate cause is either lack of insulin because the pancreas produces none or not enough, or the failure of the body to make proper use of the insulin that is available. Diabetes may be called 'secondary' when the failure to produce or utilize insulin is a symptom of some other trouble. Most

hormones interact with others, and hormones from the thyroid, adrenal and pituitary glands, and even one (glucagon) from the pancreas itself, either suppress or neutralize insulin. Thus a disease primarily of some other gland can lead to secondary diabetes. Damage to the pancreas itself can have the same effect; mumps can affect the pancreas and diabetes is sometimes reported as a complication. But even considered as a single group, these secondary cases make up only a very small fraction of all instances of diabetes. The real concern is with a very common disease, of which the causes are understood either not at all or only vaguely.

1. TYPES OF DIABETES

Diabetes may first appear at almost any age, but most often starts either before 25 or after 40. The first group used to be classified as 'juvenile', and the second as 'maturity-onset' diabetes, with the first afflicting thin youngsters and the second overweight, middle-aged people. While the two types follow different courses, the more important distinction is between diabetics who must be given injections of insulin to control the disorder (insulin is not effective if taken orally), and those who can usually manage without them. Therefore, diabetes is now classified as *insulin-dependent* (type I) or *non-insulin-dependent* (type II). Nearly all juvenile cases are of type I, but while not all cases arising later in life can be treated without insulin injections, most can. This is reflected in a subgrouping of 'maturity-onset' patients into *obese* (the majority, and almost sure to be non-dependent), and *non-obese* (likely to be insulin-dependent).

Types I and II differ in several ways. Clinically, it is the insulin-dependent type I diabetics who are liable to develop *ketosis* (>'Course and Management', below), and whose symptoms progress rapidly unless brought under control. Type II is usually insidious, the diabetes often passing unnoticed while serious damage to arteries, nerves and other structures is being done. The causes of the two types also apparently differ. Contrary to expectation, the genetic origin is clear with type II, although this is associated with an opulent diet and the patient being overweight. It is as though these people do not inherit actual diabetes, but rather are predisposed to an inability to control metabolism in the presence of middle-age spread. Thus they can usually remain well simply by careful attention to diet. On the other hand, type I diabetics, whose condition owes less to genetic factors, not only have to be given insulin, but may need doses far greater than someone whose pancreas has been removed (e.g. for cancer) and has no insulin of his own. Type I diabetes, then, displays signs of there being some inactivation of the already inadequately formed insulin. This could be an autoimmune reaction (>*immunity* (7)), and in fact antibodies against both insulin and the pancreatic islet cells have been found in these patients, of whom many have family histories of other endocrine disorders.

2. COURSE AND MANAGEMENT

All digestible carbohydrate is converted in the liver to glucose, which is stored in the form of glycogen or released into the blood-stream as required, to be taken up by the body cells as fuel. Insulin facilitates the passage of glucose from the blood into the cells. If insulin is not available, or not being utilized, glucose simply accumulates in the blood. In the ordinary way, the kidneys conserve glucose by returning it to the circulation, but

allow an excessive amount in the blood to escape in the urine. Thus sugar in the urine, shown by a very simple test, may be the first indication of diabetes. (On its own, this test does not prove anything because sometimes a perfectly healthy person has glucose in the urine. Diabetes is proved by testing the level of glucose in the blood over a period.)

A high concentration of glucose in the blood is itself a hazard: by disturbing the osmotic pressure of the blood (>*osmosis*) it can lead to coma. The glucose shed by the kidneys also has an osmotic effect, causing increased flow of urine (literally diabetes), which may be the patient's first symptom.

Without insulin glucose cannot be used as fuel, so fat has to be used instead. But the combustion of fat can be completed, i.e. resulting in the end-products carbon dioxide and water, only with the help of intermediate products of glucose combustion. Without this help, the combustion of fat stops with the formation of acidic ketones, which can reach a poisonous concentration and cause *ketosis*, leading to acidosis, and, unless treated with insulin injections, coma and death. This complication is characteristic of type I rather than type II diabetes.

A typical effect of either type of diabetes is the degeneration of small arteries. Since every part of the body depends on its arteries the possible symptoms are almost limitless. The eyes and kidneys are particularly vulnerable; uncontrolled diabetes is a common cause of blindness and also of serious kidney disease.

Larger arteries may also be involved, partly because their walls are thick enough to depend on very fine arterial twigs (vasa vasorum) to nourish them, and these are likely to be damaged. But diabetes also predisposes to arteriosclerosis (*atheroma*) and its complications such as high blood pressure, heart attacks and strokes.

The nerves, especially in the legs, are subject to diabetic neuropathy (*neuritis*), with various disturbances of sensation. Many patients suffer from sore feet, and if loss of sensation is added to defective circulation, ulcers of the lower part of the legs may form.

Infection of the skin is common, and a crop of boils is sometimes the first sign of diabetes.

However, as stated earlier, many cases of diabetes, especially in older patients, first come to light when a routine examination shows glucose in the urine; the importance of this is that immediate treatment may prevent serious damage. At one time many physicians believed that if the patient was reasonably free of symptoms, precise regulation of his carbohydrate metabolism was superfluous. It now seems clear that precise regulation is justified.

All diabetics need to pay careful attention to diet. There is no point in discussing details as the needs of patients vary widely. In general, energy (calorie) content has to be adjusted closely to maintain ideal body-weight, while allowing for the demands of exertion, which can vary from time to time. Most type II patients will need an initial period of reduced calorie intake to bring them down to their ideal weight. The carbohydrate (starch and sugar) content must be restricted; the carbohydrate intake for type I patients is adjusted to the insulin provided, and for type II sufferers to the amount the patient can manage, preferably without insulin supplements. Finding the correct dose of insulin for those patients who need it

(about a quarter of all diabetics) needs a period of close observation, with frequent laboratory checks to establish that sugar metabolism is under control. Some type II cases not easily controlled by diet alone respond to *oral hypoglycaemic agents*. These drugs are of two kinds: sulphonylureas, such as chlorpropamide, which promote the secretion of insulin if the pancreas still functions to some extent; and, if these fail, biguanides, such as metformin, which enhance the effect of insulin. Neither kind of drug is a substitute for insulin, nor are they suitable for type I, insulin-dependent patients. But they do save many type II patients from needing injections.

All diabetic patients are taught as far as possible to keep a constant check on their health, to watch that their weight is constant, and to report at once any untoward symptoms. Regular urine tests for glucose are as simple as dipping a strip of litmus paper into a school test-tube and give a rough-and-ready check. For more accurate and better information a simple test of the amount of sugar in the blood can be carried out by the patient. The latter test gives the state of affairs at the moment of testing, but a better progress report is given by testing the amount of glucose bound to the blood-protein haemoglobin.

If insulin were taken by mouth it would be destroyed by digestion, so it must be injected. However, not all patients tolerate injected insulin equally well. Some suffer from allergic reactions or hypoglycaemia (a condition which is potentially lethal unless the patient receives glucose or ordinary sugar at once). Insulin for the treatment of diabetes is usually derived from highly refined extracts of either pork or beef pancreas, but now that the chemical formula has been elucidated (>*insulin*), the molecules of these animal insulins can be modified to an exact match of the human variety.

The many available forms of insulin include plain insulin, which acts quickly but which only lasts for 6–8 hours. If the insulin is combined with zinc, and suspended rather than dissolved, the action is delayed but the duration of its effect is doubled. Combinations with zinc and protamine act for 24 hours or longer. In their usual form, all these products contain at least a trace of protein, to which some patients are sensitive. Special preparations, free of protein, are available for these individuals.

3. HISTORY

The term diabetes was first recorded by Aretaeus in the 2nd century AD, and the sugary taste of the urine by Thomas Willis in the 17th. Claude Bernard's research on sugar in the body in the mid-19th century was the start of a proper understanding of diabetes, and in 1889 von Mering and Minkowski proved the association of diabetes with a deficiency of the pancreas. But severe diabetes remained an incurable disease until 1921, when Banting and Best isolated fairly pure insulin. Insulin was crystallized in 1926, and its formula was established in 1959 (>*insulin*).

It is often pointed out that insulin is no cure, because the patient needs daily injections for the rest of his life. This is a very pessimistic view. To be sure, a dose of insulin is no more a *permanent* cure of diabetes than a drink of water is a permanent cure of thirst; but while the effect lasts the cure is complete and the patient is in all respects healthy.

More than any other class of patient, diabetics have to be their own physicians, and their doctors have become advisers and teachers rather than custodians of esoteric knowledge.

diagnosis. The identification or recognition of diseases. The methods are precisely those of detectives in novels (and no doubt of real detectives too). Apart from a few cases where the culprit practically gives itself up (e.g. a text-book history of migraine; an unmistakable rash of chicken-pox) it is a process of elimination from a group of suspects, starting with the premise that anyone might have any conceivable disease.

The first piece of evidence is the patient's own statement of his troubles – the case-history. Here the physician's skill lies in getting the facts without putting ideas into the patient's head, and in judging the patient's reliability as a witness. His problem is not with blatant liars (about age, habits, or disabilities), who are easily recognized, but with honest people who hide symptoms to avoid making a fuss or hearing bad news, or invent symptoms to rationalize their anxieties. The patient's account of previous illness and family history often gives important clues.

Physical examination is a well rehearsed routine. To record a medical history and make a complete examination would take at least an hour, but even a short history narrows the field of inquiry and indicates which parts of the examination need special care. Although physical examination occasionally reveals something quite unexpected, its main value is in confirming or refuting suspicions aroused by the history.

Finally, special investigations may be needed, such as chemical tests, microscopical study of blood cells or other tissues, and X-ray examination. A few such investigations are done routinely and count as part of an ordinary examination: simple chemical tests of the urine, for example. The current emphasis on early recognition of diseases that cause few symptoms until they reach a dangerous stage is bringing various 'special' investigations into routine practice. But as a rule patients are subjected to X-rays, blood tests and the rest only when the possible diagnoses have been reduced to two or three suspects, or when a provisional diagnosis needs elaboration – e.g., *pneumonia*, but which antibiotic drug will deal with it best?

The level of diagnosis varies greatly. Until fairly modern times diagnosis was almost always *symptomatic*. A diagnosis of gout (*podagra*) put into a word what the patient had described – the sensation that his foot was caught in a trap. It did rather more, because by naming the disease the physician was putting it in the same class as other cases he had seen or heard of, and on the basis of past experience he could predict and prescribe. Today, obvious examples of symptomatic diagnosis would be *asthenia* or *debility* (weakness), *constipation*, *dyspepsia* (indigestion), *hypertension* (high blood pressure). None of these diagnoses says anything about the real nature of the trouble. Less obvious examples include *asthma*, *epilepsy*, *neurosis*, and *rheumatism*. Any of them can be qualified in at least some cases to give a more complete answer. Thus nobody would settle for 'constipation' without asking why, or 'rheumatism' without trying to say which of the several types. But when known causes of a disease have been ruled out the symptomatic diagnosis has to be qualified by an adjective ('essential', 'idiopathic', 'primary'), meaning only that the trouble seems to have started of its own accord. 'Epilepsy' means that the pa-

tient has fits; 'idiopathic epilepsy' means that nobody knows why.

The next step is an *anatomical* diagnosis to define the exact site of the trouble. This is obvious enough when a patient breaks his leg; but injuries apart, anatomical diagnosis was hardly possible until medicine began to be founded on a thorough knowledge of anatomy in the 16th century, and it was unusual until pathology – the processes of disease – came under serious study in the 18th and 19th centuries. The change makes the difference between the superb *symptomatic* accounts of Sydenham (17th century), and descriptions by Addison and Bright (early 19th) of the precise location of diseases. From the symptomatic diagnosis *dropsy*, Bright distinguished cases where the primary trouble was heart disease from those where it was in the kidneys, the one responding to treatment with digitalis and the other not. Bright's colleague Addison, investigating cases of progressive and fatal debility, defined two diseases: one of the blood (pernicious anaemia) and one of the adrenal glands (Addison's disease).

When the site of a disease has been defined, something can usually be discovered about its nature (*pathological diagnosis*) and cause (*aetiological diagnosis*). Only then can the treatment be wholly rational. Addison could only describe pernicious anaemia as ' "idiopathic", to distinguish it from cases in which there existed more or less evidence of some of the usual causes or concomitants of the anaemic state'. But he had shown his successors where to look, and in the present century pernicious anaemia and Addison's disease have both been brought under control, the one with liver extract (later vitamin B_{12}) and the other with adrenal hormones. Each was due to deficiency of an essential factor. The diagnosis was still not complete, for the deficiency was unexplained. It so chances that both are now ascribed (at least by some investigators) to allergic reactions to parts of the body's own tissues (►*auto-immunity*). If this should be proved, the next question will be: why the reaction? Probably no diagnosis will ever be complete. The problem is simply pushed further back; and that is really all that any science achieves.

The level of a diagnosis depends not only on how much is known of the disease, but also on what is necessary or practicable in the particular case. Complete investigation of every illness is out of the question – half the population would be admitted to hospital and the other half would be attending to them, and most of the patients would either die or recover before their diagnoses were complete. In practice a diagnosis is taken far enough to show what has to be done for the patient; only in selected cases does it need elaboration. A fundamental difference between general practice and the narrower specialities is that the general practitioner has to make some sort of diagnosis, however superficial, in every kind of case, and from this rapid diagnosis decide whether detailed investigation is really needed; whereas the specialist meets cases that have already been selected, and is always expected to attempt a complete diagnosis.

For instance, a patient may be sent to hospital with the vague diagnosis 'acute abdomen', meaning that he has one of half a dozen conditions, any of which needs urgent surgical attention. To carry the diagnosis further before getting him to hospital would only waste precious time. Or an undiagnosed fever may have to be treated as typhoid until further notice, because to prove the diagnosis takes time in which the condition could become dangerous.

Sometimes new forms of treatment demand new methods of diagnosis. Until recently, 'stroke' was an acceptable diagnosis. The kind of stroke did not matter because in any case there was nothing to be done about it. Now that some kinds can be treated by surgery and others by drugs, it is often necessary to decide which blood vessel is involved and in what way.

In the past, diagnosis has been static and qualitative: it has tried to answer the question: what is the abnormal condition? The present trend is towards dynamic and quantitative diagnosis: how far has the trouble advanced, and what progress is it likely to make? This is dictated by recent developments in the treatment of disease. When people with symptoms from high blood pressure could only be given advice and sedatives, a diagnosis of 'hypertension' was enough. Now that there are highly potent drugs for controlling blood pressure, with undesirable as well as desirable effects, each case has to be accurately assessed: the degree of hypertension, its rate of progress, and the risks of withholding treatment have to be accurately balanced against the properties of the various drugs.

It is too soon to say much about diagnosis by computer, which is still in the experimental stages. Most people find the idea repugnant because it seems inhuman, but they may be missing the point. A diagnosis is made by sifting evidence and deciding which of the suspects is the likeliest culprit in the light of one's past experience of similar cases and of other people's published reports. As in crime detection, the first and most important step is to *suspect* the right answer;

proving it is generally a matter of routine. The usual reason for completely missing a diagnosis is not suspecting it. No doctor is likely to overlook malaria in the tropics, because there it is the prime suspect in every case of fever and the parasites can be seen in the blood if they are sought. But outside the tropics a patient who develops malaria may wait for days before the possibility enters anyone's mind, though when once the question is raised it can be answered almost at once. With rare diseases, or unusual manifestations of common ones, the diagnosis may lie outside the physician's experience or reading, and it might take weeks to find the answer in a library. These are the errors that a properly programmed computer can avoid. It can automatically 'suspect' everything that has been fed to it, and assess the chances that a given set of symptoms are due to a particular disease, or that a given case will respond to a particular form of treatment – according, of course, to the information it had been given previously. Nobody has seriously suggested that computers could assume all the responsibilities of physicians, but there is no doubt that they can become most valuable tools as a sort of instant reference library. (➤*Scanning* techniques, which are useful and versatile aids to diagnosis, depend on a computer to decode the readings.)

dialysis. Selective diffusion through a membrane serving as a molecular filter: small molecules, e.g. salts, pass through, while large ones, e.g. proteins, do not. The principle is described in more detail under ➤*osmosis*. It is applied in the artificial kidney: a membrane divides a stream of the patient's blood, taken from an artery and returned to a vein,

from a prepared solution of salts, glucose etc. in the same concentrations as those of healthy blood. Since these substances are balanced across the membrane there is no effective traffic in them. The protein molecules and corpuscles of the blood are too large to pass through. But waste products such as urea flow from the zone of high concentration (the blood) to the low concentration of the prepared solution and are washed away. The apparatus is designed to take over the work of incompetent kidneys, but it may also be life-saving in some types of poisoning, e.g. overdoses of sleeping pills.

Peritoneal dialysis is a simpler if less efficient method. A plastic tube is inserted into the abdominal cavity. The *peritoneum*, the membranous lining of the abdominal cavity, acts as the filter as the prepared solution is run in, left to take up waste products, and replaced with fresh solution. The cycle is repeated hourly.

diamorphine. Diacetyl morphine; ➤*heroin*.

diaphragm. Sheet of muscle separating the thorax from the abdomen. Its fibres arise from the lumbar vertebrae, the lower ribs, and the lower end of the sternum. They converge on a flat sheet of dense fibrous tissue, the central tendon. The whole structure forms a sort of dome.

When the muscle contracts, the central tendon is pulled down, the thorax is enlarged, and air is drawn into the lungs to fill the extra space. This is the most important mechanical factor in ➤*respiration*. Since the thorax is enlarged at the expense of the abdomen, the muscles of the abdominal wall simultaneously relax. If they do not relax, the diaphragm raises the pressure in the abdomen, e.g. during defecation.

The origin of the diaphragm is in the neck, from which it has descended in the course of evolution, and in the development of the individual embryo. Any organ that migrates keeps its original nerve. The *phrenic* nerve on each side is formed from spinal nerves in the neck, above the origin of the nerves of the arm. It runs downwards among the neck muscles, into the thorax beside the heart, and through the diaphragm to branch out on its under surface.

Because the phrenic nerve takes this remarkable course one may survive disruption of the spinal cord at any but the highest level. Though the whole body from the shoulders down is paralysed the diaphragm continues to work. A broken neck is fatal only if the spinal cord is torn in the upper part of the neck. On the other hand poliomyelitis may sometimes affect cells in the upper cervical region while sparing the cord lower down; then the patient needs an iron lung although his trunk and limbs are unaffected.

The phrenic nerve is easily accessible in the neck. A small operation to paralyse it prevents one side of the diaphragm from moving and so rests the lung. This used to be a common operation to give tuberculous lungs a chance to heal, but with effective drug treatment of tuberculosis it is now seldom necessary.

Diaphragmatic or hiatus ➤*hernia* is a protrusion of part of the stomach through the opening for the oesophagus.

diarrhoea. Frequent passage of watery motions. The contents of the small intestine are always liquid. The main function of the large intestine is to absorb most of the water, leaving a soft but not watery residue of faeces to be passed. If the passage through the large intestine is unduly delayed too much water is absorbed and the faeces become dry and hard and difficult to pass; that is constipation. But if the passage is too rapid, or if there is an excess of water, the faeces are still liquid when they reach the rectum and defecation is urgent and frequent.

Most diarrhoea is due to inflammation of the intestine, with excessive production of watery mucus and overactivity of the intestinal muscles both contributing to the symptoms. Inflammation can be caused by viruses (many outbreaks of gastroenteritis, especially in children), bacteria (bacterial food poisoning, bacillary dysentery), or larger parasites (amoebic dysentery, worm infestation); by irritant drugs and poisons; or by allergic reactions (food allergy, and possibly ulcerative colitis).

A saline purge (e.g. Epsom salt) works by ➤*osmosis*, retaining water in the large intestine. Inability to digest sugars or other foodstuffs causes diarrhoea in the same way (➤*carbohydrate intolerance*). In other types of malabsorption – e.g. sprue, deficiency of the pancreas – fat is not digested and causes a sort of diarrhoea.

The functioning of the intestine is much influenced by the nervous system and endocrine glands (thyroid, adrenal), and disturbances of these may cause diarrhoea. Sustained fear or anxiety can lead to overactivity of the intestine.

'Irritable colon' is a common complaint, especially of people who worry about their bowels and take laxatives. In essence it is a failure to keep a regular bowel habit, tackled by laxatives instead of a mixed diet, daily exercise, setting a regular time for opening the bowels, and ignoring an occasional failure. The rectum is irritated by hard faeces and forms too much mucus, which the constipated sufferer regards as diarrhoea.

Most of the common types of diarrhoea clear up in a day or two. The old treatment of a dose of salts or castor oil was rational because it helped to remove irritants, and by emptying the large intestine left the patient constipated for a while. It is seldom used now that most bacterial infection responds to sulphonamides or antibiotics.

Sustained diarrhoea demands attention because unless the cause is correctly treated the patient rapidly develops dehydration (especially if he vomits as well), and acidosis from loss of alkali (bicarbonate).

Whatever the cause, the first priority in treating diarrhoea is to prevent dehydration and depletion of salt and other minerals. This may be done with frequent small drinks of water, with some added sugar and a small pinch of salt, or better a prepared mixture of sugar and minerals in the correct proportions, which is sold by chemists. Drugs such as morphine and codeine to suppress bowel movement are not as much used as they once were, though with chronic diarrhoea *loperamide* is sometimes prescribed.

Traveller's diarrhoea, also known by a variety of geographical insults, often spoils a few days of a holiday. It is especially associated with warm climates and deficient hygiene. As a rule, no precise cause is established and the diarrhoea clears up in a day or two without special treatment except plenty of fluid to drink. More severe and persistent diarrhoea is likely to be caused by bacterial infection, and calls for expert advice and antibiotic therapy. Any patient unable to keep

fluids down and showing signs of dehydration (e.g. thirst, dry skin, a drawn look) probably needs hospital treatment.

A changed bowel habit always needs investigation (►*constipation*).

diastole. Phase of relaxation of the heart muscle during which the cavities of the heart are filled with blood (to be pumped out during the alternate phase, *systole*).

diathermy. Production of heat in a tissue by means of a high-frequency electric current, used for the relief of symptoms due to inflammation or stiff and painful muscles and joints.

diathesis. Hereditary or constitutional tendency to a particular type of disease. ►*predisposition.*

diet. Food is needed as fuel (►*energy*) and as raw material for growth and maintenance of the body. Even in adult life most tissues are continuously broken down and replaced, and although some of the material can be resynthesized and used again much of it is lost.

The three principal foods are *protein, fat,* and *carbohydrate.* All three can be used as fuel. Protein and carbohydrate supply the same amount of energy – about 4 Calories per gram. Fat provides 9.3 Calories per gram. But whereas fat and carbohydrate can be freely burnt, a good deal of the protein in the diet must be conserved as building material. In general, the chemical arrangement of foodstuffs differs from that of the body's own components. Digestion breaks down the food into simple compounds that are then rearranged as specifically human materials.

In addition to the three basic components, essential substances that cannot be synthesized in the body have to be supplied ready-made (►*vitamin*). The diet must also provide all the chemical elements ('minerals') found in living matter – some in minute amounts (e.g. copper, fluorine) and some in sizeable quantities (e.g. iron, calcium). Many of these minerals are poisonous in excess.

Undigested ballast (roughage) such as vegetable fibre improves the mechanical efficiency of the intestine. The great importance of this dietary factor has been generally accepted only since the mid-1970s (>fibre).

1. BALANCED DIET

The diet must provide enough fuel. At complete rest, an average man needs 1,700 Calories daily. A sedentary worker needs some 2,500 Calories, and heavy manual labour may call for twice as much. The principal ingredients of a proper adult diet are:

(a) Protein. The minimum may be below 35 grams daily. This amount of protein is found in a quart of milk, or 5 eggs, or ¼ lb of meat, fish, or cheese, or 1 lb of bread, or 2 lb of cooked peas, beans, or spinach, or 5 lb of cooked potatoes. But the bare minimum suffices only if there is enough other food to save protein from being consumed as fuel, and if the quality of the protein is right, i.e. if the amino-acids of which protein is composed are in the correct proportions. In practice these conditions are seldom met, and a reasonable diet contains twice the theoretical minimum of protein. Many proteins lack one or more amino-acids of the nine or ten that cannot be synthesized in the body (essential amino-acids), and in this respect animal foods are better than vegetable. A vegetarian diet must be well varied so that one food makes up the deficiencies of another. Because protein is used for building new tissue, children (weight for weight) need

more than adults; and at any age lost protein has to be replaced after prolonged illness, or loss of blood.

(b) Carbohydrate. Carbohydrates (starch, sugar) can theoretically provide all the body's fuel, and with few exceptions (e.g. Eskimos, who live mainly on fat and protein) a starchy staple is the main item of food, with the more expensive proteins and fats as relish. Since all digestible carbohydrates are converted to glucose in the body, the particular form of starch or sugar in the diet ought not to matter, but it has been suggested that refined sugar hastens arterial disease (>artery (1)).

(c) Fat. A diet without fat is insipid and difficult to cook. Fat provides more than twice as much energy as other foods and reduces the bulk that has to be eaten. People who live almost entirely on carbohydrate have to consume very large quantities. But fats (the term includes oils) cannot provide all the energy because the combustion of fat stops halfway unless there is also a supply of carbohydrate. Fuel in the body is ultimately oxidized to carbon dioxide and water. But this does not happen in one stage, as it would in a fire. It involves a long chain of chemical reactions. Some of the intermediate products of fat become poisonous if they are allowed to accumulate, as in >diabetes mellitus. In the presence of the products of carbohydrate breakdown, they are promptly converted to harmless substances; but in the absence of these products they persist. With severe diabetes, when carbohydrates cannot be broken down, this kind of acidosis from fat becomes dangerous.

Certain components of fat (essential fatty acids) which cannot be synthesized are needed in the same way as essential amino-acids. Vegetable oils are a better source than animal fat. Lack of essential fatty acids is another factor in arterial disease, which is much less prevalent in people whose dietary fat is mainly vegetable.

The fat-soluble vitamins (A, D, K) are found mainly in fats and oils, and a fat-free diet is likely to be deficient in them.

(d) *Vitamins.* A mixed diet generally contains enough of all the vitamins, but the unvaried diet of poor communities in many parts of the world often lacks one or more of them (►*vitamin*).

(e) *Minerals.* Any sort of diet provides most of the minerals needed, but a few of these essential ingredients are sometimes lacking. Anyone can become short of ►*salt* if he sweats much, unless salt is added to his food (some miners put salt in their beer). Most diets contain only enough ►*iron* to meet normal demands, and not enough to make up losses from bleeding. Milk and vegetables contain plenty of ►*calcium.* Deficiency of calcium is more often due to lack of vitamin D (needed for assimilation of calcium) than to shortage of calcium in the diet. Small amounts of ►*iodine* and ►*fluorine* are needed, and in many parts of the world food and drinking water do not supply enough.

The principle, discussed under ►*vitamin*, that a surplus contributes nothing useful applies to all ingredients of the diet. A varied Western diet, including animal and vegetable foods, is unlikely to lack anything important except *fibre.* It more often contains a dangerous excess of some ingredients.

2. MALNUTRITION

Millions of people in underdeveloped countries suffer from an inadequate diet. The commonest deficiency is of good protein, because the supply is limited and expensive. Clear-cut diseases are associated with lack of each of the vitamins. But a poor diet is generally poor in several respects, and malnutrition usually involves several ingredients of an adequate diet. The commonest state is not so much positive illness as failure to be really healthy, with vague symptoms such as apathy and weak resistance to infection. Malnutrition is especially serious in children, millions of whom die of what should be relatively mild infections of the intestine or lungs. ►*kwashiorkor* is a vicious form of malnutrition of children in many tropical countries.

In most of Europe, North America and other industrialized areas, malnutrition is more often due to illness than to lack of food. Failure to assimilate food from the intestine (►*malabsorption*) is a symptom of various disorders. Chronic infection makes added demands, while impairing appetite and digestion. Protein and vitamins need special attention during pregnancy and lactation. Young women occasionally develop severe malnutrition from *anorexia nervosa*, an emotional disorder with complete absence of appetite.

Old people living alone who could afford to eat well may develop malnutrition from neglecting their diet.

3. SPECIAL DIETS

There is little to recommend the traditional insipid slops of 'invalid cookery', seemingly based on a belief that enjoyable food must be harmful. Modern cookery books properly advise attractive food for the sick, a better prescription than discouraging an already depressed appetite. But bulky or flatulent foods are uncomfortable bed-fellows, and during almost any illness the sight of an overloaded tray can be nauseating. The only valid principle seems to be that sick people can best manage small, varied, and agreeable meals; quantity can be made up by eating more often than usual. This may call for much patience and ingenuity.

All kinds of unusual diets are said to promote fitness. They succeed because they encourage people in the habit of eating too much to eat less.

Indiscriminate slimming can be harmful unless the reduced diet is planned to include essentials. ▸*obesity*.

Several diseases need very special attention to diet. With some (e.g. coeliac disease, gout) certain foods are not tolerated. Some people are allergic to particular foods such as shellfish or eggs and must avoid them unless they can be desensitized by a course of injections. With diabetes the diet is planned to meet the various chemical disturbances affecting fat and carbohydrate. With all digestive disorders the diet is dictated by what the patient can manage. Special diets for kidney disease minimize the waste products to be excreted in the urine.

A major problem in dietetics is to fulfil the medical requirements of a diet while keeping a proper balance of essential ingredients. A second problem is to make the diet palatable: for instance heart disease may call for severe restriction of salt (and also of the size of meals), and salt-free food is extremely uninteresting. It is neither easy nor wise to plan special diets without the help of a dietitian.

differential diagnosis. Distinguishing between conditions with similar symptoms.

differentiation. The process in the development of living cells by which a cell acquires the special characteristics and functions of a particular tissue or organ. The cells of cancers are often poorly dif-ferentiated, like those of an early embryo; generally, speaking, the less dif-ferentiated its cells, the more dangerous the cancer. Julius Cohnheim suggested (1877) that cancers grew from remnants of undeveloped embryonic tissue. This is probably true of a kind of infantile tumour (teratoma), but most cancer probably grows from adult tissue that re-gresses to a more primitive type.

diffusion. Movement of molecules in a fluid from a zone of high concentration to one of low concentration, tending to produce an even concentration throughout, like a drop of ink in a glass of water.

digestion. Chemical rearrangement of food, essentially a breaking down of large molecules into small ones that can be absorbed through the lining of the intestine, carried in the blood to the liver, and reassembled as needed.

Carbohydrates in the diet are sugars or starches. The common unit is a *monosaccharide* with the formula $C_6H_{12}O_6$ arranged as glucose, fructose, or galactose. Ordinary sugar (sucrose) is a *disaccharide* formed by the fusion of one molecule each of glucose and fructose. Milk sugar (lactose) is a disaccharide from glucose and galactose, and maltose is formed from two molecules of glucose. Starches have large molecules which are chains of glucose molecules.

An enzyme in the saliva, *ptyalin*, begins the digestion of starch by splitting off glucose molecules from the chain two at a time – i.e. as maltose. This is unimportant. Acid in the stomach splits sucrose into glucose and fructose. In the small intestine, the enzyme *amylase* from the pancreas completes the conversion of starch to maltose. For each disaccharide, the lining of the small intestine contains an enzyme to convert it to mono-saccharides. These, and only these, are actively assimilated into the blood. In the liver, fructose and galactose are converted to glucose, which is therefore the final form of all dietary carbohydrate.

Fats are compounds of glycerol with fatty acids. The enzyme *lipase* from the pancreas splits fat into these components. The process, once thought to be complete, is now known to be only partial. Much of the dietary fat is assimilated unchanged. But first it must be made into a very fine emulsion, and this requires firstly that *some* of the fat should be split, and secondly that bile salts from the liver should be present. Both pancreas and liver must therefore be working properly for fat to be absorbed. Most of it is taken up not by the blood-stream but by the lymphatic vessels of the small intestine (lacteals) and delivered straight to the general circulation without passing through the liver, to be stored or consumed all over the body.

Protein is broken down to its component amino-acids partly in the stomach by hydrochloric acid and the enzyme *pepsin*, and partly in the small intestine by enzymes from the pancreas (trypsin) and lining of the intestine (erepsin).

Vitamins are assimilated unchanged – they have to be, for by definition they cannot be synthesized in the body. Vitamin B_{12} is not absorbed unless it is accompanied by 'intrinsic factor', formed by the normal stomach. If fat absorption is defective the fat-soluble vitamins A, D, and K may not be absorbed. In particular, vitamin K deficiency follows obstruction of the bile (obstructive jaundice).

➤*stomach*; *intestine*; *diet*.

digitalis. Foxglove and related plants: source of the most valuable drugs for the treatment of heart failure. It was known to medieval herbalists as an emetic and purgative. Only when ➤*Withering* investigated it properly in the late 18th century were these actions recognized as danger-signs of overdosage. After that it was regarded as primarily a diuretic – a drug for promoting the flow of urine – because in cases of dropsy the urine increased and fluid retained in the body vanished. The direct action of digitalis on the kidneys is now known to be of secondary importance. It is the action on the heart that really matters. Fluid retention (dropsy) is a result of inefficient work by the heart (➤*heart failure*). Digitalis increases the efficiency of the failing heart and so relieves the pressure and congestion in the veins that cause fluid to accumulate, at the same time improving the circulation of blood through the kidneys and so enhancing their output of urine. The useful actions of digitalis are firstly that it slows the heart beat, so that each beat is given time to be effective, and secondly that it strengthens the contraction of overtaxed heart muscle (though not of a healthy heart). Few drugs need more careful supervision than digitalis, because it is eliminated so slowly that doses accumulate. Overdosage makes the heart rate dangerously slow and may completely derange its rhythm.

digitoxin; digoxin. Pure substances extracted from *digitalis*, used in preference to the older preparations of digitalis leaves because the dose can be more accurately controlled.

dilatation. Widening or stretching, e.g. the reflex widening of blood vessels to increase flow, or of the pupils to admit more light to the eyes; or mechanical stretching to relieve abnormal narrowing (stricture) of a tubular organ such as the urethra. *Dilatation and curettage* is a common gynaecological procedure: under anaesthesia the muscle of the cervix uteri (normally a closed valve separating the uterus from the vagina) is gently stretched until it relaxes enough to admit a small instrument with which the lining of the uterus is peeled off. This lining is in any case only temporary: it is shed at each period and re-formed. The operation is especially valuable for diagnosis of gynaecological disorders, since microscopical examination of the lining membrane is an accurate guide to the function of the uterus and ovaries.

dimercaprol. ➤*BAL*, an antidote to certain metallic poisons.

Dioscorides (1st century AD). Greek physician in Rome. His *Materia medica* was the greatest compendium of drugs of antiquity. It remained the standard text until pharmacopoeias began to be compiled about AD 1600. And these early pharmacopoeias were little more than commentaries on Dioscorides with a few additions from Arabian and Indian sources.

diphtheria. An acute infection, nearly always of the throat but occasionally of other mucous membranes, by the diphtheria bacillus (*Corynebacterium diphtheriae*; Klebs-Löffler bacillus). In the tropics this bacterium has been known to infect the skin.

The disease is caught either from a patient or a carrier. Within a week, and sometimes after only two or three days, the patient develops fever and sore throat. The typical sign is a soft crust (membrane; pseudomembrane) that forms over the affected mucous membrane. The inflamed tissues are swollen and painful, and the lymph nodes at the sides of the neck are commonly involved, but the infection spreads no further. These bacteria stay close to their point of entry; they never invade the bloodstream. However, they release virulent toxins into the circulation, which can seriously damage the heart, the kidneys, and the nervous system. These toxins can be lethal, in addition to the danger of suffocation by the local inflammation which can obstruct the throat.

The infection responds to antibiotics, but when urgent treatment is required antitoxin is used to neutralize the toxins. The disease has been virtually eradicated by routine immunization in many countries where diphtheria was once a major cause of death among children.

diphyllobothrium. Giant tapeworm of Scandinavia, Japan and parts of North America. ➤*worms*.

diplegia. Paralysis of both arms or both legs.

diplopia. Double vision; failure to superimpose the images recorded from the two eyes, nearly always due to imbalance of the eye muscles, which should automatically keep both eyes fixed on the same object. A childhood squint does not cause diplopia because when the child is learning to interpret vision he ignores messages from one or other eye; in time the suppressed eye becomes 'lazy' and its image is no longer consciously perceived even if the squint is corrected.

dipsomania. A manifestation of alcoholism: instead of the regular daily drinking of most alcoholics the dipsomaniac has episodes of uncontrolled drinking alternating with periods of relative sobriety.

disaccharide. A sugar of which the molecules are made up of two simple sugars, e.g. *sucrose* or cane sugar, composed of glucose and fructose (➤*carbohydrate*).

disc. The intervertebral discs are tough fibrous pads with soft centres joining the individual bones of the backbone (vertebrae), making the whole structure flexible yet strong. ➤*vertebra* (1).

disinfectant. Substance used for destroying harmful microbes. The term is generally applied to chemicals used for treating things such as apparatus, sickroom furniture or drains, in contrast with ➤*antiseptics*, used on people: the only difference is that disinfectants need not be harmless to human tissue and are cheaper.

dislocation. Displacement of the moving parts of a joint, with the result that the joint is either immobilized or completely unstable.

The muscles and ligaments that hold a joint together are generally more resilient than the bone to which they are attached, and an injury is more likely to break a bone than to dislocate the joint. In most joints, dislocation is uncommon except as a complication of fracture of one of the bones forming the joint. The two main exceptions are the shoulder and the lower jaw. In the shoulder, instability is the price of extreme mobility. There is very little support below the joint, and the upper end of the humerus is easily twisted out of its shallow socket when the arm is extended above the head, e.g. in self-defence when one is thrown forwards and liable to land on one's head. It is a proverbial hazard of horse-riding. The lower jaw sometimes slips forward in its sockets at the base of the skull during a deep yawn. Injuries of the jaw push it in the opposite direction and are more likely to break the bone.

Sometimes the hip is dislocated from birth, and early treatment is required to prevent permanent disability; ➤*hip*. Dislocation of the fully developed hip is an uncommon and severe injury. Only great violence will displace this very stable joint.

The small joints of the fingers are occasionally dislocated.

Other dislocations are nearly always accompanied by fractures. They include the two best known of all fractures. Colles' fracture is essentially a fracture of the radius just above the wrist, but there is also displacement of the inner (little-finger) side of the joint. Pott's fracture is a dislocation of the ankle, a joint that cannot be dislocated without breaking one of its supporting bones.

Within a few hours of the injury it is seldom difficult to replace a dislocated bone, even, on occasion, without anaesthetics. But if treatment is delayed the surroundings swell, tissues stick together, and the condition is as hard to correct as any fracture. Mere replacement is not all, for no joint can be dislocated without tearing ligaments, and these need time – sometimes several weeks – to heal. The joint may be weakened and liable to repeated dislocation. Various operations have been evolved for strengthening or replacing weak ligaments.

disseminated sclerosis = ➤*multiple sclerosis*.

dissociation. A hysterical reaction: the patient as it were disowns what is going on in his (or more often her) mind, and may be found sleepwalking or wandering with apparent loss of memory. The multiple personalities occasionally reported are almost certainly reactions of the same type, thought to result from painful memories such as child abuse.

distal. Peripheral; further from the centre of the body or from the trunk (as opposed to *proximal*).

diuresis. Flow of urine; artificially increased flow of urine.

diuretic. Any drug used to promote a flow of urine. The kidneys filter a huge quantity of water from the blood. Most of it is reabsorbed and returned to the blood along with salt and other essentials; unwanted waste products remain in the small amount of water that is passed as urine. An excess of salt acts as a diuretic by ►*osmosis*, and in diabetics the excess of sugar has the same effect. Most diuretic drugs impede the reabsorption of salt in the kidneys. The increased output of salt carries with it a corresponding amount of water.

Diuretics are successfully used for treating heart failure, high blood pressure and many other conditions where fluid and salt are retained in the body.

diverticulitis; diverticulosis. *Diverticulosis* is the presence of small bulges or pockets at weak points in the large intestine. X-ray examination reveals such diverticula in many middle-aged people and most old people. The condition is harmless. *Diverticulitis* is inflammation of a diverticulum, with symptoms like those of appendicitis but in the wrong place, usually on the left side of the abdomen. Surgical treatment is seldom necessary; antibiotics generally control the infection.

If the inflammation persists and chronic diverticulitis develops, the symptoms may be very like those of cancer of the large intestine: changed bowel habit (sometimes diarrhoea, more often constipation), vague abdominal pain, occasionally bleeding from the rectum, and, rarely, complete obstruction. The condition has to be distinguished from cancer by X-ray investigation and direct inspection of the lower part of the intestine with a lighted tube (sigmoidoscopy). Until recently most commentaries advocated a diet with a minimum of undigested residue in order to rest the affected intestine. There is now overwhelming evidence that this was wrong and that, on the contrary, a diet with plenty of residue is needed (►*fibre*). Surgical treatment – removal of the affected segment of intestine – is reserved for severe or complicated cases.

diving. Some medical aspects are considered under ►*compressed-air sickness*.

DNA. Deoxyribonucleic acid. ►*genetics* (1).

doctor. Literally = teacher; since the 13th century, one who has attained a teacher's degree at a university. The first doctorates were conferred at Bologna. Other universities soon followed suit, and throughout Europe 'doctor' soon became synonymous with 'doctor of medicine', perhaps because he had to be distinguished from practitioners with no degree, whereas other learned professions had no untrained competitors. In most of Europe this is only colloquial usage and there is in addition a correct term for a practitioner of medicine (*médecin*, *Arzt*, *médico*, etc.). Britain is one of the countries where a doctorate is not automatically awarded on qualification; most 'doctors' have either a bachelor's degree from a university or a diploma from one of the other recognized institutions, and for them 'doctor' is a courtesy title. A doctorate in medicine can be had only some years after qualification, in recognition of research or specialized studies. Yet there is no convenient title other than *doctor* for all the people officially known as registered medical practitioners. The word should be *physician* – it is still so in America – but unfortunately this title is reserved in Britain for specialists in internal medicine (who are known in America as *internists*). The reason seems to be that three professions evolved that were not fused until the 19th century: *physicians* (the real doctors), *surgeons* (barbers), and *apothecaries* (druggists). As each attained professional status, the surgeons, having been denied recognition in the past, refused to accept the title when it was theirs and with nicely inverted snobbery clung to the title *Mr* as a mark of distinction. The apothecaries, who for centuries had been the real family doctors, had no title at all. Their own name had gone to the pharmacists; and they held licentiates and not degrees. But the courtesy title *Dr* has legal sanction. All examining bodies in Britain have to maintain standards set by the General Medical Council, and the Law recognizes only the Council's registration, not the degree or diploma by which it was obtained. To call oneself a doctor is taken to mean that one claims to be qualified and registered.

Domagk, Gerhard (1895–1964). German pathologist. From 1928 he studied hundreds of chemicals to find one which would kill invading bacteria without harming the patient. The only success of the kind had been Ehrlich's use of arsenic against syphilis. Although the germ of syphilis was delicate, the margin between poisoning the germ and poisoning the patient was narrow. Domagk was tackling a much hardier microbe, the streptococcus. Anything capable of destroying a streptococcus must, it seemed,

also destroy the patient. The solution was to interfere with a chemical process vital to the bacterium but not used by the patient's cells. This was the effect of Domagk's *prontosil*, the first ►*sulphonamide*. Domagk's new method of testing drugs in live mice was the key. With the conventional test-tube methods prontosil would have been inactive. Sulphonamides would not have been discovered, and neither would the ►*antibiotics*, because everyone would still have assumed that bacteria could not be attacked in a living patient – as Fleming, the discoverer of penicillin, pointed out.

Domagk later discovered that tuberculosis, which the sulphonamides do not affect, could be treated with ►*isoniazid*. He was awarded a Nobel Prize in 1939, but was unable to take it up until after the defeat of the Nazis, who disapproved.

dominant. Character that need be inherited only from one parent, whereas a *recessive* character does not appear unless it is inherited from both parents. ►*genetics* (2).

dopa. Dihydroxyphenylalanine, an intermediate in the natural synthesis of adrenaline, and incidentally of the pigment melanin. In the nervous system, dopa is converted first to dopamine and then to noradrenaline and adrenaline.

A derivative of dopa, methyl-dopa, is a useful remedy for high blood pressure, which is caused partly by constriction of small arteries by noradrenaline. Methyl-dopa partly replaces the usual dopa in the synthetic process, and is converted to methyl-noradrenaline. This comparatively inert substance dilutes the active noradrenaline and so reduces the constriction of arteries.

In parkinsonism (shaking palsy) there is a deficit of dopamine in the affected part of the brain. Giving dopamine or adrenaline has little effect on the disease, perhaps because they are dispersed and destroyed without reaching the target. On the other hand, *levodopa* does reach the brain, where it is converted to dopamine, and in about 75 per cent of cases it relieves the symptoms. That it does not work in 25 per cent suggests two different types of disease. Levodopa has been in use since 1968, and at present appears to be one of the most effective ways of treating parkinsonism. Levodopa is often combined with *benserazide*, which blocks the destruction of dopa by tissue enzymes.

Doppler shift. (J. C. Doppler, 1803–53, Austrian scientist.) The apparent change in frequency of waves emitted by an object that is moving in relation to an observer (e.g. the change in pitch of the sound of a motor cycle as it passes by, or the shift of colour towards red of a receding star) is a valuable aid to diagnosis. It is used to observe the flow of blood through a partly obstructed vessel or a suspect heart valve, by recording the changes in frequency of ultrasound waves as they are reflected from the moving bloodstream.

dorsal. Relating to the back.

dorsiflexion. Bending backwards; of the ankle – raising the front of the foot (plantar flexion is pointing the foot).

dose. The official dose of a drug, set out in the pharmacopoeia, is a range within which a suitable dose for most adults will be found. The correct dose in a particular case is the least that will produce the desired effect. Theoretically the dose of a drug should be related to the patient's own body weight, but in practice such accuracy is often unnecessary. And

with many drugs the size of patients varies less than individual response, which has to be gauged by trial and error, starting with a small dose. If the patient is abnormally susceptible, a dose large enough to be useful may be toxic, and another drug has to be tried.

double-blind. A technique for assessing the effects of a drug. The response of patients to the drug is compared with the response of other patients (or the same ones on another occasion) to either another drug or an inert preparation made up to look like the drug. Neither the patients nor the physician know which preparation is which, because the knowledge can falsify the experiment. ▸*research.*

Down's syndrome. A genetic disorder affecting about 1 in 700 live births, characterized by defective physical and mental growth, first described in 1866 by J. L. Down (1828–96). The straight hair, flat, sloping face and fold of skin over the inner corner of the eye suggested the name *mongolism*, now fortunately obsolete.

The condition arises when by some accident the fertilized ovum begins with 47 instead of the normal 46 chromosomes. The extra chromosome, one of the smallest (group G, number 21 or 22), is usually contributed by the mother, but occasionally by the father. The tendency of this aberration increases with maternal age. Down's syndrome affects less than 1 in 2,000 children born to mothers under 25, but about 1 in 100 to mothers over 40. Affected children are vulnerable to infection; in the past few survived childhood but nowadays about half grow up. All suffer from mental handicap, but most can be educated to look after themselves, and many to occupy themselves usefully. They are likely to do better in the country than in towns and often they have a special aptitude for looking after animals.

Chromosome tests of the parents will show whether a subsequent child is likely to be affected. Amniocentesis or similar tests early in pregnancy, whereby the embryonic chromosomes can be tested, establish the diagnosis in time for an abortion if the parents choose.

dracunculus. A kind of parasitic worm; the ►*Guinea worm.*

drainage. A common surgical procedure: provision, e.g. with a rubber tube, of a way of escape for pus or other fluid from an abscess, operation wound etc.

dream ►*sleep.*

dressing. Covering applied to a wound to protect it from further injury or infection and give it a fair chance to heal itself. Paré's dictum (16th century) still holds: 'I dressed him. God cured him.'

A gauze dressing helps to stop bleeding by providing a framework for blood-clot, with the disadvantage that it is difficult to remove the dressing without disturbing the clot. Where dry gauze would be especially liable to stick (e.g. burns) dressings impregnated with soft paraffin are useful.

The first requirement of any dressing is that it should be sterile – free from bacteria. Hospital dressings are sterilized in bulk. For domestic use, sterilized dressings with an adhesive backing are convenient. In an emergency, an inner surface of a laundered handkerchief is reasonably safe, because a hot iron destroys bacteria.

dropsy. Excess of water in the tissues; ►*oedema.*

drowning. Suffocation by water. In the ordinary sense, drowning is due to inhaling water, but a rather similar condition can arise if water from the body's own fluids accumulates in the lungs as a result of disease. An unconscious patient with a full stomach (e.g. after heavy drinking) risks inhaling fluid regurgitated from the stomach.

Drowning by sea-water has the special danger that a concentration of salt in the lungs attracts water from the blood, so that a comparatively small amount of inhaled sea-water can lead to the accumulation of a larger amount of fluid.

Often the amount of water inhaled is too little to kill the victim simply by displacing air from the lungs, and sometimes people drown without inhaling any water at all. This is because a reflex, designed to prevent foreign matter from blocking the air-passages, holds the larynx closed against the water, and the victim chokes. But these muscles of the throat relax soon after consciousness is lost, and the victim recovers if he is given a chance to breathe.

►*Artificial respiration,* mouth-to-mouth for choice, is the principal means of saving the victim's life. But neither this nor any other treatment is of the least use unless the air-passage is free of mechanical obstruction. The mouth and throat have to be cleared of weeds etc., and the patient's jaw has to be held forward to draw his tongue away from the back of his throat (this manoeuvre is the most important first-aid for unconsciousness from any cause).

drug. In non-technical language, *drug* has come to suggest a narcotic or habit-forming substance. In the technical sense, a drug is any substance taken medicinally to help recovery from sickness or relieve symptoms, or to modify any natural process in the body.

Vitamins are on the border between drugs and foods: given to improve a defective diet they are presumably foods, but in other circumstances they may count as drugs. Other substances given to make up a deficiency include *iron* for some types of anaemia, and *hormones* for disorders of glands. These relatively few drugs given to make up deficiencies of substances essential to health are perhaps the only ones that can be said to improve function directly and without risk of ill effects, because they do no more than restore the normal chemical balance. If there is no deficiency, such drugs can do no possible good, and an excess may be harmful. An overdose of iron is poisonous, and the action of most hormones is dangerously exaggerated by overdosage.

Other drugs – the great majority – act by disturbing the function of a particular tissue or organ or by interfering with a particular chemical process. The immediate effect is nearly always negative, though the result as far as the body as a whole is concerned may be positive and beneficial. It is rather like crime prevention: imprisonment is no boon to criminals, but it helps the rest of the community.

Many drugs are chemically similar to active components of living tissues. The similarity can work in at least three ways, which can be illustrated by drugs related to adrenaline, a substance concerned in the natural function of many organs. First, *isoprenaline* is an effective alternative to adrenaline; the two have similar chemical actions on the cells of the body. Second, *amphetamine* has little direct action on the cells, but the enzyme that serves to destroy adrenaline when it has served its purpose will as readily take up amphetamine, leaving any adrenaline in the tissues to continue its work; thus the net effect of isoprenaline or amphetamine is to reinforce adrenaline, though the methods are quite different. Third, *methyl-dopa* is probably taken up by other enzymes needed for the synthesis of adrenaline, which then waste their effort in synthesizing an inert compound; the net effect of this drug is to suppress the action of adrenaline.

Many widely different kinds of drug depend for their action on their ability to impersonate a natural reagent in the body. It is often impossible to say in advance whether a new product of research will reinforce or suppress the action of the substances that it resembles.

An important class of drugs is directed not at the human body but at its parasites. An ideal drug of this kind would kill bacteria etc. without any effect on human tissue. The trouble is that all life, whether human or bacterial, depends on very similar chemical processes. These drugs depend on relative rather than absolute differences – on disturbing processes that are vital to the parasite but of minor importance to man. Some of the older anti-parasitic drugs, e.g. arsenic compounds for syphilis, are poisonous to all living matter, but the parasite is rather more susceptible than the patient.

All substances – even water and oxygen – are poisonous in the sense that a gross excess is harmful. With few exceptions, all drugs are poisonous when the useful dose is exceeded, because even a 'safe' dose has unwanted effects in addition to the desired effect, and if more than the necessary dose is taken the unwanted effects mount up without any benefit to compensate for them.

The ill effects of a drug may be simply too much of what the drug is intended to do. Digitalis is given to slow a racing heart to an efficient rate. Too much digitalis slows the heart to a dangerous rate. Secondly, a drug given for its action on one organ usually affects other organs, and these secondary actions are as a rule undesirable. They have, however, led to some useful discoveries. Sulphonamides, given to control bacterial infection, have a secondary action on the amount of sugar in the blood, and another on the flow of urine. Research into these actions has produced drugs derived from sulphonamides with, respectively, a useful effect on diabetes and a powerful diuretic action, greatly increasing the amount of urine produced. In general, however, the secondary actions or side-effects of a drug are tiresome and sometimes dangerous. Thirdly, drugs can provoke allergy in the same way as other substances introduced into the body. And finally, an extremely undesirable property of many drugs is discussed in the next entry (>*drug dependence*).

The flood of new and highly active drugs since the Second World War has improved the treatment of countless diseases but has also brought new problems. Early in the 16th century, Paracelsus warned against the possible danger of giving combinations of drugs that might conflict with each other, and the danger is now very real – prescribers have to be constantly on their guard against incompatible mixtures. One drug may be a kind of antidote to another. At the best this prevents the other drug from having the desired effect, and at worst it can be dangerous. For instance, anticoagulant drugs are used to prevent blood clots from forming with arterial disease. Barbiturates inhibit anticoagulants and so increase the required dose. If the patient stops taking the barbiturate, he finds that he is then getting an overdose of the anti-coagulant. Another risk is potentiation of one drug by another, where the combined effect is greater than the sum of the two when the drugs are taken alone. This can be valuable, as with cotrimoxazole, a mixture of small doses of two antibacterial drugs which is far more active than a large dose of either ingredient alone. But other mixtures, such as pethidine with certain anti-depressants, can be lethal.

Another problem that has always existed but is much more serious with modern drugs is the difference between patients in their response to some drugs. Some people have a hereditary deficiency of an enzyme needed for inactivating a particular drug, and are unduly sensitive to the drug. This applies to several drugs used in psychiatry, which therefore have to be given very cautiously at first. Similarly a patient may develop an allergy to a drug. Such individual differences are in themselves a justification for having several drugs with similar actions on the market.

The term *bioavailability* has been coined to describe a matter of particular concern to pharmacists. It can safely be taken for granted that manufacturing and dispensing pharmacists will supply the prescribed dose of a drug, within the strict limits of accuracy and purity laid down by the Pharmacopoeia. Unfortunately it does not always follow that the correct dose will find its way into the circulation. The size of the particles of a drug affect the ease with which they are absorbed from the stomach, and it can even happen that a supposedly inert substance used to bind the particles into a tablet may react with them. Thus there are sometimes real differences between 'identical' drugs prepared by rival manufacturers.

The introduction of new drugs is discussed under ➤*research*. ➤*homoeopathy*; *naturopathy*; *placebo*.

drug dependence. This term is now preferred to *abuse*, *habit*, or *addiction* to signify a kind of illness brought on by repeated doses of certain drugs, including ill effects of the drug, a compulsive urge to go on taking it, and either demonstrable physical sickness or serious distress if the supply is cut off. With some drugs, tolerance develops so that the victim takes larger and larger doses, often far in excess of the amount that would kill anyone not used to the drug.

Clearly, this is far more than a mere *habit* which could be broken without grave trouble: for instance, some people smoke from habit, but find no difficulty in stopping, and others drink regularly from social custom, but feel no great deprivation if they go without alcohol. They may be habitual smokers and drinkers, but they are not dependent. Some other people are not so lucky, and for them giving up can be really unpleasant.

Drug *abuse* is the standard term in some countries, but sometimes a drug used quite properly can induce dependence. A patient suffering severe pain may need the relief of opiates; after a while he may become dependent, so that the drug can be discontinued only with patience and skill. This is not abuse of a drug; on the other hand, taking or prescribing any drug without good reason is, regardless of dependence.

Some years ago, *addiction* was defined too narrowly. It was said to include increasing tolerance, and physical effects (i.e. objectively demonstrable illness) of withdrawal. This definition excluded many drugs that should be considered alongside the narcotics.

Current practice is to recognize drug dependence of several types; this emphasizes the wide differences between drugs and avoids, for the time being, the stigma implicit in the terms 'abuse' and 'addiction'.

Opiates, the narcotics, are the most complete drugs of addiction and are either extracted from opium, e.g. *morphine* and *codeine*, or are chemically derived from these, e.g. *heroin* (diacetylmorphine), or are synthetically derived but related, e.g. *pethidine* and *phenazocine*. They induce a characteristic state of intoxication; the taker can tolerate larger and larger doses; the craving or urge to continue is strong enough to incite serious crime to get either the drug or the money to buy it; if the supply is suddenly cut off the victim becomes physically and even dangerously ill. Furthermore, nobody is exempt from these effects. Many kinds of drug induce true dependence in some people, but opiates can affect anyone.

Barbiturates were for many years the most widely used sedative and hypnotic drugs, and are still among the best for treating epilepsy. After regular prolonged use they tend to lose their effect and many patients can take these drugs in proper doses for years without becoming dependent. However, people who take them in increasing doses as intoxicants develop a physical dependence worse than that associated with the opiates. The symptoms include anxiety, restlessness, and epileptic fits that are sometimes fatal.

Benzodiazepines have advantages over barbiturates but induce the same kind of dependence. Alcohol is in the same category (►*alcoholism*).

Amphetamines produce a sense of elation, physical over-activity, including dangerous over-stimulation of the heart, and mental aberration, including hallucinations and occasional violence, in much the same way as *cocaine* does. However, unlike cocaine, as tolerance to amphetamines increases, the doses taken become progressively larger. There are few withdrawal symptoms with either type of drug, but cocaine addicts who stop are often profoundly depressed for a time, while amphetamine addicts sometimes develop a kind of insanity like paranoid schizophrenia. Overdoses of either can cause sudden heart failure and death.

Hallucinogens include *mescaline* from peyote (a Mexican cactus); *phencyclidine*, a veterinary anaesthetic (PCP, Angel Dust); *lysergic acid dethylamide* (LSD, acid), a synthetic drug that has been used without important results for studying schizophrenia, which its effects resemble; and *bufotenin*, a poisonous extract from South American toads. All these substances cause physical symptoms such as over-activity of the heart, blurred vision, 'shakes' and nausea. Recorded mental changes include irrational thinking, elation alternating with depression. Sometimes hallucinations, paranoia and suicidal tendencies are experienced. Advocates of hallucinogens call these effects 'psychedelic' or 'mind expanding'; to anyone else they look like self-inflicted insanity. Although the effects are so serious – they can even include lasting insanity – withdrawal symptoms are not usual. It is not unusual for the victims of these drugs to have been receiving psychiatric help before becoming drug dependent.

Glue-sniffing is a particularly distressing occurrence because many of the victims are very young. Organic solvents such as those in glue-aerosols are often closely related to anaesthetics such as chloroform, and are even more toxic. Inhaled, they induce a fleeting dream-like state of mind, followed by stupor. Over a period they cause mental deterioration and possibly fatal damage to the liver and kidneys. The habit may be difficult to break but there does not appear to be any physical dependence to cause withdrawal symptoms.

Hemp (cannabis, marihuana, etc.) is, next to alcohol and tobacco, the most popular of all habit-forming drugs. The desired effect is, like that of alcohol, to set aside harsh reality. Thought seems to be brighter but is in fact dulled and neither time nor distance can be judged. Thus anyone under the influence of hemp at the wheel of a car, for example, is very nearly as accident-prone as if he were drunk, though he is much less likely to be aggressive. There are no known withdrawal symptoms.

Tobacco is often absent from lists of drugs inducing dependence, although it must kill more people than all the other drugs listed here together, and for some, although not all, smokers it is as addictive as a narcotic. All smokers develop some tolerance to nicotine, but only some become physically dependent on it; if they stop smoking they suffer for a while from physical symptoms such as disturbed sleep and digestion in addition to more subjective changes such as irritability, depression and lack of concentration. But unlike the symptoms of withdrawing some other drugs, none of these is dangerous to health or life. However disagreeable it may be to give up smoking, it is not risky.

This list is far from complete. It includes most of the worst offenders, but any drug that modifies emotion, mood, level of consciousness or any other brain function could probably induce some degree of dependence. Beyond these, drugs that suppress or enhance any bodily function might, given time, become almost indispensable.

Of the drugs considered here, only the narcotics seem to be absolutely addictive, in that anyone taking them over a period *must* become physically dependent. The others affect only some people (admittedly a majority in the case of nicotine), which does suggest some kind of predisposition. Whether this is genetic or environmental is still open to doubt, but it does seem that some people are far more vulnerable than others.

If the drugs evoking physical dependence and, consequently, withdrawal symptoms share a common factor, it is that they resemble naturally occurring chemical transmitters of impulses in the brain, and can deputize for them, or else they can obstruct their action. In either case the natural balance is upset, and the normal supply of transmitters is adapted to the change. For example, *endorphins* are substances formed within the nervous system, of which the functions appear to include the suppression of some of the incoming signals that would otherwise evoke pain. Endorphins have been isolated and experiments have shown that they suppress pain. The narcotic drugs, such as morphine, are chemically related to endorphins and may well act by mimicry. But throughout the body, feed-back mechanisms maintain chemical equilibrium. Excess of an active substance suspends the formation of more. If, then, certain functions of endorphins are usurped by related drugs, the natural endorphins are likely to be suppressed. If the drugs are then abruptly withdrawn, functions that normally fall to endorphins are not performed at all and the patient suffers a sort of negative poisoning. Numerous habit-forming drugs can be linked in this way to substances that occur naturally in the nervous system and are presumably essential to health. All this is largely hypothetical, but there seems to be a reasonable analogy with inflammatory disorders treated with regular doses of steroids: if the doses are withheld the patient's glands stop making natural steroids, and the complete deprivation puts his life at risk.

Apart from alcohol, tobacco and glue solvents, the types of drugs mentioned here are legally available only on prescription. In many countries, including the USA, heroin is absolutely forbidden, although the ban has not stemmed illicit distribution. In Britain it can be prescribed for heart-attack victims because many physicians find that heroin does not depress the heart as morphine does, and that it can be administered over a short period without causing dependence. Heroin is also prescribed to patients with painful terminal illnesses, where dependence no longer matters, as it has fewer unpleasant effects than other drugs. But neither heroin nor cocaine may be prescribed for addicts except by specially authorized doctors in approved clinics.

The treatment of severe dependence has to be carried out under close supervision. In Britain, if a doctor thinks that a patient is addicted to a narcotic drug he must notify the responsible Chief Medical Officer at the Home Office, who keeps an index of all notified addicts. (Any doctor may refer to the index as a safeguard against prescribing narcotics for patients who are already getting them from another doctor.) Despite careful treatment, many patients relapse and some die. Quite apart from any physical effects of the drug or the means of taking it (e.g. contaminated needles), there are often grave psychological disturbances to be overcome. Of these, some may be caused by the drugs, but others may account for the patient's becoming addicted in the first place.

duct. A tube for carrying the fluid secreted by a gland.

ductless gland. Gland of which the secretion (a hormone) passes straight into the circulation; i.e. an ►*endocrine* gland, as opposed to *exocrine* gland, which has a duct to carry its secretion to a particular region, e.g. saliva to the mouth.

ductus arteriosus ►*heart* (1, 4).

dumbness. In childhood the commonest cause is deafness, which stops the child from learning to speak. Any mental disturbance that impedes learning may affect speech. In later life, a stroke may disturb either the mechanics or the mental process of speech.

Dumdum fever = ►*kala-azar*.

dumping syndrome. (More elegantly but much less often called *postcibal syndrome*.) A term applied to two conditions that sometimes complicate operations on the stomach. The contents of an intact stomach pass through the outlet (*pylorus*) at a steady pace, like a crowd at a turnstile. Some operations change this, so that the stomach deposits a meal into the small intestine too quickly, somehow causing transient discomfort, faintness, palpitations and other symptoms.

The other complication is due to an increased level of sugar in the blood following over-rapid digestion of the dumped food. The automatic response to this excess of sugar is a release of insulin to adjust the level; this may be so abrupt as to overdo the effect and leave the patient with an attack of faintness and other symptoms while the sugar returns to its normal level.

duodenal ulcer ►*peptic ulcer*.

duodenum. The first part of the ►*intestine*, between the stomach and the jejunum. The name ('twelve') refers to the length, twelve finger-breadths.

Dupuytren, Guillaume (1777–1835). French military surgeon. His name is given to a fracture of the radius a hand's breadth above the wrist with dislocation of the lower end of the ulna, a very unstable combination of injuries often needing operation; and to the contracture described below.

Dupuytren's contracture. Thickening of the fibrous lining of the palm (the *palmar aponeurosis*) which makes it impossible to straighten the fingers. Earlier surgeons had mentioned the condition, but Dupuytren gave the first full account of it in 1831. It is commonest in elderly men; it may be associated with other disorders of fibrous tissue or rheumatism. Many causes have been suggested, including pressure on the palms and alcoholism, but none has yet been proved. It is probably a symptom of a systemic disorder rather than a purely local condition. It can be relieved by removing the aponeurosis, but the present trend is towards less drastic measures.

dura mater. Parchment-like covering of the brain and spinal cord; the outer layer of the ►*meninges*.

dwarf. On average, children grow to a

height half-way between their parents and the average of the population, but there is wide variation, and even tall parents may have a small but perfectly normal child. A true dwarf is abnormally small because of some defect. The most familiar type – the circus midget – has ►*achondroplasia*: the growth of his long bones is defective, but he is normal in all other respects. A much rarer type is due to disorders of the ►*pituitary* gland with lack of growth hormone. In addition, almost any chronic disease of childhood may interfere with normal growth.

dys-. Prefix = 'bad'; in many medical terms the implied sense is *difficult* or *deformed*. *Dys*-compounds not separately defined below include dys-*arthria* (impaired speech), -*chezia* (constipation), -*kinesia* (inco-ordination), -*pepsia* (indigestion), -*plasia* (defective development), -*tocia* (difficult labour), -*trophy* (defective nutrition of an organ).

dyscrasia. In classical medicine: faulty balance of the four humours, supposed to be the fundamental cause of illness. Later: a constitutional disorder.

dysentery. The original meaning is diarrhoea with blood and mucus, together with pain and *tenesmus* (unproductive straining). In this sense of the word, dysentery is a collection of symptoms indicating severe irritation of the large intestine, of which the possible causes might range from food poisoning to cancer.

In current usage, dysentery means infection of the large intestine either by a protozoon, *Entamoeba histolytica* (amoebic dysentery), or by bacteria of the genus *Shigella* (bacillary dysentery). These infections do not necessarily produce all the symptoms of the first definition.

The large protozoon *Balantidium* is a rare cause of dysentery. The intestinal forms of ►*bilharzia* are common in many warm countries; this infection may be called chronic dysentery. Malaria is often blamed for dysentery, but what appears to be malarial dysentery is more likely to be bacillary dysentery added to an attack of malaria.

1. AMOEBIC DYSENTERY

Entamoeba histolytica resembles the amoeba of the school biology class. It is just sufficiently evolved to count as an animal; a creature consisting of a single cell about 25 microns (1/1000 in) in diameter, which is little more than a living blob of jelly with a nucleus. It feeds by engulfing particles of human tissue, red blood cells for choice, and it can broach and enter the lining membrane of the intestine. It reproduces by splitting into two halves, each of which grows into a mature amoeba. This easy life is possible only while the parasite is inside a human body. During an attack of amoebic dysentery large numbers of amoebae are ejected in the stools and most of them must die. But as the attack settles and the stools become less fluid, amoebae which have not already invaded the mucous membrane may be unable to do so. These take on a new form. They become *cysts*, like the spores of some bacteria and other simple plants. A cyst is a round, inert body, usually with several (2–4) nuclei. It makes no demands on its environment, for it neither feeds nor reproduces. In this form the parasite can live for weeks without human company.

The disease is contracted by swallowing food (e.g. raw vegetables) or water contaminated with these cysts. This is most likely to happen in places where human excrement is used as manure, but unless ideal standards of hygiene are maintained amoebic dysentery can occur anywhere. It is common in the tropics and subtropics, and fairly rare elsewhere.

The natural history varies greatly from case to case. Most of the people who are infected – in some areas over 50 per cent of the population – have no symptoms at all. They come to light only when cysts are found by microscopic examination of the stools, which in the tropics is as much a routine test as measuring the blood pressure. The cysts which they pass can be carried by flies, or, when they have dried, as dust in the wind. When someone else has swallowed them the cysts emerge from their 'hibernation' and become active amoebae again.

Comparatively few people suffer a full-blown attack of dysentery. Usually the symptoms are much vaguer: aches, which may suggest appendicitis; feeling off-colour; occasional diarrhoea; even constipation. The patient may go on like this for years, never really ill but never quite well; or he may have attacks of real dysentery from time to time. This, then, is one of several diseases which can keep people who live in the tropics constantly below par (▸*tropical diseases*).

The most important complication is infection of the liver by amoebae which enter the veins of the intestine and are carried to the liver in the portal vein. Amoebic abscesses may be formed, causing fever, and pain over the liver. Spread of infection from the liver to more distant organs (e.g. lung) is possible but rare.

Prevention is the best remedy for this disease. Proper sanitary facilities and habits and care in the handling of food prevent the transmission of the amoebae, but against the social and economic background of many tropical countries amoebic dysentery is unlikely to be eradicated for a long time.

Various drugs can be used for treating the infection. Two or more, acting against the amoebae in different ways, are commonly given. One of the oldest and most effective is *emetine*, derived from ipecacuanha. But emetine is safe only in small doses. *Metronidazole*, originally meant for treating *trichomonas*, is the best available drug against amoebic dysentery.

Intestinal bacteria which are normally harmless can set up severe infection in a mucous membrane already damaged by amoebae, and many of the symptoms of amoebic dysentery are due to secondary infection of this kind. It is often impossible to eradicate the amoebae until the secondary infection has been cured. This can be done with sulphonamides, but certain antibiotics, notably the tetracyclines, are effective not only against these bacteria but against the amoebae themselves. Certain drugs used against malaria can also be used here. Of these, chloroquine is especially successful with amoebic disease of the liver.

2. BACILLARY DYSENTERY

The intestinal bacilli are a large family of microbes adapted to a parasitic life in the large intestine. Some are quite harmless as long as they remain in the intestine; in their countless millions they form a large part of its normal contents. The colon bacillus, which everyone harbours from early infancy, is dangerous only if it strays, e.g. to the kidneys. But two groups cause disease in the intestine itself. These are *Salmonella*, of which different species are responsible for typhoid fever and much bacterial food poisoning, and *Shigella*, the germs of bacillary dysentery. An important distinction is that infection with *Salmonella* may be widespread in the body, whereas *Shigella* infections are confined to the intestine.

The severity of bacillary dysentery varies with the species of *Shigella*. The worst type, Shiga dysentery, is common in the Far East. This can be a fulminating disease almost as violent as cholera, with profuse diarrhoea, bleeding, and dehydration. Flexner dysentery is rather less severe. It is common in all warm countries, and there are occasional outbreaks in Britain, most often in institutions. The usual dysentery of temperate climates is the Sonne type, which is much milder than the others. In a typical case the only symptom is diarrhoea lasting at the most a few days.

An attack may last only a day or two with a Sonne infection or some weeks with the severer types, but even without treatment a healthy adult nearly always recovers, though he may be very ill for a while. Dysentery in small children is a different matter, for their reserves of water and salts are quickly depleted. In tropical countries dysentery is a leading cause of death among children.

In Britain dysentery is important mainly as a cause of outbreaks of diarrhoea in schools. The children carry the infection on their fingers; insuring that they wash after using the toilet guards against spreading the trouble.

The first consideration in treating dysentery is to replace lost water and salts, by mouth for choice, by injection if needed. Antibacterial medication is usually reserved for the more serious cases.

dyslexia. Word-blindness: failure to relate spoken to written words. Typical symptoms are writing letters or words backwards, slow reading, poor handwriting and chaotic spelling, all despite otherwise average or high intelligence. There appears to be faulty communication between the left and right sides of the brain. Some 4 per cent of children are said to be dyslexic, boys outnumbering girls by 3 to 1.

Although dyslexia was first identified in 1883, until quite recently the affected children were often subjected to punishment, ridicule, and 'could-do-better' reports. But with expert tuition many can reach their full potential. It may console them to know that two of the greatest geniuses in history, Leonardo da Vinci and Albert Einstein, had the same trouble.

dysmenorrhoea. Pain with menstrual periods, mainly in the lower abdomen or the small of the back. Secondary (symptomatic) dysmenorrhoea in women who have previously had normal periods can arise from a whole range of gynaecological disorders, and is treated by identifying and dealing with the cause. Much the commoner disorder is *primary dysmenorrhoea*, affecting girls from their first period or soon after. Neither the cause nor even the source of the pain is known, although this must be the commonest ailment (except perhaps acne) of adolescent girls and young women. Pain at the start of a period is vaguely ascribed to reduction of blood-flow by spasm of the uterus (a sort of anginal pain), and pain that comes on later to congestion, and it is true that the early type of dysmenorrhoea is sometimes relieved by drugs that relax spasm, and the later type by lying down, which may help to prevent blood from gravitating to the pelvis. Many cases respond to treatment with hormones, especially those that prevent ovulation (the contraceptive pill). This suggests defective balance of the sex hormones as an underlying cause.

Severe primary dysmenorrhoea can be incapacitating at the height of the attack, but it does not lead to any worse trouble, and its tendency is to get gradually better. Few cases persist after the birth of the first child, and some improve after marriage but before pregnancy. This could be an argument in favour of a hormonal cause or, as some people believe, of an emotional cause. In fact it could be either or both, because the production of hormones and the emotional state are inextricably tangled. Considering that emotional disturbance can completely stop the menstrual periods it would not be surprising if it contributed to painful periods. Although the pain certainly has a physical basis, the amount of distress it causes may well depend on emotional factors. Anything to do with sex is emotionally charged, and if dysmenorrhoea is commoner and more severe in our society than in others, our social taboos and religious teaching may well be to blame.

dyspareunia. Painful coitus. The condition may be secondary, i.e. a symptom of some other disorder, such as inflammation or a structural defect. In men this is the only kind of dyspareunia, the likeliest cause being inflammation of the foreskin. In women there are many causes of secondary dyspareunia, such as an unusually well-developed hymen, inflammation of the vagina or urinary bladder, and shrinkage of the lining of the vagina after the menopause. All these conditions are amenable to treatment, and when the cause of the difficulty has been dealt with, the symptom itself can be expected to disappear.

Primary dyspareunia is due to involuntary contraction to the muscles around the vagina, sometimes making coitus not just difficult but physically impossible. It is a defensive reflex, perhaps the aftermath of painful experience, perhaps due to conscious or unconscious aversion to sex. The ignorance and clumsiness of a young husband is a common cause. Patience and tact are needed to allay the patient's fears – with, of course, adequate medical investigation to exclude physical causes.

dysphagia. Difficulty in swallowing, a symptom of blockage or muscle spasm in the throat or gullet.

dyspnoea. Difficulty in breathing; undue shortness of breath; sometimes defined as awareness of the effort of breathing. Its essential character is that the effort is inappropriate. Nobody is more short of breath than a runner at the end of a race, but that does not count as dyspnoea because the effort is appropriate, it quickly passes, and it causes no real distress. Dyspnoea arises if the circulation through the lungs is sluggish, so that the lungs are not given a chance of oxygenating the blood at the required rate (as with heart failure); if the flow of air in and out of the lungs is impeded (asthma, bronchitis); if the blood cannot carry enough oxygen (anaemia); if the supply of oxygen is limited (high altitudes).

E

ear

1. OUTER (EXTERNAL) EAR

The *auricle* or *pinna* – the visible part of the ear – has a core of elastic cartilage, which does not extend down to the lobe (lobule). Several vestigial muscles are attached to the auricle; they represent muscles which other animals use to amplify and locate sounds. The canal (*external auditory meatus*) is directed inwards and forwards. It is about 3 cm long, and ends at the ear-drum. Since the canal is not quite straight the auricle has to be pulled back and up before the drum can be examined. The canal is widest where it meets the drum; thus the objects which children push into their ears can be difficult to remove. The sweat glands of the canal are modified to secrete a kind of wax.

Much nonsense has been talked about the shape of the auricles, which does not often indicate anything of importance. But protruding ears can be a source of real misery to a child, and the appearance can be greatly improved by plastic surgery.

The three common afflictions of the canal are small boils, which can be extremely painful; accumulation of wax causing temporary deafness; and foreign bodies such as beads. All are easy enough to manage given the right tools; but the ear-drum is delicate, and unskilled probing in the canal can do irreparable harm.

2. MIDDLE EAR

The middle ear is a cavity in the temporal bone, a part of the skull. Its outer wall is the tympanic membrane, the fibrous drum-head of the ear-drum. The cavity is bridged by three tiny bones which transmit the vibration of the membrane to the inner ear. At the back of the cavity is a small hole leading to the *mastoid antrum*, a hollow in the bone immediately behind the ear. In front is the opening of the *Eustachian tube*, leading to the back of the nose, by which the middle ear communicates with the outer air. This communication ensures that the air pressure is the same inside and outside the drum.

Inflammation in the nose causes the mucous membrane of the tube to swell. If the tube is completely blocked hearing is impaired and the ear aches. More seriously, infection can spread up the tube to the middle ear. Pus cannot escape by the congested tube, and the pressure rises and causes a violent earache (➤*otitis media*). The infection may spread still further back and involve the ➤*mastoid* antrum. Untreated, these are very dangerous conditions. They usually respond to antibiotics, but may need prompt surgery. Earache, especially in a child, is an emergency.

➤*Otosclerosis* is a familial disorder in which an abnormal deposition of bone in the middle ear interferes with the movement of the small bones – it is treated surgically.

3. INNER EAR

(i) *Hearing*. The inner ear is a small but very elaborate structure deeply embedded in the temporal bone. It includes two distinct organs, one for hearing and the other for balance. The first is the *cochlea*, a snail-shaped container for the *organ of Corti*, in which vibration (sound) produces nervous impulses for transmission to the brain. The receiving cells are arranged on a flat membrane which divides the cochlea into two spiral compartments. The fibres of this membrane gradually increase in length towards the apex of the spiral, which suggested to Helmholtz that they acted as resonators like the undamped strings of a piano – if the dampers of a piano are raised with the pedal the appropriate strings will take up their note from another instrument or a voice. This theory was accepted for about a century, but has lately been rejected.

The slightest movement of the organ of Corti initiates an electrical current. The greater the movement, the higher the voltage, up to about 5 mV. This is quite unlike a nervous impulse, which is a single or repeated discharge of fixed amplitude.

High notes, i.e. rapid vibrations, die out near the beginning of the spiral. The lowest notes are carried the length of the organ of Corti to the apex of the spiral. A note of any given pitch always dies out at the same level, opposite the same cells. The sum of the electrical currents produced is an electrical replica of the vibrations of the original sound: the organ of Corti behaves exactly as a microphone or a pick-up. But this electrical record cannot be relayed directly to the brain, if only because a nerve fibre can transmit only a few hundred impulses per second whereas a high note would need several thousand. What the brain apparently identifies is the distance that a particular sound travels along the organ of Corti. Each level in the organ has a corresponding pathway (nerve fibre) to the

brain, so different pathways from the ear transmit different frequencies. Louder sounds produce more impulses per second. Low notes stimulate not only the cells to which they are carried, far round the spiral, but also the cells on the way. Higher notes, which do not travel so far in the cochlea, stimulate fewer cells. The brain evidently gets much more information than it needs, and there must be some still unidentified means of suppressing unwanted impulses.

The range of a young ear is about 10 octaves, say from ½ octave lower than a piano to 2½ octaves higher. It is most sensitive to the upper 3 octaves of the piano, and it can also best distinguish pitch in this range. (The fundamental tone of a 64-foot organ pipe is too low to be heard; it is the harmonics that are audible.)

Throughout adult life even a healthy ear becomes gradually less sensitive and it is the highest notes – which stimulate the fewest cells – that are most affected. The fundamental tone of a woman's speaking voice is around middle C; of a man's, an octave lower. Both are below the most sensitive range of the ear and well below the range that is normally lost with age. But the quality or *timbre* of a sound depends not on the fundamental but on higher pitched accompanying sounds. Without these it is impossible to distinguish between vowels. And consonants, on which intelligible speech so much depends, are very high-pitched. Thus, if the higher frequencies are lost, speech may be heard but not understood.

(ii) *Balance*. The part of the inner ear concerned with balance, the *vestibular apparatus*, is in two parts. The sensitive cells of the *otolith organ* have fine hairs with chalky particles suspended from

external ear | middle ear | inner ear

incus

stapes

malleus

semicircular canals (balance)

temporal bone

auditory nerve

cochlea (hearing)

Eustachian tube

tympanum

external auditory meatus

Ear (diagrammatic)

them. They record the gravitational pull on the hairs, which varies in different groups of hairs with different positions of the head. This information is analysed in the cerebellum to give the position of the head, and collated with information from other sources such as eyes and joints.

Secondly, the *semicircular canals*, three on each side, lie in three planes at right angles to each other, and also have cells with fine hairs. They record not position but movement of the fluid in the canals. This takes place when there is acceleration in the plane of the canal. In view of the position of the canals acceleration in any direction must affect at least one pair. Rotary movements have the greatest effect. When the rotation stops the fluid in the canals continues to move, giving

the sensation that the head is being turned in the opposite direction. In trying to correct this apparent disturbance of balance the subject may fall down. This type of giddiness, with a false sense of movement, is called *vertigo*.

The most important function of these balance organs is to regulate the eye muscles so that an object can be held in view despite movement of the head. Balance itself is also important, but there are several other mechanisms involved (>*posture*). The impression with vertigo that the surroundings are moving comes from the disturbed reflexes between ear and eye. The ear signals, wrongly, that the head is turning, and the eyes flicker in an attempt to keep the passing scene in focus. The flickering movement is called *nystagmus*.

4. AUDITORY NERVE

Hearing and balance are conveyed in the acoustic and vestibular divisions of the auditory (8th cranial) nerve. The nerve runs across the floor of the skull into the brain-stem just below the pons. Here the impulses are relayed to consciousness and to various reflex pathways.

Disorders of this nerve cause symptoms such as vertigo, hissing or ringing in the ear (*tinnitus*), and deafness, which are also common symptoms of trouble in the ear itself. The diagnosis of these symptoms is briefly discussed under ►*deafness*.

The auditory nerve is easily damaged by pressure with head injuries, meningitis, or bleeding, abscess, or tumour of the brain. It can be affected by various drugs, including *aspirin*, *quinine*, and *streptomycin*. Certain viruses have a special affinity for the auditory nerve: nerve-deafness is a rare complication of *measles* (which can also give trouble by way of the Eustachian tube); and *German measles* in a pregnant woman can destroy the auditory nerves of the embryo.

earache. A bad earache is one of the most distressing of all symptoms. The membrane of the ear-drum is very sensitive. If the Eustachian tube is blocked, e.g. with a cold in the nose, the air pressure inside the drum cannot be balanced with the atmospheric pressure. Changes of atmospheric pressure, as in mountain railways or aircraft, may then be painful. Similarly the pressure of wax or a foreign body such as a bead in the ear can cause earache, especially after unskilled attempts to remove the obstruction. Even a very small boil in the canal of the ear is enough to cause severe pain, from spread of the inflammation to the drum rather than from direct pressure.

The most violent earache is due to inflammation inside the drum (*otitis media*), which nearly always arises from spread of infection along the Eustachian tube from the nose. Pus is formed under pressure which may be enough to burst through the inflamed membrane, in which case the ear discharges and the pain is relieved; otherwise the pus may spread to the *mastoid* bone behind the ear.

Pain apparently in the ear may in fact arise in a diseased tooth or still further afield.

All the conditions likely to cause earache respond well to early treatment, but little can be done for an earache until the cause has been determined. Since one of the conditions – acute otitis media – is extremely dangerous a painful ear needs to be examined as soon as possible.

Eaton agent. A kind of *mycoplasma*, a very simple bacterium previously classified as a virus, causing a common type of pneumonia formerly known as *primary atypical pneumonia*. Unlike true virus infections this disease responds to treatment with some antibiotics. Even without treatment it is much less dangerous than other types of pneumonia.

ecchymosis. Bruise; bleeding into the skin either from injury or from spontaneous leaking of blood as in the rashes of some fevers and in disorders of blood-clotting.

ECG = ►*electrocardiogram*.

ECHO. A group of viruses (Enteric Cytopathic Human Orphan). ►*virus* (1).

echography ►*scan*.

eclampsia. Convulsions occurring at the end of pregnancy as a result of toxaemia. ►*toxaemia of pregnancy*.

ECT = ▸*electroconvulsive therapy*.

ectoderm. Layer of cells in an ▸*embryo* from which the skin and nervous system develop.

ectopic. In an abnormal anatomical situation. *Ectopic pregnancy* occurs when a fertilized ovum, instead of passing down the Fallopian tube and implanting itself in the lining of the uterus, settles in the tube or elsewhere. Such a pregnancy seldom lasts more than 2 or 3 months, though cases have been reported in which an infant has survived in the cavity of the abdomen for long enough to be born live – of course by Caesarean section. In most cases the embryo dies early and is absorbed. Occasionally the Fallopian tube bursts and bleeds, and an immediate operation is needed to repair the damage.

ectopic beat = extrasystole; ▸*arrhythmia*.

eczema. A group of diseases, with inflammation of the skin, itch, vesicles or bullae (small or large blisters) that may at some stage exude fluid, and scale formation. Inflammation due to infection by viruses, bacteria or fungi (e.g. herpes, impetigo, ringworm) is not included. Most authorities consider eczema as identical with ▸*dermatitis*. The convention of separating the two, adopted here, may avoid the popular fallacy of regarding all dermatitis as an occupational disease. The term eczema as used here applies only to disorders thought to be constitutional rather than due to contact with particular agents. Some common patterns are:

1. *Atopic eczema*, which means practically the same as allergic eczema, is often associated with allergic conditions such as hay fever and asthma, but has not itself been proved to be an allergy. It commonly starts in infancy, and although as a rule it clears up before puberty it sometimes persists into adult life. Infants with atopic eczema could not be vaccinated against smallpox because of violent, sometimes fatal reactions. With the worldwide eradication of smallpox the problem no longer arises, but these children still have to be kept away from anyone with herpes simplex (cold sores), to which they are also vulnerable. As the skin tends to dry out, emollient creams and ointments are needed, generally reinforced with steroids.

2. *Seborrhoeic eczema* usually confines itself to the scalp, with the formation and shedding of greasy scales (dandruff). In only a few severe cases it spreads to involve the eyebrows, sides of the nose, ears and front of the chest. Various forms of treatment are mentioned under ▸*dandruff*.

3. *Nummular (discoid) eczema* affects middle-aged or elderly people, men more than women. The typical lesions are reddish discs 1–2 cm across, symmetrically on the limbs and, rather less often, on the trunk. Though they may remain dry, some cases are complicated by oozing and secondary infection. Some itching is usual though not necessarily constant. This type of eczema is apt to vanish as rapidly and mysteriously as it appeared, though it may return later. The cause is unknown, but it may follow emotional or physical stress. Steroid ointments are usually effective.

4. *Varicose eczema*, more correctly *hypostatic* or *stasis* eczema, is a mild inflammation and scaling with brown discoloration of the skin of the lower legs, especially around the ankles. If neglected

this can lead to bacterial infection and ulceration. It appears to arise from poor circulation, with stagnation of blood. Though it is often associated with varicose veins this is not always the case. Support such as elastic stockings is usually added to treatment of the skin itself.

5. *Lichen simplex* (neurodermatitis) appears as patches of thickened, sometimes pigmented skin. The main symptom is itch, and most of the skin condition is caused by constant rubbing and scratching. It seems to be due mainly to emotional stress.

EEG = ►*electroencephalogram.*

effort syndrome (Da Costa's syndrome, 'disordered action of the heart'). A form of anxiety neurosis, with symptoms suggestive (at least to the patient) of heart disease: pain over the heart, palpitation, breathlessness, fatigue. The pain is due to tension of the pectoral muscles, and the other symptoms are familiar accompaniments of anxiety. The heart is normal, and the symptoms vanish with the source of anxiety, if it can be eradicated. This was a common complaint during the First World War, but is now a rarity. However, many patients complain of chest pain, which they assume to be cardiac, for which no physical cause can be found; perhaps this is sometimes a modification of the same syndrome.

effusion. Leakage of fluid into a body cavity (chest; abdomen) due to inflammation or congestion.

ego. According to ►*Freud*, that part of the self or personality that keeps in touch with the material world; the conscious mind. It holds the balance between instinct (the *id*) and conscience (the *superego*).

Ehrlich, Paul (1854–1915). German scientist. One of the pioneers of bacteriology, he also distinguished himself in several other branches of medical science. Ehrlich's discoveries included:

1. A method of staining and identifying the bacilli of tuberculosis;

2. A method of assaying the potency of diphtheria antitoxin, essential to correct dosage;

3. A rational theory of how the antitoxin worked, and arising from this study a theory to explain the whole process of ►*immunity* to infection as a chemical combination of antigens and antibodies, for which he received a Nobel Prize in 1908;

4. The drug salvarsan (606), later modified to the safer compound neosalvarsan, the first drugs to be prepared for treating the cause of a disease – in this case, syphilis.

All subsequent work on immunity and allergy springs directly from Ehrlich's research, and his salvarsan is the prototype of scores of drugs now used against infection.

Einthoven, Willem (1860–1927). Dutch physiologist, of Leyden, awarded a Nobel Prize in 1924 for his invention of the electrocardiogram.

elastic tissue. Ordinary connective tissue with the addition of many fibres of the protein *elastin*; it is like draper's elastic in which cotton weave is laced with rubber threads. This tissue is found in some ligaments and in the walls of arteries.

elbow. Two joints are combined at the elbow: a hinge between the humerus and ulna, and a ball-and-socket between the humerus and radius. A notch in the shaft of the ulna turns on a fixed roller (*trochlea*) at the lower end of the humerus, and a shallow socket at the top of the radius moves round a fixed ball (*capitulum*) at the outer side of the trochlea. The ulnar joint can only be bent or straightened. The ball-and-socket allows the radius to be twisted at the elbow in pronation of the forearm. This movement is described under ►*radius*.

Fractures and dislocations of the elbow are common, singly or together. The notch in the ulna is deep, and if it is wrenched free of the humerus one or other bone is likely to be damaged. Usually the ulna, carrying the radius with it, is forced backwards. The vessels and nerves in front of the joint are then stretched against the lower end of the humerus and may be injured. A fracture of the lower end of the humerus with backward displacement has the same effect. Thus the complications may be more serious than the original injury. If the upper end of the ulna is fractured and the radius remains intact, the deformity of the ulna dislocates the radius; this injury may be harder to treat than fracture of both bones. This joint is more liable than any other to remain stiff after treatment. The correct anatomical position of the bones can usually be restored, by manipulation or operation, but the functional result is often disappointing.

electrocardiogram (ECG). A record of the electrical changes in the heart muscle. The currents are very small and can be detected only with a highly sensitive galvanometer. Such an instrument was invented in 1903 by Einthoven, who was awarded a Nobel Prize in 1924.

Currents were originally recorded across three pairs of electrodes: both wrists; each wrist in turn with left ankle. The tracings from these three standard leads give a good impression of the heart as a whole. The most important refinement of Einthoven's work is the use of additional electrodes placed on the chest wall; these may pick up small defects which would be obscured with the standard leads, and also localize them.

Although the ECG shows no more than the intermittent passage of electrical impulses in the heart, the tracings provide detailed information about the physical condition and functioning of the heart muscle. Disturbances of the natural rhythm are precisely shown, and damage to the muscle, e.g. caused by disease of the coronary arteries, can be localized. It is one of the most useful diagnostic aids after a suspected heart attack, both in the early stages to show whether and to what extent the heart is affected, and later to indicate the patient's progress. An ECG recording made during graduated exertion, e.g. on a static bicycle or treadmill, is a valuable test of fitness and may expose abnormalities not seen on the resting cardiogram.

electroconvulsive therapy (ECT). Treatment of mental illness by applying a small electric shock to the scalp. This causes a brief loss of consciousness and, with the original method of applying the treatment, a convulsion like an epileptic seizure. The convulsion had nothing to do with the efficacy of the treatment, and though the patient remembered nothing of it, there was a risk that it might cause him to injure himself while unconscious. Furthermore, the very idea of ECT alarms most patients. The present method is to give a light anaesthetic and a muscle relaxant, which suppress the convulsion but preserve the useful effect of the treatment. Nobody knows how ECT works, but it remains one of the best ways of treating severe depression, and it is sometimes effective with other types of mental illness.

electroencephalogram (EEG). A record of electrical events in the brain. Nerve cells generate small electric currents that can be picked up from the surface of the scalp and shown on a cathode-ray tube. By using several leads from different parts of the scalp the electrical patterns from different regions of the brain can be studied.

The interpretation of the EEG is still empirical. Certain patterns are regularly found with normal brains, and other patterns suggest some interference with normal function. So far, the greatest value of the EEG has been in confirming the diagnosis of epilepsy and distinguishing between certain types of epilepsy. In some other disorders of the brain it may help to locate the trouble.

electrolyte balance. Strictly speaking, electrolytes are compounds such as acids, bases and salts that can be decomposed by an electric current into electrically charged particles (*ions*), but the term is loosely applied to the ions themselves: e.g. positively charged *cations* of sodium and potassium and negatively charged *anions* of chloride and bicarbonate. These are all essential to life, and their concentration in the body fluids has to be kept constant by balancing intake with output.

In health this should look after itself. A reasonable diet provides the necessary intake, and the kidneys eliminate any surplus. With impairment of the kidneys, including failure by the heart to maintain an adequate circulation through them, sodium is retained, together with water. Sweating and vomiting deplete the store of sodium. Vomiting, and especially diarrhoea, can cause severe loss of potassium, as can some drugs used to eliminate an excess of sodium and water. Loss of water, sodium and potassium is what kills people with cholera; infusions to replace them are life-saving.

Other essential electrolytes include the cations calcium and magnesium and the anions bicarbonate and phosphate. *Acidosis* and *alkalosis* are largely expressions of disturbed balance of bicarbonate ions and carbon dioxide.

electromyogram (EMG). A record of nerve impulses to muscles and the response of the muscle, for the diagnosis of faults of nerve conduction and muscle contraction.

elephantiasis. Gross thickening of the skin and underlying connective tissue due to chronic obstruction of the lymphatic vessels, usually by thread-worms (▶*filaria*).

embolism. Blockage of an artery by an *embolus* (fragment of blood-clot, air bubble etc.) carried in the blood-stream. The effect of embolism depends on the size of the obstructed vessel, the presence or absence of alternative routes for the circulation of blood beyond the stoppage, and most of all on the importance of the tissue, if any, deprived of blood. Embolism of a small artery in an area with a good network of arteries has no ill effects. Embolism of an artery of the brain is one of the causes of *stroke*.

Embolism is commonly due to a fragment of clotted blood from a vein, carried through the heart to a lung. The usual effect is a kind of pneumonia in the affected zone; but a blockage of a main artery may be rapidly fatal. Some lives have been saved by surgical removal of large fragments of blood-clot from arteries in the lungs. ▶*end-artery*.

embolus. Clot, bubble etc. blocking an artery, causing ➤*embolism.*

embryo. In human biology: an unborn offspring from the time of fertilization until the time, some two months later, when it is sufficiently developed to be unmistakably human. (For the rest of pregnancy it is known as a foetus.) During the first month a human embryo much resembles that of any other vertebrate; during the second month, that of any other mammal.

An embryo starts as a fertilized *ovum,* a single cell 0.1 mm in diameter, just large enough to be seen with the naked eye. This small object is much larger than other cells of the human body. By the time it has travelled down the Fallopian tube and implanted itself in the lining of the uterus it is about a week old. Until then it has no means of growing larger, but its one large cell divides into two smaller cells, then the two into four and so on until a colony of 100 or more cells has been formed, the whole mass (*blastocyst*) the size of the original ovum. From now on the embryo can be nourished by diffusion of raw materials (water, oxygen, glucose, amino-acids, salts etc.) from the mother's blood, and it grows very quickly.

The embryo gets its nourishment from the mother through the outer layer of cells of the blastocyst. Later, this layer forms the *placenta* and one of the enveloping membranes of the foetus, the *chorion.*

In the *inner cell mass* of the blastocyst, two bubbles are formed side by side, with a double layer of cells between. One bubble will form the inner enveloping membrane of the foetus, the *amnion.* (The two membranes, chorion and amnion, make up a two-layered

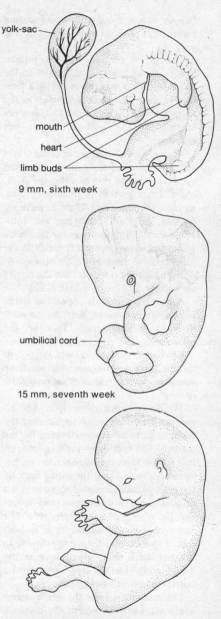

yolk-sac

mouth
heart
limb buds

9 mm, sixth week

umbilical cord

15 mm, seventh week

30 mm, end of eighth week

215

bag in which the foetus floats during pregnancy.) The second bubble is the *yolk-sac*.

The embryo proper – the new human being – grows from the cells between the two bubbles. At first this is simply a two-layered disc. The layer belonging to the amnion forms the *ectoderm*. The layer belonging to the yolk-sac forms the *endoderm*.

At a very early stage the mid-line – longitudinal axis – of the embryo is marked off by a straight rod of cells, the *notochord*. Later growth is practically symmetrical on either side of the notochord. In man, as in all vertebrates, the notochord mostly disappears as the backbone grows (►*skeleton*) but traces persist in the intervertebral discs. For a time the developing backbone is longer than the rest of the embryo and forms a distinct tail.

A new layer of cells appears at either side of the notochord, between the ectoderm and endoderm. This is the *mesoderm*.

Ectoderm, mesoderm, and endoderm are the three germ-layers, discovered by von Baer, from which all other tissues are derived.

The disc now has three layers. The ectoderm grows fastest and spills over the edges to form an outer wrapping for the embryo. The endoderm curls to form an inner tube. The mesoderm remains between the two. Along the future back of the embryo a deep groove appears in the ectoderm, which then grows over to convert the groove into the *neural tube*. The front end of the neural tube is later folded and expanded to form the brain; the rest keeps its original shape as the spinal cord. Thus the ectoderm provides both skin and nervous system.

The endoderm lines the whole digestive tract. Offshoots form the digestive glands (liver, pancreas etc.) and also lungs.

Muscles, bones, connective tissue and blood vessels are all derived from mesoderm. The heart is formed in mesoderm at the head of the embryo next to the developing brain; it is displaced towards its final position as the mouth grows between heart and brain.

In the first few weeks, nerves grow outwards from the developing brain and spinal cord. As the various parts of the body take up new positions they keep their original nerves. In adult anatomy, the source of a nerve indicates the origin of the part it supplies. For example, the diaphragm – a muscle separating the heart from the abdomen – gets its nerves from the spinal cord high in the neck, because this muscle is first formed just below the original position of the heart.

By the end of the second month all of the main structures of the body are more or less in place. The proportions are strange: the head is relatively huge and the legs are small, while some organs are still rudimentary. There is little bone, but the whole skeleton is already formed in cartilage. The backbone no longer extends beyond the buttocks as a tail. The embryo is now about 4 cm (1½ in) long. Its further development is considered under ►*foetus*.

embryology. Natural history of animals (generally vertebrates) from conception until birth; in particular the study of the development of the various tissues and organs.

In general biology, embryology helps to explain the course of evolution and the relations between different species of animal; for although the old dictum that the development of the individual recapitulates the evolution of the species has been much overworked, it is still true that the embryos of very different species are very similar, and that in its early stages an embryo almost certainly imitates the embryos (not the adults) of its remote ancestors.

Medical students learn embryology to bring order to the seeming chaos of adult anatomy, and to understand how congenital defects arise.

Embryology, like several other sciences, began with Aristotle in the 4th century BC. His biological studies included an investigation of the developing chick – a most convenient subject, for one has only to set a clutch of eggs and remove and open one each day. He left a good account of development from the third day of incubation, when the embryo becomes visible to the naked eye. He found that the organs are formed in succession, not all at the same time. He regarded reproduction as a purely female function; the male only set the process in motion.

No further progress was made until the 17th century, when embryology was revived by the great anatomists of Padua, such as Fabricius and Harvey. A fellow-student of Fabricius, Volcher Coiter, wrote the first treatise on embryology since Aristotle. But since none of these men had a microscope they could not add much to Aristotle's account.

The development of the chick as seen through the microscope was described in 1673 by Malpighi. This work was a great step forward, but introduced a serious fallacy that was to last until the 19th century. Malpighi's earliest embryos had already been incubated for several hours; long enough for him to see the rudiments of organs that Harvey and others had missed. He concluded that all the organs were present in miniature from the start.

Aristotle's view that the organs were formed in succession was fully restored 150 years later by Saint-Hilaire in France and von Baer in Germany. Von Baer, perhaps the greatest of embryologists, identified the egg or ovum of a mammal in 1827, and showed the development of all tissues and organs from the primary germ layers, ectoderm, endoderm, and mesoderm. He formulated the *biogenetic law*, foreseen by Aristotle and Harvey, that all embryos are alike.

A detailed account of embryology would be out of place here. There are short notes under ➤*embryo* (early stages) and *foetus* (later stages).

emetic. Drug given to cause vomiting. In former centuries, emetics were very widely used as an alternative or addition to purging, blood-letting, sweating – anything that would allow noxious matters to escape. They still have a limited use in treating recent poisoning.

Emetics are of two kinds. Some act by irritating the stomach; they include the household standby – common salt – ammonium carbonate, and ipecacuanha. Small doses of the last two, not enough to cause vomiting, were said to stimulate mucous glands in the lungs and were used in cough mixtures to loosen sputum. A second type of emetic stimulates a reflex centre in the brain. Morphine sometimes does this, which is why a few people cannot tolerate it. A related drug, *apomorphine*, regularly acts as a powerful emetic. In the past it has been used to create an aversion to alcohol in alcoholics who have not responded to more humane methods.

EMG = ➤*electromyogram.*

emollient. A term to describe ointments, creams, lotions, etc., for softening,

217

soothing and moisturizing inflamed or dry skin, used either on their own or with appropriate medicinal supplements.

emotion. The great obstacle to rational discussion of the emotions is that sooner or later one's own emotions enter the fray at the expense of reason. People have always paid lip-service to ideas like 'worried sick' or 'broken-hearted', and they have always accepted in principle that emotion and physical health or sickness are related. But as soon as it comes down to cases a barrier descends. The barrier may be of disbelief ('he's putting it on'), exasperation ('he should pull himself together') or even sympathy ('poor fellow'). Any of these may happen to be the right answer in a given case, but the choice depends not on the merits of the case but on the mood of the speaker.

Much misunderstanding comes from supposing that emotions are (or should be) the same for everyone, or that normal and abnormal physical responses to emotion can be defined: 'if I can suffer frustration without getting a duodenal ulcer, so can he.' But both his frustration and his physical reaction may be quite different from mine.

Civilization demands self-control, and self-control is learning not to act as emotion dictates. Even this is more than anyone can manage at all times, and reflex physical responses to emotion can hardly be controlled at all. A man can more or less learn not to punch someone on the nose whenever he is angry, but he cannot stop his pulse from racing, or a host of internal adjustments of which he is not even aware. It is these adjustments – disturbances of equilibrium – that can in time lead to physical illness, and self-control does not improve them. (If anything, it may make them worse. Properly controlled emotion is more likely to upset digestion, blood pressure and the rest than savagery.) This is the fallacy behind 'pull yourself together'. If, for example, a man is ill because he is constantly afraid, 'pulling himself together' may stop him from running away, that is from *behaving* fearfully. But it does not always stop him from being afraid, and it is the internal and uncontrollable effects of fear that make him ill. Only if not running away teaches him that there was nothing to be afraid of can pulling himself together cure him; but as long as his fear lasts, self-control cannot help him. It may, of course, make him a more useful citizen, but that is a social and not a medical cure; he is still not healthy.

The emotional background to particular kinds of illness is discussed under ➤*psychosomatic disease*; ➤*anxiety*.

Empedocles (5th century BC). Greek philosopher whose theory that all matter was compounded of four elements (earth, air, fire, water) remained the basis of theoretical medicine for some 23 centuries.

emphysema. *Pulmonary emphysema* involves the essential function of the lungs: the distension of the small air-spaces during which oxygen and carbon dioxide are passed into and out of the bloodstream. In lungs afflicted with emphysema, the small air sacs are first distended and then destroyed as their walls give way. The condition arises rarely from a hereditary defect; more often it is associated with occupational diseases such as miner's lung. But most emphysema is linked to the chronic cough of bronchitis, or to asthma, or both. Definitions vary in different countries, and rather than separate chronic bronchitis, bronchial asthma and emphysema, most people now prefer to regard them as factors of a single condition, *chronic airflow obstruction*, considered under chronic ►*bronchitis*.

Nothing can be done to restore the damaged lung tissue. A bronchodilator, such as a salbutamol inhaler, may improve function. To prevent further damage, smoking is absolutely banned, cold and damp have to be avoided, and infection (bronchitis) should be treated at once with antibiotics.

empyema. A kind of abscess: with most abscesses the infection excavates a cavity in the tissues, but with an empyema the pus occupies a natural cavity in the body. The term is most often applied to a collection of pus in the pleural space, between a lung and the outer wall of the chest. Before the discovery of antibiotics, empyema was a frequent and dangerous complication of pneumonia. In the influenza pandemic of 1918 and 1919 many people died after the sequence of influenza, pneumonia and empyema.

Empyema has to be treated surgically. The pus is first drawn off with a hollow needle and syringe. Later, when as a result of inflammation the lung is firmly stuck to the chest wall around the abscess, an opening can be made for the pus to drain away completely. A London physician in 1919 found that his patients with empyema died much more often than those of his assistant. This, it turned out, was because he was the better diagnostician and able to recognize an empyema at an earlier stage. It was then the practice to operate as soon as the diagnosis was made, and with early diagnosis the operation was being done too soon, and the lung collapsed like a pricked balloon. The assistant diagnosed his cases only at a later stage,

when the adhesion to the chest wall kept the lung inflated.

enamel. The coating of the crown of a tooth; it is mainly a complex of phosphate and fluoride of calcium, like the mineral component of bone but with a much denser crystalline structure. ►*teeth*.

encephalitis. Inflammation of the brain; the infectious agent is nearly always a virus. (Bacterial infection is usually confined to the coverings of the brain: ►*meningitis*.)

Perhaps the only virus that invariably settles in the brain is that of *rabies*, a fatal but fortunately rare disease occasionally transmitted from animals to man. In many parts of the world (Russia, N. America, Japan) local forms of virus encephalitis are carried by insects. These are mostly diseases of animals, only accidentally affecting man. They are seldom dangerous.

Even *poliomyelitis*, the best known form of encephalitis, is not primarily an infection of the brain. In the great majority of cases it is a harmless infection of the intestine, and involvement of the brain is a dangerous but unusual event. Most other viruses can cause encephalitis, but only very rarely. The severity of the disease varies widely: anything is possible from a transient headache to paralysis or death, but, apart from poliomyelitis, lasting ill effects are unusual when the infection has passed.

The encephalitis that follows some of the common infectious fevers has not yet been explained. It appears to be not an actual infection of the brain, but an allergic reaction to the virus. But these cases are so rare that it is difficult to study them.

Encephalitis lethargica was a widespread epidemic in the closing years of the First World War and some time after. It was also known as 'sleepy sickness' (nothing to do with African sleeping sickness). Many of its victims were left with a severe disturbance of muscular coordination (post-encephalitic parkinsonism). At the time there was no known way to isolate a virus, and after about 1923 the disease vanished; but everything about the epidemic suggests a virus infection. Historically, it is an interesting example of a serious disease that has appeared from nowhere and mysteriously departed, like some of the plagues of antiquity.

encephalopathy. Any disease of the brain, especially with physical changes from causes other than inflammation, e.g. lead poisoning.

endarteritis. Inflammation of the lining of an artery.

end-artery. A terminal branch of an artery that does not communicate with other branches. The importance of end-arteries is that if one is blocked, the tissue it supplies is completely deprived of fresh blood and dies.

End-arteries are found particularly in the brain, kidneys and heart muscle, which are thus vulnerable to ►*embolism.*

endemic. (Disease) always present in a given region or population (whereas an *epidemic* arrives, spreads, and disappears).

endocarditis. Inflammation of the lining of the heart, especially that of the heart valves. This tissue is unaffected by most diseases, but it becomes involved in rheumatic fever (rheumatic endocarditis), ►*mitral stenosis.* Heart valves deformed by congenital defects or rheumatic fever are sometimes infected with strepto-cocci or other bacteria (bacterial endocarditis). This is dangerous, because fragments of the infected tissue are carried in the blood and can cause blockage of arteries (embolism) anywhere in the body. Rheumatic endocarditis does not always need treatment, but seriously damaged valves can often be repaired surgically. Bacterial endocarditis, formerly incurable, responds to antibiotic drugs.

endocrine (a Greek form of Claude Bernard's term 'internal secretion' (1885)). An endocrine or ductless gland is one which releases its product (a *hormone*) directly to the bloodstream to act on other parts of the body. It is distinguished from an *exocrine* gland, of which the secretion (e.g. sweat, digestive juice) flows into a duct to be used locally.

The *pituitary, thyroid, parathyroid,* and *adrenal* glands are purely endocrine. The *pancreas* is an exocrine gland of digestion, with a duct leading to the duodenum, and also an endocrine gland releasing insulin into the blood. The *ovaries* and *testicles* produce eggs and sperms and are also endocrine glands; their hormones regulate sexual functions throughout the body.

No other organs are generally regarded as endocrine glands, though several might be added to the list. The kidney produces a hormone which affects the blood pressure, and another controlling the formation of red blood cells, and the duodenum produces *secretin,* which stimulates the pancreas. ►*Prostaglandins,* which are formed in most tissues; the numerous chemical transmitters released at nerve-endings to pass on impulses to the next stage; ►*endorphins*; and other substances under investigation can also be regarded as hormones.

The particular functions of hormones

are described with the glands which produce them. Here, it need only be stressed that none of the glands acts independently of the others. There are feed-back mechanisms between the pituitary and most of the other glands. The pituitary can secrete *trophic* hormones to stimulate these glands, and the hormones from the glands suppress the corresponding trophic hormones. If, for example, the thyroid is not secreting enough thyroxine, the pituitary hormone stimulates more secretion. An excess of thyroxine suppresses the pituitary; the thyroid is thus deprived of its stimulus and the balance is restored. In this way the amount of various hormones in the blood is kept at the right level. But the 'right' level depends on circumstances, and the setting of the feed-back mechanism is determined by the nervous system acting on the pituitary. Thus the nervous and chemical functions of the body are closely interrelated.

Several glands may be involved in a single function. Growth, for example, depends on the pituitary acting in its own right (growth hormone) and also on hormones from the thyroid and sex glands under pituitary control. The combustion of sugar involves both parts of the adrenal (two distinct glands), the pancreas, the thyroid, and the pituitary.

1. HISTORY

The workings of the endocrine glands could not be studied until chemistry was well advanced, in the late 19th century, though the glands themselves had long been known. The anatomists of antiquity thought that the pituitary secreted mucus to cool the blood, and that the thyroid lubricated the larynx. Galen recognized that ovaries corresponded with testicles (which is by no means obvious).

The adrenals were first described in the 16th century; the little parathyroids only in the 19th.

In the 12th century Roger of Palermo treated goitre with burnt seaweed – a rich source of iodine and an admirable remedy (►*thyroid* (2)). Paracelsus (1516) found many cretins where goitre was common. The first account of toxic goitre was by Caleb Parry of Bath, published posthumously in 1825, and followed in 1835 and 1840 by the reports of Graves (Dublin) and Basedow (Berlin). The function of the thyroid was fairly well understood by the end of the 19th century, and in 1915 E. C. Kendall announced his discovery of its hormone, thyroxine.

Thomas Addison described adrenal failure (Addison's disease) in 1849. Exactly a century later Kendall and his colleagues opened a new field of medical treatment by treating rheumatic and other diseases with adrenal hormones.

Thomas Bartolin of Copenhagen (1616–80) found an association of diabetes with pancreatic disease. The pancreatic origin of diabetes was proved by von Mering and Minkowski at Strasbourg in 1889, but the hormone, *insulin*, was not isolated until 1921, by Banting and Best at Toronto. One of their collaborators in this work, Collip, isolated the parathyroid hormone in 1925.

Sex hormones were first isolated in about 1930. For this work Butenandt of Berlin and Ruzicka of Zurich shared a Nobel Prize in 1939. The study of these hormones is complicated by the fact that they are formed in the adrenals as well as in the sex glands.

The pituitary has set physiologists more problems than any other gland. Defects of the pituitary cause several completely different types of illness: diabetes insipidus, major disorders of growth giving rise to giants or dwarfs, the diseases named after Cushing, Fröhlich, and Simmonds, and probably certain types of goitre and of diabetes mellitus. The pituitary is not a uniform structure but a mosaic producing at least half a dozen unrelated hormones. Fairly pure extracts of several have been made, and ACTH, first isolated by Collip, has been synthesized.

One more name must be mentioned: in 1775 a Paris physician, Théophile de Bordeu, suggested that the bodily changes which follow castration must be due to the loss of some substance formed by the testicle and passed into the blood-stream. He thought that other organs might behave in the same way, each making its special contribution to the general economy. Bordeu's shrewd guess was the beginning of endocrinology.

endoderm. A layer of cells at a very early stage in the development of an ►*embryo*, the inner of the three germ-layers. The digestive organs and lungs are derived from it.

endometriosis. The presence of fragments of mucous membrane of the same kind as the lining of the uterus in other situations – either embedded in the muscle of the uterus or in other organs, especially the ovaries. The fragments of membrane pass through the same monthly cycle as the normal uterine membrane: they swell before a period and then bleed, but they have no outlet, and therefore cause severe pain for several days before a period. The symptoms disappear during pregnancy and after the menopause. In effect, this is a severe form of dysmenorrhoea.

In mild cases, analgesic drugs (aspirin etc.) may suffice. Sometimes, but not often, the offending tissue can be found and removed surgically. All symptoms are relieved by bringing on the menopause by irradiation or removal of the ovaries, so that the uterus and the abnormal tissue cease to be stimulated by ovarian hormones. But the hormone pills used for contraception may work as well without sterilizing the patient. Since she may well need hormonal replacement if her ovaries are removed, hormones instead of operation are a good bargain.

endometrium. The lining of the uterus.

endorphin. A class of substances, chemically polypeptides, which together with related substances known as *enkephalins* are found throughout the nervous system. They are most abundant in a zone of the spinal cord (substantia gelatinosa) concerned with sensation and appear to modify the sensation of pain. The pain-killing action of opium narcotics such as morphine may be due to their imitating the natural effect of endorphins, to which they are chemically related. Endorphins are produced in response to painful stimuli and also to neutral stimulation such as rubbing a sore place. Hippocrates observed that one source of discomfort could be relieved by another. The release of endorphins offers a plausible explanation of the relief of pain by acupuncture: this possibility is under investigation in China and elsewhere.

endoscopy. Internal examination by direct vision through a lighted tube, generally with a system of lenses – e.g. gastroscopy (stomach); cystoscopy (bladder). The traditional straight viewing-tubes for endoscopy are now giving way to fibroscopic instruments which are flexible, allowing the examiner to look round curves and greatly extending the usefulness of the method.

endotoxin. A poison (toxin) forming part of a bacterium and damaging only tissues in the infected area. (An *exotoxin* is released into the circulation and affects distant organs.)

enema. Medication injected into the rectum (1) to relieve severe constipation or wash out the colon before an operation, (2) to instil water and nutrients, for which it is not a very satisfactory method, (3) to get an effective concentration of a drug to the large intestine, e.g. corticosteroids for the treatment of ulcerative colitis.

energy. A word with different meanings to different people and sometimes to the same people at different times.

In a scientific context energy is a property of matter or a system that enables it to do work, such as moving an object or bringing about certain chemical changes (other chemical changes *provide* energy, e.g. the burning of fuel to release the energy that it derived from the heat or light of the sun and stored). Energy actually engaged in work is said to be *kinetic*, and stored energy is *potential*. Energy can exist in many forms, such as heat, light, electricity, chemical energy or radiation, and any form can be converted to any other. Thus the potential energy of water behind a dam can become the kinetic energy of a mill or the electric power of a dynamo – which in turn can become light, heat or the motion of an express train. In the living body, energy is derived from the combustion of proteins, fats and carbohydrates, commonly expressed in terms of heat as *calories*, or of energy in general as *joules*. The break-down of fuel in the body is not an abrupt change to carbon dioxide and water vapour as though it were ignited, but a complex series of changes, some yielding energy and others requiring it. But the end result, and the net amount of energy released, are the same in either case. A gram of fat ultimately yields 9 Calories regardless of intermediate changes; ➤*muscle* (1).

Theoretical science apart, personal energy more often means vitality, enthusiasm, the urge to be up and doing: a quality that cannot be expressed in figures. The lack of energy that many patients report to their doctors has nothing to do with calories; rather it is a symptom of less than perfect health, including not only physical illness from infection, injury, etc., but also fatigue, boredom, worry and ageing.

A third meaning is increasingly prevalent in association with several kinds of alternative medicine. This 'energy' is a kind of vital force, said to circulate in the body by invisible channels or meridians and subject to blockages that cause disease but can be relieved by the initiated.

enkephalin ➤*endorphin*.

Entamoeba. A genus of protozoon (amoeba). *Entamoeba coli* is a harmless inhabitant of the large intestine. A related species, *E. histolytica*, causes amoebic ➤*dysentery*.

enteric. Of the intestine. Enteric coated drugs are formulated so that they are not released until they reach the intestine, either to prevent them from irritating the stomach or because the acid and enzymes there would destroy them.

enteric fever. A group of infectious diseases including typhoid and paratyphoid fevers; or simply typhoid fever.

enteritis. Inflammation of the intestine, a symptom of many diseases, including infection with bacteria or viruses and allergic reactions. The commonest types – the digestive upsets of summer holidays, and a distressing illness of babies – include inflammation of the stomach and count as ▸gastro-enteritis.

Regional enteritis (Crohn's disease) is a disease of unknown cause, with inflammation confined to one segment of intestine, often the last part of the small intestine. It can cause vague pain, or diarrhoea, or symptoms suggesting appendicitis or even obstruction. Treatment includes adequate relaxation, drugs of the belladonna type to relieve spasm, and a well planned diet. Corticosteroids sometimes give complete relief. The affected intestine may have to be removed surgically.

enuresis = ▸bed-wetting.

enzyme. An enzyme (or ferment) is a substance produced by living cells which promotes chemical change. Since each enzyme is responsible for only one type of change the number of different enzymes in the body is large, perhaps several thousand. The properties of a living organism largely depend on the chemical reactions it can perform and so on the enzymes it can produce. Differences between species or between members of the same species are generally speaking differences between their enzymes. Heredity transmits the ability to form particular enzymes *(▸genetics)*. An enzyme is a highly specific *catalyst*. The following section simply expands this statement.

1. CATALYSIS

A chemical reaction is a rearrangement of atoms to form new compounds. Thus a metal, zinc, and an acid, hydrochloric acid, react to form a white salt, zinc chloride, and an inflammable gas, hydrogen:

$$Zn + 2HCl \rightarrow ZnCl_2 + H_2.$$

The atoms are unchanged, but they are rearranged by transferring chlorine (Cl) from the acid to the metal. The change is fairly rapid, but it is not instantaneous; the mixture does not explode.

A spark causes hydrogen and oxygen to react, forming water:

$$2H_2 + O_2 \rightarrow 2H_2O.$$

This is a very fast reaction, and the mixture does explode.

Similarly hydrogen and nitrogen combine, to form ammonia:

$$3H_2 + N_2 \rightarrow 2NH_3.$$

But this reaction is so slow as to be useless. The gases can, however, be attracted to the surface of specially prepared iron. Held to the iron, the atoms of hydrogen and nitrogen react quickly. Ammonia is formed and released, leaving the iron free to take up a fresh batch of hydrogen and nitrogen. This is the Haber process for manufacturing ammonia. A small quantity of iron changes a very slow reaction into a reasonably fast one, and the iron undergoes no chemical change. This is *catalysis*; iron is a catalyst to the reaction.

The equation shown above implies that all the hydrogen and nitrogen combine to form ammonia. This is untrue, for the reaction can take the opposite direction, when ammonia breaks down to hydrogen and nitrogen:

$$2NH_3 \rightarrow 3H_2 + N_2.$$

This latter reaction is favoured by high temperature or low pressure. But at any temperature and pressure the two reactions take place simultaneously. While there is little ammonia in the mixture, the first reaction predominates. If there is much ammonia to be broken down the second predominates. At a critical concentration the two reactions balance, and although the three constituents are constantly reacting ammonia is re-formed as fast as it breaks down:

$$3H_2 + N_2 \rightleftharpoons 2NH_3.$$

The catalyst works equally well in both directions. Therefore it cannot affect the point of balance. It accelerates both the formation and the destruction of ammonia to the same extent. But removing the ammonia as it forms shifts the balance in favour of its continued formation.

One more example from inorganic chemistry shows how a catalyst may act by forming an *intermediate compound*. Sulphuric acid (H_2SO_4) is readily formed from sulphur trioxide (SO_3) and water. The equation is a simple addition:

$$SO_3 + H_2O \rightarrow H_2SO_4.$$

Sulphur *dioxide* (SO_2) is easy to get, but it is very reluctant to take on a third oxygen atom to form SO_3. On the other hand nitric oxide (NO) easily takes on oxygen to form a dioxide (NO_2). This compound reacts, again easily, with sulphur dioxide:

$$NO_2 + SO_2 \rightarrow NO + SO_3.$$

Thus the difficult conversion of SO_2 to SO_3 is done in two easy stages by means of a catalyst, NO. The catalyst acts as vehicle for conveying oxygen. The intermediate compound, NO_2, promptly reverts to NO in the second stage, so that at the end the catalyst is intact. The equation may be written:

$$2SO_2 + O_2 \xrightarrow{NO} 2SO_3.$$

In the body, a substance which would normally react very slowly if at all forms with its enzyme an intermediate compound which can react quickly.

2. Nature of Enzymes

Like any other catalyst, an enzyme acts in very small quantities; it is unchanged at the end of the reaction on which it works; it affects only the speed and not the nature of the reaction; it facilitates the converse reaction to the same extent.

Carbon dioxide (CO_2) combines with water to form carbonic acid (i.e. to make soda-water). It is a slow process. A sparklet siphon needs a good shake before any appreciable amount of carbonic acid is formed after the CO_2 has been released. In the living body CO_2 is a by-product of many vital reactions, and it must be removed by the blood and taken to the lungs to be exhaled. The blood cannot convey it as a gas; the CO_2 must form soluble carbonic acid and bicarbonates, and it must do so quickly as the blood flows past. The enzyme carbonic anhydrase in the red blood cells increases the speed of this reaction 18,000 times: an hour's work is done in a fifth of a second.

The converse reaction (carbonic acid to CO_2) is equally possible. But the continual production of CO_2 in the tissues keeps the balance tilted in favour of forming carbonic acid. In the lungs, on the other hand, CO_2 is continually removed by breathing, which favours the breakdown of carbonic acid to release more CO_2. And the same enzyme accelerates this breakdown to the same extent as it did the formation.

Enzymes are highly selective. A given enzyme will catalyse one kind of reaction and no other. But since it works by forming an intermediate compound with the substance to be transformed it may well form similar compounds with other closely related substances. The importance of this is explained in section 3 below.

Since living chemistry is largely a matter of compounding substances in one place and decomposing them in another (as carbonic acid in the example given) most enzymes have the double function of promoting both forward and backward reactions.

All known enzymes are proteins, and all proteins are very sensitive to changes of acidity and changes of temperature. Only a few, such as pepsin in the stomach, can act in an acid medium. All are destroyed by heat. They work best a little above normal body temperature (37°C). But at, say, a temperature of 50°C the enzymes are put out of action, and with them the whole body chemistry. Thus the principle that chemical reactions are accelerated by warmth is true of living reactions only within narrow limits.

3. ENZYME POISONS

Some chemicals attach themselves almost indiscriminately to others, including catalysts. If this happens the catalyst is unable to work, because the part of its molecule which should be forming an intermediate compound (section 1, above) is already occupied by the invading chemical. Chemicals of this type include cyanides, and many compounds of arsenic and mercury. These are, of course, among the deadliest of mineral poisons. Cyanides have a remarkable affinity for iron. The enzyme *cytochrome oxidase*, by means of which oxygen is used in the body cells, contains iron, and if this iron is occupied by a cyanide the enzyme ceases to act. Death is almost immediate.

The poison gas lewisite and other arsenic compounds behave in the same way as cyanides, though with less immediately vital enzymes. The antidote, British anti-lewisite (BAL), has the same structure as the vulnerable portion of the enzymes. Arsenic attaches itself to BAL, leaving the enzyme free to do its work.

Other poisons act because they closely resemble the compound on which an enzyme usually works. Many bacteria need a supply of para-amino-benzoic acid in order to grow. But the bacterial enzymes will accept instead a similar but useless compound, para-amino-benzene sulphonamide (sulphanilamide). This compound therefore prevents the bacteria from growing, and is a valuable drug. Many drugs act against human enzymes in this manner. Their effect may be to suppress some activity, or it may be to stimulate by preventing an enzyme from destroying an active natural substance too rapidly.

4. PRECURSORS AND CO-ENZYMES

Some enzymes are not wanted in the cells which produce them. Powerful enzymes for digesting proteins are formed in the pancreas, but the pancreas is not intended to digest itself. These enzymes are inactive until they join other enzymes formed in the intestine, where they can act on food; the intestine is protected from them by a film of mucus. Similarly the enzymes which clot blood are in the blood all the time. Circulating blood does not clot because the enzymes are inactive until they are joined by substances only released when there is an injury to be repaired. Such enzymes are like bombs which do not receive their war-heads until they are ready for action. They are not strictly enzymes but only precursors.

A co-enzyme is a substance needed to activate an enzyme and usually serving as a bridge between two enzymes: it may be the end-product of one reaction and the starting point of the next. Nearly all of the ▸*vitamins* help to form co-enzymes.

5. ENZYME DEFICIENCIES

In general, hereditary characters reflect the ability to form particular enzymes. Differences between healthy individuals could probably be traced to slight differences in unimportant enzymes, and inherited illness to greater differences or defects. In some disorders a missing enzyme has been identified. A small amount of the amino-acid *phenylalanine* in the diet is necessary to health, but if large amounts are allowed to accumulate they are harmful. Any excess of phenylalanine is normally converted to its hydroxide, *tyrosine*, by means of an enzyme. Children born without this enzyme become mentally defective. The condition is known as *phenylketonuria*. If phenylalanine is almost excluded from the diet these children can develop normally. At the next stage, tyrosine is partly converted to the pigment *melanin*. *Albinos* lack an enzyme needed for this conversion. Other enzymes convert tyrosine to thyroid hormone (▸*thyroid gland*); if one of these is missing the child will be a *cretin*. Many other disorders, most of them rare, have been traced to particular enzymes, and it becomes increasingly clear that some common diseases are of the same type, though why some of them remain dormant until adult life has not been explained.

Enzyme poisons have already been mentioned. One can guess that many common symptoms of disease are due to suppression of enzymes. Vitamin deficiencies deprive enzymes of essential co-enzymes. Viruses, which cause more illness than any other agent, live at the expense of their host's enzymes. Some bacteria may do the same, and many bacteria produce harmful enzymes of their own. Cancer is a disorder of cell growth and therefore, presumably, of enzymes. But this sort of argument can be extended until it becomes sterile: all illness disturbs normal function; function is orderly chemical change, and chemical change depends on enzymes. So illness is a matter of disturbed enzymes – this is a truism, and it hints at knowledge of cause and effect which nobody yet has. One thing, however, is certain: that the next major advance in medicine is as likely to come from the study of enzymes as from any other field of research.

eosin. A red acidic dye, much used in staining biological specimens for microscopic examination, usually with a contrasting blue alkaline dye; different components of the specimen take up one or other colour.

eosinophil. A kind of white blood cell, containing granules readily stained with eosin. The number of circulating eosinophils increases during illness due to allergy.

ephedrine. A drug originally extracted from a plant *Ephedra* or *ma huang*, used in China for many centuries but not adopted by Western medicine until about 1930.

The chemical structure and behaviour of ephedrine resemble those of ▸*adrenaline*, but adrenaline is inactive when taken by mouth whereas ephedrine is active. Disorders such as asthma which respond to adrenaline can be treated with ephedrine without the need for injections. However, ephedrine has been superseded in the treatment of asthma by more selective bronchodilators, usually taken by inhalation.

The enzyme ►*monoamine oxidase* decomposes adrenaline and also ephedrine; it may be that ephedrine acts not directly but by drawing the fire of this enzyme and so enhancing the effect of the patient's own adrenaline.

epicanthus. Vertical fold of skin at the inner corner of the eye, usual in Mongolians but uncommon in other races.

epidemic. (Disease) introduced to a region or population, spreading, and apparently disappearing until the next outbreak. (cf. *endemic*, always present in the region.)

epidermis. The outer layer of the skin.

epidural blockade. Anaesthesia in the lower part of the body, by injecting a local anaesthetic around the spinal nerves; especially useful during childbirth.

epigastrium. The upper part of the abdomen, in the angle of the ribs over the stomach.

epiglottis. A flap of cartilage behind the tongue; at rest it is upright and the breath passes behind it between the vocal cords. During swallowing the epiglottis drops back to cover the vocal cords and prevent food from being inhaled.

epiglottitis. Inflammation of the epiglottis, mainly affecting children. The symptoms include rapid onset of fever, sore throat, croup and severe difficulty in breathing. The underlying infection is nearly always due to *Haemophilus influenzae*, which responds well to antibiotics such as chloramphenicol. But the danger is that the child may suffocate before the

treatment has time to work; therefore at the first suspicion of epiglottitis the child must be admitted to hospital where an airway can be maintained either by an anaesthetist's tube which is passed into the trachea or by opening the trachea below the obstruction (tracheostomy).

epilepsy. An ill-defined group of disorders characterized by fits (seizures). A fit is an episode of disorganized and excessive activity in some part of the brain, causing disturbances of sensation, movement, or consciousness according to the area of the brain that is involved. With *petit mal* epilepsy the only symptom is fleeting loss of consciousness. The patient – usually a child – may even be unaware that anything has happened. *Grand mal* is the well-known type of fit in which the patient – sometimes warned by preliminary symptoms – falls unconscious, often with a cry. His muscles stiffen and then twitch violently, often causing him to bite his tongue. His bladder may empty. The attack lasts a couple of minutes. Some patients then go into a deep sleep. A few patients, instead of sleeping the attack off, pass into a trance-like state in which they behave unaccountably and in some cases antisocially.

The preliminary symptoms or *aura* indicate the area of the brain where the disturbance begins, before spreading to other parts. The aura may be an uncontrolled movement in some part of the body, or a sensation, or even, in very rare cases, a bizarre pattern of behaviour. There is no aura if the attack starts in a 'silent' area of the brain – one that is not concerned with perception or action – and in many cases the disturbance spreads so rapidly that the patient is unconscious before he has time to notice anything. In *focal* (Jacksonian) epilepsy the aura is the most prominent part of the attack: it generally starts with localized twitching that rapidly spreads to more and more muscles, and may or may not culminate in a *grand mal* attack.

No other disease arouses as much superstition as epilepsy, for none is quite so suggestive of 'possession'. Hippocrates' treatise *On the Sacred Disease*, probably written about 400 BC, tried to debunk the superstition indicated by the title and present epilepsy as a disease like any other, a result of natural causes. Yet even now many people are uneasy in the presence of epileptics, and not only in primitive societies.

In discussing the nature of epilepsy, the first point to be made is that anyone can have an epileptic fit. A head injury, an electric shock, various drugs, asphyxia, or a severe bout of fever can all cause fits. These fits are not merely *like* epilepsy; they *are* epilepsy, as defined in the first two sentences of this article. The only difference between an epileptic and anyone else is that he is unduly liable to this kind of disturbance.

In *symptomatic epilepsy* the fits are set off by a detectable physical agent such as a blood-clot or displaced fragment of bone after an injury, a tumour, pressure of oedema (excess of fluid, e.g. with very high blood pressure), or infection. Children often have fits (convulsions) at the beginning of a fever such as measles; their brain cells are more sensitive than adult cells to a rising body temperature. The location of the cause can often be inferred from the type of fit, since the origin of a particular movement or sensation is a known area of the brain. If the cause can be dealt with, symptomatic epilepsy is of course curable.

Idiopathic epilepsy – apparently spontaneous, without detectable cause – is the commoner type, and what most people mean by epilepsy. Either the brain cells are unduly susceptible to minor irritation, or there is an unrecognized agent setting off fits. In support of the former idea, idiopathic epilepsy generally starts in childhood and the children often gradually improve, just as children soon stop having convulsions in response to fever. But even if this should be so it cannot be the whole story, and many neurologists believe that *all* epilepsy is symptomatic, though the centre of the disturbance may be no more than a minute scar, too small ever to be traced.

Epilepsy, then, is no more a disease in its own right than high blood pressure or fever. It is a reaction that can be evoked in many ways. It is called symptomatic when a cause can be found, and idiopathic when the cause is unknown.

Since most epilepsy is 'idiopathic' only the symptom can be treated, not the cause. But most epileptics can be kept free from attacks, and many remain well after all treatment has been given up; the young epileptic has the best chance of complete recovery.

The unsuitability of certain jobs has been exaggerated. Employers and workmates are naturally anxious about the risk, but in fact there are very few jobs that are wholly unsuited to epileptics. People subject to epileptic fits may not drive in the UK and other countries until they have not had a fit for one year. If they still have some fits, but only during sleep, they may drive after three years without a waking fit.

Many drugs are used to suppress the symptoms of this condition. Bromides are obsolete, but after more than half a century phenobarbitone is still in use. The chief objection to it is that it is a powerful sedative and causes drowsiness. Newer drugs for *grand mal* include phenytoin and carbamazepine. Patients differ, and the best drug or mixture has to be found by trial and error. The right dose is the least that will keep the patient free from attacks. In time – it may be several years – the dose can often be reduced and finally given up. If fits start again the dose has to be increased again. Such disappointments are inevitable because the only way to find out whether it is safe to reduce the dose is to try. Patients who have gone two years with neither drugs nor fits are generally regarded as cured.

Petit mal is treated with a different type of drug, e.g. ethosuximide. It is essentially a disorder of childhood, and complete recovery is the rule, especially if there has been no associated *grand mal*.

Hereditary factors play only a minor role in epilepsy, and the disease is not a reason for not having children. On the other hand an intending marriage partner has to know what is involved; marriages have been dissolved on the grounds of unrevealed epilepsy.

Epilepsy is commonly thought to be associated with mental defect. Probably one reason for this belief is that injury to the brain in infancy can cause both epilepsy and mental defect. But most epileptics are normal people in all other respects.

epinephrine. Official name in USA for ►*adrenaline*.

epiphysis. Accessory part of a bone, developed in infancy as a separate bone and later joining the main structure. Until a year or two either side of puberty, epiphyses (mainly the ends of the limb bones) are joined to the shafts of bones by cartilage. The age at which a particular cartilaginous bridge is converted to bone is more or less constant; this sometimes gives the age of a skeleton at the time of death.

episiotomy. Surgical division of the perineum to enlarge the outlet of the birth-passage in cases of difficult birth.

epistaxis. Bleeding from the nose. ►*nose* (1).

epithelium. Coating or lining tissue; skin or mucous membrane.

Erasistratus (3rd century BC). Physician of Antioch and Alexandria, regarded as the founder of scientific physiology. He and his contemporary Herophilus established a school in Alexandria that was not surpassed until the rise of the Italian universities after the Middle Ages. Erasistratus made experiments to show the motor and sensory functions of nerves and their dependence on the brain.

Erb's palsy. (Wilhelm Erb, German physician, 1840–1921.) Partial paralysis of the arm from stretching the nerves at the root of the neck during a difficult birth. As a rule the infant recovers quickly with gentle physiotherapy.

erection. Engorgement of penis or other sex organs with blood: it is a reflex action depending on parasympathetic nerves. Muscles around the veins contract and prevent blood from leaving, and the erection is maintained by the pressure of blood in the arteries.

erector spinae. Complex system of muscles supporting the backbone, forming a rounded ridge at either side of the midline where the spinous processes of the *vertebrae* separate the two halves of the system.

erepsin. Intestinal enzymes for digesting protein.

ergot. The fungus *Claviceps purpurea*, a parasite of rye. It contains numerous alkaloids, which account for its poisonous properties and its medicinal uses.

Ergot interferes with the stimulant action of adrenaline on the muscle of arteries and on some other tissues, but itself directly stimulates involuntary muscle. The net effect of these contrary actions is unpredictable, and therefore crude extracts are no longer used. Some of the pure alkaloids have a more limited and manageable action. *Ergometrine* acts mainly on the muscle of the uterus. Injected immediately after childbirth, it causes the uterus to contract firmly and so stops bleeding. *Ergotamine* acts on blood vessels in the head and sometimes prevents migraine.

Outbreaks of ergot poisoning have been due to bread made from contaminated rye. Many victims have died. Others have lost fingers and toes from gangrene due to sustained constriction of the arteries, and still others have had convulsions and mental derangement.

The alkaloids of ergot are compounds of lysergic acid and thus related to the hallucinogen LSD.

erysipelas. A severe, contagious infection of the skin with streptococci, causing diffuse, spreading inflammation, high fever, and sometimes grave complications such as pneumonia and nephritis. Until the discovery of sulphonamides, erysipelas was a dangerous and fairly common disease; but now it is seldom seen and rapidly cured. Penicillin is now the treatment of choice.

erythema. Reddening (inflammation) of the skin. *Erythema nodosum*, with red lumps in the skin, is an uncommon complication of various types of infec-tion; it probably represents an allergic reaction.

erythrocyte = red blood cell (>*blood*). *Erythrocyte sedimentation rate* (ESR) is a clinical laboratory test: the rate at which the red cells settle in a column of blood in a glass tube is measured. Rapid sedimentation suggests that the disease under investigation is still active.

erythromycin. An antibiotic with similar activity to penicillin, used especially for patients who are sensitive to penicillin.

erythropoietin. A hormone secreted by the kidney to promote the formation of red blood cells. The anaemia following failure of the kidneys can be treated with regular injections of it.

Escherichia. A genus of bacteria, of which one species, *E. coli*, is a normal inhabitant of the human intestine. Although usually harmless, if allowed to contaminate food or drinking water some strains cause food poisoning (traveller's diarrhoea). *E. coli* infection of the urinary tract can cause pyelitis or cystitis, and in infants it is an occasional cause of meningitis.

ESR >*erythrocyte.*

essential. 1. (nutrients) necessary for health, which the body cannot synthesize for itself, e.g. essential >*amino-acids* and fatty acids, >*fat*.

2. (disease) arising without evident cause = *idiopathic* or *primary*. Thus *essential* hypertension as opposed to symptomatic or secondary hypertension due to, e.g., kidney disease.

ethanol. Ethyl >*alcohol*; spirits of wine.

ether. A group of chemical compounds derived from alcohols; usually *diethyl* *ether*, $C_2H_5.O.C_2H_5$, a volatile anaesthetic. Ether was one of the first general anaesthetics to be used. It was difficult to administer because it made the patients choke, and it was soon replaced by chloroform. But chloroform was more insidiously dangerous and ether came back. It was easy enough to handle if the early stages of anaesthesia were done with another agent – chloroform or nitrous oxide, and it was safe. In recent years, less irritant anaesthetics have superseded ether, to avoid post-operative vomiting and coughing.

ethical. A term used to describe medicines, not necessarily those of which the sale is controlled by law, that are advertised only to the medical and allied professions. Reputable companies back the advertisement of their ethical products with information about the underlying research, references to published reports, and warnings of known risks. Products advertised to the general public are described as 'over-the-counter'. By maintaining this distinction the manufacturers have undoubtedly saved a good deal of disappointment, embarrassment and confusion between doctors and patients. ➤*research*.

ethics. Many people, including some doctors, are baffled by the intricacies of medical ethics.

Doctors everywhere are supposed to accept a code of conduct more or less based on the ➤*Hippocratic Oath*. In many countries they have to take an oath when they qualify, though not in Britain, where a partly unwritten code should be taken for granted.

The Hippocratic Oath was not only an undertaking to act in the best interests of the patient; it was also an initiation to a guild. Some of its provisions lay down the doctor's behaviour towards his patient, and others, his behaviour towards his colleagues. This division has remained, and it is with the rules about ethical procedure between two doctors that the general public mostly quarrels, feeling that the profession is concerned mainly with its own interests.

Misbehaviour by a doctor may be a criminal offence, or malpractice, or negligence, or a breach of ethics, or a combination of the four. Before the laws in England were relaxed, abortion was, with a few exceptions, a crime. If it was carried out regardless of the patient's best interests, purely for the sake of a large fee, it was also unethical, and if it was decidedly the wrong treatment for the particular case (e.g. a young married woman wanting a child but afraid of pregnancy and needing only reassurance) then it was malpractice as well. Professional abortionists, sometimes erring in all these ways, went to prison for breaking the law, and lost their right to practise for their unethical behaviour ('infamous conduct'). But there were also doctors who performed abortions for a reasonable fee or sometimes without charge because, despite the law, they thought the operation medically justified. Some of these went to prison too. The operations were illegal, but were they unethical? Adultery with a patient, on the other hand, is not a crime in law, but it is highly unethical and can cost the doctor his right to practise.

Incompetence is unethical in that a doctor has a moral duty to know his own job. It is most likely to be penalized when a patient is awarded damages because of wrong or inadequate treatment. On the whole, the Courts are reasonable in their demands on doctors. They do not expect a country practitioner to have the special skills of a brain surgeon, nor a brain surgeon to be an expert on antenatal care. Each is expected to provide the skill normally expected from someone working in his chosen branch of medicine.

Negligence means falling below this standard. In most cases, including some incurring very heavy damages, negligence arises from a lapse of attention, such as failing to check a dose or taking a telephone message too lightly.

Among the skills required of any doctor is a knowledge of his own limitations. A country doctor doing his best in an emergency is not blamed if *his* best is not as good as the best of a specialist in that particular operation. But a town doctor would be negligent if he attempted the same operation knowing that a specialist was within easy reach. This is the modern equivalent of the Hippocratic clause that forbids inexperienced doctors to operate. It extends far beyond surgery. Medicine is now so specialized that nobody can be expert in all its branches, and every doctor meets a variety of cases that need a second opinion.

Malpractice can mean the same as negligence, but it is often used in a much wider sense to include deliberate wrong treatment, such as unjustified surgery, and unethical behaviour such as breach of confidence.

This matter of confidence or professional secrecy raises problems. In principle, anything that a doctor learns about his patients is to be kept secret. It may be in the patient's best interests for the doctor to discuss the case with the wife or husband, but he is not supposed to do so without the patient's permission. More than one doctor has paid heavy damages for an unguarded word to a patient's spouse. Many parents feel that they have an absolute right to know what

their children have told the doctor. But what if an adolescent consults a doctor precisely because he trusts him not to talk to his parents? Sometimes it is clearly ethical for the doctor to discuss a patient with the family, e.g. with mental disorders where the patient cannot reasonably be asked for permission, or with a gravely ill patient. A doctor called as a witness does not have the same privileges as a lawyer: he cannot withhold information on the grounds that it is confidential. This can put ethics in direct conflict with the law. To make it still worse the enforced breach of confidence may be actionable unless the doctor first insists that he is giving evidence under protest.

As regards the behaviour of doctors towards each other, the first cause of misunderstanding is that etiquette is often confused with ethics. To advise a patient (except in an emergency) knowing that he is under the care of a colleague is usually more a breach of etiquette than of ethics. Blatant advertising, on the other hand, is unethical. Another breach of ethics that, like advertising, can cost a doctor his licence is 'covering', which means using a medical qualification to shield an unqualified practitioner, e.g. by signing certificates or prescriptions on his behalf. Some unqualified practitioners may be very good at their job, but professional standards have been established to protect the public, and it is not surprising that doctors should be penalized for undermining them.

A set of written and unwritten rules discourages doctors from stealing patients from one another, and these are the ones that most annoy the public. Some of them surely started as measures to protect the guild rather than its clients, but as they now stand they do serve – perhaps clumsily – to protect the patient. It is at best undesirable, and at worst really dangerous, for two doctors, unknown to each other, to be treating the same patient. Alternative forms of treatment, both justifiable, may be dangerously incompatible. And, for all the advances of scientific medicine, confidence is still an important factor in most cures. A patient who plays one doctor off against another presumably distrusts both, and neither is likely to do him much good. People often ask doctors whom they meet on holiday or over a dinner table for advice about their health, often with the implication that their own doctors are wrong. When they get a non-committal answer, they complain about stuffy medical etiquette. To give a detailed opinion in these circumstances would be a breach of etiquette; it would make difficulties for the other doctor. But it would also be, as often as not, a breach of ethics because any such opinion would be based on insufficient information and therefore negligent. If a patient loses confidence in his doctor, it is much better for him to change doctors completely than seek casual advice.

A word is needed here about the relation of specialists and hospital doctors to general practitioners. In Britain the specialist is traditionally a *consultant* whose primary function is to advise general practitioners rather than patients. In principle it is the practitioner, the family doctor, who calls him in, rather as a solicitor takes counsel's opinion on his client's behalf. In practice, the consultant usually advises the patient directly, if only to save time, but he does so on behalf of the family doctor, to whom he returns the patient when he has given the advice or treatment that he was asked to give. In many other countries the patient is transferred rather than referred to a specialist. Events there may take the same course as in Britain, but without the feeling that the patient's own doctor is still his doctor even if for the time being he is in the background. The British system gives the family doctor a most valuable function – that of a kind of referee who in an age of over-specialization can still see the wood for the trees.

Historically, this is why a specialist will often refuse to see a patient without a letter from his doctor. Pressure of work is perhaps a stronger reason in hospitals, but it is not the original one, which is basically a rational division of labour.

The system is open to abuse by doctors who refer patients without sufficient thought, and by consultants who do not send adequate reports to the doctor, but that does not condemn the system. Nor does the form of abuse known as dichotomy, where an unscrupulous doctor refers a patient to an expensive specialist and then shares the fee, an offence for which both can be immediately struck off the Register.

Professional standards are maintained in several ways. The most important is undoubtedly the long and closely supervised training, during which approved behaviour is instilled like a series of conditioned reflexes. By the time that they are ready to qualify, most medical students find that pretty women who are also patients no longer disturb them, and that to discuss patients in public would be gross blasphemy: this can happen even if in all other ways they are still lecherous and garrulous.

The General Medical Council, a statutory body, keeps the Medical Register, which is the official list of people licensed to practise as doctors. Its disciplinary committee deals with breaches of ethics (infamous conduct). It is perhaps unfortunate that there is no intermediate penalty between warning an offender and depriving him of his livelihood by striking his name off the Register. Formerly, doctors had no right of appeal against decisions of the GMC and no right to legal representation before it, but this has now changed. A doctor who has been struck off can apply for readmission to the Register. He can be struck off for any serious breach of ethics. An alcoholic doctor may be let off with a warning, subject to his undergoing treatment, and a drug addict may be allowed to practise but forbidden to prescribe certain drugs.

A doctor convicted of any serious crime can also be struck off when his conduct has been reported to the GMC. Negligence can bring him to the Civil Courts with a claim for heavy damages. Doctors employed by the National Health Service can be fined by their local committees for not looking after their patients, and also for over-prescribing, or for prescribing needlessly expensive remedies against public funds.

Contrary to what many people think, the British Medical Association has no powers to discipline its members other than that of persuasion. But it has an ethical committee to advise doctors on questions of professional ethics. Most doctors subscribe, as professional insurance, to one of the organizations that offer legal advice and indemnity against the costs of legal actions. These organizations also keep a close watch on professional standards.

All the professions allied to medicine, such as dentistry, nursing, and pharmacy, are subject to similar codes and disciplinary bodies.

ethmoid. A small bone of the skull, forming the roof of the nose. Its name (= sieve-like) refers to the large number of holes for the olfactory nerves, carrying the sense of smell, which led the anatomists of antiquity to suppose that mucus was formed inside the skull in the pituitary gland and flowed down to the nose.

ethyl alcohol ►*alcohol* (1).

ethyl chloride. An anaesthetic agent similar to chloroform but with a more rapid action. It is very volatile, and when sprayed on the skin it evaporates so quickly that the skin is cooled to the point of insensibility. Thus it can also be used as a local anaesthetic.

eu-. Prefix = 'good', 'easy' (the converse of *dys*-; e.g. *eupepsia*, healthy digestion, as opposed to *dyspepsia*, indigestion).

euphoria. Abnormal elation.

Eustachian tube. Narrow passage between the cavity of the ear-drum and the back of the nose. Its opening in the side of the naso-pharynx is above the soft palate (►*pharynx*). Eustachius described the tube in 1562 in the first detailed account of the ear, but Alcmaeon of Croton had mentioned it 2,000 years before.

Eustachius (Bartolomeo Eustachio) (?1520–74). Anatomist in Rome; physician to the Pope. One of the few great anatomists of the time who did not work at Padua (►*Vesalius*). He was a more accurate but less imaginative worker than his contemporary Vesalius: he recorded details which Vesalius missed, but he did not see the body as a dynamic, integrated system. His accounts of particular organs – ear, larynx, kidney, nervous system – are admirable, but few were published in his lifetime. By the time they appeared (1714) they were no longer needed; the successors of Vesalius at Padua had already stolen Eustachius's thunder.

evolution. The derivation of different species from common ancestors; a process of gradual change from generation to generation.

Although no general theory of evolution was formulated until the 19th century (▸*Lamarck*; *Darwin*), scientists had toyed with the idea since the time of ▸*Aristotle*. Darwin not only produced convincing evidence that species were not ready-made but had evolved from simpler forms of life; he also indicated that change was established by 'natural selection'. If in any way an individual is better adapted to its environment than its fellows, and can transmit the advantage to its offspring, then in time the descendants of the new type outnumber and ultimately supersede the older type. The process is summed up in Herbert Spencer's phrase 'survival of the fittest'. Darwin could not offer any explanation of how changes had taken place, because nothing was known of genetics. It is now clear (▸*genetics*) that change occurs by mutation, which as a rule is harmful but occasionally confers an advantage that can be transmitted to the offspring.

The theory of evolution is important to medical science in several ways. Firstly, it brings order to biology, of which rational medicine is a branch. Many of the puzzles and seeming illogicalities of anatomy make sense in the light of the past history of the race, and the growth of an embryo from a single cell to a fully developed infant is like an epitome of the evolution, over millions of generations, of the human race from

the first living cells. Physiology deals with the working of the body and its component organs, and everything in physiology can be seen as a means of adaptation to the environment. The 'fittest' that survive are those that are best adapted.

As regards hereditary ailments, most of which take the form of enhanced liability to a disease, effective treatment tends to neutralize the effect of natural selection and so, in a sense, weaken the population. But this is a very slow process, and if the diseases can be cured it does not matter. And in advanced human society mere physical fitness – the ability to hunt and fight – is no longer a measure of adaptation to the environment. What distinguishes man from other animals is his ability to use his brain to adapt the environment to suit him. In his struggle for survival, ingenuity is a much more important factor than strong teeth.

A disquieting form of evolution takes place at the other end of the natural scale among the microbes that cause infectious diseases. Successful treatment of infection can encourage the rapid evolution of modified microbes that resist the treatment (▸*antibiotic*). This has occurred mainly among bacteria, but malaria is showing a similar tendency.

exanthem(a). 1. Skin rash as a symptom of an infectious fever (chickenpox, measles, typhus etc.). **2.** The disease itself.

excretion. Elimination of by-products of digestion and body chemistry, also of excess requisites such as salt. The principal organs of excretion are the *kidneys* (water, nitrogen compounds, salts, acids), the *lungs* (carbon dioxide, water), the *skin* (water, salt), and the *liver* (bile pigments and salts, extraneous poisons).

Technically speaking, the undigested food waste in the faeces is not excreted, because the body has never assimilated it; it is merely in transit.

exercise. Although few people would deny that exercise promotes health there is not much evidence to show that it does so; nor is it quite clear what the evidence ought to show, because nobody can define 'health' and 'fitness' or say whether they mean different things. Since most people feel fitter with regular exercise than without it there is not much need for scientific proof that they are materially better off for a daily walk. It is by no means clear that *being* fit is any different from *feeling* fit.

Exercise strengthens muscles, and disuse causes them to waste. This is only one example of the general principle that tissues with no work tend to shrink, presumably because a decreased supply of blood keeps them undernourished.

Training is more complex. Increased bulk and strength of muscle is only one part of it. Improved skill is of course another, but in unknown ways exercise also increases mechanical efficiency – the amount of work from consuming a given amount of fuel.

But health cannot be measured as muscular strength, and exercise must have more subtle effects. For example, among people with high blood pressure the mortality is highest in those who take least exercise (but it is influenced by many other factors such as overeating and smoking, and causes are hard to distinguish from effects or from mere coincidences). A muscle at rest needs very little blood. Even the heart can carry on with a very poor circulation in its coronary arteries when there is no exertion. During exercise, the amount of blood

flowing through a muscle increases at least ten-fold. This is achieved partly by widening the vessels, partly by raising the pressure, and partly by opening up new channels. If these auxiliary channels are in regular use, they are always available for emergencies. But if muscles, especially the heart, have not worked hard for years, then when their arteries begin to degenerate there is nothing in reserve.

Although the main purpose of exercise would be to forestall damage to the heart as the arteries age, it also helps even when some damage is already done, and nowadays patients with angina are treated with carefully graded exercises.

The effect of exercise on the state of mind is quite as important as its effects on the muscles and circulation. In fact, mental and physical effects are not really distinct, because exercise promotes mental relaxation and thus helps to overcome stresses that contribute to physical illness.

exocrine. An exocrine gland is one with a duct to carry its secretion to its site of action, e.g. saliva to the mouth or enzymes from the pancreas to the duodenum (cf. *endocrine*, having no duct and secreting into the bloodstream).

exophthalmic goitre = toxic goitre with protruding eyes as a symptom. ➤*thyroid gland* (2).

exophthalmos. Protruding eyes. There are many possible causes, e.g. injuries and diseases of the orbit, but the only common one is exophthalmic goitre.

exostosis. Superfluous mass of bone. ➤*osteoma*.

exotoxin. Poison released by bacteria into the circulation and causing damage away from the site of infection. For instance, tetanus bacilli do not stray from the wound where they have a foothold, but their exotoxins injure the central nervous system.

expectorant. Medicine to loosen mucus in the lungs and facilitate coughing. ►*cough medicines.*

extension. 1. The movement of straightening a joint (opposed to flexion). **2.** Treatment of a broken bone by a steady pull on the limb. The purpose is to overcome the tendency of the patient's muscles to contract automatically and cause overriding of the broken ends of bone. ►*fracture.*

exteroception. Sensation or perception of things other than one's own body – the 'five senses', as opposed to *proprioception*, which informs about the position of joints, balance etc.

extrasystole. A common irregularity of the heart beat ('dropped beat'). ►*arrhythmia.*

extravasation. Leakage of fluid from a vessel into the surrounding tissues, as a result of injury. Internal bleeding is the obvious example, but the term may apply to urine, bile or other fluids.

exudation. Seepage of watery fluid from the blood through intact vessels, e.g. as a result of inflammation.

eye

1. STRUCTURE

The eye is a sphere with a slight bulge in front and a stalk behind, a little to the inner side of the mid-line. It has a firm shell, the *sclera*, with a transparent bulge in front (*cornea*). The stalk at the back carries the *optic nerve*, transmitting visual impulses to the brain.

The sclera is lined first with a pigmented layer of fine blood vessels (*choroid*) and second with a mesh of nerve fibres and their light-sensitive endings (*retina*).

Behind the cornea is a pigmented diaphragm supported by muscle (*iris*), and behind the iris, again supported by muscle, is the *lens*. The *pupil* is a hole in the middle of the iris.

The space between the cornea and the lens is filled with watery fluid (*aqueous humour*), and the rest of the eye is filled with a clear jelly (*vitreous humour*).

Light passes freely through cornea, aqueous humour, pupil, lens, and vitreous humour to the sensitive retina. The pigmented choroid behind the retina prevents reflection of light.

The *orbit* is a socket in the skull considerably larger than the eye. The dead space is filled with loose fat, leaving the eye free to move. Six small muscles attach the sclera to the orbit.

A thin membrane, the *conjunctiva*, lines the eyelids and covers the front of the eye. The conjunctiva is constantly lubricated and washed with tears. The tears are secreted by the *lacrimal gland* under cover of the outer part of the upper lid, and drain into the nose through a small opening at the inner corner of the eye.

2. FUNCTION

The optical system of the eye, that is, the arrangement for focusing a sharp image on the retina, is simple. The 'lens' is only a minor component of the effective lens, for most of the work is done by the curved cornea, which on its own (with its backing of water) is a powerful fixed-focus lens. The named lens behind it is flexible; its curvature is adjusted by its surrounding muscle. It is supplementary

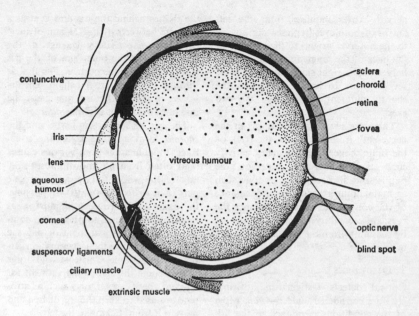

Eye (diagrammatic)

to the cornea, and the means of varying the focus.

The iris contracts or relaxes to adapt the size of the pupil to the amount of light. It incidentally constricts the pupil when the eye is focused for near vision.

The sensitive nerve-endings in the retina are of two kinds: *cones*, which function in good light and register colour, and *rods*, which need very much less light but are colour-blind. As in colour photography, all colours are recorded as different mixtures of three primary colours, perceived by three kinds of cone. Again as in colour photography, vision depends on chemical reactions promoted by light; the rods and cones are sensitive to the products of the reactions.

The cones are most sensitive to yellow, which therefore seems brighter than other colours of the same intensity. The rods are sensitive only to blue and green: hence the apparent brightness of grass by moonlight.

Rhodopsin (visual purple) is the light-sensitive chemical of the rods. It is inactivated by bright light, and thus the rods are switched off when the light is good enough for the less sensitive cones (otherwise the glare would be intolerable). Adaptation to night-vision depends on the slow resynthesis of rhodopsin. The process requires vitamin A, and night-blindness is an early symptom of vitamin A deficiency.

Impulses from the retina are carried back to the brain in the optic nerve. A cross-over system between the two optic nerves carries impulses from the left halves of both eyes (representing objects to the observer's right) to the left side of the back of the brain, and from the right halves to the right side. The brain takes several years to learn to interpret the slightly different images from the two eyes.

There are several relay stations in the nerve-path from the eyes to the back of the brain, concerned with reflex activity such as focusing and adjusting the pupils, and also remoter functions such as maintaining the posture and balance of the body. As an organ of balance the eyes are secondary to reflexes governed by sensation from the muscles and joints of the limbs.

3. DISORDERS

Optical defects (astigmatism, myopia etc.) are considered under ►*vision*. Most of the conditions mentioned in the following notes are described further under their own headings.

Working from front to back: the *conjunctiva* is protected from injury by the eyelids and the very rapid blink reflex, and from infection by the flow of tears. Infection, leading to *conjunctivitis*, is nevertheless very common. Even very slight injuries are troublesome if they involve the *cornea*. Small foreign bodies in the eye – and unskilled attempts to remove them – may cause ulcers on the cornea. These small wounds heal only slowly because the cornea has no blood supply, and if they are at all deep they may leave opaque scars that interfere with vision. An eye can be blinded by severe scarring of the cornea. This is the type of blindness that can be cured by grafting a cornea from someone who has bequeathed his eyes to a hospital.

The *aqueous humour* is secreted from the tissues behind the iris and kept at a pressure between 10 and 24 mm of mercury by compensatory leakage in the angle between the outer rim of the iris and the back of the cornea. The flow is through the pupil from behind. Disturbances of this mechanism may cause the pressure to rise: this is *glaucoma*.

The *iris*, its supporting tissue, and the *choroid* form a single layer, the uveal tract. Inflammation from various causes (and often from no known cause) may involve the whole tract (*uveitis*) or one part of it (*iritis*, *choroiditis*). If possible, the cause is treated, but in most cases treatment is directed to preventing complications such as glaucoma or damage to the retina, while the inflammation settles in its own time. Corticosteroid drugs have become the standard treatment for most of these cases. Drugs such as atropine are used to keep the iris dilated and prevent it from sticking to the lens.

The one common disorder of the *lens* is *cataract* or opacity, which can be due to congenital defect, injury, or ageing. Cataract is treated by removing the useless lens and compensating for its loss with glasses or contact lenses, or by replacing it with an artificial implant.

The *retina* cannot function unless it is evenly applied to the back of the eye. *Detachment* of the retina may follow injury or may occur spontaneously; it occasionally complicates other conditions such as *choroiditis*. Vision is lost in the affected area. Detachment is treated by making minute injuries to stick the retina in place, by heat, cold, or other means. Inflammation – *retinitis* – may complicate inflammation elsewhere in the eye; other cases are ascribed to various more general ailments including diseases of blood vessels, chronic alcoholism, and nutritional deficiencies. Much the commonest retinal disorders are due to diabetes and high blood pressure. In all these cases it is the underlying disease that is treated.

The *optic nerve* arises in an area to the inner side of the mid-point of the retina; there are no rods or cones in this area (optic disc) and it is therefore a blind spot. (Since the image on the retina is reversed, the blind spot corresponds with a small area in the field of vision to the *outer* side of centre.) The nerve is liable to damage by increased pressure within the eye (glaucoma) or inside the skull, by the same conditions as cause retinitis, and by *multiple sclerosis*, a disease of various parts of the nervous system.

Squint is a failure to balance the muscles controlling movement of the eyes. Since the eyes do not point in the same direction the images do not correspond. With the common squints of childhood, the brain resolves the conflict between disparate images by ignoring one. If the squint is neglected, the habit of ignoring impulses from one eye becomes fixed and the eye – although perfectly healthy – is in effect blind. It is for this reason, and not for the sake of appearance, that child-hood squints need to be treated early. The much less common squints that come on in adult life, after the brain has learned to resolve the two images, cause double vision.

eyelid. An eyelid is a crescent of rubbery cartilage, covered with skin and lined with conjunctiva. The muscles are mainly under conscious control, but the muscle raising the upper lid also responds to involuntary stimulation from sympathetic nerves.

Small glands in the lid margins may become blocked and form painless cysts, easily removed, or they can be infected by bacteria in the same way as skin glands elsewhere – a *stye* (hordeolum) is a boil on an eyelid.

eye-strain. Working in a poor light is inefficient and tiring but unlikely to do physical harm to the eyes. Much of the fatigue and discomfort can be ascribed to bringing the work too close in an attempt to compensate for bad lighting. Uncorrected optical defects – not wearing glasses when they are needed – have much the same effect.

F

Fabricius ab Aquapendente (Girolamo Fabrizio d'Acquapendente) (*c.* 1537–1619). Professor of anatomy and surgery at Padua (1565–1604); pupil of Fallopius. He continued the detailed study of anatomy that had begun with Vesalius, and picked up ►*embryology* more or less where Aristotle had left it. In a detailed account of the formed human foetus he described the two short-circuits in the foetal heart (►*heart* (1)).

He also described the valves which allow blood in the veins to flow only towards the heart, but did not recognize their function. He accepted Galen's theory that blood flowed in the other direction, and thought the valves ensured that the small branches should be fed, by checking the flow. The mistake did not matter, for Fabricius inspired his pupil Harvey to find the correct answer.

Fabricius Hildanus (Wilhelm Fabry (Faber)) (1560–1634). German anatomist and surgeon; a founder of the medical renaissance in Germany, often compared with Paré in France. He introduced the new anatomical learning from Italy and added important studies of congenital abnormalities. His classification of ►*burns* (3 degrees) still stands, as do his principles of amputation for gangrene.

facial. Of the face.
Facial artery. A branch of the external *carotid* artery. Its pulse can be felt at the side of the jaw.
Facial nerve. The 7th cranial nerve: it sends branches to all the muscles of facial expression. The sensory nerve of the face is the *trigeminal* (5th cranial).

Paralysis of the facial nerve is common; ►*Bell's palsy*.

facies. The face; or the appearance of the face as a clue to diagnosis. The *Hippocratic facies* of grave illness is described in the *Prognostics*; ►*Hippocrates*.

faeces. Rejected waste from the intestine, consisting of the undigested remains of the food (largely cellulose), bacteria, and a variable quantity of water and mucus. The colour is due to bile pigment (a breakdown product of blood pigment), and the odour mainly to nitrogen compounds produced by bacterial action. Examination of the faeces is important for the diagnosis of diseases of the intestine. Blood is not necessarily due to piles: traces detectable only by chemical tests may be highly significant, for any blood in the faeces is abnormal. It may be the earliest sign of cancer, at a curable stage. There are of course many other possible causes, but they have to be positively identified before cancer can be excluded.

Chemical examination may indicate faulty digestion if substances that should have been assimilated are found. Infection of the intestine is identified by studying the bacteria of the faeces, and worms and other parasites, or their eggs, are recognized by microscopy.

failure. The word is much used in a relative sense, when it may alarm the uninitiated who take it in an absolute sense. Failure of an organ (heart, lungs, a gland) seldom means that it has ceased to work. It means that the organ does not fully meet the demands made on it, and if performance cannot be improved it may still be possible to relieve failure by reducing the demands. (➤e.g. *heart failure*.)

faint (syncope). Sudden unconsciousness from lowered blood pressure in the arteries of the brain. A faint is a reflex effect. Over-activity of the vagus (parasympathetic) nerves, from emotional or other causes, slows the heart and at the same time relaxes blood vessels in the abdomen, to which much of the blood promptly gravitates. As soon as the subject's head comes down to the level of his heart, as it must if he falls or lies down, the flow of blood to his brain is restored.

Faintness from standing to attention is due to pooling of blood in the legs. It can be relieved by twitching the muscles. Faintness on suddenly standing is due to delay in the reflex adjustment of the blood vessels to the new position.

Fallopian tubes. A pair of tubes open at one end to the cavity of the abdomen and at the other to the upper part of the uterus. The abdominal end, which looks not unlike a sea anemone, is next to the ovary. It collects the ovum that is shed each month and conveys it to the uterus. Sperms swim up the tubes from the uterus, and fertilization takes place in the Fallopian tube; the fertilized ovum begins to develop into an embryo before it reaches the uterus.

Occasionally an embryo remains in the tube instead of migrating to the uterus (➤*ectopic* pregnancy).

Inflammation of a Fallopian tube (*salpingitis*) is due to bacterial infection. An abscess may form and need surgical treatment. In some cases the inflammation causes scarring and obstruction of the tube; if both tubes are so affected the

woman is sterile. The tubes can be closed surgically in order to sterilize a woman.

Fallopius (Gabriele Fallopio) (1523–62). One of the great school of anatomists at Padua, a pupil of Vesalius. He added numerous details to his teacher's work, including the first good description of the tubes named after him.

Fanconi syndrome. (Described in 1936 by G. Fanconi, Swiss paediatrician.) A congenital disorder of the kidneys, as a result of which various essential nutrients pass into the urine along with waste products, causing malnutrition and especially weakness of the bones. A very carefully balanced diet helps, but affected children cannot always be kept free from symptoms.

farmer's lung. An allergic reaction to fungal spores in mouldy hay, with symptoms of bronchitis: fever, cough, wheezing, and, after repeated attacks, loss of weight. The symptoms respond to corticosteroid treatment, but to avoid further damage the patient has to avoid any contact with mouldy hay in future.

fascia. Fibrous tissue wrapped round muscles and other organs; the packing material of the body. A bewildering array of different layers can be described, but the arrangement seems simple if one imagines that the organs grow into a pool of connective tissue and compress it into thin sheets between them. The fibrous covering of bones (*periosteum*) merges with the fascial sheaths of the neighbouring muscles.

The fascia covering the body just under the skin is said to be in two layers, deep and superficial; but the superficial 'fascia' is simply a layer of fat divided into compartments by fibrous strands. The deep fascia is rudimentary over the chest and abdomen to allow for expansion, but elsewhere it is tough and unyielding. A layer of fascia is an effective barrier against the spread of infection through the tissues, but pus very readily tracks along a fascial plane. Thus although in itself fascia is the least interesting of tissues it is important to the surgeon.

fat. The oils and fats of living creatures, and of our diet, differ only in their melting points. Strictly speaking all are triglycerides (see below). Associated compounds such as *cholesterol*, often called fats, are more strictly ►*lipids.*

Fat is incorporated into the fabric of all parts of the body. Globules of fat enmeshed in the loose network of fibrous tissue underlying the skin serve as insulator, packaging and fuel store. Some internal organs, notably the kidneys, are supported by buffers of a more solid kind of fat, familiar in the kitchen as suet. The liver maintains a store of chemically processed fat as a source of ►*energy.* Vitamins A, D, E and K are insoluble in water and have to be dissolved in fat to be circulated. Some components of fat (essential fatty acids) are needed for synthesizing a versatile group of hormones, the *prostaglandins.* Although most fats can be synthesized in the liver from carbohydrates, the essential fatty acids have to be provided ready-made in the diet like vitamins.

1. CHEMISTRY

The true ('neutral') fats and oils are *triglycerides*, i.e. compounds of glycerol with fatty acids. Glycerol is an alcohol, which means no more than that its molecule includes a hydroxyl radical (an atom of oxygen linked to one of hydrogen, —OH), which can combine with an

acid to form an *ester*, just as an alkali, also with an —OH radical, forms salts, thus:

$$HCl + NaOH \rightarrow H_2O + NaCl$$
acid   alkali   water   salt

$$CH_3COOH + C_2H_5OH \rightarrow H_2O$$
acid   alcohol   water
$$+ CH_3COOC_2H_5$$
ester

Glycerol differs from ordinary alcohol, above, in having three hydroxyl groups: $CH_2OH—CHOH—CH_2OH$. One molecule combines with three of acid to form a fat molecule, a *tri*glyceride.

A fatty acid is a hydrocarbon, i.e. composed of hydrogen and carbon, linked to a *carboxyl* radical, —COOH. Acetic acid, shown above as $CH_3.COOH$, is an example. The first carbon atom is linked to three of hydrogen, its fourth link going to the other carbon atom. This in turn gives its remaining three to the oxygen atoms: O=C–O–H. Carbon atoms always make four links; i.e. the *valence* of carbon is four. The valences of oxygen and hydrogen are shown to be two and one respectively (cf. H_2O).

Butane is a hydrocarbon with 4 atoms of carbon and 10 of hydrogen: C_4H_{10}. The structural formula shown opposite shows 4 linked carbon atoms with all their remaining bonds taken up by hydrogen atoms. Such a compound is said to be *saturated*.

In a derived fatty acid, butyric acid, a CH_3 group is replaced by a carboxyl radical. This, too, is a saturated compound. But *crotonic acid* sheds two hydrogen atoms. The two middle carbon atoms are now linked by a *double bond* so that each still uses its four bonds, but the resulting acid has room for two more hydrogen atoms, and is said to be *unsaturated*.

```
  H H H H                H H H
  | | | |                | | |
H–C–C–C–C–H          H–C–C–C–C=O
  | | | |                | | | |
  H H H H                H H H O–H
    butane                butyric acid
                 H H H
                 | | |
             H–C–C=C–C=O
                 |     |
                 H    O–H
               crotonic acid
```

Some of the higher fatty acids – with a longer chain of carbon atoms – are *polyunsaturated*, having more than one double bond. Of the three essential acids, linoleic has two, linolenic three, and arachidonic four double bonds.

The distinction of saturated from unsaturated fatty acids is important not only because the essential acids are unsaturated. A diet rich in saturated fats predisposes to atheroma and the resulting heart disease, while a preponderance of unsaturated fats gives some protection; ►*cholesterol*; *atheroma*.

2. DIETARY FAT

An adequate diet needs a modicum of fat, not only to provide the essential acids and carry vitamins, but because with no fat at all it would be so unappetizing as to be indigestible. On the other hand an excess of fat is nauseating, and more importantly it is the easiest way to put on unhealthy weight Any source of energy in the diet that the body does not immediately need is set aside for another day as deposited fat, like coal in the cellar. All surplus food can be converted to fat, but suet and butter need no conversion – and they carry more than twice the potential energy of carbohydrate or protein. Being overweight increases the risk of getting diabetes, heart attacks and other hazards, and too much fatty food is a leading cause.

The kind of fat eaten is almost as important as the amount. Animal fats are richest in saturated fatty acids, and vegetable fats (oils) in unsaturated; therefore the risk of developing heart disease is less with a predominantly vegetable diet. The foods richest in cholesterol, to be avoided in excess, include egg yolk, butcher's offal and some shellfish. (►*diet.*)

fatigue. The body-systems likely to suffer fatigue are the muscles and the nervous system.

Under experimental conditions a muscle can be tired by rapidly repeated stimulation, when the by-products of muscle chemistry accumulate faster than they can be carried away in the veins. To what extent, if any, this accounts for the fatigue of ordinary exercise is not known, but swelling from seepage of fluid is probably a more important factor. But during sustained exercise, tired muscles often recover to some extent. This, and the whole phenomenon of second wind, is still unexplained.

Again under experimental conditions, reflexes become sluggish after prolonged repetition. This is a sort of fatigue, but it cannot be equated with ordinary tiredness. Yet no amount of artificial stimulation impairs the efficiency of nerves, under laboratory conditions.

Mental fatigue is often associated, and perhaps identical, with boredom; and even fatigue that seems purely physical comes on much sooner with dull tasks than with interesting ones. Drugs such as amphetamine that give temporary respite from fatigue may do so simply by elevating mood.

The healthy tiredness at the end of a busy day cannot be properly explained. It has to be largely mental, because typically it does not come on until a satisfying task is completed. And in every sport it is the loser who feels exhausted. But to say that this kind of fatigue is mental is to state the obvious: it is a feeling and like any other feeling can only be defined as a state of mind. The origin of the feeling is still a mystery.

Extreme tiredness stops all activity, and sleep becomes imperative. Until more is known of sleep and the reasons for it, tiredness has to be defined as need of sleep, and sleep as that which relieves tiredness.

fatty degeneration. A disorder of nutrition in various tissues, notably liver and heart muscle. If these tissues are deprived of certain foods, or of oxygen (e.g. because of anaemia or poor circulation), their cells are unable to dispose of fats. As a result fat accumulates in the affected tissue and impairs its function. Hence an excess of useless fat in the liver is sometimes a result of starvation.

Poisons such as alcohol interfere with the consumption of fat throughout the body so that fat is deposited in the liver and elsewhere.

fauces. The back of the throat; the region between the mouth and the pharynx, containing the tonsils.

favism. Poisoning by a kind of bean, *Vicia fava*, found in Italy. It affects people with hereditary deficiency of the enzyme G6PD, who develop diarrhoea and anaemia from destruction of red blood cells. Blood transfusion is sometimes needed.

febrile. Affected with, or related to, ►*fever*.

feedback. A term borrowed from electronics: numerous systems in the body are kept constant by using a product of the system to regulate its own output. For example, the adrenal glands are stimulated to produce cortisol by a hormone, ACTH, from the pituitary. But an excess of cortisol suppresses the release of ACTH and so inhibits the production of more cortisol until the level returns to normal. ►*biofeedback*.

felon. A common type of septic finger, with the infection confined to the pad (pulp) of the finger-tip.

femoral. Of the femur (thigh-bone), or of the thigh as a whole.
Femoral artery. Main artery of the lower limb, the continuation of the *external iliac* artery. It enters the front of the thigh halfway along the fold of the groin, where its pulse can be felt. The femoral artery runs between muscles to the back of the knee, where it continues as the *popliteal* artery. A large branch, the *profunda femoris*, is the main artery of the thigh itself; the femoral is more concerned with the parts below the knee.
Femoral nerve. Nerve of the extensor muscles (*quadriceps*) at the front of the thigh. It is formed from the lumbar spinal nerves, and enters the thigh at the outer side of the artery.
Femoral vein. The vein corresponds closely with the artery.

femur. The thigh-bone; a massive column of bone, with a slight forward curve, and a girder-like ridge behind. At the hips the two femora are separated by the width of the pelvis. At the knees the femora come together. Hence the bones are set at an angle in the form of a V. The upper end of the femur is turned inwards and forwards; the *neck* is set at an angle of about 130° with the *shaft*. The angulation is more pronounced in women than in men, to compensate for the broader V of the shafts made by a woman's relatively wide pelvis and short thighs. The *head* of the femur is almost a perfect sphere to fit the hemispherical socket (*acetabulum*) of the hipbone. The lower end of the femur is widened to form two projections, the *condyles*, on which the ►*tibia* slides when the knee is flexed.

The femur is very strong, but it may be subjected to great strains, and fractures are common. Loss of blood may be severe with no external wound, for there is room in and among the muscles for profuse bleeding. Very rarely the nerves behind the knee are involved in a fracture of the lower end of the femur, but usually the problem with a broken thigh is the fracture itself. The muscles pulling the broken ends are so powerful that displacement, overlapping, and shortening can be difficult to overcome. If the bone is correctly set, a plaster cast cannot be trusted to keep it in place because there is so much room for play in the yielding mass of muscle. With few exceptions, these fractures need either a continuous pull, maintained by a system of weights and pulleys while the bone heals, or internal fixation by splints screwed to the bone or inside the medullary cavity.

The neck of the femur is especially vulnerable in elderly people, who can sustain a fracture here from an apparently trivial fall. The head of the bone can be held in place with a fluted nail driven into the neck from the outside. But with this treatment the patient has to remain in bed while new bone forms round the nail, which brings a risk of pneumonia and other complications. This risk can be overcome by removing the head of the femur and fitting a metal replacement, or fitting a complete artificial joint. The patient is able to stand within a day or two of the operation.

►*hip*; *knee*; *fracture*.

fenestration. A surgical operation for the relief of deafness due to advanced ►*otosclerosis*: an artificial window is made between the middle ear and the organ of hearing of the inner ear. Fenestration is now largely superseded by less drastic and more reliable operations.

Fernel, Jean (1497–1558). Professor of medicine in Paris; author of a treatise on medical practice that was a standard work of reference for two centuries. He divided his work into three parts: physiology, pathology, and treatment, in the manner of a modern text-book. Pathology – the nature of disease – was his special study. He summarized current views and added many observations of his own, including one of the few descriptions of appendicitis before the 19th century. He made no startling discoveries but he was the first to classify medical knowledge in a way that made scientific progress possible; in other words he formulated the problems that his successors were to solve.

ferric; ferrous. Iron compounds are ferric or ferrous, according to the electrochemical state of the iron. Both sorts have been used for treating iron-deficiency anaemia, but ferrous salts are preferable because they are better assimilated. Ferrous sulphate is cheap and effective, but a few people do not tolerate it well, and other salts, e.g. ferrous gluconate, have to be used instead.

fertility. Though most married couples produce children without undue difficulty, some manage only after years of

247

disappointment and some not at all. Medicine cannot always help, but every case is worth investigating.

In the first place it is the couple that needs attention and not one or other member. Some husbands resent any suggestion that they should be examined, as though it were an insult to their manhood. In fact, infertility has little to do with impotence, of which they think they are accused, and among civilized people neither diagnosis need be taken as an insult.

Even in these enlightened times a few infertile couples need no more than simple instruction about sex. And apart from mere technique, the timing of coitus is important. A woman is most likely to conceive when ovulation occurs, a fortnight before a period.

If it is hard to see what the emotional climate can have to do with fertility, the fact remains that the successful treatment of a neurosis may incidentally cure infertility. Sometimes adopting a child seems to have the same effect. All kinds of physical ill health tend to reduce fertility.

Examination of the seminal fluid may show that the number or the motility of the sperms is abnormally low. Measures to improve the man's general health, and perhaps a brief term of abstinence followed by coitus timed to coincide with ovulation, may help, and artificial insemination from the husband (AIH) is sometimes advised. A recently developed ingenious refinement of AIH is to fertilize and incubate the ovum in laboratory conditions ('test-tube baby') before implanting it in the uterus. This has provided normal children for a few couples for whom natural fertilization and implantation failed consistently.

Another method that has been tried

when the prospective mother's uterus could not nurture an embryo to maturity is to remove the fertilized ovum and re-implant it in the uterus of another woman, a 'surrogate mother'. This involves difficulties that may be unforeseen at the outset. The surrogate has no control over the natural effect on her of nine months' gestation, and simply handing the baby to its legitimate parents may prove an intolerable emotional strain.

Various gynaecological disorders that impair fertility can be treated surgically. But sometimes the ovaries fail to release an ovum each month because of a deficiency in the pituitary gland. This gland below the brain should secrete a hormone to stimulate the ovaries. If this mechanism fails the patient can be given injections of the hormone or the synthetic substitute *clomiphene*, with a warning that the treatment sometimes leads to twins, triplets or more.

In a few cases where both partners are normal there seems to be some chemical antagonism between sperms and uterine secretion. In these cases, as in those where the sperms are defective, the question of artificial insemination from a donor other than the husband (AID) may arise. This is technically simple, but it presents grave ethical and legal problems.

There remains a large group of couples in whom no treatable cause of infertility can be found. For them, adoption is often an acceptable remedy.

fertilization. The union of male and female germ cells (sperm and ovum). In the ordinary way, cells multiply by splitting (binary fission). When the cell splits the complete set of 23 pairs of chromosomes is duplicated. But when the immediate precursors of the germ cells split, one member of each chromosome-pair goes to a finished germ cell. A sperm or ovum therefore has 23 single chromosomes. ►*genetics*.

Each month an ovum leaves an ovary and is picked up by the Fallopian tube to be fertilized if sperms swim up the tube from the uterus, and one of them fuses with the ovum. The fertilized ovum then has 23 pairs of chromosomes, one member of each pair from either parent. Later events are described under ►*embryo*.

fetishism. A form of anomalous sexual behaviour, where the patient is sexually excited by an object such as an article of clothing, his fetish, in preference to more conventional sources of excitement. ►*sex*.

fever. Raised body temperature (= *pyrexia*), or any disease of which pyrexia is a leading symptom.

Fever is usually associated with infection, but is also a symptom of other kinds of illness.

The normal body temperature is maintained by a centre in the brain, which meets any threatened alteration with appropriate reflexes: reduced flow of blood through the skin and shivering to conserve heat, or increased flow (flushing) and sweating to lose heat. The critical temperature to which the centre is adjusted varies slightly during the day, and in women also during the month. The body temperature may rise by several degrees after a hot bath or strenuous exercise because the reflexes for cooling cannot keep pace, but the centre is unaffected and the temperature is quickly brought back to normal. But with fever the setting of the centre is altered, apparently by the chemical action of substances formed either by the destruction

of bacteria or by damage to the body's own tissues.

When fever comes on rapidly it is often accompanied by a *rigor*, an attack of violent shivering, and in children by a convulsion like an epileptic seizure. If the fever subsides rapidly (i.e. by *crisis*) the patient sweats profusely. A typical attack of malaria is a series of short periods of fever alternating with periods of normal temperature, with a rigor at the beginning of each outburst and sweating at the end.

Fever increases the pulse rate and most other processes in the body. The accelerated chemical turnover may contribute to natural defence against infection, but the value of fever is uncertain. ►*temperature*.

fibre. As an ingredient of a wholesome diet, this was formerly known as *roughage*. It is almost entirely the parts of fruits and vegetables that, since we have no way of digesting them, are passed on to the large intestine, where they add to the bulk of the faeces to be voided. This gives the intestinal muscles something to grip, much increasing their efficiency and preventing the need to strain, and so reducing the risk of diverticulosis, piles, some hernias, and perhaps varicose veins and appendicitis. Numerous other diseases have, with some controversy, been blamed on lack of fibre in the diet.

The value of roughage was accepted in the 19th century; then, in an era concerned only with *nutrition*, it was forgotten until T. L. Cleave, a British naval surgeon, revived interest during the Second World War. Fibre was again forgotten until 1970, since when numerous books on the subject have appeared. The importance Western society attributes to dietary fibre nowadays is attested to by the number of foodstuffs which advertise their fibre content as part of their sales pitch.

fibrillation. Rapid unco-ordinated twitching of muscle fibres.

➤*arrhythmia.*

fibrin. An insoluble protein, the basis of blood-clot; ➤*blood* (4).

fibrocystic disease = ➤*cystic fibrosis.*

fibroelastosis. Proliferation of elastic connective tissue in the lining of the heart, leading to serious heart disease in infancy. The cause is unknown, and no cure has yet been found.

fibroid (fibromyoma). A tumour of the uterus, forming a round fibrous lump, or more often several distinct lumps. Fibroids can cause excessive menstrual bleeding, sometimes discomfort, and sometimes fairly severe pain. They are not a danger to life and are in no way associated with cancer. Untreated fibroids can grow so large as to become a serious physical burden. Some fibroids can be shelled out, leaving the uterus intact and still capable of child-bearing, but more often the uterus has to be removed entire. The only after-effect of the operation is that the woman cannot have children, but in many of these cases the fibroids themselves would have made pregnancy unlikely, and most patients are near the end of or past the age of child-bearing.

fibroplasia ➤*retrolental fibroplasia.*

fibrositis. A vague but convenient term for ill-defined pain in and around muscles – 'muscular rheumatism'. The pain comes and goes for no apparent reason. Most sufferers are without symptoms for long periods; this enhances the reputation of whatever remedy was last tried. In many but not all cases the pain is confined to one group of muscles. Movement may be restricted, but by pain rather than real stiffness.

Apart from the minority of cases where 'fibrositis' is a symptom of some recognized disease, this complaint is an unsolved puzzle. Some authorities deny that it exists, i.e. that the pain has anything to do with inflammation of connective tissue (fibrositis) or of muscle (myositis). Explanations include localized muscle spasm, squeezing a nerve and causing further spasm; weak spots in the fibrous coating of muscles, allowing tissue to be pinched as it bulges through; and minor disorders of the back-bone, interfering with nerves as they emerge between vertebrae and causing referred pain in the muscles to which the nerves are destined. This last certainly accounts for many cases.

Faulty posture (which could affect either the backbone or the muscles where the pain seems to be) is an important factor in bringing on attacks. Sitting in an awkward position, or sitting *tensely* in any position, can start the pain. Tension, in turn, has many causes, including all kinds of anxiety. In treating this disorder, relaxed and mechanically efficient posture generally does more good than aspirin and massage. The remedy may be as simple as using a different chair for typing, or wearing glasses to avoid having to sit hunched over a book.

➤*backbone.*

fibula. A slender bone at the outer side of the leg. Its upper end does not quite reach the knee, but its lower end takes part in the ankle, where it forms the outer side of a square socket. The fibula takes no weight, but it is an important anchorage for muscles.

Both ends of the bone lie under the skin. The lower end is the *lateral malleolus*, the knob at the outer side of the ankle. The *lateral popliteal nerve* passes from behind the knee round the upper end of the fibula to reach the peroneal and extensor muscles.

The fibula is easily broken. It seldom remains intact with a fractured tibia, and the two bones may break at quite different levels. A bad 'sprain' of the ankle is often in fact a fracture of the lower end of the fibula, but since bones heal better than ligaments a fracture may be preferable to a sprain. The fibula is fractured in Pott's fracture-dislocation (►*Pott, Percival*).

Rarely, a fracture of the upper end involves the lateral popliteal nerve, which is also liable to compression by a tight bandage.

filaria. A very slender parasitic worm of the tropics. Several kinds affect man. *Wucheria bancrofti* is fairly common in Africa. It is transmitted by a mosquito, and grows in the lymphatic vessels, where it sets up inflammation. The infection also causes occasional attacks of fever. After years of repeated infection the skin and connective tissue of the legs or the genitals may become grossly thickened, a condition known as *elephantiasis*.

Onchocerca, a Central American and African filaria, has a predilection for the eyes and can cause blindness ('river blindness'). Some other species confine themselves to the skin.

Most filariae are killed by the drug diethylcarbamazine. Ivermectin is used to treat onchocerciasis.

fissure. A split in skin or mucous membrane; it is really a very narrow ulcer.

Anal fissure, at the junction of skin and mucous membrane of the anus, probably results from straining because of constipation. It is painful and therefore encourages further constipation. It is one of the comparatively few really good reasons for taking laxatives. An anal fissure may require a small surgical operation.

fistula. A penetrating wound or ulcer, creating an abnormal passage between two body surfaces (body surfaces include the skin and the linings of hollow organs). For instance a stab-wound of the belly may create a fistula between the intestine and the skin, or a surgeon may make an artificial temporary fistula between the bladder and the skin to relieve obstruction in the bladder. Such fistulae usually close themselves if they are kept free from bacterial infection, and if they are not acting as safety valves to an obstructed passage. A spontaneous fistula is nearly always due to infection of a minor injury. An example is *fistula-in-ano*, between the rectum and the skin. This kind of fistula starts with infection of a small blemish in the mucous membrane of the rectum or anus. It does not heal on its own because of constant reinfection by faeces; but it can be cured by a surgical operation to open the track and convert it into a shallow groove: despite contamination, open wounds of the anus heal well.

fit ►*epilepsy*.

flagellate. A minute, single-celled animal (protozoon) able to swim with one or more whip-like structures (flagella). Several kinds are parasites of man. Some cause serious disease, e.g. *trypanosomes* (sleeping sickness). Others cause only local irritation, e.g. *trichomonas* in the vagina, and *giardia* in the intestine.

flat foot ►*foot* (2).

flatulence. Gas in the stomach and intestine causes a good deal of discomfort. Most of it is swallowed, but some is produced in the lower part of the intestine by fermentation, especially in constipated people. Air is swallowed by gulping food or drink and by unsuccessful attempts to belch, and some nervous people do it at any time. Recognizing that these habits exist is the most important step towards breaking them.

flea. Kinds of blood-sucking insect, lacking wings but able to jump. Most fleas live primarily on domestic or other animals, and afflict man only as second choice. Fleas are usually no more than a nuisance to be controlled with insecticides, but some species, especially those that infest rats, carry serious diseases including plague and one kind of typhus.

flexion. The movement of bending a joint (opposed to *extension*).

flexure. 1. A bend such as the hepatic and splenic flexures where the large intestine abruptly changes direction. **2.** Line along which skin folds when a joint is flexed.

fluorine. A chemical element with similar properties to chlorine, found in many minerals and in the human body as an ingredient of bones and teeth. Although the amount in these tissues is small – about 1 part in 10,000 – it is essential to their stability.

During the 19th century there were numerous suggestions that fluorine might protect the teeth against caries (decay), but a report from Naples in 1901 that fluorine actually *caused* disfigurement of the teeth discouraged further inquiry for a time. In 1939 a study carried out in four towns in Illinois showed that too little fluorine in the drinking water was associated with frequent caries, but that too much caused unsightly mottling of the teeth. With about one part per million of fluorine in the water, there was enough to keep down the incidence of caries but not enough to cause mottling. These findings were confirmed in other surveys, and in 1946 fluorine was added to the water supply of Grand Rapids, Mich. At once there were complaints of ill-effects from the 'adulterated' water, but it transpired that the fluoridation had had to be delayed, and the ill-effects arose before any fluorine was added. After a quarter of a century of fluoridation in towns all over the world there is still no evidence that it is harmful, and countless children have escaped dental fillings and extractions. But some people still oppose fluoridation – in Antigo, Wisconsin, so strongly that it was stopped in 1960. All school children were examined at once and the prevalence of caries was recorded. By 1966, the prevalence among Second Grade children had more than trebled, and the opponents of fluorine were overruled. It is, however, true that fluorine is more important to children whose teeth are still developing. Fluoridation of the water supply means that everyone gets the same treatment, including adults who may not need it, and some of them object. Direct application of fluorides to the teeth in a mouthwash or toothpaste also seems to help.

Fluorine in any form does not abolish dental caries, but in places where the water contains enough fluorine, either natural or added, there is less than half as much caries as in places where the water lacks fluorine.

fly. The common house-fly contaminates food by carrying bacteria from animal or human excrement on its feet. The danger is slight where there is efficient waterborne sanitation but very real under more primitive conditions. Apart from intestinal infection such as bacillary dysentery, flies may be involved in the spread of wound infection, conjunctivitis (pinkeye), and poliomyelitis. Even in countries with a high standard of hygiene it is worth while to keep flies away from food. In the tropics, houses are usually sprayed with insecticides to prevent mosquitoes from spreading malaria; this also keeps down flies, which in tropical countries can be a serious menace.

A few tropical and subtropical fevers are transmitted by the bites of flies. They include sandfly fever and African sleeping sickness. In these cases the flies are actually infected by sucking blood from someone with the disease, unlike house-flies, which merely have dirty feet.

foetus. Unborn infant that has developed from an ►*embryo* to a stage where it is recognizably human, i.e. from about the eighth week of pregnancy.

At this time the foetus is about 4 cm long, measured from crown to rump. Nearly half of it is head, and the limbs are very small. The skeleton is of cartilage – gristle – but the first flecks of bone are just appearing. Its heart is pumping blood through its body and out of the placenta to receive the ingredients of growth filtered from the mother's blood. The lungs are still rudimentary. Neither they nor the intestine serves any purpose until birth. The liver grows quickly: as the main centre of chemical synthesis and storage it has much to do. For a time the liver is so large relative to the abdomen that part of the intestine is pushed through the umbilical cord.

The various organs grow at different rates and the proportions of the foetus gradually change to those of a new-born baby. At 16 weeks, the foetus is about 10 cm long, crown to rump, and weighs about 100 g (4 in and 3½ oz). At 24 weeks it has grown to 20 cm and 650 g, and it is approaching the stage at which it would stand a chance of survival if it should be born early. At 24 weeks from the start of the mother's last period – until recently after 28 weeks – it is considered viable under English law, though in practice it would still be dangerously premature and would survive only with expert nursing. A foetus of this age has very little fat, and therefore great difficulty in keeping warm, and very little stored fuel. Its reflexes for breathing and other vital functions are not yet wholly reliable.

During the last ten weeks of pregnancy the foetus – now definitely a baby – grows about 50 per cent longer and increases its weight five-fold.

The next stage in development is described under ►*birth*.

folic acid. A vitamin of the B group, present in all green plants; ►*vitamin B*.

folie à deux. Symptoms of mental disorder, usually paranoid, affecting two closely associated people at the same time. The patients are most often sisters. Although both seem equally deranged the primary disorder is always with the dominant one; the 'junior partner' adopts her delusions and as a rule recovers as soon as they are separated.

follow-up. Periodic examination of a patient after the completion of a course of treatment. Naturally, it is in the patient's interests that a surgeon who has operated on him, or a physician who has treated him for a serious illness, should see him from time to time to ensure that his recovery is maintained or suggest further treatment if necessary. But follow-up examinations are also an important part of clinical research. It is not enough to know that an operation or a new drug gives temporary relief; the long-term results may be equally important, and the possibility of delayed complications has to be considered. Often an extensive follow-up study is needed before a new treatment can be assessed in relation to older methods.

food ▸*diet*.

food poisoning. This account does not include infections such as ▸*typhoid fever* and *cholera*, conveyed by drinking water or food but not usually classified as food poisoning.

1. *Contamination by microbes*. Most food poisoning is caused by microbes that, having contaminated food, breed in the intestine and set up inflammation (gastro-enteritis) with diarrhoea and vomiting. Common bacterial causes include kinds of *Salmonella*, *Escherichia*, and the more recently identified *Campylobacter*. As often as not no organism is identified, and many cases are presumed to be caused by viruses. As a rule this kind of infection clears up on its own, but with continued diarrhoea or vomiting the lost water and salts must be replaced, if possible by mouth. Pharmacies supply preparations to be dissolved in water and drunk to keep pace with the fluid loss. Routine use of antibiotics is not recommended because they are useless against viruses, and most bacterial food poisoning clears up quickly without them; but with severe bacterial infection there is certainly a place for them.

Some bacteria infect the food rather than the consumer, and leave undetected toxins that may resist cooking. Staphylococci, e.g. from a food handler with a septic finger, are a common cause of this kind of trouble. The most dangerous condition of this kind is ▸*botulism*: its lethal toxin has the sole merit that it is destroyed by cooking.

2. *Other natural contaminants*. Foodstuffs infected by moulds cause localized outbreaks of poisoning, ▸*ergot*, *aflatoxin* (affecting rye and peanuts respectively). Fish in tropical waters may feed on a kind of plankton that without harming the fish makes it poisonous to humans. PSP (paralytic shellfish poisoning) is an instance.

3. *Poisoning by the food itself*. Quite apart from poisonous plants mistaken for edible ones, e.g. ▸*mushrooms* and various berries, perfectly respectable foods can at times be harmful. Occasional poisons include *oxalic acid* in sorrel and the green leaves of rhubarb, and *solanine* in the green parts of sprouting potatoes. *Lathyrism* is a paralysis caused by certain vetches eaten in times of famine in India and elsewhere.

4. *Artificial contaminants*. Chemical spraying of fruit trees to kill parasites can leave poisonous deposits that must be washed off before the fruit is fit to eat. Chemical fertilizers are unlikely to carry any such risk; manure is no healthier for being processed by a cow rather than a chemist.

Food additives (flavouring, colouring, preservatives, etc.) may well be inferior in appearance or taste to the real thing, but there is little evidence that they do much harm. They include vitamins A, C, and E, or substances derived from them, to prevent spoiling by the action of air; vitamin A is also a colorant. But some people are sensitive to additives such as the colorant tartrazine, which they have to avoid. And various symptoms are blamed on an excess of monosodium glutamate (MSG).

A serious outbreak of poisoning ascribed to contamination of colza oil by mineral oils occurred in Spain in 1981.

5. *Idiosyncrasy*. Individuals may be allergic to certain foods (>*immunity*), or they may have an inborn lack of a particular enzyme (>*carbohydrate intolerance, coeliac disease, favism*).

foot. In principle, the anatomy of the foot is almost identical with that of the hand. Only the proportions differ.

The 7 *tarsal* bones correspond with carpal bones of the hand. Only one takes part in the ankle joint, the *talus*. The *calcaneum*, on which the talus rests, is the largest bone in the foot. The 5 metatarsals correspond with the metacarpals. As in the hand, the 1st (big) toe has two phalanges, and the others each have three.

The weight of the body is taken by the calcaneum and the heads of the metatarsals. The other bones are raised from the ground as an arch. Since the first 3 toes are supported by the talus, which is above the calcaneum, the arch rises higher on the inner than the outer side. These are the *longitudinal* arches. With the feet together the metatarsals of each side form half of a *transverse* arch. The shape of the bones does little or nothing to maintain the arches, but the very strong ligaments of the sole are an important factor. Most of all, the arches depend on the support of the muscles, of which the strongest are those of the big toe. If these muscles are flabby the ligaments stretch and the arches are flattened.

As in the hand, the most important muscles arise higher in the limb: the *extensors* beside the shin, and the *flexors*

Bones of the foot

deep in the calf. A third group, the *peronei*, joins the fibula to the outer side of the foot. In addition there is a complex system of small muscles in the foot, arranged as those of the hand but to less purpose. They are presumably inherited from ancestors which used their feet for grasping. The really significant movements of the foot are inversion and eversion, and the powerful flexion of the big toe which gives the final thrust to the forward stride.

1. INJURIES

Fractures of the *toes* are nearly always due to direct violence, e.g. by a heavy object falling on the foot, which also crushes the soft tissues of the toe. Such fractures are less important than the damage to the toe as a whole. They are troublesome only if it is the big toe that is broken; any other toe can be lost without disability. *March fracture* is of a metatarsal, usually the 2nd. Since a metatarsal is firmly splinted by its neighbours the fracture heals quickly and well.

In contrast, fractures of the tarsal bones are always serious, both in themselves and because the violence needed to produce them is likely to cause other injuries. Hippocrates in the 5th century BC singled out fractured calcaneum as one of the most difficult fractures to treat, and the same can be said today. Manipulation is seldom easy, and some form of surgical operation is often needed to replace the fragments. Even with perfect alignment, tarsal fractures can be troublesome, because one or other of the many joints between the bones is often involved, and a broken joint surface does not readily recover its smoothness. Thus the patient may be left with a stiff and painful foot. An operation (*arthrodesis*) to seal off the affected joint, converting the components to a single bone, restricts movement but leaves the foot painless and stable. Paradoxically, arthrodesis may render the foot *more* supple, by relieving the pain that had made any movement intolerable.

2. DEFORMITIES

Various congenital defects are known as ➤*club-foot* or talipes. Of the acquired deformities – due mainly to unsuitable footwear – the commonest is *hallux valgus* or bunion. The big toe is inclined towards its neighbour. Once this happens the tendons, which should pull straight along the line of the toe and its metatarsal, pull somewhat across this line and increase the deformity. Thus the head of the meta-

tarsal protrudes, and the overlying skin becomes calloused in response to the unaccustomed pressure. If splinting and a change of shoes fail, the deformity can be corrected by a small operation.

Flat foot is incompetence of the arches. Anyone who stands still for long enough will find that his soles begin to ache, because the muscles tire and allow too much of the load to fall on the ligaments. If the muscles are weak or the person is unduly heavy, the ligaments become stretched and cannot recover. A greater load is then thrown on the already overloaded muscles. Treatment is largely a matter of educating the muscles, and it is obviously most likely to succeed if it is started before the condition has become serious. On the other hand, the importance of flat feet can be exaggerated. Some good athletes appear to have very flat feet, which give them no trouble, perhaps because their muscles are sound enough to prevent symptoms. When flat feet ache, either the muscles need to be stronger or the weight which they support needs to be less.

foramen (anat.). Hole or passage through a bone or other structure.

forearm. The forearm extends from ➤*elbow* to ➤*wrist*. The skeleton is two parallel bones, the ➤*radius* on the side of the thumb, and ➤*ulna*. The muscles are in two groups, both extending from the front of the humerus (i.e. above the elbow) to the wrist and hand. The flexors spring from the inner side of the humerus and the front of the forearm bones; the extensors from the outer side of the elbow. The rather unexpected attachment of the extensors in front of the humerus leads them straight to the back of the hand when the limb is in the natural working position, with the elbows bent and the palms facing each other.

The three main nerves are ►*radial*, ►*ulnar*, and ►*median*. The arteries are ►*radial* and ►*ulnar*. Veins accompany the arteries, but there are also large veins under the skin. From the veins of the back of the hand the *cephalic* vein follows the line of the radius and the *basilic* vein that of the ulna.

Movements are described under ►*radius*, ►*elbow*, and ►*wrist* ►►*skeleton*.

forensic medicine. Medical science (especially pathology) applied to jurisdiction.

foreskin ►*circumcision*.

forme fruste. An attack of a disease without the usual or expected symptoms – an abortive form of the disease.

Fracastorius (Girolamo Fracastoro) (1478–1553). Physician and all-round scholar of Verona, author of the earliest rational account of infectious disease (►*microbe*) and of a poem which includes the first treatise on syphilis, a disease which he named.

fracture. A broken bone. Healthy bone is extremely strong. The construction is generally tubular, and parts liable to special stress are often supported by ridges in the form of buttresses or girders. The thinner bones may be broken by a direct blow, but unless the initial force is very great the thicker bones seldom break without leverage. If a bone does break it usually snaps completely; only young bones break partly (green-stick fracture). The break is often transverse if it is close to the actual injury, e.g. Colles' fracture just above the wrist from a fall on the palm. But the line may be oblique or spiral with a less direct injury, e.g. a fracture half-way up the shin from a fall with the foot caught in an obstruction.

Many terms have been applied to different types of fracture. A *compound* fracture is one in direct communication with an open wound, as opposed to a simple or closed fracture. The distinction matters because a compound fracture is likely to be contaminated with bacteria, and infection of bone is dangerous. Until Lister's discovery of antiseptic surgery, compound fractures were usually fatal, and as recently as the First World War amputation was often the only way to save the patient's life. The antibiotic drugs have very greatly reduced the danger.

A *complicated* fracture is one where the broken ends of bone injure other organs (nerves, arteries etc.). A *comminuted* fracture is splintered. A *spontaneous* or *pathological* fracture is due to an injury that would not be enough to break a normal bone but breaks one that is abnormally weak.

The commonest sites of fracture are the clavicle (collar-bone), the radius at the wrist (Colles' fracture) and the ankle (Pott's fracture). In old people whose bones are weakened by osteoporosis (a loss of bone-substance) fractures immediately below the hip are also very common. Other sites of fractures are mentioned under the names of the various bones.

The principles of treatment apply to all fractures, and they have not changed since medical knowledge began to be recorded. First, the fracture is *reduced*, i.e. the broken ends are restored as nearly as possible to their natural position. Second, the reduced fracture is held in position while it heals.

When these two principles are applied, bone heals like any other tissue. The process begins with ►*inflammation*. The flow of blood increases, and fluid, protein and white blood cells are extruded from the blood vessels. The blood-clot at the site of the fracture is gradually removed and replaced firstly with the same kind of delicate spongy tissue as precedes the formation of a scar in the skin. Secondly, this tissue is hardened by chalky deposits to form *callus*, a firm, but not rigid, structureless mass. Thirdly, the callus is replaced by fully developed bone. When a fracture can be exactly reduced the final result is indistinguishable from the uninjured bone; in fact bone is the only tissue that is invisibly mended.

In practice not every fracture needs to be perfectly reduced. The pull of muscles makes the broken ends overlap, but if the ends are in the same mass of blood-clot, callus and ultimately bone will fill the gap. In the leg the bone needs to be pulled out to its original length because shortening impairs function. But in the arm a little overlap and shortening may not matter if the line of the bone is preserved. There are a few situations where perfection matters. Colles' fracture is so close to the wrist joint that any displacement interferes with the mechanical efficiency of the joint, and as a general rule fractures near joints need more exact reduction than others. With any fracture, reduction should obviously be as near perfect as is practicable, but too much manipulation can do more damage than leaving a slight deformity. If for any reason a fracture has to be exposed surgically it is seldom necessary to accept less than perfect reduction.

Most fractures stay in position when they have been reduced if they are kept still, e.g. in a plaster-of-paris cast. A few do not. The thigh is so heavily padded with muscle that no external cast prevents the broken ends from overriding with consequent shortening of the leg. In some other situations an oblique fracture tends to slip inside a cast. The problem can be overcome by continuous *traction*, usually with a system of weights to balance the pull of the muscles. Alternatively the fracture can be held in place by a splint fixed directly to the bone or passed down the middle of the shaft as a dowel.

Movement prevents a fracture from healing because the callus breaks before it has time to consolidate. If it continues, the broken ends become sealed with hard bone and healing is then impossible. Instead, a mobile joint forms between the fragments.

Natural healing is also prevented if one fragment loses its blood supply as a result of the injury.

Surgical repair of fractures is generally reserved for cases where natural healing is unlikely, or where the fracture cannot be adequately reduced by manipulation, or the reduction cannot be maintained.

The rate of healing depends on the site of the injury (the thigh may take two or three times as long as the collar-bone, and the shin still longer), and on the patient's age and general health. But even extreme old age does not prevent bones from healing; it only delays the process.

fragile X syndrome. Mental retardation, with physical anomalies including exaggerated forehead, jaws and ears. It is associated with a defective X-chromosome and so sex-linked (▸*genetics*), but some female carriers are also retarded, and the chromosomal defect is occasionally found in normal males.

Freud, Sigmund (1856–1939). Viennese physician; a pioneer of modern psychiatry and psychology. Freud had already achieved some distinction as a neurologist, i.e. as an expert on the physical properties of the nervous system, before turning his attention to psychology. He founded the analytical school of psychiatry (▸*psychoanalysis*).

Few men have been more misunderstood than Freud, and few have less deserved to be misunderstood, because he explained his doctrines in several good books addressed to the general public. Much of his work dealt with the conflicts between the conscious mind and the unconscious instincts, suppressed memories and so on; and the effect of these conflicts on behaviour and health.

Freud's influence is very great, even on people who think they disagree with everything he said. Most of his ideas were not exactly new – 'conscience' is an older word than Freud's 'superego'. His great contribution was to crystallize ideas that had always lurked at the back of people's minds without finding expression. *Ego*, *id*, *libido* are now household words.

More than anything else it was Freud's insistence on sex as the mainspring of behaviour that turned people against him. His opponents (some of whom had never read a word of his writings) thought he saw a wanton or a rapist in every cradle, that he was blaspheming against the innocence of childhood. In point of fact, Freud was endearingly sentimental about children. 'Sex' is an unfortunate word in Freud's context. It arouses emotion rather than thought if only because it is taken to mean adult sex. Perhaps 'sexuality' would be better, or some word that would imply an instinct of which sex is one expression. And sex may not be the real stumbling block. The resentment may well arise not from Freud's mentioning things that were not mentionable, but from the implication that a thinking man is sometimes

at the mercy of his instincts. In the 17th century Spinoza (with whom Freud had much in common) had been reviled for much the same reason, though he thought the driving force behind human behaviour was the respectable motive of self-preservation.

frigidity. Lack or inhibition of sexual feeling, sometimes amounting to aversion. ▸*sex*.

frontal. Of the forehead. The two *frontal bones*, left and right, are usually, though not invariably, fused during infancy to form a single bone (▸*skull*).

The *frontal lobes* are the part of the brain covered by the frontal bone, and extending back some little way into the territory of the parietal bones. The part under the parietal bones controls voluntary movement. The rest, the prefrontal area, has less clearly defined functions. It is concerned with learning, judgement, and behaviour, but in adults it can suffer severe injury without great inconvenience to the patient. In the operation of prefrontal leukotomy (▸*psychosurgery*) the nerve fibres from this part of the brain are cut for the relief of certain mental disturbances.

frostbite. Damage to skin and sometimes deeper tissues by freezing. Prolonged exposure to cold even without actual freezing can seriously damage the skin by interfering with the circulation of blood (▸*trench foot*), but with true frostbite ice crystals are formed and some loss of tissue is inevitable. The effect is very similar to burning.

The safest way to warm frostbitten skin is in water at blood-heat. Anything warmer is very liable to cause burns. Friction is also wrong. It warms living tissues by stimulating the circulation, but since frostbitten tissues have no circulation to stimulate, friction can only add to the damage.

Frostbitten skin needs to be covered with the cleanest possible dressing, because like burnt skin it is vulnerable to infection, having lost all resistance to bacteria.

frozen shoulder. Pain and stiffness of the shoulder, probably due to inflammation of a ►*bursa* that normally prevents friction between the joint and the surrounding structures. Recovery often takes several months, but in the meantime the symptoms can be relieved with analgesics and cautious physiotherapy.

fructose. A simple sugar in fruits; cane sugar is a compound of fructose with glucose. Fructose is assimilated as easily as glucose. Its molecule contains the same atoms as glucose ($C_6H_{12}O_6$) but differently arranged. It is converted in the liver to glucose.

fugue. An episode of apparently automatic behaviour which the patient cannot later remember, most often a symptom of hysteria, but sometimes associated with epilepsy.

functional. A term applied to various disorders, sometimes with misleading effect. The body is conventionally studied in terms of its structure (anatomy) and function, i.e. how it works (physiology). The same division has been applied to the study of its ailments. If symptoms are accompanied by detectable changes in an organ, such as injury, inflammation, faulty development or a chemical anomaly, the disorder might be called structural, but the correct term is *organic*. But, if the working of an organ is disturbed without apparent physical cause, the dis-

order is said to be *functional*. If a muscle is tense because an adjacent structure is inflamed, the tension is organic. If it is tense because the patient is anxious, the tension is functional. An unusual sound (murmur) heard over the heart is organic if it arises from a faulty heart-valve, but functional if it is due to the normal eddying of blood through a healthy valve. Epileptic seizures caused by a head injury are organic, but if the momentary disturbances of the normal working of the brain cells have no apparent cause the seizures are functional – until someone points out that they are probably due to a birth injury too slight to be detected. So 'functional' comes to mean little more than 'of unknown origin' or even neurotic (hysterical) or imaginary, and a useful word is corrupted.

fundus. The part of a hollow organ remotest from its opening: e.g. *fundus oculi*, the back of the eye; *fundus uteri*, the top of the uterus, the furthest part from the *cervix* or neck of the womb (it is shaped like an inverted flask).

fungus. A very simple kind of plant. Fungi lack the green pigment, chlorophyll, that enables other plants to form carbohydrates (sugar, starch, cellulose) from the carbon dioxide of the air. They are more closely related to bacteria than to green plants, but whereas a bacterium grows to form a colony of individual bacteria, most fungi form a network of branched threads – a *mycelium*. The usual method of reproduction is by forming *spores*. A spore is a minute body, no larger than a bacterium, able to start a new mycelium elsewhere. These tiny seeds can be carried great distances in the air. All dust contains them, and any suitable breeding ground such as exposed food is bound to be contaminated in time and grow a *mould*, which is simply a kind of mycelium. Some fungi with their mycelium in the soil grow large fruiting bodies, e.g. *mushrooms*, from which spores are scattered. *Yeasts* differ from other fungi in that they form no mycelium; like bacteria they form colonies of separate micro-organisms.

Fungi are medically important in several ways:

1. A few kinds of ►*mushroom* are very poisonous, and although accidents are rare those that do happen can be serious.

2. Certain moulds and yeasts cause infection in the same way as bacteria; indeed the distinction between these fungi and bacteria is vague.

The commonest fungal diseases (mycoses) are superficial infections of the skin (►*ringworm*) and mucous membranes (►*thrush*).

Ordinary 'household' moulds are mostly harmless, but cases have been reported of infection of the lungs and other organs by such law-abiding moulds as *Aspergillus* and *Mucor*. *Actinomyces*, which can be regarded either as an elaborate bacterium or a simple fungus,

causes 'lumpy jaw' in cattle and sometimes infects man. Some uncommon but dangerous fungal infections, e.g. with *Blastomyces*, *Histoplasma*, have been seen more often in the Americas than elsewhere. All these internal infections have been rare in the past, but they are on the increase, and this is not simply an apparent increase due to better diagnosis. Much of it is a real increase due to better treatment of bacterial infection. For bacteria in the body compete with fungi, and when bacteria are eliminated with drugs the field is open to fungi that would otherwise be harmless.

Some fungi provoke allergic reactions; for instance, *farmer's lung* is a form of allergy to moulds in contaminated hay.

3. Some important drugs are obtained from fungi. Yeast is a good source of the B vitamins. ►*penicillin* and other ►*antibiotics* are produced by moulds.

furuncle = ►*boil*.

furunculosis. A crop of boils.

fusion. Surgical fixation of a joint, e.g. *spinal fusion*, bridging adjacent vertebrae with a bone-graft to prevent movement of a chronically inflamed joint.

G

galactose. A simple sugar, combined with glucose to form *lactose* or milk sugar. Galactose is converted in the liver to glucose. Infants with a very rare congenital defect (absence of the necessary enzyme) cannot convert galactose: it accumulates in the blood and causes persistent and sometimes fatal vomiting. They remain perfectly well as long as they are given no milk products.

Galen (Galenos) (*c.* AD 130–200). Greek physician and biologist, 'the Prince of Physicians', the most influential man and one of the most prolific writers in medical history. For fifteen centuries after his death, Galen's doctrines carried almost the authority of scripture. A few pioneers of the Renaissance committed the heresy of questioning Galen – Paracelsus condemned him along with all other medical writers except himself, and Vesalius made a list of Galen's anatomical errors, both in the 16th century, but neither managed to reduce his stature. Even Harvey, in the 17th century, accepted Galen's authority in most things, and tried to show that his own great discoveries had all been anticipated by Galen. In our own century doctors have prescribed remedies that have stood the test of time – but could have stood no other test – since the 2nd century.

Galen was brought up in Pergamon, near the Aegean coast of modern Turkey, then a great centre of learning. There, and later in Smyrna and Corinth, he studied philosophy. He took up his real profession in Alexandria, then the leading medical school in the Empire,

carrying on the tradition laid down in the 3rd century BC by Herophilus and Erasistratus. These two men were the real founders of human anatomy and physiology and so of scientific medicine, and our knowledge of them is due largely to Galen. Indeed, Galen's readiness to acknowledge these predecessors, and above all Hippocrates, does much to redeem his self-satisfaction. At times he tried to debunk these great men – not always wisely, for his own theories were apt to be further from the mark than theirs. Unfortunately for posterity it was Galen's theories that prevailed.

The greatness of Galen lies not in his theories but in his observations. He wrote an exhaustive account of human anatomy. There had been nothing like it before, and there was to be nothing like it again until 1543 when Vesalius published the *Fabrica*. The mistakes in Galen's anatomy are of two kinds. Firstly, his dissections were of animals. He did not go far wrong when he used monkeys, because their anatomy differs from ours only in matters of detail, but sometimes he used other animals. Secondly, if what he saw conflicted with his preconceived ideas he described what he thought he should have seen. Nevertheless, Galen's anatomical errors are nothing beside the wealth of accurately recorded fact.

Galen carried out some important experiments. He showed conclusively that the arteries contain blood and not, as had been supposed, air. He studied the functions of the spinal cord, showing the effects of injury at various levels. 'The experimental path', he said, 'is long and arduous but leads to the truth.' It was a path that he did not take often enough. When he made experiments they were usually good, but his philosophical training was apt to be too much for him and then he fell back on theorizing. And unlike the real philosophers he presented his theories as established facts. He had an elaborate theory to explain the movements of the blood (>*circulation* (2)). The body was pervaded by three kinds of vapour or spirit: natural spirit, formed, with the blood, in the liver; vital spirit, formed in the heart; and animal spirit, formed in the brain and distributed by the nerves. These spirits had their origin in the inspired air. We see Galen the observer at his best when he says that the nerves carry something from the brain: he had made experiments to prove it. And we see the theorist at his worst when, having examined the nerves and found them solid, he states that they are tubular because it suits his theory. (Centuries later we find a much greater thinker than Galen, >*Descartes*, doing the same kind of thing.)

As a physician Galen was the most successful of his day. He travelled widely, but spent most of his professional life in Rome, where he looked after Marcus Aurelius and his son Commodus. Galen's clinical methods were more or less those of Hippocrates five centuries before him, but without the compassion and humility of Hippocrates. In his travels Galen built up a great store of drugs, which he listed and recommended quite uncritically.

The tragedy of Galen was that he needed a successor, and there was none. If someone more self-critical had been there to continue Galen's experiments, scientific medicine might have begun in earnest in the 2nd instead of the 16th century. But in all history there is no full-stop more emphatic than the death of Galen. When he died, rational medicine was extinguished for fourteen centuries. The nature of some of his theories contributed to the eclipse. He tried to show that every detail of the human body was perfectly adapted to the body's needs and a part of a preordained plan, in other words an expression of God's will (>*teleology*). It is all very well for a scientist to have this idea in mind, but stated so baldly it stifles all further inquiry. This was the part of Galen's work that the Dark Ages and Middle Ages preserved, together with the interminable catalogue of drugs, in garbled Latin translations of Galen's Greek. His experiments, and his priceless accounts of earlier doctors whose works had been lost, were all forgotten. But they did not altogether vanish. The Nestorian heretics translated them into Syriac, which Moslem scholars put into Arabic. They returned to Western Europe at the end of the Middle Ages, in Latin translations from the Arabic made in Cordoba.

galenical. Unrefined, vegetable drug, or crude extract of a plant used medicinally; e.g. opium is a galenical, but morphia is a refined active principle. Now that the active principles of most vegetable drugs can be isolated and purified, galenicals are seldom used, because doses are difficult to standardize.

In many countries, 'galenical' means much the same as 'pharmaceutical' – concerning the preparation of drugs.

gall = >*bile*.

The *gall bladder* is a small bag attached to the under-side of the liver, in which bile is stored and concentrated. When food passes from the stomach to the intestine the gall bladder contracts and ejects bile into the duodenum.

The common disorders of the gall bladder are inflammation (*cholecystitis*) and *gall stones*, which are insoluble deposits precipitated from the bile. The two are often associated. They cause pain and indigestion, easily confused with stomach disorders; intolerance of fatty food (because fat needs bile for its digestion and stimulates the gall bladder); sometimes jaundice. Occasionally gall stones are found by chance, having caused no symptoms. Troublesome gall stones are removed surgically, together with the gall bladder. Many attempts have been made to dissolve gall stones by medical treatment, to avoid an operation. A course of *chenodeoxycholic acid* is said to dissolve cholesterol stones, the commonest type, but the treatment is expensive and tedious.

It is much less used now that gall stones and even the whole gall bladder can be removed through a laparoscope, requiring a minimum of surgery (►*laparoscope*). Some stones can be destroyed by ►*lithotripsy* without any surgical intervention at all.

gamete. A sex-cell, either ovum or sperm.

gamma-globulin. Class of blood proteins: the *immunoglobulins*. They are the antibodies responsible for immunity to specific infections. Gamma-globulins can be separated from the other proteins in the blood of someone who has previously recovered from an infection, and used to boost the resistance of others who are at special risk from the same disease. People exposed to infective hepatitis can be protected for a month or so by an injection of gamma-globulin.

Unlike the other blood proteins, which are formed in the liver, gamma-globulins are formed in the lymphatic system.

ganglion. 1 (anat.). A collection of nerve cells, a relay station, in the course of a nerve.

2 (surg.). Cyst of a tendon sheath or joint capsule, producing a tense, round, usually painless swelling. Ganglia are seen almost only on the back of the hand or wrist. They are quite harmless, but if a ganglion is unsightly or large enough to be a nuisance it can be removed. The time-honoured method of squashing a ganglion with a heavy object (the family Bible was preferred) achieved temporary success but the ganglion usually reappeared.

gangrene. Mortification; death and decay of part of the body. The usual cause is loss of the supply of blood through injury or disease of the artery of the region. Not all localized death of tissue is gangrene; the dead tissue may be replaced by a scar, without any decay (which is due to bacterial action). If, for example, part of the heart muscle loses its blood supply through coronary thrombosis, there is no decay because there are no bacteria in the heart. True gangrene involves body surfaces where there are bacteria. ►*infarct*.

Blood supply can be lost through injury to an important artery where the alternative channels for the circulation are inadequate; frostbite; obstruction by clotting of blood in a diseased artery (thrombosis); severe spasm of arteries (e.g. ergot poisoning) and so on. By definition, some tissue must be lost. The great danger is that bacteria in dead tissue multiply without opposition; natural defences and drug treatment are equally powerless against them, and gangrenous tissue is a focus from which infection may spread to and kill healthy neighbouring tissue. It always has to be removed surgically.

Gas gangrene is a complication of severe wounds where tissue is crushed or torn. The bacteria (*clostridia*) breed in damaged tissue and spread to healthy tissue, which they rapidly decompose, with formation of gas. Clostridia form at least half a dozen different lethal toxins, of which the effect is mitigated by giving antitoxic serum. Penicillin destroys the bacteria at the margins of the gangrene, but tissue already affected has to be removed. These bacteria breed only in the absence of oxygen – they are *anaerobic* – and the treatment of gas gangrene has been much improved by maintaining a high concentration of oxygen in the affected area.

gastrectomy. Surgical removal of (part of) the stomach. Partial gastrectomy involves only the lower part of the stomach, subtotal gastrectomy all but the uppermost portion in contact with the diaphragm, and total gastrectomy the whole organ.

Gastroenterostomy is making an artificial passage between the stomach and the intestine, e.g. when the natural passage is blocked or (less often now than formerly) for the treatment of an ulcer. Some form of gastroenterostomy is of course needed after gastrectomy: when part of the stomach has been removed the remainder has to be joined to the intestine.

The operation has been used for duodenal and gastric ulcers (>*peptic ulcer*) and for cancer of the stomach. With duodenal ulcer the object is to remove the part of the stomach in which excessive acid is being formed, but less drastic

methods are now used, because acid secretion can be inhibited with drugs such as cimetidine; with gastric ulcer it is to remove the ulcer itself if it will not otherwise heal, and with it the part of the stomach in which new ulcers are likely to appear or in which a cancer may develop; with cancer it is to remove the growth together with the surrounding tissue which may be invisibly affected.

The stomach, considered as a digestive organ, is not essential to life, even to satisfactory digestion. Protein can be digested in the intestine without the normal preliminary breakdown by acid and enzymes in the stomach. But if the whole stomach has to be removed the intrinsic factor by means of which vitamin B_{12} is absorbed is lost, and the vitamin may have to be injected. The intact stomach is useful as a reservoir from which a large amount of food can be passed to the intestine in small quantities. After gastrectomy the whole meal arrives in the intestine at once, and this can lead to the >*dumping syndrome*.

Many patients escape all these complications of gastrectomy and manage a completely ordinary diet. Others suffer some inconvenience, if only for a time, but at the worst they have only to make their meals smaller and more frequent, and perhaps take supplementary vitamins and iron.

gastric ulcer. Ulcer of the stomach; >*peptic ulcer*.

gastrin. A hormone released into the blood by cells in the lower end of the stomach in response to protein foods such as meat. It stimulates the flow of acid from the upper part of the stomach.

gastritis. Inflammation of the lining of the stomach; a rather vague term covering a range of disorders from mild indigestion to a dangerous emergency.

Unlike most parts of the body, the stomach is rarely inflamed from direct invasion by microbes, because its acid secretion is strongly antiseptic. Gastritis may, however, complicate infection centred elsewhere; and in cases of *achlorhydria* (absence of acid) swallowed bacteria may get a foothold.

Some gastritis is due to *allergy*, e.g. to shellfish. But the likeliest cause is simple chemical irritation. The common irritants include alcohol, tobacco smoke, and many drugs.

➤*gastro-enteritis.*

gastrocnemius. Prominent muscle of the calf.

gastro-enteritis. Inflammation of stomach and intestine; a group of diseases characterized by vomiting, abdominal pains, diarrhoea, and in severe cases prostration. Bacterial food poisoning, poisoning with heavy metals, infections such as typhoid and dysentery, and food allergies can all be included, but unspecified gastro-enteritis is usually a virus infection – 'summer diarrhoea', 'gastric flu', and the sometimes dangerous diarrhoea and vomiting of infancy. As with most virus infections, the cause cannot yet be dealt with: symptoms have to be treated on their own merits while the infection subsides. Infants have limited reserves of water and are quickly dehydrated by diarrhoea and vomiting. Their stores of bicarbonate and salt are easily depleted. In infants, as in severely affected adults, treatment is mainly a matter of replacing these vital substances. If fluids cannot be kept down when given by mouth, they have to be injected. Painful spasm of the intestinal muscle is relieved by drugs that depress parasympathetic nerves, of which the prototype is belladonna. The diet has to be sloppy and bland.

➤*food poisoning.*

gastro-enterostomy ➤*gastrectomy.*

gastroplasty. Surgical reconstruction of the stomach. (➤*obesity.*)

gastroscope. A lighted tube passed down the oesophagus for inspecting the lining of the stomach. With the back of the throat anaesthetized this procedure is much less distressing than one would suppose.

Gaucher's disease. A rare disorder of ➤*lipid* metabolism.

general paralysis of the insane (GPI). (*General paralysis*; dementia paralytica.) Widespread involvement of the nervous system at a late stage of untreated ➤*syphilis.*

genetics. The study of heredity.

If there is a single property that distinguishes living matter from any other, it is the ability to synthesize proteins. These very complex substances, produced from the simplest raw materials, are the chemical basis of life. All living processes depend on a class of proteins, the *enzymes*, because every process represents chemical changes promoted by particular enzymes. This is equally true of breathing or growing red hair or suffering from gout.

Some proteins are common to all living creatures, some to a large category such as animals or mammals, and some to a single species. Some are peculiar to races, families, or individuals within a species. The difference between a man and an oak tree or a typhoid bacillus, or between two men, is largely the difference between the proteins that they can make. This is what they inherit from their forebears, and all that they inherit, and it is all that they transmit to their offspring.

The business of genetics is to show how the pattern is passed on more or less intact from generation to generation, and to explain how it comes to vary in its finer details.

1. GENES AND CHROMOSOMES

Every living cell includes a quantity of *nucleic acids.* One type, DNA (deoxyribonucleic acid), is enclosed in the central *nucleus* of the cell. The other, RNA (ribonucleic acid), is more widely distributed.

A molecule of DNA is a chain with four kinds of link. Any combination or sequence of links is possible, each sequence giving a different DNA. Since there is apparently no limit to the possible length of the chain, there could be an infinite number of different kinds of DNA.

To every kind of DNA there is a corresponding RNA. In some way, a molecule of DNA evokes equivalent units of RNA, which pass to the cell-substance.

The RNA then becomes a mould for the synthesis of a protein.

A molecule of protein is also a chain, but with twenty different kinds of link (amino-acids). Each of the amino-acids is attracted to a particular sequence of three links in a molecule of RNA. The properties of a protein depend on the sequence of amino-acids, which is determined by the sequence of links in the RNA chain, or ultimately by the kind of DNA in the nucleus of the cell. Therefore the whole nature of a cell, and of the body, which is composed of cells, depends on the kinds of DNA at its disposal.

DNA has a second unique property: it can make an exact copy of itself. Cells multiply by splitting into halves, and in the process the entire complement of DNA is duplicated. All the millions of cells of a human body arise by division and subdivision of the single cell formed by the fusion of an ovum from the mother and a sperm from the father; and every cell includes a replica of the DNA of the fertilized ovum.

Before a cell divides, its DNA is organized into paired structures called *chromosomes.* Human DNA forms 23 pairs of chromosomes. The two members of a pair are very similar but not identical (except that the sex chromosomes form a dissimilar pair in the male: see below). During division of a cell, each chromosome splits down its length as the DNA duplicates itself.

But when the germ cells (ovum or sperm) are formed, the chromosomes do not split. Instead, only one member of a pair goes to a germ cell, which then has 23 *single* chromosomes. When the ovum is fertilized, new pairs are formed with one member from either parent.

The body contains thousands of different kinds of protein, each determined by its own unit of DNA. One such unit, governing the synthesis of one protein (usually an enzyme, promoting one chemical process), is a *gene.*

A chromosome is an assembly of hundreds of genes. A gene is a unit of DNA.

2. DOMINANT AND RECESSIVE CHARACTERS

The two members of a pair of chromosomes correspond very closely. In all major respects, any two creatures of the same species are alike, and to this extent their genes are identical. Each parent contributes one member of a pair of chromosomes, and in everything that makes the chromosomes merely human the contributions are alike. But in many points of detail, individuals differ, and the genes that determine these points differ. At a particular point on a chromosome there may be a gene that determines the colour of the eyes. One parent may contribute a gene for blue eyes, and the other for brown eyes. If this happens, the child's eyes will not be of an intermediate colour; they will regularly be brown. The 'brown' gene in some way suppresses the 'blue' gene, and brown eyes are said to be *dominant* while blue are *recessive*. Only if both parents contribute a 'blue' gene will the child's eyes remain blue. A recessive character will appear only if it is represented by both chromosomes of a pair, but a dominant character needs only one. There is no difference to be seen between the brown eyes where both parents contribute brown and those where only one does so. (This example is taken only because it is so familiar: in fact eye colour is rather more complicated and may involve more than one pair of genes.)

The colour of the parent's eyes does not always indicate what gene the child will receive. A brown-eyed parent may well have one blue and one brown gene in his pair, and the germ cell that he passes to the child will have one or the other; the chances are even.

If both parents have the same *recessive* character, both must have a pair of identical genes, and their children have no choice but to take after them as regards that character.

If one parent has inherited a *dominant* character from both of his parents, then he must pass it on to all his children. But if the children get the dominant gene

from one parent and the recessive gene from the other, they are 'hybrids'. Although they outwardly show the dominant character, *their* children have an even chance of getting the recessive gene from them.

If two 'hybrids' (both of course showing the dominant character) marry, there are four possible combinations for their children: (1) dom./dom., (2) dom./rec., (3) rec./dom., (4) rec./rec.

Of these possibilities – all equally likely – only (4) will show the recessive character.

In human genetics, matters are not always so simple. Many characters depend on the interaction of several genes. For instance, the original discovery of dominant and recessive characters (Gregor Mendel, 1866) was made with garden peas, which grew either very tall (dominant) or very short (recessive). But normal men are not either tall or short; they are of all heights from about 20 per cent above to 20 per cent below the average, because so many genes are involved that there can be no simple 'either-or'. Most human characters are of this kind. Secondly, alternative genes are not always dominant or recessive. One may *tend* to dominate the other, rather than do so completely. And with some characters the hybrid is in a sense intermediate between pure dominant and recessive.

3. SEX CHROMOSOMES AND LINKAGE

A woman has 23 matched pairs of chromosomes in each cell. In a man, the 23rd pair do not match: instead of two large X chromosomes he has one large X and one small Y chromosome. Evidently the Y chromosome carries a gene for maleness, and this acts as a dominant character. When the germ cells are formed in the ovary or testis, each getting only one member of a pair of chromosomes, the mother *must* contribute an X chromosome to the child, but the father has an equal chance of contributing X or Y. The effect of the Y chromosome is that a testis develops in the embryo instead of an ovary; the hormones formed by the testis account for other male characters.

The X chromosome carries many genes that have nothing to do with sex, but the small Y chromosome does not. For example, colour vision depends partly on a gene of the X chromosome. Red-green colour-blindness is a recessive character determined by a variant of this gene. If a man has this abnormal gene on his one X chromosome, he is colour-blind, because he has nowhere to carry the corresponding normal, dominant gene. But if a woman inherits the colour-blind gene its effect is suppressed by the normal gene on her other X chromosome, unless she is unlucky enough to inherit the same gene from both parents.

A man contributes an X chromosome to a daughter and a Y chromosome to a son. Therefore a colour-blind man cannot pass the defect to a son. If his son should be colour-blind the gene must come from the mother, who is a 'carrier', i.e. she has the abnormal gene on one X chromosome, but a normal and dominant gene on the other; her vision is normal. Any daughter of a colour-blind man *must* be a carrier.

Recessive characters determined by genes on the X chromosome are described as *sex-linked*.

4. GENETIC VARIATION

In principle, a molecule of DNA is everlasting: 'The germ cell is immortal' because DNA, while on the one hand setting the pattern for the living individual,

on the other hand goes on replicating itself for succeeding generations. The genes that are common to most creatures must have persisted unchanged for hundreds of millions of years. But if genes never changed at all there could be no evolution and no different species. In fact, accidents can happen to DNA, so that its self-made replica is not exact. If one of the thousands of links in a DNA chain is altered there will be a corresponding alteration in the protein directed by that gene. If the DNA of a germ cell is affected, the alteration is perpetuated (supposing that the offspring survive).

As a rule, a change or *mutation* is a disadvantage. It decreases the chance of survival; either it is promptly lethal, in which case it eliminates itself at once, or the affected individuals fall behind in the evolutionary struggle and are gradually eliminated. But from time to time a mutation confers an advantage in the struggle for survival, and the mutants thrive at the expense of their 'normal' fellows. This is the likeliest explanation of evolution.

The people of West Africa show an instructive example of mutation. A defective recessive gene causes a minor chemical change in the blood cells. Anyone who inherits this gene from both parents develops sickle-cell anaemia and is unlikely to survive till puberty. In the course of generations the gene should gradually disappear unless fresh mutations of the same kind occur, because it confers a disadvantage.

But the gene is not wholly recessive. The 'hybrid' carriers, with the sickle-cell gene on only one chromosome of a pair, have slightly affected blood cells. It is not enough to cause a fatal anaemia, but what it does do is enhance their resistance to malaria. The carriers therefore have a better chance of survival than people with completely normal blood cells, and this advantage outweighs the disadvantage of losing some children from anaemia. Thus the abnormal gene has become very common in West Africa. It can be expected to decrease when malaria is eliminated.

5. MEDICAL GENETICS

Many human disorders are due to defective (mutant) genes. They are seldom very common because the ordinary process of evolution tends to eliminate them but a fresh mutation may occur at any time and a hereditary type of disease then appears for the first time in a family. For instance, the best known type of dwarfism, *achondroplasia*, is a dominant character. As such, it should be transmitted only by a parent who is a dwarf because one cannot carry a dominant gene without showing its effect. But more often than not the parents of an achondroplastic dwarf have normal bones, and the child is affected by mutation in an ovum or a sperm. The mutant gene is a part of the child's make-up; half of his germ cells will carry it and, on average, half of his children will be affected. His unaffected children have escaped the mutant gene – they got the other chromosome of the pair – and cannot transmit the defect to the next generation. But the gene is not part of the make-up of the normal parents of this dwarf; it affected one group of germ cells, not the whole testis or ovary; and there is no reason why their later children should be affected.

In Britain, the commonest disease due to a single pair of *recessive* genes is *cystic fibrosis*, which is a serious danger to life. Both parents must transmit the abnormal gene for the disease to appear, and it must be assumed that both are 'hybrid' carriers of the gene. The gene may have passed harmlessly down their families for many generations: there is no knowing, because actual cases appear only when two carriers happen to marry. Any child of such a marriage has one chance in four of getting the disease, two chances of being a carrier, and one chance of getting normal genes from both parents. Parents of a child with cystic fibrosis have to decide whether to risk having another child, knowing that it will have three chances of being healthy to one of inheriting the disease.

In these two examples the arithmetic is simple. It is often more complex. The odds have been worked out for many genetic disorders, and the geneticist can help prospective parents to decide whether to have children of their own or to adopt. Known risks are often no worse than the unknown risk that all parents must run: the chance that *any* child will be born with a serious genetic defect is about one in fifty. If a known risk is no greater than this it is best ignored – or nobody would dare to have children.

Healthy people with a family history of a genetic disorder may seek advice before marrying. With a dominant condition such as achondroplasia there is no problem: the normal brothers and sisters cannot possibly have the abnormal gene, and their children are as safe as anyone else's.

With a recessive condition such as cystic fibrosis, normal brothers and sisters have two chances in three of carrying the abnormal gene. In the population at large, one person in twenty-five carries it. If two carriers marry, the chance that a child will be affected is one in four. Taking these factors together, the chance that any child of a person whose brother has cystic fibrosis will inherit the disease is $2/3 \times 1/25 \times 1/4$, or $1/150$. And in Britain this is the *commonest* recessive disorder. With all others, the odds are even longer. With recessive disorders, then, healthy relatives do well to ignore the slight risk, except that first cousins, or other couples who both have a family history of the disease, have to reckon with a greater risk.

In some parts of the world, there are harmful recessive genes so common as to present a major hazard to the public health. Sickle-cell anaemia in Africa is one, and a very similar disease, Cooley's anaemia in southern Italy, is another. ►*haemoglobin*. Carriers can be identified and advised not to marry each other, and this measure, together with the eradication of malaria, has already made Cooley's anaemia less common in Italy.

Carriers of a few other recessive disorders can be identified and advised; or at least the risk to their children can be recognized so that treatment is not delayed. Research in this important branch of genetics has still a long way to go. An example of the need is *haemophilia*, transmitted by a sex linked gene, and therefore practically confined to males. The sister of a haemophiliac has a 50/50 chance of being a carrier. If she is one, then there is a 50/50 chance that any son will be a haemophiliac and any daughter a carrier. But she has no means of telling in advance whether she is a carrier or not; hence many perfectly normal people are discouraged from having children.

Some genetic disorders can be cured, e.g. *pyloric stenosis*, a constriction of the outlet from the stomach causing fatal vomiting. After a simple operation the affected baby is normal, but there must be no delay. If the risk is known in ad-

vance, precious hours may be saved in making the diagnosis. *Phenylketonuria* is a rare cause of mental deficiency due to a recessive gene. The patient has no enzyme for disposing of the amino-acid *phenylalanine*, of which small amounts are a necessary ingredient of the diet but large amounts poison the nervous system. If the condition is recognized at birth the child develops normally on a diet with little phenylalanine, and a chemical test shows whether the parents are carriers.

A few diseases are due to faulty allocation of whole chromosomes. Such defects are usually lethal to the embryo, but some can be survived. These include a wrong number of sex chromosomes (►*hermaphrodite*), and ►*Down's syndrome*, in which one of the smaller chromosomes appears in triplicate instead of in duplicate. Such disorders cannot yet be corrected, but now that the site of the trouble is known research workers at least know which way to look.

By means of ►*amniocentesis* some serious defects can be diagnosed, and ultrasonic scanning reveals numerous kinds of malformation, some needing treatment at birth, others warranting abortion.

The examples so far have been of wholly genetic disorders, which follow well-defined rules. A much larger group of diseases is only partly genetic; environment does the rest. Such diseases tend to run in families without observing any known rules of inheritance, and the effects of heredity and environment cannot always be distinguished. Tuberculosis is caused by a known bacterium. It can affect several members of a family because they catch it from each other. Or men whose fathers died of coronary thrombosis are more liable than average to die of the same thing; but that could be because they often lead similar lives. In both cases, however, the family tendency persists even if the environment is quite different. Both diseases are precipitated by external factors: bacteria, rich living and so on. But a greater than average ▸predisposition is inherited. The same is true of many of the commonest diseases, including cancer. Even with the little that is known, one can go some way to avoiding some of them. People with a family history of heart disease can take special pains to keep fit, and people with a family history of lung cancer to avoid cigarettes. It may be just enough to tip the uncertain odds in their favour.

Genetic engineering is a very young science, but with intensive research worldwide it is growing at a remarkable rate. If the chemical structure of a protein is known, as is that of insulin, the structure of DNA corresponding to it can be deduced and a gene prepared. Given this artificial gene a suitable bacterium will reproduce the protein – for the genetic code is the same for all living creatures. Relatively huge molecules of DNA can be broken down by bacterial enzymes to yield single genes; these in turn can be introduced into other bacteria or viruses to be processed. There is every hope that it will become possible to prepare replicas of healthy genes with which to treat patients with faulty genes.

Ethical problems that could arise from this source are under constant scrutiny.

genital. Concerning reproduction; or (more often) the organs of reproduction (*genitalia*).

genu. Knee. *Genu valgum* = knock-knee; *genu varum* = bow-leg. ▸*valgus*.

genus. Category in biological classification, embracing closely related species – e.g. *Felis*, the cats (*Felis leo*, lion; *Felis pardus*, leopard; *Felis catus*, wild-cat).

geriatrics. Medical care of old people.

germ ▸*microbe: infection*.

German measles (rubella). A very common virus infection in childhood, with slight fever, swollen lymph nodes, and a rash. It is a much milder illness than true measles (*rubeola*, *morbilli*). After an incubation of 2–3 weeks, the attack starts with headache, fretfulness and a rising temperature, followed a day later by a pink rash spreading from the face. Lymph nodes – typically, behind the ears – are enlarged and sore. The symptoms seldom last more than 3 or 4 days. The patient is infectious from the day before symptoms begin until the day after they disappear.

German measles was thought unimportant until in 1941 it was shown that if a woman contracts it early in pregnancy, the developing infant adopts the virus instead of rejecting it. This may cause stillbirth, or serious defects – deafness, blindness and disorders of the heart, lungs, nervous system and other organs. Some 40 per cent of such babies are likely to be affected, so that German measles in pregnancy is widely held to justify abortion.

For some time after 1941 many parents took the precaution of deliberately exposing girls to infection so as to get German measles out of the way while they were young enough for it not to matter; a vaccine became available only later. The present policy is to give all children MMR (measles, mumps, rubella) vaccine at 12–15 months old.

germ cell. Cell by which an organism reproduces itself; sperm or ovum. That the germ cell is (potentially) immortal is one of the fundamental principles of biology.

gestation. Pregnancy, especially duration of pregnancy. Human gestation lasts on average 38 weeks from conception to confinement, but is more easily measured from the beginning of the last menstrual period as 40 weeks. It varies much more than in other animals.

giant. Growth is determined by a hormone of the ➤*pituitary* gland. The normal limits are very wide, and even small parents sometimes have very large and perfectly normal offspring. True giants, i.e. people who grow *abnormally* large, have an excess of growth hormone from an over-active pituitary gland. This condition (*gigantism*) is rare. If the trouble starts in adult life when the bones cannot grow longer, characteristic deformities appear (➤*acromegaly*).

giardia. A microscopical parasite of the intestine; it is a ➤*flagellate*. Infestation (giardiasis) is so common in healthy children that some experts have doubted whether giardia does any harm at all. But it is now recognized as a cause of chronic diarrhoea and failure to thrive because of malabsorption. It responds to treatment with metronidazole.

gibbus. Hunch-back; forward angulation of the backbone. It was a common deformity when tuberculosis of the backbone (Potts' disease) was a common disease.

gigantism ➤*giant*.

gills. Respiratory organs in various aquatic animals. Small and primitive creatures breathe through the skin. Larger and more complex animals cannot get enough oxygen in this way and have evolved more efficient systems.

At a fairly early stage of evolution gill-slits appeared as openings from the side of the pharynx. Their original function is to filter off food from water taken through the mouth, but as fish advanced from a diet of micro-organisms to larger prey the gills were adapted to taking oxygen dissolved in the surrounding water into the blood. Land-dwelling vertebrates breathe with lungs, but the gills of their aquatic ancestors have persisted in a modified form. Gills can be recognized at some stage in the growth of every vertebrate, including man. In amphibia, e.g. frogs, the gills are actually used for breathing, but when a tadpole becomes a frog the lungs take over and the gills vanish.

In all but the most primitive vertebrates the forward gills are adapted for use as jaws. In land-dwelling vertebrates the remaining gills have been put to various uses. The larynx, the inner ear, and the thyroid and parathyroid glands are derived from them.

(Strictly speaking it is from the branchial arches and pouches, which support the gills proper, that these structures are derived: real human gills do not appear.)

gingiva. The soft tissue of the gums. *Gingivitis* is inflammation from bacterial infection of the gums. The mouth teems with bacteria, and its tissues are highly resistant to infection. Accumulation of food particles and a chalky deposit from the saliva (tartar, calculus) seem to provide a refuge from which bacteria can infiltrate the gums. Neglected gingivitis loosens the teeth; probably more teeth are lost from this cause than from decay.

gland. 1. An organ that forms and releases (secretes) substances that act elsewhere; if the secretion is carried to the surface of the body or the lining of a hollow organ the gland is *exocrine* (e.g. sweat glands, digestive glands); if it is carried in the blood-stream, the gland is *endocrine* (e.g. pituitary, thyroid).

2. A ►*lymph* node; these small bodies are collected in the neck, armpits, groins and elsewhere, and are an important factor in resistance to infection. 'Enlarged glands' are swollen lymph nodes, e.g. in the neck responding to infection of the throat or scalp, or in the armpit to a septic finger.

glandular fever (infectious mononucleosis). An infectious disease, or perhaps group of diseases, of which the agent is the Epstein-Barr virus, which is also associated with ►*Burkitt's tumour*, and with some cases of leukaemia. As its more common name suggests, it is a fever with which the glands (lymph nodes) are particularly involved. The alternative name, *infectious mononucleosis*, refers to characteristic forms of white cell found in the blood. The attack may take various forms: the main symptom may be enlarged lymph nodes without much else, or digestive upset, or sore throat; skin rashes sometimes occur. Serious complications are most unusual, but some cases drag on for several weeks before complete recovery and leave the patient feeling exhausted. Convalescence lasts longer than after most other infections. ►*myalgic encephalomyelitis.*

glaucoma. Abnormally high pressure within the eye, causing disturbances of vision and ultimately, unless the condition is treated, blindness. Acute (sudden) glaucoma is painful, but the commoner chronic type is insidious and may pass unnoticed until there is permanent damage to the optic nerve.

The part of the eye in front of the lens contains a watery fluid, the aqueous humour. It is divided by the iris into two compartments: the anterior chamber in front of the iris and the posterior chamber behind. The aqueous humour is secreted behind the iris and circulates through the pupil to be absorbed in the narrow gutter between the rim of the iris and the back of the cornea or window of the eye. If for any reason aqueous humour is secreted faster than it can be reabsorbed into the veins, the pressure rises and glaucoma develops.

In the cases where a cause can be found, it is obstruction to the outlet of fluid rather than excessive production. The filtration angle between the iris and the cornea is never very wide, and in some eyes it is so narrow that bunching of the iris, when the pupil is widely dilated, may be enough to block it. In other cases, the pores in the angle are deficient. Some glaucoma follows inflammation of the iris (*iritis*), and rare cases are due to congenital defects of the eye. Diabetes and myopia are among the predisposing factors. But the cause of most glaucoma is unknown.

Acute glaucoma is usually recognized from the symptoms, but chronic cases with few if any early symptoms may need careful investigation. A *tonometer* is a simple instrument like a tiny letter-balance that measures the resistance of the eyeball to light pressure and shows at once whether the pressure in the eye is raised.

Pilocarpine and other drugs that constrict the pupil often relieve the congestion in the filtration angle and allow the excess of fluid to drain normally. Acetazolamide inhibits the formation of aqueous humour. But most types of glaucoma need surgical treatment. The simplest operation is a small hole near the rim of the iris, allowing fluid to drain from the posterior chamber directly to the filtration angle. This can be done with a laser beam.

glioma. A tumour of *neuroglia*, the connective tissue of the brain. (The actual nerve cells do not form tumours, because they are unable to multiply.) Glioma differs from the cancers of other parts of the body in that it does not spread to other tissues or organs, but it is equally dangerous because of its situation.

globulin. A class of protein found in the blood and elsewhere. The molecules are relatively large (molecular weight upwards of 150,000). The antibodies responsible for immunity to infection and for allergic reactions are globulins.

glomerulus. Tangle of minute blood vessels in the ►*kidneys*, from which fluid is filtered to form urine.

gloss(o)-. Prefix = 'of the tongue'.

glossitis. Inflammation of the surface of the tongue. The tongue is so resistant to infection that glossitis is unusual in otherwise healthy people, but it is a common complication of anaemia and malnutrition.

glottis. Entrance to the main airway from the pharynx, i.e. the gap between the vocal cords. Oedema of the glottis – swelling due to the inflammation of allergy – is a serious emergency (►*pharynx* (1)), since the airway is liable to be obstructed.

glucose. A simple sugar; its combustion with oxygen to form water and carbon dioxide is the principal source of energy in the body. Even without oxygen, some energy is got by converting glucose to lactic acid.

Food contains little if any glucose as such, but all starch and sugar in the diet is changed to glucose by digestion. Glucose can also be synthesized in the liver from protein or fat. Hence glucose has no special advantage over ordinary foods. But when a patient has to be fed through a vein, glucose must be used, because the processes of digestion are bypassed and other carbohydrates would not be converted for use.

glue ear. Serous otitis; ►*otitis media*.

glue sniffing. ►*solvent abuse*.

gluten. A component of various cereals: oats, rye, and especially wheat. It is a mixture of proteins, including *gliadin*, which people with ►*coeliac disease* have to avoid.

gluteus. *Gluteus maximus* is the principal muscle of the buttock and the most powerful in the body. *Gluteus medius* and *gluteus minimus* are smaller muscles covered by gluteus maximus.

glycogen. A complex carbohydrate, *animal starch*, similar to ordinary vegetable starch. Its large molecules are chains of glucose molecules.

All carbohydrates in the diet are first digested to glucose; later, much of this glucose is recombined to form glycogen, which is stored in the liver and muscles as a reserve of energy to be called on as needed. The glycogen stores are broken down to glucose at the same rate as glucose is burnt to provide energy, so that the concentration of glucose in the blood and tissue fluid remains fairly constant. The process is regulated mainly by the hormones of the pancreas: *insulin* promotes, and glucagon inhibits the deposition of glycogen. Several other hormones act: *adrenaline* and *thyroid* hormone accelerate the breakdown of glycogen, and *corticosteroids* increase its synthesis, via glucose, from protein.

glycoside. A class of substances extracted from certain plants, including the active principles of digitalis.

goitre. Enlargement of the thyroid gland; ➤*thyroid gland* (2).

gold. Dentists have used gold since very early times for splinting or replacing teeth. The soluble compounds of gold, like those of all heavy metals, are indiscriminately poisonous to proteins and therefore to all tissues, and the effect of all such compounds is cumulative because the body has no ready means of excreting them. Chronic poisoning with heavy metals is successfully treated with chelating agents such as BAL. The medicinal uses of gold are very limited. Only a few of its salts are soluble and stable enough to be used, e.g. sodium aurothiomalate. These preparations were strongly recommended for *rheumatoid arthritis* around 1930, fell into disrepute, and have recently been restored to favour for the treatment of certain cases. Their action is not known: perhaps they act as *cytotoxic* agents to depress a kind of allergic reaction that is a factor in this disease.

gonad. Primary sex organ: ovary or testis.

gonadotropin. Hormone formed in the pituitary gland and acting on the gonad. *Chorionic gonadotropin* is supposedly formed by the embryo to suppress its mother's menstrual cycle during pregnancy.

gonococcus. *Neisseria gonorrhoeae*, the bacterium of gonorrhoea.

gonorrhoea. A common venereal disease; a bacterial infection due to the gonococcus, which invades the mucous membranes of the urethra and uterus. After a short incubation period (2–10 days; as a rule 3 days) a man develops pain and discharge of pus from the urethra; a woman may have the same, but she may feel no symptoms, in which case she can pass the infection on without being aware of it. Untreated infection can be protracted and lead to obstruction of the flow of urine in the male and sterility in either sex. The later complications include arthritis and infection of the eyes. Although gonorrhoea does not infect an unborn infant in the uterus, the infant's eyes are liable to infection while it is being born; and this can cause blindness.

Because strains of gonococci resistant to sulphonamides have evolved the usual treatment is with penicillin or another antibiotic such as spectinomycin. A single dose usually suffices.

There is little natural immunity to gonorrhoea; it can be caught again as soon as an attack has been cured. Because a woman with gonorrhoea often has no symptoms she may not seek treatment, and reinfection of the man who has been treated is all too likely.

Contraceptives are a very unreliable defence against gonorrhoea.

➤*venereal disease.*

gout. A kind of chemical arthritis caused by deposits around joints of monosodium urate crystals. These arise from an excess of uric acid.

There are numerous sources of the uric acid in the body. It is a breakdown product of nucleic acid, an essential component of all living matter. All foods contain some. The highest concentrations are in animal products such as kidney and liver, and vegetable seeds such as peas. A more important source than the diet is the regular breakdown of the body's own cells; and uric acid is also synthesized from ammonia formed in the body. In a healthy person the concentration in the blood and tissue fluids is kept to about 0.02 per cent by excreting any excess in the urine. The solubility of urate is about 0.06 per cent. Above this level, crystals may be precipitated and gout develops. The excess could arise in three ways: too much in the diet, too much synthesized in the body, and too little excreted by the kidneys. Unfortunately, diet is usually the least important, otherwise gout could be controlled simply by cutting out unsuitable food. Over-synthesis, due to an inherited biochemical anomaly, is much more significant. Defective excretion may arise from a similar fault, and also gout is occasionally a complication of kidney disease.

A classic attack of gout begins without warning, often in the middle of the night. A single joint, proverbially at the base of the big toe, is suddenly inflamed and extremely painful. After a day or two the symptoms vanish, but the attack may be repeated at any time, not necessarily in the same joint. Injury predisposes a joint to gout. A bout of heavy drinking can set off an attack by interfering with the excretion of uric acid, but as often as not there is no evident reason for the attack to start.

After many attacks a joint can become permanently deformed, with large deposits of urate (*tophi*) in the bones, e.g. of the knuckles. A tophus in the skin of the ear is sometimes seen with long-standing gout.

Many cases of gout take the form of a grumbling arthritis without acute attacks.

Although the main symptoms arise from affected joints, the real danger of gout is damage to the kidneys by uric acid crystals, which can ultimately lead to failure of the kidneys. Untreated gout is also associated with degeneration of arteries (>*artery* (1)) and its complications. Many people with a persistent excess of uric acid have few if any symptoms, and now that suitable drugs are available it may be that they should be treated in order to protect their kidneys. The question still awaits a clear answer.

The shower of crystals that causes an attack acts as a foreign body in the tissues, and is dealt with by phagocytes (wandering scavenger-cells, like white blood cells), which attempt to engulf the crystals. The resulting damage to the phagocytes causes them to release toxic substances which cause the actual symptoms; the crystals on their own would not be painful.

Colchicine, extracted from autumn crocus, the oldest and still one of the best drugs for relieving an attack, seems to act by inhibiting the phagocytes. Its effect is confined to gout and used to be taken as proof of the diagnosis. Other analgesics such as *indomethacin* are also effective. But *aspirin* is unsuitable.

Between attacks, steps can be taken to lower the concentration of uric acid in the body fluids. Drugs to enhance the excretion of uric acid by the kidneys include *probenecid* and *sulphinpyrazole*. In the early stages of this treatment, while deposits of uric acid are being mobilized, acute attacks are very apt to occur, but the final result is usually good.

The penultimate stage in the synthesis of uric acid in the body is a harmless substance, *xanthine*. The drug *allopurinol* is related to xanthine. It diverts the enzyme that oxidizes xanthine to uric acid, so that less uric acid can be formed. In this way the amount of uric acid in the blood can be kept within the limits of its solubility, and gout is then controlled. The only known drawback of this treatment is that it usually has to be continued for life, but most people who have experienced severe attacks of gout accept this price.

People with gout do well not to look for trouble by heavy drinking or overeating, and many of them can afford to lose some weight; also the most unsuitable foods (liver, kidney, meat extract) are easily avoided. But strict dieting is no longer essential with adequate treatment, and many patients controlled by the new drugs find that they can eat more or less to please themselves.

GPI ➤*general paralysis of the insane*.

graft. Most tissues can be transferred from one part of the body to another if a blood supply is provided; but they can be transferred from one person to another only if steps are taken to prevent rejection of the 'foreign' substance by the recipient's tissue (➤*transplantation*).

Skin is grafted to a new site much more often than other tissue. A skin-graft is an ideal dressing for injuries such as deep burns where an area of the original skin is lost. It shortens the time of healing, is much stronger than the scar that would gradually form if no graft were done, does not contract like a scar (burn scars can seriously restrict movement), and looks better than a scar.

A split-skin (Thiersch) graft is cut from a suitable donor area thinly enough for the blade to cut across the hair follicles, which are small pits in the surface of the skin. Fresh skin grows from the follicles to cover the donor area, and the graft is nourished by minute blood ves-

sels in the raw recipient area. Full-thickness grafts are used where there is much wear and tear or where a split-skin graft would not look well. The vessels of the recipient area will not usually suffice for these thicker grafts for a time while new vessels grow; therefore the graft is left attached to the donor area by a stalk carrying a few blood vessels. This is separated after a couple of weeks when the graft has had time to establish itself. The donor area is covered with a split-skin graft unless it is narrow enough for its edges to be stitched together.

Another tissue sometimes grafted is bone. A bone-graft may encourage an indolent fracture to heal by acting as a live scaffolding into which new bone can grow.

granulation tissue. Delicate tissue composed mainly of minute blood vessels and fibres, formed at the site of a wound or bacterial infection as the first stage in healing.

granulocyte. A kind of white blood cell; ➤*blood* (3).

granuloma. A superfluous mass of granulation tissue formed at the site of a protracted, localized bacterial infection such as tuberculosis. *Granuloma inguinale* is a tropical venereal disease caused by a bacterium, *Donovania*.

gravel. Small deposits in the urine of the same nature as the bigger 'stones' (➤*calculus*).

Graves' disease (toxic goitre). (Robert Graves 1797–1853, Dublin physician.) ➤*thyroid* (2).

grey matter. Cellular tissue in the nervous system. The brain and spinal cord are composed mainly of nerve cells and their conducting fibres. The actual cells are gathered into well-defined zones which have a pale muddy colour, in contrast with the pure white of the nerve fibres in the remaining zones. The two kinds of tissue are known as grey matter (or substance) and white matter. In the spinal cord the grey matter is gathered into a central column, surrounded by white matter. In the brain, this central grey matter is clumped into *nuclei*, and there is an additional grey zone (cortex) over the surface of the cerebrum and cerebellum.

griseofulvin. An antibiotic from the mould *Penicillium griseofulvum*, chemically unrelated to penicillin. It is effective against certain fungal infections of the skin (ringworm), and is a valuable standby if simpler and older remedies fail.

groin. The junction of the muscles of the belly-wall with those of the thigh; the fold in front of the hip-joint. It is a weak point in the structure of the abdomen because the femoral nerve and blood vessels need a free passage from the pelvis to the thigh, and in the male the duct and vessels of the testis also pass through the muscles. A structure that belongs to the abdomen, such as a loop of intestine, may bulge through the gap provided for one of these vessels; this is the commonest type of ➤*hernia*.

group therapy. A form of psychotherapy where a group of patients with similar problems meet to discuss them and the therapist plays an unobtrusive role as chairman. When group therapy works it makes better use of the psychiatrist's limited time than individual psychotherapy, and it is a way round one of the central problems of psychiatry, that the patient so easily becomes as dependent on the psychiatrist as an addict on a drug. In fact, group therapy is sometimes better than individual psychotherapy. People with emotional disturbances are almost bound to feel isolated, and the sense of isolation adds to the anxieties. As one would expect, group therapy works best with neuroses (disorders where the patient's insight is not impaired), but there are also encouraging reports with conditions where conventional psychotherapy often fails, including personality disorders and schizophrenia. Much depends on choosing the right patients for the treatment. Some of the most spectacular successes of psychotherapy have been achieved with a kind of group therapy for treating alcoholism (➤*Alcoholics Anonymous*).

Guinea worm (*Dracunculus medinensis*). A long slender worm, parasitic to man. The larvae enter the body in infected drinking water and migrate from the intestine. The female worm settles under the skin, often near the ankle, and emerges to lay eggs when the patient stands in water. The traditional remedy is to pull her slowly out by winding her round a stick over the course of a week or more. Or the worm can usually be eradicated with metronidazole.

The disease is confined to West Africa and a few other tropical regions.

gullet = ➤*oesophagus*.

gum ➤*gingiva*.

gynaecology. Medicine and surgery of the female reproductive system. Obstetrics – the management of pregnancy – is generally counted as a separate speciality, though often practised by the same specialists.

gynaecomastia. Enlargement of the male

breasts. It can be induced in any man by giving female sex hormones. Since small amounts of these hormones are part of the normal male complement (as normal women have male hormones: the difference is only proportional), the balance is easily upset, and some degree of gynaecomastia is common in adolescence. Except that it may embarrass a young man it does not matter and does not usually last.

A few drugs can cause gynaecomastia.

gypsum. Calcium sulphate; plaster-of-paris.

gyrus. A natural fold on the surface of the brain.

H

habit. A habit is much the same as a conditioned reflex – an action that has become an automatic response to a given stimulus. It may be watering of the mouth at the sight of food or lighting a cigarette in response to boredom or worry. A *habit spasm* or *tic* is an involuntary, purposeless movement, probably representing a movement that once had a purpose. For *drug habit*, ▸*addiction*.

haematology. Study of blood and its disorders.

haematoma. Swelling from bleeding into the tissues.

haematuria. Blood in the urine, a symptom of injury or disease of the kidneys or bladder. The source has to be identified as soon as possible. Most of the causes, including cancer of the bladder, are curable at an early stage. The cause may be obvious from the other symptoms. In doubtful cases examination of the bladder by cystoscopy usually provides the answer.

haemoglobin. The red pigment of the blood, carried by the red blood cells (▸*blood* (2)). It is composed of a protein, *globin*, and an iron compound, *haem*. It is the means of transporting oxygen from the lungs to the rest of the body.

Very primitive microscopical animals can get their oxygen by diffusion from the surrounding air or water. But even an insect cannot get enough oxygen in these ways, and all but the simplest creatures have evolved *respiratory pigments* which form loose chemical compounds with oxygen. Human blood carries about sixty times as much oxygen as can be dissolved in it. In the lungs, where breathing provides a constant supply, haemoglobin takes up oxygen. In the rest of the body, where combustion creates a deficit, this oxygen is released. Since the tissues are never wholly depleted of oxygen, haemoglobin never gives up its whole supply. Five litres of blood – the total amount of the body, and also the amount circulating through the lungs in one minute at rest – carry one litre of oxygen, but only a quarter of this is actually used. During exertion, the rate of circulation is increased, and at the same time a larger proportion of the oxygen is given up, because the carbon dioxide which accumulates in working tissues promotes the release of oxygen from haemoglobin.

The structure of this highly complex substance was established in 1960 by Perutz at Cambridge (Nobel Prize 1962). Globin consists of two alpha chains of 141 amino-acids, and two beta chains of 146 amino-acids. Each chain carries a molecule of the iron compound, haem, which can take up and release one molecule of oxygen.

This is normal adult haemoglobin (HbA). Other haemoglobins are known in which the amino-acids of globin are differently arranged from those of HbA. (Haem does not vary.) Before birth, globin is formed from alpha and gamma chains, in which some 30 of the amino-acids differ from those of adult beta chains. This gives foetal haemoglobin (HbF), which is able to work at a lower concentration of oxygen than HbA.

Since the foetus gets its oxygen second-hand via the mother's blood and the placenta, this property of HbF would be an advantage. During the first four years of life HbF is gradually replaced by HbA.

Certain hereditary forms of anaemia are due to faulty synthesis of globin. In the haemoglobin of *sickle-cell anaemia* (HbS) a single amino-acid in the beta chain is out of place. This causes distortion and fragility of the red cells, which are liable to break up more rapidly than they can be formed. If a child inherits the faulty gene from both parents he is unlikely to live long enough to pass the disease on to the next generation. If he has it from only one parent, his red cells carry a certain amount of HbS, but not enough to harm him. If, however, he marries someone of the same type a quarter of their children will have the disease, and a further half will be able to transmit it like their parents. Only one child in four will be quite free of it.

The statistics of evolution and heredity are such that a gene which confers even a marginal disadvantage remains rare. Yet in parts of Africa no less than 40 per cent of the population have the HbS gene, of which a double dose is lethal. This is more than a marginal disadvantage, and after a few generations it should almost obliterate the disease. But malaria is the commonest disease in these regions. The malaria parasite lives off its victim's red blood cells, and in some obscure way the parasite seems to dislike HbS. This protects carriers of the disease, and the lessened chance of dying of malaria outweighs the disadvantage of the HbS gene.

Cooley's anaemia (thalassaemia) is found mainly around the Mediterranean. The haemoglobin is normal except that HbF still exceeds HbA after childhood;

the trouble is inability to make enough HbA. The effects are similar to those of sickle-cell anaemia: why these cells should be abnormally fragile is not known. A similar relation to malaria has been suggested but the evidence is not as strong as with sickle-cell anaemia.

Carbon monoxide is poisonous because haemoglobin takes it up in preference to oxygen, and does not readily release it. In fact, carbon monoxide usurps the place of oxygen and makes haemoglobin useless. A concentration of more than 0.1 per cent in the air is quite rapidly lethal, and much lower concentrations are dangerous if breathed for a long time.

The *colour* of haemoglobin is bright scarlet when it is saturated with oxygen, as in the arteries. As the oxygen is released the colour becomes more and more blue. The blood in the veins is normally still about 70 per cent saturated with oxygen, and the colour is a rich red-purple. But if blood stagnates because of impaired circulation, heart failure etc., or if the lungs are deprived of oxygen, the blood becomes much bluer and this colour is seen through the skin (>*cyanosis*). The compound with carbon monoxide is a vivid cherry red, and people with carbon monoxide poisoning have a bright pink complexion although they are in effect asphyxiated.

haemolysis. Breakdown of red blood cells. Each cell is a parcel of the oxygen-carrying pigment haemoglobin. When the enclosing membrane gives way, haemoglobin is spilled into the plasma. Some very simple animals have their haemoglobin dissolved in the plasma, but not nearly enough can be dissolved for the needs of a warm-blooded animal such as man; hence the red blood cell.

Haemolysis may be due to destruction of red cells by parasites (malaria), or allergic reactions. ▸*anaemia* (A.2).

haemophilia. An uncommon familial disease, one of the ▸*bleeding disorders*, due to absence of one of the factors needed for normal clotting of the blood. The missing factor (factor VIII) is a protein, which haemophiliacs are unable to synthesize. The symptoms are prolonged bleeding from the least injury, and a tendency to bleed internally without any obvious cause. Firmly applied dressings may stop external bleeding, and several preparations which promote clotting, including the venom of Russell's viper, are useful. Transfusion of healthy blood or plasma, which of course contains factor VIII or a factor VIII concentrate, is needed to control severe bleeding. Many haemophiliacs die in childhood; but under treatment they can achieve a normal life-span.

Blood, or any products of blood for injection, must be meticulously screened to avoid the risk of transmitting virus infections such as hepatitis or AIDS.

Haemophilia is inherited as a *sex-linked recessive character* (▸*genetics*). This means that an affected woman 'carries' the disease without suffering from it, but that affected men are actual haemophiliacs. Children of female carriers have a 50 per cent chance of inheriting the defect – girls as carriers, boys as sufferers. If a male haemophiliac marries, all his daughters will be carriers, and all his sons will be normal. A girl can have true haemophilia only in the extremely unlikely event that her parents are a carrier and a sufferer. But girls can inherit some very rare deficiencies of other clotting factors.

Several royal families have been afflicted with haemophilia.

Haemophilus. A genus of small, mostly harmful bacteria. One species, *H. ducreyi*, causes the sexually transmitted disease *chancroid*. Another, *H. influenzae*, is often to be found in healthy throats. First recognized in 1882, before viruses were known, it was long thought to cause influenza. In fact it can cause pneumonia and, jackal-like, takes advantage of a virus infection to complicate influenza. One strain, *H. influenzae B*, is dangerous to children, in whom it can cause meningitis, and a dangerous throat infection (▸*epiglottitis*).

haemoptysis. Blood-spitting; a symptom that calls for prompt investigation because the possible causes include tuberculosis and cancer of the lung. It can also occur with infection in any part of the air-passages and with heart disease (from raised blood pressure in the lungs).

haemorrhage = ▸*bleeding*.

haemorrhoids (piles). Distended (varicose) veins at the junction of rectum and anal canal, about an inch above the opening of the anus. (The word haemorrhoids is used here in preference to the simpler *piles* only because other disorders in the same region are also commonly called piles. *Haemorrhoids* is from the Greek of Hippocrates. The obsolete *emerods* is a French corruption of the same word.)

Straining because of constipation may arise from a shortage of dietary ▸*fibre*. If this should happen, the discomfort of haemorrhoids encourages constipation and so the two disorders aggravate each other. Of other causes that can be defined, compression of veins in the pelvis by a pregnant uterus is the commonest. Cirrhosis of the liver restricts the normal flow of blood from the intestine to the liver and overburdens the alternative routes by the veins of the rectum and oesophagus.

The name haemorrhoids implies the main symptom, bleeding. There is usually some discomfort, but true haemorrhoids are seldom really painful. Even a small daily loss of blood is enough to deplete the body's reserves of iron in time, and anaemia is a common symptom of longstanding haemorrhoids.

Small haemorrhoids often subside with suppositories to reduce congestion, and mild laxatives. Larger ones can be treated by injection of an irritant fluid that causes a scar to obstruct the distended vein.

The definitive treatment of severe haemorrhoids is a surgical operation, much as Hippocrates described 24 centuries ago. The affected veins are isolated and closed off with ligatures. But simple stretching of the anal sphincter under anaesthesia, of which the rationale is not obvious, cures many cases.

Another method is to put an elastic band round the base of the haemorrhoid, causing it to wither by cutting off its blood supply.

All haemorrhoids are worth treating because correct treatment relieves much needless distress; but that is not all. The great danger of this condition is that cancer of the rectum at an early, curable stage gives similar symptoms, and unless the diagnosis is proved as soon as possible, a cancer may be neglected until it is no longer curable.

Hahnemann, Samuel (1755–1843). German physician, founder of ➤*homoeopathy*.

hair. A hair, like a fingernail, consists mainly of a dense form of the same substance (keratin) as the outer layer of the skin. Dark hair contains a central core of pigment. The follicle from which a hair grows is a small pit in the surface of the skin. In the side of each follicle is a sebaceous (grease) gland.

The growth of hair alternates between an active phase when the hairs lengthen and a resting phase at the end of which hairs are shed and new ones grow from the same follicles. In animals that moult with the seasons the phases are obvious. In man, the phases of individual hairs are not synchronized: while some are active others are resting and still others are moulting.

In the last three months of pregnancy an infant develops a profuse down of very fine hair (*lanugo*). Except in premature babies most of it is shed before birth, to be replaced by rather stronger hairs. The distribution of hair is under the influence of hormones, mainly the sex hormones. Unwanted hair, e.g. on a woman's face, may be no more than an inherited tendency; but a serious excess is due to a faulty balance of hormones.

Despite popular belief, cutting hair has no effect on its growth. Shaving is thought to thicken hair only because recently shaved stubble feels rough.

➤*baldness.*

Hales, Stephen (1677–1761). English parson and scientist; a pioneer of experimental physiology. He showed that some reflexes were mediated by the spinal cord, independently of the brain; and he measured the pressure and rate of flow of the blood in various animals. He also campaigned for better hygiene in ships, hospitals, and prisons.

Haller, Albrecht von (1708–77). Swiss biologist, physician and writer; a pupil of Boerhaave at Leyden, he taught at Göttingen and Berne. Haller was a distinguished botanist; his many contributions to anatomy included a correct explanation of hernia; but most of all he is remembered as a physiologist. His particular concern was the response of living tissue to stimulation – *irritability*.

hallucination. Sensation without physical origin, as 'hearing voices' or 'seeing things', or a waking dream. Hallucinations that the subject insists are real may suggest mental disturbance; they are commonly associated with schizophrenia but can occur with hysteria or mere fatigue, and with physical illness such as alcoholism (delirium tremens) and fever of any kind.

hallucinogen. Drug that causes hallucinations. The hallucinogens include *cannabis* (hemp, marihuana, dagga, bhang), *mescaline*, from a Mexican cactus, *bufotenin*, a toad poison, and *LSD* (lysergic acid diethylamide), a synthetic alkaloid related to ergot. In the past, cannabis has been used as a narcotic, and originally LSD was used for studying mental disorder, but none of these drugs has any proven medical value. Probably none is a true drug of addiction. Their devotees take them because they enjoy the episodes of temporary insanity. Mescaline and LSD seem to interfere with the natural action of *serotonin* in the brain, and this might suggest that schizophrenia, of which the symptoms resemble those of the drugs, has the same cause.

hallux. The big toe. *Hallux valgus* is a common deformity: tight shoes deflect the big toe across the next toe, and a ►*bunion* develops over the protruding joint.

halothane. Anaesthetic related to chloroform. It is a volatile liquid, $CHClBr.$ CF_3. Halothane is among the safest of the known general anaesthetics that are powerful enough for major surgery. Like all chlorine-containing anaesthetics, it can damage the liver. The risk is mainly with repeated use, and with successive operations halothane is avoided. An alternative anaesthetic has to be chosen for patients with any past history suggesting liver disease.

hamartoma. A tumour-like mesh of small blood vessels, probably a minor congenital malformation rather than a true tumour.

hammer toe. A common deformity, most often of the second toe, due sometimes to crowding of the toes in unsuitable footwear, and sometimes to the pressure of a deformed big toe, but in many cases without apparent cause. The toe is sharply bent down, with a corn over the resulting 'knuckle'. If simple chiropody fails the deformity may need surgical correction.

hamstring muscles. The group of muscles at the back of the thigh: *semimembranosus*, semitendinosus, and *biceps femoris*. The muscles flex the knee and also help *gluteus maximus* to extend the hip.

hand

1. STRUCTURE

The framework of the hand consists of (1) a cluster of 8 small *carpal* bones meeting the lower end of the radius to form the wrist joint, (2) the 5 *metacarpals*, which fan out to support the thumb with 2 *phalanges*, and the fingers each with 3.

The principal muscles of the hand make up the fleshy mass of the forearm. Their tendons pass in front of and behind the wrist, where they are held in

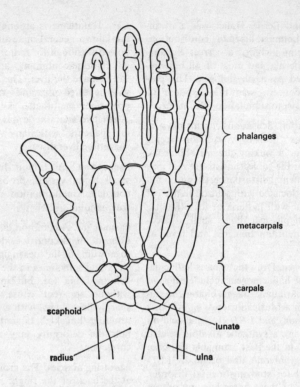

phalanges

metacarpals

carpals

scaphoid

lunate

radius

ulna

Bones of the hand

position by a system of fibrous bands. Friction is prevented by the slippery synovial sheaths, like the linings of joints, that envelop the tendons.

In addition there are numerous small muscles within the hand. One group forms the ball of the thumb (thenar eminence), and there is a smaller corresponding group for the little finger (hypothenar eminence). Many other slips of muscle arise in the palm and control fine movements of the fingers.

Flexion of the fingers – grasping – is a much stronger and better controlled movement than extension: a musician's problem is not striking the notes but raising his fingers in time to play the next note.

The hand is well supplied with blood by the 2 arteries at the front of the wrist: the ulnar artery leading towards the little finger, and the radial towards the thumb. It is the radial artery that is felt when the pulse is examined. The 2 arteries join in the palm, and if either is obstructed the other can provide a sufficient flow. If the veins accompanied the arteries in the usual way they would be squeezed flat whenever the hand was used for gripping. Blood therefore returns from the hand in large veins on the back of the hand and wrist.

The median nerve supplies the muscles of the thumb, and the ulnar nerve the remaining muscles. Sensation is shared between branches of these nerves and the radial nerve.

2. DISORDERS

Injuries of the hand are commoner than any others, for by nature man uses his hands to explore his surroundings: they are his antennae. They are also his first line of defence. In nearly all other vertebrates the head serves these functions.

In proportion to the amount of actual damage, injuries of the hand are much more disabling than any others. Injuries of the thumb are especially serious, because half the value of the hand is lost if the thumb cannot be brought to bear on the fingers. On the other hand the loss of a single finger need not greatly impair function.

Infection may follow very slight injuries. Because the skin is tough and unyielding there is little room for swelling; therefore a small pocket of inflammation can easily cause enough pressure to stop the circulation in, for example, an infected finger-tip. There is also the danger that infection may pass rapidly up the sheath of a tendon from a finger to the palm. An infected finger is thus an emergency. In most cases, antibiotics will overcome the infection, but if pus begins to form it must be released surgically without delay.

With all kinds of injury or infection of the hand, much care is needed to preserve function, for even a single stiff joint can be a great nuisance. Physiotherapy to keep the joints mobile is often the most important part of the treatment.

Rheumatic diseases commonly affect the hands: in particular, *rheumatoid arthritis* has a predilection for the bases of the fingers and the wrists.

Other disorders of the hands described elsewhere are *ganglion*, *Dupuytren's contracture*, and the *carpal tunnel syndrome*.

Hansen's bacillus. The leprosy bacillus, discovered by Gerhard Hansen (1841–1912), a Norwegian physician, in 1868, 14 years before Koch's discovery of the closely related tubercle bacillus.

hapten (haptene). A substance, other than a protein, that arouses allergy. The discovery of haptens did not invalidate von Pirquet's theory that allergy was always a reaction to a protein foreign to the tissues: haptens probably act by modifying a protein in the tissues so that it becomes 'foreign'. ▸*allergy* (1).

harelip ▸*palate*.

Harvey, William (1578–1657). English physician. He studied at Caius College, Cambridge, and later under the great anatomist Fabricius at Padua; he was physician to St Bartholomew's Hospital, London, and, as Lumleian lecturer at the College of Physicians, the equivalent of a professor of medicine (London had then no university).

In showing that the blood circulated constantly through the body Harvey made the most important discovery in the history of scientific medicine; almost everything else that is known of the workings of the body depends on it. The place of Harvey in medical science is like that of Newton in physics.

His work on the circulation (see *De Motu Cordis*, below) is so great that

Harvey's distinction on several other counts is overshadowed and often overlooked. His appointments at St Bartholomew's and the College of Physicians suggest that he was a highly esteemed practising doctor; he was also physician to the royal family and as near as any commoner could get to being a friend of Charles I. If Harvey's colleagues thought little of his prescriptions (Aubrey) that may well be because in an age of gross over-prescribing Harvey tried not to order treatment that could do no good. He was an able surgeon and obstetrician; he was one of the first Englishmen to study the nature of disease by post-mortem examination. In his own opinion his most important work was his treatise on embryology (*De Generatione Animalium*, 1651). This book is based on extensive studies of embryos of various species. It offers few facts that were not known to Harvey's teacher Fabricius or indeed to Aristotle, for until the advent of good microscopes embryology could scarcely advance. But Harvey was more careful than any earlier scientist to argue only from the evidence before him, and to avoid pure speculation. By sticking to the facts Harvey was able to draw several conclusions that were confirmed in later centuries. He inferred that every animal begins as an egg, though he was not able to find the egg of a mammal (nor was anyone else for the next 200 years). Since an egg might be too small to be seen, there was no need to suppose that insects and the like arose spontaneously; Harvey was an early opponent of the theory of spontaneous generation, still widely held until Pasteur disproved it.

Harvey correctly stated that the various structures of the body are not all present in miniature from the time of conception, but are formed in sequence.

This had been Aristotle's teaching, but Harvey's contemporaries and most of his successors until the 19th century rejected it. Again in the steps of Aristotle, and anticipating von Baer (1792–1876), Harvey noted the close similarity between embryos of widely different species.

1. DE MOTU CORDIS

Harvey's greatest work was published at Frankfurt in 1628. Its full title is *Exercitatio Anatomica de Motu Cordis et Sanguinis in Animalibus* (Anatomical Treatise on the Movement of the Heart and Blood in Animals).

In Harvey's day, Galen's teaching was still generally accepted, and Harvey himself scrupulously followed Aristotle and Galen except when he had clear proof that they were wrong. Galen had said that the purple blood in the veins was formed in the liver and enriched with 'natural spirit' derived from the food. Some of this blood found its way into the arteries by seeping through invisible pores in the dividing wall of the heart; it was enriched with 'vital spirit' from the lungs to become bright scarlet. Veins and arteries carried their respective spirits away from the centre to the rest of the body as the blood in them ebbed and flowed. The heart served only to warm the blood. Its beat and the pulse in the arteries were due to alternating expansion and collapse of the whole apparatus as vital spirit was released and then absorbed.

Since this account was wrong in every particular, and since Galen's opinions were almost a religion for doctors, Harvey's task was comparable with that of the astronomers of his day in proving and persuading others that the earth was not the centre of the universe.

Only a few small cracks had begun to

appear in the crust of the old doctrines. Vesalius and the other Paduan anatomists had rightly denied that blood could get through the dividing wall of the heart, but could not explain what it did instead. Ibn-an-Nafis in the 13th century and Servetus and Columbus in the 16th had suggested that blood from the heart might percolate through the lungs and return to the heart. Cesalpino and Leonardo da Vinci both suggested that blood left the heart by the arteries and returned by the veins, and Leonardo recognized the heart as a muscle (but thought its action was to generate heat). None of these men realized that the heart was a pump, or that the blood circulated continuously and rapidly through the body. Even Cesalpino, the only one to use the word 'circulatio', was apparently thinking of occasional seepage rather than a steady flow. And apart from Leonardo none of them supported speculation with evidence. Each has been credited at some time or other with 'discovering' the circulation, but this is like saying that a man who writes science fiction about trips to Mars has invented an interplanetary rocket.

Each step in Harvey's argument was carefully reasoned and then demonstrated by experiment and observation ('first I shall show that this may be so, and then I shall prove that it is so in fact').

He found that the heart is a muscle like any other, and that its beat is due to muscular contraction. The muscle encircles the blood in the heart, and by contracting it squeezes the blood out.

The valves of the heart are so arranged that the blood can be expelled in only one direction: into the arteries but not into the veins. Having entered the arteries, the blood is prevented from returning to the heart.

The valves of the veins allow blood to flow only towards the heart.

From the evidence so far it might be argued that the blood sent out by the arteries is used up in feeding the body, and that the veins bring newly formed blood to the heart for transmission to the arteries. Harvey refuted this theory by pointing to the quantity of blood involved. At the lowest possible estimate the whole mass of blood must pass through the heart in half an hour (we now know that it does so in a minute or less) and this least possible rate of flow greatly exceeded the rate at which new blood could be formed from the food, or at which blood could be used to feed the body. The veins would rapidly be drained, and the arteries would burst 'unless the blood should somehow find its way from the arteries into the veins, and so return to the right side of the heart; I began to think whether there might not be a motion, as it were, in a circle'.

Harvey made countless simple but irrefutable experiments to show that the blood did in fact circulate: that the heart sent a continuous and rapid stream of blood into the arteries and that the same blood returned from all over the body in the veins. In snakes, with their sluggish circulation, he watched the action of the heart in slow motion; in mammals he observed that a part becomes distended with blood if its veins are blocked, and drained of blood if its arteries are blocked and its veins left open. In various dissections he injected water into arteries and recovered it from veins. Anyone can repeat his best-known experiment. The arm is bound above the elbow so that the veins stand out, and their valves are seen as knots or swellings. A vein is compressed with a finger, and the blood is milked upwards to the next valve. The vein between the finger and the valve remains empty until the finger is released; the vein then fills from below. This may be repeated until so much blood has passed along the segment of vein, always in the same direction, that 'you will be convinced of the fact that it circulates'.

2. HARVEY'S INFLUENCE

Harvey had less trouble than most pioneers in persuading his contemporaries that he was right. A few would not listen, but most schools accepted the new doctrine within Harvey's lifetime. But for a long time nobody but Harvey seems to have appreciated the importance of his discovery. He saw that it must affect every part of medicine; yet it hardly began to do so for over a century.

One obstacle was that nobody could explain why blood should circulate until body chemistry, and especially oxygen and its function, began to be understood. Anyone but Harvey would have put forward a theory (masquerading as established fact) 'proving' the need for the circulation, for science was still called 'natural philosophy'. Not even Descartes, the best philosopher since Aristotle, was fully aware of the gulf between philosophical argument and scientific experiment. Harvey is perhaps the first modern scientist in the history of medicine. He concerned himself solely with what he could prove by repeated demonstration. Of reasons for the blood to circulate he said, 'I am of opinion that our first duty is to inquire whether the thing be or not, before asking wherefore it is.' No physician had ever spoken in such terms before, and what to us may seem a commonplace remark can have had little meaning for Harvey's contemporaries.

Harvey could find no path to carry blood from the smallest twigs of the arteries to the smallest veins, because he had no microscope and he was looking for vessels much less than 1/1000 inch across. Centuries before, Galen's theory of the blood had required small holes in the dividing wall of the heart. Therefore, said Galen, there are such holes; and everyone believed him, in just the same way as they believed him when he *demonstrated* the presence of blood in the arteries and disproved the old theory that arteries contained air. Until Harvey, doctors did not make any clear distinction between things inferred and things demonstrated by experiment. Anyone else would have said that since blood evidently flowed from arteries to veins there were passages to carry it. Harvey described at length how in one experiment after another he had utterly failed to find any such passages. As later in the century Newton ended his work on optics with a list of problems still to be solved, so Harvey set out more clearly than his critics the questions that he had failed to answer.

Some historians have blamed Harvey for being too conservative, too ready to rely on Aristotle and other ancient authorities. He was a complete teleologist – the ultimate reason for all things was that it was right for them to be so – and his practical medicine was that of Galen. One may as well blame him for being called Harvey and not Darwin or for living in the 17th instead of the 19th century. And in a sense Harvey's conservatism is a very modern trait, arising from the impact of pure science on practical medicine. A pure scientist can afford to reject all previous theories and start afresh, like Descartes. But a scientific physician has to look after sick people who cannot wait for new theories to mature. Today as 300 years ago his best guide is Harvey's doctrine that he must stick to established methods until he can prove that they are wrong.

Hashimoto's disease. Inflammation of the thyroid gland, a case of ➤*autoimmunity*, leading to thyroid deficiency. ➤*thyroid gland* (2).

hashish = ➤*hemp*.

hay fever. A common form of ➤*allergy*; strictly speaking hay fever is a seasonal complaint due to grass pollens, but the term can be stretched to include any allergic reaction involving the lining of the nose. Tree pollens cause hay fever in the spring, grass pollens in summer; anything to which a person happens to be allergic in the dust of the air can set off an attack at any time. Occasionally stimulation by hot or cold air seems to produce the symptoms of hay fever. Emotion plays some part in most forms of allergy, but is much less important with hay fever than with asthma or allergic skin disease. A few people appear to sneeze with emotion, but generally hay fever is a straightforward response to contact with a particular substance to which the patient is sensitive.

The symptoms are those of an acute inflammation in the nose, often spreading to the throat and the covering membrane of the eye (conjunctiva). Tickling at the back of the nose is followed by sneezing and watering of the eyes and sometimes headache. An attack seldom lasts long, but in some cases where the irritant is perennial a chronic disorder, with the nose always more or less blocked, may develop. Over-enthusiastic use of nose-drops for treating hay fever

is one cause of chronic inflammation and catarrh.

The immediate cause of the symptoms is *histamine*, a product of the allergic reaction, and most cases respond well to antihistamine drugs. The particular irritant can often be identified by sensitivity tests. Avoiding it would solve the problem, but that is seldom possible. Desensitization by a rather tedious course of injections works in some cases. Many patients do well with insufflation of ➤*cromoglycate* to prevent attacks, and of ➤*corticosteroids* to arrest them.

HCG = human chorionic gonadotrophin, a hormone produced by the placenta, said to cause some early symptoms of pregnancy (breast engorgement, occasional nausea). Its presence in the urine is among the earliest indications of pregnancy.

head. The head accommodates the brain, several sense organs, and inlets for air and food. In most animals other than man it is also the part of the body that leads the way; but man explores and defends himself with his hands, and in comparison with other mammals his face is rudimentary. With the recession of his nose, his eyes have been able to take a position where they work as a single, stereoscopic unit. He compensates for a rather narrow visual field with a very mobile neck.

The underlying structure is briefly discussed under ➤*skull*. The soft tissues (nerves, blood vessels, muscles etc.) form a most intricate pattern. All the nerves are derived directly from the brain and not the spinal cord (➤*cranial nerve*). Blood is delivered by three pairs of arteries: *external carotid* for the face and scalp, *internal carotid* and *vertebral* for the brain. It returns by the *jugular* veins.

291

Apart from the tiny bones for conducting sound in the inner ear, the only mobile joint in the head is the temporo-mandibular joint between the lower jaw and the base of the skull. It is provided with the powerful muscles of *mastication*. In addition, there is a complex array of muscles in the face and scalp. Unlike most voluntary muscles, they are attached to bone only at one end; the other end merges with the skin.

headache. Headache is perhaps the commonest and certainly the least informative of all symptoms. It may accompany almost any general illness, including all kinds of acute infection from a boil on the back to malaria, poisons such as alcohol, tobacco and many drugs, high blood pressure, decayed teeth, and anxiety. The source of the pain is seldom clear. Even the severe pain of migraine has not been fully explained, beyond saying that it has something to do with blood vessels inside the skull. The brain itself is surprisingly insensitive, but its covering membranes, the *meninges*, perceive pain, and headaches arising from disorders within the skull are often due to irritation of the meninges. The skull itself is the source of the pain of *sinusitis*. The headaches of worry and fatigue – the commonest of all – may arise from tension of the muscles of the neck and scalp.

Persistent headaches, and headaches that do not respond to mild analgesic drugs, need to be investigated; but the mere statement 'I have a headache' gives little more clue to the diagnosis than 'I do not feel well'.

head injury. Hippocrates, who devoted a whole treatise to the subject, observed that while even very grave head injuries were not always hopeless, none was so trivial that it could be ignored.

The special danger is that the skull allows no room for expansion. A small amount of blood is enough to irritate or compress the brain. Although actual damage to the brain cannot be repaired, much can be done to prevent further harm, or to avoid any harm.

A second's unconsciousness is proof of concussion. As a rule there are no after-effects, but repeated concussion such as a boxer may suffer inevitably does permanent damage; and anyone who has been concussed needs to be watched for signs of further trouble, especially slow bleeding, which may need prompt surgical attention.

Suffocation is the commonest cause of death after head injuries. The tongue is slung from the lower jaw. If a man is deeply unconscious his jaw may be so relaxed that the back of his tongue blocks his throat; and because his protective reflexes are suppressed he cannot breathe. Anyone can put two fingers at the angle of the jaw and two more under the point of the jaw, and bring the jaw gently upwards and forwards. The tongue comes with it and the patient can breathe.

It is essential to be sure that the space behind the tongue is not blocked by false teeth or a particle of food. Many lives can be saved if the first person on the scene of an accident gently explores this space with a finger. Any unconscious patient is liable to vomit, and may suffocate from inhaling fluid from the stomach. The danger is largely averted if he is laid on his side with his mouth downwards – provided that the jaw is drawn forwards to keep the tongue clear of the back of the throat.

After severe head injuries some patients develop a kind of ►*epilepsy*. Taking all head injuries into account, this is a very rare complication, but after localized damage to certain areas of the brain surface, e.g. by a fragment of the skull, it is not uncommon. The attacks may persist despite surgical treatment of the apparent source of irritation, in which case they are treated in the same way as the usual type of the disease.

Fractures are further discussed under ➤*skull*.

healing. The processes by which tissues damaged or destroyed by injury or disease are restored. Depending on the extent of the damage and still more on the kind of tissue involved, healing may restore the tissue to its original state or may only patch up the damage.

Repair starts with ➤*inflammation*, which is the natural reaction to damage of any kind. The inflammatory fluid which gathers at the site of injury contains not only phagocytes – cells for removing debris and dealing with infection – but also connective-tissue cells that can be modified to form new blood vessels set in a fibrous mesh (*granulation tissue*). This new tissue advances in the wake of the phagocytes involved in removing blood-clot and damaged tissue, to form a temporary bridge across the gap and restore the circulation of blood across it. The granulation tissue is delicate and vulnerable, but it acts like a dressmaker's tacking stitches while the definitive repair is carried out.

In most parts of the body at least some of the original tissue is replaced by regeneration, although the remainder may be repaired by scar tissue, consisting mainly of strong but inert collagen fibres. A clean wound such as a surgical incision should as a rule heal with a minimum of inflammation and granulation, resulting in no more than a line of scar

tissue joining normal tissues on either side; this is known as healing by first intention. Healing by second intention differs in degree: if much tissue has been lost, or healing has been impeded by, e.g., infection, the amount of granulation tissue may be too large to be spanned by regeneration spreading from the healthy tissue around the injury, and a relatively large scar will remain in the middle. Scar tissue always has a tendency to contract, so that a large scar may be not only unsightly but also deforming. For instance, the scar of a large burn in front of the elbow can make it impossible to straighten the arm. Preventing or correcting such deformity is one of the most important tasks of plastic surgery.

Healing is impeded, of course, while the cause of the injury persists, or if fresh injury or infection arises. In the early stages the newly formed tissue is very fragile and vulnerable to any but the slightest movement. On the other hand, free circulation of blood is a prerequisite and is promoted by the use of nearby muscles that do not disturb the injured part. Cold, anaemia and malnutrition delay healing. Lack of vitamin C (scurvy) is notoriously bad, although it does not follow that a properly nourished person can accelerate healing by taking extra vitamin C. Anything that suppresses inflammation, especially corticosteroid hormones, must also suppress healing.

The healing of broken bones is further discussed under ➤*fracture*.

heart. All but the very simplest organisms circulate fluids to deliver nutrients and remove waste. Plants do so with very fine tubes that rely on the forces of osmosis and surface tension, but animals use muscle fibres in the walls of tubular vessels to pump fluid (blood) round their bodies. At a fairly early stage of evolution, and in the growth of a human embryo, the muscle is concentrated at a central point to form a heart. The vessels leaving the heart become arteries; those returning, veins. Blood from the veins is received by an antechamber, the *atrium*, and passed to a more heavily muscled chamber, the *ventricle*, to be pumped by way of the arteries round the body (*>circulation*).

1. DEVELOPMENT

The primitive atrium and ventricle each become divided by a partition or *septum* into right and left halves, the right to receive used blood from the great veins (superior and inferior vena cava) and deliver it to the lungs by the *pulmonary artery*, and the left to receive freshly oxygenated blood from the pulmonary veins and pump it into the *aorta* for distribution around the body.

Until birth the developing infant receives its oxygen and food from the mother by way of the umbilical cord. The refreshed blood is diverted from right to left, bypassing the lungs, by way of an opening in the atrial septum, the *foramen ovale*, and a vessel joining the pulmonary artery to the aorta, the *ductus arteriosus*. As the unexpanded foetal lungs resist the flow of blood the pressure is higher in the right side of the heart than the left, and this keeps the bypasses open. The first breaths after birth expand the lungs and the pressure in them falls. Now the higher pressure on the left pushes the foramen ovale to, and it is soon sealed. The ductus constricts and then withers.

2. ANATOMY

In the early stages the heart is in the mid-line, pointing forwards. As it grows it turns to the left, so that the 'right' side comes to lie in front of the 'left'. When fully grown it extends from the right side of the sternum to the *apex* roughly below the left nipple. It is about the size of its owner's clenched fist.

The heart is simply a hollow muscle, the *myocardium*, divided by the now intact septa into left and right parts, each of two chambers lined with a smooth membrane, the *endocardium*.

At the outlet of each chamber flaps of endocardium form one-way *valves* to restrict the flow to one direction: on the right the *tricuspid* from atrium to ventricle, and the *pulmonary* from ventricle to pulmonary artery and lungs; on the left the *mitral* from atrium to ventricle, and the *aortic* valve from ventricle to aorta and so to the general circulation.

A membrane around the heart, the *epicardium*, corresponds with the pleura around the lungs and the peritoneum of the abdomen. Its two slippery layers prevent friction with the enclosing fibrous sheath, the *pericardium*.

Like any working muscle, the heart needs a good supply of oxygen and nutrients. The blood constantly flowing through it does not serve because the endocardium is impermeable, but immediately beyond the aortic valve the two *coronary arteries* leave the aorta and encircle the heart to provide its needs.

3. PHYSIOLOGY

Heart muscle differs from ordinary voluntary muscles in that its fibres are not separate entities but are fused to form a single meshwork that automatically contracts to expel blood (*systole*) and relaxes to receive it (*diastole*).

Left to their own devices the atria would contract about 140 times a minute and the ventricles at about 30. Contractions are initiated in a part of the right atrium, the sinu-atrial node (*S-A node*). As each wave spreads through the atria the impulse is carried to the ventricles in a leash of nerve-like fibres, the *bundle of His*; thus the action of the four chambers is synchronized.

The heart rate at rest is kept down to about 70 (with much individual variation) by a constant stream of negative impulses (*vagal tone*) carried from the cardiac centre in the lowest part of the brain, the *medulla oblongata*, to the S-A node by the vagus nerve. In response to the added demands of physical or emotional stress vagal tone is decreased. This could leave the S-A node to its built-in rate of 140, which positive impulses in sympathetic nerves to the node can increase still further. Adrenaline released from the adrenals in response to sudden demand has the same effect.

These actions are enhanced by inherent properties of the heart muscle. Stretching by increased flow of incoming blood causes the S-A node to accelerate the beat, and the ventricle to contract more powerfully. According to ►*Starling's law* the heart will meet (reasonable) added demand by added effort.

To provide the brain and other organs with enough oxygen is the immediate function of the heart, and its regulation is closely linked with that of breathing: the respiratory centre in the brain is adjacent to the cardiac centre. ►*circulation*.

4. CONGENITAL DEFECTS

The development of the heart can go wrong in many ways, some comparatively harmless, some lethal. Although an otherwise normal infant may have a defective heart, these anomalies more often accompany other congenital disorders such as Down's syndrome.

The commoner defects include *patent ductus arteriosus* or failure of the ductus to close, often after premature birth. It allows blood to escape from the aorta to the pulmonary artery, which may raise the blood pressure in the lungs and increase the burden on the heart. Until birth the ductus is kept open by the action of *prostaglandin* hormones, and a patent ductus can sometimes be persuaded to close by a prostaglandin antagonist such as indomethacin. Or it may in time close spontaneously; if not it can be corrected surgically. This is usually advised even if the defect is causing no trouble, because a patent ductus can later become a haven for bacterial infection.

Coarctation (congenital constriction) of the aorta has the effect of a finger under a running tap, making it squirt – but also jeopardizing the washer by raising the pressure. In these cases a patent ductus can act as a safety valve, which may be kept open by giving a suitable prostaglandin until the infant is fit for surgery.

Persistent gaps in the septa between atria or ventricles, and defective valves are among other developmental errors, and the aorta and pulmonary artery can be out of place. Congenital defects may be multiple, e.g. *Fallot's tetralogy*: obstructed pulmonary artery causing dilatation of the right ventricle, misplaced origin of the aorta and a defective septum between the right and left ventricles. A 'blue baby' is cyanosed, i.e. has a bluish complexion because a defective heart allows unoxygenated venous blood to enter the general circulation; Fallot's tetralogy is a common cause of this condition.

Although some congenital heart disease is beyond repair, many serious defects, including Fallot's tetralogy, are amenable to surgery.

5. ACQUIRED HEART DISEASE

The commonest type of heart disease, at least in developed countries, arises from disease of the coronary arteries, depriving the heart muscle of an adequate supply of fresh blood; ►*ischaemic heart disease* and *atheroma*.

The countless other causes of diseased heart muscle (*cardiomyopathy*) include all kinds of infection, rheumatic fever, thyroid disease, diabetes, obesity and chronic poisoning, of which alcoholism is the commonest example.

The *valves*, especially the aortic, may be abnormally tight (*stenosed*) from birth without giving trouble until late in life, when the defect is exaggerated by atheroma. Disease of the mitral valve is generally due to past rheumatic fever. Before the introduction of penicillin, syphilis was a common cause of valvular disease. Valvular disease was virtually untreatable until advances in surgery and anaesthesia made open-heart surgery possible, with refashioning or replacement of damaged valves.

Although the healthy endocardium is practically immune to infection, *bacterial endocarditis* can affect abnormal valves and require urgent treatment with antibiotics. The infecting organism is often *Streptococcus viridans*, a normal inhabitant of the mouth that can enter the bloodstream after dental extraction.

6. INVESTIGATION

Much can be learnt about the heart from the patient's account of his symptoms and routine clinical examination. A simple X-ray picture reveals significant enlargement or displacement, and may show calcification due to atheroma in the aorta or a valve. Radioactive tracers may be used to give a more detailed picture. An ►*electrocardiogram* (ECG) is an invaluable guide to the actual working of the heart. Other tests include *echocardiography*, which demonstrates the actual flow through the valves and chambers, and scanning techniques such as *magnetic resonance imaging* show details of structure. Cardiac *catheterization* involves passing a fine tube to the heart via an accessible vein or artery in order to inject a 'dye' visible by X-rays; this is a prerequisite of surgical reconstruction of blocked coronary arteries.

heart failure. The word 'failure' is misleading, for it suggests that the heart no longer works and that the patient ought to be dead. This can of course happen, but in the medical sense failure is usually only relative: the heart works, but not as effectively as it should.

As fast as blood arrives from the veins a healthy heart pumps it into the arteries. The heart is in 'failure' when it does not pump the blood quite as fast as it arrives. As a result the veins become congested with blood and the pressure in them rises. The circulation then goes on as before, but with a constant backlog of accumulated blood. The heart no longer empties itself with each beat. Because its muscle is stretched it actually beats harder than a healthy heart (as a stretched spring pulls harder), but without increasing its output. The situation is familiar to anyone who has allowed correspondence to pile up: he may answer letters as fast as they arrive, but he remains a week behind with his work. This inefficient person often works longer hours than his more productive colleagues. He has neither time nor

subclavian artery
subclavian vein
superior vena cava
pulmonary arteries
pulmonary veins
pulmonary valve
right atrium
tricuspid valve
right ventricle
inferior vena cava

jugular veins
carotid arteries

subclavian artery
subclavian vein
aorta
aortic valve
pulmonary veins
left atrium
mitral valve
left ventricle

Section of heart, slightly modified to show the four chambers;
in fact the right ventricle lies in front of the left

energy for recreation. Since he hardly manages his routine work he cannot take on extra duties at busy times.

The symptoms of heart failure are in two groups: those due to poor output (forward failure) and those due to congestion in the veins (backward failure). Forward failure affects the whole body: all tissues need an adequate supply of fresh blood, and when the supply is reduced nothing in the body functions quite as well as it should.

The left side of the heart receives blood from the lungs and pumps it to the whole body. If this side fails, the burden of backward failure falls on the lungs. If the right side of the heart, which receives blood from the whole body, fails the con-

gestion is spread throughout the body. In health, the blood vessels of the lungs contain only half a pint of blood, whereas those of the rest of the body contain a gallon. A small amount of extra fluid is enough to embarrass the lungs, and thus the laboured breathing of left-sided failure comes on quickly, sometimes without warning. The swollen feet and other symptoms of congestion due to right-sided failure are much more insidious because so much more space is available.

The symptoms of congestion are due not so much to over-filling of the veins as to leakage of water into the tissues, causing *oedema* (dropsy). The various ways in which tissues can become waterlogged are considered under ►*oedema*. At least three mechanisms operate in heart failure. The most obvious is the raised pressure in the veins, which raises the pressure in the capillaries and prevents them from absorbing water from the tissues. Secondly, poor circulation deprives the capillaries of their full quota of oxygen and causes them to leak. Thirdly, poor circulation in the kidneys causes too much salt to be retained in the body; since the concentration of salt is automatically kept constant, any excess of salt is automatically accompanied by an excess of water.

The relation to other disease is very complex, for on the one hand heart failure lowers the efficiency of other organs and on the other hand chronic disease in other organs, especially the lungs and kidneys, can lead to heart failure.

The performance of a failing heart can often be improved by drugs, of which the most important is ►*digitalis*. Many causes of heart failure can be treated directly: high blood pressure, disorders of the thyroid gland, anaemia, and various kinds of defective heart valve are treatable and in some cases completely curable. Chronic bronchitis is among the commonest causes of heart failure, at least in Great Britain, and if it cannot be cured much can be done to prevent it from becoming worse. Accumulated fluid can be removed by ►*diuretic* drugs, which increase the amount of urine, or simply by restricting salt in the diet (since the excess of water in the body is partly due to an excess of salt). A salt-free diet is insipid, but many patients gladly put up with it when they have once experienced its good effect. The demands made on the heart have to be limited to what it can manage. With severe or sudden failure this may mean complete bed-rest. Here we meet a paradox: severe attacks of difficulty in breathing due to heart failure (cardiac asthma) are most likely to occur when the patient is asleep in bed, probably because during the day any excess of fluid tends to gravitate to the legs, but in bed it is free to overload the lungs. Therefore some patients with heart failure sleep best sitting upright.

Adapting a patient's mode of life to the limits set by an inefficient heart often needs delicate judgement and the closest cooperation between patient and doctor. It must be repeated that failure is a relative term. If the patient's activities are within the set limits, so that the heart can work without a backlog, then he cannot be said to suffer from heart failure. All the other forms of treatment serve to extend the limits. But to restrict activity too much – for instance, to stay in bed when he might be in the garden or to stay at home when his heart would let him be at his office – does no good to a man's heart and does great harm to the man as a whole. Carefully graded exercise may be the best treatment of some types of heart disease.

heat exhaustion; heatstroke. An excessively hot environment can cause various kinds of trouble. Miners and others who have to work in an overheated environment such as a ship's engine room can develop painful muscular spasms, known as *miner's cramp*, from loss of salt. This is corrected by taking in extra salt.

Heat exhaustion is weakness, faintness and possibly collapse from loss of body fluid with excessive sweating. The patient has to be kept at rest, as cool as practicable, with frequent sips of water with a little salt.

Heatstroke is a dangerous result of failure to sweat enough and consequent overheating of the body (*hyperpyrexia*), leading to extreme discomfort, disorientation and sometimes convulsions and unconsciousness. It is a matter of urgency to bring the body temperature down to normal by any means, such as covering the patient with a wet sheet in a draught and getting him to hospital as soon as possible. Delay can result in death or permanent brain damage.

hebephrenia. A severe mental disorder; adolescent ➤*schizophrenia*.

Helicobacter pylori. Duodenal ulcers are commonly associated with infection by this microbe. Though it cannot be definitely said to cause the ulcers, removing it with antibiotics much improves the chances of healing.

hemiplegia. Paralysis of one side of the body (from interference with the opposite side of the brain).

hemp. *Cannabis sativa*, a plant valued commercially for its fibre and socially for drugs derived from it (marihuana, bhang, dagga, hashish). Its effects – a sense of well-being, escape from reality, hallucinations – are mostly due to an alkaloid, tetrahydrocannabinol (THC). But as with alcohol and other drugs affecting mood, the effect is much influenced by the circumstances in which the drug is taken.

Hemp has been used medicinally since antiquity in Asia. In the 19th century it appeared in the *British Pharmacopoeia* as a milder narcotic than opium, recommended for dysmenorrhoea. As the effects were unpredictable, and it lingered for too long in the body, its use was discontinued. It is still under research in the

USA and elsewhere, and may yet return to favour as an anti-emetic with cancer therapy and in terminal care.

There is still no consensus about whether it causes brain damage, or is addictive, and whether its abuse leads to more dangerous drugs. While these questions remain open governments are reluctant to legalize it.

heparin. A substance extracted from liver and other tissues that delays the clotting of blood.

hepatic. Of the ➤*liver* (Lat. *hepar*).
Hepatic artery. The liver receives a large supply of blood from the *portal vein*; this is the raw material on which it has to work. But the portal blood has already given up its available oxygen to the intestine, and like any other organ the liver needs oxygenated blood. As the lungs have a private supply from the ➤*bronchial* arteries, so the liver has from the hepatic artery, which comes from the aorta via the *coeliac* artery. Its branches in the liver accompany those of the portal vein.
Hepatic coma. Coma from liver failure, due to poisoning by substances (especially ammonia) which a healthy liver destroys.
Hepatic duct. Channel into which bile flows from the liver. Left and right ducts join to form the common hepatic duct; this is joined by the duct of the gall bladder to form the common bile duct, which opens into the duodenum.
Hepatic flexure. Part of the ➤*colon*, where it turns to the left under the liver.
Hepatic veins. Blood from the portal vein and hepatic arteries (see above) irrigates the cells of the liver and leaves by a single system of veins, which open straight into the inferior vena cava at the back of the liver.

hepatitis. Inflammation of the liver; the term is usually limited to inflammation without fibrous scarring (i.e. not *cirrhosis*).

Viral hepatitis, type A is an acute infection, often occurring in small epidemics, e.g. in schools. The infection can be carried in food or water. An incubation period of 2–6 weeks is followed by feverish illness with nausea and vomiting, swelling and tenderness of the liver and, after a few days, jaundice. Most patients recover within 2 or 3 weeks although a few take rather longer, but lasting effects and complications are very rare. An attack confers lasting immunity. No special treatment is required, but patients are advised to avoid alcohol for the next year.

Viral hepatitis, type B (formerly serum hepatitis) is usually a blood-borne infection and can be transmitted sexually. The virus is identifiable in the serum by the presence of a specific antigen (Australia antigen). Until blood could be screened for this, the usual means by which the disease was spread was by blood transfusion. Since the incubation period can be as long as 6 months it was easy to take infected blood from apparently fit donors. Kidney dialysis may also be an occasional source, and many cases now arise among drug addicts who use infected syringes. The symptoms are like those of type A, but tend to be more protracted. Unlike type A, type B does sometimes lead to a chronic hepatitis, which may lead to cirrhosis and even to liver cancer. Perhaps because their resistance is lowered by drugs, a significant number of heroin addicts die of liver failure following hepatitis. About 10 per cent of patients remain carriers and must be considered potential sources of infection, while a few are liable to relapse into active hepatitis.

Type C virus (quaintly named 'non-A, non-B', until types C and D were identified) is now recognized as the principal cause of transfusion hepatitis. It follows a similar course to type B. Type D virus has been found only as an accompaniment to type B, and a possible type E is under investigation.

Other viral infections that can inflame the liver include ➤*yellow fever* and ➤*glandular fever*.

Numerous more elaborate organisms may infect the liver as well as other organs. Two that deserve special mention are *leptospira* (➤*Weil's disease*) and *entamoeba histolytica*, the cause of amoebic ➤*dysentery*, of which amoebic hepatitis is a common complication.

Chronic hepatitis, apart from being an occasional sequel to type B acute infection, can arise as an autoimmune reaction (➤*immunity* (7)), or in response to various drugs. However, much the commonest cause among those with active acute hepatitis is *alcohol*.

Vaccines against types A and B viruses are available for people exposed to special risk of infection, e.g. frequent travellers to exotic destinations, people needing regular blood transfusions, promiscuous homosexuals or certain health workers. After vaccination immunity takes a few months to develop. For immediate though transient protection human immunoglobulin is given. Persistent hepatitis B can be treated with ➤*interferon*.

hermaphrodite. A true hermaphrodite is both male and female. This is the natural state of most plants and a few animals, but true hermaphroditism in man is mythical. Nearly all so-called human hermaphrodites are people with the wrong number of sex chromosomes

(>*genetics*). They have the primary sex organs (ovaries or testes) of one sex but many secondary characters of the other, or their external appearance is ambiguous.

There have been rare accounts of an ovary and a testis in the same person, presumably from the formation of one embryo from the elements of two. This is as near as one gets to a true human hermaphrodite; but neither organ is fertile.

Adrenogenital syndrome (>*adrenal*) can cause a sort of hermaphroditism in girls, but the ovaries are normal and if the condition is treated the girls develop normally.

Newspaper accounts of sex-change operations refer to plastic surgery done at the request of people with male sex organs to give them the outward appearance of females. These are people whose emotional make-up is female and who wish to equate their physical state with their feelings.

Homosexuality is a matter of emotion and behaviour and bears little relation to physical constitution. >*sex*.

hernia. Protrusion of an organ from one compartment of the body into another, e.g. of a loop of intestine into the top of the thigh, or of an intervertebral disc into the canal for the spinal cord.

Common types of hernia include the following:

Diaphragmatic (hiatus) hernia. The diaphragm is a strong layer of muscle and fibrous tissue separating the cavities of the chest and the belly. Its weakest point is the opening (*hiatus*) for the oesophagus to enter the stomach. Sometimes part of the stomach bulges up through the opening. This kind of hernia is so common as to be almost the rule after middle age, especially in fat people.

Generally it gives little if any trouble, but it can cause indigestion and, rarely, symptoms confused with gastric ulcer or even angina. Adjustment of diet to avoid irritating or over-filling the stomach is often enough to relieve the symptoms. Surgery is very seldom needed.

Femoral hernia. A loop of intestine can bulge into the groin alongside the blood vessels to the thigh. The effect is very similar to an inguinal hernia.

Inguinal hernia. This is the commonest form of 'rupture'. The weak point is the small gap in the abdominal muscles where the testis descended to the scrotum. Its vessels pass through the gap, which therefore cannot be sealed off. In older men, coughing or straining may cause a bulge at the gap. In some boys and young men the hernia enters a preformed space: the testis during its descent drags with it a pocket of peritoneum – the lining of the abdominal cavity. This normally withers, but it may persist like the finger of a glove, and a loop of intestine or other abdominal structure easily slips into it.

A femoral or inguinal hernia sometimes causes little trouble, but it can be uncomfortable, and it is always a source of anxiety because without warning it can become *strangulated*: a loop of intestine is pinched at the entrance to the hernia. Its contents are obstructed, and worse still fresh blood no longer reaches it. Prompt operation is needed to save the patient's life. The usual practice is to repair inguinal and femoral hernias, without waiting for trouble. A *truss* is simply a pad held firmly against the weak point to stop any organ from entering the hernia. It does not cure, and is seldom really comfortable. Unless there are strong reasons against surgery in a particular case, the best treatment is to repair the defect surgically, either by bringing its margins together or by covering it with a graft of the patient's own fibrous tissue or a synthetic support.

Umbilical hernia. Many babies have a hernia at the navel. These usually close themselves in a year or two without any trouble; but umbilical hernias that develop later need surgical repair.

heroin. Diamorphine; diacetyl morphine; a synthetic derivative of morphine intended to have the pain-killing properties of morphine without causing addiction. It turned out to be even more addicting than morphine, but was nevertheless used because in some cases of severe pain it was more effective.

The use of heroin is prohibited in the United States and some other countries, because of the very serious risk of addiction. In Britain it is still occasionally prescribed for intractable pain, but doctors are not encouraged to use it. Under the latest regulations (1973) only designated specialists can treat heroin addicts.

Herophilus (3rd century BC). The first anatomist in history; a native of Chalcedon in Asia Minor, and with Erasistratus one of the founders of the great medical school of Alexandria. He paid particular attention to the nervous system, distinguishing nerves from blood vessels and sensory from motor nerves, and giving a detailed account of the brain. His works have been lost, but were much quoted by Galen in the 2nd century AD.

herpes. Two distinct virus infections, *herpes simplex* and *herpes zoster*; both cause clusters of sore blisters on the skin, and both, once established, lie dormant waiting to erupt.

Herpes simplex involves two types of infection caused by slightly different strains of the virus. *Type 1* is the well-known cold sore. The original infection is usually in childhood, but although one attack seldom lasts more than a week or two the patient remains liable to a fresh crop of blisters at any time, usually when resistance is lowered by infection such as a common cold. The eruption may appear anywhere, but is commonest around the nose and mouth. Although this is usually a harmless though tiresome complaint, two associated conditions are serious. Babies with atopic eczema may react violently to infection with herpes simplex. Secondly, any involvement of the eyes can endanger the *cornea*; in extreme cases infection can obscure vision and necessitate corneal grafting. There is not much that need be done for uncomplicated herpes simplex except try to keep the lesions dry and clean. *Acyclovir* may help if applied from the first signs. This infection is transmitted by simple contagion, i.e. physical contact or, probably, by fomites such as infected tableware or towels. The virus embeds itself, apparently, in nerve ganglia for life and emerges if resistance is lowered at any time.

Type 2 herpes simplex causes similar lesions to type 1 but usually affects the sexual organs and is transmitted sexually. In a few years, instead of being a comparative rarity, herpes simplex has become a major venereal epidemic. In the USA, new cases diagnosed approach a million a year. The initial attack usually subsides in a week or 10 days, but the virus remains and may flare up again at any time, especially after coitus. No cure has been found yet.

Herpes zoster (shingles) is caused by the virus of chickenpox. After an attack of chickenpox, or perhaps a symptom-free infection, the virus may lurk unnoticed for many years. Then, perhaps at a time of stress but often for no apparent reason, the patient feels vaguely but increasingly unwell and develops localized pain. The virus is established in one or more sensory nerves, to which the painful area is confined. The characteristic rash, starting as a patch of inflammation with a lumpy texture and rapidly turning to clusters of blisters, appears in this area. A typically infected area lies along the course of one or two intercostal nerves, following exactly the line of the ribs round the chest wall and ending abruptly at the mid-line; but almost any nerve might be the one involved. The most important is the ophthalmic branch of the 5th cranial nerve, which carries sensation from around the eye. This type of herpes demands expert advice to protect the eye from injury.

Unlike herpes simplex, herpes zoster is extremely unlikely to recur after the first attack: although the virus may have been dormant in the tissues for many years without eliciting any immunity, the actual attack does elicit an effective defence against future attacks. The one complication that may arise is that a few patients are left with a persistent neuralgia.

Until lately, no drugs worked against these or any other virus infections. But *idoxuridine* for local application, *acyclovir* and *inosine*, both taken by mouth, are now available.

hiatus ►*hernia.*

hiccup. Abrupt spasm of the diaphragm, with reflex closure of the vocal cords blocking the expected intake of air, due to irritation of nerves that control breathing. Hiccups can be a symptom of countless disorders of the digestive or respiratory organs, also of poisoning by alcohol or, with failure of the kidneys, by the body's own waste products (*uraemia*). But more often than not there is no apparent cause.

Holding the breath can help by retaining carbon dioxide; breathing into a paper bag to recycle expired carbon dioxide has the same effect (but *not* a plastic bag, which can easily suffocate the victim!). Drinking a glass of cold water rapidly, swallowing crushed ice, and various drugs are among other remedies, and severe cases can require hospital treatment.

hip. Ball-and-socket joint between the spherical head of the *femur* (thigh-bone) and the cup-like *acetabulum* at the side of the pelvis. The acetabula face outwards and are tilted slightly downwards and backwards, which helps to take the powerful thrust of the thigh in walking.

In contrast with its counterpart the shoulder, the hip is extremely stable. The head of the femur is firmly seated in the deep socket, and the joint is reinforced by stout ligaments, especially in front. The surrounding muscles, those of the buttock and thigh, are the strongest in the body. The price of stability in a joint is limitation of movement, yet the hip is surprisingly mobile in all directions except backwards (extension). When the hip seems to be extended, as in swinging the leg back before taking a kick, it is the whole pelvis that swings on the opposite hip.

Dislocation of a fully developed hip is unusual. It requires great force, such as a collision on the road, and is likely to be only one of several injuries.

Congenital dislocation of the hip is also rather uncommon, but it is important because it can usually be prevented.

303

The primary disorder, present at birth, is no more than a laxity of the ligaments that allows the as yet unformed joint to slip in and out of place. If this state continues, the bones fail to develop and when the child begins to walk a permanent deformity is established. But if the instability is recognized soon after birth and the hip is splinted in the correct position, the bones develop normally and there is no further trouble. Until about 1960 these dislocations were ascribed to faulty development of the acetabulum, but this was putting the cart before the horse: the acetabulum develops only if the head of the femur lies in it.

The only common *fracture* near the hip is of the neck of the ➤*femur*, an inch or two from the joint. This occurs mostly in old age.

Children sometimes suffer from a deformity of the head of the femur, ➤*Perthes' disease*.

The hip is subject to great mechanical strain, and ➤*osteoarthritis* commonly affects it, causing pain, stiffness, and sometimes great disability. In most cases, treatment is conservative (rest, analgesic drugs, physiotherapy, etc.), but there is also a place for surgery for relieving severe pain or restoring function. The oldest method is to immobilize the joint (arthrodesis). This at least stopped the pain, but it left a considerable mechanical defect. In recent years hip replacement has all but superseded other surgical procedures (➤*joint replacement*).

Hippocrates of Cos (around 400 BC). By common consent the greatest physician of all time; 'the father of medicine'.

He was probably born in 460 BC and lived to a notable age – over 100, some say. He was venerated in his lifetime, and has been held up ever since as the model of what a doctor should be, almost as a religious leader or patron saint. Many legends have grown around him, but that does not justify the belief sometimes expressed that he never existed, that he is an imaginary ideal. Several early writers, including his young contemporary Plato, describe him as a real person. Nor need we insist that Hippocrates wrote none of the many books traditionally ascribed to him. He could not have written them all: some are more recent and some older than Hippocrates, and some of the doctrines are incompatible with others. But half a dozen or more of the finest seem to be the work of one man of Hippocrates' time. Somebody had to write them, and there are no other claimants. They do not reflect the philosophy that Plato has put into Hippocrates' mouth, but this means nothing, for writers of the time often used real people as pegs for their own ideas. Plato's Socrates talks differently from Xenophon's, and perhaps neither is much like the real Socrates. But these are problems for classical scholars. As far as medicine is concerned Hippocrates was a practising physician and surgeon, the leader of a medical school and guild based on the island of Cos, and the author of some of the medical writings of the school. The content of the books, the wealth of original observation, the unerring sense of what is relevant, would set them among the great works of genius. What makes them unique is the spirit in which they are written. They establish for all time how medicine ought to be practised and what doctors should try to be. The superstition and magic of primitive medicine are rejected, and the doctor is no longer a priest or benevolent sorcerer but a humane observer, counsellor and servant of the sick.

The whole collection of seventy or

more books known as the *Hippocratic Corpus* represents the teaching of one school and not of Greek medicine in general. Other schools kept the old superstitions alive, much as astrology and the flat-earth theory survive alongside scientific astronomy. In succeeding centuries the Hippocratic ideals were more and more obscured; they all but vanished 600 years later when Galen died, and medicine deteriorated until they were restored in the 16th century.

The book *On Ancient Medicine* says that history is shaped by man's search for food and congenial surroundings, and that medicine is an extension of this search – a means of adapting ourselves to our environment. It therefore concerns everyone.

'Whoever treats of this art should treat of things which are familiar to the common people. For of nothing else will such a one have to inquire or treat, but of the diseases under which the common people have laboured, which diseases and the causes of their origin and departure, their increase and decline, illiterate persons cannot easily find out for themselves, but still it is easy for them to understand these things when discovered and expounded by others.'

So much for the mystery of health and sickness and for trade secrets in medicine. And this doctrine – that the physician should explain things to his patients – has lain dormant until the present century, and it still has some way to go. To clear up any lingering doubt, Hippocrates continues:

'For it is nothing more than that everyone is put in mind of what has occurred to himself. But whoever does not reach the capacity of the illiterate vulgar

and fails to make them listen to him, misses his mark.'

The same idea appears in the first and best known of the *Aphorisms*:

'Life is short, and the Art long; the occasion fleeting; experience fallacious, and judgement difficult. The physician must not only be prepared to do what is right himself, but must also make the patient, the attendants, and externals co-operate.'

Nothing could be further from the aloof oracular physician-priest. Here, the doctor enlists the patient's help, and that of the 'externals' – the forces of Nature.

Death and disease arise from natural causes. *On the Sacred Disease* is a treatise on epilepsy, of all diseases the most likely to be blamed on supernatural causes. The theme of the book is that epilepsy is no more 'sacred' than any other disease; it is a natural event, and epileptic patients are to be studied and cared for like any others.

Diseases have many causes. Any theory that tries to explain disease and death on the basis of one or two causes must be false. Most present-day systems of unorthodox medicine are nonsensical because they ignore this fundamental truth. Hippocrates taught that diseases were disturbances in the balance of the four ►*humours* (a view not seriously challenged for more than 20 centuries). The balance might be disturbed by all manner of external factors, especially diet and climate.

From a study of carefully recorded case-histories, Hippocrates identified many predisposing factors. *Airs, Waters and Places* deals with environment. In places with a warm southerly exposure people tend to be fat and sluggish, and they are prone to dysentery but not pneumonia. In places that face north it is the other way round. Foggy regions are the unhealthiest. This book is incidentally one of the earliest on anthropology and psychology. Mountainous country, it says, breeds enterprising and warlike people; in warm low-lying countries the men are small and dark and peace-loving: 'courage and laborious enterprise are not in them'.

'A climate which is always the same induces indolence, but a changeable climate, laborious exertions both of body and mind.'

'It is changes of all kinds which arouse the understanding of mankind, and do not allow them to get into a torpid condition.'

The *Aphorisms* mention various predisposing causes to particular diseases and to illness in general. From a list like Shakespeare's seven ages we learn that babies are prone to sore mouths, vomiting, disturbed sleep, discharging ears. With teething come irritable gums, fevers, convulsions, and diarrhoea. Later come tonsillitis, asthma, worms, goitre. The catalogue takes us through adult life to old age with shortness of breath, urinary troubles, insomnia, and poor sight and hearing.

Strokes are commonest between the ages of 40 and 60.

Fat people are apt to die before slender people.

Consumption is commonest between the ages of 18 and 35.

Hippocrates is much concerned with prognosis – predicting the course of an illness. It may not seem a very useful occupation, but he explains why it is necessary:

'for by foreseeing and foretelling ... he will be the more readily believed to be acquainted with the circumstances of the sick; so that men will have confidence to entrust themselves to such a physician. And he will manage the cure best who has foreseen what is to happen from the present state of matters.'

The most famous passage in the *Prognostics* describes the appearance of someone likely to die, known as the Hippocratic facies: 'a sharp nose, hollow eyes, collapsed temples; the ears cold, contracted, and their lobes turned out; the skin about the forehead being rough, distended [taut] and parched; the colour of the whole face being green, black, livid, or lead-coloured'. It is finely observed, but Hippocrates does not allow his reader to form an opinion yet, for the patient's grim appearance could be explained in more than one way. Other symptoms have to be considered: lack of sleep, diarrhoea, starvation, any of which might show the same picture. And the patient must be watched for a time for any sign of improvement. The physician does not speak of impending death until he has ruled out the other possibilities. All this is presented as prognosis, but in forming his prognosis the physician has to make a diagnosis – to identify the patient's ailment. No other medical writer before the 18th century approached Hippocrates as a diagnostician. He studied each patient and related what he found to what he had learnt of other patients, and that is the whole science of diagnosis.

Another lesson that was to be slowly forgotten during the next 2,000 years was that medicine, like all science, cannot advance unless it is honest with itself. Prognosis is important here, because the doctor is forced to commit himself openly and expose his mistaken opinions. The test of a theory is to use it to predict an event.

All other medical writers until quite modern times dwelt on their successes. The case-histories of Hippocrates are mostly accounts of patients who died under his care, written for others to learn from his failures.

Treatment is almost disappointingly simple, because it is based on the two principles that Nature will cure most ailments if she is given a chance, and that if a doctor cannot do good he must at least do no harm. Diet and general hygiene take first place. Under-feeding is as bad as over-feeding, especially with children, and the foods that the patient enjoys do him more good than those that he dislikes – on the other hand a change of diet may help.

Drugs are used sparingly, mostly for the relief of pain, flatulence, and constipation (real or supposed). Surgery is reserved for cases where drugs will not help; but when he has to operate the doctor must be bold, quick, and neat. Fractures, dislocations, and wounds are treated by the methods handed down from ancient Egypt and still, in principle, used today. The chapter on the surgical treatment of piles could be slipped into a current textbook without much editing.

From the book *On Regimen* one can put together the elements in the management of a typical case, say of a severe cold or influenza. The patient and his family are exhaustively questioned about the symptoms and circumstances of the illness. The doctor inspects the patient, with special attention to the eyes and mouth, and asks to see the urine and stools. The patient is put to bed, and a hot-water bottle is ordered with strict instructions about protecting the skin from

burns. He is given a dose of hellebore as a purgative, and oxymel (honey and vinegar) to soothe his throat. He must drink plenty of *ptisan* (something like barley-water), and is allowed wine within reason as a sedative; for the night he may have a small dose of opium. He is to have light but appetizing meals, and stay where he is while the fever lasts.

If we replace hellebore with a milder purgative, or leave it out altogether, and put the oxymel and opium together in the same bottle of linctus, this could be an account of good practice in the 19th or 20th century. The patient is better cared for than he would have been at any time between the age of Hippocrates and the modern era. In Galen's time he would have been filled with nasty and useless drugs, and later he would have been starved, purged, sweated or bled according to the fashion.

The code of behaviour named after Hippocrates is set out in the next entry, ►*Hippocratic Oath*.

It would be silly to pretend that Hippocrates or anyone else achieved single-handed all that is in these immortal writings; they are obviously distilled from centuries of experience. One need not insist that he invented anything at all, for his is not that kind of fame. Other great medical pioneers are remembered for particular and tangible contributions to medical science.

Hippocrates gave medicine a soul.

Hippocratic Oath. The best known of the Hippocratic writings. Its origins may be Egyptian, and the early Indian physicians had a similar oath. The Oath as we know it was presumably taken on admission to the medical school and guild of Cos.

'I swear by Apollo the physician, and

by Asklepios, Hygeia, and Panacea[1] and all the gods and goddesses, and call them to witness that I will keep this oath and contract[2] to the best of my ability and judgement: to regard him who teaches me this art as equal to my own parents; to share my living with him, and provide for him in need; to treat his children as my own brothers, and teach them this art if they wish to learn it, without payment or contract; to give guidance, lectures, and every other kind of instruction to my own sons and those of my teacher, and to students bound by contract and oath to medical law, but to nobody else.

'I will prescribe treatment to the best of my ability and judgement for the good of the sick, and never for a harmful or illicit purpose. I will give no poisonous drug, even if asked to, nor make any such suggestion; and likewise I will give no woman a pessary to cause abortion. I will both live and work in purity and godliness. I will not operate, not even on patients with stone, but will give way to specialists in this work.[3] I will go into the houses that I visit in order to help the sick, and refrain from all deliberate harm or corruption, especially from sexual relations with women or men, free or slave. Anything I see or hear about people, whether in the course of my practice or outside it, that should not be made public, I will keep to myself and treat as an inviolable secret.[4]

'If I abide by this oath, and never break it, let all men honour me for all time on account of my life and work; but if I transgress and break my oath, let me suffer the reverse.'

1. Asklepios (Aesculapius) was a real physician, later deified as a son of Apollo. His daughters Hygeia and Pan-

acea personify health and healing. He is the patron of the guild of Cos.

2. 'Contract' (*syngraphe*) might be 'articles of apprenticeship'. The Oath appears to be both a general code of ethics and an initiation to the guild, the Asklepiades.

3. The prohibition of all operative surgery cannot apply to all physicians, as many critics have suggested. Medieval physicians chose not to operate, but until the time of Galen, 600 years after Hippocrates, surgery was a part of medicine. The Hippocratic writings include detailed and competent surgical instruction. The suggestion that only the operation for stone was forbidden is not justified. The Oath says literally 'I will not cut, not even sufferers from stone'. This particular operation may have been mentioned because a stone in the bladder was a common and excruciating illness (as it was until the 19th century) that might tempt a student or young doctor to operate without the necessary surgical training. Instead, he must call in an experienced colleague.

4. For the second time, the doctor is reminded that he is never off duty. He must both live and work in purity, and he may not discuss secrets that he learns outside his practice.

Hirschsprung's disease = ➤*megacolon*.

histamine. A simple nitrogen compound found in many tissues but especially abundant in the granules of *mast cells*, which are wandering tissue cells resembling the basophil white cells of the blood. Histamine is released from these cells in response to irritation, injury and to some immune responses to infection or allergy (➤*immunity*).

Essentially, the function of histamine is to promote inflammation, which in turn initiates both defence against invasion of the tissues and healing of injury. This it does by dilating blood vessels in the affected area to increase the flow of blood, and by making the capillary vessels more permeable and so promoting the access of blood cells to the tissues. The action of histamine is rapid and generally short-lived: its effects are continued by other mediators such as kinins, perhaps serotonin, and prostaglandins. Histamine was once thought to initiate pain, but in fact it arouses only itch. Pain probably arises from one or more of the other mediators. (➤*neuro-transmitters*).

Histamine circulating in the blood-stream has various effects. It lowers *blood pressure*, stimulates movement of the *stomach* and the formation of *acid* there, and constricts the *bronchi*. These four actions respectively explain an association of histamine with a dangerous form of *shock* (anaphylaxis, a violent allergic reaction), with *gastric ulcers*, and with *asthma*. These widespread effects of histamine are usually associated not with useful defence but with *allergy*, which is a sort of biological mistake where reactions that could be effective against infection are both misapplied and distorted.

During the 1940s drugs that would compete with histamine were introduced to treat symptoms of allergy. Scores of compounds with many chemical differences have since appeared, but all have one part of a molecule that resembles a part of the histamine molecule. Presumably this allows these antihistamine drugs to compete with histamine for histamine *receptors* (chemical features in susceptible tissues adapted to receive histamine molecules) so that these can exert their effects. In short, the drug *blocks* the action of histamine: it is a pharmacological squatter. Such drugs are effective only against symptoms wholly or mainly due to histamine. These include many though not all cases of hay fever, most acute allergic skin reactions (urticaria or nettle-rash) and some chronic ones, and itching due to histamine, e.g. from insect bites. The effect on asthma is disappointing because histamine is only one of several factors involved.

Most of these drugs also have an atropine-like effect, blocking some effects of acetylcholine. This, rather than antihistamine action, may explain their value against sea-sickness, and also their questionable inclusion in various common-cold remedies. These drugs nearly all have some sedative action: indeed, the first tranquillizers were based on this effect. As a rule, therefore, it is better not to drive when taking them, while a mixture of antihistamines and alcohol is especially dangerous if taken before driving a car.

For many years nobody understood why, although histamine is the most potent stimulus to acid secretion in the stomach, with a consequent association with gastric ulcers, antihistamine drugs had no effect on these functions. It was then found that there are two kinds of receptor for histamine, of which the drugs affected only one (H_1 receptors). The H_2 receptors, those of the stomach, receive a different unit in the histamine molecule. *Cimetidine* is a drug that competes for H_2 receptors and can therefore block stimulation of gastric acid by histamine. Practice has justified theory, and cimetidine is now a valuable drug for the treatment of peptic ulcers. An alternative to cimetidine is *ranitidine*.

Adrenaline is not an antihistamine drug as it does not obstruct histamine. However, it has numerous effects exactly opposite to those of histamine, though by different pathways; these are sometimes more effective than blocking histamine.

histology. Study of ►*tissue*. Traditional anatomy is concerned with organs, and histology with the fabric of the organs. Anatomy would see a building as a system of rooms and corridors; histology would see it as brickwork, woodwork, plaster, and paint.

In effect, histology is anatomy with a microscope, although the first man to recognize that all the organs of the body are arrangements of the same few tissues (M. F. X. Bichat, 1771–1802) worked without a microscope, which he despised as a toy.

The study of the individual cells of which tissues are largely composed is *cytology*, but this science need not be distinguished from histology.

An average human cell is about 1/1000 inch (0.02 mm) across. The standard light microscope has a useful magnification of 1000 diameters, and shows cells as fairly large objects, containing numerous smaller structures. No details smaller than about 1/100 of the cell diameter can be distinguished, because light waves cannot be used to distinguish objects smaller than the waves themselves. Ultraviolet waves are shorter; they are invisible but can be photographed and used to double the effective magnification. The electron microscope gives magnification up to 1/4 million or more. This brings objects as small as the larger molecules into view, so that histology and chemistry now overlap.

Little detail can be seen by looking at the surface of a lump of tissue. One has to examine a thin slice with a light shining through it. Even this shows only a shadowy pattern of pale greys, unless the specimen is first stained. Two or more dyes may be used together; some structures will take up one dye in preference to the other. For routine work a blue alkaline dye, haematoxylin, is used with a pink acidic dye, eosin. The nuclei of the cells attract haematoxylin and are stained blue, while most of the other structures are stained pink. Special stains are used for studying particular chemical components: starch gives a blue compound with iodine; iron can be converted to prussian blue, and so on.

Certain dyes can be applied to living tissue without killing it (*intravital staining*). Unstained living tissue is examined with oblique lighting against a dark background, which greatly increases contrast (as a shaft of sunlight in a dark room reveals dust particles).

Histology has greatly enhanced our understanding of anatomy and physiology, and in the hands of Rudolf Virchow (1821–1902) it became the principal source of information about the underlying processes of disease. In clinical medicine, it is a most valuable method of diagnosis. Only a very minor surgical operation is needed to remove a small piece of suspect tissue, in which a histologist can identify abnormalities. This technique (*biopsy*) is much used for the early detection of cancer.

histoplasma. A microscopical fungus, common in parts of America where it can cause a fairly harmless 'flu'-like infection, or serious disease of the lungs resembling tuberculosis. It can also set up a lethal kind of blood poisoning, involving various vital organs. The infection can be treated with the antibiotic *amphotericin*. Histoplasmosis is especially dangerous to people with AIDS.

HIV (human immunodeficiency virus).
Previously known as human T-cell lymphotrophic virus type III (HTLVIII) or lymphadenopathy associated virus (LAV). The virus invades T-lymphocytes, a type of white blood cell on which cellular immunity depends. Can cause PGL (persistent generalized lymphadenopathy – chronic swelling of the lymph glands), ARC (AIDS-related complex – PGL plus night sweats, diarrhoea, weight loss and malaise) or ►*AIDS*.

HLA. Human leukocyte antigens, so named because they were first identified in human leukocytes (white blood cells), while an antigen is a substance able to provoke a defensive or immune reaction. The antigens that determine blood groups (►*blood* (5)), which are found on the surface of red blood cells, are analogous. The slight differences between individuals, who may inherit any one of four possible blood groups (A, B, AB, or O) while forming antibodies to destroy cells of an alien type, explain why the donor's blood must match that of a patient having a transfusion. But the HLA system, which is distributed throughout the body, offers thousands of different and more or less incompatible patterns, so that except between identical twins an exact match is unlikely. When an organ such as a kidney is to be transplanted a reasonably close match is usually as much as can be hoped for, leaving some risk that the graft will be rejected.

A second reason for intense study of HLA is that certain patterns are statistically linked to particular disorders, especially those thought to arise from attack by the patient's own defences against his own tissues (►*transplantation*; *predisposition*).

Hodgkin, Thomas (1798–1866). Physician at Guy's Hospital (►*Cooper*), specializing in pathology – the study of the underlying processes of disease rather than of their outward symptoms. There were great pathologists before Hodgkin (e.g. Morgagni, Bichat, Hunter), but doctors in general did not recognize the practical as opposed to purely scientific value of their work. Hodgkin's appointment as pathologist to Guy's marks the beginning of the present era, in which the pathologist is an essential member of the clinical team, working in the direct interests of individual patients.

Hodgkin's account of what is now known as Hodgkin's disease appeared in 1832.

Hodgkin's disease. An uncommon disorder of the lymph nodes and spleen, and occasionally of other organs. Strictly speaking, it is a disorder of lymphoid tissue, found mainly in the lymph nodes and spleen but also in bone marrow and elsewhere, and concerned with defence against infection. The cells of this tissue proliferate, and the affected nodes become much enlarged. Fever and other symptoms of ill-defined sickness are usual. The patient may die of a chance infection, to which his resistance is lowered (the proliferating lymphoid tissue does not function); or from pressure on vital organs by enlarged lymph nodes; or from exhaustion, for the disease is slowly progressive.

Chronic infection such as widespread tuberculosis can produce a very similar picture, but no microbe has been incriminated in Hodgkin's disease. For the present it has to be regarded as an unusual form of cancer. Although rare, it is important firstly in the diagnosis of the many other diseases which can mimic it, and secondly because although in the long run it may not be curable, it is by no means untreatable. Most cases respond to X-ray treatment and to chemotherapy, usually as a combined attack with 3 or 4 drugs acting in different ways. Some patients have been kept in fair health for as long as 25 years.

homeostasis. The processes of maintaining constant physical and chemical conditions within the body despite external change. It is the primary function of most organs. (➤'*milieu intérieur*' under *Bernard, Claude.*)

homoeopathy. A method invented by Samuel Hahnemann at the end of the 18th century, based on the principle that like cures like. Hahnemann observed (inaccurately) that an overdose of quinine causes symptoms like those of malaria. But a moderate dose of quinine cures malaria. Therefore, he argued, small doses of a drug cure symptoms like those that larger doses would cause. The smaller the dose, the greater this paradoxical effect. Homoeopathic drugs are diluted by *trituration* with milk sugar. A 1:10 mixture is finely ground. Of the resulting powder, a fresh 1:10 mixture with sugar is made, and at each subsequent step the drug is diluted a further 10 times. At the 30th dilution or 'potency' there is one part of drug to 10^{30} parts of milk sugar. With the supposedly most potent remedies it is only by an outside chance that the patient will get a single molecule of the drug.

Homoeopathy is not concerned with the processes and causes of disease, but with its symptoms. Perhaps its greatest merit is that it compels the doctor to study all the personal idiosyncrasies of the patient – to regard him as a unique individual and not as just another 'case' of some kind.

Although the theory of homoeopathy does not stand scientific inquiry, Hahnemann was no charlatan. He was a sincere and able physician, disgusted by the excessive, sometimes brutal treatment meted out by his orthodox colleagues.

homosexuality. Sexual desire for members of one's own sex. But it would be absurd to call everyone who has such feelings, even if they lead to homosexual acts, a homosexual. In adolescents a homosexual phase is so common that it must be considered part of normal development. And the heterosexual (towards the opposite sex) feelings of adults are very often at least faintly tinged with homosexual feelings. There are all grades, including some people who seem equally attracted to either sex. American and British surveys suggest that about 4 per cent of men in those societies remain predominantly homosexual through adult life. The condition seems to be less common in women.

There have been many attempts to find a constitutional basis for homosexuality, but so far there is little evidence that physical make-up plays more than a small part. The popular image of a typical homosexual as a parody of the opposite sex applies only to a minority, and these are not in any physical sense intermediate: they affect mannerisms copied from the other sex.

Nor is there general agreement about the psychological background. It has probably been a mistake to look for a single cause when homosexuality may well arise in more than one way. The condition is itself an anomaly of behaviour or personality, and it is very often associated with other anomalies. Thus homosexuals as a class (not necessarily as individuals) include more people who are too easily swayed by their own feelings, insecure, or discontented than one would find among heterosexuals. All these tendencies may well have been exaggerated by centuries of systematic persecution. Incidentally they are not far removed from a kind of artistic temperament, and all the arts owe a great deal to homosexuals. In a way, homosexuality is like promiscuity with the opposite sex, also common among artists, in that it reflects an immature, adolescent pattern of behaviour. And if maturity means the ability to settle down and form a stable marriage, then a touch of immaturity is perhaps the price of being able to achieve anything out of the ordinary. Creative men are seldom ideal husbands. As Francis Bacon, a noted homosexual, put it, 'wife and children . . . are impediments to great enterprise, either of virtue or mischief.' It does not, of course, follow that enterprising men have to be bachelors, less still homosexuals, but it is true that such men are in many ways more childish than their fellows. If we could analyse personalities like fingerprints, we should probably find that a completely mature, rounded, 'normal' personality was so rare as to be almost abnormal, and we should still not know why some people fail to develop a stable heterosexual relationship. The advances of a homosexual adult to a child are often said to cause the child to become homosexual, but there is little evidence to support this view. Indeed, one might expect this to put a child off homosexuality. A much likelier theory is that the wrong kind of parental authority is a cause: in males, overdependence on the mother, and in females, fear of a bullying father. The most constructive suggestion in recent years is that at least some homosexuality is not a positive urge towards one's own sex but a kind of phobia about the opposite sex. Young adolescents of both sexes are notoriously scared of each other, and in this view homosexuality is a projection of this kind of anxiety into adult life. It does not conflict with earlier theories but merely suggests a way in which early influences might work.

Attempts to treat homosexuality often fail. Unless the subject strongly wishes to change, they are bound to fail. Many adult homosexuals resent the suggestion that homosexuality calls for any treatment. They insist that it is a normal state, a simple alternative to heterosexuality. It is a difficult argument to follow, because it implies that sex is not primarily concerned with reproduction. This over-reaction to popular censure is understandable, but it may discourage youngsters who could be helped from seeking advice. Despite the propagandists, homosexuality is a handicap, and many of those affected never really come to terms with it. With young subjects (say, within 10 or 12 years of puberty) there is at least some chance that ▸*behaviour therapy* may succeed.

Female sex hormones have been given to male homosexuals to suppress their sexual urges. This does not make them heterosexual. It is no more than a method of crime prevention to be used with people who, e.g. cannot stop themselves from assaulting children. The same treatment could be given to heterosexual rapists. Some German surgeons have performed minor operations on the brain to suppress certain reflex centres thought to govern homosexual behaviour, again in the hope of keeping persistent offenders out of prison. They claim that some of their patients are not only cured of their criminal tendencies but have become heterosexual. For the present, this cannot be regarded as more than an interesting experiment.

hookworm. A parasite of the duodenum, common in tropical countries more because of poor hygiene than climate. ►*worms*.

hordeolum = ►*stye*.

hormone. A substance released into the blood-stream by one organ to regulate the function of others. ►*endocrine*.

host. Animal or plant at whose expense a parasite lives.

human leukocyte antigens ►*HLA*.

humerus. The bone of the upper arm. The *head* is a smooth hemisphere, facing inwards and backwards to fit a shallow socket in the scapula at the shoulder. Below the head, the bone forms a straight cylinder, the shaft. The lower end is flattened, splayed out, and curled forwards like a scroll. It is widest just above the elbow, where on either side an *epicondyle* can be felt through the skin. The lower joint surfaces articulate with the radius and ulna (►*elbow*).

Three nerves lie directly on the bone: the *circumflex* nerve, running below the head of the humerus to reach the deltoid muscle, the radial nerve round the back of the shaft, and the ulnar nerve at the inner side of the elbow (the 'funny bone').

Several kinds of fracture are common. The tendons of the scapular muscles serve the shoulder as ligaments, and if the joint is wrenched they may be torn as sprained ligaments are torn. But they are strong, and sometimes it is not the tendon but the bone to which it is anchored that gives way. This is not as bad as it sounds, for broken bones heal better than ruptured tendons or ligaments.

Fractures of the humerus may be com-plicated by injury to any of the nerves mentioned; with fractures just above the elbow there is some risk to the brachial artery. Such complications are more troublesome than the actual fracture.

Fractures at the upper end of the humerus are often *impacted*, i.e. the fragments are driven together. Otherwise the scapular muscles twist the upper fragment so that it points outwards. It is too small and inaccessible to be manipulated, so the rest of the arm has to be brought into line with it by splinting with the arm raised. When the fracture is lower down the much stronger pectoralis major and latissimus dorsi pull the upper fragment inwards, and the arm has to be splinted in adduction, i.e. across the front of the chest.

Exact reduction of a fracture is much less important in the arm than in the leg. Angulation or shortening of a leg interferes with walking. In the arm, even fairly obvious deformity need not disturb function if the muscles are intact and the joints are mobile. A surgeon may settle for a poor-looking result, which would be unacceptable with a fractured femur, if striving for anatomical perfection means that the return to active movement will be delayed.

humours. Four fluids, supposed to permeate the body and determine the state of its health. This idea was the basis of medical theory from the earliest historical times until the 17th century of our era. It still survives in the language and perhaps in popular myth. The adjective *humoral* is still current as a term to describe chemicals such as hormones and antibodies that circulate and affect the functions of the body.

According to Empedocles (5th century BC) all matter consisted of four elements: earth, air, fire, and water. There were also four qualities: hot, cold, dry, and wet. Earth was cold and dry, air was hot and wet, fire was hot and dry, water was cold and wet.

In the body, four humours were thought to correspond with the elements: *black bile* with earth, *blood* with air, *yellow bile* with fire, and *phlegm* with water. Each had the qualities of the corresponding element.

Each element in turn corresponded with a temperament.

Black bile, hot and dry, was formed in the spleen (which in fact contains dark, tarry material formed by the destruction of spent blood cells), and the associated temperament is *melancholy* (or perhaps splenetic).

Blood, hot and wet, was associated with a *sanguine* temperament, and yellow or real bile, cold and dry, with a *choleric* temperament.

Phlegm (*pituita*; mucus), cold and wet, was supposed to be formed in the brain and especially in the pituitary body attached to the underside of the brain, and its temperament was *phlegmatic*.

The state of health depended on the balance between the four humours. A perfect balance of hot against cold, wet against dry (*eucrasia*) ensured good health. Illness was due to imbalance (*dyscrasia*) from excess of one of the humours, of which the most dangerous was black bile. The usual methods of treatment, such as emetics, purges, and blood-letting, were attempts to expel a harmful surplus of a humour.

There is a fairly close analogy between the humoral theory in Europe and the traditional medicine of China (►*Chinese medicine*).

hunch-back = ►*gibbus*.

hunger ►*appetite*.

Hunter, John (1728–93). Scottish surgeon and naturalist; he studied, taught and practised in London from 1748, first as pupil, later as partner, of his elder brother William.

If genius is a capacity for hard work then Hunter was a genius of the first water. He summed up his philosophy in the question '*Why think? Why not try the experiment?*'; he was a necessary antidote to the sterile theorizing that typified much of 18th-century science. As to theory, he simply accepted that Nature knew best. His task was to observe and record. He was a prodigious anatomist, dissecting every creature he could lay hands on, and collecting specimens to illustrate the nature of every kind of disease. He did not even stop at biology; he is regarded as the founder of scientific geology as well. His many contributions to medical science include the first satisfactory account of ►*inflammation*, a fine work on gun-shot wounds, and a brilliant but ill-fated study of venereal disease – to find whether syphilis and gonorrhoea were separate diseases he infected himself from a patient with gonorrhoea; unknown to him the patient had syphilis as well, and when Hunter developed both he concluded that they were two forms of a single disease.

hyaline-membrane disease. A dangerous condition of new-born – especially premature – babies, now classified as ►*respiratory distress syndrome*.

hydatid disease. Infection with a kind of tapeworm, *Echinococcus*. The adult worm is an intestinal parasite of dogs. Human hydatid disease is due to the larvae of the worm, which form cysts in muscle, liver and other tissues, sometimes needing surgical removal. The infection is acquired from food contaminated by dogs.

hydrocarbon. A chemical compound of hydrogen and carbon, e.g. paraffin, benzene (cf. *carbohydrate*, a compound of carbon and water, e.g. starch, sugar).

hydrocele. A collection of watery fluid in the membranous sac (tunica vaginalis) around the testicle. The fluid is easily removed with a hollow needle, but it is apt to return. If it is a nuisance to the patient a hydrocele can be cured surgically.

hydrocephalus. Enlargement of an infant's head by accumulation of cerebrospinal fluid, due to blockage of its normal circulation in and around the brain and spinal cord. Various surgical operations have been devised to relieve the pressure and prevent damage to the brain.

In later life, when the skull cannot expand, a form of hydrocephalus expands the hollow ventricles of the brain at the expense of brain tissue, leading to dementia and various disorders of the nervous system unless corrected by surgical diversion of the surplus fluid.

hydrocortisone. Cortisol, a hormone of the ►*adrenal* cortex.

hydrogen peroxide. A potent antiseptic that is not inactivated by pus.

hydronephrosis. Distension of a kidney by retained urine, with progressive loss of function, due to obstruction to the flow of urine.

hydrophobia = ►*rabies*. The word 'hydrophobia' ('fear of water') refers to the patient's inability to swallow even fluids.

hydrotherapy. Treatment of illness by water; spa treatment. It is difficult to be-

lieve that the mineral content of drinking water cures anything, or that bathing in the waters of one spring is better than in any other. However, most European spas have been used since Roman times, and for centuries have attracted physicians with special knowledge of the diseases that the waters were said to suit. Therefore, water or no, many famous spas earn their reputations by having the best staff and equipment.

The term also means restoring function by exercising in water which takes most of the weight of a limb: a good form of therapy. ►*baths*.

hymen. A membrane partly covering the opening of the vagina, torn when a woman loses her virginity. Rarely it closes the opening and has to be cut when the girl begins to menstruate.

hyoid. Small U-shaped bone in the neck, immediately below the jaw and above the larynx; it is an anchorage for numerous muscles.

The hyoid is important in forensic medicine, because a fracture of it is good evidence of manual strangulation.

hyoscine (scopolamine). A drug extracted from belladonna, hyoscyamus and other plants. It has similar actions to ►*atropine*, but is rather more narcotic and less liable to cause excitement.

hyoscyamine. A drug extracted from belladonna and stramonium; it is a form of ►*atropine*.

hyoscyamus (henbane). A plant related to ►*belladonna* (deadly nightshade), with similar poisonous and medicinal properties.

hyper-. Prefix = 'above'; 'too much'. Some of the uglier *hyper-* words in medical jargon are unnecessary or would be better with *over-*; e.g. hyperactivity, hyperventilation (overbreathing). Common words not listed separately include *hyperaemia* (congestion with blood), *-aesthesia* (abnormal sensitivity of nerve-endings), *-chlorhydria* (excess of acid in the stomach), *-metropia* (long-sightedness), *-pnoea* (needlessly deep or rapid breathing; overbreathing, a neurotic symptom), *-thyroidism* (overactivity of the thyroid gland; toxic goitre).

hyperemesis gravidarum. Severe vomiting in pregnancy, a kind of toxaemia, distinct from morning sickness, which is a nuisance but seldom serious. Antihistamine drugs or tranquillizers may stop the vomiting, and pyridoxine (vitamin B_6) has been tried; but some of these patients need to be in hospital on a carefully controlled diet, or no diet with the necessary fluids given into a vein. The pregnancy may have to be artificially ended.

The cause is not known.

hyperlipidaemia. Excess of ➤*fat* or fat-like substances in the blood.

hyperpiesia. High blood pressure. This word has been offered in place of *hypertension* because it is all Greek instead of mixed Greek and Latin. But a vocabulary that admits *antibody*, *antigen*, and *roentgenoscopy* is unlikely to reject *hypertension*.

hyperplasia. Excessive or increased growth of tissue by multiplication of its cells (cf. ➤*hypertrophy*). Hyperplasia is generally due to stimulation by hormones, e.g. the growth of the uterus and breasts during pregnancy, or overgrowth of the thyroid gland in response to excessive activity of the pituitary gland. It may also be a response to excessive demands on an organ such as the liver

when part of it has been destroyed by disease. Hyperplasia differs from neoplasia (tumour formation) in that the new cells are perfectly normal.

hyperpyrexia. Extreme fever, where the body temperature is so high as to be itself a danger to life, regardless of its cause.

hypersensitivity ➤*allergy*; *immunity*.

hypertension. High blood pressure, which may be a symptom of a recognized disease such as inflammation of the kidneys (*secondary hypertension*), or apparently a disease in its own right, i.e. one of which the cause is unknown (*essential hypertension*). Essential hypertension is divided into *benign* hypertension, with few symptoms and a prolonged course, and the much rarer *malignant* hypertension, with rapid deterioration unless treated.

These terms are necessarily vague, because nobody knows the limits of normal blood pressure.

➤*blood pressure* (1).

hypertrophy. Excessive or increased growth of tissue by enlargement, without multiplication, of its cells (cf. ➤*hyperplasia*). It is characteristically the response of muscle to work. Muscle cells (fibres) have little if any capacity for reproduction, but they are enlarged and strengthened by exercise, and shrink (*atrophy*) if they are not used.

hypnosis. State of mind induced by ➤*hypnotism*.

A technique requiring further study is *autogenic training*, by which the patient is taught to put himself into a brief, light hypnotic trance. While in this state he reinforces suggestions originally implanted by the therapist, directed against irrational fears, ingrained habits such as smoking and the like. It is reminiscent of ancient crafts such as yoga and transcendental meditation.

hypnotic. Drug used to promote sleep. The effect is intermediate between that of a sedative (minor tranquillizer, anxiolytic) and a narcotic; the difference may be only a matter of dosage. The barbiturates, which used to be the principal drugs of this group, were used for daytime sedation, e.g. small doses of phenobarbitone, for sleeping, e.g. moderate doses of amylobarbitone, and as anaesthetics given by injection.

At present, the benzodiazepines such as nitrazepam are by far the most widely used hypnotics, since they are less poisonous and less dangerously addictive. But they, too, can set up a degree of dependence, with withdrawal symptoms when they are stopped after prolonged use. It thus remains true that hypnotics are better used occasionally than regularly, and best not used at all unless they are really needed.

hypnotism. Hypnotism is an extreme form of suggestion, where within limits the subject abandons his initiative to the operator. First, the subject must be willing to be hypnotized and to obey the operator. Second, the operator must hold the subject's attention absolutely. If either lets his thoughts wander, nothing happens. Many techniques are possible, but all are based on the same principle: the subject's attention is fixed by a simple, monotonous stimulus until he ignores all other sensation. It is rather like counting imaginary sheep in order to sleep; but the hypnotic state is not sleep. A susceptible subject with a good operator may go into a deep trance in which he is unaware of anything except the operator's voice; he can make no movement unless told to, and all his muscles are held as stiff as boards (a condition otherwise seen only in severe mental disorder). At a word from the operator the subject returns to normal consciousness, but is not aware of anything that has happened during the trance. Most subjects, however, cannot be hypnotized so deeply, and some cannot be hypnotized at all, perhaps because they do not wish to be. The hypnotist has no mysterious powers. Some are better at it than others but most people can learn.

During a hypnotic trance the subject's mind is closed to all incoming sensations except the operator's voice, and also to the countless distractions and inhibitions that circulate in the waking brain. Memory then turns out to be a much fuller store than one would have supposed. We do not forget the past, but we store it in a library with no index and the keys to half the rooms hidden. Under hypnosis, events long 'forgotten' are accurately recalled, if the operator asks for them. And new instructions can be learnt that in waking life would be confused in a welter of second thoughts; conditioned reflexes can be established because the instructions are not questioned. It is claimed that if the instructions are morally repugnant to him the subject will not obey.

The first practising hypnotist was the Austrian physician Mesmer (1734–1815). He thought hypnosis was a kind of celestial magnetism, and established a cult in Paris that earned him a great deal of money and probably cured some cases of hysteria.

Many painless surgical operations have been done on hypnotized patients, but the method has not been widely adopted, because quite apart from the personal objections of patients and doctors it is too unreliable. No surgeon would be happy with a substitute for anaesthesia that might or might not work.

Some kinds of neurosis respond quickly to hypnotism. The repressed memories that psychoanalysis brings into the open can be revived more quickly than by analysis, and the patient may accept suggestions that he would be unable to take in if he were wide awake. But again the method is unreliable. Even when it seems to work it does not always solve the patient's problem. Neurosis may be regarded as an unconscious, perhaps misguided, attempt at self-defence. A person who develops a stammer to cover a sense of inadequacy is no better off if the stammer is cured while the underlying trouble is ignored; he will probably develop a new neurosis. But provided that the hypnotist is aware of this objection, hypnotism can be a valuable short cut in treating neuroses. Merely to suppress symptoms without considering their causes is bad practice in any branch of medicine, but that does not condemn all suppression of symptoms. Morphia would be poor treatment for a broken bone, but it can be a valuable adjunct to setting and splinting the fracture. Similarly hypnotism may not be the whole answer to illness due to emotional disturbance, but it is a useful tool.

hypo-. Prefix = 'below'; 'too little'. It is the converse of *hyper-* and most technical terms with *hyper-* have their opposites with *hypo-*.

hypochondria(sis). Undue preoccupation with one's real or supposed ailments; it is more of a hobby than an illness. It differs from malingering and hysteria. The malingerer may say he has a headache when he has none, in order to evade work or responsibility; the hysteric does something similar at an unconscious level and gets a real headache without physical cause; the hypochondriac spends a happy day trying new remedies for the headache that might come on.
➤*hypochondrium.*

hypochondrium (= below cartilage). The part of the abdomen covered by the cartilages of the lower ribs, once thought to be the seat of hypochondria, perhaps because it contains the liver on one side and the spleen on the other, respectively the supposed sites of biliousness and melancholy.

hypodermic. Under the skin; subcutaneous.

hypoglycaemia. Deficiency of sugar in the blood. Normal blood contains about 0.1 per cent of glucose. Numerous mechanisms interact to keep the level constant despite great variation of both intake and disposal of glucose. All carbohydrate absorbed from the diet is converted to glucose, which is then stored in the liver and muscles in the form of animal starch – *glycogen*. As glucose is consumed to provide energy, fresh supplies are released from the glycogen stores. Several hormones are concerned in keeping the balance between storage and combustion of glucose. The most important is insulin (➤*diabetes*), and the usual cause of hypoglycaemia is too much insulin. In diabetics this can arise from overdosage or wrong diet. In others, it is due to over-activity of the insulin-forming tissue of the pancreas. The excess of insulin removes glucose from the blood by increased combustion, and also increases the storage of glycogen at the expense of the blood.

The brain has no reserve of fuel; it depends entirely on a constant supply of glucose from the blood. Hypoglycaemia promptly impairs the efficiency of the brain. The symptoms vary greatly. They include uneasiness, hunger, sweating, and unaccustomed churlishness. If the blood-sugar is still further reduced, the patient may have an epileptic fit or simply lose consciousness; he may even die.

Rare causes of hypoglycaemia include failure to store carbohydrate with severe liver disease, and disturbances of other glands concerned with the distribution of glucose.

People who are prone to attacks of hypoglycaemia learn to recognize the symptoms and stop the attack by eating sugar.

hypophysis. The ›*pituitary* gland.

hypothalamus. A region of the brain below the third ventricle, i.e. in the floor of the front part of the brain between the cerebral hemispheres. It is connected by nerve fibres with most other parts of the nervous system, and its functions are bewilderingly diverse. They include:

1. Regulation of the autonomic nervous system, and so of the heart and abdominal organs, especially their response to emotion;

2. The emotions themselves, and mood (excitement, depression etc.);

3. Regulation of the body temperature;

4. Appetite and thirst;

5. The increased flow of blood through muscles during exercise, which is independent of the control of blood vessels in general to maintain the blood pressure – a function of the medulla oblongata;

6. Control of the pituitary gland, which in turn controls the output of the other endocrine glands and the kidneys.

Thus the hypothalamus is the link between the central and autonomic nervous systems and between the nervous system and the endocrine glands.

hypothermia. Fall of body temperature to a potentially dangerous level. Babies (especially if premature) and old people have difficulty in maintaining the nearly constant body temperature (36–37.2 °C) on which health depends. Babies are usually cared for, but all too often old people are not. In old age the circulation of blood is often weak, and the reflexes that should adjust body temperature become less and less efficient. Even at normal room temperature, say 18 °C, an old person whose natural functions are failing can easily and insidiously fall below the lower safe limit of body temperature (35 °C). If this should happen, the temperature continues to fall until, at around 25 °C, the patient dies. Nobody knows how many people die simply of hypothermia because they may have been dead for hours or days before they are found, and the precise cause of death is no longer clear.

The treatment of an old person found cold and confused is carried out in hospital and as soon as possible; it involves *gradual* warming, not by external means so much as by conserving the body's heat with blankets in a warm room. *Rapid warming* can be lethal.

Prevention is a major public health problem with no obvious solution. Ideally, old people should not live alone. Their surroundings should be warmer than a younger person might think necessary; they should have an adequate diet, and regular medical attention. In country districts where family life is still intact there is a chance, but in modern cities, where people are crowded in one sense and completely isolated in another, the problem grows worse.

Controlled hypothermia is an adjunct to heart surgery: all functions are markedly slowed at low temperatures, and oxygen consumption is reduced. By deliberately lowering temperature under strict controls, the time during which the circulation is interrupted can be safely prolonged, giving the surgeon invaluable time in which to operate.

hyster(o)-. Prefix = 'of the uterus'; e.g. *hysterectomy*, surgical removal of the uterus.

hysteria. A kind of neurosis, most often affecting women and once thought to arise in the uterus. Sustained anxiety, usually with little foundation, expresses itself in physical symptoms vaguely resembling those of physical illness of the part of the body that the patient associates with her worries. The hysterical fit, simulating epilepsy, has been out of fashion for many years.

➤*anxiety* (3).

I

iatrogenic. Caused by doctors: iatrogenic diseases are those that result from the treatment of other diseases. If the term is extended to all the possible ill-effects of medical and surgical treatment, the list becomes so long as to be meaningless, because effective medicines and operations have always entailed some risk. There is no need to give a special name to side-effects of a drug that are known to be the price of the cure. 'Iatrogenic' is best reserved for illnesses, often unrelated to the original illness or to the expected effect of the treatment, arising from treatment and sometimes persisting after the treatment has been stopped. Even with this limitation the list is formidable. Some can be regarded as unexpected poisoning, either because the patient is unusually susceptible to a drug or because the drug is more dangerous than anyone had suspected. For example, phenacetin was a household remedy for aches and pains second only to aspirin in popularity, for three quarters of a century before it was found to cause irreparable damage to the kidneys. The most notorious case of this kind was that of ➤*thalidomide*. Some drugs occasionally appear to cause metabolic diseases such as diabetes, gout, and porphyria. It is likely that the patient was predisposed and would have developed the disease sooner or later, but one cannot be certain. A serious complication of antibiotic treatment is ➤*superinfection*, when the antibiotic cures the original infection but also kills useful bacteria that normally compete with yet other microbes: the field is then clear for these last to set up a new infection. A common type of iatrogenic illness is produced without the help of drugs. A patient who misunderstands what a doctor tells or does not tell him may develop unfounded but serious anxieties about his health, a kind of iatrogenic neurosis.

Ibn-an-nafis (1210–88). Arabian physician. He appears to have discovered that blood circulates through the lungs some centuries before anyone else, but his work attracted no attention.

icterus = ➤*jaundice*.

icthyosis. A hereditary defect of the skin: the sweat and grease glands are fewer than normal and the skin has a dry, scaly appearance. Icthyosis in childhood sometimes improves at puberty. Greasy ointments help, but a complete cure is unlikely.

ictus. A sudden attack of illness such as a stroke or fit.

ICU ➤*intensive care unit*.

id. According to ➤*Freud*, the instinctive element of the personality.
Id reaction: ➤*ringworm*.

idiocy. The severest degree of mental deficiency, where the mental age is 2 years or less, and the subject cannot guard himself against common physical dangers. In English law the term was given up in 1960; idiocy is now included in 'severe subnormality'.

idiopathic. A term applied to diseases seeming to arise of their own accord and not as a result of some recognized cause such as infection or injury. The terms *primary* and *essential* are also used in this sense.

idiosyncrasy. This word is sometimes used in the limited sense of allergy to a particular substance. Since we already have the word *allergy*, it is better to keep *idiosyncrasy* for cases where the patient is abnormally susceptible to a substance for some other reason, such as deficiency of an enzyme needed for disposing of the substance or inability to excrete it.

idoxuridine (IDU) >*virus* (2).

IHD = >*ischaemic heart disease.*

ileitis. Inflammation of the ileum; Crohn's disease (>*enteritis*).

ileostomy. Surgical operation to bypass the large intestine by bringing the end of the ileum to the surface, used in treating severe ulcerative >*colitis*. An ileostomy is managed in the same way as a >*colostomy*.

ileum. The lower part of the small intestine.

iliac. Of the >*ilium*.
Iliac arteries. The *aorta* divides in front of the 4th lumbar vertebra into left and right *common iliac* arteries. Each of these divides into an *internal iliac* artery, which supplies the pelvic organs, and an *external iliac* artery, continued as the *femoral* artery, the main vessel of the lower limb.
Iliac fossa. Part of the abdomen immediately above the groin, of which the concave inner surface of the ilium, covered by the *iliacus* muscle, is the floor.
Iliac veins. The veins corresponding with the iliac arteries. They join to form the inferior *vena cava*.

ilium. The haunch-bone, a part of the >*pelvis*.

imbecility. Mental deficiency where the mental age reaches a level of 3–6 years and the subject is likely to need special care, now classified in English law as 'moderate subnormality'.

Imhotep (27th century BC). The first physician named in history; he was also prime minister under the 3rd Egyptian dynasty and the architect of the Step Pyramid. Imhotep was later deified as god of healing.

immersion foot = >*trench foot*.

immunity, immunology. The system of reactions to alien substances that enter the body is adapted in particular to protecting the body from infection by invading microbes. The word was first medically defined as the resistance to subsequent attacks conferred by one attack of an infectious disease, or by a simulated attack such as vaccination. In current usage, immunity includes not only this kind of healthy resistance, but also the various effects, some of them harmful, that occur when these reactions go astray.

1. GENERAL PRINCIPLES

The first principle of immunity is the distinction between 'self' and 'non-self'. *Self* refers to any of the numerous chemical ingredients of the body, and *non-self* to any substance different from these. Though all living organisms are in many ways similar, there are chemical differences not only between species but between individuals (except perhaps identical twins). The proteins that are characteristic components of all living matter are made of molecules each containing hundreds or even thousands of amino-acids, of which there are about 20 kinds; there is no reasonable limit to the possible sequences of these acids. The slightest difference results in a distinct protein. The precise ingredients of one body differ from those of another, much as the finger-prints of two people differ although the fingers work in identical ways. Such subtle chemical differences between an individual's components and another's are recognized as non-self, and may provoke the reactions of immunity and rejection, as though they had not learned a password.

Two kinds of immunity are recognized: *natural* or inborn immunity, which is not as a rule directed against exactly defined targets but against alien substances in general, and *adaptive* or acquired immunity, which fights against a specific threat such as a particular kind of infection. In fact natural and adaptive immunity are not completely distinct, and the two are closely interdependent.

Although immunity must have evolved as a means of surviving infection by dangerous parasites, the same reactions may be evoked by harmless substances. In people afflicted with ill-adjusted (hypersensitive) defences, the eating of wholesome foods may even lead to allergic and other illnesses. Worse still, sometimes a normal component of the body is attacked as if it were an invader. This is the principle of *autoimmune* disease.

Immunity may be *cellular* or *humoral*, i.e. mediated by active cells such as the white cells of the blood, or by protective substances circulating in the blood or tissue fluid. The humoral agents may be released by the defensive cells, so that the distinction is not absolute.

The cellular agents of immunity include the *white blood cells*, and the *mast cells* and *macrophages* of the tissues in general. Of the white blood cells, the *granulocytes* are mostly confined to the blood unless they are drawn to a seat of trouble, but the *lymphocytes* move freely from blood to tissues at all times as though policing the whole body.

The humoral agents include two *natural antibiotics*. These are *lysozyme*, which attacks the walls of many bacteria and kills them, and *interferon*, which inhibits the reproduction of viruses in infected cells. Lysozyme is secreted by macrophages, which are the main scavenging cells of the tissues. Like the granulocytes of the blood, they are *phagocytes*, i.e. they can engulf and digest foreign matter such as bacteria – especially those already disabled by lysozyme or other agents. Interferon is formed by various cells in response to virus infection; its inhibiting effect can then be exerted on viruses anywhere else in the body. This is why once it is brought into action by a particular virus the patient is for a time relatively immune to attack by other viruses, e.g. he is unlikely to develop measles during an attack of chickenpox.

Complement is a series of substances, consisting of 9 major components subdivided to make at least 15, which circulate in the blood. They form a *cascade*, a kind of system common in biology. The system remains inert until one unit is stimulated – in this case by injury, infection etc. – to act on the next unit, which in turn acts on the next until the whole system is *activated*. Activated complement is concerned in both natural and adaptive immunity.

Antibodies are proteins circulating in the blood (plasma proteins); formerly known as gamma-globulins, they are now renamed *immunoglobulins*. Five classes of immunoglobulin (Ig) – IgA, IgD, IgE, IgG and IgM – are subdivided into numerous varieties. The function of antibodies is to combine with and inactivate non-self substances. Any substance that can provoke antibody activity is called an *antigen*. Ideally, antigens would be only such things as viruses and bacteria, but unfortunately harmless or even beneficial substances can also mobilize the forces of immunity.

2. NATURAL (INBORN) IMMUNITY

Intact skin is almost impermeable to infection by viruses and bacteria (though some larger parasites, e.g. bilharzia and hookworm, are able to penetrate the skin). On the other hand, the mucous membranes lining the digestive, respiratory and urogenital systems are more vulnerable to invaders. The secretions of both skin and mucous membranes are mildly antiseptic, while other defensive agents include the normal bacteria (commensals) of the skin and some mucous membranes, which live at peace with the human body and pay for their lodging by keeping at bay some hostile bacteria and fungi. The value of these microscopical watch-dogs is all too apparent if they are removed by antibiotic therapy or debilitating disease, and germs that are not normally dangerous become lethal.

Most parasites afflict only certain species; e.g. leprosy and syphilis are almost exclusively human afflictions, whereas humans are by nature immune to many diseases that infect other species. Some races of man are more susceptible than others to particular infections (but here environment may be as important as heredity), and, with the same proviso, some families are more or less susceptible than others.

The immediate response to invasion by hostile microbes is the same as the response to injury, namely ▸*inflammation*. This defensive reaction is precipitated by chemical mediators such as histamine and serotonin, which are released from mast cells, and allows the agents of natural immunity to escape from the blood into the affected tissues. Complement plays an essential part in promoting inflammation. It can be activated directly by some bacteria, or indirectly by the interaction of antigens entering the system with antibodies adapted to engage them. Some components of complement can, when activated, release the mediators of inflammation. Others act as *opsonins*, i.e. they modify invading germs to facilitate their destruction by white cells. Still others are directly lethal to bacteria.

The *natural antibiotics* lysozyme and interferon are also important agents of natural immunity; the former damages bacteria, either killing them or rendering them defenceless against the voracious phagocytes, while the latter impedes the spread of viruses.

3. ADAPTIVE (ACQUIRED) IMMUNITY

Natural and adaptive immunity overlap, having several agents in common: complement, a major factor of natural immunity, is also often needed for the fusion of antigen with antibody, which is the characteristic of adaptive immunity. In return, this fusion enhances natural immunity. Furthermore, a considerable measure of adaptive immunity is inborn, as some maternal antibodies can enter the baby's blood through the placenta and protect the baby during its early months. An advantage of breast-feeding is that other antibodies can be passed to the baby in the mother's milk.

Adaptive immunity may be *active*,

meaning that the body makes its own antibodies in response to infection or the simulated infection of vaccination, or it may be *passive*, whereby ready-made antibodies, such as the mother's in a baby, or antitoxins injected against, e.g., tetanus or diphtheria, are introduced. With active immunity, the information is stored in specialized B-lymphocytes, *memory cells*, and at any subsequent exposure to the same antigen a corresponding antibody can be provided without the delay that followed the first exposure. Passive immunity, on the contrary, is transient and leaves no cell-memory. ➤*immunization*.

The elaboration of *antibodies*, the agents of adaptive immunity, is the main task of the *lymphocytes*. The complex protein molecule of an antibody can be subtly modified so that it will fit and engage a molecule of a particular antigen. A lymphocyte that has once done this can multiply rapidly to form an effective supply of the specific antibody. The number of distinct antibodies thus made available to a normal adult runs into thousands. Their functions include neutralizing bacterial toxins, preparing bacteria for destruction by phagocytes (opsonic action) and similarly preparing infected cells, direct immobilization and destruction of bacteria, and, when they have engaged corresponding antigens, promotion of inflammation and the effects of 'natural' immunity. One type of antibody (IgE) acts specifically on mast cells, causing histamine and other agents to be released – an effect more likely to cause damage than prevent it.

Two distinct types of lymphocyte are known: T-cells, primarily associated with the thymus, and B-cells, associated with the bone marrow of mammals. The B-cells form and secrete antibodies which then circulate in the blood and body fluids. The T-cells are of several kinds. Some (helper cells) appear to recognize strange antigens and then prompt B-cells to make suitable antibodies. Others (cytotoxic, or killer T-cells) do the work of antibodies against microbes that become incorporated into the cells of the body's own tissues where they are not vulnerable to the circulating antibodies made by B-cells. A cytotoxic T-cell is adapted to attack and kill an infected cell which is of no further use to the body. Less is known about a third type, the 'suppressor cell'. It appears to inhibit excessive or misplaced activity of other lymphocytes. A fourth type is concerned with chronic inflammation and delayed hypersensitivity, one of the undesirable kinds of immune response.

4. DEFECTIVE IMMUNITY

Immunity is relatively weak in the very young (apart from passive immunity; ➤'Adaptive (Acquired) Immunity', above) and in the old. It is also weak in people who are in any way debilitated, e.g. by chronic illness or, especially, by malnutrition. Disorders of the lymphatic and blood-forming tissues, such as Hodgkin's disease and leukaemia, naturally impair resistance to infection. Certain forms of medical treatment are designed to suppress immunity. These include treatment to prevent the rejection of grafted organs (an immune reaction), treatment of certain adverse and dangerous immune reactions (➤'Immunopathology', below), and treatment of certain cancers and other diseases of the blood-forming tissues. Immunosuppression is also an undesirable effect of some drugs that might otherwise be useful for their other actions.

Congenital deficiencies of nearly all of

the many factors of normal immunity have been reported. Depending on which factor is missing the effects range from undue susceptibility to certain types of infection, which are not necessarily dangerous, to an inability to survive infancy. Some of these defects can be treated by supplying the missing factor from a compatible donor, e.g. by infusion of immunoglobulins or lymphocytes, or transplants of bone marrow or immature thymus gland. Some cases can be treated with *transfer factor*, a substance extracted from normal lymphocytes, which may enhance the patient's own immune response; this does not require a compatible donor (who may be extremely difficult to find).

About one person in a thousand has an identifiable type of immunodeficiency, but it seems likely that there are more types still to be discovered. Not only are some people, for no apparent reason, more liable than others to minor infections, but far more serious diseases are also to be considered. Any living cell is a potential antigen. This must include cancer cells, but unfortunately they seldom induce much of an immune reaction. Much current research is directed at the possibility of initiating or enhancing such reactions.

An important kind of immunodeficiency was first reported in 1980 and named 'acquired immunodeficiency syndrome' or ▶*AIDS*.

5. IMMUNOPATHOLOGY

Until not long ago *allergy* seemed a fairly simple matter, but in the light of recent findings the subject has become very complex and only a superficial review is feasible here.

Like any defensive weapon, the processes of immunity have to be potentially dangerous. They are designed to eliminate one kind of living matter – the infecting microbe – but do so, to some extent, at the expense of the body that they are defending, just as an army cannot repel an invader without some damage to its own environment. Many symptoms of infection are due more to defensive reactions than to the infection itself, but that may be the price of recovery.

Adverse effects beyond the normal symptoms of infection are *immunopathological reactions*. These may be simple exaggeration of normal reactions, or the spread through healthy tissues of reactions normally associated with threatened tissues, or destructive reactions against antigens that present no threat. A bee-sting is a small but genuine threat, and a person stung by a whole swarm of bees can get a dose of venom as lethal as that of a cobra bite. A defensive reaction to the venom is thus appropriate, but with some unlucky people the reaction to a single sting is so violent as to be itself a threat to life. Some people react as violently to substances that present no threat at all, such as penicillin. Streptococci are among the most virulent of infecting bacteria, and immune responses to them are lifesaving. However, after recovering from an acute streptococcal infection a few people are left with permanently damaged hearts or kidneys; these sequels seem to be due more to the body's defences than to the infection. Some of the worst ill-effects of immunity are those arising from immune reactions to some part of the body's own fabric (*autoimmune disease*, below).

The great problem of grafting tissues or organs from other people (not to mention other species) is that the proteins of one individual are 'non-self' to another and may act as antigens. Unless the graft matches the recipient's tissues it provokes immune reactions and is rejected. Blood is the easiest tissue to match, because it includes only a few potential antigens that may differ among individuals (▸*blood* (5); *transfusion*). While many proteins throughout the body are common to everyone, and indeed to other mammals, there is enough variation to make perfect matching unlikely except between identical twins. The important differences appear to be concentrated in one chromosome, forming a group of genes of which some 50 have been identified. These genes determine a group of tissue proteins, of which each individual inherits his own particular selection, which must match as closely as possible that of the recipient if an organ transplant is to succeed. The system of genes is known in general biology as the major histocompatibility complex (MHC, tissue-compatibility), but in humans as the ▸*HLA* system. Any one person, of course, accepts his own HLA antigens as 'self' and leaves them alone. Their value is that they are altered by virus infection; the infected cell is then 'non-self' and liable to attack by T-lymphocytes. It is pure misfortune that their presence impedes transplant surgery. Incidentally, and for no known reason, the pattern of HLA antigens is associated with liability to certain diseases (▸*predisposition*).

6. HYPERSENSITIVITY

An abnormal tendency to excessive or misplaced immune responses was named allergy by von Pirquet in 1905. The term is still current, but many immunologists now restrict it to a range of phenomena collectively known as *hypersensitivity*.

Depending on which of the various defence mechanisms is mainly concerned, four types of hypersensitivity are recognized. Many immunologists now restrict the term *allergy* to *type I*, acute, immediate or anaphylactic hypersensitivity. *Localized type I hypersensitivity, atopy*, includes *hay fever*, some (perhaps most) cases of *asthma*, and some cases of *urticaria* (nettle-rash). The antigens are substances that are innocuous to most people, e.g. pollens, various ingredients of house-dust and foods such as shellfish. Antibodies, usually IgE, against these become attached to mast cells, which on subsequent contact with the allergen release histamine and other mediators causing the characteristic symptoms. While the sensitized mast cells causing asthma and hay fever occur in the lungs and nose, those connected with food allergies appear in the intestine and cause digestive symptoms such as vomiting. Sometimes mast cells in the skin are sensitized by circulating IgE, causing a rash when the patient eats a particular food.

Rarely, the sensitized mast cells are widespread: this can follow exposure to insect stings and also to drugs such as penicillin. In these cases, later contact can cause a *generalized* reaction (*anaphylactic shock*), with an urticarial rash, a precipitate fall of blood pressure and an extreme asthmatic spasm of the bronchi which, as it can cause swelling at the back of the throat, can suffocate. ▸*allergy*; *histamine*.

Type II or cytotoxic hypersensitivity arises from the destructive interaction of a circulating antibody (IgG or IgM) with antigens on the surfaces of cells. For instance, people with group A blood have antibodies against group B antigens. If they are given transfusions of group B blood, their antibodies attack the 'invading' blood cells, which not only invalidates the transfusion but seriously endangers the patient.

Type II reactions include destruction of blood cells by various drugs, and also some *autoimmune diseases* (►'Autoimmunity', below).

Type III, complex-mediated reactions occur when an antibody combines with an antigen but instead of disposing of the antigen remains as an active *complex* able to set up destructive inflammation. The effects resemble somewhat those of type I reactions, because some of the symptoms are due to activation of complement by the complex, which causes mast cells to release histamine.

When horse serum was commonly used as a vehicle for antitoxin, many patients reacted some 10 days later with *serum sickness*, which is a type III reaction with skin eruptions, joint pains, fever and other symptoms. Nowadays, this type of reaction more often follows the administration of penicillin or other drugs. These reactions are unpleasant but seldom serious. Their importance is that the patient remains sensitized, and may react violently to any subsequent exposure.

Numerous other instances of type III hypersensitivity, or something very like it, include *farmer's lung*, a reaction to a mould found in hay, and many analogous occupational hazards. Connective-tissue diseases, including *lupus erythematosus*, *polyarteritis nodosa*, and *rheumatoid arthritis*, may also be type III reactions: the evidence is strong but not conclusive. Autoantibodies, antibodies active against 'self' (►'Autoimmunity', below), are usually abundant, but there is still some doubt whether they are cause or effect.

Antibody complexes with strepto-cocci, following acute sore throat, scarlet fever etc., appear to cause both injury to the kidneys and *rheumatic fever*, with the risk of permanent damage to the heart.

Type IV, cell-mediated or delayed reactions are determined by T-lymphocytes. Instead of releasing antibodies into the circulation as do B-lymphocytes, these cells interact with other cells (including B-lymphocytes) to promote various defensive reactions. Once adapted to an antigen, those cells concerned with type IV hypersensitivity respond to any subsequent contact by releasing *lymphokines*, substances with numerous actions: they attract various types of white cell and set up protracted inflammation. Reactions of this type are a part of normal resistance to various infections, including tuberculosis and leprosy. Sometimes it is excessive, e.g. in causing cirrhosis of the liver in response to bilharzial infection, and sometimes it is both harmful and purposeless, as with *contact dermatitis*. The antigens of contact dermatitis are sometimes substances to which the patient has been exposed for years without trouble, quite distinct from obvious irritants such as acids or organic solvents. They include metals, drugs, epoxy resins, and many chemicals used in processing rubber, plastics, clothing, and countless industrial materials. Some plants are notorious, e.g. poison ivy in America and members of the primula family in Europe. Contact dermatitis shows itself as an inflamed rash, nearly always itchy and often persistent until the cause is identified and removed. Many of the agents of type IV hypersensitivity are not, on their own, antigenic. They act as *haptens*, i.e. they combine with an innocent tissue protein, changing its nature enough for it to be treated as 'non-self'.

There are probably still more types of hypersensitive reactions to be classified.

7. AUTOIMMUNITY

The danger of immune reactions being directed against an individual's own tissues, causing disease by treating 'self' as 'non-self', has been mentioned several times. In the normal or, rather, ideal state, every constituent of the body would be recognized before or soon after birth as 'self' and exempted from defensive reactions. However, it is possible for some to escape recognition, and later in life be discovered and attacked. In fact, though, this does not seem to happen often, unless a particular protein is sheltered from the ever-patrolling lymphocytes, e.g. within the lens of the eye. If an eye is injured and some of this protein escapes, it is liable to be stigmatized as 'non-self' and provoke the formation of antibodies able to attack the other eye. This is called *sympathetic ophthalmia*.

A similarly sheltered protein confined to the interior of heart-muscle cells apparently has an antigen resembling one carried by some streptococci. If these bacteria infect the throat, the antibodies mustered to deal with them can also attack the heart muscle, causing the heart disease of *rheumatic fever*.

Body proteins may be altered by infection so that they are open to attack by T-lymphocytes. They can also be altered by inert substances (haptens), leading to type IV hypersensitivity as described in the previous section.

Antibodies active against 'self' formed in any of these ways are known as *autoantibodies*.

Whether autoimmune diseases are due to autoantibodies evoked by the effects of haptens (especially drugs) and infec-

tion on normal body proteins, or whether autoantibodies are normally present and cause trouble only because mechanisms for restraining them are deficient is an unresolved question. There is also disagreement over when autoantibodies are the cause of a disease, and when they are an effect.

Beyond dispute is that autoantibodies are associated with many diseases characterized by chronic, destructive inflammation with no proven cause. They affect kidneys (glomerulonephritis), thyroid and adrenal glands, blood cells, stomach, intestine (Crohn's disease and ulcerative colitis), skin, blood vessels, joints and connective tissues: almost any tissue or organ, in fact. Until autoimmunity was recognized recently the common factors of this large group of seemingly unrelated diseases were that they were serious, incurable, and labelled 'idiopathic', which meant they appeared to happen of their own accord. ('Incurable' does not necessarily mean untreatable: in this group e.g., pernicious anaemia can be controlled with vitamin B_{12}, while failure of the pancreas, adrenals or thyroid can be treated with the appropriate hormone; however, the damage cannot yet be repaired, and treatment is lifelong.) All these conditions respond to some extent to drugs that suppress immune responses, but that does not prove that the conditions are due to autoimmunity. The drugs might act merely by suppressing inflammation.

8. IMMUNITY AND THERAPEUTICS

Medical treatment directed at immune responses is of two opposite kinds: it may either stimulate natural defences or it may suppress them.

The best-known stimulant of immunity is vaccination, which is one of several methods of ➤*immunization*. Actual deficiency of one or other part of the normal system of defence is considered in 'Defective Immunity', above. Where possible the missing factor is provided in the same way as some diabetes is treated by supplying the insulin that the patient lacks.

Many substances have been used to stimulate the various activities of lymphocytes and macrophages. This work, still mostly experimental, is directed particularly at cancer. The component cells of a cancer are certainly abnormal, and for many years pathologists have felt that cancer should act, therefore, as an antigen and provoke attack by antibodies like any other parasite. In fact many cancers are now known to do just this, but so weakly that the body's defences seldom prevail. One cancer – ➤*Burkitt's tumour* – is associated with the virus of glandular fever. This tumour was almost confined to people in Central and E. Africa who were underfed and chronically infected with malaria, bilharzia, hookworm and other debilitating diseases. It seemed more than likely that these people, with their immune responses undermined, developed cancer from an infection that caused only a harmless if tedious fever in healthier people, who could build up adequate reserves of antibodies. This theory is very strongly supported by the fact that previously fit people who contract the acquired immune deficiency syndrome (➤*AIDS*), and so lose the ability to elaborate antibodies, die of Burkitt's tumour if they are infected with glandular fever. This is only a single example of apparent immunity to a cancer, and an uncommon cancer at that, but the same type of virus (Epstein-Barr) is under suspicion in con-

nection with other cancers. Perhaps some cancer never comes to light because the immune response can deal with it, as some people completely resist ordinary infections without ever showing symptoms. It is already certain that people who in general are unusually susceptible to infection are also more liable than others to develop cancer. Although it is far too soon to start holding out hope, we can at least watch with interest the search for ways of enhancing immune responses.

Immunosuppression is the logical answer to undesirable immune responses, in particular the rejection of grafted tissues as well as severe hypersensitivity and autoimmunity. The most potent drugs are *cytotoxic* agents, a varied group of drugs that in one way or another inhibit the multiplication of cells. Some of the drugs are especially active against lymphocytes, which must be the target, but none are free of adverse effects on other cells and tissues; they all cause unpleasant symptoms and are not advisable if they can be avoided. To a large extent their immunosuppressive action depends on their affinity for rapidly multiplying cells, such as those concerned with immunity. This is why the same drugs have a selective action against various kinds of cancer cell, which multiply more rapidly than normal ones.

Since inflammation is a phase of immunity, ➤*anti-inflammatory* drugs are, to some extent, immunosuppressive. The most powerful of them, the *corticosteroids*, have widespread effects on other phases of immunity, and one of their disadvantages is that they make the patient vulnerable to infection of any kind.

The ideal treatment would suppress only the particular antibodies or activated lymphocytes causing trouble, but this line of research is still at an early stage.

immunization. Artificially providing antibodies to deal with antigens such as bacteria or their toxic products, to confer the immunity that would follow a real infection without the same risk to health and life.

Immunization may be *active* or *passive*. Active immunization mimics infectious disease by introducing a relatively harmless antigen sufficiently like the real one to generate antibodies against either. The immunity is retained, leaving the subject able to resist the real infection. The original vaccine was the live virus of vaccinia, a mild infection so closely related to smallpox that it confers immunity to both (▸*Jenner*). Most of today's vaccines are prepared from microbes processed to disarm them yet preserve their antigens. Some are effective after a single dose, others only after two or three.

Passive immunization is a temporary measure against existing infection or the immediate threat of exposure. Antibodies are given in the form of immune globulin from people known to be immune to common infections. This gives immediate protection, lasting for some weeks, but no immunity to later exposure.

Routine protection of children includes vaccination against diphtheria, tetanus, pertussis (DTP), *Haemophilus influenzae* B, and poliomyelitis in their first year, and measles, mumps and rubella (MMR) in their second. Some of these vaccines are to be repeated when the child first goes to school. Girls aged 10–14 who are not immune to rubella should be immunized against it, and at the same age children susceptible to tuberculosis may be offered BCG vaccination.

Adults may need to be immunized against occasional risks associated with their work, or with foreign ▸*travel*.

immunoglobulin ▸gamma-globulin.

impaction. A fracture is said to be impacted when the broken ends of bone are driven together and firmly interlocked. Colles' fracture above the wrist is usually impacted, but the fragments are nearly always far enough out of line to need resetting.

An impacted tooth is one that has grown out of line and become wedged in the jaw and unable to come through.

impetigo. Infection of the outer layers of the skin by staphylococci, forming clusters of small abscesses. It is contagious, especially among children, and from the original site other areas of the patient's own skin can be infected by contact. Antibiotics applied to the surface usually clear up impetigo in a few days, but with spreading infection and in the case of small children the drug may have to be given by mouth or by injection.

implantation. Embedding of an embryo in the lining of its mother's uterus, about 6 days after conception.

impotence. Inability to perform coitus; in the main it is a disorder of men from failure of erection, but it may also occur in women from structural anomalies or painful inflammation with spasm of the muscles around the vagina; the spasm can also be due to anxiety.

There are many possible physical causes, none of them except ageing very common, such as disorders of the sex organs and of the glands and nerves that control them. But more often than not there is no physical defect, and the problem is psychiatric. When a husband is impotent his wife naturally supposes that he has an aversion to her, but his real trouble is as likely to be lack of confidence in himself. Some men are potent with prostitutes but not with their wives because with prostitutes they have no worries but with their wives they are over-anxious to succeed. Worry suppresses sexual reflexes as readily as it suppresses appetite for food.

incision. Wound made by cutting, e.g. in a surgical operation (as opposed to *laceration*, a torn wound, or *abrasion*, a graze).

incisor. Chisel-like front tooth, of which there are two pairs in each jaw.

incontinence. Inability to control reflex emptying of rectum or bladder, sometimes because of a disorder of the organ itself but more often from loss of co-ordination in the nervous system, e.g. with brain damage or senility. The best treatment would be to deal with the cause, but that is not always possible. Even, however, when voluntary control is irretrievably lost the reflexes, controlled by the spinal cord, can often be educated so that they operate at reasonably spaced intervals and the patient knows when to take steps to avoid soiling himself.

incubation. The *incubation period* of an infectious disease is the interval between infection and the first symptoms. The period may be as short as a few hours with bacterial food poisoning or as long as several years with leprosy, but for a given disease its limits are fairly well defined. With a few diseases the incubation period hardly varies, e.g. smallpox (12 days); chickenpox (14 days). With most, however, there is some variation between cases.

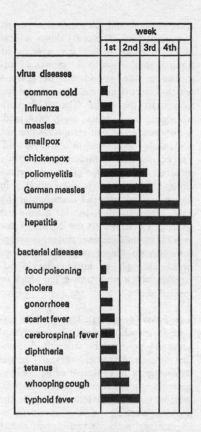

Average incubation periods

The chart shows that virus diseases do not usually appear until more than a week after infection. A virus has first to find its target organ and then establish itself before it can multiply and cause symptoms (▸*virus*). In the two exceptions shown, common cold and influenza, the portal of entry is also the affected tissue; the virus has no journey to make.

Bacteria do not have to establish themselves before they can multiply; they can start at once, and the incubation period is usually short. The chart shows several apparent exceptions. The symptoms of tetanus are due not to the growth of microbes in the wound but to poisons which travel from the wound up the nerves to the brain. The delay with whooping cough is less easily explained: it may simply be that symptoms are not noticeable until the infection is advanced, for many children are certainly infected without ever showing obvious signs. Typhoid is a special case. It is in fact a typical bacterial disease, starting soon after infection, but for a time the trouble is confined to the depths of the small intestine. The fever and other symptoms do not begin until the microbes break through to invade the bloodstream, which may take a few days or several weeks.

indigestion (dyspepsia). The term indigestion (dyspepsia) includes various symptoms arising from the stomach: discomfort or pain, flatulence, nausea. There is sometimes a recognizable cause such as gastritis or a gastric ulcer, but often indigestion is due to interference with the normal working of the stomach by overeating, eating when appetite has been suppressed by worry, anger, drugs, heavy smoking, unsuitable diet, the common habit of swallowing air, or hurried, unattractive meals.

Any number of drugs can be used to relieve the symptoms; an aperitif occasionally helps by imposing a few minutes' rest before eating, encouraging appetite, and allaying anxiety; but alcohol on an empty stomach would aggravate conditions such as gastritis or ulcer.

indomethacin. A drug used to relieve pain and inflammation. It is generally re-served for rheumatic symptoms too severe to be relieved by milder drugs such as aspirin, e.g. those of an attack of gout.

induction. *Induction of labour* is the use of artificial means to start the process of childbirth if there has been undue delay or the health of mother or child is at risk. The hospital routine of warm bath followed by enema, followed if necessary by injections of a pituitary hormone to stimulate the uterus, often works. If this fails, releasing a little fluid from the membranous bag surrounding the baby may set off contractions of the uterus. Injections of *prostaglandins* can also be used to induce labour.

infarct; infarction. Congestion and blockage of a blood vessel on which a part of an organ depends, with death and scarring of the affected tissue. It differs from gangrene in that there is no bacterial infection to spread the damage. The segment of lost tissue may be called an infarct. In general, if one artery is blocked, neighbouring arteries, with communicating branches, take over the work. Infarction occurs in places where small arteries do not communicate with each other, such as the kidney; or where the arteries together supply only enough blood for the whole organ, with little in reserve, as in the brain; or where alternative arteries to the blocked one are also unhealthy and cannot take over, as in many middle-aged hearts. If one were to simulate coronary thrombosis (clotting in an artery in the heart muscle) by artificially closing an artery in a healthy heart, probably nothing untoward would happen because the other coronary vessels would suffice. Post-mortem studies have shown that people who have died from other causes have at some time had a coronary thrombosis without symptoms. In this disease it is the infarction that matters, and it can arise from narrowing of the vessels without actual thrombosis.

infection. The countless microbes that surround us include *protozoa*, small *fungi, bacteria* and *viruses*. Some are essential to health, but a few are pathogenic – able to infect the tissues of the body, multiply and cause trouble. The mere presence of microbes does not constitute infection. The skin and inner linings such as those of the mouth, throat and large intestine all teem with microbes, many of them necessary to health.

Microbes do not penetrate intact skin. Either they enter a wound (an invisible scratch or pinprick will do) or they are injected by the bites of insects etc. (>*insect*). The mucous membranes lining the mouth, air-passages, and digestive and urinary tracts are much more vulnerable, and many kinds of microbe pass through them without trouble. Particular species have their chosen portals of entry: typhoid and dysentery bacilli penetrate the lining of the intestine but not of the lungs, and they do not infect wounds; the natural inhabitants of the intestine seldom cause trouble there but will set up infection if they find their way into the urinary tract. Infection of the intestine is transmitted by food or drink, and infection of the nose, throat and lungs as a rule by droplets from coughs and sneezes.

How the nature of infection was discovered is summarized under >*microbe*. Before Pasteur's work (1861 onwards) on the role of microbes in disease there could be no concerted attack against either wound infection (including the inevitable infection that made surgery so dangerous) or specific infectious diseases, though there were flashes of inspiration. A few surgeons had insisted on cleanliness, e.g. Henri de Mondeville (14th century) and Ambroise Paré (16th century); and in 1861 Semmelweis published his great work on the control of infection in childbirth. Jenner introduced vaccination against smallpox in 1796, and in 1854 Snow stopped an outbreak of cholera by tracing an infected water supply. The only effective drugs were mercury against syphilis (16th century) and quinine against malaria (17th century).

As soon as Pasteur had published his findings the English surgeon Lister began to apply them to operative surgery and to the treatment of wounds. Compound fractures, where the broken bone is exposed to direct contamination from a wound, had usually called for amputation, and even if the operation was done promptly half the patients died (without operation they nearly always died). In view of Pasteur's proof that fermentation, putrefaction, and infection were similar processes, and of the fact that carbolic acid rendered sewage innocuous, Lister dressed compound fractures with carbolic acid, and found that many cases recovered without amputation. If he still had to amputate, then carbolic dressings made the operation much safer. This work was published in 1867. Three years later, Lister introduced the carbolic spray. It squirted a mist of carbolic acid over the field of a surgical operation in order to prevent infection from bacteria in the air. For the first time patients could submit to major operations with no great risk of dying a week or two later from spreading infection, introduced by the surgeon or caught from the person in the next bed. And surgeons could safely operate in regions such as the abdomen, where hitherto surgery had been unthinkable.

Since the other great obstacle to surgery had just been removed by the discovery of anaesthetics, surgery took one stride from antiquity into modern times.

Within a few years the spray was found to be unnecessary if everything that was to come into contact with the patient was sterilized before the operation; thus antiseptic surgery gave way to aseptic surgery. (►*surgery*; *antiseptic*; *wound*).

While the surgeons were revolutionizing their craft, Pasteur and other bacteriologists were applying to other diseases than smallpox the principle of vaccination. Early hopes that all infection might be controlled by vaccines were not fulfilled, but by the turn of the century people could be protected against several epidemic diseases, and there were effective antidotes to the bacterial toxins of diphtheria and tetanus (►*immunity*; *immunization*).

In the 20th century the most important development has been the discovery of drugs that will destroy bacteria in the body without harming the patient. In 1911 Ehrlich (who already had a Nobel Prize for his work on immunity) introduced an arsenic compound safe enough to be used against syphilis – salvarsan (606). Other drugs of the same type followed, then in 1935 Domagk discovered that sulphonamides cured a wide variety of infections. Penicillin and other antibiotics introduced since 1941 provide effective treatment for virtually all infections caused by bacteria.

The search for drugs effective against virus infections has met with little success. The few 'viruses' that respond to antibiotics are mostly not viruses but primitive bacteria. With true virus diseases, prevention by some form of vaccination is still the best hope. Poliomyelitis has become a rare disease in countries where vaccines are widely used, and measles is likely to follow suit.

Besides prevention and treatment of particular diseases, general hygiene has advanced greatly since the 18th century. Decent housing, sanitation, clean drinking water and clean and sufficient food all contribute to the reduced incidence of infectious diseases, even if the effect of any one factor cannot be assessed. Since 1950, when effective drugs against tuberculosis came into general use, the death rate from tuberculosis has fallen dramatically. But it had been falling gradually for many years. With good drugs, people who already have tuberculosis are less likely to die of it. With good general hygiene, they are less likely to catch it in the first place. Cure and prevention interact. If the sick are cured they can no longer infect the healthy.

inferiority complex. The 'complex' is not diffidence ('pardon me for living'), but the group of traits such as assertiveness and aggression unconsciously assumed to compensate for real or imagined inferiority.

infertility ►*fertility*.

inflammation. Response of any part of the body to insult or injury, such as wounding, burning, infection by microbes or intrusion of any other matter recognized by the tissues as foreign.

Acute inflammation is the first stage both of healing and of fighting infection. The outward signs were described by Celsus in the 1st century AD: *rubor et tumor cum calore et dolore*: redness and swelling with heat and pain.

Specialized cells in connective tissues

and in blood start the process by releasing or activating histamine, serotonin, prostaglandins and other substances. Under the influence of these *mediators* small blood vessels in the area are dilated, and their walls, normally permeable only to the relatively small molecules of water, salt and nutrients such as glucose and amino-acids, allow large protein molecules to pass. The proteins in the blood normally restrict, by ►*osmosis*, the amount of fluid allowed to escape into the tissues. With this restraint lifted, fluid (inflammatory exudate) accumulates.

The increased flow of blood accounts for Celsus' redness and heat, and the fluid for the swelling. The pain is due partly to the swelling (hence the relief of having an abscess lanced) and partly to stimulation of nerve endings by one or more of the mediators. To the four classical signs may be added impaired function: no inflamed organ works well. Common accompaniments are fever, headache and simply feeling ill. The number of white cells in the blood is increased.

The pattern of inflammation varies according to the tissues involved and the nature of the injury. Fluid often predominates with inflammation of lining membranes in joints (*synovitis*), in the chest (*pleurisy*) and elsewhere. Infection by streptococci, staphylococci and other bacteria attracts white blood-cells, leading to the formation of pus. With diphtheria the exudate characteristically forms an adhesive fibrous membrane over the lining of the throat. No sign of inflammation is more familiar than the outpouring of watery mucus with a cold or hay fever.

Persistent *chronic inflammation* ensues if the original cause persists, e.g. when ill health impairs resistance to infection, when a foreign body prevents healing or when a component of the body itself sets up a defensive reaction (►*autoimmunity*). Some kinds of infection, e.g. tuberculosis, regularly evoke a smouldering chronic inflammation. Deposits of fibrous scar tissue result from an attempt to wall off the infection.

Some of the proteins and cells in the inflammatory exudate take part in the repair of damaged tissues (►*healing*); others in resisting infection (►*immunity*). These desirable outcomes are necessary to health, but the mediators of inflammation are not selective. Like the people of whom they are components they readily treat unfamiliar visitors as hostile merely because they are foreign. These undesirable responses, hypersensitivity and autoimmunity, are discussed under *immunity*.

The suffix -*itis* conventionally signifies inflammation.

►*anti-inflammatory drugs*.

influenza (grippe; flu). A common infectious disease appearing in epidemic form every few years and worldwide (pandemic) at rather longer intervals. The virus is spread by airborne infection from coughs and sneezes. After a short incubation there is an abrupt onset of fever, with aching head, back and limbs. Although this is primarily an infection of the airways, respiratory symptoms are seldom prominent at the start, when they are often limited to a tight sore throat and a dry cough. Nasal catarrh, sore eyes and a looser cough with sputum may appear a day or two later. As a rule the symptoms abate within a few days, to vanish by the end of a week; but occasionally the attack is followed by a long spell of lethargy and other symptoms (>*myalgic encephalomyelitis*). Although the virus itself can be dangerous, especially at the height of an epidemic, bacterial infection of tissues already weakened by the virus poses the greater threat. Most of the 20 million deaths in the great pandemic of 1918–19 were from pneumonia arising in this way (>*empyema*). One culprit was *Haemophilus influenzae*, a bacterium for many years mistaken for the actual cause of influenza. The pandemic of 'Asian flu' in 1957 carried a far lower death rate, due at least in part to the use of antibiotics, unknown in 1918. Though ineffective against the virus these could deal with secondary bacterial infection.

At all times there are sporadic cases and local outbreaks of influenza. These can be mild, easily passing as common colds or nondescript virus infections ('there's a bug going around'). In this way the virus lives on, its fires banked, until the next epidemic.

Sympathetic nursing, perhaps with aspirin to alleviate some of the symptoms, is usually the basis of treatment; but for secondary infection by bacteria antibiotics may be needed. An antiviral drug, *amantadine*, is of some use, especially as a prophylactic in selected cases.

Influenza vaccines are used to protect people at special risk such as asthmatics and diabetics. There is more than one strain of influenza virus, and a given vaccine is effective against only one. In addition the virus undergoes slight changes from year to year, so that a vaccine that is effective against one epidemic may be less so against the next. WHO maintains a constant watch and provides information worldwide about currently active strains.

inguinal. Of the groin – the fold in front of the hip-joint where the muscles of the abdomen and thigh meet.

injection. Administration of a fluid such as a solution of a drug directly into a tissue or organ by means of a syringe. Related procedures include instillation (dropping fluid, e.g. into the eye), and infusion (allowing a fluid to flow into the body, e.g. saline solution to correct dehydration).

Intradermal injection, into the skin itself, is used to test the patient's reaction to a substance: if he is sensitive to it a red flare will appear. *Subcutaneous* injection, into the layer of fatty tissue, allows a drug to be absorbed into the circulation at a moderate rate. This route is not suitable for irritant substances. *Intramuscular* injections are given with a larger needle into the depths of a muscle at a selected point where there are no blood vessels or nerves to be injured, such as the upper and outer quadrant of the buttock. This is perhaps the commonest site for injections. *Intravenous* injection, directly into a vein, is used either for very rapid effect or to dilute an irritant drug with the large volume of circulating blood and prevent it from damaging the tissues.

In addition, drugs are sometimes injected straight into the affected part of the body, such as a joint.

innocent. Benign (of tumours that have no tendency to invade neighbouring tissues and are not cancerous).

innominate (Lat. = unnamed). Several anatomical structures are illogically so named.

Innominate artery. A large branch of the arch of the *aorta*; it divides into right *subclavian* and *common carotid* arteries (on the left these arteries are separate branches of the aorta).

Innominate bone. The hip-bone or *coxa*: ➤*pelvis.*

Innominate vein. Large vein formed from the *subclavian* and *internal jugular* veins. The left and right innominate veins join to form the *superior vena cava.*

inoculation. Deliberate infection from a mild case of a disease in order to confer immunity, a method used against smallpox before the discovery of vaccination. ➤*immunity* (1).

insect. A six-legged *arthropod.* Insects play an important part in human illness. Some arthropods that are not strictly insects (e.g. ticks and mites, related to spiders) also carry disease; in this context they need not be distinguished from true insects. Arthropods cause trouble in several ways.

Contamination. Flies are the main offenders. They are dirty feeders with sticky feet, and they cause much illness simply by carrying bacteria from one place to another. Intestinal infection is often transmitted in this way where sewage disposal is deficient. In hot countries one of the most useful health precautions is to protect food from flies.

Infestation. Sometimes the insect is itself the disease. Infestation with lice or fleas should count as a disease in its own right, and *scabies* is the presence of itch-mites in the skin. The tropical tumbu-fly produces grubs that hatch in the skin, causing an unpleasant but fairly harmless sort of boil.

Poisonous bites and stings. Bees (➤*bee sting*), wasps and hornets inject minute doses of poisons resembling snake venoms, but the real danger is a severe allergic reaction in sensitized people (➤*allergy*). ➤*Scorpions,* ➤*spiders,* centipedes,

and many other arthropods have similar venoms, and a few species can inject enough to be dangerous to human victims, especially children.

Transmission. Numerous diseases are transmitted by insect bites. The responsible microbes can infect either the insect or man, sometimes in different phases of a complex life-cycle (e.g. malaria parasites undergo sexual reproduction in mosquitoes but not in man). An insect that transmits a disease is the *vector* of the disease. Common vectors include *mosquitoes* (malaria, yellow fever, filariasis); *fleas* (plague, typhus); *lice* and *ticks* (typhus, relapsing fever); and numerous tropical insects. Parasites have a strictly limited choice of victims, and particular vectors carry only particular diseases. Fleas, lice and ticks each transmit their own particular kind of typhus, and the mosquitoes of malaria are not those of yellow fever.

Most insect-borne diseases are tropical, and most tropical diseases are insect-borne. An important factor in the eradication of tropical disease is the control of insects, and the 1948 Nobel Prize for Medicine rightly went to the Swiss chemist Paul Müller for his work on DDT and other new insecticides.

insomnia ➤*sleep.*

insufficiency. In the sense of impaired function, a term less open to misunderstanding than ➤*failure.* But to English ears *cardiac insufficiency* sounds cumbersome and alien, though in French *insuffisance cardiaque* is fine.

insulin. A hormone formed in the pancreas and released into the bloodstream. It promotes the uptake of glucose from the blood by the body cells; without it, glucose is neither consumed as fuel nor adequately stored, but simply accumulates in the blood until it spills over into the urine (►*diabetes*). An excess of insulin dangerously decreases the amount of glucose in the blood (►*hypoglycaemia*).

Insulin is thought to act by facilitating the passage of glucose through the outer membranes of cells. Chemically, it is a lightweight protein; its molecule is a chain of 51 amino-acids. F. Sanger received the 1958 Nobel Prize for Chemistry for establishing the exact structure.

intensive care (therapy) unit (ICU, ITU). A hospital department providing constant nursing care, with running records of heart, circulation, breathing and other functions, and facilities for immediate action in case of emergency.

intercostal (Lat. = between ribs). The space between any two ribs is bridged by two layers of intercostal muscles, and contains intercostal nerves and blood vessels.

intercurrent. (Illness) arising in the course of another illness; e.g. serious injury may lower a person's resistance so that he is an easy prey to intercurrent pneumonia.

interferon. A factor in the normal system of defence against virus infection: a 'natural antibiotic'. Interferons are proteins formed in response to viruses and other agents, including some bacterial toxins. They in turn induce the formation of substances that inhibit the replication of viruses (and also, probably, of some other alien nucleic acids).

Early hopes that interferon might be as valuable against viruses as penicillin against bacteria have not been realized, but human interferons prepared by genetic engineering are finding a place in the treatment of some cancers (notably Kaposi's sarcoma complicating AIDS), and of chronic active hepatitis B. Intensive research into other possible uses is going on.

intertrigo. Soreness where two areas of skin rub together and sweat collects, a particular nuisance to fat people. Most of the trouble is due to bacteria. Intertrigo is treated with dusting powders and mild antiseptics, and to some extent prevented by losing weight and keeping cool.

intervertebral disc ►*vertebra* (1).

intestine

1. STRUCTURE

The greater part of the digestive tract, a tube some 7.5 m long to the anatomist, but in life shortened by the tone of its muscles to 5 m. The small (narrow) intestine accounts for 80 per cent of its length, and the large (wide) intestine for the final 20 per cent.

The *small intestine* begins as the *duodenum* at the outlet of the stomach (pylorus), its 20–25 cm making a C-shaped curve in front of the right kidney. Two offshoots from it, the liver and pancreas, have ducts opening together into the duodenum. The next two fifths of its length, the *jejunum*, is continued as the *ileum*. This leads to the lower right side of the abdomen where the small intestine enters the large.

The *large intestine* consists of a short cul-de-sac (*caecum*), the *colon*, running upwards to the liver, turning sharply across the abdomen towards the spleen, then down the left side to the pelvis, where it becomes the *sigmoid colon*, and finally the *rectum*, leading to the short anal canal.

The digestive tract starts life as a straight tube down the middle of the embryo, growing from behind into the abdomen and pushing ahead a fold of the lining of the cavity (*peritoneum*). This finally forms a sling or hammock for the jejunum and ileum (*mesentery*). As the intestine outpaces the growth of other organs, the mesentery fans out like a kilt with a short waistband but a long hem.

Between its coating of peritoneum and its lining of mucous membrane the intestinal wall is composed largely of muscle fibres. These can help digestion with a churning action, or push the contents with waves of contraction (*peristalsis*). The muscles are subject to a network of nerves, *parasympathetic* to stimulate and *sympathetic* to inhibit.

The lining membrane of the small intestine has a velvety surface; seen under a microscope it rather resembles a rubber suede brush. The little projections (*villi*) together present an enormous surface for absorbing nutrients. Small glands between the villi secrete *enzymes*, each adapted to the processing of a particular nutrient (▸*digestion*).

The duodenum also functions as an endocrine gland, in that it responds to the arrival of the acid contents of the stomach by secreting into the bloodstream a hormone, ▸*secretin*, which stimulates the release of alkali (bicarbonate) from the liver and pancreas; this enters the duodenum by the pancreatic and bile ducts to neutralize the acid.

The intestinal contents are completely liquid as they pass from the small intestine to the large, and the principal function of the large intestine is to recover water and salt, so preventing the body from becoming dehydrated. With a disease such as cholera this function is practically bypassed, and in a matter of hours fatal dehydration can set in. By absorbing most of the water the colon creates a semi-solid mass that can be retained until it can conveniently be voided.

Unlike the small intestine, which is virtually sterile, the colon teems with bacteria. Most are harmless where they are, though potentially dangerous to other parts of the body if they stray. Some kinds are useful, e.g. for synthesizing vitamin K. Antibiotics can upset the balance of power by killing some of the bacteria and so giving others a chance to take over and cause trouble.

2. EXAMINATION

Most intestinal diseases cause symptoms which point to the intestine as the affected organ; in other words one usually knows where to look for the trouble. Almost the whole of the intestine can be felt through the soft belly-wall.

The last 12 in of the large intestine can be inspected with a lighted tube (*sigmoidoscope*). A light anaesthetic is sometimes needed for this rather disagreeable examination, but it is the only certain way of identifying some important disorders of the large intestine. If the diagnosis is still uncertain after looking at the inside of the intestine a small specimen of the lining can be taken for microscopic study.

X-rays are used in the same way as for the stomach. The patient swallows fluid (barium meal) which is opaque to X-rays, such as a suspension of barium sulphate. The intestine can then be shown in silhouette as the fluid passes along it. Similar fluid injected into the rectum (barium enema) gives a picture of the large intestine.

A specimen of the fluid in the small intestine can be taken with a syringe attached to a long, soft rubber tube. The end of the tube is swallowed and passes along the stomach to the duodenum or beyond. Its position can be determined with X-rays. A small device for taking a sample of the lining of the intestine can be introduced in the same way. Various scanning techniques are increasingly used in the diagnosis of intestinal disorders.

Laboratory examination of the stools is an important guide to the state of the intestine. Chemical analysis reveals defective breakdown or absorption of foods. Intestinal parasites are identified by microscopy; in hot countries where this kind of infection is rife microscopic examination of the stools is a matter of routine. Bacteriological investigation of the stools is needed for the exact diagnosis of intestinal infection, for tracing the source of infection, and for the proper control of people whose work involves handling food or drinking water.

Sometimes the only way to make a diagnosis is to operate and look at the intestine. This is less drastic than it sounds. An exploratory operation carries little risk, and certainly less risk than the sort of suspected trouble that calls for it. Most abdominal operations are in a sense exploratory. What looks like acute appendicitis may turn out to be a leaking duodenal ulcer or a twisted ovarian cyst. These, and several other disorders with similar symptoms, could probably be distinguished without operation if there were time, but most of them require immediate surgical attention. The provisional diagnosis 'acute appendicitis' may be a convenient abbreviation of 'case for urgent abdominal operation, probably but not necessarily appendicitis'. Suspected cancer often needs the same approach: if the patient is kept waiting until the diagnosis is proved beyond doubt it may be too late to operate. Seen

in this light, the risk of an unnecessary operation seems reasonable enough. ➤*abdomen* (1).

3. Disorders

There are many different ailments of the intestine, and the patient usually has symptoms to indicate *something* wrong in the intestine. But the symptoms alone may not show precisely *what* is wrong, because widely different causes produce similar effects. The intestine is a very simple apparatus in which only a few things can go wrong. Intestinal disease may impair the absorption of food (➤*malabsorption*), or it may disturb the purely mechanical function of moving the contents along the tube: they can be moved too quickly, with ➤*diarrhoea*; too slowly, with ➤*constipation*; or not at all if the tube is blocked.

Pain from the intestine is felt when the nerve-endings are stretched. This will obviously happen when the intestine is distended with gas or overloaded with food. The pressure also increases if it is blocked or if its muscle is over-active. When the intestine is inflamed it becomes over-sensitive and the normal pressure changes become painful. In one way or another, then, almost any intestinal disorder may be painful.

Bleeding is a common symptom of many disorders. Blood undergoes chemical change in the intestine and becomes black. It is recognizable as blood only if the bleeding is from low down, e.g. from piles or cancer of the rectum. Otherwise it merely darkens the stools. Significant amounts of blood may be passed without being noticed: the loss of a teaspoonful of blood daily can cause serious anaemia in time. Anaemia of this type is very common (duodenal ulcer, hookworm disease, piles, regular use or abuse of aspirin), but perhaps intestinal bleeding is even more important as a warning sign. Most cancers of the intestine can be removed if they are recognized in the early stages, and a trace of blood may be the first sign.

The actual diseases are discussed under their own headings; what follows is no more than a crude attempt at classifying some of the important ones.

Emotion and mood play a large part. Fear or misery can cause sustained overactivity of the intestine. This does not always lead to diarrhoea. Often the activity is not co-ordinated and the result is constipation and discomfort. Symptoms ascribed to constipation such as headache and lethargy are more likely to be an accompaniment than a real consequence of constipation. The intestine reacts to any emotion, but it reacts most to emotion centred on itself. Some people seem to be obsessed with their digestive organs. This is perhaps because so much of an infant's earliest training has to do with the action of his bowels. Nothing is more likely to disturb this action than the constant fear that it might be disturbed. Finally, physical disease of the intestine can cause anxiety and so set up a vicious circle. It is sometimes impossible to distinguish cause from effect.

Malabsorption may occur simply because there is not time for complete absorption, either because the intestine is inflamed and over-active or because it is too short, usually as a result of surgical removal of an irreparably damaged section. Secondly, it may be due to a defect of the lining which reduces its ability to absorb, e.g. ►*sprue*, ►*coeliac disease*, intestinal tuberculosis. Thirdly, it may be due to the absence of digestive enzymes, e.g. with disease of the pancreas or with

congenital defects such as ►*carbohydrate intolerance*.

Over-activity, apart from the emotional factors already discussed, is usually due to inflammation. Inflamed mucous membranes pour out fluid; therefore the contents of the intestine are increased. The muscles and their nerves are irritated, and the contractions are exaggerated. Both fluid and contractions contribute to diarrhoea. But violent contractions are not always co-ordinated. Instead of a smooth, orderly progress along the intestine, one section may contract before the following section has had time to relax: it is then pushing against an obstruction, which causes distension and pain. Inflammation of the intestine (*enteritis*) is most often due to infection. The agent may be a virus ('summer diarrhoea', 'gastric flu'), a bacterium (food poisoning, dysentery, cholera, typhoid and paratyphoid fevers), or a more highly developed creature (amoebic dysentery, worm infestation). Many poisons cause symptoms like those of bacterial infection. Purgative drugs may act by irritating the intestine to greater activity, by 'drawing' an excess of fluid into the intestine, by increasing the bulk of the contents, or (which may come to the same thing) by lubrication.

Crohn's disease and *ulcerative colitis* are perhaps autoimmune reactions (►*immunity* (7)) provoked by infection, as yet unidentified.

Activity may be *impaired* in two ways. If the nerves fail, the muscle ceases to contract and there is stagnation. Or there may be a mechanical blockage. Lack of coordination of the intestinal muscles can cause constipation; this never amounts to a stoppage but only to impaired efficiency. When the peritoneum is inflamed (*peritonitis*) the intestine ceases to contract; it becomes an inert tube, unable to propel its contents. This condition, known as *ileus*, appears to be a reflex by which the nerves of the intestine are inhibited. The same thing may happen after a serious injury or operation. There is no need for the whole intestine to be paralysed. If only a short section goes out of action it acts as a barrier to the passage of the contents. This may follow interference with the blood supply, e.g. by thrombosis of an artery or pressure on the mesentery, or severe localized inflammation. In a rare congenital disorder, *megacolon*, certain nerves fail to grow into a section of the large intestine. Since the affected section cannot squeeze its contents along it is in effect a barrier, and the intestine above it becomes more and more distended.

Actual blockage (*intestinal obstruction*) can arise in several ways. Congenital defects include *atresia*, when a part of the intestine – usually the junction of the rectum with the anus – remains solid, without a canal; and faulty development of the mesentery can result in twisting or *volvulus* of the intestine. Volvulus can, rarely, occur even with a normal mesentery. It causes obstruction of the blood vessels rather than of the intestine itself, but either condition is equally lethal unless promptly relieved by surgery. Another cause of obstruction in early childhood (sometimes later) is *intussusception*: a section of intestine is sucked into the section beyond.

The commonest cause of obstruction is *hernia*, which arises where a weak point in the muscles of the abdomen allows a loop of intestine to slip between the muscle fibres. In most cases it comes to no great harm, but there is always a danger that it will be constricted. A similar condition arises within the abdomen if a loop of intestine is trapped behind a fibrous band (*adhesion*) joining two organs. The band may be a congenital anomaly or a result of scarring after inflammation, injury, or surgical operation.

All types of intestinal obstruction need surgical treatment.

Tumours are very rare in the small intestine but two types are common in the large intestine: *polyp*, which is usually harmless but occasionally leads to the other type, *cancer*. Most intestinal cancer, however, is without apparent cause apart from a tendency to run in families. Constipation used to be blamed, but without evidence. Piles most emphatically do not cause cancer. Their importance is that bleeding from a curable cancer is all too often ascribed to piles until the cancer has become incurable.

About a sixth of all cancers reported in Great Britain affect the large intestine, and in many countries the proportion is still higher. The usual treatment is to remove the affected section and repair the cut ends. When the rectum is involved normal function cannot often be restored without the risk of leaving some of the cancer behind, and an artificial anus (*colostomy*) has to be made. Even when a cure seems unlikely the operation is usually worth trying, if only to prevent the misery of obstruction. And in some 50 per cent of cases the disease can be cured. This figure is very much higher in cases where unexplained bleeding and above all a *change of bowel habit* have been investigated as soon as possible. The kind of change is immaterial; any change – more frequent motions, less frequent, less regular – calls for full examination. The cause may be entirely innocent, but it has to be ascertained.

Other important disorders of the intestine, not mentioned above but discussed under their own headings, are *duodenal ulcer* (►*peptic ulcer*), *appendicitis*, and *diverticulosis* – small pockets or diverticula in the lining of the large intestine, harmless in themselves but apt to become inflamed. These three are among the commonest causes of *perforation* of the intestine with leakage of its contents into the peritoneal cavity and peritonitis; this highly dangerous condition calls for immediate operation.
►*abdomen* (1); *stomach*; *rectum*.

intrauterine device ►*contraception*.

intravenous. In or into a vein. *Intravenous injection* is the quickest way to get a drug into the circulation in an emergency and is also used with drugs such as aminophylline to avoid the irritation that might follow injection into a muscle.
Intravenous infusion by continuous drip-feed is used to restore or maintain vital stores of water, salts and nutrients during recovery from injuries and other disturbances.
Intravenous pyelography ►*kidney* (4).

intussusception. A cause of blockage of the intestine: a length of the tube is telescoped into the next section, and drawn further and further in by the action of the intestinal muscles. It is rare in adults, but is not uncommon in the first year of life. The condition needs urgent attention, usually surgical.

involution. Shrinkage, in particular of the uterus after pregnancy: this organ takes several weeks to return to its former size. Also (mainly in psychiatry) the period of life when one has at last to accept that one is not getting any younger. In women, the menopause is an abrupt reminder.

involutional melancholia. Depression, severe and irrational enough to count as a form of insanity or psychosis, at the time of the menopause. ►*depression*.

iodine. A very small amount of this element is necessary to health because it is a component of thyroid hormone. In most places, the diet and drinking water supply enough, but in some areas there is hardly any in the soil and the inhabitants are subject to goitre – enlargement of the thyroid gland – showing as a rounded swelling of the front of the neck. This represents, so to speak, an attempt by the gland to make bricks without straw. If iodine is provided the swelling subsides.

A solution of iodine is a powerful antiseptic, suitable for sterilizing intact skin before a surgical operation but too corrosive for use in wounds.
►*isotope*.

iridectomy. Surgical operation on the eye: a small hole is made near the margin of the iris to allow fluid trapped in the front of the eye to circulate in case of *glaucoma*. The raised pressure is thus relieved and the danger to sight is overcome.

iris. Flat ring of pigmented tissue in the front of the eye, between the cornea and the lens. Its muscle fibres widen the hole in the middle, the pupil, in poor light and constrict it in bright light. The dark pigment, melanin, is common to everyone apart from some albinos. Diffraction through the opalescent outer layers (the stroma) of the iris makes this dark-brown pigment on the inner surface appear blue. However, scattered deposits of pigment in the outer layers give the appearance of brown, hazel, green etc.

iron. A healthy adult body contains 3–4 grams of iron; enough for a 2-inch nail. Most of it is combined with protein to form ►*haemoglobin*, the oxygen-carrying component of the red blood cells. Some is held in storage, in the reticulo-endothelial cells of the liver and other organs. Small amounts are needed by enzymes concerned with the use of oxygen throughout the body.

The outermost layer of the skin and mucous membranes is continuously shed (the extent is seen when a limb has been in plaster for a few weeks and the shed layer has had time to accumulate). In this way, the body loses about 1 mg of iron daily, and in healthy men this is the only loss, and all that the diet has to replace. A balanced diet contains at least ten times this amount of iron, but only 10 per cent is absorbed. The amount absorbed can be increased to 30 per cent if the body is short of iron, or slightly decreased if there is a surfeit; but the mechanism, still unknown, cannot cope with large discrepancies. If the stores have been depleted they are only slowly replenished. If, as rarely happens, there is a gross excess of iron, the body dutifully stores it and it becomes a nuisance.

Normal menstruation costs about 30 mg of iron per month, so that a woman loses and needs twice as much iron as a man. If her loss is at all heavy her intake may not keep pace; then she has not enough to replace the lost haemoglobin and she becomes anaemic (►*anaemia* (B.2)). Pregnancy makes special demands. A new-born baby has 300 ml of blood, containing 150 mg of iron, and a further 250 mg in store, all provided by the mother. To maintain her store during pregnancy, she needs three times as much iron as a man. Her milk also contains a little iron, but not much more than she would lose by menstruation if she were not feeding a baby.

Growing children have not only to maintain the store of iron; they must steadily increase it as the volume of blood grows.

In all these cases of extra demand there is unlikely to be much spare iron to meet emergencies, and any continued bleeding will cause anaemia. Even in grown men, the store can be depleted in time by quite trivial losses. 2 ml of blood – half a teaspoonful – contains 1 mg of iron, and a daily loss of this amount doubles the requirement.

1. SUPPLY OF IRON

Most foods contain some iron. Liver is an excellent source; meat, eggs, and cereals are good; most vegetables are fair (spinach is commonly over-rated); milk is poor, which is why new-born babies need a large store. In societies where toddlers are breast-fed, e.g. parts of China and Africa, children are often anaemic. Vitamin C, present in fruit and vegetables, improves the absorption of iron from the intestine, and the anaemia of scurvy (lack of vitamin C) is partly due to poor absorption. Any mixed diet has enough iron for normal requirements, but a generally poor diet will not meet the extra demands described above. If the stores have been depleted even a very good diet will not replenish them. An artificial supply is needed.

In Greek mythology the seer Melampus treated impotence with a decoction of iron rust. But the first person to record the true value of iron, in the treatment of anaemia, was the English physician Sydenham (1624–89). Many salts of iron are suitable. Solutions are unpleasant to take, but coated tablets are generally acceptable. People whose stomachs are upset by one preparation may have no trouble with another. Overdosage is a mistake. Only a limited amount can be absorbed, and the percentage falls as the dose is increased. Impatient people who take two or three times the standard dose do not assimilate two or three times as much iron, and the unabsorbed portion upsets the digestion.

If the deficiency is due to inability to absorb iron, or if the iron is needed in a hurry, injections can be given.

2. IRON POISONING

The body has no natural means of getting rid of excess iron; it goes on storing it. In a very rare disease, *bronzed diabetes*, far too much iron is absorbed from the food and deposited all over the body. The skin becomes 'bronzed' with iron salts, and the damage to the pancreas causes diabetes. Ultimately the liver fails. A similar condition can affect people who have had scores or hundreds of blood transfusions (►*anaemia* (A.2)). This sort of chronic poisoning is uncommon.

Although the proportion of a dose of iron which can be absorbed becomes smaller as the dose increases, enough is absorbed from a really massive dose to be dangerous. Furthermore a very high concentration of iron in the stomach has a corrosive action. A bottle of 50 tablets contains enough iron to kill a small child, and in fact a number of children have died after swallowing a handful of iron tablets. When children are around, these preparations have to be kept out of reach as carefully as any other drug.

The compound *desferrioxamine* readily assimilates iron to form a new compound, ferrioxamine, that can be excreted by the kidneys. This is an effective means of treating all forms of iron poisoning.

irritability. The ability of living tissues to respond to change, in particular the response of nerve and muscle to stimulation. Haller (1708–77), one of the founders of modern physiology, taught that irritability was the characteristic property of living matter.

irritable bowel syndrome. Spastic colon: ►*constipation.*

ischaemia. Insufficient supply of blood to a part of the body, e.g. to the heart muscle, causing angina.

ischaemic heart disease (IHD). The heart muscle, like any other tissue in the body, needs a constant supply of blood to provide oxygen and other nutrients. IHD is the result of failure by the coronary arteries to meet the demand. It may show itself either as ►*angina pectoris*, or as ►*myocardial infarction* (coronary thrombosis). Angina is the response of a muscle forced to work with insufficient oxygen, and myocardial infarction is the loss of a segment of muscle lacking enough oxygen to keep it alive. In Western society the former is an all-too-common disability of middle and old age, and the latter is a leading cause of death.

In the normal way a working muscle gets its energy from the combustion of glucose and oxygen, forming water and carbon dioxide. Without enough oxygen, incomplete combustion leaves irritant end-products such as lactic acid. If diseased arteries in the legs cannot deliver enough blood, walking causes pain in the leg muscles (intermittent claudication) in the same way as with diseased coronary arteries angina follows exertion.

The possible causes of IHD include

shortage of oxygen in the air, or in the blood with severe anaemia. A narrowed valve at the outlet from the heart (aortic stenosis) may so impede the flow of blood that the heart overworks to maintain an adequate circulation even at rest, and cannot meet additional demands. In practice, though, IHD is usually associated with disease of the coronary arteries resulting from ➤*atheroma*.

ischium. The rump-bone, a part of the ➤*pelvis*.

islets of Langerhans. Clusters of cells scattered through the pancreas in which *insulin* is formed.

isoimmunity. Immune (allergic) response to tissue from another member of one's own species. An important instance is incompatibility between the blood of an unborn baby and that of its mother (➤*rhesus factor*).

isolation. Patients may need isolation to prevent their infecting others or to protect them from infection. The latter reason has been recognized only in recent years; it can apply to premature babies, patients whose natural defences have been suppressed by drugs in order to prevent tissue grafted from another person (e.g. a kidney) from being rejected after the operation, and patients with certain blood diseases that make them unduly vulnerable to infection.

To be effective, isolation demands a complex ritual that needs a special hospital unit, where everything that has been in contact with the patient is disinfected on its way to the outside world and vice versa.

With many common infectious diseases the need for isolation is much less than it was before there were antibiotics to cure the diseases, but antibiotics have

introduced a new class of disease that needs the strictest isolation: infection with newly evolved strains of microbe that resist the usual antibiotics. It is precisely in hospitals, where antibiotics are in constant use, that these strains are likely to appear.

isomer. Any of two or more compounds with different arrangements of the same atoms. Thus two atoms of carbon, six of hydrogen and one of oxygen (C_2H_6O) can form an alcohol (C_2H_5OH) or an ether, (CH_3-O-CH_3), with quite different properties.

isoniazid. Isonicotinic acid hydrazide (INH), shown by Domagk to inhibit the growth of tubercle bacilli; it has been used since 1952 for treating tuberculosis, combined with an antibiotic. It is closely related to the vitamin nicotinamide, which also has some effect against tuberculosis in animals.

Many patients treated with isoniazid have found that it raises their spirits. As a result similar compounds in which this action is enhanced have been prepared for the treatment of ➤*depression*.

isotope. One of two or more forms of a chemical element with similar chemical properties but different atomic weights. Isotopes are used in medical research for tracing the movements of chemical substances in the body. A substance can be labelled by incorporating in its molecules an unusual isotope which can later be identified. Radioactive isotopes are easily traced by recording their radiations. ➤*scan*.

Radioactive isotopes can be used for diagnosis, and have a limited place in the treatment of disease. If diseased tissue has a special affinity for an element, a radioactive isotope of the element can be used to suppress or destroy the tissue. For instance, the thyroid gland collects nearly all the iodine in the body, and a dose of radioactive iodine should suppress cancer of the thyroid; unfortunately the cancer cells are abnormal and do not necessarily assimilate iodine.

itch. 1. = ➤*scabies*.
   2. A little understood sensation. No nerve-endings have been identified as 'itch endings' in the way that special endings for pain, touch, heat, and cold, and the pathways that carry these sensations to the brain, can be at least provisionally identified. There is evidence that itch may be carried by the same nerve fibres as pain, but it is not conclusive. Since 1830 it has been generally accepted that one nerve fibre does only one job, but it is possible that slight stimulation might cause one sensation and stronger stimulation another. Scratching temporarily replaces itch with slight pain. Why itch should so readily arise without any stimulation at all, merely from thinking about it, remains a mystery.

IUD. Intrauterine device; ➤*contraception*.

IVP. Intravenous pyelography. ➤*kidneys* (3).

J

Jacksonian fit. (J. Hughlings Jackson, 1834–1911, British neurologist.) Focal *►epilepsy.*

jalap. Drug extracted from a Mexican plant, strongly purgative.

Jarisch-Herxheimer reaction. An abnormal response, with inflammation and fever, to the injection of drugs against syphilis and perhaps other infections; variously explained as stimulation of the parasites by inadequate dosage, and as a sudden release of poisons by killing large numbers of parasites.

jaundice. Yellow discoloration of the skin and mucous membranes by excess of the bile pigment in the blood.

Bile pigment is an end-product of haemoglobin, formed as worn-out red blood cells are destroyed. There is always a small amount in the blood. The liver disposes of it and excretes it into the bile, which passes down the bile ducts to the gall bladder and finally into the intestine. Bile pigment accumulates in the blood: (1) if too much is formed; (2) if the liver cells do not dispose of it; or (3) if the bile ducts are obstructed.

Too much pigment is formed with certain types of anaemia, due to excessive destruction of blood cells (*►anaemia* (A. 2)).

The working of the liver cells is impaired by infection (*►hepatitis*), various poisons, and rare chemical defects.

Obstruction of the flow of bile from the liver cells, with reabsorption of pigment into the blood, may occur within the liver from inflammation (hepatitis again; reaction to certain drugs; congestion due to heart failure), or in the larger ducts leading from the liver (diseases of the gall bladder; gall stones).

When jaundice is due to obstruction, no pigment reaches the intestine, and the stools are therefore uncoloured. On the other hand, a large amount of pigment is filtered from the blood by the kidneys, and the urine is dark.

Of the symptoms that may be associated with jaundice, itching is actually due to jaundice, whereas nausea and inability to tolerate fatty food have the same causes as the jaundice itself.

Bile pigment stains connective tissue, and the yellow colour persists for some days after an attack of jaundice is really over.

A trace of jaundice is common in the first few days of life and is not a serious matter. But a severe and dangerous jaundice arises from incompatibility between the baby's blood and the mother's; *►rhesus factor.*

jaw *►maxilla* (upper jaw); *mandible* (lower jaw).

jejunum. Part of the small intestine, from the duodenum to the ileum.

Jenner, Edward (1749–1823). English country practitioner, a pupil of John Hunter. He invented vaccination. For half a century, *inoculation* had been used to prevent dangerous attacks of smallpox. The principle, known for centuries in Asia, was to infect people deliberately from mild cases of smallpox, because as a rule the disease breeds true: mild cases cause mild cases. The person is then immune to all smallpox. Inoculation worked well as regards conferring immunity, but it meant having smallpox and there was no certainty that the attack would be mild or even that it would not be fatal.

Jenner took up a popular belief that people who had had cow-pox, a mild disease, were safe from smallpox. In enough cases to prove the matter, he found that: (1) people who had had cow-pox escaped smallpox during outbreaks in the area; (2) they could not be infected even by inoculation with smallpox; and (3) the same protection could be safely conferred by inoculation with cow-pox, which he called vaccination. The work was published in 1798.

jet lag ►*travel.*

joint. Joints between bones may be fixed (fibrous) or mobile (synovial). The bones of the skull are firmly bound together by fibrous tissue, and no movement between them is possible. The lower ends of the tibia and fibula are similarly joined by fibrous tissue, but this joint allows a small amount of play.

The bodies of the vertebrae are joined by thick pads of fibrocartilage, which are flexible enough to allow some movement without impairing the stability of the column. A similar joint at the angle of the sternum allows the angle to be increased when a deep breath is taken. The symphysis pubis, also a fibrocartilaginous joint, does not move.

A much commoner type is the *synovial joint.* Where the bones touch each other they are coated with smooth and slippery cartilage. The joint is hermetically enclosed by the tough fibrous *capsule,* which is lined with the slippery *synovial membrane.* This membrane exudes clear,

viscous *synovial fluid,* which keeps the joint surfaces moist. The capsule is a continuation of the periosteum, the fibrous sheath of the bones. It becomes considerably thicker than the periosteum, and where it is subject to particular stresses its fibres are arranged in stout bands or *ligaments.* Beyond these *capsular* ligaments, the joint may be strengthened by *accessory* ligaments spanning the bones. A ligament is effective only when it is taut. It serves to limit movement in a particular direction, rather than to support the joint in any position. For instance, the thrust from the hip in striding forwards would be less effective if the joint could be bent backwards as readily as it can be flexed. When the thigh is fully extended, the strong ligament down the front of the hip-joint is tightened and so ensures that the body is pushed forwards and not the thigh backwards. In other positions of the hip, this ligament is slack and does not support the joint. The stability of most joints depends more on muscles than on ligaments. A muscle acting on a joint is anchored to bone on either side of the joint. Its obvious function is to contract and so bring its two points of attachment closer together. But even at rest a muscle exerts a gentle pull, and this pull is maintained in any position, and counteracted by the equal pull of muscles on the other side of the joint. Thus the muscles are adjustable guy-ropes. The principle can be seen at work in the 'Anglepoise' table lamp, which has a jointed skeleton supported by accurately balanced springs.

A ►*sprain* is the result of forcing a joint beyond the limit set by its ligaments, when a ligament becomes torn. A ►*dislocation* is an actual disruption of the joint; the joint surfaces become separated from each other. Any kind of inflammation in a joint is ►*arthritis*. Disorders of particular joints are discussed under the names of the joints (►*shoulder*, *knee* etc.).

joint replacement. For half a century surgeons had considered the possibility of replacing irreparably damaged joints with artificial ones, but the technical problems could not be solved. Live tissues can deal with wear and tear by replacing themselves; artificial ones cannot and so must be extremely durable. They must also be biologically inert, i.e. they must be accepted by the host tissues and not rejected as foreign bodies. In the highly successful artificial hips designed by Sir John Charnley (1911–82) a stainless steel ball articulates with a polyethylene socket that provides at least some of the elasticity of live bone. These parts are anchored with acrylic cement. With a more recent version under trial they are coated with hydroxyapatite, a normal component of bone that might be not merely accepted but actually incorporated into the living structure.

Artificial knees were for a time less successful than hips, but with recent improvements have been doing well. Shoulders and elbows are replaced much less often.

joule. International unit of energy or work, approximately 0.239 calories (1 calorie = 4.187 joules).

jugular veins. Large veins of the neck. Most of the venous blood from the brain leaves the skull by an opening to each side of the foramen magnum, the *jugular foramen* (►*skull*), and enters the *internal jugular vein*. This very large vessel runs vertically down the side of the neck at the outer side of the carotid arteries and under cover of the sterno-mastoid muscle. It ends behind the sterno-clavicular joint, where it meets the *subclavian* vein to form the *innominate vein*.

The *external jugular vein* is a much smaller vessel, receiving blood from the face and the side of the scalp. It runs down on the surface of the sterno-mastoid, to the subclavian vein. The slight bulge of this vein can sometimes be seen through the skin at the side of the neck. A tributary, the *anterior jugular vein*, runs down the front of the neck.

Jung, Carl Gustav (1875–1961). Swiss psychiatrist, ►*psychoanalysis*.

juxtaglomerular apparatus (JGA). A structural unit of the kidneys. It is a group of cells around the arteriole entering each glomerulus; collectively these units form an endocrine gland secreting *renin*, a hormone involved in regulating the blood pressure (►*kidney*; *blood pressure*).

K

kala-azar (Dumdum fever). A tropical fever due to a kind of ►*Leishmania* transmitted by sandflies. The infection is mainly in the bone marrow and lymphatic system. The symptoms include fever, anaemia, and enlargement of the spleen and liver. In untreated cases, the disease is commonly fatal, but there are several effective drugs, mostly compounds of antimony.

Kala-azar is confined to dry regions of north-east Africa and southern Asia.

kaolin. Powdered aluminium silicate, a bland substance used to absorb fluid and irritants from the intestine in the treatment of diarrhoea; also applied externally as a poultice because it retains heat.

Kaposi's sarcoma. (M. K. Kaposi, 1837–1902, Austrian dermatologist.) An uncommon cancer-like disease of the skin, usually of the legs, with lesions resembling blood-blisters. Small isolated lesions may be treated surgically or by irradiation. With more widespread lesions, ►*interferon* therapy is giving encouraging results. This strange condition has recently come to the fore because it is one of the leading causes of death from ►*AIDS*. There is at least a statistical association of Kaposi's sarcoma with lymphoma, a cancer of which one type (*Burkitt's tumour*) also afflicts patients with AIDS. Until the advent of AIDS Kaposi's sarcoma was considered a rarity in developed countries, but was seen more often in poor regions such as Central Africa, where most people suffered from more than one chronic infec-

tion and resistance was low. As with Burkitt's tumour, which was unknown outside Central Africa until it became a complication of AIDS, we may reasonably suspect a virus disease that people with an intact immune system can resist.

keloid (cheloid). Tough lump of fibrous tissue at the site of a scar: it is like an ordinary scar but there is too much of it. Keloids are very unusual on fair skins, but dark-skinned people and especially negroes are prone to them. They are harmless but disfiguring, and although they are easily removed, the operation leaves a scar in which new ones may form.

keratin. A protein; the main component of finger-nails, hair, and the thin, tough outer layer of the skin.

keratitis. Inflammation of the *cornea* (round window at the front of the eye).

kernicterus. Jaundice of new-born infants so severe as to damage the brain. ►*rhesus factor*.

ketosis. Poisoning by ketones (acetone and related substances). These are intermediate products in the combustion of fat in the body. Normally they are quickly broken down to harmless substances – ultimately carbon dioxide and water. But when the chemical disposal of fat is disturbed, as in severe diabetes or starvation, ketones accumulate in the blood. They can then be identified in the urine as a sign that diabetes is not being controlled by treatment, and the breath

353

may smell of acetone. The 'odour of sanctity' may have been the odour of ketosis, due to starvation from prolonged fasting.

kidneys. The adjective *renal* and compounds of *nephr-* refer to these organs (*renal calculus* and *nephrolith* are the same as *kidney-stone*).

1. STRUCTURE

Man has two kidneys, one at each side of the backbone between the thick muscles of the back and the abdomen. A kidney is in fact 'kidney' shaped, like a bean (unlike the heart, which is by no means 'heart' shaped). It is the size of a cupped hand, about 12 cm from top to bottom and 6 cm from side to side; it is 3 cm thick. The concavity or *hilum* faces inwards, forwards, and slightly downwards.

The urine formed by the kidney enters the *renal pelvis*, a funnel-shaped structure in the hilum which narrows to a slender tube, the *ureter*. The ureter passes straight down the back of the abdomen to the bladder, a distance of about 25 cm.

The principal artery and vein of the body, the aorta and the inferior vena cava, lie between the kidneys. From either side of the aorta a very large renal artery enters the renal pelvis; between them these arteries carry about a quarter of the total blood circulating when the body is at rest. (The flow through the kidneys, about 70 litres or 15 gallons an hour, remains constant during wide fluctuations of the total blood-flow.) The blood returns to the vena cava by the renal veins.

The kidneys are embedded in a special kind of fat: ordinary fat is liquid at body temperature, but this is firm. Hence the tendency of the kidneys to slip downwards ('floating kidney') in people who have lost much fat.

Behind, the kidneys are well protected by muscles, and in their upper halves by the 11th and 12th ribs. The liver pushes the right kidney a little lower than the left. The spleen, pancreas, and stomach lie in front of the left kidney, and the duodenum and several loops of intestine in front of the right. An important gland (▸*adrenal*) is perched on the top of each kidney.

The working unit of the kidneys is the *nephron*. Each kidney contains about a million nephrons. Each nephron begins with a small twig from the renal artery. This arteriole breaks up to form a minute tangle of capillary vessels: a *glomerulus*. The capillaries reunite to form small arterioles which make up the *renal tubule*, a long, winding tube headed by a goblet-shaped extension, *Bowman's capsule*, which completely surrounds the glomerulus. The capsule is permeable and serves as a collecting chamber for the fluid extruded from the glomerulus which is to be converted to urine in the tubule. The tubules lead to collecting ducts, which carry the urine to the renal pelvis.

2. PRIMARY FUNCTION

No living cell can withstand much change in its environment. Even slight changes in chemical composition will kill a highly developed structure such as a human nerve cell. The organs mainly responsible for preventing such changes are the kidneys.

Like all capillaries, the glomerulus is permeable and acts as a filter. The blood reaches it at a high enough pressure for some 10 per cent of its volume to be forced into Bowman's capsule and the renal tubule through pores too small to allow blood cells and the large molecules

labels: capsule, glomeruli, tubules, renal vein, renal artery, renal pelvis, ureter

from renal artery, Bowman's capsule, glomerulus, renal tubule, collecting tubule, loop of Henle, to renal vein

(Left) *section of kidney*;
(right) *enlarged diagram of nephron*

of most proteins to pass. The fluid entering Bowman's capsule – the glomerular filtrate – thus consists of everything in the blood except cells and proteins, namely water, salts, nutrients such as sugar (glucose) and the amino-acids of which proteins are built, and waste products. It is filtered at a rate of 120 ml per minute, which would dispose of all the water in the body in about 5 hours, together with a couple of ounces of sugar and half a pound of salt.

In the tubules this large volume of filtrate is changed to a small volume of urine. Of the 120 ml of water, all but 1 ml is returned to the blood. In general, nutrients are also reabsorbed. The tubules can return nearly all of the glucose in a normal glomerular filtrate to the blood, but they cannot deal with an overload. People with diabetes have an excess of glucose in their blood, and therefore in the glomerular filtrate; some of the excess passes along the tubules to be lost in the urine.

355

There is a special arrangement for salt: reabsorption is adjusted to need. If the body is short of salt, hardly any reaches the urine, but if there is an excess the concentration of salt in the urine can reach 2 per cent. This is an important figure, because sea water averages 3 per cent. Therefore if a man drinks a pint of sea water he must pass a pint and half of urine to get rid of the salt, and so runs a greater risk of dying from lack of water than a man who drinks nothing.

Waste products tend to remain in the tubules to be excreted in the urine. The most abundant is urea, an end-product of protein breakdown. About half of the urea in the glomerular filtrate returns to the blood and half reaches the urine. Since over 99 per cent of the water in the filtrate is returned, the net effect is that urea is concentrated 60-fold: in other words, 1 ml of urine contains as much urea as 60 ml of blood.

In addition to the useless and potential waste products of the body's own chemistry, the kidneys excrete alien substances such as drugs. Many are inactivated in the liver before reaching the kidneys, but some drugs are concentrated in the tubules and may damage them. Notorious among these are commonplace analgesics such as phenacetin, and some antibiotics.

The kidneys also help to regulate the acidity of the body fluids. In health, this is very slightly alkaline (pH about 7.4). Small changes are harmful, and large changes are lethal. Because many by-products of body chemistry are acidic a constant tendency to acidosis has to be overcome. The first line of defence is elimination of carbon dioxide, equivalent to carbonic acid, from the lungs (►*respiration* (2)). But this mechanism is suitable only for immediate adjustments. It is soon exhausted if there is no other means of getting rid of acid. The kidneys provide two or three pathways. They form ammonia, which neutralizes acids to form ammonium salts. They receive alkaline phosphate (Na_2HPO_4) from the blood but excrete acid phosphate (NaH_2PO_4) into the urine; in effect the phosphate takes up acid. And there are probably other mechanisms.

Regulation of tubular reabsorption. As a rule a man passes about 1.5 litres of urine daily, but this amount can vary greatly in accordance with demand. The amount of the glomerular filtrate – 120 ml per minute or 160 litres daily – is almost constant, but the proportion of this huge quantity of water reabsorbed in the tubules can be adjusted. Normally, over 99 per cent returns to the blood. Thus reabsorption need only be reduced by 1 per cent for the amount of urine to be more than doubled. A sensory organ in the hypothalamus, in the floor of the brain, responds to slight changes in the dilution of the blood. This organ governs the release of anti-diuretic hormone (ADH) from the pituitary gland. ADH promotes reabsorption in the tubules, thus conserving water and reducing the volume of the urine. By curbing it the rate of urine formation can be increased tenfold or more. People with the uncommon disease *diabetes insipidus*, who lack ADH, may pass as much as 20 litres of urine (about 4 gallons) in 24 hours, because instead of 99 per cent they can reabsorb only 90 per cent or less of the glomerular filtrate.

While the amount of urine can be increased to meet any likely excess of water, it cannot be safely reduced to less than about 600 ml, say a pint, per day. This is the least amount that will carry away waste products.

Factors other than a relative lack of water can stimulate release of ADH and so diminish the volume of urine. These include severe emotional upsets, and normal sleep.

The amount of salt in the urine is determined by a hormone from the adrenal glands, *aldosterone*. This hormone increases the reabsorption of sodium in the tubules. It is released in response to lack of salt, and also to lowered blood pressure. Indirectly, it affects the volume of urine, because a large amount of salt excreted in the urine requires a large amount of water to dissolve it. Conversely, if an excess of salt is retained in the body, water is also retained. This is why abnormal collections of fluid in the body, e.g. with heart disease, can be dispersed by reducing the amount of salt in the diet.

3. SECONDARY FUNCTIONS

The kidney is also an endocrine gland, i.e. it secretes *hormones*. Some of the endocrine tissue is found in the *juxtaglomerular apparatus* (JGA). This consists of cell clusters around the arterioles entering the glomeruli. The clusters respond to decreased blood pressure in the arterioles by releasing a hormone, *renin*, into the circulation. Renin activates a protein in the blood, angiotensinogen, to form *angiotensin*, which raises the blood pressure by constricting arteries elsewhere. Angiotensin also stimulates the adrenals to release *aldosterone*, which causes salt and water to be retained, thereby increasing the blood volume, and so contributes to raising the blood pressure. There are probably several other factors which contribute to this elaborate mechanism for maintaining a constant flow of blood to the kidneys. Sometimes the pressure has to be raised to a level that endangers other organs and, in fact, the kidney itself may be damaged by the high pressure that it has promoted.

The hormones secreted by the kidneys also include *kinins*, which dilate blood vessels and reduce blood pressure, and *prostaglandins*, which have a similar effect. They presumably serve to balance the action of renin, but the interactions are not fully understood.

Erythropoietin, a hormone that stimulates the formation of red blood cells, is secreted by the kidneys in response to a lack of oxygen in the blood, e.g. due to anaemia, severe bleeding, or high altitudes.

4. EXAMINATION OF THE KIDNEYS

The symptoms of renal disturbances are often too vague to suggest any precise diagnosis. They do not necessarily point to the kidneys at all, and indeed the kidneys can be seriously impaired before there are any symptoms. Nor does routine clinical examination shed much light, because the kidneys are almost out of reach. Examination of the urine, on the other hand, provides much information about the kidneys and there are simple bedside tests which reveal protein, blood and other abnormal constituents. If these give positive results, laboratory analysis will provide more detailed information. The microscope may show blood cells, bacteria, or fragments of tissue shed from the kidneys. Examination of the urine is complemented by blood tests to show whether, and to what extent, the kidneys are allowing waste products to accumulate.

Simple X-ray examination does not give a good picture of the kidneys, but the image can be much intensified by *intravenous pyelography* (IVP), when a 'dye' is injected into a vein to prepare the patient. The dye, a compound of iodine which casts a shadow on X-ray film, is rapidly concentrated and excreted by the kidneys. This method not only gives a clear image of the kidneys (if they are working well enough to concentrate the dye) but the rate of excretion roughly indicates their efficiency as well. An alternative method, *retrograde pyelography*, is to inject the dye upwards from the bladder by way of a ►*cystoscope*. This gives a clear image of the renal pelvis even if the kidney is not able to concentrate dye injected intravenously.

Of the more modern techniques, ultrasound (►*ultrasonic waves*) is the simplest for visualizing the kidneys, but does not give any information about their efficiency (unlike IVP). CT and MRI ►*scans* are also useful.

5. DISORDERS

One normal kidney is enough to maintain good health; two kidneys can tolerate a good deal of damage. Even with advanced kidney disease the symptoms are often mild and vague until a very late stage. If the kidneys stop working altogether the patient quickly succumbs to acidosis and poisoning by waste products unless he can be treated.

The effects of disease of the kidneys are more easily classified than the causes.

The symptoms of which the patient is aware are few, and none is specific. Even quite advanced loss of renal function may cause no more than a sense of not being well, with perhaps loss of appetite and, therefore, weight, tiredness and pallor, due mainly to anaemia and acidosis.

Pain is usually experienced in the back below the 12th rib and sometimes spreads to the lower abdomen. It may be associated with inflammation, e.g.

pyelonephritis (see below) although more severe pain can arise from a kidney-stone. Intermittent pain – renal colic – from this cause can be excruciating, making diagnosis fairly straightforward. Other renal pain may be hard to distinguish from other kinds of backache.

Fluid retention, causing increased body weight and later swelling of the tissues or *oedema*, can arise not only from disordered kidneys, but from numerous other causes. Renal oedema is mainly due to loss of protein, which dilutes the blood and reduces the osmotic gradient between the tissue fluid and the plasma (►*oedema* (2)), through leaky glomeruli. This oedema is aggravated by failure of the kidneys to excrete surplus salt. Gross oedema, resulting from heavy loss of protein, is described as the *nephrotic syndrome*.

Altered *output of urine*, either more or less than normal, may point to disturbed renal function. Healthy kidneys keep pace with the body's needs, putting out more or less urine in order to keep the total volume of water in the body constant. With various disorders the kidneys fail to concentrate urine when they should, and the output increases. Normally less urine is formed during sleep than when the subject is awake, which is why healthy people generally sleep through the night without having to wake to pass urine. This ability may be lost with renal disease. Excessive volume of urine (*polyuria*) is distinct from frequent passage of small amounts of urine, which is a common symptom of irritation in the bladder, e.g. inflammation (*cystitis*), or of an enlarged prostate, or simply of anxiety. An abnormally low output of urine (*oliguria*) or no output (*anuria*) at all may be due to acute renal disease, or to mechanical obstruction to flow.

Blood in the urine is a symptom that always needs prompt investigation. The possible causes include most disorders of the urinary system.

High blood pressure, which so often accompanies renal diseases, is sometimes blamed for headaches or other unhelpful symptoms, but more often it causes no definite symptoms at all.

Disorders of the kidneys range from congenital defects to tumours and infection.

Congenital defects are commoner in the kidney than in any other part of the body. Structural anomalies range from absence of kidneys, which the baby does not survive, to simple misplacements, fusion of the two kidneys, and unusual arrangements of the renal pelvis, which are seldom important. Anomalies that need surgical correction include those that interfere with the flow of urine, and occasionally those that cause high blood pressure by disturbing the renal blood-vessels. Other congenital disorders, chemical rather than structural, affect the renal tubules, causing them to excrete substances into the urine that should return to the blood. Substances affected by disorders of this kind include glucose, various aminoacids and phosphates (causing renal *rickets*); most or all of these are affected in the *Fanconi* syndrome. An entirely different type of congenital lesion is faulty development of microscopic structure, resulting in the gradual formation of cysts which spread through the kidney like bubbles.

Injuries of the kidneys are not very common, because they are well protected. But a heavy blow directly over a kidney can bruise or even tear it, and like any part of the body the kidneys can be damaged by gunshot or stab wounds. Bleeding is the danger. Blood in the urine after an injury is an obvious pointer, though it can just as easily come from a severe bruise as from an actual wound. Damaged kidneys are likely to heal without intervention, but close and continuous observation is essential. A badly torn kidney may have to be removed to stop dangerous loss of blood, but one intact kidney is more than enough to maintain health.

Tumours of the kidney include benign growths that cause little or no trouble, and cancers that, taken in time, can be removed with a fair chance of success. These include one of the few cancers of infancy, *nephroblastoma* or *Wilms' tumour*.

Systemic ►*lupus erythematosus*, which can lead to the degeneration of small arteries and connective tissues in many parts of the body, is especially liable to damage the kidneys.

Stones, or calcium deposits, often form with or without symptoms in the kidneys (►*calculus*).

Infection is very common. The agent, usually *E. coli*, a normal inhabitant of the lower intestine, infects the bladder (►*cystitis*), from which it goes up the ureters to infect the renal pelves of the kidneys (►*pyelitis*). Infection can also be carried to the kidneys from other parts of the body in the blood-stream, and is liable to cause abscesses. Infection of this later type includes tuberculosis.

Nephritis, or inflammation of the kidney, includes a very wide range of conditions, some of which should perhaps not be so called. For more than half a century the whole group was simply known as *Bright's disease*. Then it became nephritis and was broken down into 3 groups – acute, subacute and chronic; then chronic nephritis itself was divided into 3 types. With more and more understanding of the nature of nephritis its classification has become less and less understandable. When involving inflammation of the kidneys, the pyelitis of the last paragraph is rightly renamed *pyelonephritis* because the infection always involves the *kidney substance* as well as the *renal pelvis*. As the elements most involved are the tubules and the supporting interstitial tissue, the condition is also called *tubulointerstitial nephritis*, at least in its later stages when it exists as an aftermath of an acute infection. But a similar condition may follow *gout*, of which it is the most serious complication, and chronic poisoning by various agents, including analgesic drugs.

More often, the most seriously affected elements are the glomeruli, and *glomerulonephritis* accounts for most cases of the Bright's disease of past generations. The effect of this inflammation or degeneration of glomeruli (associated with some damage to other elements) is to produce any or all of the symptoms listed above, or in some cases no symptoms until the disease is advanced. *Acute glomerulonephritis* is a severe illness, with a frequently sudden onset of blood in the urine, followed by oedema, raised blood pressure, and sometimes loss of renal function. In most cases it is a reaction to streptococcal infection such as scarlet fever or sore throat. The antibodies produced in the body to combat the streptococci react, in a few unlucky patients, with kidney cells in the same way as they react with the heart muscle to cause rheumatic fever in other patients. Most people recover completely; the younger the patient the better the outlook. But sometimes there is lasting damage to the kidneys.

Chronic glomerulonephritis is an end-result of many different kinds of renal disease. It is so insidious that many cases remain undiagnosed until the kidneys almost cease to work. The first indication may be the chance discovery at a routine medical examination of protein or blood cells in the urine. The condition may be subdivided into different microscopical pictures, showing proliferation of cells in the vessels of the glomeruli, or thickening of the surrounding membrane, or very little change to account for the poor renal function. Often circulating antibodies react to some element of the nephrons, but while this strongly suggests an autoimmune disease (►*immunity* (7)), it does not quite amount to proof.

6. TREATMENT OF KIDNEY DISEASE

Some kidney conditions can be treated specifically by methods designed to attack causes. Infection responds to the same measures as infection elsewhere and often requires less than the usual doses of antibiotics because they are concentrated in the kidneys. Injuries are managed like any other internal injuries, loss of blood being the first concern. Tumours and obstruction, e.g. by a stone or an enlarged prostate, are usually treated surgically.

The causes of many disorders of the kidney are still unknown or incompletely understood, or, if they can be identified, sometimes no means of attacking the cause has been found. Since renal function has to be seriously impaired before there are any symptoms, early diagnosis is difficult and, unlike the liver, the kidneys cannot regenerate lost tissue.

Renal failure, i.e. impairment enough to cause symptoms, can be treated in one of three ways, regardless of the underlying cause.

A patient with renal failure is poisoned by waste products from the breakdown of protein in the diet, by imbalance of inorganic components of the body fluids (salts etc.) and by accumulation of acids in the body. A diet can be devised to contain only those substances that will be utilized, leaving no waste, and with salts and sources of acid adjusted to maintain the correct balance. Water is limited to the patient's output.

The introduction of treatment by ➤ *dialysis* has meant that it is possible to live even if the kidneys are not working at all. The method depends on the fact that if fluids are separated by a porous membrane, substances dissolved in the fluid on one side will, if their molecules are smaller than the pores, migrate to establish similar concentrations on either side of the membrane. In the tubules of a healthy kidney, this process is supplemented by active retention of necessary substances and rejection of unwanted ones. With a passive membrane this can be imitated if a body fluid is on one side and a solution of the desirable substances on the other. Then only unwanted matter leaves the body fluid. The patient's own peritoneum, lining his abdominal cavity, is a suitable membrane, and a dialysing solution can be run into the cavity through a tube. But for long-term treatment *haemodialysis* is usually preferable to peritoneal dialysis. Haemodialysis employs an artificial kidney, i.e. a machine with a synthetic membrane over which a stream of the patient's blood, taken from an artery, flows so that waste products pass into the dialysing solution before the cleansed blood is returned to a vein. Generally treatment involves three 3-hour sessions a week, although there is some variation between both centres and individual patients.

Renal failure may be accompanied by severe and intractable anaemia, because the kidneys no longer secrete erythropoietin to promote the formation of red blood cells. Until recently this was untreatable, but by genetic engineering erythropoietin is now available for correcting the deficiency.

The ideal treatment of renal failure is a successful *transplant*. Although there are still many problems to be solved, mostly concerned with rejection of the transplant by the body's defence mechanisms, many thousands owe a new lease of life to this procedure. Fortunately diet and dialysis can keep the patient going while a suitable donor is sought. The use of the antibiotic *cyclosporin* to prevent rejection has greatly improved the prognosis.

Klinefelter's syndrome. A congenital anomaly: a boy grows to become an unusually tall man with defective testes, enlarged breasts and occasional learning problems. The condition arises from having a superfluous X chromosome: XXY instead of the usual male XY; ➤*genetics* (3).

knee. The knee joint is formed between the lower end of the *femur* and the upper end of the *tibia*. The *fibula* plays no part. The joint between the femur and the knee-cap (*patella*) shares the synovial membrane and capsule (➤*joint*) of the knee. The surfaces are by no means a perfect fit, but the disparity is largely overcome by a cartilage or *meniscus* on each side of the joint. A meniscus is a flattened crescent of springy fibrous tissue, thick at the rim and wafer-thin at the inner edge.

The ligaments of the knee are very strong. They are at both sides, behind, and, most unusually, inside the joint. These last are the *cruciate* ligaments, stout bands from the tibia to the notch between the two condyles of the femur. In front, the knee is supported by the *quadriceps* muscle. This huge muscle, forming the front of the thigh, ends as a flat tendon spread over the knee and anchored to the front of the tibia. The patella is a disc of bone embedded in the tendon which slides up and down on the femur as the muscle acts.

The only deliberate movements of the knee are the pendulum-like flexion, by the hamstring muscles, and extension, by the quadriceps. But when the knee is straightened the ligaments are not all pulled taut at the same moment. Those which are still lax allow a slight inward twist of the femur; then all ligaments are tight and the knee is said to be locked. (Locking the knee has a second meaning, defined below.) The beginner on skis disobeys the instruction to bend his knees partly because he is unconsciously bracing them against a fall, but also because by 'locking' his knees he transfers the strain from his tired muscles to his ligaments.

Fractures of the tibia or femur which involve the joint surfaces often need operative treatment, for unless the fragments are exactly replaced the joint is bound to become stiff. Some fractures of the patella give little trouble, but after some bad fractures the patella has to be removed. This operation causes remarkably little disability.

Dislocation of the knee is very unusual, but torn ligaments are common. A complete tear of any of the main ligaments renders the knee unstable, and surgical repair may be needed.

The commonest disorder of the knee is a torn meniscus, usually at the inner side of the joint. A sideways jolt to the slightly bent knee is the usual cause. If the torn meniscus lies flat it gives no trouble, but the torn part tends to curl and block the joint. The knee is then painful and cannot be completely straightened. This limitation of movement is called 'locking' (see above). The patient often acquires a knack of twisting and straightening his knee to replace the tear, but the meniscus is still torn, and lacking a blood supply it cannot heal. The trouble therefore recurs, and the only cure is to remove the meniscus. A knee can function well without menisci, but the success of the operation depends largely on the condition of the muscles: indeed this is true of all surgery of the knee. The ligaments are very strong, but they are effective only when the knee is straight. In all other positions the strength of the knee is the strength of the quadriceps.

The knee is commonly a site of rheumatoid arthritis and also of osteoarthrosis; either can be crippling. Early attempts at replacing the joint, following the spectacular success of hip replacement, often failed. But with the technical problems largely overcome, replacing the damaged knee joint with an artificial one is now a standard procedure.

Koch, Robert (1843–1910). German physician and pathologist. If Pasteur laid the foundations of microbiology, Koch was the principal builder of this science. Much of his early work on bacteria was done while he was a busy general practitioner in Prussia. Pasteur had proved in general terms that bacteria could cause disease. Koch showed which types of bacteria caused particular diseases. He found methods of identifying and classifying bacteria, of growing them in pure culture (i.e. without contamination by other species), and above all of proving whether they were true causes of a disease or mere bystanders. ➤*microbe* (1).

Kocher, Theodor (1841–1917). Swiss surgeon. His career is a bridge between the hazardous and limited surgery before Lister's use of antiseptics and present-day methods. He advanced many branches of surgery, but is especially remembered for his work on the nature and treatment of goitre, for which he received a Nobel Prize in 1909. In recent years, surgery has been more and more divided into specialities, and more and more a team effort. Kocher was for years undoubtedly the best surgeon in the world, a distinction that no one surgeon could claim today.

koilonychia. Thin, concave fingernails, due to lack of iron.

Koplik's spots. (H. Koplik, 1858–1927, American physician.) Very small red spots with white centres, on the inner lining of the cheeks, a characteristic and early sign of measles.

Korsakow's syndrome. (S. S. Korsakow, 1853–1900, Russian neurologist.) Deterioration of the function of nerves and brain, with loss of memory and poor mental co-ordination, sometimes with disturbed sensation or muscular action. Elaborate lies, perhaps to compensate for loss of memory, may be a symptom. The cause is deficiency of B vitamins, often due to chronic alcoholism.

kuru. A lethal infection of the nervous system by a *prion* (➤*slow virus*) confined to a New Guinea tribe. Apparently transmitted by ritual cannibalism, it has become rare now that the rituals have been largely abandoned.

kwashiorkor. A severe form of malnutrition first recognized among children in West Africa but now known to be widespread in the tropics. The condition sets in after weaning, which is sometimes delayed until the age of 2 years. An affected child does not look thin at first sight, because the skin and abdomen are distended with retained water. A swollen liver may add to the pot-belly. There is loss of pigment in the skin and often the hair, which becomes sandy and brittle. The skin changes have been confused with those of *pellagra*. These children have little resistance to other illness, and often die of what should be minor ailments. The digestive organs may become so impaired that the child can no longer absorb good food even if it is provided.

Kwashiorkor was formerly regarded as a pure protein deficiency, but it now seems that the limited supply of protein might suffice if there were enough other food to spare the protein from being squandered as fuel: hence the term *protein-energy malnutrition*. Why these very poor diets afflict some children with kwashiorkor and others with the more predictable emaciation of *marasmus* is not clear. Failure to digest other foods than protein because of intestinal infection may be a factor.

kyphosis. Curvature of the spine producing convexity or arching of the back. The natural curve in the thoracic region of the spine is a slight kyphosis, as opposed to the *lordosis* or hollowing of the lumbar region below.

L

labial. Of the lips.

labium. Lip. *Labia majora, minora*: outer and inner folds of skin of the vulva.

labour. The process by which a pregnant woman is delivered of her baby. (The infant is considered under ▸*birth*.)

The baby in the uterus is surrounded by watery fluid in a closed bag of membrane. He is nourished by the *placenta*, a thick disc attached to the inside of the uterus, where it draws supplies from the mother's blood, and joined to the baby by blood vessels in the *umbilical cord*. The uterus is a hollow muscle with a downward extension, the *cervix*, in the vagina. The cervix is a muscular ring, tightly closed during pregnancy.

In the *first stage* of labour the muscle fibres leading down to the cervix contract at intervals of a few minutes, while those of the cervix itself relax. The effect is to open the cervix and create a passage from the uterus into the vagina. The cervix is drawn up over the lowest part of the baby, normally the head. In advance of the baby's head, a pocket of fluid is trapped; after a time the membrane bursts and the fluid escapes. This may be a signal for the contractions to become stronger and more frequent. With a first baby, this stage can last all day, but it tends to be shorter with later pregnancies. It cannot be timed, because often it has no definite beginning. All through the latter part of pregnancy the uterus contracts and relaxes, and labour is only an intensification of the process.

The *second stage* is the descent of the baby and its actual birth. As soon as the cervix is wide enough the character of the contractions changes. They become more purposeful, and the woman instinctively helps by pushing. The muscle fibres of the uterus remain a little shorter after each contraction, and the baby is pushed down the vagina. There are two obstacles: a sharp bend forwards from uterus to vagina, and the muscles, connective tissue and skin of the floor of the pelvis at the outlet from the vagina, which take some time to stretch.

After the birth of the baby, the *third stage* of labour is a few contractions to expel the placenta and leave the uterus as a tight knot of muscle. There may be waves of contraction (after-pains) for some time after delivery.

Nobody knows why, some 38 weeks after conception, labour should begin. It is probably set off by a chemical stimulus – a hormone, oxytocin, from the pituitary, but why the hormone should suddenly become active remains a mystery. The duration of pregnancy varies more in humans than in other animals, but more than a couple of weeks either side of the average entails risks for the baby. What really matters is not an exact number of days, but the stage of development of the baby at birth. A premature baby has difficulty in surviving as an independent being until it reaches the stage of growth at which it should have been born; and if labour is unduly late the baby may no longer be getting enough nourishment from the placenta, and labour has to be started artificially (▸*induction*).

Contractions of the uterus in the first

stage of labour are often no worse than rather uncomfortable. If there is pain, it is a sort of colic from stretching involuntary muscle; like other internal organs, the uterus does not transmit any other sensation (it is wholly insensitive to cutting or heat). The source of pain in the second stage is more obvious: a large baby is pushed through a narrow and sensitive passage, and although continued pressure tends to numb the skin of the outlet it cannot do so completely.

The amount of pain suffered by any individual woman in labour is partly dictated by her expectations and frame of mind. The uterus transmits signals up the spinal cord, but the interpretation of those signals is the function of the brain. They may be differently perceived by different people. Certainly a woman who expects to suffer (having been filled with tales of horror by relatives and friends) is likely to do so. Equally certainly, by setting up muscular tension which resists the process of birth, the suffering itself is likely to increase.

Training throughout pregnancy (it is useless to wait until confinement), usually by a physiotherapist, teaches women to relax the muscles of the outlet from the pelvis while pushing with their abdominal muscles, making labour quicker and easier. In good hands, this sort of training does much more: it helps to establish confidence and mental relaxation when the time comes. This method has sometimes been derided, perhaps because its merits had been exaggerated, but most women who have given it a serious trial have found it helpful.

When antenatal training achieves its object, 'natural childbirth', there is no need for drugs to relieve pain, but not all women have received this training and those who have do not all find that it

works. The treatment of pain in childbirth is always a compromise. In the first stage, a large enough dose of an antispasmodic drug might take away all pain, but by taking away the spasm would bring labour to a halt. *Pethidine* is both pain-killing and antispasmodic and therefore perfectly suited to relieving the symptom, but it has to be used very cautiously in order not to prolong labour. The second stage brings a new hazard: if the baby is still under the influence of a narcotic drug when he is born, his breathing will be depressed, and his most urgent need in the first few minutes of life is a few deep breaths. Also, during the second stage the attendant needs the mother's cooperation. Hence the caution with which doctors and midwives give analgesic help such as gas and air. Unless delivery is to be assisted by forceps anaesthetics cannot be used until the last few contractions, when they can guide the baby into the open air without help from the mother. Many women find the second stage of labour much less distressing than the last part of the first. Any pain brings with it the irresistible urge to push the baby towards its exit. The pushing, having something to do to help the birth along, makes the pain seem more tolerable: it is positive effort with a recognizable end in view.

Various types of spinal anaesthesia can be induced by injecting a local anaesthetic into the spine. Techniques of this kind can be used either throughout labour, the local anaesthetic being topped up whenever needed, or only in the second stage. Many obstetricians (and mothers) believe that this is the ideal form of childbirth analgesia, giving, in expert hands, a totally pain-free labour to a fully conscious woman. But there are technical problems to killing pain without killing muscular effort, and thus slowing labour down. And the method demands skilled anaesthetists. Only a few hospitals can as yet offer this method to any woman who wants it.

By far the greatest hazard used to be infection (►*puerperal* fever). Now that this is a rarity, labour is usually a safe venture. The remaining dangers are largely mechanical. Most babies are born head first, with the back of the head to the mother's front. Any other position is more difficult, and if possible the baby is manipulated into the natural position before birth.

Delay in the first stage does not matter if the baby's heart beat indicates that it is well; but if either mother or child is distressed Caesarean section may be needed. Delay in the second stage may be due to mechanical obstruction: the baby is too big for the passage, or in the wrong position. If the disparity is obvious, the trouble can be avoided by Caesarean section before labour begins. The *obstetric forceps*, giving a firm but gentle grip on the baby's head, can be used to ease the baby's head past the outlet. Although the midwife tries to prevent injury to the mother's skin and muscles if she can do so without delaying the birth, it is sometimes necessary to make a deliberate cut (*episiotomy*) that can be neatly stitched after the birth; this does much less harm than allowing the tissues to be torn.

Ergometrine, a drug derived from *ergot*, stimulates contraction of the uterus. It is often given at the end of labour to tighten the uterus and prevent bleeding.

It is easy to understand that many women would rather give birth in their own homes than in hospitals. All things being equal nobody could argue with them. But things are not always equal. Although complications are rare nowadays they can occur without warning, and a hospital has the means of dealing with them that nobody's home could provide. Many problems can be predicted, in which case delivery in hospital is mandatory, but sometimes there is no warning of the need for an emergency Caesarean section, or instant resuscitation of a distressed baby. Many drawbacks of hospital confinement, such as rigidly limited visiting hours and keeping mothers apart from their hard-earned babies except at feeding times, are now past history, and inviting husbands to attend confinements, unusual a generation or so ago, is now common practice.

labyrinth. The inner ear, embedded in the temporal bone of the skull, consisting of the organs of balance and hearing.

laceration. An irregular, torn wound (as opposed to an incision or cut).

lacrimal. Of tears, e.g. *lacrimal gland*, where tears are formed, under the upper lid. (There is no need for the fussier spelling *lachrymal*, which seems to have crept into English usage by mistake. At least in technical senses, *lacrimal* has international sanction and a proper pedigree.)

lactation. Formation of milk. ►*breast*; *milk*.

lactose. Milk sugar, a compound of the simple sugars *galactose* and *glucose*, to which it is broken down in the intestine. After assimilation, galactose is converted to glucose.

Laënnec,   René-Théophile-Hyacinthe (1781–1826). French physician with an unsurpassed genius for diagnosis, a pupil of Corvisart. He wrote admirable studies of numerous disorders of the heart and lungs, in particular of tuberculosis, about which he left little to be said until the discovery of the causative microbe at the end of the century. His own early death was due to this disease.

Laënnec is best remembered as the inventor of the ▸*stethoscope*, with the help of which he was able to recognize disorders in the chest much more accurately than anyone before him – indeed quite as accurately as anyone since, given the same equipment. Improvements since his time are due to laboratory investigations, X-rays and the like; not to better clinical technique. The great diagnosticians of the 19th century, of whom Laënnec may be counted the first, used their eyes, ears, and hands to make correct and confident diagnoses that seem to us almost impossible without elaborate technical methods.

The most remarkable feature of Laënnec's discovery was that he himself said practically all that was to be said about its use: his descriptions of normal and abnormal sounds from the heart and lungs might have been written yesterday.

Lamarck, Jean-Baptiste (1744–1829). French naturalist; remembered more for two theories which were discredited (spontaneous generation, and inheritance of acquired characters: ▸*Pasteur*; *evolution*) than for the fact that he was the first man to put forward a theory of evolution.

laminectomy. Surgical operation: removal of a plate of bone (lamina) at the back of one or more vertebrae to expose the spinal cord.

Langer's lines. (Carl von Langer, 1819–87, Viennese anatomist.) Lines along which most of the supporting fibres in the skin are arranged. They determine the direction in which the skin folds if lightly pinched, and they concern the surgeon because incisions along them are less likely to stretch than those across them. Thus an appendix scar running almost transversely, a little tilted down towards the mid-line, may be almost invisible, while a vertical one would be obvious. The surgeon's choice, however, is not always free since access must, for the patient's safety, take precedence over the cosmetic result.

lanolin. Wool fat, a bland substance used on its own to soften hard skin, or mixed with more active ingredients as the basis of various ointments.

laparoscope. A lighted tube with an optical system by which the abdominal organs can be examined. The instrument is inserted through a 6 mm (¼ in) incision to give information that without it would probably need a full-scale abdominal operation. The laparoscope can be used not only for diagnosis but for quite elaborate surgery such as removing gall stones or even the whole gall bladder.

laparotomy. Literally: cutting the flank or loin. The accepted meaning is any surgical operation in which the abdomen is opened, especially in the sense of *exploratory laparotomy*, when the exact diagnosis is still in doubt until the abdominal organs are inspected.

lardaceous disease ▸*amyloid disease.*

laryngitis. Inflammation of the larynx caused by spread of infection either downwards from the nose and pharynx or, less often, upwards from the lungs or trachea. Sore throat, dry cough, and hoarseness are the symptoms; apart from infection they can arise from any irritation of the vocal cords such as excessive smoking or shouting. An attack of laryngitis seldom lasts more than a few days, and since there are various other causes of hoarseness (►*larynx*) persistent symptoms need to be investigated.

Inhaled air is normally warmed and moistened in the nose before it reaches the larynx. When the nose is blocked, e.g. by a common cold, air breathed through the mouth is still cold and dry when it reaches the larynx. This seems to irritate inflamed vocal cords, and is a good reason for staying indoors with laryngitis. Inhaled steam helps because it is moist and warm. Menthol, friar's balsam and other traditional adjuncts to the steam have a medicinal aroma which assures the patient that the treatment is doing him good. Perhaps the more important effect of the inhalation is on the nose; it may clear the airway.

There is no evidence that gargling has any effect on laryngitis.

laryngoscope. Instrument for examining the inside of the larynx. For *direct laryngoscopy* an illuminated tube or half-tube is passed behind the tongue, and behind the epiglottis: this is possible only if the parts have been anaesthetized and the patient is in exactly the right position on an operating table, because the epiglottis is very sensitive and the axis of the larynx is at right angles to that of the mouth.

The usual and older method is *indirect laryngoscopy*. A dentist's angled mirror is held against the soft palate and used to reflect light into the larynx and an image of the larynx to the surgeon. The lamp can be worn on the surgeon's forehead or placed beside the patient and reflected into the patient's mouth by a mirror with a hole through which the surgeon peers.

This method gives an excellent view of the parts behind the tongue, including the vocal cords. If the mirror is turned upwards the nasopharynx, above and behind the soft palate, can be examined.

Manuel Garcia, a teacher of singing who studied the movements of his own vocal cords, is usually credited with the invention of laryngoscopy (1854), and the Hungarian surgeon Czermak with introducing it to medical practice (1858). But the method had already been discovered, and ignored, at least three times: by Levret (Paris, 1743), Bozzini (Frankfurt, 1807), and Senn (Geneva, 1827).

larynx. The voice-box at the entrance to the windpipe (*trachea*) in the front of the neck. The trachea and lungs arise in the embryo as an offshoot from the pharynx, which is a part of the digestive tube. At the entrance to the trachea from the pharynx a valve has been evolved, to be closed during swallowing. The voice is a secondary function; birds have a larynx but their voices come from the *syrinx* further down the trachea.

The larynx is enclosed by cartilages. Below it is supported by a firm ring, the *cricoid cartilage*, which is the entrance to the trachea proper. The much larger *thyroid cartilage* is perched on top of the cricoid. It is shaped like a snow-plough, with its two halves widely separated behind and meeting in front to form the Adam's apple. From inside the Adam's apple two fibrous ridges run back; these are the *vocal cords*. Each cord is attached behind to a small, mobile triangle of cartilage (*arytenoid cartilage*). The arytenoids slide on the cricoid, between the two halves of the thyroid cartilage.

The cartilages of the larynx have a complex set of muscles to move them. At most times the arytenoids are kept apart and the vocal cords, joined in front, form a V-shaped opening, the *glottis*, through which one breathes. For swallowing, the arytenoids are drawn together and the gap is closed. At the same time a flap of cartilage behind the tongue, the *epiglottis*, drops like a hinged lid over the larynx. For speech, the arytenoids are also drawn together, but the epiglottis stays up. The thyroid cartilage is tilted on the cricoid to vary the length and tension of the vocal cords and so adjust the *pitch* of the voice. The *volume* of sound depends on the amount of air delivered from the lungs (▶*respiration* (1)). The *timbre* or quality of sound, which makes the difference between the vowels, depends on the configuration of the upper air-passages, including the nose and its sinuses. It is adjusted by changing the shape of the mouth.

1. Disorders

A blow on the Adam's apple can fracture the thyroid cartilage. This is a serious injury because it jeopardizes the airway. An artificial inlet for air in the trachea (tracheostomy) may be needed at once, and the fracture itself may need surgical repair.

The vocal cords can be damaged by the strain of shouting or singing; the usual injury is rupture of a small blood vessel. This may cause a swelling (*polyp*) like a small berry on the cord. A polyp causes hoarseness or even temporary loss of the voice, but fortunately it is easily removed without ill effects.

Acute inflammation of the larynx (▶*laryngitis*) often follows infection elsewhere in the air-passages, e.g. a common cold above or acute bronchitis below the larynx. ▶*Diphtheria* is especially dangerous if it involves the larynx, for the airway is liable to be blocked. When diph-

theria was common this was the usual reason for tracheostomy. Tuberculosis occasionally spreads from the lungs to cause chronic laryngitis.

The muscles of the larynx are supplied by the recurrent laryngeal nerves. These are branches of the vagus nerves. They run down into the root of the neck – the left nerve well into the thorax – and then up, alongside the trachea, to enter the larynx from below. Both nerves are exposed to injury during operations on the thyroid gland, in which they are practically embedded as they run upwards, and the left nerve may be involved in disease such as cancer of the left lung, causing paralysis of the left vocal cord and hoarseness.

A cancer of a vocal cord the size of a pin's head is enough to cause hoarseness. At this stage the chance of removal and complete cure is extremely good. If the cords are not involved, cancer of the larynx is less obvious and the outlook is less good. The necessary operation can be anything from a nick in the vocal cord which heals completely to removal of the whole larynx. Even after the most drastic operations patients can learn to speak at least enough to make themselves understood by swallowing air and talking in controlled belches.

▶*pharynx*; laryngoscope.

laser. Light Amplication by Stimulated Emission of Radiation, a means of intensifying and concentrating light. Ordinary light is comparable with a leaderless mob, and a laser beam with a column of trained soldiers. Light is as much a form of energy as heat, electricity or the potential (stored) energy of water behind a dam or of fuel, and like them can be converted to any other form. The organized energy of a laser can be precisely directed to a target without disturbing adjacent structures.

Several kinds of laser are used medically. The simplest is as a ►*cautery*, converting the energy of light to heat that coagulates and seals damaged tissues in the same way as boiling an egg causes it to set. As the energy is strictly localized adjacent tissues are unaffected; a suitable laser can make clean and bloodless incisions. Skin blemishes such as the congenital 'port-wine stain' often respond to laser therapy.

More destructive lasers cause solid matter to disintegrate. Possible uses include clearing blocked blood vessels and destroying calculi such as gall stones.

Light can promote chemical change (as shown by photography). Converting an inert drug to a form able to attack cancer cells at the exact site of the disease is an exciting prospect.

Lasers are especially valuable in eye surgery. They can seal a torn or detached retina, or disperse clusters of vessels or fibrous tissue that threaten sight with conditions such as diabetic retinopathy and ►*retrolental fibroplasia*; in many cases of ►*glaucoma* they can replace open surgery, and lasers can even correct optical defects by reshaping the cornea, thus obviating the need for spectacles.

Lassa fever. A severe virus infection, first observed at Lassa, Nigeria, in 1969. The virus is carried by a rat, which is thought to spread it by contaminating food. Symptoms are most obvious in the throat and chest, but the virus infects the bloodstream and may attack almost any organ. In some outbreaks the death rate has been over 40 per cent. No specific treatment is effective, but good nursing improves the outlook.

lathyrism ►*food poisoning* (3).

latissimus dorsi. Large flat muscle of the back; its fibres arise from the spines of the vertebrae from the 7th thoracic downwards, and from the back of the pelvis. They converge on a small flat tendon attached to the humerus a little below the shoulder.

The muscle forces the arm down and back, as in swimming or climbing.

laudanum. Tincture of opium; an alcoholic extract of opium formerly much used as a narcotic.

Laveran, Alphonse (1845–1922). French army doctor. He discovered the parasite of ►*malaria*.

laxative = ►*purgative*.

LE = ►*lupus erythematosus*.

lead. Salts of lead, e.g. lead acetate, have been used as astringents on the skin. A lotion of lead acetate is supposed to be cooling and good for sprains, but cold water probably does as well without being poisonous.

Lead and its compounds have many industrial uses, and in the 19th century lead poisoning was a common and serious occupational disease. The body has no means of getting rid of lead. Small amounts regularly inhaled or swallowed accumulate, and in time large amounts may be stored, mostly in bone in the place of calcium. Symptoms vary from case to case. The commonest is *lead colic*, a severe abdominal pain; others are anaemia, and damage to nerves or the brain. The precautions now used in all industries involving lead have made poisoning a rarity. Large supplements of calcium in the diet help to displace lead from the bones, and the chelating agent EDTA forms an inert compound with lead that is excreted in the urine.

Leeuwenhoek, Antony van (1632–1723). Draper, of Delft, Holland; in his spare time the most celebrated of all microscopists.

The compound microscope, invented some years before Leeuwenhoek's birth, had technical faults that were not overcome until the 19th century; it was then less efficient than the simple magnifying glasses that Leeuwenhoek ground for himself. With the aid of a tiny biconvex lens, Leeuwenhoek accurately observed and described details that a beginner with an expensive modern microscope can easily overlook.

He showed that muscles are composed of fibres, and recorded the alternating light and dark bands or stripes across the fibres (the bands are about 1/20,000 inch wide). He gave the first descriptions of spermatozoa, studied the flow of blood through capillary vessels (first seen by Malpighi), studied red blood cells of various species, noticing that those of fish had nuclei whereas human red cells had none, and in 1675 observed microbes (protozoa) in water. In a report published by the Royal Society, London, in 1683, he described bacteria from his mouth (▸*microbe*).

leg. In descriptive anatomy the leg is only the part of the lower limb between the knee and the ankle, as distinct from the *thigh*.

The skeleton of the leg is the ▸*tibia*, which carries the weight, with the slender ▸*fibula* attached at each end to its outer side. Unlike the radius and ulna in the forearm, these two bones are rigidly joined to each other; there is no significant movement between them.

There are three groups of muscles: the *extensors* of the ankle and foot between the two bones in front, the *flexors* behind, forming the bulge of the calf, and the *peroneal* muscles at the outer side. At the inner side the flat surface of the tibia – the shin – is covered only by skin and fibrous tissue. The actions of the muscles are described under ▸*ankle* and ▸*foot*.

The nerves are branches of the ▸*sciatic* nerve. The ▸*popliteal* artery runs behind the knee, below which it divides into anterior and posterior tibial arteries. These are deeply buried in the extensor and flexor muscles, but they emerge near the ankle and their pulses can be felt on the top of the foot and immediately behind the lower end of the tibia. The veins accompanying these arteries are rather small, and much of the blood returns by the ▸*saphenous veins* just below the skin.

In comparison with other parts of the body the circulation of blood in the legs is precarious, and very little interference with it can be tolerated. Gravity resists the return of blood and can be overcome only if the valves in the saphenous veins are competent. If they fail, blood collects in the veins and stagnates, and the nutrition of the skin is impaired (▸*varicose veins*). Widespread disease of the arteries usually shows itself first in the legs and feet. Elsewhere the reduced flow of blood does not cause symptoms for a long time, but here there is little margin of safety.

Legionnaires' disease. A kind of pneumonia first recognized in 1976 among members of the American Legion at a convention in Philadelphia, though with hindsight it is clear that there had been earlier unrecognized outbreaks. The cause is a bacterium, *Legionella pneumophila*. The disease usually affects groups of people sharing a building such as a hospital or a hotel. The bacteria tend to lurk in places such as water-tanks, air-conditioning units and other static or sheltered water.

The infection is most obvious in the lungs, but often involves other organs. Many patients have died before the disease has been identified because *L. pneumophila* is difficult to isolate. The diagnosis is proved by a sharp increase of antibodies to the bacteria in the patient's blood, but this does not happen for 3 weeks or more after infection. Therefore the first victims of an outbreak may not be recognized until it is too late.

Several antibiotics have been used to treat this disease. The most successful has been erythromycin.

Leishman, Sir William (1865–1926). British army doctor; a pioneer of tropical medicine.

Leishmania. A microscopical parasite similar to that of sleeping sickness; transmitted by sandflies, and causing either localized infection (Delhi boil or ►*oriental sore*) or a dangerous fever (Dumdum fever or ►*kala-azar*).

lens. The lens of the eye is a flexible structure the size and shape of a lentil. Most of the refraction is done by the rounded *cornea* at the front of the eye, which is a fixed component. The lens itself adjusts the focus as the surrounding muscle increases or decreases its curvature.

Leonardo da Vinci (1452–1519). Florentine artist and scientist. Modern medicine begins with the accurate observation of how the human body is constructed, and the first men to reject the anatomical dogma and superstition of the Middle Ages were not the doctors but the artists. Foremost among these was Leonardo, perhaps the first man in 13 centuries to

dispute the doctrines of Galen and trust the evidence of his own eyes. He left incomparable drawings of his dissections of every part of the body, in which he corrected many of the fallacies that had prevented medical science from advancing. As an engineer he was especially interested in the action of muscles, and he came as near as anyone before Harvey to understanding the circulation of blood.

Leonardo's discoveries were not directly helpful to medicine, because they were not published; but the example of the artists encouraged doctors to study anatomy in the only rational way: from the human body and not from ancient texts.

leprosy (lepra). A disease once found in all countries but now almost confined to the tropics, due to *Mycobacterium leprae* (►*Hansen's bacillus*), a microbe almost indistinguishable from that of tuberculosis. The infection is confined to the skin and nerves.

One form, *lepromatous* leprosy, causes raised blotches and lumps on the skin (including the well-known leonine facies or lion-face). The surfaces of the blotches may break down to form ulcers. The other common form, *tuberculoid* leprosy, affects nerves, causing patches of skin to lose all sensation, or sometimes only the sense of pain. There are also visible changes in the skin, more or less coinciding with the loss of sensation; they include loss of hair and, in dark skins, of colour. These areas of paler than normal skin are as near as one gets to the 'white as snow' of biblical lepers.

There are also *indeterminate* and *borderline* cases, which may develop into either lepromatous or tuberculoid forms.

The crippling deformities of advanced

leprosy are due to the involvement of nerves. They include damage to joints by paralysis of muscles, and loss of tissue (notably fingers and toes) from both paralysis of blood vessels and unnoticed burns or other injuries.

Only the florid lepromatous form of leprosy is infectious, and even this is difficult to contract. Leprosy is very rare except among people who live in the closest contact with lepers. It is quite exceptional even for doctors and nurses in leprosaria to catch the disease.

Until about 1947 the standard drug for leprosy was chaulmoogra oil, which was not very effective. But research to find a sulphonamide to cure tuberculosis produced *dapsone* and other sulphone drugs. They do not cure tuberculosis, but they work well against leprosy. The drawback is that treatment has to be prolonged (two years or even longer), and the patient's bacteria may develop resistance to the drug. The antibiotic *rifampicin* is now routinely added to dapsone, and with more virulent cases *clofazimine* is added as well. The treatment must still be prolonged.

Even if current drugs do not always cure leprosy they at least check its progress, and they make the patient non-infectious, thus protecting the next generation. If the ten million or so lepers scattered through many of the warmer parts of the world could have even an incomplete course of drugs this disease could probably be eradicated, and the campaign to do so is high on the list of priorities of the World Health Organization. The traditional leprosarium where lepers live and work and marry away from the world is already giving place to dispensaries where lepers attend for treatment while living safely with healthy people.

Leptospira. A *spirochaete* or spiral bacterium. Several species cause disease in animals that occasionally spread to man; the best known is ►*Weil's disease.*

lesion. Disturbance of the structure or function of a part of the body, such as a wound, abscess, tumour, or chemical abnormality.

leuc(o)-; leuk(o). Prefix = 'white' (blood cell, matter in the brain, as opposed to grey matter, etc.).

leukaemia. Leukaemia is a cancer-like disease of the white blood cells. Whereas most cancer grows and spreads from a single focus, leukaemia is a widespread affection of the bone marrow and other blood-forming tissue. The essential disorder seems to be failure of developing white cells to mature. Fully developed, effective white cells cannot reproduce themselves; after a life-span of a few days or weeks they are replaced by new cells. But leukaemic cells retain the ability to multiply, and they do not develop to a stage at which they can function as a defence against infection. As the disease progresses, these useless immature cells displace normal white cells, and the patient is as much at the mercy of infectious diseases as someone with no white cells at all. The abnormal activity in the bone marrow also encroaches on the formation of red blood cells and platelets, so that the patient becomes anaemic, and his blood does not clot properly. Although in some very acute cases the patient may live only a few months, it may be many years before serious symptoms appear – in the most chronic cases, 20 years or more. Unhappily, it is often in children that leukaemia progresses most rapidly. This is one of the forms of cancer that is becoming commoner, especially in the most developed countries.

The term leukaemia is a Greek rendering of 'white blood', Virchow's description of a case in which there were so many white cells that the blood had a milky appearance. In health, the number of these cells is not more than 10,000 per cubic millimetre. With leukaemia, counts up to 300,000 have been recorded.

Leukaemia is easier to study than other forms of cancer, because so much can be learnt from a drop of blood. Even with the recent increase, leukaemia is not very common, but many of the lessons learnt from it can be applied to cancer in general.

In some animals, leukaemia can be caused by a virus; this form of the disease can be transmitted to other animals. It is now practically certain that virus infection also plays a part in human leukaemia.

Leukaemia is slightly commoner among the relations of people with leukaemia than in the general population, but the difference is not enough to prove a hereditary basis. On the other hand, structural changes in one of the ►*chromosomes* are regularly found, but these could be a result rather than a cause of the disease. The affected pair of chromosomes (no. 21) is the pair which is abnormal in ►*Down's syndrome* – a disorder often associated with leukaemia.

Some apparent recoveries in the past were probably misdiagnosed cases of glandular fever, but with chemotherapy complete recovery, at least from some forms of leukaemia, is possible nowadays. Even when a cure is not possible, life may be prolonged or at least its quality may be improved. The object is to suppress the division and reproduction of cells. The rapidly dividing leukaemic cells are more susceptible than healthy cells, so that the treatment can be adjusted to suppress their activity without greatly damaging healthy cells. A wide range of drugs is now available, variously suited to the different types of leukaemia and also to individual patients. Effectiveness has always to be balanced against side-effects. In the end, leukaemic cells may adapt themselves to the treatment, but it may be many years before this happens, and in the meantime the patient remains fit; the healthy elements of his bone marrow have a chance to maintain a complement of normal blood cells.

►*cancer*.

leukocyte. White blood cell. ►*blood* (3).

leukoderma. Patches of skin without pigment; ►*vitiligo*.

leukoplakia. Small white patches on a mucous membrane; they are areas where the outer layer is unduly thick. Leukoplakia in the mouth follows prolonged irritation, e.g. from heavy pipe-smoking, poor dental hygiene or chronic infection. A similar condition of the female genital organs is apparently due to deficiency of sex hormones after the menopause. The former condition is treated by removing the cause; the latter by supplying appropriate hormones.

Leukoplakia needs attention because it may be a precursor of cancer.

leukorrhoea. Excess of white or colourless secretion from the vagina; it may be only an exaggeration of the normal secretion, or a symptom of irritation anywhere in the genital organs, such as the common infections with *trichomonas* or *candida*.

leukotomy ➤*psychosurgery*.

LGV = ➤*lymphogranuloma venereum*.

libido. Freud's term for the instinctive sexual drive, which may conflict with civilized behaviour, causing emotional tension.

lichen. Several skin diseases with raised blotches: with *lichen planus* the blotches have a violet sheen, and itch. The cause is unknown, but emotional upsets seem to play some part.

ligament. Fibrous band between two bones at a ➤*joint*. Ligaments are flexible but inelastic; they come into play only at the extremes of movement, and cannot be stretched when they are taut. Any intermediate position of a joint is held entirely by the muscles, which in any case are its main supports. The ligaments set the limits beyond which no movement is possible. 'Double-jointed' simply means that the ligaments are longer than usual and allow a larger range of movement.

A joint can be forced beyond its normal range only by tearing a ligament; this is a *sprain*. Fibrous tissue heals reluctantly, and a severe sprain can be quite as incapacitating as a fracture.

limb. All vertebrates have two pairs of limbs slung from the backbone. The pattern of two fore-limbs and two hind-limbs attached respectively to pectoral and pelvic girdles must have been laid down early in evolution. In birds, reptiles, and mammals even the components of the limbs correspond closely between species, although the proportions are adapted in ways that make external appearances widely different (➤*skeleton*).

Excepting modifications to do with walking upright, human limbs have evolved little from the basic pattern: a girdle composed of three bony elements on either side (fused in the shoulder-blade and hipbone); an upper segment with one long bone (*arm* with humerus, *thigh* with femur); next a segment with parallel long bones (*forearm* with radius and ulna, *leg* with tibia and fibula); next a cluster of small bones (*carpus, tarsus*); five straight bones protruding (*metacarpals, metatarsals*); and from each of the five a digit, four digits preserving the primitive three segments and one (thumb, big toe) with only two segments. Because the limbs are twisted during early growth out of their lizard-like position, the back of the arm finally corresponds with the front of the thigh, and the radius and thumb with the tibia and big toe. Most of the muscles correspond fairly closely between the limbs, and the nerves and vessels are roughly alike.

linctus. Medicine to be licked or sipped; a syrupy cough mixture.

lingual. Of the tongue.

liniment. Liquid preparation rubbed into the skin to relieve stiff muscles or aching joints, mainly by ➤*counter-irritation*, but perhaps also by some local effect of drugs absorbed through the skin.

lip(o)-. Prefix = 'fat'.

lipid. A term applied to fat and related substances, including fats and oils (➤*fat*), ➤*cholesterol*, glycolipids, which are the main components of the ➤*myelin* (insulating) sheaths of nerves, and phospholipids, which are distributed throughout the body but principally in brain tissue.

The commonest disorders involving lipids are ➤*obesity* and ➤*atheroma*, which leads to arteriosclerosis. Loss of myelin is an important factor in diseases of the nervous system such as ➤*multiple sclerosis*.

Uncommon congenital disorders arise from lack of an enzyme to dispose of a particular lipid, of which a harmful excess is then deposited in the nervous system and elsewhere. The least rare of these is Gaucher's disease, with abnormal storage of glycolipids.

lipoma. A harmless tumour composed of fat cells, easily removed if it becomes unsightly.

lipoprotein. A compound of a ▸*lipid* with a protein, the lipid using the protein as a vehicle to carry it in the circulation (▸*fat, cholesterol*).

liquorice. The root of the plant *Glycyrriza*, mentioned as a drug by Dioscorides in the 1st century AD and in use ever since as a digestive, laxative, and flavouring agent. A suggestion that liquorice might promote the healing of gastric ulcers was fully confirmed by 1965. A pure substance extracted from the root, carbenoxylone, seems to increase the resistance of the lining of the stomach to erosion by acid, and some other drugs with a similar effect have also been extracted. However, liquorice and its derivatives can cause fluid retention, and also cirrhosis of the liver. A newer drug, *sucralfate*, is preferable, and in any case the principal treatment of peptic ulcers is now with *cimetidine* or *ramitidine*.

Lister, Joseph (Lord Lister) (1827–1912). English surgeon; professor of surgery in Glasgow (1860), Edinburgh (1869), and London (1877); perhaps the most important figure in the history of surgery. By preventing bacterial contamination (▸*infection*), Lister converted surgery from something hardly less dangerous than the diseases it tried to cure into a relatively safe form of treatment: a medieval craft into a modern science. It was

no chance discovery. From his student days Lister had studied the processes of inflammation, and he had already established himself as one of the great surgical investigators before 1867, when he published his first paper on antiseptic surgery. Almost as soon as Pasteur showed how infection took place, Lister showed how it could be avoided.

In addition, Lister made numerous advances in operative technique, including the introduction of satisfactory catgut ligatures.

listeriosis. Infection by a bacterium, *Listeria*, transmitted by various animals and causing meningitis and occasionally other disorders. These respond to treatment with antibiotics.

lithium. Metal of the same class as sodium, with the ability to displace sodium from compounds in solution. Some types of mental disorder are associated with an excess of sodium in the brain cells. These disorders are relieved by giving the patient lithium carbonate, presumably because lithium replaces some of the sodium. The treatment is used mainly with *manic-depressive psychosis*, especially in the manic phase, but good results have also been claimed in some cases of schizophrenia.

lithotomy. Removal of a stone (calculus) from the urinary bladder, one of the oldest surgical operations, prohibited in the Hippocratic Oath (because it was to be done only by specialists). Before the discovery of antiseptics made abdominal surgery safe, the operation had to be done by approaching the bladder from below, between the thighs. The patient lay on his back with hips and knees flexed, like a trussed fowl. The position is still called the *lithotomy position*; it is used mainly for gynaecological examinations and operations.

lithotripsy (extracorporeal shock wave therapy, ESWT). A method of disintegrating stones in the gall bladder, kidney or urinary bladder by focusing shock waves or a laser beam on them.

lithotrite. An instrument for crushing a stone in the bladder.

Little's disease. Cerebral palsy (>*spastic paralysis*).

liver

1. STRUCTURE

The liver, like the salivary glands and pancreas, is an outgrowth of the digestive tube: it is a very large gland opening off the beginning of the small intestine (*duodenum*). In the embryo it is at first a mid-line organ, but its right side soon outpaces the left. At birth, three quarters of the liver is to the right of the mid-line, and in an adult, seven eighths. The liver completely fills the part of the abdomen that is covered by the right side of the diaphragm and rib-cage.

All the blood from the spleen and from the stomach and intestine is passed to the liver by the *portal vein*. It seeps through the substance of the liver and returns to the general circulation by way of the *inferior vena cava*. In the process the liver cells take up materials digested and absorbed from the food.

The blood from the portal vein is the raw material on which the liver works. In addition, fresh blood is supplied by the *hepatic artery*.

The digestive secretion of the liver, the *bile*, flows through small channels to the common bile duct, which opens into the duodenum. Bile is formed continuously but is most needed when there is a meal

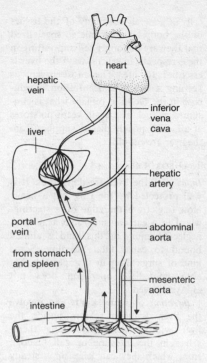

Diagram of portal circulation

to be digested. Between meals most of it is stored in the *gall bladder*, a bag projecting from the bile duct and stuck to the underside of the liver, able to contract and eject bile when stimulated by the presence of food in the duodenum.

2. FUNCTION

The liver is an organ of *digestion*, and of *excretion* (>*bile*).

Its many other functions include *synthesis* of proteins and other substances needed elsewhere, such as glucose, amino acids, and the proteins of the blood; *storage*, especially of glucose (in the form of *glycogen*); and *neutralization* of poisons. These are functions of living

377

cells in general, but many of the tissues of the body have become so specialized that they are no longer self-supporting in these respects. In several ways the liver is essential to life. The most urgent is keeping a steady concentration of glucose in the blood to replace what is consumed as fuel. The brain keeps no stores at all, and quickly dies if supplies from the liver are cut off.

3. DISORDERS

Injuries of the liver are dangerous. It is well protected by the ribs, but a heavy blow (e.g. from the edge of a steering-wheel in a car collision) may tear it. A neglected injury of this kind is almost bound to cause fatal bleeding. Some kind of surgical repair is imperative, but even immediate operation does not always succeed.

Infection of many kinds can involve the liver. Bacteria seldom invade the liver without first establishing themselves in the intestine or gall bladder, from which they can keep up a steady attack. Some viruses, on the other hand, attack the liver directly (►*hepatitis*). The liver is commonly involved in diseases due to more highly developed parasites, e.g. amoebic *dysentery*, *bilharzia*, *hydatid disease*, *malaria*, and *Weil's disease*.

Poisoning of the liver is common, because anything absorbed from the stomach is carried first to the liver, which therefore gets a higher concentration than other organs and is often damaged in the process of neutralizing poisons to protect the rest of the body. Much the commonest poison is alcohol, and many drugs and industrial chemicals can damage the liver.

Impaired circulation in the liver is a common effect of heart disease; it can also arise from disorders of the liver itself.

Tumours of the liver are common for the same reason as poisoning: they are carried from the stomach and intestine. Cancer in these organs sooner or later spreads to the liver unless it is checked. Cancer that begins in the liver is rare in most countries, though it is very common in tropical Africa, where it appears to be associated with hepatitis B.

The *effects* of liver disease are comparatively few. A healthy liver has much more capacity than is ever needed at one time: nothing goes wrong until at least three quarters of its cells are out of action. The minor upsets popularly ascribed to the liver – biliousness, feeling liverish, and the *crises de foie* of French drug advertisements – are usually upsets of the stomach and not of the liver.

If the liver is damaged enough to cause symptoms the symptoms are widespread. With acute hepatitis, ►*jaundice* usually suggests the diagnosis. But with chronic liver disease the symptoms are often vague – feeling unwell, indigestion, perhaps loss of weight – and the liver may not come under suspicion for some time.

But the liver has great power of recovery. If the disease is neither progressive nor so severe that it overwhelms the patient, lost or damaged liver cells regenerate. This is as well, for medical treatment does not greatly affect the liver. As a general rule, treatment is designed to keep symptoms at bay and reduce the demands on the liver to a minimum while it restores itself.

The liver is a much more complex organ than the heart or kidneys, and nobody is likely to devise a machine to take over its many functions. There is a much better chance of overcoming the technical problems of transplanting a whole liver, and some successful transplants of healthy livers have now been performed.

Surgery, transplants aside, has only a small place in the management of liver disease, apart from repair of injuries and drainage of abscesses. But ➤*cirrhosis*, an effect of several kinds of disease, sometimes obstructs the flow of blood through the liver, with damage by backpressure. This can be overcome by an operation to divert some of the blood to the vena cava or some other large vein, leaving enough flow through the liver for its work to continue. These are hazardous operations, but they can be lifesaving.

4. EXAMINATION

The functions of the liver are so diverse that a complete assessment is seldom practicable. Because of the considerable reserves of functional capacity, minor disturbances cause few if any symptoms and are difficult to detect.

Ordinary clinical examination will detect an excess of bile pigment in the blood sufficient to cause jaundice, and show whether this is accompanied by leakage of bile pigment into the urine; but jaundice does not appear until the blood contains several times the normal amount of bile. Chemical study of the blood is needed to reveal a small excess of bile pigment, and whether the excess is due to overproduction or defective excretion.

An enlarged liver can be felt through the abdominal wall, and one can usually get some impression of the texture. The patient's symptoms may suggest the diagnosis, but special tests are often needed. The gall bladder can be examined by X-rays: a drug is given that is excreted in

the bile and is opaque to X-rays, and the gall bladder then throws a shadow. The portal blood vessels can be shown by an analogous method.

There are many chemical tests of liver function, each measuring a single process. Usually several are done at the same time, because one function can be depressed while others remain normal.

When other methods have failed to give an answer, a minute specimen of liver tissue can be taken for microscopical examination through a hollow needle passed between the ribs into the liver.

Various kinds of ➤*scan* are used to get detailed images of structural change in the liver.

loa. A kind of threadworm (➤*filaria*) in West Africa, transmitted by the bite of a fly. It causes severe itching by burrowing under the surface of the skin.

lobar ➤*pneumonia*.

lobectomy. Surgical removal of one of the lobes of a lung, e.g. for cancer or localized chronic infection. Each lobe of a lung is a structural unit that can be removed without disturbing the rest of the lung and with the minimum of risk.

local anaesthetic ➤*anaesthetics*.

lockjaw = ➤*tetanus*.

lordosis. Curvature of the spine convex towards the front, e.g. the natural lordosis in the lumbar region which produces the hollow of the back. (Cf. *scoliosis, lateral curvature*; *kyphosis*, the opposite to lordosis.)

louse. A kind of small insect; several species are parasitic to man. Given decent living conditions and ordinary cleanliness, infestation is not usual, but a louse may transfer itself to anyone and where there is overcrowding or lack of hygiene it may be difficult to prevent lice from thriving. Warfare and natural disasters produce such conditions.

Two of the major epidemic diseases that are notifiable to the World Health Organization are transmitted by lice: typhus and relapsing fever.

LSD ➤*hallucinogen.*

Ludwig's angina. A kind of abscess in the floor of the mouth.

lumbago. Persistent ache in the small of the back, often associated with pain down the leg (*sciatica*). When these two occur together they are generally due to pressure on nerves by a 'slipped disc' (➤*vertebra* (1)). Lumbago alone may have the same cause, or any of the other structures of the back may be strained by faulty posture. ➤*backache.*

lumbar. Of the part of the back between the lowest pair of ribs and the top of the pelvis. The lumbar region is supported by the five lumbar *vertebrae.*

lumbar puncture. Insertion of a hollow needle between two of the lumbar vertebrae (usually the 3rd and 4th) into the spinal canal. The method is used to take a specimen of cerebrospinal fluid for the diagnosis of meningitis and other disorders affecting the brain or spinal cord, or to inject drugs into the spinal canal – e.g. antibiotics for treating meningitis, or anaesthetics for operations on the lower half of the body.

lung

1. STRUCTURE

The two lungs fill most of the ➤*thorax,* which is a smaller cavity than it appears

to be. The heart, which separates the lungs, encroaches more on the left lung than the right. The lower surfaces of the lungs are concave to fit the dome of the ➤*diaphragm.* The lowest limit of the lungs is some 4 fingers' breadth above the margin of the ribs. The narrow apex of each lung rises above the level of the clavicles into the neck. The root or *hilum* of a lung faces inwards to the heart. It contains an array of tubes: the air-passages (main bronchi) and numerous blood vessels. Deep fissures divide the right lung into three *lobes* and the left into two.

The main *bronchus* divides into a branch to each lobe; these divide into segmental bronchi, ten on the right and nine on the left. A *segment* of the lung is roughly a pyramid with its apex to the hilum. The segmental bronchus divides and subdivides into smaller and smaller tubes. The narrowest and most numerous – comparable with the twigs of a tree – are the *bronchioles.* The terminal bronchioles open into small cavities, the air-sacs, each with several compartments called *alveoli.* The whole surface of the alveoli is some thirty times that of the skin.

2. FUNCTION

The bronchi serve merely to carry air to and fro. Their walls are strengthened with rings of cartilage, and contain muscle fibres which adjust their calibre. Their lining membrane secretes mucus; it keeps itself clean by the undulation of hair-like processes (*cilia*) which sweep any fine particles that are breathed in towards the trachea and away. Larger particles set up a cough reflex and are removed more rapidly.

The lining of the terminal bronchioles and alveoli allows gases to pass between the inspired air and the blood in the pulmonary capillaries. This exchange of oxygen and carbon dioxide is the primary function of the lungs; ➤*respiration*.

In addition to respiration, the lungs have certain minor functions. Nearly half a litre of water is lost daily by evaporation into the expired air, an important factor in the fluid balance of the body. This evaporation causes the loss of about 250 Calories, a significant amount of heat but one that cannot be adjusted (➤*temperature*). Animals which do not sweat, such as dogs, depend on this type of heat loss to keep the body temperature down after exertion. When a dog pants, water evaporates from the surface of the tongue, and excess heat is eliminated. Certain volatile substances such as alcohol, and of course carbon dioxide, are excreted through the lungs. A sudden excess of acid in the blood, such as the acid formed in working muscles, can be eliminated as carbon dioxide by deeper breathing.

3. PLEURAL CAVITY

Each lung is wrapped in two layers of thin membrane, the *pleura*. The outer, *parietal* layer lines the inside of the thorax. The inner, *visceral* layer coats the outside of the lung. The two layers merge at the hilum of the lung; elsewhere they are quite separate and free to slide. They are lubricated by tissue fluid. There is thus no friction between lung and ribs. In health the pleural cavity does not really exist, but with disease or injury the layers may be separated, e.g. by watery fluid (*effusion*), air (*pneumothorax*), or pus (*empyema*).

4. EXAMINATION

Common symptoms such as shortness of breath, cough, and pain in the chest can all arise from causes beyond the lungs. The symptoms of a few conditions –

pneumonia, bronchitis, asthma – are sometimes almost unmistakable, but more often than not the exact diagnosis of lung ailments needs various objective tests.

A complete study of the lungs needs the resources of a research laboratory, but much can be discovered by simpler means, e.g. testing resonance (➤*percussion*) and listening to the sounds of breathing (➤*stethoscope*). But these methods do not always suffice. The stethoscope is still a most useful instrument, but for many purposes X-rays are more reliable.

X-rays pass freely through air, less freely through liquids and soft tissues, and hardly at all through bone. In a healthy chest the backbone and ribs throw heavy shadows, and the heart is massive enough to be opaque, but the lungs are transparent apart from the tree-like pattern of their blood vessels. In nearly all disease of the lungs air is displaced by liquid or solid matter which is less permeable to X-rays and therefore throws a shadow.

Direct examination of a part of the lungs is possible by *bronchoscopy*: a lighted tube is passed down the trachea into a bronchus. This method is no part of the routine examination of the lungs, but occasionally it is valuable for establishing a diagnosis. Sometimes minor surgery can be carried out through the bronchoscope, e.g. removal of a fragment of tissue for microscopical examination.

The mechanical efficiency of the lungs can be studied in a laboratory, but few tests are simple enough for general use. Chest expansion means little, for the most important muscle of respiration, the diaphragm, does not move the ribs. A much more useful measurement is the volume of air which can be blown out in one second; time is as important as quantity because the important factor is the rate at which air can be exchanged. This is tested by a *peak flow meter*, which has a mouthpiece and a dial. The patient blows into it, and the reading gives a good estimate of how hard he can blow, indicating the severity of any airflow obstruction (e.g. asthma, bronchitis). Serial readings show progress under treatment. Some patients do this at home, just as diabetics check their own urine or blood.

5. DISORDERS

No precise classification can be simple enough to be useful. What follows is merely a guide to some other entries in this book.

Injuries. The lungs may be injured by penetrating wounds or by a fragment of a broken rib. Bleeding into the pleural cavity (*haemothorax*) may be severe, but continued bleeding is usually from other structures than the lung. A punctured lung loses air and, since it is elastic, collapses like a balloon. As the lung shrinks the bleeding stops. In fact, the air in the pleural cavity may be a greater embarrassment than the blood (►*pneumothorax*).

Infection. Even in health the airpassages carry potentially dangerous bacteria, and the lungs are continually exposed to infection by micro-organisms in the air. Nothing happens unless resistance is lowered, as by illness, or an unfamiliar organism to which the subject has never acquired resistance arrives – or perhaps a familiar one in unusually large numbers. In such circumstances the lungs are very vulnerable. Infection primarily of the trachea and bronchi causes ►*bronchitis*; infection in the remoter parts of the lung causes ►*pneumonia*. An ►*abscess* may be formed in the lung as a result of stagnation beyond a blocked bronchus. Most lung abscesses respond to antibiotics, but surgical drainage is sometimes needed. Certain types of microbe are peculiarly liable to attack the lungs, e.g. ►*tuberculosis*.

Mechanical disorders. ►*Asthma* is cramp in the muscles of the bronchi, obstructing the free passage of air. ►*Bronchiectasis* is abnormal distension of the bronchi. ►*Emphysema* is loss of the elasticity of the alveoli, resulting in overdistension of the lungs. ►*Atelectasis* is failure of the lung or some part of it to take in air after birth, or loss of air with collapse of the lung. ►*Respiratory distress syndrome* is a cause of death of newborn babies.

Occupational diseases. Several diseases are due to inhaling dusts associated with particular jobs: ►*pneumoconiosis*; *farmer's lung*.

Tumours. Benign tumours of various kinds are found. They usually have to be removed because there is no other way of telling that they are not cancerous. Much the commonest tumour is ►*cancer*, either originating in the lung (*primary*) or seeded off from a cancer elsewhere (*secondary*). The enormous increase in primary lung cancer during the 20th century has made it a leading cause of death in many countries. The increase is mainly due to cigarettes but atmospheric pollution is also a factor. The only effective treatment is removal, which may be impossible by the time the disease is recognized, for in the early, curable stages there may be no symptoms. But as many as half of the cases found by chance at an X-ray examination are operable – a strong argument for routine chest X-ray. ►*pleura*.

lupus erythematosus (LE). One (or probably more than one) of the disorders formerly known as collagen diseases or connective-tissue diseases; the group also includes rheumatoid arthritis. There are grounds for regarding all these diseases as instances of *autoimmunity* (➤*immunity* (7)), a sort of allergic reaction to one of one's own tissues.

Discoid LE is a degeneration of connective-tissue elements of the skin. It takes the form of red, often scaly patches on exposed skin, aggravated by strong sunlight. Screening ointments against ultraviolet light help to prevent it, and chloroquine (a drug more often used against malaria) may clear up the skin trouble. Most cases improve with time.

Systemic LE (SLE) can affect any part of the body, with deposition of fibrous matter and inflammatory changes resulting in the degeneration of small arteries and connective tissue. It causes various skin rashes and damage to joints, heart and lungs, kidneys, and the nervous system. The most serious damage is usually to the kidneys.

As with rheumatoid arthritis, antiinflammatory drugs ease joint symptoms, and the anti-malarial drug chloroquine may help. Corticosteroids, given in quite small doses, greatly improve the prognosis.

lupus vulgaris. Tuberculosis of the skin, mainly of the face, formerly a common and disfiguring disease but now rare. It responds well to the drugs used for tuberculosis in general.

luxation. Dislocation of a joint.

Lyme disease. Infection by a spirochaete, *Borrelia*, transmitted from other mammals by ticks. First reported in 1975 in Lyme, Connecticut, it has since been recognized in many parts of the world. The disease begins with a nondescript fever, often followed by a rash lasting 2– 3 weeks. Months later many of the patients develop symptoms of arthritis. In a few the nervous system or the heart are also involved. Lyme disease usually responds to antibiotics, but some patients continue to have symptoms on and off for years.

lymph. Part of the ➤*tissue fluid*, which instead of returning to the blood in the capillaries enters the lymphatic vessels (➤*lymphatic system*). The small amount of protein in the tissue fluid is concentrated in the lymph; otherwise the two fluids are alike. In the intestine, fat is absorbed into the lymphatic vessels and not the blood capillaries. This gives lymph from the small intestine a milky appearance, from which these lymphatic vessels are known as *lacteals*.

In addition to molecules (e.g. protein) too large to return to the circulation by the capillaries, particles such as bacteria leave the tissue spaces in the lymph, to be filtered off in the lymph nodes.

Lymph nodes (also called *lymph glands*, or simply *glands*) are small bean-like bodies in the course of the lymphatic vessels. Several small vessels enter the periphery and a single larger vessel leaves the concavity of the node. The distribution is described under ➤*lymphatic system*.

The *lymphoid tissue* of which the nodes are mainly composed forms lymphocytes (a type of white blood cell concerned with ➤*immunity*). Similar tissue is found in the *tonsils* and *adenoids* and along the rest of the digestive tract, and in the *spleen*.

lymphadenoma = ➤*Hodgkin's disease*.

lymphangiitis. Inflammation of lymph vessels from spread of infection, usually from a septic wound, seen as red lines in

lymph nodes:
cervical
axillary
mediastinal
abdominal
inguinal

deep lymph nodes

Principal groups of lymph nodes

the skin between the wound and the nearest lymph nodes, e.g. from a sore finger to the armpit. It is generally due to infection by *streptococci*. Lymphangiitis (often misnamed *blood-poisoning*) is not to be neglected, because if the infection has spread so far it may pass the barrier of the lymph nodes and set up a real blood-poisoning or septicaemia. A sulphonamide or antibiotic drug usually suppresses it promptly.

lymphatic system. A network of thin-walled vessels found in all parts of the body except the central nervous system. The vessels carry ►*lymph* from the tissue spaces. Small vessels unite to form larger vessels until finally the lymph is drained into the *innominate veins* at the root of the neck by two large lymphatic vessels: the *right lymphatic duct* from the upper half of the right side of the body and the *thoracic duct* from the rest. The vessels have valves like those of the veins, which prevent backflow.

The vessels are interrupted by ►*lymph* nodes which filter off bacteria and other foreign particles, and contribute lymphocytes and antibodies.

If the lymphatics are obstructed protein is not drained from the tissues, and fluid collects (►*oedema*) because the osmotic pressure falls (►*tissue fluid*).

The lymph nodes are a barrier, preventing bacterial infection from spreading from the tissue spaces into the blood-stream. Unless a focus of infection is contained and eradicated by local defence mechanisms (►*inflammation*) the lymph nodes for the area swell, and if the infection is ►*acute* the vessels feeding them may become inflamed (►*lymphangiitis*). The nodes are collected in fairly well-defined groups, at the sides and back of

the neck, in the armpits and groins, at the roots of the lungs, and in the vicinity of the large veins of the abdomen and pelvis. The lymph nodes may become inflamed before the original source of infection is apparent or only after it has subsided. Similarly the nodes are a barrier, though a less effective one, against the spread of cancer. Fragments which break away from a cancer are treated as foreign bodies in the tissue spaces and carried to the nearest lymph nodes. If these nodes can be removed or destroyed with the original cancer the condition may still be curable, but as more distant nodes become involved the outlook deteriorates.

The cells in the nodes which engulf foreign particles – the phagocytes – form part of a larger organization, not directly concerned with lymph. This is the *reticuloendothelial system*, which includes similar cells in the liver and bone marrow, and at large in the tissues and blood. The whole of this system becomes involved in diseases such as generalized infections, and some tumour-like disorders such as ►*Hodgkin's disease*. ►*immunity*.

lymph node ►*lymph*.

lymphocyte. A kind of white blood cell. ►*blood* (3).

lymphogranuloma venereum (LGV). A venereal disease, causing enlargement of lymph nodes in the groins and thickening, sometimes ulceration, of the surrounding skin; in some cases there is a more generalized illness with fever. LGV is most often seen in the tropics, where it may be almost as common as syphilis and gonorrhoea. It is due to a virus-like microbe ►*Chlamydia*, similar to the causes of trachoma and psittacosis, which are probably very small bacteria. Unlike true virus diseases, these all respond to treatment with antibiotics.

lymphoma. Cancer-like growth originating in lymphatic tissue. There are many types, differing in structure and virulence, but most respond at least for a time to anti-tumour therapy. Some are curable. The group includes ➤*Hodgkin's disease* and ➤*Burkitt's tumour.* ➤*AIDS*.

lysergic acid diethylamide ➤*hallucinogen.*

lysis. 1. Disintegration of blood cells (haemolysis; ➤*anaemia* (A.2)) or bacteria.

2. Gradual subsidence of a fever, as opposed to *crisis*, sudden recovery.

M

Mackenzie, Sir James (1853–1925). General practitioner in Burnley, later a heart specialist in London. With the help of a device that he called a ➤*polygraph*, which made simultaneous recordings of the heart beat and of pulses in veins and arteries, he was able to explain all the common disturbances of the heart beat (➤*arrhythmia*). Einthoven's invention of the electrocardiograph drew attention from Mackenzie's work rather too soon, for the possibilities of the polygraph were never sufficiently explored.

macro-. Prefix = '(*unusually*) large'; e.g. *macrocyte*, abnormally large red blood cell; *macrophage*, large scavenging cell in the tissues; *macroscopic*, seen with the naked eye.

macula (macula lutea). The yellow spot, the centre of the retina at the back of the eye where vision is sharpest and colour best perceived. Lesions of the macula are the commonest cause of registerable blindness in the Western world.

macular degeneration. Gradual loss of central vision of no known cause, but possibly hereditary, affecting elderly people.

macule. Spot or blemish, level with the surrounding skin; as opposed to *papule*, a raised spot.

maduromycosis (Madura foot). A chronic infection of the foot, seldom seen outside the tropics, by any of several agents on the borderline between microscopical fungi and bacteria, mostly *Nocardia*, but sometimes *Actinomyces* (➤*actinomycosis*). Over the course of years the infec-tion, if untreated, gradually destroys all the tissues of the foot including the bones. Some of the agents respond to antibiotics; otherwise the only remedy is to remove the affected tissues.

Magendie, François (1783–1885). French physiologist. Anticipating his still greater disciple Bernard, he rejected the academic speculation and near-mysticism that still clouded scientific thought, insisting that the human body obeyed the same natural laws as everything else in nature. He was the first to describe the separation of nerves joining the spinal cord into sensory and motor roots, and the pathway of reflex action from a sensory organ along a nerve, to the spinal cord by the sensory (posterior) root, then from the spinal cord by the anterior root and lastly to the responding (effector) organ.

Magendie's experiments with diet established the main ingredients needed, in particular the very different food value of different proteins. He was also a founder of modern pharmacology; he isolated the active principles of many plant drugs and described their actions.

magnesium. A metal essential to all but the most primitive forms of life. An atom of magnesium lies at the centre of a molecule of *chlorophyll*, the green pigment that enables plants to use the energy of sunlight to synthesize from carbon dioxide and water the carbohydrates that are the basis of all the other components of animals, including ourselves; for we all live on either plants or on other animals that eat them (➤*energy*).

In the human body magnesium is involved in the structure of bones and teeth, and with numerous enzymes. Almost any diet contains enough, but deficiency of magnesium can be a part of severe malnutrition or malabsorption, with disturbances of muscle action.

Magnesium compounds used medicinally include carbonate and trisilicate (antacids), and citrate, hydroxide and sulphate (laxatives). A paste of magnesium sulphate and glycerol is a time-honoured dressing for boils and the like. Injections of magnesium sulphate are sometimes given for treating ►*eclampsia*.

magnetic resonance imagery (MRI) ►*scan*.

malabsorption. Failure to assimilate essential ingredients from the diet, leading to symptoms of malnutrition.

In a normal person, each of the chemical ingredients of the food is broken down by particular enzymes to small, simple molecules. Only these can pass through the lining of the intestine into the circulation, to be resynthesized and incorporated into the tissues.

If an enzyme is lacking, the corresponding food substance cannot be broken down and is not absorbed. Examples are ►*cystic fibrosis*, where several enzymes from the pancreas are lacking and several kinds of food are affected, and ►*carbohydrate intolerance*, where a particular sugar (usually milk sugar) remains in the intestine.

Alternatively, the intestine may fail to absorb the products of digestion although the enzyme system is intact. After drastic operations on the intestine, food may pass through too quickly to be completely absorbed, and with defects of the mucous membrane of the intestine absorption may be delayed. Undue haste

and poor absorption are combined with chronic inflammation of the intestine (►*enteritis*). ►*Coeliac disease*, a kind of malabsorption in childhood, is due to a defect provoked by the protein *gluten*, found in certain cereals. ►*Sprue*, a similar disease affecting adults in the tropics, may be caused by damage to the lining of the intestine by vitamin deficiency (but cause and effect are difficult to distinguish).

Malabsorption can lead to malnutrition, amounting in the worst cases to starvation. It may also cause diarrhoea, because unabsorbed fats and sugars in the intestine have a purgative action. With sprue and coeliac disease, diarrhoea is the leading symptom. With chronic inflammation of the intestine, the diarrhoea of malabsorption is added to that of the primary disease.

malaria. An infectious disease due to a minute animal parasite (protozoon) transmitted by female mosquitoes, one of the commonest causes of sickness and death in the world.

A mosquito sucks blood from an infected person. The parasites breed in the stomach of the mosquito, and after about 10 days their offspring invade the salivary glands. The mosquito is then infectious, and everyone she bites gets an injection of parasites in a droplet of saliva.

The young parasites are carried in the patient's blood to the liver and other organs, where they multiply without causing symptoms. After a variable incubation period – often a fortnight but sometimes much longer – parasites return to the bloodstream and invade red blood cells, where they multiply rapidly. The infected red cells are soon destroyed, setting free countless parasites to invade other red cells. When this happens the patient has an attack of fever. The attack commonly begins with headache and violent shivering (*rigor*). After anything from an hour to a day the symptoms vanish until the next batch of parasites is released, with further destruction of red cells. All types of malaria cause attacks of fever at more or less regular intervals, and increasing anaemia from loss of blood cells.

There are four known types of malaria parasite, all species of the protozoon *Plasmodium*. *P. malariae* causes quartan fever with attacks every 3 days (the 'four' implied by *quartan* are counted from 1, not 0). These parasites may hibernate in the liver for many years and cause occasional attacks long after the patient has left a malarial region. Quartan malaria is common in subtropical countries.

P. vivax causes tertian fever, with attacks on alternate days. It, too, may persist for some time after the original bout. This type of malaria used to be common in the temperate zone, as far north as Finland.

P. ovale causes tertian malaria in parts of Central Africa.

P. falciparum causes subtertian (malignant tertian, MT) fever, the most dangerous kind of malaria. The attacks are frequent and irregular, at intervals from a few hours to two days; or the fever may simply persist. All types of malaria can cause diverse symptoms, and MT is notorious for imitating every other acute illness. Many of the symptoms are due to congestion of the blood vessels in an affected organ by masses of damaged blood cells. MT malaria can cause a kind of *dysentery*, and also *cerebral malaria* (invasion of blood vessels in the brain), which kills many thousands of children. A rare but equally dangerous complica-

tion, *blackwater fever*, seems to be an abnormal response to treatment of MT malaria with quinine. This parasite does not hibernate in the body; when a bout is over it does not recur. But the patient can start a new attack if another infected mosquito bites him. MT malaria is the commonest type in tropical Africa and also occurs in the hotter parts of Asia and South America.

If malaria – even MT – is untreated, most patients recover after anything from two or three to a dozen episodes of fever. The complications of MT malaria are often fatal, but much of the large death rate (and far larger sickness rate) is due to the anaemia and sheer exhaustion of repeated infection. Children in the tropics die of what should be trivial complaints because they no longer have any natural resistance.

An attack of malaria does not confer immunity, but after repeated attacks with the same strain of parasite the attacks become less and less severe, in those who survive.

Quinine, introduced to Europe from Peru in the 1630s, was for two centuries the only known remedy for attacks of malari and also, with a small daily dose, a means of preventing them. Synthetic antimalarials such as *chloroquine* are preferred to quinine, having fewer side-effects; but as subtertian parasites in many areas have developed resistance to chloroquine there is still a place for quinine. Residual parasites causing recurrent malaria can be eradicated with *primaquine*. Drugs to be taken regularly for prophylaxis in infected areas include *proguanil* and *mefloquine*. Quite as important as prophylactic drugs is avoiding mosquito bites, e.g. by sleeping under a net and using insect repellents; ►*travel*.

Ideally there should be no need for

treatment, because malaria can be prevented and, in time, eradicated. If every case could be treated, mosquitoes could not become infected and their bites would be harmless. This is the situation in most of Europe: mosquitoes of the right sort are not uncommon but there is nobody to infect them. Small outbreaks can still occur when someone imports active malaria.

Hippocrates advised people recovering from malaria to retire to the hills, where the disease did not occur, and a close association between malaria and a wet environment must have been obvious from early times. Marshes were supposed to exude noxious vapours that caused the disease (*malaria* = 'bad air') until Laveran's discovery of the parasite in 1880. In 1894 Manson suggested that the infection might be transmitted by mosquitoes (which of course flourished in the places where malaria was commonest, the marshes); and in 1897 Ross proved Manson's theory.

All malaria is carried by mosquitoes of the genus *Anopheles*. These can be distinguished by their posture when they settle. Other mosquitoes settle with their bodies level; *Anopheles* at an angle, head down. They can breed only where there is standing fresh water, in which they lay their eggs and their larvae develop.

If the cycle is broken at any point, malaria disappears. The first method has been mentioned: it is to treat all the patients.

Secondly, the mosquitoes can be prevented from biting. Houses are cleared of adult mosquitoes with insecticides. People in malarial regions avoid sitting out of doors in the early evening when the mosquitoes bite most; they may be able to cover their windows with gauze; they sleep under nets.

Mosquitoes are prevented from breeding by attention to their breeding places. This includes anything from drainage of vast swamps to proper disposal of discarded cans where rain might collect, clearing the banks of streams and stagnant backwaters (running water is no danger), and spreading a film of oil over the surface of pools to suffocate the larvae. Prevention of breeding is the most effective means of malaria control, but it can be very expensive.

Finally, people exposed to infection can protect themselves by taking regular small doses of an antimalarial drug.

By such methods many circumscribed areas have been freed from malaria. Even in heavily infected regions most large towns are now safe. But rural areas, especially the huge and sparsely populated plains of Africa, present special problems. To deal with breeding places – and it must be done regularly – would need more money and staff than could be found. The only hope is to apply long-acting insecticides to every dwelling and offer treatment to every patient. It will take a long time.

malignant. A term used to distinguish severe or progressive forms of a disease from mild or self-limiting (*benign*) forms. A malignant tumour is cancerous, whereas a benign tumour is a simple growth that does not invade other tissues. Malignant malaria is the subtertian form associated with the highly dangerous blackwater fever and with fatal involvement of the brain; benign malaria is tertian or quartan and does not have these complications.

malingering. Deliberate feigning of illness; doubtless a common condition, but a diagnosis that can seldom be made with certainty. A man may claim to have hurt his back at work in the hope of compensation. It is one thing to prove that he has broken no bones, but quite another to say that he is lying about what he feels.

malleolus. Knob of bone at either side of the ankle.

malleus. One of the three small bones that conduct sound from the ear-drum to the organ of hearing in the inner ear.

malnutrition. Deficiency of any essential component of a proper ▸*diet*. Malnutrition can be due either to illness where food is not assimilated (▸*malabsorption*) or, much more often, to poor diet. Anyone whose health could be improved by more or better food is suffering from malnutrition, and this is surely the state of more than half the people in the world.

Some effects of particular deficiencies are mentioned under ▸*vitamins* and ▸*kwashiorkor*; but single deficiencies are not as common as general malnutrition. If a diet is inadequate in one respect it is likely to be so in others. The commonest picture is a negative one: failure to thrive, failure to resist trivial infection, lack of energy or initiative.

Even in wealthy communities where the average diet is more than enough (and a surplus contributes nothing to health) there can be under-nourished individuals. The great risk is to lonely old people who cannot be bothered to feed themselves properly even when they can afford to. It is a vicious circle, for malnutrition makes them more apathetic than ever.

Civilization tends to spread malnutrition by enlarging the population without increasing the production of food. One dose of quinine will save a child from dying of malaria, but it may take years

to grow new crops for him to eat. Scientific medicine is a doubtful blessing without scientific agriculture and, above all, education in the uses of both.

malocclusion. Faulty alignment of the teeth, causing an inefficient bite.

Malpighi, Marcello (1624–94). Physician and anatomist; professor at Bologna and Pisa; the first professional anatomist to work with a microscope. He greatly extended the science of embryology, which had of necessity been rather crude while such a small object as an early embryo could be studied only with the naked eye. Here, his work was a direct continuation of that of Harvey a generation before him. A still more important extension of Harvey's work was Malpighi's discovery of capillary blood vessels, of which Harvey could only infer the existence when he proved that blood must find some pathway between arteries and veins. Malpighi left accurate descriptions of most of the organs and tissues of the body, and half a dozen or more of the minute structures of the body are still named after him.

malpractice ▸*ethics*.

Malta fever. A kind of ▸*undulant fever*, primarily an infection of goats but often transmitted to man.

maltose. A compound sugar obtained from starch; its molecule consists of two units of glucose.

malunion. Healing of a fracture with the broken ends of the bone out of their true line. If the deformity is enough to interfere with function the bone may have to be broken again and reset.

mandible. Lower jaw; a single bone loosely jointed with the skull at the temporomandibular joints in front of the ears. Its movements are described under ►*mastication*. The upper jaw, the *maxilla*, is a component of the skull proper.

The development of jaws from the forward gills was one of the decisive steps in evolution; with jaws an animal is better equipped for self-defence and for extending its diet, two cardinal factors in the struggle for survival. But as regards evolution the human jaw served its purpose long ago. The hands have taken on many of its primitive functions, and the modern human mandible is a poor thing in comparison with that of less advanced creatures.

mandragora (mandrake). A plant of the same family as belladonna and with similar effects as a drug; used as a narcotic in ancient Egypt and, until recently, in Western Europe. During the Middle Ages its forked root was thought to resemble a man and to imprison a lost soul. The plant was uprooted by tying it to a dog's tail, so that nobody should die from the horror of hearing it scream.

mania. Mental disturbance with aimless and ungovernable excitement.

manic-depressive psychosis. One of the two common types of severe mental disturbance (the other is schizophrenia); also called *affective psychosis*, because the apparent disorder is of ►*affect* – the patient's ideas and emotions and their expression are all of a piece, instead of being incongruous as in schizophrenia.

The illness may take the form of *mania*, when the patient is endlessly busy, talks for the sake of talking, seems full of ideas that he never pursues because he is so soon involved in the next pointless task; he may be too busy to eat or sleep. These symptoms would pass for *hypo-*

mania, a sort of harmless eccentricity, except that the absurd over-activity of true mania is neither rational nor open to discussion, and interference may be violently opposed.

Or the patient may be profoundly melancholic, in extreme cases to the point of mute immobility.

The two kinds of attack do not at first appear to have any similarity but the common factor is that the patient is helplessly at the mercy of his confused emotions.

After an attack, which without treatment may last weeks or months, most patients are perfectly normal, though they may have further attacks later. In some cases, attacks of mania and depression alternate.

With either type of attack the patient may need a spell in hospital. Mania can now be treated with large doses of tranquillizers – too large to be given without constant supervision – and melancholy with various drugs (►*depression*). This psychosis can also be treated with ►*lithium*. When drugs fail, electro-convulsive therapy often cuts an attack short. Neither type of patient is often dangerous to others, though neither is easy to live with. But they can be a great danger to themselves. An untreated maniac can exhaust himself with his unceasing activity, and he can starve for lack of time to eat. A depressive can also starve for lack of any wish to eat or even live. At the depth of his attack he may lack the determination to kill himself, but there is real risk of suicide when he is recovering and can find the energy to do it.

The outlook is much better than one might suppose from seeing a patient at the height of an attack. The personality does not deteriorate, even after repeated attacks; and with modern treatment most attacks can be shortened or controlled. ➤*depression*.

manipulation. Replacing dislocated joints and setting broken bones must be among the oldest of medical procedures, and in principle the methods described in Egypt 3,500 years ago have not changed. Dislocated joints are manipulated to replace the moving parts of the joints and restore their function. Fractures are manipulated to put the broken ends in the best position for healing. Thus far, there is no disagreement. The manipulative treatment of supposed partial dislocations does, however, arouse differences of opinion, because more often than not the dislocation or displacement cannot be demonstrated. Two systems of treatment outside orthodox practice make much use of this kind of manipulation. *Chiropractic* is based on the theory that diseases are caused by pressure on nerves and are cured by manipulating the backbone. *Osteopathy* holds that partial dislocations (osteopathic lesions) interfere with the circulation of blood. Neither theory is accepted by orthodox medicine, but it may be in order to manipulate joints for the purpose of breaking down adhesions, though when it comes to demonstration the adhesions are apt to be as elusive as osteopathic lesions or the compressed nerves of chiropractic. In a given case, practitioners of all three schools might offer the same treatment for three different reasons. Perhaps this need not worry the patient if he is relieved of his symptoms.

It has often been argued against chiropractors and osteopaths, not to mention untrained bone-setters, that they could endanger a patient's life by failing to recognize a condition such as a tuberculous joint, and causing a violent reaction by manipulation; but trained chiropractors and osteopaths are well aware of this, and are taught to avoid such mistakes.

Even such a seemingly clear-cut diagnosis as a slipped disc can be a matter of conjecture. In some cases there is no doubt at all, but in others it is by no means clear what, if anything, is going on between the vertebrae to cause symptoms such as pain round the shoulder or stiffness of the neck. Some of these cases respond well to manipulation, though opinions differ about what the manipulation actually does.

In the treatment of stiff joints after injury or operation, manipulation takes second place to active movement by the patient himself.

Mantoux test. Injection into the skin of a minute dose of *tuberculin*, a substance extracted from tubercle bacilli; a reaction indicates that the subject has at some time been infected with tuberculosis or immunized against it. The test is used to show whether immunization is needed, and less often as a help in diagnosis.

MAO = ➤*monoamine oxidase*.

marasmus. Extreme emaciation, particularly in infancy. Marasmus is now taken to mean wasting as a result of gross malnutrition in infancy. It has been ascribed to lack of fuel (Calories), but recent evidence suggests that like ➤*kwashiorkor* it is a form of *protein-energy* malnutrition.

march fracture ➤*stress* fracture.

marihuana ➤*hemp*.

marrow. 1. *Bone marrow*; the soft core of a bone. At birth, all the bones are filled with *red* marrow, a highly active tissue in which most blood cells originate. In adult life, the red marrow of the limbs is replaced by *yellow* marrow, consisting largely of fat; in the rest of the skeleton the red marrow persists.

2. *Spinal marrow* = ►*spinal cord*.

massage ►*physiotherapy*.

masseter. A powerful muscle of mastication at the side of the jaw.

mastectomy ►*breast*.

mastication. The lower jaw (*mandible*) is slung by powerful muscles from the base of the skull, with which it forms a loose joint in front of the ear.

In biting, the jaws are pulled together by the powerful *temporalis* and *masseter* muscles, arising respectively from the sides of the skull and the cheek bones. The muscles below the chin which open the mouth are weak: gravity does most of the work. In carnivores, the jaws can carry out only this hinge-like movement. In other mammals, including man, the mandible is free to slip backwards and forwards and from side to side, which makes the rotary action of chewing possible.

Mastication breaks up food and mixes it with saliva to facilitate swallowing. It may also stimulate the flow of saliva. Otherwise it is not very important from the point of view of digestion. But it seems to preserve the teeth, and much dental decay is ascribed to the soft diet of Western civilization.

mastitis. Inflammation of the ►*breast*.

mastoid. Breast-shaped; the *mastoid process* is the knob of bone projecting down from the skull behind the ear, to which is attached the front part of the sternomastoid muscle. The *mastoid antrum* is a cavity in the bone above the process and a finger's breadth from the surface. It communicates by a small opening with the cavity of the eardrum or middle ear (►*ear* (2)) which lies in front of it, and the mastoid process is honeycombed with small air-cells which open off the antrum. The mucous membrane lining the antrum and air-cells is a continuation (by way of the Eustachian tube and middle ear) of the mucous membrane of the nose.

Acute inflammation of the mastoid antrum was a common and serious complication of infection of the nose or throat, such as measles or tonsillitis, until the discovery of sulphonamides and antibiotics. It is now rarely seen. If an abscess does form in the antrum the bone has nearly always to be opened surgically. Without operation the pus may find its own way out, and the path of least resistance is to the inside of the skull. Meningitis and brain abscess are uncommon but very dangerous complications of untreated mastoid infection. The more usual outcome is chronic infection with a steady trickle of pus through a hole in the ear-drum and increasing deafness. In this chronic state, which may last indefinitely, pain is unusual but a continuous hissing or ringing sound (*tinnitus*) can be almost as disturbing as pain. Treatment is aimed not only at relieving these tiresome symptoms but also at reducing the danger of a sudden flareup with further spread of the infection. Antibiotics and patient cleansing may serve, but a fairly extensive operation is often the only cure. The thick bony cover of the antrum has to be removed, together with the small conducting bones of the middle ear and the membrane of the eardrum. The ear often works surprisingly well after this rather drastic treatment, and in any case the operation does less to restrict hearing than untreated infection, which would end in complete deafness.

masturbation. So many children and adolescents play with their own genitalia at times that the practice cannot seriously be called abnormal. Nor is there the least evidence that it is dangerous or harmful. At the worst, persistent masturbation may be a symptom of insecurity comparable with, say, nail-biting. Because of a misinterpretation of Genesis xxxviii, where the Lord slew Onan for failing to impregnate his brother's widow, masturbation has been branded as a sin; and the uninhibited masturbation of certain mentally deranged people has been mistaken for a cause of their madness.

materia medica. Substances used to treat illness, i.e. drugs in the widest sense. Also the study of drugs, pharmacology.

maxilla. Upper jaw; a component of the skull extending from the orbit to the roof of the mouth. It is the principal element of the skeleton of the face. The bone is hollowed out by the *maxillary sinus* or *antrum*, which opens into the nose.

ME ►*myalgic encephalomyelitis.*

measles (rubeola; morbilli). One of the most widespread and contagious of all infections; due to a virus spread from case to case by air-borne droplets. Major outbreaks are to be expected every two or three years.

After an incubation period of 7–14 days, the attack begins with fever and running nose and eyes, followed by sore throat. A day or two later small red spots with white centres (Koplik's spots) can be seen on the lining of the mouth. The typical blotchy skin rash appears about the fourth day and spreads down from

the face. In an uncomplicated case the temperature soon begins to subside. The whole attack lasts about a week.

By itself, the measles virus is not often dangerous; but during the attack the patient is abnormally vulnerable to all sorts of bacteria. Most deaths from measles are in fact due to secondary bacterial infection. The commonest complications of this sort are pneumonia and infection of the middle ear. Antibiotic drugs have no effect on the virus, but greatly reduce the danger from bacteria.

An effective vaccine against measles was not discovered until 1960, and a suitable one for routine use only in 1964. The present policy is to give all children MMR (measles, mumps, rubella) vaccine at 12–15 months old.

meatus. Canal or passage; e.g. *external auditory meatus*, ear-hole.

Meckel's diverticulum. (J. F. Meckel, 1714–74, German anatomist.) A protrusion from the small intestine; it is a vestigial structure representing the yolk-stalk, found in about 2 per cent of people. It resembles the *appendix*, and can be inflamed with symptoms like those of appendicitis.

meconium. Greenish fluid, mostly bile and mucus, in an infant's intestine, passed soon after birth (or before birth if labour is difficult and the infant is distressed).

medial. Towards the mid-line (in anatomical description).

median. 1 (anat.). In the mid-line. The *median plane* divides the body into left and right halves.

2 (statistics). The middle value of a series, e.g. the 3rd of 5 or the 11th of 21. The median is sometimes a more useful

'average' in medical statistics than the usual arithmetic mean.

Median nerve. A branch of the brachial plexus; it is motor to most of the flexor muscles in the forearm and to the small muscles of the thumb, and carries sensation from the radial (thumb) side of the hand. It lies superficially at the wrist, and is liable to injury when the wrist is cut, as by pushing the hand through a pane of glass. ➤*carpal tunnel.*

mediastinum. Compartment between the lungs, containing the heart, major blood vessels, trachea, oesophagus, etc.

medicine. 1. Drug or mixture of drugs.

2. Any science or practice concerned with sickness and health.

3. In England, also the more specialized field of practice that excludes surgery and obstetrics, formerly called *physic* and practised by physicians, whose social status was higher than that of the surgeons. Elsewhere, this speciality is called *internal medicine*, and its practitioners are *internists*.

medulla = ➤*marrow*, or the central zone of a gland or other organ.

medulla oblongata. The lowest part of the brain; in other words, the upward continuation of the spinal cord into the skull. It contains the *vital centres* which govern the reflexes for breathing, heart rate, and blood pressure. If the impulses from these centres stop, the heart can still beat at its own rate, but breathing is impossible; serious injury to the medulla oblongata is immediately fatal.

megacolon (Hirschsprung's disease). A congenital defect of the large intestine, where the network of nerves in a segment of the intestine is incomplete and therefore the muscles do not work. The contents of the intestine are held up at this point, and the intestine becomes enormously distended. The child is cured by removing the affected length of intestine and joining the cut ends.

Meibomian glands. (H. Meibom, 1634–1700, German anatomist.) Sebaceous (grease) glands at the edges of the eyelids. Inflammation of one of these glands causes a kind of *stye*. Simple blockage causes a *Meibomian cyst*, a painless round lump that is easily removed.

melaena. Blackened faeces, from the presence of iron compounds (usually derived from blood, e.g. from a bleeding gastric ulcer).

melancholia. Severe ➤*depression.* (= black bile, one of the four ➤*humours* of the classical theorists.)

melanin. The dark brown pigment of the hair, skin, and eyes, present in blue or brown eyes (➤*iris*) and, in different amounts, in the skin of people of all races. Chemically, it is derived from the same raw material as adrenaline.

An ➤*albino* is unable to synthesize melanin.

melanoma. Pigmented tumour, containing melanin, such as a mole; also a rare kind of cancer. The latter, *malignant melanoma*, is becoming commoner and needs prompt and complete surgical excision, in order to catch it before it has had time to set up secondary tumours (*metastases*) elsewhere in the body. Some melanomas are sensitive to radiation, but surgery comes first. There is growing evidence that these tumours may in future be susceptible to some form of immunization, but this is still speculative.

menarche. Onset of menstruation at puberty.

Mendel, Gregor (1822–84). Austrian monk; Abbot of Brünn (Brno). By numerous experiments in cross-breeding, mainly with pea plants, Mendel founded the science of ►*genetics*.

Ménière's syndrome. (P. Ménière, 1799–1862, French neurologist.) An affection of the inner ear, with disturbance of both its functions – hearing and balance. Typically, the patient has attacks of deafness with *tinnitus* (a ringing or hissing sound in the ear), accompanied by giddiness which may be severe enough for him to fall down or to vomit.

Ménière's syndrome resembles migraine in the periodic attacks, the frequent absence of demonstrable cause, the number of theories to explain it, and the various forms of treatment offered. A disturbance of blood-flow, with altered pressure, seems the likeliest explanation of most though not all cases.

Several different kinds of drugs are used, and the most suitable for a particular case is found by trial and error. Incapacitating one-sided attacks can be treated, as a last resort, by an operation to put the inner ear out of action. Loss of the balance organ is unimportant, because balance is maintained by several other mechanisms. A selective operation that preserves the hearing organ may be possible. Such drastic treatment is not often justified.

meninges (pl. of *meninx*). Membranes enclosing the ►*brain* and ►*spinal cord*. Three layers are described. The innermost, the *pia mater*, is like tissue paper stuck to the outside of the brain and cord, dipping into the various folds and crevices. The outer layer, the *dura mater*, is a parchment-like membrane applied to the inside of the skull and spinal canal. Folds of dura mater partly separate the cerebral hemispheres and the cerebrum from the cerebellum; there is a smaller fold between the cerebellar hemispheres. Otherwise the dura mater does not leave the bone. The intermediate layer, the *arachnoid mater*, is a filmy membrane attached to the inner surface of the dura mater. The arachnoid and pia are joined by fine threads (arachnoid = 'like a cobweb'). The *subarachnoid space* between arachnoid and pia is filled with cerebrospinal fluid (CSF).

Inflammation of the meninges, usually from bacterial infection, is known as ►*meningitis*.

meningismus. Stiff neck and other symptoms resembling those of meningitis, such as may occur at the start of many kinds of fever although the meninges are not involved.

meningitis. Inflammation of the *meninges* from infection by viruses or bacteria.

According to the type of infection, meningitis ranges from a mild, fleeting disturbance to a rapidly fatal disease. Common to all types are fever and a disproportionately severe headache. Inflammation anywhere causes reflex tightening of surrounding muscles, and with meningitis spasm of muscles in the neck and back is usual. With the more severe types, there may be convulsions, vomiting, and delirium.

The diagnosis is confirmed by examining the *cerebrospinal fluid*, which shows characteristic chemical changes, often with turbidity from the presence of numerous white blood cells. The infecting microbe can usually be identified.

Many of the common viruses occasionally cause meningitis. Except in rare cases where the brain is also infected, there is little danger – fortunately, for drugs have no effect on viral meningitis.

A common bacterial cause of meningitis is the *meningococcus*, which many healthy people carry in their throats. Infection with meningococci can be mild and transient. Sometimes it spreads to the blood-stream to cause fever and rash (one of several diseases formerly called 'spotted fever'); however, it can also cause a serious form of meningitis, which can start an epidemic in crowded conditions. Meningococcal meningitis responds to prompt treatment with penicillin. Many other bacteria can infect the meninges, generally by spreading from another infected organ, e.g. as a complication of pneumonia. These are dangerous diseases, but as a rule they respond to treatment with antibiotics.

Tuberculous meningitis was invariably fatal until the discovery of streptomycin in 1944. It is a fairly unusual complication of tuberculosis elsewhere in the body. Treated early, it is now a curable disease; but it starts so insidiously that serious harm can be done before it is recognized.

meningococcus. *Neisseria meningitidis*, the cause of epidemic meningitis (cerebrospinal fever).

meningocoele. Bulging of meninges through a gap in a defective vertebra (►*spina bifida*).

meniscus. A slip of cartilage at either side of the ►*knee* joint, separating the joint surfaces.

menopause (change of life; climacteric). The time when a woman's ovaries cease to set free an ovum every 4 weeks and she is no longer fertile. Menstruation stops because there is no stimulus from the ovaries. The usual age is in the middle or later forties, but there is much individual variation.

The accompanying changes are due to readjustment of pituitary and ovarian hormones.

The onset is often gradual, the periods becoming less and less regular, or it may be quite sudden.

Although many women accept unpleasant symptoms as inevitable, by no means all women suffer. Some, especially when the onset is gradual, have no symptoms except lack of menstrual periods.

Many of the symptoms blamed on the menopause are not due to it, and there is a very real danger of neglecting other disorders that could and should be treated, by putting them down to the change of life. Disorders of blood vessels, digestive organs, joints and other organs may well happen to start at about the same time as the menopause. More perhaps than any other symptom, *depression* is wrongly, or no more than half rightly, regarded as a direct result of the menopause. The altered balance of sex hormones may well cause some emotional instability and so prepare the soil for depression, but the immediate causes are only coincidental. A man is allowed to age gradually and adapt himself to the inevitable changes, but a woman is suddenly, perhaps brutally confronted with middle age at a time when children leave home and husbands no longer look forward to promotion. The blackest of all moods is a sense of being unwanted.

The direct symptoms of the menopause are relatively few. With luck, there may be none at all. Disturbed reflexes of blood vessels can cause hot flushes, palpitations or other odd sensations. Mucous membranes, especially those of the sex organs, may become dry and inflamed. Later effects include weakening of bone and hardening of arteries. These are all mitigated by small doses of sex hormones: it is simple replacement therapy, comparable with giving insulin for diabetes or vitamins for malnutrition.

menorrhagia. Excessive bleeding with menstruation.

menses. Menstrual (monthly) periods.

menstruation. Periodic bleeding in women of childbearing age. When a girl is born her ovaries contain the rudiments of up to half a million eggs (*ova*), which lie dormant until puberty. From then until the menopause some 30 years later, an ovum is released each month from one or other ovary (*ovulation*), and finds its way to the adjacent Fallopian tube. Before it is released an ovum ripens in a sort of shell, the *Graafian follicle*. Only the ovum, a single cell, is released. The follicle remains in the ovary and grows into a small endocrine gland, a *corpus luteum*.

The corpus luteum produces a hormone, *progesterone*, that stimulates the lining of the uterus to form a thick layer, with an abundant circulation of blood, ready to receive an embryo if the ovum becomes fertilized.

An embryo forms a hormone that keeps the corpus luteum in being and so preserves the enriched lining of the uterus. But if the ovum is not fertilized, the corpus luteum withers in 2 weeks, and the uterus, deprived of progesterone, sheds its lining. The process is spread over a few days. The raw surface left behind bleeds a little: the average loss during a menstrual period is about 2 ounces (60 ml) of blood.

As soon as the bleeding is over the lining of the uterus regenerates, and some 2 weeks later the cycle begins again with the release of another ovum.

The interval between ovulation and menstruation – i.e. the life-span of the corpus luteum if there is no pregnancy – is nearly always 2 weeks. But the interval between menstruation and the next ovulation varies from person to person, and also from month to month in the same person. The whole cycle may last from 3 weeks to 5 or more.

➤*dysmenorrhoea.*

mental handicap (mental defect, mental retardation). Subnormal development of the mind from the time of birth or infancy, the intelligence quotient failing to reach 70. In these terms some 3 per cent of the population count as retarded, but as many pass unnoticed. Older classifications (moron, imbecile, idiot, in descending order of development) have been abandoned. Handicap is now classified as *profound* (IQ below 20), *severe* (20–29), *moderate* (30–49) and *mild* (50–69). Children in the first two groups usually have well-defined brain damage; the others only seldom, many of them being merely at the lower extreme of the normal range. With expert teaching and a sympathetic background at home mildly handicapped children may do well enough to join an ordinary school.

Many children of average – even above-average – intelligence are thought to be subnormal because of an unrecognized handicap such as defective hearing or eyesight, or word-blindness.

True subnormality implies that the mind has not developed as it should have done because of some defect. Rarely, the trouble starts some time after birth from some such cause as tuberculous meningitis, but nearly always the defect arises at birth or before.

Congenital syphilis, once the commonest cause, is now very rare. German measles during pregnancy is prevented by vaccination.

Premature birth, poor nutrition from a defective placenta, or serious difficulties during labour can affect the brain cells. Harmful disorders of body chemistry include severe jaundice in infancy, lack of thyroid hormone (cretinism), and phenylketonuria.

Down's syndrome is due to a fault in the fertilized ovum at the time of conception.

None of these defects is very common. There are many others that are extremely rare.

Some types of mental deficiency, e.g. cretinism, can be cured, and others, e.g. those caused by German measles, poor nutrition, severe jaundice (►rhesus factor) and difficult labour can often be prevented with good antenatal supervision. In other cases – admittedly still the majority – treatment means making the best of what the child has. The outlook is generally better than it appears to be. Only a small minority of defectives are really incapable of learning anything useful; these will always need protection. The majority can be taught at least to look after and occupy themselves, and many can earn a living. In particular, people suffering from Down's syndrome are often *better* than others at caring for animals; and any subnormal person gets a sense of achievement from work that better-endowed people would find boring. It is difficult for a normal person, anxious to help, to imagine what would keep a subnormal person happy. What seems tragic to a normal parent or teacher may be nothing of the kind to the subnormal child.

mental illness. Illness, as opposed to deficiency, of the mind cannot be defined except as abnormal working of the mind, of which normal working cannot be defined. Serious illness is at least recognizable, but minor disorders merge imperceptibly into normality; where the line is to be drawn is purely a matter of opinion.

Some general patterns are more or less recognizable.

Various physical diseases affect the brain. A patient who is delirious at the start of a fever is for the time being insane. Similarly, acute intoxication with alcohol or any of a large number of drugs and poisons causes temporary insanity. More lasting injury to the mind can be due to gradual and continued poisoning, e.g. with alcohol (*Korsakow's syndrome*), mercury, or lead. Degeneration of arteries in the brain and ► *Alzheimer's disease* are among the commonest causes of mental deterioration in middle age and later. ►► *dementia.*

But no physical cause can be shown in most cases of mental illness. They fall roughly into three groups: *neuroses*, *psychoses*, and *personality disorders*.

The common view that a neurosis is less serious than a psychosis is no more than half true. The essential difference is that neurosis does not affect ordinary reasoning, and however disturbed the emotions may be, the conscious mind keeps touch with reality; whereas psychosis distorts conscious reasoning. The neurotic is fully aware of his abnormality (though he may not be able to identify it), but the psychotic is not, because he cannot distinguish fantasy from reality.

Two examples may illustrate the difference. First, a clerk in a large firm is overanxious about his work and afraid of being dismissed. He disapproves of his own weakness and tries to suppress his fears, but instead of tackling them at source by ensuring that he satisfies his employer, he pushes them to the back of his mind – sweeps them under the carpet. Although he is no longer consciously aware of fear as such, his emotional tension remains to affect his behaviour or his bodily health. He is all too aware that he is unwell. He may complete the circle by regarding his poor health as the cause of his inefficiency – real or supposed – as a clerk. This man is *neurotic*. The fears at the root of his trouble may have been ill-judged, but they were not nonsensical. Like anyone else he must have had his faults, and bad clerks can lose their jobs. His neurosis is an exaggeration of normal responses.

Second, another clerk is delighted with his work but is unshakeably convinced that the management committee meets solely to discuss plans for getting rid of him. This man is *psychotic*. His belief is irrational, yet he sees nothing wrong with it, and is not open to argument.

Neuroses are considered further under ➤*anxiety*, ➤*depression*, *neurosis* and ➤*psychosomatic disease*.

A psychosis may be either *organic*, where the brain is physically damaged, or *functional*, where the mind is disturbed without any recognizable physical cause. Organic psychoses include those due to injury, arterial disease, infection (e.g. syphilis), and poisons such as alcohol and numerous drugs. The two common types of functional psychosis are ➤*schizophrenia* and ➤*manic-depressive psychosis*. The distinction between organic and functional psychosis does not mean much. In this context, 'functional' means no more than that the cause is not yet known, but it seems more and more likely that physical causes for these diseases will be found.

Some of the conditions described as *personality disorders* should not really be counted as mental illnesses. Nobody achieves perfect harmony with his neighbours and surroundings, but some do better than others. The ones who do less well are said to have personality disorders, but there is no clear dividing line.

Some types of personality are associated with particular types of mental illness – e.g. a cold, withdrawn type with schizophrenia, or an easy-going, rather irresponsible type with manic-depressive psychosis, or emotional instability with various forms of neurosis – but these are no more than pointers to what *might* happen if the person should ever become mentally ill.

But one group of personality disorders – *psychopathic personalities* – amount to diseases, though it is the neighbours rather than the patients who suffer. These are the social misfits, a most varied collection of drug addicts, alcoholics, drifters, perverts, and habitual criminals. Psychopathic behaviour of one sort or another can be a symptom of mental deficiency or illness, but the term ➤*psychopath* is usually restricted to people who seem normal apart from their behaviour. In some 'problem families' it is difficult to say whether heredity or upbringing is the main factor.

mental subnormality ➤*mental handicap*.

mepacrine. A synthetic drug introduced as an alternative to quinine for treating malaria, also effective against some intestinal worms. For many years it was the standard anti-malarial drug, but less toxic substances have superseded it.

mercury. The metal itself, and its chlorides *calomel* (HgCl) and *corrosive sublimate* ($HgCl_2$) are fairly ancient remedies. Until the present century they were the only drugs with any effect on syphilis; and calomel and grey powder (mercury and chalk) were widely used purgatives until very recent times.

Compounds of mercury still in occasional use include diuretics such as mersalyl, and numerous antiseptics.

Mercury is as poisonous as ►lead, with similar symptoms and treatment. Its industrial uses are now carefully controlled, but mercury poisoning was once common in some trades, including the preparation of felt: 'mad as a hatter' and 'hatter's shakes' are reminders of the effect of mercury on the nervous system.

mesenteric. Of the *mesentery*.

The *mesenteric arteries*, branches of the aorta, supply blood to the intestine. Since there are no effective communicating vessels between their small branches, there is no alternative supply if a branch is blocked by a clot (*thrombosis*), and the affected segment of intestine is deprived of blood. This is a dangerous situation requiring prompt surgery.

The *mesenteric veins* carry blood from the intestine to the *portal vein* and so to the liver.

mesentery. A pleated membrane in which the intestine is loosely slung from the back of the abdomen, with the mesenteric blood vessels and lymph nodes between its two layers.

Mesmer, Anton (1734–1815). Austrian physician. ►*hypnotism*.

mesoderm. Layer of cells in an ►*embryo* from which muscle, bone, blood, connective tissue and some other structures grow.

metabolism. The chemical changes by which foods are converted into compon-ents of the body or consumed as fuel, the chemical structure of the tissues is modified, and waste-products are broken down to substances that can be eliminated. Metabolism consists of *catabolism*, the breakdown of large, unmanageable molecules into small components (e.g. proteins to amino-acids), and *anabolism*, the reconstruction of large molecules.

metacarpus. The middle of the hand, from wrist to fingers. The 5 *metacarpal* bones radiate from the wrist (*carpus*); their rounded ends form the knuckles.

metastasis. Migration of disease (infection, cancer etc.) from its original site to another part of the body by carriage of bacteria, diseased cells etc. in blood or lymph.

metatarsus. Part of the foot corresponding with the *metacarpus* of the hand.

Metchnikoff, Ilya (1845–1916). Russian biologist in Paris; he did much to elucidate the mechanism of immunity against infection, in particular the role of the white blood cells in destroying bacteria. He shared a Nobel Prize with Ehrlich in 1908.

meteorism. Painful distension of the intestine with gas.

methadone. A synthetic substitute for morphine.

methanol. Methyl alcohol; wood spirit. It is used as a solvent and in methylated spirit. It causes extreme drunkenness and a coma from which the drinker may not recover. Blindness is a common sequel.

methotrexate. A drug chemically related to folic acid. Folic acid is a reagent in the growth of tissue by multiplication of cells. Methotrexate interferes with this action, and is used to discourage abnormal cells from proliferating in some types of cancer and also in certain skin diseases.

methyl alcohol = ➤*methanol.*

methyl-dopa. A drug used to suppress the synthesis of noradrenaline. ➤*blood pressure* (1); *dopa.*

methyl salicylate. Oil of wintergreen, derived from various plants or synthetically. It is among the oldest and most popular of external applications for stiff or painful muscles or joints. It acts mainly by ➤*counter-irritation*, but it may be that enough is absorbed through the skin to act in the same way as other salicylates such as aspirin.

It is too strong an irritant to be applied to injured or very young skin, and is a corrosive poison if swallowed.

microbe. A microbe or micro-organism is a living creature too small to be seen with the naked eye. A germ or *pathogen* is one of the relatively few types of microbe that can cause disease by ➤*infection* of an animal or plant. It is with these that medicine is directly concerned.

Some microbes, the *protozoa*, are animals. The pathogens of this type include the parasites of malaria and amoebic dysentery. Others, such as the microscopic *fungi* which cause ringworm, are plants. The *bacteria* resemble plants in some ways and animals in others; at this very low level there is no clear boundary between animals and plants. Lower still, the *viruses* are on the border between living and inanimate matter. These four groups are discussed separately under ➤*protozoon*, ➤*fungus*, ➤*bacterium*, and ➤*virus*. But even with this broad classification there are doubtful cases. The cause of actinomycosis is a microbe which could be an underdeveloped fungus or an advanced bacterium. The 'bacterium' of typhus and the 'virus' of trachoma both fall somewhere between bacteria and viruses.

1. HISTORY

The discovery of microbes and the gradual recognition of infection as a cause of disease are two separate chapters which did not come together until the middle of the 19th century.

No medical writer before the 16th century went beyond a vague idea that some diseases might be spread by contagion, though many described epidemics in great detail. Thucydides, describing the pestilence of 430 BC, says that people were afraid of catching the disease from each other but that those who had recovered were in no danger of catching it again – surely the first mention of immunity in history. In the 2nd century AD Galen ascribed fevers to disorders of the 'humours', blood, phlegm, yellow bile, and black bile, without mentioning the possibility of contagion; he nevertheless removed himself from plague-stricken areas on two occasions. During the Black Death (1346–9) Guy de Chauliac reported that many physicians would not visit patients for fear of catching the plague, and Boccaccio, in the introduction to the *Decameron*, said that the plague was caught not only by associating with the sick but by touching anything that they had touched. But in general, infectious disease was not recognized as such; rather it was supposed that a stricken region was subject to some climatic or other influence, and when people fled from epidemics it was from these influences that they fled. Since environmental factors are important in the spread of infection, the theory was reasonable. Its greatest exponent was Hippocrates, who accurately described conditions which would favour particular diseases. Malaria prevailed in low-lying regions (where as we now know mosquitoes that transmit the disease are found), and diarrhoea in hot places (where there are most flies and not enough rain to wash the place clean).

The first general account of infection was by Fracastorius of Verona. In *De Contagione* (1546) he correctly ascribed numerous diseases to infection, and said that the 'seeds of contagion' could be transmitted by direct contact with a patient, by contact with articles that the patient had touched, or at a distance. He recognized that the seeds of a particular contagion could produce only that disease, and that infection and putrefaction were similar processes.

The first suggestion that germs might be small living creatures came from a German priest, Athanasius Kircher, in about 1650; he claimed to have seen plague germs with his microscope, but since he advised killing them by lighting fires to burn off their wings and feet it seems unlikely that he saw actual bacteria.

Microbiology really began in Holland with the work of Leeuwenhoek, published in 1683. Protozoa and bacteria of various kinds are easily recognized from his descriptions and drawings. But no microbe was shown to cause disease until 150 years later.

In 1835 Bassi showed that a minute fungus caused muscardine, a disease of silk-worms, and suggested that human diseases such as smallpox and plague had similar causes. The first of these to be identified was the fungus which causes favus (a kind of ringworm), by Schönlein in 1839. In the next few years many other

microbes were associated with different diseases.

A great problem was that an *association* of a microbe with a disease did not prove that the microbe was the *cause* of the disease, and it was later found that many of the microbes blamed for diseases were innocent bystanders. The bacterium still known as *Haemophilus influenzae* was discovered in 1892; 40 years later it was shown that influenza was in fact due to a virus. Koch (see below) showed how to avoid such misattribution.

Worse still, there was little proof that microbes were ever the cause of disease, however strong the circumstantial evidence, while there was still a possibility that the disease produced the microbes. Many good biologists believed in spontaneous generation – in the formation of new life in decaying matter. In their view the bacteria found in diseased tissues had appeared as a result of the disease, just as maggots in rotting organic matter were a result of the rotting. In fact, the Italian physician Francesco Redi had disposed of the maggots in 1668 by showing that if meat was shielded with gauze from egg-laying flies, no maggots would grow, but his work was ignored. An English priest, John Needham, published in 1745 the results of careful experiments which seemed to show that all living matter was able to generate microbes, but he had not managed to prevent his specimens from being contaminated by bacteria in the air. An Italian priest, Spallanzani, refuted this theory by heating the air surrounding his specimens and excluding other air: no bacteria appeared. Needham replied that Spallanzani's rough treatment had spoiled the specimens and invalidated the experiment. For a century scientists were divided between the two schools of thought. The question was argued most fiercely in France, where Buffon and later Lamarck supported Needham, and Spallanzani found an unexpected ally in Voltaire; and it was a French chemist, Pasteur, who found the answer.

Pasteur proved that fermentation of wine and beer, souring of milk and similar processes depended on living microbes – yeasts (fungi) or bacteria. If the microbes in a specimen were destroyed by heat there would be no fermentation and no new microbes would appear unless the specimen was then contaminated by untreated air. He devised a simple trap which allowed air to reach his specimens, but not microbes; still there was no fermentation. As soon as the trap was removed microbes found their way in and multiplied, and fermentation began. Pasteur then showed that fermentation, putrefaction, and infection were all due to contamination by microbes – that the microbes were the cause and not the effect of these processes. One of the first doctors to see the importance of Pasteur's work was the English surgeon Lister, who took steps to exclude bacteria from wounds and so initiated safe surgery (►*infection*).

The relation of microbes to disease was finally and fully established by Pasteur's German contemporary Robert Koch. If Pasteur had proved that microbes in general could cause disease, it was still necessary to show which particular microbe was responsible for a particular disease. For instance, sputum from a case of tuberculosis would contain half a dozen or more different kinds of bacteria, and the specimen might be contaminated by still other types on its way to the laboratory; but only one type had anything to do with the disease, and

in practice it was usually outnumbered by harmless types. Before anything could be proved the different types had to be separated and studied individually. To this end Koch prepared a solid medium, originally of gelatin, later of agar jelly with added nutrients. A specimen wiped over the surface of the medium left a trail of bacteria, each free to multiply on its own. After incubation for a day or two the medium was peppered with visible colonies, each composed of the progeny of one bacterium from the original specimen. By sowing a sample of a colony on a fresh medium 'a pure culture' of one species of bacterium could be established.

Koch then set out the following rules to be observed before ascribing a disease to a particular microbe:

1. The microbe must be regularly associated with the disease;

2. It must be isolated in pure culture;

3. Microbes from the pure culture must reproduce the disease in animals and be recovered from the infected tissues.

These rules were a restatement of rules proposed as early as 1840 by the anatomist Henle, but it was Koch who showed how they could be fulfilled. They are known as *Koch's postulates*, and they established medical bacteriology as a proper science with Koch as its founder. In the two decades between Koch's announcement of his postulates and the end of the 19th century most of the bacteria involved in common diseases were identified by Koch or one of his many pupils.

There remained the problem of diseases that were obviously due to infection for which no microbe could be found. Bacteria will not pass through the finest filters (hence the use of filters to purify drinking water). Fluid extracts from tissues infected by these obscure diseases were still infectious after filtration; therefore the agents had to be smaller than bacteria and too small to be seen with the microscopes then available. The name 'filterable virus' was coined for them; later they became known simply as viruses. They could not be demonstrated; their existence had to be inferred from the infectivity of the extracts. Nor could they be grown in pure culture, because, as we now know, a virus can multiply only when it is incorporated into a living cell. Therefore Koch's postulates could not be met, and the study of viruses had to be based on circumstantial evidence. The first disease to be ascribed to a virus in this way was the mosaic disease of tobacco plants (Ivanowski, 1892), and the next was foot-and-mouth disease of cattle (Loeffler and Frosch, 1898).

In 1931 Goodpasture evolved a method for making pure cultures of viruses in chick embryos. This work, carried out at Nashville, Tennessee, was a development of a method suggested 50 years earlier by Ogston, the discoverer of staphylococci. More recently other methods of tissue culture, by which fragments of tissue removed from living organs can be kept alive almost indefinitely, have been used for growing viruses. Since 1938 it has been possible to make detailed photographs of viruses with the electron microscope. With very few exceptions the earlier inferences about virus diseases have been confirmed in accordance with Koch's postulates, and many unsuspected virus diseases have been identified.

Although the 'germ theory' of infectious disease has been proved beyond doubt, a microbe is not necessarily the sole cause of a disease associated with it. Like other accidents, infection has not only an immediate cause – the specific microbe – but also, as often as not, contributory causes. Tuberculosis is directly due to the tubercle bacillus, but poor standards of living, other sorts of illness, and even mental stresses can all make an actual attack more likely. Hereditary factors probably count as well; they are difficult to assess because members of a family are liable to infect each other. The essential point is that nearly everyone is exposed to infection by tubercle bacilli at one time or another, but most people escape the disease. Some contributory causes of infectious disease are evident from individual cases, but others are recognized only from the statistical study of large numbers of cases, which is *epidemiology*.

Some of the tributaries of microbiology have become almost as important as the main stream. The study of *immunity* to infection has provided effective vaccines against many of the most dangerous microbes, and also shed light on certain processes of disease such as *allergy*. Successful transplantation of organs from one person to another depends on controlling the 'immune response' by which the body rejects transplanted organs as though they were microbes.

The development of *antibiotics* for the treatment of infection is among the most valuable contributions of microbiology to medicine.

microbiology. The study of microbes, until recently generally called bacteriology; but since bacteriologists have to deal with all kinds of minute creatures, not only bacteria, the term microbiology is more appropriate.

microcephaly. Abnormally small head,

with incomplete development of the brain and mental deficiency.

micro-organism = ➤*microbe*.

microscope. The founders of medical microscopy, Leeuwenhoek (1632–1723) and Malpighi (1628–94), used *simple* microscopes, i.e. powerful magnifying glasses, yet they managed to describe most of the structures that a present-day medical student is expected to see with an elaborate modern instrument. The *compound* microscope now used was invented by Galileo some years before Malpighi's birth, but the technical problems of lighting and correcting distortion of the image were not overcome until much later.

Objects smaller than the wave-length of light cannot be seen, because the waves pass them by. This limits the useful magnification of an optical microscope to about 1000 diameters. Cross-lighting may reveal smaller objects, rather as a shaft of sunlight in a shaded place reveals particles of dust in the air. But to show detail at higher magnification, something smaller than light waves must be used. The electron microscope gives several hundred times the magnification of an optical microscope.

➤*histology*; *microbe*.

microsporum. A minute fungus, causing *ringworm* of the scalp.

micturition. Urination; act of passing urine. ➤*bladder*.

midbrain. Part of the brain-stem, between the *pons* and the *hypothalamus*. Its primitive function, to control the movements of the eyes, is retained in the human brain, but most of it is occupied by enormous bundles of nerve fibres connecting the cerebral cortex with lower centres. The most interesting structure in the midbrain is the *reticular formation*, a collection of nerve cells interspersed among a network of nerve fibres; it extends downwards from the midbrain to the upper end of the spinal cord. It appears to be a switching station in which sensations from the periphery are diverted either to consciousness or to reflex paths, and impulses to suppress or to stimulate muscles are sent to the periphery. Consciousness is an active process depending on impulses from the reticular formation. Sleep is a passive state in which these impulses are reduced.

midwifery = ➤*obstetrics*.

migraine. A common and distressing kind of headache, with no evident cause. Attacks last a few hours. They may be frequent, but some people have only one or two typical attacks in a lifetime. Warning symptoms such as a sense of flickering before the eyes are common; during the attack the patient cannot stand bright light. Most patients feel nauseated during or after the attack, and some actually vomit. The classic accounts of migraine describe the headache as one-sided: this is quite common but by no means the rule.

The site of the trouble seems to be the arteries inside and outside the skull, but the nature and cause of migraine are still unknown. It has no lasting effects, and the attacks become less frequent with time. Interference with substances such as *serotonin* that affect the relaxation and contraction of arteries is the likeliest explanation of migraine. Emotional upset, perhaps acting through such substances, plays some part but is not the main factor. Some patients find that particular foods or medicines provoke attacks.

Conventional analgesics (aspirin, paracetamol) may suffice with mild attacks. Ergotamine, with or without caffeine, has a more specific action. Antihistamine drugs, or antiemetics such as metoclopramide, can help to suppress nausea. At present the best remedy for acute attacks appears to be sumatryptan, which mimics serotonin. It is not to be combined with other drugs.

Apart from any medication, complete relaxation at the first warning signs can thwart some attacks, and techniques such as ►biofeedback may also be effective.

Drugs to reduce the frequency of attacks include *pizotifen* and some beta-blockers and calcium-channel blockers.

miliaria = ►*prickly heat*; minute sweat-blisters like *milia* – millet-seeds.

miliary tuberculosis. Small, widely scattered points of tuberculous infection.

milieu intérieur. Internal environment; the tissue fluid, a watery solution derived from the blood, in which the cells of the body lead their aquatic existence. ►*Bernard, Claude.*

milk. Human milk differs considerably from cow's milk in the proportions of its main ingredients: it contains about the same amount of fat, but twice as much sugar (lactose) and half as much protein. Human milk contains only just enough calcium and iron for the baby's needs.

For a few days after the birth of a baby, a woman forms a special kind of milk known as *colostrum*, corresponding with the beestings of cows. Colostrum contains about 8 per cent of protein, 2.5 per cent of fat, and 3.5 per cent of sugar (compared with 2 per cent, 4 per cent, and 8 per cent in ordinary human milk).

The vitamins in milk depend on the mother's diet, but the other components are maintained, if she is underfed, at the expense of her tissues, at least for a while. But after a few weeks the supply of milk fails if the mother has a poor diet or is ill, or even if she is emotionally disturbed.

A few drugs can affect the baby by way of the milk, but most, including alcohol, pass from the mother's blood-stream into the milk only in very small amounts. ►*breast.*

minim. In the apothecaries' measures, 1/60 drachm or 1/480 fluid ounce; roughly one drop.

miosis. Contraction of the pupil of the eye; *miotic* is a drug to cause this.

miscarriage ►*abortion.*

mite. A kind of small insect, e.g. *Sarcoptes scabei*, the itch-mite, which burrows into the skin and causes scabies.

mithramycin. An antibiotic, too poisonous to be used for treating infection, but (like actinomycin) more poisonous to certain cancer cells than to healthy tissue. It has a limited place in the treatment of cancer.

Mithridates (*fl.* 100 BC). King of Pontus. As a precaution against murder (for which he gave cause in plenty) he built up a resistance to poison, probably arsenic, by taking a small daily dose.

mithridaticum. The universal antidote, a favourite medieval remedy with scores of unpleasant and useless ingredients. Its name is derived from ►*Mithridates.*

mitosis. Reproduction of a cell, with duplication of the chromosomes so that each of the two new cells has all the properties of the original one; it is the normal process by which tissues grow.

mitral stenosis. Narrowing of the *mitral valve* by inflammation; the cause is nearly always rheumatic fever. As a result of scarring, the valve is shrunken but leaky, and the efficiency of the heart is impaired. In some cases the heart muscle compensates for the defect by pumping harder, but this may not be possible if the muscle itself has also been damaged by rheumatic fever or if the valve is much affected, and the condition then leads to disability.

A narrow mitral valve can be much improved by plastic surgery, or by implanting a synthetic valve.

mitral valve. Passage between the left atrium and left ventricle of the heart. ➤*valve.*

Mittelschmerz. Pain mid-way between menstrual periods, at the time of ovulation.

MMR (measles, mumps, rubella) vaccine. These common infections of childhood all carry their own risks, mentioned under those headings. MMR vaccination could, if widely enough distributed, eliminate all three as worldwide vaccination has eliminated smallpox, and this is among WHO's objectives. The policy is to give MMR vaccine to children at 12–15 months of age, unless there are contra-indications such as impaired immunity or certain allergies.

mole ➤*birth-mark.*

molecule. The smallest complete unit of a substance; a molecule can be broken down to smaller molecules or to its component atoms, but the substance then loses its identity.

Mondino de Luzzi (d. 1326). Anatomist at Bologna; the 'restorer of anatomy'. ➤*anatomy.*

mongolism ➤*Down's syndrome.*

Monilia ➤*Candida.*

Moniz, Egas ➤*psychosurgery.*

monoamine oxidase (MAO). An ➤*enzyme* which promotes the oxidation of adrenaline and similar substances (pressor amines), rendering them inactive. These amines transmit impulses from certain nerve fibres to adjoining nerve cells; if they were not promptly destroyed they would set off unwanted nervous activity. ➤*Depression* appears to be associated with a deficiency of some pressor amine in the brain. Drugs which suppress MAO activity (MAO-inhibitors) and so prolong the life of the amines relieve depression. Special precautions are needed with these drugs, because MAO is needed for inactivating various substances that are dangerous if they are allowed to accumulate. Patients taking MAO inhibitors have to avoid numerous other drugs and also certain foods including cheese: ➤*depression.*

monocyte. A large white blood cell. ➤*blood* (3).

mononucleosis ➤*glandular fever.*

Monro, Alexander (1697–1767). Scottish anatomist. He studied under Boerhaave at Leyden, a school that had become the leading centre of medical science. Monro returned to Edinburgh and brought its medical school into the front rank, where it has remained. He was succeeded in the chair of anatomy by his son (1733–1817) and grandson (1773–1859). These three Alexanders held the chair from 1720 till 1846.

morbilli = ➤*measles.*

Morgagni, Giovanni-Battista (1682–1771). Professor of anatomy at Padua from 1715 until his death; the last of a dynasty of geniuses that had begun in 1538 when Vesalius, the founder of scientific anatomy and therefore of modern medical science, was appointed to this chair. Morgagni's fame rests not on any particular discovery, but on a new approach to the problem of disease. He applied the detailed knowledge of his illustrious predecessors to the symptoms of disease, and related symptoms to the alterations of normal anatomy that could be found either by clinical observation or by post-mortem examination. His masterpiece *De Sedibus et Causis Morborum* is a series of accurate case-histories with the patients' symptoms related to the site and nature of the disease.

morning sickness. A common, tiresome, but seldom serious condition in the early part of pregnancy. The cause is not known. A very light snack (e.g. a few biscuits) before rising may be enough to allay the symptoms. No drugs are recommended. The trouble usually clears up in a few weeks.

More serious and persistent vomiting (*hyperemesis gravidarum*) is probably a different kind of disorder.

Moro reflex. (Ernst Moro, 1874–1951, German physician.) A reflex of early infancy: if the bed on which it lies is rapped, the baby protects itself by clutching its arms across the chest.

morphia; morphine. The main active principle of opium. The alkaloid morphine is used in the form of compounds such as the hydrochloride or the sulphate. The term 'morphia' includes all these. Their effects are identical.

Morphine and its derivatives (heroin etc.) suppress pain better than any other drugs except general anaesthetics. Very large doses of morphine actually induce anaesthesia, but they are too near to lethal doses to be safe.

Small doses probably do not interfere with the transmission of pain impulses to the brain, but they so alter the state of mind that these impulses cause little distress. Whether this is the same as suppressing pain depends on the definition of pain; according to the point of view taken here (▶*pain*) it is the same. Without the element of distress, pain has little meaning.

Larger doses depress the whole brain, and especially the vital centres for the regulation of breathing and circulation. Slight depression of the cough reflex is sometimes useful; for this purpose *codeine* (methyl morphine) is better and safer than morphine itself.

Morphine causes spasm of some involuntary muscles, e.g. in the intestine, and in this way can aggravate colic. Constipation is a tiresome side-effect. A few people complain of nausea. Continued administration of morphine inevitably induces ▶*drug dependence*.

For all its drawbacks, morphine is among the most valuable drugs. Apart from synthetic drugs closely related to morphine (e.g. pethidine) there is nothing to take its place, and Sydenham's dictum that nobody ought to be a physician without opium still holds good.

Morphine antagonists, such as naloxone, are drugs chemically related to morphine but lacking its depressant action on the brain. Nerve cells take them up instead of morphine, and cannot then take up morphine, because they can accommodate only a limited amount of either. These drugs have some value in treating overdosage of morphine, and especially in protecting new-born infants from narcotics given to the mother during labour (**>***endorphin*).

morphology. Comparative anatomy; the study of similarities and differences between species. The word was coined by Goethe; it took on new significance half a century later with Darwin's theories of evolution.

mosquito. Kinds of flying insect; the females of several species transmit infectious microbes by sucking blood. *Anopheles*, the carrier of malaria, can be distinguished from other mosquitoes by its slanting posture when it settles.

Other mosquito-borne diseases include *dengue* and *yellow fever* (*Aëdes* mosquitoes), and some types of virus *encephalitis* and *filariasis* (*Culex* mosquitoes).

Since mosquito-borne diseases are not contracted in any other way they can be eradicated by control of mosquitoes (**>***malaria*).

motion sickness = **>***travel sickness*.

motor neurone disease. An uncommon and mysterious degeneration of groups of nerve cells in the spinal cord and brain, with loss of function in the corresponding muscles. Neither cause nor remedy has yet been discovered.

mouth. Entrance to the digestive tract. In lower animals, the mouth is often no more than a hole at the front. In all vertebrates, one of the gill-openings is modified to form a movable jaw, and this is one reason for the dominance of these animals over other types. With this kind of mouth an animal can choose its food instead of merely accepting what comes, and the mouth can also be a weapon of defence or attack. Man has to rely much less on his mouth than other vertebrates, because he can do even better with his hands.

The mouth extends from the lips to the back of the tongue where the pharynx begins. The roof (hard palate) and the arch of the lower jaw are rigid; otherwise the mouth is surrounded by muscles. These muscles act in concert with the tongue during the mastication and swallowing of food, and they are essential to articulate speech.

The whole of the cavity is lined with a mucous membrane. Small mucous glands are scattered throughout the membrane except on the outer surface of the lips. The mucus from these glands, together with the saliva, keeps the mouth clean and lubricated.

Specially modified nerve-endings, the taste-buds, are found on the surface of the tongue and palate.

In the embryo, the tissues of the mouth grow from each side into the gap between the brain and the heart and meet in the mid-line. Incomplete fusion results in various degrees of harelip and cleft palate (**>***palate*).

The mouth teems with bacteria, yet although minor injuries to the lining are very frequent, serious infection is quite uncommon. Most of the bacteria, but not all, are harmless, and there seems to be far more resistance to infection than most mucous membranes have. Even severe wounds of the mouth generally heal without much trouble – whereas human bites on the skin, which must be contaminated with the same bacteria, nearly always develop serious infection and are notoriously slow to heal.

But if the general health is poor because of malnutrition or chronic poisoning (e.g. alcohol, lead), or especially with fevers when the flow of saliva is reduced, infection of the mouth is very common. Keeping the mouth clean and moist is an important part of general nursing with any severe illness.

moxibustion. Treatment of disease by burning a *moxa*, a small heap of dried mugwort, on the skin to raise a blister. The method differs from the use of poultices in that the moxa is not necessarily applied over the affected organ, but at some point from which the organ is said to be influenced. ➤*Chinese medicine*.

MRI (magnetic resonance imaging) ➤*scan*.

mucopus. Mucus contaminated with pus, e.g. sputum with bronchitis.

mucosa. Mucous membrane.

mucous. Associated with *mucus*. A *mucous membrane* is a delicate skin-like layer containing glands that secrete mucus, e.g. the linings of the air-passages and digestive tract.

mucoviscidosis = ➤*cystic fibrosis*.

mucus. A clear viscous fluid, forming a protective barrier on the surfaces of lining membranes.

Müller, Johannes (1801–58). German philosopher and medical scientist; a physiologist with whom only Claude Bernard (1813–78) stands comparison. Müller was a late product of the Renaissance: Bernard, with his insistence on arguing from nothing that had not been demonstrated, was a specialized scientist of our own time. Most of the current concepts of normal and abnormal bodily function can be traced directly to the work of one or the other.

Müller put every known science to the service of medicine, and himself contributed a most versatile imagination. He is best known for his theory of *specific nerve energies* – a given sensory nerve conveys only a single kind of sensation, regardless of how it is stimulated, and our awareness of the world therefore depends on the properties of our nerve-endings. This has the profoundest implications for psychology as well as for the mere mechanics of the nervous system. Possible exceptions to the theory (➤*taste*) do not affect its value as a working hypothesis, a starting-point for research.

His studies embraced far more than one man could develop in a lifetime, but fortunately he was among the greatest of teachers, and there was no shortage of younger men to extend his work. Müller's pupils included the physicist Helmholtz, who explained the mechanisms of vision and hearing, Henle and Schwann, who brought microscopic anatomy up to date, and the greatest of pathologists, Virchow.

multiple sclerosis (disseminated sclerosis). A chronic disease of the central nervous system in which small, scattered areas of the brain and spinal cord degenerate and nerve fibres lose their insulating myelin sheaths and their ability to conduct impulses. The *sclerosis* resembles scarring after a virus infection such as poliomyelitis; but there is no evidence of infection or any other cause.

The symptoms depend entirely on where the patches of sclerosis appear, and they can therefore mimic those of almost any disorder of the nervous system. This is an episodic disorder: symptoms come and go, and between episodes the patient may be well for months or years. As a result, the most extravagant claims have been made for all manner of remedies; but at present no treatment is of lasting value.

mumps (epidemic parotitis). A common virus disease to which most people acquire immunity through a childhood attack.

The virus, which resembles that of influenza, is air-borne. An attack begins 2–4 weeks after exposure with mild fever, followed by painful swelling of the parotid salivary glands lasting a day or two. As a rule the symptoms then vanish, but sometimes the infection spreads to other salivary glands or, less often, to the testes or pancreas. Like other virus diseases, mumps can involve the nervous system, but the symptoms are nearly always mild and short-lasting.

In grown men, mumps occasionally causes sterility; and a few cases of diabetes from involvement of the pancreas have been recorded.

murmur. Any sound from the heart additional to the normal heart sounds. ►*stethoscope.*

muscarine. A highly poisonous alkaloid from the mushroom *fly agaric* (*Amanita muscaria*); both chemically and in its effects it resembles *acetyl choline.* The effects are abolished by atropine.

muscle. Muscle is the most abundant tissue in the body; it accounts for some two fifths of the body weight. The specialized component is the *muscle fibre*, a long slender cell or agglomeration of cells which becomes shorter and thicker in response to a stimulus. These fibres are supported and bound together by ordinary connective tissue, and are well supplied with blood vessels and nerves.

The chemical components include *actomyosin*, a protein responsible for the actual contraction; *myoglobin*, which resembles the haemoglobin of blood and maintains the store of oxygen; *phos-*

phates for transferring energy; and glucose, stored as *glycogen*, for fuel.

There are 3 types of muscle: striated, smooth, and cardiac.

Striated (= striped, voluntary, skeletal) muscle is the flesh or lean meat. The 'stripes' are bands across the fibres about 1/1000 mm wide produced by regular alternation of the actin and myosin components of actomyosin. Nearly all striated muscle is under conscious control, but also takes part in unconscious reflexes (►'Mechanics', below).

Smooth (= plain, involuntary, visceral) muscle is found in the walls of the digestive and urinary tracts and other hollow organs, and of the blood vessels. Its fibres, each a single cell, are much shorter than striated fibres. All smooth muscle is controlled unconsciously through the ►*sympathetic* and ►*parasympathetic* nervous systems, usually together, one stimulating and the other inhibiting.

Cardiac muscle, the substance of the heart, can be regarded as an enormously developed involuntary muscle in the wall of a blood vessel, but it differs from any other muscle. Its fibres are short and thick, and form a dense mesh. They contract rhythmically without any nervous impulse; the nerves only modify the rate of contraction (►*heart*).

1. NATURE OF MUSCLE CONTRACTION

Within a muscle fibre threads of the two proteins actin and myosin are arranged in interlocking bundles. When the protein actomyosin is formed the bundles of actin are drawn further into the bundles of myosin, so that the fibre is shortened. The energy for this chemical reaction is provided by the breakdown of adenosine triphosphate (ATP) to adenosine

trapezius

deltoid

triceps

latissimus dorsi

extensors
of wrist
and hand

flexors
of wrist
and hand

gluteus
maximus

hamstrings

gastrocnemius

Achilles tendon

sterno mastoid

pectoralis major

biceps

serratus anterior

extensors of
wrist and hand

flexors of
wrist and hand

rectus abdominus

sartorius

quadriceps

extensors of foot

Superficial muscles, back and front

diphosphate (ADP). Myosin is itself the enzyme which promotes this breakdown.

Energy is then needed to convert ADP back to ATP. The ultimate source is the combustion of glucose (stored in the muscle as ►*glycogen*) with oxygen to form carbon dioxide. But oxygen may not be immediately available – it is quite usual to hold the breath during brief exertion such as a short sprint where the deep breathing comes after the race. The conversion of glucose to lactic acid provides some energy without using any oxygen at all: $(CH_2O)_6 \rightarrow 2(CH_2O)_3$. This mechanism cannot, however, be used for long, because if lactic acid accumulates muscle quickly tires. It simply delays the moment when oxygen must be brought in to complete the conversion to carbon dioxide, with further release of energy: $2(CH_2O)_3 + 6O_2 \rightarrow 6CO_2 + 6H_2O$. In the meantime there is a state of *oxygen debt*.

The motor nerve joins the muscle fibre at the motor end-plate. An impulse in the nerve causes release of *acetyl choline*, which triggers off the conversion of ATP to ADP. How this 'pulls' the bundles of actin and myosin together is not yet known.

Some impulses to smooth muscle are transmitted by noradrenaline instead of acetyl choline. Heart muscle gets energy from fat rather than glucose and so is undisturbed by variations in the amount of glucose in the blood.

2. CONTROL

Smooth muscle fibres are so arranged that some bundles encircle the organ and others run the length of it. The former squeeze, while the latter shorten a segment of the organ, pushing the contents forward to the next segment, which is re-laxed to receive them. Waves of contraction flow along the organ. This activity is called *peristalsis*. Most smooth muscle has a double nerve supply: one causes contraction and the other actively promotes relaxation.

Striated muscle has only one set of motor nerves, originating in the spinal cord, and relaxation is merely the absence of contraction. But the motor nerve cells in the spinal cord are connected with other nerves of which some stimulate (for instance those under conscious control from the brain) and others inhibit.

The conscious will determines the kind of movement to be made, *and no more*. Even a simple movement needs several muscles to contract, not all by the same amount, and other muscles to relax. This is all reflex action. A man decides to drive a screw home. Having placed the screwdriver he must grip it and turn it clockwise. He grips with the flexor muscles to his fingers, but most of them arise in the forearm and also flex the wrist. The wrist is kept straight by simultaneous action of its extensors. He twists mainly with his biceps. The muscles for twisting the forearm anticlockwise must be inhibited. On its own, the biceps would also bend the elbow; therefore its antagonist the triceps also contracts to steady the elbow. To prevent the thumb side of the hand from being turned outwards away from the screw the whole limb must be rotated inwards by the shoulder muscles. If the man has to exert pressure on the screw the muscles joining the shoulder-blade to the trunk come into play. All this activity is unconscious and reflex except the intention to turn a screw.

3. MECHANICS

Even at rest a muscle is not completely

flabby. Continuous activity of the nerve cells maintains a slight tension or *tone*, which causes no movement because it is balanced by the tone of the opposed muscles. The engine is kept permanently ticking over, never switched off. If anything tends to stretch a muscle, the tone is automatically increased to resist the tendency. An increase of tone without shortening is called *isometric* contraction. In the example of the screwdriver, the triceps contracts isometrically. If on the other hand a muscle pulls, i.e. shortens, against a steady resistance, the tone is constant while the length changes; this is *isotonic* contraction. In practice most activity is a mixture of the two.

The action of a particular muscle is usually described in terms of the movement when it contracts isotonically – its attachments to the skeleton are brought closer together. Thus the quadriceps muscle in front of the thigh straightens the bent knee by pulling the front of the tibia up towards the femur, a kicking movement. But when the opposing hamstring muscles bend the knee, the quadriceps is stretched. The reflex of muscle tone would resist this, and has to be suppressed by a contrary reflex action.

A man standing at the alert with his knees slightly bent uses the isometric contraction of quadriceps to hold the position against gravity. This kind of static or postural action is the most important function of many muscles, especially in a precariously balanced animal such as man.

4. DISORDERS

There are few common diseases of muscle. Tumours are very rare excepting an innocent tumour of the uterus (►*fibroid*). Primary infection of muscle is also rare (the muscle abscesses seen in tropical Africa are thought to arise from malnutrition).

Several hereditary diseases affect the growth and function of muscles (►*myopathy*). Apart from familial periodic paralysis, a disturbance of potassium balance, they are little understood.

The balance of potassium and sodium is upset by loss of salt from severe sweating or diarrhoea, and this interferes with the transmission of impulses in muscle.

Some bacterial toxins and chemical poisons appear to affect muscle directly, but the motor nerves are much more vulnerable. In ►*poliomyelitis* motor nerve cells in the spinal cord are destroyed, and all activity in the corresponding muscles ceases as though the nerves had been cut. On the other hand ►*tetanus*, like strychnine poisoning, stops inhibition of the motor cells, throwing the muscles into uncontrolled contraction.

Calcium plays some part in muscle action, perhaps in triggering the breakdown of ATP (►'Nature of Muscle Contraction', above). If the calcium balance is disturbed, e.g. by ►*rickets*, ►*parathyroid* disease, or ►*alkalosis*, the muscles become irritable and over-active, a state known as *tetany*.

Impulses from nerve to muscle are transmitted by the release of acetyl choline. ►*Myasthenia gravis* is a disease in which this mechanism fails from time to time. Poisoning with ►*curare* prevents acetyl choline from acting on the muscle fibres; this is a useful means of relaxing muscles to facilitate surgery.

muscle relaxants. Drugs that prevent nerve impulses from being transmitted to muscle fibres. The muscles are thus as effectively paralysed as an electric light with a blown fuse.

The principal use of temporary paralysis is for surgical operations, where the complete relaxation makes the surgeon's work easier (and therefore safer), and reduces the dose of anaesthetic. The same principle can be applied to diseases in which violent muscle spasm is a threat to life, such as tetanus. The original drug of this type is ►*curare*.

Drugs used for treating the chronic muscular spasm of some disorders of the nervous system include *baclophen*, which acts on the nerves, and *dantrolene*, acting on the muscles themselves. Benzodiazepines, e.g. *diazepam*, have some relaxant action even in the customary dosage, which accounts for some of their tranquillizing effect. Large doses have been successfully used for treating tetanus (►*relaxation*).

muscular atrophy ►*myopathy*.

muscular dystrophy ►*myopathy*.

muscular rheumatism ►*fibrositis*.

mushroom. Kinds of large fungus. The mushroom itself is the spore-bearing or reproductive part of the fungus.

There are many species, some edible and some poisonous, and the differences are not always obvious. The only safe rule is to eat no fungus that one cannot positively identify. Accidents are uncommon, but when they do happen they are serious.

Some poisonous varieties are made relatively safe by their disgusting taste. The two most dangerous kinds of poison are *muscarine* and *phallin*. Muscarine occurs in several species, notably *Amanita muscaria*, a red toadstool with white spots. It resembles ►*acetyl choline*, and has similar effects: diarrhoea, vomiting, and

depression of the heart. Atropine is an effective antidote. Phallin behaves like a snake venom. The symptoms are delayed for some hours. They include severe dysentery, and damage to the nervous system, blood cells, liver, and kidneys. Many of the patients die a few days later from liver failure and general exhaustion. The main source of phallin poisoning is *Amanita phalloides* (death cap), which bears a superficial resemblance to the common mushroom.

Edible mushrooms are an attractive garnish and flavouring, but the food value is negligible.

mutation ►*genetics* (4).

myalgic encephalomyelitis (ME syndrome). The name is a massive overstatement. Encephalomyelitis means inflammation of the brain and spinal cord, a serious and sometimes fatal result of infection. ME is an ill-defined collection of symptoms that include aching muscles, lassitude and depression. It may linger for months before complete recovery. It commonly follows a virus infection, notably glandular fever. *Post-viral fatigue syndrome* is a better name for it.

myasthenia gravis. An uncommon disease, affecting voluntary muscles. The characteristic symptom is rapid weakening of muscles when they are made to work, with slow recovery at rest. An affected muscle does not respond to stimulation by the trace of acetyl choline released from its controlling nerve, exactly as though it were poisoned with curare. The drug *eserine* increases the effect of acetyl choline and restores a normal response. More effective drugs with similar action, such as neostigmine and pyridostigmine, are now used. Corticosteroids also help.

Myasthenia gravis is often associated with disease of the thymus gland, and it is now regarded as an autoimmune disease (*immunity* (7)) with circulating antibodies that act against both the receptor for nervous impulses in muscle fibres, and the thymus. Some patients improve if the thymus is removed.

mycobacterium. A genus of bacteria slightly resembling minute fungi, including the bacilli of tuberculosis and leprosy.

mycoplasma. A kind of microbe, seemingly between a bacterium and a fungus, causing 'atypical' ➤*pneumonia.*

mycosis. Disease caused by a ➤*fungus.*

myelin. A greasy substance forming an insulating sheath around nerve fibres. In many diseases of the nervous system the fibres lose their myelin sheaths and fail to conduct impulses.

myelitis. Inflammation of marrow: an ambiguous term because *marrow* can mean bone marrow or the spinal cord.

myelocoele. Protrusion of spinal cord through a defect in a vertebra. ➤*spina bifida.*

myelography. X-ray examination of the spinal cord.

myeloma. A tumour of bone-marrow cells, with a tendency to appear simultaneously in several places. There are several types, corresponding with the various types of cell in bone marrow. Some are comparatively harmless, but some are progressive in the manner of *leukaemia.* All are rare.

myocardial infarction (MI). Suffocation of a segment of the heart muscle by blockage of an artery. Deprived of its supply of oxygen, the segment is at once put out of action. This can be rapidly fatal, but with any luck the damaged muscle is replaced in time by a firm puckered scar. The blockage is usually by a blood clot (thrombus) stuck to the lining of a coronary artery already damaged by *atheroma* (blood will not normally clot in a healthy vessel). Most heart attacks are of this kind. *Coronary thrombosis* is a less accurate term because MI is sometimes due to narrowing of the artery by atheroma without thrombosis.

With hindsight the patient may recall premonitory symptoms such as vague chest pains or simply feeling off colour, but the first symptom to be reported is usually an abrupt onset of gripping pain in the chest (sometimes shoulder, neck, arm or back) like that of ➤*angina* but persistent. The degree of pain varies greatly; it can be agonizing or so mild as almost to pass unnoticed. The patient is likely to be pale, clammy and anxious. A blood test reveals characteristic changes in the levels of certain enzymes, and an electrocardiogram serves not only to confirm the diagnosis but to show the location and extent of the damage.

The immediate danger is that the normal pumping action of the heart may give way to a futile seething motion (ventricular fibrillation) or stop altogether. In this case the chance of recovery depends on immediate ➤*resuscitation.*

The intensive care unit of a modern hospital has facilities for continuous monitoring of the heart action and other vital functions, and for dealing at once with any threat to them. The danger to life decreases rapidly after the first 2–3 hours. As a rule the patient is reasonably safe after 2–3 days, and ready to recuperate at home a week or so later, with every hope of resuming a normal life in 2–3 months.

The point has often been raised that the stresses of being bundled into an ambulance, rushed to a strange hospital bed and festooned with wires and tubes could do an already alarmed patient more harm than good. Against this may be set the reassurance of knowing that everything possible is on hand for keeping him out of further danger.

In the early stages pain is often (not always) the dominant symptom; a narcotic such as morphine may be needed. In Britain, unlike many countries, diamorphine (heroin) is not outlawed and many physicians prefer it as having fewer side-effects. It is given for too short a time for any risk of dependence.

In some cases an enzyme such as streptokinase given within a few hours of the attack may dissolve the clot (thrombolysis). Small doses of aspirin reduce the risk of further clotting, and more powerful anticoagulants such as heparin are also used during the early stages of recovery. Drugs are available for dealing with irregularities of the heartbeat after MI, and some patients may still need treatment for angina.

(►*angina*; *atheroma*; *ischaemic heart disease*.)

myoglobin. Oxygen-carrying pigment in muscle, similar to *haemoglobin* in blood.

myoma. Tumour of muscle; a very rare condition (because muscle cells cannot normally multiply), except for the innocent tumours of the uterus known as ►*fibroids*.

myopathy. Literally, any disease of muscle; in practice, any of a group of rare diseases of which inadequate func-tion of voluntary muscles is the principal or only symptom.

The various myopathies affect different parts of the *motor unit*. This consists of a *nerve cell* in the spinal cord or brain, with a long thread-like extension, a *nerve fibre*, leading to a muscle. There is a kind of junction box between the nerve fibre and its subordinate *muscle fibres*, which complete the unit. A defect anywhere in the unit has much the same effect: the muscles are inefficient.

Numerous types of myopathy have been described, according to the part of the motor unit that is defective or, less logically, to the groups of muscles that are weak. The rarest types have the longest names.

A muscle without a nerve does not thrive. Myopathy of this type is known as *muscular atrophy*. With congenital types where the original number of nerve cells is defective, the corresponding muscle fibres never develop. Where groups of nerve cells degenerate in adult life (*motor neurone disease*) the affected muscles waste. With different types of muscular atrophy the disability may be anything from trivial to incapacitating. No effective treatment has been found because lost nerve cells do not regenerate.

►*Myasthenia gravis* is a defect of transmission across the gap between nerve and muscle.

Muscular dystrophy includes several uncommon disorders in which muscles waste away for no known reason. The muscle fibres behave as though their controlling nerves have been put out of action (as with the muscular wasting of poliomyelitis), but the nerves appear to be normal. All forms of muscular dystrophy are hereditary. They are distinguished by severity, age of the patient at onset, and distribution of affected muscles.

The *Duchenne* type of muscular dystrophy is the least uncommon, and unfortunately the most severe. It is inherited as a sex-linked recessive character (like haemophilia), carried in the female line and affecting males. Muscular weakness sets in during childhood, starting in the hips and spreading upwards and downwards. Walking is affected from the start and in time becomes impossible. Patients cannot be expected to live beyond about 20 years. So far, no effective treatment has been found, but at least there is a good chance of identifying carriers and warning them that, should they have children, their sons would have a 50 per cent chance of developing the disease. Other forms of muscular dystrophy are much less dangerous, and some do not affect life expectancy.

Myotonia is abnormal tension of resting muscles. It is seldom a serious affliction.

Familial periodic paralysis behaves as the name suggests. The periodic attacks of paralysis are due to inability to keep a constant concentration of potassium in the blood; they are treated by adjusting the intake and output of potassium.

Lastly, some disorders of endocrine glands, especially over-activity of the thyroid, may cause a kind of myopathy, treated by treating the primary disorders.

myopia. Short sight. ➤*vision*.

myositis. Inflammation of muscle. Bacterial infection is not usual in muscle, but one type – gas gangrene – is extremely dangerous if it does occur. Natives of tropical Africa commonly suffer from large abscesses in muscle (*pyomyositis*) without evidence of infection.

Myositis ossificans is a very uncommon disorder where bony deposits appear in muscle.

Some rheumatic diseases may affect muscles as well as joints, and this can be regarded as a sort of myositis (or fibrositis).

myotonia ➤*myopathy*.

myringotomy. Surgical perforation of the ear-drum to release pus from the middle ear with *otitis media*.

myxoedema. Coarsening of the skin with other symptoms of failure of the thyroid gland in adult life. ➤*thyroid* (2).

N

naevus ►*birth-mark*.

nagana. A disease of cattle in tropical Africa, carried by tsetse flies and closely related to human sleeping sickness. ►*trypanosome*.

nail-biting. This very common habit appears to be a symptom of insecurity.

nails. A nail grows from a tuck in the skin. It is composed of *keratin* like that of the outermost layer of the skin and the hair. The small patch of skin covered by the tuck forms the *matrix* from which the nail grows. The rest of the nail-bed – under the exposed part of the nail – does not contribute. If the matrix is seriously damaged, the whole nail is lost.

Ill health, especially when there is an element of malnutrition, commonly affects the growth of the nails. Iron deficiency causes softening and concavity of the nails. But the commonest defect – splitting – has no apparent cause.

Small injuries at the side of a fingernail are easily infected, and the infection may get between the nail and its bed to form a kind of whitlow (*paronychia*). Acute paronychia is a painful condition, often needing a minor operation to release a bead of pus. If the infection has already spread for any distance part of the nail may have to be removed.

Chronic paronychia is common among housewives, because constant immersion in hot water makes the skin of the fingertips soggy and vulnerable to mild infection. There is little swelling or pain, but the trouble persists and the nail may become deformed. Antibiotics are used to overcome the infection, but the most effective treatment is keeping the hands dry.

Ringworm of the nails, usually associated with 'athlete's foot', is a minor but tiresome complaint. In the past an affected nail had usually to be removed before the infection could be eradicated, but the antibiotic *griseofulvin* now provides an effective remedy without surgery.

Psoriasis, a common disease of the skin, often causes small blemishes on the fingernails.

narcolepsy. A rare disorder: the patient is normal except for fits of uncontrollable sleepiness and sudden waves of muscular weakness. The cause is unknown. Amphetamine and similar drugs generally ward off the attacks.

narcosis. Dulling of consciousness ('a drowsy numbness'); also = *anaesthesia*.

narcotic. Any drug producing narcosis, especially morphine and similar drugs of addiction.

The word *narcotic* illustrates the difficulty of classifying drugs. Many drugs conventionally placed in other categories act as narcotics, and their classification depends on the dose. *Hemp* (cannabis) has a narcotic effect, but its devotees take it not so much for this effect as for the mental derangement, including hallucinations, which releases them from reality. Hence this drug is often classified as a *hallucinogen*, along with other drugs that excite rather than benumb the brain. *Hyoscine* antagonizes the parasympathetic nervous system, like ➤*atropine*, but unlike atropine it has a narcotic action that has been used to produce 'twilight sleep', a state of incomplete anaesthesia. All ➤*anaesthetics* are narcotic, and in current German usage narcotic and anaesthetic are practically syonymous. To increase the confusion, the term narcotic is sometimes applied to drugs of addiction in general, though some of these have little or no narcotic action.

In this book, *narcotic* refers to a group of drugs used to relieve pain, that also sedate and, in larger doses, stupefy the patient. Drugs that relieve pain without this narcotic effect are classed as ➤*analgesic*.

The prototype of narcotic drugs is ➤*morphine*, extracted from opium, and the other members of the group have similar actions to morphine. *Codeine*, also found in opium, is intermediate between the narcotics and the simple analgesics. *Heroin* was first synthesized from morphine in the hope that it would be less addictive, but in fact it is even more so.

The numerous synthetic narcotics include *pethidine*, which does not depress respiration as much as morphine, and relieves rather than aggravates colic; *methadone*, sometimes given as an alternative to morphine or heroin as a first step in the treatment of addiction; and *pentazocine*, which is said to be less addictive than some of the others.

All drugs of this class are potentially lethal, and all must be regarded as addictive. ➤*drug dependence*.

nasolacrimal duct. Passage for drainage of tears into the nose. The eyes water with a cold in the nose or hay fever, when the duct is blocked by swelling of the mucous membrane at its outlet.

nasopharynx. Region behind the nose, above and behind the soft palate. ➤*pharynx*.

naturopathy. A system of preserving health by means of a simple diet, regular exercise, and the avoidance of drugs or anything that seems artificial. It is based on the principle that natural processes will keep the body in health if they are given a fair chance instead of being constantly thwarted by unnatural foods, customs, and medicines.

Naturopathy has no need to justify itself – that is amply done by the known results of overeating, smoking, lack of exercise and the rest. The difficulty arises from not knowing what is natural. People who think it natural to wear no clothes forget that *Homo sapiens* is a subtropical species that has adapted itself to other climates by having the ingenuity to dress. Other species depend for survival on physical attributes, but man lives by his wits. He avoids starvation by farming – which is systematic interference with Nature – and by cooking and preserving some of his food. Muck-spreading is no more 'natural' than spreading accurately measured chemical fertilizers.

Purists in this cult avoid all drugs or medicines. They miss the chance of curing some eminently curable diseases, but they also avoid dangers such as poisoning their stomachs with aspirin, their kidneys with phenacetin, or their intestines with purgatives. It is harder to justify a belief that some medicines are natural and good, while others are artificial and bad. All effective medicines are potentially dangerous, and in fact the chemists have yet to produce anything as lethal as the 'natural' poisons of some medicinal plants. All chemicals must be made from naturally occurring raw materials, and many synthetic drugs are only slight modifications of substances found in living matter. Cinchona bark is a natural remedy for malaria. It has the disadvantage that different samples contain different amounts of the active principle, quinine. Therefore quinine, unnaturally extracted from cinchona, is a better drug: the dose can be measured exactly. Even refined quinine is neither as safe nor as effective as the newer synthetic drugs of the same chemical family. The raw material is coal tar. But coal tar is itself derived from plants; it is as natural as cinchona bark.

To object, as the strictest naturopaths do, to all medicines, and even to food grown with the aid of artificial fertilizers, is to deprive man of the one thing that has enabled him to survive – his ability to devise methods of adapting his environment to his needs, which he has evolved while other creatures have wings or claws or long legs as their means of survival. But only fools would argue with naturopaths about walking rather than driving, and moderation in diet, and escaping from large towns whenever possible, and eating fresh vegetables rather than slimming pills.

nausea. Sensation of being about to vomit; either an inborn ➤*reflex* from irritation of the vagus nerves in the stomach, or a conditioned reflex from stimulation of the same nervous pathways, e.g. by disgusting sights or smells, when a sort of overspill of nervous activity triggers off impulses in the brain that are usually associated with overactivity of the stomach muscle.

navel = ➤*umbilicus.*

necator. A kind of hookworm. ➤*worms.*

neck. The core of the neck is the column of 7 *cervical vertebrae* encased by a com-

plex system of muscles which move the vertebrae or maintain their posture. The neck serves to direct the main sensory organs and weapons without the need for cumbersome movements of the whole body. Man lives more by his hands than by his ears, nose, and teeth, and in this sense has less use for a neck than other animals. On the other hand his highly developed, stereoscopic vision requires a mobile neck, as anyone knows who has tried to play tennis with a stiff neck.

In an early human embryo only the mouth separates the head from the heart. At about 3 weeks rudimentary ➤*gills* appear in the mouth region, pushing the head and heart further apart. Most of the face and neck, and also the lungs, arise from these gills. The heart and lungs migrate to the ➤*thorax*, dragging with them the various structures still joining them to the head and neck. Thus there are two groups of organs in the front of the neck: structures in transit to the thorax, and structures properly belonging to the neck.

1. STRUCTURES IN TRANSIT

In the mid-line the ➤*pharynx* lies immediately in front of the vertebrae. It is the continuation of both nose and mouth, and starts as a channel common to breathing and eating. At the level of the Adam's apple the air-passage becomes separated from the digestive tube as the ➤*larynx*. The pharynx continues downwards behind the larynx; here it is concerned only with swallowing, and the larynx with breathing and speaking. In the lower part of the neck the pharynx continues as the ➤*oesophagus* – still lying on the vertebral column – and the larynx as the ➤*trachea*.

At either side of the pharynx, mostly

under cover of the sternomastoid muscle, the ►*carotid artery* runs up to the head with the internal ►*jugular vein* beside it. The ►*vagus* nerve accompanies the artery, and the ►*sympathetic* nerve chain runs behind, on the transverse processes of the vertebrae.

Spinal nerves emerging from the sides of the vertebrae between the muscles of the neck are distributed to the neck itself and to the upper limbs (►*brachial* plexus).

Since the ►*diaphragm* first arises in this region and migrates with the heart to the thorax, it derives its nerve from the neck.

The vertebral column protects the ►*spinal cord* and the two *vertebral arteries*, which share the supply of the brain with the internal carotid arteries.

2. LOCAL STRUCTURES

The salivary glands (►*saliva*) at the rim of the lower jaw are on the boundary of neck and face. The ►*thyroid* gland is at the front and sides of the larynx and trachea. The 4 ►*parathyroid* glands are behind the thyroid gland.

Lymph nodes are widely distributed in the neck. One chain encircles the neck from nape to chin; another runs down alongside the internal jugular vein.

3. DISORDERS

With so many vital structures at risk, *injuries* are obviously more serious than in most parts of the body. Fractures and dislocations (►*vertebrae*) may cause paralysis or, if the uppermost part of the spinal cord is torn, death. The fractures are not in themselves important; what matters is the extent to which the cord is involved.

The neck is crowded, and *swellings*, whether from bleeding, inflammation, or tumours, may interfere with swallowing or breathing.

The gills disappear long before birth, leaving only the structures derived from them (e.g. jaws, tongue, thyroid, parathyroids, ear, larynx). But occasionally a gill remains, either as a cyst or as an opening at the side of the neck. These anomalies can be corrected surgically. *Torticollis* (wry-neck) may be due to injury of a sternomastoid muscle at birth.

Other disorders are discussed under the names of the various structures.

necropsy. Post-mortem examination.

necrosis. Death of some portion of an organ, e.g. from damage to its blood supply or poisoning by bacteria.

necrotizing enterocolitis. A disease of very young, especially premature, babies. Bacteria invade the wall of the intestine, causing severe damage and sometimes perforation. The affected infants are mostly delicate from the start, and nearly a third of them succumb. Because the bacteria thrive on normal feeds the patient has to be fed by infusion while the infection is treated with antibiotics. Perforation or gangrene of the intestine requires immediate surgery.

Neisseria. A genus of bacteria, including those of epidemic meningitis and of gonorrhoea. They are fragile organisms, difficult to grow in the laboratory, and unable to survive long in the open air.

nematode. Roundworm. ►*worms*.

neomycin. An antibiotic extracted from the fungus *Streptomyces fradiae*.

neonatal. Of new-born babies, conventionally limited to the first 4 weeks of life.

neoplasm. New growth; a useless proliferation of tissue (= ►*tumour*).

nephrectomy. Removal of one kidney. Provided that the other kidney is healthy, the operation does not cause disability; a single kidney has enough functional reserve to take on the work of two.

nephritis. Literally the word means inflammation of the kidneys, but it is, or has been, applied to many conditions that are not inflammatory. It replaced the older term *Bright's disease* without clarifying it. Several types of nephritis are considered under ►*kidneys* (5).

nephroblastoma (Wilms' tumour). Cancer of the kidney in infancy. ►*kidneys* (5).

nephrolithiasis. Stone in the kidney; renal ►*calculus*.

nephrosis. Any disease of the kidney with *oedema* (dropsy, retention of water in the body) as the main symptom. The term *nephrotic syndrome* is more usual, because it implies that the condition is a symptom of something else and not a definite disease.
    ►*kidneys*.

nerve. A nerve is a bundle of conducting fibres, a cable. Motor fibres conduct impulses *from*, sensory fibres *to* the brain or spinal cord. Nearly all nerves include both kinds.

Twelve pairs of ►*cranial nerves* arise from the brain and pass through the skull, and 31 pairs of ►*spinal nerves* arise from the spinal cord and pass between the vertebrae. All other nerves are branches of these; some are formed from the union of several branches.

The conducting fibres are projections (axons) of cells in the brain or cord. A nerve fibre in the foot is part of a cell which has its nucleus at the level of the lowest ribs. Since lost nerve cells cannot

be replaced, and nerves are easily injured, it is well that the vital part of the cell is out of harm's way.

Each fibre is enclosed in an insulating tube of myelin, an arrangement like a telephone cable. If a nerve is injured these tubes must first heal before the conducting fibres can be restored. With a crushing injury the tubes may still be intact although the fibres within are broken, in which case healing is no problem. New fibres can grow down the tubes from the nerve cells. This regeneration may take many weeks but it is likely to be complete. When a nerve is cut the ends can be sewn together and will heal, but the thousands of fibres cannot all be expected to grow down the right tubes. A fibre from a motor nerve cell which grows down a tube leading to a sensory organ in the skin cannot function. Thus even after prompt and careful surgery a cut nerve seldom recovers completely, but with luck the results can be surprisingly good. The brain seems to learn to interpret signals arriving by new paths.

Nerve fibres within the brain and spinal cord are equipped with a simpler kind of myelin sheath which is not restored when it is damaged, and here injured fibres do not recover.

Conduction in nerves can be interrupted in several ways. Cold, lack of oxygen, pressure, and local anaesthetic drugs all block nerves. They are effective wherever along the course of the nerve they are applied. A local anaesthetic may be injected at the root of the neck to paralyse the nerves of the hand during an operation, and the pressure of a bone or tendon in the same region may cause numbness of the fingers.
    ►►*nervous system*; *neuralgia*; *neuropathy*.

nervous system

1. CENTRAL NERVOUS SYSTEM

Even the simplest animal – a protozoon made of a single cell – responds to a stimulus by withdrawing itself. In more advanced creatures some of the cells in the outer layer of the body are adapted to receive stimuli and transmit them to other cells adapted for movement. Cells that transmit impulses to other cells are called nerve cells or *neurones*. In all higher animals the neurones are gathered together to form an anatomical unit, the *nervous system*, derived entirely from the outermost layer of the embryo (*ectoderm*), which also forms the outer coat of the skin.

In the embryo of a vertebrate (such as man) the future neurones are gathered in the mid-line of the surface of the back. This strip, running the length of the embryo, is first depressed to form a groove and then submerged, as the tissues of the back close over it, to form a tube. Later this *neural tube* is surrounded by the skull and vertebrae, to form the ►*brain* and ►*spinal cord*, together making the *central nervous system*.

A neurone consists of a cell-body with several thread-like projections or *processes*. There are generally several branched processes, *dendrites*, and a single long process, the *axon*, which is the main conducting fibre. An axon may be very long – extending, for instance, from a cell-body in the spinal cord at the small of the back to a muscle in the foot. Similarly, sensory processes extend from the periphery to their parent cells in the nerve roots (►*spinal nerves*). The nerves of the body are simply bundles of conducting fibres, each with its parent cell in the central nervous system. Each fibre has a coat of *myelin*, a fatty insulating substance. The myelin sheath accelerates conduction and is essential to repair if the fibre is damaged. Fibres within the central nervous system have rudimentary myelin sheaths and no power of healing (►*nerve*).

Twelve pairs of ►*cranial nerves* spring from the under-surface of the brain and 31 pairs of ►*spinal nerves* from the spinal cord. Their parent cells are only the outer links of complex chains of neurones within the central nervous system. A group of muscle cells is activated by a single motor neurone in the spinal cord, but this neurone may receive impulses through its dendrites from hundreds of other neurones, of which some stimulate and others inhibit. Only a few of these, in the upper part of the brain, are involved in conscious activity or sensation. The rest operate ►*reflex* actions.

Herophilus (Alexandria, 3rd century BC) recognized the nerves had to do with sensation and movement, and he described the brain in some detail. His contemporary Erasistratus taught that the nerves were hollow and acted by transmitting vital spirit, a belief that was not seriously challenged until late in the Renaissance. Vital spirit flowed through nerves into the muscles and caused them to swell and shorten. Two thousand years later Descartes was expounding the same theory – he even described and drew valves within the 'hollow' of the nerves. Swammerdam disproved the theory in the 17th century, but his work was not published until 1737. The first modern account of the nervous system was by Albrecht von Haller in 1766. Having shown the tendency of muscle fibres to contract in response to stimuli, Haller proved that some nerve fibres carried impulses from the central nervous system which stimulated the muscles, while others carried sensory impulses to the brain. Although the idea that nerves might be sensory or motor was very ancient – it was put forward by Herophilus and elaborated by Galen (2nd century AD) – sensation as a property of the brain and not of the organ stimulated was a revolutionary concept. A pricked finger does not feel pain; it only transmits an impulse along a nerve to be interpreted in the brain.

The nervous system functions largely by ►reflex action. Descartes was the first to suggest this. It was a lucky guess with no shred of evidence behind it. Descartes was concerned not with the workings of the body but with the human soul. Having denied the existence of a soul in animals he had to postulate something like reflex action to explain animal behaviour. Descartes's theory was confirmed by the experiments of Hales, published in 1761, showing that the withdrawal of a limb when the skin was pricked was determined by the spinal cord. Marshall Hall (1833) described spinal reflexes and their modification by impulses from the brain. The current view of the nervous system as an integrated whole is largely due to Sherrington's work around the turn of this century.

Johannes Müller's discovery (c. 1830) that a given nerve fibre, however stimulated, can produce only one kind of effect was the first step towards understanding the nature of nervous impulses, though it now appears that there are exceptions to Müller's rule. In 1852 Helmholtz recorded the speed of conduction in a nerve. Later knowledge is due largely to Lucas, Sherrington, Dale, Adrian, Hodgkin, and Huxley in England, and to Erlanger and Gasser in America. Excepting Lucas, all these physiologists have been awarded Nobel Prizes.

2. Autonomic Nervous System

In all vertebrates a special system of nerves regulates the organs of blood-circulation, respiration, digestion, excretion, and reproduction. Since its activity is wholly reflex and appears to be independent of the brain it was named the autonomic system by J. N. Langley (Cambridge, 1898). Functionally the system is in two parts: the ►sympathetic system, arising from the thoracic and upper lumbar spinal nerves, and the ►parasympathetic system from certain cranial nerves, of which the most important is the ►vagus, and from the sacral nerves. The autonomic motor nerve cells are in groups or ganglia outside the central nervous system. The sympathetic ganglia form a chain at either side of the backbone, and the parasympathetic ganglia are actually on the organs supplied.

When the neural tube is formed in the embryo (see above) some of the developing neurones are stranded between the tube and the back of the embryo. They form the neural crest. These neurones migrate, some to become the autonomic nerves and the medulla of the ►adrenal gland (which is a modified sympathetic ganglion) and others to the sensory ganglia of the spinal nerves.

Despite appearances the workings of the autonomic and central nervous systems are intimately related. Autonomic activity is determined partly by the ►vital centres in the brain-stem and partly by centres in the floor of the forebrain which are also concerned with emotion – the outward signs of emotional changes such as blushing, pallor, sweating, palpitation, are autonomic reflexes.

Galen described the vagus nerve as part of a single nerve comprising the 9th, 10th (vagus) and 11th cranial nerves. The error is to his credit because it proves that he had studied the matter: the three nerves are quite distinct in the neck, but if they are traced back to their origin in the brain-stem they are seen to be intimately related. Galen also gave some account of the sympathetic nerves and their ganglia, but the first accurate description of this system was by Eustachius in the 16th century. Numerous physiologists, notably Claude Bernard, studied the autonomic system during the 19th century; the first to recognize it as a co-ordinated system was W. H. Gaskell of Cambridge, who named it the *involuntary nervous system*. More recent studies have been mainly concerned with the connections of the system in the ➤*brain*, where autonomic and central nervous systems are no longer distinct.

3. THE NERVOUS IMPULSE

A living nerve fibre at rest is electrically charged. The potential difference between the inside and outside of the fibre is about 80 millivolts. It depends on the different concentrations of potassium inside and outside: the ratio is about 30:1. The two elements potassium and sodium are more or less interchangeable in a dead structure. If a nerve fibre were inert, both would diffuse freely until their concentrations were the same inside and out. But the living fibre actively rejects sodium by some unknown mechanism (the 'sodium pump'). The chemical stability of the cell requires one or other element – which one does not matter – and since sodium is lacking, potassium is retained and with it an electric potential.

If the electric potential is lost the nerve is said to be *depolarized*. This happens if the lining membrane becomes freely permeable: sodium then enters and the surplus of potassium is released. A

nerve impulse is simply a wave of depolarization, started by various kinds of stimulus, e.g. an electric current, heat, pressure, or certain chemicals. Once the process has begun, the depolarization of any part of a neurone is a sufficient stimulus to depolarize the next segment. Thus the impulse travels to the end of the nerve fibre. This is quite different from ordinary electrical conduction, and much slower. The thickest fibres conduct at a rate of 100 metres per second, and some very slow fibres at only about 1 metre per second. This is easily demonstrated because pain is conveyed in fast and slow fibres. A mildly painful stimulus such as a pinprick or touching a hot kettle causes an immediate rather indefinite sensation, followed a second or so later by a slowly conducted but precise sense of pain.

When the impulse reaches the end of the fibre it has to be passed to the next nerve cell (for all activities depend on more than one neurone) or to an effector organ such as a muscle (➤*reflex*). This is done by releasing a *chemical transmitter* from the nerve-ending. The gap between a nerve-ending and its target is a *synapse*. Some chemical transmitters are known. Muscle fibres and most autonomic nerve cells respond to *acetyl choline*. Sympathetic nerve-endings usually release *noradrenaline*. Within the central nervous system there are certainly other transmitters as well as these. *Serotonin* appears to be one. And since there are inhibitory nerves there are presumably inhibitory transmitters. It now seems clear that gamma-amino-butyric acid (GABA) is one of these ➤*neuro-transmitters*.

Two kinds of mechanism control bodily functions: nervous activity, and chemical activity by *hormones* released from glands such as the pituitary and thyroid. The distinction is convenient, but less clear-cut than it appears to be, for the function of a nerve is to release a chemical transmitter when it is stimulated. The difference between a nerve and a gland is that a nerve releases its chemical transmitter at a given point, where it is destroyed as soon as it has acted, whereas a gland releases its transmitter into the blood-stream to act throughout the body. The adrenal medulla is a collection of sympathetic nerve cells behaving as a gland; it releases adrenaline into the blood-stream to activate other sympathetic nerves in distant organs.

A nerve cell returns to its resting state almost immediately after transmitting an impulse. Within one or two milliseconds its charge is restored and ready to be fired again. The process can be repeated indefinitely. Waking or sleeping, the nervous system is constantly active throughout life. No fresh cells, it seems, are formed after birth. The original stock serves for a lifetime, and the cells that wear out and die are not replaced.

4. SUPPORTING STRUCTURES

The central nervous system is protected by the skull and backbone and their lining membranes, the ►meninges, which enclose the ►cerebrospinal fluid. The fluid acts as a shock-absorber.

A neurone is the most helpless of living cells. It is like the proverbial genius, pre-eminent in his chosen specialty but incapable of looking after himself. A neurone keeps no stores. If it is deprived of blood, and so of glucose and oxygen, for more than a few seconds it dies. If the blood stops flowing, the stagnant blood in the vessels carries enough supplies to keep nerve cells alive for a few minutes.

There is no ordinary connective tissue in the nervous system. Instead the neurones are supported by a network of spidery cells, the *neuroglia*, which appears to do for them most of the routine chemical work that less delicate cells in other tissues do for themselves.

Nerve fibres are insulated with a layer of myelin. In the actual nerves, outside the brain and spinal cord, the myelin is formed by *Schwann cells*, which wrap each fibre in layer upon layer of myelin. If a nerve fibre is cut, the Schwann cells can form a new tube into which a new fibre can grow, provided that the cell-body of the neurone is intact. But in the brain and spinal cord the myelin is laid down by the neuroglia, which does not lay down new paths for damaged fibres. Here, then, any damage is permanent.

5. DISORDERS

Localized disorders are discussed elsewhere (►brain; spinal cord; nerve). ►Mental illnesses are presumably disturbances of the brain (a few are known to be), but this is open to dispute because nobody can say where or what the mind is.

Disease of the nervous system is usually disease of its supporting structures. Since nerve cells cannot divide they cannot form tumours. Apart from the tumours of embryonic nerve cells, occurring very rarely in infancy, tumours of nervous tissue arise from the neuroglia.

Diseases as different as syphilis, arteriosclerosis, and diabetes affect the nervous system by injuring its small blood vessels (diabetes probably has other effects as well).

If the myelin sheaths are damaged conduction is impaired. Many disorders are of this kind, including damage to nervous tissue by diphtheria, alcohol, and multiple sclerosis. The actual nerve cells remain healthy, but they are ineffective unless the myelin recovers.

All parts of a neurone are vulnerable to pressure. Even slight pressure on a nerve disturbs sensation and causes tingling or 'pins and needles', and if the pressure continues the fibres cease to conduct – everyone has experienced numbness in a limb after sitting awkwardly. Nerve fibres recover when the pressure is relieved, but the cell-bodies in the central nervous system can be killed by pressure. Normally the cerebrospinal fluid is kept at a constant pressure, but a part of the brain or spinal cord may be compressed by bleeding, abscess, tumour, or fractured bone. If the compression is not relieved there is liable to be permanent damage.

neuralgia. *Neuralgia, neuritis,* and *neuropathy* have become almost synonymous, though they should mean different things. All refer to affections of *peripheral nerves.*

Neuritis is inflammation of a nerve. *Neuropathy* means any disorder of a nerve, or perhaps any disorder other than inflammation. *Neuralgia* is a pain originating in a nerve. For instance, the pain of sciatica, arising in the roots of the sciatic nerve, is neuralgic, but the pain of a decaying tooth, which is merely conducted by a nerve, is not.

Trigeminal neuralgia, or *tic douloureux,* is a severe pain on one side of the face, in an area corresponding with a branch of the trigeminal (5th cranial) nerve. A typical attack is severe for a minute or so, but it is soon over and the patient is completely well until the next attack, which may not be for several weeks. In more advanced cases attacks become more frequent, and adequate treatment is imperative.

Trigeminal neuralgia is permanently cured by cutting the nerve near its origin. This is a drastic remedy, but a priceless refuge if milder treatment should fail. An injection of alcohol into the nerve usually stops the symptoms for a year or more. Some cases are cured by an operation to allow more room for the nerve as it passes through the floor of the skull. Such methods as these have been necessary because the usual pain-killing drugs have so little effect, but an antispasmodic, *carbamazepine*, has a curious affinity for the trigeminal nerve, and often relieves the symptoms.

neurasthenia. A kind of neurosis, with tiredness as the main symptom; also a convenient label for lassitude not due to anaemia, infection, malnutrition or other recognized disease.

neuritis. Inflammation of a nerve (mononeuritis) or several nerves (polyneuritis). Most of the conditions called neuritis do not involve inflammation, and are better classified as ►*neuropathy* (►*neuralgia*). True inflammation can be due to infection by viruses (e.g. herpes) or bacteria (e.g. leprosy), but often the cause is obscure.

neurodermatitis. Atopic ►*dermatitis*; atopic eczema.

neurofibromatosis (von Recklinghausen's disease). A rare hereditary disorder, with fibrous swellings of nerves and dark blotches on the skin.

neuroglia. The connective tissue of the ►*nervous system.*

neurology. Study of the nervous system and its disorders.

neuroma. Tumour of nerve tissue. A mature nerve cell, unlike most other cells in the body, cannot reproduce itself. A rare kind of neuroma is made of embryonic nerve cells; most tumours of the nervous system arise from the *neuroglia*, the connective tissue that supports the active nerve cells.

neurone (neuron). A nerve cell with its conducting fibres. ►*nervous system.*

neuropathy. Any disorder of peripheral nerves (cf. ►*neuralgia*), especially one without inflammation. The symptoms of disturbed function are much the same whatever the cause: tingling, numbness, sometimes pain, muscular weakness, sometimes poor condition of the skin (from deficient regulation of its blood vessels), all in the area to which the affected nerve is destined. The commonest cause is *pressure*, which impairs conduction; e.g. ►*carpal tunnel* syndrome and 'slipped disc' (►*vertebra* (1)). Other common causes include diabetes, disorders of the circulation (both, probably, by decreasing the supply of blood to nerves), and numerous poisons including lead and other metals and some drugs. Lack of vitamins, especially of B_{12} (pernicious anaemia), niacin (pellagra) and B_1 (beri-beri), can cause severe neuropathies, advancing to paralysis of the affected regions if they are untreated. Vitamin B deficiency is an immediate cause of neuropathy with chronic alcoholism.

neurosis. A large and ill-defined group of mental disturbances, merging on the one hand with normality and on the other with real derangement of the mind. Probably no boundary can be drawn between normality and neurosis: one man's due regard for detail is another man's obsession. There is a clearer distinction between neurosis and derangement (psychosis): the neurotic is all too aware that

something is wrong, and the psychotic is not; and the neurotic's reason is not impaired.

Most if not all neurosis can be ascribed to ►*anxiety* in one form or other; the symptoms appear to be modifications of normal responses to real or imaginary danger met in the past and unconsciously recalled. Some psychiatrists prefer the term *anxiety disorder* to neurosis.

With *panic attacks* the pulse quickens, sometimes with angina-like pain and sweating, simulating a heart attack. Overbreathing (hyperventilation) washes carbon dioxide out of the body fluids, altering their acidity and causing dizziness, tingling sensations, muscular cramps, even unconsciousness, all increasing the sense of panic. *Chronic anxiety* causes milder symptoms of the same kind for long periods at a time.

Such obvious symptoms of anxiety may accompany *phobias*, in particular *agoraphobia*, neurotic fear of open or public places. Other phobias or irrational fears may be directed at meeting people, or at harmless animals such as cats or earthworms.

Obsessions (recurrent thoughts that the subject knows to be irrational but cannot shake off) and *compulsions* (repetitive actions of the same kind, such as Lady Macbeth's hand-washing) are thought to symbolize past fears or unacceptable memories.

With *conversion disorder* (hysteria) buried memories emerge in the form of physical symptoms, usually involving the nervous system, such as loss of sensation or muscular power in a limb. The symptoms are what the patient thinks they should be, and may well not correspond with the facts of anatomy. But unlike those of malingering they are real to the patient. If he says he is blind then although the nerve pathways are demonstrably intact the sensation is not being consciously registered. A similar effect can be induced in a hypnotic trance.

Hypochondriasis differs from conversion disorder in that the patient exaggerates the importance of real sensations rather than unconsciously creating symptoms. He can persuade himself that the gurgling of his intestine or the palpable beat of his heart are signs of deep-seated mischief. His obsession with ill health is often linked to depressive neurosis. (➤*depression.*)

Dissociative disorders are similar to conversion disorder but much less often seen. A *fugue*, literally 'flight', is indeed a flight from reality: the patient wanders away like a sleepwalker and for a time loses his memory of who or where he is. In the extreme, *multiple personality* is occasionally reported, with episodes of 'being' someone else of whom in lucid intervals the patient has no knowledge or recollection. These conditions may symbolize escape from abuse during childhood.

neuro-transmitters. Impulses or messages are carried in the nervous system by relays: from a nerve cell along its fibre to a synapse or junction box, where they are passed to the next nerve cell and on. The end of the nerve fibre acts as a minute endocrine gland. When stimulated this releases a hormone which acts on the adjacent nerve cell to send the message to the next stage. The first transmitter to be recognized was ➤*adrenaline* (1894), followed by ➤*acetyl choline* (1914), and these, with noradrenaline, are the main transmitters outside the brain. But recent research has shown that within the brain numerous substances act, or may act, as transmitters. Two closely related amino-acids – L-glutamic and gamma-amino-butyric acids – respectively stimulate and suppress nerve cells. But these simple on-or-off effects are subject to modification by many other substances, of which over 40 are under intensive study. They include dopamine, serotonin, enkephalins, pituitary hormones, and both acetyl choline and noradrenaline, which apparently perform subtler tasks than the mere switching on and off which they perform outside the brain. The interaction of some of these substances appears to affect behaviour, emotion and mood, as well as physical performance. A better understanding of them should lead to important advances in the understanding of conditions as diverse as slow learning, Parkinsonism, behavioural disturbances and psychoses.

neutrophil. The most numerous of the white blood cells. ➤*blood* (3).

niacin; nicotinamide ➤*vitamin B.*

nicotine. An alkaloid in tobacco. Small doses stimulate nerve-endings in the sympathetic and parasympathetic systems, with reflex effects such as constriction of blood vessels, nausea or vomiting, alteration of the heart beat. With novices to smoking, parasympathetic reflexes (slow pulse, faintness, nausea) often predominate; with habitual smokers, sympathetic reflexes (quick pulse, raised blood pressure, impaired appetite and digestion). Larger doses suppress these reflexes and then cause convulsions, paralysis, and death.

Bronchitis and cancer from smoking are due to tobacco tar, but nicotine accounts for the headache and also for the liability of smokers to heart attacks and strokes. And it is nicotine that causes the dependence on tobacco that causes sane people to smoke although they fully understand the risks (►*tobacco*).

nipple ►*breast*.

nit. A louse's egg, firmly adherent to the hair or clothing of an infested person.

nitrite. A salt of nitrous acid (HNO_2). Nitrites are used medicinally to dilate small arteries, e.g. in treating ►*angina*. Some compounds that are not strictly nitrites but have the same effect, such as glyceryl trinitrate (nitroglycerin), are included in the group. Although these drugs have been given for many years to dilate narrowed coronary arteries they probably work by relaxing other arteries, lowering the pressure and taking the load off the overworked heart muscle.

nitrogen. The principal component of air; an essential element in all living matter. No animal can use the pure nitrogen of the air, but bacteria in the soil and in certain plants synthesize nitrogen compounds that other creatures can assimilate. By far the most important nitrogen compounds are the *proteins*, the basic stuff of a living organism. Nearly all the nitrogen of the diet is in animal or vegetable proteins, which are broken down by digestion to *amino-acids* and then resynthesized. Waste nitrogen in the body is excreted by the kidneys, mainly as *urea*.

nitrous oxide (laughing gas). N_2O; the first general anaesthetic and still one of the most useful. ►*anaesthetics* (2).

Nocardia. A genus of soil-dwelling microbes, classified as bacteria, that, like *Actinomyces*, seem closer to fungi. They can cause dangerous infection of the lungs, sometimes spreading to the skin, brain and elsewhere, calling for intensive treatment with penicillin or sulphonamides. Nocardia can also contribute to *maduromycosis*.

noma. *Cancrum oris*; a dangerous infection of the mouth leading to gangrene, usually a complication of some other illness in severely under-nourished children. It was often fatal until the discovery of antibiotics. These drugs generally cure the disease rapidly, but there is nearly always severe malnutrition to be treated at the same time. Noma is still common in the poorer parts of the tropics.

noradrenaline. Arterenol; norepinephrine ►*adrenaline*.

normal. Since medical practice aims to prevent or correct departures from normal functioning of the body we should be able to recognize normal people when we see them. We cannot in fact do so with any confidence, and common sense may be as good a guide as science.

For many purposes, normal means average. A normal man weighs 70 kg, has 5 litres of blood and a body temperature of 37°, and an intelligence quotient of 100. His blood contains 0.1 per cent of glucose, and his kidneys produce 1.5 litres of urine every 24 hours. Figures such as these are needed whenever one has to generalize, but nobody supposes that they are anything more than typical values. Absolute values belong to physics, not biology. Nearly all biological measurements follow a Gaussian or normal distribution, i.e. most individuals are clustered around the average value for the whole population, and the further one gets from the average, the fewer individuals one finds. Thus most healthy adult men are found to weigh, say, between 60 and 80 kg; some weigh as little as 55 and some as much as 85; and a few are outside these limits. None of them is necessarily abnormal. If a man is seven feet tall *and* has a pituitary tumour to explain his unusual size, then his height is truly abnormal. But if he has no tumour and no sign of illness then his height can only be called unusual.

But the average can be misleading. For many years medical students learnt that normal women had less haemoglobin in 100 ml of blood than normal men – about 13.5 g against nearly 16. It now seems that so many women are anaemic that the average is depressed. If iron lost by excessive bleeding is replaced there is little difference between the sexes. When the amount has been brought up to a maximum between 15 and 16 g iron does no further good. This, then, is apparently the ideal value, and it is a more realistic normal than the average. Similarly, a peasant in a poor tropical country is average if he has malaria, worms and malnutrition, but it will be a bad day for humanity if he is counted as normal.

This kind of thing leads to very serious difficulties. In Western society it is widely considered normal to have a smoker's cough, to put on weight in middle age or to need aspirin. Medical diagnosis is confused because normal values are not the same for everyone. Among healthy people, blood pressure may vary by as much as 20 per cent either side of the average for the population, and it may be impossible to say whether a rather high pressure is at the upper limit of the normal range or the lower limit of hypertension, i.e. of disease. In this as in many other cases (e.g.

the instance of the very tall man) normal and abnormal are not set figures but ranges of values, and they may overlap. This, of course, is one of the great advantages of the family doctor over the consultant: the family doctor may know what the patient's blood pressure was a couple of years ago, and an increase is much more significant than today's high reading.

More than anything else it is the uncertainty about what is normal that makes medicine a very inexact science and sets experience at such a premium. Even such apparently precise investigations as X-ray films and blood chemistry have to be judged and often their interpretation is open to argument. If it were not so, there would be little need of specialists, and doctors could be trained in half the time. We are still with Hippocrates in 400 BC: 'Life is short, and the Art long; the occasion fleeting; experience fallacious, and judgement difficult.'

nose. The projection on the front of the face is only a small part of the nose. That the human nose projects at all does not mean that it is important but that the

Side wall of the nose; the conchae are partly removed

upper jaw has receded in the course of evolution.

The bridge of the outer nose, between the eyes, is supported by the nasal bones. The cavity, extending to the back of the hard palate, is completely divided into left and right halves by the nasal *septum*. This is a thin sheet of bone behind and of cartilage in front. The cartilaginous septum supports the outer nose below the nasal bones.

At the back of the hard palate the two halves of the nose open into a single cavity, the nasal part of the ➤*pharynx*. At each side the *maxilla* forms the wall of the nose; the floor is the *palate*, and the roof is the base of the skull. Three small flaps of bone, each with its lower edge curled under, protrude from the side-wall into the cavity of the nose. These *conchae* (turbinate bones) increase the surface area of the cavity, and shield the openings of the sinuses.

The bones surrounding the nose are hollow. Their cavities, the (paranasal) *sinuses*, communicate with the nose by small openings in the side-wall. Two other openings are important: that of the *nasolacrimal duct*, by which tears flow down (hence blowing the nose to get rid of a foreign body in the eye), and the *Eustachian tube*, connecting the middle ear with the pharynx immediately behind the nose proper.

The mucous membrane of the nose also lines the various extensions of the nasal cavity. It is a lax membrane, easily distended by blood and tissue fluid; when inflamed by infection (e.g. common cold) or allergy (e.g. hay fever) it can quickly swell until the nose is blocked. In health it is kept moist by mucus, secreted by its many tiny glands. Its surface is covered with *cilia*, microscopic hair-like structures which undulate and keep the mucus moving towards the back of the nose. When the membrane is inflamed the cilia can no longer cope with the excess of mucus which is formed, and in any case the sinuses could not be cleared because their openings are blocked by the swollen membranes. This gives a simple mechanical explanation of the watering eyes, headache, faceache, and earache which may accompany a severe cold in the nose. The stagnation brings a risk of more serious infection of the sinuses or ear (➤*sinusitis*; ➤*otitis*).

The nose warms and moistens the inhaled air. Even on a cold day the air is saturated with water and within a few degrees of body temperature when it reaches the trachea. To some extent the nose also acts as an air-filter. The sense of smell is discussed in section 2 below.

1. DISORDERS

The commonest disorders – common cold, hay fever, and sinusitis – have been mentioned and are further discussed under their own headings.

Inflammation of the nasal mucous membrane, of which the common cold and hay fever are acute instances, is called *rhinitis*. Chronic rhinitis, with a more or less permanently running nose, is usually associated with a stagnant focus of infection: sinusitis, a polyp, or, in children, tonsillitis with swollen adenoids. A nasal polyp is a soft, round protrusion from the mucous membrane, looking rather like a pearl. It is a result of inflammation which then keeps the infection going. A large one may completely block its side of the nose. The removal of nasal polyps is a simple and satisfactory operation. Less often, rhinitis may be dry or *atrophic*. The mucous membrane is then shrunken and does not secrete enough mucus; the patient is troubled by dry crusts which collect in the nostrils. Such patients are often subject to hay fever.

Nose-bleed (epistaxis) may be caused by an obvious injury or by an utterly trivial injury to an exposed vessel weakened by past inflammation. It is a common symptom of many fevers, including the fevers of childhood and typhoid. Sometimes it is due to high blood pressure or to disorders of the blood. The bleeding vessel is most often near the front of the septum, just inside the nostril, and the bleeding can be stopped by pinching the nose for a few minutes. In most cases, of course, the bleeding stops on its own; but a nose-bleed has to be treated with some respect. If it continues, the loss of blood can be serious. Skilful packing of the nose with gauze will stop almost any bleeding, but unskilful attempts are more likely to make matters worse.

A broken nose is a common sporting injury. The fragments are replaced by gentle leverage through the nostril, under local or general anaesthesia.

The shape of a nose can be changed by plastic surgery, approaching the supporting cartilage and bone through a nostril. New bone can be grafted in, or excessive bone or cartilage removed. This kind of operation can greatly improve the appearance after serious accidents. In countries where leprosy is common a cured leper may be rejected by the community because his collapsed nose marks him out. Many such patients have been made acceptable by operations to restore the lost tissue. This kind of surgery has been practised for centuries in India. In modern times many healthy people have operations to change the shape of the nose.

2. SENSE OF SMELL

The nerve-endings for perceiving smells are confined to a small area at the top of the nasal cavity. The nerves pass through small holes in the ethmoid bone to join the olfactory (1st cranial) nerves. The part of the brain concerned with smell (rhinencephalon) is prominent in lower vertebrates, but in man it is completely overshadowed by more recently evolved structures.

Although carried in quite different paths the senses of smell and *taste* are closely related. Taste is a very crude sensation; all subtleties of flavour depend on smell. This is evident when the narrow slit at the top of the nose is obstructed with a cold, and the tongue (which is not really affected) seems to lose most of its sensibility.

The mechanism of smell is unknown, and it is difficult even to suggest a working theory. The nose can distinguish more smells than the ear can distinguish sounds. But all sounds are simply vibrations. They differ only in the rate and the amount of vibration, and it is easy enough to suppose that different nerves respond best to different frequencies. Taste and vision are even simpler. Only four tastes can be distinguished, and colour vision can be explained in terms of only three types of nerve-ending, each responding to a particular range of wave-lengths. But the nerve-endings in the nose, which appear to be all alike, convey thousands of distinct sensations from stimuli that do not appear to be related as sounds or colours are related. Yet there must be a common factor; one cannot suppose that the nose contains 10,000 different kinds of sensory organ. The size and shape of the incoming molecules seem to affect their odour, and it has been suggested that the characteristic vibrations of molecules are what the sense of smell actually records.

nosology. Nomenclature and classification of diseases (Gk *nosos* = 'disease').

notifiable diseases. In all countries certain diseases have to be reported to the public health authority, in order that preventive measures against spread can be taken, or to provide statistics from which the behaviour of diseases in the community can be studied. The diseases specified are not necessarily the same in all countries or at all times. In Britain, notifiable diseases are reported to the public health physician either by the attending doctor or by the head of the family (in practice, nearly always the doctor). The public health physician sends a weekly return to the Department of Health, and informs the Department at once of anything urgent.
International rules. Four quarantinable epidemic diseases are notified to the WHO: *cholera, plague, smallpox,* and *yellow fever.* In addition, louse-borne typhus and relapsing fever, malaria, influenza and poliomyelitis are reported to WHO by national health authorities.
National rules. Other infectious diseases are notifiable within a country. In Britain they include the more serious childhood fevers, and tuberculosis, pneumonia, puerperal fever, and infections liable to be carried by food or drinking water, in all some 20 diseases. In the United States about 40 diseases are notifiable in addition to the international ones. In many other countries the lists are much shorter.
Regional and other rules. In many countries state or provincial authorities draw up additional lists in accordance with local conditions. In Britain, a County Council can make any disease temporarily notifiable.

The Factories Act requires notification to the Department of Employment of certain diseases arising from the patient's work, including *anthrax* (also notified to the Department of Health) and numerous industrial poisons.

Hospitals in Britain inform the Registrar-General of all cases of cancer and their progress. This information provides a national register from which the various types of cancer and the effects of treatment can be studied.

notochord. The simplest form of backbone, found in some primitive fish-like creatures; it is a rod of connective tissue to give the muscles purchase. In all vertebrates a notochord appears in the embryo, to be replaced by a vertebral column. Small remnants of the notochord persist in an adult human in the centres of the intervertebral discs; ►*vertebra* (1); *skeleton* (1).

NSAID (Non-Steroidal Anti-Inflammatory Drug). This important group includes aspirin and later introductions such as indomethacin and ibuprofen. They suppress inflammation by inhibiting certain ►*prostaglandins,* and may prove to be useful for suppressing other unwanted effects of these hormones.

nucleic acids ►*genetics* (1).

nucleoprotein. A compound of a nucleic acid with a protein.

nucleotide. A link in the chain of a nucleic acid molecule, composed of a purine or pyrimidine base, the sugar ribose, and phosphoric acid.

nucleus. The kernel of a living cell; it is composed largely of nucleoprotein, the structure of which determines what proteins the cell can make and thus determines the biological properties of the cell.

nursing. The general care of sick people, as opposed to medical attention to their diseases, was not suddenly invented during the Crimean War. Hippocrates had plenty to say about what is now called nursing, and even when medical practice fell to its lowest ebb in the Middle Ages several religious orders provided and staffed hospitals. After the Renaissance new orders were founded especially for the care of the sick and needy. The greatest of these was St Vincent de Paul's order, the Sisters of Charity, founded in Paris in 1634. But the Renaissance coincided with the Reformation and in Protestant countries there was nobody to take the place of the monks and nuns, and the care of hospital patients was left to untrained domestic servants.

Even the few nurses that there were – lay or religious – had no special training. The doctors prescribed medicines of which the patients' attendants understood nothing. The first person to act on the principle that spiritual care was not enough was Theodor Fliedner, a German clergyman, who established the world's first school of nursing at Kaiserswerth in 1833. In 1851 Florence Nightingale took a course of training at Kaiserswerth. Three years later she led a team of nurses to the Crimean War and transformed military hospitals from squalid prisons into decent places where the wounded stood a reasonable chance of recovery.

In 1860 Florence Nightingale established at St Thomas's Hospital, London, the school that became the model for schools of nursing everywhere. After three years of properly supervised training and experience, her nurses were entitled to regard themselves as members of a new profession, no longer the well-meaning amateurs of earlier times. In the 20th century, laws have been passed in nearly all countries to regulate the training and registration of nurses.

Nursing was defined in Florence Nightingale's *Notes* (1859):

'I use the word nursing for want of a better. It has been limited to signify little more than the administration of medicines and the application of poultices. It ought to signify the proper use of fresh air, light, warmth, cleanliness, quiet, and the proper selection and administration of diet – all at the least expense of vital power to the patient.'

Even at that time, accurate observation could have been added to the list, and today a nurse has to be skilled in the use of all manner of scientific apparatus for diagnosis and treatment, in addition to the duties that Miss Nightingale laid on her. Indeed, nursing now calls for so much technical knowledge and skill that like medicine and surgery it has become divided into specialities far beyond the long-standing division into general nursing and midwifery. After qualification nurses may well choose to specialize in the care of children or old people, or intensive care, operating-theatre work, psychiatric nursing, caring for handicapped patients, or any number of areas.

nutrition ▸*diet*; *digestion*; *malnutrition*.

nux vomica. The seed of a tropical tree from which the poisonous alkaloid *strychnine* is extracted. It has a long history as a tonic: since large doses cause violent and fatal convulsions, small doses were supposed to stimulate the nervous system in a more modest way. In fact it has no medicinal value.

nystagmus. A reflex scanning movement of the eyes to keep moving objects in view. It can be observed when someone watches the scenery from a moving vehicle. The reflex is partly under control of the balance organ of the middle ear. If co-ordination between this organ and the eyes is disturbed, e.g. by alcohol, disease of the inner ear, work in a cramped position and a poor light (miner's nystagmus), or certain disorders affecting the brain, nystagmus occurs when the eyes should be still. The subject may have the illusion that everything is spinning round him (vertigo), but some people are unaware of their nystagmus. ➤*ear* (3,ii).

nystatin. An antibiotic from the mould *Streptomyces noursei*, used to treat *thrush*, i.e. infection of mucous membranes with the fungus *Candida*.

O

obesity. Unhealthy excess of body weight, with the emphasis on the first word, may be as good a definition as any of this ill-defined disorder. For anyone there is a limit beyond which any added weight makes him less fit than he might be, if only by imposing an unnecessary burden on joints and muscles. The heart has not only to work harder; its efficiency suffers from fat deposited in its muscle. The chances of developing diabetes and hypertension are also increased.

Tables of ideal weight are usually based on height and sex. At 175 cm (5 ft 9 in) tall a man might be rated at 68 kg (150 lb) and a woman at 64 kg (140 lb), but these are no more than average values. Some people have heavier frames and some carry more muscle than others. The crucial factor is the amount of fat, and especially the fat belly. The characteristically feminine fat deposits around the thighs and buttocks (▸*cellulite*) do not threaten health.

Even allowing for individual variation, an excess of 20 per cent over the accepted ideal weight is regarded as mild obesity but enough to damage health and shorten life. Over 50 per cent is regarded as moderate, and 100 per cent as severe.

To stay alive the body needs energy, derived from food, to maintain a constant temperature and keep heart, lungs, brain and other systems ticking over. This ▸*basal metabolism* is a more or less fixed quantity, amounting for an average man to some 1700 Calories (7100 kJ) per day. The energy to be added for daily activities varies widely. With a completely sedentary occupation it might bring the total daily requirement to 2200 Calories; with heavy manual labour to over 3000. Small people use less than large, and, apparently, women less than men.

Food, once eaten, is chemically processed and then either oxidized (burnt) to provide energy or stored. As only enough is burnt to supply the energy needed, any surplus is automatically added to the body weight. Thus, in the simplest terms, obesity is a result of eating too much.

How supply balances demand to keep a constant body weight is not fully understood. The sensations of appetite and satiety depend on the interaction of nerve centres in the brain with hormones from the thyroid and other glands; the intestine itself works as an endocrine organ, secreting hormones that respond to the presence or absence of food.

(It is of course possible to eat without being hungry, or not to eat without feeling full – just as for a time one can overrule the reflexes that govern breathing by holding breath or overbreathing. But in due course reflexes are restored, with a return to normal.)

A current theory suggests that the various mechanisms act to set a threshold at which weight remains steady, and that fat people overeat because the threshold is somehow advanced.

Heredity plays an important part. Fat parents tend to breed fat children only partly by their example: children brought up away from fat parents still tend to become fat adults.

Environmental factors other than up-bringing include social pressures: most people are bound by convention, and keeping up with people who overeat may advance the threshold of hunger, as associating with heavy drinkers can lead to alcoholism.

Compulsive overeating is seen with some kinds of *neurosis*, but it is hard to distinguish cause from effect. A person might become neurotic because he is fat and dislikes himself for it. To insist that it is his own fault only makes matters worse.

Serious *glandular* disorders are popularly supposed to be a leading cause of obesity. In the severest cases they almost certainly are, but in the great majority their role is not at present clear.

TREATMENT

In theory unwanted weight could be shed by either increasing the demand for calories or decreasing the supply: more exercise or less food. But even strenuous exercise uses surprisingly few calories: someone has estimated that running a full marathon would shed only a single pound. The professional jockey jogging in a sweatshirt is beside the point: he is simply losing a pound or two of sweat before being weighed, and the fluid will replace itself within hours.

So the only satisfactory remedy is to eat less. The question is how to set about it. Losing weight is one thing; maintaining the loss is another. Countless programmes and special diets have been devised, many of them ill-informed and none that will meet every case. Therefore a sensible first step towards losing weight is to consult someone who knows what he, or more often she, is talking about.

Professional dietitians are trained to assess the need to reduce, and how to meet the particular case.

The problem is in many ways similar to that of an alcoholic who can cut down his drinking for weeks or months, but then relapses. Almost any of the countless reducing diets works for a time but the lost weight all returns. The best ones are based not on what food is forbidden but on what a person *should* eat. The whole idea of 'dieting' is questionable, because it implies a temporary state, where what is needed is a permanent change of eating habits. The most successful treatment of alcoholism is offered by Alcoholics Anonymous, where people share a common problem and help each other to solve it. In the same way losing weight is often best tackled in a group. Continuing support is needed and that of fellow sufferers is best of all.

In a minority of cases, weighing 50 per cent or more over the ideal, more drastic dietary restriction may be needed for a while, and this is best done under expert supervision in hospital.

There is only a limited place for drug treatment. Earlier attempts with thyroid hormone, then amphetamines, have been abandoned because either seriously damages the heart. Newer appetite suppressants are better, but need close supervision. Despite popular superstition there is no place for diuretics; they only eliminate water and salt, which are not implicated.

In very severe cases, 100 per cent or more overweight, when all else fails surgery may be needed. The preferred operation is gastroplasty, which fashions a partial barrier in the stomach to restrict the amount of food that can be taken in at a time. Although, like any major operation, it involves a certain risk the results can be spectacular, with sustained loss of weight and improved health.

obsession ▸*neurosis.*

obstetric forceps. Tongs ending in curved loops, shaped to hold a baby's head firmly but safely; used to ease the head past a resistant outlet when birth is delayed at the final stage; invented in about 1600 by an English obstetrician, Peter Chamberlen, and kept as a family secret for more than a century.

obstetrician. Specialist in the management of childbirth.

obstetrics. Midwifery; medical care in pregnancy and childbirth. Progress was much hindered in the past by superstition and taboo. Until modern times most Englishwomen had misgivings about allowing a physician – a man – to attend them in labour, and the midwives had little or no training. Although physicians had studied obstetrics since the time of Soranus (2nd century BC) their knowledge did not often reach the patients. In many parts of the world the old taboos live on: men are excluded from midwifery, and few women are trained.

Many surgeons in the 17th and 18th centuries wrote good accounts of the mechanics of labour, but the turning-point for obstetrics did not arrive until the 19th century when Semmelweis overcame the great hazard, infection (▸*puerperal* fever). This work was soon followed by the discovery of anaesthetics. In the 20th century, the midwives have become an organized profession with prescribed courses of training and examination.

▸*labour; pregnancy; Caesarean section.*

occipital. Of the back of the head; the *occipital bone* is the back of the floor of the skull. It forms a movable joint with the backbone. The brain-stem passes through a large hole in the occipital bone (*foramen magnum*) to become the spinal cord.

The *occipital lobe* is a part of the brain at the back of the skull above the cerebellum. It records and interprets vision.

occupational disease. Paracelsus, in the 16th century, seems to have been the first physician to recognize a trade as the cause of a disease. He described chronic inflammation of the lungs in miners, and poisoning by heavy metals in smelters.

The systematic study of occupational disease began with Ramazzini, whose *De morbis artificum diatriba* was published in 1700. He correctly identified most of the typical ailments of the trades of his time and suggested ways of avoiding them, such as cleanliness, ventilation, and better posture. To the questions that doctors had asked patients since the time of Hippocrates he added: *What is your job?*

The Industrial Revolution introduced new kinds and conditions of work, and with them many new diseases. The pioneer of modern industrial medicine was C. T. Thackrah (1795–1833) of Leeds, whose work was the inspiration of a series of Factories Acts for protecting the health of workers.

If many of the old hazards have been overcome by safer machinery, better designed factories, protective devices and so on, new hazards are always likely to arise; and even when safeguards are available there is no guarantee that they will always be used.

Injuries and skin troubles are by far the commonest of occupational hazards (▸*accidents; dermatitis*). Others are lung diseases from inhaled dust (>*pneumo-coniosis*), and many kinds of poisoning.

People working with animals or animal products are exposed to kinds of infection that other people escape, such as anthrax and undulant fever. Doctors and nurses can get diseases such as tuber-culosis from their patients – less often than one might expect because they ac-quire immunity to most common infec-tions during their apprenticeship.

occupational therapy. A valuable method of treating various chronic and disabling illnesses. The original idea was surely to relieve boredom, but reading to patients and bringing them jigsaw puzzles is more than simple kindness: it is a positive factor in their recovery. A patient who is bored and miserable does not recover as quickly as one who is interested in life. He may even abandon a course of treat-ment or discharge himself from hospital before he is ready to go. An occupational therapist, though, is much more than a reliever of boredom with a box of em-broidery wool and raffia. She is a *therap-ist*, i.e. she has an active part in the treatment of patients, and a detailed knowledge of their abilities and handi-caps. Finding suitable diversions and re-creations, which may range from garden-ing to drama, is only a part of the work. This new profession overlaps two others. On the one hand, a patient who will be left with a lasting physical or mental dis-ability may need either to relearn lost skills or to acquire new ones so that he will be ready for a job in keeping with his abilities. Here, occupational therapy merges into industrial therapy (some long-term hospitals have elaborate work-shops where patients are taught to earn a living again), and vocational training. On the other hand, occupational therapy

overlaps physiotherapy by giving the pa-tient interesting or rewarding tasks that also restore the function of muscles, nerves or joints. It has lately been sug-gested that these two professions might unite.

Any patient facing a long spell of con-finement in hospital or at home is likely to find occupational therapy helpful. Those who need it most are the mentally sick. When the symptoms of a severe dis-order such as schizophrenia have been controlled with drugs, occupational therapy becomes the most important part of the treatment. When the patient can take a pride in what he is doing, he is well on the way to resuming his place in society.

oculist. Eye specialist; ophthalmologist.

oculomotor nerve. Third cranial nerve, controlling movements of the eye.

odontology. Study of the teeth.

oedema. Excess of tissue fluid, either throughout the body (dropsy) or around some local disturbance. About 60 per cent of the body weight is water, making some 40 litres. The water is divided be-tween the blood (3 litres of plasma), the body-cells (25 litres), and the *tissue fluid* (12 litres). The tissue fluid permeates all the minute spaces and crevices of the body; it is the environment in which the cells live like fish in the sea.

Tissue fluid is derived from the blood. The arteries and veins are waterproof, but the microscopical capillary vessels that carry blood from the arteries to the veins allow water to leak from blood to tissue fluid and back. The pumping pres-sure from the heart drives water out of the capillaries. But protein dissolved in the blood cannot easily escape from the capillaries, and it draws water in, from the tissue fluid, by ►*osmosis*. These two opposing forces balance, so that the amount of tissue fluid remains more or less constant. Oedema or waterlogging of the tissues occurs either when the mechanical pressure in the capillaries is too high, or when the osmotic pressure is too low. In either case the balance is upset and water is forced out of the blood faster than it can return. (The blood does not become depleted, because its volume of water is maintained by the balance between the amount drunk and the amount passed in the urine.)

1. MECHANICAL OEDEMA

High blood pressure in the ordinary sense does not cause oedema, for only the pressure in the arteries is high. It is kept high by constriction of the smallest arteries; beyond them, in the capillaries, the pressure is normal. If you tread on a hose-pipe the pressure rises between you and the tap, not beyond you. It is when the veins beyond the capillaries are congested that the pressure in the capillaries rises and oedema develops.

Thus tight garters cause swollen feet, and so do *varicose veins*, in which the flow may be severely impeded.

By the time blood reaches the veins, the impetus of the heart beat is spent. The squeezing action of the leg muscles is needed to push the blood up the veins of the legs towards the heart. The imperceptible automatic movements of keeping the balance are usually enough, but if one stands perfectly still for long periods the feet may swell because of stagnation and raised pressure in the leg veins. Soldiers kept standing at attention are taught to work the muscles of their calves without appearing to move, and stationary household chores might be less tiring if housewives learnt the same

trick. These forms of oedema are due only to gravity. They are promptly corrected by raising the feet. Five minutes of lying down with a pillow under the feet does more than an hour in a chair.

A good example of mechanical oedema can be seen at the end of an all-night journey by air. The passengers take off their shoes and sleep. Their legs are relaxed and still, and the seat-fronts gently compress the veins of their thighs. In the morning they can hardly get their shoes on, but the oedema subsides quickly when the blood-flow in the veins has been restored by working the leg muscles – wiggling the toes, stretching, walking down the cabin.

A more serious type of mechanical oedema is due to ►*heart failure*. The essence of heart failure ('failure' means inefficiency, not collapse) is that instead of emptying the veins that enter it the heart allows them to become engorged. This creates back-pressure on the capillaries and causes oedema. The excess of tissue fluid will collect wherever gravity is added to the back-pressure from the veins, not only in the legs but also in the cavity of the belly (►*peritoneum*), where there is almost unlimited space for water to accumulate. Oedema within the peritoneum is known as *ascites*. Obstruction to the veins in the liver, e.g. with cirrhosis of the liver, causes severe ascites without much oedema elsewhere.

The oedema of heart failure is not all mechanical; it is partly osmotic as described below.

2. OSMOTIC OEDEMA

Water can pass freely in and out of the capillaries, but only small amounts of protein get through, and these are carried away in the lymphatic vessels. Thus tissue fluid is a very weak solution of protein, whereas blood is a concentrated solution. The difference in concentration determines the amount of osmotic pressure for drawing water back into the blood from the tissue fluid.

If there is either too much protein in the tissue fluid or too little protein in the blood, the osmotic pressure is no longer high enough to oppose the mechanical pressure from the heart beat, and an excess of water remains in the tissue fluid as oedema.

Damaged capillaries allow too much protein to escape into the tissue fluid. The causes include infection, allergy (nettle-rash), and physical injury such as scalding or bruising.

If the lymphatic vessels are obstructed, the normal traces of protein are not removed from the tissue fluid, and their concentration rises until the osmotic pressure is impaired. This type of oedema may follow surgical operations for cancer, where lymphatic vessels are closed to prevent spread of the disease. A tropical parasite, *filaria*, lives in lymphatic vessels and occasionally causes massive swelling (*elephantiasis*) of the legs or scrotum.

The oedema of starvation is due to lack of protein: there may not be enough in the diet to supply the blood proteins. And lack of vitamin B_1 causes oedema through heart failure. With severe liver disease the synthesis of blood proteins is deficient. With kidney disease, protein is lost in the urine.

A different kind of osmotic oedema is due to retention of *salt*. In health, the kidneys remove any excess of salt from the blood and pass it into the urine. But if the kidneys are defective, or if the circulation of blood through them is sluggish, salt begins to accumulate. Instead of going into the urine, it passes into the

tissue fluid, and it 'draws' water with it. This is the main cause of oedema with kidney disease (>*nephritis*), and one of the causes with >*heart failure*. The rate at which salt is passed in the urine (given properly functioning kidneys) is determined by hormones from the adrenal glands. The balance of these hormones is altered by menstruation and by pregnancy, and much of the associated discomfort, e.g. premenstrual tension, is probably due to slight oedema from salt retention.

oesophagus. The gullet; it is the downward continuation of the >*pharynx*. The oesophagus is a strong muscular tube, flattened from front to back when empty. In the neck it lies behind the trachea immediately in front of the backbone. Behind the heart, it crosses in front of the aorta from right to left and passes through the diaphragm to widen out into the >*stomach*.

The sole function of the oesophagus is to convey food and drink from the pharynx to the stomach, which it does by means of waves of muscular contraction along its walls. In man, gravity usually helps, but the oesophagus can easily maintain a flow against gravity, as when a quadruped drinks. The action is controlled by the >*vagus nerves*.

Blood is supplied by the nearest vessels along the course of the oesophagus; at the lower end these are branches of the gastric vessels of the stomach. The blood in the gastric veins flows to the >*portal vein* and so must traverse the liver before reaching the heart. Blood from the rest of the oesophagus flows straight to the heart by tributaries of the superior vena cava. The two systems communicate, and thus the oesophageal veins offer a bypass for blood from the stomach if the portal vein is obstructed.

1. DISORDERS

Congenital defects arise mostly from incomplete development: at some point the passage may be too narrow (*stricture*) or completely absent (*atresia*). A stricture can often be stretched, but complete atresia is always serious, because it needs a major operation on a baby which may be in no condition for heroic surgery. There may be other congenital defects, or the baby may develop pneumonia from inhaling milk. Nevertheless, operations for atresia offer a 70 per cent chance of complete recovery as against no chance without operation.

Stricture later in life may be a congenital defect which at first gave no trouble, or the result of injury (e.g. by swallowing corrosive liquids) or of pressure by a tumour. *Cardiospasm* causes the same difficulty with swallowing as a stricture. Though the word implies tightening of the outlet to the stomach (cardiac sphincter), the fault is probably not a tight sphincter but a lax oesophageal wall due to a congenital defect of the nerve endings. The oesophageal muscles are thus unable to push food past the normal resistance of the sphincter.

With ➤*cirrhosis* of the liver the portal vein may be obstructed; the veins of the oesophagus (see above) are then overloaded and liable to bleed.

oestrogen. A kind of female *sex hormone*. *Oestradiol* is the most important natural oestrogen. For medicinal use it has the disadvantage that it is ineffective when taken by mouth; but closely related synthetic drugs can be so used. Synthetic oestrogens that are not derived from oestradiol include *stilboestrol* and *dienoestrol*. ➤*sex hormones*.

olecranon. Upper end of the *ulna*, forming the point of the elbow.

olfactory. Concerned with the sense of smell. ➤*nose* (2).

olig(o)-. Prefix = 'few', 'little'; e.g. *oligaemia*, insufficient volume of blood (cf. anaemia, defective quality of blood); *oligophrenia*, mental deficiency; *oliguria*, diminished flow of urine.

omentum. A loose fold of membrane (peritoneum), heavily impregnated with fat, hanging from the stomach and colon in front of the small intestine.

onchocerca. A kind of parasitic worm (➤*filaria*).

oncology. Study of tumours.

onychia. Infection under a fingernail. The nail often has to be removed so that the infection can be cleared up to allow a fresh nail to grow. Otherwise the infection may destroy the growing tissue under the base of the nail so that the nail is permanently lost.

oophor(o)- (oöphor(o)-). Prefix = 'of the ovaries'; e.g. *oophorectomy*, removal of an ovary.

ophthalmia. Conjunctivitis (inflammation of the covering membrane of the eyelids and front of the eye). The term is generally confined to certain types of conjunctivitis.

Ophthalmia neonatorum, conjunctivitis of the new-born, is due to contamination during birth. When it is caused by *gonorrhoea* it can lead to blindness, but with the use of antibiotics this has become a rare complication.

Sympathetic ophthalmia is inflammation of an eye due to injury to the other eye, apparently an instance of auto-immunity (>*immunity* (7)). It is fortunately very uncommon.

Egyptian ophthalmia = >*trachoma*.

ophthalmic surgery; ophthalmology. Medical and surgical care of the eyes; ophthalmologists are medical practitioners specializing in disorders of the eyes (cf. *optician*).

ophthalmoscope. Instrument for inspecting the inside of the eye. Its primary use is the diagnosis of eye diseases; but the lining of the eye is the one part of the body where blood vessels can be directly inspected, and the ophthalmoscope gives valuable evidence of disorders as various as high blood pressure, diabetes, and kidney disease. Also, the optic nerve is the only part of the nervous system that can actually be seen. Since the patient's own lens acts as a powerful magnifying glass the structures can be seen in great detail.

opiate. Narcotic; drug that dulls the senses, especially drugs derived from opium.

opisthotonos. Muscle spasm with extreme arching of the back, from widespread irritation of the nervous system e.g. by *tetanus*.

opium. Drug extracted from the seeds of a kind of poppy, *Papaver somniferum*. In the past it was given as a crude powder or as an alcoholic solution, *laudanum*; but as with most vegetable drugs the purified active principles are now preferred. The most important of these, on which the effect of opium largely depends, is >*morphine*. Opium also contains > *apomorphine*, >*codeine* (methyl morphine) and >*papaverine*.

opposition. Action of turning the thumb to face the other fingers and provide a firm and sensitive grip, much better developed in man than any other animal; it is one of the features that has enabled the human race to evolve beyond other species. >*skeleton* (4).

opsonin. A substance in blood that enables white blood cells to engulf bacteria.

optic atrophy. Degeneration of the optic nerve, with loss of vision. It can be due to injury or poisoning of the nerve, or interference with its blood supply.

optician. Designer or maker of optical instruments, especially spectacles and other aids to vision. A *dispensing optician* makes lenses to the prescription of an ophthalmologist (oculist). A *sight-testing* (ophthalmic) optician prescribes and supplies glasses.

optic nerve. Bundle of nerve fibres, carrying impulses from the *retina* – the light-sensitive lining of the eye – to the base of the brain. The optic nerves join inside the skull to form a cross, the *optic chiasma*, whence impulses from the right halves of both eyes are transmitted to the right side of the brain and from the left halves to the left side.

oral. Of the mouth.

orbit. Eye-socket. >*skull*.

orchi(o)-. Prefix = 'of the testicle (testis)'; e.g. *orchidectomy*, removal of the testis; *orchiopexy*, surgical fixation of an undescended testis in the scrotum; *orchitis*, inflammation of the testis, a painful complication of mumps and sometimes of gonorrhoea; *orchis* = testis.

orciprenaline. Drug related to adrenaline, used as a >*bronchodilator*.

organ. A distinct, more or less separate structure in the body, serving particular functions; e.g. the brain, a kidney, a muscle. Organs are composed of various *tissues* (which may be similar in different organs). The supporting structure of an organ is its *stroma*. The elements that give it its special function are its *parenchyma*.

organic. Related to organs or to living creatures (organisms) in general. *Organic chemistry* was at first thought to be the chemistry of organisms: the carbon compounds with which it dealt could be made only by some vital process. This was found not to be strictly true, and the term *biochemistry* had to be coined. But in fact the raw materials of organic chemistry – coal tar and the like – were formed in the first place by the decay of animal and vegetable matter.

Organic diseases are those in which structural changes in organs can be found. They are contrasted with *functional* diseases, in which function is disturbed without apparent alteration of structure. This is an unfortunate division, because it too easily implies that if a disease is not organic it is probably imaginary.

organotherapy. Treatment of disease with substances extracted from organs, usually from endocrine glands; now almost entirely superseded by treatment with purified or synthetic hormones.

oriental sore (Baghdad button; Delhi boil; etc.). Infection of the skin with a protozoon, *Leishmania tropica*, transmitted by a sandfly. A boil at the site of inoculation is followed by an open sore that may take several months to heal. The condition is fairly common in many of the drier regions of the tropics.

ornithosis. A kind of pneumonia transmitted to man by several species of bird: the term includes *psittacosis*, transmitted by parrots and budgerigars. It is a fairly dangerous disease, but the agent – formerly regarded as a virus but now as a ►*Chlamydia* – is usually overcome with tetracycline antibiotics.

oropharynx. The lower part of the pharynx, below the *nasopharynx*, behind the tongue.

orthodontics. Correction of faulty position of the teeth.

orthopaedics. Literally, the correction of deformities of children, such as abnormal curvature of the spine and clubfoot; as now used, the term embraces the whole surgery of bones and joints, including the treatment of injuries (fractures; dislocations).

orthoptics. Training of eye-muscles, e.g. for the correction of squint.

os (oris). Mouth.

os (ossis). Bone.

osmosis. Selective migration of molecules through semi-permeable membranes. Most living membranes – animal or vegetable – behave as molecular sieves. Small molecules pass through; large ones do not. Such membranes are called *semi-permeable*.

The molecules of a liquid are in constant, rapid and haphazard motion like a cloud of gnats. Because their motion is haphazard they tend to become evenly distributed, as a drop of ink will spread itself evenly through a bucket of water, given time. This tendency of a solution to become uniform persists when a semi-permeable membrane separates a strong solution from a weak one. If water can pass through and the substance dissolved cannot, the traffic is in one direction: water from the weak solution passes through the membrane to dilute the stronger until both are of the same strength, and in so doing can build up a considerable pressure. The process is called osmosis, and the pressure is called osmotic pressure. This is one of the ways in which plants draw water from the soil.

The semi-permeable membranes of the human body, e.g. the walls of the cells, generally give free passage to water, salts, sugars, and the amino-acids of which proteins are built, but they block the large molecules of completed proteins. Thus the proteins exert osmotic pressure.

Blood is pumped from the heart at an average pressure of about 100 mm of mercury (0.13 atmosphere). By the time it reaches the minute capillary blood vessels the pressure has fallen to 32 mm, and at the further end of the capillaries it is about 12 mm. This pressure tends to force water etc. out of the capillaries into the tissues. But the proteins of the blood exert osmotic pressure at about 25 mm in the opposite direction. Therefore water leaks out of the capillary at one end and in again at the other. The cells get a regular supply of their chemical needs from the blood, but the total volume of the blood is kept constant.

ossification. Deposition of new bone. ➤*bone* (2).

osteitis. Inflammation of bone. True inflammation of bone is almost always a result of bacterial infection, involving the marrow: ➤*osteomyelitis.*

Osteitis deformans = ➤*Paget's disease.*

Osteitis fibrosa is thinning of bone from loss of the hard calcium salts, due to over-activity of the *parathyroid* glands.

osteoarthritis (osteoarthrosis). Degeneration of joints, with some loss of the almost frictionless cartilage linings and formation of rough deposits of bone. Since there is no inflammation, 'osteoarthrosis' is the better term. It is one of the seemingly inevitable processes of ageing, affecting mainly the joints subject to most wear and tear from weight-bearing – those of the legs and spine. Joints that have been subjected to abnormal stresses by faulty posture, injury, or deformity are especially vulnerable and may develop osteoarthrosis before middle age.

Much osteoarthrosis is discovered by chance from X-ray pictures made for some other reason, the joint having given no trouble. In such cases the condition is ignored for osteoarthrosis is no threat to health. Its symptoms – if any – are strictly confined to affected joints. They are discomfort or pain, and limitation of movement.

Since this is in no way a dangerous condition, treatment need go no further than the patient's comfort requires. Mild analgesic drugs, warm applications, or support for aching joints may be enough.

Surgery has much to offer in advanced cases. Becauses the pain comes from movement, a completely fixed joint is better than one with very limited and painful movement. Surgical fixation of the hip used to be the best treatment of severe osteoarthrosis of the joint. Later, various methods of realigning the joint were devised. But the best results at present follow replacement of the joint with an artificial ball and socket.

osteoblast. Bone-forming cell (➤*bone* (2)); cf. ➤*osteoclast.*

osteochondrosis (osteochondritis). Defective growth of part of a bone. Numerous types have been named, e.g. Perthes' disease (hip), Scheuermann's disease (one or more vertebrae), Schlatter's disease (below the knee), and others. At least some of these disorders arise from minor fractures; perhaps they all do.

osteoclast. Bone-absorbing cell (▸*bone* (2)). (Bone grows and is maintained by simultaneous deposition of new bone by osteoblasts and absorption of old bone by osteoclasts.)

osteoclastoma. Kind of bone tumour. ▸*osteoma.*

osteoma. Tumour of bone. The term could be applied to any tumour arising from bone, but is generally restricted to benign, i.e. non-cancerous tumours. A true osteoma is an uncommon tumour, most likely to arise from the skull and jaw. Benign tumours in other bones are usually mixed tumours of bone and cartilage, osteochondromas. Commoner than either is an *exostosis*, which is a superfluous lump of bone near a joint or at the attachment of a muscle; this is not a real tumour but an overgrowth of normal bone. All these conditions are cured by simply removing the lump.

Osteosarcoma (osteogenic sarcoma) is a cancer of bone-forming cells with a tendency to form deposits in the lungs.

Osteoclastoma is a tumour arising from osteoclasts, the cells responsible for removing old bone to make way for new. They destroy bone substance in their neighbourhood, but have little tendency to disseminate themselves.

osteomalacia. Softening of bones from lack of vitamin D in adult life, a similar disease to *rickets* in childhood, but rickets also impedes growth. Osteomalacia affects mainly the weight-bearing bones: the vertebrae are compressed and the legs bowed.

Since enough vitamin D is formed in the skin under the influence of sunlight, osteomalacia does not affect people who are able to get into the open, and is unknown in sunny regions. Except during and after pregnancy adults do not need much vitamin D in the diet, even if they live indoors, and deficiency is most often due to intestinal disease, with failure to assimilate the vitamin from the food.

The condition is cured with supplementary vitamin D.

osteomyelitis. Infection of bone, with abscess formation in the marrow. Since bone is rigid, the pus of the abscess has no chance to escape and therefore spreads along the length of the bone. The pressure interferes with the circulation and may deprive parts of the bone of their blood supply. A fragment of dead bone (sequestrum) will harbour bacteria indefinitely, because it is no longer accessible to the defence mechanisms (or drugs) carried in the blood. Established osteomyelitis usually needs surgery to open the cavity and remove dead bone.

The infection can follow a compound fracture (a fracture with the broken ends of bones exposed to contamination), but it is more often carried by the bloodstream from a site of infection elsewhere, such as a septic throat. The warning symptoms are pain and tenderness, fever, and more or less severe general illness. X-rays do not show any change in the early stages, and the diagnosis has to be made by inference.

Since the discovery of antibiotics, osteomyelitis has become much less common because the primary infection can be arrested before it spreads to bone; and the condition itself has become much easier to treat. The infection can usually be controlled before the need for surgery arises.

Chronic osteomyelitis used to be a common sequel, with a persistent leakage of pus from an ulcer in the overlying skin and slow deterioration of the patient's health; several operations were sometimes needed. Few cases now reach this stage, and although they all need surgery to clear away dead and infected bone, antibiotics greatly hasten their recovery.

The usual microbes are streptococci and staphylococci. Tuberculosis and syphilis used often to cause kinds of smouldering infection of bone, but all tuberculosis other than that of the lungs is now rare, and syphilis is seldom allowed to reach this late stage.

Typhoid and relapsing fevers occasionally lead to a mild, persistent osteomyelitis.

osteopathy. A system of medical practice, founded by A. T. Still (1828–1917), an American country doctor. Its principles are that the body will look after its own ailments if it is given a chance, and the usual hindrance is a structural defect such as a displaced bone that can be corrected by manipulation. The defect or *osteopathic lesion* is said to affect neighbouring organs by disturbing their blood supply. Still taught that all disease was caused in this way, but present-day osteopaths regard osteopathy as an addition to orthodox medicine rather than an alternative to it.

➤*manipulation.*

osteoporosis. Thinning of the texture and weakening of bone; a condition so common in old people that it seems an inevitable process of ageing. There is evidently some association with decreased production of sex hormones: women whose ovaries have had to be removed may develop osteoporosis at any age unless artificial hormones are given. An excess of adrenal hormones has the same effect; osteoporosis is one of the complications of ➤*corticosteroid* treatment if it is prolonged. Any bone that is completely immobilized develops osteoporosis in time, and the whole skeleton is weakened after a long period in bed.

One factor is loss of calcium from bone, and it has been suggested that old people would be less liable to osteoporosis if they took more calcium in their food. Milk is the most convenient source.

otitis externa. Inflammation of the skin of the external ear (including the canal or *meatus*), due to infection with bacteria or fungi. The irritation of wax in the canal seems to facilitate infection. The ear-drum is an effective barrier to spread into the middle ear, but if the drum is perforated by previous injury or infection the middle ear is likely to become involved.

Some people are prone to otitis externa after swimming, and have to protect their ears with plugs or bathing caps. The condition generally responds quickly to expert cleansing; antibiotic drugs are sometimes needed.

otitis interna. Inflammation of the inner ear (labyrinth), from spread of infection either inwards from the middle ear or outwards from within the skull. In other words it is a possible complication of either otitis media or meningitis. The treatment with antibiotics of the primary disorder also deals with the otitis interna, but there is a danger of permanent damage to the hearing organ.

otitis media. Inflammation of the middle

ear, from infection within the ear-drum. The infection nearly always comes from the back of the nose by way of the Eustachian tube, a direct passage from the ear to the nose. The usual sequence is a virus infection of the nose (e.g. measles, common cold) making the mucous membrane vulnerable to bacteria that would normally do no harm, with spread of bacterial infection up the tube to the middle ear.

Acute otitis media causes violent earache, often with fever and other constitutional symptoms of infection. Unless the attack is cut short with antibiotic drugs the earache persists until the pus in the middle ear escapes. The drum may perforate spontaneously; otherwise it has to be punctured surgically. When the infection has cleared up the drum generally heals and there is no further trouble. Occasionally the pus, instead of escaping safely to the outer ear or down the Eustachian tube, seeps into the mastoid bone behind the ear or, still worse, into the skull-cavity. These complications need urgent operation. They used to be common, but thanks to sulphonamide and antibiotic drugs are now rare.

Chronic otitis media represents a kind of stalemate between acute infection and natural resistance: the severe symptoms of an acute attack are overcome, but the infection smoulders for months or years. The perforation of the drum fails to heal, there is a slight discharge of pus, and hearing is usually affected. With patient cleansing the infection can often be controlled, but if the bone is involved a surgical operation may be needed. Large defects in the drum, with serious loss of hearing, can often be repaired by grafting when the infection has been successfully treated.

Serous otitis ('glue ear') is a common cause of deafness in children. The middle ear becomes filled with clear, sticky fluid which prevents the transmission of sound. This form of otitis may follow blockage of the Eustachian tube by minor infection such as a cold, but by the time symptoms arise there is generally no sign of infection. As a rule, the fluid drains itself through the Eustachian tube. Glue ear usually needs hospital treatment. It is occasionally necessary to puncture the drum and wash the fluid away.

otolith organ. The balance mechanism of the inner ear. ➤*ear* (3, ii).

otology. Study of the ears.

otorhinolaryngology. Branch of medicine dealing with ear, nose and throat (ENT).

otosclerosis. A hereditary defect of the middle ear, with formation of superfluous bone that may prevent the slight movements of the small bones that transmit vibration from the drum membrane to the sensory organ of the inner ear. In most cases the condition is harmless, but if the abnormal bone blocks transmission to the inner ear hearing is lost. This kind of deafness is treated surgically. *Fenestration* – making a new opening to the inner ear – has now been superseded by replacement of the immobilized conducting bone by a synthetic substitute (➤*stapedectomy*). On the whole the results of surgery are good, but some patients still need hearing aids even after operation.

ovary. The primary female sex organ, homologous with the male testis. A woman has two ovaries, one at each side of the uterus immediately below the opening of the Fallopian tube. The ovary is the only organ in the abdomen and pelvis that has no coating of peritoneum. Instead, it is covered with germinal epithelium, of which some cells form *ova* (eggs). The cells destined to form ova pass from the surface into the substance of the ovary where each is surrounded by a membrane to make a primitive (primordial) follicle. When a girl is born, her ovaries contain some hundreds of thousands of primordial follicles, of which only a few hundred will ever mature.

After puberty, a single follicle matures every month. The surrounding membrane grows rapidly and bursts on the surface of the ovary. The ovum – a single cell – is released and enters the Fallopian tube, where it may become fertilized. The rest of the follicle continues to grow into a small gland, the corpus luteum. If the ovum is fertilized, the corpus luteum continues to grow and secrete hormones that maintain pregnancy. If the ovum is not fertilized the corpus luteum withers, and menstruation occurs. The cycle continues until the menopause, some thirty years after puberty.

In addition to forming ova, the ovary serves as an endocrine gland, secreting the *sex hormones* that determine various female sex characters.

The activities of the ovary are governed by hormones of the pituitary gland. Sterility from failure to release ova for fertilization is more often due to deficiency of a pituitary hormone than of the ovaries themselves.

The common disorders of the ovaries are various types of abnormal growth. These swellings are often filled with fluid, and are then known as *ovarian cysts*. Many of these are practically harmless in themselves, but any ovarian cyst is liable to bleed, or to become twisted at its base and therefore congested and painful. Some ovarian swellings grow so large as to be a nuisance. A few are found to be cancers when they are examined by surgical operation. For these reasons it is standard practice to remove a defective ovary, regardless of the kind of disorder – it is seldom possible to identify the disorder without operation. Removal of one ovary has no ill effects. If both have to be removed the patient is then sterile, but in such circumstances she is likely to have been already sterile before the operation, because an ovary that needs removal has usually ceased to provide ova. Menstruation ceases after removal of both ovaries. Symptoms associated with this artificial menopause are controlled in the same way as those of the natural menopause, by regular small doses of oestrogens to replace the lost hormones.

oxalic acid. Oxalic acid and its salts (*oxalates*) are found in sorrel, rhubarb tops and other plants, and are synthesized for various industrial uses. Oxalic acid is extremely poisonous in two ways. It corrodes the lining of the mouth and stomach; and it interferes with the working of nerve and muscle fibres by neutralizing the active calcium of the body fluids, which is essential to nerve conduction and muscle contraction. Calcium compounds – e.g. chalk – are used as antidotes.

oxidant. Oxidizing agent; a substance transferring oxygen to another, removing hydrogen or introducing an electron with its negative electrical charge. Burning is rapid oxidation of fuel, converting stored chemical energy to heat. Most life on earth depends on the energy released by gradual oxidation of glucose. Oxidation can also be damaging, as witness fire or the rusting of iron. Wine left open to the air is spoilt as alcohol (C_2H_6O) loses hydrogen to form acetaldehyde (C_2H_4O)

and gains oxygen to form acetic acid ($C_2H_4O_2$).

The tiny cells of which the body is made up are enclosed by delicate membranes. The unsaturated fatty acids that maintain the stability of these cell membranes are vulnerable to attack by oxidants, and the resulting damage to the cells apparently predisposes them to serious disorders including ➤*atheroma*, which leads to strokes and heart attacks, and probably cancer.

The processes of body chemistry – metabolism – often involve a number of stages. Oxidizing glucose forms carbon dioxide and water: $C_6H_{12}O_6 + 6O_2$ ➤$6CO_2 + 6H_2O$. But this represents only the first and last stages of a series of reactions. The intermediate products of some processes include oxidants such as peroxides and hypochlorites, both familiar domestic bleaches. *Free radicals* consisting of one or more atoms are transient products of chemical change, actively seeking other radicals with which to form stable compounds. An isolated atom of oxygen with its negative electrical charge is incomplete in this sense, and during its brief life is a highly active and potentially destructive oxidant. The white blood cells that proliferate in response to infection release oxidant enzymes.

In addition to these and other endogenous oxidants, the environment contributes ozone, ultraviolet radiation, tobacco smoke and exhaust fumes.

Reducing agents have the opposite effect to oxidants and are a defence against harmful oxidation. Several enzymes act in this way, but alone they are not enough; they need additional help from the diet. The principal dietary antioxidants are *beta-carotene* (a plant pigment from which vitamin A can be derived), *vitamin C* and *vitamin E*.

oxygen. One of the most widely distributed elements; it constitutes about one fifth of the air. All known forms of life except a few bacteria depend on a constant supply of oxygen to provide energy by combustion of glucose or other fuel. Some tissues can work for a short time without oxygen, but the deficit has to be made up later (➤*muscle* (1)).

Oxygen is taken into the lungs and combined with the haemoglobin of the blood to be carried to every part of the body (➤*blood* (2); *haemoglobin*; *respiration*).

Oxygen has many medicinal uses. It is given to enrich the air when either breathing or circulation is impaired. This is of the greatest value when the lungs are unable to take up enough oxygen from the air, e.g. with severe bronchitis, but cannot help much if the lungs are healthy but oxygen is poorly distributed because the flow of blood is limited, e.g. with heart failure. But oxygen still has a place in the treatment of heart failure, because some of the trouble is due to congestion of the lungs. Oxygen is a necessary adjunct to many anaesthetics.

Oxygen under high pressure (hyperbaric oxygen) is under trial for resuscitation from severe shock and other states of collapse, and the promotion of healing. It is an effective remedy against infection with bacteria that live without air (gas gangrene; tetanus).

oxyntic. Acid-forming; the oxyntic cells in the lining of the stomach secrete hydrochloric acid.

oxytocin. A hormone of the ➤*pituitary* gland; it stimulates contraction of the uterus, which is especially sensitive to its action at the end of pregnancy. Oxytocin can be synthesized. It is used to start contraction of the uterus if labour is delayed.

Oxytocin also stimulates the muscle fibres around the milk ducts of the breast, and is given (by nasal spray) to facilitate lactation.

oxyuris. Pin-worm, an intestinal parasite.

ozone. An unusual form of oxygen, with molecules of 3 instead of 2 atoms. Its characteristic smell can be recognized near an electric motor. Ozone is a powerful antiseptic, and high concentrations are poisonous to all forms of life. The healthy ozone of seaside air is a myth. ➤*oxidant*.

P

pacemaker. The natural pacemaker of the heart is the *sinu-atrial node*, from which a wave of contraction spreads through the heart muscle with each beat (➤*heart* (3)).

When the natural heart beat fails with certain types of heart disease the beat can be started again with an artificial pacemaker if one can be provided within a very few minutes. This apparatus delivers small regular electric shocks. It can be life-saving, e.g. when a patient who has had a coronary thrombosis has a second, potentially fatal attack in hospital where a pacemaker can be applied at once.

Patients in whom the conducting mechanism of the heart has broken down (heart block, ➤*arrhythmia*) used to be in considerable danger, but they can now live normal lives when a small battery-driven pacemaker has been attached to the heart. The simplest and most reliable type acts at a fixed frequency of 70 beats per minute. Other types, not suitable for all cases, pick up the natural impulse from the sinu-atrial node and deliver it to the ventricles. With this type the rate is regulated by the patient's own nervous system.

Pacinian corpuscles. (F. Pacini, 1812–83, Italian anatomist.) Minute round organs at the ends of some nerve fibres in skin and tendons, receiving the sensation of pressure.

paediatrics. Medical care of children. Paediatrics was a recognized specialty before the era of medical specialization began in the latter part of the 19th century. Some of the classical writers (e.g. Celsus; Soranus) drew attention to important differences between children and adults in their responses to illness and its treatment. The first book entirely devoted to paediatrics, by Paolo Bagellardo, appeared in Padua in 1472. But this, like other medical books of its time, was little more than an appraisal of ancient authorities. Paediatrics really began with the publication in 1765 of a treatise on children's diseases and their treatment by Nils Rosen von Rosenstein of Uppsala in Sweden. It is a record of careful observation and sensible inference. For instance, when Rosen described the ill effects of teething (which he overstated), he started with a stern warning against putting other ailments down to teething, instead of making 'a diligent inquiry into the real cause of the disease'. Today's paediatricians still have to sound the same warning, for it is all too easy to blame on teething any illness that happens to arise at the same time. Older children may find their ailments blamed on 'growing'. (For a similar danger in later life, ➤*menopause*.)

Paget's disease. (Sir James Paget, 1814–99, English surgeon.) Two diseases are named after Paget.
1. *Osteitis deformans* is a disorder of the skeleton. The normal processes of absorption and renewal of bones become disturbed and no longer co-ordinated. Some bones may lose calcium and with it their rigidity, and as a result they are deformed by weight-bearing. Later too much calcium is deposited and the bones are thickened. Paget's disease can be con-

fined to a single bone or affect several, e.g. legs, skull, vertebrae. It is a very slow process and comparatively harmless. The cause is unknown. Most cases are discovered by chance, e.g. after a routine X-ray examination. Sometimes the affected bones ache, and in advanced cases the patient's activity may be restricted. X-ray treatment often relieves pain, and the hormone ►calcitonin has recently been used with success. Disodium etidronate also gives relief.

2. Paget's disease of the nipple looks like a harmless eczema of the nipple, but is in fact associated with an uncommon type of breast cancer and needs prompt surgical treatment.

pain. Pain is distinct from other sensations (except, perhaps, itch) and is carried by its own nerve fibres. These fibres follow two pathways: one, with fast conduction, carries a 'sharp' sensation; the other, a slower and duller sensation. The two components can be distinguished when the hand is pricked or pinched.

It is worth insisting that pain is not an event in the part of the body that is hurt, nor in the nerves that conduct impulses from the part, but in an area of the brain where the impulse is translated into a conscious feeling. If no feeling is aroused, one cannot say that there is pain. On the other hand, if the feeling is aroused there is pain. Whether or not pain is felt does not depend only on the nature and extent of the stimulus. It also depends on frame of mind. A man who is preoccupied may hardly notice an injury that he would find painful at another time. Another man who is expecting an injury and anxious about it may feel more pain than the injury would normally be worth. 'Imaginary pain' is almost meaningless. All pain is in the mind; it has no other

existence. Colours, sounds, smells, textures and other things of which we are aware are our interpretation of real, measurable events around us. Pain has no such counterpart in the outside world.

The use of pain as a warning is obvious: it can prevent further injury by discouraging the activity that aroused it. But as often as not, pain is unpleasant to no good purpose.

The first aim in treating a disease is to remove its cause; to relieve pain is often a close second. The two may go together. Setting and splinting a broken bone deals with the injury itself and also stops painful movement of the broken ends. But in this as in many other instances there may be delay before definitive treatment, and the treatment itself is painful. With many other conditions, pain persists during the cure. For the patient himself the strict medical priorities are often reversed: treatment of causes takes second place. Many painful conditions resolve themselves, and some cannot yet be cured. In either case the sole object of treatment is to relieve pain.

The humane motive is the principal reason but not the only one for treating pain, for there is more than mental suffering at stake. Severe or protracted pain has physical effects. It provokes various reflex actions, of which sweating, nausea, and faintness are familiar examples. By disturbing the heart and circulation, pain contributes to shock (failure of the circulation), a sometimes fatal complication of extensive injury or severe acute illness. Anaesthetics have made surgery safer as well as less unpleasant.

Most pain arises from direct mechanical injury to the specific nerve-endings, such as a blow, a wound, or a burn, but pain can also be due to chemical irritation. When the flow of blood through a muscle is restricted, e.g. the heart muscle in angina, by-products of incomplete combustion accumulate and cause pain.

Not all tissues are sensitive to pain. In the skin and its underlying connective tissue many kinds of stimulus cause pain; in muscle, pressure or defective blood supply; in most abdominal organs, distension or muscle spasm. The linings of the abdomen and chest (peritoneum and pleura) and the membranous coating of bone are very sensitive; bone itself is not, nor is the interior of solid organs such as the liver, nor, surprisingly, the brain. The majority of the internal organs can be cut or burnt without sensation.

For drugs used against pain ►*anaesthetics*; *analgesic*; *narcotic*.

►*counter-irritation*; *referred pain*.

palate. Roof of the mouth, divided into the hard palate in front and the soft palate behind the back teeth. Most of the hard palate is formed by the floor of the maxilla (upper jaw-bone); behind it are small *palatine* bones. The soft palate is a fibrous arch equipped with muscles which draw it up to close the back of the nose during swallowing. Behind the tongue the pillar at each side of the arch of the palate divides to embrace the *tonsil*. The downward projection from the centre of the arch, the *uvula*, does not appear to be useful. An unduly long one may cause a child to cough when lying down; it can be removed without ill effects.

The mucous membrane coating the soft palate contains a few taste-buds; they are much less important than those of the tongue.

The palate develops in two halves which normally fuse in the mid-line. Cleft palate, a common congenital defect, is incomplete fusion of the two sides. It is often associated with *harelip*, which is a similar failure of the two halves of the upper lip to join. The extent of the defect can be anything from a groove at the edge of the lip or in the uvula to complete separation of the two sides of palate and lip. Some degree of cleft is to be expected in 1:750 of babies, but if an immediate relation is affected the chance is about 1:20.

These defects can always be greatly improved and often made completely good by plastic surgery. Timing the operation can be more difficult than doing it. If the operation is likely to be prolonged it may have to be postponed until the baby is older and stronger. On the other hand if the defect makes it impossible for the baby to suck some kind of repair has to be done. If the operation is delayed until the child has learnt to speak the speech defect may be difficult to correct. The compromise is an early operation to establish the function of the palate or lip and a later operation to improve the child's appearance.

palliative. Treatment to suppress symptoms rather than the underlying disease. The word is often given a rather derogatory sense, as though palliation were bad practice; but this is not justified unless treatment of causes is neglected. It would be deplorable to suppress the cough of pneumonia or the pain of appendicitis and do nothing to control the infection, but the relief of symptoms is an important adjunct to curative treatment. And with many diseases the whole treatment is palliative – for instance, no known treatment will shorten a cold, but much can be done to make it less unpleasant while it lasts.

pallor. The pale complexion of sick people is usually due to constriction of blood vessels in the skin, which conserves heat by preventing blood from being cooled on the surface of the body. Pallor may also be due to a shortage of the red blood-pigment haemoglobin, i.e. anaemia.

palpitation. Awareness of the heart beat, either because the heart is in fact beating more forcibly than usual or because the subject pays undue attention to it.

palsy. Paralysis.

paludism. Malaria (*palus* = swamp, where mosquitoes are likely to breed and carry malaria).

panacea. Greek goddess of healing; cure-all.

pancreas. A broad strip of soft glandular tissue across the back of the abdomen, mostly under cover of the stomach. It is broadest on the right where it nestles in the curve of the duodenum, wrapped round the portal vein and closely applied to the arteries of the liver and the bile duct. From here it tapers away, upwards and to the left, between the stomach and the left kidney to reach the spleen. The pancreas receives blood from the cocliac artery (which also supplies the stomach, liver, and spleen), and returns it to the portal vein.

This is a dual-purpose organ. It is an offshoot of the intestine, and primarily a digestive gland. In this respect it is analogous to the salivary glands – in German it is known as the abdominal salivary gland. Most of its cells are arranged around branches of the pancreatic duct, into which they secrete the pancreatic juice. The duct enters the duodenum in company with the bile duct; in other words the pancreas and liver share the same opening into the intestine, and are both apt to suffer if the opening is blocked (e.g. by a gall stone or a tumour). The pancreatic juice is alkaline, and neutralizes the acid entering the intestine from the stomach. It contains numerous digestive enzymes – catalysts by which complex substances in the food are broken down to simple chemicals which can be absorbed from the intestine into the blood-stream (>*digestion*).

Apart from its primary digestive function the pancreas is concerned with the chemical control of sugar in the body. Scattered through the gland are small clusters of specialized cells which do not communicate with the duct and contribute nothing to the pancreatic juice. These are the *islets of Langerhans*. They produce two hormones, *insulin and glucagon*, which are released directly into the blood-stream. Their functions are complementary. Insulin promotes the uptake of sugar from the blood by the tissues, for storage and combustion. Glucagon promotes the release of sugar from the tissues (mainly the liver) into the blood. (>*carbohydrate*; *diabetes*).

1. DISORDERS

By far the most important disease involving the pancreas is *diabetes mellitus*. Diabetes is discussed under its own heading; it is not a single disease but a collection of symptoms due to failure to use insulin, either because the pancreas is not making enough or because the demand is abnormally great. Some diabetes is caused by disorders of the pancreas, but in many cases the pancreas is healthy.

Pancreatitis – inflammation of the

pancreas – may be mild and transient, but at its worst it can be very dangerous with a clinical picture suggesting either severe disease of the gall bladder or perforation of a duodenal ulcer. Sometimes the diagnosis can be made only by surgical operation. If digestive enzymes leak into the abdominal cavity they set up a violent peritonitis with the same symptoms as peritonitis from any other cause. Most cases are due to, or associated with, obstruction of the pancreatic duct as it enters the duodenum, for instance by a gall stone blocking both pancreatic and bile ducts, or by swelling of the mucous membrane from heavy drinking.

Mild attacks of pancreatitis sometimes complicate mumps, not surprisingly because the virus of mumps has a predilection for the salivary glands, which closely resemble the pancreas.

Chronic pancreatitis is an uncommon cause of poor digestion and pain. Its origin is usually obscure, but since the islets of Langerhans escape damage while the digestive part of the gland is slowly destroyed the trouble probably begins in the pancreatic duct, with which the islets are not concerned. The loss of pancreatic enzymes leads to ➤*malabsorption.*

Cancer of the pancreas is for no obvious reason becoming more common. At present the only treatment is removal, but diagnosis is often late, and the operation is difficult because the organ is not easily accessible; the outlook is not good.

pancreatitis. Inflammation of the ➤*pancreas.*

pandemic. Outbreak of infectious disease, more widespread than an epidemic (e.g. over a whole continent or even, as in some outbreaks of influenza, around the world).

pannus. Opaque inflamed membrane spreading over the front of the eye and obscuring vision; a complication of ➤*trachoma.*

papaverine. An alkaloid extracted from opium, not related to morphine; it relaxes involuntary muscle and has been used for treating spasm in blood vessels and other organs. Its action is brief and not very reliable, and it has been superseded by synthetic drugs.

papilla. Small projection from the surface of a tissue, such as one of the minute structures that cover the tongue.

papilloma. Abnormal growth of papillae; wart.

papule. Pimple; raised spot on the surface of the skin.

Paracelsus (Philipp Theophrastus Bombast von Hohenheim, 1493–1591, nicknamed Aureole; he does not appear to have adopted the name Paracelsus before about 1540). Paracelsus was born at Einsiedeln of a Swabian father and a Swiss mother. He was brought up in Austria and later travelled throughout Europe, never settling for more than a year or two. He studied with equal enthusiasm theology, chemistry, and medicine, and their shadier counterparts necromancy, alchemy, and quackery. He had the learning and imagination to be one of the great reformers of all time, yet he achieved little. He has been called the medical Luther, but he was nothing of the kind. At the outset, Luther asked no more than that the established church should set its own house in order, and almost by accident found half Europe at his feet. Paracelsus set himself to reform the whole of medicine (and much besides), but converted nobody and changed nothing. His greatest opportunity came in 1526 when he was appointed town physician and professor in Basle. From this eminent post he could have influenced all Europe, but he so alienated his colleagues that he had to leave Basle after only a year. Publicly burning the works of Galen and Avicenna was good theatre, but tactless. Paracelsus might just have been forgiven for this, but not for claiming precedence over all other doctors, including his contemporaries.

Paracelsus intended to 'purify medicine of errors' by accepting only rules that had been proved by experiment. Here was the true scientific method; unfortunately Paracelsus did not follow it. He demolished the old, unproven theories, only to replace them with wilder fantasies of his own. He wrote a curious mixture of Latin with his native dialect. When he was short of a word he invented one, often without defining it. Throughout, his brilliant observations lie half submerged in mystical jargon.

His attitude to theology throws some light on this weird genius. He was a fiercer critic of orthodoxy than Luther. Men were being burnt at the stake for less – Paracelsus may have escaped because he was so unlikely to influence anyone else. Yet when leaders of the new Reformation approached him as a possible ally, he rudely told them that he was a good Catholic and had no time for their heresies.

Nobody need blame the doctors of his time for rejecting Paracelsus; he compelled rejection. But his patients loved him. With them he was considerate and even courteous.

Some of Paracelsus's discoveries were acceptable in the 16th century. He was the first man to describe miner's lung (>*pneumoconiosis*), the relation of cretinism to goitre, the distinction between mental defect and insanity, and the proper use of opium. He introduced chemistry to medicine with compounds of lead, iron, copper, and mercury, and he was the first to use sulphur and antimony as drugs. He believed in simple, clean dressings for wounds.

In other matters Paracelsus was centuries ahead of his time. Surgery was still considered an ungentlemanly craft, but Paracelsus believed that surgeons should have the same status as physicians and work closely with them. He insisted that anatomy should be studied and taught in relation to the living body – a view only now being adopted by medical schools. He detested polypharmacy, the giving of half a dozen remedies in the hope that one would work, for he maintained that one drug was as likely to cancel as to reinforce another. He said that talking to a patient and letting him talk might be the best treatment. None of these doctrines could hope to be accepted at the time. For this was the voice of Hippocrates, calling across 20 centuries. Men still shaking the dust of the Middle Ages from their ears could not possibly hear it.

paracentesis. Release of fluid from a tissue or body cavity by insertion of a drainage tube.

paracetamol >*analgesic*.

paraesthesia. Abnormal sensation without external cause, e.g. tingling, 'pins-and-needles', a common symptom of compression or irritation of a nerve. >*neuropathy*.

paraffin. A series of compounds of carbon with hydrogen, including gases, liquids and solids.

Liquid paraffin is a clear, inert, almost tasteless fluid; it is not absorbed from the intestine and therefore passes through as a lubricant. It has been much used as a mild laxative.

Soft paraffin (petroleum jelly; petrolatum) forms a good barrier to protect superficial injuries of the skin such as burns; it prevents dressings from sticking to raw areas. It is the basis of many ointments.

paralysis. Loss of voluntary movement; failure of nervous impulses to reach muscles; it can be a symptom of almost any disorder of the nervous system. *Infantile paralysis* = ►*poliomyelitis. Paralysis agitans* = ►*parkinsonism.*

parameter. A fairly recent addition to medical language, borrowed from geometry. It is used of quantities that can be measured and compared in different individuals, such as body weight, blood pressure, or the concentration of sugar in the blood.

paranoia. A kind of mental disorder, with delusions of persecution and self-importance. On its own it is rare – some psychiatrists deny that there is such a disease. But paranoid symptoms are common in schizophrenia.

paraphimosis. Painful constriction of the tip of the penis by retraction of an abnormally tight foreskin, usually an indication for circumcision.

paraplegia. Paralysis of the lower part of the body, usually from injury to the spinal cord (cf. *hemiplegia*, paralysis of one side of the body).

parasite. A creature that lives at the expense of another living creature, its *host.* Human parasites include *viruses, bacteria, fungi, protozoa,* and *worms.* Nearly all parasites injure the health of the host to some extent, and many cause serious illness. Harmless parasites, such as the bacteria of the healthy intestine, are called *commensals.*

parasympathetic. One of the two divisions (cf. ►*sympathetic*) of the autonomic or vegetative nervous system, which are responsible for the automatic, unconscious regulation of bodily function. Most parts of the body receive twigs from both of these divisions, generally with opposite actions.

Two groups of nerves form the parasympathetic system. The *cranial* outflow arises from the lowest part of the brain. Several cranial nerves include parasympathetic fibres; the *vagus* (10th cranial) nerve carries most. The *sacral* outflow arises from the lower end of the spinal cord as the two sacral nerves (nervi erigentes).

Parasympathetic nerves have the following actions:

Fibres in the 3rd cranial (ophthalmic) nerve constrict the pupils and focus the lens of the eye.

Fibres in the 7th (facial) and 9th (glossopharyngeal) nerves stimulate the salivary glands. These nerves also carry the sense of taste, making a simple pathway for the reflex by which the taste of food stimulates the flow of saliva.

The vagus nerves are widely distributed. In the *heart* they slow the beat and reduce its force. The various reflexes that accelerate the heart act more by withdrawing the inhibition by the vagus than increasing stimulation by sympathetic nerves. In the *lungs*, they reduce the flow of air. They increase the activity of the *digestive* organs.

The pelvic nerves stimulate emptying of the bladder and rectum. They are also responsible for erection of the penis (but orgasm depends on sympathetic nerves).

To some extent, autonomic nerves act independently of the brain – hence their name – but the activity of the whole system is modified and co-ordinated in the brain, mainly in and around the hypothalamus. This part of the brain is also concerned with the emotions, which have their physical expression in reflexes of the autonomic system (widening of the pupils, sweating, quickened pulse, blushing, blanching, digestive disturbance etc.).

All the actions of parasympathetic nerves are due to the substance *acetyl choline*, which is released from the nerve-endings and activates the 'target organs'. The effects of an impulse in a particular nerve are confined to its own area, because acetyl choline is very rapidly destroyed.

Drugs, such as *carbachol*, that imitate acetyl choline, or *eserine*, that prevent its destruction, have similar actions to the parasympathetic nerves. Drugs such as *atropine*, that interfere with acetyl choline, suppress parasympathetic action.

parathyroid. One of several (usually 4) small glands behind or embedded in the thyroid gland. The parathyroids produce a hormone, *parathormone*, which regulates the concentration of calcium in the blood. If this concentration falls the parathyroids are thereby stimulated to release more of the hormone, which increases the solubility of calcium in the bones and so restores the amount in the blood.

Deficiency of the parathyroids is rare. It may occur for no known reason, or may follow injury to the parathyroids during surgery of the thyroid gland. The result is *tetany* – over-excitability of

nerve and muscle, with twitching, cramp, and tingling sensations. Tetany is controlled by injecting either calcium or the hormone.

A tumour of a parathyroid may produce an excess of parathormone. Too much calcium is then withdrawn from the bones, which become fragile. The surplus of calcium in the blood is excreted in the urine; it may form stones in the kidneys. These tumours are not malignant. They can be removed surgically and usually cured. If after the operation there is too little parathormone the deficiency can be made up by injections, but this is seldom necessary.

The ►*thyroid gland* produces a hormone (*calcitonin*) to combat excessive calcium in the blood, as a counterpart to parathormone.

paratyphoid fever. A group of infectious diseases related to ►*typhoid* fever but generally milder. Of the three types, only paratyphoid B is common in Western Europe. A and C occur mainly in the tropics and subtropics.

Most outbreaks are spread by contamination of food or drinking water by infected people, who may have long recovered from the illness. In hot, dry climates infection may be spread by dust or flies. Hygienic water supplies and food-handling greatly reduce the incidence.

Symptoms are of two kinds. Some cases are like typhoid fever: the patient is obviously ill without signs to incriminate any particular organ, and the diagnosis depends on identifying the bacteria in the laboratory. In other cases the trouble is confined to the intestine, and the main symptom is diarrhoea.

The bacteria of paratyphoid fever are species of *Salmonella*, a group that includes the bacteria of typhoid fever on the one hand, and of bacterial food poisoning on the other. Paratyphoid is intermediate between the two, or rather can take either form.

Paré, Ambroise (1510–90). French surgeon; one of the greatest figures in the history of surgery. Inspired by the anatomical work of Vesalius, he more than anyone else led surgery out of the Middle Ages. Vesalius had said that one of the main reasons for the decline of medical practice between the 2nd and 16th centuries was that by delegating all surgical work to uneducated barbers the physicians had lost touch with anatomy as the basis of rational medicine. Paré founded his practice and teaching on Vesalius's anatomical studies. He was a barber-surgeon who raised himself to the highest ranks of the scholarly medical profession – without learning to write Latin.

Paré was the first to treat serious bleeding by finding the cut artery and tying a ligature round it, instead of burning it. He also abolished the use of boiling oil to take the 'poison' from gunshot wounds. The cruelty of it horrified him. It chanced that in 1536, when attending a French force sent to relieve Turin, Paré had no oil. Instead he applied a bland dressing of egg-yolk, oil of roses, and turpentine. In the morning his patients were comfortable and their wounds not inflamed. Other patients, treated with boiling oil, were in great pain from their festering wounds.

The most famous sentence in Paré's extensive works summed up his principle of letting well alone: 'I dressed him. God healed him' (*Je le pansai. Dieu le guérit*).

paregoric. Compound tincture of camphor; camphorated tincture of opium. Paregoric contains about 1 per cent of morphine. It was a favourite household remedy in the 19th century, much used to calm fretful children – an undesirable practice, for children would have been better off without opium, and doping them must often have masked symptoms of illnesses that needed attention.

parenchyma. The working tissue of an organ. All organs have a framework (*stroma*) of unspecialized connective tissue, supporting the specialized tissue that gives the organ its distinctive character (*parenchyma*), e.g. the contractile cells of a muscle or the secreting cells of a gland.

paresis. Partial paralysis.

parietal. 1. Of the wall of a body cavity as opposed to its contents. The parietal pleura lines the inside of the thorax; the continuation of this membrane over the surface of the lungs is the *visceral* pleura. Similarly the abdomen is lined with the parietal peritoneum, and the abdominal organs are coated with the visceral peritoneum.

2. Of the side of the cranium or brainbox. The parietal bones cover about the same area as a cardinal's skullcap. The *parietal lobes* are the corresponding part of the brain. The front part of these lobes, immediately behind the part of the frontal lobes concerned with movement, records conscious sensation.

parkinsonism (shaking palsy; paralysis agitans). A disturbance of voluntary movement: muscles become stiff and sluggish, movement becomes clumsy and difficult, and uncontrollable rhythmic twitching of groups of muscles produces the characteristic shaking or tremor, which may be widespread or limited to one group of muscles. Mental faculties are not affected; they may seem to be if the patient cannot control the muscles of speech.

The site of the disorder is the *basal ganglia* – groups of cells in the centre of the brain where deliberate impulses to move, from conscious areas of the brain, are transmitted to nerves that direct the appropriate muscles. The basal ganglia can be affected in many known ways (poisoning, injury, stroke), but these are all rare. The pandemic of ➤*encephalitis* lethargica that began in 1917 was complicated by parkinsonism. But in most cases, no cause for the degeneration of the basal ganglia can be found; the term Parkinson's disease is confined to these cases.

Voluntary movement is co-ordinated by a balance of opposing nerve actions, some exciting movement and some inhibiting it. In parkinsonism, it is as though these two actions were not equally impaired – unwanted excitation of muscle is not inhibited as it should be, and muscles contract without any conscious intention that they should do so. The inhibiting nerve cells in the basal ganglia have degenerated and cannot be repaired, while many exciting cells are still intact.

The effect of most forms of treatment of parkinsonism is to put all the nerve cells of the affected region equally out of action; then some kind of balance is restored. The drugs used probably act in some such way. Belladonna (atropine) is the prototype, but it has many other actions, some of them unpleasant. Synthetic drugs with a more selective action are available. Surgery gives more lasting and generally more reliable results. Stereotactic surgery – a sort of three-dimensional geometry – makes it possible to coagulate a minute cluster of cells in the centre of the brain without

other damage. It is a negative and destructive approach to a disease of which the cause is still unknown, but in some cases the results justify it. Surgery is especially effective against the tremor, but it usually has some effect on the other symptoms, and has enabled many patients to write legibly again, or handle a knife and fork.

As with several other disorders involving the brain (➤*depression, schizophrenia*) chemical anomalies that cannot be called causes are at least associated with parkinsonism. There appears to be a deficiency of *dopamine*, a chemical precursor of adrenaline, in the basal ganglia. Most of the drugs used act indirectly to counteract such a deficiency, but levodopa (➤*dopa*) probably has a direct action in replacing the missing dopamine. This drug is especially useful for improving muscular coordination. It is not only a valuable form of treatment, very largely superseding surgery, but its effect sheds much light on the nature of the disease.

Parkinson's disease. (James Parkinson, 1755–1824, London physician.) The commonest form of ➤*parkinsonism*.

paronychia. Small abscess at the side of a fingernail. ➤*nails*.

parotid gland. Salivary gland behind the jaw. ➤*saliva*.

parotitis. Inflammation of the parotid gland. It is occasionally due to bacteria, in which case an abscess may form and need surgical treatment, but the usual cause is the virus of ➤*mumps* (epidemic parotitis).

paroxysm. A fit or convulsion, or any sudden, violent attack of illness.

parturition. Childbirth. ➤*labour*.

Pasteur, Louis (1822–95). French chemist; professor in Strasbourg, Lille, and Paris. His most important chemical discovery was that certain compounds exist in two forms, the molecules of one being mirror images of those of the other. Many ingredients of the body – e.g. glucose, amino-acids, adrenaline – are of this type, and although the two forms seem identical by ordinary chemical tests only one form is active in the living body.

Pasteur's greatest work was in biology, where he established the relation of microbes to fermentation, putrefaction, and infectious disease, as described under ➤*microbe* (➤*infection*). This discovery was one of the major turning points in medical history.

pasteurization. Pasteur's method of preventing the transmission of disease by infected milk (tuberculosis, typhoid etc.).

The milk is heated either to 65 ° C (149 ° F) for 30 minutes or to 72 ° C (162 ° F) for 15 seconds and then rapidly cooled. This does not sterilize the milk, but it kills the kinds of bacteria liable to cause disease.

Pasteurization is obviously useless unless the treated milk is protected from contamination.

patella (kneecap). A thick disc of bone set in the tendon of the ➤*quadriceps* muscle in front of the knee. There is a general tendency for small bones to be formed in tendons which are pressed directly against bare bone; several of these *sesamoid* bones are found in the hand and foot. The patella is simply a large sesamoid. It may slightly increase the mechanical efficiency of the quadriceps by acting as a fulcrum, but the knee functions well without it.

The pull of the quadriceps is some degrees off vertical. Its tendency to dislocate the patella sideways is overcome by muscle fibres attached to the inner side of the patella. If these fibres are injured, or weakened by inflammation in the knee joint, the patella is unstable. Occasionally, repeated dislocation of the patella becomes such a nuisance that an operation is needed to repair the damaged fibres.

Sudden and powerful contraction of the quadriceps may snap the patella across, but a direct blow is more likely to break it into several fragments. If the fragments are held in place by the tendon, these fractures heal well in a plaster cast. But if the tendon is badly torn the patella must either be held together with sutures or, if there are several small fragments, removed. The loss of the bone is less disabling than a roughened joint surface.

patent. Open. *Patent ductus*: ➤*ductus arteriosus*.

path(o)-. Prefix = 'disease'; 'suffering'.

pathogen. Microbe capable of causing disease.

pathogenesis. The processes by which a disease develops.

pathognomonic. (Symptom etc.) peculiar to a particular disease, sufficient in itself to establish the diagnosis.

pathology. Natural history of disease; study of abnormal changes in the body and their causes. While clinical medicine deals mainly with the effects of disease, pathology deals with the underlying processes.

Of necessity, pathology is a modern science: abnormalities in the body cannot be usefully discussed until normal structure and function (anatomy and physiology) are understood, and no clear idea of function was possible until

1628 when Harvey discovered the circulation of the blood. Diseases had previously been described in terms of their symptoms, and attributed to disordered balance of the ►humours. The humoral theory was so deeply ingrained that few people even looked for evidence of disease beyond the obvious outward signs. Two who did so were Antonio Benivieni of Florence (1443–1502), apparently the first man to do necropsies (post-mortem examinations) in search of the true causes of disease, and Jean Fernel of Amiens (1497–1558), who broke new ground by devoting a section of his medical textbook to pathology.

Scientific pathology really began in 1761 with the publication of Morgagni's *De sedibus et causis morborum*, a large collection of case-histories in which patients' symptoms are related to disorders of particular organs found by necropsy.

John Hunter (1728–93) applied the experimental method to pathology and amassed a store of accurate observations, including thousands of specimens of diseased organs, many of them still preserved. But even at the end of the 18th century pathology had progressed no further than showing where in the body the trouble lay with various diseases. The actual processes remained a mystery, and the humoral theory was hardly less credible than some of the rival theories that sprang up. Hunter did, however, produce a substantially correct account of inflammation, one of the fundamental processes of disease. Under the influence of scientists such as Hunter, pathology came to rely more and more on observed facts and less on philosophical speculation. One other pioneer of the 18th century must be mentioned: Bichat focused attention not on whole organs but on their constituent *tissues* as

the sites of disease. Although Bichat himself was not a microscopist it was his doctrine that led others to study disease with the microscope. The flood of pathological discovery in the 19th century came largely from microscopical examination of diseased tissues.

Full-time professional pathologists began to appear early in the 19th century. One of the first was Hodgkin in London. The busiest was Rokitansky in Vienna. By this time, complete postmortem examination was the rule when the cause of death was in any doubt, and Rokitansky attended some 70,000. His procedure for these examinations is still standard. More important, his unequalled experience and accuracy enabled him to leave precise descriptions of most of the known diseases. This great scientist suddenly clouded his reputation with a general theory that might have put pathology back into the Middle Ages if it had been accepted. When medicine had at last broken away from sweeping, unfounded generalizations Rokitansky revived the old humours in a new guise. All diseases were affections of the circulating blood – crasis or dyscrasis, terms that seem to mean no more than normal or abnormal tendencies – and they were as ill-defined as the humours of 500 BC. To be fair, Rokitansky may have meant no more than that chemical abnormalities determined the processes of disease; if this is so he was quite right regarding some diseases, and only putting the cart before the horse regarding others.

The greatest of all pathologists was Rudolf Virchow, a pupil of the physiologist Müller. As a young man, Virchow demolished Rokitansky's theories and set pathology back on the path of observation and experiment. His colleague Schwann had taken anatomy one step further than Bichat and shown that the fundamental unit was not the tissue, but the *cells* that composed it. Virchow showed that diseases were best explained in terms of changes that took place within the cells. This was almost as important to medical science as was the study of molecules rather than substances to chemistry. Excepting some very recent discoveries, most current ideas of pathology spring from the work of Virchow and of his contemporaries who discovered the nature of ►*infection*.

Pathology has come to deal with smaller and smaller units: from a vague concept of the whole person with the classical study of humours to the study of particular organs, then tissues, then cells, and, finally, molecules. In Virchow's day, only a few diseases such as diabetes and gout, involving the simple molecules of glucose and uric acid, could be studied chemically. But all processes in the body – normal or abnormal – are in a sense chemical, and in theory all disease might be expressed in terms of disturbed chemical reactions. Pathologists are now beginning to study these disturbances, and Rokitansky's theories seem rather less absurd than they did a century ago.

In the past, post-mortem studies were the only possible way of learning about the nature of disease, and they are still very important for both research and teaching. But they reveal disease at a stage where it is beyond the help of medicine, and they reveal established, static conditions, not the dynamic processes that concern practical medicine. For all its great achievements, 19th-century pathology often seemed remote from the problems of living patients. It described in great detail what had gone wrong with a patient's anatomy, but it had little to say about his physiology – the workings of affected cells, tissues, and organs.

In the 20th century pathology has been coming to life by dealing more with active processes and less with fixed states. Techniques such as X-ray examination and biopsy – the study of small samples of living tissue – show what is going on while the patient is still alive and perhaps curable instead of waiting until he is dead to find out what is wrong. The chemistry of the living body can also be studied in detail. A department of pathology now accommodates half a dozen different sciences, all involved not only in research but in the investigation and treatment of patients. Like other sciences, pathology is becoming on the one hand more specialized, and on the other hand more closely integrated with its neighbours.

Pavlov, Ivan Petrovich (1849–1936). Russian physiologist. He was originally concerned with the physiology of digestion, in particular the regulation of flow of saliva and digestive juice in the stomach. During his experiments, mainly with dogs, he found that salivation was induced not only by stimuli directly concerned with eating but by any stimulus (e.g. the ringing of a bell) that the dog had learned to associate with food. These learnt responses he called *conditioned reflexes* (►*reflex*). In 1904 Pavlov received a Nobel Prize for his work on digestion. But his discoveries have a much wider significance; they shed new light on the whole study of learning and behaviour. If it is true, as many psychiatrists hold, that neuroses are ill-formed conditioned reflexes, then Pavlov helped to elucidate one of the commonest of all ailments (►*anxiety*).

PCA. Patient-controlled ►*analgesia*.

pectoral. Of the chest. The pectoral muscles are *pectoralis major* and *pectoralis minor*. Pectoralis major is a large fan-shaped muscle covering much of the front of the chest, and converging on the humerus a little below the shoulder. It swings the arm across the body, and is highly developed in birds as a muscle of flying. In man it acts with *latissimus dorsi*, a large muscle of the back, to pull the arm down as in swimming breast stroke, or pull the body up as in climbing. Pectoralis minor is an unimportant muscle covered by pectoralis major.

pediculus. Louse. *Pediculosis* = infestation with lice.

pellagra. A form of malnutrition, very common among people whose staple diet is maize, due primarily to deficiency of *niacin*, a vitamin of the B group.

The tissues mainly affected are skin, mucous membranes, and nerve. Exposed areas of skin develop a sort of eczema with roughening and darkening of the surface (*pellagra* = 'rough skin'). Changes in the mucous membranes cause a sore tongue and, more seriously, chronic diarrhoea. Various symptoms of disturbance of the nervous system can arise, including severe mental derangement.

As with other vitamin deficiencies, the symptoms vanish with a mixed diet and supplements of the appropriate vitamin.

The association of pellagra with a maize diet is so common that a positive toxic action of maize has been sought. The explanation may be that the amino-acid *trytophan*, found in most protein, much reduces the need for niacin. Maize contains very little trytophan. Therefore maize-eaters need more niacin than other people, while as often as not they

get less because the rest of the diet is poor.

pelvis. Lower limb-girdle, composed of the lower part of the backbone and the two hip-bones. (Also *renal pelvis*: the outlet of the ►*kidney*.)

The pelvis is a firm ring of bone. The centre-piece is the *sacrum*, consisting of

female

sacroiliac joint

sacrum

coccyx

male

ilium

sacrum

ischium

pubis

female   male

Front and right side of pelvic bones

5 vertebrae fused into a single bone, broad and massive in its upper part and tapering to a point below, to which the rudimentary tail (coccyx) is attached. The hip-bones (haunches) are attached to either side of the sacrum at the rigid *sacroiliac joints*. In front the hip-bones meet at the symphysis pubis, where they are bound together with tough fibrous tissue. In the male, these joints are practically rigid; in the female they allow slight adjustment of the pelvis during childbirth.

Each hip-bone consists of three elements. The largest, the *ilium*, forms a barrier between the abdomen and the muscles of the buttock and thigh, and supports the sides of the abdomen. The *ischium* is the rump, on which one sits. The smallest element, the *pubis*, meets its fellow in the mid-line to complete the ring of bone in front. These three elements all contribute to the *acetabulum*, the socket of the hip-joint at the side of the pelvis. In contrast with the mobile shoulder-girdle, the characteristic of the pelvis is its great stability.

In the middle of the pelvis is a large opening spanned by a flexible diaphragm of muscle, through which the outlets of the reproductive, digestive, and urinary systems pass. The region below this diaphragm is the *perineum*.

1. PELVIC ORGANS

The cavity of the pelvis is merely the lower part of the abdomen, and the attempt to distinguish abdominal from pelvic organs is not very useful. For instance, the urinary bladder is within the pelvis when it is empty but mainly in the abdomen when it is full.

The large intestine enters the pelvis on the left side and crosses to the mid-line where its penultimate segment, the rectum, lies on the front of the sacrum

and passes through the pelvic diaphragm to become the anal canal.

The urinary bladder rests on the pubic bones at the front of the pelvic cavity. In the female, the vagina and uterus are between the bladder and the rectum.

The principal nerves and blood vessels of the pelvis lie close to the bone. The femoral nerve and blood vessels pass over the front of the pelvis into the thigh; in the male they are accompanied by the vessels and duct (vas deferens) of the testis. The sciatic nerve enters the back of the thigh through a gap between the sacrum and hip-bone, below the sacroiliac joint.

2. DISORDERS

Deformity of the pelvis, however slight, is important to women because it may cause difficulty with childbirth – even a normal pelvis leaves little room to spare. The so-called *contracted pelvis* is not deformed but simply the relatively small pelvis of a woman with small bones, which may cause trouble if she has a large baby. A more real and serious deformity is caused by rickets in childhood, or any other illness that interferes with the growth of bones. In all these cases, Caesarean section solves the problem.

If the sacrum and hip-bone were completely united like the vertebral elements of the sacrum, the sacroiliac joint would cause no trouble. But since the joint allows some slight movement it is prone to the ailments of joints in general, such as rheumatic diseases. Sacroiliac strain is a difficult diagnosis to prove, but what appears to be a strain of this joint is common, especially in women.

Fractures of the pelvis are a result of considerable violence, usually crushing injuries, associated with serious damage elsewhere. As a rule the fracture itself heals without difficulty, but there is a danger of injury to the underlying organs by fragments of bone. The bladder is especially vulnerable, and needs prompt surgical repair if it is damaged.

pemphigus. A name applied to several skin diseases, none of them common, characterized by blisters.

Acute (contagious) pemphigus is a sort of impetigo, caused by streptococci or staphylococci and treated with penicillin or sulphonamides. *Pemphigus neonatorum* is a similar condition in small babies.

Pemphigus vulgaris is a rare generalized disease in which the blisters are an incidental symptom; it is an autoimmune disorder (>*immunity* (2)) and responds to treatment with corticosteroids.

Types of pemphigus related to many infections (diphtheria, syphilis, leprosy) have been described.

penetrance. The extent to which an inherited character or *gene* manifests itself. This concept is needed because one can inherit, for instance, a tendency to gout without ever having symptoms of the disease. An inherited tendency that only seldom reveals itself is said to be of low penetrance; one that regularly does so is of high penetrance. This is a much more complex affair than the simple binary arithmetic of theoretical genetics. >*genetics*.

penicillin. The first antibiotic to be used (1941), and still one of the most valuable. The discovery and action of penicillin are described under >*antibiotic*.

Since the original discovery of *penicillin G* many closely related antibiotics have been isolated. They are all compounds of 6-aminopenicillanic acid. In addition to natural penicillins several useful derivatives of this acid have been synthesized; the acid itself being first extracted from moulds.

Penicillin G has to be injected, but penicillin V is active when taken by mouth.

Some of the newer penicillins such as ampicillin destroy not only bacteria sensitive to penicillin G but also several other types including intestinal bacteria.

The names of penicillins are distinguished by the suffix *-cillin*.

penis. Male copulatory organ. The penis is constructed of 3 columns of erectile tissue: the two *corpora cavernosa* placed side by side, and the *corpus spongiosum* below them. The end of the corpus spongiosum is enlarged to form the conical tip (glans penis). Erectile tissue consists mainly of a labyrinth of blood vessels. Erection is simply distension of the tissue with blood: the veins are compressed by reflex contraction of muscle fibres around them while the arteries are dilated.

The urethra, a tube for the passage of urine or semen, traverses the corpus spongiosum. The muscles that close the veins during erection also close the outlet from the urinary bladder.

The *prepuce* is a loose fold of skin partly covering the glans (>*circumcision*).

pentamidine. A synthetic drug for treating sleeping sickness and related diseases (>*trypanosomiasis*).

pentose. A sugar with 5 carbon atoms in its molecule, e.g. *ribose*, a component of nucleic acids.

pepsin. An enzyme formed in the stomach for the digestion of protein.

peptic ulcer. Erosion of a small patch in the lining of the stomach (gastric ulcer) or duodenum (duodenal ulcer), or occasionally of other parts of the digestive tract. It is easy enough to see that this might happen, and rather surprising that it does not happen all the time. People manage to digest tripe, and tripe is very like their own stomachs.

Several factors normally prevent the stomach from digesting its own lining.

The enzyme pepsin is secreted as *pepsinogen*, which is inactive until mixed with acid. The acid is formed in different cells from pepsinogen. The active mixture of the two is not formed until they are free in the cavity of the stomach.

The mucous membrane is protected from this destructive mixture by a layer of mucus.

Acid is not normally formed unless there is food in the stomach to absorb it.

As soon as the acid contents of the stomach flow into the duodenum the acid is neutralized by the alkaline secretion of the duodenum.

Even with these safeguards the mucous membrane suffers considerable injury, but damaged cells are very quickly replaced, probably within 24 hours. Small breaches are very common, but they seldom lead to ulcers.

If the regulation of movement and secretion of the stomach (►*stomach* (1)) is disturbed, a small breach of the surface may erode the deeper layers and form a definite ulcer. Excess of acid, and especially the secretion of acid when the stomach is empty, is an important factor in duodenal ulceration. Gastric ulceration may be related to delayed emptying and stagnation of digestive secretions in the stomach. Emotional stress can promote secretion of acid and is almost certainly a cause of peptic ulcers, and certain types of physical stress, e.g. extensive burns, can have the same effect. But for the most part the causes of this disease are unknown. Faulty diet is easy to accuse and hard to convict.

Pain is usually the first symptom and may be anywhere in the upper part of the abdomen, but is usually in the midline. If the patient happens to vomit the pain generally goes, and it is nearly always relieved by food or antacid drugs such as magnesium trisilicate; these are all ways of dealing with excess acid, the immediate cause of the pain. Heartburn and nausea are other common symptoms. Most if not all peptic ulcers bleed from time to time and can cause anaemia.

Duodenal ulcers are commonly accompanied by infection of the stomach with ►*Helicobacter pylori*.

Serious complications include sudden and severe bleeding, perforation of the stomach or duodenum with leakage into the abdominal cavity and peritonitis, and narrowing of the outlet of the stomach. These complications are, as a rule, treated surgically.

Nearly all peptic ulcers can be persuaded to heal by medical (i.e. non-surgical) treatment. The first objective of most treatment is to reduce the amount of acid and of digestive enzymes in the stomach; hence the success of antacids such as magnesium trisilicate. Drugs opposing the stimulation of the stomach by its vagus nerves in order to reduce its secretion of acid (of which the prototype is atropine) used to be the only other form of medication; more recently *poldine* represented this class of drug. *Carbenoxolone*, a derivative of liquorice, enhances the resistance of the mucous membranes to attack by gastric secretions. It effectively promotes the healing of ulcers, but sometimes causes fluid retention, and, in a few cases, cirrhosis of the liver;

therefore, it must be administered with caution.

All other treatment is now overshadowed by two drugs, *cimetidine* and *ranitidine*, that prevent ►*histamine* from stimulating gastric secretion, a method closer to tackling the cause of these ulcers than any previous therapy. These drugs may be supplemented with *pirenezapine*, which acts like poldine, or sucralfate, which has similar effects to carbenoxolone.

Newer introductions include *omeprazole*, which inhibits the actual formation of acid, and there are promising results from the use of *prostaglandins*.

Surgery is much less often needed than formerly, and the operations are much less drastic.

There is no sound evidence that peptic ulcers turn to cancer. Duodenal ulcers certainly do not do so: cancer of the duodenum is practically unknown. Cancer of the stomach is so common that mere coincidence might account for an apparent association with gastric ulcer, but a likelier explanation is that some gastric cancer begins with the symptoms of an ulcer. This may be playing with words, and the practical conclusion is that anything that looks like a gastric ulcer needs investigation and treatment.

Some methods of investigation are discussed under ►*stomach* (2).

peptone. Partly digested protein.

percussion. A method of examining the chest and other parts of the body by tapping them and listening to the quality of sound, as an inn-keeper judges the amount of beer in a cask from its resonance; described by Auenbrugger in 1761.

Healthy lung tissue emits a clear, resonant sound; a pocket of air, as in the stomach, sounds like a drum: solid tissue such as the heart or other muscle sounds dull. Thus the outlines of various organs can be roughly plotted by percussion. If part of a lung is not properly ventilated, or there is fluid between the lung and the chest wall, resonance is lost.

Tapping the skin with a bare finger does not give a very distinctive sound. Auenbrugger overcame this difficulty either by percussing through the patient's shirt or by wearing a glove. A better method is to lay a finger of the other hand on the chest and lightly tap that.

perforation. Piercing of an organ by disease, e.g. of the ear-drum by an abscess (otitis media) or the wall of the stomach by a peptic ulcer.

pericarditis. Inflammation of the pericardium, sometimes a complication of infectious diseases, rheumatic fever and other conditions; sometimes the cause is unknown. Many cases need no special attention beyond the treatment of the primary disease. If fluid collects (pericardial effusion) the heart may be embarrassed and the fluid has to be removed with a hollow needle. But the commonest cause is virus infection. Pericarditis may also follow myocardial infarction (coronary thrombosis), kidney disease, and invasion by cancer.

Pericardial effusion can be diagnosed by ultrasound (►*echography*). Large effusions can be drawn off, although constrictive pericarditis, a complication of tuberculosis now seldom seen in developed countries, requires surgery to relieve pressure on the heart.

pericardium. Fibrous sheath of the heart, enclosing a lubricated membrane like the lining of a joint and allowing the heart to beat almost without friction.

perilymph. Fluid surrounding the organs of hearing and balance in the inner ear.

perinatal. Of the period shortly before, during and shortly after birth. An international standard has not yet been laid down, but the period is roughly from the 28th week of pregnancy until the infant is a month old.

The perinatal mortality rate is the sum of stillbirths and neonatal deaths.

perineal. Of the perineum.

perineum. The external aspect of the outlet of the pelvis, i.e. the region enclosed by the thighs and the lower part of the buttocks, including the external genital organs and the anal canal (►*pelvis* (1)). The term is often – especially in midwifery – limited to the bridge of muscle and fibrous tissue between the genital organs and the anus, which is very liable to be injured during childbirth.

periosteum. Fibrous coating of a bone; it carries a network of nerves and blood vessels and is essential to the nutrition of the bone, and is also the sensitive part of the bone. When growth is complete, the periosteum is the one place where new bone can be formed. Fractures do not heal if the periosteum is destroyed. When this happens (it is fortunately a rare occurrence) a graft has to be taken from another bone.

peripheral nerves. Cords of nerve fibres, radiating from the central nervous system (brain and spinal cord) and conducting impulses to and from all parts of the body – usually called simply *nerves*.

peristalsis. Rhythmic squeezing movements, flowing along tubular organs such as the intestine and propelling the contents. The rate and force of the contractions is regulated by autonomic (sympathetic and parasympathetic) nerves, but peristalsis itself is an intrinsic property of the muscles in the walls of these organs.

peritoneum. The lining membrane of the abdominal cavity; it forms a thin, transparent layer over the walls of the cavity and the abdominal organs. In effect it is a single closed bag, completely empty. The organs said to be within the cavity – stomach, intestine, liver, spleen etc. – are in fact *behind* it, but they grow forwards, pushing the peritoneum ahead of them. The intestine wanders so far forwards that the two layers of peritoneum join behind it to form the *mesentery*, in which the intestine hangs as if in a fold of a curtain.

The peritoneum is provided with blood vessels, which enable it to exude a thin film of fluid, so that the abdominal organs are lubricated in the same way as the moving parts of a joint. Its nerves convey a sensation of pain if it is stretched or inflamed. Sensation from the peritoneum over the organs is ►*referred* to various places, e.g. from any part of the stomach or intestine to the mid-line of the abdomen; but sensation from the peritoneal lining of the belly-wall is correctly localized. Hence with appendicitis the pain from the appendix itself is felt at the navel, but as the inflammation spreads to the abdominal wall the pain seems to move to the actual site of the appendix, below and well to the right of the navel.

With failure of the heart or kidneys, when fluid tends to leak away from the blood, large quantities may collect in the peritoneal cavity. This type of dropsy is known as *ascites*. Similarly, fluid collects if the peritoneum itself is inflamed.

The peritoneum has remarkable

powers of healing. When a section of the intestine is surgically removed and the cut ends have been stitched together, the peritoneal coating forms a watertight seal within a few minutes. When the peritoneum is inflamed (*peritonitis*), for instance after perforation of a diseased appendix, the great danger is that the whole peritoneum will be involved – a most lethal condition. This danger is greatly lessened by the tendency of the inflamed surfaces to stick together – in other words to heal – and so wall off the trouble. This readiness to heal may be a nuisance. Any disturbance such as injury, operation, or infection, may cause two surfaces which should be separate to stick together. Adhesions formed in this way interfere with the normal movements of the intestine or even cause obstruction.

peritonitis. Inflammation of the peritoneum, the result of irritation within the abdominal cavity. The intestines and other organs are regarded as lying outside the true cavity, separated from it by their coating of peritoneum. As long as this coating remains intact it is almost impossible for peritonitis to develop. But if the peritoneum is punctured in any way it is extremely vulnerable. The cavity is a perfect incubator for bacteria, and infection spreads very rapidly from an abdominal wound or from the intestine if, for instance, the appendix is inflamed and bursts. Until the discovery of antiseptics abdominal surgery was so dangerous as to be virtually impossible, because every attempt was bound to cause peritonitis, which at that time few survived.

Peritonitis can be severe even without bacteria. Acid leaking from a perforated gastric ulcer or bile from a duodenal ulcer irritate and inflame the peritoneum.

Chemical inflammation of this kind is soon followed by bacterial infection.

The surface area of the peritoneum is very large. If much of it is inflamed the effect is similar to that of a very extensive burn with profound ►*shock*. The abdominal muscles tighten, as muscles over an inflamed area always do, but the intestine is paralysed while the inflammation lasts. The whole abdomen is painful. Fortunately, inflamed surfaces of peritoneum tend to adhere and so to restrict the spread of peritonitis. If this were not so, untreated peritonitis would almost always be fatal within a day or two. As it is, the condition is serious enough, but with the help of antibiotics and surgical operations to deal with the source of the trouble (e.g. repair of perforated intestine, removal of appendix) most cases can now be controlled.

The formation of an abscess – a localized collection of pus – is usually described as a complication of peritonitis. It is certainly a common sequel, but on the whole a desirable one because it is much less dangerous than diffuse inflammation throughout the peritoneum. The usual site is the pelvis, whence the pus can be released into the rectum. The patient with peritonitis is often nursed sitting rather than lying so that if pus should be formed it will gravitate to the pelvis. If infection is allowed to spread upwards a less accessible abscess may be formed between the liver and the diaphragm.

Women are more exposed to peritonitis than men because their Fallopian tubes open directly into the cavity, and infection in the female reproductive organs can spread by the tubes to the peritoneum. This type of peritonitis nearly always results in a pelvic abscess.

Occasionally tuberculosis causes

chronic peritonitis. This is not a violent illness like the acute condition described above; it causes ill-defined abdominal symptoms of which the nature is often discovered only at operation. Tuberculous peritonitis is now much less common than it used to be.

pentonsillar abscess. Abscess around a tonsil; quinsy. ➤*pharynx* (1).

pernicious anaemia (Addisonian anaemia). Defective formation of red blood cells through lack of vitamin B_{12}. ➤*anaemia* (B.2).

pernio = ➤*chilblain.*

peroneal. Of the ➤*fibula*; of the outer side of the lower leg. The peroneal muscles, attached to the fibula, run to the outer side of the foot and are concerned with tilting the foot outwards, an important movement when walking on rough or sloping ground and also in adjusting the balance.

perspiration. Since the two words are available, it seems worth while to keep a distinction between perspiration and sweating. Perspiration (insensible perspiration) is passive transudation of almost pure water from the surface of the body at a constant rate of 500–700 ml daily – a considerable loss to anyone deprived of water. Perspiration is 'insensible' because the water immediately evaporates.

(Cf. ➤*sweat* – an active secretion of salt water for the regulation of body temperature.)

Perthes' disease. (Georg Perthes, 1869–1927, German surgeon.) Osteochondrosis of the hip; a deformity of the head of the femur (the ball of the ball-and-socket hip-joint) in children, commoner in boys than girls. The cause is unknown, but may be interference with the blood

supply by injury. Movement of the affected joint in certain directions, especially outwards, is limited and uncomfortable. The bone can usually be persuaded to grow normally by splinting.

pertussis = ➤*whooping cough.*

pes cavus. Abnormally high arches of the foot, the opposite condition to flat foot.

pes planus. Flat foot. ➤*foot.*

pessary. 1. Soluble gelatinous preparation for introducing antiseptic or other drugs into the vagina; vaginal suppository.
2. Appliance inserted into the vagina to support weak ligaments or as a contraceptive.

petechia. Minute fleck of blood in the skin from a bleeding capillary vessel, e.g. with the rashes of some fevers.

pethidine. A synthetic drug related to morphine, with similar pain-relieving properties but less tendency to depress respiration.

petit mal. A minor form of ➤*epilepsy.*

petrous. Rock-like: the petrous temporal bone houses the inner ear.

pH. A measure of acidity or alkalinity. It is derived from the concentration of hydrogen ions in solution (cH), which itself gives unwieldy figures, e.g. the cH of a standard solution of caustic soda is 1/10,000,000,000,000 or 10^{-13} – which is much more conveniently expressed as pH 13; or a similar solution of hydrochloric acid as pH 1. Distilled water, pH 7, is neutral. Human blood is normally slightly on the alkaline side, pH 7.4.

phaeochromocytoma. A rare tumour of the medulla of the ➤*adrenal* gland.

phagocyte. Cell able to engulf and digest bacteria, dead cells etc. The white cells of the blood and certain mobile cells at large in the tissues are phagocytes.

phalanx. A segment of a digit, or the bone of the segment. The thumbs and big toes have each 2 phalanges; the other fingers and toes have each 3. ➤*hand; foot.*

phantom limb. The illusion that a limb is still present, and sometimes even painful, after it has been amputated. Nerves in the remaining part of the limb contain fibres that used to serve the amputated part, and if these fibres are stimulated the sensation is still ➤*referred* there.

pharmaceutical. Concerning pharmacy.

pharmacology. Scientific study of drugs – their chemistry, effects on the body, useful and dangerous actions, dosage – including research into new drugs. It is distinct from pharmacy, though the two overlap. Pharmacology is a fairly young science. Until the 19th century it was generally enough to know that a drug was good for this or that disease. Critical studies were rare, and most drugs were given for no better reason than that they were traditional. Withering's study of digitalis (1785) and Jenner's of vaccination were among the very few scientific assessments of methods of treatment before experimental chemistry and biology had advanced far enough for pioneers like Magendie (1783–1855) in France and Buchheim (1820–79) in Germany to make a systematic study of drugs.

pharmacopoeia. List of approved drugs, with notes on their preparation, standards of purity, doses etc.

Between the beginning of the 16th century and the middle of the 19th many academic centres had their own pharmacopoeias for the guidance of local physicians and apothecaries. One of the most useful functions of these books was to ensure that a prescription meant the same thing to the man who wrote it and the man who dispensed it.

From the middle of the 19th century, official national publications began to replace local pharmacopoeias. The London Pharmacopoeia, first published in 1618, gave way in 1864 to the first British Pharmacopoeia, published under government authority by the new General Medical Council. The United States Pharmacopeia, first published in 1820, became official in 1907. The World Health Organization publishes an International Pharmacopoeia, which has no statutory authority but is a valuable guide to national compilers.

pharmacy. Preparation and care of drugs; it is an applied science, related to pharmacology in much the same way as building to architecture. ➤*apothecary.*

pharynx. Muscular back-wall of the nose, mouth, and throat, extending from the base of the skull to the entrance of the oesophagus (gullet) half-way down the neck. Its muscle fibres are attached to the under-side of the skull, to the ➤*hyoid* bone, and to the sides of the *thyroid* and *cricoid* cartilages (➤*larynx*). The fibres curve back to meet in the mid-line in front of the backbone.

As regards function the pharynx is in three parts. Above the level of the palate it is the back of the nose, the *nasopharynx,* and concerned only with breathing. During swallowing this part is closed off by raising the soft palate. The lowest part, the *laryngeal pharynx,* behind the larynx, is only for swallowing. Between the two, from the palate to the opening of the larynx, the *oropharynx* is a passage for both air and food.

Swallowing begins as a voluntary action of the tongue and cheek muscles. When they have pushed food to the back of the tongue the action becomes reflex, though all the muscles involved are structurally voluntary muscles (*>muscle*). The palate is raised to close the back of the nose, the epiglottis covers the entrance to the larynx, and the vocal cords close (*>larynx*). Waves of contraction then push the food down to the oesophagus. Gravity plays little part.

The nasopharynx opens into the cavity of the middle *>ear* by the *Eustachian tube*. This is a narrow channel about 4 cm long. From the side of the nasopharynx above the soft palate it runs between walls of cartilage to enter the temporal bone of the skull. It serves to balance the air pressure at the two sides of the eardrum. A slip of muscle joining the tube to the larynx contracts during swallowing; this pulls the entrance to the tube and allows air to pass if the pressure inside the ear-drum differs from that of the outside ear.

The pharynx is encircled with lymphoid tissue (*>lymph*) of which two collections are large enough to deserve names. These are the *adenoids* at the back of the nasopharynx, and the *tonsils* between the pillars of the arch of the *>palate*. Similar clumps of lymphoid tissue are scattered through the length of the digestive tract. Like the spleen and lymph glands they set up resistance to infecting microbes (*>immunity*). It has been said that the tonsils and adenoids sample the microbes in the inhaled air and form suitable antibodies. This they may well do, but there is little evidence that it is a very useful occupation. In fact, no special function can be ascribed to them.

1. Disorders

Pharyngitis or sore throat is among the commonest of all infections, and fortunately one which usually resolves itself. Bacteria, notably streptococci, tend to be more harmful than viruses in this area. *Scarlet fever* is infection of the pharynx with streptococci which happen also to cause a rash. In children, *>rheumatic fever* is preceded by a streptococcal infection, usually of the pharynx. This type of pharyngitis responds quickly to penicillin and other antibiotics.

Tonsillitis, inflammation of the tonsils, is common in children but not in adults, because the tonsils usually shrivel and virtually disappear in late childhood. So far from combating streptococcal infection some tonsils seem to nurture it, perhaps because their defensive function has been destroyed by previous infection. Surgical removal of the tonsils and adenoids is done much less than it used to be, but it still has a place in the treatment of recurrent sore throat in childhood when the tonsils are obviously unhealthy. Between the two World Wars tonsils were removed wholesale. That the operation has since fallen from favour is partly due to penicillin, but also to the length of hospital waiting-lists. After several months' delay many children have been found not to need the operation after all, and the tendency now is to reserve it for selected cases.

Spread of infection from the pharynx to the surrounding tissues causes unpleasant and possibly dangerous abscesses. The usual site is around the tonsil: this is a *quinsy*. In addition to antibiotics to control the infection a minor operation is often needed to release the pus and prevent it from spreading.

Oedema of the glottis is distension by

tissue fluid of the mucous membrane around the entrance to the larynx. It may follow infection but typically it is an allergic reaction like nettle-rash. Anywhere else it would be a minor nuisance, but here it is dangerous because the swelling may be enough to obstruct the airway. Prompt injection of adrenaline or of corticosteroids may reduce the swelling, but an artificial airway may be needed for a time.

phenacetin; phenazone. Two of the earliest synthetic drugs. ➤*analgesic.*

phenobarbitone. A hypnotic and sedative drug, with a more sustained action than other barbiturates. To a great extent it superseded the bromides, and in the first half of the 20th century was the most popular drug for relieving anxiety. It is still used in the treatment of epilepsy.

phenol (carbolic acid). The prototype of antiseptics and disinfectants: with it, Lister revolutionized surgery. ➤*infection; antiseptic.*

phenolphthalein. An irritant purgative.

phenothiazine. Originally intended as an insecticide, this compound was found almost accidentally to have exceptional pharmacological properties when routine tests showed an ability to counteract histamine, as well as a remarkable calming effect on emotional activity. Derivatives of the original insecticide form two chemically similar but biologically very different types of drug, both of the highest importance. The ➤*antihistamine* drugs are used to treat various allergic disorders, as well as to inhibit vomiting and to prevent sea-sickness. A drawback is that they sometimes cause drowsiness, but this property has been put to good use in a completely different field. Phenothiazine

is also used in the major ➤*tranquillizers* which are used for the relief of grave mental disorders including schizophrenia, for which there was little, if any, effective treatment before the introduction of one of these drugs, chlorpromazine.

phenylalanine ➤*phenylketonuria.*

phenylketonuria. A rare cause of mental deficiency. It is an inherited recessive character – i.e. both parents must carry the abnormal gene, with a 1:4 chance that a child of theirs will develop the disorder. The actual defect is absence of an enzyme for dealing with the amino-acid *phenylalanine,* which is a component of proteins. An excess of phenylalanine accumulates, and in some unknown way this affects the nervous system.

The condition can be detected soon after birth by chemical analysis of the urine. If the affected child is fed on protein foods from which phenylalanine has been removed, his brain develops normally.

phenytoin. A drug used to control epilepsy.

phimosis. Abnormally tight foreskin, sometimes requiring circumcision.

phlebitis. Inflammation of a vein, generally associated with blockage of the vein by a blood-clot (*thrombosis*). A healthy vein has a smooth, unwettable lining on which blood cannot clot. If the lining is damaged or irritated the surface is roughened and clots can form on it. In fact, one way of treating varicose veins is to inject an irritant, which sets up a mild phlebitis and closes the vein. But with spontaneous phlebitis, such as may occur in the legs after childbirth or surgical operations, the sequence is probably reversed: the first event is thrombosis, and phlebitis follows as an effect and not a cause. The term *thrombophlebitis* describes the condition and leaves open the question of which comes first.

After an injury such as an operation blood clots more readily than usual – a protective mechanism – but the main reason for thrombophlebitis as a complication of childbirth and operations is immobility, which allows blood to stagnate. The risk has been much less since surgeons gave up insisting on prolonged and complete rest in bed.

The readjustment of a woman's sex hormones in pregnancy causes blood to clot more readily. Oral contraceptives cause a similar readjustment, which may account for the slightly increased tendency to thrombophlebitis among women who take these drugs.

Circulation of blood is impaired only if a very large vein is involved. The part beyond the obstruction (nearly always a leg) then swells, and may remain swollen for weeks or months while new channels are established. A more serious risk is that a piece of clot may be dislodged and travel to the lungs and obstruct a branch of the pulmonary artery. This condition, *pulmonary embolism*, is a danger to life if the piece of clot is large enough to block a major branch of the pulmonary artery. Smaller clots cause a kind of pneumonia; very small ones probably pass unnoticed.

The use of anticoagulant drugs to discourage clotting has lessened the dangers of thrombophlebitis. Occasionally an affected vein has to be sealed with a ligature to prevent the clot from moving. The affected part may need complete rest during the attack, but on the other hand the most effective treatment has been prevention of the attack by precisely the opposite means – avoiding complete immobility – for the flow of blood in veins depends largely on the squeezing action of the neighbouring muscles.

Phlebotomus fever ►*sandfly* fever.

phlebotomy. Venesection; withdrawal of blood from a vein. ►*blood-letting.*

phlegm ►*mucus*; one of the four humours of classical medical theory.

phobia. A kind of neurosis, in which symptoms of ►*anxiety* are aroused by a particular object or situation.

phocomelia. A grave congenital defect of the limbs: the hands and feet are fairly normal, but the arms and legs fail to grow. The hands and feet spring from the shoulders and hips like the flippers of a seal. This rare deformity suddenly became much commoner when the drug ►*thalidomide* was on the market.

phonocardiogram. Recording of heart sounds.

phosphorus. A non-metallic element, one of the components of living matter. Most of the phosphorus in the body is combined with calcium in bone, and the balance of assimilation and excretion of phosphorus is closely linked to that of calcium.

Certain phosphates, e.g. those of adenosine and creatine, are readily broken down, with release of energy, or reformed with storage of energy. These reactions play an important part in body chemistry (►*energy*).

Most tissues incorporate small amounts of phosphorus. The presence of phosphorus compounds in the insulating sheaths of nerves led to the absurd belief that phosphates must be good for nerves, and to the prescription of 'tonics' containing wholly useless doses of phosphorus compounds.

The pure element is a most dangerous poison. There are several forms or allotropes (as pure carbon can be charcoal or diamond), of which the white and yellow are dangerous and the red fairly safe. Phosphorus poisoning has been rare since the prohibition of yellow phosphorus in matchheads.

photophobia. Intolerance of bright light, a common symptom of inflammation of the eyes, of dilatation of the pupils (e.g. by drugs), of migraine, and of meningitis.

photosensitivity. Increased sensitivity of the skin to light, usually of a particular wavelength; exposed areas become inflamed after a very brief spell of direct sunlight. This is an exaggeration of a reaction that anyone suffers with sufficient exposure. ►*sunburn*. Numerous drugs, including barbiturates and sulphonamides, can cause photosensitivity to develop.

phrenic. Of the diaphragm. The *phrenic nerve*, the nerve of the diaphragm on which breathing largely depends, has to traverse the length of the neck and chest before reaching its destination (►*diaphragm*). Before the introduction of effective drugs for tuberculosis around 1950, surgical interference with this nerve was often used to paralyse one side of the diaphragm in order to prevent the affected lung from moving while it healed.

Many ancient Greek philosophers regarded the diaphragm as the seat of the mind, and *phren* meant either diaphragm or mind. The second meaning still appears in *schizophrenia*.

phrenitis (archaic). Delirium, frenzy (if the word were used now it would mean inflammation of the diaphragm as such

and not of the supposed seat of the disordered mind).

phrenology. An attempt to study the brain from the outward shape of the skull. It was introduced by an able Viennese physician and anatomist, Franz Josef Gall (1758–1828). Phrenology has no basis in fact, but besides this lapse Gall made several valid observations on the anatomy of the brain.

phthisis. Consumption; pulmonary ►*tuberculosis*.

physic. The practice of medicine (in the limited sense, excluding surgery and obstetrics); also medicine in the sense of a remedy to be taken.

physician. Medical doctor; specialist in internal diseases. ►*doctor*.

physiology. Study of function of living organisms and their different parts. It is the companion of anatomy, which deals with structure. 'Function' is meant in the widest sense, including everything that happens in a living body and how it happens. Physiology is concerned with normal, healthy function, but the boundary between normality and abnormality – the concern of pathology – is not always clear. Similarly, function is so closely related to structure that physiology and anatomy are not as distinct from each other as one might suppose.

Ancient physiology was based largely on speculation, and while serious errors about anatomy persisted, speculation was almost bound to go astray. The early Greek philosophers evolved variations on the theory of ►*humours* as the basis of life and matter. None of these was related to fact.

Erasistratus (*c.* 300 BC) is generally regarded as the first man to have studied physiology as opposed to thinking about it. He was a junior colleague of Herophilus (>*anatomy*) in Alexandria. Erasistratus recognized the main functions of the nervous system and muscles, and came closer than anyone in the next 2000 years to understanding the action of the heart.

After Erasistratus, the next man who might have extended physiology was Galen (2nd century AD); but Galen was so wedded to his own mistakes that he made little progress. After Galen, all science came to a halt until the Renaissance.

Of necessity, all other medical sciences had to wait for anatomy to be revived. As the anatomists of Padua revealed structure, so their successors were enabled to make the first proper studies of function.

The earliest of the Paduan physiologists was Sanctorius (1561–1636), who introduced measurement to medical science. (It has been argued that science *is* measurement. By this definition, Sanctorius's studies of pulse rate, body temperature, and diurnal variation of body weight would make him the originator of modern scientific medicine.) But the turning-point was the discovery by another graduate of Padua – Harvey – of the circulation of the blood, published in 1628. Without this knowledge one can make little sense of the human body: it is like trying to account for the electrical fittings in a modern home without having heard of electricity.

After a considerable pause for Harvey's discovery to sink in, physiology took shape in the hands of scientists such as Hales and Haller in the 18th century, Magendie and Müller in the early 19th century, and Magendie's illustrious pupil Bernard.

The subject is discussed further under the names mentioned in this article, and under such headings as >*circulation*; *endocrine*; *nervous system*; *stomach*; *vitamins*.

physiotherapy. Treatment of illness by physical means such as massage, exercise, heat and electricity. Massage is a very ancient craft, but it has only recently had much recognition in orthodox medical practice. In Britain, it was not an officially recognized and chartered profession until 1920, and the Chartered Society of Physiotherapy replaced the Chartered Society of Massage and Medical Gymnastics in 1943.

The scope of physiotherapy is now very wide. Its traditional role – the palliative treatment of rheumatic aches and stiff joints – is only one of many, including maintenance or restoration of function after injury (there is not much point in setting a broken bone if the limb is allowed to become stiff and useless), attention to breathing with bed-ridden patients who would otherwise be liable to pneumonia, and training of joints and muscles to be of at least some use after nerve injuries, strokes etc. This last is perhaps the most rewarding part of physiotherapy. Even people with very severe physical disability can be educated to independence, including many with complete paralysis below the level of a spinal injury.

Massage is a feature of numerous varieties of >*alternative medicine*: shiatsu, aromatherapy, etc.

pia mater. Gossamer membrane over the brain and spinal cord, the innermost of the 3 *meninges*.

pica (>*magpie*). Eating earth or other unsuitable material; a habit of early childhood with obvious dangers. It is generally regarded as a sort of neurosis aroused by insecurity, but some cases have been attributed to iron deficiency.

piles. An *external pile* is a blood-blister at the margin of the anus, which arises from bursting a small vessel while straining. It is harmless but very painful. The pain is promptly relieved by opening the blister, and releasing the clot of blood.
Internal piles: ➤*haemorrhoids.*

(Other conditions such as *fistula* and *fissure* of the anus are sometimes misnamed piles.)

pilocarpine. Alkaloid extracted from a Central American shrub, with similar actions to *acetyl choline*, occasionally used to constrict the pupil of the eye in treating ➤*glaucoma.*

pilonidal sinus. A trivial malformation, representing a minor degree of ➤*spina bifida.* The sinus is a pit in the skin at the base of the spine containing a tuft of hair. As a rule it is harmless. If it becomes a nuisance by getting infected it is easily removed.

pineal body. A small protrusion from the centre of the brain. Its function in man is not known. The pineal body has evolved from a primitive central eye. In a few reptiles it still responds to light and may control the darkening of the skin when the animal is in a bright light. It may also be associated with sexual development. There is some evidence in mammals that chemicals concerned with transmitting impulses in the brain are formed in the pineal body.

Descartes insisted that the soul resided in the pineal body.

pink disease. A rare disease of infants, with redness of hands and feet, neuritis and other symptoms, probably due to

mercury poisoning (e.g. from teething powders).

pink-eye ➤*conjunctivitis.*

pinna. The visible part of the ear; the auricle.

pinta. A skin disease of tropical America, due to infection with a spirochaete similar to those that cause syphilis and yaws.

piperazine. Synthetic drug for treating intestinal worm infestation.

pituitary body (pituitary gland; hypophysis). The most complex of the ➤*endocrine* glands; consisting of two distinct organs, the anterior and posterior lobes.

The *anterior lobe* (adrenohypophysis) develops in the embryo from the roof of the mouth. It is a typical endocrine gland, composed of hormone-secreting cells of several kinds. The *posterior lobe* is a downgrowth from the floor of the brain, and is a modified part of the nervous system, in effect, a protrusion of the *hypothalamus.* The two lobes grow together and hang like a berry from the underside of the brain, occupying a small hollow in the floor of the skull.

The hormones of the anterior lobe regulate growth and the activity of several other endocrine glands. The following hormones have been identified:

1. ACTH (*adrenocorticotrophic* hormone; corticotrophin) stimulates the adrenal cortex to secrete cortisol (➤*adrenal*; *corticosteroid*).

2. *Thyrotrophic* hormone stimulates the ➤*thyroid gland.*

3. Two *gonadotrophic* hormones stimulate the gonads (ovaries or testes). One, the follicle-stimulating hormone, controls the formation of ova by the ovary or sperms by the testis. The other, the

luteinizing hormone, controls the secretion of sex hormones by the gonads. The gonadotrophic hormones are the same for either sex.

4. *Growth hormone* is the principal factor for maintaining growth in childhood and adolescence. It promotes the synthesis of protein and other components of tissues. In adult life the pituitary still secretes small amounts of growth hormone, which influence the control of sugar in the body by the pancreas.

5. *Lactogenic hormone* (prolactin) regulates the secretion of milk.

6. *Melanophore-stimulating hormone* acts on melanophores (pigment cells) in the skin. It forms part of the *endorphin* system.

The hormones of the anterior pituitary are themselves regulated by the *hypothalamus*, a part of the brain immediately above the pituitary. The hypothalamus thus provides a link between the nervous system and the endocrine glands.

Growth hormone and lactogenic hormone act, probably through intermediaries, on the tissues. The 'trophic' hormones act through other glands, and are regulated by feed-back mechanisms. For instance, ACTH stimulates the adrenals to secrete cortisol. But as soon as there is enough cortisol in the blood, this suppresses the formation of ACTH, by its effect on the hypothalamus, and the stimulus to the adrenals is removed until the concentration of cortisol in the blood falls again. The amount of cortisol needed varies according to factors such as stress, and the circuit pituitary/adrenal/hypothalamus/pituitary is adjusted in the hypothalamus, which in turn responds to other parts of the brain.

Glands that are regulated by trophic hormones cease to work if the pituitary fails. Conversely, if these glands fail, the pituitary pours out more and more trophic hormones to no purpose.

Complete failure of the anterior pituitary causes *Simmonds' disease*. The symptoms are those of simultaneous failure of thyroid, adrenal, and sex glands, which are very like those of extreme senility. This disease – fortunately rare – is fatal unless regular doses of the missing hormones are provided. Sometimes only one pituitary hormone is lacking, and the symptoms are those of deficiency of the associated gland. Lack of growth hormone in childhood causes *pituitary dwarfism*; these people generally develop normal intelligence but their bodily growth is arrested in childhood unless hormone supplements are given early. Growth hormone has no effect unless it is given early in life.

An excess of growth hormone from a pituitary tumour in childhood causes *gigantism*: the bodily proportions are normal but the dimensions are too big. A similar excess in adult life causes ►*acromegaly*.

Prolactinoma is a pituitary tumour secreting prolactin, causing inappropriate lactation and stopping menstruation. *Bromcriptine* is used effectively for treating this condition in selected hospital units.

Cushing's syndrome, an excess of adrenal hormones, can arise from overactivity of the pituitary, with too much stimulation of the adrenals by ACTH.

The *posterior lobe* secretes two hormones:

1. Oxytocin stimulates contraction of the uterus at the end of pregnancy and initiates labour. It also promotes the secretion of milk. This seems to be partly a direct action on the breast and partly an

indirect action by stimulating the anterior lobe to secrete lactogenic hormone.

2. Antidiuretic hormone (ADH) causes water to be retained by the kidneys and restored to the blood, preventing excessive loss of water in the urine. When the blood is slightly diluted after drinking water this hormone is suppressed and the control over the kidneys is relaxed until the surplus of water has been eliminated. A larger amount of ADH than the pituitary normally forms increases the blood pressure, and for this reason the hormone is also called *vasopressin*. Preparations of ADH or a synthetic substitute can be used to sustain the blood pressure in states of collapse.

A deficiency of ADH causes excessive flow of urine with constant thirst, i.e. ➤*diabetes insipidus.*

pityriasis. Any skin disease with which dandruff-like scales are shed. *Pityriasis rosea* is a common and harmless rash which clears up in a few weeks, possibly due to a mild infection of the skin surface. Generally a single oval spot, the 'herald patch', appears a week before the main crop of smaller spots.

placebo. A remedy without any direct action on a disease, given to keep the patient happy, or to persuade the prescriber that he is doing something positive and useful, or both. Many carefully conducted trials have shown that some three quarters of all patients feel better after taking placebos (provided that they believe the placebos to be active medicines), and objective tests show that many of them are in fact better. This makes the assessment of a new drug difficult: if the drug is completely inert it will still seem effective. To get a true picture one must compare the new drug either with an old one or with a placebo, given to a similar group of patients. Even toxic effects of new drugs have to be studied with the placebo effect in mind: many of the control subjects given only a placebo (e.g. coloured water) find that the 'medicine' causes drowsiness, insomnia, nausea etc.

placenta. Organ by which an unborn infant gets nourishment from its mother. The placenta develops from the layer of cells surrounding those destined to form the body itself (➤*embryo*). It is a part of the growing infant's tissues, not the mother's, and its dense network of blood vessels communicates by way of the umbilical vein and arteries with the circulation of the infant. The placenta is firmly attached to the lining of the mother's uterus, but no blood passes between the two. Dissolved oxygen and nutrients diffuse from the mother's blood to the placenta, and carbon dioxide and other waste products diffuse in the opposite direction.

The placenta is released shortly after the birth of the infant, to whom it is still joined by the umbilical cord. At this stage it forms a thick disc, some 15 cm across, weighing about a pound.

In addition to its main functions as an organ of respiration, nutrition, and excretion for the infant, the placenta acts as an endocrine gland for the mother, secreting hormones that diffuse into her circulation and maintain pregnancy.

placenta praevia. An unusual situation of the placenta, which lies across the opening of the uterus instead of high up and out of the way during birth. It is a cause of bleeding before or during labour, and may necessitate Caesarean section.

plague. A severe infectious fever, due to a

bacterium *Yersinia* (formerly *Pasteurella*) *pestis* transmitted by rat-fleas. The disease is primarily one of rats and other rodents, but spreads to man in times and places where rats and men are in close contact. As rats die of the disease, so their parasites the fleas seek other hosts. The pneumonic form of plague can be transmitted from man to man by coughing.

Bubonic plague is the common form. In addition to the symptoms of any severe infection (fever etc.), buboes appear after a few days. A bubo is a swollen, acutely inflamed lymph node. These painful swellings occur in the armpits and groin and at the sides of the neck. Dark blotches from bleeding into the skin are one reason for the name *black death*.

Pneumonic plague is a fulminating pneumonia due to infection of the lungs with these bacteria. The slate-blue complexion of sufferers from this form of plague was a second reason for calling it the black death.

Without treatment, bubonic plague is fatal in well over 50 per cent of cases, and pneumonic plague in 100 per cent. But streptomycin and other antibiotics control the infection, and if they are given without delay the outlook is good.

At present plague is a rare disease, but it still smoulders in some hot countries, and rats and their fleas are ubiquitous. When sanitary services are disrupted, e.g. by warfare or natural disasters, major outbreaks are still possible. A specific vaccine, repeated yearly, gives good protection.

Some of the great epidemics of antiquity may have been plague, but they cannot be identified with certainty. About the Black Death of 1346–9, the eye-witness accounts of Guy de Chauliac (a physician who had the disease and recovered), Boccaccio (in the introduction to the *Decameron*) and others leave no reasonable doubt: this was wave upon wave of bubonic and pneumonic plague. It killed perhaps half the population of Europe. For the next 3 centuries, plague swept across Europe at intervals, then mysteriously receded. Since the Great Plague of 1665 there have only been local outbreaks.

plantar. Of the sole of the foot. *Plantar warts* are like any others, probably due to a virus infection, but they are more troublesome because of their position. They may disappear if pads are applied to take the weight off them, but a caustic of some kind is often needed to destroy them. Occasionally they have to be cut away.

plasma. The fluid component of blood. ➤*blood* (1).

Plasmodium. A genus of protozoa, including the parasites of ➤*malaria*.

plastic surgery. Plastic surgery includes the well-known cosmetic operations such as face-lifting and modifying unshapely noses, but it also deals with repair of lost or damaged tissue. Skin-grafting (➤*graft*) after extensive burns or other injuries is not done merely to improve the final appearance. It provides the best possible dressing to protect exposed areas from infection and loss of body fluid; it prevents shrinkage of large scars, with deformity and loss of movement, and greatly hastens recovery. Nor is cosmetic surgery only a means of satisfying a patient's whims. It often relieves very real distress.

platelet (thrombocyte). The smallest of the solid particles suspended in the blood, formed by the fragmentation of large cells in the bone marrow and necessary to the clotting of shed blood and the sealing of injured blood vessels. ➤*blood* (4).

platysma. A thin sheet of muscle fibres under the skin of the neck.

pleura. A double layer of thin membrane surrounding the lungs, analogous with the *pericardium* round the heart and the *peritoneum* in the abdomen, and resembling the *synovial membranes* of the joints. ➤*lung* (3).

pleurisy. Inflammation of the pleura, practically always due to infection by bacteria or viruses. *Dry pleurisy* causes a characteristic pain on coughing or taking a deep breath. *Pleurisy with effusion*, where fluid accumulates in the space between lung and chest wall, is painless because the fluid protects the inflamed membrane from friction. *Empyema* is pleurisy with effusion of heavily infected fluid, i.e. pus; it is a kind of abscess.

Bacterial pleurisy is a common accompaniment of underlying infection in the lung, especially of pneumonia. The lungs themselves are insensitive, and the typical pain of pneumonia is entirely due to pleurisy. Pleurisy without apparent cause, especially where there is a large effusion, needs thorough investigation, because it may be the first indication of serious underlying disease.

Epidemic pleurisy is a virus infection (➤*Bornholm disease*).

Treatment of pleurisy itself is mainly palliative: analgesic drugs, warmth, restricting movement of the affected side to relieve pain; removal of fluid, etc. The bacterial types subside as the underlying infection is treated, and virus pleurisy subsides of its own accord. ➤*empyema*.

pleurodynia. Pain such as that of pleurisy; epidemic pleurisy (➤*Bornholm disease*).

plexus. Network of veins or nerves. Nerve plexuses include the *brachial* plexus, a system of communicating branches between nerves destined for the arm, at the root of the neck; the *lumbo-sacral* plexus, a similar arrangement for the leg; the *coeliac* (*solar*) plexus of sympathetic nerves in the upper part of the abdomen, and the *cardiac* plexus next to the heart.

Pliny the Elder (AD 23–79). Roman civil servant and writer; author of a massive compendium of scientific knowledge and superstition, which included several books on medical matters. Pliny had no personal knowledge of medicine, but because he wrote so much about it he was approved as an authority for many centuries.

plumbism. Chronic poisoning by ➤*lead*.

pneumoconiosis. A group of occupational diseases caused by inhaling noxious dusts at work. The various types are named after the particular dust to which the worker is exposed.

Silicosis afflicts various miners and stone-workers. Silica dust (in effect, very fine sand) provokes small concentrations of inflammation and scarring, which may join to form larger masses of useless fibrous matter in the lungs. In time this leads to shortness of breath, and the patient becomes increasingly vulnerable to infection of the lungs. The only remedy is prevention by adequate ventilation at the place of work, protective masks where needed, and regular checks to ensure that anyone showing early signs can be removed from the risk: this probably means a change of job, which may be very difficult.

Asbestosis is similar, but asbestos fibres are especially noxious. They can cause a kind of fibrosis more like a chronic allergic reaction than a simple response to irritation, and, in some cases, lung cancer. They can also cause a cancer of the pleura that is otherwise a rarity.

Anthracosis, caused by inhaling coal dust, is more liable to certain complications than simple silicosis; in particular, it can lead to the formation of massive lesions resembling a slowly progressive tuberculosis. In the end, the circulation of blood through the lungs may be so impaired that heart failure results.

➤*bagassosis*; *byssinosis*; *farmer's lung.*

pneumocystis. A microscopical parasite found in healthy lungs but causing pneumonia when resistance is undermined by AIDS. The infection can often be suppressed with trimethoprim.

pneumonia. Inflammation of the lungs from infection by viruses or bacteria. It is quite distinct from bronchitis, with which the lining of the main air-passages is inflamed and swollen; with pneumonia the trouble is further down, in the tiny pockets (*alveoli*; see *lung* (1)) at the ends of the air-passages. The walls of the alveoli have to be thin enough to allow oxygen to pass freely from the air to the blood, and they are also thin enough to allow inflammatory exudate – the fluid that leaks from blood vessels during any inflammation – to pass into the alveoli. The distinguishing feature of pneumonia is waterlogging of the alveoli in the affected part. Inflammatory exudate can form a solid clot, so that the part has the consistency of liver, as first described by Morgagni (1761).

Pneumonia can be classified by the distribution of the affected alveoli. In *lobar* *pneumonia* the whole of one lobe or segment is involved. *Broncho-pneumonia* affects groups of alveoli close to the larger air-passages, so that small patches of inflammation are scattered through the lungs. In a third type, *hypostatic pneumonia*, gravity determines the pattern. In this type of pneumonia the alveoli in the lowest parts of both lungs collect fluid because of poor circulation, just as the feet swell when blood does not circulate properly in the legs. Stagnant fluid in the lungs is a good breeding-ground for bacteria, and hypostatic pneumonia is bacterial infection of fluid already there, unlike other types of pneumonia where the fluid is the result of infection. It is seen only as a complication of other diseases, when an already sick person lies still in bed for a long time.

Since the discovery of antibiotic drugs for treating infection there has been less emphasis on the various patterns of pneumonia and more on the species of microbe, which determines the choice of drug. The commonest bacterial causes of pneumonia are streptococci (including the *pneumococcus* which is the usual cause of lobar pneumonia), staphylococci, and the 'influenza bacillus' (which does not cause influenza). Viruses can be the sole cause of pneumonia, or they can pave the way for bacterial infection, as when pneumococci take over from a common-cold virus.

A text-book case of lobar pneumonia starts either without warning or after a short minor illness with sudden fever, pain in the chest (from inflammation of the ➤*pleura* or coating of the lung; there is no feeling in the lung itself), and a cough with blood-tinged sputum. (There is no pain if the trouble is in the centre of the lung far from the pleura, and for a time the pneumonia is almost unrecognizable.) After a few days any pain goes, because the inflamed pleura is cushioned by fluid, the cough becomes easier and more effective, but the fever persists. After a week or so the patient may undergo a *crisis* when the fever vanishes almost as suddenly as it appeared together with the other symptoms; or the fever goes by *lysis* (gradually); or the infection spreads outside the lung (▸*empyema*); or the patient dies. But textbook cases are no longer the rule. With antibiotic drugs the symptoms of bacterial pneumonia usually begin to improve soon after the start of treatment. Whereas previously some 20 per cent of the patients died (in some series as many as 40 per cent) nearly everyone who is reasonably fit before the attack now recovers. Furthermore bacterial pneumonia is less common than it was; it seems to be giving place to virus pneumonia, which is much less dangerous and runs an altogether less dramatic course.

Despite antibiotics, pneumonia is still a fairly common cause of death, but not among the young and middle-aged who used to be its principal victims. The people still apt to succumb are those who are already debilitated by chronic disease and put up no natural resistance – not even, in some cases, a raised temperature. In them, pneumonia is not so much the true cause of death as the mode of dying from some disease such as failure of the heart, liver, or kidneys.

Until recent years, pneumonia was a common and dangerous complication of major operations, especially operations on the abdomen. Anaesthetics certainly prepared the ground by irritating the lungs, but the main cause was prolonged and complete immobilization in bed, often with tight bandages (to support the wound – and impede breathing). Improved anaesthetics, breathing exercises, and above all a minimum of complete bed-rest have now made post-operative pneumonia a rarity.

Several other types of pneumonia should be mentioned. 'Atypical' pneumonia is usually caused by mycoplasma, an organism on the borderline between bacteria and viruses. It starts with an indeterminate fever, followed by cough, pain in the chest, and sometimes anaemia and other complications. It does not usually respond to penicillin, but tetracycline is effective. *Ornithosis*, carried to man by birds (especially parrots: ▸*psittacosis*), is caused by a rather similar organism, *Chlamydia*. This also leads to a kind of pneumonia responding to tetracycline.

'Opportunist' pneumonia is caused by organisms not normally harmful, but able to infect people whose immunity has been suppressed either by chemotherapy to prevent rejection of transplanted organs, or by infection with AIDS (▸*pneumocystis*).

pneumothorax. Air in the pleural cavity, between the lung and the chest wall, preventing normal expansion of the lung and so impairing respiration.

Pneumothorax is a complication of penetrating injuries of the chest and of disease of the lungs – in the latter case the air leaks out from the affected lung. Some cases arise without any apparent cause (spontaneous pneumothorax); these may be due to congenital weaknesses in the outer walls of the lungs.

As soon as the leak heals, the air is gradually absorbed until the lung can expand fully again. Sometimes the air may be actively withdrawn. In the past, a pneumothorax was sometimes deliberately induced in order to collapse and so rest a lung affected with tuberculosis, but this procedure is now obsolete.

podagra = ►*gout*.

poison. Water, oxygen, and the ingredients of a good diet are all poisonous in excess, but the term has to be limited to substances that are harmful in small quantities. If the toxins of bacteria and the venoms of insects, snakes etc. are excluded the list of poisons is still very long. It includes practically all drugs and many minerals and synthetic substances. As a rule, poisons and drugs extracted from plants are dangerous in smaller doses than mineral poisons, but not in quite such minute doses as toxins and venoms.

Corrosive poisons such as acids, alkalis, and many disinfectants alter the chemical state of proteins and therefore indiscriminately damage all living matter. Other poisons interfere with particular chemical reactions in the body; for instance, cyanides prevent the transfer of oxygen in living cells and produce chemical suffocation. Vegetable poisons are often chemically related to substances in the body, which they displace in vital reactions. Their use as drugs depends on these effects, and poisoning is generally an exaggeration of the medicinal effect.

Some of the commoner poisons are described under their own headings. Only a few generalizations can be made here.

Irritants may help to eliminate themselves by causing vomiting or diarrhoea before all the poison has been absorbed from the stomach and intestine. Occasionally the stomach may have to be emptied by means of an emetic such as ipecacuanha or, better, a stomach tube – but this needs expert handling. With corrosive poisons, recognized by staining or burning of the mouth, emetics and purgatives only make matters worse; and if a patient who is not fully conscious is given an emetic he may inhale vomited fluid and so die of the remedy rather than of the poison.

General antidotes include charcoal, which takes up many kinds of poison, and tannic acid (e.g. as strong cool tea), which neutralizes some vegetable poisons by making them insoluble. White of egg may protect the stomach from further damage by corrosive poisons. Milk is probably as good a household antidote as any.

Specific antidotes for some poisons are mentioned under the names of the poisons. Very few are completely effective. More than anything else it is skilled nursing that saves lives after severe poisoning, and all but the most trivial cases are safest in a hospital. The full effects of poisoning may not develop for some hours, and the victim may need continuous artificial respiration or even, with some poisons, the use of an artificial kidney in which the poison is washed from the blood.

poison ivy. *Rhus toxicodendron*, a potent instigator of contact ►*dermatitis* in many parts of the world, especially the USA.

policlinic. A clinic or health centre in a town, generally dealing only with outpatients (cf. ►*polyclinic*).

poliomyelitis (acute anterior poliomyelitis; infantile paralysis). A virus infection of grey matter in the front part of the spinal cord, affecting the nerve cells responsible for stimulating contraction of muscles. If some of these cells are damaged by the infection the corresponding muscles can no longer work.

The virus is fairly common. In the great majority of cases infection is confined to the throat and intestine, and the symptoms – if any – are those of a minor digestive upset. In a few cases, perhaps only 1 per cent, the spinal cord is involved and groups of muscles are weakened or paralysed. Sensation is not affected. There is little danger to life unless the muscles of the throat and of breathing are paralysed, but in about a quarter of all cases with involvement of the spinal cord there is some permanent loss of muscle power, sometimes confined to small groups of muscles, sometimes more widespread.

Since the virus can be carried by human excrement, good sanitation reduces the risk of infection. This has not been an advantage. Where sanitation is poor, most people are infected in infancy, when paralysis is unusual. In more hygienic surroundings there are enough children and adults who have never been infected, and therefore have no immunity, for epidemics to occur; and these older patients are more prone to serious effects of the disease. But even during an epidemic paralysis is rare in comparison with the numbers who either escape all symptoms or recover completely.

In view of good evidence that fatigued muscles are the most likely to suffer, children under the slightest suspicion of poliomyelitis are kept as quiet as possible. It is usual to close schools, swimming baths etc. during an epidemic, but since most cases are without symptoms and cannot be traced such measures have little effect; they may, however, help to prevent some of the children at risk from over-exertion. Much the most important method of prevention is the routine use of vaccines. With these, poliomyelitis can be virtually exterminated. Two kinds of vaccine are available, one given by mouth (➤*Sabin*) and the other by injection (➤*Salk*).

pollex = thumb.

polyarteritis nodosa. A rare disease, with inflammation of small arteries and impaired circulation in the tissues that they supply, which may be anywhere in the body; thus polyarteritis may show itself as a disease of skin, kidneys, joints, lungs etc. Cases associated with rheumatic fever or tuberculosis may be allergic reactions to some product of the primary disorder. Other cases show many signs of a protracted allergic reaction though no cause can be found. The most successful treatment is with corticosteroid drugs.

polyclinic. Hospital with various specialist departments (cf. ➤*policlinic*).

polycystic kidney. A developmental disorder, with the formation of cysts or bubbles in the substance of the kidneys. This is seldom apparent until adult life when the enlarged kidneys may ache, bleed or become infected. As with other disorders of the kidneys the blood pressure is often high. Serious impairment of function may need treatment by dialysis (artificial kidney) or a transplant operation.

polycythaemia. Excess of red blood cells. The number of these cells is normally about 5 million per cubic millimetre of blood (➤*blood* (2)), with fairly wide variation among healthy people. A figure below 4 million is proof of ➤*anaemia*, and above 6 million of *polycythaemia*.

Relative polycythaemia is seen with dehydration: the total number of red cells in the circulation is still normal, but they are suspended in a smaller volume of fluid. This state often follows severe injuries, especially burns where large amounts of fluid are lost into the damaged tissues.

Absolute polycythaemia – more cells

than usual in the normal volume of fluid – is a natural response to prolonged shortage of oxygen. People who live at very high altitudes have it to compensate for the rarefied atmosphere, and it is also seen with chronic disease of the heart or lungs when oxygen is not delivered to the body at the normal rate.

Polycythaemia vera is a very rare disease in which for no known reason the patient has too many red cells, sometimes as many as 9 million per cubic millimetre. The blood can become so thick that it does not flow properly, and the patient has then to be treated either by blood-letting or by suppressing the formation of new cells with drugs or radiation.

polygraph. An apparatus for simultaneous recording of pulses, invented by ➤*Mackenzie* for studying heart disease, and later reintroduced in a modified form as a 'lie-detector'.

polymorph (polymorphonuclear leukocyte). A white blood cell with a segmented nucleus. ➤*blood* (3).

polymyalgia rheumatica. A kind of muscular inflammation affecting women more than men, seldom starting before the age of 60. The symptoms include stiffness and pain, often severe, around the neck and shoulders or occasionally in other groups of muscles. The disease is associated with an obscure type of inflammation of arteries, sometimes affecting the temporal artery at the side of the scalp, from which it may spread to the arteries of the eyes. The condition responds well to small doses of corticosteroids, and treatment not only relieves the muscles but prevents damage to the eyesight.

polyp (polypus). A tumour, usually harmless, attached to a mucous membrane by a stalk, like a berry. Polyps are common in the large intestine, where they need surgical attention because some intestinal polyps are precursors of cancer. Polyps of quite a different type are often found in the nose. These are not real tumours but simply swellings of the mucous membrane caused by infection or allergy (hay fever).

polypeptide. A compound of two or more amino-acids joined by peptide bonds. The amino (NH_2) group of one joins the acid (COOH) group of the next, with the loss of water. Thus alanine, $CH_3.CH(NH_2)COOH$, and glycine, $CH_2(NH_2)COOH$ (which may be written $HNH.CH_2COOH$), form alanylglycine:

$$CH_3.CH(NH_2)CO/OH + H/NH.CH_2COOH$$
alanine ↓ glycine
$$CH_3.CH(NH_2)CO.NH.CH_2COOH + H_2O$$
alanylglycine water

A ➤*protein* is simply a polypeptide in which hundreds of amino-acids are joined in this way.

When proteins are digested they are broken down to individual amino-acids.

Several hormones are polypeptides. For instance, ADH and ACTH (➤*pituitary body*) are respectively chains of 8 and 39 amino-acids; insulin, of 51.

polyposis. A hereditary tendency to form numerous polyps in the large intestine.

polysaccharide. A compound sugar, of which each molecule is made up of several molecules of simple sugars; e.g. *starch*, a long branching chain of glucose molecules. Polysaccharides are the principal carbohydrates and main source of energy in most normal diets.

polyuria. Formation of an excessive

volume of urine. The word *diabetes* has much the same meaning.

pompholyx. A kind of ►*eczema* of the hands or feet, with small itching blisters that sometimes merge and become infected.

pons (pons Varolii). Part of the brainstem, above the *medulla oblongata* and below the *midbrain*; it appears to be a broad horizontal band of nerve fibres across the front of the brain-stem. The nerve cells of the 5th, 6th, and 7th cranial nerves are in the pons. Many of the transverse fibres enter the *cerebellum*, which protrudes from the back of the brain-stem at this level.

Bleeding in or around the pons upsets the regulation of the body temperature. Some of the highest fevers are from this cause; on the other hand the patient's temperature may fall to that of the surroundings. But the centre for regulating temperature is not in the pons. This strange effect may be due to compression of fibres passing through the pons from the real centre in the *hypothalamus*.

The name *pons Varolii* ascribes the discovery of the pons to Costanzo Varolio (1543–78) of Bologna. In fact it is clearly shown in earlier drawings of Eustachius, but Varolio was the first to name it.

popliteal. Of the back of the knee. The *popliteal fossa* is a lozenge-shaped space bounded by the tendons of the hamstring muscles above and the calf muscles below. It contains the *popliteal artery* and *vein*, which are the continuation of the femoral vessels into the calf, and the *popliteal nerves*, which are the two terminal branches of the sciatic nerve.

porphyria. A group of hereditary disorders of body chemistry, with excessive production of *porphyrins*, which appear in the urine either as red pigments or as colourless compounds that blacken on exposure to light. All types of porphyria are rare.

In the type with red urine the other important symptom is sensitivity of the skin, especially to sunlight. Disturbances of skin pigmentation and hair growth can also occur.

Other types of porphyria cause episodes of abdominal pain, mental confusion, and skin disorders. Sometimes attacks are precipitated by other illnesses or by drugs.

porphyrin. A substance combined with iron and protein to form the oxygen-carrying blood-pigment *haemoglobin*. Similar porphyrins are found in most living organisms, e.g. in the green pigment of plants, chlorophyll.

portacaval shunt. Surgical operation to establish a short-circuit between the portal vein and the inferior vena cava, for treating obstruction of veins in the liver. ►*portal vein.*

portal vein. A large blood vessel formed from the veins of the stomach, intestine, and spleen. It enters the liver and distributes the materials assimilated from the diet (►*digestion*) to the cells of the liver to be stored or resynthesized. The blood is returned to the general circulation by the hepatic veins, which enter the inferior vena cava. The portal vein is an ordinary vein as far as the intestine is concerned, removing blood that has already circulated; but to the liver it behaves as an artery delivering blood.

Until birth an infant has no need of its own liver because it has nothing to digest, and the portal circulation is bypassed by the *ductus venosus*, a vessel passing straight from the portal vein to the inferior vena cava. At birth this vessel closes.

Disease of the liver, especially *>cirrhosis*, may impede the flow of blood in the small branches of the portal vein and raise the pressure (*portal hypertension*). This causes leakage of fluid (*>oedema*), and large amounts of water may accumulate in the abdominal cavity. The small veins at the entrance to the stomach, where tributaries of the portal vein communicate with veins belonging to the general circulation, become overloaded and may bleed dangerously.

A rare form of portal hypertension arises in infancy from thrombosis (clotting) in the portal vein, probably caused by infection of the umbilical cord.

Portal hypertension can be successfully treated by surgery. Several operations have been devised for diverting some of the blood in the portal vein into the general circulation without its passing through the liver. This relieves the pressure and symptoms, and since the liver has a considerable reserve of function there is little impairment of nutrition.

postmaturity. Condition of an infant at birth after unduly prolonged pregnancy. If labour is delayed beyond a week or two after the normal time for pregnancy to end, the risk to the child may be almost as great as that of prematurity, because the placenta is no longer able to nourish the child sufficiently. The mother's difficulties may be increased if the child's bones begin to harden. Postmaturity is treated either by artificial *>induction* of labour, or by Caesarean section.

posture. In physiological terms, posture is a complicated system of reflexes. The muscles used to maintain posture are the

same as those used for voluntary movements – mainly those of the backbone and legs, but also many others – but their governing nerve cells receive unconscious as well as conscious stimuli. These are co-ordinated by the cerebellum and other unconscious parts of the brain, responding to unconscious sensation such as imminent loss of balance. Normally, the muscles of posture are so nicely balanced that they do practically no work. Some muscular pain ('fibrositis') is possibly due to abnormal posture, e.g. the slumped posture of depression or the taut posture of anxiety.

Pott's fracture-dislocation. The supporting bones at each side of the ankle are broken and the foot is displaced outwards

potassium. Metallic element, similar to sodium. In test-tube chemistry these two elements are almost interchangeable, but in the body life itself depends on the correct balance between a high concentration of potassium inside the cells and a high concentration of sodium in the surrounding fluids. Nerve impulses are transmitted by electrical currents associated with a momentary exchange of sodium and potassium. A small excess or deficit of potassium interferes with the action of the heart and larger changes are enough to stop it. When fluid is lost from the body, e.g. from diarrhoea or burns, or when the balance between intake and loss of potassium is disturbed by certain drugs, the correct amount of potassium may have to be maintained artificially. Most fruits provide a good supply, but sometimes potassium salts have to be given medicinally.

Pott, Percivall (1714–88). London surgeon; he gave the first description of the injury since known as *Pott's fracture*. With this serious injury of the ankle, the foot is twisted outwards (in the opposite direction to the common sprain). The fibula, at the outer side of the leg, is broken above the ankle joint, and at the inner side of the joint either the lowest part of the tibia breaks or the ligament binding it to the foot tears. The ankle joint is then unsupported and becomes dislocated. Pott is usually said to have suffered this fracture himself when crossing London Bridge, but it seems that his leg was broken higher up. He bought the front door of the nearest house for a stretcher and had himself carried to Guy's Hospital, saying that the only good surgeon at his own hospital, St Bartholomew's, had just broken his leg.

Pott's disease is paralysis of the legs through damage to the spinal cord by tuberculosis of the backbone.

Pott was the first man to identify a cause of cancer: chimney-sweep's cancer of the scrotum from repeated contamination with soot.

poultice. A kind of dressing applied hot to inflamed areas to relieve pain by *counter-irritation* and perhaps to increase resistance to infection by increasing the flow of blood. The objection to poultices is that they tend to make the skin soggy and liable to harbour further infection.

predisposition. There is nothing new in the idea that patterns of health and sickness are to some extent influenced by race, build, social background, occupation, personal habits, and family history. The links may be strong, as with some purely genetic disorders, or only tenuous, but in the past they have tended to be more interesting than useful. Such information could not make a diagnosis, though it might suggest to a potential patient that he might be prone to particular diseases, thereby giving him the chance to do something about the situation.

Since the middle of this century, developments in three seemingly unrelated medical specialties have changed the whole picture: these are genetics, statistics and organ transplantation. Within a few years, the study of predisposition seems likely to become a very important branch of practical medicine. The understanding of *genetics* has advanced very quickly, especially since the discovery and solution of the genetic code. The nature and distribution of hereditary traits can now be studied in great detail. Medical *statistics*, after Doll and Hill proved that smoking is a direct cause of lung cancer, have been applied widely to the study of other causes of ill health. For example, several 'risk factors' in addition to smoking have been proved to predispose to heart attacks: overeating, lack of exercise, and high blood pressure are among them. But it is common knowledge that some people are overweight, take little exercise, and drink and smoke without troubling their hearts at all (the term 'Churchill syndrome' has been suggested). Similarly, in some people, alcohol seriously damages the liver, while others drinking as much or more may escape harm. In addition, an excess of salt in the diet leads to high blood pressure in some people, but not all. Until quite recently there was little hope of knowing which people were most at risk. But with the advent of *transplantation* of organs such as kidneys some unexpected information came to light. Since 1900 it had been known that blood for transfusion must be compatible with the patient's own blood, compatibility being determined mainly by the major blood groups A, B, AB, and O. These groups depend on certain *antigens* on the surface of red blood cells, and an individual's pattern of these antigens (i.e. blood group) is inherited. But for a transplanted organ to be compatible with the patient, an analogous set of antigens on the surface of body cells should match, or at least nearly match. These ➤*HLA* antigens can form not four, but thousands of individual patterns, and new patterns are still being identified. For some time an association of duodenal ulcers with blood group O has been recognized. It now appears that many disorders are associated with particular HLA patterns. Only one, *ankylosing spondylitis* (a crippling affliction of the backbone), is almost constantly related to a known pattern, but with many others a particular pattern is found much more often than pure chance would allow. These include *rheumatoid arthritis* and the whole range of autoimmune diseases, in which some

part of the body is damaged by the patient's own defences (➤*immunity* (7)). Another is *alcoholic cirrhosis* of the liver: this gives hope that in time it may be possible to warn people in advance of risks to which they are unduly susceptible. More than this, these findings may bring us nearer to finding the causes of many serious and baffling diseases.

prednisolone; prednisone. Synthetic derivatives of ➤*corticosteroid* hormones.

prefrontal lobe. The foremost part of the brain; apparently concerned with intellect and personality. Some severe forms of mental disorder have been relieved by operations to isolate the prefrontal lobes (➤*psychosurgery*).

pregnancy. Pregnancy lasts from conception until labour. It lasts, on average, for 38 weeks. Because the date of conception is often uncertain, it is convenient to date pregnancy from the first day of the last menstrual period, which is likely to be a fortnight before conception, making a total of 40 weeks. Towards the end of pregnancy it becomes important for the welfare of both mother and child to know as accurately as possible how long the pregnancy has lasted. No single piece of evidence is conclusive, but the date of the last period is valuable information: ➤*postmaturity*; *prematurity*.

The many changes that occur – provision for nourishing the developing baby, cessation of menstrual periods, growth of the uterus, development of the breasts – are brought about by a hormone, progesterone, formed in the early stages by the *corpus luteum* in the ovary, later by the placenta. The ending of pregnancy, formation of milk, and labour depend on hormones from the pituitary, but the mechanism is not fully understood.

A missed period is usually the first indication of pregnancy, but it is not completely reliable. The diagnosis can be made with some confidence by clinical examination of the uterus a few weeks later, and it is absolutely proved when the heart beat of the foetus is heard half-way through pregnancy (much sooner with an electronic stethoscope) or movements are felt; the woman herself is aware of these movements some weeks before the examining doctor or midwife. The characteristic hormones in the urine can be detected about a month after conception by tests with animals: Aschheim-Zondek (mice), Friedman (rabbits), or Hogben test (xenopus toads).

Biologically it can be argued that child-bearing is the normal condition of fertile women. This at least gets away from the idea of pregnancy as a sort of illness – a puritanical idea that accounts for some of the disagreeable symptoms associated with pregnancy. Symptoms such as nausea, fainting (commoner in fiction than fact), and emotional instability are due in the first place to incomplete adaptation to the altered output of hormones. They seldom last more than a few weeks, but they can be aggravated and prolonged by worrying about them. Protracted and serious nausea and vomiting, requiring hospital treatment, are fortunately rare: >*hyperemesis gravidarum*.

A pregnant woman can easily eat more than she needs, either because she is anxious not to deprive the baby or simply because she feels hungry, and afterwards it may be difficult to lose the extra weight. In fact, the *quantity* of food she needs is not much increased, but the *quality* needs attention. In particular she may need supplementary iron and vitamins.

Although pregnancy is normally a healthy state, certain precautions are needed. With adequate antenatal care the risks of pregnancy and labour can mostly be overcome, because the more dangerous complications can be anticipated and dealt with (>*toxaemia of pregnancy*). Careful explanation is almost as important as the routine check of progress of the developing infant and health of the woman; her labour is much easier if she knows exactly what will be expected of her.

Any untoward symptoms during pregnancy, including even unrelated minor ailments, should be reported at once. Although not very many drugs have been *proved* to harm the foetus, all medicines must be regarded with suspicion and taken only under qualified supervision. >*Benzodiazepines* may produce lethargic babies, while the effects of narcotics on the foetus are far worse. The baby may fail to breathe or may be born as an addict needing treatment for withdrawal symptoms. Alcohol, except in extreme moderation, and smoking both put the foetus at risk. In particular, alcohol can cause a well-defined foetal alcohol syndrome (FAS), and the affected child may be undersized, lethargic or mentally retarded.

prematurity. An infant used to be 'premature' if its birth-weight was less than 2.5 kg (5½ lb). This was an unsatisfactory definition because it suggested that new-born babies should all be the same size. In fact, small parents can expect to have perfectly healthy babies that would be premature according to the definition, and other people may have babies of 'normal' weight that are underdeveloped at birth and need special care. What matters is the stage of the baby's development at birth. A baby that is born too soon is not yet able to maintain a normal body temperature, mainly because the protective fat develops only in the final weeks of pregnancy. The truly premature baby is also more vulnerable to temporary lack of oxygen than a full-term baby. A normal full-term baby can manage without oxygen for some minutes, presumably by converting glucose to lactic acid (►*muscle* (1)); but a premature baby cannot because he has no store of glucose. Other complications associated with premature births include an immature nervous system, kidneys and other organs. In addition, premature babies have often not fully developed the ability to suck and swallow, and need special feeding methods. They are unusually vulnerable to infection and to cold; ►*brown fat*. Congenital abnormalities are commoner than among full-term babies: they may sometimes cause the premature birth.

A premature baby is better defined as one born three or more weeks too soon. Assessment is made easier by an accurate record of the last menstrual period. Routine antenatal examination does not give a precise indication of how long a pregnancy has lasted while an X-ray picture does, by showing the development of the bones from which the status of the baby as a whole can be inferred. But exposing an unborn baby to radiation is most undesirable, and the same information can be obtained safely by ►*echography*.

Infants born at full term (40 weeks after the last period), yet small enough to suggest prematurity, are described as *small-for-dates*.

premenstrual syndrome. Various symptoms which occur a few days before a menstrual period are collected under this name. Whether they represent a single disorder or more than one is not clear.

'Syndrome' seems preferable to 'tension' because 'tension' presupposes more than is known. This syndrome is to be distinguished from ►*dysmenorrhoea*, which is pain and other symptoms experienced mainly during periods.

The possible symptoms include fatigue, painful breasts, headache, and various emotional disturbances, often exaggerations of the patient's normal character traits. As retention of water may be a feature, some patients are aware of putting on weight before their periods.

The cause or causes of the premenstrual syndrome are not fully understood. The balance of hormones is evidently disturbed, and the symptoms have been ascribed to periodic shortages of progesterone with consequent fluid retention. But if this were all, treatment with hormone supplements and with diuretics to remove surplus water should give more consistent relief than in fact they do. There is clearly more to be learned. The symptoms and their severity vary widely. Each patient has to be treated on the merits of her particular case. Although a specialist's opinion may be helpful, this syndrome calls for a family doctor who knows and understands the patient.

presbyacusis. Loss of hearing in old age – a gradual process that starts in adolescence. High-pitched sounds are most affected, so that consonants are not distinguished though vowel sounds can still be heard.

presbyopia. Loss of the ability to focus the eyes in old age.

prickly heat (miliaria). An itchy rash due to blockage of sweat glands, with the formation of minute blisters, commonest among newcomers to tropical climates. Various lotions are used and may help, but the only completely effective treatment is to keep cool. Light clothing – cotton for choice – is essential.

prion ►*slow virus.*

probenecid. A drug that interferes with the passage of certain substances from the kidneys to the urine or vice versa. It prevents the excretion of penicillin into the urine, and so enhances the effect of a dose of penicillin. On the other hand it prevents the kidneys from reabsorbing uric acid into the bloodstream from the urine, and is therefore used to eliminate uric acid in the treatment of gout.

procaine. One of the most successful local anaesthetic drugs.

proctology. Study and treatment of disorders of the rectum.

prodrome. A symptom appearing before an illness is manifest, e.g. Koplik's spots in the mouth a day or two before the rash clinches a diagnosis of measles.

progesterone. A hormone secreted by the *corpus luteum* i.e. the small gland that develops in an ovary each month at the site from which an ovum or egg has been released. Progesterone stimulates development of the uterus to receive a fertilized ovum and nourish the embryo. If the ovum is fertilized and pregnancy occurs, the corpus luteum and later the placenta continue to form progesterone, which prevents menstruation and the release of more ova. If pregnancy does not occur, the corpus luteum withers.

The action of progesterone in preventing ova from being shed suggested the idea for the contraceptive pill.

prognosis. Prediction of the course of an illness.

progressive muscular atrophy. A form of ►*motor neurone disease.*

prolactin. Lactogenic hormone, formed in the anterior lobe of the pituitary and stimulating the formation of milk.

prolapse. Displacement of an organ from its normal position, usually by gravity as a result of weakness of the supporting tissues. Prolapse of the rectum – extrusion of a segment of bowel through the anus – is not uncommon in children. Most cases respond to simple measures such as holding the buttocks together with adhesive plaster and education of the muscles, but a few need surgical reconstruction.

Prolapse of the uterus is common in women who have borne several children, especially if the supporting muscles and ligaments have been badly stretched or torn. Sometimes prolapse is due to a congenital weakness of the pelvic muscles and ligaments, which should normally sling the uterus in a sort of muscular hammock. The earliest sign of prolapse of the uterus is bulging of the vaginal walls by pressure either from the bladder in front (*cystocoele*) or the rectum behind (*proctocoele*). True prolapse is descent of the uterus into the vagina, causing severe discomfort, difficulty in retaining urine and other symptoms. At a later stage, the uterus may actually protrude from the vulva. In the early stages a ring pessary helps. This device is placed in the vagina and serves to prop the uterus against the firm base of the pubis, i.e. the bony ridge forming the front of the pelvis. Many patients find this objectionable and choose surgery, which is in any case the only useful treatment for more advanced prolapse. A conservative operation shortens the supporting ligaments and muscles of the uterus, in the manner of a facelift. If childbearing is no longer a consideration, the certain cure is to remove the uterus, which incidentally relieves older women of some of the worries usually associated with menopause.

pronation. Turning the hand palm downwards; the opposite movement is *supination.*

prontosil. The precursor of the ▸*sulphonamides*, and indirectly of penicillin and other antibiotics.

prophylaxis. Prevention of disease: anything from vaccination to a daily walk.

propranolol. A drug used to impede certain effects of adrenaline and of sympathetic nerves. ▸*beta-blockers.*

proprioception. Sensation from muscles, joints, etc., conveying information (not always consciously perceived) about their position in relation to the rest of the body so that posture is maintained by reflex movement.

prostaglandins. A group of chemically similar substances first identified in 1935 in extracts of prostate glands, but now known to occur in most tissues and organs. All are derived from essential fatty acids (▸*fat*), but their biological actions are very diverse. Some are concerned with inflammation, and the anti-inflammatory effect of drugs such as aspirin appears to be due to suppression of these. Other prostaglandins affect the clotting of blood, the elimination of water and salt in the kidneys and (presumably in consequence) the blood pressure, the air-passages in the lungs, the processes of immunity to infection and

hence allergic reactions, the behaviour of the stomach and intestine, and the reproductive organs. This last provides the first known clinical use of prostaglandins, namely the induction of labour or of abortion. Natural labour is apparently started by prostaglandins that act on the uterus. They also keep open the *ductus arteriosus* (▸*heart* (1)), by which the foetal blood bypasses the lungs until after birth, when breathing can start. Thus anti-inflammatory drugs (NSAIDs), which act by suppressing prostaglandins, are avoided in late pregnancy: they not only delay and prolong labour but also jeopardize the baby's circulation by letting the ductus close too soon.

NSAIDs, used to suppress inflammation with conditions such as rheumatoid arthritis, can cause gastric ulcers, and prostaglandins protect the stomach lining from this effect.

Other uses include the prevention of blood clots during dialysis, and there is intensive research into the possible use of prostaglandins in the treatment of high blood pressure, asthma and arterial disease.

prostate gland (prostata). One of the male sex organs: it is a rounded mass of muscle fibres and small glands immediately below the urinary bladder, surrounding the outlet of the bladder (urethra). It secretes a part of the seminal fluid in which sperms from the testis are suspended.

Inflammation of the prostate is an occasional complication of infection elsewhere in the urinary system (tuberculosis, gonorrhoea etc.). The prostate can be injured by a blow between the buttocks, and it may be irritated by continuous pressure – e.g. in a long-distance lorry driver with a badly sprung seat. With all disorders of the prostate a firm seat is more comfortable than a soft one that can press upwards between the buttocks.

Much the commonest disorder of the prostate is overgrowth of its glandular elements in middle or old age. The ill effects are purely mechanical. Because the enlarged gland causes a sensation of pressure at the outlet of the bladder, the patient has a frequent urge to pass water (as a patient with large piles feels that he has to open his bowels). And the encroachment on the urethra tends to obstruct the flow of urine. In time, it may be impossible to empty the bladder completely, and the stagnant remainder of urine is liable to become infected with bacteria and damage the bladder and kidneys. If a large amount of urine is retained, the added pressure is a further embarrassment to the kidneys.

Removal of the enlarged part of the prostate is a fairly simple operation. Most surgeons advise early operation, because the risk is much increased if the kidneys are already damaged. If the operation is done when the symptoms first become a serious nuisance the results are extremely good.

Another reason for early attention is that a few cases of enlarged prostate are due to cancer, which becomes incurable if treatment is delayed. The best treatment of cancer of the prostate is to remove it, but if this is not possible or not advisable the cancer can be effectively discouraged by removing the testes or giving drugs such as stilboestrol.

prosthesis. Artificial substitute for a part of the body (e.g. false teeth, glass eye, wooden leg).

protein. Proteins are essential ingredients of all living matter. They make up about 12 per cent of the weight of the human body (water is 70 per cent, fat 15 per cent). A molecule of protein is a chain of several hundred amino-acid molecules (*>polypeptide*). Amino-acids are composed of carbon, hydrogen, oxygen, nitrogen, and sometimes sulphur. Some 22 different kinds of amino-acid are involved. The biological properties of a protein depend on the exact sequence of different amino-acids in the chain (primary structure), their orientation (secondary structure), and the shape of the chain as a whole (tertiary structure). Small differences make for totally different proteins, and the possible permutations are almost unlimited. Other components of living matter vary little; it is in the arrangement of their proteins that species and individuals differ.

The proteins of the food (*>diet*) have to be broken down so that the amino-acids can be rearranged as specifically human proteins. A non-human protein introduced into the tissues provokes a defensive reaction (*>immunity; allergy*) and is rejected. Similarly a human protein that differs in any respect from the recipient's proteins is treated as non-human: this is the obstacle to transplantation of organs from one person to another.

Most of the protein dissolved in the blood (plasma protein) is assembled in the liver. The cells of the various tissues form their own proteins from amino-acids that diffuse from the blood into the tissue fluid. The exact structure of a protein is determined by the particular nucleic acid, in the cell nucleus, responsible for its synthesis. Nucleic acids for the synthesis of all the proteins of the body are determined at the time of conception, and hereditary characters depend on their precise nature. In essence, what parents pass to their children is the ability to form particular proteins. Many proteins are common to the whole race, but many show minor individual variations. Apart from identical twins, no two people are likely to have an exactly similar set of proteins.

Protein is mainly used in the structure of tissues. Any surplus can be used as fuel (►*energy*). The nitrogenous portion of amino-acids is converted to *urea* and excreted by the kidneys, and the residue is oxidized to carbon dioxide and water. If the diet does not contain enough ordinary fuel (carbohydrate and fat) the subject may be short of protein because he burns it instead of using it for growth and repair of tissue. *Protein-energy malnutrition* is thought to arise in this way. Two severe and superficially very different forms are ►*kwashiorkor* and ►*marasmus*. Treatment with a high-protein diet is not enough; the other ingredients of the diet also need attention, as do concurrent infections.

Proteus. A genus of bacteria: as a rule they are harmless but they can cause serious trouble when other bacteria have been eliminated from wounds, etc., with antibiotics.

prothrombin. A substance dissolved in blood, necessary to clotting. Prothrombin itself is inactive, but when blood is shed prothrombin is converted to *thrombin*, which together with several other factors causes blood to clot. The *prothrombin time* is a laboratory test of blood-clot formation. It can be used to measure the effect of anticoagulant drugs (i.e. drugs used to prevent clotting).

protoplasm. The characteristic material of most living tissue, based on a jelly-like suspension of protein in water.

protozoon. The protozoa are the smallest and simplest creatures that can be called animals. They form a diverse group with the common characteristic that their bodies are not divided into separate functional units or cells. They differ from simple plants such as algae in depending on other living creatures for their food; but the distinction between plants and animals at this low level is vague, and there are many border-line cases. The sizes of protozoa lie between 0.005 and 0.5 mm.

In general protozoa reproduce themselves by dividing into two equal parts, each of which grows to a replica of the original organism, able to divide again when it is large enough. In some species there is also a kind of sexual reproduction. At its simplest this is merely a fusion of two seemingly identical 'parents' which later split into 'offspring'. Some protozoa, such as the malaria parasite, have an elaborate life-cycle in which male and female forms appear.

A few species of protozoa are parasitic to man: ►*dysentery*; *giardia*; *leishmania*; *malaria*; *toxoplasmosis*; *trichomonas*; *trypanosome*.

proximal. Nearer to the centre of the body or to the trunk (as opposed to *distal*).

pruritus = ►*itch*.

pseudarthrosis. False joint, resulting from failure of a broken bone to heal: instead of joining, the broken ends become sealed with hard bone, and the fracture cannot then heal without a surgical operation. ►*fracture*.

pseudocyesis. False pregnancy, with symptoms of a real pregnancy. The basis is emotional, but emotion affects the formation of hormones by the pituitary gland, with physical effects like those of pregnancy. This is a rare neurosis in Western society, but much commoner where husbands may disown barren wives.

pseudomembrane. A skin of dried secretion at the back of the throat, as in diphtheria.

pseudomembranous colitis. A complication of treatment with certain antibiotics occasionally used for refractory bone infections. All broad-spectrum antibiotics carry some risk of killing the natural bacteria and allowing alien species to invade the intestine, but here infection with a species of ►*clostridium* (*C. difficile*) can cause violent diarrhoea and even death. A characteristic pseudomembrane forms over the lining of the large intestine. As with all severe diarrhoea, fluid replacement is the first consideration, together with treatment with various drugs including metronidazole.

Pseudomonas. A genus of bacteria. One species, *Ps. aeruginosa*, can cause very troublesome infection, especially in hospital wards. It forms a characteristic blue pigment. This organism was formerly called *Ps. pyocyanea* with reference to the bluish pus.

psittacosis. Pneumonia due to Chlamydia carried by birds of the parrot family; a kind of ►*ornithosis*.

psoas. A large muscle attached to the front of the lumbar vertebrae and passing in front of the hip-joint to the femur. It flexes the hip-joint, i.e. draws the thigh forwards and upwards.

psoriasis. A common disorder of the outer layer of the skin. The typical appearance is of thickened red blotches with a scaly surface, most often on the scalp, back, and arms. Fortunately the face is hardly ever affected, even when the blemishes are very widespread. In most cases the blemishes are the only symptom. Itching is unusual, and the general health is affected only in rare cases where the disease spreads rapidly and becomes dangerous unless treated. What distresses the patient is the disfigurement and the feeling – associated with any obvious skin disease – that he is somehow 'unclean'. In the past this feeling was wholly justified, because psoriasis was confused with leprosy and syphilis, both considered marks of divine disapproval.

Contagion plays no part in this disease. Only people with a hereditary predisposition ever suffer from it. Probably 2 per cent of people have psoriasis at some time in their lives; the true figure may be much higher because not every sufferer has it badly enough or for long enough to get medical advice. An actual attack can be precipitated by injury, acute illness, or, it seems, by emotional upsets.

Skin is adapted to wear and tear by continuous replacement of its surface. The tough protective outer layer consists of dead, flattened cells like scales. As these are shed the next layer of cells is adapted to take their place on the surface, to be replaced by fresh living cells from still deeper in the skin. New cells are formed in the deeper layer as fast as dead cells are shed from the surface, and the thickness of the skin remains constant. In psoriatic skin the whole process is accelerated; new cells are formed more quickly than dead cells are being shed, and the living undercoat of the skin becomes too thick. Various abnormalities of microscopical structure and tissue chemistry have been described, but whether they are causes or effects of the visible changes is not known. The primary defect may be in the capillary blood vessels of the skin, which are abnormally tortuous and dilated in predisposed people whether or not psoriasis has developed.

Psoriasis may be accompanied by a peculiar form of arthritis resembling but distinct from rheumatoid arthritis.

Even without treatment psoriasis tends to come and go. With treatment it can nearly always be cleared up, at least for a time. But the predisposition remains, and more often than not the trouble returns and has to be treated again and again. The simplest remedy is sunlight or artificial ultraviolet radiation, and it improves all but a few psoriatics who cannot tolerate it and are made worse. Coal tar acts by sensitizing the skin to light. Corticosteroid ointments are still widely used, though with some caution to avoid side-effects. *Dithranol* has a similar effect to coal tar but is much more powerful. *Calcipotriol*, which is related to vitamin D, is a promising newcomer. More drastic methods, needing close supervision by specialists, include *PUVA* (a combination of ultraviolet radiation with a sensitizing drug *methoxsalen*), and certain highly active derivatives of vitamin A. *Cyclosporin* and *methotrexin* suppress immune reactions and are used only with severe psoriasis.

psychiatry. Study and treatment of mental and emotional disorders; it is related to *psychology* as surgery to anatomy. (For a general discussion and references to particular disorders, ►*mental deficiency*; *mental illness*.)

psychoanalysis. A method of investigating and at the same time treating neuroses (►*anxiety*) evolved by ►*Freud* and modified by some of his followers, notably Jung and Adler. Nobody doubts that there is much mental activity of which we are unaware most of the time but which comes to the surface in dreams and, Freud argued, in slips of the tongue. Conflict within this *unconscious* could lead to neurosis, and psychoanalysis aims first to find out the nature of the conflict, which the patient resolves when he can recognize and understand it. Initially Freud thought this could be achieved by hypnosis, but he gave this method up in favour of simply letting the patient talk about his problem with only a little unobtrusive guidance from the analyst. The main cause of schism was Freud's doctrine that the developing sex instinct was of primary importance as a source of inner conflict. His disciple *Adler* thought that a stronger motive was the need to be as good as the next man. Adler also thought that free will played a greater part than Freud would allow. A third school was founded by *Jung*, who added the words introvert and extrovert to the language, and who propounded the esoteric notion of a collective unconscious.

Today psychoanalysis tends towards a less doctrinaire technique, concentrating on the patient's particular worries rather than his whole past life, with the analyst offering more positive guidance; ►*psychotherapy*.

psychology. Study of the mind – of perception, thought, emotion, learning, behaviour. No simple definition is possible, because not all psychologists agree about what, precisely, they are studying. It is perhaps best to leave the word *mind* out, because it is itself such a vague concept. Modern psychology is mainly concerned with behaviour and the factors that determine it. *Behavioural psychology* is in one sense the part of psychology that deals with responses that can be observed and objectively recorded, but in another sense it is the whole of scientific psychology, because science is a matter of observations and the conclusions that can be logically drawn from them. Psychology approached from this direction claims ➤*Pavlov* rather than ➤*Freud* as its patron, and is a part of general physiology. *Experimental psychology* is of necessity based largely on behavioural studies, because the Freudian and other analytical schools of thought are concerned with abstract concepts that are not open to subjective experiment.

Psychiatry is a part of medical practice, the speciality that is concerned with mental abnormality exactly as cardiology is concerned with the heart. *Clinical psychology* is not quite the same thing as psychiatry. A clinical psychologist usually works with psychiatrists, but does not necessarily hold a medical qualification. He may be involved in psychiatric research, in specialized forms of diagnosis such as testing intelligence, or in treatment such as behavioural therapy or analysis (which is diagnosis and treatment combined).

psychoneurosis = ➤*neurosis*.

psychopath. A term that embraces anyone whose behaviour is unacceptable to the society in which he lives; a psychopath might be defined as someone with a defective conscience – leaving conscience still to be defined.

The Mental Health Act of 1959 defines *psychopathic disorder* as 'a persistent disorder or disability of mind (whether or not including subnormality of intelligence) which results in abnor-mally aggressive or seriously irresponsible conduct on the part of the patient, and requires or is susceptible to medical treatment'.

Psychopaths include road-hogs, moral delinquents, and violent criminals. The common factor is lack of regard for others, of a social sense. They may require, but are not always susceptible to, medical treatment. Their trouble (or rather the trouble that they give to society) is said to arise from emotional isolation in childhood, a lack of warmth or affection. Better training in parenthood would be a hopeful prophylactic. But in some cases there may also be a constitutional defect. A significant number of habitual criminals have abnormal sex chromosomes (an additional X chromosome), and some show a characteristic anomaly in the electroencephalogram.

psychosis. Severe mental disorder involving loss of touch with reality; insanity as ordinarily understood. ➤*mental illness*.

psychosomatic disease. Any illness in which disturbance of the mind causes physical changes in the body.

Emotion is expressed in the conscious mind, and also at a completely unconscious level of the brain where it stimulates reflex action in the sympathetic and parasympathetic nerves, which are distributed throughout the body and regulate functions such as rate of blood-flow and digestion. Emotion also affects the activity of the ➤*pituitary* gland, which in turn regulates several other glands.

Few if any physical diseases are due entirely to emotional upset; what emotion does is to exaggerate the effects of physical causes. Individual cases of a disease differ widely in the relative importance of physical and emotional causes.

For example, *asthma* is a narrowing of the air-passages in the lungs. Emotion may cause reflex spasm of the muscle fibres in the walls of these passages and so precipitate an attack of asthma – but it can do so only in someone who is liable to asthma because of a physical anomaly. There is an emotional element in asthma, absent in some cases, important in others; but it is combined with allergy and other physical elements.

Diseases in which emotion can play a major part include various disorders of the skin, where blood vessels and sweat glands can both be affected; digestive disorders including overeating, duodenal ulcer, colitis with chronic diarrhoea; migraine; high blood pressure and perhaps other disorders of the heart and circulation. For many experts (if there can be experts in such an ill-defined branch of medicine) even this short list is too long; for others the list should be expanded to include dozens of diseases that might appear to have purely physical causes.

If conditions ascribed to ➤*stress* are included, then psychosomatic diseases are a very large group. It is a commonplace that tuberculosis and other infections can light up under emotional strain. After severe injuries, the patient's anxiety contributes to the danger. It has been suggested that in these and similar situations emotional stress overworks the adrenal glands and lowers resistance, with serious, even lethal physical effects.

psychosurgery. Treatment of mental disorder by operating on the brain, introduced in 1935 by the Portuguese neurosurgeon Egas Moniz (1874–1955). Moniz treated severe disorders such as suicidal depression by *prefrontal leukotomy*, which disconnected the brain cells at the very front of the brain, the area suppos-edly concerned with intellect and personality. He recorded many successes in otherwise hopeless cases, and received a Nobel Prize in 1949. But the operation had serious drawbacks. The patients, while relieved of their distress, often ceased to care about anything, and some developed epilepsy. The original operation has been superseded by more precise and less destructive procedures with few adverse effects. Even so, psychosurgery remains controversial, for although it often works well it lacks rational basis, and its effects are irreversible. Some psychiatrists do not believe that there is any place for it, but others regard it as valuable when other treatment fails.

psychotherapy. Treatment of mental disorders, especially by teaching as opposed to drugs or physical interference. Examples of large-scale psychotherapy are ➤*behaviour therapy* and ➤*psychoanalysis*. But nearly all forms of treatment include an element of psychotherapy. A physician making brief notes of a patient's symptoms is establishing the facts from which he will infer a diagnosis, but at the same time he is allowing the patient to unload some of his worries. And even the most useless prescription (➤*placebo*) conveys a measure of confidence.

ptomaine. A product of decomposition of protein by bacteria, i.e. of putrefaction. Ptomaines are poisonous and were once thought to be a main cause of ➤*food poisoning*. In fact it is the bacteria, not the ptomaines, that cause the trouble.

ptosis. Sagging or drooping of an organ, especially of the upper eyelid from weakness of its muscle.

ptyalin. An enzyme in saliva, promoting the conversion of starch to sugar.

puberty. Onset of sexual maturity or fertility, brought about by stimulation of the gonads (ovaries or testicles) by hormones from the pituitary gland. The gonads begin to form fertile ova or sperms, and also to secrete hormones that promote adult sexual characters (body hair, female breasts, male voice etc.). The time of puberty is established in girls by the first menstrual period, following the first ovulation; in boys there is no such precise moment.

For a year or two after puberty the whole body seems to be adjusting itself to the altered system of hormones – not surprisingly, since the whole body chemistry is affected to some extent. The difficulties of puberty are mainly emotional. Physical readjustment is seldom a problem, except that a sudden burst of activity in the grease glands of the skin causes *acne* at precisely the time of life when a disfiguring skin complaint is hardest to bear.

The age of puberty varies widely among perfectly normal children; and even when it is several years away from the average there is generally no abnormality. Delayed puberty may sometimes be due to a relative deficiency of pituitary hormones; but the causes of puberty – normal or abnormal – are not really known.

It is not true that puberty occurs at a younger age in the tropics or in dark-skinned people. It is, however, true that the average age of puberty in Western Europe has decreased considerably in the past century – from over 15 to about 13 in girls, and a year or two later in boys. The reason is not known. It may simply be that the average child of a century ago was underfed and therefore underdeveloped; this would also explain why the average English boy now grows an inch or two taller than the average boy of 100 years ago.

pubis. A bone forming part of the ➤*pelvis*.

puerperal. Related to childbirth; affecting a woman who has recently given birth.

Puerperal fever (puerperal pyrexia) can mean any high temperature following childbirth, but is generally taken to mean infection of the birth-passage as a result of childbirth.

No child is born without some injury to the mother. The soft linings of the uterus and vagina are at least bruised by the head and shoulders of the child, and the placenta, having been firmly stuck to the inside of the uterus, leaves a raw area when it is expelled. If labour is difficult, more extensive injury is likely; but these tissues heal quickly, and as a rule are repaired within a couple of weeks. But until healing is complete the birth-passage is vulnerable to infection. What was an ideal incubator for the baby becomes an ideal incubator for bacteria. Streptococci cause some of the worst cases, but in such an environment most kinds of bacteria can set up rapidly spreading and dangerous infection.

Until the mid 19th century death from puerperal fever was appallingly common, and the growth of hospitals was making matters worse because infection was carried from patient to patient. Estimates run as high as one death among every 4 nursing mothers in some hospitals. ➤*Semmelweis* in Vienna wrote that until he insisted on routine disinfection of the attendants' hands, patients whose labour was prolonged nearly all died of puerperal fever. But by that one simple precaution, Semmelweis brought the mortality below one in 100. By the turn of the century the figure had fallen to one or two per thousand, where it remained until effective drugs were found – sulphonamides in 1935, penicillin in 1941. In recent years, mortality from puerperal fever has fallen almost to vanishing point: it has been of the order of one in 100,000 births in England.

In the United Kingdom and some other countries puerperal pyrexia (high temperature after childbirth, regardless of cause) is a ➤*notifiable disease*.

pulmonary. 1. Of the lung (e.g. pulmonary tuberculosis). **2.** Of the pulmonary arteries (e.g. pulmonary embolism, stenosis).

Pulmonary artery. The right ventricle of the heart pumps blood from the veins into the right and left pulmonary arteries, to be circulated through the lungs and replenished with oxygen. Because these vessels carry dark blood, depleted of oxygen, unlike the bright red oxygenated blood of other arteries, Galen called them the *venous arteries*.

Pulmonary embolism. A clot of blood in a vein has a clear passage through the right side of the heart to the pulmonary arteries, if it is dislodged. The original site of such a clot is usually a vein of the pelvis or lower limb. A clot large enough to rest at the division of the pulmonary trunk can be rapidly fatal unless it is surgically removed within a few minutes; this is among the most urgent of all surgical operations. Pulmonary embolism has never been a common disaster. It used sometimes to follow surgical operations, but with the practice of getting patients out of bed as soon as possible, so that blood does not stagnate in the veins, it is now very rare.

Pulmonary oedema. The pulmonary veins open into the left side of the heart. With left-sided ➤*heart failure* the pulmon-

ary veins become congested with blood that a healthy heart would pump away; the pressure in them rises, and fluid is forced out of the capillaries into the lungs, which become waterlogged (➤*oedema*). Any other cause of oedema can affect the lungs, but pulmonary oedema is typically due to heart failure.

Pulmonary stenosis. Abnormally narrow pulmonary artery. ➤*heart* (4).

Pulmonary veins. Two large veins leave each lung and enter the left atrium of the heart. These veins carry arterial (oxygenated) blood; Galen called them the *arterial veins*.

pulmonic. Pulmonary (US more than UK).

pulse. Pressure-wave in an artery, corresponding with the heart beat. Arteries are elastic and therefore expand with each wave; it is this rhythmic expansion that is felt. The main beat is followed by a rebound wave, which is easily recorded mechanically but scarcely possible to feel.

The pulse in an artery surrounded by soft tissues (muscle, fat) can seldom be detected, but a pulse can be felt wherever an artery can be lightly compressed against a bone. These are the pressure points, familiar to first-aiders, where arteries can be compressed to stem heavy bleeding.

In most people the resting pulse rate is between 60 and 70 beats per minute, but in individual cases rates as slow as 50 or as fast as 100 may be normal. Changes in pulse rate are much more significant than the precise rate at a given moment. For instance, when a patient is first seen after an injury a pulse rate of 90 means very little, but an increase from 80 to 90 may be the only clue to internal bleeding. The force of the pulse is even more significant

than the rate as an index of the state of the circulation.
➤*arrhythmia.*

pupil. Circular hole in the centre of the iris, by which light reaches the back of the eye. The iris consists largely of muscle fibres. They are controlled by *sympathetic* nerves, which cause the pupil to enlarge, and *parasympathetic* nerves, which cause it to contract. The pupil is reflexly contracted in bright light and also when the eye is focused on close objects. Excitement and fear increase the flow of adrenaline into the bloodstream, which dilates the pupils in the same way as stimulation of the sympathetic nerves. Drugs such as belladonna dilate the pupils by abolishing the action of the parasympathetic nerves, leaving the sympathetic unopposed.

purgative; purge. Any drug given to induce opening of the bowels (defecation).

The terms aperient, laxative, purgative, and cathartic have been used in ascending order of severity, but they are not very useful because the classification of a particular drug may depend on the dose as much as the nature of the drug. Purges are better classified by the way in which they act.

Some of the most effective purges act solely by their bulk. The intestine will usually empty itself regularly if its muscles have something to grip. A good diet ought to contain enough undigested residue (roughage), mainly vegetable fibres, to provide this. A diet of milk and eggs is constipating because it is wholly digested. Bulk purges include methylcellulose and agar-agar, and also salts such as magnesium sulphate, which draw an excess of water into the large intestine by *osmosis*.

Indigestible oily fluids such as liquid paraffin act partly by their bulk but mainly by simple lubrication. However, for lubricating the stools emulsifying agents such as dioctyl are less troublesome. Purgative enemas and suppositories (e.g. glycerine) act partly as lubricants and partly by increasing bulk as glycerine attracts water into the rectum.

Most other purges stimulate the intestine by irritating its lining. The vegetable laxatives such as senna, cascara, and rhubarb all contain irritant compounds of anthracene. Jalap and colocynth contain more violent irritants; they act partly by direct stimulation and partly by causing inflammation with exudation of fluid from the lining of the intestine. They are unpleasant and seldom used. Castor oil is itself bland, but the acid of the stomach decomposes the oil and releases the irritant ricinoleic acid. All irritant purges cause griping if the dose is at all excessive, and the right dose for an individual has often to be guessed. The synthetic irritant bisacodyl is less troublesome in this respect than the older drugs.

In general, purgatives of any type are mainly for occasional and not regular use. If one seems to be needed, the cause should be identified before choosing a remedy; in other words, ➤*constipation* calls for a professional opinion.

purpura. Spontaneous bruising of the skin. ➤*bleeding disorders.*

purulent. Containing pus.

pus. A by-product of ➤*inflammation*, especially local inflammation due to certain bacteria. It is commonly a thick yellow fluid, but may be watery or almost solid. The physical properties – consistency, colour, smell – depend on the kinds of bacteria.

During inflammation, fluid and white blood cells leak from the blood vessels. These are the main components of pus. To them are added living and dead bacteria and the remnants of tissue damaged by infection.

pustule. Small abscess in the surface layer of the skin; a small pus-blister.

Malignant pustule = ➤*anthrax* of the skin.

putrefaction. Decomposition of animal or vegetable remains by bacteria.

pyaemia. Spread of bacterial infection by the blood-stream, usually from an abscess, with the formation of new abscesses.

pyelitis (pyelonephritis). Inflammation of the renal pelvis, i.e. of the receptacle at the outlet of the ➤*kidney*. The pelvis is a hollow cone into which urine formed in the kidney flows. From the apex of the cone a slender pipe, the *ureter*, conveys the urine to the *bladder*.

Pyelitis is due to bacterial infection, often by bacteria which occur in great profusion in the healthy large intestine and cause trouble only if they stray from their natural habitat. It is possible for them to be carried straight to the renal pelvis in the blood, but usually the infection spreads up the ureter from the bladder. The female bladder with its short outlet (*urethra*) is not nearly as well protected from extraneous contamination as the male bladder, and pyelitis is much commoner in women than in men.

Stagnant urine is very liable to infection. Any impediment to the flow of urine predisposes to pyelitis, which often complicates pregnancy, stone in the kidney or bladder, enlargement of the prostate gland, and narrowing of the ureter or urethra. (A stone may be the result of infection.)

A valve where the ureter enters the bladder normally prevents urine from flowing in the wrong direction when the bladder is full, and is a fairly effective barrier against the spread of infection in the bladder (cystitis) to the ureters and pelvis. In children with pyelitis this valve is often defective. Infection might well injure the valve, but it seems likelier that the defective valve precedes the infection. Operations for repairing these valves have been devised.

Acute pyelitis need not cause much in the way of symptoms. In children particularly it can be a very vague illness, recognized only when the urine is found to harbour large numbers of bacteria. More often, however, there is a high temperature with pain over the affected kidney(s) or in the lower part of the abdomen (right-sided pyelitis can mimic appendicitis). The accompanying cystitis causes frequent and painful passage of urine.

Chronic pyelitis is the same disease continuing for months or years, with attacks of acute pyelitis at intervals and few if any symptoms between attacks. It accounts for a good deal of vague ill health, especially in middle-aged women.

Pyelonephritis (inflammation of renal pelvis *and* kidney) describes the condition better than the older term, *pyelitis*, because the kidney substance is also affected to a greater or lesser extent. The distinction is worth making because it draws attention to the potential danger of the disease. Pyelitis pure and simple would be unpleasant but fairly harmless, and in the past few doctors took it very seriously. It is now clear that if chronic pyelonephritis is not treated the kidneys may gradually approach a kind of severe glomerulonephritis, with a danger of kidney failure (►*kidneys* (5)). The usual treatment is with trimethoprim or amoxycillin. Predisposing factors such as obstruction to the flow of urine may need surgical correction.

pyelography. X-ray examination of the kidneys (1) by injecting into a vein a substance opaque to X-rays that is concentrated by the kidneys and passed into the urine (intravenous pyelography), or (2) by injecting a similar substance into the ureters towards the kidneys by way of a cystoscope passed into the bladder (retrograde pyelography). Method (1) works only if the kidney is functioning and able to concentrate the substance. It is therefore a test of function as well as of structural defects. Method (2) shows the outlet of the kidney regardless of function.

pyelonephritis ►*pyelitis*.

pyknolepsy. An uncommon form of epilepsy in childhood, with repetitive fleeting loss of consciousness. The distinction from *petit mal* is not clear.

pyloric stenosis. Narrowing of the outlet from the stomach. In adults this may be due to scarring from a duodenal ulcer, but the term is usually reserved for a disorder of infancy, congenital hypertrophic pyloric stenosis. This condition afflicts boys more than girls (3 or 4:1), and is said to be commonest in first-born children. The condition is simply overdevelopment of the muscle in the wall of the pylorus. It is a genetic disorder, but nothing more is known of the cause.

A few weeks after birth the baby begins to vomit. The vomiting, described as 'projectile', is quite different from the spilling-over of feeds that most babies show from time to time: the milk is really ejected. The baby loses weight and dies if not treated. The standard treatment is Ramstedt's operation, by which the constricting muscle fibres are split longitudinally. This operation is safe and completely effective.

Some babies appear to recover without operation if given drugs which act like atropine to suppress stimulation of the stomach muscle by the vagus nerves. Many surgeons would insist that these are not true cases of pyloric stenosis. It is difficult to argue the point without arguing in a circle, but since pyloric stenosis is a definite structural fault it may well be that every true case needs operation.

pylorus. Outlet from the stomach; narrow muscular tube joining the stomach to the beginning of the intestine (duodenum).

pyo-. Prefix = 'pus'.

pyorrhoea. 1. Any discharge of pus. **2.** *Pyorrhoea alveolaris*, infection of the gums. ►*gingiva; teeth*.

pyrexia = ►*fever*.

pyridoxine = ►*vitamin B₆*.

PZI. Protamine-zinc insulin, a compound of insulin with a more delayed action than ordinary insulin. It enables some diabetics to manage with one injection instead of two or three in a day.

Q

Q-fever. An infectious disease very like a virus pneumonia, due to a similar microbe (*Rickettsia*) to that of typhus. It is carried by sheep and other livestock, which themselves suffer no ill effects. Like other rickettsial diseases, Q-fever responds well to treatment with antibiotics.

quadriceps (quadriceps femoris). The large (four-headed) muscle of the front of the thigh: its 4 heads are *vastus lateralis*, *vastus intermedius*, and *vastus medialis*, all arising from the shaft of the femur, and *rectus femoris*, arising from the pelvis above the hip-joint. The whole mass is attached to the front of the tibia by a broad tendon. A bone set in this tendon, the knee-cap (*patella*), acts to some extent as a fulcrum, but the muscle works well after loss of the patella.

The muscle serves to extend or straighten the knee, and is perhaps the most important of the various supports of the knee joint. A healthy quadriceps is essential to recovery from injuries of the knee.

The kind of sudden jerk that in a younger person might fracture the patella sometimes tears the quadriceps in middle-aged or elderly people.

quarantine. Originally an attempt to prevent plague from spreading: at Mediterranean seaports (Ragusa, Rhodes, Venice) incoming ships were isolated, and their crews forbidden to disembark, for 40 days. The system started in the 14th century and had been adopted in most European ports by the 16th. There was no sort of agreement between countries until the advent of cholera in the 19th century brought governments together. Even then, discussions lasted from 1851 till 1903, when the first international regulations were drawn up. By that time it was clear that control was needed only when there was good reason to suspect cholera or plague on board. Later, yellow fever, smallpox, and louse-borne relapsing fever and typhus were added to the list of diseases subject to international regulations

Quarantine is now seldom rigidly enforced, and the period of 40 days has been shortened to a time corresponding with the known incubation period of each disease. It is nearly always safe to keep people who have been in contact with infection under medical supervision, without strict isolation unless symptoms develop; but with several types of infection contacts may have to be kept away from places such as schools, cinemas, and public transport.

quartan fever. ➤*Malaria*, with a bout of fever every 4th day by the old notation (1st, 4th, 7th . . .) or every 3rd day as one would now say.

quinidine. An isomer of quinine used to curb the response of heart muscle to overstimulation with certain irregularities of the heart beat (➤*arrhythmia*).

quinine. An alkaloid in ➤*cinchona* bark, for many years the only remedy for malaria. It cures falciparum (subtertian) malaria, and suppresses the other kinds, but without preventing recurrences. For three centuries quinine was regarded primarily as a febrifuge, for dispelling fever (high body temperature) in general, regardless of the kind of fever. This was reasonable at a time when the causes of fever were still unknown, but well into the 20th century quinine was still being used 'to bring down the temperature' with any febrile illness, though it should have been obvious that its only real value was for treating malaria.

From the mid 20th century various synthetic drugs with fewer side-effects, or a wider range of action, almost made quinine obsolete; but in some areas, especially in Africa, strains of malaria parasite that resist these have appeared, and quinine has regained favour.

Like quinidine, quinine slows the response of muscle to stimulation, which explains its value in preventing nocturnal cramp.

quinsy. Abscess round the tonsil; an occasional complication of a sore throat. ►*pharynx* (1).

R

rabbit fever = ➤*tularaemia.*

rabies (hydrophobia). A virus infection,
unusual in its severity and in the number
of different kinds of animal that it can
affect. Human rabies is fortunately rare
even in countries where the virus is
common among wild animals. When it
does occur it is nearly always the result
of a bite from an infected dog. The virus
enters the skin and slowly travels along
nerves to the spinal cord and brain. The
incubation period between infection and
first symptoms lasts between 10 days and
several months. The actual illness, with
fever, delirium, muscle spasms, and
paralysis, is fatal within a few days. The
patient may be unable to drink because
of painful spasm of the throat muscles:
hence the alternative name *hydrophobia.*

The first step in treating rabies is
thorough cleansing of any bite from a
suspect animal. Pasteur, in 1885, produced an effective vaccine, of which
various modifications are still used.
Though given after the patient has been
infected, the vaccine usually has time to
work before symptoms develop, because
of the long incubation period. Until very
recent times, there was no chance of recovery from established rabies, but with
modern life-support therapy there have
been cures.

Prophylactic vaccination can be used
to protect people whose work may
expose them to rabies although there
may be unpleasant side-effects.

rachis. Spine; backbone. (The word is
seldom used except as an element of compound words such as the following.)

rachischisis. A congenital defect of the
backbone; = ➤*spina bifida.*

rachitis = ➤*rickets.* Literally, rachitis
means inflammation of the backbone
(*spondylitis*), which rickets is not. The
word appeared in one of the first scientific accounts of the disease, by Francis
Glisson (1650), who adopted it as a
Latin name for 'the disease of children
commonly known as the rickets'. A few
years later, John Aubrey insisted that the
disease was named after a Dr Ricketts of
Newbury, who specialized in its treatment, adding 'and now 'tis good sport to
see how they vex their Lexicons, and
fetch from it the Greek *rachis,* the backbone' (*Aubrey's Brief Lives,* ed. O. L.
Dick, Secker & Warburg, 1960, p. xlvi).
Or the word may be much older and related to 'wrick' (twist, sprain).

radial. Of the radius, the outer of the
two bones of the forearm.
Radial artery. In front of the elbow
the brachial artery divides into two
branches, *radial* and *ulnar.* The radial
artery runs down the forearm to the
thumb side of the wrist, where it can
easily be felt for examining the pulse. It
curls round the base of the thumb, and
rejoins the ulnar artery in the palm.
Radial nerve. A branch of the brachial
plexus, supplying branches to the
muscles and skin of the back of the
upper limb. It winds round the back of
the shaft of the humerus, where it is
liable to injury if the bone is broken.

radiation sickness. All living creatures receive constant radiation from outer

space (cosmic radiation) and radioactive deposits in the soil, but the dose is too small to have any obvious effect. It is possible, however, that natural radiation may play a part in evolution by causing mutation (>*genetics* (4)).

With the discovery of X-rays in 1895 and radium in 1898 two potentially dangerous sources of ionizing rays were uncovered, and the new uses of atomic energy in war and peace have added greatly to the dangers.

All forms of life are destroyed by large enough doses of radiation. The main effect is on cell division, the process by which tissues reproduce themselves or grow. Therefore a growing child is more susceptible than an adult, and an embryo even more than a child. The most susceptible parts of the body are those that grow or replace themselves most rapidly; blood-forming tissues and sex glands, followed by lining membranes and skin. The constantly multiplying cells of a cancer are more susceptible than healthy tissue – hence the treatment of cancer with radium, X-rays etc.

People far enough from an atomic explosion or a major accident in a nuclear reactor to escape immediate death from burning can still get a rapidly lethal dose of radiation. The brain is among the least susceptible organs; if the dose is enough to damage brain cells the victim dies within a few hours. People a little further from the disaster die in a few days from damage to the lining of the intestine, and those in the next zone die in a few weeks from failure of the blood-forming tissues. Some in this third group may be saved by a graft of healthy bone marrow.

A far commoner hazard is lasting damage to a single tissue. This can happen not only to the remoter victims

of atomic explosions, but to people overexposed to X-rays or radioactive matter used in medicine and industry. Irradiation of the sex glands causes sterility; but a rather smaller dose may disturb the sex cells without destroying them and so cause deformity in the next generation. Disturbance of other tissues can make them liable to cancer, especially of the skin and of the blood cells (leukaemia). Before suitable precautions were enforced many X-ray workers developed cancer of the skin.

Whether radiation arrests or causes cancer depends on whether the dose is enough to destroy or merely disturb the parts of a cell concerned in growth. Some of the drugs for treating cancer have a similar effect.

radioactive isotopes >*isotope*.

radiography. Examination by X-rays.

radiology. Study of radiation, especially its medical uses for diagnosis and treatment of disease >*X-rays*.

radiotherapy. Treatment of disease with ionizing radiation from radioactive substances or X-rays. The earliest form of radiotherapy was the treatment of cancer with radium, which has given place to substances such as radioactive cobalt (^{60}Co) that are easier to get and to handle. An alternative is exposure of the cancer to high-voltage X-rays. Useful as these measures are, they have the disadvantage that sufficient radiation to suppress a cancer often has ill effects on the body as a whole; but some surface cancers are cured by radiotherapy without upsetting the patient at all.

Other uses of radiotherapy include the treatment of *polycythaemia vera*, an abnormal proliferation of red blood cells, with radioactive phosphorus (^{32}P), and that of toxic *goitre* with radioactive iodine (^{131}I). Ankylosing ►*spondylitis* can be treated with X-rays. Skin diseases characterized by proliferation of the surface layer of the skin used often to be treated with small doses of X-rays, but this technique is now thought too drastic for all but a few cases.

radium. Radioactive element, discovered by Marie and Pierre Curie in 1898; used for destroying cancer cells near the surface of the body.

radius. One of the two bones of the forearm; the other is the ulna.

With the arm down and the palm of the hand facing forwards the two bones are parallel, the radius on the outer side. At the elbow the ulna takes most of the strain, but at the wrist the strain falls on the radius. The ulna is the longer of the two because it extends beyond the elbow joint to form the *olecranon*, the point of the elbow. The two bones form joints with each other at each end.

At the upper joint the head of the radius turns in a notch on the side of the ulna. At the lower joint the arrangement is reversed: a notch at the lower end of the radius fits the rounded lower end of the ulna. Rotation of the forearm is a movement of the radius around the ulna. In *supination* the bones are parallel, the palm faces forwards or upwards. In *pronation* the bones are crossed; the head of the radius is still in its notch at the outer side of the ulna, but the lower end has rolled over the ulna to lie on its inner side, and the palm faces backwards or downwards.

Because supination brings the powerful biceps muscle into play it is a stronger movement than pronation. If the right hand is turned clockwise as in driving a screw the biceps can be felt to contract.

1. INJURIES

It is difficult to break one bone of the forearm without disturbing the other. Often both are fractured. With fracture of the radius alone the ulna is likely to be dislocated at the wrist and with fracture of the ulna the radius may be dislocated at the elbow. Such injuries are unstable and difficult to manipulate. They often need surgical operation and internal fixation (►*fracture*).

The commonest fracture of the forearm is ►*Colles' fracture*, in which the lower end of the radius is displaced backwards by a fall on the palm of the hand. In Smith's fracture the broken end is displaced forwards; this is also called chauffeur's fracture because it can be caused by a blow on the back of the wrist from a starting handle.

With all these injuries, unless the alignment of the bones is restored rotation of the forearm is disturbed. This can be a serious disability.

Ramazzini, Bernardino (1633–1714). Italian physician; professor of medicine at Modena, Padua, and finally Venice. Famous in his own time as an authority on epidemics, he is now remembered mainly for the first systematic account of the relation between diseases and trades (►*occupational disease*).

rat. Rats live as close to man as they can safely get, and share several of his nastier diseases. These include a common type of bacterial food poisoning, and Weil's disease, rat-bite fever, flea-borne typhus, flea-borne relapsing fever, and plague.

rat-bite fever. Fever with swollen lymph

nodes, from infection either with the spiral bacterium *Spirillum minus* or the mould *Streptobacillus moniliformis*, both of which are common in rats. Human infections are rare only because rat-bites are rare. Neither form is very dangerous. Both respond to penicillin.

rauwolfia. A plant of which the root is an ancient Indian remedy for insomnia and mental disturbance, first introduced to Western medicine in 1953. Its active principle, *reserpine*, was not a very good tranquillizer, but found a place in the treatment of high blood pressure.

Raynaud's disease. (M. Raynaud, 1834–81, French physician.) A disorder of small arteries, especially in the hands and feet, with sudden attacks of pallor and coldness of the fingers or toes, lasting from a few minutes to an hour or more. The attacks are due to reduction of the flow of blood by spasm of the arteries.

Contraction of arteries near the surface of the body is a natural response to cold. By restricting the flow of blood through the skin it prevents loss of heat. These arteries also contract when blood is diverted to the muscles to prepare for physical exertion, e.g. in response to fear or anger. In people with Raynaud's disease the natural response of the small arteries is grossly exaggerated. Attacks may be brought on by slight cold, emotion or stimuli such as vibration. Sometimes Raynaud's disease is a symptom of a disorder of the nerves or endocrine glands; in these cases it clears up when the primary disorder is treated. But more often the defect seems to be in the arteries themselves. Drugs that dilate blood vessels may help, and in severe cases cutting the sympathetic nerves to the affected limb, to prevent reflex contraction of the arteries, alleviates the symptoms.

The most effective treatment is to identify the factors that precipitate attacks and avoid them.

receptor. 1. Nerve-ending adapted to a particular kind of sensation.

2. Chemical component of a living cell (a part of a much larger molecule), with which a foreign substance combines to alter the functioning of the cell. The idea of chemical receptors was first suggested by Ehrlich to explain the interaction of antigens and antibodies to neutralize the effects of bacteria in the body (>*immunity*), but it can be extended to explain the effects of many hormones and drugs.

recessive >*genetics* (2).

rectum. The last few inches of the large >*intestine*, terminating in the anal canal.

The rectum is likely to be involved in diseases of the large intestine such as dysentery or ulcerative colitis. It is the commonest site of cancer in the intestine. The early symptoms – passage of blood or mucus, or a change in the usual bowel habit such as unaccustomed constipation or diarrhoea – often bring the patient to a surgeon in time for this type of cancer to be cured.

Haemorrhoids (piles) are swollen veins at the junction of the rectum with the anal canal.

rectus. Straight (muscle), e.g. *rectus abdominis*, a strap-like muscle at each side of the mid-line at the front of the abdomen; *rectus femoris*, a vertical muscle at the front of the thigh, forming part of the quadriceps muscle.

reduction. Restoration of the natural position of a displaced organ, e.g. setting a broken bone, or replacing an organ that has protruded into a hernia.

referred pain. Pain felt in a different part of the body from the site of injury. A blow on the inner side of the elbow causes pain in the little finger, which has not been touched. This is because the pain is neither in the finger nor the elbow; it is awareness that a nervous impulse has reached the brain by a particular pathway. In this case the pathway is by certain fibres of the ulnar nerve, which run from the little finger up the inner side of the arm and ultimately via the spinal cord to the brain. The brain 'knows' only that it has received a signal from somewhere on the pathway, and it always interprets the signal as an insult to the little finger. It would still do so if the finger had been amputated.

Some pathways from different organs converge in the spinal cord and brain. Many of the internal organs first appear in one part of the embryo and later migrate to another part, trailing their original nerves with them. Pain signals in these migrant nerves are interpreted as coming from the original site of the organ. For instance, the diaphragm, separating the heart and lungs from the stomach and liver, first grows in the same part of the embryo as the shoulders. Irritation of the diaphragm by pleurisy, or inflammation of the liver, causes pain to be felt in the shoulder – it is 'referred' to the shoulder.

reflex (adj., or n. = reflex *action*). Involuntary response to a stimulus, determined by impulses in nerves. There are three components: the *receptor* reacting to the stimulus, the *effector* responding, and the *reflex arc*, the pathway of the nervous impulse. A familiar example is the *knee-jerk*. The quadriceps muscle of the thigh is slightly stretched by a tap with a rubber hammer on its tendon. The receptors are the muscle-spindles, sensory organs in the muscle which set off a nervous impulse in response to stretching. The impulse passes up the femoral nerve to the spinal cord. Here it is transmitted to motor nerve cells and down their fibres to the effector organ, the muscle itself, which contracts.

The knee-jerk is an instance of the general principle that muscles automatically resist any tendency to stretch them. This is how balance is maintained: any disturbance of position is resisted unless a movement is actually needed. Even voluntary movements include a reflex element. The will determines what movement is to be made, but the choice of which muscles are to contract, and the inhibition of the opposing muscles that have to be stretched in the process, are reflex.

Many reflexes, including the knee-jerk, are *inborn*. They have evolved just as ears and fingers and kidneys have evolved, and are part of everyone's hereditary constitution. Most bodily functions are controlled mainly by inborn reflexes. The effectors are either muscles or glands; receptors are more diverse. Dilatation of blood vessels in the skin and sweating are responses to heat; constriction of the vessels and shivering, to cold; deep breathing, to acidity of the blood; slowing of the heart beat, to increased blood pressure; passage of urine, to distension of the bladder; constriction of the pupils, to bright light; salivation, to eating. Some reflexes, such as breathing and passing urine, can be modified for a time by nerves under voluntary control, but in the end reflex action is stronger than will. Nobody can hold his breath or his water for ever. Reflex actions effected by ➤*sympathetic* or ➤*parasympathetic* nerves may be greatly modified by emotion; this is the basis of most ➤*psychosomatic* illness.

Only two nerve fibres are involved in the knee-jerk. Most reflex arcs are more complicated, several nerve cells intervening between receptor and effector; and a number of reflexes may combine to produce a single effect. A man keeps his balance by adjusting the tension of muscles in his trunk and legs, a reflex action determined by sensations from muscles, joints, eyes, and the balance organs of the ears. The transmission of the impulse is discussed under ➤*nervous system*.

Not all reflexes are inborn. *Conditioned* reflexes are either modifications of inborn reflexes or completely new automatic responses, developed as a result of the individual's experience. Such reflexes were first demonstrated by Pavlov at the end of the 19th century. By an inborn reflex a dog's mouth waters when it eats. But the sight of food also stimulates a flow of saliva, before eating begins. This, Pavlov argued, cannot be a predetermined inborn reflex, because the dog must learn to recognize food before the stimulus can work. Next, Pavlov taught a dog to associate the ringing of a bell with food. In time the bell alone, without food, made the dog's mouth water. This is still a pure reflex – there is no question of the dog's deliberately producing saliva – but it has to be learnt. Actions as varied as fainting at the sight of blood and stopping a car at a red traffic light may be reflexes of the same type: an involuntary response to a learned stimulus.

A different type of conditioned reflex is acquired by learning that some action has a particular consequence. A rat in a cage seems to move aimlessly, but learns to repeat a movement that releases food into the cage. Here there is no external stimulus as there is in the first type, unless hunger or merely enjoying food is

regarded as a stimulus. The response has no counterpart among inborn reflexes.

Conditioned reflexes do not override the principle that a reflex arc is invariable; they are new reflexes added to existing ones. Pavlov's bell did not replace food as a stimulus. The inborn reflex worked as before, and the bell was a new stimulus operating a new reflex. Indeed, the response differed slightly: saliva after the bell had not quite the same chemical composition as saliva when eating.

Inborn reflexes, then, are standard equipment which everyone inherits and transmits to his offspring. Conditioned reflexes are optional extras to be acquired by each generation in response to the environment. The extent to which learning is merely the acquisition of conditioned reflexes is still open to speculation.

refraction. Deflection of light at the interfaces of glass, water etc., which accounts for the action of lenses. In medical usage, refraction refers to the focusing mechanism of the eye, or to the testing of this mechanism before prescribing spectacles.

refractionist. A person who tests the refraction of the eye.

regime; regimen. In French, the word *régime* must do duty for both, and many writers make it do so in English. Since English has the two words it is worth preserving the distinction: *regime* in the political sense; *regimen* in the medical sense of a set of rules prescribed for treating illness or preserving health.

regional enteritis. Regional ileitis; Crohn's disease. ➤*enteritis*.

registrar. In British hospitals, a junior specialist, the first assistant to a consultant physician or surgeon.

Reiter's disease. A feverish illness, characterized by inflammation of the urethra, sore eyes, and painful joints resembling those of rheumatoid arthritis. The pattern of the illness strongly suggests an infection, and in the past cases of Reiter's disease have been ascribed to gonorrhoea, which can cause the same symptoms. But although from circumstantial evidence Reiter's disease appears to be a venereal infection this has not been proved, and no infecting organism or germ has been definitely identified. The current view is that this is essentially an unusual reaction to various kinds of infection, and that urethritis may be coincidental. It is also thought that Reiter's disease should be classified as a reactive arthritis.

relapsing fever. Intermittent fever caused by a spiral bacterium, *Borrelia*. One type is carried by lice, the other by ticks.

About a week after infection, the patient has a severe attack of fever, which completely subsides after a few days, to return a week or ten days later. There may be as many as 10 of these relapses if the infection is not treated. It is believed that several strains of bacteria infect the patient together, or that fresh strains evolve from those originally injected by the insect, and that the patient has to acquire immunity to each strain in turn before he finally shakes the disease off. Though very debilitating, relapsing fever is seldom fatal even without treatment, and the infection responds well to antibiotics.

Louse-borne relapsing fever (famine fever), like louse-borne typhus and plague, typically follows a breakdown of hygienic services, e.g. in wartime or after natural disasters. All three of these diseases are internationally ►*notifiable*.

Tick-borne relapsing fever is common in some tropical countries. The ticks live in crevices in the walls of mud huts. The disease can be controlled by spraying houses with insecticides.

relaxant. Drug used for relieving spasm of muscles, or for preventing muscles from contracting. ►*muscle relaxants*.

relaxation. Literally speaking, relaxation is the condition of muscles not actively contracting or tense, but in the present context it is taken in a wider sense that includes a tranquil state of mind.

Purposeless contraction or tension of muscles is a familiar sign of emotional stress such as frustration, anger, fear or even pleasant anticipation. As the tense muscles are not trying to move anything the opposing muscles must contract to balance them. Thus a boy showing off his biceps unconsciously tenses his triceps as well: otherwise the unopposed biceps would simply bend his elbow without showing a manly bulge. A real expert in any field of activity, be it music, sport or typing, illustrates the point: muscles not actively engaged are relaxed.

Emotional tension often shows itself in the muscles of the shoulder girdle, neck and jaw. It is self-defeating in that it is itself a kind of stress in a vicious circle, aggravating or even causing headache, backache and other symptoms.

Clenching one's teeth and fists does not dispel anger – but taking deep breaths and counting to ten (or more) proverbially does. Consciously relaxing muscular tension can relieve other effects of stress, including more remote symptoms such as increased pulse rate and raised blood pressure. Although it seems to be putting the cart before the horse, consciously relaxing muscles can evidently work backwards to relieve the unconscious disturbance that caused them to contract in the first place.

Sitting quietly and comfortably for fifteen minutes or so, letting the whole body relax one part at a time, may forestall or at least mitigate attacks of migraine, asthma and other troubles associated with stress – and persistent stress may aggravate almost any disorder.

Many kinds of therapy succeed largely through relaxation. They include methods as diverse as meditation, hypnosis, autogenic training, massage, icthyotherapy (watching exotic fish in an aquarium), soothing music and simple reassurance. (►*alternative medicine.*)

relaxin. A hormone that loosens the ligaments of the pelvis at the end of pregnancy and facilitates birth. It is known to be important in some animals, but whether relaxin plays any part in human labour is uncertain. The laxity of the baby's ligaments associated with congenital dislocation of the ►*hip* is possibly an effect of this hormone.

REM. Rapid eye movement; ►*sleep.*

remission. Temporary freedom from symptoms in the course of a disease.

renal. Of the kidney. The *renal arteries,* one for each kidney, are very large branches of the aorta; between them, they receive about a quarter of the output of the heart. Congenital anomalies of these arteries are occasionally troublesome. An abnormally narrow renal artery is a rare cause of high blood pressure; and an abnormally situated branch of the artery may pinch the ureter and impede the flow of urine from the kidney, a condition needing surgery.

Renal hypertension: high ►*blood pressure* caused by disease of the kidneys.

Renal rickets ►*rickets.*

renin. A hormone formed by the kidneys, concerned with the regulation of blood pressure. ►*circulation* (1).

rennin. An enzyme that clots the protein *casein* as the first step in the digestion of milk, found in the stomachs of most young mammals, including human babies.

repetitive strain injury. A recent addition to the list of occupational disorders: aching and weakness of muscles constantly involved in monotonous tasks such as working with the keyboard of a typewriter or computer.

research. Medical science, which is applied human biology, is a branch of natural science in general, and research in any branch of science is apt to affect any other branch. Basic medical research is research in the theoretical sciences on which medical practice is based: ►*anatomy*, ►*physiology*, ►*pathology*, ►*pharmacology* and others. This entry is concerned with clinical research, or the application of the results of basic research to sick people, and in particular with the problems of trying out new drugs.

In principle, basic research is the concern of universities, and investigation of new drugs is that of the chemical and pharmaceutical industries. The two fields overlap considerably, and all research is becoming so expensive that few universities can manage without some financial help from industry or elsewhere. Basic research indicates the kind of substance that is likely to turn into a useful drug, and, coupled with clinical observation, the actions that should be sought in new drugs. A manufacturer often has to start from the other end. His plant is adapted to the synthesis of certain classes of compound. It is no mere chance that most of the early synthetic drugs were related to dyestuffs: the modern chemical industry began in the second half of the 19th century with dyes and other substances needed by the textile industry. As chemists began to see the possibility of synthesizing new drugs, with the advantages over the old herbal remedies that they could be exactly standardized, modified, and produced in the required amounts, they naturally turned first to the substances on hand or to compounds easily derived from these. There is no theoretical limit to the number of different substances that might be synthesized, but even the largest chemical plant cannot attempt more than a few of them without heavy capital expenditure. Therefore a manufacturer, whether capitalist or state-controlled, has to be fairly sure of his ground before starting work on a new type of chemical compound.

Often the starting point is a known drug, and many new drugs are simple modifications of old ones, in which a change of chemical structure has enhanced the desired effect or decreased the toxicity. Or a chemist may synthesize a new substance and pass it to the biologists to see whether it has any potential as a drug. This all sounds like a hit-or-miss research, but there is no alternative while so little is known about how drugs work. Two closely related compounds may have similar, or opposite effects. Thus isoprenaline and methyl-dopa are both related to adrenaline. One is a useful alternative to adrenaline in the treatment of asthma, whereas the other is a direct antidote, used for lowering high blood pressure.

The first step in testing a possible new drug is to give it to small animals such as frogs and mice, and test its effect on each of the organs in turn, to see whether the compound shows any promise or whether it is too toxic to be worth further study. Most compounds are rejected at this stage. Sometimes there are wholly unexpected rewards. In the late 1950s, when a series of compounds was being studied in the hope of finding a new treatment for worms, one of them (guanethidine) did not cure the rats of their worms but caused an alarming fall in their blood pressure. The research changed course, and later guanethidine emerged as one of the most valuable remedies for high blood pressure.

If the new compound promises to be useful, it is tested with higher animals (e.g. dogs, monkeys) including – since the disaster with thalidomide – pregnant animals, with particular attention to the margin between effective doses and dangerous doses, the *therapeutic index*. Unless the index is reasonably high the research is discontinued. Otherwise, the compound can be tested for untoward effects on healthy human volunteers, usually members of the research team.

From this point, in many countries further research comes under official scrutiny: in Britain by the Committee on Safety of Drugs, and in the United States by the Food and Drugs Administration. The clinical trials, i.e. tests on actual patients, are conducted under an agreed code of practice, with these government agencies to arbitrate. The manufacturer must satisfy the agency that his drug is likely to be useful and reasonably safe, and he must then find a physician with facilities for clinical research who is willing to conduct the first trials, usually one working in a large hospital attached to a university, for only a large medical unit has the laboratories and other elaborate diagnostic aids for recognizing ill effects before serious harm is done. And, apart from safeguards, the manufacturer's claims will have to be supported by unimpeachable authority when he comes to market his new product.

Only rarely can a new drug be assessed from its effect on a handful of patients. An example was the first treatment of tuberculous meningitis with streptomycin in 1944. The mortality from this disease had been 100 per cent; no patient had ever recovered. A single patient cured was virtual proof that the new drug worked. But this is quite exceptional. With most other diseases, the patient might have recovered without the drug. This problem can be overcome by comparing the new drug with the results of giving no active treatment. A valid comparison needs a large enough series of cases to exclude, within reason, the workings of pure chance – another reason for choosing a large hospital: ► *statistics*.

Two groups of patients are studied together. They are matched as nearly as possible for age, sex, severity of illness, race, social background and other factors that might affect the outcome. Ideally, the only difference between the groups would be the drug itself.

To give one group the new treatment and the other no treatment at all would not serve, because the patients who knew that they were being treated would inevitably do better than the others. So the control (untreated) group must be given medication that looks like the real thing, a ► *placebo*, and none of the patients is told until later to which group he belongs. Neither should the physician be told, because knowing which patients are getting the drug can affect both his manner with them (and therefore their response) and his judgement of the results. The trial is then *double-blind*, with neither the doctor nor the patients knowing how the two groups are allocated. The hospital pharmacist does know, and breaks silence if there is any sign of trouble.

In a *cross-over* trial, the two groups, still without knowing, change sides at half-time, so that all the patients at one stage or the other receive the drug. With chronic disorders needing prolonged treatment, the patients thus serve as their own controls.

Several ethical questions arise. The physician must be sure that the trial is justified. In 1865 Claude Bernard summed this up by saying that a trial likely to make the patient worse was forbidden, one likely at least to do no harm was permissible, and one likely to make the patient better was obligatory. This does not go quite far enough. To justify a clinical trial, a new drug should offer some prospect not merely of working, but of being better than existing and tried remedies. 'Better' need not mean more efficient: it can also mean safer, or more convenient. For example, many drugs derived from adrenaline are offered for the relief of asthma. Probably none of them stops an asthmatic attack more efficiently than adrenaline itself. The first of them, ephedrine, is much less efficient, but it is safer and has the great advantage that it can be taken by mouth instead of by injection. Because its action is slow, ephedrine is better for preventing attacks than for treating them. A later development, isoprenaline, is taken under the tongue or inhaled and works quickly enough to stop an attack. But all these drugs irritate the heart. The latest ones, such as salbutamol, are much safer in this respect. Thus all these drugs justify themselves, though none is more efficient than the prototype. Often, though, a new drug offers no advantage other than circumventing a rival's patent; this is a common source of discord between doctors and manufacturers. On the other hand, a drug that is neither better nor worse than another, but cheaper, would be justified.

Next, the patients have to be told exactly what is happening. Unless they fully understand the nature of the trial and agree to take part, it is unethical to include them. With children, the parents' consent is needed, and with mentally deranged patients, that of the relatives. In both cases the doctor has to some extent to accept the responsibility of acting *in loco parentis*, which poses its own ethical problems.

There is then the question of treating dangerous illness. If, for example, a new treatment for typhoid fever is proposed, to give half the patients a placebo would be grossly improper because their lives would be in danger. In such cases, the new drug is compared not with a placebo but with an established remedy such as chloramphenicol. In this instance, the new drug could be only marginally more effective since chloramphenicol is highly active against typhoid bacilli, and a large series of cases would have to be studied to show a statistically significant advantage. But a slightly less active drug might be acceptable if it proved to be safer. Hundreds of cases might have to be studied before one could be sure.

If the first trials are successful, the drug is tested at other centres before the Committee on Safety of Drugs makes its recommendations to the medical profession in general.

It should be mentioned that only about one compound in every 200 studied ever reaches the stage of being given to patients, so that the cost of the research leading to one new drug is enormous. Even among the few that find their way into clinical practice there are many disappointments. New drugs often seem better than they really are. It may be months or years before their drawbacks come to light, and despite all the precautions doctors have to be constantly on guard when handling new remedies. Alexander Pope was no pharmacologist, but in one couplet he summed up this problem:

'Be not the first by whom the new are tried
Nor yet the last to lay the old aside.'

resection. Excision, surgical removal. The suffix *-ectomy* denotes resection: *appendicectomy* = resection of the appendix.

reserpine. Active principle of ►*rauwolfia*.

respiration. Exchange of gases between an organism and its environment. All living tissues need a constant source of energy, which is supplied by burning fuel (carbohydrate, fat, or protein) – i.e. combining fuel with oxygen. Fat in the fire or fat in the body produces exactly the same amount of heat when it is oxidized; only the rate of oxidation differs. An average man at complete rest needs about 1.2 Calories per minute, and to generate this amount of heat he uses 250 ml of oxygen.

A man at rest breathes in about 3.75 litres of air per minute. This air contains 750 ml of oxygen of which he uses a third, or 250 ml.

With deep and rapid breathing he takes in about 15 times as much air, and during exertion he takes up more oxygen from it. Thus the *oxygen* uptake can be increased about 30 times.

The end-products of oxidation in the body are energy, water, and *carbon diox-*

ide. Oxygen is carried by the blood to the tissues, where it is exchanged for carbon dioxide, which the blood carries to the lungs. This exchange of gases in the body is called *internal respiration*. The opposite exchange in the lungs, where oxygen is taken in and carbon dioxide is breathed out, is *external respiration*. A third term, *tissue respiration*, is applied to the actual process of oxidation inside the living cells.

1. MECHANICS OF BREATHING

The lungs are elastic bags, together holding about 6 litres of air when fully expanded and about half this amount at rest. During quiet breathing the air in the two lungs fluctuates between, say, 3 and 3.4 litres. The extremes, during forced breathing, are 1.5 and 6 litres.

Air is inhaled when the diaphragm and intercostal muscles enlarge the cavity of the chest, and atmospheric pressure forces air into the empty space provided.

The diaphragm is a sheet of muscle attached to the lower ribs and the lumbar vertebrae and rising in the centre to form a dome. As the muscle contracts the centre is pulled down, and the thorax is enlarged at the expense of the abdomen. The belly bulges to make room for the displaced abdominal organs.

The intercostal muscles span the gaps between the ribs. By contracting they make the chest deeper from front to back by raising the front of the ribs, and also wider by splaying the ribs. This enlargement of the rib-cage makes more room for the abdominal organs and so draws the belly *in*. During quiet breathing the opposed actions of the diaphragm and the intercostals on the abdomen about cancel each other. When breathing is distressed the muscles of the neck and shoulders reinforce the usual respiratory muscles.

Expiration, on the other hand, is mainly passive. The lungs and chest wall are elastic. When the pull of the muscles is relaxed, the recoil is enough to expel the air. But during forced breathing the abdominal muscles are used to compress the belly and push the diaphragm up.

A *cough* works like an air-gun: the chest is 'loaded' with compressed air by contracting the abdominal muscles while the outlet – the ►*larynx* – is held firmly shut. The gun is fired by sudden relaxation of the larynx.

Singing makes very special demands on breathing. The singer breathes as much as possible with his diaphragm, which contracts more rapidly than the intercostals, and is thus a better means of snatching a quick breath. But a more important part of singing is controlled breathing *out*, and again the diaphragm is a better mechanism than the intercostals. If a singer tries to breathe with his intercostals – i.e. from the ribs – he has to control the out-flow by constricting the throat (as in 'loading' the lungs for a cough), and this produces the strangled tone of a bad singer. But if he breathes in with his diaphragm he distends the abdominal muscles, which he can then balance against his diaphragm to regulate the out flow. The stream can be a torrent or a trickle, and the larynx plays no part in its regulation; its muscles need be used only to determine the pitch of the note. The same principles apply to public speaking. The medical significance is that people who have trouble with breathing, such as asthmatics, or people who run a risk of infection of the lungs, such as patients recovering from major operations, can be taught better breathing. This is an important branch of physiotherapy.

2. REGULATION OF BREATHING

Breathing appears to be a deliberate action, and the muscles are voluntary muscles under conscious control. But free will in this respect is largely an illusion. Only a particular breath or short series of breaths can be adjusted at will; breathing as a whole is a reflex action. A given demand for oxygen may be satisfied by 20 moderate breaths in a minute. A sobbing child may take twice as many shallow breaths, or a singer half a dozen deep ones, but neither changes the volume of air exchanged in the given time. This balance can be deliberately upset by holding the breath or over-breathing, but only for a very short time; the subject's will is soon overruled by mechanisms outside his consciousness.

The process is co-ordinated by the *res-piratory centre*, a group of nerve cells in the lowest part of the brain. Lack of oxygen in the blood is at best only a weak stimulus to the respiratory centre, and severe shortage of oxygen *suppresses* the centre. The really important factor is the acidity of the blood. This depends on the ratio of circulating bicarbonate (alkaline) to carbon dioxide (acidic). An excess of carbon dioxide makes the blood less alkaline, and stimulates the respiratory centre. Breathing becomes deeper and faster, and more carbon dioxide is expired. Any acid in the blood (e.g. lactic acid formed in the muscles during exercise) has the same effect. The more acidic the blood, the greater the stimulation.

There is an important difference between *anoxia* (lack of oxygen) and *asphyxia* (suffocation). With asphyxia, the blood is short of oxygen and at the same time carbon dioxide formed in the tissues is not eliminated. This carbon dioxide stimulates breathing and so tends to correct both faults. With anoxia, for example at very high altitudes, there may be just enough oxygen in the air to keep a man alive if he breathes rapidly and deeply, but he lacks the stimulus. At first, the *slight* shortage of oxygen may provide a weak stimulus. But deep breathing eliminates carbon dioxide – and with it the most effective stimulus to the respiratory centre. The centre is then inhibited both by lack of carbon dioxide in the blood and *severe* lack of oxygen, and breathing stops. Lack of oxygen also depresses the brain, so that even if an oxygen mask is to hand the man quickly becomes too dazed to use it.

respiratory distress syndrome. The infantile form of this dangerous condition is described under ➤*hyaline-membrane disease*. The adult form is a complication of severe injury or acute illness, either of which may cause blood or plasma to seep into the lungs. Unless the condition is treated promptly the patient is likely to suffocate. The treatment includes oxygen therapy, assisted respiration, and attention to the underlying injury or illness.

respiratory syncytial virus (RSV). A virus first identified in 1954 but not recognized as a cause of human illness until 10 years later. When RSV is grown in tissue culture there is a tendency for the cells of the culture to merge with each other and form a conglomerate or *syncytium*. RSV infection is common in the first two years of life. Older children and adults are generally immune.

Most RSV infection is mild and confined to the nose and throat, and the illness is exactly like a common cold. In some cases it is more like influenza.

Less commonly, RSV infection causes *bronchiolitis*. This is a severe illness of early childhood, with symptoms suggesting both pneumonia and asthma. The importance of bronchiolitis was not recognized until the mid-1960s, and before then it was surely the cause of some mysterious 'cot-deaths', apparently from suffocation. An antiviral agent, *ribavirin*, can be given by aerosol to infants at special risk. Drugs that relieve the spasm of asthma have no effect because the bronchioles are blocked not by spasm but by inflammation. In severe cases the child needs oxygen and artificial respiration, and also constant supervision of the fluid intake to avoid dehydration. In practice this means that he has to be treated in hospital.

rest. Until recently, rest was regarded as a sort of panacea, or at least as a necessary supplement to all other medical treatment. Its most famous champion was a London surgeon, John Hilton (1804–78), whose *Rest and Pain* was among the most influential medical books of the 19th century. Hilton did more than anyone else of his time to teach surgeons to let well alone. His doctrine that diseased parts need rest – for many years a medical axiom – is still accepted, but only with some reservations. Where there is definite inflammation, or where damaged tissues are healing, movement delays or prevents healing, and also encourages the spread of infection to neighbouring tissues if bacteria are the cause of the trouble. To some extent, rest is automatic, because loss of function is one of the effects of inflammation. With pneumonia, for instance, the chest fails to expand on the affected side and breathing is one-sided. One cannot use a septic finger or a badly sprained ankle. Nobody with a fever wishes to exert himself.

Sometimes it is necessary to help. A broken bone does not heal unless the ends are held in place. Before effective drugs were found, prolonged rest was the most hopeful treatment of an organ affected with tuberculosis, and surgical methods were used to prevent a severely affected lung from being used. An inflamed joint may need a splint not only to prevent the pain of movement but to allow the inflammation to subside. In these and many other cases there are definite reasons for encouraging rest, and nobody doubts its value.

But rest for its own sake is no longer accepted as good medicine. Until about 1950, candidates for medical degrees could safely begin an answer to almost any question by saying that they would order a bland diet, a laxative, and complete rest. Today, they would be expected to say why, and also what they meant by rest.

The surgeons were perhaps the first to recognize that rest could be overdone, when they discovered that many of the complications that arose while their patients spent a mandatory fortnight in bed after operations arose precisely because the patients *were* in bed, and could be avoided by getting the patients up as soon as possible. In fact, many patients are able to walk around a few hours after major surgery, without ill effects. And loss of function after injuries can often be blamed on failure to get the injured part moving as soon as possible.

Much the same is true of other branches of medicine. If there is no definite reason for patients to rest, they are no longer forced to do so. Even those who do not feel well enough to get up are, with few exceptions, at least encouraged to move around in bed. In defiance of all that was taught traditionally, exercise is prescribed in certain cases of serious heart disease. It has to be closely supervised, because over-exertion would be dangerous, but exercise is now an accepted part of the treatment of established heart disease and of the prevention of heart attacks.

Rest does not necessarily mean physical rest. Much illness is largely due to mental stress. This calls for rest, but of a kind that may be better taken behind a lawn-mower than in bed.

resuscitation. Revival of patients who appear to be dead, e.g. from drowning, electrocution or heart attacks. By any definition, death is irreversible, and anyone who can be resuscitated is still alive, however desperate his condition. But to decide whether a person is dead and beyond resuscitation or still alive may be very difficult indeed; and the decision has become much harder in recent years. When resuscitation meant only artificial respiration it was hard enough to decide when further attempts would be useless. Now that a heart can be kept beating with an electrical impulse, while the lungs are ventilated mechanically, or the whole work of heart and lungs can be done by a machine, it may be almost impossible to say whether someone is alive or dead. One can remove an animal's heart and keep it beating almost indefinitely with a supply of oxygen and other essentials: in a sense the heart still lives while the animal is undoubtedly dead. Similarly it may be possible to keep most of a patient's organs 'alive' long after he has ceased to be a living person in any complete sense.

➤*artificial respiration*; *cardiac massage*.

reticular formation. A tangle of nerve cells and fibres in the brain-stem in which impulses between the brain and the periphery are switched into appropriate pathways (➤*midbrain*).

reticulocyte. A newly formed red blood cell, distinguished from mature cells by a fine network revealed by staining. An unduly large proportion of these cells is evidence that red cells have been rapidly replaced, e.g. after bleeding.

reticuloendothelial (RE) system. A community of cells scattered around the body. They are *phagocytes*, i.e. they can engulf and destroy foreign matter, such as bacteria, or worn-out tissue due to be replaced, such as blood cells that have served their useful term. Stationary RE cells line blood-spaces in the bone marrow, spleen and lymph nodes, and are also found in the liver and other tissues. Some authorities limit the RE system to these cells, but others include cells wandering at large in the blood and connective tissues. RE cells are closely related to blood cells.

The RE system seems to play an essential though ill-defined part in immunity to infection.

➤*spleen*; *lymph*.

reticulosis. Any disorder mainly affecting the reticuloendothelial system, including infections such as typhoid and malaria with a predilection for RE cells, and conditions such as Hodgkin's disease.

retina. Light-sensitive membrane lining the back of the ➤*eye*.

retinaculum. Retaining band of connective tissue, such as the *flexor retinaculum* at the front of the wrist (➤*carpal tunnel*).

retinitis pigmentosa. A degenerative disorder of the retina, with characteristic abnormalities of retinal pigmentation. The first symptom, which may appear in childhood, is poor night vision. In later life the field of vision is progressively restricted, and ultimately some victims become blind. Retinitis pigmentosa appears to be a result of various hereditary traits, of which the modes of inheritance have not all been elucidated. There is still no effective treatment.

retinoblastoma. A tumour of the retina; one of the rare cancers of infancy.

retinol = ►*vitamin A*.

retinopathy. Any disease of the retina. It is a better word than the widely used 'retinitis' for conditions without inflammation, such as the damage to the retina by severe diabetes or high blood pressure arising from degeneration of small arteries in the retina.

Retinopathy of prematurity is associated with the oxygen supplements needed to keep some premature babies alive.

The blood vessels of the retina are not completely formed until a late stage of pregnancy. If the infant is born while the vessels are still being formed, a surfeit of oxygen may inhibit their growth. When the supplementary oxygen is later withdrawn there is a tendency for new and defective vessels to proliferate; these may settle down but sometimes cause trouble by bleeding or forming fibrous deposits (fibroplasia).

retrobulbar neuritis. Inflammation of the optic nerve at the back of the eye, with pain and loss of vision. Spontaneous recovery is the rule, though the condition may recur later. This is sometimes an early sign of multiple sclerosis, but often there is no apparent cause.

retroflexion ►*retroversion*.

retrolental fibroplasia ►*retinopathy*.

retroversion. Backward displacement of an organ, especially the uterus. A normal uterus slopes downwards and backwards; a retroverted one may lie vertically or slope downwards and forwards. *Retroflexion* is a somewhat different condition: the uterus is arched backwards. Both conditions are so common among healthy women that one may doubt whether they should be regarded as abnormalities. Nevertheless, symptoms such as backache and menstrual disturbances are sometimes relieved by correcting the position of the uterus.

retrovirus. A kind of virus that can invade living cells and convert its RNA into DNA (►*genetics* (1)) to be incorporated with the DNA of the invaded cell. The affected cell replicates in its new, altered form, which may now be cancerous or otherwise diseased. HIV, the agent of AIDS, is a virus of this kind.

Reye's syndrome. A disorder of uncertain origin causing damage to brain and liver, affecting children and adolescents, usually after a virus infection such as influenza. Many of the reported cases have been associated with the use of aspirin, which is therefore best avoided under the age of 18 unless there is a special reason, such as rheumatic fever.

rhesus factor (Rh factor). A factor in blood determining one of the systems of blood groups (►*blood* (5); *transfusion*).

An independent system of blood groups discovered in 1940 in experiments with rhesus monkeys has been named the *rhesus system*. It involves half a dozen factors, of which one ('D') is especially important. In 85 per cent of people the red blood cells carry factor D; these people are rhesus (Rh) positive. The 15 per cent without D are Rh negative.

If Rh-positive red cells find their way into a Rh-negative person's bloodstream, their D factor excites a defensive reaction: it is a 'foreign' substance, and an *antibody* is formed to neutralize it, exactly as though it were a harmful bacterium. The effect of this reaction is to destroy the foreign red cells. If a Rh-negative person is given a transfusion of Rh-positive blood, antibodies are formed too slowly to cause much trouble. But the person is then *immune* to D, and remains so. If he ever has another transfusion of Rh-positive blood, his antibodies will promptly destroy the foreign cells, just as antibodies first formed during an attack of measles will ever afterwards destroy the virus of measles and prevent a second attack (▸*immunity*).

Like all blood groups, the Rh group is inherited. If a Rh-negative woman marries a Rh-positive man, there is a fair chance that her children will be Rh-positive. Since blood cells are too large to pass from the baby to the mother during pregnancy, his Rh-positive red cells have no chance of making her form antibodies, and unless she has previously had a Rh-positive blood transfusion all is well. But at the time of birth the mother bleeds from the uterus and the baby bleeds through the placenta. If some of the baby's cells get into the mother's veins, she forms antibodies against them. She is then immune to D, and if she has another Rh-positive baby her antibodies filter across the placenta and damage the baby's red blood cells.

Although 15 per cent of women are Rh-negative, and 85 per cent of their husbands are Rh-positive, only about one baby in 200 is affected by Rh-incompatibility. Firstly, not all babies of these mixed marriages are Rh positive, and the negative ones run no risk. Secondly, most women do not actually form the antibodies, or they do so only after two or three successful pregnancies. Thirdly, even when there are antibodies the damage to the baby's red cells may not be enough to give serious trouble. But in a few babies this is a fatal disease. Some are stillborn, some are born with heart failure due to profound anaemia, and some develop severe jaundice soon after birth, because broken-down blood-pigment forms bile-pigment, and jaundice is simply an excess of bile-pigment. The babies with heart failure seldom live more than a few hours, but after the first day the jaundice becomes more lethal than the anaemia. Bile-pigment is highly poisonous to the new-born baby's nervous system, much more so than in older children or adults. The *untreated* babies who survive may have permanent damage to the brain (▸*spastic paralysis*).

The standard treatment is *exchange transfusion*. An ordinary transfusion might help the anaemia but would do nothing to lessen the destruction of the baby's own red cells and the resulting jaundice. Exchange transfusion is done with a large hypodermic syringe and a three-way valve with leads to (1) the baby, (2) a supply of Rh-*negative* blood, (3) waste. Blood is drawn from the baby a syringeful at a time and replaced with the fresh blood which, being Rh-negative, cannot be harmed by the mother's antibodies still in the baby's blood. By the time half a litre of blood (twice the volume of the baby's blood) has been withdrawn both antibodies and bile-pigment are usually reduced to safe levels. By this means some 95 per cent of affected babies can be saved. If the condition is diagnosed by ▸*amniocentesis* during pregnancy, it is possible to transfuse healthy blood into the foetus's abdominal cavity, from where it is taken into the blood-stream. An antibody against the D factor is used to prevent Rh-negative women from developing antibodies of their own that would be a danger to a subsequent baby. The immunization is carried out immediately after the first confinement. If any Rh-positive cells have entered the mother's blood, they are neutralized by the injected antibody before they have time to do any harm. The patient develops no lasting immunity to Rh-positive cells.

rheumatic fever. An acute illness, commonest among children and adolescents, with raised temperature, and centres of inflammation arising and subsiding unpredictably in connective tissues. The tissues most affected are those of the larger joints and the lining and valves of the heart. Characteristically, one joint after another becomes swollen and painful for a few days.

Sometimes the disease seems to run a very mild course with little or no fever, and only fleeting pains in the limbs. In the past such cases have been lightly dismissed as 'growing pains', but growing pains are a myth.

Many children develop curious involuntary movements during an attack of rheumatic fever, a condition known as Sydenham's ►*chorea*.

The joints always recover completely, and chorea always subsides. But the heart may be permanently affected. Inflammation of the heart valves may leave scars that deform the valves. The *mitral valve*, which allows blood to flow from the left atrium to the left ventricle but prevents flow in the opposite direction, is most often damaged. There may be narrowing of the valve (mitral stenosis) and also leakage (mitral incompetence). Both

defects increase the work to be done by the heart, sometimes to a point where the heart muscle (which may itself have been weakened by rheumatic fever) can no longer meet all normal demands (►*heart failure*).

The cause of rheumatic fever is still not known. It is always preceded by infection with the same species of bacterium, the haemolytic streptococcus (severe sore throat, scarlet fever etc.), the rheumatic attack coming on a week or two after recovery from the infection.

In some ways, rheumatic fever resembles an allergic reaction. It does not seem to arise from allergy to streptococci, but the trouble might be caused by the antibodies that the patient himself forms to destroy the streptococci. If the precise nature of the disease remains a mystery, it is at least clear that rheumatic fever is prevented by prompt and adequate treatment of streptococcal infection. This has been possible since the discovery of sulphonamides, and since 1936 the disease has become less and less common.

Salicylates such as aspirin control the symptoms of rheumatic fever. Corticosteroid hormones are equally effective, but they have numerous drawbacks and have not replaced salicylates as the routine treatment. Penicillin is given prophylactically for some years to prevent recurrence.

The treatment of late complications – rheumatic heart disease – has been greatly improved by operations for restoring the efficiency of damaged valves.

rheumatism. Any painful disorder of joints or muscles not directly due to infection or injury. This rather ill-defined group includes rheumatic fever (acute rheumatism), rheumatoid arthritis, osteoarthritis, gout, and 'fibrositis' – itself an ill-defined group of disorders in which pain felt in muscles is the common factor.

rheumatoid arthritis. A chronic disease of connective tissue, commoner in women than men. In Britain at least one person in 20 has it at some time; the figure may be much higher because mild cases are not reported.

The characteristic feature is a small knot or nodule of inflamed fibrous tissue; these tender nodules are often just under the skin. Any organ may on occasion be affected, but most of the symptoms arise from inflammation of the fibrous connective tissue around the joints. Any joint may be affected but the knuckle-joints and wrists tend to suffer most.

The course of the disease varies widely. In some cases the inflammation subsides without doing much damage, though further attacks are possible. Less often a sort of grumbling inflammation persists and the affected joints are stiffened by damage to their linings of smooth cartilage. In severe cases joints may become crippled. This is partly due to direct damage to the joint linings, and partly to the action of muscles around the joint. The muscles over any seat of inflammation tighten as a defensive reaction, and when this happens around a damaged joint the joint may in time be deformed or even dislocated.

In rare cases, rheumatoid arthritis takes the form of a generalized feverish illness like a protracted attack of rheumatic fever.

The cause of rheumatoid arthritis is not known. It is probably an auto-immune disease (>*immunity* (7)), i.e. one in which the patient's natural defence against infection attacks his own tissues. Physical and emotional stresses play some part in setting off attacks, and there may also be hereditary factors. The immediate damage to joints is probably due to the release of destructive enzymes from inflamed cells, and some research is directed at the source of these.

Rheumatoid arthritis is not likely to be completely curable until more is known of its causes, but much can be done to alleviate it. Pain and inflammation can be controlled with various drugs such as aspirin, ibuprofen and indomethacin (>*anti-inflammatory drugs*), and in most cases this is enough.

Compounds of gold are sometimes given to suppress the underlying process rather than the symptoms of rheumatoid arthritis. The results are often good, but the dose is not easy to regulate, and the treatment is suitable only for selected cases. The anti-malarial drug chloroquine is also sometimes effective. How these drugs work is unknown.

Steroid hormones (>*corticosteroid*) give quite dramatic relief in severe cases. This disease was the first for which these drugs were used, and for a short time it seemed as though a cure had been discovered. But it soon became clear that the disadvantages of the treatment outweighed the benefits except in severe, progressive disease; in such cases these hormones are invaluable.

Acutely inflamed joints can be protected from harmful wear and tear and from deformity by splinting, but as inflammation subsides controlled exercises are used to preserve function. Patients who have lost the use of one joint are taught to make the best use of unaffected joints, and many ingenious gadgets have been devised to assist severely handicapped patients. Devices as simple as a higher toilet seat or a knife and fork with handles large enough to be grasped by stiff fingers may be enough to restore a patient's independence.

Some joints can be treated surgically. Surgery can be used to correct deformity, to immobilize a badly damaged joint and prevent painful and useless movement, or to construct an artificial joint.

rhinitis. Inflammation of the lining of the nose, e.g. by common cold or hay fever.

rhodopsin. Light-sensitive pigment in the retina. ➤*eye* (2).

rhythm method. Safe-period method of birth control. ➤*contraception*.

rib. The rudiments of a pair of ribs project from the sides of every ➤*vertebra*. As a rule only those of the 12 thoracic vertebrae form separate bones, but an additional pair may be attached to the 7th cervical or 1st lumbar vertebra. These are unimportant unless a cervical rib compresses one of the nerves to the arm.

The ribs have rounded heads to fit shallow sockets on the vertebrae, and each makes a second joint with the transverse process of the vertebra. The front part of each rib is of cartilage, not bone. The cartilages of the upper seven ribs are directly attached to the sternum, and the next three each join the cartilage above. The last two ('floating ribs') end blindly in the muscles of the back.

A rib is easily broken and easily mended. The fracture is effectively splinted by the adjacent ribs. The object of strapping fractured ribs is not so much to promote healing as to relieve the pain of breathing. If the ribs are held firmly respiration is carried on by the diaphragm. The danger of a fractured rib is

injury to the underlying organs – lungs, liver, spleen – with internal bleeding. But apart from small punctures of the lung (➤*pneumothorax*) which usually heal well, these complications are rare except in cases of severe multiple injuries. Some of the worst are caused by the impact of the steering wheel in motor accidents, with fractures of the ribs or costal cartilages on both sides and depression of the sternum against the heart.

riboflavin = ➤*vitamin B₂*.

rickets. Defective growth of bone due to lack of vitamin D. The vitamin is formed in human skin exposed to sunlight. Children deprived of sunlight need vitamin D in their diet (fish, milk, eggs). Rickets affects those who lack either source. It was therefore rife among poor children in English towns during the Industrial Revolution. In many countries it is known as the English disease.

Without vitamin D, not enough calcium salts are deposited in bone to make it rigid. The cartilage at the growing ends of long bones is enlarged, e.g. at the front ends of the ribs and at the knees; and weight-bearing bones are twisted out of shape.

A rare condition, *renal rickets*, is due to incompetence of the kidneys, which allow phosphates to escape in the urine in such amounts that not enough calcium phosphate can be deposited in the bones.

Neither sunlight nor a normal diet provides enough vitamin D to cure rickets; a concentrated supply such as halibut-liver oil or synthetic vitamin D is needed.

For the origin of the word, ➤*rachitis*.

Rickettsia. A genus of small bacteria, responsible for typhus and several other fevers transmitted by insects.

Rift Valley fever. An influenza-like illness, due to a virus found in East Africa. It is transmitted from animal to man by mosquitoes.

rigor. Violent attack of shivering at the start of a fever, indicating a rapid rise of body temperature.

ringworm. One of the commonest skin diseases; it is an infection of the outer layer of the skin with a microscopical fungus or mould. With certain types the infection tends to spread outwards as a disc; the centre heals while the circumference is still active, forming a ring.

Common sites are the scalp (true 'ringworm'), the groin ('dhobie itch'), and between the toes ('athlete's foot').

Itching is common to all forms. With ringworm of the scalp, small patches of hair are temporarily lost. The nails of the fingers or toes may harbour the fungus and become deformed, often in association with athlete's foot.

Sometimes small itchy blisters appear at some distance from the site of infection, e.g. on the fingers with athlete's foot. This *id reaction* is not a spread of the infection, but an allergic reaction to it.

Many ointments and lotions can be applied to the affected skin, including preparations of salicylic acid, antiseptic dyes, aluminium acetate, and undecylenic acid. There are many species of fungi among the causes of ringworm and they respond to different remedies, but even when the fungus has been identified the best treatment may have to be found by trial and error.

The antibiotic griseofulvin, taken by mouth, cures cases of ringworm that resist all local treatment. It is most often needed with infection of the hair and nails, and renders unnecessary the older, drastic remedies which involved removing large areas of hair or infected finger-nails.

river blindness. A result of invasion of the eye by the larvae of *onchocerca*, a kind of ►*filaria*.

RNA. Ribonucleic acid. ►*genetics* (1).

Rocky Mountain spotted fever. A potentially dangerous fever, resembling a severe attack of measles, first reported from the Rocky Mountains but later over much of North America. It is caused by a kind of *rickettsia*, carried from various animals to man by tick bites. Prompt treatment with antibiotics is usually effective.

rodent ulcer. A kind of cancer of the skin, practically confined to the face and scalp. It starts as a small, round, painless hard lump in the skin. As the lump grows its centre tends to break down, forming an open sore (ulcer) with a raised circumference. Like any cancer, a rodent ulcer destroys any healthy tissue in its path. Unlike most other cancers it is nearly always restricted to the area in which it is seen. If, therefore, it is removed surgically or destroyed with drugs or radiation it is almost certainly cured. This property, together with the fact that the disease occurs where it is easily noticed, makes rodent ulcer the least dangerous of cancers.

Roentgen, Wilhelm Conrad (1845–1923). German physicist, awarded the first Nobel Prize for physics in 1901 for his discovery of X-rays. When studying the behaviour of electricity in a vacuum in 1895, Roentgen found that a covered photographic plate had been exposed. He made a rapid yet thorough investigation of the event, and within a few weeks was able to publish an account of the physical properties of the new rays, the use of photographic plates or fluorescent screens to observe them, and the degree of transparency to them of different substances including human tissues.

Roentgenography. Radiography; the use of X-rays to reveal internal structure.

Rokitansky, Carl von (1804–78). Viennese pathologist; the most indefatigable observer of the processes and physical effects of disease. He personally made and described more than 30,000 post-mortem examinations, and directed twice that number. This mass of reports is a foundation-stone of modern pathology. Rokitansky was no experimental scientist, and he was an unlucky theorist (➤*pathology*), but it was on his observation of fact that scientists like Virchow were to build.

rosacea. A chronic eruption confined to the front of the face, mostly affecting middle-aged, fair-skinned people. The skin is reddened, with clusters of small veins and blotchy thickening.

In the past rosacea has been ascribed to over-indulgence in alcohol or tea or spicy food; but there is little evidence to inculpate any of these and the cause remains unknown. Although no microbes are known to be involved, rosacea usu-ally responds well to local application of *metronidazole*, a drug used against amoebic infections, or to *tetracycline*, an antibacterial agent.

roseola. Any pink rash, but especially that of measles (rubeola).

Ross, Sir Ronald (1857–1932). British physician, in the Indian Medical Service; he proved that malaria was transmitted by mosquito bites. Ross was awarded a Nobel Prize in 1902.

roundworm. A common parasite of the intestine. ➤*worms*.

RSV = ➤*respiratory syncytial virus*.

rubefacient. Medication applied to the skin to increase its flow of blood and redden it. ➤*counter-irritation*.

rubella = ➤*German measles*.

rubeola = ➤*measles*.

rubor. Reddening (of the skin) as a sign of inflammation.

rugae. Wrinkles or folds, e.g. those of the lining of the intestine and some other mucous membranes.

rupture. 1. Bursting of a hollow organ such as an inflamed appendix. **2.** = ➤*hernia*.

S

Sabin vaccine. A vaccine against poliomyelitis, prepared by growing the virus under artificial conditions until it loses its ability to cause the disease. When this attenuated virus is taken by mouth it confers immunity in the same way as an attack of poliomyelitis, but without causing symptoms.

sac. A pocket or bag of tissue, e.g. *amniotic sac*, the fluid-filled membrane surrounding an unborn baby; *hernial sac*, a protrusion of peritoneum (lining membrane of the abdomen) through a gap in the muscles (>*hernia*).

saccharose. Ordinary sugar; sucrose.

sacral. Of the sacrum.

sacroiliac joint. Joint at the base of the spine between the sacrum and hip-bone (>*pelvis*).

The sacroiliac joints carry the weight of the body to the legs; the sacrum belongs to the backbone and the ilium to the lower limb. The joint surfaces do not interlock, and since the plane of the joint is almost vertical there is a considerable shearing strain. Unlike most joints, the sacroiliac joint gets little support from muscles. This is one of the few joints supported almost entirely by ligaments, and since there is virtually no movement between the bones the ligaments are all taut the whole time. Yet there is a real joint-space, lined with cartilage, as though this were a movable joint. Towards the end of pregnancy the ligaments of the sacroiliac joint may loosen, allowing the baby's head to push the sacrum back a little and so enlarge the birth-passage. The strain on the slackened ligaments would explain the dull ache at the base of the spine so often felt in the last weeks of pregnancy.

Inflammation of these joints is a characteristic symptom of *sero-negative arthritis*, a progressive disorder resembling rheumatoid arthritis and ankylosing spondylitis. While the condition lacks a factor in the blood usually found in rheumatoid arthritis patients, a tissue group regularly associated with ankylosing spondylitis is sometimes associated with sero-negative arthritis.

sacrum. The continuation of the backbone below the lumbar vertebrae; it consists of 5 vertebrae joined together. The sacrum is the central bone of the >*pelvis*.

safe period >*contraception*.

St Anthony's fire. 1. >*Erisypelas*. **2.** Ergot poisoning.

St Louis encephalitis. A virus disease, affecting the brain, occasionally carried from animals to man by mosquitoes.

St Vitus's dance. Sydenham's >*chorea*, a complication of rheumatic fever.

saline. A common abbreviation of 'normal (or isotonic) saline solution', a solution of sodium chloride in water in a concentration, about 0.9 per cent, which balances the osmotic action (>*osmosis*) of the body fluids, so that it can be injected without disturbing the amount of water inside the cells of the body. A stronger (hypertonic) solution would draw water out of the cells, and a weaker (hypotonic) one would waterlog them. In this context, 'normal' means physiological; it has nothing to do with the normal solution of chemistry, which is nearly 7 times stronger.

Normal saline solution is used in large quantities to replace fluid in cases of dehydration, and in small quantities as a vehicle for drugs to be injected. There are several more elaborate variations in which a part of the sodium chloride is replaced by other salts of which the body has been depleted, or by glucose. In addition to their clinical uses, these are used in the laboratory for keeping alive fragments of tissue to be studied.

saliva. Watery fluid secreted by the salivary glands into the mouth. The flow of moisture keeps the mouth clean, facilitates speech, and makes it possible to ▸*taste* solids (the nerve-endings for taste respond only to dissolved substances). One phase of ▸*digestion* begins in the mouth: saliva contains an ▸*enzyme, ptyalin*, which splits starch into smaller molecules to be broken down in the intestine to simple sugars.

There are 3 pairs of *salivary glands*: parotid, submandibular, and sublingual. The *parotid* gland extends from the root of the cheek bone in front of the ear down to the angle of the jaw, which it overlaps. The external carotid artery and the facial nerve are embedded in the gland. The duct runs forwards to open inside the cheek. The *submandibular* gland lies under the jaw, below the back teeth, and the *sublingual* in the floor of the mouth behind the chin. The ducts of both open at either side of the *frenulum* of the tongue.

Salivation is a ▸*reflex* carried by ▸*parasympathetic* nerves. The stimulus may be food in the mouth (inborn reflex) or mere anticipation of food (con-

ditioned reflex). The very opposite of appetite – nausea – can also cause salivation, but this is only a part of widespread over-activity of reflexes.

By far the commonest disorder of the salivary glands is ▸*mumps*, a virus infection which may involve other glands.

Like all glands the salivary glands can be affected by cancer, but most salivary tumours are not cancerous and are easily cured by surgical removal.

The duct of a salivary gland may become blocked by a *calculus*, a deposit of insoluble chalky matter. Small calculi are easily removed; with large ones the whole gland may have to be removed – no great loss since it has probably ceased to work, and the remaining 5 are more than enough.

Salk vaccine. A vaccine against poliomyelitis, prepared by killing the virus with formaldehyde and adding a small amount of penicillin. When the dead virus is injected it cannot cause the disease but confers immunity to infection by a live virus.

Salmonella. A genus of bacteria, including the causes of typhoid and paratyphoid fevers and some common types of food poisoning.

salpingitis. Inflammation of the Fallopian tubes from infection with gonococci, streptococci or other bacteria. The infection may be carried to the tubes in the blood-stream, but more often reaches them by direct spread from the vagina and uterus. An acute attack causes severe pain in the lower abdomen like that of appendicitis, and like appendicitis it can lead to widespread and serious infection of the peritoneum.

Probably most cases subside if they are treated promptly with antibiotics, but quite often the affected tube has to be removed, because the trouble is not reported until an abscess has formed. If both tubes are seriously inflamed they may remain blocked by scar tissue; the patient cannot then conceive.

salt. 1. Any compound formed by replacing the hydrogen of an acid with ammonium or a metal, i.e. neutralizing an acid with an alkali.

2. Sodium chloride; common salt. Salt is an essential component of all living matter. Life began in the sea, and living cells still need an immediate environment very like sea water, although diluted.

The concentration of salt in the body fluids is kept steady by the kidneys. If the concentration rises the salt passed in the urine can reach 2 per cent; if it falls no salt is allowed to escape in the urine. But some salt is inevitably lost in sweat, and this must be replaced in the diet.

If too much salt is retained, e.g. because of deficient flow of blood through the kidneys with heart disease, or with deficiency of the kidneys themselves, the correct dilution of the body fluids is maintained by keeping an equivalent excess of water (►*oedema* (2)). It is only in conditions such as these that the intake of salt may have to be restricted. A healthy person can deal with any amount of salt that he is likely to eat. But the gross excess taken by drinking sea-water is poisonous, because sea-water is 3 per cent salt and the most concentrated possible urine only 2 per cent. To get rid of the salt in a pint of sea-water the kidneys must pass a pint and a half of water, and if this goes on the body becomes dehydrated.

If too much salt is lost, e.g. by heavy sweating, vomiting, or leakage of body fluids as a result of burns or other injuries, the correct concentration could be maintained only by reducing the amount of water in the body. What in fact happens is that the concentration is allowed to fall. Salt depletion is quite common after exertion in hot surroundings. The victim feels unduly weary and incompetent, and he is apt to suffer painful muscular cramps, or even prostration. The condition is often mistaken for heatstroke. The remedy is salt. Anyone who is short of salt can drink a solution of salt in water that would make him vomit in ordinary circumstances.

sal volatile. Ammonium carbonate, used as smelling salts. The pungent smell of ammonia is supposed to revive people who faint, but lowering the patient's head is more effective.

Sanctorius (Santorio) (1561–1636). Italian physician; professor of medicine at Padua; one of the first men to apply science, in the modern sense of drawing inferences from exact observation and measurement, to the study of the human body. He used a cumbersome thermometer to measure the temperature of the body (a practicable instrument was not devised until the 19th century), compared the pulse rate with a pendulum of variable length, and spent many hours of his life suspended from a balance, estimating the fluctuations of his body weight. This was a completely new approach to physiology: it marked the transition from believing in what ought to happen to observing what does happen in the healthy body.

sandfly. A small insect, *Phlebotomus*, of which different species carry the two forms of Leishmaniasis (►*kala-azar*, ► *oriental sore*) and sandfly fever.

Sandfly fever (three-day fever, Pappataci fever), transmitted by the bite of *Phlebotomus paptasi*, occurs in the countries around the Persian Gulf and the eastern Mediterranean. The patient has aches all over the body and sore eyes, but the disease is not dangerous and does not last long. It is due to a virus.

saphenous veins. Superficial veins of the lower limb; they include the *long* or *great saphenous vein*, which runs from the base of the big toe up the inner side of the limb to the groin, where it joins the femoral vein, and the *short* or *small saphenous vein*, which runs up the back of the calf to enter the popliteal vein behind the knee. There are communicating branches between the two, and between them and the deep veins. The usual one-way valves ensure that the flow is upwards, and valves in the deep branches open inwards so that the flow is from the saphenous to the deep veins under the muscles. If any of these valves fail the saphenous veins become engorged: ➤*varicose veins*.

The saphenous veins are easily accessible, and a segment of one of them is commonly used to bypass a blocked coronary artery. The relatively thin walls of a vein respond to the new environment and pressure by thickening and taking on the aspect of an artery.

sarcoid; sarcoidosis. A sarcoid is a small focus of chronic inflammation without evidence of infection; the name implies a similarity to sarcoma (a kind of cancer) but the two are quite unrelated. *Sarcoidosis* is the disease in which sarcoids occur. They may be scattered throughout the body. Often they cause no trouble, but when they happen to be concentrated in particular organs or tissues they can imitate many diseases, including disorders of the skin or the lymph nodes,

bronchitis, and rheumatism. The liver, nervous system, and blood-forming tissues may also be involved.

Sarcoidosis commonly first appears as *erythema nodosum*, a skin condition that represents a kind of allergic reaction to an infection or an alien substance such as a drug. Enlarged lymph nodes at the roots of the lungs accompany the condition, as do fever and other symptoms on occasions. Such enlarged nodes may appear on routine X-ray examination as the only sign of the disease, but later examination may show fibrous changes in the lungs. Inflammatory changes in the eye call for prompt treatment, usually with corticosteroid drops, in order to protect sight.

Some cases of sarcoidosis gradually deteriorate, but the trend is either recovery, or at least for the disease to become stationary. When treatment is needed, corticosteroids are usually given: small doses generally suffice.

The cause is not known. For many years, sarcoidosis was thought to be a reaction to tuberculosis, but this view is no longer tenable. There is evidently a disorder of immunity, but its nature has yet to be defined.

sarcoma. Cancer arising in bone, connective tissue or muscle, i.e. the tissues mainly derived in the embryo from mesoderm (as opposed to *carcinoma*, arising in covering or lining membranes). Sarcoma is much less common than carcinoma. ➤*cancer*.

sarcoptes. Acarus, a mite, of which one species causes ➤*scabies*.

sartorius. A very long strap of muscle at the front of the thigh, attached to the pelvis above the hip-joint and the upper part of the shin. Its action is to flex both hip and knee, as when sitting cross-legged, tailor-fashion.

scabies (the itch). A minor but distressing skin disease caused by the itch-mite (*Sarcoptes scabei*), of which the female burrows just under the surface of the skin to lay her eggs. The usual sites are soft moist skin, as in front of the elbows or in the groins. The main symptom is itching, which may be complicated by infection of scratch marks with bacteria.

Lotions of insecticides such as lindane or malathion usually clear up the trouble with a single application.

scalp. The skin over the vault of the skull; it is peculiar in several respects. It is extremely tough and inelastic, and it is firmly attached to an underlying muscle, the *epicranius*. This muscle extends as a thin sheet (*frontalis*) from the eyebrows over the forehead and (*occipitalis*) from the nape of the neck over the back of the skull; the central portion is a broad, flat tendon joining the two sheets of muscle. The connective tissue between the epicranius and the skull is very loose and flimsy.

Because the scalp is unyielding, a blow with an instrument as blunt as a rubber truncheon or a boxing glove splits it as cleanly as a knife. The pull of the attached muscle causes the wound to gape, and the blood vessels, of which there are many, are held open. The arteries of the scalp intercommunicate freely, so that there may be arterial bleeding from both sides of the wound. The bleeding can be stopped either by firm pressure over the whole injured area or by stitching the wound.

The loose tissue under the muscle allows bleeding to seep under the whole scalp (whence the black eye from a blow on the forehead). Similarly, pus spreads easily, and abscesses under the scalp are especially dangerous. The flimsiness of the tissue makes it possible for large areas of the scalp to be torn off, e.g. if the hair is caught in machinery.

scan. Any of several methods of portraying internal structures with little or no intervention, giving information that could otherwise be got only by exploratory surgery. Types of scan include:

1. *Scintigraphy*. A radioactive ►*isotope* is artificially incorporated into a substance that the body accepts as it would the ordinary inactive form. Acting as a bugged undercover agent it emits rays that when analysed give information about the organs in which it circulates. Introducing radioactive matter to the body may seem objectionable, but the dose of radiation is usually less than that of an ordinary X-ray examination, and only isotopes that rapidly shed their activity are used.

2. *Echography* (ultrasonography). Bats recognize obstacles by picking up the reflections of their own squeaks. In the same way *sonar* registers the depth of the sea-bed and detects shoals of fish, and echography analyses the reflections of sound waves to provide images of internal organs and tissues. The method can be used for locating gall stones, obstructed arteries and many other abnormalities. It can also measure the flow of blood through a heart valve (echocardiography) and depict a pregnant uterus without incurring the risks to the unborn child that preclude X-ray examination during pregnancy. ►*Doppler shift*.

3. *Computerized tomography* (CT) is a refined form of X-ray photography. A narrow beam of X-rays is swung in an arc around the part to be examined, and

a computer is set to receive and analyse the rays that emerge. Different tissues are more or less opaque to X-rays, and their various degrees of opacity give a picture of a slice through the body like a specimen in an anatomical museum.

4. *Magnetic resonance imaging* (MRI) is the newest form of scan. Under the influence of a magnet atoms, especially those of hydrogen, line themselves up like iron filings in a schoolroom demonstration of a magnetic field. The pattern is analysed by means of radio waves fed into a computer and presented as a picture like that of a CT scan of the organs to be studied. The only objections to this brilliant aid to diagnosis are that the apparatus is very expensive, and that some patients dislike the sensation of being investigated in a drainpipe.

scaphoid. A small bone in the wrist, at the base of the thumb. It is the most easily broken of the carpal bones (the 8 small bones in the ball of the hand), and the fracture is often difficult to recognize in an X-ray picture. As a rule, a fractured scaphoid heals if the wrist is kept in plaster for a few weeks, but in some cases a surgical operation is needed.

scapula (shoulder-blade). A flat, thin triangle of bone about the size of a hand which covers the back of the upper ribs. It has various irregular protrusions for the attachment of muscles, and a shallow socket to receive the rounded upper end of the humerus which forms the *shoulder-joint*.

As it is padded by thick muscles and is very mobile, the scapula is seldom broken. The rare fractures are usually associated with other, more serious injuries.

scapular (adj.). Of the scapula. (The noun 'scapular' has no anatomical meaning: it is a garment.)

scarlatina = ►*scarlet fever*.

scarlet fever (scarlatina). An infectious fever, mainly of childhood, caused by the bacterium *Streptococcus pyogenes*. It is a streptococcal sore throat with the addition of a scarlet rash.

Scarlet fever is spread from case to case by coughing, but many healthy people carry the bacterium and can infect others at any time. The infection can also be spread by contaminated milk or other food.

The symptoms begin about 4 days after infection with fever, sickness, and sore throat. The face is very flushed except that the skin round the mouth remains pale. A day or two later a rash of tiny raised spots, redder than the surrounding skin, spreads over the body.

Apart from the rash, which is unimportant, scarlet fever is no different from any other streptococcal infection. It responds to the same treatment – usually penicillin – and unless treated threatens the same complications (►*streptococcus*).

scavenger cells. Specialized white blood-cells (phagocytes) and wandering cells anywhere in the body (macrophages) that collect the remains of outworn tissues, dead bacteria and the like.

Schick test. A test of susceptibility to diphtheria: a minute dose of diphtheria toxin is injected into the skin, where an inflamed spot appears if the person is susceptible. The test can be used to show whether people exposed to diphtheria need to be immunized.

Schistosoma = ►*bilharzia*.

schistosomiasis. Bilharzial disease.

schizoid personality. A term applied to

people who avoid emotional involvement with others and tend to be aloof, withdrawn, over-sensitive, and sometimes decidedly eccentric. Although 'schizoid' implies 'like schizophrenia', and schizophrenia is a sort of caricature of a schizoid personality, the two conditions are quite distinct. The most that can be said is that if a schizoid person should ever become mentally deranged he would be more likely to develop schizophrenia than any other psychosis.

Schizomycetes. A class of microbes to which bacteria belong.

schizophrenia. A kind of psychosis or mental derangement; it is probably a pattern of symptoms with various causes rather than a single disease, and some psychiatrists therefore prefer the term 'schizophrenic reaction'.

If one symptom can be said to typify schizophrenia it is the impossibility of making any emotional impact on the patient. The term schizophrenia (split mind) does not mean dual personality, but dissociation of the patient's thoughts from the physical reality of his own body and surroundings – it is no mere slip of the tongue when a schizophrenic refers to himself as 'he' and not 'I'.

When once thought is divorced from reality all kinds of mental symptoms can arise. A healthy mind seems to filter a mass of impressions, and pass to full awareness only those that appear to make sense. To a schizophrenic, sense and nonsense may be all one. The jumbled fantasies, the absurd patterns of words and half-formed ideas that most people have when falling asleep give some hint of what may go on in a schizophrenic's mind. His delusions (e.g. of his own importance, or of persecution by others) and hallucinations (e.g. 'hearing

voices') are as real to him as anything else, for he accepts everything that comes into his mind as valid. His intellect is not impaired, but he fails to apply it.

The causes of schizophrenia are largely unknown. To call it an abnormal response to intellectual or emotional conflict only pushes the question one step backwards: why should a few unfortunate people respond in this way? Heredity certainly plays some part but not, it seems, the leading part; it is hard to distinguish hereditary from environmental factors because families tend to share the same environment. Several chemical abnormalities in the brain have been identified. They relate to *adrenaline* (and drugs such as amphetamine that mimic adrenaline can cause an illness like schizophrenia), *serotonin* (and hallucinogenic drugs such as LSD cause symptoms like those of schizophrenia, and they interfere with serotonin), the copper-containing protein *ceruloplasmin*, and many others. But these changes could as easily be effects of the disease as causes. At least some of them are sure to be effects, for the mental turmoil of schizophrenia must be reflected in chemical changes. The idea of schizophrenia as a chemical anomaly like diabetes or gout is attractive, and would hold out better hopes of cure than any other explanation, but much more evidence is needed – especially about the detailed chemistry of the healthy brain.

Until recently, most schizophrenics were certified insane and confined to mental hospitals until they recovered. Many did not recover or if they improved enough to be released they had been in hospital so long that they were unable to cope with the outside world and soon relapsed. It is now known that apart from a minority of severe progressive cases there is no need to keep schizophrenics in hospital for long periods, and that the atmosphere of an institution can easily make them worse by depriving them of their remaining shreds of identity. All schools of psychiatry agree that these patients should and can be integrated with the general public like any others with noninfectious illnesses. Since progress in treatment has made this policy possible it has been found that most patients are soon able to live and work with other people – a normal job of work is itself a useful form of treatment. Some patients relapse, but can be expected to recover after further treatment. A few remain ill, but even these seldom need special hospitals. While the illness is at its height, schizophrenics can be difficult to live with, but they are only seldom dangerous.

Psychological treatment such as psychoanalysis has its advocates among those who regard schizophrenia as the patient's attempt to adapt himself to conflicts that he cannot resolve. Freud, the founder of psychoanalysis, said that it would be an error in schizophrenia. There is even a possibility that analysis may make things worse, and most psychiatrists feel that the place for psychotherapy is in helping the patient to readjust himself when the worst of his symptoms have been allayed by other means.

➤Electroconvulsive therapy is sometimes used. It is not as dramatically helpful with schizophrenia as with severe depression, but it is effective in some cases.

Much the most important advance in the drug treatment of schizophrenia was the introduction in 1954 of the potent tranquillizer, chlorpromazine. This drug, or newer ones of the same type, has made it possible to return severely disturbed patients to their homes in a few weeks instead of years, and with this form of treatment many patients lead normal working lives instead of being restrained in institutions.

Schwann, Theodor (1810–82). German anatomist, a pupil of Müller in Berlin; later professor of anatomy at Louvain. He was the first to recognize that animal tissues were composed of ➤cells, and so paved the way for his colleague Virchow to establish the modern science of pathology.

The *sheath of Schwann* is a membrane around a nerve fibre.

sciatic. Of the *ischium* (rump), one of the bones of the pelvis. The *sciatic nerve* is the principal nerve of the lower limb, the largest nerve in the body. It is formed in the pelvis from branches of several of the lumbar and sacral spinal nerves, passes below the sacroiliac joint to the buttock, then behind the hip-joint to the back of the thigh. It is deeply buried in muscles throughout its course. Above the knee it divides into tibial and peroneal branches, which between them supply all the structures below the knee. Above this division, small branches of the sciatic nerve go to the muscles and skin of the back of the thigh.

sciatica. Persistent pain in the area of the sciatic nerve, i.e. the back of the thigh, calf, and foot; the whole area is not necessarily or even usually involved.

Sciatica is a symptom and not a disease, and in each case it is the cause that has to be identified and treated, and not the sciatica itself. The commonest cause is pressure on a spinal nerve destined for the sciatic nerve, usually by an intervertebral disc ('slipped disc'; ➤vertebra (1)). Less often sciatica is due to pressure on the nerve in the thigh from a bad sitting posture or a badly designed seat. Any disease that causes irritation of nerves, e.g. diabetes, alcoholism, may involve the sciatic nerve and cause a kind of sciatica.

scintigram ➤*scan*.

sclera (sclerotica). The white shell of the eye.

scleroderma. An uncommon disorder of connective tissue, tending to start with thickening and hardening of the skin. Later it may spread to internal organs and impair digestion, breathing and other functions. The cause is unknown. Most symptoms can be treated, but the course of the disease is so unpredictable that the value of treatment is difficult to assess.

sclerosis. Thickening or hardening of tissue; e.g. *arteriosclerosis*, hardening of the arteries; *multiple (disseminated) sclerosis*, deposits of abnormal connective tissue in the central nervous system.

scoliosis. Sideways curvature of the spine (cf. *lordosis*, forward curvature; *kyphosis*, backward curvature).

Scoliosis may be due to weakness of the muscles of one side of the back, e.g. as a result of poliomyelitis; to disease of the vertebrae such as rickets; to chronic disease of one lung, when the muscles on the affected side are held taut; to sciatica or disease of a hip-joint, when the pelvis is tilted to relieve strain on the painful side and the spine is bent in the opposite direction to compensate; or to no apparent cause.

scorbutic. Affected with scurvy (lack of vitamin C).

scorpion. Scorpions are found in most hot countries. They are related to spiders, but whereas a spider injects poison by biting, a scorpion has a poisonous sting in its tail. Scorpion venom is a nerve poison as strong as cobra venom, but the quantity is much less.

A scorpion sting is painful and may be followed by transient weakness of the muscles in its vicinity, but there is little danger except to small children; a child stung by a scorpion is a case for hospital. An antivenene can be given in serious cases. Local anaesthetics are sometimes injected to relieve pain. A dressing soaked in a cold solution of epsom salt or even cold water may help, and the injured part (usually a leg) needs to be kept still. Pain-killing drugs and alcohol do more harm than good.

scotoma. A blind spot in the eye.

scrofula. Tuberculosis of lymph nodes at the side of the neck with ulceration of the over-lying skin; the King's evil, supposed until the time of the Stuarts to be cured by the Royal Touch.

scrotum. A loose bag of skin containing the testes, which function at a few degrees below the temperature of the rest of the body.

scurvy. A defect of the substance that binds cells together, especially in connective tissue and capillary blood vessels, due to lack of vitamin C. The usual cause is lack of fresh vegetables or fruit; but healing of severe injuries or inflammation makes heavy demands on the supply of vitamin C and may cause a relative deficiency even with an average diet. The symptoms include bleeding into the skin, around bones, into joints, and from the gums. The teeth become loose and misshapen. Resistance to infection is lowered. ➤*vitamin; vitamin C*.

sea sickness ➤*travel sickness*.

sebaceous. Of *sebum*, a greasy substance formed by the sebaceous glands of the skin. A *sebaceous cyst* or *wen* is a lump in the skin, often at the back of the neck or on the forehead, filled with sebum because of blockage of one of these glands. If the cyst is unsightly or in any other way a nuisance it is easily removed.

seborrhoea. Excessive activity of the sebaceous glands, often associated with acne or dandruff. A kind of eczema, *seborrhoeic dermatitis*, sometimes develops in greasy skin, especially on the scalp. It consists of small, inflamed, itchy spots, with a tendency to form loose scales. Seborrhoeic dermatitis usually responds to simple lotions and dusting powders, but the spots are prone to bacterial infection, and affected skin has to be kept very clean.

sebum. A greasy substance formed by the sebaceous glands around the roots of hairs. It keeps the skin supple.

secretin. A hormone secreted into the blood by the duodenum in response to the arrival of food from the stomach; this prompts the pancreas to secrete its digestive hormones.

secretion. The formation by an organ (a gland) of a substance that is needed by some other organ or by the body as a whole. The secretions of *exocrine* glands are carried away in tubes (ducts), or poured straight into the place where they are to be used; e.g. the secretions of the digestive glands and the glands of the skin. The secretions of *endocrine* glands – hormones – are released into the blood.

sedative. A medicine for soothing a patient or making him drowsy. The older sedatives are simply small doses of hypnotics, i.e. of drugs that would send the patient to sleep in larger doses. A newer class of drugs, the tranquillizers, allay anxiety without much dulling the patient's general awareness.

semen. Seed; the secretion of the testes, consisting largely of sperms, to which is added fluid from the prostate and other smaller glands opening into the urethra.

seminoma. A cancer of the testis.

Semmelweis, Ignaz Philipp (1818–65). Hungarian obstetrician, a pioneer in the prevention of ➤*puerperal fever*, then a very common cause of death after childbirth, due to bacterial infection of the birth-passage.

Before Semmelweis, Charles White (Manchester, 1773) and Alexander Gordon (Aberdeen, 1795) had written of puerperal fever as a form of contagion; Gordon actually recognized that doctors and midwives could carry the infection on their hands and clothes. Next, Oliver Wendell Holmes (Harvard, 1843) wrote a paper in which he stated: 'The disease known as puerperal fever is so far contagious as to be frequently carried from patient to patient by physicians and nurses.' He warned against the possibility of carrying infection from post-mortem room to labour ward. Nobody paid him the least attention.

In about 1847 Semmelweis, an assistant in the university department of obstetrics in Vienna, noticed firstly that puerperal fever was commoner in his wards (where 10 per cent of the women admitted died of it) than in the wards where the midwives were taught; and secondly that a colleague who died of blood-poisoning after doing a post-mortem examination had the same symptoms as the women. He then realized that his students were in the habit of going straight from the post-mortem room to attend confinements, and he inferred that they carried the infection.

The role of microbes in causing infection was not yet known; nevertheless Semmelweis insisted that everyone attending a confinement should first wash in chlorine water, an efficient antiseptic. The death rate fell at once. Only 1 per cent of the patients still died. Semmelweis published an account of his work in 1861. His views were not only not accepted; he was so abused by his colleagues that he left Vienna and went back to Hungary. He fared better overseas. As early as 1855, Holmes heard of his success and wrote a second paper, to which American doctors did begin to pay attention. A few years later Pasteur and then Lister set the control of infection on a scientific basis and the doctrine of Semmelweis became generally accepted as one of the most important advances in the whole history of medicine.

senility. Although it could mean the sum of all the changes due to old age (>*ageing*), senility is generally taken to mean the changes in the brain (>*dementia*; *Alzheimer*).

sensation. There are several kinds of *receptor*, each responding to a particular kind of stimulus by starting an electrical impulse in an adjacent nerve fibre. The receptors include the rods and cones in the retina of the eye, responding only to light, the organ of Corti in the ear, responding to sound, the taste-buds, the olfactory nerve-endings responding to smells, structures in the skin responding to touch, pressure, and temperature, and receptors for unconscious sensations such as balance and blood pressure. The nerve impulses for all these sensations are identical. They are carried to the brain, where impulses in particular fibres are identified with their sources and translated into information about the environment. Unconscious sensation is conveyed to outgoing (motor) nerve fibres to evoke reflex actions that adjust the body to meet change. Some conscious sensation is also diverted to reflex action, e.g. a bright light is consciously perceived but also causes the pupil to constrict so that the eye is not over-stimulated.

Sensations are essentially events in the brain. If an impulse reaches the brain by a particular sensory nerve then the sensation associated with that nerve is evoked. Dreams and hallucinations must represent spontaneous activity without the usual stimulus to the appropriate receptors, but as far as the brain is concerned the sensations are real.

➤*referred pain.*

sepsis. Destructive infection of tissue by bacteria such as streptococci or staphylococci.

septicaemia. Spread of sepsis by carriage of bacteria in the blood; blood-poisoning.

septum. A partition such as the sheet of bone and cartilage between the nostrils.

sequestrum. A loose fragment of dead bone, formed as a result of infection of bone (osteomyelitis) and then providing a safe shelter for bacteria so that the infection persists until the sequestrum is removed.

serology. The study of serum, especially of the reactions of serum with microbes. If serum from a person's blood contains antibodies that react with a particular species of microbe, that is good evidence that the person is or has been infected with the same kind of microbe – a useful aid to diagnosis of infectious diseases. Conversely, microbes can be identified from their reactions with sera containing known antibodies.

serotonin. 5-Hydroxytryptamine (5-HT); a substance found in many tissues; it is released from blood platelets at a site of bleeding and helps to control the bleeding by causing constriction of small blood vessels. It is concerned with the working of the brain, where it has been identified as a ▸*neuro-transmitter*. Some hallucinogenic drugs interfere with the action of serotonin.

serratus anterior. A large muscle arising from the sides of the ribs and drawing the shoulder-blade forwards, as when punching. If the arms are fixed, the muscle lifts the ribs and helps breathing. A person out of breath will therefore clutch a fixed object.

serum. Clear yellow fluid that separates from clotted blood. ▸*blood* (1; 4).

Servetus (Miguel Servet y Reves) (1511– 53). A Spanish theologian sometimes credited with the discovery of the circulation of blood through the lungs.

Galen's doctrine that blood passed from the left to the right side of the heart through holes in the dividing wall had been accepted for 13 centuries. Servetus said that the blood passed not through the middle wall of the heart but 'by a very ingenious arrangement' through the lungs. He proposed a similar arrangement between the arteries and nerves in the brain. The first theory is correct; the second is nonsense. Neither is based on observation, but the first may have been inspired by a similar suggestion in the 13th century by Ibn an-Nafis.

Servetus's fellow-student Vesalius, a scientific observer, merely said that he could find no holes and that he did not see how Galen's theory could work. Servetus, a dreamer, proposed the right theory without evidence. The real discovery, i.e. demonstration, of the pulmonary circulation was by Vesalius's pupil Colombo. Servetus was concerned not with the flow of blood but with how the Divine Breath reached the remoter parts of the body. Another passage in the same book, *Christianismi Restitutio*, questioned the doctrine of the Holy Trinity. Servetus fled from the wrath of the Spanish Inquisition to the protection of Calvin in Geneva, but Calvin also thought him a heretic and had him burnt at the stake.

sesamoid. A bone formed in a tendon at a point of great friction, e.g. the patella (knee-cap) in the tendon of the quadriceps muscle in front of the knee.

sex. Most bodily functions are concerned with the survival of the individual. Sex ensures the survival of the species. The central event is the *fertilization* of an *ovum* by a *sperm*, and the primary sex organs are the *ovary* and the *testis* in which these germ cells are formed. The accessory sex organs facilitate fertilization and the development of the fertilized ovum. The principal ones are the *Fallopian tubes, uterus* and *vagina* in the female, and the *vas deferens, prostate* and *penis* in the male. These organs are described under their own headings, and the physiology is further considered under *puberty, pregnancy, labour, menopause, sex hormones, genetics*.

Sexual intercourse, or coitus, the process by which fertilization occurs, is based on a simple reflex action: continued stimulation of the penis causes waves of contraction in the involuntary muscles along the urethra, and the ejaculation of a few ml of semen containing some hundreds of millions of sperms, swimming in all directions. One of these may find its way into the uterus, and along a Fallopian tube to penetrate the waiting ovum. Ejaculation is determined at a very primitive level of the nervous system: the nerves involved go no further than the spinal cord. But, like many other reflex actions, it is influenced and modified by many conscious and unconscious factors, and it is preceded and accompanied by many other inborn and conditioned reflexes. These are concerned mainly with the arousal of sexual desire, which prepares the accessory organs for coitus. Unless the male is aroused coitus is not possible, and if the female is not aroused it may be possible but it gives her no pleasure and may be painful. The essential physical changes are erection of the penis by distension with blood, and a similar swelling of tissues at the entrance to the vagina together with secretion of a lubricant fluid. These effects are reflex actions governed by ➤*parasympathetic* nerves, but they are affected by all the senses, and by memory, fantasy, the mood of the moment, moral and aesthetic feelings, and idiosyncrasy. Only a few of these responses appear to be instinctive, e.g. those of certain smells or to contact with lips, breasts or genitalia, and even these few are profoundly affected at higher levels of consciousness: thus intimate contact that by instinct should excite may embarrass or repel if the other person is unattractive or the circumstances are inappropriate.

Most sexual stimuli are learnt and become conditioned reflexes. When skirts reached the ground the sight of a woman's ankles was exciting. In modern western society, breasts have usurped ankles – but in societies where breasts are normally bare the men are not disturbed by them. Kissing is an expression of love, but only among people who are brought up to this idea. And, within a society, individuals differ very widely in their acquired tastes, which may have their origins in infancy or early childhood.

Sexual arousal, if it is continued, culminates in *orgasm*, a sudden burst of activity in the ➤*sympathetic* nervous system, of which the effects in the male include ejaculation of semen, and in both sexes a kind of pleasurable convulsion followed by a profound sense of release and satisfaction. Thus one half of the involuntary (autonomic) nervous system, the parasympathetic, prepares for the climax, and the other half, the sympathetic, achieves it. But the division is not so clear; the two systems work together throughout, and their activity is influenced by hormones and by the conscious elements of the nervous system.

Before considering one or two of the more common medical aspects of the sexual act it may be worth noting the analogy between sexual appetite and the much less complicated appetite for food. At its most primitive, the desire to eat arises from having an empty stomach. The desire is reinforced by the taste or smell of food. That is about all that is inborn or instinctive. The rest has to be learnt, as Pavlov's dogs learnt to associate a bell with food until the bell alone stimulated appetite and they had acquired a conditioned ➤*reflex*. We learn to respond with appetite to the sight of food, talk of food, the trimmings of a well served meal, or merely knowing that it is dinner time. Appetite is enhanced by pleasant surroundings, congenial company and a relaxed mood. Unattractive-looking food, wholesome as it may be, worry, or illness suppress appetite. A delicacy in one society may disgust another. Religions lay down dietary rules that other religions think absurd. Unhappy associations can create dislikes and fads, and within a social group individual tastes differ greatly for no apparent reason.

Sexual feelings develop in the same way and under similar influences, but they are subject to far more public and private censure than tastes in food. A man who eats peanut butter with smoked salmon may seem eccentric, but nobody fetches a psychiatrist or a policeman to him. Even in sexual matters, what matters most is not what society really thinks, but what the individual supposes that society thinks. One of the commonest sources of unhappiness in sex is the fear of falling below a required standard. The conflict between instinctive sexual desire and indoctrinated moral standards is, according to Freud and his disciples, a common source of anxiety and neurosis in general. This may or may not be true, but the conflict is undoubtedly a source of trouble with sex itself. Even in these days of open discussion, people still marry believing, consciously or not, that sex is dirty and wrong. But prudery is not the only tyrant. Permissiveness also has its tyrannies, and girls whose great-grandmothers worried themselves into a decline over losing their virtue are now apt to worry if they remain virgins, or are less promiscuous, or more conventional, than seems right to them. The leaders of subcultures sometimes forget that there are people who prefer simple home cooking to the exotic fare that they advocate.

Inadequacy, real or supposed, is the commonest reason for people to consult their doctors about sex. *Frigidity* is lack of sexual desire, sometimes amounting to positive aversion. The term is nearly always applied to women rather than men, perhaps because the medical vocabulary has been coined by men, and frigid men prefer to call themselves continent. *Impotence* is inability to perform coitus. A woman can be impotent if physical obstruction at the entrance to the vagina makes coitus impossible: ➤*dyspareunia*. But impotence is primarily a male disorder, usually a failure of the penis to erect, but it can also take the form of premature ejaculation, when orgasm occurs and erection subsides either before or at the moment of entry.

These conditions can have physical causes. Sexual activity, like other physical functions, is depressed by general ill health, and by various drugs. Heavy drinking is a common cause of impotence; on the other hand a reasonable drink at bedtime (which in this context does not have to be any fixed hour) can allay the anxiety that is causing the trouble. Hence the reputation of alcohol as an aphrodisiac. Most impotence and most frigidity are emotional states or frames of mind. It is relevant that a few men are impotent with their wives yet potent with prostitutes. This has been rather pompously ascribed to an incest-taboo, the man unconsciously identifying his wife with his mother. A simpler explanation might be that he loves his wife and is afraid of hurting her, physically or mentally. Clear thinking would tell him that his going with prostitutes would hurt her more, but logic has no place in sexual behaviour. Similarly, frigidity has been ascribed to anxieties arising from psychological trauma in childhood, but often it would be simpler and clearer to blame shyness, from which either sex can suffer. And pretended frigidity is natural in women, as in females of other species. A woman is seldom aroused as quickly as a man, and her apparent disinclination is sometimes an invitation to woo her. Unless both partners are prepared for it, coitus is not as satisfying as it should be to either, and may be positively distasteful to the woman.

Most people do not discuss the details of their sex-life, even with their best friends, and those who do are not always truthful. (This casts doubt on some surveys of sexual behaviour.) Young couples disappointed by their first attempts would do well to ignore the glowing accounts that other people offer them. They can take it that most honeymoons are something of a fiasco. A few couples achieve sexual harmony at once, but many more need months or even years. It requires patience and above all consideration. This may sound sanctimonious, but it is true. Instinctive sex is a selfish urge, but civilization is largely a process of modifying and subduing instinct, and civilized sex is a partnership. Professional help is needed if neurosis or physical illness interferes with sex, but in the countless cases where the trouble is ignorance, thoughtlessness or shyness the remedy is largely, perhaps literally, in the partner's hands. It is silly to pretend that sex is not important to a stable marriage. It is supremely important, but not so important that it can never be ridiculed. Laughing at it, and at ourselves for taking it too seriously, often brings it comfortably to earth.

Some other medical aspects of sex are briefly discussed under ➤*contraception, fetishism, homosexuality, masturbation.*

sex chromosomes ➤*genetics* (3).

sex hormones. A person's sex is determined by the sex chromosome from the father at conception. With an X chromosome the gonads become ovaries; with a Y chromosome they become testes. All the other distinguishing marks of sex (sex characters) are determined by hormones formed by the gonads. These hormones are all closely related *steroids*. There are three groups: *androgens, oestrogens*, and *progestogens*. Both sexes have all three, but the proportions differ.

If androgens predominate, male characters (broken voice, facial hair, muscular physique etc.) develop. These characters can be induced in females by giving the hormones artificially, or with certain disorders of the adrenal glands where an excess is produced. In the absence of androgens, female characters develop. Androgens promote the synthesis of protein and the growth of muscle and bone. After puberty the increase of sex hormones causes the ends of the bones, where most growth occurs, to harden, and growth ceases. Because they lack hormones with this effect, eunuchs tend to grow unusually tall.

Oestrogens are the primary female hormones. They influence bodily character less than androgens, because female characters seem to represent the basic human form; it is the male who is a modification. But without these hormones a female remains immature. Their action is more concerned with function than structure; they determine the female sexual cycle, on which fertility depends.

Progestogens are much more specialized hormones, concerned with the preparation and maintenance of pregnancy.

In the body the androgens are represented mainly by *testosterone*, the oestrogens by *oestradiol*, and the progestogens by *progesterone*. The actions of oestradiol and progesterone are considered further under ➤*menstruation* and ➤*ovary*.

Many related hormones have been synthesized for medicinal use. Most are derived from the natural hormones, but synthetic oestrogens such as stilboestrol are not steroids. They are used to make up deficiencies, e.g. of oestrogens after the menopause or of progesterone in some women who tend to miscarry. Some cancers of the reproductive organs can be held in check by altering the balance of sex hormones. Some of the modified androgens promote growth of muscle and bone without stimulating the sex characters.

The sex hormones formed by the gonads are supplemented by varying amounts formed in the cortex of the adrenal glands, which accounts for abnormal sexual development in some disorders of these glands.

The formation and release of sex hormones by the gonads is governed by other hormones from the pituitary gland. If the pituitary is defective there is no stimulus to the gonads and therefore a deficiency of sex hormones.

shaking palsy ➤*parkinsonism.*

shell shock. A very severe form of anxiety neurosis among soldiers exposed to trench warfare in the First World War. The term was dropped because the blast of shells was no more than a contributory cause; but at least it was better than the term thrown up by the Second World War – *lack of moral fibre* – with its implication that the patient and not the war was to be blamed.

shingles ➤*herpes* zoster.

shock. Failure of the circulation of blood when the blood pressure is too low to maintain an adequate flow through the tissues and back to the heart; often the immediate cause of death from injury or acute illness. The lethal factor is a reduced flow of blood through the brain. Other organs can manage for a while with a reduced supply, but the brain cannot.

In health, the calibre of the blood vessels is such that they offer a steady resistance to flow. As a result, an even pressure is maintained, enough to ensure that sufficient blood is pumped through the vessels of the brain to keep up a supply of oxygen and glucose and to remove waste.

Unless some compensating mechanism operates, the pressure must fall if (1) the volume of blood is decreased, or (2) the capacity of the vessels is increased, or (3) the heart pumps less vigorously. All three can contribute to shock. A fourth but less likely cause of a fall in blood pressure would be decreased viscosity of the blood.

1. When someone donates a pint of blood his vessels contract so that the remaining 7 pints still fill them at the original pressure. Later, the volume is restored from the tissue fluid, and the lost protein and cells are replaced more gradually. But after more serious bleeding, with the addition of damage to tissue, the vessels cannot contract enough, and the pressure falls. The bleeding need not be apparent. Enough blood can be lost into the muscles of the thigh around a fractured femur to cause shock. A very large amount of fluid, much of it derived from the blood, can accumulate in a burn, with similar effects on the circulation to severe bleeding. Diarrhoea or vomiting can be so profuse that all the

tissues, including the blood, are short of water; for instance if people die of cholera they are in effect killed by shock.

2. An ordinary faint is due to reflex activity including sudden widening of blood vessels to internal organs. The simultaneous constriction of vessels in the skin, causing pallor, does not nearly compensate, and for a moment – until he lies down – the patient is in a state of shock. A similar reflex may operate after injury, and increase the effect of bleeding. Pain and anxiety make it worse. Anything done to relieve pain or calm fear is more than mere kindness – it may be life-saving. With some very severe infections and some types of chemical poisoning the control of blood vessels by the nervous system may become so disorganized that shock develops. It is in this type of shock that the corticosteroid drugs are sometimes very helpful.

3. The efficiency of the heart may suddenly fall off after damage to the heart muscle, e.g. by coronary thrombosis, causing the blood pressure to fall to a dangerous level.

Two or three of these types of shock can occur together. If the circulation is impaired for any reason the heart and blood vessels are deprived of oxygen like any other organs, and this causes the blood vessels to dilate and the heart to beat less effectively. A very dangerous vicious circle is then established, and without prompt treatment the patient is unlikely to live.

The treatment of shock obviously depends on the cause. With injuries the first step is to ensure that no further injury is done. Many people who might have survived their original injury are killed by unskilful attempts to move them. Bleeding has to be stopped if replacing lost blood is to do much good. Quite light pressure over an artery or around the edges of the wound is enough, or a well applied bandage. When bleeding has stopped, interference with the wound may start it again.

Movement of broken limbs increases the damage and the pain; both contribute to shock.

In the past great stress was laid on the value of warmth, but in fact warmth can do harm by dilating the blood vessels of the skin. It is enough to keep the patient comfortable and prevent him from shivering; cooking him does no good.

Morphine or some such drug may help by relieving pain and calming the patient. Alcohol, on the other hand, promptly lowers the blood pressure and is dangerous. Anything at all given by mouth has to be avoided until it is certain that none of the digestive organs is damaged.

With most types of shock the definitive treatment is to replace lost fluid, with blood or plasma transfusion if possible, though other kinds of fluid are also valuable. Drugs to raise the blood pressure, such as noradrenaline and angiotensin, are occasionally helpful but their usefulness is limited.

shock therapy. Treatment of severe mental disorder by abrupt stimulation of the brain cells sufficient to cause a kind of epileptic seizure. Nobody knows how this works, but in practice it often gives quick and lasting relief from severe depression and some other disorders. Various drugs have been used for the purpose, but their effects are difficult to control, and at present the standard method is by applying a small electric current to the scalp (>*electro-convulsive therapy*).

shoulder

1. STRUCTURE

The shoulder is a ball-and-socket joint between the rounded head of the ►*humerus* and the glenoid fossa of the ►*scapula*.

The shape of the bones lends little stability to the joint, for the glenoid fossa is small and shallow. While in the hip the head of the femur sits like an egg in an egg-cup, in the shoulder the head of the humerus is more like a golf ball on a tee. Like all movable joints, the shoulder is enclosed in a fibrous capsule, but the capsule is slack and gives little support. Nor is there much support from accessory ligaments. The stability of the shoulder depends almost entirely on muscles.

Fan-shaped muscles from both surfaces of the scapula converge on the upper end of the humerus, to which they are attached behind, above, and in front of the joint. Their tendons merge with the joint capsule, and serve as adjustable ligaments, of which the tension can be maintained in any position.

The deltoid muscle covers the joint and its scapular muscles. Below the joint the nerves and vessels of the arm are close enough to be involved occasionally in fractures or dislocations.

2. MOVEMENTS

The shoulder has a wide range of movement in all directions.

In all but slight movements of the shoulder the scapula moves with the arm. A straight punch is ineffective if the shoulders are braced back. But if the scapula is swung round so that the glenoid fossa looks forwards, the humerus has a firm backing.

When the arms are raised above the head through 180 °, about 90 ° of the

Dissection of left shoulder

movement takes place at the shoulder-joint itself, and 90 ° comes from rotation of the scapula. If for any reason the shoulder-joint should become immobilized there may still be a good deal of useful movement from the scapula.

3. DISORDERS

The shoulder is more readily *dislocated* than any other joint in the body. This is the price of mobility. It is embraced by muscles on three sides, but below there is little to keep it in place. Dislocation of the head of the humerus is nearly always downwards and forwards. Hippocrates rightly said that dislocation in other directions seemed possible, but he added that he had not seen a case. Simple manipulation is usually all that is needed, but occasionally there are complications.

The nerves and vessels below the joint may be involved. The tendons that merge with the capsule may be torn, in which case the dislocation will be liable to recur. There may be an associated fracture, especially since the tendons may be more resilient than the bone to which they are attached. But a fracture is less troublesome than a torn tendon, because bone heals better than fibrous tissue.

These tendons lie in a narrow gap between the joint and an overhang of the scapula, the acromion process. Injury or inflammation of the tendons, or of the subacromial bursa, leads to painful friction when the shoulder is abducted, and sometimes to the painful stiffness known as ►*frozen shoulder*.

shoulder-blade ►*scapula*.

sickle-cell anaemia. A hereditary defect of red blood cells. ►*haemoglobin*; *genetics*.

side-effect. Unwanted action of a drug, e.g. drowsiness from an antihistamine given to relieve allergic symptoms, or acceleration of the heart by a drug given for asthma. The term is not usually applied to the toxic effects of an overdose, but to an effect of a standard therapeutic dose. ►*drug*.

sidero-. Prefix = 'iron', e.g. sideropenia, iron deficiency; *siderosis*, deposition of excess iron of the tissues.

SIDS. Sudden infant death syndrome; ►*cot death*.

sigmoid. S-shaped. The sigmoid colon is the last part of the large intestine before the rectum, lying in the left side of the pelvis.

sigmoidoscopy. Direct examination of the rectum and sigmoid colon with a lighted tube.

sign. Objective indication of disease, i.e. one found by examining a patient, as opposed to a ►*symptom*, reported by the patient himself.

silicosis. Deposition of silica dust in the lungs, an occupational disease of miners. ►*pneumoconiosis*.

silver nitrate. Dilute solutions or suspensions of silver salts were formerly much used as antiseptics in the treatment of infected mucous membranes, and for preventing infection in the eyes of new-born babies. Penicillin generally superseded them.

Simmonds' disease. (Morris Simmonds (1855–1925), German physician.) Failure of the ►*pituitary* gland.

Simpson, Sir James Young (1811–70). Scottish gynaecologist; a pioneer of anaesthesia. ►*anaesthetics* (2).

sinew. Tendon or ligament.

sinus. 1 (path.). Burrowing ulcer in the form of a blind tube, usually a track by which pus formed at the blind end reaches a body surface. A *fistula* is similar but open to body surfaces at both ends (a body surface may be the skin or the lining of a hollow organ).

2 (anat.). (a) Recess or cavity opening off a hollow structure, e.g. the *air sinuses* around the nose; (b) natural bulge in a tube, e.g. the *carotid* sinus, a dilated segment of the internal carotid artery, sensitive to pressure changes; (c) blood-space with inelastic walls, e.g. the *venous sinuses* around the inside of the skull carrying blood from the brain to the jugular veins; (d) any cavity not otherwise classified.

The *paranasal air sinuses*, or simply 'the sinuses', are extensions of the cavity of the nose into the surrounding bones.

The largest is the maxillary sinus or antrum, which occupies most of the bone between the floor of the orbit and the roots of the upper teeth. The maxilla looks solid but is only a shell of bone, lined with an extension of the mucous membrane of the nose. There are similar sinuses over the eyebrows (frontal), in the roof of the nose (ethmoid), and at the back of the nose (sphenoid). All open by narrow channels into the side of the nose, and all are in effect extensions of the nose. The middle ear and ►*mastoid* antrum communicate with the nose by the Eustachian tube and are part of the same system.

The sinuses act as resonators for the voice; otherwise they have no known function, except to reduce the weight of the skull.

The mucous membrane of the nose swells quickly when it is inflamed with a common cold or hay fever, and may block the openings of the sinuses. A sudden change of air pressure, e.g. with change of altitude, is then painful because the air trapped in the sinuses is still at the original pressure. The discomfort is usually worst in the ears because the ear-drums are very sensitive to differences of pressure inside and out, but the maxillary and frontal sinuses can also be painful. Even at ground level air is slowly absorbed from the sinuses into the blood, and cannot be replaced if the openings are blocked. The partial vacuum is as uncomfortable as raised pressure.

Inflammation of the sinuses (►*sinusitis*) is discussed below.

sinusitis. Inflammation of the mucous membranes lining one or more sinuses of the nose due to spread of infection from the nose, often a complication of allergy (hay fever). Since the sinuses are merely a continuation of the cavity of the nose some degree of sinusitis accompanies every cold. The condition becomes troublesome when the infection is trapped and persists. The passages from the nose to the sinuses are narrow at the best of times, and when the mucous membranes are congested and swollen these passages are easily blocked by quite small quantities of mucus. Any deformity of the cartilages of the nose increases the chance of blockage.

Sinusitis causes moderate to severe headache or faceache with an unpleasant sense of stuffiness in the nose. In an acute attack the patient may be ill and feverish for some days. With chronic sinusitis the nose always feels blocked, and acute attacks may be precipitated by colds, hay fever, damp foggy weather or even emotional upsets.

Acute sinusitis needs thorough treatment, not only because it is disagreeable, but to avoid the remote danger that the infection might spread inwards and cause meningitis. Antibiotics are used to clear up infection in the sinuses and have largely overcome the need for surgical treatment. Nasal drops to shrink the mucous membrane give prompt but temporary relief. After their brief effect has worn off the condition may be worse than it was beforehand, especially if they are used habitually. Bland solutions, e.g. of sodium bicarbonate, are used to rinse out infected sinuses.

skeleton. The highest status reached by animals without some sort of rigid framework is that of the earthworm and the octopus.

Skeletons are of two kinds: a shell of hard, inert material exuded by the skin (*exoskeleton*), and an inner framework of living tissue (*endoskeleton*). An exoskeleton is a good passive defence, but

skull

7 cervical vertebrae

sternum

clavicle

scapula

12 thoracic vertebrae

humerus

5 lumber vertebrae

pelvis

ribs

sacrum

ulna

radius

coccyx

femur

patella

tibia

fibula

leaves little scope for initiative. It is a dead thing that has to be cast off to allow growth, leaving the animal helpless until another is formed. If a shell is heavy enough to protect, it is also cumbersome.

All creatures that can be called higher animals have an internal framework. The simplest endoskeleton is the *notochord*, a crude, unjointed forerunner of a backbone. This is an improvement on the condition of the spineless worm, for it enables muscles to work without contracting the whole body – a worm trying to advance on a smooth surface only manages to squirm.

On its own, a notochord is by no means better than a shell. The defenceless owners of these primitive skeletons, such as the lancelet, bury themselves in tidal sand with only their mouths protruding to gather such food as comes their way; they seldom risk a nocturnal swim. In comparison, the swift and voracious lobster seems a very lord of creation. But the humble lancelet, or a similar creature some 500 million years ago, was the ancestor of all vertebrates – fish, flesh, fowl. The notochord has all but disappeared in these more complex animals, but even in man it is important to the embryo, where it precedes the vertebral column. Traces of it persist into adult life in the intervertebral discs.

From the forward end of the notochord a living skull, able to grow with the brain, has been evolved. The addition to the skull of a mobile lower jaw is among the most important steps in evolution, for more than anything else it marks the transition from passive to active existence.

Limbs within shells can be serviceable, as the claws of a lobster or the hind legs of a grasshopper, but they are not as versatile as limbs built round a central core – wings, fins, hooves, hands.

Even a vertebrate may have a supplementary exoskeleton. Tortoises have an obvious one, and the skin of a shark is like a flexible shell. A man's hair, finger-nails, and dental enamel are derived from his skin, of which the horny outermost layer (stratum corneum) is a thin, flexible shell.

Vertebrate skeletons are all based on the same plan: an *axial* skeleton consisting of skull, backbone, ribs and tail, and an *appendicular* skeleton consisting of pectoral (shoulder) and pelvic (hip) girdles each bearing two limbs. Species differ from each other mainly in proportions.

Some human characteristics are related to man's unique upright stance; others, to the use of the forelimbs for feeding, for defence, and above all for learning.

The *skull* has to house a relatively enormous brain, and the cranium is accordingly much larger than the face. With the great development of the frontal lobes of the brain, the large forehead forms a shelf above the eyes. As in other primates, but not in lower orders, the deep eye-sockets are walled off from the temples by bone. The nose is prominent not because it is important, but because the teeth below it have receded. For the same reason man (alone among animals) has a chin.

The *backbone* is composed of 33 vertebrae. The first 24 make a flexible column from the nape of the neck to the small of the back; the next 5 are fused to form the sacrum, to which the pelvic girdle is attached; and the last 4 form a vestigial tail, the coccyx. The vertebrae are separated by discs of very tough fibrocartilage, which between them account for about a quarter of the height of the whole column.

When it is first formed, the whole backbone is curved in a single arc, convex backwards. It is so in a new-born baby. But this curvature would make an upright stance impossible. As the baby begins to move its head and use its eyes, the curve in the neck is reversed, to become convex forwards, and the same thing happens with the lumbar vertebrae when the baby begins to stand. The adult pattern is thus a forward curve in the neck, a backward curve from the root of the neck to the last rib, a forward curve between ribs and pelvis, and lastly a backward curve of the sacrum and coccyx.

The *ribs* project from the sides of the vertebrae and curve round the body-wall to enclose the heart and lungs, sloping downwards at about 45 °.

In front the bone of a rib gives way to cartilage. The upper 7 cartilages join a flat bone at the front of the chest, the *sternum*. The next 3 join the cartilage above but do not reach the *sternum*. The last two are unattached.

The elements of the primitive pectoral girdle are fused to form the *scapula* or shoulder-blade, which with its attached muscles is free to slide over the upper ribs, carrying the arm with it. A ridge of bone projects from the back of the scapula above and beyond the shoulder-joint. To it is attached the outer end of the *clavicle* or collar-bone. This is a simple strut, joined at its inner end to the sternum. Animals which use their forelimbs only for running, and so need only a pendulum movement at the shoulder, have a rudimentary clavicle or none (e.g. dog, horse). The clavicles allow muscles to move the arms in various directions without simply displacing the shoulders.

The *upper limbs* follow the most primit-

ive pattern with only slight, but important modifications. The radius and ulna are about equally massive, whereas in more specialized limbs the ulna tends to degenerate. In man, joints between these two bones at either end (additional to the elbow and wrist proper) allow the forearm to twist through almost 180 ° (➤*radius*). This allows objects to be picked up and then turned over for study.

Except for a single feature the human hand is very primitive. It looks much like that of a lizard, and the type is common to many tree-dwelling animals. We may suppose that vertebrates took very early to the trees, where the simple 5-fingered hand was a good instrument for climbing. It needed modification only in animals that returned to the ground and had to run, or in those that took to the air. Man's latest ancestors were surely tree-dwellers, and they left him the priceless heritage of an unevolved carpus with 5 intact digits: priceless, because unspecialized and therefore adaptable. The one special feature of the human hand is the extreme mobility of the thumb, or more strictly of the 1st metacarpal at the base of the thumb. This little bone is so jointed at the carpus that it can be swung from its 'natural' position, in line with the other 4 metacarpals, across the palm so that the thumb is *opposed* to the fingers. The tip of the thumb can thus be brought to bear on the tip of any of the fingers. Many animals can oppose their thumbs, but none to anything like the same extent as man. This movement accounts more than any other for man's dexterity, and so, to a great extent, for his general pre-eminence among animals.

The pelvic girdle is a rigid structure, firmly attached to the backbone. The last 5 vertebrae (excluding the rudimentary tail) are fused to form the sacrum. To either side of this massive bone is attached a hip-bone which curves round to meet its fellow in front. On the outer side of each hip-bone is a deep socket (contrasting with the very shallow cup on the scapula) into which the head of the femur fits to make the hip-joint. Since the hips are widely separated by the pelvis, whereas the knees are together, the two femora are set at a V-shaped angle.

Throughout the lower limb, mobility is sacrificed to stability. It is much more specialized than the upper limb. The hip, as a ball-and-socket joint, has some movement in all directions, but movement at the knee and ankle is limited to one plane. The fibula is no more than an appendage of the tibia, and no movement between the two is possible. The bones of the foot are jointed to allow twisting movements. They are arranged to form flexible arches along and across the foot; man thus walks on springs. No other creature has arched feet, just as no other creature walks quite upright.

The 206 bony elements of the skeleton are held in place by tough fibrous bands called *ligaments*, but the stability of the system depends much more on the interaction of the muscles, which serve not only to move the joints but also to maintain their posture.

➤*bone*; *joints*; and the bones and joints named above.

skin. The two principal layers of the skin are the *dermis*, composed of tough, elastic connective tissue with a rich network of blood vessels and nerves, and the *epidermis*, a protective outer layer without blood vessels. The epidermis has a deep layer of growing cells and a covering of dried dead cells that are constantly shed and replaced from the growing layer.

The sweat glands are curled tubes of epidermis that grow down into the dermis. The nails and hair are also derived from epidermis. Like sweat glands, hair follicles (roots) grow down into the dermis. Each follicle gives rise to a few sebaceous or grease glands.

The skin is more than a waterproof jacket for the body. It is an active and versatile organ of sensation and of adaptation to a changing environment.

Since it is almost waterproof, the skin prevents rapid absorption or evaporation at the surface of the body and so helps to keep the amount of water in the body constant. It is a fairly good shield against injury – after all, it is leather – and it heals quickly if it is damaged, unless a large area is lost. Sweat and sebum are both mildly antiseptic.

The sensations of touch, pressure, warmth, cold, and pain provide much information about the environment and provide warning of certain dangers. Sometimes they evoke protective reflexes.

The most elaborate function of the skin is to keep the internal ➤*temperature* of the body constant.

1. DISORDERS

Hundreds of different skin diseases have been described. Many are analogous with diseases of other organs. The skin suffers far more injuries than the rest of the body, and although it is a fairly good barrier to infection it is so much exposed that many types of infection are common. They include virus infections (e.g. *warts*), bacterial infections (*boils*; *erysipelas*; *impetigo*), and fungal infections (*ringworm*), and also infestation with larger parasites such as *scabies*. Fleas and lice can be dangerous because they can transmit infectious disease.

Congenital defects of the skin include

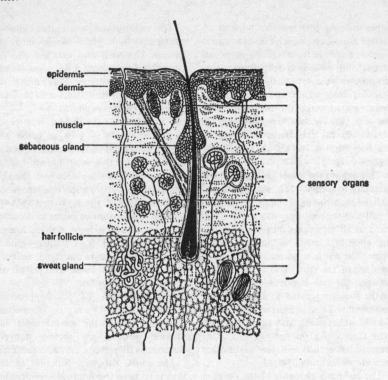

Section of skin, magnified

the various kinds of *birth-mark*, and some very rare disorders such as *icthyosis* and a congenital lack of sweat glands that makes it impossible to live in a hot climate.

Cancer of the skin is generally safer than most forms of cancer, partly because it is noticed while it is likely to be curable, and partly because one form, the rodent ulcer, does not migrate to other parts of the body.

Allergy and irritation by noxious substances cause many kinds of *dermatitis* (eczema). These are the commonest of all occupational diseases.

Because it is open to inspection, the skin often shows signs of illness of the body as a whole; e.g. the rashes of many fevers or the skin changes of vitamin deficiencies.

The skin has more unexplained diseases than other organs, perhaps because disorders that would be too slight to arouse comment in any other organ are enough to irritate the skin and – which is much more important – arouse a sense of disgust. *Acne*, for instance, brings great distress to adolescents, yet in purely physical terms it is hardly worth calling a disease. Even *psoriasis*, which most people would regard as a fairly serious skin disease, may be no more than a rather unusual response to some form of irritation.

Emotional distress is often out of all proportion to the real severity of a skin disease, and the feeling that he is 'unclean' outweighs any other symptoms the patient may have. The specialist in skin diseases has to be something of a psychiatrist as well. To complicate matters, most skin diseases are aggravated by anxiety. Some have been blamed entirely on worry ('neurodermatitis') but in such cases there is probably an underlying physical disorder that flares up at times of emotional stress.

skull. The skull includes more than 20 named bones, some of them with several components, all firmly interlocked. There are movable joints with the neck and the lower jaws, but the components of the skull itself are so tightly joined that they can be considered as parts of a single bone, comprising the brain-box (*cranium*) and the face, which is suspended from the front half of the cranium.

The cranium is moulded to the contours of the brain; it is the growth of the brain that determines the shape of the bones and not vice versa. The vault of the skull (*calvarium*) is rounded. It is made up of the *frontal bones* in front, *parietal* at the top and sides, *temporal* around the ears, and *occipital* at the back. These consist of two thin sheets of ivory-like bone separated by a spongy layer, the diploë. Although the structure appears flimsy, the round form gives it considerable strength.

The floor or base of the cranium includes parts of the frontal, temporal, and occipital bones joined to a bridge, the *sphenoid bone*, which spans the skull behind the eyes. The floor is arranged in descending tiers or *fossae*. The foremost

is the anterior *fossa*, supporting the frontal lobes of the brain and roofing the orbits and nose. Next, the middle fossa behind the eyes supports the temporal lobes, and below and behind is the posterior fossa containing the cerebellum. On the underside, the front part of the floor of the cranium forms the roof of the face, and the back part is the anchorage of the muscles of the neck.

A large hole in the centre of the floor, the *foramen magnum*, allows the stem of the brain to enter the spinal canal, where it is continued as the spinal cord. There are numerous smaller holes for the passage of nerves and blood vessels.

The bones of the face are arranged round the openings for the eyes, nose, and mouth. The centre-piece on either side is the maxilla, which provides the floor of the orbit, the side of the internal part of the nose, the base of the cheek, and the upper jaw. It appears to be massive, but it consists mainly of a thin-walled cavity, the maxillary sinus (antrum). Several of the other bones are hollowed out by sinuses, all opening into the nose. The cheek bone (zygoma) forms an arch,

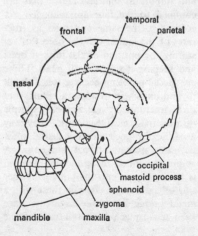

fastened like the handle of a jug to the maxilla in front and the temporal behind.

1. DISORDERS

Various congenital malformations are occasionally seen. Because the development of the skull follows that of the brain, a deformity of the skull does not affect the brain. One type of mental defect, microcephaly, is associated with an abnormally small head, but the primary defect is in the brain; and because the brain fails to grow properly the skull remains small. With hydrocephaly, when an excess of fluid accumulates around the brain, the skull enlarges to accommodate the excess; this is no problem because the bones of the calvarium are separate in early life, and the fibrous bridges between them can expand. With the hereditary type of dwarfism, achondroplasia, the bones of the limbs and face are underdeveloped but the cranium grows to the normal size, and the brain is not affected.

Fractures of the skull are common and important injuries. Those that are confined to the face are managed according to the same principles as fractures of the limbs, with the object of restoring the position of the broken bone and keeping it still while it heals. There are special problems because it is difficult to find anywhere to apply a splint, and these fractures provide a good example of modern surgical teamwork. They may need the combined efforts of dental, plastic, and nose-and-throat surgeons. A common method of temporary fixation is to insert pins into the bone on either side of the fracture and join these with a metal bridge when the fragments have been set in place. With fractures of the jaws a method described by the ancient Egyptians is still in use: that of joining the teeth with wires so that the intact jaw splints the broken one.

With fractures of the cranium, the fracture itself is of little importance. The complications are all that matters. The underlying vessels are likely to be damaged, and the bleeding is extremely dangerous to the brain. There is no room for expansion in the skull, and quite a small amount of blood can cause fatal pressure on the brain. If the signs are recognized at once it is usually possible to operate and stop the bleeding. If the fracture is associated with an open wound there is a danger of infection inside the skull, which again can be dealt with if it is recognized in time. Hence when there is the least suspicion of a fractured skull the patient needs to be under close supervision.

A depressed fracture – a dent in the bone – is treated by lifting the fragment, which may otherwise cause localized pressure. The method was described by Hippocrates (5th century BC).

➤*head injury*.

sleep. Although we spend about a third of our lives asleep, and it is apparently necessary to health that we should do so, we know little of the nature of sleep and almost nothing of its purpose.

The activity of the brain, as shown by the electroencephalogram, is altered but not suppressed. The cerebral cortex, where most of the conscious activity of the brain seems to take place, is still electrically active during sleep, but the activity is unconscious because the impulses from the reticular formation of the midbrain are cut off. The reticular formation acts as a switching station between the highest levels of the brain and the rest of the nervous system, and it seems to have the power of determining whether one is awake or asleep. When the reticular formation is switched to sleep, nervous impulses continue to circulate in the cortex and the rest of the brain, but they are no longer dependent on incoming impulses from the sense organs.

The electrical waves from the waking brain are rapid and irregular, averaging about 10 per second. In very light sleep the waves become smaller and rather slower. In deep sleep the waves are slow and regular, about 1 per second, and much larger than the waking waves, from large numbers of nerve cells acting synchronously. The depth of sleep varies in different parts of the brain.

In the course of a night's sleep there are episodes of electrical activity in the cortex associated with rapid eye movements (REM). An average period of REM sleep is 15 or 20 minutes, followed by 70–90 minutes without REM. Everyone, including people who say that they never dream, probably dreams during REM sleep. But a dream is remembered only if one wakes almost at once. The 'non-dreamers' are the people who sleep on. If they are deliberately woken while their eyes are seen to be moving they remember dreaming like anyone else.

The factors determining whether the reticular formation is switched to sleeping or waking are complex and poorly understood. The formation seems to have its own day-and-night rhythm, but this is readily modified. Habit (conditioned reflex) has a considerable influence. It is reinforced by lack of strong sensations – i.e. by comfort, darkness and silence – or by monotonous, rhythmic sensations such as a steadily flashing light or a repetitive sound, even

a loud one. Tiredness, whatever that may be, is obviously important.

The changes during sleep are not confined to the brain. The chemical processes of the body are slowed, and the flow of saliva, tears, mucus, and urine decreases.

It may seem almost self-evident that the body needs a rest from time to time, but in fact it is nothing of the kind. Nobody knows why the brain or any other organ should need rest, nor what happens to the brain during sleep that does it good. Only one thing is certain: that sleep is necessary. The desire to sleep is almost overwhelming after 2 or 3 days without sleep. If the subject is forced to stay awake he behaves as though he was drunk, with the difference from the drunkard that he can usually pull himself together and behave normally for short periods. Deprivation of sleep is an effective technique of brain-washing. It can produce distinct alteration of personality. When normal sleep is restored, the subject sleeps longer and deeper than usual for some nights, with frequent long periods of REM sleep.

The subject can be selectively deprived of REM sleep by waking him as soon as his eyes begin to move, and although he is allowed his usual hours of sleep the loss of REM sleep has similar effects to depriving him of all sleep. This rather suggests that dreaming is a necessary function.

Insomnia is a very common symptom. It can be a direct result of physical symptoms such as pain, itching, or indigestion. Anxiety makes it difficult to go to sleep, and depression causes early waking, but here one may confuse cause with effect. A person who thinks that he does not sleep enough develops anxiety about it. Many people feel tired because they cannot cope with their affairs, and persuade themselves that they cannot cope because they are tired. They therefore take sleeping pills that make them still less able to cope. There is a clear analogy between insomnia and constipation, where worry about a supposed disorder becomes a real disorder.

None of the time-honoured rules about hours of sleep is valid, except that everyone needs what is enough for *him*. Most children sleep a good deal longer than adults, but there are healthy children who sleep much less than most. A child in good physical health is unlikely to go short of the sleep that he, individually, needs. Old people tend to sleep less, but they are apt to get too little sleep because of depression arising from loneliness or physical ailments.

sleeping sickness. An infectious disease confined to tropical Africa, transmitted by tsetse flies. ►*trypanosomiasis*.

sleepy sickness ►*Encephalitis* lethargica, an epidemic virus infection.

slipped disc ►*vertebra* (1).

slough. A fragment of dead tissue cast off from living tissue, e.g. the core of a boil.

slow virus. Because it is not certain that these should have been classified as viruses they are also known as *prions*. They are mutations of certain normal cell proteins, smaller than any known virus, and lacking DNA or RNA. They apparently replicate by means of the DNA of cells that they have invaded. After a long interval (hence 'slow') they cause serious disorders of the brain (spongiform encephalopathy). These include Creutzfeld–Jakob disease in humans, scrapie in sheep, and 'mad cow disease' in cattle.

small-for-date ►*prematurity*.

smallpox (variola). A dangerous and highly contagious viral disease, formerly a worldwide scourge. As affluent countries adopted routine vaccination after 1800, smallpox became mainly a tropical disease, and was still rife in most poor countries until well into the second half of the 20th century. A determined campaign led by the World Health Organization now seems to have relegated smallpox to medical history, making it the first disease ever to be eradicated.

The symptoms of smallpox begin with a severe fever 12 days after exposure to infection, followed 3 days later by a rash like that of chickenpox. But while a chickenpox rash is concentrated on the trunk, and fresh spots, which lie close to the surface, appear on successive days, smallpox spots tend to be dense on the face and may appear on the palms and soles and in the mouth. As they affect the deeper layers of the skin regularly some scarring is the rule rather than the exception. The mortality varied in different outbreaks, but was often high.

smoking ►*tobacco*.

snake bite. Most snakes are not poisonous, though it is wise to regard them all as dangerous until proved safe. Poisonous snakes carry venom in modified salivary glands. When they bite, the venom flows into the wound along grooved or hollow fangs.

Snake venoms are of two principal types: nerve poisons which paralyse the victim, and tissue poisons which destroy cells and interfere with the clotting of blood.

The only poisonous snake in Britain and most of Europe is the common adder. Its bite is unpleasant but seldom deadly. All the other continents have numerous species of highly poisonous snakes, mostly in tropical regions. As a rule they are timid creatures and bite man only as a last resort in self-defence, though a few seem to be aggressive, e.g. mamba (Africa), fer-de-lance (tropical America), hamadryad (Asia). Puff adders are dangerous because they are too sluggish to get out of the way, and kraits because they are too small to be noticed. More people die from snake bite in India than in the rest of the world together.

With dangerous snakes the best treatment is the appropriate antivenene as soon as possible. Hospitals in tropical countries keep a *polyvalent serum*, effective against all the local snakes, and people exposed to the risk of snake bite far from medical help carry a supply in a snake-bite kit. As symptoms may be delayed for a day or more, anyone bitten by a tropical snake is best taken to hospital even if he does not appear to be in trouble.

There is some controversy over first aid. A splint is needed to keep the limb still (it is nearly always a limb); and a tourniquet or bandage above the bite only tight enough to grip the limb *lightly* may help, but it has to be released for a full minute every half hour and reapplied higher up.

Some people cut the punctures open and rub in potassium permanganate crystals; others inject a solution of epsom salt. Unless they are done with some skill these more heroic measures (including the tourniquet) can do more harm than good, and they are useless after a few hours when the poison has spread. An important part of first aid is to give no alcohol.

Snow, John (1813–58). London physician, the first to specialize in anaesthesia. Even more celebrated than his many contributions to the technique of anaesthesia was Snow's investigation of an outbreak of cholera, worthy of the best detective fiction, which he traced to an infected water supply when nothing was yet known of infection by microbes, and everyone else thought that cholera was due to noxious vapours in the air.

sodium. A metallic element distributed throughout the body, most abundant in the body fluids outside the cells; within the cells it is largely replaced by potassium. It is taken into the body mainly as sodium chloride (common ➤*salt*). Most diets contain slightly more than is needed, and the excess is passed by the kidneys into the urine. If there is a shortage the kidneys pass none, but some salt is inevitably lost in sweat and this has to be replaced in the diet. ➤*salt*.

soft sore ➤ *chancroid*.

solar plexus ➤ *coeliac plexus*.

soldier's heart = ➤*effort syndrome*.

solvent abuse. Many common solvents, such as those used in glue for model aeroplanes, are chemically related to anaesthetics such as ether and chloroform, or to alcohol. Like these they are intoxicating. Inhaling the vapour of certain glue solvents causes fleeting excitement followed by confusion, dizziness and stupor. If, as easily happens, 'glue-sniffing' becomes a habit, the brain is liable to be permanently damaged, together with the kidneys, liver, lungs and heart. An affected child may die from failure of any of these, but is more likely to grow up with seriously impaired mental and physical health. Despite intensive propaganda addressed to both children and parents, this epidemic shows no signs of abating.

somatic. Of the body as opposed to the mind, or of the body with the exception of the reproductive cells (which are in a sense immortal).

Soranus of Ephesus (*c.* AD 100). Roman physician; by repute a prolific writer on many medical topics, but most of his work is either lost or survives only in much later translations. He is regarded as the best gynaecologist of antiquity, and the leading authority on mental illness.

spasm. Sustained involuntary contraction of muscle, often caused by inflammation in a neighbouring structure, for instance the stiffness of the jaw muscles with an infected tooth socket. Spasm can also be caused by interference with the nervous control of muscles, e.g. with ➤ *tetanus.* ➤*spastic paralysis.*

spastic paralysis. Loss of voluntary movement together with spasm of the affected muscles.

A muscle is activated by nerve cells in the spinal cord which communicate directly with the muscle by their nerve fibres. If these fibres are cut (e.g. by a penetrating wound of a limb), or if the nerve cells themselves are damaged (e.g. by poliomyelitis) the muscle ceases to act at all; it is limp and the paralysis is said to be *flaccid.*

These nerve cells are themselves activated by various other cells in the brain and spinal cord, some concerned with voluntary movement and others with reflex action, some with stimulating and some with suppressing muscular activity. If parts of the brain concerned with movement are damaged, reflex pathways

in the spinal cord are left intact with nothing to oppose them or co-ordinate their effects; the muscle is kept permanently taut, and the paralysis is said to be *spastic.*

Congenital spastic paralysis (*cerebral palsy*; *Little's disease*) in its various forms is among the commoner physical handicaps of childhood. It has come into prominence in recent years not because it is on the increase – if anything, it is becoming rarer – but because many other kinds of physical handicap that used to be common are no longer so (e.g. those resulting from poliomyelitis, tuberculosis of bone, rheumatic fever, and rickets), and because the needs of spastic children are better understood.

The paralysis is due to failure of groups of nerve cells in the brain. There are three main types. Spasm predominates if the affected cells are in the cerebral cortex, lack of co-ordination if they are in the cerebellum, and uncontrolled purposeless movements (athetosis) if they are in the basal ganglia, the grey matter in the centre of the brain. Common to all types is weakness of groups of muscles with persistent spasm that interferes with useful movement. The trouble is often confined to the legs, but in the worst cases it may be very much more widespread, even involving the muscles of speech.

Paralysis in this condition is relative. It does not mean that an affected limb cannot be deliberately moved at all, but that voluntary movement is impaired. A totally paralysed baby would be stillborn or die soon after birth. The disability varies between trivial defects that do not affect the patient's life in the mildest cases and lifelong dependence on other people's help in the severest cases.

Mental development is often but by no

means always retarded. It is difficult to assess because the physical handicap can make an intelligent child seem backward.

The cause cannot always be found, but very often it can be traced to a particular type of injury to brain cells. These include severe jaundice (>*rhesus factor*), physical injury during birth (less common than one would expect), temporary shortage of oxygen to the brain during the transition between the baby's getting oxygen from the mother's blood and breathing for himself, and lack of glucose as a result of immaturity at birth. In theory these are all largely preventable conditions.

A spastic baby cannot always be recognized at birth. All new-born babies work by reflex action, and the damage may not show itself until purposive movements should begin. This creates a false impression that the disorder is progressive, but in fact all the damage is done at or shortly after birth. From then on there is no further loss of brain cells, and the condition can only remain stationary or improve. Unlike other tissues, nerve cells cannot regenerate; but much can be done to make the most of all the unaffected areas of the brain. Healthy muscles can be taught to take on at least some of the work of paralysed muscles, occasionally with the help of surgery. Severely affected children may need special education for a time at least, and some need speech training before they can communicate and make the most of their intelligence. All this kind of work is still at an early stage, but it has been advancing rapidly in recent years.

Paralysis following a stroke is spastic because the damage is in the brain, unlike the flaccid paralysis that follows damage lower down.

species. Although the classification of animals and plants is based on the concept of species there is no exact definition. When reproduction is sexual it can be said that members of the same species can breed and produce fertile offspring, but with simple creatures such as bacteria the only criterion is very close similarity.

Related species are grouped together as a *genus*. Within a species there may be distinct races or breeds. Bacteria that are apparently of the same species may differ in such respects as the severity of the disease that they cause and may be classed as strains, varieties etc.; but the classification of bacteria and viruses is unsatisfactory and subject to frequent change.

spectacles >*vision*.

speculum. Lighted tube or other instrument for enabling openings or cavities of the body to be inspected.

speech. Words are formulated in the speech centre of the cerebral cortex, at the side of the brain. This centre lies next to the zone of cerebral cortex that controls the dominant hand. Since the main nervous pathways cross the mid-line, the speech centre is on the left side of the brain in right-handed people. The centre is closely co-ordinated with centres for hearing (comprehension), vision (reading), and hand movement (writing).

Vowel sounds are produced by the >*larynx* and shaped by the mouth, and consonants are formed by the tongue and lips.

A defect anywhere in a long and complicated chain can impair speech. To begin, a certain level of general intelligence is needed. But delayed or defective speech in childhood need not mean that the child is stupid; children of equal ability do not all develop at the same rate. Sometimes a first child does not speak as early as subsequent children because he does not hear speech going on around him all day – children learn more easily from each other than from their parents. Defective hearing, easily overlooked, is an obstacle to learning and is a common cause of backwardness in speech. Emotional disturbances and mental illness can affect speech in various ways. Their symptoms range from occasional stammering to complete failure to communicate.

The speech centre can be affected by injury or disease such as a stroke; in these cases paralysis of the right hand is often accompanied by loss of speech. Any disease of the neck or throat can affect the larynx or its nerves. Defects of the mouth affect the quality of speech.

Any illness that affects the co-ordination of movements, e.g. parkinsonism, may cause difficulty with speaking.

Speech therapy, a young and highly skilled profession, teaches patients to overcome defects that would have been thought incurable a generation ago. It embraces not only the training of children who have never learnt to speak distinctly but also the re-education of adults such as those whose speech has been impaired by injury or disease.

sperm. Male germ cell. A human sperm consists of an oval *head* about 0.005 by 0.003 mm and a slender whip-like tail about 0.05 mm (1/500 in) long. The testes produce sperms in vast numbers; some two hundred million are released in an orgasm.

spermatic cord. A bundle containing the duct of the testis (vas deferens) and blood vessels, wrapped in fibrous tissue and a rudimentary muscle (cremaster),

suspending the testis. The passage of the cord through the groin creates a weak point where a ➤*hernia* may develop.

spermatozoon (-zoön, pl. -zoa). Sperm.

sphenoid. A large bone spanning the base of the skull behind the eyes.

sphincter. Ring of muscle fibres around the entrance or exit of a hollow organ.

sphygmomanometer. Pressure gauge for measuring the blood pressure. When extreme accuracy is needed, as in some experimental work, the pressure is measured directly with a tube in an artery, but an ordinary sphygmomanometer records the pressure of air needed to stop the flow of blood into a limb. ➤*blood pressure.*

spica. Bandage applied with successive turns crossing each other; figure-of-eight bandage.

spider. Spiders bite their prey and inject poison. Only a few are dangerous to man. The worst are members of the genus *Latrodectus*, small black creatures with red markings found in most warm countries. They include the *black widow* (America), the *button spider* (S. Africa), the *karakut spider* (Russia and near East), and the *red-backed spider* (Australasia). The poison stimulates nerve cells and causes trembling, sweating, vomiting, and severe pain. If these general symptoms overshadow the pain of the bite itself the condition suggests some acute abdominal disorder, and patients unaware that they had been bitten have been subjected to abdominal operations. Severe bites from these spiders can be lethal, especially to children.

A few other kinds of spider, e.g. the funnel-web spider of Australia, are also dangerous. The tarantula and the still more alarming tropical bird-eating spiders are comparatively harmless; their bites may be painful but that is all.

Tarantism or dancing mania, a strange medieval affliction, appears to have been some kind of mass hysteria not due, as people thought, to the bite of the tarantula.

spina bifida. A congenital defect of the vertebral column or backbone. The embryonic vertebrae first appear immediately in front of the spinal cord, which is simply a continuation of the brain. Each vertebra puts out an extension on either side of the cord, and these join behind the cord to form an arch around it. Tough ligaments between the arches complete a kind of armour-plating like the shell of a lobster's tail. Spina bifida is a failure of one or more arches to develop.

With *spina bifida occulta*, the commonest form, only a single vertebra is defective, causing no trouble or needing only minor surgery. But with larger defects the membranes around the cord (meninges) bulge through the gap as a hernia or *meningocoele*; or the cord itself, or the nerves arising from it are exposed (*myelocoele*). In such cases the child is often stillborn or lives for only a few days. But with adequate treatment some children survive with degrees of paralysis varying from a localized patch of numbness to complete lack of control from the waist down. Other defects, especially *hydrocephalus* with resultant brain damage, often accompany spina bifida.

Prompt surgery may help to prevent further damage to the growing nerves, and in the less severe cases the child may grow up to be mobile and independent; but with extensive defects the outlook tends to be poor.

The condition may be detected during pregnancy by a test of the mother's blood and echography (>*scan*) in time for a safe termination of pregnancy. Though a history of one spina bifida child increases the risk of another, given the possibility of early detection the parents may well opt for trying again.

There is good evidence that an adequate supply of folic acid (>*vitamin B*) during pregnancy reduces the chances of the child developing this defect.

spinal cord. The continuation of the brain below the skull; it is a column of nervous tissue enclosed in the *spinal canal*, a tunnel in the backbone. The spinal cord is not a distinct organ from the brain. Both are parts of a single unit, made up of nerve cells (grey matter) and conducting fibres (white matter). The spinal cord is a conductor between the brain and the rest of the body, but that is not all. It deals with many reflex actions without reference to the brain: for instance, the familiar knee-jerk depends only on the spinal cord (>*reflex*). Passing urine is also a spinal reflex, though its timing is controlled by the brain.

The >*spinal nerves* carry impulses between the cord and the trunk and limbs. They leave the backbone by the gaps between the vertebrae. Originally a pair of nerves emerges from the cord opposite to each gap, but the backbone grows more than the cord. In adult life the cord ends at the first lumbar vertebra, just below the 12th ribs, and the spinal nerves for the lower vertebrae are carried down the rest of the spinal canal as a leash, the *cauda equina*.

The *meninges*, the surrounding membranes of the brain, are continued down the whole length of the spinal canal to form a waterproof sheath for the spinal cord, filled with *cerebrospinal fluid.*

1. INJURIES

The spinal cord is well protected by bones and muscles, and considerable violence is needed to damage it. The danger is from a fracture of a vertebra with displacement of the fragments. Not all injuries of the spinal cord occur at the time of the accident. Unskilful handling of the patient can displace a fracture that did not at first involve the cord to a position where a fragment of bone can do permanent damage. If there is the least suspicion of an injury to the back it is a safe policy for only people trained in this kind of first aid to move the victim.

A severe jolt may cause temporary interference with the working of the spinal cord. But nerve fibres that are cut or torn do not regenerate in the cord or brain as they can in peripheral nerves. This means that communication between the brain and the parts of the body below the injury is interrupted, with loss of sensation and voluntary movement. Below the injury the spinal cord can still maintain reflex actions.

The treatment of spinal injuries is largely a matter of making the best of the remaining function, and of preventing complications such as deformity produced by uncontrolled muscle reflexes and damage to skin that has lost its sensation. Before the Second World War cases of severe damage to the spinal cord were generally regarded as hopeless because the cord itself could not be repaired, and most of the patients died of infection within a year or two of the injury. The outlook was completely changed by surgeons such as Guttmann, who recognized that the spinal cord was only a part of the whole patient, and that with skilled training and perseverance people with spinal injuries could acquire new skills and pleasures. From the start the patient is set the objective of leading an independent life.

2. OTHER DISORDERS

Compression of a nerve fibre interferes with the conduction of impulses, and pressure on the spinal cord can cause anything from minor disturbances of sensation to complete paralysis. If the pressure is relieved without delay, normal conduction is likely to return. Sources of pressure include results of injury such as blood-clots, and abscesses and tumours. All these are amenable to surgery.

A congenital defect of the vertebrae, ►*spina bifida,* causes the spinal cord to be pinched in a gap in the backbone. With the uncommon condition ►*syringomyelia* a cyst in the centre of the cord causes pressure from within; this also is probably a congenital defect.

Infections that cause inflammation of the brain (encephalitis) may also involve the spinal cord. Many of the common viruses can do this, but in fact such infection is rare, with the exception of *poliomyelitis.* Even poliomyelitis, which has a special affinity for the motor nerve cells of the spinal cord, causes serious trouble in only a small minority of cases. *Tabes dorsalis* is involvement of the cord at a late stage of syphilis, affecting mainly the sensory fibres.

Several diseases damage the insulating sheaths of nerve fibres in the cord with loss of conduction. These include deficiency of vitamin B_{12} (pernicious anaemia), and *multiple sclerosis,* of which the cause is still unknown.

spinal nerves. Branches of the spinal cord from which the nerves of the trunk and limbs are derived. There are 31 pairs, each pair corresponding with a vertebra, and emerging from the sides of the backbone through a gap between two vertebrae. In principle the nerves encircle the body, each pair supplying a segment, but this simple arrangement is modified for the limbs. The nerves from the upper and lower ends of the spinal cord form networks, the brachial and lumbosacral plexuses, from which branches supply the upper and lower limbs; thus each limb nerve contains elements of several spinal nerves.

At their origin from the spinal cord the motor and sensory fibres are in separate bundles or roots, motor in front of sensory. The two roots merge as the nerves pass out of the backbone.

There is little room to spare in the gaps between the vertebrae, and with many disorders of the backbone the emerging nerves may be compressed, causing mainly disturbances of sensation such as numbness, tingling, or pain. The commonest source of pressure is a 'slipped disc' (►*vertebra* (1)), and the commonest sites are the lumbar and sacral vertebrae where the pressure causes lumbago or sciatica.

spine. 1. Any sharp projection from a bone, such as the spinous process (neural spine) projecting from the back of each of the vertebrae that make up the backbone. **2.** The backbone (spinal column) as a whole. ►*skeleton* (4); *vertebra*.

spirochaete. A spiral bacterium. Most spirochaetes are harmless, but the group includes Vincent's spirochaete (*Borrelia vincenti*), associated with Vincent's angina, and the causes of syphilis, yaws, relapsing fever, Weil's disease, and a kind of rat-bite fever.

spirometer. An instrument for measuring the efficiency of the lungs.

splanchnic. Of the viscera (internal organs of the abdomen and thorax).

spleen. Large purple, rubbery abdominal organ. It is the size of the whole hand, rather larger than a kidney, under the ribs on the left side between the stomach and the left kidney. The spleen is a fibrous sponge full of blood and lymphoid tissue. It is an offshoot of the supporting tissue of the stomach, and is supplied by large blood vessels branching off those of the stomach. It is an important element of the *reticuloendothelial system*, which is a collective term for scavenger cells scattered throughout the body.

In classical and medieval medicine the spleen was the seat of one of the four humours, the black bile (melancholy). The blood in the spleen is rather tarry because the lymphoid tissue acts as a filter bed, tending to concentrate the solid blood cells and let the fluid plasma pass.

An unborn infant's bone marrow does not start forming blood cells until the 5th month of pregnancy. Until this time the blood cells are all formed in the spleen, thymus, and liver, but by the time the child is born the only blood cells still being formed there are lymphocytes. In many animals the spleen continues to make red blood cells throughout life, and even in adult man it can do so if there is a sudden demand, e.g. during recovery from severe anaemia.

The spleen is also concerned with the destruction of spent red blood cells. The useful life of a red cell is 4 months. It is then broken down in the reticuloendothelial system and replaced by a new cell from the bone marrow. The spleen also appears to carry out a quality control:

faulty or misshapen red cells are removed from the circulation and destroyed.

In carnivorous animals the spleen is a reservoir of blood cells for emergencies. When the animal has to go into action the spleen contracts under the influence of adrenaline, forcing additional cells into the circulation. In man, this function is only rudimentary.

Like other lymphoid tissues (lymph nodes, thymus) the spleen forms antibodies, on which ►*immunity* largely depends.

Apart, perhaps, from the quality control of red cells, all the functions of the spleen can be carried on by other organs, though children without spleens are unduly susceptible to infection, especially with pneumococci. To a lesser extent, some adults may have the same trouble. They can be protected with pneumococcal vaccine, as can children over the age of two.

1. Disorders

The ribs and diaphragm generally protect the spleen from injury, but it can be torn by a really heavy blow on the left side, or punctured by a broken rib. It then bleeds freely into the abdominal cavity. The spleen is too spongy to be easily repaired, and the usual treatment of a ruptured spleen is to seal off its blood vessels and remove it. The operation is not difficult, because the spleen is on a sort of stalk. A ligature tied round the stalk cuts off the whole blood supply.

The spleen has few if any diseases of its own, but it is involved in various widespread disorders of the lymphoid and blood-forming tissues, e.g. ►*leukaemia*, ►*Hodgkin's disease*. In some types of anaemia due to excessive destruction of blood cells (►*anaemia* (A.2)) the spleen is enlarged, and removing it may help the patient.

Almost any kind of infection can cause the spleen to enlarge, and with some tropical diseases the spleen becomes enormous (►*malaria*, ►*bilharzia*). A diseased spleen protruding beyond the margin of the ribs is vulnerable, and ruptured spleen is a very common accident in the tropics. The large malarial spleen is packed with red blood cells damaged by malaria parasites and therefore removed from the circulation to be broken down (the spleen is carrying out its function of 'quality control'). With bilharzial disease the main reason for the large spleen is damage to the liver by the parasites.

Many chronic diseases of the liver affect the spleen, because the splenic vein is a tributary of the ►*portal vein*; therefore blood from the spleen has to pass through the liver to get back to the heart. Any obstruction in the liver causes backpressure and congestion in the spleen.

splenic anaemia = ►*Banti's disease*.

splenomegaly. Abnormal enlargement of the spleen. *Egyptian splenomegaly* is due to infection with ►*bilharzia*; it arises partly from direct involvement of the spleen and partly from interference in the liver with blood vessels that should drain the spleen. In this latter respect it is a variant of Banti's disease. In most cases the effect of malaria is added to that of bilharzia.

spondylitis. Inflammation of vertebrae. *Ankylosing spondylitis* is a rheumatic affection of the vertebrae (bamboo spine) mainly affecting young men. There is gradual loss of mobility in the joints between the vertebrae. In severe cases the normally flexible ligaments supporting these joints acquire almost the consistency of bone, and the affected part of the spine resembles a bamboo rod. The patient is liable to episodes of backache, and in severe cases breathing may be hindered. Treatment is unsatisfactory. X-rays have been used to slow the process, but may damage the bone marrow of the vertebrae, an important blood-forming tissue, and cause anaemia. In addition, the danger of leukaemia makes the use of X-rays unacceptable.

Anti-inflammatory drugs relieve pain and also facilitate physiotherapy. This is one condition for which phenylbutazone is still used.

spondyloisthesis. A partial dislocation of one of the joints of the spine; it is commonly the 5th lumbar vertebra (carrying the rest of the backbone with it) that slips forward on the top of the sacrum. The condition is associated with a congenital defect of a vertebra. The affected joint may need surgical fixation.

spondylosis. A degenerative process or ➤osteoarthritis of vertebrae and the joints between them, usually diagnosed from X-ray pictures which show narrowing of the joint spaces and small irregular protruberances of bone around the joints. Spondylosis may cause stiffness or aching in the affected segment of the spine, and spondylosis in the neck, causing pressure on the nerve roots which emerge between vertebrae, is often blamed for ➤fibrositis in the back and shoulders, perhaps for want of a more convincing cause. Though spondylosis can cause symptoms, most people over the age of 30 show signs of it without suffering any discomfort.

spongiform encephalopathy ➤slow virus.

spore. Seed of a fungus; some bacteria (e.g. that of tetanus) form spores as a kind of hibernating or dormant phase in which they are remarkably resistant to antiseptics. Bacterial spores may survive even in boiling water for half an hour or more, but they are readily killed by compressed steam in an autoclave.

spotted fever. 1. Epidemic meningitis. 2. A kind of typhus.

sprain. An injury to a joint without fracture or separation (dislocation) of bones but with torn fibres of the supporting tissue. The pain is usually enough to prevent movement that would interfere with healing. Cold compresses, or merely raising the limb, may help to reduce swelling. A skilfully applied bandage supports the joint and takes strains off the damaged ligament while it heals. The ankle is much more often sprained than any other joint. Sprains elsewhere have to be treated with suspicion because they are apt to disguise small fractures.

sprue. Chronic diarrhoea, loss of weight, and anaemia from failure to assimilate fat and vitamins from the intestine. The diarrhoea is due to unabsorbed fat, and the anaemia to lack of folic acid, which has much the same effect as the vitamin B_{12} deficiency of pernicious anaemia (➤anaemia (B.2)).

Tropical sprue occurs in parts of Asia and America. It is not clear whether lack of folic acid causes defective function of the intestine or vice versa, but treatment with broad-spectrum antibiotics may be supplemented with folic acid.

Non-tropical sprue is like the coeliac disease of infants, and is treated by excluding gluten (wheat-protein) from the diet.

sputum. Mucus (phlegm), often with pus, coughed from the air-passages. Sputum, as opposed to saliva or spittle formed in the mouth, is proof of inflammation.

Even a very small amount, which most smokers consider normal ('clearing the chest'), is a definite sign of bronchitis. Microscopic examination of bacteria, cells etc. in the sputum is helpful in the diagnosis of many diseases of the lungs.

squint. Faulty alignment of the axis of an eye. A squint may be *convergent* (inward), *divergent* (outward), or, rarely, vertical. The obvious cause, paralysis of one of the muscles of the eye, is rather uncommon, but a squint that first appears in adult life is likely to be paralytic. A paralytic squint arises from damage to one of the nerves of the eye muscles, and generally causes double vision. These squints call for prompt investigation because they are symptoms of irritation or compression of the nerve.

Congenital squint is by far the commonest type. The muscles and their nerves are healthy, but the two eyes are wrongly co-ordinated. The squint is said to be *concomitant* because the eyes move together, with the same degree of squint in all positions (whereas the degree of a paralytic squint varies with the direction of gaze). A concomitant squint may not be obvious until the child begins to use his two eyes as a unit, and not always then, for some squints remain latent for years.

Concomitant squint is often due to faulty accommodation (focusing). If the child is long-sighted, nothing is in focus with the eyes at rest. To see a distant object clearly, he has to focus the lenses as a normal child would do to see a near object. But the reflex for focusing is linked to reflexes controlling the eye muscles, so that the eyes automatically turn inwards when they are focused for near vision, like a coupled range-finder on a camera. In a long-sighted child, the two reflexes are thrown out of step. As he focuses on the horizon his eyes turn inwards as though he were looking at a near object, and he squints and sees double. But his young brain is still learning to translate nerve impulses from the eyes into pictures, and to overcome the nuisance of double vision it ignores the impulses from one eye. Unless the squint is treated, the habit of ignoring one eye becomes fixed; when the squint is finally corrected it is too late for the brain to learn and the eye remains useless. Squints have therefore to be recognized and treated early.

The treatment includes correction of focus by glasses, exercises for the eye muscles (orthoptics), and in some cases surgical adjustment of the muscles.

stapedectomy. Surgical treatment of deafness due to *otosclerosis*, an abnormal deposition of bone in the cavity of the middle ➤*ear* that interferes with sound conduction from the drum to the organ of Corti by the chain of small bones. The disease prevents the innermost of the 3 bones, the stapes, from vibrating. The operation, done with a binocular microscope, consists of removing the stapes and replacing it with a tiny plastic piston. It is both safer and more reliable than the former treatment, fenestration, which involved making a new opening to the inner ear.

stapes. One of the small articulated bones of the middle ear.

staphylococcus. A spherical ➤*bacterium*, diameter 0.001 mm (1/25,000 in); a single staphylococcus looks exactly like a ➤*streptococcus*, but a family forms a cluster instead of a chain. Two kinds of staphylococcus are important:

1. *Staph. albus* inhabits healthy skin,

seldom causing trouble. It may be the only microbe in cases of trivial infection such as pimples, but more often it merely joins in when some more virulent microbe has already started an infection. Like the bacteria of the intestine, it can become dangerous if it strays from its natural environment, e.g. into the urine.

2. *Staph. aureus* (*Staph. pyogenes*) is much more harmful. It is called *aureus* because of its yellow pigment, and *pyogenes* because it provokes the formation of pus. About half the population harbours it either in the nose or on the skin. It is the usual cause of infection in wounds and of abscesses, boils, and impetigo. Staphylococcal infection tends to be localized, but even a small abscess can cause fever and other general symptoms because staphylococci form various toxins (poisons) which circulate in the blood. If, as rarely happens, the staphylococci themselves invade the blood-stream they can cause a most lethal ►*septicaemia*.

Natural resistance to staphylococci is fairly good, considering that everyone has a boil or an abscess at one time or another, and serious complications are rare. The natural tendency for these microbes to become walled off in abscesses helps to prevent spread but hinders destruction of the microbes by white cells and antibodies in the blood. (With *streptococci*, which tend to spread, the opposite holds.) Even with drugs to assist the natural defences, a surgical operation is often needed to provide an outlet for the pus (►*abscess*).

Antiseptics readily kill staphylococci, but no drug was both safe and effective against staphylococci in the body until the discovery of ►*sulphonamides*. All sulphonamides inhibit staphylococci, but embarrassingly large doses of the earlier ones were needed. Suitable sulphonamides were overshadowed by the introduction of penicillin in 1941, since when many other effective antibiotics have been discovered. It is as well that there are many, because staphylococci are prone to become resistant to a particular drug in time, and another must be used against them. This danger is greatest in hospitals, where only the 'fittest' microbes are likely to survive.

Food poisoning by staphylococci is different from infection: it is due to chemical poisons formed by staphylococci which contaminate the food before it is eaten.

starch. A carbohydrate found in many plants; it is the basis of most diets. A molecule of starch is a long branched chain of molecules of *glucose*, to which it is converted by digestion. Starch is very similar to cellulose, but the human digestive system has no enzymes for separating the glucose molecules of cellulose and cannot therefore use foods such as grass.

Starch has no special fattening properties. Reducing the amount of starch in the diet (potatoes, bread) is merely the most convenient way of reducing the total intake of food without impoverishing the diet.

Starling's law. (Ernest H. Starling, 1866–1927, professor of physiology at University College, London.) The force with which the heart contracts is proportional to the rate at which it is filled from the veins and the resistance against which it has to pump; in other words the heart adapts itself to the needs of the moment. Heart failure means that the heart cannot comply with this law. It is only a matter of degree. No heart can obey Starling's law beyond a certain level of work, but with heart failure this level is lower than it should be.

starvation. Even when the body is at rest it needs a continuous supply of energy for chemical processes and for the work of its vital organs; and the materials of many tissues need constant replacement.

When no food is taken, the carbohydrate stored in liver and muscle as glycogen can be converted to glucose and used as fuel, but even a well-fed body has only a few hours' supply. After this, the fat deposited under the skin and elsewhere can be consumed. Complete starvation for several days – under the closest supervision – is an effective but transient method of losing weight. Fat that is an integral part of most tissues is not available as fuel.

If the store of available fat is depleted, other sources of fuel are brought in. The most important is protein; but as soon as the body begins to consume its own protein its health begins to suffer.

The heart and nervous system are spared to the end, but the rest of the body can lose up to half its weight before the victim dies of starvation. This may take a month or more, but in the meantime resistance has become so low that the least infection may be fatal. With severe starvation the digestive organs may be so injured by lack of vitamins and other necessities that they can no longer take up ordinary foods if they are provided. People in this state may need food that requires little digestion for some time.

A severely starved person may not, at first sight, look thin, because lack of protein in the blood allows water to collect in the tissues and produce a kind of ➤*oedema*.

statistics. There are two meanings, both of medical interest. The original meaning is the compiling of numerical data about populations for official use: a statist was a statesman or politician. The basic form is the census, used since the earliest historical times for taxation. Census data together with statistics such as birth-rate, death-rate, and ages and causes of dying are obviously very important in studying the health of the community, in identifying the problems to be tackled or the success with which they are being tackled, and in studying the natural history of epidemics. Causes of lung cancer and arterial disease, two of the leading causes of death, have been identified in this way. A population under study is simply all the people, or as many as can be traced, within a defined group. For example, the World Health Organization collates statistics from all over the world for studying the control of major pestilences such as malaria and tuberculosis, whilst a municipal health department may be concerned with the population of a single school.

Medical historians usually credit John Graunt of London with being the first to apply statistics ('political arithmetic') to the study of public health. He began to publish his *Natural and Political Observations made upon the Bills of Mortality* in 1662. But 50 years before this Felix Platter wrote his observations on 7 outbreaks of plague that he had lived through in Basle, including a house-to-house census of the town with notes on everyone who had caught the plague in the outbreak of 1609–11. The MS is still in the University Library; it has not been published in full.

The second meaning of statistics is the analysis of representative samples. Clinical research usually has to deal with fairly small groups of patients, i.e.

samples of the whole population. The sample is compared with a *control*, which may be a second sample differing only in respect of the factor to be studied (e.g. a new drug not given to the control group). Or the control may be the same group studied at a different time, or it may be a known standard such as an average for the population as a whole. The results are expressed in figures and analysed to show whether differences between the study group and the control are *significant*, i.e. unlikely to have arisen by pure chance. Statistical analysis never proves anything in the absolute sense of proving a theorem in geometry. It aims at the same kind of proof as a court of law. In abstract theory, the man with the jewels in his knapsack and his fingerprints on the latch could be the victim of a series of misunderstandings, but his guilt is established beyond *reasonable* doubt. In most clinical work, 'significant' means 95 per cent sure, i.e. a 5 per cent chance that the result was a fluke. With a new drug, this could justify further trials provided that no serious drawbacks had arisen, always bearing in mind the 5 per cent chance that the new will finally turn out to be no better than the old. 'Highly significant' is 99 per cent sure, and 'very highly significant' is 99.9 per cent. The greater the difference between sample and control, and the larger the sample (number of patients studied), the higher the significance is likely to be. A crude example will show the effect of the two factors.

Suppose that a man is taking bets on a 50–50 chance such as whether a card drawn from a pack will be black or red. The 'sample' is a series of consecutive draws. The 'control' is the theoretical distribution of an infinite number of draws governed by chance. The man should

win twice in a row once in 4 attempts if he bets on 2 reds (RR), since the possible results are RR, RB, BR, BB. He should win 3 in a row once in 8 attempts, 4 in 16 attempts, and 5 in 32 attempts, i.e. the odds against 5 reds in a row are 31 to 1, so we are about 97 per cent sure that this result will not arise by chance. This is more than the limit of significance, and we may suspect the man of cheating. After 7 consecutive wins, due to arise by chance only once in 128 attempts, we are more than 99 per cent sure: 'highly significant'. After 10 consecutive wins (1 in 1024 by chance) we are more than 99.9 per cent sure and may well feel that it is time to call a policeman. Thus a very small sample, only 10 draws, can give a very highly significant result if the difference from the expected result is great enough: here, it is the maximum. In medical research, this kind of thing happens only rarely, e.g. when an effective drug is discovered for a previously incurable disease. As a rule, the differences to be studied are more subtle. If our card-sharper is wise he will cheat only half the time, to win 3 draws in 4. Then his 6 wins in 8 draws will arouse no suspicion, because this would occur by chance once in about 7 attempts, whereas 8 wins would be well past the limit of 'highly significant'. Even 18 wins in 24 draws would occur by chance once in about 80 attempts, which is 'significant' but a little short of 'highly significant'. The odds against his winning all 24 would have been over 16 million to one, but at 3 out of 4 we should need a sample of more than 40 draws before the man's 3 wins out of 4 became 'very highly significant'.

When the results of a clinical experiment have been analysed, then, a statistician can say with mathematical precision how likely or unlikely it is that the results are due to pure chance, but he cannot say what, other than chance, has affected the result. A trial may appear to show that a new drug is significantly better than an old one, or that a rich diet increases the risk of heart disease, but it shows nothing of the kind unless all other differences between sample and control are considered and their effects excluded. The effect on the patients of knowing that they are getting a new and promising drug is enough to invalidate a trial (▸*placebo*; *research*). People with an over-rich diet might get heart disease because as a group they are also people who tend to go by car when a walk would do them good. It happens that both these factors, over-eating and lack of exercise, endanger the heart, but this could be established only by considering each independently of the other. The commonest fallacy in research involving statistics is to mistake association for cause and overlook the essential factor. From the figures alone one might think that hot climates encourage typhoid fever and malaria. Certainly they are associated, but only because so many of the countries that cannot afford an expensive public health service to prevent these infections happen to be hot countries.

Most people consider statistical evidence untrustworthy. This is not so. It is as precise as any other kind of evidence, but easier to misinterpret than most.

status asthmaticus. A severe and prolonged attack of asthma, persisting for 24 hours or more despite the usual remedies.

status epilepticus. A succession of epileptic attacks, or one very prolonged attack. Although status epilepticus is usually controlled by the drugs used for ordinary epilepsy, a prolonged fit needs hospital treatment because the muscle spasms may have to be controlled with drugs such as curare; breathing has then to be maintained artificially while the effects of the drug last.

status lymphaticus (status thymolymphaticus). A mythical disease formerly thought to be a cause of sudden death in childhood, in cases where the only apparent abnormality was enlargement of the thymus gland. The mistake arose because the normal weight of the thymus had been grossly underestimated. During severe illness or stress the thymus shrinks rapidly, and its average weight after death, on which the estimates were based, is much less than its average weight in life. But if death is very sudden the thymus has no time to shrink, and therefore appears to be abnormal. Most of the deaths ascribed to this 'enlargement' were really due to sudden suppression of breathing by anaesthetics.

STD. Sexually transmitted disease (= ▸*venereal disease*).

steatorrhoea. Diarrhoea due to undigested fat in the intestine, e.g. with ▸*coeliac disease* and ▸*sprue*.

stenosis. Narrowing of a tubular organ such as a segment of a blood vessel, the intestine or a heart valve.

stereoisomers. Substances identical in all respects except that their molecules are mirror images of each other, like right and left hands. They are conventionally named D- (dextro-, right) or L- (laevo-, left) isomers. In terms of ordinary chemistry there is nothing to choose between them, but the enzymes that govern living organisms such as ourselves can work on only one kind, for instance D-sugars and L-amino acids, rejecting all others.

stereotactic surgery. A method of direction finding that has much increased the scope of brain surgery, enabling the surgeon to work on areas of the brain that would otherwise be inaccessible. The exact location of the area, which may be a cluster of cells the size of a pinhead, can be inferred from the structure and dimensions of the inside of the patient's skull as shown by X-rays. These data are used to set an apparatus consisting of two arcs at right angles to each other, like the gimbals of a ship's compass, by which the point of a needle can be guided to the area within 0.1 mm. The calculations can be done by a computer, which also indicates the point at which the needle can be inserted without damaging the intervening brain tissue. A minute electric current passed down the needle then inactivates the tissue around its point. The method is mainly used for suppressing uncontrollable muscular activity such as the tremor of *parkinsonism*. It has also been used for destroying small tumours, for locating foreign bodies, and even for the treatment of serious behavioural disorders: this last is still at an experimental stage.

sterile. 1. Free from living microbes.

2. Unable to have children: not the same as *impotent* (unable to copulate). For instance, a eunuch is sterile but not necessarily impotent, and some people are impotent for psychological reasons although they are fertile if the emotional problem can be overcome. ➤*fertility*.

sterilization. 1. ➤*antiseptic*; *bacterium* (5).

2. Surgical operation to render the patient sterile. The most certain method would be removal of the gonads (castration), but this causes hormonal disturbance, because the gonads form impor-

tant hormones as well as germ cells. In practice, males are sterilized by obliterating the vas deferens on each side (a simple procedure, because the vas lies just below the skin of the groin), and females by obliterating the Fallopian tubes. Either operation blocks the passage of germ cells (sperm or ovum). Although fertility can sometimes be restored by a second operation sterilization is best regarded as irrevocable. In some countries it is illegal. On the other hand, the governments of some overpopulated and undernourished countries are doing all they can to encourage men to be sterilized while their families are still small.

sternomastoid. Large muscle at the side of the neck, extending from the top of the sternum and clavicle, to the skull behind the ear.

The sternomastoids acting together flex the neck. Either acting alone turns the head. They balance the vertebral muscles at the back of the neck, acting as guy-ropes to maintain the posture of the head.

Contracture of a sternomastoid causes a deformity, *torticollis* (wry-neck), by which the head is twisted to one side. In infants this is usually the result of injury during birth. It needs physiotherapy, or sometimes surgery to prevent further compensatory deformity such as uneven growth of the face.

sternum (breast-bone). A flat bone at the front of the chest to which the upper ribs are attached by their cartilages. The upper part or *manubrium* slopes downwards and forwards, making an angle (angle of Louis) with the more nearly vertical *body*. A joint between manubrium and body allows the sternum to straighten when the ribs rise during inspiration.

Fractures of the sternum generally heal without trouble, but since the heart lies just behind the bone they can be dangerous. They are the result of considerable violence and usually associated with other serious injuries.

steroid. A group of chemical compounds, widely distributed in nature, all with the same pattern of 17 carbon atoms arranged in 4 linked rings. Steroids with significant effects on the human body include substances as different as *vitamin D*, the drugs extracted from *digitalis*, male and female *sex hormones*, and the hormones of the *adrenal cortex*. The term is often confined to this last group, as an abbreviation of *corticosteroid*.

stethoscope. Instrument for examining the sounds in the chest (*stethos*) or other parts of the body, invented by Laënnec in 1816 and first described in his book *De l'auscultation médiate* (Paris, 1819). 'Mediate auscultation' meant listening through an instrument, as opposed to 'immediate auscultation' with an ear on the patient's chest, the method of Hippocrates. The old method had been inefficient and undignified and little attention had been paid to the sounds of the heart and lungs. The new instrument, coupled with its inventor's clinical genius, transformed the diagnosis of disorders of the heart and lungs from a guessing-game to a science.

At first Laënnec used a roll of paper. Later, after much trial and error, he devised a straight wooden tube, widened at the patient's end for picking up the soft breath sounds. An adapter screwed into this end converted the stethoscope into a tube of uniform diameter for listening to the heart. The modern binaural stethoscope, with a flexible tube to each ear, often has interchangeable wide and narrow chest-pieces for the same purpose. A flexible diaphragm may improve the acoustic properties. Some sounds, e.g. an unborn baby's heart, are heard better with the original straight stethoscope.

Electrical instruments can be used for demonstrating sounds to a class, and for recording them (phonocardiography).

A kind of electronic stethoscope, depending on the deflection of high-frequency echoes, is used for studying the flow in arteries and for detecting the foetal heart in early pregnancy.

The sounds heard in a healthy chest are the soft rustling of air entering and leaving the lungs, and. the heart sounds, two to each beat. The first heart sound is a dull thud as the ventricles, having filled, begin to contract, their inlet valves close, and blood begins to flow into the arteries. The second sound is sharper; it is heard when the ventricles have emptied themselves and the outlet valves close. Recorded tracings show third and fourth sounds, but these are faint or inaudible with an ordinary stethoscope.

If the texture of the lungs is altered by disease the conduction of sound may be enhanced or restricted and the air-stream is distorted. Different types of disease produce characteristic changes in the breath sounds, and various added sounds may be heard, such as the squeaky wheeze (*rhonchus*) of air being forced through narrowed tubes in asthma, or the crackling and bubbling sounds (*râles*) of fluid in the airpassages. Friction between inflamed membranes in pleurisy produces a sound 'like the creaking of leather', described by Hippocrates.

Disorders of the heart muscle affect the quality and timing of the heart sounds, and disorders of the valves cause added sounds (murmurs, *bruits*). The quality of an abnormal sound usually indicates the type of disorder, and the area where it is loudest indicates the site, but some sounds are almost impossible to interpret without further investigations. The murmurs that are sometimes heard from perfectly healthy hearts cause anxiety to both doctors and patients. A doctor hears a murmur that might indicate a defective valve. He cannot simply ignore it, because the heart needs attention if it is in fact abnormal. But as soon as the suspicion is mentioned the patient has something to worry about, and may go on worrying long after the heart has been proved innocent. Children are especially prone to harmless murmurs, and many healthy children have had to live like invalids because a suspicion once raised would not be stilled.

stilboestrol. A synthetic drug with similar actions to the oestrogens formed by the ovaries. ➤*sex hormones.*

Still's disease. A rare form of ➤*rheumatoid arthritis*, affecting children, with the important difference from the usual adult form of the disease that most patients recover completely.

stimulant. Drugs either increase (stimulate) or decrease (depress) the normal activity of organs. Depression is much commoner than true stimulation. This is to be expected, because healthy tissues generally perform as well as they can be made to, and unhealthy tissues can be improved only by removing the cause of ill health. Many apparent stimulants in fact depress. For instance, digitalis improves the performance of a *diseased* heart by suppressing useless activity; it does no good to a normal heart.

Alcohol needs special mention, because it is still often called a stimulant. Its sole effect is to depress all tissues, especially the nervous system; if it appears to stimulate, that is only because it suppresses inhibitions and worries.

Numerous drugs enhance the action of adrenaline and related substances that transmit impulses at relay stations in the brain. They include adrenaline substitutes such as ephedrine and amphetamine, and drugs used to relieve depression. Since they increase the activity (though not necessarily the efficiency) of the brain, any of these might be described as a stimulant. ➤*analeptic.*

stimulus. Any event outside a living cell that causes change within the cell. In general, a particular kind of cell responds only to a particular stimulus. Cells at the back of the eye respond to light, cells in taste-buds to certain chemicals, muscle fibres to acetyl choline released from nerve-endings. An electric current serves as a stimulus to most cells that are capable of being stimulated, but it may act not directly on the cell but on its controlling nerve.

Stokes–Adams attack. (William Stokes, 1804–78, and Robert Adams, 1791–1875, Dublin physicians.) Sudden unconsciousness caused by heart-block. ➤*arrhythmia.*

stomach. The part of the digestive tube between the lower end of the oesophagus and the beginning of the intestine, shaped like the bag of a bagpipe.

The first part of the stomach, the *fundus*, rises to the left of the oesophagus and forms a dome under the left side of the diaphragm. The second part, the *body* of the stomach, is a broad tube running down from the fundus. The third part, the *antrum*, is funnel-shaped. It runs upwards and to the right, and ends in the mid-line of the body at the *pylorus*, which is a muscular tube acting as a valve between the stomach and the *duodenum* or beginning of the intestine.

In very stocky people the stomach is almost entirely hidden by the left ribs, but in some thin people it hangs down in a loop like the letter J. The spleen lies to the left of the fundus, the left kidney behind the body, and the pancreas behind the antrum and pylorus.

The stomach is very muscular. Like the rest of the digestive tube it may contract in waves (peristalsis) to push its contents along but for some time after a meal the food is churned to and fro and thoroughly mixed with the digestive fluid (gastric juice) secreted by the stomach lining. The muscle is thickest at the pylorus, where it prevents food from passing too rapidly to the duodenum.

The lining membrane secretes large quantities of mucus, an effective barrier to prevent digestion of the stomach by its own enzymes. Three other important substances are formed by cells of this membrane: *hydrochloric acid*, *pepsin*, and *intrinsic factor*. The acid-forming cells are nearly all in the body of the stomach.

The *acid* is remarkably strong – gastric juice is about 0.4 per cent HCl, rather stronger than the decinormal solution commonly used in chemical laboratories. The synthesis is not fully understood; it is certainly complex. In brief, the cells take up acidic carbon dioxide from the blood, and return it to the blood converted to alkaline bicarbonate (the blood is slightly more alkaline after a meal). This active extrusion of alkali into the blood leaves the cell with a relative excess of acid to be secreted into the stomach.

Pepsin is an enzyme concerned in the digestion of protein.

Intrinsic factor is a protein without which vitamin B_{12} is not adequately absorbed.

The stomach has a good supply of blood from branches of the *coeliac* artery, which is a branch of the aorta. The blood is returned by way of the *splenic* vein to the *portal* vein and so to the liver.

1. REGULATION

The behaviour of the stomach has been directly observed in several classic studies. From 1823 to 1833 the American surgeon William Beaumont observed his patient Alexis St Martin, who had a permanent opening between his stomach and his abdominal wall after a gunshot wound. Through the opening Beaumont was able to study the secretions and movements of the stomach.

Pavlov 50 years later isolated a small pocket of a dog's stomach (Pavlov pouch) from which he could collect pure gastric juice, uncontaminated by food, and study the composition and rate of formation of gastric juice under various conditions. More recently S. Wolf and H. G. Wolff, in New York, have made detailed studies of their patient Tom. In this case an opening similar to that of Alexis St Martin had to be made surgically to relieve an obstruction.

These and other experiments have shown that:

1. Impulses in the vagus nerves stimulate movement of the stomach, dilate its blood vessels, and promote secretion.

2. The sympathetic nerves inhibit movement and constrict the blood vessels. They diminish secretion only indirectly, by reducing the blood supply of the mucous membrane. Adrenaline and similar drugs have the same effect.

3. The vagus nerves begin to stimulate

the stomach at the sight and smell or even the prospect of food. The activity is greatly increased by eating. ➤*reflex*.

4. The effects of emotional disturbances are varied, but on the whole they inhibit rather than stimulate the stomach. Symptoms with an emotional background are thus more likely to be due to stagnation than to excessive secretion.

5. Mechanical stimulation of the stomach by the pressure of food causes secretion independently of the vagus nerves. The action is indirect: *gastrin* (a polypeptide) is released from the lining of the antrum and stimulates the secreting cells higher in the stomach via the blood-stream. The gastric juice so formed is less acid than that promoted by nervous action.

6. Secretion is diminished by a high concentration of acid (a typical feedback mechanism) and also by fatty food.

2. EXAMINATION OF THE STOMACH

A patient's symptoms may be a good guide to the state of his stomach, but more often symptoms such as loss of appetite, nausea, or stomach-ache do no more than point vaguely in the direction of the upper abdomen. Ordinary clinical examination seldom establishes the diagnosis: a gastric ulcer (which is most likely to be in the part of the stomach not covered by the ribs) may be tender, but that is about all.

The stomach can be examined by X-rays. The patient takes a draught of a fluid opaque to X-rays (e.g. barium sulphate suspension). This makes it possible to study movements, shape and size of the stomach, deformities, and the pattern of the mucous membrane.

A fractional test meal is a means of studying the secretion of gastric juice. The patient swallows one end of a long rubber tube, and a syringe is attached to the other end. A sample of gastric juice is first drawn off for analysis, and further samples are taken at intervals after various stimuli. The test meal itself usually consists of gruel, and secretion can also be stimulated by drugs.

The inside of the stomach can be examined with a gastroscope, which is simply a lighted tube passed down the oesophagus, with a system of lenses at each end. This instrument can also be used to take a small piece of mucous membrane for microscopical inspection.

3. DISORDERS

Only a few diseases of the stomach are common, but these few include some of the commonest of all ailments. Those mentioned here are discussed in more detail under their own headings.

Congenital ➤*pyloric stenosis* is a hereditary affliction of babies, usually boys. The exit from the stomach is blocked by overgrowth of the muscle. It is treated surgically.

Inflammation of the stomach (➤*gastritis*), unlike inflammation elsewhere in the body, is not often caused by infection, because the acid kills bacteria. It is more often due to irritation by swallowed poisons. The poison may have been produced by bacteria growing in food before it was eaten; the harm was then done before the acid had a chance to act (➤*food poisoning*). The two commonest chemical irritants causing gastritis are alcohol and aspirin. Chronic, insidious gastritis has been attributed to every sort of dietary indiscretion. Some cases are certainly due to alcohol – all heavy drinkers are liable to chronic gastritis – but often the cause cannot be defined.

Gastric ulcer is discussed together with

duodenal and other similar ulcers under ➤*peptic ulcer*.

Cancer of the stomach is one of the commonest of cancers. In principle it should be easy to treat. The stomach is surgically accessible, and it can be removed without great danger. If, then, a cancer is recognized while it is still strictly confined to the stomach the chance of cure is good. The trouble is that these cancers are, more often than not, recognized only when surgical cure is already difficult or impossible. This is because the early symptoms are no more than those of some minor upset, and the diagnosis can be made only by one or more of the investigations described in section 2 above.

The surgical treatment of stomach cancer is not likely to be much improved, and no form of medical cure has yet been found. The high death rate from this cause can be reduced only by *early* investigation of trifling symptoms such as loss of appetite, abdominal discomfort, or 'indigestion'.

Achlorhydria is absence of hydrochloric acid from the stomach. The amount of acid is well below average in some 3 per cent of healthy people, and also in patients with chronic gastritis or cancer of the stomach. It is often reduced with gastric (not duodenal) ulcer. Complete failure to secrete acid, associated with inability to assimilate vitamin B_{12}, causes the usual type of pernicious anaemia; ➤*anaemia* (B.2).

For surgery of the stomach, ➤*gastrectomy*.

stomatitis. Inflammation of the mucous membrane of the mouth, often from invasion by types of bacteria that as a rule live harmlessly in healthy mouths. The mouth is generally resistant to infection – it needs to be, for it teems with microbes and is often injured. But stomatitis is a common complication of conditions that lower resistance, such as anaemia and vitamin deficiency. It can also follow treatment with antibiotics, which eliminate the normal bacteria of the mouth and so expose it to alien species. ➤*noma; Vincent's disease.*

stone = ➤*calculus.*

strabismus ➤*squint.*

strangulation. Cutting off the blood supply to a part of the body, e.g. to a loop of intestine pinched in the opening of a *hernia*.

strangury. Difficult and painful passage of urine, e.g. with narrowing (stricture) of the urethra (the passage from the bladder), or a stone in the bladder, or spasm of the bladder muscle due to inflammation (cystitis).

strawberry mark ➤*birth-mark.*

streptococcus. A spherical ➤*bacterium*, diameter 0.001 mm (1/25,000 in). Unlike staphylococci, which form clusters, streptococci grow in lines like beads on a string. Three types are important in human disease:

1. *Str. viridans* is normally a harmless inhabitant of the mouth and throat, which can enter the bloodstream when the lining of the mouth is damaged, e.g. when a tooth is extracted. This bacterium has little resistance to the natural defences and is quickly destroyed in the blood. But a heart valve with a congenital defect, or damaged by rheumatic fever, sometimes offers a sheltered anchorage where *Str. viridans* can multiply. The resulting *bacterial endocarditis* is a serious condition; until the discovery of antibiotics it was always fatal, but treat-

ment with penicillin is effective. Penicillin is also used to prevent the disease by giving it to people with defective heart valves before operations on the mouth.

2. *Str. faecalis* is equally harmless in its natural habitat, the large intestine, but if it contaminates the urine it can cause ►*pyelitis.*

3. *Str. pyogenes* is among the most troublesome of all microbes. About one person in 10 carries it in the mouth and throat (whereas everyone carries *Str. viridans* in the mouth and *Str. faecalis* in the intestine).

It is one of the two main causes of infection and pus formation in wounds, the other being *Staphylococcus pyogenes* (pyogenic = engendering pus). Streptococci are much less prone than staphylococci to form localized abscesses; streptococcal pus is watery and tends to spread widely through the tissues, and streptococci form a *toxin* that breaks down fibrous barriers. The lymphatic system, which serves to remove foreign matter from the tissue fluid, becomes infected, and inflamed lymphatic vessels may show as red lines joining a wound to the nearest lymph nodes. Streptococci may also enter the bloodstream and cause septicaemia.

Streptococci produce numerous other toxins, which circulate and cause a severe feverish illness in addition to damage at the site of infection. Some strains of *Str. pyogenes* form a toxin responsible for the rash of scarlet fever.

Because of their greater tendency to spread, streptococci typically cause a more fulminating type of infection than staphylococci, but for the same reason they are more exposed to natural defences and to the action of antibacterial drugs. In the great majority of cases streptococcal infection can be rapidly overcome, especially since nearly all the usual drugs (sulphonamides, antibiotics) are effective.

The commonest streptococcal disease is a sore throat, usually more severe than the still commoner type due to viruses. Scarlet fever is simply a streptococcal sore throat due to a strain which also produces a rash.

At least two important diseases – rheumatic fever and acute nephritis – appear to be after-effects of streptococcal infection, though neither is directly due to infection. They do not respond to antibiotics, but they may be prevented by prompt treatment of streptococcal disease. The mechanism is not known, but a plausible theory is that when the patient forms antibodies to combat streptococci some of the antibodies are harmful to his own tissues.

streptomycin. An ►*antibiotic,* from the soil fungus *Streptomyces griseus,* discovered by Waksman in 1944. It is lethal to many types of bacteria, including several against which penicillin is ineffective. It revolutionized the treatment of tuberculosis, against which there had previously been no specific treatment. Newer antibiotics have now restricted its usefulness.

The principal drawback of streptomycin is that it sometimes damages the auditory nerve (►*ear* (4)) which conveys the senses of hearing and balance from the ear. Poisoning by streptomycin itself causes giddiness; the closely related dihydro-streptomycin causes deafness.

stress. Any influence that disturbs the natural equilibrium of the living body. A fundamental rule of physiology is that the cells of the body need a constant environment, and that the primary function of any organ is to maintain this internal environment despite changes in the surroundings (►*Bernard, Claude*). Stresses in this sense include physical injury, exposure, deprivation, all kinds of disease, and emotional disturbance, any of which can disturb the normal regulation of the internal environment.

According to the Canadian physician Hans Selye and many others, prolonged stress provokes first an immediate reaction, then a more or less balanced state in which the stress is resisted, and finally a breakdown of resistance. Many organs are involved, but most of all stress affects the adrenal glands: ►*adrenal* (2). If the resistance to change is depleted by any one kind of stress, there is less chance of resisting other stresses. Thus a serious injury increases susceptibility to infection, and worry aggravates physical illness.

►*psychosomatic disease.*

stress fracture (fatigue fracture). Repetitive strain sometimes causes a crack in an affected bone, resulting in a sudden pain with tenderness over the fracture. The break is seldom complete and can be expected to heal within a few weeks of rest; more active treatment, e.g. with a plaster cast, is rarely needed. This type of fracture may afflict army recruits whose feet are unaccustomed to long marches (*march fracture*) or athletes making repeated demands on the same part of a limb.

stricture. Narrowing of a tubular organ, e.g. by scarring.

stroke (apoplexy). More or less sudden interference with the circulation of blood in a part of the brain, generally with some permanent damage. Nerve cells can survive only a very short time without fresh supplies of oxygen and glucose, certainly not long enough for new paths for the circulation to be established, and lost nerve cells are not replaced.

Serious strokes are of three kinds: (1) *cerebral haemorrhage*, bleeding from a weakened artery into the brain; (2) *embolism*, sudden blockage of an artery by a flake of material that has come adrift from a diseased artery or from the heart; (3) *thrombosis*, a more gradual blockage by clot-formation within a diseased artery of the brain.

Sometimes a congenitally weak spot in an artery predisposes to haemorrhage. With or without such a weak spot, high blood pressure greatly increases the risk, and one of the main reasons for treating high blood pressure is that the risk of a stroke can be greatly diminished.

A disease of arteries that predisposes to all three types is atheroma (►*artery* (1)). High blood pressure is again a contributory factor. A few strokes are due to embolism by fragments of clot formed in an unhealthy heart. A clot can find its way from a lung, through the heart to the brain. Sometimes a clot elsewhere, e.g. a vein in a leg, causes a stroke. It must reach the brain either via the lungs or through an abnormal opening between the right and left sides of the heart.

The effect of a stroke depends entirely on the size and situation of the affected area of brain. Some strokes cause no symptoms at all, and others are rapidly fatal. Between these extremes there are many degrees of impaired function, depending on the site and extent of the damage. If the patient survives the first week or two the final outcome is nearly always better than one would expect. This is partly because of a zone of temporary loss of function around the permanently damaged area, and partly because the patient can often adapt intact muscles to take over the work of muscles that he can no longer control. A physiotherapist can do a great deal to help in this way; similarly speech therapists can sometimes teach people to speak again despite serious damage to the speech centre of the brain.

Strokes due to haemorrhage can sometimes be treated surgically, by removing a blood-clot or by sealing a weak vessel. If an embolus can be traced to clotting in an accessible site such as an artery in the neck it may be possible to clear the artery surgically and prevent further attacks. Anticoagulant drugs to impede clotting are used after some types of stroke – not, of course, those due to bleeding.

Transient ischaemic attacks (TIA) are not uncommon in later life. The patient has the symptoms of a stroke for a few minutes and then recovers completely. They may be due to temporary spasm of a blood vessel in the brain, or sometimes to compression of an artery in the neck by an awkward posture. Sometimes they are due to a defect in an artery that could later cause a major stroke, unless it is corrected surgically. Therefore anyone with a history of TIA needs full investigation, in case surgery should be required. In addition, *dipyridamole* and *aspirin*, either of which should reduce the risk of clot-formation by inhibiting the blood platelets, have been used prophylactically.

stroma. The fibrous framework of a tissue (cf. *parenchyma*, its characteristic working cells).

struma = ►*goitre*.

strychnine ►*nux vomica*.

stye (hordeolum). A boil in one of the skin glands of an eyelid.

subacute. Between acute and chronic.

subacute combined degeneration of the spinal cord. A result of vitamin B_{12} deficiency, which also causes pernicious anaemia, damaging groups of both sensory and motor nerve fibres (hence 'combined') in the spinal cord. The affected sensations include that of position, which normally co-ordinates the interaction of muscles. Voluntary muscular activity is also impaired, but not reflex contraction; thus the affected muscles are stiff rather than flabby (spastic, not flaccid paralysis). Symptoms start in the legs; later the arms may be involved.

The disorder is treated like pernicious anaemia with regular injections of vitamin B_{12}.

subarachnoid. In the fluid-filled space between the coverings of the brain and spinal cord. ►*meninges*.

subclavian. Below the collar-bone (clavicle). The *subclavian artery* is a very large vessel arising on the left side directly from the aorta, and on the right from the innominate artery, a short vessel that divides into subclavian and right carotid arteries. After passing below the clavicle, the subclavian is continued as the axillary artery into the armpit.

The branches include the *vertebral artery*, which runs up the side of the backbone into the skull, and arteries to parts of the neck and chest.

The subclavian is accompanied by a *subclavian vein*, which joins the corresponding jugular to form an *innominate vein*.

subcutaneous. Under the skin.

sublimation. According to Freud, an unconscious process of diverting unseemly instincts into respectable channels.

subliminal. Term applied to sensations

too slight or fleeting to be consciously perceived, though they may be unconsciously remembered; or stimuli too small to arouse a response in a nerve.

subluxation. Partial dislocation; displacement of bones in a joint without complete separation.

subphrenic. Below the diaphragm. A *subphrenic abscess*, in the space between the diaphragm and the top of the liver, sometimes arises from infection in the abdomen. It can be difficult to recognize because although the patient is obviously suffering from severe infection there is no indication of where the trouble lies. Sometimes a gas-bubble below the diaphragm is shown by X-rays, and sometimes the diagnosis is made by excluding all other possibilities.

substrate. The substance on which an *enzyme* acts; i.e. the raw material of a chemical process in a living organism.

Substrate competition is a common way for drugs to act. The drug so closely resembles a natural substrate that the enzyme reacts with it instead. For instance, *sulphonamide* drugs closely resemble a foodstuff of bacteria. The bacterial enzymes involve themselves with the useless drug and so deprive the bacteria of an essential food.

subtertian fever. Malignant tertian; falciparum. ►*malaria.*

succus entericus. The digestive juice of the small intestine. ►*digestion; intestine.*

sudamen (pl. *sudamina*). Sweat blister; prickly heat.

sudden infant death syndrome ►*cot death.*

sudor. Sweat.

sugar ►*carbohydrate.*

suicide. About 100 people are known to commit suicide in Britain every week. The rate is higher among the well-to-do than among the poor. Comparisons between countries, indicating for instance that suicide is much commoner in northern than southern Europe, may not be valid because in some countries doctors may be reluctant to upset relatives with the stigma of a mortal sin in the family. The formula of British juries 'suicide while the balance of the mind was disturbed' is a compromise between stating the fact and saving the family's face.

But the juries have been nearer the truth than they knew. Completely rational suicides are the exceptions. As a rule, something has gone wrong with the patient's thinking – and he really is a patient. Until 1961, he was officially a criminal in English law. Most people felt that the law was absurd, but it had the merit that anyone who attempted suicide could be legally detained, while someone investigated the case and found out why the prisoner (who was in fact kept under supervision in hospital) had tried to kill himself. The great drawback of this law was that it encouraged everyone concerned to conceal the 'crime', so that nothing was done to avert a second, possibly successful, attempt.

Suicide must now be regarded as the final symptom of a common illness, or group of illnesses. If the disease has a distinguishing feature it is the patient's feeling – perhaps unfounded – that he is cut off from the society or background he regards as his. In general, the patient also has some kind of mental instability, though there are circumstances in which a mentally stable person is so isolated from society that he kills himself. In these cases the society may be at fault. In the past an officer who behaved dishonourably, like a well-born Japanese who lost face, was expected to kill himself. Such suicides, dictated by public opinion, were little different from lynchings. But in most cases the sense of isolation is coupled with (and not the direct cause of) mental depression. If the depression is severe it may be the only real factor, though the patient imagines reasons for killing himself. These are often in the form of self-condemnation ('I have sinned – I am unfit to live').

The medical significance of suicide is that many cases could be prevented if the symptoms were recognized in time; and suicides are almost as numerous and quite as futile as deaths on the roads.

Several widespread and dangerous fallacies stand in the way of a rational view of suicide:

1. 'Attempted suicide is only moral blackmail.' Attempted suicide may well be moral blackmail (whether the patient knows it or not), but it is not *only* moral blackmail. The attempt may be a cry for help, but it is a desperate cry. The patient cannot be sure of surviving. He may hope to recover after giving everyone else a fright ('look what you made me do'). But he cannot tell how many pills will make him unconscious without killing him (nor, in the individual case, can a pharmacologist); he does not know how far he can fall without breaking his neck (nor does a surgeon). He may well hope to recover and find that things are better, but he does not much care about the risk of killing himself. Anyone in this frame of mind needs expert attention.

2. 'If one attempt fails, so will the next.' The patient is all too likely to try harder next time, because nobody was sufficiently impressed by the first attempt. This time he may try it with a motor car or a fire, and kill someone else by mistake.

3. 'The ones who talk about it never do it.' This is the most dangerous medical fallacy since surgeons gave up believing that pus was a good thing. *Most* people who commit suicide have dropped a hint to someone. It is a symptom to be taken as seriously as coughing up blood.

There are social services, official and voluntary, for dealing with the purely material reasons for suicide. The mental depression that underlies practically every case is a treatable illness.

sulphonamide. 1. The chemical group – SO_2NH_2.

2. Any compound that includes this group, especially one used to treat bacterial infection ('sulpha-drug'). Some diuretics and drugs used for treating diabetes are also sulphonamides.

In 1932 ▸*Domagk* showed that the red dye *prontosil* controlled certain types of infection. The active principle of prontosil is sulphanilamide (*para*-aminobenzene sulphonamide), which was discovered in 1908 by Gelmo in Vienna and used in dyeing.

The anti-bacterial effect of sulphonamides depends on their similarity to *para*-aminobenzoic acid, which bacteria need as a vitamin. The bacteria mistake the drug for the vitamin and poison themselves.

Sulphonamides are effective against many kinds of infection, including common types of pneumonia, meningitis and cystitis, bacillary dysentery, gonorrhoea, trachoma, and streptococcal infection. Since their introduction in 1935, some of the most lethal diseases have been curable. There are now scores of drugs, of which the official names all have the prefix '*sulpha-*', derived from sulphanilamide but with fewer toxic effects, a wider range of activity, or smaller dosage. *Co-trimoxazole* is a mixture of a sulphonamide, *sulphamethoxazole*, with *trimethoprim*, which interferes with the synthesis of folic acid. This mixture thus disturbs the metabolism of bacteria at two points, and sometimes controls an infection against which neither ingredient would work on its own.

sulphone. A kind of drug related to the sulphonamides; the sulphones were investigated during a search for a sulphonamide that would cure tuberculosis, and found to be an effective long-term treatment of leprosy. *Dapsone* is the usual form.

sunburn. Anyone with a fair skin is burnt by sufficient exposure to bright sunlight, especially when reflection from snow or water is added. In the tropics, enough ultraviolet rays find their way through even an overcast sky to cause some burning.

Several common drugs (e.g. sulphonamides) and a few uncommon diseases (porphyria; lupus erythematosus) sensitize the skin to sunlight. The antimalarial drug chloroquine sometimes suppresses an abnormal sensitivity.

The best treatment is to keep out of direct sunlight or protect the skin with long sleeves and a broad hat. Various creams and lotions filter off the harmful rays. They are selective, and it may be necessary to discover the wave-length of light to which a particular skin is sensitive, or try several preparations until a suitable one is found.

sunstroke ►*heatstroke*.

superego. Freud's term for a part of the unconscious mind that acts as a censor – the conscience.

super-female. A female with 3 instead of 2 X chromosomes to a cell. Such women are often sterile but are otherwise normal.

superinfection. During the course of one infection, a second infection by a different kind of microbe. The term is generally limited to a second infection by a microbe that is resistant to drugs being used against the first; the second microbe is sometimes a resistant variant of the first, and sometimes one of a type that is harmless until other types have been eliminated by drugs.

supination. Turning the forearm and hand palm upwards (cf. *pronation*, palm downwards).

suppository. A form of medication for insertion into the rectum, solid at ordinary room temperature but liquefying at body temperature, used either for a local effect such as relief of constipation or as a means of getting a drug into the circulation. (Chemical pessaries for vaginal use are also sometimes called suppositories.)

suppuration. Formation of pus.

suprarenal ►*adrenal*.

surgery. The craft of surgery (*chirurgia* – hand-work, treatment of disease with the hands) is much older than recorded history. The Edwin Smith Papyrus, one of the earliest medical texts (*c.* 1600 BC), describes the splinting of fractures, the replacement of dislocated joints, the care of wounds – as today, contaminated wounds are left open but clean ones are stitched – and the drainage of abscesses.

Hippocrates (*c.* 400 BC) devotes one book to the treatment of head injuries and another to the surgery of piles. In a general treatise on surgery he insists on careful preparation and technical skill –

his surgeons had to be professionals in any sense – and the Hippocratic Oath makes it clear that there were specialists.

After the Graeco-Roman era surgical practice deteriorated. The pious and scholarly physicians of the Middle Ages did not soil their hands on their patients, excepting a very few great men such as Guy de Chauliac. For the most part, surgery was left to itinerant tradesmen with little if any training. But one group – the barbers – took this additional work seriously and in the end achieved something like professional status. In England, they received a charter in 1540. Three years later, Vesalius published the *Fabrica* and brought anatomy and surgery back into the realm of medical science. (➤*Paré*.)

But another 2 centuries had to pass before surgery was wholly accepted as a part of medicine, and a surgeon became first and foremost a doctor. John Hunter (1728–93) put his chosen profession in its true perspective when he taught his students that a surgical operation was a last resort, an admission that other methods had failed: 'It is like an armed savage who attempts to get that by force which a civilized man would get by stratagem.' There must always be a place for surgery in the repair of damage or deformity, but for the rest the surgeon's ultimate goal is to work himself out of a job. Until recently, many forms of tuberculosis could be cured only by drastic surgery; now, streptomycin and other drugs offer a safer and surer remedy for all but a few cases.

By the middle of the 19th century surgeons had acquired almost unbelievable skill in the few operations that were possible. But the body cavities – abdomen, chest, skull – were forbidden territory except for desperate attempts to repair wounds, because any operation was almost bound to introduce fatal infection. Operations involving bones were almost equally dangerous. And since the patient was conscious, any operation lasting more than a few minutes was unthinkable. These two obstacles, infection and pain, kept surgery more or less within the bounds that the Greek doctors of the Roman Empire had known.

Then both obstacles were overcome at almost the same time. ➤*Anaesthetics* were introduced in the 1840s, and 20 years later the principle of surgery without ➤*infection* was discovered. All the old operations became safer, and for the first time, surgeons could reasonably treat diseases of the abdomen and of the bones and joints. With time no longer the first consideration, surgeons could work more like watch-makers than inspired butchers, and even the brain came within their scope.

Between the two World Wars the technique of anaesthesia improved rapidly. All surgery became safer, and with methods of maintaining respiration while the chest wall was open it was possible to operate on the lungs and the outside of the heart. The inside of the heart remained inaccessible until the introduction of heart-lung machines to take over the work of the heart during the operation.

suture. Surgical stitching, or the material used for it. Cotton or linen threads have been used for centuries. They are strong and easy to work with, but if the wound is infected these materials provide a safe refuge for bacteria. Catgut, popularized by Lister, is broken down in the tissues and disappears, and is particularly suited to stitches that have to be buried. The disappearance of the suture does not weaken the repair, because no suture is more than a splint to facilitate healing by living tissue. Occasionally even catgut provokes an adverse reaction. The ideal suture is a strip of the patient's own fibrous tissue, but the method is not often feasible.

Synthetic fibres are now used more often than natural ones because they are stronger and easier to sterilize, and various types of wire can also be used; all these remain in the tissues except where they are used in the skin and can be removed as the wound heals. Removable metal clips are a satisfactory alternative.

swallowing. The initial stage of swallowing is a voluntary act, though it is so well learnt as to be almost automatic. As soon as the food passes the back of the tongue a series of reflexes comes into play: the epiglottis closes the larynx and the food is pushed into the oesophagus by the muscles of the larynx.

sweat. A weak solution of salt, secreted by glands in the skin. Sweating is an active process, distinct from insensible *perspiration*, which is simply evaporation of almost pure water from the surface of the skin. The evaporation of sweat takes up a great deal of heat, and sweating is one of the principal means of regulating the temperature of the body. Unless the sweat can evaporate, no heat is lost. The air can take up only a limited amount of water vapour; therefore if the surrounding air is already saturated sweat merely accumulates on the skin; an atmosphere that is both hot and humid is intolerable.

In cool surroundings no sweat at all is secreted. In very hot surroundings the sweat glands may pour out as much as 10 litres (2 gallons) in a day, together with 30 grammes (1 oz) of salt. *heatstroke*.

Newly formed sweat has little smell. The unpleasant smell of stale sweat is due to the action of bacteria. Deodorants act mainly by destroying bacteria on the skin.

sycosis barbae *barber's itch*.

Sydenham, Thomas (1624–89). 'The English Hippocrates'; next to Harvey the most celebrated of English physicians. Harvey in the laboratory and Sydenham at the bedside symbolize the two poles of the world of medicine. Sydenham was not concerned with scientific discovery for its own sake. Like Hippocrates, he was content to observe the course of illnesses, record neither more nor less than what he observed, and interfere as little as possible with the natural process of healing. Nobody has excelled Sydenham's accounts of symptoms nor his precise distinctions between various diseases.

Good remedies were few. Sydenham made the best use of those that he had, and established sound principles for treating malaria (then a common disease in England) with cinchona, syphilis with mercury, anaemia with iron, and severe pain or restlessness with opium.

His purely clinical study of disease led Sydenham to the conclusion that symptoms represent Nature's attempt to shake off disease. Although this is by no means the universal truth that Sydenham thought it to be, it remains one of the most important and most neglected principles of medical practice. Patients consult doctors to have their symptoms relieved, and every generation needs a Sydenham to point out that treating symptoms without first considering their causes may be the worst of disservices.

sympathectomy. Surgical operation to disconnect sympathetic nerves, with the object of preventing spasm of blood vessels or other effects of these nerves. Chemical sympathectomy is inhibition of sympathetic nerves with drugs; it has the advantage over surgery that it does no permanent damage and can be stopped at any time, but a drug affects the whole sympathetic system whereas surgery is confined to the particular branch that is to be put out of action.

Although sympathectomy would increase the flow of blood through healthy arteries it does not always improve diseased arteries, which may already be as wide as they can be. As a rule the operation is done only if a trial of blocking the nerve with a local anaesthetic improves the circulation.

sympathetic. One of the two divisions (cf. *parasympathetic*) of the autonomic or vegetative nervous system, which are responsible for the automatic, unconscious regulation of bodily function. Most parts of the body receive twigs from both of these divisions, generally with opposite actions.

The sympathetic nerves originate from cells in the spinal cord. These cells send fibres to relay stations (*ganglia*) which form a chain lying in front of the muscles at either side of the backbone. From the sympathetic nerves branches spread throughout the body, most of them accompanying the main arteries.

Sympathetic nerves have the following actions:

The sweat glands and the tiny muscles at the roots of the hairs (*arrectores pilorum*) are stimulated.

The upper eyelids are raised, and the pupils are dilated – the upper lids can, of course, also be controlled by voluntary nerves.

Arteries to muscles, including the coronary arteries of the heart muscle, are dilated, but other arteries (skin, abdominal organs etc.) are constricted.

The rate and force of the heart beat are increased, and more air is allowed into the lungs.

The activity of the digestive organs is suppressed.

With one exception, the sympathetic nerves act by releasing *adrenaline* and *noradrenaline*, and an injection of one of these substances has similar effects to direct stimulation of the nerves. The exception is the nerves of the sweat glands, which like parasympathetic nerves release *acetyl choline*.

Sympathomimetic or *adrenergic* drugs imitate the effects of the sympathetic nerves. Adrenaline itself is given for asthma and other severe symptoms associated with allergy. It works only if it is injected, and its action is rapid but short-lived. Many drugs have rather similar actions. *Ephedrine* can be given by mouth. It works fairly well against asthma, and is less likely than adrenaline to raise the blood pressure. But it causes unwanted mental excitement. This last effect is the principal one of *amphetamine* and related compounds, and accounts for their use by drug addicts. *Salbutamol* and *terbutaline* are especially suited to asthma because they relax the bronchi without much effect on the heart and blood vessels.

Sympatholytic drugs inhibit sympathetic nerves. The drugs used to treat high ►*blood pressure* are mostly of this type. They inhibit all the effects of adrenaline. Some others, e.g. *tolazoline*, selectively inhibit only the characteristic effects of noradrenaline (*alpha* effects) such as constriction of blood vessels, and can be used to treat spasm of blood vessels without disturbing the rest of the sympathetic system. ►*Betablockers* inhibit the other actions of the sympathetic nerves (*beta* effects) and can be used to prevent the nerves from overstimulating the heart in conditions such as angina, again without disturbing the rest of the system.

symptom. In ordinary English a symptom is any indication that something may be wrong: a manifestation of disease. Symptoms in this sense may be subjective, i.e. observed by the patient, or objective, i.e. observed by his attendants. Medical usage restricts the term to what the patient himself reports. Abnormalities found by examining the patient are *signs*.

A *presenting symptom* is one which prompts a patient to seek medical advice – not necessarily the first he notices; he may ignore a cough and some loss of weight but consult a doctor when he finds blood on his handkerchief. Bleeding is then the presenting symptoms, cough and weight loss are other symptoms, and the signs might include a slightly raised temperature and abnormal shadows in an X-ray picture of the lungs.

synapse. A junction or relay station between nerve cells. When an impulse travels down the conducting fibre (axon) of a nerve cell a chemical substance (usually acetyl choline) is released from the end of the fibre and sets off a new impulse in the next nerve cell of the chain of communication.

syncope = ►*faint*.

syndrome. A fixed pattern of symptoms, not necessarily with the same cause in all cases.

synovium. Smooth moist membrane lining a ►*joint*.

syphilis. An infectious disease caused by a spiral bacterium (spirochaete), *Treponema pallidum*. Since the spirochaete cannot withstand exposure in the open air the disease is transmitted only by close contact, nearly always sexual (but ►*yaws*). The infection enters through either a mucous membrane (vagina or male urethra) or a scratch in the skin; thus apart from frankly venereal infection there are rare cases from kissing and from touching an infectious patient with an unnoticed scratch on the hand – a risk to doctors and nurses. A greater danger is infection of an unborn infant, for *T. pallidum* is one of the very few microbes that can pass through the placenta to infect the infant.

There are no recognizable accounts of syphilis earlier than about AD 1500, but after the return of Columbus from the New World the disease spread as a plague from the Mediterranean across Europe. Nobody can prove that Columbus and his men imported syphilis, but it seems likely. There is, however, a considerable weight of contrary opinion, some of it well informed (►*yaws*). One need not take very seriously the scholars who have insisted that the leprosy of the Bible must have been syphilis because it is an apt punishment for sin, and congenital syphilis visits the sins of the fathers upon the children.

Syphilis was first named in 1530 by Fracastorius in a poem *Syphilis sive Morbus Gallicus*, where he describes the disease as hitherto unknown and gives an unmistakable account of its natural history. He then tells how an unfortunate shepherd named Syphilus cursed the Sun during a heat-wave and was promptly stricken with the new disease as a punishment.

All the protean effects of syphilis are

due to localized, subdued and chronic inflammation wherever the spirochaetes take hold. The small blood vessels are more affected than any other structures, and many of the symptoms are from impaired circulation of blood in affected areas.

The first sign is a *chancre*, a hard small lump that may break down to form an ulcer at the site of entry. The nearest lymph nodes – in the groins if, as is usual, the chancre is on the genitalia – swell. The chancre appears at any time between a week and 3 months after infection, and gradually disappears even without treatment. In a few cases there is no chancre and the disease passes straight to the second stage.

In the second stage, beginning several weeks or even months after infection, the spirochaetes have been disseminated in the blood-stream and cause general mild illness and a skin rash with swollen lymph nodes. The rash may be localized or widespread, and can take so many forms that cases of secondary syphilis have been mistaken for most of the common skin diseases. This stage also subsides even without treatment, but the infection still lurks.

The third stage of syphilis does permanent damage. The spirochaetes form established colonies in various parts of the body and start a persistent grumbling inflammation followed by obstruction of small arteries and loss of normal tissue. Any tissue or organ in the body can be affected and almost any chronic disease can be simulated. Physicians of the 19th century, when advanced syphilis was rife, taught that any student who knew syphilis knew medicine. A sort of chronic abscess (*gumma*), consisting mainly of dead tissue and overgrown scar tissue, may appear anywhere in the body and cause symptoms by compressing healthy neighbouring tissue. Mucous membranes, skin, and bones are common sites of tertiary syphilis. Syphilis of the heart can be fatal. The initial attack is on small arteries that nourish the main artery – the aorta – which loses its resilience and becomes permanently stretched by the pressure of blood (>*aneurysm*). Later the valve that prevents blood pumped into the aorta from returning to the heart leaks, so that the heart is no longer an efficient pump.

The nervous system may be severely damaged at a late stage of the disease. Again the various types of syphilis can be confused with many other diseases, but there are two characteristic types. These are *tabes dorsalis* (locomotor ataxia), with loss of reflexes that coordinate voluntary movement and posture; and *general paresis* (GPI, dementia paralytica), with deterioration of personality, delusions (often of grandeur or self-importance), and at last total insanity.

As early as 1530 Fracastorius described the treatment of syphilis with mercury. It was unreliable and dangerous but much better than nothing, and for four centuries offered the only hope of a cure. In 1910, Ehrlich discovered arsphenamine (>*arsenic*), and for the first time it became possible to kill microbes in the body without great risk to the patient. Arsenic has now given way to penicillin as the standard treatment of syphilis. In the first and second stages syphilis can usually be cured because there has been no permanent damage. In the later stages it can only be arrested, for tissues already destroyed are not restored.

Prevention would be the best answer, but this is still no more than a dream (>*venereal disease*).

595

In the early stages, the spirochaete can usually be identified. Later it becomes difficult to isolate, but its presence can be inferred from blood tests.

syringomyelia. An uncommon defect of the spinal cord. Small cavities filled with watery fluid appear in the centre of the cord and disturb conduction in adjacent nerve fibres. The fibres conducting the sensations of pain and temperature are the first to suffer, but other functions may be impaired later (sometimes after decades). The cause is unknown, but there may be a congenital fault in the spinal cord. There is no reliable treatment. Surgical operations to relieve pressure within the cord sometimes help.

system. (1) A group of more or less distinct organs with a common function, e.g. the cardiovascular system (heart and blood vessels), the digestive or alimentary system (oesophagus, stomach, intestine, liver, pancreas and other digestive glands). (2) A school of medical or pseudo-medical opinion based on a few fixed axioms, e.g. homoeopathy. (3) The whole body regarded as a functional unit, now obsolescent as a noun but still alive as an adjective: see next entry.

systemic. Applying to or affecting the body as a whole, often opposed to *local* or *topical*. Thus the local symptoms of an abscess include swelling and pain, while the systemic symptoms include fever and proliferation of white blood cells. A drug may be given systemically, e.g. by mouth or by injection into a vein, to be taken into the circulation and distributed throughout the body, or topically, e.g. in an ointment, to act only at the site of trouble.

systole. Contraction of the heart muscle, the active phase of its cycle when blood is pumped into the arteries (cf. *diastole*, the passive phase when the heart relaxes and blood flows into it from the veins).

T

TAB. Combined vaccine against typhoid, paratyphoid A and paratyphoid B fevers.

tabes (archaic). Any wasting disease. *Tabes dorsalis* = syphilis of the spinal cord. *Tabes mesenterica* = abdominal tuberculosis.

tachycardia. Unduly rapid heart beat.

tachyphylaxis. Decreasing effectiveness of a drug after repeated use; it occurs most often with drugs acting on the nervous system. ►*tobacco.*

taenia. Tapeworm. ►*worms.*

talipes = ►*club-foot.*

talus (astragalus). A bone of the foot. It fits into a mortise formed by the lower ends of the tibia and fibula to form the ankle joint.

tapeworm ►*worms.*

tarsus. 1. Base of the ►*foot.* Of the 7 tarsal bones, only one, the talus, articulates with the leg to form the ankle-joint.
2. Tough fibrous tissue in an eyelid, providing shape and support.

taste. The mucous membranes of the tongue and palate contain numerous minute sensory organs, the taste-buds. Each bud is a round cluster of spindle-shaped cells, from which nerve fibres lead to the facial and glossopharyngeal nerves. Four types of sensation are received from the taste-buds: salt, sweet, sour (acid), and bitter. Of these, only sour is obviously linked to the chemical structure of the substance tasted. The buds all look alike, but four sensations

suggest four types of bud. Furthermore some areas of the tongue are more sensitive than others to particular tastes: the tip to sweet and salt, the edges to sour and salt, and the back to bitter. There is, however, evidence that all taste-buds are able to respond to all four tastes, and that the long-accepted principle that one nerve fibre can do only one job may need modification. It may be that different tastes are transmitted by different patterns of impulses, decoded in the brain. The same applies to the different types of sensation from the skin.

This crude sensation promotes a reflex flow of saliva. But awareness of flavours depends more on smell (►*nose* (2)) and on information about consistency, texture, and even appearance.

Tay-Sachs disease. A rare genetic disorder. The affected children, mostly of E. European Jewish origin, lack an enzyme needed to decompose a ►*lipid* of which an excess accumulates in the nervous system, causing irreparable damage and early death. Carriers of the defective gene can be detected by a blood test, and if both parents are positive amniocentesis will show if the foetus is affected.

teeth

1. STRUCTURE

The exposed part of a tooth is the *crown*, the concealed part is the *root.* The slight constriction where the two meet is the *neck*, to which in health the mucous membrane of the gum is attached.

A tooth is a stout shell of *dentine*

(ivory), which is like compact bone except that it has no blood vessels. The dentine of the root is coated with a thin layer of a similar but softer material, *cement*. The crown has a thick covering of *enamel*, which is much denser and harder than dentine or than any other animal matter. The cavity of the tooth is filled with the *pulp*, soft connective tissue rich in blood vessels and nerve fibres.

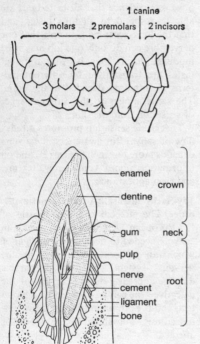

(Above) *arrangement of adult teeth;*
(below) *section of tooth (diagrammatic)*

The arrangement of the teeth is the same in upper and lower jaws. On each side, counting from the mid-line, there are 2 incisors, 1 canine, 2 premolars, and 3 molars – 8 teeth in each quadrant or 32 in all. The *incisors* are chisel-edged. The upper ones close in front of the lower; together they act as scissors. The *canines* are conical, grasping teeth, especially well developed in carnivores, which use them for seizing their prey and wrenching off lumps of meat. Premolars and molars are adapted for grinding food between knobs (*cusps*) on their surfaces. The premolars, each with 2 cusps, are also called *bicuspid* teeth. The upper molars each have 4 cusps; the lower molars have 5.

Each upper molar has 3 roots. Lower molars have 2, and the other teeth usually have single roots. The roots are deeply embedded in sockets in the jaws, to which they are fastened by ligaments (*periodontal membrane*).

2. Development

The elements of the teeth are formed before birth. The lining membrane of the mouth grows into the tissue from which the jaws are to develop, and forms the enamel. The rest of the tooth is modified connective tissue. Each tooth bud is enclosed in a little capsule or *dental follicle*. At birth the jaws are filled with these follicles.

The deciduous or milk teeth begin to erupt about half-way through the first year of life – the time varies and is unimportant. Only 20 milk teeth appear: in each quadrant 2 incisors, 1 canine, and 2 molars. The set is usually complete at about 2 years.

The first permanent teeth to erupt are the 1st molars at about 6 years. They are behind the deciduous molars, so no teeth are shed when they appear. Later the deciduous teeth are replaced by permanent teeth – deciduous molars by permanent premolars. The last milk teeth, the canines, are usually replaced in the 12th year. After that the 2nd permanent molars erupt. The 3rd molar (wisdom) teeth are delayed for a few more years and may not erupt at all.

Healthy development of the teeth obviously depends to some extent on the general health: the teeth are as susceptible as any other organ to malnutrition. Vitamin deficiencies, especially scurvy and rickets, impair the growth of the teeth. Dentine and enamel both need a supply of *fluorine*, and minute quantities of certain other elements appear to be needed – probably molybdenum and manganese, possibly vanadium and selenium.

Drugs given to pregnant women, notably tetracycline antibiotics, may affect the baby's teeth; the enamel is discoloured and sometimes defective.

3. DISORDERS

Human jaws have receded in the course of evolution, and there is now barely room for the full set of permanent teeth. But quite apart from overcrowding, teeth are apt to grow unevenly. Some of the effects are obvious: the teeth are unsightly, useless because they do not meet their opposite numbers (malocclusion), and hard to clean. The second and third effects make them liable to decay. These are more than enough reasons for energetic treatment. *Orthodontics* is the branch of dentistry which deals with misplaced teeth. It has become a very refined craft, and even quite gross deformities can be corrected if they are treated early. Some of the remote effects which have been ascribed to malocclusion, such as disorders of breathing, are open to doubt.

Tartar (calculus) is a chalky precipitate from the saliva. If it is not regularly removed it injures the gums and provides a shelter for bacteria.

Considering that the mouth teems with microbes the gums remain remarkably free from infection, but they can become infected and inflamed, especially if they are not kept clear of tartar and food residues. The inflammation – *gingivitis* – is disagreeable in itself because the gums are tender and the mouth tastes and smells unpleasant; in time the bone of the jaws recedes, the teeth become loose, and dentures may be difficult to fit. The condition of the gums deteriorates rapidly with anaemia, malnutrition, and many chronic infectious diseases.

Much the most important disease of the teeth is decay or *dental caries*. The enamel and then the dentine are dissolved from part of the tooth until the pulp is exposed and ultimately the tooth dies. The process is still not fully understood, but the usual sequence appears to be as follows. Bacteria in the mouth, perhaps lactobacilli, ferment sugar to form acids. The acids dissolve the calcium salts of the enamel and dentine to form a crevice in which the process can proceed more quickly. The bacteria are most active away from air. At first they are protected from air by particles of food between the teeth, but later the crevice that they have made protects them. Once a hole is established other types of bacteria can attack the pulp.

Enamel which lacks fluorine is especially vulnerable. Some people, perhaps 10 per cent of the population, are highly resistant to caries for no known reason. Clean teeth are safer than dirty teeth because on them bacteria are exposed to the air. The protective value of chewing is not clear. Chewing may do more for the supporting tissues than for the teeth themselves. Sugar is a better medium for the bacteria – i.e. more harmful to the teeth – than any other food, and sugar between meals is much worse than sugar with meals because saliva flows freely during a meal. Saliva itself is essential to the health of the teeth. If the saliva is deficient the teeth decay rapidly.

Next to caries the commonest cause of severe toothache is an *abscess* around a root. Such abscesses may be associated with caries or with inflamed gums, but they can also arise at the roots of healthy teeth. The tooth socket is of bone and therefore rigid, and the abscess cavity is plugged by the tooth. Since there is no room for expansion the abscess is painful even at the earliest stage, and the pus is liable to invade neighbouring tissue. The path of least resistance is usually into the mouth, but an abscess at the root of a lower back tooth may point below the angle of the jaw. The obvious treatment is to draw the tooth, which releases the pus and alleviates both pain and risk. This used to be the only way to manage an established abscess, but with antibiotics it is now possible to abort the process, at least in the early stages. Even when pus has formed it can sometimes be drained by drilling the length of the tooth and filling the cavity when it is clean.

A detailed account of dental treatment is beyond the scope of this book, but there is a historical note under ►*dentistry*. Here it may be said that modern dental treatment is governed by two principles: conservation and prevention. Caries does not attack a whole tooth at once. It starts at one point, presumably at some fault in the microcrystalline structure of the enamel. If the decayed part of the tooth is cleared away and the hole is filled the tooth is neither more nor less liable to further trouble than any other tooth. The best modern artificial teeth are excellent, both functionally and cosmetically, but nobody pretends that

they are quite as good as natural teeth. A dentist will not, then, draw a tooth if he can reasonably preserve it. Much of his skill hangs on the judgement of what is reasonable, of the moment at which a natural tooth is likely to be more troublesome than an artificial one. The deciding factor is more often the state of the gums than that of the teeth themselves.

Prevention is even more important. Most dental disease is theoretically avoidable. The mouth cannot be freed of bacteria, and indeed if most of the bacteria are destroyed by antibiotics there is a danger that other microbes, normally opposed by bacteria, will cause trouble. But the bacteria of the mouth are harmless unless they are protected by particles of food between the teeth, or by tartar; if neither is allowed to collect the teeth and gums are safe. If no food, especially no sugar, ever remains between the teeth there is nothing for the bacteria to ferment. Perfect cleaning of the teeth immediately after eating and regular scaling of tartar by a dentist ought to protect the teeth for a lifetime. Whether it would in fact do so is not known, for nobody can be sure of removing every food particle with every brushing, and a few hours are enough to establish the first crevice that is the start of caries.

Diet is important in two ways. Firstly, it must contain the factors necessary for the healthy growth of teeth, at least until growth is complete. Vitamin deficiencies are rare in prosperous communities but all too common elsewhere. ►*Fluorine* deficiency is a result of living in an area where the drinking water contains too little. Secondly, the food should need chewing. It is difficult to prove the importance of this, but most authorities agree that the soft food of an over-civilized diet is a factor in dental ill health.

Finally, the actual treatment of diseased teeth and gums is also a means of prevention, for if lost tissue cannot be restored the processes of decay can at least be arrested or greatly slowed.

teething. Children may be fretful and even feverish when they are cutting teeth, but it does not follow that these symptoms are due to teething. The first teeth erupt at an age when children are meeting infections to which they have not yet developed any immunity. The child may be teething or ill or teething *and* ill. Each case needs to be investigated before the trouble can be dismissed as unimportant (➤*paediatrics*).

telangiectasis. A cluster of small blood vessels such as one of the blotches on the face with ➤*rosacea*. Some birthmarks are of this type, and telangiectases in the nose are apt to bleed. Haemorrhagic telangiectasia is an uncommon hereditary disease that can cause anaemia from frequent bleeding.

teleology. The doctrine of final causes: the assumption that events are ultimately due to the ends which they serve. In other words, things happen because it is necessary that they should happen. This is very nearly the same as saying that they happen because it is God's will.

In essence, the doctrine must be almost as old as abstract thought. Materialism can never wholly displace it, because man's finite intelligence cannot deal with infinite problems. Science is largely a matter of determining causes and effects. Progress means advancing the frontiers of what we can rationally define, but the frontiers remain, and discussion of anything beyond them is almost bound to be teleological. Aristotle thought in terms of a planned universe in which everything had its place. To say that events are caused by the need for them is no more than to say that they must suit the plan – or the purpose of the planner. The doctrine led to error only when later and lesser thinkers than Aristotle, such as Galen, presumed to know what this purpose was. The early Christians all but canonized Galen. If they had thought more deeply they would have disowned him for supposing he was party to God's design. He was the greatest physician of ancient Rome, and a fine observer. But since he was determined that everything he observed should take its place in the grand design *as he saw it*, he was not always a reliable witness. For example, although his account of the muscles was detailed and reasonably accurate, he flouted the evidence of his own eyes by describing hollow nerves, in order to suit his theory of how muscles worked. He also described, as though he had seen them, channels between the chambers of the heart and an elaborate system of communication between the arteries and nerves at the base of the brain, because he thought that they should be there to convey the 'vital spirit'. Some of the most tenacious fallacies in medicine have arisen, and will continue to arise, in this way.

The belief that pus was necessary to the healing of wounds bedevilled surgery throughout the Middle Ages and almost into our own times. Observing that wounds usually formed pus, the surgeons argued that pus must have a useful purpose, so they irritated and infected wounds to encourage more pus to be formed. Thus they caused as much suffering as ever they relieved. Inflammation, the process by which pus arises, gives a more modern instance of the same kind of fallacy. John Hunter, who could use teleology without letting it blind him, correctly described inflammation as a means of defence and healing. From this it is all too easy to conclude that inflammation is *always* desirable, and to be encouraged. Not until the 20th century was it shown that certain types of inflammation are harmful. ►*allergy*.

Teleology, then, has no place in a 'pure' science such as physics, except as the last refuge of the man who knows that he has reached the limit of his ability to see or reason. The same is true of basic research in medicine, which has to seek out causes and not take them for granted. But in medical practice decisions have to be made which cannot be based on complete knowledge or mathematical proof. What the doctor cannot explain he must take for granted; beyond the frontiers of scientific knowledge he is inevitably a teleologist. This is the difference between the science and the art of medicine.

In speaking or writing about medicine, teleology can hardly be avoided. The critical reader will find instances on almost any page of this book. The heart *pumps* blood; the kidneys *filter* it; muscles *pull*, or *resist* gravity; white blood cells *attack* germs. All these verbs imply purpose. To a purist, each begs the question. Yet anyone who tried to avoid them would write so pedantically as to be unreadable even by a specialist. If one is to discuss these things at all one must discuss them in a language that can be understood, and as often as not this is the language of teleology. Even the experimental physiologist, running to catch his train, can be allowed to breathe fast in order to bring more oxygen to his overworked muscles. He will have time when he reaches his laboratory to reflect that he breathed fast, not *in order to* do anything, but *because* acid formed in his muscles stimulated the nerve centre controlling respiratory rate.

temperament. The four temperaments of ancient medicine were supposedly related to the four ►*humours*: *sanguine* to blood, *melancholy* to 'black bile' (the dark, viscous blood of the spleen), *choleric* to yellow (real) bile, and *phlegmatic* to phlegm or mucus.

temperature. The temperature of the body is not strictly constant, nor is it the same in all parts of the body. 'Normal' temperature, taken in the mouth, is close to the temperature of arterial blood. In the armpit the temperature is a little lower and in the rectum, higher. Most people have an average temperature in the mouth between 36 ° and 37.2 °C (97° and 99 °F), but the value fluctuates during the day (lowest in the early morning, highest in the evening), and, in women, during the month (lowest at menstruation, highest at ovulation).

The reflex control of temperature is modified by clothing. Tropical heatwaves apart, the body constantly loses heat to the environment by conduction and radiation and above all by evaporation of water from the skin. It gains heat from the combustion of fuel derived from food. Small variations are dealt with by adjusting the flow of blood through the skin. To conserve heat, the blood vessels of the skin contract and the skin pales; to lose heat they dilate and the skin flushes. Heat is gained rapidly when the muscles are made to work, for like all engines they dissipate some of the energy provided as heat. If no positive exercise is taken to work the muscles, they can work automatically to produce shivering.

Heat is lost when the sweat glands pour water on to the skin to be evaporated. If the surrounding air is moving, sweat evaporates faster. Movement of the air also increases the conduction of heat away from the body. The warmth of clothing depends on the layer of enclosed, still air.

Raised body temperature is discussed under ➤*fever*, and lowered body temperature under ➤*cold*.

temper tantrums. Most small children have occasional episodes of uncontrolled rage, but frequent tantrums may need investigation. Often a child's feelings develop faster than his ability to express them; he is like an adult who finds foreigners intolerably stupid because he cannot communicate with them. Temper tantrums may of course be straightforward blackmail, but they may also be a desperate attempt to convey some real problem such as illness or emotional starvation.

temporal. Of the side of the cranium (temple). The *temporal bone* is the part of the skull around the ear. Its outer surface gives attachment to the *temporalis* muscle.

The (superficial) *temporal artery* runs in front of the ear, where its pulse can be felt, and over the scalp. This artery is occasionally the site of painful chronic inflammation (*polymyalgia rheumatica*).

The *temporal lobe* is a part of the brain under cover of the temporal bone. It records hearing, and appears to play an important part in the storage of memory.

temporalis. Large muscle at the side of the head for closing the jaw. In many animals these muscles are so large in relation to the head that there is a crest on

top of the skull to accommodate them, much as the huge pectoral muscles of a bird raise a crest on the sternum.

tendon (leader; sinew). Fibrous cord joining a muscle to a bone. A tendon is a bundle of tough fibres of *collagen*, which are so strong that a violent jerk of the muscle is as likely to break off a piece of the bone as to snap the tendon.

An *aponeurosis* is a flat sheet of fibres representing the tendon of a flat muscle, as in the abdominal wall or scalp.

The sensory nerves in tendons transmit the unconscious sensation of stretch, setting off reflex contraction of the muscle to oppose the movement and maintain a given posture. This reflex is exemplified by the familiar knee-jerk: a tap of the examiner's hammer stretches the tendon in front of the knee and the muscle promptly responds. A tendon can also register pain if it is squeezed.

Tendons have their own blood vessels, and can heal if they are stitched together after an injury. The result is apt to be spoiled because in the process of healing the tendon sticks to neighbouring structures, and loses its mobility.

At the wrist and ankle the tendons are enclosed in slippery fibrous sheaths, which may be inflamed (*tenosynovitis*) by bacterial infection or rheumatism.

➤*trigger finger*.

tennis elbow. Pain and stiffness in the muscles below and to the outer side of the elbow joint, commonly associated with a strain on the muscles such as a hard game of tennis when out of training, or unaccustomed effort with a screwdriver. The pain is variously ascribed to a partial tear of the muscle fibres, to pinching of the radial nerve as it passes through the muscle at this point, and to bursitis. It can be relieved by an injection of hydrocortisone into the painful spot, or by manipulation. Whether treated or not the symptoms disappear in time, but they may linger for many months.

tension ➤*premenstrual tension*.

teratoma. 1. A grossly deformed foetus.

2. A kind of tumour of which the cells may develop into a semblance of almost any tissue; originating either from several different kinds of cell or from persistent embryonic cells that have kept their ability to develop in various ways.

tertian fever ➤*malaria*.

testis (testicle). The primary organ of sex in the male. Like its counterpart the ovary, the testis has two distinct functions. It forms the male germ cells – sperms – and it is also an endocrine gland, secreting sex hormones into the blood-stream.

Within its tough fibrous shell, the *tunica albuginea*, the testis contains fine coiled tubes, the *seminiferous tubules*, lined with cells that from puberty until old age can develop into sperms. The seminiferous tubules lead to the *epididymis*, a tangle of tubes in which newly formed sperms mature. The epididymis opens into the *vas deferens*, which carries the sperms through the groin, behind the urinary bladder, and through the prostate gland to the urethra.

Between the seminiferous tubules are collections of *interstitial cells* where hormones, mainly *androgens*, are formed (➤*sex hormones*).

Both components of the testis are regulated by hormones of the ➤*pituitary*.

The testes originate in the abdomen immediately below the kidneys. In fish (soft roes) and birds they remain there, but in man and most other mammals they migrate through the groins to the surface of the body where they are carried in a bag of skin, the *scrotum*. They work at a lower temperature than other organs. A testis that fails to descend to the scrotum generally fails to produce live sperms, but its output of hormones is not impaired. The testes usually descend before birth, but about 10 per cent of boys are born with one or both still on the way. In most of them the undescended testis arrives within a few weeks, but the condition has to be treated if it persists. Pituitary hormones may complete the process; otherwise the testis must be brought down surgically.

In its descent from the abdomen the testis brings with it its duct, the *vas deferens*, and its blood vessels, which arise next to those of the kidneys. All these form a leash, the *spermatic cord*. Occasionally the cord becomes twisted, causing severe pain in the testis and obstructing its supply of blood. This condition, torsion of the testis, needs prompt surgical treatment.

The passage of the cord through the muscles of the abdomen creates a weakness through which a *hernia* can protrude.

The commonest disorder in this region is ➤*hydrocele*.

Because the testes are readily accessible cancer of a testis is likely to be detected at an earlier stage than most others, and men are being encouraged to look for them in the same way as women are advised to examine their breasts regularly.

Inflammation of the testis (orchitis) is an occasional complication of mumps, gonorrhoea, tuberculosis and some other infections.

testosterone. A male sex hormone (androgen); the principal hormone of the testis.

tetanus. Spasm of voluntary muscles

with convulsions, caused by infection with the tetanus bacillus, *Clostridium tetani*. This bacillus lives harmlessly in the intestines of various animals, especially horses and occasionally man. It can multiply only in the absence of air, but when conditions are unfavourable it forms spores, a sort of hibernating phase, from which active bacilli can develop after years of inactivity. Tetanus spores are often found in soil. Many wounds must be contaminated with tetanus spores, but nothing untoward happens unless the conditions exactly suit them. For this, the spores must be embedded in tissue that has been killed, e.g. by other bacteria, injury, or chemical poisons, so that it has no oxygen supply.

Even active tetanus bacilli do not harm the tissues in which they multiply; but they produce a *toxin* that is one of the most poisonous substances known. It has a similar action to strychnine, but the lethal dose is about 100,000 times less.

The toxin released by tetanus bacilli follows the path of the nearest nerve to the spinal cord. There, it blocks the automatic impulses that restrain motor nerve cells and so allow the selective stimulation that is the basis of controlled movement. When the motor cells are freed from this restraint they bombard the muscles with impulses, and the muscles respond either with convulsive twitching or sustained contraction. Co-ordinated movement is impossible because opposed muscles pull against each other.

Trismus – a spasm of the jaw muscles – gives tetanus its alternative name, *lockjaw*. It may be the first symptom, but any group of muscles can be affected first. Later, other groups follow; the patient is severely ill and may die from inability to control breathing or from sheer physical exhaustion. Symptoms may begin at any time from a few days to a month or more after the original wound – the later, the less the danger.

Tetanus can be prevented by vaccination, which has to be repeated every 5 years and immediately after a suspect injury. People who have not been vaccinated against tetanus can be given temporary immunity after a wound with an injection of antitoxin.

The antitoxin is also used for treating an actual case of tetanus, but it neutralizes only toxin that has not yet invaded nerve cells – it prevents the disease from getting worse but does not cure symptoms that have already begun. Opening up the wound surgically exposes the bacilli to air, which they cannot tolerate. Oxygen can be used to reinforce this effect.

Since any sensation may trigger convulsions, patients with tetanus have to be nursed in quiet and shade. In addition to neutralizing the toxin with antitoxin (immunoglobulin) the patient is given vaccine to promote his own formation of antitoxin, and penicillin to attack the infecting bacilli. Muscle-relaxant drugs such as diazepam are given to control muscular spasm: even curare has been used to this end.

Untreated tetanus is often fatal, but with present-day treatment most patients recover, and suffer no lasting effects.

tetany. Twitching and spasm of muscles from any cause, e.g. disturbance of the calcium in the tissue fluid with disease of the parathyroid glands, vitamin D deficiency, or alkalosis.

tetracycline. An antibiotic prepared from chlortetracycline, which is extracted from the fungus *Streptomyces aureofaciens*. These and other related compounds are broad-spectrum antibiotics, i.e. they kill many different types of microbe. This versatility is useful with mixed infections, and when the infecting microbe cannot be identified. The disadvantage is that useful bacteria are also destroyed.

thalamus. Two masses of nerve cells, sometimes joined in the mid-line, at the headward end of the brain-stem, between the cerebral hemispheres. Sensations of all kinds are carried to the thalamus to be relayed to the cerebral cortex, where they are consciously perceived, or to lower centres where appropriate reflex actions are set in train. At least one sensation – pain – appears to be perceived in the thalamus itself, without having to be referred to the cortex. If the thalamus is damaged, pain is not so easily induced, but such pain as can be felt seems unnaturally severe.

thalassaemia. Cooley's anaemia, a hereditary anomaly of ➤*haemoglobin.*

thalidomide. Sedative drug first used in Germany in 1958, and withdrawn in 1961 because of serious deformities among babies born to women who had taken the drug during pregnancy. Thalidomide is related chemically to drugs that have been used for many years. Its advantage was that overdoses were unlikely to be fatal. A few patients taking it developed a kind of neuritis, which was mistaken for a minor side-effect.

A well known but very rare congenital defect of the limbs, *phocomelia*, suddenly became commoner, and the increase was associated with thalidomide. At that time the routine investigation of new drugs did not include tests during pregnancy, because the risk to the embryo was unsuspected. Looking back, it seems that the action of thalidomide on adult nerve

cells, which can cause neuritis, is far more injurious to the growing nerve cells of an embryo. The nerves are the first part of a limb to develop, and if their growth is impaired the bones and muscles also fail to develop.

Since 1961, drugs have been tested on pregnant animals before being considered for human use.

theine. Caffeine extracted from tea.

thenar. Of the ball of the thumb. ➤*hand* (1).

theophylline. An alkaloid resembling theine. ➤*aminophylline.*

therapeutics; therapy. Therapeutics is the science of treating disease; therapy is the treatment itself.

thermometer. Sanctorius measured the body temperature before 1612 with a cumbersome modification of Galileo's thermometer, but for two and a half centuries no further progress was made for want of a convenient instrument. The 19th-century German physicians Carl Wunderlich and Ludwig Traube were the first to make any systematic study of the temperature in health and sickness. The modern clinical thermometer was designed by Sir Clifford Allbutt (1836–1925) in 1867.

A half-minute thermometer registers in half a minute under laboratory conditions but takes rather longer in the mouth and much longer under the arm. If the reading is going to be wrong, it will be too low – unless the thermometer has been rinsed in warm water or not shaken down.

The arrow indicating 'normal' (37 ° C; 98.4 ° F) is no more than a guide to an average temperature. A single reading is not usually as important as the progress of the temperature. As with a barometer, the rise or fall is more significant than the exact level.

thiamine = ►*vitamin B₁*.

Thiersch graft. (Karl Thiersch, 1822–95, German surgeon.) ►*graft*.

thigh. Region from hip to knee; functionally it includes the buttock.

The skeleton of the thigh is the ►*femur*, which for most of its length is surrounded by large muscles. These muscles are in four main groups: those of the buttock (*gluteus*), the *quadriceps* at the front of the thigh and the *hamstrings* at the back, and the adductor muscles of the inner side of the thigh.

The *gluteal* nerves and arteries arise within the pelvis and pass under the hipbone to supply the buttock. The *sciatic* nerve takes the same route, and then runs down the back of the thigh, giving branches to the hamstring muscles. The *femoral* nerve enters the thigh in the middle of the groin and supplies the quadriceps and adductor muscles. It accompanies the femoral artery, which is the main source of blood for the whole limb.

thiopentone. A short-acting barbiturate drug, injected into a vein as a general anaesthetic.

thiouracil. A drug that suppresses overactivity of the thyroid gland, used for treating toxic goitre.

thoracic duct. The largest vessel of the ►*lymphatic system*.

thoracoplasty. A major operation on the chest wall in which several ribs are removed to allow the wall to collapse and close the cavity of a large abscess. With

effective antibiotics against tuberculosis and other lung infections this drastic operation is now seldom used, but in the past it saved many lives.

thoracotomy. Any surgical operation that involves opening the thorax.

thorax. Compartment of the body enclosed by the ribs, extending from the first rib above to the diaphragm below. The word 'chest' generally means the same, but it has no clear anatomical definition.

The thorax is smaller than it appears to be. The shoulders fill out the contour of the living body, but the thorax itself is conical, and at the top it is no wider than the neck. Its floor is higher than the limit of the ribs, because the diaphragm is a dome, and the upper part of the abdomen is also enclosed by the ribs.

The thorax is divided by fibrous partitions into three compartments. The central compartment, the *mediastinum*, contains the *heart*, with the *oesophagus* behind it, and in its upper part the *trachea*, with the *thymus* gland in front of it. In addition, the mediastinum contains the blood vessels entering and leaving the heart, and several important nerves.

The two lateral compartments are the *pleural cavities*, which contain the *lungs*.

All three cavities are lined with slippery membranes to prevent friction: the mediastinum with the *pericardium*, and the pleural cavities with the *pleura*.

1. THORACIC SURGERY

Penetrating wounds of the thorax always need attention, for two reasons. Firstly, if air can get between the chest wall and the lung, the lung may collapse like a balloon (►*pneumothorax*). Secondly, there is little to prevent infection from spreading throughout the pleural cavity. To prevent air from getting in, the wound needs to be tightly covered, e.g. with a strip of sticking plaster, until it can be stitched; and anything lodged in the wound is best left until the patient reaches an operating theatre.

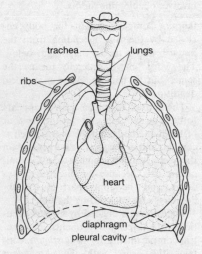

Principal thoracic organs, with part of the right lung removed

Apart from the repair of wounds, only one operation on the thorax was feasible until modern times. This was the drainage of pus from an abscess of the pleural cavity (►*empyema*). There was no danger that the lung would collapse, because the tissues round the abscess were stuck together by inflammation.

Now that infection can be controlled, and adequate breathing artificially maintained, the lungs are as accessible to the surgeon as any other organ, and with the invention of a heart-lung machine to act for the heart as well, the surgery of the heart has also advanced.

►*heart*; *lungs*.

throat. The word has no precise ana-

tomical meaning: 'cut throat' refers to the front of the ►*neck*, and especially the carotid and jugular blood vessels; to throttle someone is to squeeze his windpipe (►*trachea*); a sore throat is inflammation mainly of the middle part of the ►*pharynx*, at the back of the mouth, spreading downwards to the voice-box or ►*larynx*.

Food passes through the mouth, pharynx, and oesophagus to the stomach; air passes through the nose (or mouth), pharynx, larynx, and trachea to the lungs. The pharynx thus serves both swallowing and breathing. Its continuation behind the larynx is a flat tube, of which the back wall (in contact with the backbone) and the front wall (which is the back of the larynx) are held together except during actual swallowing. The larynx, on the other hand, has a shell of cartilage which ensures that the airway is held open. Various reflexes ensure that food shall not be inhaled. The swallowing reflex is coupled to reflexes which stop breathing, draw the vocal cords together as a shutter across the larynx, and drop the epiglottis as a lid over the vocal cords. If a particle of food passes these barriers it stimulates nerve-endings in the larynx or trachea and sets off the cough reflex which expels it.

If an object such as a fish-bone sticks in the throat instead of being swallowed it may sustain the reflexes which prevent breathing: the subject chokes. As soon as the object is dislodged and returned to the mouth or swallowed, or at least moved to a less sensitive area, breathing is resumed. The usual first-aid methods – thumping the patient's back, holding him head down, hooking a finger behind the tongue – are attempts to move the object into a safer place. The rare cases in which choking persists are serious emergencies, because it may be impossible for the patient to breathe properly until the airway is cleared by means of surgical instruments, a simple procedure in an operating theatre but difficult elsewhere. There is less immediate danger from inhaling an object down the larynx and trachea into a lung. It is likely to be coughed up. If it is not it has to be removed through a bronchoscope – a lighted tube passed down the trachea – to prevent an abscess from forming beyond it.

thromboangiitis obliterans = ➤*Buerger's disease*.

thrombocyte. Blood platelet. ➤*blood* (4).

thromboendarterectomy. Surgical treatment of thrombosis in an artery by stripping the diseased lining of the artery together with the clot, leaving a free passage for the blood.

thrombophlebitis. Inflammation of a vein with obstruction by clotted blood. ➤*phlebitis*.

thrombosis. Clotting of blood in an artery or vein, with partial or complete blockage of the circulation in the area. Although blood clots almost at once if it is shed, it cannot normally do so inside an intact blood vessel. But if the lining of the vessel is unhealthy and loses its water-repellent sheen a fibrous clot may form on it and increase until the vessel is obstructed. Thrombosis in veins is generally associated with inflammation (➤*phlebitis*), and thrombosis of arteries with ➤*atheroma*.

Thrombosis causes little trouble if there are adequate alternative (collateral) vessels to maintain the circulation in the area; if there are not, some tissue is inevitably damaged. Death of a segment of a

tissue from blockage of its artery (e.g. of a segment of heart muscle after a coronary thrombosis) is *infarction*.

A second danger of thrombosis, whether or not there is any local damage, is *embolism*, when a fragment of the clot (embolus) breaks off and blocks a vessel further along. Some strokes are due to thrombosis in the heart or in a carotid artery, when there is no significant blockage but a small embolus lodges in one of the arteries of the brain.

The enzyme *streptokinase*, injected into the affected vessel, may dissolve a recently formed thrombus. *Anticoagulant* drugs help to prevent thrombi from forming. An obstructed artery can sometimes be cleared by a surgical operation, *thromboendarterectomy*, or even bypassed with a graft.

thrombus. A clot formed on the lining of a blood vessel.

thrush. Infection of a mucous membrane, usually in the mouth, with the fungus *Candida albicans*. ➤*Candida*.

thymus. A kind of gland in the root of the neck, mostly under cover of the upper part of the sternum. It consists largely of developing lymphocytes, the white blood cells concerned with immunity to infection. In relation to the size of the body, the thymus is largest around birth. Between birth and puberty it only doubles its size, and after puberty it very gradually shrinks. The residue of the thymus can be removed in adult life without known ill effects.

The thymus is concerned with cellular immunity, i.e. resistance to infection (especially by viruses) and to at least some kinds of cancer, as well as with adverse immune reactions such as rejection of grafts and allergic reactions. These effects are due to T-lymphocytes, a type of white blood cell originally processed by the thymus. This complex subject is discussed under ►*immunity*.

A tumour of the thymus, *thymoma*, may be associated with a disorder of muscle action, *myasthenia gravis*, which is sometimes cured by removing the enlarged thymus.

►*status lymphaticus*.

thyroid cartilage. The shell of the ►*larynx*; its protrusion in the front of the neck is the Adam's apple.

thyroid gland. Endocrine gland in the front of the neck. It consists of two lobes, one at either side of the Adam's apple, joined at their lower ends by a bridge of glandular tissue across the upper part of the trachea. Although it lies near the surface the normal gland is small and soft and can scarcely be felt through the skin.

1. FUNCTIONS

The principal hormones of the thyroid are *thyroxine* (T_4) and *tri-iodothyronine* (T_3), derivatives of the amino acid tyrosine with respectively 4 and 3 atoms of iodine in their molecules. When released into the circulation they promote the synthesis of proteins throughout the body, and they increase the rate at which oxygen is used to consume fuel reserves and with it the output of energy. The release of these hormones is controlled by feedback mechanisms: if the level in the blood falls, *thyroid stimulating hormone* (TSH) from the pituitary acts to raise it, and vice versa.

A second thyroid hormone, *calcitonin*, restricts the concentration of calcium in the blood, in opposition to the hormone of the ►*parathyroid* glands.

2. DISORDERS

In the embryo the thyroid grows downwards to the neck from the back of the tongue. Occasionally a fragment is left behind and forms a cyst. But the most important congenital disorder of the thyroid is *cretinism*, failure of the gland to develop. The new-born cretin is usually a normal baby, presumably because he has been able to use thyroxine from his mother's thyroid. After birth his physical and mental development are retarded. The child's appearance is characteristic: coarse hair and skin, protruding tongue, and pot belly. The untreated cretin remains under-sized and below the mental level at which formal education is possible. If he is given thyroxine from an early age he develops normally. Unfortunately cretinism is difficult to recognize in the first few months, and if treatment is delayed the patient may not quite catch up with normal children.

Thyroid deficiency starting in adult life causes *myxoedema*. The patient, often a middle-aged woman, loses energy and appetite; the body temperature is low; the skin is dry and puffy; the mind is dulled. All these changes are completely reversed by giving thyroxine. Some cases of myxoedema are due to ►*autoimmunity* (►*immunity* (7)): a defence mechanism for rejecting invasion by parasites is directed against one of the body's own tissues. Rejection of an essential protein of the thyroid (Hashimoto's disease) was the first proven instance of autoimmunity.

Goitre is any enlargement of the thyroid gland. *Simple goitre* arises from lack of iodine in the diet. Deprived of its most important raw material, the thyroid is constantly stimulated to produce more thyroxine. It responds by overgrowing, and may become enormous. Only about

0.2 mg of iodine is needed daily. In most parts of the world this is provided by sea-food, vegetables, or drinking water. Where the soil lacks iodine – usually in mountainous regions – goitre is endemic. This happens in the central parts of all the continents, and even in England a 'goitre belt' stretches from Derbyshire to Somerset. In many countries the prevalence of goitre has been much reduced by adding traces of iodine to table salt. Large goitres may have to be removed because neighbouring structures (trachea, veins, nerves) are compressed or because they are unsightly. Kocher was the pioneer in this branch of surgery.

With *toxic goitre* (thyrotoxicosis) symptoms arise from an excess of circulating thyroxine. Women are affected much more often than men.

Of several types only two are common. With *Graves' disease* the gland is uniformly and seldom greatly enlarged. A *toxic nodular goitre* on the other hand is lumpy, and may grow to a considerable size. Occasionally a thyroid adenoma, a benign tumour, forms a single nodule secreting an excess of hormone. A patient with thyrotoxicosis feels like an overheated engine (which in effect she is). Symptoms include a fast, occasionally irregular pulse, restlessness, sweating in cool surroundings and loss of weight despite increased appetite. Nodular goitre is a local phenomenon with symptoms only of overactivity of the thyroid. But Graves' disease is due to abnormal antibodies that stimulate the gland and also account for the bulging eyeballs that give the disease its alternative name *exophthalmic goitre*.

A dilute solution of iodine taken by mouth allays symptoms at least for a time. It is not suitable for long-term therapy, but is one way of making the patient fit for surgery if that is the chosen treatment. Beta-blockers, though they have no direct action on the thyroid, can also relieve most of the symptoms. Drugs that directly suppress over-activity include *carbimazole* and *propylthiouracil*: to some patients these may give lasting relief.

Surgery to remove surplus thyroid tissue was for many years the only definitive treatment, and in selected cases still has its place. Alternatively the surplus tissue may be inactivated with radioactive iodine, and in many cases this is the treatment of choice. Because virtually all the iodine in the body is stored in the thyroid gland, the small doses of radioactive iodine do not affect other organs.

thyroiditis. Inflammation of the thyroid gland, sometimes due to a virus infection. Bacterial infection is rare in the thyroid. Thyroiditis is more often due to auto-immunity (►*immunity* (7)).

thyrotoxicosis. Abnormal and excessive activity of the thyroid gland; toxic goitre. ►*thyroid gland* (2).

thyrotrophic hormone. The thyroid-stimulating hormone (TSH) of the pituitary gland.

thyroxine. Hormone formed in the thyroid gland.

tibia. The shin-bone, one of the two parallel bones in the lower leg, corresponding with the ►*radius* in the forearm (the fibula corresponds with the ulna). The two forearm bones are equally important, but in the leg the tibia carries all the weight and is much more heavily built than its companion.

A flat surface of the tibia, from the front of the knee to the inner side of the ankle, lies immediately under the skin.

The large muscles of the foot and ankle are attached to the other surfaces.

The commonest fracture involving the tibia is ➤*Pott's* fracture-dislocation of the ankle.

Because the tibia is covered only by skin, fractures of the middle of the bone are more often compound than fractures of any other bone – a broken end is forced through the skin and the fracture is contaminated with bacteria from outside.

An intact fibula is a good splint for a fractured tibia, and fractures of the tibia alone are usually easy to manage. But an injury severe enough to break the tibia is unlikely to spare the fibula, and fractures of both bones together can be very unstable. If they are broken straight across, as by a direct blow, a plaster cast may hold them in place; but if the fracture is oblique or spiral the broken ends are liable to slip inside a cast, and a continuous pull against the muscles has to be maintained. This can be done by weights suspended from a wire passed through the heel. Otherwise, the fracture can be splinted internally with a metal pin down the centre of the shaft.

The blood supply of the tibia is not very good, and healing of fractures may be slow.

tic. Habit spasm; a purposeless stereotyped movement such as screwing up the eyes, shrugging the shoulders, or a 'nervous' cough. Most if not all tics have their origin in a deliberate and significant movement, which later becomes unconscious, like a conditioned reflex. Tics most often affect insecure children. They generally vanish in time, but if a tic becomes a nuisance it may have to be treated as a neurosis.

Tic douloureux (trigeminal neuralgia) is not really a tic (➤*neuralgia*).

tick. A small creature like a wingless insect, related to the spiders; a few species attach themselves to human skin and transmit varieties of typhus and relapsing fever.

tincture. Alcoholic solution of a drug.

tinea. Fungal infection of the skin; ➤*ringworm*.

epithelial tissue

connective tissue

bone

tinnitus. Ringing, buzzing, or hissing sound in the ear; it can arise from almost any disorder of the ear or its nerve. Wax in the ear-hole, blockage of the Eustachian tube with a common cold, and irritation of the auditory nerve by an overdose of aspirin are among the commonest causes, and often no cause can be found. The patient's distress is not relieved by being told that the symptom is imaginary. Hearing is awareness that nervous impulses have reached a particular area of the cerebral cortex. The impulses are no less real for having originated within the ear and not from vibrations of the outside air which others can also hear. There is no sort of connection between tinnitus and auditory ➤*hallucination.* ➤*Ménière's syndrome.*

tissue. Living matter of any one particular type, both structural and functional; a tissue is composed of more or less uniform *cells* which may or may not be surrounded by a homogeneous ground-substance or *matrix*. The cells of blood are suspended in a fluid matrix, *plasma*; those of bone in a hard solid.

An *organ* is a distinct structural unit (e.g. muscle, gland, eye), made of different kinds of tissue: the *parenchyma* is the specialized working tissue of the organ, and the *stroma* is the less evolved supporting tissue which holds the parenchyma together.

The many tissues of the body appear to be derived from four primitive cell-types: epithelial, mechanical, amoeboid, and nerve cells (but they can be classified in other ways).

Epithelial tissues include true epithelium such as the outer layer of the skin (*epidermis*) and the lining membranes of hollow organs, and also the parenchyma of glands. The cells are closely packed, with little if any ground-substance.

The mechanical tissues include muscle with its highly specialized cells, and various tissues in which the ground-substance is more important than the cells which produce it, such as bone, cartilage, and connective tissue.

The characteristic of amoeboid cells is independent movement in a fluid medium, and the tissues with which they are associated are the body-fluids blood and lymph.

Nerve cells arise in the embryo from the same layer of tissue as the outer skin, but they behave so differently from any other cells that they must be separately classified.

Tissues were first described by ➤*Bichat* in 1800.

➤*histology.*

tissue fluid. Watery fluid percolating all the minute spaces among the cells of the body. Chemical supplies for the cells diffuse out of the capillary blood vessels into this fluid, from which they are absorbed by the cells. Waste products are transferred from the cells via the tissue fluid to the blood. The walls of the cells and of the capillaries act as filters, impermeable to anything as large as a protein molecule but allowing free passage to smaller molecules.

A solution in which the molecules are free to move tends to become uniform; in other words dissolved substances diffuse from zones of high concentration to zones of low concentration. Supplies, e.g. of oxygen, diffuse from the blood where they are concentrated to the cells where they are lacking. Waste products, e.g. carbon dioxide, diffuse in the opposite direction. If the blood ceases to flow the concentrations become balanced

613

and diffusion stops: the cells can no longer be kept alive.

If all the molecules are not free to move the solution still tends to become uniform, but the movement is in only one direction and therefore exerts pressure. Protein cannot diffuse out of the capillaries in any quantity, but water from the tissue fluid can diffuse in to dilute it creating an osmotic pressure (►*osmosis*) of about 25 mm of mercury.

Blood is pumped from the heart at a pressure of around 100 mm of mercury, reduced in the arterioles to 32 mm. This exceeds the osmotic pressure; therefore at the entrance to a capillary water is forced out. As blood flows through the capillary the pressure falls to 12 mm. Since this is less than the osmotic pressure, water now returns to the capillaries. Thus the tissue fluid circulates, leaking from one end of the capillaries and returning to the other end.

Not all of the fluid returns to the capillaries. Some enters the thin-walled ►*lymphatic* vessels and is ultimately returned to the blood in the veins at the root of the neck. This part of the fluid, the ►*lymph*, carries away the small amounts of protein that leak from the capillaries, and any solid particles (e.g. bacteria) that find their way into the tissue spaces.

The tissues become swollen by an excess of tissue fluid if the hydrostatic pressure in the capillaries rises, or if the osmotic pressure falls (►*oedema*).

tobacco. The catalogue of diseases said to be caused or made worse by tobacco is so long and varied as to be unconvincing at first sight. Most people would be willing to blame tobacco for one or two diseases but will not accept a crimesheet that includes indigestion, blindness, bronchitis, heart failure, gangrene of the feet, and several kinds of cancer; and because the campaign against smoking sounds like hell-fire propaganda or an advertisement for a quack remedy it is apt to be rejected. Yet each item on the list is backed by very sound evidence.

Tobacco smoke has at least three highly poisonous ingredients, each with complex effects on the body: tar, carbon monoxide, and nicotine.

Tobacco tar is an irritant. It causes chronic inflammation of mucous membranes, and is the most important of the various factors that lead to chronic bronchitis. In this condition the lining of the air-passages not only produces more mucus than it should but loses the ability to clear the passages of mucus and dust particles. The heavy smoker can inhale smoke in comfort only because the protective cough reflex is suppressed. The devitalized mucous membranes are an easy prey to bacteria. In time, breathing becomes so inefficient that the patient becomes a respiratory cripple. The condition of the lungs puts an increasing strain on the heart and may cause it to fail.

The degenerative change in mucous membranes is in some unknown way a precursor of cancer. The chance of developing lung cancer is in strict ratio to the amount of smoking. Nobody smokes enough or lives long enough to be quite certain of developing a tobacco cancer, but one can paint enough of the tar on a mouse's ear to be certain of producing cancer. Smoking does not make lung cancer inevitable, nor is it the sole cause of lung cancer. What it does is to convert a rare disease into a very common one.

Some tobacco cancers arise in the mouth or throat instead of the lungs.

Carbon monoxide displaces oxygen from the blood. In heavy smokers it may reduce the efficiency of the blood by about 10 per cent, so that in effect the patient is slightly anaemic. This would not ordinarily be enough to cause symptoms, but must aggravate shortness of breath from bronchitis. Carbon monoxide may be partly responsible for the defective eyesight (*tobacco amblyopia*) of some heavy smokers.

Nicotine interferes with the ganglia (relay stations) of the autonomic nervous system. Since this system is distributed throughout the body and is responsible for the reflex control of most organs, nicotine has very widespread effects. Small doses stimulate these nerves indiscriminately. The possible effects include the faintness and nausea of the novice, from stimulation of parasympathetic nerves; but as the habit develops these effects are largely superseded by stimulation of sympathetic nerves, causing over-activity of the heart, suppression of appetite, and constriction of small blood vessels near the body surface.

A rare form of arteriosclerosis, *Buerger's disease*, seems to be a direct result of smoking added to some unknown predisposing factor. This disease can cause gangrene of the feet, treatable only by amputation, when a susceptible person continues to smoke.

It is not certain whether tobacco contributes to the usual form of arteriosclerosis with *atheroma*, but people with atheroma (i.e. most of the population) greatly increase the risk of its more dangerous complications, such as coronary thrombosis, by smoking. The reason is not known, but nicotine is the likely cause.

The effect of nicotine on mood is hard to define. Most habit-forming drugs produce drowsiness or some kind of elation, or both – alcohol, for instance, elates by dulling the higher levels of consciousness with their uncertainties and inhibitions. But nicotine in the doses that can be got from smoking neither stupefies nor cheers. It has none of the soothing effects that are sometimes attributed to it. At the most it causes a fleeting confusion and a vague, equally fleeting sense of excitement. Even these trivial effects can only be produced after some hours' abstinence, e.g. with the first cigarette of the day, for nicotine is subject to *tachyphylaxis*: doses repeated at short intervals have less effect than the first dose.

A habitual heavy smoker gets little positive pleasure from the habit. The only obvious effect is the morning cough that he may call clearing his throat but is in fact a sign of bronchitis and serious trouble to come. The pleasure is negative; it is a very brief respite from the sense of physical deprivation that the smoker feels when he has not smoked for a while. This is the 'soothing' effect of tobacco. In other words some (though not all) regular smokers depend on tobacco for their sense of well-being. To insist, as some purists do, that these people are not addicted is quibbling. Addicted or only 'habituated', the majority of heavy smokers can give up smoking only with the greatest difficulty. It may take them several months to feel at ease without tobacco, and even years later a single lapse may be enough to restore the old habit. The one certain remedy is not to start in the first place. As to giving up an established habit, any chest clinic or psychiatric department will offer advice and moral support, but everything depends on the smoker's determination to give it up completely – cutting down is almost bound to fail.

Cigarette smoke is more noxious than

cigar or pipe smoke. This is partly because pipe and cigar smokers tend to inhale less and partly because of chemical differences in the smoke, but as regards heart attacks the difference is so great that some ingredients of cigarettes other than tobacco may play a part.

Snuff and chewing tobacco cause some chronic irritation of the nose or mouth, but most of their ill effects are confined to the actions of nicotine. ⮞*addiction*.

tocopherol = ⮞*vitamin E.*

tolerance. Gradually increasing resistance to the effects of a drug given over long periods, typically seen with drugs of addiction such as morphine.

tomography. A technique of X-ray examination: the X-ray tube is moved during the exposure in such a way that only structures in a selected plane of the body cast clear shadows. ⮞*scan*.

tongue. The tongue consists almost entirely of muscles, attached to the base of the skull below the ears, to the lower jaw, and to the hyoid bone above the larynx. These muscles are controlled with remarkable precision to adapt the shape and position of the tongue to the needs of eating or speech. From their attachments it will be clear that the tongue is much larger than it appears to be – an important matter for an unconscious patient, whose tongue can easily obstruct his airway. But because of the attachment to the inside of the jaw the airway can be kept clear by drawing the chin forwards.

Quite apart from the special sense of ⮞*taste* the ordinary senses of touch and temperature are more acute on the surface of the tongue even than on the finger-tips.

Minute projections (*papillae*) from the surface give the tongue a velvety texture. Like all the other covering membranes of the body, that of the tongue is constantly shed and replaced. The debris, together with dried mucus and food particles, is more liable to accumulate on the tongue than on the perfectly smooth membranes of the rest of the mouth. Normally it is cleared by the saliva, but if the flow of saliva is deficient the tongue becomes coated or 'furred'. Fever, thirst, or merely loss of appetite reduce salivation, and a furred tongue is therefore a poor guide to the state of a person's health.

The tongue is seldom infected by microbes: competition from harmless bacteria in the mouth, the antiseptic action of saliva, and a very rich blood supply all contribute to this immunity. On the other hand the tongue is very sensitive to deficiency of iron or of various vitamins, of which a smooth, sore tongue may be an early symptom. The two commonest types of anaemia are due to lack of iron and lack of vitamin B_{12}, so that a sore tongue often accompanies anaemia.

The tongue is susceptible to syphilis, but now that this disease is regularly treated with penicillin syphilis of the tongue is no longer common.

About 1 per cent of all cancers are found in the tongue. Syphilis used to be an important cause. Irritation from a rotten tooth has often been blamed, but there are many more rotten teeth than cancers of the tongue and the association need not be causal. Generally speaking the further forward the cancer the better the outlook. A cancer near the tip of the tongue is recognized early and is easily accessible for surgery or radiation. If treatment is sought at the first sign of trouble – pain, swelling, ulceration – the chance of cure is good.

tonsil. A mass of lymphoid tissue, in health about the shape and size of an almond (and called *almond* in many languages), at either side of the back of the mouth: the soft palate rises as an arch of which the supporting columns are split to embrace the tonsils. ▸*pharynx.*

tonsillar. Of the tonsil.

tonsillectomy. Surgical removal of the tonsils.

tonsillitis. Inflammation of the tonsils, usually from infection by streptococci. ▸*pharynx* (1).

tooth ▸*teeth.*

tophus. A chalk-like deposit in the tissues, consistingly mainly of uric acid or its salts, characteristic of *gout.*

topical (of medication). Applied directly to the affected part, e.g. ointments, eye drops, injections into painful joints; as opposed to *systemic* medication, where the drug is given by mouth, by injection, by inhalation etc. so that it will enter the circulation to be distributed throughout the body.

torticollis. Wry-neck. ▸*sternomastoid.*

torulosis (cryptococcosis). A rare but dangerous infection with a kind of yeast; similar to *blastomycosis.* Cases are occasionally reported from most parts of the world. The antibiotic amphotericin-B has much improved the outlook.

tourniquet. A constricting band placed tightly enough round a limb to stop the entry of blood in case of severe bleeding. Its use has been discouraged because a tourniquet left in place for more than half an hour is likely to destroy the limb.

If possible it is better to control bleeding either by compressing the edges of the wound or by direct pressure over the artery. If a tourniquet is applied in desperation it must be as broad as possible – a scarf, not a piece of string. It must be no tighter than is needed to stop the bleeding – but if it is not tight enough it may increase bleeding from veins without checking the flow in the arteries; and it must *unconditionally* be completely released at intervals of not more than half an hour, preferably less, and only reapplied when the limb is seen to be flushed with blood. Since cut vessels usually seal themselves fairly quickly, it will often be found that the tourniquet is no longer needed, but in that case the wound has to be constantly watched for renewed bleeding.

toxaemia. Literally: blood poisoning; illness due to *toxins* in the blood-stream, usually toxins formed by bacteria in some localized seat of infection. The fever and general illness with an abscess are due to this type of toxaemia. Some bacteria, e.g. those of diphtheria and typhoid, cause severe toxaemia while themselves confined to a relatively small area of tissue, and the symptoms of tetanus are due entirely to toxins, the bacteria themselves doing no apparent harm to the tissue where they establish themselves.

toxaemia of pregnancy. A mysterious and, it seems, exclusively human ailment affecting many women during pregnancy and disappearing as soon as the pregnancy is over. The term toxaemia implies more than is known, because although the symptoms suggest it, no toxin has been identified. *Pre-eclampsia* is now the preferred name, because if neglected it may in a few cases lead to ▸*eclampsia.*

The symptoms are very like those of nephritis (►*kidney* (5)) – accumulation of water in the tissues, first noticed as undue swelling of the ankles; loss of protein in the urine; and high blood pressure. Because of water retention the patient gains more weight than she would be expected to. At this stage the patient is carefully watched for any increase in the symptoms, or new symptoms, and kept quiet; most cases settle down and the pregnancy runs its normal course. Salt rather than water has to be restricted because the retention of water is an effect of failure to eliminate salt from the kidneys. The danger is that if the trouble progresses the patient may develop *eclampsia* at the end of pregnancy; this is a kind of epilepsy that can be fatal to the baby and sometimes to the mother too. If there is any threat of eclampsia, hospital treatment becomes mandatory: the pregnancy may have to be terminated at short notice, and intensive treatment may be needed to prevent fits.

toxic goitre ►*thyroid* (2).

toxic shock syndrome. A rare but lethal reaction to staphylococcal infection, usually associated with the incorrect use of sanitary tampons.

toxicology. Study of poisons.

toxin. A poisonous protein, such as many bacteria form. Bacterial toxins are roughly divided into *endotoxins*, incorporated in the bacteria and damaging tissues in the immediate vicinity of the infection, and *exotoxins*, which are released by the bacteria and pass into the bloodstream or elsewhere and produce harmful effects remote from the site of infection. Toxins act as *antigens*, i.e. antibodies are formed to neutralize them as a natural defence against disease (►*immunity*).

toxoid. A toxin extracted from bacteria and chemically modified so that it loses its poisonous effect but keeps its ability to evoke immunity. Diphtheria toxoid is injected to confer immunity to diphtheria.

toxoplasmosis. Infection with the protozoon *Toxoplasma gondii*, passed to man either from undercooked, infected meat or from live pets (kittens). It is usually harmless, or causes only minor, self-limiting illness, but occasionally causes a sort of glandular fever which can be treated with pyrimethamine and sulphonamides. If the infection passes from a woman to her unborn child, congenital toxoplasmosis can injure the nervous system and, in particular, the eyes.

trachea (windpipe). A straight vertical tube extending from the larynx to the level of the angle of the sternum, immediately above the heart, where the trachea divides into the two main *bronchi*, one to each lung. It is an elastic tube, held open by hoops of cartilage. A gap at the back of each hoop is bridged by muscle; only the uppermost cartilage, the *cricoid*, is a complete ring. The lining membrane of the trachea secretes mucus, which keeps it moist and traps inhaled dust. The mucus is constantly moved upwards by the undulation of the *cilia*, fine processes which give the lining a velvety pile.

The trachea lies immediately in front of the oesophagus. Behind the sternum, the innominate artery and vein cross in front of it. In the neck, the trachea lies under the skin except at the upper end where the thyroid gland intervenes.

Inflammation of the mucous membrane, *tracheitis*, often accompanies bronchitis, causing soreness in the mid-line.

The trachea itself is seldom blocked, but the larynx may be obstructed by injury, inflammation (e.g. diphtheria), or paralysis, or, in an unconscious patient, simply by the dead weight of the tongue against the back of the throat. Since the tongue is attached to the jaw, it can be drawn out of harm's way by pulling the jaw forwards – often a life-saving measure. During anaesthetics and with other types of unconsciousness an adequate airway can be ensured with a rubber tube passed between the vocal cords into the trachea.

Tracheostomy is an operation to bypass the larynx. The trachea is opened and a metal tube is inserted. This operation is used when the larynx is blocked or liable to become blocked, as in diphtheria, and also when a patient is unable to cough because of severe coma or paralysis and the trachea must be cleared of mucus by mechanical suction.

tracheal. Of the trachea.

tracheitis. Inflammation of the ▸*trachea*.

tracheostomy. Surgical operation, opening the ▸*trachea* to relieve an obstruction and maintain a clear airway.

tracheotomy. 'Cutting the trachea': ▸*tracheostomy*, 'making an opening (mouth) in the trachea', describes the operation better.

trachoma. Severe and prolonged inflammation of the membrane lining the eyelids and covering the front of the eye (conjunctivitis), due to a microbe resembling a virus but probably a degenerate bacterium (▸*Chlamydia*). The microbe is closely related to that of the 'swimming-bath conjunctivitis' or pink-eye of temperate climates, but real trachoma is a disease of hot, dry regions. It leads to scarring of the eyelids; the lashes may turn inwards and constantly irritate the eyes, or the patient may be unable to close his eyes properly, or a *pannus* – an opaque membrane of inflammatory tissue – may encroach on the cornea and obstruct vision. Although the infection tends to burn itself out, the victim is often partly or totally blind by the time it does so. The number of people blinded by trachoma runs into millions.

Unlike the true virus diseases, trachoma responds well to treatment with sulphonamides or antibiotics. Deformity of the eyelids in advanced cases may need surgical correction. Blindness is of the type that can be treated by corneal grafting. The problem is not how to cure the disease but how to provide treatment for several hundred million patients in underdeveloped countries.

tranquillizer. A kind of drug, used to calm the emotions. Emotional agitation is a common symptom of ailments ranging from minor anxiety states to severe episodes of mania or schizophrenia. Until 1953 the only drugs that helped were *sedatives* such as bromides and barbiturates. A sedative was merely a small dose of a hypnotic drug generally used in larger doses to procure sleep. If the dose was large enough to relieve agitation it was also large enough to make the patient drowsy and inefficient. Agitated schizophrenics had to be almost anaesthetized before they were effectively calmed.

In 1953, *rauwolfia* was introduced to Western practice from traditional Indian medicine, and became the first of a new class of drugs, the tranquillizers or

619

ataractic drugs. These induced a calmer mood without making the patient sleepy. Rauwolfia, however, was soon superseded by other drugs.

Some of the antihistamine drugs used to control allergy were found to calm the patient's mood. This effect was investigated, with a view to finding a compound of which it would be the main effect, and in 1954 a *phenothiazine* compound, *chlorpromazine*, was introduced. With this or one of the many other phenothiazine drugs very severe mental disturbances can be controlled, and patients such as advanced schizophrenics, hitherto kept for years in mental hospitals, can lead ordinary lives. *Haloperidol* is unrelated to the phenothiazine tranquillizers, but it has similar effects and is used in the same way. There is now a wide range of newer drugs, many of them derived from the two already mentioned. The class as a whole is known as *major tranquillizers*.

A further class of drugs, the *minor tranquillizers*, are used for controlling tension in less serious conditions such as anxiety states. Some of them probably relax physical, muscular tension as well as emotional tension. The first of them, *meprobamate*, introduced in 1955, is derived from mephenesin, a drug intended to be a muscle relaxant. The ►*benzodiazepines*, of which *chlordiazepoxide* was the first to become popular and *diazepam* is now the most widely used, have practically superseded all other drugs of this class.

Major tranquillizers are also called *neuroleptics* or *anti-psychotics*, and minor tranquillizers are also known as *anxiolytics*.

transfusion. The transfer of blood from a healthy person to a sick one is an ancient and fairly obvious idea. It is in this sense that the word 'transfusion' is used here. A similar use of salt or sugar solutions is an 'infusion'.

Nobody would have known where to put the blood until Harvey's discovery of the circulation (1628) showed that it must be injected into a vein. The architect Wren suggested the injection of drugs into veins, and two other early Fellows of the Royal Society, John Wilkins and Richard Lower, carried out blood transfusion between dogs. A French physician, Jean-Baptiste Denys, successfully gave lamb's blood to a human patient in 1667, but soon after a second patient died, and no further attempt was made for 150 years.

Then James Blundell of Guy's Hospital, London, showed that blood could not be safely transfused from one species to another. He gave several of his patients human blood, the first in 1818, and transfusion became an accepted if unusual form of treatment.

Two problems remained. Firstly, the blood was apt to clot while it was being given. This can be prevented by adding a small amount of sodium citrate, which diverts calcium, an essential factor in clotting. Secondly, many of the patients had severe reactions, sometimes fatal. This was not overcome until Landsteiner discovered blood groups in 1900 (►*blood* (5)).

Some of the chemical components of the shell of a red blood cell differ slightly in different people. A particular factor and its two or three variants form a *system*. People whose red cells have the same variant belong to the same *blood group* as regards that system (though they may belong to different groups as regards other systems).

The most important blood-group

system was the first to be discovered. There are three variants: A, B, and O. Everyone inherits a gene for one variant from each parent. O behaves as a blank, simply as absence of A or B. A man who inherits A from each parent, and one who inherits A from one and O from the other both belong to group A. Thus the 6 possible pairs (AA, AO, BB, BO, AB, OO) resolve themselves into 4 groups (A, B, AB, O).

A positive factor, A or B, that the blood does not contain is treated as a foreign substance which has to be neutralized. This is done by an *antibody*, a protein in the blood whose sole function is to react with that particular foreign substance. In the ordinary way, antibodies are formed only when a foreign substance has found its way into the body. They are a defence against infection by bacteria (>*immunity*). These blood group antibodies are unusual in that they are present at birth. All group A people have antibodies against B, group B against A, and group O against both. Group AB people have, of course, neither antibody – otherwise they would destroy their own blood cells.

If a patient is given blood against which he has antibodies he will destroy the transfused blood. Not only is the transfusion useless, but the destroyed red cells set up a severe reaction, occasionally leading to kidney failure and death. If the patient can be tided over, e.g. with an artificial kidney, the kidneys usually recover.

The dangerous reactions are between *patient's antibodies and transfused cells*. Transfused antibodies seldom do much damage to the patient's cells because they are rapidly diluted in the patient's body. Hence group AB people, having neither antibody, are universal recipients, and group O people, having cells against

which neither antibody can act, are universal donors. But other groups than one's own are not entirely safe, and in practice a donor of the same group is always sought.

In Britain the distribution of groups is O 46 per cent, A 42 per cent, B 9 per cent, AB 3 per cent. The figures are very different in some parts of the world.

Another system of blood groups (>*rhesus factor*) is important because incompatibility of rhesus groups between husband and wife may endanger their new-born children. This danger is much increased if a rhesus-negative mother has ever had a rhesus-positive transfusion.

Blood groups are determined by mixing the cells with serum known to contain antibodies against A and against B. If the cells stick together in clumps in both samples they must be group AB, because both antibodies react with them. If they clump only with the anti-A serum, they are group A. If both samples are unaffected, they are group O.

Blood can be stored for about 3 weeks at 4 °C, the temperature of a kitchen refrigerator. It cannot be actually frozen without damaging the red cells.

For some years it has been known that a donor may carry the virus of a kind of infectious jaundice (hepatitis) in his blood; now it is also necessary to screen blood for the far more dangerous virus of AIDS. In the tropics there is the same risk with malaria. Syphilis was a worry in the early days of transfusion. It is much less common today; all blood banks test blood for syphilis before storing it; in any case this infection does not survive refrigeration.

In cases such as severe anaemia with heart failure, blood transfusion may overload the circulation. The risk is overcome by separating the blood cells and giving them without the plasma, the fluid portion of blood. On the other hand with severe ►*shock*, e.g. after extensive burns, plasma leaks out of the patient's blood vessels leaving the cells with too little fluid. In this case, plasma without cells is transfused. Plasma can be stored for months as a dried powder.

transplantation. The transfer of a tissue or organ from one subject to another, as opposed to simple grafting of tissue from one part to another of the same person.

With the exception of the nervous system, where function depends on strict continuity between the centre and the periphery, almost any part of the body could be successfully grafted. The surgeon has only to ensure an adequate circulation of blood in the new site, and the technical problems of doing so can be overcome.

An organ can be grafted from one to another of identical twins with no more trouble than simple grafting. But a transplant from anyone other than an identical twin meets a hostile reaction from the recipient's tissues. This is due to the trivial chemical differences between different people. Any protein introduced to the tissues that differs, however slightly, from its counterpart in the recipient's body is liable to be destroyed by *antibodies*. This is the ordinary mechanism for dealing with unwelcome invaders such as bacteria (►*immunity*). After a technically successful transplantation of, say, a kidney the recipient's blood flows freely through the vessels of the new organ; it is alive and begins to form urine. It may be threatened at once by the sort of destructive reaction that any foreign body in the tissues

might provoke, but it is likely to survive this initial attack. The real danger comes some days or weeks later, when antibodies have been formed specifically to react with any of its proteins that are strange to the recipient. If the differences are extensive, the transplanted organ is likely to be rejected – it ceases to function and dies.

The easiest tissue to transplant is blood (►*transfusion*). There is the same possibility that transfused blood will be rejected, but the important points of difference between bloods have been identified, and a donor can be chosen whose blood is sufficiently like that of the patient to be accepted: the donor and recipient belong to the same group.

The chemical make-up of other tissues is more complex. The factors analogous with blood groups that cause one person's tissues to be incompatible with another's are very numerous, so that a suitable donor may be hard to find: ►*HLA*. But it is already possible to choose donors from whom an organ stands at least a fair chance of surviving in the patient's tissues. Steps can then be taken to minimize the patient's reaction. These include giving corticosteroids and drugs that interfere with the formation of new antibodies. A class of white blood cells, the *lymphocytes*, are especially concerned with immunity and the rejection of foreign substances. When a transplanted organ seems likely to be rejected it may be saved by suppressing the lymphocytes, either by X-ray treatment or by drugs, or by removing the thymus gland and spleen where many of the lymphocytes are formed. Two newer preparations, an anti-lymphocyte serum and an antibiotic, *cyclosporin*, which inhibits rejection without injuring the bone marrow, have much improved the chances of safe and successful transplantation.

Even when the problems of transplanting organs are solved, the problem of finding donors will remain. But the science of typing and matching the tissues of donor and recipient is advancing rapidly. Kidneys were the first major organs to be successfully transplanted, followed by heart, liver, pancreas and now heart-and-lung transplants.

The cornea at the front of the eye is a special case. It has no circulation; lymphocytes and antibodies do not invade it, and a cornea from anyone who has given permission for his eyes to be used after his death can be grafted without any problems of immunity and rejection. These tissues can be preserved in banks and used to restore sight lost from damage to the front of the eye.

Some burns are so extensive that it is impossible to find enough intact skin on the patient to prepare ordinary skin-grafts. In such cases, skin can be transplanted from someone else although it will later be rejected: in the meantime it has provided a scaffolding where the patient's own new skin can grow. This compromise has to be accepted because any measures to prevent rejection would also suppress the process of healing, and also make serious infection of the raw areas a certainty.

transposition. Transposition of the great vessels is an uncommon fault in the development of the heart: the aorta arises from the right side of the heart instead of the left, and the pulmonary artery from the left instead of the right, and the circulation of blood is ineffective. The condition can now be corrected by an extremely elaborate operation.

Transposition of all the organs from left to right is interesting but unimportant (>*dextrocardia*).

trapezius. Large triangular muscle of the back; the two trapezii together are kite-shaped. The muscle rotates the shoulder-blade when the arm is raised (>*shoulder*). At rest the trapezius muscles are important in maintaining the >*posture* of the shoulders.

trauma. A wound; damage to the tissues by any physical agency (burns, fractures etc.); emotional upset as a cause of mental illness.

travel. Travelling to far places can involve several matters of medical concern. One, *travel sickness*, is considered in the next entry. Another is the risk of contracting exotic diseases, and anyone planning a journey to, for instance, the tropics, should get up-to-date information about required immunization and advisable prophylaxis. WHO regularly circulates bulletins worldwide about these matters. Health centres and pharmacies can supply the latest information.

Travel agents should be able to provide the same information but in any case a medical check-up is a wise precaution before a long journey, remembering that facilities in remote places can be primitive and medicines unobtainable.

Even where the facilities are good they can be cripplingly expensive, and adequate insurance is essential.

Long flights involve special problems. Changes of time zone are usually blamed for 'jet-lag', but fatigue and dehydration by pressurized and conditioned air contribute. Free alcohol is another possible cause, with a hangover mistaken for jet-lag. Swollen ankles can be more than a mere nuisance, because they can lead to thrombosis of the veins (especially during pregnancy). Every chance to leave one's seat and take a few paces is worth taking: this also applies to train and bus journeys. If it is impossible or inconvenient to walk around, isometric exercises may serve instead.

travel sickness. The motion of ships, cars, aircraft, swings etc. disturbs the balance organ of the inner ear and sets up a chain of reflex action that may radiate to the vomiting centre in the *medulla oblongata*, the lowest part of the brain. The same reflex can be set off by artificial stimulation of the balance organ, e.g. by squirting cold water into the ear. The reflex appears to be a pure accident; one can hardly suppose that it was useful to some remote ancestor.

Travel sickness may become a conditioned reflex: a person who has learnt to expect it may be sick before the ship moves. But it cannot, as is sometimes suggested, be wholly psychological because it affects babies and animals. On the other hand the psychological or emotional element is not to be lightly dismissed. An attack can often be averted by occupying the patient's mind – in small boats a spell at the tiller can work wonders, or in larger boats a walk on deck, provided that the patient keeps warm – but if the attack has already begun the patient can seldom think of anything else.

In a ship or aircraft the see-saw motion is least at the point of balance, amidships. The view through a porthole is distressing, because the conflict of sensation between a deck that should be horizontal and a swinging horizon contributes greatly to the sickness. The ears are disturbed least with the head tilted back as in a dentist's chair. Aircraft seats can nearly always be adjusted to the right position, and car-sick passengers are more comfortable with head-rests.

Small but frequent snacks are better than no food. Alcohol is a traditional stand-by. It does nothing to help the physical factor of motion sickness but may allay the emotional factor. People who do not normally drink are better without it.

Of the many drugs that relieve travel sickness, *hyoscine* is the oldest and still among the most effective. Some of the antihistamine drugs and tranquillizers (the groups overlap) are also effective and cause less drowsiness than hyoscine – they include cyclizine, dimenhydrinate, promethazine and cinnarizine. All these drugs are better at preventing than curing motion sickness: they work best when the first dose is taken an hour or so before the journey begins.

People who use car ferries may need to be reminded that any of the drugs can make them temporarily unfit to drive.

tremor. Trembling or shaking of a part of the body; a symptom of many disorders, trivial and serious. Occasionally the kind of tremor is a clue to the diagnosis, e.g. the rather slow shaking of parkinsonism (shaking palsy) or the fine quivering of the hands with an over-active thyroid gland; but often a tremor is no more than a hint that the case warrants further investigation.

trench fever. An epidemic disease among infantry in the First World War, probably a kind of typhus.

trench foot (immersion foot). A result of prolonged exposure to cold, especially to cold water. Water conducts heat away from the skin and aggravates the effects of a cold environment so that temperatures well above freezing become harmful. The natural response to cold is for blood vessels in the skin to contract, reducing the flow of blood and thus the loss of heat. If the reaction has to be sustained the skin suffers; it becomes waterlogged and numb and is then an easy prey to slight injury or infection.

trench mouth ➤*Vincent's disease.*

trepan; trephine. A trepan is a very ancient instrument for cutting a round hole in the skull; it is simply a cylindrical or crown saw. A trephine is a trepan with a central pin to guide the saw.

Prehistoric skulls have been found with signs of successful trepanning – when the margins of the hole are sealed with compact bone the patient must have survived the operation – and some primitive modern people still do the same operation to let evil spirits out of the head.

The ancient Greek surgeons used the operation as it is still used, to relieve pressure on the brain from bleeding after severe head injuries. Hippocrates gave detailed instructions in a treatise on wounds of the head, explaining how to avoid any risk of damaging the brain.

To avoid leaving a large hole in the skull, which would not heal, surgeons expose the brain by using a very small trephine at several points and joining the holes with a wire saw, so that a small trap-door can be raised.

Treponema. A kind of spirochaete or spiral bacterium. Species include *T. pallidum,* the cause of syphilis.

For other diseases caused by species of Treponema ➤*yaws.*

triceps. The muscle of the back of the arm: its three 'heads' (➤*biceps*) arise (1) from the scapula just below the shoulder joint, and (2) and (3) from the back of the humerus. The whole mass is attached below to the olecranon process of the ulna, which juts out behind the elbow. Triceps extends (straightens) the elbow. ➤*shoulder.*

trichiniasis (trichinosis). Illness due to a very small worm, *Trichinella*; this is a common parasite of pigs passed to man in undercooked pork. A week or two after infection, when the parasites breed, there is a feverish reaction, often with sore eyes and a variety of other symptoms that may represent a kind of allergy. The tiny larvae find their way into the circulation. Most of them, together with the parent worms, die and cause no further trouble, but some become embedded in muscles and may persist for months or even years, causing rather vague aches and pains. Trichiniasis is only rarely a serious disease. Treatment with *thiabendazole* is generally effective.

triglyceride. A compound of three molecules of fatty acid with one of glycerine. Animal and vegetable fats and oils are all triglycerides; ➤*fat.* (Mineral oils are hydrocarbons.)

Trichomonas. An animal microbe (➤*flagellate*) that commonly infects the mucous membrane of the vagina and causes irritation and discharge; since it can also infect the male urethra the patient's partner may also need treatment to prevent reinfection. Various antiseptic local applications may cure the condition, but the best drug seems to be *metronidazole,* which is taken by mouth.

trichophyton. Kind of fungus with an affinity for hair, causing some forms of ➤*ringworm.*

trichotillomania. A bizarre neurosis: the patient pulls out tufts of his own hair.

Trichuris. An intestinal parasite, the whipworm. ➤*worms*.

trigeminal. The *trigeminal nerve* (5th cranial nerve) emerges from the root of the brain and crosses the floor of the skull to a point close to the inner ear, where it bulges to form the *trigeminal ganglion*, a relay station for its sensory fibres. The 3 branches of the nerve spring separately from the ganglion. They are (1) the *ophthalmic nerve*, carrying sensation from the upper part of the face, (2) the *maxillary nerve*, carrying sensation from the middle of the face, and (3) the *mandibular* nerve, carrying sensation from the lower part of the face and also controlling the jaw muscles.

Trigeminal neuralgia (tic douloureux): ➤*neuralgia*.

trigger finger. A thickened sheath of a flexor tendon to a finger impairs movement, so that when the flexed finger is to be extended it is uncomfortably restrained, and then abruptly released as if flicking a pellet. Sometimes this accompanies a rheumatic disorder but usually there is no apparent cause. The disorder can be corrected surgically by slitting the sheath.

trinitrin. Glyceryl trinitrate, nitroglycerin; a standard remedy for angina pectoris.

trismus. Spasm of the jaw muscles, e.g. as a result of inflammation from an abscess around a tooth or a throat infection.

Trismus can also arise from irritation of the nerve cells controlling the muscles – this is the symptom that gives *lockjaw* (tetanus) its name.

trisomy. A congenital anomaly: a superfluous chromosome is added to a normal pair, making three instead of two of a kind. Triplication of one of the smallest chromosomes accounts for Down's syndrome.

trochanter. One of two large knobs (greater and lesser trochanter) near the upper end of the femur, to which are attached various muscles acting on the hip.

tropical diseases. A few diseases can flourish only in a tropical climate, usually because they are transmitted by creatures confined to the tropics. For instance, the tsetse fly that carries sleeping sickness does not tolerate temperatures much below 25 °C (77 °F), and the snails that carry bilharzia have to live in fairly warm water. But most of the important tropical diseases are tropical mainly because the countries of the temperate zones have had the resources needed to eradicate them, while most tropical countries have not. In the past, malaria, leprosy, smallpox, plague and cholera have all been pestilences in Western Europe.

Preventive medicine cannot claim all the credit for confining these diseases to hotter and poorer countries. Nobody has the least idea why plague suddenly retreated in the 17th century, or why cholera waited until the 19th century before invading Europe. Epidemics are unpredictable. But there is not much doubt that vaccination eradicated smallpox, and hygienic water supply and sewage disposal prevented intestinal infections from spreading.

Practically all tropical diseases are infectious, and most are curable, and can be eradicated by treating every case. For example, mosquitoes able to transmit malaria can be found in most of Europe, but they are harmless while there is no untreated malaria for them to transmit.

Simultaneous treatment of the millions of people with malaria in the tropics would be impossible, and in practice malaria has to be tackled mainly by controlling mosquitoes. Large areas have been freed from malaria in recent years.

With the drugs now available for arresting leprosy it should be possible to reduce the number of active, infectious cases to a level where the disease can no longer flourish. But while leprosy recedes, a closely related disease – tuberculosis – advances, and tuberculosis could be on the way to joining the other numerous diseases that have been more or less relegated to hot countries. Similarly yaws has been much reduced by effective drugs, while syphilis, which may well be a variant of the same disease, has increased.

Visitors to the main towns of tropical countries now run little risk of catching 'tropical' diseases, thanks to clear water, proper sewage disposal, control of insects and rodents, routine vaccination, and treatment of the sick. But in the poorer suburbs and in the vast rural areas these services are at best rudimentary. The greatest obstacle is lack of money: not only are most tropical countries poor, but the greater distances between settlements tend to make health services more costly than in industrial countries.

Most people in the tropics are underfed. Malnutrition is the greatest of all tropical diseases, and because of it people are less able to resist infection than they should be, and epidemics thrive.

Shortage of water is a common problem, making it difficult for people to keep themselves – let alone their environment – clean. At the other end of the scale, torrential rain may wash away filth only to deposit it in the regular source of water. As often as not, villagers depend on a single stream for all their needs; they may even share it with their herds.

Polluted water can be made safe to drink simply by boiling it, but people will not always be persuaded to do so. The same obstacle, ignorance, stands in the way of all progress in preventive medicine. People readily accept curative medicine because it makes immediate sense – hospital beds do not stand vacant in the tropics – but the doctrines of hygiene make little impact, and may well conflict with cherished traditions. Health education is as necessary as clean water or insect control.

tropical ulcer. Chronic open sore, usually on the leg, common in the tropics. The ulcer begins with a minor injury and is infected with bacteria similar to those of ►*Vincent's disease*. Small, recent tropical ulcers heal if the infection is controlled with antiseptic dressings, but large ones often need skin-grafting.

Trueta, Josep (1897–1977). Spanish surgeon in Barcelona during the Spanish Civil War. After his escape from Spain, Trueta was invited to Britain, primarily because a world war was imminent and he had recently acquired unique experience in treating air-raid casualties. At Oxford, as a professor of orthopaedic surgery, he developed the method of treating severe wounds by surgical cleansing followed by encasing the damaged part in plaster and leaving it. The plaster stank, but the wound healed cleanly. He also promoted important research into surgical shock, and the blood supply of the kidneys.

truss. An appliance consisting of a pad and some means – a spring or an

627

arrangement of straps – of holding it in place at a weak point in the abdominal muscles where internal organs are liable to protrude, i.e. to control a *hernia*. A truss is useful when there is some reason for not operating but as a rule hernias are best treated surgically.

trypanosome; trypanosomiasis. A trypanosome is a kind of *protozoon* or animal microbe, of which several species cause disease in men and animals. All types of trypanosomal infection (trypanosomiasis) are transmitted by insects confined to the tropics. Trypanosomes are related to the protozoa that cause leishmaniasis (kala-azar; oriental sore).

Sleeping sickness – African trypanosomiasis – is of two kinds. West African sleeping sickness is due to *Trypanosoma gambiense*, and is transmitted by the bite of a tsetse fly, *Glossina palpalis*. This fly breeds in damp forest near river-banks, and bites man for choice. Where the disease is endemic it may affect most of the population. After about a fortnight the site of the infection is marked by a firm lump, violet on a white skin but hardly visible on a dark skin; the patient is ill and feverish for some days; lymph nodes swell, first in the area of the bite, later in all areas (armpits, neck, groins). A rash appears on a white skin but is seldom seen on African patients. In a week or two the patient seems to recover, and for many months or even years he suffers no more than an occasional bout of fever. Some patients probably overcome the infection, but in some the trypanosomes ultimately invade the nervous system. The drowsiness that gives the disease its name then follows. Often the patient sleeps little, but day and night he is dull and apathetic. He may starve for want of the energy to eat, or die of any passing infec-

tion. This disease is confined to the belt of rain forest along the West African coast and through the Congo basin to the Great Lakes.

East African sleeping sickness occurs in low-lying areas (below about 2000 ft) between Lake Victoria and S. Africa. It is due to *T. rhodesiense*, and transmitted by several species of tsetse fly, notably *G. morsitans*. These flies breed in open country or sparse bush, generally away from human habitation; they bite antelopes and other wild animals for choice, and man only by chance. Infection is therefore sporadic. Even in the worst affected areas it is unusual for as many as 5 per cent of the population to be infected. The disease runs a much more rapid course than the West African type. Many patients die within a few months of infection. There is no 'sleeping' stage; in fact many patients are agitated.

Sleeping sickness is curable in the early stages before the nervous system is involved, but in the later stages the chance of cure diminishes rapidly, especially with the East African type. The drugs used include pentamidine, suramin, and various compounds of arsenic – these last offer the best hope in the late stages, but the doses required are themselves dangerous. Pentamidine has been used to protect people exposed to infection. The essential problem of treatment is that most of the patients are so used to fevers of one kind or another that they do not seek help until too late. The best chance of early diagnosis is to examine everyone in an infected area. Better still is to eradicate the tsetse flies.

Chagas' disease – South American trypanosomiasis – is due to *T. cruzi*, and is transmitted in the excreta of various bugs. After the initial fever, Chagas' disease often runs a fairly harmless course, but the trypanosomes may invade muscle and other tissues and cause them to be replaced by thin scars. If this happens to the heart, the disease is fatal. There are still no effective drugs.

Animal trypanosomiasis affects horses in South America and cattle and many other animals in Africa. One type, *nagana*, due to *T. congolense*, makes cattle farming impossible in much of tropical Africa. The relation of animal to human trypanosomiasis is not clear. Wild animals are often said to harbour *T. rhodesiense*, but opinions differ. These antelopes do not appear to develop any disease from their trypanosomes, but there is no reason why they should not act as a reservoir for the parasite. On the other hand nagana, which is deadly to cattle, does not seem to affect man. Attempts to control East African sleeping sickness by wholesale slaughter of wild animals have not succeeded.

trypsin. An enzyme from the pancreas for digesting protein.

tsetse fly. Blood-sucking insect of tropical Africa, like a small horse-fly, easily recognized by its fast, straight flight and abrupt landing, and the position of its wings at rest one over the other. Two species, *Glossina palpalis* in West Africa and *G. morsitans* in East Africa, transmit most cases of sleeping sickness, but at least a dozen other species are occasionally responsible.

TSH. Thyroid-stimulating hormone. ►*thyroid gland* (1).

tsutsugamushi fever. A kind of ►*typhus* transmitted by mites in parts of Asia.

tubal pregnancy. Pregnancy occurring in a Fallopian tube instead of the body of the uterus (►*ectopic*).

tubercle. 1. Small focus of inflammation and tissue destruction, the characteristic lesion of tuberculosis. **2.** Small natural promontory on a bone.

Tubercle bacillus: the bacterium that causes tuberculosis.

tuberculin. A protein derived from tubercle bacilli, used in various diagnostic tests. A small amount is injected into the skin; a patch of inflammation indicates that the subject reacts to tuberculin and therefore has some immunity to tuberculosis, either from previous or current infection or because he has been artificially immunized.

tuberculosis. A common and dangerous infectious disease. A cautious estimate by WHO puts the number of new cases of tuberculosis in the world at 2–3 million and the deaths from tuberculosis at 1–2 million every year.

1. Causes

The immediate cause of tuberculosis is infection by the tubercle bacillus, *Mycobacterium tuberculosis*. There are five known variants of this bacterium: human, bovine, avian, murine, and piscine. The first two are common parasites of man.

Human bacilli are spread by coughing. Still air may remain contaminated for several hours. The bacilli are killed by sunlight, but in damp dark surroundings they may live in dust for weeks. The bacilli are inhaled, and the infection begins in the lungs.

Bovine bacilli infect cattle, and are passed to man in milk (or, rarely, through handling infected animals). The infection spreads from the intestine or, less often, the throat. It may be carried to any part of the body, most often to lymph nodes or bones.

Avian bacilli are adapted to the high body temperatures of birds and seldom trouble man, and piscine bacilli are adapted to the low temperatures of fish and are harmless to man. Murine bacilli (vole bacilli) do not cause human disease but confer immunity to the harmful variants; they can be used as a vaccine in the same way as the cowpox virus was used to protect against smallpox in the original method of vaccination.

There is no tuberculosis without tubercle bacilli, but most people who are infected never develop the disease. A generation ago, most people in industrial countries and nearly everyone in the cities had been infected in childhood or adolescence. The number has declined recently, but even in the fortunate countries where active tuberculosis is becoming a rare disease millions of people show clear evidence of having had a mild, possibly symptom-free attack. The predisposing causes that make the difference between a trivial unnoticed incident and protracted, often fatal illness are as important as the bacillus itself.

1. Although in theory a single bacillus could multiply and spread infection throughout the body, in practice many bacilli are more likely to take hold than a few, and repeated exposure is more dangerous than a single exposure. The main danger of *overcrowding, bad ventilation* and *lack of sunlight* lies in the number of infecting bacilli.

2. The *hereditary factor* has been overestimated. Tuberculosis runs in families mainly because families live together and infect each other. Like all infections, tuberculosis is especially violent in populations to which it is new, as in some tropical countries; but many natives of the tropics are an easy prey because their resistance is lowered by malaria and malnutrition rather than because of their race.

3. Resistance changes with *age*. It is low at birth, but a baby is seldom infected unless its mother has active disease. After a few months resistance develops, but it falls off at puberty, especially among girls. 'Phthisis [pulmonary tuberculosis] most commonly occurs between the ages of 18 and 35 years' (Hippocrates, *Aphorisms*, 5th century BC). Old people are also susceptible, probably because their resistance is lowered by other illnesses.

4. *General health* at the time of infection is perhaps the most important factor of all. Tubercle bacilli thrive in the presence of malnutrition, or infection by other bacteria. Whooping cough is a notorious precursor of tuberculosis. In most people who have overcome an initial infection without apparent illness a few tubercle bacilli probably remain alive and may suddenly become active under the influence of illness, injury, or severe emotional strain – i.e. of *stress* in the widest sense.

5. *HIV and AIDS* have increased the incidence in many countries; the lowered resistance to infection of all kinds has made the victims extremely susceptible to tuberculosis.

2. EFFECTS

(i) *Pulmonary tuberculosis* (phthisis: consumption) is the commonest form of the disease. The *primary focus* is a small patch of inflammation in a lung, usually near the top. This forms a small abscess, with a central zone where tissue is destroyed surrounded by inflammation and healing. The lymph nodes at the root of the lung are also inflamed. In most cases the trouble goes no further. The focus dwindles to a small scar. The scar is revealed by X-rays, and a *tuberculin* skin test proves that the person has developed a defensive (allergic) reaction to tubercle bacilli.

In a few cases, the primary focus spreads and causes a fever lasting some weeks, from which the patient generally recovers even without special treatment. The dangers with this type of tuberculosis are (1) rapid and fatal spread through both lungs (the 'galloping consumption' of 19th-century writers), (2) dissemination of bacilli throughout the body in the bloodstream (miliary tuberculosis), and (3) tuberculous meningitis.

The usual adult disease may not begin in earnest until months or years after the primary infection. It may be either a revival of the primary focus or a fresh infection. The defensive reaction – immunity or allergy to tubercle bacilli – acquired from the primary infection confines the disease to the lungs and prevents any rapid progression, but like an ill-disciplined army of liberation it does as much damage to the infected lung as the tubercle bacilli themselves. Pockets of infection enlarge and form cavities – chronic abscesses – in the lungs. Healing more or less keeps pace with the damage that is being done, but the balance is delicate. Any of the predisposing causes described above can tilt it in favour of the bacillus, or by dealing with the causes the disease can be arrested.

The symptoms may include fever, sweating at night, cough, blood-spitting, and loss of weight. None of these is peculiar to tuberculosis, and any may be absent from a particular case. Continued ill health is probably the most constant symptom, but some cases of active disease are discovered by chance during a routine X-ray examination. X-rays give the best evidence of the extent of the dis-

ease. The presence of active pulmonary tuberculosis is proved by finding tubercle bacilli in the sputum.

(ii) *Miliary tuberculosis* is spread of infection from the primary focus by transport of bacilli in the blood-stream. In some cases the patient is quickly overwhelmed. In others, the bacilli establish small colonies, and signs of tuberculosis appear simultaneously in various parts of the body with the formation of very numerous small abscesses (*milia* = millet-seeds). Or the disease may settle in one or two organs – bone, joint, kidney, nervous system, lymph nodes. In some cases, miliary tuberculosis settles with few if any symptoms.

(iii) The *lymph nodes* are to some extent involved in all forms of tuberculosis. If the bacilli are swallowed and not inhaled (usually from milk infected with bovine tubercle bacilli) the disease may be confined to lymph nodes in the neck after infecting the throat, or to abdominal lymph nodes after infecting the intestine. Tuberculous glands in the neck used to be a common disease of childhood. The *scrofula* (king's evil) of earlier centuries was a spread of this infection to the overlying skin.

(iv) *Tuberculous meningitis* arises only as a complication of other forms of the disease. It was invariably fatal until the discovery of streptomycin in 1944.

(v) *Tuberculosis of bones and joints* is usually a very slow process, but since even in favourable cases the structures are gradually replaced by unstable fibrous tissue it always led to disability before the discovery of effective drugs: the least movement kept the infection alight and the best treatment was to immobilize affected joints. Tuberculosis of a vertebra (Pott's disease) leads to collapse of the bone, angulation of the spinal column, and injury to the spinal cord unless it is treated.

(vi) *Tuberculosis of the skin*, of which the commonest form is *lupus vulgaris*, a destructive inflammation of the skin of the nose and cheeks, is a reminder that the tubercle bacillus is closely related to the leprosy bacillus.

(vii) *Abdominal tuberculosis*, affecting intestine and lymph nodes (tabes mesenterica), and sometimes leading to a low-grade inflammation of the whole peritoneal lining of the abdomen, can arise either from drinking infected milk or from the patient's own infected sputum, some of which anyone with pulmonary tuberculosis must swallow. The disease is often surprisingly free of symptoms: the patient is vaguely unwell with some sort of digestive disorder, and loses weight, but the diagnosis is sometimes made almost by intuition, or by chance when the infection is discovered during an abdominal operation. Any of the abdominal organs can be infected on occasion, particularly the kidneys, bladder, and reproductive organs.

3. TREATMENT

Until 1944 there was no means of attacking the tubercule bacillus, and treatment was directed at the contributory or predisposing causes. Since nobody knows how these causes act it is not possible to say why the older methods worked, or which were the effective ingredients, but with careful, sometimes prolonged nursing many patients recovered or at least improved who would certainly have died without treatment. The balance could be tilted against the disease and in favour of the patient. But many patients seemed to recover only to relapse later, and in some the disease could

be slowed but not stopped. If the bacilli were already firmly established, as with tuberculous meningitis or any rapidly spreading infection, the case was hopeless from the start.

Rest is probably the most important of the older remedies. Sanatorium treatment relies greatly on physical rest, but the emotional rest of a calm, ordered environment could be as valuable, for in essence rest is absence of *stress*.

Anyone with tuberculosis needs a good mixed diet with enough protein and vitamins. The continuous process of healing has to keep ahead of damage to tissue, and makes its own demands on the diet; and the raised body temperature means that food is consumed at more than the normal rate.

Fresh air is a traditional cornerstone of the treatment. Its greatest value may be to lessen the risk of infection to others. *Climate* has little if any direct influence, but a *change* of climate can make it much easier for the patient to relax.

Tuberculosis of lymph nodes in the neck, a single kidney, or a joint, often due to bovine (milk-borne) tubercle bacilli, was formerly known as 'surgical tuberculosis' because it could be cured, if the disease was inactive elsewhere, by removing the affected glands or kidney or by immobilizing the joint.

Excepting cases where the patient's natural resistance is clearly getting the upper hand, all types of tuberculosis are now treated with drugs acting directly against tubercle bacilli. The first to be used was streptomycin (1944). It was followed by para-aminosalicylic acid in 1946 and isoniazid in 1952. More recent additions to the list include rifampicin, ethambutol, pyrazinamide and many others. The simultaneous use of two or more drugs makes it less likely that the bacilli will become resistant to treatment.

The effect of drug treatment has been remarkable. Even the severest types of infection can usually be arrested. In countries with effective medical services the remaining deaths from tuberculosis are mostly among older patients. For instance, in England and Wales in 1946, when streptomycin was still confined to a few experimental units and the other drugs were unknown, 900 girls aged 15–19 died of tuberculosis. In 1961, 9 died.

4. PREVENTION

Since many (in some places most) people are likely to be infected at some time, but only a minority will develop the illness, anything that increases people's resistance to the point where they can be infected without symptoms is in effect prevention. In English cities *infection* was still almost universal in 1910, but the *death rate* had been since 1860. In the next 35 years it was halved again despite the setbacks of two World Wars. No single factor can explain the decrease (as vaccination explains the decrease of smallpox, or clean drinking water that of typhoid). Better diet, better housing, better working conditions, and better care of the sick must all have contributed. Recent campaigns against tuberculosis all over the world have shown that as long as people suffer from malnutrition nothing has much effect on the disease.

Infection of the lungs can be prevented only to a limited extent. But the greatest danger is from a sudden heavy infection, and this can be reduced by treating the source – the people with severe disease. In the past, hospital treatment automatically took these people out of the community and helped to reduce the danger. At present drug treatment renders nearly all patients noninfectious after a short time. An important element in any campaign is that as far as possible it should cover the whole community, which not only ensures that people who themselves need treatment will get it but protects those who are not yet infected.

For many years before the discovery of the new drugs, the number of new cases notified in Britain did not vary much. Probably a real decrease was cancelled by increased accuracy of diagnosis. The number of deaths had been falling steadily but slowly, and seemed to be levelling out at some 20,000 deaths annually. During the few years since the drugs have been in general use, this figure has fallen to 2000, and most of the deaths are of older people. At the same time, with fewer active cases to spread infection, the number of new cases has been halved.

Bovine tuberculosis can be eradicated by eliminating tuberculous cows from dairy herds, or by pasteurizing all milk. Pasteurization has practically eradicated bovine tuberculosis in much of Western Europe and the United States, and nonpulmonary tuberculosis has become fairly uncommon, occurring only as a complication of pulmonary disease.

Vaccination with a modified bacillus that evokes immunity without causing disease (BCG; *bacille Calmette-Guérin*) is now a part of all major campaigns. Vaccination does not entirely prevent tuberculosis, but it greatly reduces the risk of a dangerous attack. A simple skin test (▸*tuberculin*) shows which people have no immunity and need to be vaccinated.

tularaemia. An infectious disease related to *plague* but affecting rabbits instead of rats. Human cases have occurred in the USA, Japan, and Russia, mostly from handling wild rabbits.

tulle gras. Netting impregnated with petroleum jelly and sterilized; a useful non-adhesive dressing for burns and wounds.

tumour. Any swelling, but especially a *neoplasm* (new growth), which is a collection of cells that have, as it were, seceded from the general community of cells that make up the various tissues and organs of the body, no longer serve any purpose useful to the rest of the body, and grow at the expense of their healthy neighbours.

A *benign* tumour is simply a growing mass of useless but essentially harmless tissue. It keeps within its own bounds, and becomes a nuisance only if it is unsightly or if it obstructs or otherwise interferes with neighbouring tissue. It is cured by removal. A common example is the ►*fibroid*.

A malignant tumour is the same thing as a ►*cancer*.

twins. *Fraternal* (dizygotic, binovular) twins develop when two ova are fertilized at the same time. As a rule a woman's ovaries release only a single ovum each month, but if two or more happen to be released together they can be fertilized together. A tendency to shed more than one ovum can be inherited, so that fraternal twins occur more often in some families than others. If pituitary hormones or the synthetic drug clomiphene are used to stimulate the ovaries in case of infertility several ova may be released.

Identical (monozygotic, monovular) twins develop from the two halves of a single ovum, formed as the first step in the growth of an embryo.

About one pregnancy in 90 produces twins: and according to Hellin's law one in 90^2 produces triplets and one in 90^3 quadruplets.

tympanic. Of the (ear-)drum.

tympanities. Flatulent distension of the abdomen.

typhoid. Prostrated and mentally numbed by fever. The *typhoid state* occurs in many acute diseases and differs from *delirium* in the absence of excitement.

Typhoid fever is an infectious disease due to *Salmonella typhi* (typhoid bacillus), a bacterium of the same genus as those of paratyphoid fever and various types of food poisoning. Unlike the salmonellae of food poisoning, *S. typhi* seems to be exclusively a parasite of man, and the infection is always acquired from someone else. The usual source is drinking water or food that has been contaminated from someone either suffering from typhoid or harbouring the bacteria without symptoms (i.e. a carrier). In countries with poor sanitation, flies may carry the bacteria from excrement to food or water.

After infection the bacteria invade the wall of the small intestine and multiply in collections of lymphoid tissue (Peyer's patches) there, at this stage causing no symptoms. After 1–2 weeks they invade the blood-stream and cause fever, often with severe but ill-defined illness. Many patients develop a rash of pink spots about a week later when the fever is at its height. Without the help of a laboratory, typhoid can be indistinguishable from other severe fevers. Since the bacteria circulate in the blood they may settle anywhere and cause symptoms of inflammation in any organ. They have a particular affinity for the spleen and bones. Other species of salmonella regularly cause diarrhoea and vomiting, but neither is typical of typhoid; constipation is seen twice as often as diarrhoea. Yet the greatest danger is from the intestine, where the infection may erode a blood vessel and cause profuse bleeding, or perforate the wall and cause leakage into the abdominal cavity and peritonitis. Without treatment, at least 10 per cent of patients die. The others recover gradually. They may not completely overcome the infection, and second attacks are not uncommon; or they may remain symptomless carriers of the bacteria. Some people become carriers without going through any obvious illness.

The diagnosis is confirmed by finding the bacteria in the blood in the early stages or in the stools or urine later – these are the source of infection to other people. From about the second week of the attack, *antibodies* against typhoid can be demonstrated in the blood.

Nearly all cases respond well to treatment with chloramphenicol or some other antibiotic.

Typhoid can be prevented in the community by proper sewage disposal, controlled water supply, and clean food-handling. The system breaks down when an unsuspected carrier handles food or drinking water.

The individual can be protected by vaccination, usually with a combined vaccine (TAB) against typhoid and paratyphoid.

typhus. A group of infectious diseases caused by very small bacteria of the genus *Rickettsia*. Typhus was first distinguished from typhoid fever by an American physician, W. W. Gerhard, in 1837. There is still confusion with the names: in German, typhoid is *Typhus*, and typhus is *Fleckentyphus* or *Fleckenfie-*

ber (spotted fever). And in English spotted fever can mean either typhus or epidemic meningitis.

Louse-borne typhus affects only man. It is transmitted by body-lice, and outbreaks can occur whenever people are dirty and crowded together. It is rare in times of peace and plenty, but devastating epidemics can occur during wars or famines or after natural disasters, anywhere in the world.

The related diseases include *Rocky Mountain spotted fever* and several kinds of *tick fever*, transmitted from rodents to man by tick-bites; *murine typhus*, transmitted from rats by fleas; and *tsutsugamushi fever* (scrub typhus), transmitted from rodents by mites. These cause sporadic cases in infected regions (generally hot countries), but not major epidemics.

All forms of typhus cause a prostrating fever within a fortnight of infection, lasting one or two weeks. Skin rashes are common: red spots followed in some types of disease by pin-point bleeding into the skin. Many patients develop a kind of pneumonia. Some of these diseases are not very dangerous, but with untreated louse-borne typhus and Rocky Mountain spotted fever as many as 20 per cent of the patients die.

Fortunately all these infections respond well to good nursing and treatment with antibiotics.

tyramine. A substance found in cheese and some other foods. It imitates the effects of adrenaline in the body, perhaps by increasing the natural secretion of adrenaline in the nervous system. This may explain why cheese disturbs sleep in some people.

A class of drugs (monoamine oxidase

inhibitors) given for ►*depression* increases the available adrenaline. The effect of tyramine added to that of these drugs sometimes causes a dangerous excess of adrenaline activity, with a sharp rise of blood pressure. Cheese is therefore forbidden to patients taking the drugs.

U

ulcer. A persistent breach in a body surface (skin or mucous membrane) that fails to heal because of defective circulation (e.g. ulcer of the leg with varicose veins), continued injury (e.g. an ulcer on the tongue beside a jagged tooth) or irritation (e.g. duodenal ulcer from an excess of acid), tumour formation (e.g. rodent ulcer), or infection – which can be the primary cause or can be added as a complication of any other. The primary cause of some ulcers, e.g. those of the intestine with ulcerative colitis, is unknown.

For gastric and duodenal ulcers ➤*peptic ulcer.*

ulcerative colitis ➤*colitis.*

ulna. The inner of the two bones of the forearm. Its upper end is the point of the elbow, and it can be felt under the skin throughout its length to the little-finger side of the wrist. Since the ulna and radius work in all ways as a unit they are discussed together under ➤*radius.*

ulnar. Of the ➤*ulna.*
Ulnar artery. In front of the elbow the brachial artery divides into two branches, *radial* and *ulnar*, which run parallel courses to the hand, roughly following the lines of the two bones of the forearm (radius and ulna). Of the two, the ulnar is more concerned with the blood supply of the forearm and the radial with the hand.
Ulnar nerve. One of the two nerves of the front of the forearm and hand; the other being the *median* nerve. The ulnar nerve enters the forearm by passing behind the elbow, where it is exposed to injury. Even a slight jar to the bone ('funny bone') at this point is very painful.

ultrasonic waves (ultrasound). Vibrations of the same kind as sound waves, but too rapid to be heard (above 20,000 cycles per second). Ultrasound is increasingly used in diagnosis, for examining internal structures by the principle of radar (➤*echography; scan*). In the treatment of disease, an ultrasonic beam can be focused at a given depth below the surface of the skin, where the energy of the vibrations is dissipated as heat; the method is used for relieving pain in joints and muscles. A more intense beam can be used to destroy very small segments of tissue. For instance, in disease of the inner ear with disturbance of balance (vertigo) ultrasonic waves have been successfully used to put the balance organ out of action without disturbing the adjacent organ of hearing.

ultraviolet radiation. Waves of the same kind as light, but with a higher frequency than the visible spectrum (but a lower frequency than X-rays).

Ultraviolet radiation in sunlight converts inactive steroids in the skin to vitamin D, but unless there is a deficiency of this vitamin (rickets) it does nothing to promote health. Artificial ultraviolet radiation is used for treating skin diseases (*acne; psoriasis*). It increases the rate at which the outer layer of the skin is shed and replaced.

An excess of ultraviolet is harmful; it can provoke severe inflammation and, in time, even cancer of the skin. Protective lotions can be had to filter off the radiation.

Bacteria are quickly destroyed by ultraviolet radiation.

umbilical cord. A bundle of two arteries and a vein and some vestigial structures, surrounded by a clear gelatinous material and a thin membrane, connecting an unborn infant with its placenta. The cord is normally sealed with a ligature and cut soon after birth, and the remaining stump withers and falls off.

umbilicus (navel). The scar in the centre of the abdomen where the umbilical cord entered.

A weakness in the muscles at this point may allow a bulge (umbilical hernia) to appear. ➤*hernia*.

Infection of the umbilicus at birth is unusual with proper midwifery, but is common with primitive methods. In parts of West Africa many babies die of tetanus contracted in this way.

unconscious. The unconscious (subconscious) mind is a fundamental concept in Freud's psychology and, in one form or another, in most other schools. The mind is said to work at different levels. The conscious mind, i.e. the mind in the ordinary sense, examines events in the light of reason and experience. The unconscious mind is a great store of events that are forgotten as far as the conscious mind is concerned, and perhaps of events or impressions that have never reached consciousness. But it is not a passive store; it is continuously active, and its activity modifies the conscious mind, and it affects the functions of the body in similar ways to conscious thoughts and emotions. At times it may be in direct conflict with the conscious, rea-soning mind. Such conflict is thought to be a major source of disturbed behaviour and physical ill health.

➤➤*anxiety*; *psychoanalysis*; *psychosomatic disease*.

unconsciousness ➤*coma*.

undine. A vessel like a small retort, for rinsing the front of the eye.

undulant fever. An infectious disease due to the bacterium *Brucella abortus*; this is primarily a parasite of cattle, in which it causes *contagious abortion*. Human disease is contracted either from handling infected cattle or from milk. Where milk is pasteurized, the disease is rare.

Two other species of *Brucella* are occasionally transmitted from animals to man: *Br. melitensis* from goats (Malta fever) and *Br. suis* from pigs.

Often the disease is so mild as to pass unnoticed unless a bacteriological examination for some other purpose shows that the patient has been infected with *Brucella*. In an average case an intermittent fever lasts 2 or 3 weeks and then clears completely. The disease gets its name from a tendency for episodes of fever to recur, sometimes over several months. There are no characteristic signs, and the diagnosis is impossible without the help of a bacteriological laboratory.

Although it can be a great nuisance, undulant fever is seldom dangerous. Most cases respond to treatment with antibiotics.

The commonest complication is chronic inflammation of a bone. Human infection does not cause habitual abortion.

unsaturated fat ➤*fat*.

uraemia. Excess of urea in the blood,

from defective function of the kidneys. Urea is not itself poisonous, but an excess of it implies an excess of other waste products that are poisonous. ➤*kidneys* (5).

urea. Carbamide; $CO(NH_2)_2$, an end-product of the chemical breakdown of protein in the body, excreted in the urine at a rate of 20–30 g daily.

ureter. Tube leading from kidney to bladder. ➤*kidneys* (1).

urethra. Tube carrying urine away from the bladder. The female urethra is short, passing below the pubis to open in front of the vagina. The male urethra passes downwards through the prostate gland before turning forwards to run the length of the penis. Because of the long urethra the male bladder is better protected against infection (*cystitis*) than the female.

urethritis. Inflammation of the urethra, sometimes caused by *gonorrhoea*. But many other kinds of infection, not necessarily venereal, can also cause urethritis. They include the organism *Chlamydia*, which also causes ➤*trachoma*, infection with *Candida* (thrush) and with *trichomonas* (both common and tiresome afflictions of women, which can be transmitted occasionally to their partners), and other causes, sometimes unknown, classified as non-specific urethritis (NSU). The female urethra is much more vulnerable than the male.

uric acid. An end-product of the digestion of nucleic acids, excreted in the urine at a rate of about 0.6 g daily. People with ➤*gout* either have an abnormality of body chemistry that causes them to form more uric acid than can be easily disposed of by the kidneys, or one

that prevents them from getting rid of uric acid at the normal rate.

urine. A watery fluid formed by the kidneys as described under ➤*kidneys* (2).

Normal urine is a solution in water of numerous waste products of body chemistry, and of necessary substances (including water itself) of which there is at the time an excess. The principal waste products are from the digestion of protein and other nitrogen compounds. They are urea, uric acid, and creatinine. (The only waste product of fat and carbohydrate is carbon dioxide, which is excreted by the lungs.) In addition there is a variable amount of sodium chloride and other salts. If the body is short of salt, e.g. after profuse sweating, there may be none at all in the urine, but if there is an excess the amount in the urine can be increased to 2 per cent. By selective excretion of acid or alkaline salts the slight alkalinity of the blood is kept constant. The urine is usually, but not always, slightly acid. The yellow colour of urine is due to a substance *urochrome*, of which neither the source nor the composition is known.

Abnormalities of the urine are often valuable clues in diagnosis. Even a very simple examination can give much information.

The *colour* can be affected by bile pigments, which do not normally appear in the urine but may do so with some disorders of the liver (➤*jaundice*); or by blood with disorders of the kidneys or bladder. A few coloured substances in foods or medicines find their way into the urine.

Normal urine has only a faint *smell*. The unpleasant ammoniacal smell of stale urine is due to the action of air and bacteria. If there is infection in the bladder (cystitis), the urine may have an offensive smell.

The *concentration*, estimated by measuring the specific gravity, does not usually signify much in a single specimen, but inability to vary the concentration at different times is a sign of defective kidneys.

Normal urine contains no *protein*. The presence of albumin, of which a crude test is to curdle it by boiling, does not indicate any particular diagnosis, but does show that there is something to be investigated further.

Most simple tests for *sugar* (glucose) depend on the change of colour when a blue copper salt is reduced by glucose to red-brown copper. The chance finding of a small amount of glucose in the urine does not prove that anything is wrong, but the likeliest reason for it is diabetes, and many cases needing treatment are first recognized in this way.

urticaria (nettle-rash (*urtica* = stinging-nettle); hives). One of the commonest manifestations of ▸*allergy*.

Nettles release *histamine* and other poisons that cause the capillary blood vessels to leak fluid (but not blood cells) into the tissues, and also evoke sensations such as itching or burning. An allergic reaction against a substance to which the patient is sensitive (usually a food) causes similar poisons to be formed in certain tissues, and as a result itchy blotches appear on the skin. Typically they are fleeting, and disappear from one part of the skin only to reappear in another.

Urticaria usually responds to antihistamine drugs. In severe cases, adrenaline or corticosteroids may be needed. If the irritant can be identified and avoided,

so much the better; but this is not always easy.

uterus (womb). A hollow muscle about the size of a duck's egg, lying in the pelvis immediately behind the bladder. The narrow lower end is the *cervix* (neck), which opens into the vagina. The upper part or *body* of the uterus opens at each side into a *Fallopian tube*, like an outspread arm above the ovary.

The uterus is slung from various ligaments, none of them efficient. Its real support is the muscular floor of the pelvis.

The lining of the uterus (*endometrium*) is shed each month during the thirty-odd years of fertility, and replaced by a new endometrium, which rapidly grows thick enough to provide a bed for the fertilized ovum if pregnancy occurs (▸*menstruation*; *pregnancy*). During pregnancy, menstruation stops and the endometrium remains intact.

The muscle fibres that form the bulk of the uterus have a remarkable ability to adapt themselves. During pregnancy their weight increases from about 30 g (1 oz) to 1 kg (2 lb), and their automatic contractions during labour exert a force of some 10 kg (which a strong woman may double by voluntary contraction of her abdominal muscles). After pregnancy the uterus reverts to little more than its original size in a few weeks.

The embryonic uterus grows in two halves, each with its own Fallopian tube and ovary. In some mammals the later fusion of the two halves is incomplete, so that the cavity of the uterus is Y-shaped (bicornuate); and occasionally a human uterus develops in this way. This particular anomaly does not matter, but some others may interfere with conception or pregnancy and need surgical correction. The most difficult cases are those where the uterus is simply under-developed. Hormone treatment may encourage it to grow to a normal size, but the patient's chances of bearing children are not good.

Two common disorders peculiar to the uterus are ►*prolapse*, from weakening of its muscular support after childbearing, and ►*fibroids*, a sort of benign tumour.

The uterus is one of the commonest sites of cancer in women. This type of cancer is among the few that can usually be prevented. Most uterine cancer starts in the cervix, and for a long time (probably 10 years) before anything dangerous happens, characteristic changes can be detected in the lining of the cervix if a few cells are scraped off and examined microscopically. The operation takes only seconds and is painless. If these changes – *carcinoma-in-situ* – are found, the affected part of the cervix can be removed and no cancer develops. The

woman can still bear children. Less often than the cervix, the body of the uterus can give rise to cancer. The first symptom is usually unexpected bleeding or discharge. With early surgery, sometimes with hormone therapy, the chances of cure are high.

Since the uterus has no function but childbearing, its removal for certain disorders does not affect general health.

uveitis. Inflammation of the *uveal tract*, a layer of tissues in the eye comprising the *iris* and its supporting structures and the *choroid* membrane behind the retina. ►*eye* (3).

uvula. The small projection of the soft palate in the mid-line. An irritating cough at night is sometimes attributed to a long uvula that tickles the back of the throat, and is treated by removing the uvula. This sort of cough is more likely to be due to a trickle of infected mucus from the back of the nose.

V

vaccination. The original meaning was infection with vaccinia (cow-pox) to confer immunity to smallpox, introduced in 1796 by Jenner (►*immunity*). About a century later Pasteur suggested that as a tribute to Jenner the term should be applied to the principle of using modified germs to confer immunity to more dangerous ones. Vaccination is now synonymous with ►*immunization*.

vaccine. A virus or bacterium so modified (e.g. by culture in an unnatural environment or treatment with formaldehyde) as to be no longer dangerous, yet able to confer immunity in the same way as infection with the actual disease.

vaccinia. 1. Cow-pox: a contagious disease of cattle that can cause a mild infection in man. The virus is so like that of smallpox that an attack of one confers immunity to the other.
2. An attenuated form of smallpox, produced by infecting calves with the virus, which then undergoes some modification that makes it comparatively harmless; used in preference to natural cowpox for vaccination. A few people have an attack of vaccinia after vaccination. It is usually like mild chickenpox – but it is dangerous to people with eczema.

vagina. Passage from the uterus to the vulva, behind and below the bladder: it is a tube surrounded by muscles, normally flattened to form a transverse cleft at right angles to the vertical cleft of the vulva. It is adaptable, allowing free passage to the baby during childbirth (the obstacles are at the entrance and exit of the vagina).

The lining membrane is controlled by *oestrogens* (sex hormones). In women after the menopause the lining may become thin and fragile, and in girls before puberty it is vulnerable to bacterial infection. In either case medication with oestrogens strengthens it.

Bleeding from the vagina other than normal menstruation always requires investigation. During pregnancy it may be the first indication of a threatened or inevitable miscarriage. At the end of pregnancy, it is likely to be a sign of ►*placenta praevia*. Bleeding after confinement may be due to a fragment of placenta that has remained in the uterus, or to an injury of the cervix. All these conditions need treatment to prevent further and possibly serious bleeding. Bleeding between menstrual periods, or after the menopause when the periods have stopped, has many possible causes, some trivial and some, such as cancer, very serious. This is a symptom that calls for expert advice as soon as possible.

vaginismus. Spasm of the muscles around the vagina, making coitus difficult or impossible (►*dyspareunia*).

vaginitis. Inflammation of the vagina. During the years of fertility the sex hormones seem to protect the vagina from most of the common bacteria, and the likely causes are *Trichomonas*, and *Candida*. Girls and older women are more liable to bacterial infection.

vagus nerve. Tenth cranial nerve; the

most important component of the ►*para-sympathetic* nervous system.

The nerve arises from the brain-stem, passes through the base of the skull, and accompanies the internal jugular vein down the neck. In the thorax the vagus nerves run down the sides of the oeso-phagus. In the abdomen their branches are distributed to the main digestive organs. On its way the vagus gives branches to the heart and lungs.

The *sensory* fibres convey (uncon-scious) sensations of *stretch* from the lungs, of *pressure* from the heart and aorta: these initiate appropriate reflexes to modify breathing and circulation. The *motor* fibres constrict the bronchi, slow the heart, and stimulate the digestive organs (►*respiration; heart; digestion*).

In addition the vagus conveys ordin-ary nerve fibres, unconnected with the parasympathetic system, controlling speech and swallowing.

Numerous drugs modify the activity of the vagus (►*parasympathetic*). *Vago-tomy* is the operation of cutting the nerves for the relief of ►*peptic ulcer*.

valgus; varus. In Latin, *valgus* is bowlegged and *varus* is knock-kneed; but in current usage the meanings have changed places. The words are now used to describe several kinds of congenital de-formity of the limbs. *Valgus* has the gen-eral meaning of outward angulation and *varus* of inward angulation: thus *coxa valga*, splayed hip; *genu valgum*, knock-knee, with the lower leg splayed out-wards; *talipes valgus*, clubfoot with the sole turned out in an exaggeration of flat-foot; and corresponding *varus* de-formities in the opposite direction.

Valsalva, Antonio Maria (1666–1723). Professor of anatomy at Bologna; the teacher of Morgagni and a pupil of Mal-

pighi. He was among the first to recog-nize the importance of studying the ap-pearance of diseased organs after death, and many of his observations are re-corded in Morgagni's great text-book on the sites and causes of disease.

Valsalva's experiment: inflation of the Eustachian tubes by holding the nose and trying to blow down it.

Valsalva manoeuvre: if the pressure in the chest is raised by blowing hard against resistance or by a static muscular effort such as straining at stool, blood is prevented from returning to the heart; the output of the heart is thus reduced and the subject may faint (►*Starling's law*).

valve. Several body-tubes are provided with valves which restrict flow to one di-rection. The important ones are the valves of the heart and of the veins.

A valve consists of two or three *cusps* or flaps attached to the vessel wall like pockets. The flow of blood in the right direction presses the cusps flat against the wall. Reflux opens the pockets, brings their edges together, and blocks the vessel. The valves between the atria and ventricles of the ►*heart* (right: *tricus-pid*; left: *mitral*) are prevented from turning inside out like an umbrella in a storm by strong threads attached to muscles which contract with the ventricles.

Disorders of the heart valves are de-scribed under ►*heart* (5). Failure of the valves in the veins causes ►*varicose veins*.

valvular disease ►*heart* (5).

varicella = ►*chickenpox*.

varicocele. Varicose swelling of the veins from a testis, usually the left side, perhaps because the left spermatic vein joins the renal vein at an awkward angle so that the circulation of blood is less efficient than on the right. Most varicoceles are of no significance. A few ache, especially if the patient's attention has been drawn to them; removal of the redundant veins is then a simple and harmless operation.

varicose veins. Abnormal swelling of veins, usually in the legs. Blood is returned from the legs in two groups of veins. The *deep* veins accompany the arteries. They are surrounded by muscles, which support them and squeeze the blood along them. The ➤*saphenous veins* lie directly under the skin, and at intervals communicate with the deep veins. A system of one-way ➤*valves* ensures that the flow is *upwards* in the principal veins and *inwards* in the communicating branches. If these valves are defective, the blood stagnates, the pressure in the saphenous veins rises, and the veins become swollen and tortuous. Aching and fatigue are the commonest early symptoms. Because of back-pressure on the ➤*capillary* blood vessels fluid collects in the feet and causes them to swell. The skin above the ankles may become thin and discoloured and even break down to form a varicose ulcer.

The weakness of the valves which leads to varicose veins is sometimes hereditary, but the most important direct cause is prolonged standing – not walking, but standing still. Policemen and housewives are especially vulnerable. Obesity is a contributory cause; pregnancy has the same effect with the addition of pressure on the veins in the pelvis. Obstruction of the deep veins (e.g. with ➤*phlebitis*) causes overloading of the saphenous veins.

Supporting bandages or elastic stockings relieve the swelling and discomfort, but to cure varicose veins surgery is needed. Either the vein is sealed off with ligatures or, more drastically, it is actually removed. Small varicosities can be treated with injections of irritant fluids which cause their walls to stick together. A first operation may be disappointing because other veins, previously unsuspected, may swell when the principal vein has been closed.

variola = ➤*smallpox. Variola minor* = alatrim, a mild variant of smallpox.

variolation. Deliberate infection from a mild case of smallpox to confer immunity, superseded by ➤*vaccination.* ➤➤*immunity* (1).

Varolio, Constanzo ➤*pons.*

varus ➤*valgus.*

vascular. Of vessels, especially blood vessels.

vas deferens. The duct of the testis; it carries spermatozoa by a tortuous route up the neck of the scrotum, obliquely across the groin, through a gap in the abdominal muscles, behind the bladder and through the prostate gland to the urethra. In the groin the vas deferens lies directly under the skin, where it is easily accessible to the surgeon, and male sterilization by sealing it with a ligature is a very simple operation.

vasectomy. The operation of closing the vas deferens. ➤➤*sterilization.*

vasoconstriction; vasodilatation. Reflex narrowing or widening of blood vessels; the principal means of regulating blood pressure. Selective constriction or dilatation of vessels in the skin adjusts the body temperature.

vasomotor nerves. ➤*sympathetic* nerve fibres regulating the calibre of blood vessels. They are controlled by nerve cells in the *vasomotor* centre in the brain-stem.

vasopressin. The *anti-diuretic hormone* (ADH) of the ►*pituitary*.

vector. Animal – often an insect – transmitting infection from person to person or from infected animals to human beings. Mosquitoes are vectors of malaria and yellow fever, lice of typhus, and tsetse flies of sleeping sickness.

vegetarian diet. Man has evolved as an omnivorous animal; his 'natural' diet contains both animal and vegetable foods. A good mixture provides all the necessities that cannot by synthesized in the human body (vitamins; essential amino-acids). All these things can be found in vegetable foods, but to avoid deficiency of one or other the diet must be as varied as possible. A well-balanced vegetarian diet avoids many if not all of the dietary hazards that contribute to disease of the heart and blood vessels, among others.

vein (Lat. *vena*). Vessel by which blood returns from the periphery to the heart. The high pressure of the blood in the arteries is expended by the time the blood has passed through the capillaries to reach the veins, and the average pressure in the veins is very close to atmospheric pressure, i.e. effectively nil. The veins accordingly have much thinner walls than arteries, but their diameter is much greater to accommodate the more leisurely flow. Veins are both wider and more numerous than arteries, but their structure is similar. Their thin walls contain a few muscle fibres, activated by sympathetic fibres, which enable them to contract in response to diminished return of blood and so ensure that the flow is maintained.

A vein is thin-walled only because there is little pressure to stimulate growth of muscle. If a length of vein is grafted into an artery to pass an obstruction its walls thicken under the pressure of arterial blood and in a short time it takes on the structure of an artery.

The column of blood in a vein is broken into short segments by valves which prevent any back-flow. Each consists of two opposed flaps like a pair of sluice gates. The continuous, imperceptible activity of muscles all over the body gently squeezes the veins and keeps the blood moving from valve to valve. If part of the body has been perfectly still for a time the blood tends to stagnate, but movement such as stretching or shifting the weight from heels to toes restores the flow.

An artery is usually accompanied by two veins, its *venae comitantes*. Strangely, the very largest of the arteries are accompanied by single veins (jugular, subclavian, iliac, venae cavae). In the limbs, the principal veins are supplemented by large subcutaneous veins.

1. DISORDERS

An injured vein bleeds much more slowly than an artery of the same size, but it is less muscular and cannot retract so well. On the other hand, the lightest pressure is enough to stop the bleeding while the blood clots. The *average* pressure in the veins is atmospheric, but gravity creates a positive pressure in veins below the heart and a negative pressure – suction – in veins above the heart. If the injured part is raised to the level of the heart there is no pressure in the veins, which stop bleeding. Above the heart the air pressure outside the vein is greater than the blood pressure within: the veins on the back of the hand collapse when the arm is raised. If a vein in this position is cut it usually closes, but with a hole in a large vein (jugular) air may be sucked in. This is more dangerous than bleeding for a large air-lock can stop the circulation in some vital organ. Serious cases are rare. Small quantities of air must often get into veins without harm.

The commonest disorder of veins is failure of the valves in the veins of the leg; the resulting back-pressure stretches the vessels and causes ►*varicose veins*. Varicose veins in the rectum are ►*haemorrhoids*.

Inflammation of a vein (►*phlebitis*) is important because it is associated with obstruction by clotted blood (►*thrombosis*). Obstruction of a small vein does not matter. There are plenty of others. But if a very large vein is blocked by a clot, the part which it should drain becomes congested. The clot may break away and be carried through the heart to create a blockage (►*embolism*) in an artery of the lung. In the normal way, however, the clot is slowly absorbed, and either the vein resumes its function or a neighbouring vein takes over.

►*circulation*; *portal vein*.

vena cava. One of two great veins opening into the right atrium of the heart: the *superior vena cava* above, and the *inferior vena cava* below. Between them they receive the whole of the circulating venous blood (except the blood from the heart muscle, which drains directly into the atrium).

The superior vena cava is formed from the two ►*innominate* veins, by which it receives blood from the ►*jugular* and ►*subclavian* veins. It also receives the *azygos* vein; thus it drains the head, upper limbs, and thorax.

The inferior vena cava is formed from the two common ►*iliac* veins. It lies in front of the lumbar vertebrae, to the right of the aorta. Its largest tributaries are the ►*renal* and ►*hepatic* veins, from the kidneys and liver.

venene = ►*venom*.

venereal disease. Infectious disease usually transmitted by sexual contact. Also known as *sexually transmitted disease* (STD). Any infection can be and presumably is transmitted sexually on occasion. The peculiarity of venereal diseases is that they are seldom transmitted in any other way. The common ones are *gonorrhoea* and *syphilis*, both world-wide, and *chancroid* and *lymphogranuloma venerum*, seen mostly in the tropics but increasing in temperate climates. To the list must now be added AIDS, at present the most serious of all, and also herpes and chlamydial infection.

Apart from AIDS and herpes, venereal diseases are usually curable with antibiotics or sulphonamides, but when treatment is delayed, established damage may not be reparable. The early signs, especially among women, may be so slight as to pass unnoticed, unless the patient undergoes medical examination. Treatment of one partner without attention to the other is largely a waste of time, and one of the unsolved problems is how to trace and treat the patient's contacts.

Both World Wars greatly increased the incidence of venereal diseases. After the second, the incidence declined under the influence of effective drugs; but since the late 1950s venereal diseases have become commoner in most countries. One of the worst features of the newest epidemic is that the average age of the patients has steadily fallen, especially among girls.

venesection. Cutting a vein to draw off blood. ►*blood-letting*.

venom (venene). Poison injected by an animal by stinging or biting. Venomous animals include various insects (bees etc.), spiders, scorpions, reptiles, and fish.

Venoms are proteins. They can be neutralized by *antibodies* (antivenenes) in the same way as bacterial poisons (toxins), and effective preparations are available against most of the common and dangerous ones.
➤*insect*; *snakebite*.

ventricle. A cavity, especially (1) in the ➤*brain* or (2) in the ➤*heart*.

1. The nervous system is developed from a simple tube. This structure persists in the spinal cord with its narrow *central canal*, but as the more highly developed parts of the brain grow the canal expands into a series of bubbles connected by narrower passages. In each cerebral hemisphere is a lateral *ventricle*, opening into the *third ventricle* at the centre of the brain. The cavity of the midbrain is a slender tube (*aqueduct of Silvius*), which broadens in the hind brain into the *fourth ventricle*, between the cerebellum and the brain-stem. The fourth ventricle narrows to the central canal of the spinal cord. The system is filled with cerebrospinal fluid, and communicates with the space around the brain and cord (➤*meninges*) by holes in the roof of the 4th ventricle.

2. The two major compartments of the heart are the right ventricle, pumping blood through the lungs, and the left ventricle, pumping blood through the rest of the circulation.

venule. Minute vein, receiving blood from capillary vessels (cf. ➤*arteriole*, delivering blood to capillaries).

vermifuge. Any drug used to expel intestinal ➤*worms*.

vernix caseosa. A greasy substance covering the skin of a new-born baby.

verruca = ➤*wart*.

vertebra. Segment of the backbone (vertebral column). The human backbone has 33 vertebrae, of which the upper 24 are separate bones, the next 5 are fused to form the *sacrum*, and the lowest 4 form the *coccyx*, which represents the tail.

There are 7 *cervical* vertebrae in the neck, of which the uppermost, the *atlas*, makes a joint with the base of the skull. Then come 12 *thoracic* vertebrae, each carrying a pair of ribs, and 5 *lumbar* vertebrae. The backbone is described as a unit under ➤*skeleton* (4).

The weight-bearing *body* of a vertebra is roughly cylindrical. An arch of bone, the *neural arch*, projects from the back of the body to enclose the *spinal canal*, which protects the spinal cord. Three projections from the neural arch provide anchorage for the muscles of the back: the *spinous process* in the mid-line and the *transverse processes* at the sides. The neural arch forms interlocking joints with the vertebrae above and below.

1. INTERVERTEBRAL DISC

The flexible pads between the bodies of the vertebrae, or intervertebral discs, make up a quarter of the length of the backbone. Each disc consists of a jelly-like core, the *nucleus pulposus*, enclosed by dense fibrous tissue, which is firmly attached to the bodies of the vertebrae. This arrangement allows a certain amount of movement without loss of strength, and the discs are effective shock-absorbers.

The tough shell of a disc is weakest behind. Severe strain may cause a bulge here. The nucleus pulposus is squeezed into the bulge and causes symptoms from pressure on nerve fibres. If the bulge is to one side of the mid-line the pressure is on the nerve roots; if it is in the mid-line the spinal cord itself is affected.

This disorder is known as *slipped disc*, prolapsed disc, or hernia of the nucleus pulposus.

The usual cause of a slipped disc is strain while the backbone is flexed, e.g. bending forwards with the legs straight to lift a heavy object. This is a common type of industrial injury. Housewives suffer a similar type of back-strain from constantly working with their backs bent, e.g. working at a sink that is too low, leaning across a bed to tuck in the far side, or bathing the baby. The discs injured by this kind of strain are those between the lumbar vertebrae. The symptoms include backache and ▸*sciatica* from compression of nerves running from the lumbar region to the leg. Weight-lifters avoid strain by keeping their backs straight, squatting, and lifting by straightening their legs.

The thoracic vertebrae are so well splinted by the ribs that their discs are unlikely to be strained. But the cervical discs are commonly damaged, perhaps by a combination of faulty posture (letting the neck sag and jutting the chin) and the processes of ageing. This is one of the many causes of pain, tingling, and numbness in the hand or higher up the arm, and also of some of the aches round the shoulder-blades that pass for 'fibrositis'.

A slipped disc is a mechanical defect, and its treatment is also mechanical. Postural training and manipulation may be enough. In acute cases the patient may have to lie flat for some weeks, or the affected part of the spine may have to be splinted, e.g. with a surgical collar. When simpler treatment fails, the protrusion of the disc can be removed surgically.

2. MOVEMENTS

The two uppermost vertebrae are very mobile. The joint between the atlas and the base of the skull is adapted to nodding the head. The next joint down, between the atlas and the second cervical vertebra (axis), is for shaking the head (rotation).

The movements of the other joints are comparatively slight, but added together they give the backbone a good range of movement. If a few of the joints become fixed as a result of disease, injury or surgery, the effect on the backbone as a whole may not be serious. Flexion (bending forwards) and extension (straightening or bending backwards) take place mainly in the cervical and lumbar regions, and rotation in the thoracic region, where the ribs prevent flexion.

3. INJURIES

Since the joints between the vertebrae interlock, and the fibrous part of the discs is very tough, it is easier to break these joints than to put them out of joint. But a kind of dislocation does occur between the 5th lumbar vertebra and the sacrum or between two lumbar vertebrae (▸*spondylolisthesis*).

A direct blow or a sudden wrench can crack a spinous process or a transverse process. But the serious fractures are those of the vertebral bodies. If the body of a vertebra is broken it is liable to collapse. The backbone then bends forwards at a sharp angle, over which the spinal cord is stretched. This can cause paralysis below the level of the fracture. The damage to the spinal cord may occur not at the time of the original injury but as a result of attempts to move the victim.

When there is even a suspicion of injury to the back it is safest to leave all movement of the victim to trained first-aiders. If he has to be moved before expert help arrives it is best to carry him in the position in which he was found, or else face down so that any accidental movement of the backbone will tend to straighten it rather than increase the angulation.

These fractures heal well when they are immobilized, but a torn spinal cord cannot be repaired.

4. OTHER DISORDERS

The most important congenital disorder of the vertebrae is ►*spina bifida*, a defect of the neural arches.

Deformities are very common. They can be caused by faulty posture (when cause and effect are hard to distinguish); by defective muscles, e.g. after poliomyelitis; by deformity elsewhere, e.g. lateral curvature to compensate for deformity of one hip; or there may be no apparent cause.

With advancing years some degree of *osteoarthritis*, a degenerative condition, seems almost inevitable. Many old people have *osteoporosis*, which is a loss of bone substance.

Pott's disease, tuberculosis of the vertebrae, was once a common cause of hunchback. The damage to the vertebral bodies caused angulation and injury to the spinal cord in the same way as a fracture.

Ankylosing spondylitis is a kind of inflammation affecting the backbone (and sometimes the sacroiliac and other joints). The typical symptoms are pain and extreme stiffness of the backbone.

The cause is not known, and treatment is purely symptomatic.

vertebral artery. An artery running up from the root of the neck to the skull, tunnelling through the sides of the vertebrae. The left and right vertebral arteries join to form the *basilar* artery, which, together with the carotids, supplies the brain.

vertebro-basilar insufficiency. Partial obstruction of the blood-flow in the vertebral arteries, causing symptoms, usually transient, of a ►*stroke*.

vertigo. Giddiness with a definite sensation of movement; the subject feels that he or his surroundings are rotating. The ill-defined dizziness that many people feel if they suddenly stand up, or if they are tired or feverish, is not vertigo.

True vertigo arises from disturbances of the organ of balance (►*ear* (3, ii)) or its nerve (►*ear* (4)).

Vesalius (van Wesel), Andreas (1514–64). The most celebrated of all anatomists. Born in Brussels, he studied in Louvain and Paris, and became professor of anatomy in Padua at the age of 23.

Vesalius found anatomy more or less where Galen had left it in AD 200, and in 5 years of careful dissection and experiment he established anatomy as a modern science. He wrote several minor works, and one towering masterpiece, *De humani corporis fabrica*, published at Basle in 1543. This work, generally known as the *Fabrica*, is said to be the first modern treatise in any science – the first account of things actually seen – after centuries of arid speculation. Since no rational medicine is possible until the structure of the body is understood, the *Fabrica* was a turning-point for all branches of medicine. Vesalius knew that this would be so. He ascribed the decadence of medicine to the fact that the physicians of the Middle Ages had delegated to menials all surgical work and with it all knowledge of anatomy. He set himself two tasks: first, to revert to Galen by making anatomy the foundation of all medicine, and second to correct Galen's anatomical errors, of which he mentions over 200. He succeeded almost beyond belief.

The *Fabrica* is systematic, not regional anatomy, i.e. it deals with the organs according to type and not situation. Its 7 books describe (I) bones, (II) muscles, (III) blood vessels, (IV) nerves, (V) abdominal organs, (VI) heart and lungs, (VII) brain. Modern reference books are arranged in much the same way, as opposed to practical manuals or guides to dissection which describe the arrangement of organs in the various regions of the body. And Vesalius insisted that his book was for reference. Like any professor of anatomy today, he told his students that they would learn anatomy only by doing their own dissections and seeing for themselves, not from books or lectures.

The superb illustrations, drawn from Vesalius's dissections, are matched only by Leonardo's anatomical drawings, which remained hidden for 200 years.

Vesalius was the most practical of scientists. In his work, perhaps for the first time, natural science was divorced from philosophy. He decided what he was to investigate and described what he found, presenting unadorned facts for others to interpret. He produced no theories to obscure the truth, and perhaps that is why for once the truth was readily accepted by other scientists. Having completed his life's work at the age of 29, Vesalius resigned his post and became court physi-

cian to Charles V, later to Philip II of Spain. He founded a dynasty of brilliant anatomists at Padua, culminating in Fabricius and his pupil Harvey.

vesical. Of the bladder.

vesicle. Blister.

Vibrio. Genus of curved (comma-shaped) bacteria, including the cause of *cholera*.

villus. Minute finger-like protrusion from the lining of the intestine. The millions of closely packed villi give the lining a velvety surface.

Electron microscopy has shown that the villi are themselves coated with *microvilli*.

Vincent's disease (Vincent's angina; trench mouth). (H. Vincent, 1862–1950, French physician.) A bacterial infection of the gums, occasionally spreading to the throat. The bacteria are *Fusiformis* and a species of *Borrelia* resembling the spirochaete of relapsing fever. Both can often be found in healthy mouths, and it is not certain whether they cause the ulceration and inflammation or merely thrive in the presence of some undiscovered infection. Vincent's disease is associated with poor general health and physical exhaustion (hence 'trench mouth' in the First World War). The condition may clear up with simple cleansing and attention to general health, but it responds more quickly to treatment with metronidazole or with penicillin.

Virchow, Rudolf (1821–1902). Prussian pathologist, anthropologist and statesman, a pupil of Müller in Berlin. For some years after taking his degree (1843) Virchow worked as a pathologist in Berlin. In 1847 he and his colleague Reinhardt founded what is still a leading medical journal, now known as *Virchow's Archiv*. A year later he investigated an epidemic of typhus, and his report strongly criticized the living conditions of the people affected. The government of 1848 was having more than enough trouble with revolutionaries, and Virchow was promptly dismissed. He became professor of pathology at Würzburg. In 1855 he returned to Berlin as professor, and held the chair for the rest of his life.

In politics he kept his liberal views. He was a co-founder and for many years the leader of the Progressive Party. He sat in the Prussian Parliament from 1862 until his election to the Reichstag in 1880. For what it was worth he opposed many of Bismarck's policies. With considerably more success he put the public health service of Berlin on a sound basis.

Virchow published numerous works on anthropology, and he assisted the archaeologist Schliemann in the exploration of Troy.

His detractors criticized him for opposing new ideas other than his own, such as Darwin's theory of evolution and some of the new discoveries about bacteria and infection. In fact he did nothing of the sort. He merely insisted that new theories should be proved before being allowed to displace the old ones, and he asked no less of his own theories.

Virchow's great fame rests on a simple principle: *omnis cellula e cellula*, every cell comes from a cell. From this germ a new science of pathology, a new understanding of all medical science and indeed all biology were to grow.

Until about 1850 pathology had been content to record the appearances of disease: this heart was enlarged, that liver was scarred, those kidneys were pale. It was an extension of the work of Morgagni in the previous century.

Another pupil of Müller, Theodor Schwann, made the important discovery that animals, like plants, were composed of living cells, which he thought arose spontaneously in a formless ground substance or *blastema*. Schwann's theory was published in 1839. The great Viennese pathologist Rokitansky concluded that disease caused the blastema to produce abnormal cells and tissues.

During his short exile at Würzburg, Virchow recognized that every cell in the body, healthy or diseased, was derived from an earlier cell and, at many removes, from one cell, the fertilized ovum – itself derived from cells of parents and ancestors. All diseases were manifestations of changes, active processes, that had taken place in cells derived from cells. This was like discovering for the first time that the population of a country is composed of individual people who are the children and parents of other people, who eat, sleep, grow, work, help each other, commit crimes against each other, and finally die yet still live in their offspring. It is only in such terms as these that history makes sense, and it was only in Virchow's terms that pathology at last began to make sense.

Virchow's greatest work was published as early as 1858 with the title *Cellular-Pathologie*. For the rest of his life he developed his theme. Every known disease had to be studied afresh. Instead of the old question 'what has already happened to this organ?' pathology had to ask 'what is at present going on in these cells?' It was no longer a static science, but a dynamic one.

virus. The smallest microbe and the

smallest known living creature – if indeed it is living. Viruses can be examined with an electron microscope, but most types are too small to be seen with an ordinary microscope. In size, they range between 0.0005 mm, about half the size of a small bacterium, and 0.00001 mm, the size of a very large molecule.

All viruses are totally parasitic. An isolated virus is an inert speck of matter. It cannot feed, grow, or multiply; it shows no more sign of life than a doornail. A few very small viruses have actually been crystallized. But when a virus becomes attached to a living cell of an appropriate organism (like other parasites, it can live on only one or two species of animal or plant) it diverts the cells' functions to its own needs and can multiply.

The essential difference between a virus and an undoubtedly living creature such as a bacterium or a plant or an animal is that a virus is not equipped with all the chemical components needed for life. It cannot provide its own energy, but must borrow from a better endowed organism. What every virus does contain is nucleic acid. The smallest viruses are parcels of nucleic acid and nothing else; it is because they are pure substances that they can be crystallized. Nucleic acids are the substances that control the synthesis of living matter: they are the very essence of life. All nucleic acids are made up of the same few substances strung together to make relatively huge molecules. The sequence of submolecules in the chain determines the kind of living matter that will be formed in the cell. Differences between species, between individual members of a species, and between the various types of cell in an individual represent differences in the structure of their nucleic acids.

Given a supply of chemical energy and raw material, a nucleic acid can form an exact replica of itself.

When a cell is infected with a virus, its resources are squandered in helping the invader to reproduce itself and prepare fresh virus particles to invade neighbouring cells. This futile activity is harmful to cells. A few viruses can produce toxins or poisons, in the manner of bacteria, but on the whole it seems that the harmful effects of virus infection are due to the mere presence of the virus.

It is impossible to say whether a virus is a living creature or not. Self-reproduction is characteristic of life. Viruses could be said to reproduce themselves, in which case they are alive. Or they could be considered as inanimate objects of which living cells make copies, in which case they are not alive.

1. TYPES OF VIRUS

No rational classification of viruses is yet possible. They are usually named after the diseases they cause or the sites where they are found. Animals, plants, and even bacteria are subject to virus infections, so the number of different viruses must be very great.

Human virus diseases include the common cold, influenza, measles, mumps, chickenpox, smallpox, poliomyelitis, herpes, intestinal upsets, and many others.

Obviously no virus can be grown like a bacterium on an artificial medium; a preparation of living tissue is needed. Certain viruses, e.g. smallpox, can be identified by their mode of growth in fertile eggs. More often they have to be identified by showing whether they react with ►antibodies isolated from men or animals who have developed immunity to them.

Some important virus diseases can be caused by several distinct types of virus, and infection confers immunity only to the one type. Furthermore viruses may change their character in the course of time by mutation: they are subject to evolution, and the diseases they cause can change their character.

A few groups have names unrelated to diseases. Among the enteroviruses (viruses found in the intestine) are Coxsackie viruses, named after the town in which they were first discovered, and ECHO (enteric cytopathic human orphan) viruses, called orphans with inappropriate pathos because for some time no disease could be found for them. This has been put right – various fevers have now been ascribed to them.

Myxoviruses, which include those of influenza, have an affinity for mucus. Arbor viruses are arthropod-borne, i.e. transmitted by insects and the like. They include those of yellow fever and dengue (mosquitoes), sandfly fever, and tick fever.

Some larger organisms formerly known as viruses, include those of trachoma (a common cause of blindness in hot dry countries), and ornithosis (a kind of pneumonia transmitted to man by certain birds). These are chemically more complete than true viruses, and have now been reclassified as ►*Chlamydia*, an intermediate form between viruses and bacteria.

The gradation from tiny viruses such as poliomyelitis virus to large viruses (smallpox), chlamidia, bacteria, and fungi might suggest that evolution has followed a similar path, but this is unlikely to be so. Certainly viruses as we know them cannot be the earliest form of life, because they cannot live without higher forms.

2. Virus Diseases

Some of the common virus diseases have already been mentioned. They are considered further under their own headings. In addition, many ill-defined fevers are caused by viruses. What used to pass for pneumonia in infants, unexplained diarrhoea at any age, and vague, short illnesses are often virus infections. True influenza is a serious epidemic disease due to a known group of viruses. The word 'flu' is loosely applied to common colds and other minor virus diseases. Purists object, but since the particular virus is not likely to be identified in such cases 'flu' is as good a word as any, as long as it is not confused with true influenza.

Most viruses have an affinity for a particular type of cell, in which they produce a characteristic type of damage, with recognizable symptoms. One case of measles is very like another. Like bacteria and other foreign matter in the body, viruses provoke ►*immunity* by causing antibodies to be formed; these chemical substances inactivate present infection and prevent future infection. Some symptoms of virus disease are due to the body's defensive reaction and not directly to the virus. Viruses may stray from their usual haunts with serious results. Poliomyelitis is a common and mild infection of the intestine, but in 1 per cent of cases it involves the nervous system.

Most virus infections confer lasting immunity to later attacks by the same kind of virus. Vaccines (►*immunization*) have the same effect – which needs time to develop. Antibodies from people who are already immune (immunoglobulins) confer immediate immunity lasting for a few weeks.

Antibacterial drugs such as penicillin

have no effect on viruses. The antiviral agent ▸*interferon*, an element of the body's own response to infection, has a limited use but more general application awaits further research. *Ribavirin* can be given to children to suppress severe bronchiolitis caused by *respiratory syncytial virus*. It is also given for Lassa fever. *Acyclovir* and *amantadine* are among the drugs used against herpes infections, especially if the eyes are threatened; amantadine also gives some protection against influenza A. *Ganciclovir* is too toxic for general use, but may save the sight in some cases of secondary infection in people with AIDS. *Zidovudine* (ZDU; formerly AZT) is used in some cases of AIDS. It is not a cure but may check the progress of the disease.

3. VIRUSES AND CANCER

Cancer is abnormal behaviour of cells, especially as regards multiplication. While reproducing themselves excessively, cancer cells tend to lose the functions of their healthy neighbours. But some viruses cause cells not only to produce more viruses, but to multiply themselves, all at the expense of their normal functions. The common wart is an abnormal proliferation of cells in the skin, caused by a virus. A wart is by no means a cancer, for it has no tendency to spread beyond the skin or set up colonies in remote parts of the body.

A few types of cancer in animals are certainly caused by viruses, e.g. the Rous sarcoma of fowls, but these are rarities. One form of human cancer, Burkitt's sarcoma, first reported in Uganda, may be due to a virus transmitted by mosquitoes.

Against any general virus theory is the lack of evidence that cancer is infectious:

people simple do not catch cancer from each other. But this does not rule out the theory. If cancer were an occasional effect of a virus that most people carried it would be impossible to trace infection. Nearly all of us have chickenpox at some time. Only the unlucky few later develop shingles from the same virus, and if the virus had not been positively identified with that of chickenpox nobody would suspect shingles of being an infectious disease.

For viruses to cause cancer they would have to induce permanent changes in the nucleic acids of the infected cells, for one of the features of cancer is that the change in cell behaviour is irreversible. Studies of bacteria infected with bacterial viruses (bacteriophages or *phages*) show that this can happen. Changes induced by phages are transmitted to succeeding generations of bacteria. So it is quite conceivable that viruses might induce cancerous changes in human cells that would be transmitted to the successors of these cells. Burkitt's tumour is closely associated with the Epstein-Barr virus (which causes glandular fever), and little doubt remains that the relationship is of cause and effect. There are analogous relationships between cancer of the uterine cervix and *herpes simplex* (type II), and between liver cancer and viral *hepatitis* (type B).

▸*cancer*; and the historical note under ▸*microbe*.

viscus (pl. *viscera*). Any of the specialized internal organs – heart, lung, stomach, liver, kidney etc., but not muscles, bones, nerves or other parts of the general framework of the body.

vision. The structure, function, and common diseases of the eyes are considered under ▸*eye*. The following notes are concerned only with refraction, on which sharpness of vision (visual acuity) depends.

Light entering the eye is refracted, and so brought to a focus, by the *cornea* – the window at the front of the eye, which cannot be adjusted – and the *lens* behind the pupil, which is flexible and can be adjusted.

When this optical system is correctly adjusted (*emmetropia*) a healthy eye can resolve two points subtending an angle of about one minute. The limiting factor is the distance apart of the sensitive nerve-endings (rods and cones) of the retina at the back of the eye, exactly as the resolution of a camera, however good its lens, is limited by the grain of the film.

The standard lettering used for testing visual acuity is made up from units subtending an angle of one minute at a known distance. The line of type for 'normal' vision is what an emmetropic eye can easily read at the prescribed distance of the chart, often 6 metres. On a 6-metre chart the line above should be legible at 9 metres, and the next at 12 metres. If this is the smallest type that the patient can read his vision is 6/12, or 0.5 in metric notation. With a 20-ft chart it would be 20/40. People with very sharp vision can do rather better than the arbitrary standard, and most charts include smaller type representing 6/5 and 6/4 (1.5 metric).

A common cause of poor visual acuity is a slight asymmetry of the cornea (▸*astigmatism*), which is corrected with lenses that are asymmetrical in the opposite sense. More serious deformity of the cornea can be corrected with contact lenses.

The common defects of focusing arise from discrepancies between the focal length of the lens system and the actual length of the eye, causing short or long sight.

Short sight (*myopia*) is due to too strong a lens (or too long an eye). Distant objects are focused at a point in front of the retina. Near objects, which need a stronger lens, can be focused on the retina and seen sharply.

Long sight (*hypermetropia*) is caused in the opposite way. With the eye at rest, even distant objects are focused behind the retina. The muscles of the lens can shorten its focal length, i.e. strengthen it, and if the discrepancy is not too great distant objects can be focused sharply; but the lens is not so adaptable that near objects can be focused on the retina. (▸*squint*.)

Presbyopia is a normal process of ageing. From childhood the lens gradually becomes less flexible, so that the muscles can adapt it less and less. In old age it is virtually a fixed-focus lens set at infinity.

A child with normal refraction can focus objects held a few inches in front of his eyes. This distance, the near point, gradually increases. In middle age he may be holding his book at arm's length to focus the print, which is then too far away to be read. Distant objects can still be focused because the lens does not have to be adapted for them. Short-sighted people, on the other hand, may still be able to read comfortably in old age.

All these defects are corrected by suitable glasses: short sight by concave (negative) lenses to weaken the refraction of the eye, and long sight by convex lenses to strengthen it. Presbyopes need separate glasses for distant and near vision.

These are the usual causes of poor

eyesight. But it must be emphasized that many other disorders, needing treatment very different from glasses, can interfere with vision. All defects of vision therefore require expert examination before glasses are even considered.

visual acuity. Sharpness of ▸*vision*.

visual field. The area in sight when looking straight ahead. The eyebrows limit the field above, and the nose restricts the field of binocular or 3-dimensional vision. By comparing the patient's field with his own an examiner can get a rough idea of any defect. A *perimeter* provides an accurate picture: the patient fixes his gaze on a central point, and the positions at which he first sees a bright spot moved around the periphery are plotted. Defects in the field give clues to the location of damage to the nerve pathways from the eyes to the visual area at the back of the brain.

vital centre. Collection of nerve cells by which some activity immediately essential to life is regulated, e.g. the respiratory, cardiac, and vasomotor centres which govern breathing, heart rate, and blood pressure. These centres are in the *medulla oblongata*, the lowest part of the brain immediately above its junction with the spinal cord. Serious injury to the vital centres is instantly lethal, whereas life may continue after loss of higher parts of the brain.

vitamin. Essential accessory to the main ingredients of the diet. A proper diet contains the raw materials of which the body is made and continually remade, together with fuel to provide energy. The main ingredients are protein, fat, and carbohydrate. Smaller quantities of inorganic matter are also needed: sodium, potassium, calcium, iron, and traces of several other metals; phosphates, chlorides, iodides, and fluorides. In addition, certain compounds are needed which the body cannot make from their raw materials (i.e. it lacks the enzymes needed for their synthesis); these are the vitamins. Only small amounts are needed. Most of them serve as minor reagents in major chemical reactions (▸*enzyme* (4)). The system might be compared with the workshop of a versatile carpenter. He can fashion all the parts of a piece of furniture and makes his own glues and varnishes. But he cannot make screws; these he must buy ready-made. If he cannot buy screws he turns out rickety furniture held together only with glue and nails.

Some of the diseases due to lack of particular vitamins have been known for a long time, such as beri-beri in Asia, rickets in England, and scurvy among sailors. The 16th-century explorer Jacques Cartier cured his crew of scurvy with leaves, a remedy he learnt from the Canadian natives. In 1753 James Lind of Edinburgh showed that scurvy could be prevented or cured by fruit juice: '. . . as greens or fresh vegetables, with ripe fruits, are the best remedies for it, so they prove the most effectual preservatives against it.' No other 'deficiency disease' was recognized as such until the end of the 19th century, when Takaki in Japan and Eijkman in Batavia showed the connection between beri-beri and diet. Children with rickets were given cod-liver oil in the 19th century, but nobody knew why until after the First World War.

That deficiency diseases were due to lack of 'accessory factors' was first suggested by (Sir) Frederick Gowland Hopkins of Cambridge in 1906. Later Funk named the factors 'vitamines' (because he thought they were chemically amines;

when they were found not to be the 'e' was dropped).

As each new vitamin was discovered it was given a letter. It is not a very good notation, because several of the original vitamins were later found to be groups of different compounds. Now that all the known vitamins have been analysed they are often given their chemical names.

To return to the metaphor of the carpenter, doubling the number of screws would not make the furniture twice as good; similarly forcing cod-liver oil on an adequately fed child does not make him even healthier – in fact a glut can be toxic.

Ideally the diet should provide enough of all the vitamins, but there are growing doubts about what is enough. Currently accepted standards are based on the amounts needed to prevent known deficiency diseases, but there is evidence that some the estimates may be too low for the best of health.

vitamin A (retinol). A complex alcohol found in fish oils, butter, and meat. Plant pigments include *carotenes*, from which vitamin A is formed after digestion; hence carrots and other vegetables are a rich source. Since vegetable oils contain little or none, vitamin A is added to margarine.

Vitamin A forms part of the pigment *visual purple* in the eye and is essential for seeing in poor light. Night blindness is the earliest symptom of deficiency. With severe deficiency the skin and mucous membranes become dry and hard. The conjunctiva – the transparent membrane in front of the eye – may become opaque.

With severe malnutrition the cornea and finally the eye itself are involved,

and in deprived communities vitamin A deficiency is a leading cause of blindness.

Deficiency can be due to very poor diet but is more likely to arise with diseases such as coeliac disease which interfere with the digestion of fat; vitamin A is absorbed from the intestine only together with fat.

Overdosage of vitamin A is potentially harmful, especially to an unborn child. During pregnancy women are being advised to avoid supplements including fish-liver oil and liver products.

Carotene, on the other hand, does not appear to be toxic, so that green and yellow fruits and vegetables are preferable to liver, eggs and butter as a main source. In addition to being a precursor of vitamin A, carotene is an antioxidant, one of a group of substances of which the importance to health has only recently come to light; ▸*oxidants*.

Some derivatives of vitamin A have a place in the treatment of ▸*acne* and some other skin complaints.

The Ebers papyrus (16th century BC) recommends liver – a good source of vitamin A – for night blindness.

vitamin B complex. At first named simply vitamin B, the factor that prevented *beriberi*, this was later shown to be a group of water-soluble substances found together in foods such as whole-grain cereals. As one by one the components were isolated they were successively named B_1, B_2 etc. When a dozen or more had been so named some were found not to be vitamins after all. Though now officially known by their chemical names, informally four of them (1, 2, 6 and 12) have kept their numbers.

All the B vitamins are *co-enzymes*: like warheads they activate enzymes that without them would be inert proteins.

The members of the group, and the effects of lacking them, have been studied individually, but in practice deficiency of a single B vitamin (apart from B_{12}) is unlikely, because a diet lacking one is almost certain to lack others.

Vitamin B_1 (thiamine) is widely distributed. Rich sources include cereals, yeast, some meat and many vegetables. Thiamine is involved in carbohydrate metabolism, and deficiency injures nerve cells and heart muscle. These effects are not confined to beri-beri; they can also arise from the malnutrition caused by chronic alcoholism. Supplements of this vitamin are required in the treatment of recovering alcoholics, generally along with other vitamins of the group.

Vitamin B_2 (riboflavin) is involved in the metabolism of carbohydrates and proteins. Shortage damages the mucous linings of the mouth and the surrounding skin. In severe cases the eyes may also be involved.

Vitamin B_6 (pyridoxine) is in fact a group of chemically related co-enzymes needed in many reactions with proteins and their by-products. It incidentally promotes the synthesis of another vitamin, nicotinic acid, from tryptophan (an essential amino-acid). Deficiency, seldom seen on its own, causes anaemia and damage to nerves and skin.

Vitamin B_{12} (cyanocobalamine) is a very elaborate compound, apparently the only one in the body to need an atom of cobalt. It is present in meat, eggs and dairy produce. Dietary shortage is uncommon except with unnatural diets, e.g. strict veganism. Deficiency, resulting in pernicious ➤*anaemia* and ➤*subacute combined degeneration of the spinal cord*, is usually a result of failure to absorb the vitamin.

Nicotinic acid (niacin) is chemically related to nicotine, but has none of the biological actions of that alkaloid. Lack of this vitamin is the main cause of *pellagra*, with symptoms including a kind of eczema involving mucous membranes as well as skin, diarrhoea and mental disturbance.

Folic acid is concerned, like vitamin B_{12}, with pernicious ➤*anaemia*, though not with the damage to the spinal cord (subacute combined degeneration) that may accompany anaemia due to B_{12} deficiency. But lack of folic acid during pregnancy is a factor in a congenital defect of the backbone; ➤*spina bifida*.

Other vitamins classified with this group include *biotin* and *pantothenic acid*, of which a deficiency is seldom reported.

vitamin C (ascorbic acid). Scurvy, a disease characterized by spontaneous bleeding, loss of teeth, anaemia and impaired healing, is prevented by eating fruit or vegetables. These provide ascorbic acid (ascorbic: no scurvy). Chemically this resembles glucose, from which most mammals can derive it. But primates such as ourselves have to eat it ready-made.

The defect underlying most if not all the features of scurvy is in the synthesis of the packing and binding material of the tissues, in particular collagen, for which ascorbic acid is a prerequisite. The capillary vessels become fragile and leaky; injuries are easily incurred and heal slowly and inadequately. Resistance to infection is also impaired.

Any diet that includes fresh vegetables, raw or lightly cooked, is likely to provide enough vitamin C to obviate any risk of scurvy. The healing of injuries, including burns and operations, makes extra demands, and many surgeons prescribe supplements of vitamin C almost as a routine in such cases.

For more than half a century the possible use of vitamin C against the common cold has been debated, and many experienced physicians remain unconvinced of its value. One objection to the large doses proposed is that any surplus is simply passed in the urine. But a cold, like any other infection, increases the demand for vitamin C. Several studies have suggested that supplements, while not affecting the likelihood of catching a cold, may shorten the attack and alleviate the symptoms. Other studies, though, show no significant benefit.

In chemical terms, vitamin C is a powerful reducing agent, i.e. it can take up oxygen from another substance and replace it with hydrogen. This is the opposite to an oxidizing agent, and vitamin C is important as an antioxidant; ►*oxidants*.

vitamin D. A factor necessary to the formation of healthy bone. Rickets, a disorder of bone formation, was treated with cod-liver oil as early as 1782, but the practice was not widespread – surprisingly, for no better medicine could have been found. As late as 1918, when Mellanby clearly proved that some factor in cod-liver oil (not then separated from vitamin A) cured rickets, many people were unconvinced. It had been shown in Glasgow that lack of sunlight was the cause of rickets: how, then, could fish oil be of any use? In 1919 Dame Harriet Chick studied the severe outbreak of rickets in Vienna, and found that either cod-liver oil or sunlight would cure it. The explanation is that cod-liver oil and other foods contain a true vitamin – i.e. one which the body needs but cannot

make for itself – and that sunlight transforms an inert substance in the skin (ergosterol) into *calciferol*, which is one form of the vitamin, known as vitamin D_2. Cholecalciferol in fish liver is D_3. Vitamin D_1 was an early mistake which proved not to be a vitamin.

Vitamin D promotes the absorption of calcium from the intestine and its excretion in the urine, but its most important effect is on the movement of calcium in bone. The hard substance of bone is composed of insoluble calcium salts. As bone grows these salts are removed from the inside and deposited on the outside. Lack of vitamin D impairs the process.

All the effects of this vitamin – absorption, excretion, bone growth – can be described as *mobilizing* calcium, which amounts to making it soluble. Calcium dissolved in the body-fluids is in two forms. Most salts of calcium, and of any other metal, dissociate when dissolved in water into electrically charged particles (*ions*). Calcium ions have important effects on muscle contraction; if their concentration in the body-fluids varies, the performance of muscle is seriously impaired. The ►*parathyroid* hormone maintains a constant level of calcium ions. But *calcium citrate* is a soluble salt which does not dissociate and so has no electrical properties. In this form, calcium is merely a passenger in the blood. The amount can be varied to suit the needs of the moment.

Vitamin D is known to prevent citrates from being destroyed in the tissues. Its other effects could well be due to maintaining an adequate supply of citrates.

A gross excess of vitamin D causes too much calcium to be mobilized; this unwanted calcium may form bony deposits in the kidneys and elsewhere.

In summer, butter and eggs are good sources, and vitamin D is usually added to margarine. Fish oils contain very large quantities. But sunlight is the most reliable source.

▸*rickets*; *osteomalacia*.

vitamin E (tocopherol). From animal experiments the existence of this vitamin was inferred in 1922 and confirmed when it was isolated in 1936. Rats deprived of it were shown to become sterile, and later studies showed that depriving some animals of tocopherol appeared to injure nerves and muscles. Although many possible functions of tocopherol in human metabolism were suggested and investigated, for half a century none could be found.

Like vitamin C, vitamin E is a reducing agent, and both of them are used in the food industry as antioxidants. Recent research has shown that this is the principal, perhaps only function of vitamin E in the body; ▸*oxidants*.

vitamin K. A vitamin required for the formation of the enzyme thrombin, without which blood cannot clot. Two equally effective forms of the vitamin occur naturally, one in green vegetables and the other formed by intestinal bacteria. Various synthetic drugs can be used instead.

Since the vitamin is provided by food and also by bacteria a shortage is extremely unlikely; but it can be absorbed only in the presence of bile. If the flow of bile is obstructed (▸*jaundice*) vitamin K is poorly absorbed. The clotting of blood is delayed and the patient is liable to bleed heavily if, for instance, he has a surgical operation. Obstructive jaundice often needs surgical treatment, which was dangerous before vitamin K was discovered.

Drugs such as warfarin oppose the action of vitamin K. They are among those used to prevent unwanted clotting (▸*thrombosis*).

New-born babies are sometimes short of vitamin K. To prevent them from bleeding they are given the vitamin until bacteria in the intestine (there are none at birth) take over.

vitiligo. Patchy loss of pigment from the skin. The white patches are unsightly, especially on a naturally dark skin, and they are very liable to sunburn, but otherwise the condition is harmless. The cause is apparently autoimmune (▸*immunity* (7)), and no treatment except the use of cosmetics has any effect.

vitreous humour. The clear jelly filling the larger part of the eye, behind the lens. (The part in front of the lens is filled with the watery *aqueous humour*.)

vivisection. Surgical operation on a living animal for experimental purposes. This highly emotive word is applied by opponents of animal experiment to any procedure, even dietary experiments.

In all civilized countries, these experiments are subject to laws about who may do them, compulsory anaesthetics and so on. The argument that they are scientifically unsound is not really valid, because nobody is more aware than the biologists who do them of their limitations – what is true of one species may not be true of another. But without animal experiments there would be little scientific background to medicine. (▸*research*.)

Some people would like to see all animal experiments banned. Without accepting this extreme view, many people feel that stricter controls are needed to ensure that only experiments of real practical value are allowed, and that those of which the outcome is already known should be forbidden.

vocal cord ►*larynx.*

Volkmann's contracture. (R. v. Volkmann, 1830–99, German surgeon.) A degeneration of muscles, e.g. of the hand, with scarring and contracture, resulting from loss of blood supply. It can arise from constricting a limb in a plaster cast that is too tight to allow for swelling.

volvulus. Twisting of a loop of intestine so that its contents are obstructed and, if it is tightly twisted, the blood is prevented from flowing through its vessels. It is most likely to occur if the *mesentery* – the fold of tissue in which the intestine hangs – is unusually long. Volvulus has to be treated by immediate operation to untwist the loop and, in some cases, stabilize it to prevent a recurrence. If the circulation has been obstructed for any length of time the loop may be irreparably damaged; it has then to be removed.

vomiting. A reflex action with reversal of the normal movements of the muscles in the wall of the stomach; at the same time the voluntary muscles of the abdomen are brought under reflex control to hasten emptying of the stomach.

The reflex is clearly protective when it is set off by an irritant in the stomach, or by overloading. Vomiting can also be set off by over-activity of the intestine further down; hence anything that causes diarrhoea may incidentally cause vomiting. This can be regarded as a sort of radiation of impulses in branches of the *vagus* nerve, which controls both intestine and stomach. The nausea, salivation, pallor, and sweating that often precede vomiting are not governed by the vagus nerve. The whole system of reflexes is controlled by a centre in the brain, which evidently has a complex set of relays. It can be activated by conscious centres of the brain in some emotional states – disgust in adults, or mere excitement in many children.

Repeated or sustained vomiting is always a serious symptom. On the one hand, the causes include emergencies such as obstruction of the intestine and poisoning. On the other hand the vomiting itself can quickly lead to a dangerous loss of water and salt.

Vomiting can often be controlled by the anti-emetic drug *metoclopramide.* ►*travel sickness; hyperemesis.*

von Graefe, Friedrich Wilhelm Ernst Albrecht (1828–70). The son of a professor of surgery in Berlin, Albrecht von Graefe became the greatest pioneer of eye surgery. He devised operations and the necessary instruments for their execution for cataract, glaucoma, squint and other disorders. Many of his techniques and instruments are still in use.

von Recklinghausen's disease. (F. von Recklinghausen, 1833–1910, German pathologist.) = ►*neurofibromatosis.*

vulva. Female external genitalia, bounded at the sides by the *labia majora.* These thick folds of skin and fat enclose two smaller folds, the *labia minora,* which in turn enclose the clitoris and the openings of the urethra and vagina.

W

wart. Small, rough tumour of the outer layer of the skin. Warts are of great theoretical interest because they are the only human tumours that are certainly caused by virus infection, and this might throw some light on the origin of cancer: ▸*cancer* (1); *virus* (3).

The most important difference between warts and other tumours is their habit of disappearing spontaneously. But when a wart does disappear, the virus sometimes lies dormant and resumes its activity later. This unpredictable behaviour makes it difficult to assess the value of treatment. Warts are often 'charmed' away by people who claim special gifts for the work, but one can never be sure that the wart was not about to vanish of its own accord.

Warts can be cut out or destroyed by freezing or corrosive fluids. Skill and experience are needed, for unless the treatment is applied correctly it may cause the virus to spread and set up new warts.

As a general rule, warts are best left alone to vanish in their own time. But those on the sole of the foot (plantar wart, verruca plantaris) are painful and have to be treated.

Wasserman reaction (WR). A blood test for the diagnosis of syphilis, now superseded by more reliable tests. When the bacterial cause of syphilis was discovered in 1905, several kinds of infection could be diagnosed by showing a characteristic reaction between the patient's blood and a preparation of the appropriate species of bacteria. The reaction showed that the patient had acquired immunity to the bacteria as a result of infection. In 1906 the German bacteriologist August von Wasserman (1866–1925) introduced such a test for syphilis, using tissue from a patient who had died of congenital syphilis as the reagent. The test gave reliable results, but for the wrong reason. The effect of the reagent depended not on syphilis in the tissue but on the tissue itself, for by pure chance healthy liver and heart muscle contain a substance that reacts with the blood of a person who has syphilis.

The Wasserman reaction does not distinguish syphilis from yaws or other diseases due to species of *Treponema*, but nor does any other known test apart from observing the course of the disease. A few other infectious diseases also give a weakly positive WR.

The similar, more recently introduced *Kahn test* is considered to be more reliable.

water. Water accounts for about 60 per cent of a man's body weight and 50 per cent of a woman's. The difference is due to the average woman's larger proportion of fat, which contains no water.

Of an average man's 40-odd litres (9 gallons) of water, the *plasma* of the blood contains rather more than 3 litres, and the *tissue fluid*, permeating the whole body and bathing each of its millions of cells, about 12 litres. Together, these 15 litres make up the *extracellular fluid*. The rest of the water, the *intracellular fluid*, is incorporated in the cells.

Although the balance between blood, tissue fluid and cells remains almost constant there is a rapid and continuous

exchange of water between them
(>*tissue fluid*).

The body inevitably loses about 1–5
litres of water daily. The kidneys *must*
form at least 600 ml of urine to get rid of
poisonous waste products. Evaporation
from the skin (insensible perspiration)
takes 500 ml, and evaporation from the
lungs 300 ml. Only a small amount is
lost in normal faeces, say 100 c.c.

Eating replaces some of the lost water.
All food contains water. An average diet
may provide 600 ml of free water, and in
addition the end-products of combustion
are carbon dioxide, excreted by the lungs,
and water, say 300 ml. The remaining
600 ml – a pint – is replaced by drinking.
This pint is the very least that must be
drunk daily in cool surroundings.

Sweating can greatly increase the loss.
In extreme conditions the sweat glands
can pour out as much as 10 litres in a
day.

The balance is regulated almost automatically. Any reasonable excess passes
into the urine, and a deficit arouses the
sensation of thirst.

Shortage of water begins to cause obvious changes when the water in the
body is reduced by about 10 per cent (4
litres). The plasma suffers least, because
a deficit lowers the blood pressure and,
by concentrating the plasma, increases
its osmotic pressure. Both effects tend to
keep water in the plasma at the expense
of the tissues by the mechanism described under >*tissue fluid*. The skin looks
dry and pinched, and loses its elasticity.
When the deficit reaches 25 per cent (10
litres) the blood is so viscous and the
blood pressure so low that the circulation
stops. Even under ideal conditions water
is lost at a rate of 1.5 litres daily, so a
man can live only a few days without
drinking.

The commonest danger arises from
diarrhoea and vomiting, to which sweating is often added. Severe vomiting makes
drinking impossible, and the nausea that
accompanies many illnesses makes it difficult. The extreme case is >*cholera*, which
can be fatal in a matter of hours. In all
these conditions the associated loss of
salt makes matters very much worse.

Children are particularly susceptible to
loss of water; sick children may not feel
thirsty although they are short of water,
and they need encouragement to drink.
Any child losing fluid needs the closest
attention.

There are many situations in which
drinking does not suffice, and fluid has
to be injected. It is usually given into a
vein. As well as ensuring that the right
amount of water is replaced, injected
fluids can also be made up to restore lost
salts and other necessities.

It is possible to take in too much
water, but water intoxication is a rare accident. On the other hand an excess of
tissue fluid is a fairly common symptom
(>*oedema*).

Waterhouse–Friderichsen syndrome. (Described in 1911 by R. Waterhouse, English pathologist; in 1918 by C. Friderichsen, Danish paediatrician.) Sudden collapse during an acute infection, especially meningococcal meningitis, supposedly from bleeding into the adrenal
glands, causing them to fail.

Weil's disease (leptospirosis). (Adolf Weil,
1848–1916, German physician.) An infectious disease of animals occasionally
transmitted to man, caused by various
species of *Leptospira*, a spirochaete
(spiral bacterium).

The usual form is due to *L. icterohaem-
orrhagiae*, a common parasite of rats.
The rats seem to carry the spirochaetes

without being sick, as some humans carry diphtheria. The infection is mainly in the rats' kidneys, and is acquired by contact with anything (usually water) contaminated with rat's urine. Weil's disease is an occupational risk of sewermen, ratcatchers and miners, and cases occur from bathing in rat-infested canals and rivers.

Other species of leptospira infect dogs and farm animals and are sometimes passed to man.

Weil's disease is an acute fever, usually lasting a week or 10 days. In severe cases the liver, kidneys, and heart muscle may be heavily infected, and the combination of jaundice, nephritis, and heart failure can be fatal. Some patients have a tendency to bleed into the skin and elsewhere.

The variants of the disease caught from dogs and farm animals cause meningitis rather than jaundice. They are seldom if ever fatal.

Unlike other spirochaetal diseases (syphilis, yaws, relapsing fever, Vincent's disease), leptospirosis responds poorly to penicillin unless it is given promptly. It is best dealt with by prevention: rubber boots and gloves for workers unavoidably exposed to rats; rodent control; surface drainage; and not bathing in dubious waters.

wen ➤*sebaceous* cyst.

Wernicke's syndrome. (K. Wernicke, 1848–1905, German physician.) Brain damage, with dizziness, mental confusion and stupor. Like ➤*Korsakow's syndrome* it is caused by lack of vitamin B₁, most often as a result of chronic alcoholism.

whiplash injury. A popular term covering a variety of injuries to the neck of driver or passenger when a car stops abruptly, as in a collision. The damage ranges

from a lethal fracture to relatively minor injury and sprains of ligaments or muscles, but even with apparently slight damage pain and stiffness can persist for some time even with rest and physiotherapy.

white matter. Parts of the brain and spinal cord composed mainly of nerve fibres. ➤*grey matter*.

whitlow. Septic finger-tip, especially *paronychia*, a small abscess at the side of the ➤*nail*, with a tendency to creep under the nail. If this happens part or all of the nail may have to be removed to release the pus.

whooping cough (pertussis). An acute infectious disease of childhood. The main symptom is coughing, in violent and uncontrollable outbursts, often followed by vomiting. The ➤*incubation* period varies, but is commonly about a week. An attack confers immunity, and most children are exposed to infection at some time. The disease is thus rare in adults.

In the ordinary way, anyone about to cough first takes a deep breath. The cough of pertussis comes on so suddenly that the child may be caught at the end of expiration with no time to breathe in. The cough reflex closes the glottis, and the child cannot take a breath until the outburst is over; he thus appears to be suffocating. He then learns the trick of drawing in air against the resistance of the glottis, which produces the 'whooping' sound. With a mild attack, there is no need to whoop, and the disease may pass for a bad cold. Small babies sometimes fail to learn the knack of whooping and get no air while the outburst lasts.

Pertussis is seldom dangerous in older children, but may be serious in babies, both in itself and in its complications such as pneumonia and mechanical damage to the lungs. A child with whooping cough is unusually susceptible to tuberculosis.

A small bacillus, *Bordetella*, formerly classified as *Haemophilus*, is the supposed cause, but its relation to the disease is less clear-cut than, say, that of the haemolytic streptococcus to scarlet fever. It is a difficult organism to grow in the laboratory, and its effects are not easy to prove. Other organisms are probably involved as well.

Immunization against *B. pertussis* does not entirely prevent attacks, but since it makes them less likely and less serious it is well worth doing. Pertussis is a component of a *triple vaccine* (the other components being diphtheria and tetanus) which is usually given at 3 months and twice more in the first year of life. For children who react badly to the first dose, pertussis is omitted for the later doses, thereby limiting protection. During an epidemic, the antibiotic erythromycin can be given prophylactically.

The infection responds to antibiotics, which probably have more effect on other germs complicating the disease than on *B. pertussis* itself. Even with the best treatment, pertussis can be a protracted and debilitating illness.

Wilms' tumour. (Max Wilms, 1867–1918, German surgeon.) Nephroblastoma. ►*kidneys* (4).

Wilson's disease (hepatolenticular degeneration). (A. Kinnear Wilson, 1878–1937, British neurologist.) A rare hereditary disease with cirrhosis of the liver and disordered control of movement of the same kind as parkinsonism (shaking palsy).

Certain tissues need a trace of *copper*. All diets contain the minute amount required; copper deficiency is unknown in man, though it has been described in sheep. The fundamental disorder in Wilson's disease is deficiency of *caeruloplasmin*, a blood protein that regulates the distribution and storage of copper, resulting in abnormally large amounts of copper being deposited in the liver and parts of the brain, causing local poisoning.

Drugs such as penicillamine take up an excess of copper and are used to prevent further damage to brain cells.

withdrawal symptoms ►*drug dependence*.

Withering, William (1741–99). English physician. He practised in Birmingham. His *Account of the Foxglove* (1785) is among the most celebrated of all medical texts.

In 1775, Withering was asked for his opinion of a family receipt for the cure of the dropsy, long kept a secret by an old woman in Shropshire. It was said to act by producing violent vomiting and purging. It contained 20 or more herbs, but Withering quickly identified the root of the foxglove (*digitalis*) as the active herb.

At that time there was no science of pharmacology. Drugs were used because they had always been used or because someone of importance had recommended them. No drug had ever been properly studied – a bare handful of the hundreds of remedies used would have withstood even cursory investigation.

Having shown that the drug had powerful effects, Withering set about finding a way of preparing it that would allow accurate dosage. The leaves were more reliable than the root, and because their properties changed during the year they had always to be collected when the plant flowered.

Withering soon recognized that purging and vomiting were not the useful actions of the drug but symptoms of overdosage. He recorded every known symptom of digitalis poisoning: 'sickness, vomiting, purging, giddiness, confused vision, objects appearing green and yellow; increased secretion of urine, with frequent motions to part with it; and sometimes inability to retain it; slow pulse, even as slow as 35 in a minute, cold sweats, convulsions, syncope, death'. He gave detailed instructions to avoid these dangers – 'the effects of our inexperience'. He recognized the important peculiarity of digitalis that its action is slow and sustained, so that repeated doses have a cumulative action.

Far ahead of the times is Withering's insistence on a large number of observations before drawing conclusions. This was made possible by his setting aside an hour or more each day for giving free advice to the poor – two or three thousand of them annually. He also drew many of his colleagues into the investigation.

Withering was unusual in trusting his chosen drug and giving it alone. Any ordinary prescription of the time contained a score or more of ingredients, and there was no way of knowing which, if any, of them had helped the patient. Withering added no more than flavouring to his digitalis, or occasionally a small dose of opium 'to restrain its action on the bowels'.

Not content with setting a standard for all future studies of drugs, Withering pointed out that chemistry (then in early infancy) might in the future come to the prescriber's aid, and that the actions of drugs on 'insects and quadrupeds' might be studied with profit.

World Health Organization (WHO). Founded in 1946: an agency of the United Nations dedicated to the principle that health is 'a state of complete physical and social well-being, and not merely the absence of disease or infirmity' which should be the right of all people. WHO supervises international quarantine rules and the notification of serious epidemics. Its publications include detailed bulletins of medical data from most countries, and international exchange of new discoveries. WHO sponsors regular meetings between health authorities of member countries and, in the poorer countries, it promotes campaigns for controlling specified diseases. It does not, on principle, conduct these campaigns, but it can offer experts to plan them, and, if necessary, share the cost of implementing them. The first objective of WHO, to eliminate smallpox, was achieved in 1980. This must count as one of the greatest triumphs of human endeavour. The next targets are malaria and leprosy.

worms (helminths). A diverse and ill-defined collection of primitive animals. Many species are parasites, and some cause human ailments. The mere presence of a parasite need not denote illness. Some parasitic worms live at peace with their hosts and cause no disturbance. Nearly all worm infestations clear up in time, though it may be a long time.

The worms to be considered here are those that live in the intestine. Some worms that live in other parts of the body are discussed under ▸*bilharzia*; *filaria*; *Guinea worm*; *hydatid disease*; *trichiniasis*.

The common intestinal worms of

childhood are passed from person to person: faeces contain the eggs; a child's fingers become contaminated; he swallows the eggs and the cycle is repeated. The worms of this type include the roundworm *Ascaris*, the threadworm *Enterobius* (both worldwide), and the whipworm *Trichuris* (mainly tropical). The eggs of the threadworm are laid on the skin around the anus, where they cause itching. The child scratches and reinfects himself when he sucks his fingers. Otherwise these worms cause little trouble, except that rare cases of blockage by a tangle of worms in the intestine are described.

Hookworms (*Ankylostoma duodenale*; *Necator americanus*) can occur in most parts of the world, but because of the mode of infection they are common only in warm countries. The larvae live in soil contaminated by faeces, and enter the body through the skin of the feet. Therefore the infection thrives only where sanitation and personal hygiene are defective, and people walk bare-footed. Under these conditions, whole populations suffer from hookworm disease. The worms attach themselves to the lining of the duodenum and cause very slight but persistent loss of blood. The resulting anaemia is not severe, but it is enough to keep the patient's general condition below what it should be.

Of the tapeworms – long segmented ribbons – *Taenia saginata* is a parasite of cattle, *Taenia solium* of pigs, and the very long *bothryocephalus (diphyllobothrium latum)* of fish, mainly in the Baltic. With adequate meat inspection these parasites do not often reach the consumer, and with thorough cooking even infected food is rendered harmless. Most tapeworm infections cause few symptoms, but all kinds of intestinal disturbance are

ascribed to the first two on occasion, and the third is said to cause a sort of pernicious anaemia.

Drugs used to eradicate intestinal worms include *mebendazole, piperazine, niclosamide* and *praziquantel.*

wound. The traditional classes of wound are *contusion* (bruise), *abrasion* (graze), *laceration* (tear), and *incision* (cut). Perhaps *puncture* should be added. A *penetrating* wound is one that enters a body cavity (skull, chest, abdomen). No such classification is of much use. What matters is which particular structures have been damaged (e.g. whether nerves or vital organs are damaged) and the effect of the local injury on the body as a whole.

With most wounds the most urgent problem is bleeding, discussed under its own heading. Broken bones and damaged nerves can wait; bleeding cannot.

With multiple injuries and unconscious patients, even the control of bleeding is less urgent than ensuring that the patient can breathe. In these circumstances his tongue may fall back and completely block his throat. But the tongue is attached to the jaw, and drawing the chin forwards and upwards clears the airway. This simple manoeuvre is more important than artificial respiration.

Apart from the control of bleeding by firm yet gentle pressure around the wound or on the appropriate artery the only essential first aid is to avoid infection. Antiseptics are only of limited value; a clean dressing does all that can usefully be done. Further treatment of all but minor wounds needs an operating theatre where the damage can be assessed, the wound thoroughly cleaned, and injured tissues repaired.

wrist. The joint formed by the ➤*radius* and 3 of the small bones of the ➤*hand*. The lower end of the radius is hollowed out to receive the *scaphoid* at the base of the thumb, the *triquetral* at the base of the little finger, and the *lunate* between them. These three bones are firmly bound together by ligaments and move as one in their socket. The ulna, which at the elbow is more important than the radius, does not take part in the wrist joint. Its joints with the radius are described under ➤*radius*.

The capsule is reinforced by ligaments at the sides and in front of the joint. More than 20 tendons on their way from the forearm to the hand surround the wrist. Most of them are bridged over by strong fibrous bands attached to the bones. These bands prevent the tendons from straightening like bow-strings as the wrist bends. Under them the tendons move in lubricated sheaths like the synovial membranes of joints.

Sprain (torn ligament) is not very common in the wrist, but other injuries are easily mistaken for sprains. The small bones – especially the scaphoid – are liable to fractures which are little more than cracks and are difficult to see in an X-ray film. Such fractures cause no deformity, but roughen the joint surface and so cause pain and stiffness. Part of the bone may be cut off from its artery and die. This is less likely to happen if the fracture is immobilized, because arteries then have a chance to grow across from the sound fragment, but even with the best treatment fractures of the scaphoid are sometimes troublesome. The lunate bone may be dislocated forwards, and this injury is sometimes complicated by pressure on the median nerve. Manipulation is usually easy, but if the artery to the bone is damaged there may be some lasting disability. Removing the bone relieves the pain but weakens the wrist. The ligaments around the wrist are apt to be stronger than the bones to which they are attached, and a sudden strain may tear off a chip of bone. These small fractures generally heal quickly if they are immobilized.

The commonest injury at the wrist is fracture of the lower end of the radius, ➤*Colles' fracture.*

There is only just enough room for the ➤*tendons* as they pass under their fibrous bands. Any inflammation of their sheaths (*tenosynovitis*) is immediately painful. The band across the base of the palm encloses the median nerve with a leash of tendons, and pressure here involves the nerve (➤*carpal tunnel syndrome*).

wry-neck. Torticollis. ➤*sternomastoid.*

X

xanthoma. Small soft yellow deposit of cholesterol and other fatty substances in the skin, especially common in diabetics and people with a tendency to *atheroma* (arteriosclerosis) and its complications. With a rare hereditary disorder these deposits occur all over the body; but the common type is confined mainly to the eyelids. The exact significance of these deposits (except that they indicate an excess of cholesterol in the blood) is not known, but in view of the association with arterial disease many physicians advise reducing the cholesterol in the diet (restricted animal fat and eggs). ►*artery* (1).

X-chromosome. Chromosome 23, present in duplicate in the female sex; ►*genetics.*

xeroderma. Abnormal dryness of the skin; ►*icthyosis.*

xerophthalmia. Dryness and, in extreme cases, opacity of the front of the eye, from deficiency of *vitamin A.*

X-rays. Electromagnetic radiation of shorter wave-length than ultraviolet rays (►*Roentgen.*)

1. DIAGNOSIS BY X-RAYS

X-rays differ from light only in their much shorter wave-length. As some kinds of matter are translucent and others are opaque, so some kinds of matter allow X-rays to pass while others obstruct them to a greater or lesser extent. Dense, heavy substances are the most impermeable to X-rays (*radiopaque*). For instance, lead glass is radiopaque because it contains a heavy metal.

Radiopacity is a matter of degree, and different textures can be distinguished by the density of their shadows on a photographic plate or a fluorescent screen.

Bones are so much denser than other tissues that they can be examined in great detail. On the other hand the lungs, consisting mainly of air, cast very little shadow, and therefore abnormalities such as patches of inflammation are easily distinguished. With accurately judged exposure the shadows of many other tissues and organs can also be distinguished, though in much less detail.

Many organs can be examined with X-rays after suitable preparation. Barium sulphate casts a heavy shadow, and is so insoluble that it can be swallowed with no risk that any will be absorbed from the intestine. When a suspension of barium sulphate has been swallowed a series of X-ray pictures will show its progress along the oesophagus, stomach, and intestine. With a fluorescent screen the movements of these organs can also be studied.

Compounds of iodine are also radiopaque and can be used to study many organs. Those that are excreted into the urine cast shadows of the kidneys. Others, excreted into the bile, are used for examining the gall bladder. These methods not only provide clear silhouettes of the urinary passages or bile passages; they also indicate the efficiency of these systems by the rate at which the radiopaque substance is excreted.

Instead of a radiopaque substance, air can be injected into a space to provide contrast. Scanning by computerized tomography shows far more detail than any other X-ray technique (>*scan*).

2. X-RAY THERAPY

X-rays are used in the treatment of cancer. Some superficial cancers can be cured in this way. With deeper cancers, X-rays can be focused to a determined depth below the surface. They are used alone or as an adjunct to surgery, with the objects of picking off cancer cells at the periphery of the field of operation, reducing the risk of mechanical spread of cancer cells by the operation, and reducing the amount of tissue that needs to be removed. The X-rays used for this purpose are generated at a much higher voltage than those used for diagnosis.

In the past small doses of X-rays were much used for treating skin diseases, in the same way as ultraviolet rays, and also to remove hair for the treatment of ringworm, but this is no longer common practice. The use of X-rays to suppress over-activity of an organ such as the thyroid gland is practically obsolete, but there may still be a place for X-ray treatment of a few diseases in which a tissue tends to proliferate, e.g. to suppress the overgrowth of red blood cells in >*polycythaemia*. When an organ has been transplanted, the natural process by which it tends to be rejected can be suppressed by treating areas of bone marrow with X-rays, but this technique is being superseded by less harmful methods.

➤*radiation*.

Y

yaws (framboesia). An infectious disease of humid tropical regions, due to *Treponema pertenue*, a spiral bacterium indistinguishable from that of syphilis.

The early stages resemble syphilis, except that there is no history of venereal infection, and the primary lesion may be anywhere on the body. In the late stages the infection is practically confined to the skin, where it forms unsightly excrescences and ulcers, and the bones.

Yaws always responds quickly to treatment with penicillin, and in many areas where it was once common it has now become a rare disease – only to be replaced by syphilis.

The infection is transmitted either by direct contagion or on the feet of flies.

The relation of syphilis to other diseases caused by species of *Treponema* is not known. Only syphilis is regularly transmitted venereally. *Bejel*, a disease confined to small areas of North Africa and the eastern shores of the Mediterranean, cannot be distinguished from syphilis, yet it runs through families and communities without sexual contact. *Pinta*, a South American skin disease without serious complications, is a similar kind of infection. It is strongly argued by opponents of the theory that Columbus imported syphilis from the New World (➤*syphilis*) that the four conditions, with their different natural histories, are variants of a single disease, and that the other three have evolved from yaws, which originates in the African rain-forest. From the rain-forest to the northern desert there is said to be a gradual transition from yaws to bejel; and apart from the mode of transmission there is no difference between bejel and syphilis. Against the theory that bejel and syphilis are modifications of yaws, and in favour of the Columbus theory, is the absence of any reference to syphilis before Columbus's voyage and the sudden epidemic immediately after his return.

Y-chromosome. Chromosome 23, paired with an X-chromosome in the male sex; ➤*genetics*.

yeast infections ➤*fungus*.

yellow atrophy. Rapidly fatal damage to the liver by, e.g., poisoning or overwhelming infection.

yellow fever. A dangerous infection of tropical Africa and America, due to a virus transmitted by *Aëdes* mosquitoes. It is primarily a disease of monkeys and other forest creatures, but has caused epidemics in towns.

The liver bears the brunt of the infection, and may fail at the end of a short, violent fever with profound jaundice. The kidneys and heart are also affected. Mild cases are common among people who live in the forests where yellow fever is endemic; but during urban epidemics the death rate has been very high.

Mosquito control and vaccination have made yellow fever a rare disease, but public health departments throughout the tropics remain vigilant. An infected traveller, or an infected mosquito carried by aircraft, could start a disastrous epidemic. In 1940, thousands of people died in the Sudan during such an epidemic, and yellow fever had previously been unknown there. There has never been a case in Asia, but Aëdes mosquitoes abound. New arrivals must prove that they have been vaccinated. Yellow fever vaccine affords complete protection from getting the disease or carrying it.

Yersinia. (Alexandra Yersin, 1863–1943, Swiss microbiologist.) Genus of bacteria of which one, *Y. pestis*, formerly classified as *Pasteurella*, causes ►*plague*.

Z

zinc. A small trace of zinc is among the essential ingredients of the body. An enzyme concerned with the use of carbon dioxide incorporates an atom of zinc in its molecule. Deficiency of zinc is a rare complication of malnutrition, malabsorption, or severe injuries.

Zinc oxide is a bland, mildly antiseptic substance much used in ointments and lotions to protect inflamed skin. *Calamine* is a preparation of zinc oxide or zinc carbonate.

Zollinger-Ellison syndrome. Peptic (duodenal) ulcer caused by over-activity of the digestive part of the pancreas, which stimulates the glands of the stomach to secrete an excess of acid.

zoonosis (zoönosis). Any infectious disease of animals that may affect man. Most parasites have a preferred host but occasionally infect another species. A few appear to have no difficulty in changing their allegiance. The many zoonoses mentioned in this book include *anthrax, cat-scratch fever*, kinds of bacterial *food poisoning, ornithosis, plague, rabies*, kinds of *relapsing fever, tuberculosis* and *typhus, undulant fever, Weil's disease*, and many kinds of *worm* infestation.

zoster. Herpes zoster: shingles. ➤*herpes*.

zygoma. Cheek-bone; a bridge of bone from the *maxilla*, below the eye, to the *temporal* in front of the ear.

zygote. Cell produced by fusion of male and female germ cells; fertilized ovum.

zymosis (archaic). Contagious or epidemic disease (literally = fermentation; the secondary meaning recognizes the similarity of infection and fermentation, finally explained by Pasteur's research into both phenomena).

Visit Penguin on the Internet
and browse at your leisure

◆ preview sample extracts of our forthcoming books
◆ read about your favourite authors
◆ investigate over 10,000 titles
◆ enter one of our literary quizzes
◆ win some fantastic prizes in our competitions
◆ e-mail us with your comments and book reviews
◆ instantly order any Penguin book

and masses more!

'To be recommended without reservation ... a rich and rewarding on-line experience' – Internet Magazine

www.penguin.co.uk

READ MORE IN PENGUIN

In every corner of the world, on every subject under the sun, Penguin represents quality and variety – the very best in publishing today.

For complete information about books available from Penguin – including Puffins, Penguin Classics and Arkana – and how to order them, write to us at the appropriate address below. Please note that for copyright reasons the selection of books varies from country to country.

In the United Kingdom: Please write to *Dept. EP, Penguin Books Ltd, Bath Road, Harmondsworth, West Drayton, Middlesex UB7 0DA*

In the United States: Please write to *Consumer Sales, Penguin USA, P.O. Box 999, Dept. 17109, Bergenfield, New Jersey 07621-0120*. VISA and MasterCard holders call 1-800-253-6476 to order Penguin titles

In Canada: Please write to *Penguin Books Canada Ltd, 10 Alcorn Avenue, Suite 300, Toronto, Ontario M4V 3B2*

In Australia: Please write to *Penguin Books Australia Ltd, P.O. Box 257, Ringwood, Victoria 3134*

In New Zealand: Please write to *Penguin Books (NZ) Ltd, Private Bag 102902, North Shore Mail Centre, Auckland 10*

In India: Please write to *Penguin Books India Pvt Ltd, 706 Eros Apartments, 56 Nehru Place, New Delhi 110 019*

In the Netherlands: Please write to *Penguin Books Netherlands bv, Postbus 3507, NL-1001 AH Amsterdam*

In Germany: Please write to *Penguin Books Deutschland GmbH, Metzlerstrasse 26, 60594 Frankfurt am Main*

In Spain: Please write to *Penguin Books S. A., Bravo Murillo 19, 1° B, 28015 Madrid*

In Italy: Please write to *Penguin Italia s.r.l., Via Felice Casati 20, I–20124 Milano*

In France: Please write to *Penguin France S. A., 17 rue Lejeune, F–31000 Toulouse*

In Japan: Please write to *Penguin Books Japan, Ishikiribashi Building, 2–5–4, Suido, Bunkyo-ku, Tokyo 112*

In South Africa: Please write to *Longman Penguin Southern Africa (Pty) Ltd, Private Bag X08, Bertsham 2013*

READ MORE IN PENGUIN

A SELECTION OF HEALTH BOOKS

Food for Thought David Benton

There has been an explosion of interest in the possibility that what we eat affects our behaviour. *Food for Thought* steers a path through the sensational claims to a series of well-researched and sensible conclusions.

Children First Penelope Leach

Penelope Leach argues that society today leaves little time or space for children and no easy way for adults – especially women – to be both solvent, self-respecting citizens and caring parents. *Children First* is her call to action.

Woman's Experience of Sex Sheila Kitzinger

Fully illustrated with photographs and line drawings, this book explores the riches of women's sexuality at every stage of life. 'A book which any mother could confidently pass on to her daughter – and her partner too' – *Sunday Times*

The Effective Way to Stop Drinking Beauchamp Colclough

Beauchamp Colclough is an international authority on drink dependency, a reformed alcoholic, and living proof that today's decision is tomorrow's freedom. Follow the expert advice contained here, and it will help you give up drinking – for good.

Living with Alzheimer's Disease and Similar Conditions
Dr Gordon Wilcock

This complete and compassionate self-help guide is designed for families and carers (professional or otherwise) faced with the 'living bereavement' of dementia.

Living with Stress
Cary L. Cooper, Rachel D. Cooper and Lynn H. Eaker

Stress leads to more stress, and the authors of this helpful book show why low levels of stress are desirable and how best we can achieve them in today's world. Looking at those most vulnerable, they demonstrate ways of breaking the vicious circle that can ruin lives.

READ MORE IN PENGUIN

A SELECTION OF HEALTH BOOKS

Back in Ten Minutes Dr Mary Rintoul and Bernard West

Millions of people suffer from back pain at some time in their lives. In the majority of cases, the cause is poor posture, over-lifting, injury or stress, and damage can be prevented or alleviated by following this simple but effective programme of exercise and self-help.

Anorexia Nervosa R. L. Palmer

Lucid and sympathetic guidance for those who suffer from this disturbing illness and their families and professional helpers, given with a clarity and compassion that will make anorexia more understandable and consequently less frightening for everyone involved.

Medicines: A Guide for Everybody Peter Parish

The use of any medicine is always a balance of benefits and risks – this book will help the reader understand how to extend the benefits and reduce the risks. Completely revised, it is written in ordinary, accessible language for the layperson, and is also indispensable to anyone involved in health care.

Other People's Children Sheila Kitzinger

Though step-families are common, adults and children in this situation often feel isolated because they fail to conform to society's idealized picture of a normal family. This sensitive, incisive book is essential reading for anyone involved with or in a step-family.

Miscarriage Ann Oakley, Ann McPherson and Helen Roberts

One million women worldwide become pregnant every day. At least half of these pregnancies end in miscarriage or stillbirth. But each miscarriage is the loss of a potential baby, and that loss can be painful to adjust to. Here is sympathetic support and up-to-date information on one of the commonest areas of women's reproductive experience.

READ MORE IN PENGUIN

A SELECTION OF HEALTH BOOKS

Infertility Elizabeth Bryan and Ronald Higgins

Positive and sympathetic, this book will guide infertile couples, questioning health workers and the concerned general reader alike through a maze of fascinating new issues involving medicine, technology, counselling, ethics, law and health economics. It frankly confronts all the painful medical and moral choices while celebrating dramatic new hopes for the childless.

Mixed Messages Brigid McConville

Images of breasts – young and naked, sexual and chic – are everywhere. Yet for many women, the form, functions and health of our own breasts remain shrouded in mystery, ignorance – even fear. The consequences of our culture's breast taboos are tragic: Britain's breast-cancer death rate is the highest in the world. Every woman should read *Mixed Messages* – the first book to consider the well-being of our breasts in the wider contexts of our lives.

Defeating Depression Tony Lake

Counselling, medication and the support of friends can all provide invaluable help in relieving depression. But if we are to combat it once and for all, we must face up to perhaps painful truths about our past and take the first steps forward that can eventually transform our lives. This lucid and sensitive book shows us how.

Freedom and Choice in Childbirth Sheila Kitzinger

Undogmatic, honest and compassionate, Sheila Kitzinger's book raises searching questions about the kind of care offered to the pregnant woman – and will help her make decisions and communicate effectively about the kind of birth experience she desires.

The Complete New Herbal Richard Mabey

The new bible for herb users. It is authoritative, up-to-date, absorbing to read and hugely informative, with practical, clear sections on cultivation and the uses of herbs in daily life, nutrition and healing.